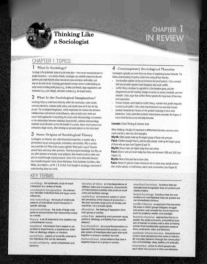

S0-AGZ-319

Chapter In Review Cards at the back of the Student Edition provide students a portable study tool containing all of the pertinent information for class preparation.

THE

SOC
Are you in?

SOLUTION

ONLINE RESOURCES INCLUDED!

CourseMate Engaging. Trackable. Affordable.

Sociology CourseMate brings course concepts to life with interactive learning, study, and exam preparation tools that support SOC2.

FOR INSTRUCTORS:
- Custom Options through 4LTR+ Program
- Instructor's Manual
- Test Bank
- PowerPoint® Slides
- Instructor Prep Cards
- Engagement Tracker

FOR STUDENTS:
- Interactive eBook
- Auto-Graded Quizzes
- Flashcards
- Games: Crossword Puzzles, Beat the Clock
- Videos
- Student Review Cards

Students sign in at
login.cengagebrain.com

YOUR FEED-BACK YOUR BOOK

Our research never ends. Continual feedback from you ensures that we keep up with your changing needs.

SOC 2

Student Registration Edition

Nijole V. Benokraitis

CENGAGE
Learning·

Australia • Brazil • Japan • Korea • Mexico • Singapore • Spain • United Kingdom • United States

SOC 2; Student Registration Edition

SOC 2
Nijole V. Benokraitis

© 2012, 2010 Wadsworth, Cengage Learning. All rights reserved.

Executive Editors:
Maureen Staudt
Michael Stranz

Senior Project Development Manager:
Linda deStefano

Marketing Specialist:
Courtney Sheldon

Senior Production/Manufacturing Manager:
Donna M. Brown

Production Editorial Manager:
Kim Fry

Sr. Rights Acquisition Account Manager:
Todd Osborne

For product information and technology assistance, contact us at
Cengage Learning Customer & Sales Support, 1-800-354-9706

For permission to use material from this text or product,
submit all requests online at **cengage.com/permissions**
Further permissions questions can be emailed to
permissionrequest@cengage.com

This book contains select works from existing Cengage Learning resources and was produced by Cengage Learning Custom Solutions for collegiate use. As such, those adopting and/or contributing to this work are responsible for editorial content accuracy, continuity and completeness.

Compilation © 2012 Cengage Learning
ISBN-13: 978-1-285-13617-2

ISBN-10: 1-285-13617-9

Cengage Learning
5191 Natorp Boulevard
Mason, Ohio 45040
USA
Cengage Learning is a leading provider of customized learning solutions with office locations around the globe, including Singapore, the United Kingdom, Australia, Mexico, Brazil, and Japan. Locate your local office at:
international.cengage.com/region.

Cengage Learning products are represented in Canada by Nelson Education, Ltd.
For your lifelong learning solutions, visit **www.cengage.com/custom.**
Visit our corporate website at **www.cengage.com.**

Printed in the United States of America

BRIEF CONTENTS

CONTENTS

1 Thinking Like a Sociologist   1

2 Examining Our Social World   20

3 Culture 38

4 Socialization 60

5 Social Interaction and Social Structure 80

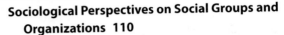

12 Work and the Economy 214

13 Families and Aging 232

14 Education 254

15 Religion 274

16 Population, Urbanization, and the Environment 292

17 Social Change: Collective Behavior, Social Movements, and Technology 312

A sociological imagination can give you more control over your life.

1

Thinking Like a Sociologist

According to a highly publicized recent study, text messaging is associated with the highest risk of car crashes, and headset cell phones aren't much safer than handheld cell phones. In effect, text messaging equates to a driver traveling the length of a football field at 55 miles per hour without looking at the road, and using a cell phone almost triples the risk for being in a car accident (Hanowski 2009). Almost 92 percent of American drivers consider someone talking on a cell phone while driving a serious threat to safety, and 97 percent say the same about texting while driving. However, 67 percent admit using cell phones, and at least 15 percent send text messages while driving (AAA Foundation for Traffic Safety 2008).

Why is there such a disconnection between many Americans' beliefs and behavior? And why, despite the evidence of the risk for accidents, have only 18 states and the District of Columbia passed laws that ban texting while driving (Hanes 2009)?

This chapter examines these and other questions. Let's begin by looking at what sociology is (and isn't) and how a "sociological imagination" can inspire us to have more control over our lives. We'll then look at how sociologists grapple with complex theoretical issues in explaining human behavior.

> **sociology** the systematic study of social interaction at a variety of levels.

what do you think?

Basically, sociology is just common sense.

1 2 3 4 5 6 7
strongly agree   strongly disagree

1 What Is Sociology?

Sociology is the systematic study of social interaction at a variety of levels. *Social interaction* is the process by which we act toward and react to people around us (see Chapter 5). When sociologists talk about the *systematic* study of social interaction, they mean that social behavior is regular and patterned, and that it takes place between individuals, in small groups (such as families), large organizations (such as IBM), and entire societies (such as between the United States and other countries). But, you might protest, "I'm unique."

ARE YOU UNIQUE?

Yes and no. Each of us is unique in the sense that you and I are like no one else on earth. Even identical twins, who have the same physical characteristics and genetic matter, usually differ in personality and interests. One of my colleagues tells the story about his twin girls who received the same doll when they were 3 years old. One twin chattered that the doll's name was Lori, that she loved Lori and would take good care of her. The second twin muttered, "Her name is Stupid," and flung the doll into a corner.

Despite some differences, identical twins, you, and I are like other people in most ways. Around the world, we experience grief when a loved one dies, participate in rituals that celebrate marriage or the birth of a child, and want to have healthy and happy lives. Some actions, like terrorist attacks, are unpredictable. For the most part, however, people conform to expected and acceptable behavior. From the time that we get up until we go to bed, we follow a variety of rules and customs about what we eat, how we drive, how we act in different social situations, and how we dress for work, classes, and leisure activities.

So what? you might shrug. Isn't it "obvious" that we dress differently for classes than for job interviews? Isn't all of this just plain old common sense? Before reading further, take the quiz in *Figure 1.1*.

ISN'T SOCIOLOGY JUST COMMON SENSE?

No. Sociology goes well beyond what we call common sense in several ways:

- *Common sense is subjective.* If a woman crashes into my car, I might conclude, according to the common-sense statements that I've heard over the years, that "all women are terrible drivers." In fact, most auto crash drivers are men—especially teenagers and those age 70 and older (Insurance Institute for Highway Safety 2008). Thus, *objective* sociological data show that many men are worse drivers than women.

- *Common sense ignores facts.* Because common sense is subjective, there is little room for facts that might be disturbing or challenge cherished beliefs or ways of understanding what happens and why. For example, many Americans are most concerned about street crimes, such as robbery or murder. However, sociological data, collected since the 1970s, show that we're much more likely to be assaulted or murdered by someone we know or live with (see Chapters 7 and 13).

- *Common sense is often contradictory.* In terms of

FIGURE 1.1

Everybody Knows That...
After reading each statement, check off whether you agree or disagree.
In the United States...

		I agree	I disagree
1.	The death penalty reduces crime.	☐	☐
2.	Opposites attract.	☐	☐
3.	People age 65 and older make up the largest group of those who are poor.	☐	☐
4.	A majority of Latino families receive public assistance.	☐	☐
5.	Divorce rates are higher today than ever before.	☐	☐
6.	Among married people and unmarried couples, jealousy is a normal trait that shows love.	☐	☐
7.	The best way to get an accurate assessment of public opinion is to poll as many people as possible.	☐	☐
8.	Most child kidnappings are committed by strangers.	☐	☐

The answers are on the next page.

some of our favorite proverbs, do "opposites attract" or "birds of a feather flock together"? And should we believe "out of sight, out of mind" or that "absence makes the heart grow fonder"?

- *Commonsense perceptions vary across groups and cultures.* In the United States, it's common sense to date before choosing a marriage mate. In many other societies, however, it's common sense to marry someone that parents and relatives have selected. Thus, commonsense notions about mate selection vary considerably around the world.

- *Much of our common sense is based on myths and misconceptions.* A common myth (false notion about life that ignores evidence to the contrary) is that living together is a good way to find out whether partners will get along in marriage. Generally, however, couples who live together before marriage have higher divorce rates than those who don't live together before marriage (see Chapter 13).

Sociology, in contrast with common sense, examines claims and beliefs critically, considers many points of view, and enables us to move beyond established ways of thinking. These are some of the reasons why a sociological perspective, and especially a "sociological imagination," is important.

2 What Is the Sociological Imagination?

According to sociologist C. Wright Mills (1916–1962), our individual behavior is influenced by social factors—where and how others and we fit into the big picture. Mills (1959) called this ability to see

FIGURE 1.1

Evaluating your answers: If you agreed with one or more statements, you believe common sense fictions rather than social facts.

1. States without the death penalty have had consistently lower homicide rates than those with death penalties, and the gap has grown since 1990 (see Chapter 7).
2. Much of the research on successful dating and marriage shows that compatibility, and not that "opposites attract," is an important reason for long-term relationships (Benokraitis 2011).
3. Children under 6 years of age, and not those age 65 and older, make up the largest group of Americans who are poor (see Chapter 8).
4. About 20 percent of Latino families live below the poverty level, but less than half of them receive assistance such as cash, food stamps, and Medicaid. In fact, 40 percent of Latinos have annual incomes of $50,000 or more (U.S. Census Bureau 2010).
5. Divorce rates are lower today than they were between 1975 and 1990 (see Chapter 13).
6. Most people experience jealousy, but it is one of the most common reasons for controlling and abusive behavior (Benokraitis 2011).
7. What matters in polling is not the number of people polled, but their representativeness in the general population (see Chapter 2).
8. In most child kidnappings, the perpetrator is a noncustodial parent and not a stranger (Federal Bureau of Investigation 2009).

sociological imagination the intersection between individual lives and larger social influences.

microsociology the study of small-scale patterns of individuals' social interaction in specific settings.

world. Microsociology concentrates on the relationships between individual characteristics, whereas macrosociology examines social dynamics across the breadth of a society.

MICROSOCIOLOGY: HOW PEOPLE AFFECT OUR EVERYDAY LIVES

To some extent, we have many choices in our everyday lives. We decide, for example, where to shop, what to eat, and whether to buy a car. **Microsociology** focuses on small-scale patterns of individuals' social

the intersection between individual lives and larger social influences the **sociological imagination**. The sociological imagination emphasizes the connection between personal troubles (biography) and structural (public and historical) issues. Mills noted, for example, that if only some people are unemployed, that's a *personal trouble.* If unemployment is widespread, it's a *public issue,* because economic opportunities have collapsed and the problem requires solutions at the societal rather than at the individual level.

A sociological imagination helps us understand the relationship between individual behavior and larger societal influences. Americans have among the lowest voting rates in industrialized countries. Why? It's tempting to conclude that Americans are apathetic or satisfied with the way that government functions (i.e., individual choice). As you'll see in Chapter 11, however, and compared with many other countries, our political system often discourages voting. Examples include scheduling elections when most people work, difficulty in registering to vote, and transportation problems among many people at lower socioeconomic levels (i.e., structural factors). Thus, according to a contemporary sociologist, the sociological imagination is "a means for many eye-opening experiences" because, among other things, it "empowers people to think about themselves, others, and what life is and could be in new and liberating ways" (Dandaneau 2001: 12).

The sociological imagination relies on both micro- and macro-level approaches in examining the social

MARRIAGE WITHOUT LOVE? NO WAY!

When I ask my students, "Would you marry someone you're not in love with?" most laugh, raise an eyebrow, or stare at me in disbelief. "Of course not!" they exclaim. In fact, the "open" courtship and dating systems common in Western nations, including the United States, are foreign to much of the world. In many African, Asian, Mediterranean, and Middle Eastern countries, marriages are arranged. In these societies, marriages forge bonds between families rather than individuals and preserve family continuity along religious and socioeconomic lines. Thus, love is not a prerequisite for marriage in societies that value the intergenerational and community relations of a kin group rather than an individual's choices (see Chapters 9 and 13).

interaction in specific settings. In most of our relationships, we interact with others on a micro, or "small," level (such as members of a work group discussing who will perform which tasks). These everyday interactions involve what people think, say, or do on a daily basis.

MACROSOCIOLOGY: HOW SOCIAL STRUCTURE AFFECTS OUR EVERYDAY LIVES

Macrosociology focuses on large-scale patterns and processes that characterize society as a whole. Macro, or "large," approaches are especially useful in understanding some of the constraints—such as economic forces, social movements, and social and public policies—that limit many of our personal options on the micro level.

Microsociology and macrosociology differ conceptually, but they are interrelated. Consider divorce. On a micro level, sociologists might analyze the everyday interactions that fuel marital tension, unhappiness, and lead to divorce. On a macro level, sociologists might look at how economic factors—such as job loss, home foreclosures, and high credit card debts—affect divorce rates. Thus, examining micro, macro, and micro-macro forces is one of the reasons why sociology is a powerful tool in understanding (and changing) our behavior and society at large (Ritzer 1992).

WHY SOCIOLOGY IS IMPORTANT IN YOUR EVERYDAY LIFE

Sociology offers explanations that can greatly improve the quality of our everyday life. These explanations can influence or inform choices that range from personal decisions to expanding your career opportunities.

Making Informed Decisions

Knowing some sociology can help us make informed decisions that enrich the quality of our lives. In 1982, psychologist Carol Gilligan published an influential book that maintained that adolescent girls face a devastating drop in self-regard that boys don't experience. A decade later, clinical psychologist Mary Pipher's (1994) best seller contended, similarly, that teenage girls experience a decline in self-esteem from which many never recover. Both books, publicized by the popular press, generated considerable anxiety among parents, especially mothers, who worried about their daughters' emotional health.

Was the distress justified? No, because the conclusions were based on very small and nonrepresentative groups—Gilligan's on a private girls' school and Pipher's on a handful of troubled girls who sought counseling. In fact, well-designed studies since then have shown that the self-esteem scores of boys and girls are virtually identical (Barnett and Rivers 2004). Nonetheless, many academics and the mainstream press continue to promote the idea that girls have low self-esteem.

Consider another example. We often hear that grief

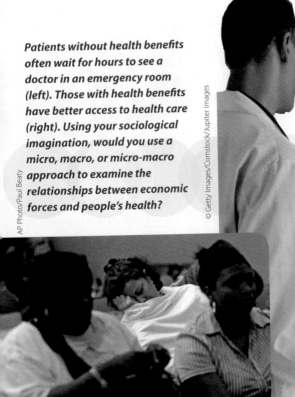

Patients without health benefits often wait for hours to see a doctor in an emergency room (left). Those with health benefits have better access to health care (right). Using your sociological imagination, would you use a micro, macro, or micro-macro approach to examine the relationships between economic forces and people's health?

AP Photo/Paul Beaty

© Getty Images/Comstock/Jupiter Images

counseling is essential after the death of a loved one. In fact, 4 in 10 Americans are better off without such counseling. Grief is normal and people work through their losses on their own, whereas counseling sometimes prolongs the feelings of depression and anxiety (Stroebe et al. 2000).

Understanding Diversity

The racial and ethnic composition of the United States is becoming more diverse. By 2015, 62 percent of the U.S. population will be white, down from 76 percent in 1990 and 86 percent in 1950 (U.S. Census Bureau 2008). As you'll see in later chapters, this racial/ethnic shift has already affected interpersonal relationships, as well as education, politics, religion, and other spheres of social life.

Recognizing and understand diversity is one of the central themes in sociology. Our gender, social class, marital status, ethnicity, sexual orientation, and age—among other factors—shape our beliefs, behavior, and experiences. If, for example, you are a white, middle-class male who attends a private college, your experiences will be very different from those of a female Vietnamese immigrant who is struggling to pay expenses at a community college.

Almost all college and university sites feature "diversity." By their senior year, 41 percent of college students have taken an ethnic studies course, 38 percent have had a roommate of a different racial or ethnic background, and 40 percent say that promoting racial understanding is a "very important" or "essential" personal goal. However, 21 percent of these students report having little knowledge of or could "get along" with people from different races/cultures (Saenz and Barrera 2007).

Increasingly, nations around the world are intertwined through global political and economic ties. What happens in other societies often has a direct or indirect impact on contemporary U.S. life. Decisions in oil-producing countries, for example, affect gas prices, spur the development of hybrid cars that are less dependent on oil, and stimulate research on alternative sources of energy.

Evaluating Social and Public Policies

Sociology is also useful in evaluating social and public policies. For example, federal, state, and local governments spend more than $30 billion each year to reduce illegal drug use. Such expensive efforts are often futile, however, because we have little reliable data on drug use, drug market economics, and enforcement activi-

ties (National Research Council 2001). Would you, the taxpayer, be better served if drug policies and budgets were based on accurate information?

Thinking Critically

Students develop a sociological imagination not just when they understand and can apply the concepts, but when they can think, speak, and write critically. Much of our thinking and decision making is often impulsive and emotional. Critical thinking abilities enhance all learning, knowledge, and problem solving (Paul and Elder 2007). "Critical sociological thinking" goes further because "students perceive and understand that their individual lives, choices, circumstances, and troubles are shaped by larger forces such as race, gender, social class, and social institutions" (Grauerholz and Bouma-Holtrop 2003: 493; see also Eckstein et al. 1995). (A *social institution,* which we'll examine in later chapters, is a set of widely shared beliefs and procedures that meet a society's basic needs).

Expanding Your Career Opportunities

A degree in sociology is a springboard for entering many jobs and professions. A national survey of the class of 2005 sociology majors found that, in full-time and the largest job categories, 30 percent were in administrative support or management positions, 27 percent were employed in social service and counseling, and more than 10 percent were in sales and marketing occupations (Spalter-Roth and Van Vooren 2008).

Many entry-level jobs are posted on popular Internet sites (such as USAjobs.gov and CollegeGrad.com). The positions include nonprofit organizations, government positions, and "everything in between," especially for applicants "with strong oral and written communication skills" (Vitullo 2009: 8).

What skills do sociology majors believe that they've acquired? Among graduating seniors, 73 percent felt they could develop evidence-based arguments, 67 percent said they could write a report that nonsociologists would understand, and 61 percent reported being able to interpret research findings (American Sociological Association 2006). In other cases, students major in sociology because they see it as a broad liberal arts foundation for professions such as law, education, medicine, social work, and counseling.

Even if you don't major in sociology, developing your sociological imagination can bring a depth and breadth of understanding to your job. Sociology courses help you learn to think abstractly and critically, formulate problems, ask appropriate questions, search for answers in the most reliable and up-to-date sources, organize material, and make effective oral presentations.

3 Some Origins of Sociological Theory

during college, most of my classmates and I avoided taking theory courses (in all disciplines) as long as possible. "This stuff is boring, boring, boring," we'd complain, "and has nothing to do with the real world." Theorizing, in fact, is part of our everyday lives. Every time you try to explain why your family and friends behave as they do, for example, you are theorizing.

As people struggle to understand human behavior, they develop theories. A **theory** is a set of statements that explains why a phenomenon occurs. Theories produce knowledge, guide our research, help us analyze our findings, and, ideally, offer solutions for social problems. (Some sociologists differentiate between *theory* and *theoretical perspective*. Most use the terms interchangeably to explain how social phenomena are related to one another.)

Sociologist James White (2005: 170–171) describes theories as "tools" that don't profess to know "the truth" but "may need replacing" over time as our understanding of society changes. Like hardware tools

Sociology and Other Social Sciences: What's the Difference?

How would different social scientists study the same phenomenon, such as homelessness? Criminologists might examine whether crime rates are higher among homeless people than those in the general population. Economists might measure the financial impact of services for the homeless in the nation and other countries. Political scientists might study whether and how government officials respond to homelessness. Psychologists might be more interested in how homelessness affects individuals' emotional and mental health. Social workers are most likely to try to provide needed services such as food, shelter, medical care, and jobs. Sociologists have been most interested in examining homelessness across gender, age, and social class, and explaining how this social problem devastates families and communities.

According to sociologist Herbert Gans (2005), sociologists "study everything." There are currently 43 different subfields in sociology, and the number continues to increase. Why do sociologists' interests range across so many areas? Probably because the discipline's origins reflect the broad interests of its founders.

Creatas Images/Jupiter Images

TOOLS = THEORIES

that change over the years, theories evolve over time to explain social phenomena. As you'll see shortly, for example, sociological theories about behavior changed considerably after the rise of feminist perspectives during the late 1960s.

Sociological theories did not emerge overnight. Nineteenth-century thinkers grappled with some of the same questions that sociologists try to answer today: Why do people behave as they do? Why is society structured like it is? What holds society together? What pulls it apart? Of the many contributors to the development of sociology, some of the most influential were Auguste Comte, Harriet Martineau, Émile Durkheim, Karl Marx, Max Weber, Jane Addams, and W. E. B. Du Bois.

AUGUSTE COMTE

Auguste Comte (pronounced oh-gust KONT; 1798–1857) coined the term *sociology* and is often described as the "father of sociology." Comte's English translator, Harriet Martineau (1802–1876), fleshed out and publicized many of Comte's ideas. "We might, say, then, that sociology had parents of both sexes" (Adams and Sydie 2001: 32).

Comte maintained that the study of society must be **empirical**. That is, information should be based on observations, experiments, or experiences rather than on ideology, religion, or intuition. He saw sociology as the scientific study of two aspects of society: social statics and social dynamics. *Social statics* investigates how principles of social order explain a particular society, as well as the interconnections between structures. *Social dynamics* explores how individuals and societies change over time. Comte's emphasis on social order and change within and across societies is still useful today because many sociologists examine the relationships between education and politics (social statics), as well as how their interconnections change over time (social dynamics).

empirical information that is based on observations, experiments, or experiences rather than on ideology, religion, or intuition.

HARRIET MARTINEAU

Harriet Martineau, an English author, published several dozen books covering a wide range of topics in social science, politics, literature, and history. Her translation and condensation of Auguste Comte's difficult material for popular consumption was largely responsible for the dissemination of Comte's work. She emphasized the importance of systematic data collection through observation and interviews, and an objective analysis of records in explaining events and behavior, and published the first methodology text for sociology (Adams and Sydie 2001).

Martineau, a feminist and strong opponent of slavery, denounced aspects of capitalism for being alienating and degrading. She was especially critical of machinery that resulted in injury and death, particularly of women and children. Martineau's suggestions for improving women's position in the workforce included education, nondiscriminatory employment, and training programs. She advocated women's admission into medical schools and emphasized issues such as the care

Father of Sociology—Auguste Comte

of infants, the rights of the aged, and the prevention of suicide and other social problems (Hoecker-Drysdale 1992). Her publications included thousands of articles and numerous books that criticized the injustices against women, slaves, children, the mentally ill, the poor, and prostitutes.

After a 13-month tour of the United States, Martineau described American women as being socialized to be subservient and dependent rather than equal marriage partners. She also criticized religious institutions for expecting women to be pious and passive rather than educating them in philosophy and politics. Most historians ridiculed and dismissed her ideas as too radical.

ÉMILE DURKHEIM

Émile Durkheim (1858-1917), a French sociologist and writer, agreed with Comte that societies are characterized by unity and cohesion because its members are bound together by common interests and attitudes. According to Durkheim, however, Comte did not show that sociology could be scientific (and ignored Martineau's contributions on this subject).

Social Facts

To be scientific, Durkheim maintained, sociology must study **social facts**—aspects of social life, external to the individual, that can be measured. Sociologists can gauge *material facts* by examining demographic characteristics such as age, place of residence, and population size. They can determine *nonmaterial facts,* such as communication processes, by observing everyday behavior and how people relate to each other (see Chapters 3 to 6). Social facts also include *social currents* such as collective behavior and social movements (see Chapter 17).

Division of Labor

One of Durkheim's central questions was how people can be autonomous and individualistic while being integrated in society. **Social solidarity**, or social cohesiveness and harmony, according to Durkheim, is maintained by a **division of labor**—an interdependence of different tasks and occupations, characteristic of industrialized societies, that produce social unity and facilitate change.

As the division of labor becomes more specialized, people become increasingly more dependent on one another for specific goods and services. Currently, for example, many couples who are planning a wedding often contract and consult specific "providers" such as a photographer, florist, deejay, caterer, bartender, travel agent (for the honeymoon), and even a "wedding planner."

Social Integration

Durkheim, perhaps more than any of the other early pioneering theorists, showed the importance of testing theory empirically. In his classic

Harriet Martineau

Spencer Arnold/Getty Images

© The Art Gallery Collection/Alamy

During his lifetime, Émile Durkheim published numerous studies on education, crime, religion, suicide, and many other aspects of society.

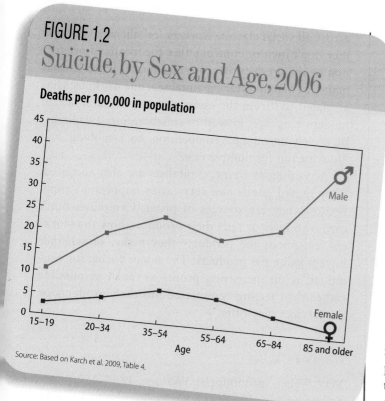

FIGURE 1.2
Suicide, by Sex and Age, 2006

Deaths per 100,000 in population

Age: 15–19, 20–34, 35–54, 55–64, 65–84, 85 and older

Male / Female

Source: Based on Karch et al. 2009, Table 4.

study, *Suicide,* Durkheim (1897) relied on extensive data collection to test his theory that suicide is related to social integration. For instance, Durkheim calculated the suicide rates of women and men, of the married and unmarried, and of Protestants, Catholics, and Jews.

He found that suicide rates reflected the degree to which individuals were integrated into family, group, and community life. Durkheim concluded that people who experience meaningful social relationships are less likely to commit suicide than those who feel alone, helpless, or hopeless. That is, many seemingly isolated individual acts, including suicide, are often the result of structural arrangements such as weak social ties.

Are Durkheim's findings on social integration dated? No. Suicide has been one of the 11 leading causes of death in the United States since 1975 (Heron et al. 2009). We typically read about the high suicide rates of teens. As *Figure 1.2* shows, however, the highest suicide rates are for people age 85 and older, and especially white males (Karch et al. 2009). Using Durkheim's analyses, the high suicide rates of older men may reflect being widowed and feeling alone, a sense of hopelessness because of terminal illnesses, and not being "connected" to support systems that women develop. Women are more likely than men to have close friends (especially other women), to maintain close ties with mothers and

sisters, and to join community groups that provide assistance during troubling times (American Association of Suicidology 2009; see also Chapters 9 and 13).

KARL MARX

Karl Marx (1818–1883), a German social philosopher, is often described as the most influential social scientist who ever lived. Marx, like Comte and Durkheim, tried to explain changes in society that were taking place during the Industrial Revolution.

The Industrial Revolution began in England around 1780 and spread throughout Western Europe and the United States during the nineteenth century. A number of technological inventions—such as the spinning wheel, the steam engine, and large weaving looms—enabled the development of large-scale manufacturing and mining industries over a relatively short period. The extensive mechanization shifted agricultural and home-based work to factories in cities. As masses of people migrated from small farms to factories to find jobs, urbanization and capitalism grew rapidly.

Capitalism

Unlike his predecessors and contemporaries, Marx (1867/ 1967, 1964) maintained that economic issues produce divisiveness rather than social solidarity. According to Marx, the most important social changes reflected the development of

capitalism an economic system in which the ownership of the means of production—like land, factories, large sums of money, and machines—is in private hands.

alienation the feeling of separation from one's group or society.

capitalism, an economic system in which the ownership of the means of production—like land, factories, large sums of money, and machines—is in private hands. As a result, Marx saw industrial society as composed of three social classes:

- *capitalists*—the ruling elite who own the means of producing wealth (such as factories)
- *petit bourgeoisie*—small business owners and owner workers who still have their own means of production but might end up in the proletariat because they are driven out by competition or their businesses fail
- *proletariat*—the masses of workers who depend on wages to survive, who have few resources, and who make up the working class

Class Conflict

Marx believed that society is divided into the haves (capitalists) and the have-nots (proletariat). For Marx, capitalism was a class system where conflict between the classes was commonplace and where society was anything but cohesive. Instead, class antagonisms revolved around struggles between the capitalists who increased their profits by exploiting workers and workers who resisted but gave in because they depended on capitalists for jobs.

Marx argued that there was a close relationship between inequality, social conflict, and social class. Thus, he maintained, history is a series of class struggles between capitalists and workers. As wealth became more concentrated in the hands of a few capitalists, he predicted, the ranks of an increasingly dissatisfied proletariat would swell, leading to bloody revolution and eventually a classless society. As you'll see in later chapters, some conflicts (such as the United States' wars in Iraq and Afghanistan, and many European countries' quotas on immigrants) reflect a struggle between the haves and the have-nots. For the most part, however, the have-not nations wield little power in resolving class conflicts.

Alienation

In industrial capitalist systems, Marx (1844/1964) contended, **alienation**—the feeling of separation from one's group or society—is common across all social classes. Workers feel alienated because they don't own or control either the means of production or the product. Because meaningful labor is what makes us human, Marx maintained, our workplace has alienated us "from the essence of our humanness." In modern language, instead of collaborating, a capitalistic society encourages competition, backstabbing, and "looking out for number one."

According to Marx, capitalists are also alienated. They regard goods and services as important simply because they are sources of profit. Capitalists don't care who buys or sells their products, how the workers feel about the products they make, or whether buyers value the products. The major focus, for capitalists, is on increasing profits as much as possible rather than feeling "connected" to their products or the services they offer.

MAX WEBER

Max Weber (pronounced VAY-ber; 1864–1920) was a German sociologist, economist, legal scholar, historian, and politician. Weber rejected the Marxian view that economics was a major factor in explaining society. Instead, Weber focused on social organization, a subjective understanding of behavior, and a value-free sociology.

Social Organization

For Weber, economic factors were important, but ideas, religious values, ideologies, and charismatic leaders were just as crucial in shaping and changing societies. A complete understanding of society, according to Weber, must analyze the social organization and interrelationships among economic, political, and cultural institutions. In his *Protestant Ethic and the Spirit of Capitalism*, for example, We-

Weber headed the first German Institute of Sociology and held a number of other prestigious university positions.

Hulton Archive/Getty Images

Is It Possible to Be a Value-Free Sociologist?

Max Weber was concerned about the popularity of professors who took political positions that pleased many of their students. He felt that these professors were behaving improperly because science, including sociology, must be "value free." Faculty must set their personal values aside to make a contribution to society. According to one sociologist who supports Weber's position, sociology's weakness is its tendency toward moralism and ideology.

Many people become sociologists out of an impulse to reform society, fight injustice, and help people. Those sentiments are noble, but unless they are tempered by skepticism, discipline, and scientific detachment, they can be destructive. Especially when you are morally outraged and burning with a desire for action, you need to be cautious (Massey 2005: B12).

Can sociologists be value free—especially when they have strong feelings about many societal issues? Should they be?

There is considerable disagreement, however, on whether sociologists can *really* be value free. Some argue that being value free is a myth because it's impossible for a scholar's attitudes and opinions to be totally divorced from her or his scholarship (Gouldner 1962). Many sociologists, after all, do research on topics that they consider significant and about which they have strong views. If you talk to your sociology instructor, for example, you'll probably find that she or he teaches and does research on topics in which she or he is intensely, and personally, interested.

Other sociologists maintain that one's values should be passionately partisan, frame research issues, and have an impact on improving society (Feagin 2001). That is, sociologists should not apologize for being subjective in their teaching and research.

ber (1920) argued that the self-denial fostered by Calvinism supported the rise of capitalism, strengthened predestination, and shaped many of our current values about working hard (see Chapters 6 and 12).

> **value free** separating one's personal values, opinions, ideology, and beliefs from scientific research.

Subjective Understanding

Unlike many of his predecessors, Weber stressed the differences, rather than the similarities, between the natural and the social sciences. Weber didn't dismiss "objective research," but he posited that an understanding of society requires a "subjective" understanding of behavior. Such understanding, or *verstehen* (pronounced fer-SHTAY-en), requires knowing how people perceive the world in which they live. Weber described two types of *verstehen*. In *direct observational understanding*, the social scientist observes a person's facial expressions, ges-

Can sociologists be value free—especially when they have strong feelings about many societal issues? *Should* they be?

tures, and listens to his/her words. In *explanatory understanding*, the social scientist tries to grasp the intention and context of behavior.

If a person bursts into tears (direct observational understanding), the observer knows what the person may be feeling (anger, sorrow, and so on). An explanatory understanding goes a step further by spelling out the reason for the behavior (rejection by a loved one, frustration when your computer crashes, humiliation if a boss yells at you in public).

Value-Free Sociology

One of Weber's most lasting and controversial views was the notion that sociologists must be as objective, or "value free," as possible in analyzing society. A researcher who is **value free** is one who separates her or his personal values, opinions, ideology, and beliefs from scientific research.

Jane Addams with a child at Hull House.

served as a community center for the neighborhood poor. An active reformer throughout her life, Jane Addams was a leader in the woman's suffrage movement and, in 1931, the first American woman to be awarded the Nobel Peace Prize for her advocacy of negotiating, rather than waging war, to settle disputes.

Sociologist Mary Jo Deegan (1986) describes Jane Addams as "the greatest woman sociologist of her day." She was ignored by her colleagues at the University of Chicago (the first sociology department established in the United States in 1892), however, because discrimination against women sociologists was "rampant" (p. 8).

Despite such discrimination, Addams published articles in numerous popular and scholarly journals, as well as a number of books on the everyday life of urban neighborhoods, especially the effects of social disorganization and immigration. Much of her work contributed to symbolic interactionism, an emerging school of thought. One of Addams' greatest intellectual legacies was her emphasis on applying knowledge to everyday problems. Her pioneering work in criminology included ecological maps of Chicago that were later credited to men (Moyer 2003).

W. E. B. DU BOIS

W. E. B. Du Bois (pronounced Do-BOICE; 1868–1963) was a prominent black sociologist, writer, editor, social reformer, and passionate orator. The author of almost two dozen books on Africans and black Americans, Du Bois spent most of his life responding to the critics and detractors of black life. He was the first African American to receive a Ph.D. from Harvard University, but once remarked, "I was in Harvard but not of it."

Du Bois helped found the National Association for the Advancement of Colored People (NAACP) and became editor of its journal, *Crisis*. He argued, unsuccessfully, that the NAACP should be led by African Americans, rather than whites.

The problem of the twentieth century, he wrote, is the problem of the color line. Du Bois was certain that the race problem

During Weber's time, the government and other organizations demanded that university faculty teach the "right" ideas. Weber encouraged everyone to be involved as citizens, but he maintained that educators and scholars should be as dispassionate as possible about political and ideological positions. The task of the teacher, Weber argued, was to provide students with knowledge and scientific experience, and not to "imprint" the teacher's personal political views. If educators introduce personal value judgments, according to Weber, a "full understanding of the facts ceases" (Gerth and Mills 1946). The box "Is It Possible to Be a Value-Free Sociologist?" examines this issue further.

JANE ADDAMS

Jane Addams (1860–1935) was a social worker who co-founded Hull House, one of the first settlement houses in Chicago that

Near the end of his life, discouraged with the ongoing discrimination in the United States, Du Bois moved to Ghana.

was one of ignorance and wanted to provide a "cure" for prejudice and discrimination. Such cures included black political power, civil rights, and providing blacks with a higher education rather than funneling blacks into technical schools.

These and other writings were unpopular at a time when Booker T. Washington, a well-known black educator, asked black people to be patient in demanding equal rights. As a result, Du Bois was dismissed as a radical by his contemporaries but rediscovered by a new generation of black scholars during the 1970s and 1980s. Among his many contributions, Du Bois examined the oppressive effects of race and class, described the numerous contributions of U.S. blacks to Western culture, advocated women's rights, and played a key role in reshaping black-white relations in America (Du Bois 1986; Lewis 1993).

All of the early thinkers agreed that people are transformed by each other's actions, social patterns, and historical changes. Most importantly, these and other early contributors shaped contemporary sociological theories.

4 Contemporary Sociological Theories

how one defines "contemporary sociological theory" is somewhat arbitrary. The mid-twentieth century is a good starting point because "the late 1950s and 1960s have, in historical hindsight, been regarded as significant years of momentous changes in the social and cultural life of most Western societies" (Adams and Sydie 2001: 479). Some of the sociological perspectives had earlier origins, but all matured during this period. Like their predecessors, modern sociologists developed theoretical explanations that reflected their social and historical contexts such as the women's rights, gay rights, and anti-Vietnam war protests during the 1960s and 1970s; the impact of popular culture; and the increasing numbers of women who entered higher education and the labor force.

Sociologists typically use more than one theory in explaining human behavior. The theories view our social world somewhat differently, but all of them try to explain why society is organized the way it is and why we behave as we do. Four of the most influential theoretical perspectives are functionalism, conflict theory, feminist theories, and symbolic interactionism.

FUNCTIONALISM

functionalism *(structural functionalism)* an approach that maintains that society is a complex system of interdependent parts that work together to ensure a society's survival.

Functionalism (also known as *structural functionalism*) maintains that society is a complex system of interdependent parts that work together to ensure a society's survival. Much of contemporary functionalism grew out of the work of Auguste Comte and Émile Durkheim, both of whom believed that human behavior is a result of social structures that promote order and integration in society. One of their contemporaries, English philosopher Herbert Spencer (1820–1903), used an organic analogy to explain the evolution of societies. To survive, Spencer (1862/1901) wrote, our vital organs—like the heart, lungs, kidneys, liver, and so on—must function together. Similarly, the parts of a society, like the parts of a body, work together to maintain the whole structure.

Society Is a Social System

Prominent American sociologists, especially Talcott Parsons (1902–1979) and Robert K. Merton (1910–2003), developed these earlier ideas of structure and function. For these and other functionalists, a society is a system of major institutions such as government, religion, the economy, education, and the family.

Each institution or other social group has *structures,* or organized units, that are connected to each other and within which behavior occurs. Education structures such as colleges, for instance, are not only organized internally in terms of who does what and when, but depend on other structures such as government (to provide funding), business (to produce textbooks and

Sociologists typically use more than one theory in explaining human behavior, all of which try to explain why society is organized the way it is.

construct buildings), and medical institutions (to ensure that students, staff, and faculty stay healthy).

Functions and Dysfunctions

Each structure fulfills certain *functions,* or purposes and activities, to meet different needs that contribute to a society's stability and survival (Merton 1938). The purpose of education, for instance, is to transmit knowledge to the young, to teach them to be good citizens, and to prepare them for jobs (see Chapter 14).

Some social patterns are **dysfunctional** because they have a negative impact on a group or society. When one part of society isn't working, it affects all of the other parts by creating conflict, divisiveness, and social problems. Consider religion. In the United States, French, Portuguese, Spanish, and British missionaries were responsible for destroying much of the indigenous American Indian culture. The missionaries, determined to convert the "savages" to Christianity, eliminated many religious ceremonies and practices that they deemed "uncivilized" (Price 1981). More recently, religious intolerance has led to wars and terrorism (see Chapter 18 online).

Manifest and Latent Functions

There are two kinds of functions. **Manifest functions** are intended and recognized; they are present and clearly evident. **Latent functions** are unintended and unrecognized; they are present but not immediately obvious. Consider the marriage ceremony. The primary manifest function of the marriage ceremony is to publicize the formation of a new family unit and to legitimize sexual intercourse and childbirth (even though both occur outside of marriage in many industrialized countries). Its latent functions include the implicit communication of a "hands-off" message to suitors, providing the new couple with household goods and products through bridal shower and wedding gifts, and redefining family boundaries to include in-laws or stepfamily members.

Critical Evaluation

Functionalism is useful in seeing the "big picture" of interrelated structures and functions. According to some critics, however, functionalism is so focused on order and stability that it often ignores social change. For example, functionalists typically see high divorce rates as dysfunctional and as signaling the disintegration of the family rather than indicating a positive change (such as people leaving an unhappy situation).

A second criticism is that functionalism often ignores the inequality that a handful of powerful people create and maintain. Instead of challenging the status quo, some contend, functionalism simply describes it. Some critics have also charged that functionalism views society narrowly through white, male, middle-class lenses. According to some feminist scholars, for example, "functionalism tends to support a white middle-class family model emphasizing the economic activities of the male household head and domestic activities of his female subordinate" while ignoring nontraditional families, such as single-parent households (Lindsey 2005: 6).

CONFLICT THEORY

Whereas functionalists emphasize order, stability, cohesion, and consensus, **conflict theory** examines the ways in which groups disagree, struggle over power, and compete for scarce resources (such as property, wealth, and prestige). In contrast with functionalists, conflict theorists see disagreement and the resulting changes in society as natural, inevitable, and even desirable.

Sources of Conflict

The conflict perspective has a long history. As you saw earlier, Karl Marx predicted that conflict would result from widespread economic inequality, and W. E. B. Du Bois denounced U.S. society for its ongoing racial discrimination that results in divisiveness. Since the 1960s, and as you'll see in later chapters, many sociologists—especially feminist and minority scholars—have emphasized that the key sources of economic inequity in any society also include race, ethnicity, gender, age, and sexual orientation.

Conflict theorists agree with functionalists that some societal arrangements are functional. But, conflict theorists ask, who benefits? And who loses? When corporations merge, workers in lower-end jobs are often the first to be laid off, whereas the salaries and benefits of corporate executive officers (CEOs) soar and the

value of stocks (usually held by higher social classes) increase. Thus, mergers might be functional for those at the upper end of the socioeconomic ladder, but dysfunctional for those in the lower rungs.

Social Inequality

Unlike functionalists, conflict theorists see society not as cooperative and harmonious, but as a system of widespread inequality. For conflict theorists, there is a continuous tension between the "haves" and the "have-nots," most of whom are children, women, minorities, and the poor.

Many conflict theorists focus on how those in power—typically white, wealthy, Anglo-Saxon, Protestant males (WASPs)—dominate political and economic decision making in U.S. society. This group controls a variety of institutions, such as education, criminal justice, and the media, and pass laws that benefit only small groups of people like themselves (see Chapters 8, 11, and 12).

Critical Evaluation

Conflict theory is important in explaining how societies create and cope with disagreements. However, some have criticized conflict theorists for over-emphasizing competition and coercion at the expense of order and stability. Inequality exists and struggles over scarce resources occur, critics agree, but conflict theorists often ignore cooperation and harmony. Voters, for example, can boot dominant groups out of office and replace them with African Americans (including the President of the United States), Asians, Latinos, and women. Critics of conflict theory also point out that the have-nots can increase their power through negotiation, bargaining, lawsuits, and strikes.

Some critics also believe that conflict theory pre-sents a negative view of human nature and neglects the importance of love and self-sacrifice, which are essential to family and other personal relationships. Because conflict perspectives examine institutional rather than personal choices and constraints, they don't give us insights on everyday individual behavior.

feminist theories approaches that try to explain the social, economic, and political position of women in society with a view to freeing women from traditionally oppressive expectations, constraints, roles, and behavior.

FEMINIST THEORIES

Rebecca West, a British journalist and novelist, once said, "I myself have never been able to find out precisely what feminism is; I only know that people call me a feminist whenever I express sentiments that differentiate me from a doormat." Feminist scholars agree with West and conflict theorists that much of society is characterized by tension and struggle between groups. They go a step further because **feminist theories** try to explain the social, economic, and political position of women in society with a view to freeing women from traditionally oppressive expectations, constraints, roles, and behavior. Thus, feminist perspectives maintain that women suffer injustice because of their sex, and that people should be treated fairly and equally regardless of their race, ethnicity, national origin, age, religion, class, sexual orientation, disability, and other characteristics.

Focusing on Gender

Many feminist scholars contend that women have historically been excluded from most sociological analyses (Smith 1987). Before the 1960s women's movement in the United States, very few sociologists published anything about gender roles, women's sexuality, fathers, or domestic violence. According to sociologist Myra Ferree (2005: B10), during the 1970s, "the Harvard social-science library could fit all its books on gender inequalities onto a single half-shelf." Since then, and be-

symbolic interaction-ism *(interactionism)* a micro-level perspective that looks at individuals' everyday behavior through the communication of knowledge, ideas, beliefs, and attitudes.

interaction action in which people take each other into account in their own behavior.

cause of feminist scholars, many researchers—both women and men—now routinely include gender as an important research variable on both micro and macro levels.

Listening to Many Voices

Feminist scholars contend that gender inequality is central to *all* behavior, from everyday interactions to organization structures and political and economic institutions. As a result, feminist theories encompass many perspectives. For example, *liberal feminism* emphasizes social and legal reform to create equal opportunities for women. *Radical feminism* sees male dominance in social institutions (such as the economy and politics) as the major cause of women's inequality. *Global feminism* focuses on how the intersection of gender with race, social class, and colonization has exploited women in the developing world (see Lengermann and Niebrugge-Brantley 1992). Whether we identify ourselves as feminist or not, most of us are probably liberal (or even radical) feminists because we endorse equal opportunities for women and men in the workplace, politics, education, and other institutions.

Critical Evaluation

Feminist scholars have been effective in challenging discrimination in employment, among other practices, that have routinely excluded women who are not part of the "old boy network" (Wenneras and Wold 1997). One criticism, however, is that many feminists are part of an "old girl network" that has not always welcomed different points of view from black, Asian American, American Indian, Muslim, Latina, lesbian, working-class, and disabled women (Almeida 1994; Lynn and Todoroff 1995; Jackson 1998).

A second criticism is that feminist perspectives tend to downplay social class inequality by focusing on low-income and minority women but not their male counterparts. Thus, some contend, feminist theories are not as gender balanced as they claim. Some, including feminists, also question whether feminist scholars have lost their bearings by focusing on personal issues such as greater sexual freedom rather than broader social issues like poverty and wage inequality (Rowe-Finkbeiner 2004; Chesler 2006).

> "I myself have never been able to find out precisely what feminism is; I only know that people call me a feminist whenever I express sentiments that differentiate **me from a doormat.**"
>
> –Rebecca West, British journalist

SYMBOLIC INTERACTIONISM

Symbolic interactionism (sometimes called *interactionism*) is a micro-level perspective that looks at individuals' everyday behavior through the communication of knowledge, ideas, beliefs, and attitudes. Whereas functionalists and conflict theorists focus on structures and large systems, symbolic interactionists focus on *process* and keep the *person* at the center of their analysis.

There have been many influential symbolic interactionists whom we'll cover in later chapters. In brief, George Herbert Mead's (1863–1931) proposal that the human mind and self arise in the process of social communication became the foundation of the symbolic interactionist schools of thought in sociology and social psychology. Herbert Blumer (1900–1987) coined the term *symbolic interactionism* in 1937, developed Mead's ideas, and emphasized that people interpret or "define" each other's actions instead of merely reacting to them, especially through symbols. Erving Goffman (1922–1982) contributed significantly to these earlier theories by examining human interaction in everyday situations ranging from jobs to funerals.

Constructing Meaning

Our actions are based on **interaction** in the sense that people take each other into account in their own behavior. Thus, we act differently in different social settings and continuously adjust our behavior, including our body language, as we interact (Goffman 1959;

Blumer 1969). A woman's interactions with her husband are different from those with her children. And she will interact still differently when she is teaching a class of students, talking to a colleague in the hall, or addressing an audience of colleagues at a professional conference.

For symbolic interactionists, society is *socially constructed* through human interpretation (O'Brien and Kollock 2001). The daughter who has batting practice with her dad will probably interpret her father's behavior as loving and involved. In contrast, she will see batting practice with her baseball coach as less personal and more goal oriented. In this sense, our interpretations of even the same behavior, such as batting practice, vary across situations and depend on the people with whom we interact.

Symbols and Shared Meanings

Symbolic interactionism looks at subjective, interpersonal meanings and at the ways in which we interact with and influence each other by communicating through *symbols*—words, gestures, or pictures that stand for something and that can have different meanings for different individuals.

After the 9/11 terrorist attacks, many Americans displayed the flag on buildings, bridges, homes, and cars to show their solidarity and pride in the United States. In contrast, some groups in Palestine and Pakistan burned the U.S. flag to show their contempt for American culture and policies. Thus, symbols are powerful forms of communication that show how people feel and interpret a situation.

To interact effectively, our symbols must have *shared meanings*, or agreed-on definitions. One of the most important of these shared meanings is the *definition of the situation*, or the way we perceive reality and react to it. Relationships often end, for example, because partners define emotional closeness differently ("We broke up because Tom wanted sex. I wanted intimacy and conversation."). We typically learn our definitions of the situation through interaction with *significant others*—like parents, friends, relatives, and teachers—who play an important role in our socialization (as you'll see in Chapters 4 and 5).

Critical Evaluation

Unlike other theorists, symbolic interactionists show how people play an active role in shaping their lives on a micro level. One of the most common criticisms, however, is that symbolic interactionism overlooks the widespread impact of macro-level factors such as economic forces, social movements, and public policies on our everyday behavior and relationships. When the U.S. economy began to plunge in mid-2008, for example, more than 75 percent of job losses were concentrated among men. Their unemployment created considerable conflict among married and unmarried couples who suddenly encountered severe financial problems (Whelan 2009). Symbolic interactionism rarely considers such macro-level changes in explaining everyday behavior.

We act differently in different situations.

WORK

PLAY

1 symbol ≠ 1 meaning

The American flag is one symbol, but it has different meanings for different groups.

A related criticism is that interactionists often have an optimistic and unrealistic view of people's everyday choices. Most of us enjoy little flexibility in our daily lives because deeply embedded social arrangements and practices benefit those in power. For example, people are usually powerless when corporations transfer many jobs overseas or cut the pension funds of retired employees.

Some also believe that interaction theory is flawed because it ignores the irrational and unconscious aspects of human behavior (LaRossa and Reitzes 1993). People don't always consider the meaning of their actions or behave as reflectively as interactionists assume. Instead, we often act impulsively or say hurtful things without weighing the consequences of our actions or words.

For a summary of all these perspectives, see *Table 1.1.*

TABLE 1.1
Leading Contemporary Perspectives in Sociology

THEORETICAL PERSPECTIVE	FUNCTIONALIST	CONFLICT	FEMINIST	SYMBOLIC INTERACTIONIST
Level of Analysis	Macro	Macro	Macro and Micro	Micro
Key Points	• Society is composed of interrelated, mutually dependent parts • Structures and functions maintain a society's or group's stability, cohesion, and continuity • Dysfunctional activities that threaten a society's or group's survival are controlled or eliminated	• Life is a continuous struggle between the "haves" and the "have nots" • People compete for limited resources that are controlled by a small number of powerful groups • Society is based on inequality in terms of ethnicity, race, social class, and gender	• Women experience widespread inequality in society because, as a group, they have little power • Gender, ethnicity, race, age, sexual orientation, and social class—rather than a person's intelligence and ability—explain many of our social interactions and lack of access to resources • Social change is possible only if we change our institutional structures and our day-to-day interactions	• People act on the basis of the meaning they attribute to others Meaning grows out of the social interaction that we have with others • People continuously reinterpret and reevaluate their knowledge and information in their everyday encounters
Key Questions	• What holds society together? How does it work? • What is the structure of society? • What functions does society perform? • How do structures and functions contribute to social stability?	• How are resources distributed in a society? • Who benefits when resources are limited? Who loses? • How do those in power protect their privileges? • When does conflict lead to social change?	• Do men and women experience social situations in the same way? • How does our everyday behavior reflect our gender, social class, age, race, ethnicity, sexual orientation, and other factors? • How do macro structures (such as the economy and the political system) shape our opportunities? • How can we change current structures through social activism?	• How does social interaction influence our behavior? • How do social interactions change across situations and between people? • Why does our behavior change because of our beliefs, attitudes, values, and roles? • How is "right" and "wrong" behavior defined, interpreted, reinforced, or discouraged?
Example	• A college education increases one's job opportunities and income	• Most low-income families cannot afford to pay for a college education	• Gender affects decisions about a major and which college to attend	• College students succeed or fail based on their degree of academic engagement

Every day, we are inundated

with information that is false, misleading, and unscientific.

2

Examining Our Social World

what do you think?

Trust your instincts, not research results.

1	2	3	4	5	6	7
strongly agree					strongly disagree	

Spring break is all about beer-fests, wet-T-shirt contests, frolicking on the beach, and hooking up, right? Maybe not. A recent survey found that 70 percent of college students stay home with their parents, and 84 percent of those who throng to vacation spots report consuming alcohol in moderation (The Nielsen Company 2008).

If you suspect that these numbers are too high or too low and wonder how the survey was conducted, you're thinking like a researcher, the focus of this chapter. We'll begin by considering what sociologists mean by social research and how the research affects our everyday lives, examine the scientific method, explore some of the major data collection methods, and end with a discussion of how ethical guidelines shape sociological research.

social research research that examines human behavior.

1 Doing Sociology: What Is Social Research?

Social research examines human behavior. The process requires curiosity and imagination, but also knowing the rules and procedures that guide research aimed at describing and explaining why people behave as they do. Because knowledge is cumulative, social researchers continuously challenge the quality of existing studies and modify their research designs.

You'll recall that sociologists debate whether the discipline can or should be value free, especially in teaching (see Chapter 1). When it comes to research, they agree that the selection of a topic may be subjective (e.g., choosing to examine immigration because of personal experiences or family background), but that the researcher should be objective in collecting, analyzing, and interpreting the data. That is, private beliefs, biases, and value judgments shouldn't intrude on the research process (Gray et al. 2007).

2 Why Is Sociological Research Important in Our Everyday Lives?

how do we know what we know? Much of our knowledge is based on *tradition,* a handing down of statements, beliefs, and customs from generation to generation ("The groom's parents should pay for the wedding rehearsal dinner" or "Flying the American flag at home shows one's patriotism."). Another common source of knowledge is *authority,* a socially accepted source of information that includes experts, parents, government officials, police, judges, and religious leaders ("My mom says that..." or "According to the American Heart Association...").

Knowledge based on tradition and authority simplifies our lives because it provides us with basic rules about socially and legally acceptable behavior. Often, however, the information is misleading or downright incorrect. Suppose a 2-year-old throws a temper tantrum at a family barbecue. One adult comments, "What that kid needs is a smack on the behind." Another person immediately disagrees: "All kids go through this stage. Just ignore it." Who's right? Much research shows that neither ignoring a problem nor inflicting physical punishment (such as spanking) stops a toddler's bad behavior. Instead, according to many researchers, most young children's misbehavior can be curbed by techniques such as making simple rules, being consistent in disciplining misbehavior, praising good behavior, and setting a good example for how to act (see Benokraitis 2011 for the review of this literature).

In contrast with knowledge based on tradition and authority, sociological research is important in our everyday lives for several reasons:

1. **It creates new knowledge that helps us understand social life.** Regarding the economy, for example, sociological research has shown that the law fails to remedy much workplace inequality because it disregards unintentional and unconscious discrimination, and that workplace diversity leads to better products and greater company profits (Berrey 2009).

2. **It exposes myths.** U.S. newspapers and television shows perpetuate the myth that suicides rates are highest during the end of the Christmas holidays. In fact, suicide rates are lowest in December and highest in the spring and fall (but the reasons for these peaks are unclear). Another myth is that more women are victims of domestic violence on Super Bowl Sunday than on any other day of the year, presumably because men are intoxicated and become abusive. In fact, intimate partner violence is common throughout the year and doesn't spike on Super Bowl Sunday (Mikkelson and Mikkelson 2005; Annenberg Public Policy Center 2008).

3. **It affects social policies.** In many states, fatal child abuse or neglect is often undercounted because agencies vary in their interpretations of what constitutes abuse and neglect. For example, a child who is killed in an auto crash because the intoxicated parent had not placed the child in a car seat may be counted as an accident rather than parental neglect (Christensen and Therolf 2009). Sociological research can uncover such systemic flaws, and provide attorneys and social workers with the data they need to change laws that prevent children's deaths because of parental abuse or neglect.

4. **It sharpens our critical thinking skills.** Many Americans, especially women, rely on talk shows such as *Oprah* for information on a number of topics. During 2009 alone, Oprah Winfrey featured and applauded guests who maintained, among other things, that children contract autism from the measles, mumps, and rubella (MMR) vaccinations that they receive as babies, that fortune cards can help people diagnose their illnesses, and that people can wish away cancer (Kosova and Wingert 2009)—all of which are false.

AP Photo/Jennifer Graylock

Oprah Winfrey has regularly featured guests, such as actress Suzanne Somers, pictured here, who dismiss scientific findings about health and endorse treatments such as taking up to 60 vitamin pills every day and wishing cancer away.

5. **It helps us make informed decisions about our everyday lives.** In 2009, 135 college presidents signed a statement asking public officials to reduce the legal drinking age from 21 to 18, primarily because they felt helpless in enforcing legal drinking laws at dorms and local establishments. However, considerable sociological research has shown that lowering the legal drinking age to 18 results in more campus rapes and fatal car accidents, especially for young males (Kaestner and Yarnoff 2009).

theory
+ hypothesis
+ variables
+ data
+ explanation of results
_____
= foundation of scientific method

Image Source/Jupiter Images

3 The Scientific Method

hundreds of thousands of U.S. veterans get treatment for post-traumatic stress disorder (PTSD), using at least 12 different drugs and a variety of psychotherapies (such as cognitive restructuring and group therapy). According to the National Academy of Sciences (2007), however, *scientific* evidence shows that only one treatment may be effective in reducing PTSD symptoms. So, how could science help inform the treatment of U.S. veterans suffering from PTSD?

SCIENTIFIC SOCIOLOGY

To discover patterns that explain behavior, sociologists rely on the **scientific method,** the steps in the research process that include careful data collection, exact measurement, accurate recording and analysis of the findings, thoughtful interpretation of results, and, when appropriate, a generalization of the findings to a larger group. Throughout this process, sociologists (like other social scientists) are interested in the relationships between variables.

Variables and Hypotheses

A **variable** is a characteristic that can change in value or magnitude under different conditions. Variables can be attitudes, behaviors, or traits such as ethnicity, age, and social class.

Scientists can simply ask a research question ("Why do people get a divorce?"), but they usually begin with a **hypothesis,** a statement of a relationship between two or more variables that they want to test ("Unemployment increases the risk of divorce."). In testing a hypothesis, sociologists predict a relationship between an **independent variable,** a characteristic that determines or has an effect, and the **dependent variable,** the outcome. In the previous example of a hypothesis, "unemployment" is the independent variable and "divorce" is the dependent variable.

Reliability and Validity

After asking a research question or stating one or more hypotheses, how do scientists measure the variables? Sociologists are always concerned about the reliability and validity of their measures. **Reliability** is the *consistency* with which the same measure produces similar results time after time. If, for example, you ask, "How old are you?" on two subsequent days and a respondent gives two different answers, such as 25 and 30, there's either something wrong with how you are asking the question or the respondent is lying. Respondents might lie, but scientists try to make sure that their measure is as reliable as possible.

Validity is the degree to which a measure is accurate and *really* measures what it claims to measure.

scientific method the steps in the research process that include careful data collection, exact measurement, accurate recording and analysis of the findings, thoughtful interpretation of results, and, when appropriate, a generalization of the findings to a larger group.

variable a characteristic that can change in value or magnitude under different conditions.

hypothesis a statement of a relationship between two or more variables that researchers want to test.

independent variable a characteristic that determines or has an effect on the dependent variable.

dependent variable the outcome, which may be affected by the independent variable.

reliability the consistency with which the same measure produces similar results time after time.

validity the degree to which a measure is accurate and really measures what it claims to measure.

deductive reasoning
an inquiry process that begins with a theory, prediction, or general principle that is then tested through data collection.

inductive reasoning an inquiry process that begins with a specific observation, followed by data collection, a general conclusion, or theory construction.

population any well-defined group of people (or things) about whom researchers want to know something.

sample a group of people (or things) that are representative of the population researchers wish to study.

probability sample a sample for which each person (or thing, such as an e-mail address) has an equal chance of being selected because the selection is random.

Consider student course evaluations. The measures of a "good" professor often include items such as "The instructor is interesting" and "The instructor is fair." Because we don't really know what students mean by "interesting" and "fair," how accurate are such measures in differentiating between "good" and "bad" professors?

Deductive and Inductive Reasoning

Deduction and induction are two different but equally valuable approaches for examining the relationship between variables. Generally, **deductive reasoning** begins with a theory, prediction, or general principle that is then tested through data collection. An alternative mode of inquiry, **inductive reasoning,** begins with specific observations, followed by data collection, a general conclusion, or theory construction (see *Figure 2.1*).

Using a deductive approach, you might want to test a theory of academic success in which one of your hypotheses is the following: "Students who study in groups perform better on exams than those who study alone." You would collect relevant data, ultimately confirming or rejecting your hypotheses and theory. On the other hand, you might notice that your classmates who participate in study groups seem to get higher grades on exams than those who study alone. Using an inductive approach, you would detect patterns (or lack of them), collect data systematically, formulate hypotheses, and suggest a theory that could then be tested deductively. Most social science research involves both inductive and deductive reasoning.

SAMPLING

Early in the research process, sociologists decide what sampling procedures they will use. Ideally, researchers would like to study all the units of the population in which they are interested—say, all adolescents who use

drugs. A **population** is any well-defined group of people (or things) about which researchers want to know something. Obtaining information from populations is problematic, however. The population may be so large that it would be too expensive and time consuming to conduct the research. In other cases—such as that of all adolescents who use drugs—it may be impossible even to identify the population.

Researchers typically select a **sample,** a group of people (or things) that are representative of the population they wish to study. In obtaining a sample, researchers must decide whether to use probability or nonprobability sampling. A **probability sample** is one for which each person (or thing, such as an e-mail address) has an equal chance of being selected because the selec-

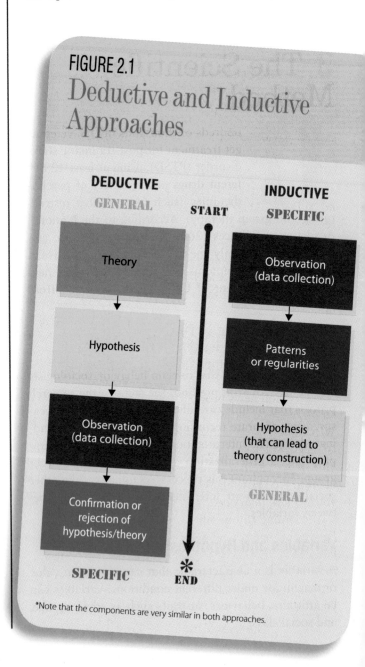

FIGURE 2.1
Deductive and Inductive Approaches

*Note that the components are very similar in both approaches.

Are American Idol voters an example of a probability or non-probability sample of the show's fans?

tion process is *random.* The most desirable feature of a probability sample is that the results can be generalized to the larger population because the people (or things) have had an equal chance of being selected through randomization.

A **nonprobability sample** is any sample for which little or no attempt is made to get a representative cross section of the population. Instead, researchers use sampling criteria such as convenience or the availability of respondents or information. Nonprobability samples are very useful when sociologists are exploring a new topic or want to get insights on how people feel about a particular topic before launching a larger study (Babbie 2002).

Television news programs, newsmagazines, and entertainment shows often provide a toll-free number or a Web address and encourage viewers to vote on an issue (such as whether U.S. troops should leave Afghanistan). How representative are these voters of the general population? And how many enthusiasts skew the results by voting more than once?

According to one observer, most Internet polls are "good for a few laughs" but are little more than "the latest in a long series of junk masquerading as indicators of public opinion because the participants aren't representative of everyone's opinion" (Wilt 1998). But, you might think, if as many as 100,000 people respond to a poll, doesn't such a large number indicate how peo-

ple think? No. Because the respondents are self-selected and don't comprise a random sample, they're not representative of the entire population.

> **nonprobability sample** a sample for which little or no attempt is made to get a representative cross section of the population.

THE RESEARCH PROCESS: THE BASICS

Hypotheses construction, establishing reliability and validity, using deductive and inductive reasoning, and sampling are some of the preliminary and often most challenging steps in the research process. The process itself involves seven basic steps illustrated in *Figure 2.2,* which outlines the scientific method using a deductive approach beginning with an idea and ending with writing up (and sometimes publishing) the results.

1. **Choose a topic to study.** Good research is generally guided by theory. The topic can be general or very specific. Some sociologists begin with a new and unexplored idea; others extend or refine previous research findings. A topic can generate new information, replicate a previous study, or propose an intervention (such as implementing a new program for children in foster homes).

2. **Summarize the related research.** In what is often called a *literature review,* the sociologist summarizes the pertinent research, shows how her or his topic is related to previous and ongoing research, and indicates how the study will extend the body of knowledge in an area. Or, if the research is applied, the sociologist demonstrates that the proposed service or program will improve people's lives. In both cases, a summary of the related research makes clear the study's theoretical base, and shows how the approach is systematic and cumulative in terms of past research.

3. **Formulate a hypothesis or ask a research question.** The sociologist next states a hypothesis or asks a research question. In either case, she or he needs to be sure that the measures of the variables are reliable and valid.

4. **Describe the data collection method(s).** In this step of the research process, the sociologist describes which method or combination of methods, sometimes called *methodology, procedure,* or *research design,* is best for testing the hypothesis or answering the research question. As you'll see shortly, each data collection technique has strengths and weaknesses that the researcher considers in deciding which data

collection method is the most appropriate. The sociologist also describes the sampling technique, the sample size, and the characteristics of the respondents.

5. Collect the data. The actual data collection might rely on field work, surveys, experiments, or existing sources of information such as Census Bureau data.

6. **Present the findings.** After coding (tabulating the results), running statistical tests, and analyzing the data, the sociologist presents the findings as clearly as possible. Because data can be interpreted in many ways, it's up to the researcher to keep the summary of findings focused and understandable to the reader.

7. **Analyze and explain the results.** After presenting the data, the sociologist explains why the findings are important. This can be done in many ways. The researcher might show how the results provide new information, enrich our understanding of behavior or attitudes that researchers have examined previously, or refine existing theories or research approaches.

In drawing conclusions about the study, the sociologist typically discusses the study's implications. For instance, does a study of juvenile arrests suggest that new policies should be implemented, existing ones should be changed, or that current police practices may be affecting the results? That is, the researcher answers the question "So what?" by showing the importance and usefulness of the study.

QUALITATIVE AND QUANTITATIVE APPROACHES

The scientific method is important in both qualitative and quantitative approaches. In **qualitative research**, sociologists examine non-numerical material that they then interpret. In a study of grandfathers who were raising their grandchildren, for example, the researcher tape-recorded in-depth interviews and then analyzed the responses to questions such as financial worries and daily parenting activities (Bullock 2005).

In **quantitative research**, sociologists focus on a numerical analysis of people's responses or specific characteristics, studying a wide range of attitudes, behaviors, and traits (such as homeowners vs. renters). In one

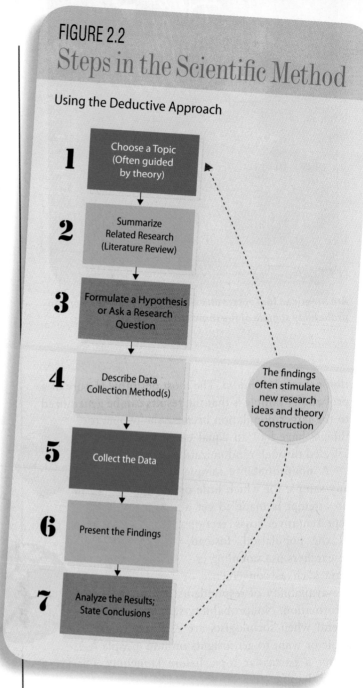

FIGURE 2.2
Steps in the Scientific Method

Using the Deductive Approach

1 Choose a Topic (Often guided by theory)

2 Summarize Related Research (Literature Review)

3 Formulate a Hypothesis or Ask a Research Question

4 Describe Data Collection Method(s)

5 Collect the Data

6 Present the Findings

7 Analyze the Results; State Conclusions

The findings often stimulate new research ideas and theory construction

study, for example, the researchers analyzed data from a national probability survey of almost 7,000 respondents to examine the influence of grandparents who live with their children and grandchildren (Dunifon and Kowaleski-Jones 2007).

Which approach should a sociologist use? It depends on her or his purpose. Quantitative data can provide valuable information on characteristics such as national college graduation rates. Qualitative data, in contrast, might yield in-depth descriptions of why some college students drop out whereas others graduate. In many cases, sociologists use both approaches.

CORRELATION AND CAUSATION

Sociologists have found that some of the best predictors of divorce include marrying at a young age, having children before marriage, and experiencing domestic violence (see Chapter 13). This does not mean, however, that these and other characteristics *cause* divorce. Instead, divorce is more *likely* or *probable* in certain situations (when the marital partners are teenagers, for example).

Because nothing in life (except death) is certain, sociologists talk about *correlation*—the extent of the relationship between variables—rather than causation. They rarely use the term *cause* when interpreting their results because they cannot prove that a cause-and-effect relationship exists. Instead, sociologists "can only *suggest,* or at most *indicate*" a relationship between variables (Glenn 2001). Thus, a researcher would say that marrying at a young age is "more likely" to result in divorce, is "associated (or correlated)" with divorce, or "contributes to" rather than "causes" divorce.

Consider another example of the difference between correlation and causation. In a recent study that received considerable media attention, the researchers recruited 510 undergraduates from five colleges. The study concluded that students living in coed dorms were far more likely than those living in single-sex residence halls to consume alcohol regularly, to have more sexual partners, to use pornography more frequently, and to have more permissive attitudes toward sexual activity. The authors found a correlation (association) between these dependent variables and choice of residence halls (the independent variable), but incorrectly implied causation with statements such as coed housing "created" risk-taking behavior (Willoughby and Carroll 2009: 245–246).

4 Some Major Data Collection Methods

during the research process, sociologists typically use one or more of the following data collection methods: surveys, secondary analysis of existing data, field research, content analysis, experiments, and evaluation research. Because each technique has benefits and limitations, a sociologist must consider which will provide the most accurate information given time and budget constraints.

SURVEYS

Every 10 years, the Census Bureau tries to count every person living in the United States, and has done so since 1790. The Census Bureau is required by law to count every person, people are legally required to fill out the census form, and the information is kept confidential. The data are important in determining the number of Congressional representatives in each state and deciding how $450 billion in federal funds will be allocated annually to state and federal governments (Hare 2009).

Despite the decennial Census Bureau count, on average only about 66 percent of Americans fill out and return the census form (Hare 2009). People don't fill out the forms for a variety of reasons: They are suspicious of how the collected data will be used, don't realize the significance of the census, experience language barriers in understanding the form, and/or believe that the census won't change their lives because they're poor or can't find jobs (Bulik 2009).

Most social scientists, including sociologists, use **surveys** to systematically collect data from respondents using questionnaires, face-to-face or telephone interviews, or a combination of these methods. Questionnaires can be mailed, used during an interview, or self-administered (such as student course evaluations). *Random sample surveys* are preferred because the results can be generalized to a larger population, but it's often difficult to determine the population from which a random sample is drawn.

Telephone interviews are popular because they're a relatively inexpensive way to collect data. Researchers can obtain representative samples through *random-digit dialing,* which involves selecting area codes and exchanges (the next three numbers) followed by four random digits. In the procedure called *computer-assisted telephone interviewing* (CATI), the interviewer uses a computer to select random telephone numbers, reads the questions to the respondent from a computer screen, and then enters the replies in precoded spaces, saving time and expense by not having to reenter the data after the interview.

Advantages

Surveys are usually inexpensive, simple to administer, and have a fast turnaround.

surveys a systematic method for collecting data from respondents, including questionnaires, face-to-face or telephone interviews, or a combination of these.

Stockbyte/Getty Images

Because the results are anonymous, respondents are generally willing to answer questions on sensitive topics such as income, sexual behavior, and the use of drugs (Hamby and Finkelhor 2001).

Face-to-face interviews have high response rates (often up to 99 percent) compared with other data-collection techniques because they involve personal contact. In-depth interviews can provide rich detail about the respondent's social world and vivid descriptions of personal experiences, such as the emotional consequences of having a baby or losing a job. People are more likely to discuss such sensitive issues in an interview than via a mailed questionnaire or a phone survey (Weiss 2004).

Interviewers can also record a respondent's body language, facial expressions, and intonations, which can be useful in interpreting verbal responses. If a respondent doesn't understand a question or is reluctant to answer, the interviewer can clarify or probe. An astute interviewer can also gather information on variables such as social class by observing the respondent's home and neighborhood.

The Internet is an increasingly popular place for surveys. It can be an inexpensive means of collecting data because no interviewer is needed. In addition, Internet surveys provide respondents with visual material, including videos, to look at and respond to (Keeter 2009).

Disadvantages

One of the major limitations of surveys that use mailed questionnaires is a low response rate, often only about 10 percent (Gray et al. 2007). If the questions are unclear, complicated, or seen as offensive, a respondent may simply throw the questionnaire away. Others give answers that conform to socially desirable standards. For example, the proportion of Americans who say they voted in a given election is always higher than the actual number of votes cast in the election (Radwin 2009).

Another problem with surveys is that people may skip questions or lie about questions that they feel are "too nosy." If respondents lie or ignore questions, the research results will be invalid or limited (because the researcher might have to exclude a key variable such as income).

Unlike questionnaires and telephone surveys, face-to-face interviews can be very expensive. Also, people may be less candid if the interviewer is of the other sex,

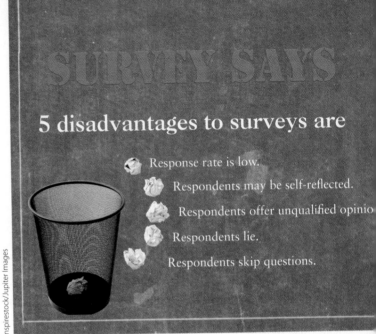

5 disadvantages to surveys are

- Response rate is low.
- Respondents may be self-reflected.
- Respondents offer unqualified opinio
- Respondents lie.
- Respondents skip questions.

InspirestStock/Jupiter Images

and the interview environment itself can affect responses. For example, women may be less willing to admit they have been raped if questioned by men, by interviewers of a different racial or ethnic background, or in the presence of family members (Herod 1993; Kane and Macaulay 1993).

Public opinion polls, common on television and in newspapers, often use surveys. Sociologist Joel Best (2001) suggests asking three basic questions about the numbers: (1) Who created these numbers? (2) Why were these numbers created? (3) How were these numbers created? Asking a few other basic questions about a survey, like those in *Table 2.1*, will help you evaluate its credibility.

SECONDARY ANALYSIS

Sociologists also rely heavily on **secondary analysis,** an unobtrusive form of data collection that examines information that has been collected by someone else. The data may be historical materials (such as court proceedings), personal documents (such as letters and diaries), public records (such as state archives on births, marriages, and deaths), and official statistics (such as health information from the Centers for Disease Control and Prevention).

Advantages

In most cases, secondary analysis is convenient and inexpensive. Census Bureau data on topics such as income and employment are readily available at public college and university libraries and online. Also, many academic

TABLE 2.1
Can I Trust These Numbers?

To determine a survey's credibility, ask:

- Who sponsored the survey? A government agency, a nonprofit partisan organization, a business, or a group that's lobbying for change?
- What is the purpose of the survey? To provide objective information, to promote an idea or a political candidate, or to get attention through sensationalism?
- How was the sample drawn? Randomly? Or was it a "self-selected opinion poll" (a SLOP, according to Tanur 1994)?
- How were the questions worded? Were they clear, objective, loaded, or biased? If the survey questions are not provided, why not?
- How did the researchers report their findings? Were they objective, or did they make value judgments?

institutions buy tapes or CD-ROMs containing national, regional, and local data that can be used for faculty or student research, or for class-related projects.

In secondary analysis, the data are *longitudinal* (collected at two or more points in time based on the same or different samples of respondents) and *cross-sectional* (collected at one point in time). Both time frames provide useful information, but longitudinal research is especially suitable in examining changes of behavior or attitudes by comparing similar populations during different years or following a particular group of people over time. Thus, secondary analysis of existing data allows researchers to examine trends, such as voting patterns or attitudes about the death penalty, as well as information that was collected once, such as during March 2012.

Disadvantages

Existing data sources may not have the information a researcher needs. For example, some of the statistics on remarriages and redivorces have been collected only since the early 1990s. Thus, it would be impossible for a researcher to compare these behaviors over decades. It may also be difficult to gain access to historical materials because the documents may be fragile, housed in only a few libraries in the country, or held in private collections.

If the existing sources don't include information the researcher is looking for, she or he may have to change the direction of the research or exclude some variables. If you wanted to find out why some mothers deliberately kill their infants, for example, you'd find very little national data (Meyer and Oberman 2001). Consequently, you'd have to rely on studies with small and nonrepresentative samples or collect such data yourself.

field research data collection by systematically observing people in their natural surroundings.

FIELD RESEARCH

In **field research,** sociologists collect data by systematically observing people in their natural surroundings. In *participant observation*, researchers interact with the people they are studying, and may or may not reveal their identities as researchers (as you'll see shortly). If you recorded interaction patterns between students and professors during your classes, you would be engaging in participant observation.

In *nonparticipant observation*, researchers study phenomena without being part of the situation. For example, child psychologists, clinicians, and sociologists often study young children in classrooms through one-way mirrors. In several studies, field researchers followed more than 400 parents and their 2- to 5-year-old children in grocery stores, noting parents' interaction with their kids. The researchers found that good-looking children, especially boys, got more attention from their parents. The "pretty" kids were more likely than the unattractive ones to be buckled into the shopping cart instead of allowed to stand up in the cart and to be held by the hand instead of being permitted to wander away (Harrell 2005; for a discussion of the variations in observational research, see Adler and Adler 1994).

In field research, some studies are short (such as the study of parents and their children in grocery stores). Others, often called *ethnologies,* require a considerable amount of time in the field. For example, Sudhir Venkatesh (2008), while a graduate student at the University of Chicago, spent more than 6 years studying the culture and members of the Black Kings, a crack-selling gang in Chicago's inner city.

Observational studies are usually highly structured and carefully designed research projects in which data are recorded and then converted to quantitative summaries. These studies may examine complex communication patterns, measure the frequency of acts (such as the number of head nods or angry statements), or note the duration of a particular behavior (such as the length of eye contact) (Stillars 1991). Thus, observational studies are much more complex and sophisticated than they appear to be to the general public or an inexperienced researcher.

Researchers sometimes combine participant and nonparticipant observation. Sociologist Elijah Anderson, for example, focused much of his research on households in West Philadelphia, an inner-city black community with high crime rates. As a nonparticipant observer, Anderson watched "decent" and "street" family members to learn how and why some poor residents take extraordinary measures to conform to mainstream values (such as maintaining a strong family life), whereas others engage in crime and violence (Anderson 1999). Over the years, Anderson's role of detached observer morphed into that of participant observer as he became personally involved with some of his research subjects. For example, he hired an ex-drug dealer as a part-time research assistant, found community members lawyers or jobs, encouraged his respondents to stay out of crime, and even loaned them money (Cose 1999).

Field researchers study a variety of topics, including how customers, cocktail waitresses, bouncers, and paid consultants often engage in deception, hustling, and bribes to help people hook up with someone at a nightclub (see Grazian 2008 for a description of this study).

© Ianni Dimitrov/Alamy

Advantages

Unlike secondary analysis and most surveys, field research provides an in-depth understanding of attitudes and behavior. Observation is also more flexible than some other methods because the researcher can modify the research design, for example, by deciding to interview (rather than just observe) key people after the research has started (see Bailey 2007 for a discussion of these and other advantages of field research).

Because observation doesn't disrupt the natural surroundings, the researcher doesn't directly influence the subjects. In *Nickel and Dimed,* a study based on participant observation, journalist Barbara Ehrenreich (2001) worked at several low-income jobs (such as waitressing in Florida and clerking in a Wal-Mart in Minnesota) to find out whether lower wage American workers could survive on their earnings. Ehrenreich's conclusion that people can't get by on a $7-per-hour job supported what sociologists had been saying for decades. Because she is a best-selling journalist, however, Ehrenreich's project has become a well-known example of field research.

Disadvantages

If a researcher needs elaborate recording equipment, must travel far or often, or has to live in a different society or community for an extended period, observation can be expensive. Researchers who study other cultures must often learn a new language, a time-consuming task.

Doing field work in a country that's wracked by war may be dangerous for both researchers and respondents. In a study of the major causes of death before and after the U.S. invasion of Iraq, for example, a team of American researchers feared the possibility of being killed or abducted. The researchers also had difficulty recruiting interviewers who were willing to travel to some of the most dangerous neighborhoods and convince subjects to participate in a study conducted by Americans (Guterman 2005).

A field researcher may also encounter barriers to collecting the desired data. Homeless and battered women's shelters, for example, are usually—and understandably—wary of researchers' intruding on their residents' privacy.

CONTENT ANALYSIS

Content analysis is a method of studying social behavior that systematically examines some form of communication. This is an unobtrusive approach that a researcher can apply to virtually any form of written

FIGURE 2.3
How Do Views of Female and Male Babies Differ?

As the cards illustrate, girls and boys are viewed differently from the time they are born. In these and other birth announcements, girls, but not boys, are typically described as "sweet" or "precious." Also, images usually show boys as active but girls as passive.

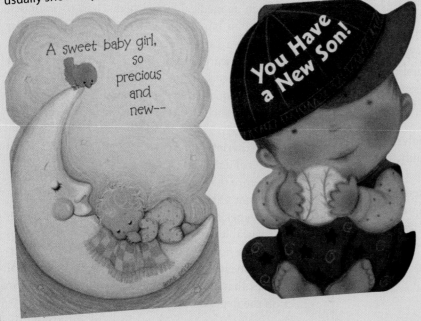

A sweet baby girl, so precious and new—

You Have a New Son!

roles? These are only two cards, but we could do a content analysis of all such cards at a particular store or of a large sample of cards from a number of stores to determine whether these kinds of cards reinforce stereotypical gender role expectations.

Sociologists have used content analysis to examine the depictions of minority groups in sociology college textbooks, media coverage of heavy metal and rap music, images of women and men in advertisements, and changes in childrearing advice in popular parenting magazines (Binder 1993; Shaw-Taylor and Benokraitis 1995; Larson and Hickman 2004; Rutherford 2009).

Advantages

A major advantage of content analysis is that it is usually inexpensive and sometimes less time consuming than other data collection methods (especially surveys and field research). If, for example, you wanted to examine the content of television commercials aimed at older people, you wouldn't need fancy equipment, a travel budget, or a research staff.

or oral communication: speeches, TV programs, newspaper articles, advertisements, office memos, songs, diaries, advice columns, poems, or e-mails, to mention just a few. The researcher develops categories for coding the material, sorts and analyzes the content of the material in terms of frequency, intensity, or other characteristics, and draws conclusions about the results.

For example, look at the two greeting cards in *Figure 2.3*. What messages do they send about gender

Counting the homeless is an ongoing research problem. Communities must provide accurate numbers to qualify for federal funds, but census takers have difficulty getting such counts because safety rules prohibit them from entering private property (such as warehouses) or dark alleys. In one approach, the YWCA in Trenton, New Jersey, gave free haircuts at a fair for the homeless to attract the city's homeless people to a place where they could be counted (Jonsson 2007). Is such field research unethical because it violates people's privacy? Or is it innovative in helping a community get more federal funding for the homeless?

AP Photo/Mel Evans

A second advantage is that researchers can correct coding errors fairly easily by redoing the work. This is not the case with surveys. If you mail a questionnaire with poorly constructed items, it's too late. A third advantage is that content analysis is unobtrusive. Because researchers aren't dealing with human subjects, they don't need permission to do the research or worry about influencing the respondents' attitudes or behavior.

A fourth advantage is that content analysis often permits comparisons over time. In one study, the researchers examined the amount and intensity of violence in children's animated movies that were released between 1938 and 1999 (Yokota and Thompson 2000). It would be very difficult, using most other data collection methods, to collect information about or analyze a phenomenon over a 62-year period.

Disadvantages

Content analysis can be very labor intensive, especially if a project is ambitious. In the research on children's animated movies, it took several years to code one or more of the major characters' words, expressions, and actions.

A related disadvantage is that coding material is very subjective. Having several researchers on a project can decrease subjectivity. Many content analyses are performed by only one researcher, however, decreasing the likelihood that the coding is objective.

Finally, content analysis often reflects social class biases. Because most books, articles, speeches, films, and so forth are produced by people in upper socioeconomic levels, content analysis rarely captures the behavior or attitudes of working classes and the poor. Even when documents created by lower-class individuals or groups are available, it's difficult to determine whether the researchers reflect social class prejudices in their coding.

EXPERIMENTS

Experiments are more common among physical scientists (such as medical researchers) than sociologists, but they are an important data collection method. An **experiment** is a carefully controlled artificial situation that allows researchers to manipulate variables and measure the effects. In the classic experimental design, there are two equal-size groups that are very similar in characteristics such as sex, age, ethnicity or race, and education.

In the **experimental group**, the subjects are exposed to the independent variable. In the **control group**, they are not. Before the experiment, the researcher measures the dependent variable in both groups using a *pretest*. After the experimental group is exposed to the independent variable, the researcher measures both groups again using a *post-test*. If the researcher finds a difference in the measures of the dependent variable, she or he assumes that the independent variable is having an effect on the dependent variable.

In a recent study, the researchers at a large public university divided their introductory sociology classes into experimental and control groups. Both groups had the same readings, lectures, instructor, films, and active learning exercises. In the experimental group, however, the professor incorporated a comedic clip, ranging from 1 to 6 minutes, toward the end of the class. The purpose of the clips (such as from Jon Stewart's *The Daily Show, The Colbert Report,* and George Carlin's sketches) was to launch a group discussion or active learning exercises that demonstrated sociological thinking and concepts

Are many sociologists, comedians, and television satirists (such as Jon Stewart, pictured here) similar in encouraging critical thinking about social life?

AP Photo/Jason DeCrow

An Experiment That Went Awry

In a well-known 1973 experiment, psychologist Philip Zimbardo created a mock prison, using 21 undergraduate volunteers as prisoners and guards. The experiment was stopped after 6 days because some of the participants experienced intense negative reactions, and the study raised several ethical questions. For more information about this study, go to Stanford Prison Experiment, at www.prisonexp.org. We'll examine this study in more detail in Chapter 6.

such as "alienation," "social class," and "conflict theory."

Compared with the control groups, the experimental groups (who viewed the clips) had higher scores and final grades, lower rates of withdrawal, and higher completion of online discussion questions. In addition, many of the students in the experimental groups began to bring in their own clips that illustrated sociological concepts. The researchers concluded that comedy is a useful tool in exploring sociological concepts because it resonates with students, and that "there is much to learn about social life by exploring what we laugh at and why" (Bingham and Hernandez 2009: 350).

Advantages

A major strength of experiments is that they come closer than any other data collection method in suggesting a cause-and-effect relationship. Experiments are usually (but not always) less expensive and time consuming than other data collection techniques (especially large surveys and multiyear field research), and there's often no need to purchase special equipment. A related strength is that because researchers recruit students or other volunteers (as in medical research) for their experiments, subjects are usually readily available and don't expect much, if any, monetary compensation.

A third advantage is that experiments can be replicated many times with different subjects. Such replication strengthens the researchers' confidence in the validity and reliability of the measures and the study's results. For example, doctors stopped prescribing hormone pills for menopausal women because better-designed experiments that replicated earlier studies found

that the pills increased the risk for breast cancer and strokes (Ioannidis 2005).

Disadvantages

A major disadvantage of laboratory experiments is that "the conditions so carefully controlled for the purpose of establishing causality may be so atypical or artificial that it becomes difficult to generalize from them to the outside world" (Gray et al. 2007: 280). Especially in laboratory settings, subjects know that they're being studied and might behave very differently than if they were in a natural setting (Babbie 2002).

A second drawback is that researchers must rely on volunteers, paid subjects, or a captive audience, such as college students who participate in faculty experiments. Students may resent being required to be in an experiment or might volunteer to do so (self-select) to win favor with a professor.

A third disadvantage is the possibility that the conclusions drawn from experiments may not be accurate. Among other problems, attrition among the subjects may be very high, the members of experimental and control groups may communicate with each other about what's going on and behave differently as a result, and the presence of a researcher may affect the behavior of the subjects (Cook and Campbell 1979; see also Chapter 6 on the Hawthorne effect).

Another limitation is that controlled laboratory settings are not suitable for studying large groups of people, a major focus in sociology. As you saw in Chapter 1, many sociologists examine macro-level issues (such as employment trends) that can't be observed in a laboratory setting.

TABLE 2.2
Some Data Collection Methods in Sociological Research

METHOD	EXAMPLE	ADVANTAGES	DISADVANTAGES
Surveys	Sending questionnaires and/or interviewing students on why they succeeded in college or dropped out	Questionnaires are fairly inexpensive and simple to administer; interviews have high response rates; findings are often generalizable	Mailed questionnaires may have low response rates; respondents may be self-selected; interviews are usually expensive
Secondary analysis	Using data from the National Center for Education Statistics (or similar organizations) to examine why students drop out of college	Usually accessible, convenient and inexpensive; often longitudinal and historical	Information may be incomplete; some documents may be inaccessible; some data can't be collected over time
Field research	Observing first-year college students with high and low grade-point averages (GPAs) regarding their classroom participation and other activities	Flexible; offers deeper understanding of social behavior; usually inexpensive	Difficult to quantify and to maintain observer/subject boundaries; the observer may be biased or judgmental; findings are not generalizable
Content analysis	Comparing the transcripts of college graduates and dropouts on variables such as gender, race/ethnicity, and social class	Usually inexpensive; can recode errors easily; unobtrusive; permits comparisons over time	Can be labor-intensive; coding is often subjective (and may be distorted); may reflect social class biases
Experiments	Providing tutors to some students with low GPAs to find out if such resources increase college graduation rates	Usually inexpensive; plentiful supply of subjects; can be replicated	Volunteers and paid subjects aren't representative of a larger population; the laboratory setting is artificial
Evaluation research	Examining student records; interviewing administrators, faculty, and students; observing students in a variety of settings (such as classroom and extracurricular activities); and using surveys to determine students' employment and family responsibilities	Usually inexpensive; valuable in real-life applications	Often political; findings might be rejected

EVALUATION RESEARCH

Evaluation research—which uses all of the standard data collection techniques described so far—assesses the effectiveness of social programs in both the public and the private sectors. Many government and non-profit agencies provide services that affect families and other groups both directly and indirectly. Examples include housing programs, programs to prevent teenage pregnancy, work-training programs, and drug-rehabilitation programs. Because local and state government budgets have been cut since the early 1980s, social service agencies have become increasingly concerned about the efficiency of their programs and often rely on evaluation research to streamline their services.

In evaluation research, sociologists use a variety of data collection methods such as examining an organization's records (secondary analysis and content analysis), surveys to gauge employee and client satisfaction, and interviews with the staff and program recipients. Unlike the other data collection methods we've looked at, evaluation research is *applied* because it compares a program's achievements with its goals (Weiss 1998). The research findings are generally used to improve the operations of the program.

Advantages

Evaluation research is important because it examines actual efforts to deal with social problems such as homelessness and poverty. If the researchers rely on secondary analysis, the data collection costs are usually low. Also, the findings can be very valuable to program directors or agency heads in showing discrepancies between the original objectives and the program's actual functioning and accomplishments (Card et al. 1994).

Disadvantages

Practitioners rarely welcome the results of evaluation research if a sociologist concludes that a particular program isn't working. For example, since its inception in 1983, the DARE (Drug Abuse Resistance Education) program—which has relied on trained volunteers from local police departments to address grade-school children on the dangers of drug use—has been popular with schools, police departments, parents, and politicians across the country. When social scientists evaluated DARE in 1994, 1998, and 1999, however, they found that there was no significant difference in the drug use of students who had completed the DARE curriculum and those who hadn't done so. When the DARE funding was threatened, its promoters dismissed the evaluation research results as "voodoo science" (Miller 2001).

RECAP OF RESEARCH APPROACHES

In summary, researchers have to weigh the benefits and limitations of each research approach in designing their studies (see *Table 2.2*). Often, they use a combination of methods because "many sociologists view the social world as a multi-faceted and multi-layered reality that reveals itself only in part with any single method" (Jacobs 2005: 4). Despite a researcher's commitment to objectivity, ethical debates and politically charged disagreements can influence sociological research.

> **evaluation research**
> research that uses all of the standard data collection techniques to assess the effectiveness of social programs in both the public and the private sectors.

5 Ethics, Politics, and Sociological Research

In a scene in the movie *Kinsey* (released in 2004), government agents seize a box of materials being shipped by Dr. Alfred C. Kinsey, the pioneering sex researcher, and confiscate the contents because they're "obscene." Have such attitudes toward sex research changed? And, if so, what other ethical and political dilemmas do sociologists (and other social scientists) encounter in conducting their research?

ETHICAL RESEARCH

Because so much research relies on human subjects, the federal government and many professional organizations have devised codes of ethics to protect the participants. Regardless of the discipline or the research methods used, all ethical standards have at least three golden rules, but their implementation is sometimes more complicated than it seems.

- First, *do no harm* by causing subjects physical, psychological, or emotional pain. Not causing physical harm is pretty obvious, but how do researchers know if the participants are experiencing emotional or psychological harm? If a subject becomes agitated in answering some questions (such as about rape or the death of a loved one), she or he has every right to not respond or drop out of the study.

TABLE 2.3
Some Basic Principles of Ethical Sociological Research

The American Sociological Association (1999) has published ethical codes and guidelines for researchers. The key elements tell researchers that they . . .

- Must obtain all subjects' consent to participate in the research and their permission to quote from their responses and comments;
- May not exploit subjects or research assistants involved in the research for personal gain;
- Must never harm, humiliate, abuse, or coerce the participants in their studies, either physically or psychologically;
- Must honor all guarantees to participants of privacy, anonymity, and confidentiality;
- Must use the highest methodological standards and be as accurate as possible;
- Must describe the limitations and shortcomings of the research in their published reports;
- Must identify the sponsors who funded the research; and
- Must acknowledge the contributions of research assistants (usually underpaid and overworked graduate students) who participate in the research project.

was jailed briefly for refusing to reveal what he knew about animal rights' groups that had vandalized a university research laboratory using animals (Jaschik 2009). *Table 2.3* provides some of the basic ethical principles in conducting sociological research.

Some disciplines seem to be more susceptible to ethical violations than others. During the last several years, medical researchers, especially, have been accused of considerable scientific misconduct. Some of the alleged violations have included changing the research results to please the corporation (usually tobacco and pharmaceutical industries) that sponsored the research, being paid by companies to deliver speeches to health practitioners that endorse specific drugs even though the medications don't reduce health problems, and attaching their names to articles in prestigious periodicals (such as *The New England Journal of Medicine*) that have been prepared by "ghost writers" who have been well-paid by pharmaceutical companies. In return, the medical researchers, who are often physicians, receive considerable financial support for their research (e.g., see Mello et al. 2005; Henschke et al. 2006; Harris 2008; Basken 2009a, 2009b; Blumenstyk 2009).

In the social sciences, some data collection methods are more susceptible to ethical violations than others. Surveys, secondary analysis, and content analysis are less vulnerable than field research and experiments because the researchers typically don't interact directly with subjects, affect them, or become personally involved with the respondents. In contrast, experiments and field research can raise ethical questions due to deception or influencing the subjects' attitudes or behavior.

POLITICAL, RELIGIOUS, AND COMMUNITY PRESSURE

The legitimacy of social science research is especially likely to be challenged when studies focus on sensitive social, moral, and political issues. Research on teenage

- Second, the researcher must get the subject's *informed consent* to be in the study. This includes the subject's knowing what the study is about and how the results will be used. Sociologists can use deception (such as not revealing that they are researchers) if doing so doesn't harm the participants, if the research has been approved by an institutional review board (usually either at the university or by the federal government), and if the researcher explains the purpose of the data collection at the conclusion of the research (American Sociological Association 1999: 14).
- Third, researchers must protect a subject's *confidentiality,* even if the participant has broken a law. Recently, for example, a graduate student in sociology

sexual behavior is valuable because it provides information that public health agencies and schools can circulate about sexually transmitted diseases, such as HIV, and contraception. Nonetheless, many local jurisdictions have refused to let social scientists study adolescent sexual behavior. Some parents believe that such research violates student privacy and might make a school district look bad (e.g., if a study reports a high incidence of drug use or sexual activity) (Kempner et al. 2005).

Moreover, some religious groups, school administrators, and politicians have opposed such studies because they believe that the research undermines traditional family values or makes deviant behavior look normal. As a result, many social scientists don't do research on some of the most controversial issues because there is no funding or because a study would be opposed by a variety of groups that get considerable media attention (Carey 2004).

Local and national advocacy groups also have a vested interest in ignoring research studies that might jeopardize their funding. For example, the National Alliance for the Mentally Ill embraces claims on the prevalence of mental disorders that are based on flawed community studies and that contend that half of Americans suffer from a mental disorder at some point, especially depression. In fact, better designed studies show that about 75 percent of depressive symptoms are normal and temporary (such as worrying about an upcoming exam or grieving the death of a family member or friend). If mental health organizations can convince politicians that mental illness is widespread, they can get more funding for mental health services. And pharmaceutical companies are eager to sell antidepressant drugs to alleviate depression. As a result, many mental health organizations and pharmaceutical companies benefit by labeling even normal depression as an "overwhelming problem" (Horwitz and Wakefield 2006: 23).

Even people who pride

themselves on their individualism conform to cultural rules.

3 Culture

what do you think?

I shape my culture;
my culture doesn't shape me.

1 2 3 4 5 6 7
strongly agree   strongly disagree

1 Culture and Society

Once when I returned a set of exams, a student who was unhappy with his grade blurted out an obscenity. A voice from the back of the classroom snapped, "You ain't got no culture, man!" The remark implied that refined people don't curse and that proper classroom behavior doesn't include using vulgar language.

As popularly used, *culture* often means appreciating the finer things in life, such as Shakespeare's sonnets, gourmet dining, and the opera. In contrast, sociologists use the term in a much broader sense: That is, culture refers to the learned and shared behaviors, beliefs, attitudes, values, and material objects that characterize a particular group or society. Thus, culture determines a people's total way of life.

Most human behavior is not random or haphazard. Among other things, culture influences what you eat; how you were raised and will raise your own children; if, when, and whom you'll marry; how you make and spend money; and what you read. Even people who pride themselves on their individualism conform to most cultural rules. The next time you're in class, for example, count how many students are *not* wearing jeans, T-shirts, sweatshirts, or sneakers—clothes that are the prevalent uniform of adolescents, college students, and many adults in U.S. society.

A society is a group of people who have lived and worked together long enough to become an organized population and to think of themselves as a social unit (Linton 1936). Every society has a culture that guides people's interactions and behaviors. Society and culture are mutually dependent; neither can exist without the other. Because of this interdependence, social scientists sometimes use the terms *culture* and *society* interchangeably.

> **culture** the learned and shared behaviors, beliefs, attitudes, values, and material objects that characterize a particular group or society.
>
> **society** a group of people who have lived and worked together long enough to become an organized population and to think of themselves as a social unit.

SOME CHARACTERISTICS OF CULTURE

All human societies, despite their diversity, share some cultural characteristics and functions (Murdock 1940). We don't see culture directly, but it shapes our attitudes and behaviors.

1. **Culture is learned.** Culture is not innate but learned, and it shapes how we think, feel, and behave. If a child is born in one region of the world but raised in another, she or he will learn the customs, attitudes, and beliefs of the adopted culture.

2. **Culture is transmitted from one generation to the next.** We learn many customs, habits, and attitudes informally through interactions with parents, relatives, friends, and from the media. We also learn culture formally in settings such as schools, workplaces, and community organizations. Whether our learning is formal or informal, we don't have to reinvent the wheel through a process of trial and error. Instead, and because each generation transmits cultural information to the next one, culture is cumulative.

3. **Culture is shared.** Culture brings members of a society together. We have a sense of belonging because we share similar beliefs, values, and attitudes about what is right and wrong. Imagine the chaos if we did what we wanted (such as physically assaulting an annoying neighbor) or if we couldn't make numerous daily assumptions about other people's behavior (such as coming to work every day).

4. **Culture is adaptive and always changing.** Culture changes over time. New generations discard technological aspects of culture that are no longer practical, such as replacing typewriters with personal computers. Attitudes can also change over time. Compared with several generations ago, for example, many Americans now feel that premarital sex is acceptable or at least not wrong (*see Figure 3.1*).

Culture reflects who we are, but remember that it's people who create culture. As a result, culture changes as people adapt to their surroundings. Since the 9/11 attacks, for example, many people worldwide, including Americans, have become accustomed to greater surveillance by the government. We don't complain at airports when we have to pass through a metal detector, when our baggage is X-rayed or searched, when items are confiscated, and, increasingly, when airlines use full-body scanners. Thus, as the dangers in society have grown, people have passed laws or implemented rules that have both increased their security and decreased their privacy.

MATERIAL AND NONMATERIAL CULTURE

Cultures that people construct are both material and nonmaterial (Ogburn 1922). **Material culture** consists of the tangible objects that members of a society make, use, and share. These creations include diverse products

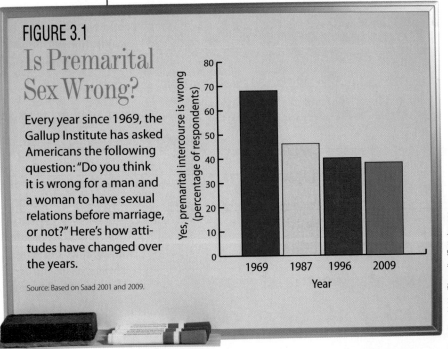

FIGURE 3.1
Is Premarital Sex Wrong?

Every year since 1969, the Gallup Institute has asked Americans the following question: "Do you think it is wrong for a man and a woman to have sexual relations before marriage, or not?" Here's how attitudes have changed over the years.

Source: Based on Saad 2001 and 2009.

Y axis: Yes, premarital intercourse is wrong (percentage of respondents)
X axis: Year — 1969, 1987, 1996, 2009

such as buildings, tools, music, weapons, jewelry, religious objects, and cell phones.

Nonmaterial culture includes the shared set of meanings that people in a society use to interpret and understand the world. Symbols, values, beliefs, sanctions, customs, and rules of behavior are elements of nonmaterial culture. Some sociologists study the material aspects of culture, such as technology, but most are interested in nonmaterial culture, such as communication patterns, attitudes, and behavior.

Material and nonmaterial culture influence each other. The automobile, for example, has changed every society that has adopted it. Among other things, cars have provided privacy during courting and dating, transported passengers relatively inexpensively, generated new laws (such as using seat belts), and created environmental problems.

2 The Building Blocks of Culture

Consider the following research findings:

- Good-looking people, especially men, earn 5 percent more per hour than average-looking people.
- Obese women, especially white women, earn 17 percent less than women of average weight.
- College students who view their instructors, especially their male professors, as good looking give them better course evaluations, which, in turn, generates more economic rewards, such as merit increases and promotions, for those professors (Hamermesh and Parker 2003; Engemann and Owyang 2005).

Such findings contradict the proverb "Beauty is in the eye of the beholder" (that someone or something is beautiful if the viewer perceives it so). How can we explain this contradiction? Why do many Americans agree on who is beautiful, average, or unattractive? Are the less attractive people victims of bias? Or do good-looking people develop self-confidence and social skills that enhance their economic opportunities?

To answer such questions, we must understand the building blocks of culture, especially symbols, language, values, and norms.

SYMBOLS

A **symbol** is anything that stands for something else and has a particular meaning for people who share a culture. In most societies, for example, a handshake communicates friendship or courtesy, a wedding ring signals that a person isn't a potential dating partner, and a siren denotes an emergency. People influence each other through the use of symbols. A smile and a frown communicate different information and elicit different responses. Through symbols, we engage in *symbolic interaction* (see Chapter 1).

> **nonmaterial culture** the shared set of meanings that people in a society use to interpret and understand the world.
>
> **symbol** anything that stands for something else and has a particular meaning for people who share a culture.

Symbols Take Many Forms

Written words are the most common symbols, but we also communicate by tattooing our bodies, getting breast implants, and purchasing goods and services that we feel might increase our social status. And gestures (such as raised fists, hugs, and stares) convey important messages about other people's feelings and attitudes.

Symbols Distinguish One Culture from Another

In Islamic societies, many women wear a head scarf (*hijab* or *hejab*) that covers their hair and neck, a veil that hides part of the face from just below the eyes (*nijab*), or a garment that covers the entire body (a *chador* or *burqa*). The variety of veils is just a piece of cloth, but mean different things to people across and within cultures.

For non-Muslims, especially Westerners, veils are often symbols of women's repression by men and religious zealotry; they conjure up images of terrorism and connote hiding something. For many Muslims, on the other hand, veiling symbolizes religious commitment, modesty, women's dress codes, and an Islamic identity. Other Muslims—including those who live in the Middle East or have immigrated to Western countries—view most veiling, especially *nijabs* and *burqas,* as "a tradition rather than an Islamic ritual or rule" that is problematic for a variety of reasons, such as discouraging face-to-face interaction (Murphy 2009: 17).

Symbols Can Unify or Divide a Society

Symbols usually unify people culturally. Every Fourth of July, many Americans celebrate the anniversary of gaining independence from Britain with parades, firecrackers, barbecues, and numerous speeches by local and national politicians. All of this symbolic behavior signifies freedom and democracy, even though few Americans know the history of the struggle for independence. Many immigrants purposely choose July 4th as the date on which to be naturalized because it represents "the land of the free."

Symbols can also be divisive. For example, some white southerners fly the Confederate flag because they see it as a proud emblem of their Southern heritage. Others have abandoned the flag because it is used by racist groups, like the Ku Klux Klan, to symbolize slavery and white domination of African Americans.

Symbols Can Change Over Time

Symbols communicate information that varies across societies and may change over time. In 1986, for example, the International Red Cross changed its name to the International Red Cross and the Red Crescent Movement to encompass a number of Arab branches, and adopted a crescent emblem in addition to the well-known cross. Israel wanted to use a red Star of David, rejecting the cross as a Christian symbol and the crescent as an Islamic one. Red Cross officials offered a red diamond as the new shape, but some countries rejected the diamond because it represents bloody conflicts in many African countries that mine diamonds (Whitelaw 2000). The red cross and crescent continue to be the organization's emblems until the issue is resolved.

LANGUAGE

Perhaps the most powerful of all human symbols is **language**, a system of shared symbols that enables people to communicate with one another. In every society, children begin to grasp the essential structure of their language at a very early age and without any instruction. Babbling leads, rapidly, to uttering words and combinations of words. The average child knows approximately 900 words by the age of 2 and 8,000 words by age 6 (Hetherington et al. 2006).

The 1994 Oregon Death with Dignity law allows physician-assisted suicide for terminally ill patients whose suffering is unbearable, who lose bodily functions, and who want control over their death. Other states have considered passing similar legislation, but it's been a divisive issue, partly because the choice of words makes a big difference in people's attitudes. In a recent Gallup survey, 75 percent of Americans agreed that doctors should be allowed by law to "end the lives" of patients. But when the question was worded to say that doctors should be permitted to "assist the patient to commit suicide," only 58 percent of the respondents agreed. Because of the stigma attached to suicide, we often use indirect language, such as "aid in dying," "choice in dying," and "end-of-life options" (Nunberg 2007). Thus, language is important.

Why Language Is Important

Language makes us human: It helps us understand our everyday experiences, conveys our ideas, communicates information, and influences other people's attitudes and behavior. Language directs our thinking, controls our actions, shapes our expression of emotions, and gives us a sense of belonging to a group.

Language can also spark anger and conflict. Recognizing this connection, two high schools in Connecticut started to fine students, up to $103, for cursing. The schools' officials hoped to decrease the fights that erupted when students used obscenities and vulgar

FABRICE COFFRINI/AFP/Getty Images / © AP Photo/Keystone/Salvatore Di Nolfi

Left: *The two emblems of the International Movement of the Red Cross and the Red Crescent.* **Right:** *The proposed red diamond emblem.*

language (Llana 2005). Language, thought, and behavior are indeed interrelated, which is especially evident when we consider gender and ethnicity.

Language and Gender

Language has a profound influence on how we think about and act toward women and men. Those who adhere to traditional usage of language contend that nouns such as *businessman, chairman, mailman,* and *mankind,* and pronouns such as *he* refer to both women and men, and that women who object to such usage are too sensitive. Suppose, however, that all of your professors used only *she, her,* and *women* when they were referring to all people. Would the men in the class feel excluded?

Many professors routinely use phrases such as "Okay, guys, in class today…" and no one objects. One of my colleagues illustrates the linkage between language, gender, and how they affect our thinking by saying, "Okay, gals, in class today…" "I always get a reaction of gaping mouths, laughs, and bewildered looks," he says. The students react differently to "guys" and "gals" because we have internalized male terms (such as *guys, policemen,* and *maintenance man*) as normal and acceptable.

Language, Race, and Ethnicity

Words—written and spoken—create and reinforce both positive and negative images about race and ethnicity. Someone might receive a *black mark,* and a *white lie* isn't really a lie. We *blackball* someone, *blacken* someone's reputation, view *blackguards* (villains) with dislike, and prosecute people who deal in the *black market.* In contrast, a *white knight* rescues people in distress, the *white hope* brings glory to a group, and the good guys wear *white hats.*

Racist or ethnic slurs, labels, and stereotypes demean and stigmatize people. Derogatory ethnic words abound: *honky, hebe, kike, spic, chink, jap, polack, wetback,* and many others. Self-ascribed racial epithets are as harmful as those imposed by outsiders. When Italians refer to themselves as *dagos* or African Americans call each other *nigger,* they tacitly accept stereotypes about themselves and legitimize the general usage of such derogatory ethnic labels (Attinasi 1994).

Through language, children learn about their cultural heritage and develop a sense of personal identity to their group. In many Latino and other immigrant families, the native language begins to disappear after just one generation, resulting in communication problems between Americanized children and their non-English–speaking kin in the homeland. To counter the loss of Spanish and other languages among their children, many bilingual parents have instituted weekend schools where children learn to speak their native language (Tobar 2009; see also Chapter 10).

Language also reflects differences in how people construct and view reality across cultures or groups. Some governments apply the label *terrorism* to just about anyone who disagrees with them to muzzle opposition. Because *terrorist* is a pejorative term, many groups use euphemisms: "freedom fighter" sounds heroic, "holy warrior" has religious overtones, "rebel" sounds noble, "guerrilla" implies making sacrifices for the "greater good," and "revolutionary" suggests that the terrorist is fighting for the homeland or freedom (see online Chapter 18).

Language and Social Change

Language is dynamic and changes over time. U.S. English is composed of hundreds of thousands of words borrowed from many countries and from groups that were in the Americas before the colonists arrived (Carney 1997). *Table 3.1* provides a few examples of English words borrowed from other languages.

In response to cultural and technological changes, our vocabulary now includes *sexting, e-book, tweet, staycation,* and *unfriend,* among other new words. And to some people's dismay and others' delight, some writers are now substituting *part-*

$*#@%**#@

Mike Kemp/Jupiter Images

ner for the traditional *spouse, wife,* or *husband.*

Language is sometimes slow to catch up with cultural changes. For example, how does one refer to a romantic partner, especially in social situations? "Significant other" can mean a parent, sibling, or close friend; "partner" or "companion" doesn't sound quite right; "lover" isn't acceptable in most social circles; "girlfriend" or "boyfriend" seems inappropriate unless you're a teenager; and "the person I'm seeing" might elicit unwanted questions about your relationship.

VALUES

Values are the standards by which members of a particular culture define what is good or bad, moral or immoral, proper or improper, desirable or undesirable, beautiful or ugly. They are widely shared within a society and provide *general guidelines* for everyday behavior rather than specific rules that apply to concrete situations. For example, when faculty members catch students plagiarizing, students often plead innocence and blame the instructor ("*You* never told us *exactly* what *you* mean by plagiarism.").

Major U.S. Values

Sociologist Robin Williams (1970: 452–500) has identified a number of core U.S. values. All are central to the American way of life because they are widespread, have endured over time, and reflect many people's intense feelings.

1. **Achievement and success.** U.S. culture stresses personal achievement, especially occupational success. Many Americans are captivated by people—including celebrities and affluent athletes—who flaunt their wealth and status.

2. **Activity and work.** Americans often seem to be in a hurry and want to "make things happen." They respect people who are focused and disciplined in their jobs, and

assume that hard work will be rewarded. Journalists and others often praise those who work past their retirement age.

3. **Humanitarianism.** U.S. society emphasizes concern for others, helpfulness, kindness, and offering comfort and support. During natural disasters—such as earthquakes, floods, fires, and famines—at home and abroad, many Americans are enormously generous, as when they contributed millions of dollars within a few days after Hurricanes Katrina and Rita in 2005, and the earthquake in Haiti in 2010.

4. **Efficiency and practicality.** Americans emphasize technological innovation, up-to-dateness, practicality, and getting things done. They are offended if described as "backward," "inefficient," or "wasting time." Many American colleges, in fact, now tout their programs or courses as being practical and useful instead of emphasizing knowledge and intellectual growth.

5. **Progress.** Americans focus on the future rather than the present or the past. The next time you walk down the aisle of a grocery store, note how many products are "new," "improved," and "better than ever." If Americans don't keep up with technological progress, they believe people in other countries will view them as "outmoded," "stagnant," and "computer challenged."

6. **Material comfort.** Americans consider it normal to want new products and services. Many work hard to pay for fancy new cars, large homes, and dream vacations (even if they can't afford them). Americans never have enough gadgets and always need more stuff. When the stuff accumulates, they buy stuff to stuff it into.

7. **Freedom and Equality.** Countless documents affirm freedom of speech, freedom of the press, and freedom of worship in the United States. Beginning

TABLE 3.1
U.S. English Is a Mixed Salad

☐ Africa: apartheid, Kwanzaa, safari	☐ Spain: anchovy, bizarre
☐ Alaska and Siberia: husky, igloo, kayak	☐ Thailand: Siamese
☐ Bangladesh: bungalow, dinghy	☐ Turkey: baklava, caviar, kebob
☐ Hungary: coach, goulash, paprika	☐ France: bacon, police, ballet
☐ India: bandanna, cheetah, shampoo	☐ Japan: geisha, judo, sushi
☐ Iran and Afghanistan: bazaar, caravan, tiger	☐ Norway: iceberg, rig, walrus
☐ Israel: kosher, rabbi, Sabbath	☐ Mexico: avocado, chocolate, coyote
☐ Italy: fresco, spaghetti, piano	☐ Germany: strudel, vitamin, sauerkraut, kindergarten

To save the native tongue—Irish Gaelic—parts of Ireland's Galway County don't translate street signs into English (the majority language). Potential home buyers must submit to a rigorous oral test to determine whether they can speak Irish Gaelic because only fluent speakers are welcomed (O'Neill 2007). Is this discrimination? Or a legitimate way to protect a linguistic heritage?

© Neil Setchfield/Alamy

with the colonists, immigrants have been drawn to this country to enjoy freedom from political persecution, economic problems, and religious intolerance. U.S. laws also tell Americans that they have been "created equal" and have the same legal rights, regardless of race, ethnicity, sex, religion, disability, age, or social class. Americans believe that if they work hard, apply themselves, and save their money, they will be successful in the future.

8. **Conformity.** Individuals don't want to be seen as "strange," "peculiar," or "different." They conform because they want to be accepted, to get social approval from those they respect, and to be hired or promoted. Striving for success often means controlling one's impulses and biting one's tongue.

9. **Democracy.** Democracy provides the average U.S. citizen with equal political rights, and distributes power and decision making across several bodies (legislative, executive, and judicial branches). Democracy emphasizes equality, freedom, and faith in the people rather than giving power to a monarch, dictator, or emperor.

10. **Individualism.** American culture sets a high value on each person's development. Thus, we try to raise children to be independent, creative, self-directed, self-motivated, and spontaneous.

Williams himself acknowledged troublesome patterns in the list because these core American values, as you may have noticed, are sometimes contradictory and don't always mesh with reality. For example, Americans value equality but are comfortable with enormous gaps in wealth and power, and continue to discriminate against people because of their ethnicity, race, sexual orientation, gender, or age. We proclaim that we respect individualism but make hurtful comments about people who are fat, thin, or have a physical disability. And we say we value responsibility but often blame television rather than parenting for children's bad behavior.

norms a society's specific rules concerning right and wrong behavior.

Values Are Emotion-Laden

Most of us are passionate about our values because they arouse strong emotions. Consider the nationwide outburst of patriotic behavior in the United States after the 9/11 attacks. When values such as democracy are threatened or assaulted, many people rally to protect them.

People who oppose widely shared cultural values, such as the freedom of expression, can be as fervent as those who defend them. Over the years, for example, small groups of parents and others have denounced books that they find objectionable (e.g., *Heather Has Two Mommies* and *The Color Purple*) and sometimes succeed in removing them from libraries and schools (American Library Association 2010).

Values Vary Across Cultures and Change over Time

As you'll see shortly, cultural values can change as a result of technological advances, immigration, and contact with outsiders. For example, the Japanese parliament recently passed a law making love of country a compulsory part of school curricula. The lawmakers and their numerous supporters hope that teaching patriotism will counteract the American-style emphasis on individualism and self-expression that they believe has undermined Japanese values of cooperation, self-discipline, responsibility, and respect for others (Wallace 2006).

In the United States, surveys of first-year college students show a shift in values. Between 1968 and 2006, for example, developing a meaningful philosophy of life plummeted in importance, whereas being rich became substantially more valued (Pryor et al. 2007). Consistent with our humanitarian values, however, a majority (70 percent) of the students surveyed in 2008 said that "helping others who are in difficulty" is essential or very important, but women were more likely to feel this way (see *Figure 3.2*).

NORMS

Values express general goals and broad guidelines for daily living, but **norms** are a society's specific rules of right and wrong behavior. Norms tell us what we *should, ought,* and *must* do, as well as what we *should not, ought not,* and *must not* do: don't talk in church, stand in line, and so on.

Norms are not universally applied to all groups, however. For example, a female professor's students sometimes comment on her clothes in their course evaluations and want her to "look like a professor." In contrast, her husband, also a professor, "has yet to hear a single student comment about his wardrobe." So, she changes her outfits every day and wears business-like clothes while her husband usually wears khaki pants (or jeans) and a polo or button-down shirt day in and day out (Johnston 2005). Thus, "her" and "his" norms differ.

Norms reflect values and, thus, are expectations shared by the members of the society at large or by the members of particular groups within a society. In the United States, where individualism is a basic value, young adults are expected to move out of their parents' home and to become independent and self-sufficient. In China, in contrast, where communal responsibility is a basic value, several generations live under the same roof, and children are expected to care for their aging parents.

Here are some general characteristics of norms:

- Most are *unwritten,* passed down orally from generation to generation (using the good dishes and tablecloth on special occasions).

- They are *instrumental* because they serve a specific purpose (getting rid of garbage that attracts roaches and rats).

- Some are *explicit* (save your money "for a rainy day"), whereas others are *implicit* (being respectful during a wake or funeral).

- They *change* over time (it's now more acceptable than in the past to have a child out of wedlock but much less acceptable to smoke or to be overweight).

- Most are *conditional* because they apply in specific situations (slipping out of your smelly shoes may be fine at home but not on an airplane).

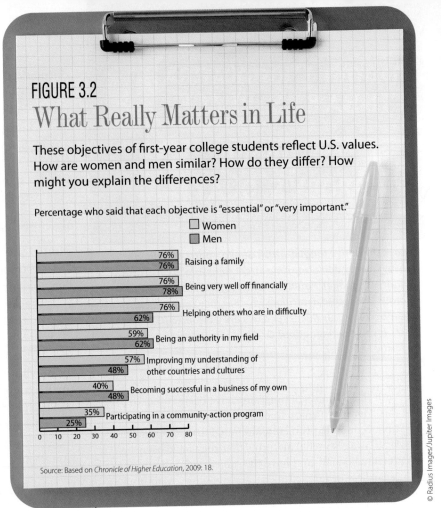

FIGURE 3.2
What Really Matters in Life

These objectives of first-year college students reflect U.S. values. How are women and men similar? How do they differ? How might you explain the differences?

Percentage who said that each objective is "essential" or "very important."

☐ Women
☐ Men

Objective	Women	Men
Raising a family	76%	76%
Being very well off financially	76%	78%
Helping others who are in difficulty	76%	62%
Being an authority in my field	59%	62%
Improving my understanding of other countries and cultures	57%	48%
Becoming successful in a business of my own	40%	48%
Participating in a community-action program	35%	25%

Source: Based on *Chronicle of Higher Education,* 2009: 18.

- Because they are situational, norms can be *rigid* ("You *must* turn in a term paper.") or *flexible* ("You can have another week to finish the paper.").

Norms organize and regulate our behavior. We may not like many of the rules, but they make our everyday lives more orderly and predictable. Imagine, for example, if your professor said, "This class meets from 2:00 to 5:00 on Tuesdays. If I'm an hour or so late, just wait for me."

Sociologists differentiate three types of norms—folkways, mores, and laws—that vary because some rules are more important than others. As a result, a society punishes some wrongdoers more severely than others.

Folkways

About 69 percent of Americans believe that people are ruder than they were 20 or 30 years ago, citing, in particular, driving aggressively, using offensive language in public, and talking loudly on cell phones ("American Manners Poll" 2005). Rudeness violates **folkways,** norms that members of a society (or a group within a society) see as not being critical and that may be broken without severe punishment. Etiquette rules are good examples of folkways: Cover your mouth when you sneeze, say "please" and "thank you," and knock before entering someone's office.

We follow a variety of everyday conventions and customs unconsciously because we've internalized them since birth. We often don't realize that we conform to norms until someone violates one, such as picking one's nose in public or eating ice cream from the carton and then putting it back in the freezer.

Folkways vary from one country to another. Punctuality is important in many Western countries but not in much of Latin America and the Mediterranean. Japan is notable for its gift giving among businesspeople, but this may be viewed as bribery in Western countries. Austrians, as well as Germans and the Swiss, consider chewing gum in public vulgar. There are also many differences in table manners: Europeans keep their hands above the table at all times, not in their laps, and Koreans frown on sniffling or blowing one's nose at the table (Axtell et al. 1997).

Most folkways are firm ("You must be at work at 9:00 a.m."), whereas others evolve over time. The growth of technology and the increase in college enrollments, and thus in the average size of classes, have changed many folkways on campuses. In the past, a syllabus was typically a few pages long, presenting course requirements and deadlines for exams and papers. Now, many syllabi—some as long as 20 pages—look more like legal documents. They describe, often in great detail, a variety of rules on civil classroom behavior and Internet plagiarism, as well as policies on disabilities, makeup exams, grading, late assignments, attendance, and laptop and cell phone use, even forbidding videos of professors that may appear on YouTube (Wasley 2008).

> **mores** norms that members of a society consider very important because they maintain moral and ethical behavior.

Mores

After some passengers complained, Southwest Airlines booted a woman off a flight for wearing a tight, low-cut blouse that showed considerable cleavage. The woman was furious, but Southwest said that its rules can deny boarding to any passenger whose clothing is "lewd, obscene, or patently offensive." As this example illustrates, mores (pronounced "MOR-ays") are much stronger than folkways. **Mores** are norms that members of a society consider very important because they maintain moral and ethical behavior. Most people believe that mores are crucial in upholding a decent and orderly way of life.

According to U.S. cultural mores, one must be sexually faithful to one's spouse or sexual partner, loyal to one's country, and must not kill another person (except during war or in self-defense). Notice that while folkways emphasize *ought to* behavior, mores define *must* behavior. The Ten Commandments are a good example of religious mores. Other mores include ethical guidelines (don't cheat, don't lie), expectations about interpersonal behavior (don't live on handouts), and rules about sexual partners (don't have sexual intercourse with children or family members).

Mores, like folkways, can change. For example, 84 percent of Americans in 1970 compared with 54 percent in 2006 viewed marijuana usage as immoral (Saad 2009). Also, until about the late 1970s, 80 percent of U.S. babies born out of

At the 60th anniversary of the liberation of Auschwitz in 2005, Vice President Dick Cheney represented the United States. The other dignitaries wore formal overcoats, "gentlemen's" hats, and dress shoes. The vice president was dressed "in the kind of attire one typically wears to operate a snow blower": a drab olive-green parka with a fur-trimmed hood, a knit cap, and hiking boots (Givhan 2005: C1). What does Mr. Cheney's attire say about how predominant casual dress has become in U.S. culture?

wedlock were given up for adoption. This rate has dropped to about 2 or 3 percent today because most unwed mothers, who are no longer stigmatized for having out-of-wedlock babies, keep their infants (Benokraitis 2011).

Laws

The most rigid norms are **laws**, formal rules about behavior that are defined by a political authority that has the power to punish violators. Unlike folkways and most mores, laws are deliberate, formal, "precisely specified in written texts," and "enforced by a specialized bureaucracy," usually police and courts (Hechter and Opp 2001: xi).

Laws change over time. Fourteen states now allow sale of marijuana for medical use, and several more are considering such legislation. And the powerful American Medical Association has called on the government to reconsider marijuana's classification as a dangerous drug until there is more research on the drug's effects (Wood 2009). It's not clear whether U.S. laws about marijuana usage are gaining momentum because of medical research, changing mores, states' enhancing their budgets by taxing marijuana as they do with cigarettes and alcohol, or a combination of these reasons.

Laws also vary across societies. Judges in Iran can order public floggings of young men accused of drinking alcohol, distributing Western music CDs, or being alone with women who are not their relatives. Singapore, where chewing gum is now legal after a 12-year ban, requires citizens who want to chew gum to submit their names and ID cards to the government (Anderson 2001; Knickerbocker 2005).

Sanctions

Most people conform to norms because of **sanctions**, rewards for good or appropriate behavior and/or penalties for bad or inappropriate behavior. Children learn norms through both *positive* sanctions (praise, hugs, smiles, new toys) and *negative* sanctions (frowning, scolding, spanking, withdrawing love) (see Chapter 4).

Sanctions vary. When we violate folkways, the sanctions are relatively mild: gossip, ridicule, exclusion from a group. If you don't bathe or brush your teeth, you may not be invited to parties because others will see you as

At the 2009 MTV Video Music Awards, country singer Taylor Swift received an award for best female video. Rapper Kanye West stormed the stage, grabbed Swift's microphone, and told the audience that the award should have been given to Beyoncé, a popular singer and actress. Which types of norms did West violate—folkways, mores, or laws?

crude, but not sinful or evil. The sanctions for violating mores and some laws can be severe: loss of employment, expulsion from college, whipping, torture, banishment, imprisonment, and even execution. The sanctions are usually harsh because the unacceptable behavior threatens the moral foundations of a society. The public floggings in Iran, you'll recall, punish offenders for their "immorality" and send a warning to others to follow the rules.

Sanctions aren't always consistent, despite universally held norms. In the United States, someone who can hire a good attorney might receive a lighter penalty for a serious crime. In some cultures, young girls and women may be lashed for engaging in premarital sex, but men aren't punished at all for the same behavior, even though they have also violated Islamic law (Agence France Presse 2001). Also, laws are sometimes enforced selectively or not at all. In the United States and elsewhere, for example, offenders who violate laws against discrimination, sexual harassment, and domestic violence are rarely prosecuted or punished (see Chapters 7 and 13).

3 Some Cultural Similarities

 ou've seen that there's considerable diversity across societies in symbols, language, values, and norms. There are also some striking similarities across and within cultures because of cultural uni-

TABLE 3.2
Some Cultural Universals

Athletics	Food taboos	Inheritance rules	Music
Bodily adornments	Funeral rites	Joking	Postnatal care
Community organization	Games	Kin terminology	Property rights
Cooking	Gestures	Language	Puberty customs
Courtship	Gift giving	Magic	Religious rituals
Dancing	Greetings	Marriage	Sexual restrictions
Division of labor	Hairstyles	Medicine	Status differentiation
Education	Hospitality	Mealtimes	Supernatural beings
Ethics	Housing	Modesty	Trade
Etiquette	Incest taboos	Mourning	Visiting
Family feasts			

Source: Based on Murdock 1945.

cultural universals customs and practices that are common to all societies.

ideal culture the beliefs, values, and norms that people in a society say they hold or follow.

real culture the actual everyday behavior of people in a society.

ethnocentrism the belief that one's culture and way of life are superior to those of other groups.

versals, real and ideal culture, ethnocentrism, and cultural relativism.

CULTURAL UNIVERSALS

Cultural universals are customs and practices that are common to all societies. Anthropologist George Murdock and his associates studied hundreds of societies and compiled a list of 88 categories that they found among all cultures (see *Table 3.2* for some examples).

Many cultural universals exist, but specific behaviors vary across cultures, from one group to another in the same society, and across time. For example, all societies have food taboos, but specifics about what people ought and ought not to eat differ across societies. About 75 percent of the world's people eat insects as part of their diet. In Thailand, locusts, crickets, silkworms, grasshoppers, ants, and other insects have become a big part of the Thai diet (Stolley and Taphaneeyapan 2002). South Korea has an estimated 6,000 restaurants that specialize in dog meat because it's easier to digest than many other meats. Increasingly, however, as many South Koreans accept Western norms, some are treating dogs as pets and members of the family rather than as nutritional food sources (Demick 2002; Stolley and Taphaneeyapan 2002; McLaughlin 2005).

IDEAL VERSUS REAL CULTURE

The **ideal culture** of a society comprises the beliefs, values, and norms that people say they hold or follow. In every culture, however, these standards differ from the society's **real culture**, or people's actual everyday behavior. For example, Americans say that they love their children, and continuously proclaim that children are their most precious resources. Every year, however, hundreds of thousands of children experience abuse and neglect on a daily basis. Indeed, 80 percent of people who abuse their children are parents (U.S. Department of Health and Human Services 2009; see also Chapter 13). Thus, ideal culture and our actual behavior are often inconsistent.

ETHNOCENTRISM AND CULTURAL RELATIVISM

When President Bush visited Queen Elizabeth II in England in 2003, he brought with him five of his personal chefs. Queen Elizabeth was offended because she has a large staff of excellent cooks ("Bush's Cooks..." 2003). Was President Bush being ethnocentric?

Ethnocentrism is the belief that one's culture and way of life are superior to those of other groups. This attitude leads people to view other cultures as inferior, wrong, backward, immoral, or barbaric. During the nineteenth and twentieth centuries, for example, there was rampant anti-immigrant sentiment toward people immigrating from Ireland, Poland, and other European countries. The Chinese Exclusion Act of 1882 barred Chinese immigrants, and the Immigration Act of 1924 used quotas to limit Italian and Jewish immigration.

Because people internalize their culture and take it for granted, they may be hostile toward other cultures. Each group tends to see its way of life as the best and the most natural. Some of my black students argue that it's impossible for African Americans to be ethnocentric because they suffer much prejudice and discrimination. *Any* group can be ethnocentric, however (Rose 1997). An immigrant from Nigeria who assumes that all native-born African Americans are lazy and criminal is just as ethnocentric as a native-born African American who assumes that all Nigerians are arrogant and "uppity."

Ethnocentrism can also be functional. Pride in one's country promotes loyalty and cultural unity. When children learn their country's national anthem and customs, they have a sense of belonging. Ethnocentrism also reinforces conformity and maintains stability. Members of a society become committed to their particular values and customs, and transmit them to the next generation. As a result, life is (generally) orderly and predictable.

Ethnocentrism has its benefits, but it's usually dysfunctional because viewing others as inferior generates hatred, discrimination, and conflict. Many of the recent wars, such as those in the former Yugoslavia and Rwanda (Africa), and the ongoing battles between Palestinians and Israelis reflect religious, ethnic, or political intolerance toward subgroups (see Chapter 15 and online Chapter 18). Thus, ethnocentrism discourages intergroup understanding and cooperation.

The opposite of ethnocentrism is **cultural relativism**, a belief that no culture is better than another and that a culture should be judged by its own standards. Most Japanese mothers stay home with their children, whereas many American mothers are employed outside the home. Is one practice better than another? No. Because Japanese fathers are expected to be the breadwinners, it's common for many Japanese women to be homemakers. In the United States, in contrast, many mothers are single heads of households who have to work to provide for themselves and their children. Also, economic recessions and the loss of many high-paying jobs in the United States have catapulted many middle-class women into the job market to help support their families (see Chapters 10, 12, and 13). Thus, Japanese and American parenting may be different, but one culture isn't better or worse than the other.

An understanding of cultural relativism is practical and productive. Businesspeople and other travelers can overcome cultural barriers and improve communication if they understand and respect other cultures.

4 Some Cultural Variations

there is considerable cultural variation *across* societies and sometimes *within* the same society. *Subcultures* and *countercultures* account for some of the complexity within a society.

SUBCULTURES

A **subculture** is a group of people whose distinctive ways of thinking, feeling, and acting differ somewhat from those of the larger society. A subculture is part of the larger, dominant culture but has particular values, beliefs, perspectives, lifestyle, or language. Members of subcultures often live in the same neighborhoods, associate with each other, have close personal relationships, and marry others who are similar to themselves.

One example of a subculture is college students. At residential campuses, most college students wear similar clothing, eat similar food, participate in similar recreational activities, and often hook up with each other. Whether students live in campus housing or commute, they share a similar vocabulary that includes words such as *syllabus, incomplete grade, dean's list,* and *core courses*. Many students are members of other subcultures as well: sororities and fraternities, sports teams, clubs, honor societies, and religious, political, and ethnic groups.

Whether we realize it or not, most of us are members of numerous subcultures. Subcultures reflect a variety of characteristics, interests, or activities:

- *Ethnicity* (Irish, Mexican, Vietnamese)
- *Religion* (Catholics, evangelical Christians, atheists, Mormons)
- *Politics* (Maine Republicans, Southern Democrats, independents)
- *Sex and gender* (gay men, lesbians, transsexuals)
- *Age* (older widows, kindergartners, middle schoolers)
- *Occupation* (surgeons, teachers, prostitutes, truck drivers)
- *Music and art* (jazz aficionados, country music buffs, art lovers)
- *Social class* (billionaires, working poor, middle class)
- *Recreation* (mountain bikers, bingo or poker players, motorcycle riders)

Some subcultures retreat from the dominant culture to preserve their beliefs and values. The Amish, for example, have created self-sustaining economic units, travel locally by horse and buggy, conduct religious services in their homes, make their own clothes, and generally shun modern conveniences such as electricity and phones. Despite their self-imposed isolation, the Amish have been affected by the dominant U.S. culture. They traditionally worked in agriculture, but as farming became less self-sustaining, many began small businesses that produce quilts, wood and leather products, and baked goods for tourists. Others, until the economy started collapsing in 2008, found steady wages in assembling recreational vehicles, local furniture jobs, and construction (Boak 2009; Mertens 2009).

To fit in, members of most subcultures adapt to the larger society. Some Chinese restaurants have changed their menus to accommodate the average American's taste for sweet-and-sour dishes but list more authentic food on a separate, Chinese-language menu. Many Middle Eastern menus routinely describe traditional dishes and mark the items as mild or spicy to cater to their customers' tastes.

Some analysts describe the popular television program **The Simpsons** *as countercultural because it ridicules the media's shallowness, portrays government in a cynical light, mocks indifferent or incompetent teachers and administrators, makes fun of stereotyping Asians who manage convenience stores, and scoffs at bungling and greedy law enforcement officers (Reeves 1999; Cantor 2001).*

In many instances, subcultures arise because of technological or other societal changes. With the emergence of the Internet, for example, subcultures arose that identified themselves as hackers, techies, or computer geeks.

> **counterculture** a group of people who deliberately oppose and consciously reject some of the basic beliefs, values, and norms of the dominant culture.
>
> **multiculturalism (cultural pluralism)** the coexistence of several cultures in the same geographic area, without one culture dominating another.

COUNTERCULTURES

Unlike a subculture, a **counterculture** deliberately opposes and consciously rejects some of the basic beliefs, values, and norms of the dominant culture. Countercultures usually emerge when people believe they can't achieve their goals within the existing society. As a result, such groups develop values and practices that run counter to those of the dominant society. Some countercultures are small and informal, but others have millions of members and are highly organized, like religious militants (see Chapter 15).

Most countercultures do not engage in illegal activities. During the 1960s, for example, social movements such as feminism, civil rights, and gay rights organized protests against mainstream views but stayed within the law. However, some countercultures are violent and extremist, such as the 926 active hate groups across the United States (see *Figure 3.3*), who intimidate ethnic groups and gays. There have been instances where counterculture members have clearly violated laws: Some skinheads have murdered gays; antigovernment militia adherents bombed a federal building in Oklahoma, killing dozens of adults and children; and anti-abortion advocates have murdered physicians and bombed abortion clinics.

MULTICULTURALISM

Multiculturalism (sometimes called *cultural pluralism*) refers to the coexistence of several cultures in the same geographic area, without one culture dominating another. Many applaud multiculturalism because it encourages intracultural dialogue (e.g., U.S. schools offering programs and courses in African American, Latino, Arabic, and Asian studies). Supporters hope that emphasizing multiculturalism—especially in academic institutions and the workplace—will decrease ethnocentrism, racism, sexism, and other forms of discrimination.

Despite its benefits, not everyone is enthusiastic about multiculturalism. Not learning the language of the country where one lives and works, for instance, can be isolating and create on-the-job miscommunication,

FIGURE 3.3
Active Hate Groups in the United States: 2008

WA 15
OR 10
MT 12
ND 1
MN 9
NH 5
VT 1
ME 2
ID 9
WY 4
SD 3
WI 8
MI 26
NY 31
MA 16
RI 3
CT 6
NV 15
UT 6
CO 17
NE 4
IA 17
IL 28
IN 17
OH 27
PA 28
NJ 44
CA 60
KS 6
MO 31
KY 10
WV 13
VA 22
MD 13
DE 4
DC 9
AZ 16
NM 2
OK 15
AR 24
TN 37
NC 29
SC 36
AK 1
TX 66
MS 25
AL 32
GA 37
LA 28
HI 1
FL 51

Source: Southern Poverty Law Center, 2010, www.splcenter.org (accessed January 18, 2010).

About 75 percent of the world's people consume insects, which are high in protein, vitamins, and fiber, and usually low in fat. More than two out of every three American adults are overweight or obese, the highest percentage on the planet (Flegal et al. 2010). Would we be healthier if we ate insects instead of gulping down hamburgers and french fries?

AP Photo/Dario Lopez-Mills

tension, and conflict. Some also believe that multiculturalism can destroy a country's national traditions, heritage, and identity because ethnic and religious subcultures may not support the dominant culture's values and beliefs (Watson 2000; Skerry 2002).

CULTURE SHOCK

People who travel to other countries often experience **culture shock**—a sense of confusion, uncertainty, disorientation, or anxiety that accompanies exposure to an unfamiliar way of life or environment. Familiar cues about how to behave are missing or have a different meaning. Culture shock affects people differently, but the most stressful changes involve the type of food eaten, the type of clothes worn, punctuality, ideas about what offends people, the language spoken, differences in personal hygiene, the general pace of life, a lack of privacy, and concern about finances (Spradley and Phillips 1972; Pedersen 1995).

To some degree, everyone is *culture bound* because they've internalized cultural norms and values. For example, an American journalist who works in Mexico City says that perpetual lateness is common: A child's birthday party may start 2 or 3 hours late, a wedding may begin an hour after the announced time, and interviews with top Mexico City officials may be up to 2 hours late or the official never arrives. These norms are changing because of the growth of Mexico's global economy, but the more relaxed attitude of time in Mexico City (and elsewhere) can be a culture shock to someone from the United States who has grown up in a "clock-obsessed" culture (Ellingwood 2009).

American students who have studied abroad often experience culture shock when they return, such as in readjusting to traffic jams, the pace of daily life, and the emphasis on work above personal life. For example, a student who studied in Ecuador said that she missed the sense of community she had felt: "Back in the United States, I noticed how separate and selfish people can be at times" (Goodkin 2005).

A major component of culture is popular culture. Popular culture has an enormous impact on many contemporary societies.

5 Popular Culture

Sociologists use the term *high culture* to describe the cultural expression of a society's elite or highest social classes. Examples include opera, ballet, paintings, and classical music. In contrast, popular culture refers to beliefs, practices, activities, and products that are widely shared within a population in everyday life.

Popular culture includes television, music, magazines, radio, advertising, sports, hobbies, fads, fash-ions, movies, as well as the food we eat, the gossip we share, and the jokes we pass along to others. People produce and consume popular culture: They are not simply passive receptacles but influence popular culture by what they buy, how they spend their leisure time, and how they express themselves.

popular culture the beliefs, practices, activities, and products that are widely shared among a population in everyday life.

mass media forms of communication designed to reach large numbers of people.

THE IMPACT OF POPULAR CULTURE

Popular culture can have positive and negative effects on our everyday lives. Most people don't believe everything they read or see on television but weigh the merit and credibility of much of the content. Most of us are highly influenced, nonetheless, by a popular culture that is largely controlled and manipulated by newspapers and magazines, television, movies, music, and ads (see Chapter 4). These mass media, or forms of communication designed to reach large numbers of people, have enormous power in shaping public perceptions and opinions. Let's look at a few examples.

Television

The top-rated television programs are what some critics call "trash TV" (such as reality shows, sitcoms, and animated shows such as *The Family Guy, American Dad,* and *South Park*) in which "the producers see nothing wrong with glorifying drunken idiocy and moral buf-

Does Pop Culture Make Kids Fat?

The incidence of obesity among American children and teenagers has more than tripled, increasing from 5 percent in the 1960s to almost 17 percent by 2006 (Ogden et al. 2008). There are many reasons for the increase, but physicians and researchers lay much of the blame on popular culture, especially the advertising industry. Marketers in the United States spend an estimated $10

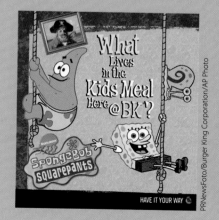

PRNewsFoto/Burger King Corporation/AP Photo

billion a year to market products to children. Much of the advertising, particularly on television, uses cartoon characters like SpongeBob SquarePants and Scooby-Doo to sell sugary cereal, cookies, candy, and other high-calorie snacks (Institute of Medicine 2006; Strasburger et al. 2006). In contrast, many European countries forbid advertising on children's television programs.

foonery in every episode" (Goldberg 2009). Many Americans believe that there is too much violence, cursing, sexual language, and explicit sexual content on TV. A bigger complaint is that the raw language (such as "bitch" and "douche bag"), violence, and sex that formerly were restricted to the 10 p.m. hour have migrated to earlier time slots when young children are watching (Wyatt 2009; see also Parents Television Council 2010).

Newspapers and Magazines

How accurate is the information we get from the mass media? Even though crime has decreased in the United States in recent years, newspapers and magazines have increased the amount of space they devote to covering violence. School violence is always a popular topic, even though most schools are safer now than they were almost 20 years ago (Dinkes et al. 2010).

In addition, the coverage can be deceptive. For example, a study of school violence concluded that six of the most influential newspapers (including the *New York Times, Washington Post,* and *Los Angeles Times*) have portrayed violence in rural/suburban and urban schools differently. The newspapers were much less likely to print stories about shootings in urban school systems even though they occur 12 times more often than in rural schools. Violence in rural and suburban schools gets more coverage because many Americans have a stereotypical picture of rural life as peaceful and tranquil (Menifield et al. 2001).

Advertising and Commercials

The average American views 3,000 ads per day and at least 40,000 commercials on television per year (Kilbourne 1999; Strasburger et al. 2006). We are constantly deluged with advertising in newspapers and magazines, on television and radio, in movie theaters, on billboards and the sides of buildings, on public transportation, and on the Internet. Our Sunday newspaper comes in two big plastic bags, but about 80 percent of the content is advertising.

Many of my students, who claim that they "don't pay any attention to ads," come to class wearing branded apparel: Budweiser caps, Adidas sweatshirts, Old Navy T-shirts, or Nike footwear. A national study of people age 15 to 26 years concluded that—regardless of gender, ethnicity, and educational level—exposure to alcohol advertising contributed to increased drinking.

Those who saw more ads for alcoholic beverages tended to drink more, and those who remembered the ads drank the most (Snyder et al. 2006).

Much mass media content is basically marketing. Many of the *Dr. Phil* shows plug his books and other products, as well as those of his wife and older son. Much of the content on television morning shows and MTV has become "a kind of sophisticated infomercial" (O'Donnell 2007: 30). For example, a third of the content on morning shows (e.g., *Early Show* on CBS, *Today Show* on NBC, and *Good Morning America* on ABC) is essentially selling something (a book, music, a movie, or another television program) that the corporation owns. One of the most lucrative alliances is between Hollywood and toy manufacturers (see Chapter 4). And according to some scholars, the U.S. mass media has expanded cultural imperialism abroad.

CULTURAL IMPERIALISM

In **cultural imperialism**, the cultural values and products of one society influence or dominate those of another. Many countries complain that U.S. cultural imperialism displaces authentic local culture and results in cultural loss.

The United States established the Internet, a global media network that uses mainly English and is heavily saturated with American advertising and popular culture (Louw 2001). Iran's government has recently denounced Batman, Spider-Man, and Harry Potter toys as a form of "cultural invasion" that challenges the country's conservative and religious values. The curvaceous and often scantily clad Barbie dolls with peroxide-blond hair have been especially singled out as "destructive culturally and a social danger." However, many of the girls who watch foreign television and (illegal) satellite want the dolls (Peterson 2008: 4).

6 Cultural Change and Technology

" adio has no future" (Lord Kelvin, Scottish mathematician and physicist, 1897).

- "Everything that can be invented has been invented" (Charles H. Duell, U.S. Commissioner of Patents, 1899).

- "Television won't be able to hold on to any market it captures after the first six months. People will soon get tired of staring at a plywood box every night"

(Darryl F. Zanuck, head of Hollywood's 20th Century Fox studio, 1946).

- "There is no reason for any individual to have a computer in their home" (Kenneth Olsen, president and founder of Digital Equipment Corp., 1977).

Despite these predictions, radio, television, computers, and other new technologies have triggered major cultural changes around the world. This section examines why cultures persist, how and why they change, and what occurs when technology changes faster than cultural values, laws, and attitudes.

CULTURAL PERSISTENCE: WHY CULTURES ARE STABLE

In many ways, culture is a conservative force. As you saw earlier, values, norms, and language are transmitted from generation to generation. Such **cultural integration**, or the consistency of various aspects of society, promotes order and stability. Even when new behaviors and beliefs emerge, they commonly adapt to existing ones. Recent immigrants, for example, may speak their native language at home and celebrate their own holy days, but they are expected to gradually absorb the new country's values, obey its civil and criminal codes, and adopt its national language. Life would be chaotic and unpredictable without such cultural integration.

CULTURAL DYNAMICS: WHY CULTURES CHANGE

Cultural stability is important, but all societies change over time. Some of the major reasons for cultural change include diffusion, invention and innovation, discovery, and external pressures.

Diffusion

A culture may change because of *diffusion*, the process through which components of culture spread from one society to another. Such borrowing may have occurred so long ago that the members of a society consider their culture to be entirely their own creation. However, anthropologist Ralph Linton (1964) has estimated that 90 percent of the elements of any culture are a result of diffusion (see *Figure 3.4*).

Diffusion can be direct and conscious, occurring through trade, tourism, immigration, intermarriage, or the invasion of one country by another. Diffusion can also be indirect and largely unconscious, as in the Internet transmissions that zip around the world.

Invention and Innovation

Cultures change because people are continually finding new ways of doing things. *Invention*, the process of creating new things, brought about products such as toothpaste (invented in 3000 BC), eyeglasses (262 AD), flushable toilets (the sixteenth century), can openers (1813), fax machines (1843—that's right, invented in 1843!), credit cards (1920s), sliced bread (1928), computer mouses (1964), Post-It notes (1980), and DVDs (1995).

Innovation—turning inventions into mass-market products—also sparks cultural changes. An innovator is someone determined to market an invention, even if it's someone else's good idea. For example, Henry Ford invented nothing new but "assembled into a car the discoveries of other men behind whom were centuries of work," an innovation that changed people's lives (Evans et al. 2006: 465).

Discovery

Like invention, *discovery* requires exploration and investigation, and results in new products, insights, ideas, or behavior. The discovery of penicillin prolonged lives, which, in turn, meant that more grandparents (as well as great-grandparents) and grandchildren would get to know each other. However, longer life spans also mean that children and grandchildren need to care for elderly family members over many years (see Chapter 13).

Discovery usually requires dedicated work and years of commitment, but some discoveries occur by chance, called the *serendipity effect*. For example, George de Mestral, a Swiss electrical engineer, was hiking through the woods. He was annoyed by burrs that clung to his clothing. Why were they so difficult to remove? A closer examination showed that the burrs had hook-like arms that locked into the open weave of his clothes. The discovery led de Mestral to invent a hook-and-loop fastener. His invention, Velcro—derived from the French words *velour* (velvet) and *crochet* (hooks)—can now be found on everything from wallets to spacecrafts.

External Pressures

External pressure for cultural change can take various forms. In its most direct form—war, conquest, or colonization—the dominant group uses force or the

> **cultural integration** the consistency of various aspects of society that promotes order and stability.

Tim Robberts/Stone/Getty Images/Jupiterimages

threat of force to bring about cultural change in the other group. When the Soviet Union invaded and took over many small countries (such as Lithuania, Latvia, Estonia, Ukraine, Georgia, and Armenia) after World War II, it forbade citizens to speak their native languages, banned traditions and customs, and turned churches into warehouses.

Pressures for change can also be indirect. For example, some countries, (e.g., Thailand, Vietnam, China, and Russia) have reduced their prostitution and international sex trafficking because of widespread criticism by the United Nations and some European countries (but not the United States). The United Nations has no power to intervene in a country's internal affairs but can embarrass nations by publicizing human rights violations (Farley 2001).

TECHNOLOGY AND CULTURAL LAG

Some parts of culture change more rapidly than others. **Cultural lag** refers to the gap when nonmaterial culture changes more slowly than material culture.

There are numerous examples of cultural lag in modern society, because ethical rules and government regulations haven't kept up with technological developments. For example, a gradu-

ate student posted a paper on a university Web site and found out later that an Internet term-paper mill was selling it without her knowledge or permission. Because intellectual property laws applying to Internet use are still being developed, the student was in court for several years before the paper mill settled for an undisclosed amount (Foster 2006).

Cultural lag often creates uncertainty, ambiguity about what's right and wrong, conflicting values, and a feeling of helplessness. According to Naisbitt and his colleagues (1999: 3), we both fear and worship technology, become obsessed with gadgets (like computers) even though they take up much of our time, don't deal

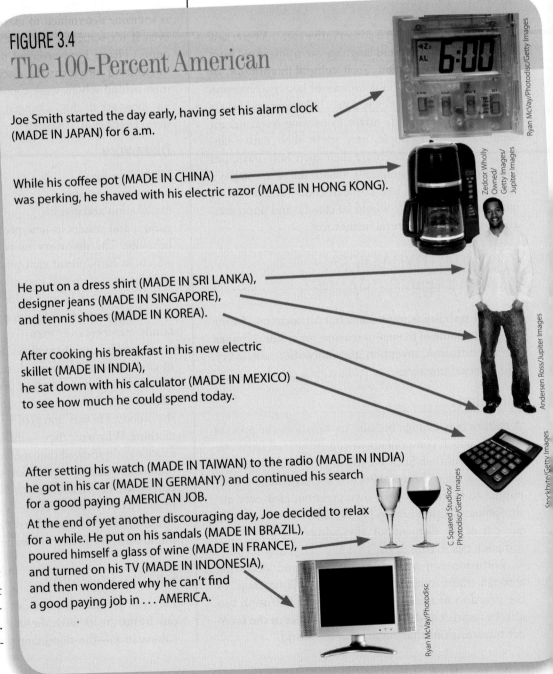

FIGURE 3.4
The 100-Percent American

Joe Smith started the day early, having set his alarm clock (MADE IN JAPAN) for 6 a.m.

While his coffee pot (MADE IN CHINA) was perking, he shaved with his electric razor (MADE IN HONG KONG).

He put on a dress shirt (MADE IN SRI LANKA), designer jeans (MADE IN SINGAPORE), and tennis shoes (MADE IN KOREA).

After cooking his breakfast in his new electric skillet (MADE IN INDIA), he sat down with his calculator (MADE IN MEXICO) to see how much he could spend today.

After setting his watch (MADE IN TAIWAN) to the radio (MADE IN INDIA) he got in his car (MADE IN GERMANY) and continued his search for a good paying AMERICAN JOB.

At the end of yet another discouraging day, Joe decided to relax for a while. He put on his sandals (MADE IN BRAZIL), poured himself a glass of wine (MADE IN FRANCE), and turned on his TV (MADE IN INDONESIA), and then wondered why he can't find a good paying job in . . . AMERICA.

Ryan McVay/Photodisc/Getty Images
Zedcor Wholly Owned/Getty Images/Jupiter Images
Andersen Ross/Jupiter Images
Stockbyte/Getty Images
C Squared Studios/Photodisc/Getty Images
Ryan McVay/Photodisc

TABLE 3.3
Sociological Explanations of Culture

THEORETICAL PERSPECTIVE	FUNCTIONALIST	CONFLICT	FEMINIST	SYMBOLIC INTERACTIONIST
Level of Analysis	Macro	Macro	Macro and Micro	Micro
Key Points	• Similar beliefs bind people together and create stability. • Sharing core values unifies a society and promotes cultural solidarity.	• Culture benefits some groups at the expense of others. • As powerful economic monopolies increase worldwide, the rich get richer and the rest of us get poorer.	• Women and men often experience culture differently. • Cultural values and norms can increase inequality because of gender, race/ethnicity, and social class.	• Cultural symbols forge identities (that change over time). • Culture (such as norms and values) helps people merge into a society despite their differences.
Examples	• Speaking the same language (English in the United States) binds people together because they can communicate with each other, express their feelings, and influence each other's attitudes and behaviors.	• Much of the English language reinforces negative images about gender ("slut"), race ("honky"), ethnicity ("jap"), and age ("old geezer") that creates inequality and fosters ethnocentrism.	• Using male language (such as "Congressman," "fireman," and "chairman") conveys the idea that men are superior to and dominant over women, even when women have the same jobs.	• People can change the language they create as they interact with others. Many Americans now use "police officer" instead of "policeman," and "single person" instead of "bachelor" or "old maid."

with ethical issues raised by biotechnology (like the implications of cloning embryos), and rely on technology as quick fixes: "We want to believe that any given solution is only a purchase away."

Cultural lags have always existed and will continue in the future. Technology is necessary, but we can make conscious choices about how and when we use technological advances. Thus, cultural lags can be viewed as opportunities for making positive changes that enhance culture.

7 Sociological Perspectives on Culture

hat is the role of culture in modern society? And how does culture help us understand ourselves and the world around us? Functionalist, conflict, feminist,

and interactionist scholars offer different answers to these and other questions about culture, but all provide important insights. *Table 3.3* summarizes these perspectives.

FUNCTIONALISM

Functionalists focus on society as a system of interrelated parts (see Chapter 1). In their analysis of culture, similarly, functionalists emphasize the social bonds that attach people to society.

Key Points

For functionalists, culture is a cement that binds society. As you saw earlier, norms and values shape our lives, provide guideposts for our everyday behavior, and promote cultural integration and societal stability (see pp. 44–48). Especially in countries such as the United States that have high immigration rates, cultural norms and values help newcomers adjust to the society.

For functionalists, all societies have similar strategies for meeting human needs. These cultural universals (see p. 49), such as religious rituals, may play out differently in different societies, but all known societies have religious rituals.

Functionalists also note that culture can be dysfunctional. For example, when subcultures such as the Amish refuse to immunize their children, some diseases can surge in the community (Brown 2005). Also, various countercultures (such as paramilitary groups) can create chaos by bombing federal buildings and killing or injuring hundreds of people.

Critical Evaluation

Functionalism is important in showing that shared norms and values create solidarity and stability in a culture. In emphasizing culture's meeting people's daily needs, however, functionalism often overlooks diversity and social change. For example, a number of influential functionalists have proposed that immigration should be restricted because it dilutes shared U.S. values, overlooking the many contributions that newcomers make to society (see Chapter 10).

CONFLICT THEORY

Unlike functionalists, conflict theorists argue that culture can generate considerable inequality instead of unify society. Because the rich and powerful determine economic, political, educational, and legal policies for their own benefit and control the mass media, the average American has little power in changing the culture—whether it's low wages, disastrous wars that taxpayers pay for, or corporate corruption (see Chapters 8 and 11).

Key Points

For conflict theorists, many cultural values and norms benefit some members of society more than others. There's nothing wrong with Americans' being hardworking and wanting to be successful, for example, but who benefits from the average worker's efforts? As you'll see in Chapters 11 and 12, American taxpayers paid billions of dollars to bail out faltering financial industries because the top leaders made bad decisions based, largely, on greed. After the bailouts, the corporate executives and many of their staff used the money to give themselves higher salaries and bonuses than ever before. Thus, those at the top of the socioeconomic ladder can benefit by breaking the rules, including honesty, that other Americans are expected to follow.

According to conflict theorists, as a handful of powerful U.S. corporations increase their global influence,

the rich get richer. The result is widespread inequality. The scientists who created the Internet opened it to the public. However, new laws (passed by wealthy politicians and attorneys) have protected the interests of profit-making cable providers over those of individual users (Lessig 2001).

Conflict theorists also point out that technology benefits primarily the rich. For example, the C-Leg is a prosthetic leg that allows users to go down slopes or staircases, to run, or to stroll on a hilly path. Because the C-Leg costs about $50,000 and is typically not covered by medical insurance, only affluent people can take advantage of this technology (Austen 2002).

Critical Evaluation

Conflict theorists have provided important insights about why U.S. society (and others) suffers from widespread inequality. For example, values such as competitiveness benefit capitalists, who can threaten to fire workers if they aren't as productive as employers expect (see Chapter 12).

According to some critics, conflict theorists often emphasize divisiveness and don't appreciate how culture bonds people to a society. Capitalism may generate widespread inequality, but many people see even low-paid work as important if it helps them climb out of poverty.

FEMINIST THEORIES

Feminist scholars, who use both macro and micro approaches, agree with conflict theorists that material culture, in particular, creates considerable inequality, but they focus on gender differences. Feminist scholars are also more likely than other theorists to examine multicultural variations across some groups.

Key Points

Gender affects our cultural experiences. When media portrayals of women are absent or stereotypical, we get a distorted view of reality. For example, hip-hop and rap music that glorifies gang rape and violence against women degrades all women (see Chapter 9). Feminist scholars also emphasize that subcultures—for example, female students or single mothers—may experience culture differently than their male counterparts do because they typically have fewer resources, such as income and power (see Chapters 11 and 12).

Unequal access to resources often results in women having fewer choices than men, and living under laws and customs that subordinate women. In the United

States, for example, an out-of-wedlock birth typically impoverishes women but not men. In Japan, where rape is often kept hush-hush, police and judges rarely take the offenses seriously (Makino 2009). In Sudan, a woman can be publicly flogged for indecent dress, including wearing trousers (McCrummen 2009). And in many Islamic societies, men dictate women's appropriate attire and behavior (Heath 2008; Zahedi 2008).

Critical Evaluation

Feminist analyses expand our understanding of cultural components that other theoretical perspectives ignore or gloss over. Like conflict theorists, however, feminist theorists often stress divisiveness rather than examining how culture integrates women and men into society. Another weakness is that feminist scholars typically focus on low-income and middle-class women as victims, overlooking the ways affluent women exploit these groups, both female and male.

SYMBOLIC INTERACTIONISM

Unlike functionalists and conflict theorists, symbolic interactionists examine culture through micro lenses. They are most interested in understanding how people create, maintain, and modify culture.

Key Points

Interactionists explain how culture influences our everyday lives. Language, you'll recall, shapes our views and behavior. People within and across societies create a variety of symbols that may change over time. They also change their communication patterns because of technology. Recently, for example, Americans have been either delighted or dismayed that they now receive more e-cards than paper cards to commemorate various holidays or special events such as birthdays and wedding anniversaries (Hendrix 2009).

Symbolic interactionists also note that our values and norms, like other components of culture, aren't superimposed by some unknown force external to us. Instead, as people construct their perception of reality, they create, change, and reinterpret values and norms through interaction with others. Remember the ex-

Muslims in the Kashmir region of India surround a groom as he goes to his in-laws' house to fetch his bride. For functionalists, such traditions reinforce cultural identity and bind people with similar beliefs.

ample of the student at the beginning of the chapter who blurted out an obscenity when he was unhappy with an exam grade? He was quickly reprimanded by a classmate for being uncivil. If the class had laughed or even applauded, my syllabus would've gotten even longer because I would've had to add rules about professional and polite classroom behavior. Instead, peer pressure was an effective sanction that discouraged such language.

Critical Evaluation

Micro approaches are useful in understanding what culture means to people and how these meanings differ across societies. However, symbolic interactionists don't offer a systematic framework for understanding how, exactly, people create and shape culture or develop shared meanings of reality. Why, for instance, are some of us less civil than others even though we share the same cultural values and norms? Another weakness is that interactionists don't address the linkages between culture and institutions. For example, it's important to recognize how language bonds people together, but interactionists say little about how organized groups (such as the English-only movement) try to maintain control over language or use language to promote their values.

Have you ever thought

about how you became the person you are today?

Socialization

1 Socialization: Its Purpose and Importance

You've probably heard the expression that humans are born with a *tabula rasa*, meaning "blank slate." Even before age 2, socialization has started to fill that slate. **Socialization** is the lifelong process of social interaction in which the individual acquires a social identity and ways of thinking, feeling, and acting that are essential for effective participation in a society. Thus, socialization transforms a naked, wet, and crying newborn into a person who becomes a social being.

> **socialization** the lifelong process of social interaction in which the individual acquires a social identity and ways of thinking, feeling, and acting that are essential for effective participation in a society.

WHAT IS THE PURPOSE OF SOCIALIZATION?

Socialization—from childhood to old age—can be relatively smooth or very bumpy, depending on factors such as age, sex, race/ethnicity, and social class. Generally, however, socialization has four key functions that range from providing us with a social identity to transmitting culture to the next generation.

Socialization Establishes Our Social Identity

Have you ever thought about how you became the person you are today? Sociology professors sometimes ask students to give 20 answers to the question "Who am I?" (Kuhn and McPartland 1954). How would you respond? You would probably include a variety of descriptions such as college student, single or married, female or male, your occupation, and family status (son or father, for example). All of your answers would reflect a sense of being someone, of your *self* (a concept we'll examine shortly). You are who you are largely because of socialization.

Socialization Teaches Us Role Taking

Why do you act differently in class than when chatting with your friends? Because we play different roles in different settings. A *role* is the behavior expected of a person in a

what do you think?

I'm always the same, no matter where I am or who's around.

1	2	3	4	5	6	7
strongly agree				strongly disagree		

particular social position (see Chapter 5). The way we interact with a parent is typically very different from the way we talk to an employer, a friend, or a professor. We all learn appropriate roles through the socialization process.

Socialization Controls Our Behavior

In learning appropriate roles, we absorb values and a variety of rules about how we should (and should not) interact in everyday situations. If we follow the rules, we're usually rewarded or at least accepted. If we break the rules, we may be punished. As a result, socialization controls our behavior.

We act in socially acceptable ways because we internalize societal values and beliefs. **Internalization** is the process of learning cultural behaviors and expectations so deeply that we assume they are correct and accept them without question. For example, several European nations provide generous employment leave for parents to care for preschool children, but fathers rarely take advantage of this benefit because most people, including women, assume that child rearing is a woman's responsibility (Forsberg 2005).

Despite our personality differences, the process of socialization teaches us to conform to societal expectations. This does *not* mean that we become programmed robots. Instead, many of our choices are shaped and limited by the cultural beliefs, values, and norms that we learn through socialization. The limits, whether we agree or disagree with them, ensure that society is orderly and predictable.

Socialization Transmits Culture to the Next Generation

Socialization is also the process of acquiring the culture in which we live. Each generation passes on the learned roles and rules to the next generation. The culture that is transmitted includes language, beliefs, values, norms, and symbols, as you saw in Chapter 3.

WHY IS SOCIALIZATION IMPORTANT?

Social isolation can be devastating. An example of its negative effects is Genie. When Genie was 20 months old, her father decided she was "retarded" and locked her away in a back room, curtains drawn and the door shut. Genie was tied into a harness and placed in a wire mesh cage. She had almost no opportunity to overhear any conversation between others in the house. Genie's father frequently beat her with a wooden stick and never spoke to her. When she was discovered in 1970 at age 13, a psychiatrist described Genie as "unsocialized, primitive, and hardly human." Except for high-pitched whimpers, she never spoke. Genie had little bowel control, experienced rages, rubbed her face frantically, and tried to hurt herself. After living in a rehabilitation ward and a foster home, she learned to eat normally, was toilet-trained, and gradually developed a vocabulary, but her language use never progressed beyond that of a 3- or 4-year-old (Curtiss 1977). (If you want to read more about Genie, see "The Civilizing of Genie," available online at http://kccesl.tripod.com/genie.html.)

The research on children who are isolated (like Genie) or institutionalized (like orphans) shows that socialization is critical to our development. Talking, eating with utensils, and controlling our bowel movements do not come naturally. Instead, we learn to do all of these things beginning in infancy. When children are deprived of interaction with other people, they do not develop the characteristics that most of us see as normal and human.

2 Nature and Nurture

biologists tend to focus on the role of heredity (or genetics) in human development. In contrast, most social scientists, including sociologists, underscore the role of learning, social-

TABLE 4.1	
The Nature-Nurture Debate	
NATURE	**Human development is . . .** Innate Biological, physiological Due largely to heredity Fairly fixed
NURTURE	**Human development is . . .** Learned Psychological, social, cultural Due largely to environment Fairly changeable

ization, and culture. This difference of opinion is often called the *nature-nurture debate* (see *Table 4.1*). Many researchers believe that heredity and environment overlap in shaping the developing person, but there is still a tendency to emphasize either nature or nurture.

HOW IMPORTANT IS NATURE?

Some scientists propose that biological factors—especially the brain—play an important role in our development. A study of brain scans, for example, suggests that increased activity in a region of the brain (the ventromedial prefrontal cortex) a few inches behind the bridge of the nose may predispose people to have a negative outlook on life. Research suggests that when activity in this region of the brain increases, people tend to be more anxious, irritable, angry, and unpleasant (Vedantam 2002). It's not clear, however, why many people have high brain activity yet remain calm, friendly, and pleasant.

How Biology Affects Behavior

Some scientists point to unsuccessful attempts at sex reassignment to show that nature is more important than nurture. John Money, a highly respected medical psychologist at Johns Hopkins University Hospital, has published numerous articles and books maintaining that gender identity is not firm at birth but is determined as much by culture and nurture as by genes and hormones (Money and Ehrhardt 1972).

Recently, several scientists have challenged such conclusions. In 1963, twin boys were being circumcised. The penis of one of the infants, David Reimer, was accidentally burned off. Encouraged by John Money, the parents agreed to raise David as "Brenda." The child's testicles were removed, and surgery to construct a vagina was planned. Money reported that the twins were growing into happy, well-adjusted children, setting a precedent for sex reassignment as the standard treatment for 15,000 newborns with similarly injured genitals (Colapinto 1997, 2001).

In the mid-1990s, a biologist and a psychiatrist followed up on Brenda's progress and concluded that the sex reassignment had not been successful. Almost from the beginning, Brenda refused to be treated like a girl. When her mother dressed her in frilly clothes as a toddler, Brenda tried to rip them off. She preferred to play with boys and stereotypical boys' toys such as machine guns. People in the community said that she "looks like a boy, talks like a boy." Brenda had no friends, and no one would play with her: "Every day I was picked on,

EMOTIONAL ATTACHMENT

Nina Leen/Time Life Pictures/Getty Images

HARLOW STUDIES

In the early 1960s, psychologists Margaret and Harry Harlow (1962) conducted several studies on infant monkeys. In one group, a "mother" made of terrycloth provided no food, while the mother made of wire did so through an attached baby bottle containing milk. In another group, the terrycloth mother provided food but the wire mother did not. Regardless of which mother provided milk, when both groups of monkeys were frightened, they clung to the cloth mother. The Harlows concluded that warmth and comfort were more important to the infant monkeys than nourishment. Since then, some sociologists have cited the Harlow studies to argue that emotional attachment may be more critical than physical nourishment for human infants. Do you see any problems with sociologists' generalizing the results of animal studies to humans? Or not?

sociobiology a theoretical approach that applies biological principles to explain the behavior of animals, including human beings.

every day I was teased, every day I was threatened" (Diamond and Sigmundson 1997: 300).

When she was 14, Brenda rebelled and stopped living as a girl: She refused to wear dresses, urinated standing up, turned down vaginal surgery, and decided she would either commit suicide or live as a male. When his father finally told David the true story of his birth and sex change, David recalls that "all of a sudden everything clicked. For the first time things made sense and I understood who and what I was" (Diamond and Sigmundson 1997: 300).

David had a mastectomy (breast removal surgery) at the age of 14 and underwent several operations to reconstruct a penis. At age 25, he married an older woman and adopted her three children. He committed suicide in 2004 at the age of 38. Most suicides have multiple motives, but some speculated that David committed suicide because of the "physical and mental torments he suffered in childhood that haunted him the rest of his life" (Colapinto 2004: 96). David's experience suggests to some scientists that nature outweighs nurture in shaping a person's gender identity.

Considerable debate continues within the medical community about whether parents should allow surgery on their children who are born with ambiguous genitals (a topic we'll examine in Chapter 9). Some physicians argue that parents should be counseled until the child is old enough to decide whether to undergo surgery, because sexual identity does not derive solely, or even primarily, from a person's genitals. Others contend that genital surgery helps establish a child's sexual identity at an early age and that it's irresponsible to do nothing (Weil 2006).

Sociobiology and Socialization

Sociobiology is a theoretical approach that applies biological principles to explain the behavior of animals, including human beings. Sociobiologists argue, for example, that evolution and genes (nature) can explain why men are generally more aggressive than women. To ensure that their genes will be passed on to offspring, males (human and animal) have to prevail over their rivals. The intense competition often includes aggression and violence (Barash 2002).

Critics reject this sociobiological explanation of male violence. If men were innately aggressive, they would be equally violent across all societies. This is not the case. The proportion of women who have ever suffered physical violence by a male partner varies considerably: 80 percent in Vietnam, 61 percent in Peru, 20 percent in the United States, and 13 percent in Japan (Chelala 2002; Rennison 2003; World Health Organization 2005). Such variations presumably reflect cultural norms and practices, and other environmental factors (nurture) rather than biology or genetics (nature) (Chesney-Lind and Pasko 2004).

HOW IMPORTANT IS NURTURE?

Most sociologists agree that nature affects human development. They maintain, however, that nurture is more significant than nature because socialization and culture shape even biological inputs.

How Behavior Affects Biology

Some research suggests that environment (nurture) influences children's genetic makeup (nature). A family history of alcoholism, for example, places a person at greater risk for development

David Reimer was raised as a girl, Brenda, until he was 14.

REUTERS/Landov

of alcohol problems. Serotonin, a brain transmitter, regulates mood, emotion, sleep, and appetite. When people abuse alcohol, serotonin's primary role as an inhibitor breaks down. As a result, alcoholics are often aggressive, depressed, and anxious (Schuckit 1999).

Children of alcoholics can inherit a malfunctioning serotonin transporter gene, become alcoholics themselves, and suffer from behavioral and emotional problems. Birth defects associated with prenatal alcohol exposure can occur in the first 3 to 8 weeks of pregnancy, before a woman even knows she's pregnant. A woman's single drinking "binge"—lasting four hours or more—can permanently damage the brain of an unborn child. A man who drinks heavily may have genetically damaged sperm that also leads to birth defects. Thus, the abuse of alcohol (an environmental factor) by either a woman or a man can have a devastating, irreversible, and lifelong negative impact on her or his child (Twitchell et al. 2001; Hetherington et al. 2006).

Adult behavior can influence a child's biological makeup in other ways. Physical, psychological, or sexual abuse can affect the developing brain during childhood, and the changes may trigger disorders such as depression in adulthood. An impaired corpus callosum—the pathway integrating the two hemispheres of the brain—can result in dramatic shifts in mood and personality, especially for children who have suffered neglect and sexual abuse (Teicher 2000). Thus, childhood mistreatment can impair biological development.

Culture and Socialization

Sociologists often point to cross-cultural data to illustrate the importance of nurture. In a well-known study, anthropologist Margaret Mead (1935) observed three tribes—the Arapesh, Mundugumor, and Tchambuli—who lived close to one another in New Guinea.

She found three combinations of gender roles. Among the Arapesh, both men and women were nurturant with their children. The men were cooperative and sensitive, and rarely engaged in warfare. The Mundugumor were just the opposite: Both men and women were competitive and aggressive, neither parent showed much tenderness toward their offspring, and both parents often used physical punishment to discipline their children. The Tchambuli reversed Western gender roles. The women were the economic providers, and the men took care of the children, sat around chatting, and spent a lot of time decorating themselves for tribal festivities. Mead concluded that attributes long considered either masculine (such as being aggressive) or feminine (such as being emotional) are culturally, not biologically, determined.

Margaret Mead (1901–1978) conducted a number of field studies in the Pacific. Many academics have described Mead as an influential feminist scholar because her work, especially her demonstration that gender roles and child-rearing practices differ in a variety of cultures, helped to break down stereotypes about what is natural (or innate).

IS THE NATURE-NURTURE DEBATE BECOMING OBSOLETE IN SOCIOLOGY?

You and your cousins, Erik and Joelle, share the same genes, but you're in college whereas they dropped out of high school. Why? A growing number of sociologists—who are calling for a "genetically informed sociology"—maintain that the nature *or* nurture debate is becoming outdated in understanding socialization processes and outcomes (Ledger 2009: 16–17). Ignoring the impact of genetics, they argue, leads to an incomplete understanding of behavior because genes

AP Photo

shape our lives and could help explain why there is so much variation across families and other groups.

People presumably have at least 52 characteristics—such as aggression, leadership traits, and cognitive ability—that are partially inherited (Freese 2008). However, our social environment can enhance or dampen these genetic characteristics, such as in the following examples:

- A gene that regulates the levels of dopamine, which affects the brain, influences sexual aggression, as well as other behaviors such as impulsivity and recklessness, is much more likely to have such negative effects if the adolescent attends a school with a student culture that endorses early sexual activity and if the adolescent has low cognitive abilities, such as reasoning and memory (Guo et al. 2008b; see also Guo et al. 2008a).

- People who have inherited a genetic predisposition for alcoholism vary depending on other social factors, especially environment. As income and education levels decrease, for example, using alcohol goes up, and as childhood deprivation and the number of "daily hassles" increases, so does alcoholism (Pescosolido et al. 2008). Thus, the environment can help one overcome genetic predispositions for alcoholism.

- Children who are genetically predisposed to obesity don't always become overweight because some parents discourage overeating and provide their kids with numerous recreational activities (Martin 2008).

Sociologists who study the relationship between genetics (nature) and the social environment (nurture) admit that their samples are small, but they maintain that research which combines genetics (nature) and socialization (nurture) can enhance our understanding of how the environment affects genetic predispositions (see Schnittker 2008 and Shanahan et al. 2008).

3 Sociological Explanations of Socialization

functionalism provides a foundation for understanding the purposes of socialization described at the beginning of this chapter. However, functionalists don't tell us *how* socialization works on a micro level, and they treat socialization as a one-way process in which people adapt to culture rather than make choices and change society. Two important approaches that examine interpersonal relationships and other micro-level factors are social learning theories and symbolic interaction theories (*Table 4.2* summarizes these perspectives). Let's begin with social learning theories.

SOCIAL LEARNING THEORIES

The central notion of **social learning theories** is that people learn new attitudes, beliefs, and behaviors through social interaction, especially during childhood. We learn how to behave both directly and indirectly, for example, through observation and reinforcement. We also learn how to act without actually performing the behavior.

Direct and Indirect Learning

In most cases, our socialization is *direct*. By being rewarded or punished, we learn many behaviors through reinforcement. A little girl who puts on her mother's makeup may be told she's cute, but her brother will be scolded ("Boys don't wear makeup!"). If a child is caught lying, she or he will be punished through a variety of sanctions, such as not being able to play with friends, not being allowed to watch television or use the computer, or having to do extra household chores.

Socialization also involves *indirect* reinforcement through *modeling* (imitating people who are important in our lives). In one study, for example, researchers observed preschoolers aged 2 to 6 who pretended to shop for a visiting friend of their Barbie or Ken doll. The pretend store stocked 133 miniature items, including meat, fruit, vegetables, snacks, cigarettes, beer, and wine. Overall, 28 percent of the children bought cigarettes, and 61 percent bought alcohol. The children whose parents smoked were almost four times more likely to buy cigarettes. The children whose parents drank at least monthly were three times more likely to buy alcohol. The researchers concluded that observing parental behavior may influence children to view smoking and drinking as appropriate, and to adopt such practices later in life (Dalton et al. 2005).

Learning and Performing

Social learning theorists often make a distinction between *learning* and *performing* behavior. Children and adults can learn to do something through observation, but they don't always imitate the behavior. For exam-

TABLE 4.2
Key Elements of Socialization Theories

SOCIAL LEARNING THEORIES	SYMBOLIC INTERACTION THEORIES
• Social interaction is important in learning appropriate and inappropriate behavior. • Socialization relies on direct and indirect reinforcement.	• The self emerges through social interaction with significant others. • Socialization includes role taking and controlling the impression we give to others.
Example: Children learn how to behave when they are scolded or praised for specific behaviors.	*Example:* Children who are praised are more likely to develop a strong self-image than those who are always criticized.

ple, children may see their friends cheat in school but don't do so themselves. Adults, similarly, may see their coworkers steal office supplies but buy their own.

Social learning theorists maintain that we behave in certain ways because of past rewards and punishments, modeling, and observation. We behave as we do, then, because our society teaches us what's appropriate and what's not (Bandura and Walters 1963; Mischel 1966; Lynn 1969).

Critical Evaluation

Social learning theories help us understand why we behave as we do, but much of the emphasis is on early socialization rather than on what occurs throughout life. Social learning theories also don't explain why reinforcement and modeling work for some children but not others, especially those in the same family. There may be personality differences, but if learning is as effective as social learning theorists maintain, siblings' attitudes and behavior should be more similar than different. This is often not the case, however, even with identical twins.

Another weakness is that most social learning theories ignore factors such as birth order, which brings different advantages and disadvantages. Except for affluent families, larger families have fewer resources for the second, third, and later children. The first child may be disciplined more but may also be encouraged to pursue interests that could lead to higher education and a prestigious career. In contrast, later-born children may enjoy less parental attention and be less likely to receive financial support to pursue a college education (Zajonc and Markus 1975; Conley 2004).

SYMBOLIC INTERACTION THEORIES

Symbolic interaction theories have had a major impact in explaining social development. Sociologists Charles Horton Cooley (1864–1929), George Herbert Mead (1863–1931), and Erving Goffman (1922–1982) were especially influential in showing how social interaction shapes socialization.

Charles Horton Cooley: Emergence of the Self and the Looking-Glass Self

Newborn infants lack a sense of **self,** an awareness of having a social identity. Gradually, they begin to differentiate themselves from their environment and develop a sense of self.

After carefully observing the development of his young daughter, Charles Horton Cooley (1909/1983) concluded that children acquire a sense of who they are through their interactions with others, especially by imagining how others view them. The sense of self, then, is not innate but emerges out of social relationships. Cooley called this social self the *reflected self,* or the **looking-glass self,** a self-image based on how we think others see us. He proposed that the looking-glass self develops in an ongoing process of three phases:

- *Phase 1: Perception.* We imagine how we appear to other people and how they *perceive* us ("She thinks I'm attractive," or "I bet he thinks I'm fat.").

- *Phase 2: Interpretation of the perception.* We imagine how others *judge* us ("She's impressed with me," or "He's disgusted with the way I look.").

- *Phase 3: Response.* We experience *self-feelings* based on what we regard to be others' judgments of us. If we think others see us in a favorable light, we may feel proud, happy, or self-confident ("I'm terrific."). If we think others see us in a negative light, we may feel angry, embarrassed, or insecure ("I'm pathetic.").

Our interpretation of others' perceptions (phase 2) may be totally wrong. The looking-glass self, remember, refers to how we *think* others see us rather than what they *actually* think of us. However, our perceptions of other people's views—whether we're right or wrong—mold our self-image, which then guides our behavior.

Cooley focused on how children acquire a sense of who they are through their interactions with others, but he noted that the process of forming a looking-glass self does not end in childhood. Instead, our self-concept may change over time because we reimagine ourselves as we think others see us—attractive or ugly, interesting or boring, intelligent or stupid, graceful or awkward, and so on.

Sometimes we're very aware of the process shaping our looking-glass self. Consider your own self-concept: If others keep telling you what a great student you are, you'll likely see yourself as intelligent. In many settings, however—such as public places, large classrooms, and sports events—the looking-glass self is irrelevant because there is relatively little interpersonal interaction and the other people are strangers or aren't very significant in our lives.

George Herbert Mead: Development of the Self and Role Taking

Cooley described how an individual's sense of self emerges, but not how it develops. George Herbert Mead, one of Cooley's colleagues, took up this task. For Mead (1934), the most critical social interaction occurs in the family, the foundation of socialization.

Our self develops, according to Mead, when we learn to differentiate the *me* from the *I*—two parts of the self. The *I* is creative, imaginative, impulsive, spontaneous, nonconformist, self-centered, and sometimes unpredictable. The *me* that has been successfully socialized is aware of the attitudes of others, has self-control, and has internalized social roles. Instead of impulsively and selfishly grabbing another child's toys, for example, as the *I* would do, the *me* asks for permission to use someone's toys and shares them with others.

For Mead, the *me* forms as children engage in **role taking,** learning to take the perspective of others. Children gradually acquire this ability beginning early in the socialization process through three sequential stages:

Parents who encourage their children to express themselves help them develop a positive self-image.

Photodisc/Getty Images

1. **Preparatory stage (roughly birth to 2 years).** An infant doesn't distinguish between the self and others. The *I* is dominant, while the *me* is forming in the background. In this stage, children learn through imitation. They may mimic daddy's shaving or mommy's angry tone of voice without really understanding the parent's behavior. In this exploratory stage, children engage in behavior that they rarely associate with words or symbols, but they begin to understand cause and effect (e.g., crying leads to being picked up). Gradually, as the child begins to recognize others' reactions (to form a looking-glass self), he or she develops a self.

2. **Play stage (roughly 2–6 years).** The child begins to use language and understand that words (like *dog* and *cat*) have a shared cultural meaning. Through play, children begin to learn role taking in two ways. First, they emulate the words and behavior of **significant others,** the people who are important in one's life, such as parents or other primary caregivers and siblings. The child learns that he or she has a self that is distinct from that of others, that others behave in many different ways, and that others expect her or him to behave in specific ways. In other words, the child learns social norms (see Chapter 3).

   In the play stage, the child moves beyond imitation and acts out imagined roles ("I'll be the mommy and you be the daddy."). The play stage involves relatively simple role taking because the child plays one role at a time and doesn't yet understand the relationships between roles. This stage is crucial, according to Mead, because the child *is learning to take the role of the other.* For the first time, the child tries to imagine how others behave or feel. The *me* grows stronger because the child is concerned about the judgments of significant others.

Also in the play stage, children experience **anticipatory socialization,** the process of learning how to perform a role they don't occupy. By playing "mommy" or "daddy," children prepare themselves for eventually becoming parents. Anticipatory socialization continues in later years, for example, when expectant parents attend childbirth classes, job seekers practice their skills in mock interviews, and many high-school students visit campuses and attend orientation meetings to prepare for college life.

3. **Game stage (roughly 6 years and older).** This stage involves acquiring the ability to understand connections between roles. The child must "not only take the role of the other…but must assume the various roles of all participants in the game, and govern his action accordingly" (Mead 1964: 285). Mead used baseball to illustrate this stage. In baseball (or other organized games and activities), the child plays

one role at a time (such as batter) but understands and anticipates the actions of other players (pitcher, shortstop, runners on bases) on both teams. As children grow older and interact with a wider range of people, they learn to respond to and fulfill a variety of social roles.

The game stage enables understanding and taking the role of the **generalized other,** people who don't have close ties to a child but who influence her or his internalization of society's norms and values. The generalized other, then, exerts control over the *I* and ensures some predictability in life. For sociologists, the development of the generalized other is a central feature of the socialization process because the *me* becomes an integral part of the self (see *Figure 4.1*).

After the generalized other has developed, the *me* never fully controls the *I,* even in adulthood. We sometimes break rules or act impulsively, even though we know better. Or, when we are frustrated or angry, we may lash out against other people even though they haven't done anything wrong.

Erving Goffman: Staging the Self in Everyday Life

Cooley and Mead described how the self and role taking emerge and develop during early socialization. Erving Goffman (1959, 1969) extended these analyses by showing that we interact differently in different settings throughout adulthood. Goffman proposed that social life mirrors the theater because we are like actors: We engage in "role performances," want to influence an "audience," and can have considerable control over the image that we project while we're "on stage." (These concepts are explored in greater detail in Chapter 5.)

In a process that Goffman called **impression management,** we provide information and cues to others to present ourselves in a favorable light while downplaying or concealing our less appealing qualities. Being successful in this presentation of the self requires managing three types of expressive resources. First, we try to control the *setting,* the physical space, or "scene," where the interaction takes place. In the classroom, "a professor may use items such as chalk, lecture notes, computers, videos, and desks to facilitate a class and show that he or she is an excellent teacher" (Sandstrom et al. 2006: 105).

A second expressive resource is controlling *appearance,* such as clothing and titles that convey information about our social status. When physicians or professors use the title "Doctor," for example, they are telling the "audience" to respond to them respectfully.

The third expressive resource is *manner*—the mood or style of behavior we display that sends important messages to the audience. For example, faculty members regularly manage their manner when interacting with students. When you e-mail a professor a question about your research project, the response is usually inviting ("I'll be happy to discuss your project.") even though the professor may actually be annoyed ("Your project has nothing to do with this course; stop wasting my time.").

Sometimes, no matter how much we try to manage setting, appearance, and manner, we slip up in our role performances. This leads to discomfort and embarrass-

anticipatory socialization the process of learning how to perform a role one doesn't yet occupy.

generalized other people who don't have close ties to a child but who influence her or his internalization of society's norms and values.

impression management the process of providing information and cues to others to present oneself in a favorable light while downplaying or concealing one's less appealing qualities.

C Squared Studios/Photodisc/Getty Images

ment for everyone involved, but the audience is typically tactful:

> Imagine that you are giving a presentation in one of your classes and, just as you make a key point, a large droplet of saliva sprays from your lips and lands near someone sitting in the front row. Although several of your classmates cannot help but notice it, none of them are likely to shout out, "Hey, you just about spit on someone in the first row!" Instead, they will probably show tact and act as if nothing unusual or embarrassing took place. (Sandstrom et al. 2006: 109)

As we move from one situation to another, according to Goffman, we maintain self-control, for example, by avoiding emotional outbursts and altering our facial expressions and verbal tones. Thus, all of us engage in impression management practically every day.

Critical Evaluation

Symbolic interactionists have provided major insights about socialization, especially of young children as they form a sense of self and learn role taking. Interactionists have also shown that fitting into our social world is a complex process that continues through adulthood. Like other theories, however, symbolic interactionism has its limitations. For example, it's not clear why some children have a more positive looking-glass self than others, even when the cues are consistently negative, as when some children who grow up in abusive homes and attend low-quality schools are successful later in life.

Some scholars have criticized the vagueness of essential concepts such as *self*, *me*, and *I*. Because the concepts are imprecise, it's difficult, if not impossible, to measure them. Some have also challenged Mead's claim that children automatically pass through play and game stages as they get older. Instead, some critics contend, the extent of socialization depends on a child's social context, such as whether parents and other primary caregivers are actively involved in the child's upbringing and provide enriching interaction. Even then, some

FIGURE 4.1

Mead's Three Stages in Developing a Sense of Self

STAGE 1: **Preparatory Stage** (under age 2)

No distinction between self and others; the child is self-centered and self-absorbed

Learns through observation

STAGE 2: **Play Stage** (aged 2 to about 6)

Distinguishes between self and others

Imitates significant others (usually parents)

Learns role taking, assuming one role at a time, in "let's pretend" and other play that teaches **anticipatory socialization**

STAGE 3: **Game Stage** (aged 6 and older)

Understands and anticipates multiple roles

Connects to societal roles through the **generalized other**

critics contend, some children never develop the role of the generalized other (see Ritzer 1992).

Other scholars have questioned the value of the concept of the generalized other in understanding early socialization processes. Because children interact in many social contexts (home, preschool, play groups), they do not simply assume the role of one generalized other, but many. That is, as children get older, they may have several **reference groups**—groups of people who shape an individual's self-image, behavior, values, and attitudes in different contexts (Merton and Rossi 1950; Shibutani 1986).

Another weakness is that interactionists credit people with more free will than they have. Individuals don't always have the power or ability to shape others' reactions or their social world. For example, impression management is a skill that is less common among lower socioeconomic groups than middle classes, whose members have internalized such expectations to be successful in jobs. Also, how people react to us may reflect our membership in a particular group or social category (e.g., because of one's sex, age, or race/ethnicity) that we can't change (Powers 2004).

A major criticism of Cooley, Mead, Goffman, and other interactionists is that they tend to downplay or ignore macro-level and structural forces that affect our development (Ritzer 1992). As the next two sections show, socialization processes are diverse, especially in multicultural countries such as the United States. Even in societies and communities that have similar characteristics, large-scale social structures (such as the economy, educational institutions, and popular culture) have a major impact on socialization. Let's begin by looking at socialization agents who play important roles in our lives.

4 Primary Socialization Agents

infants waste no time in socializing parents (and others) to be caretakers. By fretting, crying, and whining, they teach adults when to feed, change, and pick them up. Thus, even babies aren't merely passive recipients; they are also active participants in their own development. The family, peer groups, teachers, and the media are some of the primary **agents of socialization**—the individuals, groups, or institutions that teach us what we need to know to participate effectively in society.

FAMILY

Parents, siblings, grandparents, and other family members play a critical role in our socialization. Parents, however, are the first and most influential socialization agents.

How Parents Socialize Children

The purpose of socialization is to enable the child to regulate her or his own behavior and to make socially responsible decisions. In teaching their children social rules and roles, parents rely on several of the learning techniques discussed earlier in this chapter, such as reinforcement, to encourage desired behavior. Parents also manage many aspects of the environment that influence a child's social development: They choose the neighborhood (which often determines what school a child attends), decorate the child's room in a masculine or feminine style, provide her or him with particular toys and books, and arrange social events and other activities (such as sports, art, and music) to enrich the child's development.

Parenting Styles

Parents have four common parenting styles (see *Table 4.3*) that affect socialization. In *authoritarian parenting*, parents tend to be harsh, unresponsive, and rigid, and to use their power to control a child's behavior.

Authoritative parenting is warm, responsive, and involved yet unobtrusive. Parents set reasonable limits and expect appropriately mature behavior from their children. *Permissive parenting* is lax: Parents set few rules but are usually warm and responsive. *Uninvolved parenting* is indifferent and neglectful. Parents focus on their own needs rather than those of the children, spend little time interacting with the children, and know little about their interests or whereabouts (Baumrind 1968, 1989; Maccoby and Martin 1983; Aunola and Nurmi 2005).

Healthy child development is most likely in authoritative homes, in which parents are consistent in combining warmth, monitoring, and discipline. Authoritative parenting tends to produce children who are self-reliant, achievement-oriented, and successful in school. Adolescents in households with authoritarian, permissive, or uninvolved parents tend to have poorer psychosocial development, lower school grades, lower self-reliance, higher levels of delinquent behavior, and are more likely to be swayed by harmful peer pressure

> **agents of socialization** the individuals, groups, or institutions that teach us what we need to know to participate effectively in society.

During the last decade, numerous summer camps have sprung up in South Korea where children ages 7 to 19 live in military-style barracks, undergo drills and exercise from dawn to dusk, eat very simple meals, and have no access to computers, television, or cellphones. Most are sent by parents "who realize that their pampered offspring need more discipline to become better students and grow into conscientious adults" (Glionna 2009: A1). Some of the kids' offenses have included getting a low grade on an important test, accidentally breaking a window in the family's apartment, and most commonly, talking back to their parents.

AP Photo/Yonhap, Shin Young-kuyn

(e.g., to use drugs and alcohol) (Dorius et al. 2004; Eisenberg et al. 2005; Hillaker et al. 2008).

Such findings vary by social class and race/ethnicity, however. For many Latino and Asian immigrants, authoritarian parenting produces positive outcomes, such as academic success. This parenting style is also effective in safeguarding children who are growing up in low-income neighborhoods with high levels of crime and drug peddling (Brody et al. 2002; Pong et al. 2005).

Siblings

Siblings, like parents, play important roles in the socialization process. Children can bully and abuse their (usually) younger brothers and sisters through name-calling, ridiculing, destroying personal possessions, and even physical or sexual abuse. Such behavior can leave lasting emotional scars that lower a child's self-esteem, and physical abuse sends the message that violence is acceptable for resolving conflict now and in the future (Gelles 1997; Wiehe 1997).

Siblings can also be supportive: They can help younger brothers and sisters with their homework and protect them from neighborhood and school bullies. During adolescence and adulthood, siblings often act as confidantes and as role models on how to get along with people, and they often offer financial and emotional assistance during stressful times (Conger and Elder 1994; McCoy et al. 2002).

PLAY AND PEER GROUPS

Play is important in children's development because it provides pleasure, forms friendships, and builds communication, emotional, and social skills. Peer groups also play a significant role in our socialization. A **peer group** consists of people who are similar in age, social status, and interests. All of us are members of peer groups, but such groups are especially influential until about our mid-20s. After that, coworkers, spouses, children, and close friends are usually more important than peers in our everyday lives.

TABLE 4.3
Parenting Styles

PARENTING STYLE	CHARACTERISTICS	EXAMPLE
Authoritarian	Very demanding, controlling, punitive	"You can't borrow the car because I said so."
Authoritative	Demanding, controlling, warm, supportive	"You can borrow the car, but be home by curfew."
Permissive	Not demanding, warm, indulgent, set few rules	"Borrow the car whenever you want."
Uninvolved	Neither supportive nor controlling	"I don't care what you do; I'm busy."

Play and Its Functions

As you saw earlier, George Herbert Mead believed that play and games are important sources of socialization: We become more skilled in using language and symbols, learn role-playing, and internalize roles that we don't necessarily enact (the generalized other). Play serves several other important functions.

First, play promotes cognitive development. Whether it's doing simple five-piece puzzles or tackling complex video games like *Sim City* and *Roller Coaster Tycoon*, play encourages children to think, formulate strategies, and budget and manage resources. From

Rubberball/Jupiter Images

an early age, however, play is generally gender typed. In 2008, the top-selling toys for girls were Barbie dolls, followed by Hannah Montana games, generic dolls, and Nintendo Wii, a video game console. The top-selling toys for boys were video games, followed by Nintendo Wii, Lego, cars, and Transformers (Stead 2008).

Second, play—especially when it's structured—keeps children out of trouble and enhances their social development. For example, children who devote more of their free time to structured and supervised activities—such as hobbies and sports—rather than just hanging out with their friends, perform better academically, are emotionally better adjusted, and have fewer problems at school and at home. In effect, sports and hobbies provide children with constructive ways to channel their energy and intelligence (McHale 2001).

Third, play can strengthen peer relationships. Beginning in elementary school, few things are more important to most children than being accepted by their peers. Even if children aren't popular, belonging to a friendship group enhances their psychological well-being and ability to cope with stress (Rubin et al. 1998; Scarlett et al. 2005).

Peers in Children's Socialization

Peer influence usually increases as children get older. Especially during the early teen years, peers often reinforce desirable behavior or skills in ways that enhance a child's self-image ("Wow, you're really good in math!"). In this sense, to use Cooley's concept, peers can help each other develop a positive looking-glass self.

Peers also serve as positive role models. Children acquire a wide array of information and knowledge by observing their peers. Even during the first days of school, children learn to imitate their peers at standing in line, raising their hands in class, and being quiet while the teacher is speaking. Peers can also teach new skills. A child who's talented in art may help a schoolmate during art class, and one who's good in sports may teach others how to control a soccer ball or hold a baseball bat properly.

Not all peer influence is positive, however. Some cliques encourage high-risk behavior that includes sexual activity, smoking, drinking alcohol, and using other drugs. In most cases, however, peer acceptance (whether one is a jock, a computer geek, or a reporter on the yearbook staff) promotes friendship and a sense of fitting in. Thus, peer groups can be important sources of support for teens and increase their self-esteem, especially for adolescents who have poor relationships with their parents or feel insecure about their appearance or abilities (Strasburger and Wilson 2002).

TEACHERS AND SCHOOLS

Talk show host Oprah Winfrey often praises a fourth-grade teacher who recognized her abilities, encouraged her to read, and inspired her to excel academically. Have there been teachers, like Oprah's, who played a key role in shaping who you are today? Like family and peer groups, teachers and schools have a strong influence on our socialization.

The School's Role in Socialization

By the time children are 4 or 5, school fills an increasingly large portion of their lives. The primary purpose of the school is to instruct children and enhance their cognitive development. Schools do not simply transmit knowledge; they also teach children to think about the world in different ways. Because of the emphasis on multiculturalism, for example, children often learn about other societies and customs (see Chapters 3 and 14). Even outside of classes, schools affect children's daily activities through homework assignments and participation in clubs and other extracurricular activities.

Because many parents are employed, schools have had to devote more time and resources to topics—such as sex education and drug-abuse prevention—that were once the sole responsibility of families. In many ways, then, schools play an increasingly important role in socialization.

Teachers' Impact on Children's Development

Teachers are among the most important socialization agents. From kindergarten through high school, teachers play numerous roles in the classroom—instructor, role model, evaluator, moral guide, and disciplinarian, to name just a few. Once children enter school, their relationships with their teachers are important for academic success. Kindergarten and elementary-school teachers' reports of behavioral problems (such as unexcused absences) and poor grades often continue into the middle school years (Hamre and Pianta 2001).

POPULAR CULTURE AND THE MEDIA

Because of iPods, iPhones, texting, YouTube, and social networking sites such as Facebook, young people are rarely out of the reach of the electronic media. How does such technology affect socialization?

Electronic Media

The American Academy of Pediatrics (2001: 424) advises parents to avoid television entirely for children younger than 2 and to limit the viewing time of elementary school children to no more than 2 hours a day, to encourage more interactive activities "that will promote proper brain development, such as talking, playing, singing, and reading together." Still, 68 percent of children under age 2 view 2 to 3 hours of television daily, and 20 percent have a television in their bedroom, as do one third of 3- to 6-year-olds (Garrison and Christakis 2005; Vandewater et al. 2007).

The average young American now spends practically every waking minute—except for the time in school—using a smartphone, computer, television, or other electronic device. In 2009, those ages 8 to 18 spent 7.5 hours a day engaged with some type of electronic media, up from 6.5 hours in 2004. The 53 hours in 2009 were greater than the amount of time most adults spend at a full-time job. Generally, youths who spend more time with media have lower grades and lower levels of personal contentment (see *Table 4.4*). These findings are similar across all ages, for girls and boys, race/ethnicity, parents' social class, and single- and two-parent households (Rideout et al. 2010).

High media usage can decrease academic success, but two thirds of parents are especially concerned that the media contribute to young people's violent or sexual behaviors (Borzekowski and Robinson 2005;

Class field trips enhance children's socialization. Among other benefits, the field trips expand learning beyond the classroom, enrich students' understanding of subject matter, and encourage them to think about occupational choices and careers that they haven't considered.

Rideout 2007). Are such concerns justified? Many researchers agree that there are negative aspects of electronic media, such as obesity (because frequent sitting replaces playing outside and encourages eating foods advertised on children's programs that are high in fat and sugar). They contend, however, that there is still no evidence that television viewing *causes* violence. For example, violent crimes in society have decreased despite the increased depiction of violence on television and other electronic media (Powell et al. 2007; Sternheimer 2007).

A recent study found that middle-school-aged children, both girls and boys, who almost exclusively played rated M (for mature) games more than 15 hours a week were more likely than their counterparts to be bullies in school, get into fights, destroy property, and argue with their teachers. The researchers point out that it may be that more aggressive children are drawn to more violent games, and not that the games themselves are to blame (Kutner and Olson 2008).

There is growing consensus, however, that violent video games make violence seem normal. Playing violent video games such as *Grand Theft Auto: Chinatown Wars* and *God of War 3* can increase a person's aggressive thoughts, feelings, and behavior both in laboratory settings and in real life. Violent video games also encourage male-to-female aggression because much of the violence is directed at women (Anderson et al. 2003; Carnagey and Anderson 2005).

Still, it's not clear why violent video games affect people differently. Many young males enjoy playing such video games, for example, but aren't any more aggressive, vicious, or destructive than those who aren't video-game enthusiasts (Williams and Skoric 2005; Kutner and Olson 2008).

Advertising

Increasingly, advertisers are targeting children as early as possible. A new form of advertising called *advergaming* combines free online games with advertising. Advergaming is growing rapidly. Sites such as those operated by Nestlé (http://www.wonka.com), Mattel (Barbie.com), and M&Ms (http://mms.com/us/fun-games/games) attract millions of young children and provide marketers with an inexpensive way to "draw attention to their brand in a playful way, and for an extended period of time" (Moore 2006: 5).

In the print media, young people see 45 percent more beer ads and 27 percent more ads for hard liquor in teen magazines than adults do in their magazines (Strasburger et al. 2006). It's been estimated that girls ages 11 to 14 are subjected to about 500 advertisements a day on the Internet, billboards, and magazines, but that "the majority of [the models are] nipped, tucked, and airbrushed to perfection" (Bennett 2009: 43).

What effect do such ads have on girls' and women's self-image? About 43 percent of 6- to 9-year-old American girls use lipstick or lip gloss, 38 percent use hairstyling products, and 12 percent use other cosmetics. Eight- to 12-year-old girls spend more than $40 million a month on beauty products (Bennett 2009). Many women, especially white women, are unhappy with their bodies. In an analysis of 77 recent studies of media images of women, the researchers concluded that there is a strong association between exposure to media depicting ultra-thin actresses and models, and many women's dissatisfaction with their bodies and their likelihood of engaging in unhealthy eating behaviors, such as excessive dieting (Grabe et al. 2008).

Millions of others turn to cosmetic surgery. Women have 91 percent of all cosmetic procedures, and those undergoing surgery have increased 142 percent since 1997. The most common cosmetic surgery is for breast augmentation. In 2008 alone, 356,000 women had breast implants, whereas penis implants aren't even mentioned (American Society for Aesthetic Plastic Surgery 2010).

5 Socialization Throughout Life

biological aging comes naturally, but social aging is quite a different matter. As we progress through the life course—from in-

TABLE 4.4
How Does Electronic Media Affect Children?

AMONG ALL 8- TO 18-YEAR-OLDS, PERCENTAGE WHO SAID THAT THEY...

	HEAVY USERS (MORE THAN 16 HOURS/DAY)	MODERATE USERS (3–16 HOURS A DAY)	LIGHT USERS (LESS THAN 3 HOURS/DAY)
Get good grades (A's and B's)	51	65	66
Get fair/poor grades (C's or lower)	47	31	23
Have been happy at school this year	72	81	82
Are often bored	60	53	48
Get into trouble a lot	33	21	16
Are often sad or unhappy	32	23	22

Source: Based on Rideout et al. 2010: 4 (table).

fancy to death—we are expected to act our age and to learn culturally approved norms, values, and roles.

INFANCY

Some scientists describe healthy infants' brains as "small computers" because of their enormous capacity for learning (Gopnik et al. 2001: 142). Normal babies are quick learners, but many proud parents believe that their children can be brilliant. As a result, since 1997, millions of Americans have spent $200 million a year on "Baby Einstein" enrichment products such as flash cards and educational software for children as young as 6 months ("Your baby will learn the numbers 1–20!" according to some ads). Other parents have played classical music all day or cassette tapes in the baby's crib that were supposed to teach the baby French or German.

In fact, some researchers have found that baby DVDs were doing

Advergaming, which uses free video games to promote a product, keeps the brand name in front of the player at all times.

© Image copyright Zoom Team, 2009. Used under license from Shutterstock.com

more harm than good because babies 8 to 16 months old who watched these DVDs learned fewer words than those whose parents talked to them, told them stories, and exposed them to a rich vocabulary (Zimmerman et al. 2007). In 2009, when lawyers threatened a class action lawsuit for deceptive advertising because the "Baby Einstein" products (owned by the Walt Disney Company) didn't increase an infant's intelligence, parents were offered a refund (Lewin 2009).

CHILDHOOD

According to French historian Philippe Ariès (1962), childhood—viewed as a distinct stage of development— is a fairly recent phenomenon. In medieval Europe, children as young as 6 dressed like adults and took part in the same work and recreational activities as adults. In the U.S. colonies, child labor was nearly universal. At the beginning of the nineteenth century, American children began to spend more time playing than working, and adolescence became a new stage of life without adult responsibilities. More books for and about children were published, and people began to recognize children's individuality by giving them names that were different from those of their parents. In the nineteenth century, people began for the first time to celebrate birthdays, especially those of children. There was also a marked decline in the use of corporal punishment, and physicians and others began to recognize the early onset of sexual feelings in children (Degler 1981; Demos 1986). At the turn of the twentieth century, children in the United States were required to attend school until age 16, and in 1938, the federal government passed its first law forbidding child labor.

Most American children today enjoy happy and healthy lives, but many experience a rough socialization. About 1.5 million children younger than 18 (2 percent of all children) have an incarcerated parent, a number that has increased by one third since 1991. Another 510,000 are in the foster care system. And every year, at least 1 million children experience mistreatment that includes neglect and physical and sexual abuse (Mumola 2000; Child Welfare Information Gateway 2009). Thus, for millions of U.S. children, the socialization process is shaky at best.

ADOLESCENCE

In many developing countries, children still work side by side with adults. Many girls marry at very young ages, even at 9, and are often married off to men in their 50s and 60s who have several other wives and many children. A poverty-stricken father often sells off his young daughters to pay debts, educate his sons, or purchase farm animals (see Benokraitis 2011). Thus, many children, especially girls, experience a quick transition from childhood to adulthood.

In developed societies, in contrast, adolescence is prolonged. Because an industrial society needs a highly trained and educated labor force, many young adults pursue their studies well into their late 20s and, consequently, postpone typical adult responsibilities such as marrying, having children, and getting a full-time job.

Almost 90 percent of U.S. parents say that, compared with the time when they were growing up, it's harder to monitor their 12- to 17-year-olds, especially when both parents are employed (National Center on Addiction and Substance Abuse 2008). Nearly half of such parents believe that they don't spend enough time with their children, but 75 percent of children ages 8 to 17 say that working parents have a positive effect on the quality of their home life (Conlin 2007). It seems, then, that many employed parents are doing a better job in raising their kids than they think.

High-school counselors typically applaud parental involvement in their children's lives, but also dread "helicopter parents" who hover over their kids, micromanaging every aspect of their lives. Examples include verbally attacking teachers over their adolescents' low grades, demanding that their child be moved to another class before the school year has even begun, and showing up in the guidance counselor's office with college

Until 1938, young children made up a large segment of the labor force, especially in factories. They worked six days a week, 12 or more hours a day, received very low wages, and were often injured because of dangerous equipment.

applications that they have filled out for their children (Krache 2008). Helicopter parenting diminishes teens' sense of self and autonomy, ability to develop their decision-making skills, and capacity to become responsible in problem solving.

ADULTHOOD

Socialization continues throughout adulthood, the period roughly between ages 21 and 65. Most adults adopt a series of new roles—work or career, marriage, parenthood, divorce, remarriage, buying a house, and experiencing the death of a child, parent, or grandparent. We'll examine these transitions in later chapters. Two of the most important roles in adulthood are work and parenthood, but let's begin with young adults who are reluctant to leave their parent's nest.

The Crowded Empty Nest

During the 1960s and 1970s, sociologists almost always included the "empty nest" in describing the family life cycle. This is the stage in which parents, typically in their 50s, find they are alone at home after their children have married, gone to college, or found jobs and moved out. Today, however, young adults are living at home longer than was generally true in the past. The terms *boomerang children* and *boomerang generation* used to refer to young adults moving back in with their parents, but many people in their 30s, 40s, and older—often with a spouse and children in tow—are moving back home (Koss-Feder 2009). In 2008, for example, of the 20 percent of young adults ages 25 to 34 still living with their parents, 67 percent were men and 33 percent were women (U.S. Census Bureau, Current Population Survey 2009).

Macro-level factors encourage a large number of young adults to stay home or move back. Student loans, low wages, divorce, credit card debt, and jumping from job to job until they find work they enjoy have made it harder for young middle-class adults to maintain the lifestyles that their parents provided. And the transition to adulthood gets tougher the lower you go on the economic and educational ladder. Until the late 1980s, it was possible for a high-school graduate to achieve a middle-class standard of living.

Individual and macro-level variables intersect in explaining the delay of many Americans' transition to adulthood, especially living on their own. Many doting parents are willing to support their adult children financially who spend years searching for jobs they like rather than those that provide a living. Others, as you'll see in Chapter 13, are delaying marriage and don't feel a need to establish their own homes.

Still others enjoy the comforts of the coddling parental nest. According to one of my male students in his late 20s, for example, "My mom enjoys cooking, cleaning my room, and just having me around. I don't pitch in for any of the expenses, but we get along great because she doesn't hassle me about my comings and goings" (Benokraitis 2011: 335). Perhaps most important, the stigma traditionally linked to young adults' living at home has faded because the practice is widespread enough "to be considered socially acceptable rather than an indicator of the youth's personal failure" (Danziger 2008: F8).

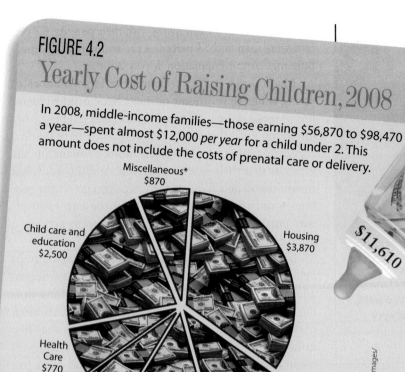

FIGURE 4.2
Yearly Cost of Raising Children, 2008

In 2008, middle-income families—those earning $56,870 to $98,470 a year—spent almost $12,000 *per year* for a child under 2. This amount does not include the costs of prenatal care or delivery.

Miscellaneous*
$870

Child care and education
$2,500

Housing
$3,870

Health Care
$770

Clothing
$740

Transportation
$1,550

Food
$1,310

$11,610

*Includes personal care items, entertainment, and reading materials.
Source: Based on Lino and Carlson, 2009, Table 1.

© Don Farrall/Photodisc/Getty Images/ Creatas/Jupiter Images

Work Roles

The average American holds at least nine jobs from ages 18 to 34 alone (U.S. Department of Labor 2002). Such job changing means that our occupational socialization is an ongoing process. Learning work roles is difficult because each job has different demands and expectations. Even when there is formal job training, we must also learn the subtle rules that are implicit in many job settings. A supervisor who says, proudly and loudly, "I have an open door policy. Come in and chat whenever you want," may *really* mean, "I have an open door policy if you're not going to complain about something." Even if we remain in the same job for many years, we must often acquire new skills, especially those related to computers, for example, or risk becoming labeled obsolete and being laid off.

As U.S. companies have transferred more jobs overseas, many workers have been fired or laid off. Being laid off can be stressful at any age. In the case of midlife men (generally defined as those aged 45–60), such changes are especially traumatic: They must learn new job-hunting skills and must often adjust to as much as a 70 percent decrease in their earnings. Instead of enjoying the security of a job in their midlife years, these men must undergo occupational socialization that assaults their self-image as good employees and family providers (see Chapter 12).

Parenting Roles

Like workplace roles, parenting does *not* come naturally. Most first-time parents muddle through by trial and error. Family sociologists often point out that we get more training for driving a car than for marriage and parenting. For example, most couples don't realize that raising children is expensive. Middle-income couples, with an average income of $77,000 a year, spend about 16 percent of their earnings on a child during the first 2 years (see *Figure 4.2*). Child-rearing costs are much higher for single parents and especially for low-income families if a child is disabled, chronically ill, or needs specialized care that welfare benefits don't cover (Lukemeyer et al. 2000; Lino and Carlson 2009).

Arguments over finances and child-rearing strategies are two of the major reasons for divorce (see Chapter 13). All in all, adjusting to marital and parental roles during adulthood requires considerable patience, effort, and work.

LATER LIFE

Later life also requires adjusting to new situations. Because we live longer, we may spend 20 percent of our adult life in retirement. When retired people are unhappy, it's usually because of health or income problems rather than the loss of the worker role. If retirement benefits don't keep up with inflation or if a retiree isn't covered by a pension plan, older people can plunge into poverty soon after retirement (Toder 2005; see also Chapter 13).

Comedian Woody Allen once quipped, "It's not that I'm afraid to die. I just don't want to be there when it happens." Older people who are in poor health and experience continuous pain sometimes welcome death. Many others reenter the labor force or volunteer in various organizations, are often involved with their grandchildren, and forge new relationships after widowhood (see Chapter 13). Thus, even in the later years, many people continue to learn new roles as they participate in society.

6 Resocialization

Socialization doesn't always occur in predictable ways. Sometimes people have to learn totally new behavior patterns, or be resocialized. **Resocialization** is the process of unlearning old ways of doing things and adopting new attitudes, values, norms, and behavior. Much resocialization takes place in what sociologist Erving Goffman (1961) called **total institutions**— places, such as military boot camps, mental hospitals, prisons, concentration camps, and some religious orders—where people are isolated from the rest of society, stripped of their former identities, and required to conform to new rules and behavior.

Some resocialization is voluntary, such as when an American wife moves to the Middle East with her Iranian husband and must follow local customs about veiling, women's submissive roles, and staying out of public life. Other examples of voluntary resocialization include entering a religious order, seeking treatment in a drug-abuse rehabilitation facility, or serving in the military.

Resocialization can also be involuntary, as when children are sent to a foster home or a juvenile detention camp. Correctional institutions especially exemplify involuntary resocialization. Prisons have buildings that are physically separated from the rest of society. Whether built in rural or urban areas, prisons have high fences, barred windows, armed corrections officers at the entrance, and the staff has almost complete control over the prisoner. The inmates are strip-searched, deloused, and fingerprinted; their heads are shaved; they are issued a uniform; they are given a serial number; and they are told what to do and when to do it.

Prisoners have almost no privacy, limited access to family and friends, and little communication with the outside world. The purpose of these practices and restrictions, according to Goffman, is to destroy any sense of individualism, autonomy, past identity, and to produce a more compliant person (we'll examine some of the effects of involuntary resocialization in Chapter 7).

As this chapter shows, socialization is a powerful force in shaping who we are. Socialization doesn't produce robots, however, because people are creative, adapt to new environments, and change as they interact with others.

> **resocialization** the process of unlearning old ways of doing things and adopting new attitudes, values, norms, and behavior.
>
> **total institutions** places where people are isolated from the rest of society, stripped of their former identities, and required to conform to new rules and behavior.

Most resocialization occurs in institutions ranging from monastic orders to the military.

All of us

conform to a cultural social structure.

5 Social Interaction and Social Structure

what do you think?

I don't mind if people stand close to me when talking.

1 2 3 4 5 6 7
strongly agree   strongly disagree

Generally, African Americans have higher death rates at an early age and tend to receive lower quality health care than whites, even when both groups are similar in family medical history, social class, and health insurance coverage (for a summary of some of these studies, see Kreps 2006). Health practitioners were puzzled by this racial difference until a groundbreaking study suggested that interaction might be a key factor. Regardless of race or ethnicity, physicians talked 43 percent more than their African American patients but only 24 percent more than their white patients, and the doctors' comments and voice tone were more positive with white patients (Johnson et al. 2004).

Subsequent studies supported the finding that doctor–patient interaction patterns frequently differ. White patients often ask more questions, whereas African American patients tend to ask fewer questions to avoid appearing stupid or to waste the doctor's time (especially when a physician hurries from one patient to another) (Perloff et al. 2006).

social interaction the process by which we act toward and react to people around us.

The doctor–patient example illustrates four critical components of **social interaction,** the process by which we act toward and react to people around us (Maines 2001; Schwalbe 2001):

- Social interaction is central to all human social activity.
- People respond differently during social interaction, depending on what they think is at stake for them ("I may seem stupid if I ask a lot of questions.").
- People influence each other's behavior through social interaction ("Mr. Smith doesn't have any questions, so I can move on to the next patient.").
- Elements of social structure, such as race and ethnicity, affect all social interaction and can produce different personal outcomes.

All of us conform to a cultural social structure that shapes our roles, status, social interaction, and nonverbal and online communication.

1 Social Structure

Social structure is an organized pattern of behavior that governs people's relationships (Smelser 1988). Because social structure guides our actions, it gives us the feeling that life is orderly and predictable rather than haphazard or random. We're often not aware of the impact of social structure until we violate cultural rules, formal or informal, that dictate our daily behavior. People may sometimes resent the impact of social structure because it limits their personal choices. But like it or not, social structure and social interaction—whether at work or a doctor's office—shape our daily lives.

Every society has a social structure that encompasses statuses, roles, groups, organizations, and institutions (Smelser 1988). We'll examine groups, organizations, and institutions in later chapters. Let's take a closer look here at statuses and roles, two building blocks of our everyday lives.

2 Status

for most people, the word *status* signifies prestige: An executive, for example, has more status than a receptionist, and a physician has a higher status than a nurse. For sociologists, **status** refers to a social position that a person occupies in a society (Linton 1936). Thus, executive, secretary, physician, and nurse are all social statuses. Other statuses that are familiar to you include student, professor, musician, voter, sister, parent, police officer, and friend.

Sociologists don't as-sume that one position is more important than another. A mother, for example, is not more important than a father, and an adult is not more important than a child. Instead, all statuses are significant because they determine social identity, or who we are.

STATUS SET

Every person has many statuses (see *Figure 5.1*). Together, they form her or his **status set**, a collection of social statuses that a person occupies at a given time (Merton 1968). Dionne, one of my students, is female, African American, 42 years old, divorced, mother of two, daughter, cousin, aunt, Baptist, Maryland voter, supervisor at a bank, volunteer at a soup kitchen, president of her homeowners association, country music fan, and stockholder. All of these socially defined positions (and others as well) make up Dionne's status set.

Status sets change throughout the life course. Because she will graduate next year and is considering remarrying and starting an after-school program, Dionne

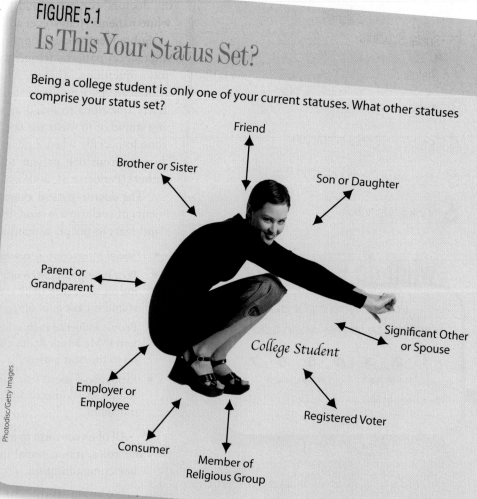

FIGURE 5.1
Is This Your Status Set?

Being a college student is only one of your current statuses. What other statuses comprise your status set?

Friend

Brother or Sister

Son or Daughter

Parent or Grandparent

Significant Other or Spouse

College Student

Employer or Employee

Registered Voter

Consumer

Member of Religious Group

Photodisc/Getty Images

will add at least three more statuses to her status set and will also lose the statuses of divorced and college student. As Dionne ages, she will continue to gain new statuses (grandmother, retiree) and lose others (supervisor at a bank, or wife, if she is widowed).

Statuses are *relational,* or complementary, because they are connected to other statuses: A *husband* has a *wife,* a *real-estate agent* has *customers,* and a *teacher* has *students*. No matter how many statuses you occupy, nearly every status is linked to that of one or more other people. These connections between statuses influence our behavior and relationships.

ASCRIBED AND ACHIEVED STATUS

Status sets include both ascribed and achieved statuses. An **ascribed status** is a social position that a person is born into. We can't control, change, or choose our ascribed statuses, which include sex (male or female), age, race, ethnicity, and family relationships. Your ascribed statuses, for example, might include *male, Latino,* and *brother*. Some argue that sex isn't really an ascribed status because people can have sex-change operations. However, a sex-change operation doesn't change the fact that someone was born a male or a female (except in a minority of cases, as you'll see in Chapter 9).

An **achieved status,** in contrast, is a social position that a person attains through personal effort or assumes voluntarily. Your achieved statuses might include college student, wife, employee, and member of the middle class. Unlike our ascribed statuses, our achieved statuses can be controlled and changed. We have no choice about being a son or daughter (an ascribed status), but we have an option to become a parent (an achieved status).

Students sometimes think that religion and social class are ascribed rather than achieved statuses. It's true that someone may be born into a family that practices a certain religion or one that is poor, middle class, or wealthy. Because we can change these statuses through our own actions, however, neither religion nor social class is an ascribed status. A Catholic might convert to Judaism (or vice versa). And thousands of Americans born into poor or working-class families become millionaires because they work hard, save, and live modestly (Stanley and Danko 1996).

MASTER STATUS

An ascribed or achieved status can be a **master status** that determines a person's identity (Hughes 1945; Becker 1963). In most societies—including the United States—one's sex, age, physical ability, and race are master statuses because they are very visible and often shape a person's entire life. Occupations are frequently a master status because they denote social class and may override an ascribed status such as one's sex ("She's a chemical engineer; she must be successful.").

A master status can be positive or negative. Many people admire Bill Gates, the founder of Microsoft, because he's a billionaire, a positive master status. Master statuses can also be negative. Instead of getting to know a person in a wheelchair, for example, we might stigmatize her or him as somehow imperfect and react to the disability rather than the person's accomplishments.

STATUS INCONSISTENCY

Because we hold many statuses, some clash. **Status inconsistency** refers to the conflict that arises from occupying social positions that are ranked differently. Examples include a computer programmer who works as a bartender or a skilled welder who stocks shelves at Wal-Mart because neither can find a better job in a weak economy.

Such discrepancies often derail our interactions. In conversation with a computer scientist or a welder, what should we do? Ask how the lower level job is going? Or avoid talking about work because it's a sensitive issue? We'll cover status inconsistency in more detail in Chapter 7. For now, you should be aware that you occupy many statuses, and some of them may clash now and in the future.

3 Role

e ach status is associated with one or more roles. A **role** is the behavior expected of a person who has a particular status. We occupy a status but play a role. In this sense, a role is the dynamic aspect of a status (Linton 1936).

College student is a status, but the role of a college student requires many *formal* behaviors such as going

ascribed status a social position that a person is born into.

achieved status a social position that a person attains through personal effort or assumes voluntarily.

master status an ascribed or achieved status that determines a person's identity.

status inconsistency the conflict that arises from occupying social positions that are ranked differently.

role the behavior expected of a person who has a particular status.

role performance the actual behavior of a person who occupies a status.

role set the different roles attached to a single status.

to class, reading, thinking, completing weekly assignments, writing papers, and taking exams. *Informal* behaviors may include joining a student club, befriending classmates, attending football games, and even abusing alcohol on weekends.

Like statuses, roles are relational (complementary). Playing the role of professor requires teaching, advising students, being present during office hours, responding to e-mail, and grading exams and assignments. Most professors are also expected to serve on committees, do research, publish articles and/or books, and perform services such as giving talks to community groups. Thus, the status of college student or professor involves numerous role requirements that govern who does what, where, when, and how.

Roles can be rigid or flexible. A person who occupies the status of secretary typically plays a role that is defined by rules about when to come to work, how to answer the phone, when to submit the necessary work and in what format, and how many sick days are allowed each year. A boss, on the other hand, usually enjoys considerable flexibility: She or he has more freedom to come in late or leave early, to determine which projects should be completed first, and to decide when to hire or fire employees.

Because roles are based on mutual obligations, they ensure that social relations are fairly orderly. We know what we are supposed to do and what others expect of us. If professors fail to meet their role obligations by missing many classes or coming to classes unprepared, students may respond by studying very little, cutting classes, and submitting negative course evaluations. If students miss classes, don't turn in the required work, or cheat, professors can fail them or assign low grades.

ROLE PERFORMANCE

Roles define how we are *expected* to behave in a particular status, but people vary considerably in fulfilling the responsibilities associated with their roles. Many college students succeed, whereas others fail; some professors inspire their students, whereas others put them to sleep. These differences reflect **role performance,** the *actual* behavior of a per-

Leslie Visser graduated from Boston College with honors, was an accomplished athlete, and has been a successful sports analyst, journalist, and sportscaster for more than 25 years. When describing Visser's achievement, writers typically focus on her gender: "The first woman to cover Monday Night Football" or "The first woman enshrined into the Pro Football Hall of Fame." Does Visser's master status diminish her achieved status?

son who occupies a status. For example, a professor may vary her or his role by demanding more of graduate students than of undergraduates. An instructor may also relate differently to male students than to female students or act differently with a 19-year-old student than with a 40-year-old student who's anxious about returning to school.

ROLE SET

We occupy many statuses, and we play many roles associated with each status. A **role set** refers to the different roles attached to a single status. Every role set includes rights and responsibilities associated with people with

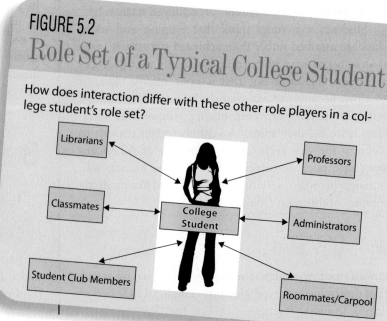

FIGURE 5.2
Role Set of a Typical College Student

How does interaction differ with these other role players in a college student's role set?

- Librarians
- Professors
- Classmates
- College Student
- Administrators
- Student Club Members
- Roommates/Carpool

different statuses and role sets. *Figure 5.2* illustrates six roles of a typical college student. Because a different set of norms governs each of these relationships, the student interacts differently with a classmate than with a reference librarian or a professor. All of these interactions, shaped by explicit or implicit rules, make up a student's role set.

These six roles reflect only one status—that of college student. If you think about other statuses that a college student may occupy (employee, son or daughter, parent, girlfriend or boyfriend, husband or wife), you can see that meeting the expectations of numerous role sets can create considerable role conflict and role strain.

TABLE 5.1
Why Do We Experience Role Conflict and Role Strain?

REASON	EXAMPLE
Because many people are over-extended, some roles are bound to conflict with others.	Students may study less than they want because employers demand that they work overtime or on weekends.
People have little or no training for many roles.	Parents are expected to live up to high standards and to turn out "perfect" kids even though they receive more training for driving a car than for parenting.
Some role expectations are unclear or contradictory.	Some employers pride themselves on having family-friendly policies but expect employees to work 12 hours a day, travel on weekends, and use vacation days to care for a sick child.
Highly demanding jobs often create difficulties at home.	Some jobs (such as being in the military, policing, firefighting, and serving on medical teams after a hurricane or flood) require people to be away from their families for extended periods of time or during crises.

ROLE CONFLICT AND ROLE STRAIN

Playing many roles often leads to **role conflict,** the frustrations and uncertainties a person experiences when confronted with the requirements of two or more statuses. College students who have a job, especially if it is full-time, often experience role conflict because both employers and professors expect them to excel, but it's very difficult to meet these expectations. The role conflict increases if the student is a parent of young children, or cares for an aging mother or father who needs help on a daily basis.

Whereas role conflict arises from tensions *between* the roles of two or more statuses, **role strain** is the stress that arises from incompatible demands among roles *within* a single status. Students experience role strain when several exams are scheduled on the same day, but they are also involved in time-consuming extracurricular activities. Faculty members experience role strain when the requirements of being a professor—teaching, research, and community service—sap their energy and time. And military chaplains report role strain in preaching about peace while blessing those about to go to war.

Almost all of us experience role strain because many inconsistencies are built into our roles. *Table 5.1* presents examples of some of the factors that create role conflict and role strain.

COPING WITH ROLE CONFLICT AND ROLE STRAIN

Role conflict and role strain can produce tension, hostility, aggression, and stress-related physical problems such as insomnia, headaches, ulcers, eating disorders, anxiety attacks, chronic fatigue, nausea, weight loss or gain, and drug and alcohol abuse (Weber et al. 1997). Some role conflict and role strain may last only a few weeks, but others are long-lived (e.g., working in a stressful or low-paying job).

To deal with role conflict and role strain, some people *deny that there's a problem.* Employed mothers, especially those who are divorced, often become super-moms—who provide home-cooked meals, attend their children's sports activities, and volunteer for a school's fund-raising campaign—even though they're exhausted, must do laundry at midnight, and neglect their health

role conflict the frustrations and uncertainties a person experiences when confronted with the requirements of two or more statuses.

role strain the stress that arises from incompatible demands among roles within a single status.

and interests. Super moms may succeed over a number of years in dealing with role conflict and role strain. Eventually, however, they may become angry and resentful, or experience health or emotional problems (Douglas and Michaels 2004). There are five other, more effective ways of minimizing role conflict and role strain.

First, we can reduce role conflict through *compromise or negotiation*. To decrease the conflict between work and family roles, for example, many couples draw up schedules that require fathers to do more of the housework and child rearing.

Second, we can *set priorities*. If extracurricular activities interfere with studying, which is more important? Succeeding in college always requires making sacrifices, such as attending fewer parties and not seeing friends as often as we'd like.

Third, we can *compartmentalize* our roles. Many college students take courses in the morning, work part-time during the afternoon or evening, and devote part of the weekend to leisure activities. It's not always easy but usually possible to segregate our various roles.

Fourth, we can decide *not to take on more roles*. One of the most effective ways to avoid role conflict is to just say "no" for requests to do volunteer work, pressure from family or friends to take on unwanted tasks (such as babysitting), or pleas to become involved in college or community activities.

Finally, we can *exit* a role or status. In most cases, we can withdraw from community activities and club offices, for example, that can decrease role conflict and role strain considerably. There's always pressure to remain in a role, but none of us is indispensable, and there are many people who are eager to replace us. Some role exits are painful and long-lived, however. Divorce, for instance, is a process, and not a quick event, that is usually spread over many years (sometimes decades), during which two people (and their children) must redefine their expectations and adjust to a different household structure (see Chapter 13).

4 Explaining Social Interaction

Statuses and roles are two critical components of social structure that shape our everyday relationships, but it is social interaction that provides the basis of these relationships and affects who you are, how you behave, and what you say. Social interaction seems natural and simple, but it's fairly complex.

Our social interaction begins in infancy and changes over time depending on the situation and our sex, ethnicity, social class, marital status, and age, among other factors. For example, many men enjoy compliments about their appearance, but they rarely ask, "Does this make me look fat?" Women do so fairly frequently. Even if the man replies, "You look fine," a woman may head for the closet to try on another outfit or worry about how she looks.

Why do we interact as we do? Why do our interaction patterns change over time? And why do people sometimes interpret the same words differently? Three micro-level perspectives—symbolic interactionism, social exchange theory, and feminist theories—provide answers to these and other questions. These perspectives offer distinctive contributions, but they have one characteristic in common: Each explains how people communicate in their daily lives (*Table 5.2* summarizes these insights).

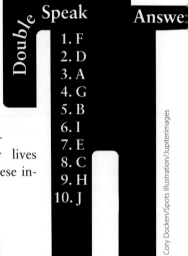

Double Speak | Answe

1. F
2. D
3. A
4. G
5. B
6. I
7. E
8. C
9. H
10. J

© Cory Docken/Spots Illustration/Jupiterimages

SYMBOLIC INTERACTIONISM

For interactionists, the most significant feature of all human communication is that people take each other and the context into account (Blumer 1969). When your professors ask, "How are you?" they expect a "Fine, thanks" and probably barely look at you. A doctor, on the other hand, usually looks you in the eye when asking "How are you?" and takes notes as soon as you start to reply. Thus, "How are you?" has different meanings in different social contexts and elicits different responses ("I'm doing okay" vs. "I've been having a lot of headaches during the last few weeks.").

How do we know how to react and what to expect from others? Interactionists say that much of the answer lies in understanding that people construct reality.

Social Construction of Reality

What people perceive and understand as reality is a creation of the social interaction of individuals and groups. "Human reality is socially constructed reality" because people impose their subjective meanings on interactions

DOUBLESPEAK

1. automotive internist	A. repairperson
2. internment excavation expert	B. bombing
3. service technician	C. spying
4. auto dismantler and recycler	D. gravedigger
5. air support	E. fake
6. previously owned	F. car mechanic
7. genuine imitation	G. junk dealer
8. surveillance	H. stock market crash
9. equity retreat	I. used
10. revenue enhancement	J. tax increase

Source: Based on Lutz 1989, and the National Council of Teachers of English Committee on Public Doublespeak 2005; answers on facing page.

to make sense of the world around them (Berger and Luckmann 1966: 172).

Our social interactions aren't isolated incidents. Instead, we produce, interpret, and share the reality of everyday life with others. This social construction of reality typically evolves through direct, face-to-face interaction, but the interaction can also be indirect, as in watching TV shows and movies or participating in Facebook or other online social networks.

Words are also important in shaping our perceptions of reality. Government officials, businesspeople, advertisers, politicians, educators, lobbyists, advocacy groups, and even social scientists use language deliberatively to shape or change our perceptions of reality. For example, doublespeak is "language that pretends to communicate but really doesn't. [It] makes the bad seem good, the negative appear positive, the unpleasant appear attractive or at least tolerable." There are several kinds of doublespeak: Euphemisms are inoffensive words or phrases that avoid a harsh, unpleasant, or distasteful reality; gobbledygook (or bureaucratese) overwhelms the listener with big words and long sentences; and inflated language makes everyday things seem impressive and makes the simple seem complex (Lutz 1989: 1–6). Take the quiz above to see how

much doublespeak you can decipher (answers on opposite page).

Social Interaction and Self-Fulfilling Prophecies

Our perceptions of reality shape our behavior. In an oft-cited statement, also known as the *Thomas Theorem*, sociologists W. I. Thomas and Dorothy Thomas (1928: 572) observed, "If men define situations as real, they are real in their consequences."

Carrying this idea further, sociologist Robert Merton (1948/1966) proposed that our definitions of reality can result in a **self-fulfilling prophecy:** If we define something as real and act on it, it can, in fact, become real. For example, a researcher who interviewed and received written accounts from adults ages 21 to 64 found that physical education teachers who publicly humiliated students often turned them off physical fitness for good. One man said, "To this day I feel totally inadequate in team-related activities and have a natural reflex to AVOID THEM AT ALL COSTS" (Strean 2009: 217; capitalization in original). Thus, gym teachers' negative comments made students feel inferior and inadequate in sports, and changed their behavior during adulthood regardless of their ability and performance.

Our perceptions of reality shape our behavior, but how do people define that reality? For interactionists, two

TABLE 5.2
Sociological Explanations of Social Interaction

PERSPECTIVE	KEY POINTS
Symbolic Interactionist	• People create and define their reality through social interaction. • Our definitions of reality, which vary according to context, can lead to self-fulfilling prophecies.
Social Exchange	• Social interaction is based on a balancing of benefits and costs. • Relationships involve trading a variety of resources, such as money, youth, and good looks.
Feminist	• The sexes act similarly in many interactions but often differ in communication styles and speech patterns. • Men are more likely to use speech that's assertive (to achieve dominance and goals), while women are more likely to use language that connects with others.

important methodological tools—ethnomethodology and dramaturgical analysis—help answer this question.

Ethnomethodology

A term coined by sociologist Harold Garfinkel (1967), **ethnomethodology** is the study of how people construct and learn to share definitions of reality that make everyday interactions possible. Reality is socially constructed because we base our interactions on common assumptions about what makes sense in specific situations (Schutz 1967; Heritage 1984; Hilbert 1992).

People make sense of their everyday lives in two ways. First, by observing conversations, people discover the general rules that we all use to interact. Second, people can understand interaction rules by breaking them. Over a number of years, Garfinkel instructed his students to purposely violate everyday interaction rules and then to analyze the results. In these exercises, some of his students went to a grocery store and insisted on paying more than was asked for a product. Others were instructed, in the course of an ordinary conversation and without indicating that anything unusual was happening, "to bring their faces up to the subject's until their noses were almost touching" (Garfinkel 1967: 72).

In these and other exercises during which students broke everyday interaction rules, they were punished. Grocery clerks became hostile when the students insisted on paying more than the marked price for a product, and people backed off when their noses were almost touching: "Reports were filled with accounts of astonishment, bewilderment, shock, anxiety, embarrassment, and anger. . ." (Garfinkel 1967: 47).

Violating interaction rules, even unspoken ones, can trigger anger, hostility, and frustration. College students become upset if professors ignore teaching norms by using sarcasm and putdowns, coming to class unprepared or consistently late, misplacing students' homework, constantly reading from the book, or discouraging students' comments and questions (Berkos et al. 2001).

Dramaturgical Analysis

Dramaturgical analysis is a technique that examines social interaction as if occurring on a stage where people play different roles and act out scenes for the "audiences" with whom they interact. According to sociologist Erving Goffman (1959, 1967), life is similar to a play in which each of us is an actor, and our social interaction is much like theater because each of us is always on stage and always performing. In our everyday performances, we present different versions of ourselves to people in different settings (audiences).

Because most of us try to present a positive image of ourselves, much social interaction involves *impression management,* a process of suppressing unfavorable traits and stressing favorable ones (see Chapter 4). To control information about ourselves, we often rely on props to convey or reinforce a particular image. For example, physicians, lawyers, and college professors may line their office walls with framed diplomas, medical certificates, or community awards to give the impression that they're competent, respected, and successful.

According to Goffman, the presentation of a performance involves front- and back-stage behaviors. The *front stage* is an area where an actual performance takes place. In front stage areas, such as living rooms or hotel restaurants, the setting is clean and the servers or hosts are typically polite and deferential to guests. The *back stage* is an area concealed from the audience, where people can relax. Bedrooms and restaurant kitchens are examples of back stages. After guests have left, the host and hostess may kick off their shoes and gossip about their company. In restaurants, cooks and servers may criticize the guests, use vulgar language, and yell at each other. Thus, the civility and decorum of the front stage may change to rudeness in the back stage.

Another example of front- and back-stage behavior involves faculty and students. Professors want to create the impression that they're well prepared, knowledgeable, and hard working. In back-stage areas such as their offices, however, faculty may complain to their colleagues that they're tired of teaching a particular course or grading terrible exams and papers, or they may confess that they don't always prepare for classes as well as they should. Students often plead with instructors for higher grades: "But I studied very hard" or "I'm an A student in my other courses." In back-stage areas such as dormitories, student lounges, or libraries, however, students may admit to their friends that

Cory Thoman

they barely studied or that they have a low grade-point average.

SOCIAL EXCHANGE THEORY

The fundamental premise of **social exchange theory** is that social interaction is based on each person's trying to maximize rewards (or benefits) and minimize punishments (or costs). An interaction that elicits a reward, such as approval or a smile, is more likely to be repeated than an interaction that brings a cost, such as disapproval or criticism (Thibaut and Kelley 1959; Homans 1974; Blau 1986).

Interactions are most satisfying when there is a balance between giving and taking. A lack of reciprocity appears unfair and threatens the continuation of the relationship: "It indicates to the person receiving less that the other really does not care enough to maintain exchanges" (Cohen 1981: 46).

People bring various tangible and intangible resources to a relationship, such as money, status, intelligence, good looks, youth, power, talent, fame, and affection. Any of a person's resources can be traded for more, better, or different resources that another person possesses. Marriages between older men and young women, for example, often reflect an exchange of the man's power, money, and/or fame for the woman's youth, physical attractiveness, and ability to bear children.

Many of our cost–reward decisions are conscious and deliberate, but others are passive or based on long-term negative interactions. For example, much of the research on domestic violence shows that women stay in abusive relationships because their self-esteem has eroded after years of criticism and ridicule from both their parents and their spouses or partners ("You'll be lucky if anyone marries you," "You're dumb," "You're ugly," and so on). In effect, the abused women (and sometimes men) believe that they have nothing to exchange in a relationship, that they don't have the right to expect benefits (especially when the abuser blames the victim for provoking the anger), or that enduring an abusive relationship is better than being alone (Walker 2000; Bergen et al. 2005).

> **social exchange theory** the perspective whose fundamental premise is that social interaction is based on each person's trying to maximize rewards (or benefits) and minimize punishments (or costs).

FEMINIST THEORIES

Feminist perspectives offer additional insights on social interaction. Two examples are emotional labor and gender roles.

Interaction and Emotional Labor

Emotions are important components of social interaction. According to sociologist Arlie Hochschild (1983), we learn *feeling rules* that shape the appropriate emotions for a given role or situation. For example, *emotional labor,* "the management of feeling to create a publicly observable facial and bodily display," is critical in many occupations that demand continuous interaction and masking of true feelings:

> *The secretary who creates a cheerful office that announces her company as "friendly and dependable" and her boss as "up-and-coming," the waitress or waiter who creates an "atmosphere of pleasant dining," the tour guide or hotel receptionist who makes us feel welcome. . . all of them must confront in some way or another the requirements of emotional labor. (Hochschild 1983: 11)*

Hochschild maintains that because many women have jobs with little power and that deal with the public, they are usually more likely than men to perform work that requires emotional labor.

The chaotic and crowded back-stage conditions in many restaurant kitchens stand in stark contrast with the efficient and relaxed front-stage behavior of its servers. Can you think of a situation where your front- and back-stage behaviors differ dramatically?

© Luca Campedri/Nonstock/Jupiter Images

© Thinkstock Images/Jupiterimages

ockphoto.com

Interaction and Gender Roles

Women and men are more similar than different in their interactions. A study that recorded conversations of college students in the United States and Mexico found that women and men spoke about the same amount—16,000 words per day. Also, an analysis of studies published since the 1960s concluded that men are generally more talkative than women, but talkativeness depends on the particular situation. During decision-making tasks, men are more talkative than women, but when talking about themselves or interacting with children, women are more talkative than men (Leaper and Ayres 2007; Mehl et al. 2007).

Other studies support the findings that cultural norms and gender role expectations shape the sexes' communication patterns. Generally, women are socialized to be more comfortable talking about their feelings, whereas men are socialized to be dominant and take charge, especially in the workplace. Because women tend to use communication to develop and maintain relationships, talk is often an end in itself because it's a way to foster closeness and understanding. Women often ask questions that probe for a greater understanding of feelings and perceptions ("Were you glad it happened?"). Women are also much more likely than men to do conversational "maintenance work," such as asking questions that encourage conversation ("What happened at the meeting?") (Lakoff 1990; Robey et al. 1998).

Compared with female speech, men's speech often reflects *conversational dominance*, speaking more frequently and for longer periods. They also show dominance by interrupting others, reinterpreting the speaker's meaning, or changing the topic (Tannen 1990; Mulac 1998). Such interaction differences aren't innate because of one's gender, however. Instead, much depends on women's and men's roles in society, their occupations, and their position and status in the job hierarchy. For example, men who do much of the parenting have communication styles that are similar to those of mothers. In the workplace, women and men who occupy high-level decision-making positions also have similar interaction styles with superiors and subordinates (Cameron 2007).

5 Nonverbal Communication

Our bodies and nonverbal messages often communicate more clearly and loudly than our words. **Nonverbal communication** refers to messages sent without using words. This silent language, a "language of behavior" that conveys our real feelings, can be more potent than our words (Hall 1959: 15). For example, sobbing sends a much stronger message than saying, "I feel very sad." Some of the most common nonverbal messages are silence, visual cues, touch, and personal space.

SILENCE

Silence transmits a variety of feelings and emotions: agreement, apathy, awe, confusion, disagreement, embarrassment, regret, respect, sadness, thoughtfulness, and fear, to name just a few. In various contexts, and at particular points in a conversation, silence means different things to different people. Sometimes silence saves us from embarrassing ourselves. Think, for example, about the times you fired off an angry e-mail or text message, regretted doing so an hour later, and then cringed at the thought of getting the person's fuming response.

In interpersonal relationships, the silent treatment can be devastating. Many of us have experienced the pain of getting this treatment from friends, family members, coworkers, or lovers. Not talking to people who are important to us builds up anger and hostility. Initially, the "offender" may work very hard to make the closemouthed person talk about a problem. Eventually, the target of the silent treatment will get fed up, give up, or end a relationship (Rosenberg 1993).

VISUAL CUES

Visual cues, another form of nonverbal communication, include gestures, facial expressions, and eye contact. Let's consider a few examples of how such body language works in our daily interactions.

Gestures in Early Life

How important are gestures in our nonverbal communication even when we're infants? A recent study found an association (not causation) between baby gestures,

Retrofile RF/Stockbyte/Getty Images

SOUTH AMERICA	UNITED STATES	JAPAN	FRANCE	GERMANY	OTHER COUNTRIES
not okay	okay	money	zero	vulgar gesture	better check first

the children's verbal ability at age 5, and the parents' socioeconomic status (SES). Parents who earned at least $60,000 a year and had a college degree or higher were more likely than those who earned less than $15,000 a year (and were often high-school dropouts) to use more gestures, such as pointing, waving, and clapping. The higher SES parents were also more likely than the lower SES parents to associate a baby's gesture with a word ("That's right, this is a doll."), which increases the child's vocabulary (Rowe and Goldin-Meadow 2009).

Gestures in Adulthood

Most of us think we know what certain gestures mean—folding your arms across your chest indicates a closed, defensive attitude; leaning forward often shows interest; shrugging your shoulders signals indifference; narrowing your eyes and setting your jaw shows defiance; and smiling and nodding shows agreement.

Finger-pointing is usually a gesture that directs attention outward, placing blame or responsibility on someone else. The common "talk to the hand" gesture sends a stronger message: "Go away!" or "I'm not listening to you." Few gestures, however, clearly convey a meaning by themselves. Instead, they must be interpreted in context. Because of habit or hearing problems, for instance, a coworker may always lean forward when listening regardless of whether he or she is interested.

The same gesture may have different meanings in different countries:

- Tapping one's elbow several times with the palm of one's hand indicates that someone is sneaky (in Holland), stupid (in Germany and Austria), or mean or stingy (in South America).
- Screwing a forefinger into one cheek signifies a dimple—a traditional sign of feminine beauty—and means, in Italy and Libya, "She's beautiful." The same gesture in southern Spain means that a man is effeminate, and in Germany, "You're crazy!"
- In many Middle Eastern countries, people consider the shoes and the soles of one's feet to be unclean. As a result, stretching out one's legs with the feet pointing at someone or crossing one's legs so that a sole faces another person is considered rude (Morris 1994; Lynch and Hanson 1999; Jandt 2001).

Facial Expressions

Facial expressions provide visual cues on how people feel, but they may be difficult to interpret. First, our facial expressions don't always show our true emotions. Parents, for example, tell their children "Don't you roll your eyes at me!" or "Look happy when Aunt Minnie hugs you." Thus, children learn that displaying their real feelings—especially when they're negative—is often unacceptable.

Second, faces can lie about feelings. Parents often know when children are lying because the children avoid eye contact, cry, swallow frequently, blink often, or start to sweat. Many adults, in contrast, monitor and control their facial expressions. They can deceive, successfully and over many years, because they have rehearsed the lies in their heads, are smooth talkers with a reputation for being trustworthy, or have gotten away with lying in the past (Ekman 1985; Sullivan 2001).

Third, our facial expressions don't always reflect how we feel because they change over time because of socialization. Consider smiling.

Infants learn very quickly that a smile will get a parent's attention and a positive response (the parent smiles back) (Jones and Hong 2001). By kindergarten, most of us have learned to smile (and not smile) only in appropriate situations ("Don't smile during Uncle Fred's funeral, dear.").

Finally, facial expressions can be deceptive because of cultural variations. American businesspeople have grumbled that Germans are cool and aloof, whereas many German businesspeople have complained that Americans are excessively cheerful and hide their true feelings with grins and smiles. The Japanese, who believe that it's rude to display negative feelings in public, smile more than Americans do to disguise embarrassment, anger, and other negative emotions (Jandt 2001).

Eye Contact

We often communicate with our eyes. Are the eyes, as a proverb says, the mirrors of the soul? Or do they hide our innermost feelings?

Rod Aydelotte-Pool/Getty Images

Pictured here are President Bush and Saudi Crown Prince Abdullah at Bush's Texas ranch in 2002. Many U.S. journalists raised questions about two men holding hands. In response, Arab Americans were quick to point out that Arab society sees the outward display of affection between male friends as an expression of respect and trust. Thus, government officials and military officers often hold hands as they walk together or converse with one another.

Eye contact serves several social purposes (Eisenberg and Smith 1971; Ekman and Friesen 1984; Siegman and Feldstein 1987). First, we get much information about other people by looking at their eyes. Eyes open wide show surprise, fear, or a flicker of interest. When we are angry, we stare in an unflinching manner. When we are sad or ashamed, our eyes may be cast down.

Second, eye contact is a potent stimulus. Speakers sometimes change their strategy when people in the audience don't look at them. Your instructors, for example, may speak louder, walk around the classroom, or revert to writing on a blackboard when they feel that students' lack of eye contact indicates boredom or texting. In contrast, people usually evade the eyes of someone whose gaze is disturbingly unbroken and direct. When two people like one another, they establish eye contact more often and for longer durations than when there is tension in the relationship.

Finally, eye contact often varies across societies. In the United States, making eye contact is a key component of effective body language. Especially during job interviews, we're told, our eyes should signal attentiveness and interest, and "blinking, staring, or looking away whenever you begin speaking makes it hard for you to connect with your interviewer" (Bohannon 2000: 22). In some Asian cultures, like Japan, in contrast, students often avoid making eye contact with their instructors as a sign of respect (Jandt 2001).

TOUCH

Touch is another important form of nonverbal communication. Touching sends powerful messages about our feelings and attitudes.

What Touching Communicates

Touching expresses our feelings toward another person. The sense of touch is activated long before birth:

> *The skin is the largest sense organ of the body. . . [and] babies are surrounded and caressed by warm fluid and tissues from the beginning of fetal life. . . [After birth], the lips and hands have the most touch receptors; this may explain why newborns enjoy sucking their fingers (Klaus et al. 1995: 52).*

Parents all over the world communicate with their infants through touch—stroking, holding, patting, rubbing, and cuddling.

Touching sends many messages, some positive (hugging, embracing, kissing, and holding hands) and some negative (hitting, shoving, pushing, and spanking). Other forms of touching are contradictory. One of my students, for example, left a boyfriend because "He said he loved me and trusted me but he gripped my arm tightly every time I talked to another guy and pulled me away." The boyfriend's touch was controlling and threatening rather than affectionate. Between intimate partners, in addition, a decline in the amount of touching may signal that feelings are cooling off.

Gendered Touching

Whether touching is viewed as positive or negative depends on the situation and one's gender. In higher education, even when the faculty member is well liked, male and female students perceive touching differently. When female professors touch male students on the arm while talking to them, the students view the gesture as friendly. When a male professor touches a female student on the arm, she may get nervous because she's afraid that the touching may escalate (Lannutti et al. 2001; Fogg 2005).

Cross-Cultural Variations in Touching

As with other forms of nonverbal communication, the interpretation of touching varies from culture to culture. In some Middle Eastern countries, people don't offer anything to another with the left hand because it's used to clean oneself after using the toilet. And among many Chinese and other Asian groups, hugging, back-slapping, and handshaking aren't as typical as they are in the United States because such touching is seen as too intimate (Lynch and Hanson 1999).

According to one scholar, compared with those in some other societies, people in the United States are "touch-deprived" because they have one of the lowest rates of casual touch in the world:

> *If you are talking to a friend in a coffee shop in the United States, you might touch each other once or twice an hour. If you were British and in a London coffee shop, you probably won't touch each other at all. But if you were French and in a Parisian café, you might touch each other a hundred times in an hour! (Jandt 2001: 117)*

PERSONAL SPACE

The distance that people establish between themselves when they interact is an important aspect of nonverbal communication. Personal space plays a significant role in our everyday nonverbal interactions, reflects power and status, and varies across societies.

When Is Our Personal Space Violated?

Our living space is public or private. In the public sphere, which is usually formal, we have clearly delineated spaces: "This is your locker," "That's her office," or "You're parking in my spot." We usually decorate our public spaces with businesslike artifacts such as awards or framed photos of an institution's accomplishments.

Private spaces send a different message. They convey informality and a relaxed feeling. Private spaces—such as homes, apartments, and dorm rooms—are often mini-museums that reflect people's interests, hobbies, and personalities. We can tell a lot about people by simply looking around their rooms or homes—the newspapers and books they read, the music they enjoy, whether they're neat or sloppy, and so on.

People sometimes invade our personal space by standing too close to us in a line, leaning against us, using all of the shared armrest in tight airline seats, or plopping their feet on the chair next to us in a classroom. Not all space intrusions are physical encroachments. Loud cell phone conversations are a good example of an auditory intrusion into our personal space.

In intimate relationships (such as between family members), our personal space is often 2 feet or less because our social interactions are comfortable and affectionate, and we're at ease with close physical proximity. In contrast, in public situations (such as someone speaking to a large audience or faculty in large classrooms), the personal space is often 12 feet or more because the speaker, who has a higher social status than the audience, has a formal relationship with the listeners and avoids close physical contact (Hall 1966).

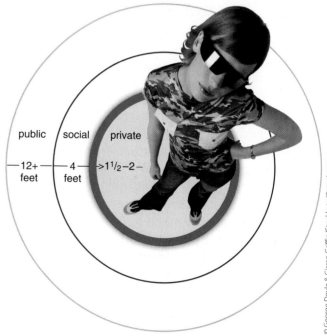

public | social | private
12+ feet | 4 feet | >1½–2

Space and Power

Space signifies who has privilege, status, and power (Chapman and Hockey 1999; Falah and Nagel 2005). Wealthy people can afford enormous apartments in the city or houses in the suburbs, whereas the poor are crowded into the most undesirable sections of a city or town or in trailer parks. Executives, including college presidents and deans, have large offices (even entire suites), whereas faculty members often share office space, even though many of their discussions with students are confidential. A receptionist's space is typically open to the public, and crowded with file cabinets and computers. Generally, the higher the SES, the greater the consumption of space, including large cars, reserved parking spaces, private dining areas, first-class airline seats, and luxurious skyboxes at sports stadiums.

Cross-Cultural Variations and Space

Cultural values and norms determine how we use space. Americans not only stand in line but also have strict queuing rules: "Hey, the end of the line is back there" and "That guy is trying to cut into the line." In contrast, "along with Italians and Spaniards, the French are among the least queue-conscious in Europe" (Jandt 2001: 109). In these countries and others, people routinely push into the front of a group waiting for taxis, food, and tickets, and nobody objects.

Americans maintain personal space in an elevator by moving to the corners or to the back. In contrast, an Arab male may stand right next to or touching another man even when no one else is in the elevator. Because most Arab men don't share American concepts of personal space in public places and in private conversations, they consider it offensive if the other man steps or leans away. In many Middle Eastern countries, however, there are stringent rules about women and men separating themselves spatially during religious ceremonies and about women avoiding any physical contact with men in public places (Jandt 2001; Office of the Deputy Chief 2006; see also Chapter 3)

6 Online Interaction

We have replaced many of our face-to-face activities with a virtual reality, where we obtain services and exchange information, ideas, and greetings in *cyberspace,* an online world of computer networks. This final section addresses two questions: Who's online and why? And is online interaction beneficial or harmful?

WHO'S ONLINE AND WHY?

The percentage of adult Americans connected to the Internet increased from practically zero in 1994 to 74 percent in 2009 (Pew Internet & American Life Project 2010). E-mail, instant messaging (IM), and text messaging are still popular, but social networking sites are becoming widespread (see *Table 5.3*).

Variations by Sex, Age, Ethnicity, and Social Class

Equal numbers of women and men (74 percent) use the Internet. There has been

---

TABLE 5.3

Usage of Some Common Internet Tools in the United States, 2009

TOOL	DEFINITION	PERCENTAGE OF ALL ONLINE ADULTS 18 AND OLDER WHO USE THIS TOOL
Blog	Website maintained by an individual with regular entries of commentary, reports, descriptions of events, or other material, including personal online diaries, photos, and videos	13
Social networking site	Website that focuses on building online communities of people who have similar interests or activities	73 (Facebook) 48 (MySpace)
LinkedIn	A business-oriented social networking site used mainly by professionals	14
Twitter	A form of social networking that enables users to send or read short messages of up to 140 characters (known as "tweets")	19

Source: Percentages based on Lenhart et al. 2010.

an enormous growth in Internet use across most age groups, but only 38 percent of Americans aged 65 and older are online compared with 70 percent of those aged 50 to 64, 81 percent of those aged 30 to 49, and 93 percent of those aged 18 to 29. Many older Americans say that they don't need the Internet, whereas others live on fixed incomes and can't afford computers or monthly charges for Web service, or both (Fox 2006; Pew Internet & American Life Project 2010).

Asian Americans are the most wired group in the United States. More than 90 percent are Internet users compared with 64 percent of Latinos, 70 percent of African Americans, and 76 percent of whites (Pew Internet & American Life Project 2010). Asian Americans are more likely to use the Internet because many parents in this group are professionals who can afford computers and online service, and encourage their children to use the Internet for education, a major avenue of upward mobility (see Chapters 10 and 14). Latinos with lower educational levels and little English proficiency are the least likely to be connected to the Internet (Livingston et al. 2009).

The biggest digital divide is between social classes. The higher a family's income, the greater the likelihood that its members are Internet users (see *Figure 5.3*). Affluent families can buy home computers, pay for Internet service, and send their children to schools that provide computer-related instruction. Thus, the children from the poorest families are the most likely to lack technological skills.

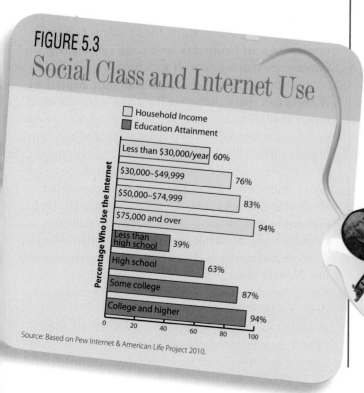

FIGURE 5.3
Social Class and Internet Use

Percentage Who Use the Internet

Household Income
- Less than $30,000/year: 60%
- $30,000–$49,999: 76%
- $50,000–$74,999: 83%
- $75,000 and over: 94%

Education Attainment
- Less than high school: 39%
- High school: 63%
- Some college: 87%
- College and higher: 94%

Source: Based on Pew Internet & American Life Project 2010.

What We Do (and Don't Do) Online

Of the more than 70 online activities that Americans participate in, the most common are sending e-mail, finding information, and reading the news (Pew Internet & American Life Project 2010). About 45 percent of users say that the Internet has played a crucial role in making a major financial decision, buying a car, choosing a college, or getting additional career training. About 61 percent look online for health information (Horrigan and Rainie 2006; Fox and Jones 2009). Thus, the Internet has an important impact on many Americans' lives.

More than one third (35 percent) of American adult Internet users have a profile on an online social network site, up from 8 percent in 2005 and compared with 65 percent of teens who use social networks. In absolute numbers, however, adults comprise a larger number of social network users than teenagers because they make up a larger portion of the U.S. population. Across all ages, people use social network sites for the same reason: to maintain contact with current friends or to locate past friends (Lenhart 2009).

Women's and men's online activities tend to differ. Both use search engines (like Google) heavily, but women are more likely to use e-mail to contact friends and family members for news and advice. Men, in contrast, are more likely to engage in financial activities (such as buying or selling stock), research products (such as cars or appliances), and get information on their hobbies or recreational activities (Fallows 2005).

Such differences aren't surprising. Gender roles have changed, but most women still have the primary responsibility for child care and domestic tasks, whereas men are more likely to make major financial decisions and, even when they're married and have children, have more time to pursue leisure interests, including Internet activities (see Chapter 13).

HOW BENEFICIAL AND HARMFUL IS ONLINE INTERACTION?

You'll see in Chapter 17 that technological changes bring both benefits and costs. The same is true of online interaction, ranging from family relationships to privacy issues.

Family Relationships

Some commentators predicted that technology would pull families apart, but 25 percent of

Stockbyte/Getty Images / Courtesy of Chapel House Photography

adults say that the new communication technology has made their families closer than when they were growing up. For example, cell phones have increased the frequency of interaction between parents, especially if both are employed, to coordinate schedules and to chat with their children. Many parents report spending more time with their children by playing video games with them at home. In the case of young adults who have moved out on their own or are away at college, parents say that family members interact more often than in the past through e-mail and instant and text messaging (Kennedy et al. 2008).

Others complain that communication technology is cutting into family time. According to one mother, she, her husband, and two sons used to have breakfast together and chat. Now, all four start the day on four computers in four separate rooms to check e-mail, Facebook, Twitter, or other social networking sites, and breakfast is rushed and silent because the boys are busy texting their friends (Stone 2009).

Other Social Connections

During the late 1990s, a number of scholars predicted that the Internet would replace close offline relationships, diminish people's involvement in interpersonal and community relationships, and isolate them socially. Contrary to such gloomy forecasts, the Internet has increased interaction, especially with people who have similar interests. Millions of Americans use the Internet to plan religious activities, arrange neighborhood gatherings, petition local politicians, and contact civic organizations. All of these activities have strengthened rather than diluted interpersonal and community ties, and now have a more diverse social network of people across social class and ethnic groups (Hampton et al. 2009).

A major disadvantage of cyberspace communication is that it's more impersonal than face-to-face interaction. According to one faculty member, for instance, e-mail has made teaching more isolating and less satisfying because face-to-face interactions have "mostly evaporated": "Students used to drop by my office all the time, and I miss that. . . After the business part of our conversation was over, we'd chat" (Connolly 2001: B5).

Some also maintain that social networking sites, especially Facebook, are superficial and give people a false sense of friendship and connection to others. You might have 400 "friends" on Facebook, but so what? How many of them really care, for example, about your cat's name, your favorite music, or are interested in viewing photos of your last vacation? (Deresiewicz 2009). Thus, according to some critics, social network-

"Didn't you get my e-mail?"

ing sites may be inflating many people's egos, but the sites are replacing the time we might take to develop relationships with the few friends that we *really* have.

Miscommunication

E-mail is supposed to make communication easier because online interaction lets us think before we speak. During face-to-face and phone discussions, we sometimes regret having been impulsive or rude. Spontaneous e-mail messages can get us into trouble, but most of us learn fairly quickly that we can compose our thoughts and formulate our ideas more clearly and persuasively in an e-mail than during many face-to-face interactions. In Goffman's terms, we can manage the impressions that we give off to others.

On the negative side, even the most neutral exchanges can spark problems. To avoid misunderstandings, e-mail users often use *emoticons* (like smiley faces or frowning ones) to convey voice inflections and facial expressions.

Still, when we don't see the other person's body language, misinterpretation is common because what we think are witty jokes may be taken as personal insults, and our matter-of-fact comments may be viewed as indifference (see Menchik and Tian 2008). For example, a simple and matter-of-fact directive from an instructor, like "I want you to rewrite this assignment and resubmit it," would usually be perceived as normal by a student in a face-to-face encounter but may be interpreted as abrupt in an e-mail. Also, people sometimes forward private e-mails to others without the writer's consent, causing embarrassment or anger.

> ## Even the most neutral [electronic] exchanges can spark problems.

Cyber Bullying and Gossip

One in three online U.S. teens, most of them girls, have experienced *cyber bullying,* which involves a wide range of annoying and potentially menacing activities, such as receiving threatening messages, having an embarrassing picture posted, or having rumors about them spread online (Lenhart 2007).

In other cases, especially at college campuses, people can post anonymous and vicious racist, sexist, or homophobic comments about students on college network sites. A dean of students has likened the sites to "the worst of junior high," but the Web site operators are protected by free speech (Yan 2009: 98). People who identify themselves can be suspended or expelled if they threaten someone with physical harm, but being nasty in cyberspace—however offensive or vicious—is legal (Kim 2009).

Work and Leisure

In 2008, 30 percent of Americans *telecommuted* (worked from home) at least 2 days a week, up from only 9 percent in 1995, but down from 32 percent in 2006. The vast majority earned $75,000 or more a year (Saad 2008).

Telecommuters cite numerous benefits: They spend less money on clothes and gasoline, and less time in traffic; have a more flexible work schedule; spend more time with children instead of using child care; and can attend many of their children's school functions. In addition, the country's almost 4 million telecommuters collectively save about 840 million gallons of gas and 14 million tons of carbon dioxide emissions a year. That's equal to taking 2 million vehicles off the road (Heubeck 2005; Jones 2006; Consumer Electronics Association 2007).

On the negative side, telecommuting often blurs the line between home life and work. Increasingly, many of us use our personal time to catch up with work-related assignments and responsibilities. Further, 60 percent of Americans work during vacations. Even at the office, the average employee has added two extra hours of work a day just to check and respond to work-related e-mail, and one out of five Americans feels that e-mail cuts into their leisure time because a coworker, supervisor, or client can contact them at any time and usually expects a quick response (Alvarez 2005).

Privacy

The Internet can expose more of our private information to the public than any technology in history. A major cost of online interaction is jeopardizing our privacy because e-mail is neither anonymous nor confidential. Many companies monitor and preserve their employees' e-mail messages and can use them to discipline or fire people. It's also becoming increasingly common for employers to search networking sites before deciding whether to make a job offer to a graduating college student. E-mails don't disappear after being deleted but may last indefinitely in cyberspace. People often say things in e-mails they would never say in person, especially when they're flirting, angry, frustrated, or tired.

Many Americans willingly give out personal information on social networking sites—photos, phone number, address, age, education and work background, political and religious views, and so on. It takes a private investigator just a few clicks to get a composite picture of someone from public records, e-mail messages, Web sites, blogs, and networking sites such as MySpace, Facebook, and LinkedIn. Also, computer-savvy individuals can use Web bugs, tags that track users as they move from Web site to Web site. The person compiles a profile of what someone likes and dislikes, and then sells the information to companies (Lamb 2009).

© Rawdon Wyatt/Alamy

Social groups

provide an important part of our social identity.

6 Social Groups, Organizations, and Social Institutions

what do you think?

It's easy to resist pressure to follow the crowd.

1	2	3	4	5	6	7
strongly agree					strongly disagree	

1 Social Groups

every Saturday night, from 75 to 100 drivers meet at a parking lot in Baltimore to show off and discuss their customized, souped-up cars. The drivers are typically men, represent a variety of racial/ethnic backgrounds, and range in age from the late teens to early 40s. Most pour their paychecks into making their cars faster, paying for wild paint jobs, and installing television sets and stereo systems. They hang out until about 2 a.m., even though these get-togethers sometimes create conflict at home: "My wife complains that I put Saturday night before her" (Mitchell 2002: A6). These car enthusiasts are a social group.

WHAT IS A SOCIAL GROUP?

A **social group** consists of two or more people who interact with one another, and who share a common identity and a sense of belonging or "we-ness." Friends, families, work groups, religious congregations, clubs, athletic teams, World War II veterans, and organizations are all examples of social groups.

Each of us is a member of many groups simultaneously. Some groups are highly organized and stable (local political parties); others are fluid and temporary (high-school classmates). Interaction, especially face-to-face interaction, is the key ingredient in creating and maintaining groups.

> **social group** two or more people who interact with one another, and who share a common identity and a sense of belonging or "we-ness."

Social groups are essential because they provide an important part of our social identity and help us understand the behavior of other people in our society. Some groups, nonetheless, are more binding and significant than others because they shape our social and moral beliefs. Our most important social groups are primary and secondary groups, in-groups and out-groups, and reference groups.

PRIMARY GROUPS AND SECONDARY GROUPS

Suppose your car's battery died this morning, your sociology professor gave a pop quiz for which you hadn't studied, your computer's hard drive crashed, and your microwave stopped working. Whom might you call to vent? Your answer reflects the difference between primary and secondary groups.

Primary Groups

A **primary group** is a relatively small group of people who engage in intimate face-to-face interaction over an extended period. For sociologist Charles Horton Cooley (1909/1983: 24), the most significant primary groups were "the family, the play-group of children, and the neighborhood or community of elders" because they are first and central in shaping a person's social and moral development.

Primary groups are our emotional glue. We call members of our primary group to share good news or to gripe. Primary group members are typically understanding, supportive, and tolerant even when we're in a bad mood or selfish. They have a powerful influence on our social

Why is the cast of characters on the television series
Glee an example of a social group?

FOX-TV/THE KOBAL COLLECTION/BAER, CARIN

© Lew Robertson/Corbis

EMOTIONAL GLUE

identity because we interact with them on a regular and intimate basis over many years, usually throughout our lives. Because primary group members genuinely care about each other, they contribute to one another's personal development, security, and well-being. Our family and close friends, for example, stick with us through good and bad, and we feel comfortable in being ourselves in their presence.

Secondary Groups

A **secondary group** is a large, usually formal, impersonal, and temporary collection of people who pursue a specific goal or activity. Your sociology class is a good example of a secondary group. You might have a few friends in class, but students typically interact infrequently and formally. When the semester (or quarter) is over and you've accomplished your goal of passing the course, you may not see each other again (especially if you're attending a large college or university). And you certainly wouldn't call your professor if you needed a sympathetic ear at the end of a bad day. Other examples of secondary groups include political parties, labor unions, and employees of a company.

Unlike primary groups, secondary groups are usually highly structured: There are many rules and regulations, people know (or care) little about each other personally, relationships are formal, and members are expected to fulfill particular functions. Whereas primary groups meet our *expressive* (emotional) needs, secondary groups fulfill *instrumental* (task-oriented) needs. Once a task or activity is completed—whether it's earning a grade, turning in a committee report, or building a bridge—secondary groups usually split up and go on to become a member of other secondary groups.

Table 6.1 summarizes the characteristics of primary and secondary groups. These characteristics represent **ideal types**—general traits that describe a social phenomenon rather than every case. Ideal types provide composite pictures of how social phenomena differ rather than specific descriptions of reality. Because primary and secondary groups are ideal types, their characteristics can vary. Thus, members of primary groups may sometimes devote themselves to meeting instrumental needs (such as creating a family-owned business), and members of secondary groups (such as military units and athletic teams) can develop a lasting personal closeness.

IN-GROUPS AND OUT-GROUPS

> *All good people agree,*
> *And all good people say,*
> *All nice people, like Us, are We*
> *And everyone else is They.*
> *—from* We and They, *by Rudyard Kipling*

Comstock/Jupiter Images

Rudyard Kipling's poem "We and They" captures the essence of in-groups and out-groups. Members of an **in-group** share a sense of identity and "we-ness" that typically excludes and devalues outsiders. **Out-groups** consist of people who are viewed and treated negatively because they are seen as having values, beliefs, and other characteristics different from those of the in-group. For example, "we" vegetarians are healthier than "you" meat eaters, "we" computer nerds are smarter than "you" fraternity and sorority "types," and so on.

Based on ascribed or achieved statuses, almost everyone sees others as members of in-groups and out-groups. From ancient times to the present, people in various parts of the world have made "we" and "they" distinctions based on race or ethnicity, gender, religion, age, social class, and other social and biological criteria (Coser 1956; Tajfel 1982; Hinkle and Schopler 1986).

Out-group members are usually aware of being outsiders. For example, overweight people are often viewed by others as lazy, unmotivated, and undisciplined. Many overweight people have internalized such negative attitudes and see themselves as part of an out-group. In a national study of overweight people, nearly 40 percent had negative attitudes about fat people (including themselves), about 33 percent would rather experience a divorce than be obese, 15 percent would give up 10 years or more of life to be thinner, and 4 percent would trade blindness for obesity (Schwartz et al. 2006).

In-groups and out-groups affect our feelings about ourselves and others, our social identity, and our life outcomes. In-groups can be a positive influence in pro-

in-groups people who share a sense of identity and "we-ness" that typically excludes and devalues outsiders.

out-groups people who are viewed and treated negatively because they are seen as having values, beliefs, and other characteristics different from those of an in-group.

TABLE 6.1
Characteristics of Primary and Secondary Groups

	CHARACTERISTICS OF A PRIMARY GROUP	CHARACTERISTICS OF A SECONDARY GROUP
Interaction	• Face to face • The group is usually small	• Face to face or indirect • The group is usually large
Communication	• Communication is emotional, personal, and satisfying	• Communication is emotionally neutral and impersonal
Relationships	• Intimate, warm, and informal • Usually long-term • Valued for their own sake (expressive)	• Typically remote, cool, and formal • Usually short-term • Goal-oriented (instrumental)
Individual Conformity	• Individuals are relatively free to stray from norms and rules	• Individuals are expected to adhere to rules and regulations
Membership	• Members are not easily replaced	• Members are easily replaced
Examples	• Family, close friends, girlfriends and boyfriends, self-help groups, street gangs	• College classes, political parties, professional associations, religious organizations

moting individuals' sense of self-worth and belonging, and increasing group solidarity and cohesion, but they can also create conflict and provoke inhumane actions, even war. For example, in-group/out-group hostilities have fueled the Palestinian-Israeli battles over the occupation of the West Bank, the eviction of white farmers in South Africa, and ongoing civil wars in some African nations (see online Chapter 18).

REFERENCE GROUPS

Besides belonging to primary groups, secondary groups, in-groups, and out-groups, we also have reference groups. A **reference group** is a group of people who shape our behavior, values, and attitudes (Merton and Rossi 1950). Reference groups influence who we are, what we do, and who we'd like to be in the future. Unlike primary groups, however, reference groups rarely provide personal support or face-to-face interaction over time.

Reference groups might be people with whom we already associate, like a college club or a recreational athletic team. They can also be groups that we admire and want to be part of, such as successful financial advisors or country club members. Each person has many reference groups. Your sociology professor, for example, may be a member of several professional sociological associations, a golf enthusiast, a parent, and a homeowner. Identification with each of these groups influences her or his everyday attitudes and actions.

Especially from kindergarten through high school, cliques typically exclude others because of social status, race, ethnicity, gender, clothes, school activities, or other characteristics, which increases campus racial tensions and promotes stereotypes. Should schools try to discourage the formation of in-groups? If yes, what might they do? If no, why not?

© F1online digitale Bildagentur GmbH/Alamy

Like in-groups and primary groups, reference groups can have a strong impact on our self-identity, self-esteem, and sense of belonging because they shape our current and future attitudes and behavior. We often add or drop reference groups throughout the life course. If you aspire to move up the occupational ladder, for example, your reference group may change from entry-level employees to managers, vice presidents, and CEOs.

GROUP CONFORMITY

Most Americans see themselves as rugged individualists who have a mind of their own and don't bow to group pressure (see the discussion of values in Chapter 3). A number of studies have shown, however, that most Americans are profoundly influenced by group pressure. Four of the best-known of these studies are by Solomon Asch, Stanley Milgram, Philip Zimbardo, and Irving Janis.

Asch's Research

In a now-classic study of group influence, social psychologist Solomon Asch (1952) told subjects that they were taking part in an experiment on visual judgment. After arranging six to eight male undergraduates around a table, Asch showed them the line drawn on card 1 and asked them to match the line to one of three lines on card 2 (see *Figure 6.1*). The correct answer, clearly, is line C.

All but one of the participants in each group—who usually sat in the next-to-last seat—were Asch's confederates, or accomplices. In the first test with each group, all the confederates selected the correct matching line. In the other tests, each of the confederates, one by one, deliberately chose an incorrect line. Thus, the nonconfederate participant faced a situation in which seven other group members had unanimously agreed on a wrong answer. Averaged over all of the trials, 37 percent of the nonconfederate participants ended up agreeing with the false judgments of the group. When those participants were asked to judge the length of the lines alone, away from the influence of the group, they made errors only 1 percent of the time.

Asch's research demonstrated the power of groups over individuals. Even when we know that something is clearly wrong, we may go along with the group to avoid ridicule or exclusion. Remember that these experiments were done in a laboratory and with groups whose members didn't know each other. A group's influence on members' judgments and behavior can be even stronger when it is a real-life primary group or a reference group.

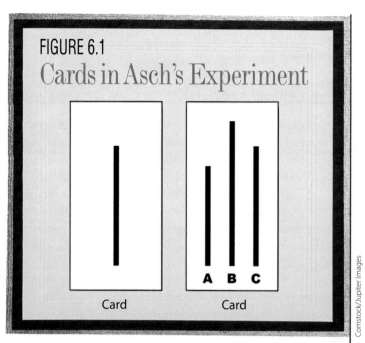

FIGURE 6.1
Cards in Asch's Experiment

Card

Card

A B C

Comstock/Jupiter Images

Milgram's Research

In a well-known laboratory experiment on obedience conducted by psychologist Stanley Milgram (1963, 1965), 40 volunteers were asked to administer electric shocks to other study participants. In each experimental trial, one participant was a "teacher" and the other a "learner," one of Milgram's accomplices. The teachers were businessmen, professionals, and blue-collar workers. The learner was strapped into a realistic-looking chair that supposedly regulated electric currents. The learner was not actually receiving a shock but was told to fake pain and fear. The teacher read aloud pairs of words that the learner had to memorize. Whenever the learner didn't answer correctly, the teacher was told to apply an electric shock from a low of 15 volts to a high of 450 volts. When the learners shrieked in pain, the majority of the teachers, although distressed, obeyed the study supervisor and administered the shocks when told to do so.

Milgram's study was controversial. Ordering electric shocks raised numerous ethical questions about the subjects' suffering extreme emotional stress (see Chapter 2). However, the results showed that an astonishingly large proportion of the subjects inflicted pain on others to obey an authority figure.

Zimbardo's Research

The Stanford Prison Experiment conducted by social psychologist Philip Zimbardo also underscores the power of groups on human behavior (Haney et al. 1973; Zimbardo 1975). Zimbardo advertised in a local California newspaper for volunteers for an experiment on prison life and selected 24 young men, most of them college students, as participants.

On a Sunday morning in August 1971, nine young men were "arrested" in their homes by police as neighbors watched. The "prisoners" were booked and transported to a mock prison that Zimbardo and his colleagues had constructed in the basement of the psychology building at Stanford University. The prisoners were searched, issued an identification number, and outfitted in a dresslike shirt and heavy ankle chains. Those assigned to be "guards" were given uniforms, billy clubs, whistles, and reflective sunglasses. The guards were told that their job was to maintain control of the prisoners but not to use violence.

All the young men quickly assumed the roles of either obedient and docile prisoners or autocratic and controlling guards. The guards became increasingly more cruel and demanding. The prisoners complied with dehumanizing demands (such as eating filthy sausages) to gain the guards' approval and bowed to their authority. (A slide show of this experiment is available online at www.prisonexp.org.)

Zimbardo's study was scheduled to run for 2 weeks but was terminated after 6 days because the guards became increasingly aggressive and humiliated the prisoners. Among other things, they forced the prisoners to clean out toilet bowls with their bare hands, locked them in a closet, and made them stand at attention for hours. Instead of

AP Photo, File

Many social scientists have used Milgram's findings to explain the Abu Ghraib prison in Iraq where U.S. soldiers abused and humiliated Iraqi prisoners because "I was just following orders."

simply walking out or rebelling, the prisoners became withdrawn and depressed. Zimbardo ended the experiment because of the prisoners' stressed reactions.

The experiment raised numerous ethical questions about the harmful treatment of participants. It demonstrated, however, the powerful effect of group conformity: People exercise authority, even to the point of hurting others or themselves, or submit to authority if there is group pressure to conform (Zimbardo et al. 2000).

Janis's Research

Sometimes intelligent people, even those in positions of high responsibility, make disastrous and irrational decisions. Why? Social psychologist Irving Janis (1972: 9) cautioned presidents and other heads of state to be wary of groupthink, a tendency of in-group members to conform without critically testing, analyzing, and evaluating ideas, which results in a narrow view of an issue. To preserve friendly relations and to remain loyal to the group, Janis argued, individuals don't raise controversial issues, question weak arguments, or probe "soft-headed thinking." As a result, influential leaders often make decisions—based on their advisors' consensus—that turn out to be political and economic fiascoes.

A United States Senate study (2004) on intelligence agencies provides an example of groupthink. The report concluded that U.S. leaders' decision to invade Iraq in 2003 was based on a groupthink dynamic that relied on unproven and inaccurate assumptions, inadequate or misleading sources, and a dismissal of conflicting information, which showed that Iraq had no weapons of mass destruction.

Janis and other researchers have focused on high-level decision making, but groupthink is common in all kinds of groups—student clubs, PTAs, search committees, professional organizations, and juries, for example. If group members are aware of the negative characteristics of groupthink, they can avoid some of the pitfalls by setting up and following democratic discussion and voting processes, hammering out disagreements, and seeking advice from informed and objective people outside the group.

SOCIAL NETWORKS

Groups exist within the context of larger social units, such as social networks. A **social network** is a web of social ties that links an individual to others. A social network may involve as few as three people or as many as millions.

Some of our social networks, such as our primary and secondary groups, may be tightly knit, involve interactions on a daily basis, and have clear boundaries about who belongs and who doesn't. In other cases, our social networks connect us to large numbers of people whom we don't know personally and with whom we interact rarely or indirectly, and the group's boundaries are fluid or unclear. Examples of such distant networks include members of the American Sociological Association and *Reader's Digest* subscribers.

The Internet, in particular, has generated numerous interlocking social networks that unite people across many states and countries who share similar concerns, interests, or characteristics that include gender, education, occupation, sexual orientation, age, religion, and/or ethnicity. Facebook, for example, is a very popular social network that includes millions of international subscribers with a broad range of characteristics (see Chapter 5).

> *Sometimes intelligent people, even those in positions of high responsibility, make disastrous and irrational decisions.*

2 Formal Organizations

from the time that you turn on the faucet to brush your teeth until you sit down in your first class, you've participated in dozens of formal organizations. A **formal organization** is a complex and structured secondary group that has been deliberately created to achieve specific goals in an efficient manner. We depend on a variety of formal organizations to provide goods and services in a stable and predictable way, including companies that supply clean water for brushing our teeth, numerous food producers who stock our favorite breakfast items, and garment industries and retailers that produce and sell the clothes we wear.

CHARACTERISTICS OF FORMAL ORGANIZATIONS

Formal organizations share some common characteristics:

- Social statuses and roles are organized around shared expectations and goals.
- Norms governing social relationships among members specify rights, duties, and sanctions.
- A formal hierarchy includes leaders or individuals who are in charge.

Two of the most widespread and important types of formal organizations in the United States are voluntary associations and bureaucracies.

VOLUNTARY ASSOCIATIONS

A **voluntary association** is a formal organization created by people who share a common set of interests and who are not paid for their participation. Unlike bureaucracies, as you'll see shortly, voluntary associations vary quite a bit in organizational structure. Some small voluntary organizations, such as book clubs, don't have a formal hierarchy, a rigid set of rules or regulations, or even specific goals. Others, like investment clubs, have a constitution, written regulations about the duties and rights of officers and members, minutes, and an agenda that's circulated before each meeting.

Helping others is a strong American value (see Chapter 3). Whether it's an earthquake in Haiti, a drought in Somalia, or a flood in New Orleans, Americans generously send money, food, and personnel. Every year, millions of Americans—many of whom have full-time jobs—are volunteers in a variety of local, regional, and national organizations. These volunteers save government agencies billions of dollars every year by providing needed services (see *Table 6.2*).

In the United States, more than 1.2 million charities, social welfare organizations, and religious congregations are voluntary associations (Independent Sector 2006). If local voluntary associations that focus on education, self-help, and environmental issues were included in the count, the numbers of groups and members would be staggering. Overall, there are four types of voluntary associations: groups that have a charitable or altruistic purpose (like the United Way), groups that focus on political issues (like the emerging Tea Party), groups that organize around occupations (like the National Association of Realtors), and groups that have a recreational orientation (like the Beer Can Collectors of America).

Who is most likely to join voluntary associations? It depends on the organization. Charitable/altruistic and recreational associations attract people from a variety of social classes, age categories, and ethnic/racial backgrounds. Political and occupation-related associations, on the other hand, are more common among people from higher socioeconomic backgrounds, who have money to fund the groups' activities and time to attend local, regional, and national conferences.

BUREAUCRACIES

When I ask my students to describe a bureaucracy, their answers often include adjectives such as "bungling," "impossible," "buck-passing," "frustrating," "hellish," and worse. Such reactions are understandable because, for most of us, dealing with a bureaucracy is synonymous with red tape, slow-moving lines, long and tedious forms, and rude employees.

For sociologists, a **bureaucracy** is a formal organization that is designed to accomplish goals and tasks through the efforts of a large number of people in the most efficient and rational way possible. Bureaucracies are not a modern invention but existed thousands of years ago in ancient Egypt, China, and Africa. Some

voluntary association a formal organization created by people who share a common set of interests and who are not paid for their participation.

bureaucracy a formal organization that is designed to accomplish goals and tasks through the efforts of a large number of people in the most efficient and rational way possible.

TABLE 6.2
Volunteering in the United States, 2009

Percentage of adults who volunteer	36
Total number of volunteers aged 16 and older	62 million
Average annual hours per volunteer	52
Percentage of volunteers who worked full time	34
Estimated hourly value of volunteer time	$20.25 per hour
Total dollar value of volunteer time	$295 billion

Sources: Based on Corporation for National and Community Service 2007; Independent Sector 2009; Lopez 2009.

bureaucracies function more smoothly than others, and some formal organizations are more bureaucratic than others. Whether they are relatively small (such as a 500-bed hospital) or huge (such as Medicare, a U.S. government agency that provides health insurance for millions of Americans aged 65 and older), bureaucracies share some common characteristics.

Ideal Characteristics of Bureaucracies

Max Weber (1925/1947) identified six key characteristics of the ideal type of bureaucracy. Remember that ideal types describe distinctive and abstract traits rather than those that fit any specific organization. In Weber's model, then, the following characteristics describe what an efficient and productive bureaucracy *should* be like:

- *High degree of division of labor and specialization.* Individuals who work in the bureaucracy perform very specific tasks.

- *Hierarchy of authority.* Workers are arranged in a hierarchy where each person is supervised by someone in a higher position. The resulting pyramids—often presented in organizational charts—show who has au-thority over whom and who is responsible to whom. Thus, there is a chain of command, stretching from top to bottom, that coordinates decision making. *Figure 6.2* shows a simplified organizational chart of a small state university of 5,000 students. If this chart included receptionists, food services, plant maintenance, libraries, human resources, student housing, and numerous other offices and staff, the bureaucratic structure would be much more complex. The shaded boxes represent the flow of authority from the top (governor of the state) to the bottom (students in the sociology department).

- *Explicit written rules and regulations.* Detailed written rules and regulations cover almost every possible kind of situation and problem that might arise. They address a variety of issues, including hiring, firing, salary scales, rules for sick pay and absences, and everyday operations. If a person has a question, all she or he has to do is look up the answer.

- *Impersonality.* There is no place in a bureaucracy for personal likes or dislikes or tantrums. Instead, employees are expected to follow the rules, to get the work done, and to behave professionally. An impersonal workplace in which all employees are treated equally minimizes conflict and favoritism and increases efficiency.

- *Qualifications-based employment.* People are hired based on objective criteria such as skills, education, experience, and scores on standardized tests. If workers perform well and have the necessary credentials and technical competence, they'll move up the career ladder.

- *Separation of work and ownership.* Neither managers nor employees own the offices they work in, the desks they sit at, the machinery they use, or the products that they make, invent, or design.

For Weber, all of these characteristics produce an efficient and rational bureaucracy. A "rational matter-of-factness," he maintained, dehumanized bureaucracies but also made them more productive by "eliminating from official business love, hatred, and all purely personal, irrational, and emotional elements

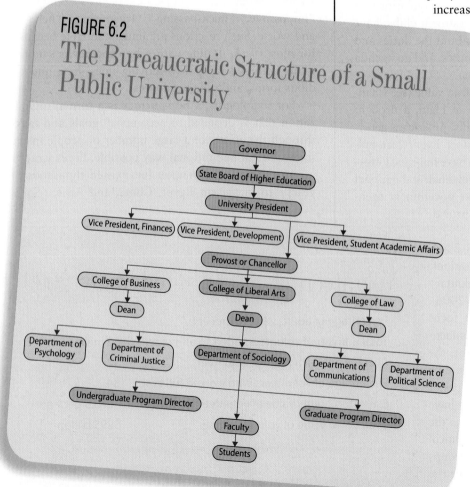

FIGURE 6.2
The Bureaucratic Structure of a Small Public University

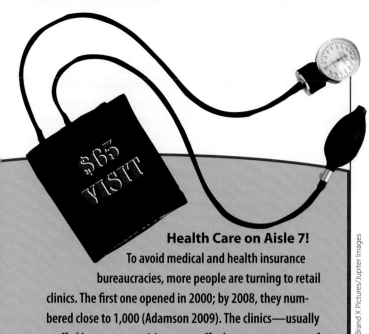

Health Care on Aisle 7!
To avoid medical and health insurance bureaucracies, more people are turning to retail clinics. The first one opened in 2000; by 2008, they numbered close to 1,000 (Adamson 2009). The clinics—usually staffed by nurse practitioners—offer low-cost treatment for more than 25 common conditions, such as strep throat and ear infections, and provide health screening tests, immunizations, and physicals. The clinics are located in pharmacies, grocery stores, and "big box" stores, such as Target and Wal-Mart. There is no need to make an appointment and minimal (if any) waiting; the patients are in and out in about 15 minutes, and most of the clinics are open evenings and weekends.

which escape calculation" (Weber 1946: 216). Weber viewed bureaucracies as superior to other forms of organization because they're more efficient and more predictable, but he also worried that bureaucracies could become "iron cages" because people become trapped in them, "their basic humanity denied."

Shortcomings of Bureaucracies

Weber described the ideal characteristics of a productive and efficient bureaucracy, but what's the reality? As you read through the following list of problems, think about the ones you've experienced while working in a bureaucracy or dealing with one.

- *Weak reward systems* reduce the motivation to do a good job, and are thus a major source of inefficiency and lack of innovation (Barton 1980). Besides low wages or salaries, weak reward systems include few or no health benefits, little recognition, unsafe equipment and work environments, and few incentives to be creative.

- *Rigid rules* discourage creativity. An employee in a bureaucracy who suggests a way to decrease red tape, for

example, will probably be criticized for being lazy or not following the rules, rather than being praised for being innovative.

alienation a feeling of isolation, meaninglessness, and powerlessness that may affect workers in a bureaucracy.

- Rigid rules create and reinforce *bureaucratic ritualism,* a preoccupation with rules and regulations rather than the organization's objectives (Merton 1968). Instead of questioning whether all the red tape is really necessary, bureaucrats are usually more concerned that people follow established procedures because "we've always done it this way."

- Rigid rules and ritualism often lead to **alienation,** a feeling of isolation, meaninglessness, and powerlessness. When people are reduced to a "small cog," they feel dehumanized and see little opportunity for advancement. Alienation—at all levels—may result in high turnover, tardiness, absenteeism, stealing, sabotage, stress, health problems, and in some cases, whistle-blowing (reporting organizational misconduct to legal authorities).

- *Communication problems* are common in bureaucracies. Because communication typically flows down rather than up the hierarchy, employees (and many managers below the highest echelons) rarely know what's going on. Supervisors and their subordinates may be reluctant to discuss problems or offer suggestions for fear of being criticized or fired. Those at the top often make ill-informed decisions based on incomplete or inaccurate information, as illustrated by groupthink (Blau and Meyer 1987; Fletcher and Taplin 2002).

- *Parkinson's Law* is the idea that work expands to fill the time available for its completion (Parkinson 1962). This means that, even if employees finish an assigned task before the deadline, they'll look busy and act as though they're still working on the task

" WHAT HAPPENED TO THAT EFFICIENCY REPORT ? I HAD IT IN MY HAND NOT TWO MINUTES AGO. "

to safeguard their jobs or to avoid getting another assignment. Parkinson's Law also explains a bureaucracy's tendency to keep getting larger. That is, bosses may not crack down on idle workers because higher productivity may reduce the possibility of increasing the budget or hiring more people.

- A related idea, the *Peter Principle,* proposes that workers are promoted until they reach their level of incompetence (Peter and Hull 1969). In many bureaucracies, employees who perform well are promoted to the next level, usually into administrative positions. Thus, project directors become managers, teachers become principals, and nurses become hospital administrators. Sooner or later, those promoted find themselves in positions for which they lack sufficient knowledge, capabilities, training, competence, or experience.

- The **iron law of oligarchy** is the tendency of a bureaucracy to become increasingly dominated by a small group of people (Michels 1911/1949). A handful of people can control and rule a bureaucracy because the top officials and leaders monopolize information and resources. As a result, those at the top maintain their power and privilege.

- The cumulative effect of these and other bureaucratic dysfunctions can result in *dehumanization* because weak reward systems, ritualism, rigid rules, and the other shortcomings limit organizational creativity and freedom. For example, sociologist George Ritzer argues that some of the problems and characteristics that dominate bureaucracies are increasingly shaping U.S. society. As the "The McDonaldization of Society" box shows, Americans' everyday life is becoming more automated, rigid, and impersonal.

Once established, bureaucracies are almost impossible to eliminate. For example, the U.S. Department of Education is a huge bureaucracy that continues to grow even though it has done little to improve the public educational system and even restricts college opportunities for many low-income students (see Chapter 14). However, most bureaucracies continue to function, largely because of the internal development of informal groups.

THE INFORMAL SIDE OF BUREAUCRACY

Informal networks develop at all levels of a bureaucracy, from the bottom to the top. At the top, a CEO or a few members of the board of directors run the organization. They often make decisions informally, and the rest of the board then rubber-stamps those decisions. And because of personal ties and connections, the top officials at large corporations often know each other, consult with each other, and serve on each other's boards. For example, George J. Mitchell, former U.S. Senator, has served on the board of directors of Disney, two large and influential law firms in Washington, DC, a large insurance company, and five large corporations such as FedEx and Staples. Such interlocking ties suggest that a small group of people holds much of the informal decision-making power across many organizations (see also Chapter 12).

Historic Studies of Informal Structures

What about informal structures at the lower ranks? For many years, and well into the 1930s, experts concentrated on organizational efficiency based on the principles of *scientific management* developed by Frederick Winslow Taylor, a mechanical engineer who wanted to improve industrial productivity.

Taylor (1911/1967) considered workers—especially those in factories and on assembly lines—mere adjuncts to machines, assumed that people don't like to work, and maintained that employees must be prodded by the promise of financial incentives, close supervision, and clear goals that they can attain with little effort. Taylor believed that the best results would come from a trained and qualified management and a cooperative workforce, but that management had to enforce the cooperation because most workers are incapable of handling even the simplest tasks.

A number of studies conducted by industrial psychologists and sociologists between 1927 and 1932 shook up Taylor's views. The research teams studied employees at the Western Electric Company's Hawthorne plant in Chicago. The *Hawthorne studies,* as they're often called, found that informal groups were critical to the organization's functioning (Roethlisberger and Dickson 1939/1942; Mayo 1945; Landsberger 1958).

Informal social groups can promote an organization's goals if they collaborate, are cohesive, and motivate each other (Barnard 1938). They can also resist an organization's goals and formal rules. In one of the Hawthorne studies, Roethlisberger and Dickson (1939/1942) spent 6 months observing a group of 14 men who wired telephone switchboards in what the company called the "bank-wiring room."

The bank-wiring room work group consisted of nine wiremen, three solderers, and two inspectors. Management offered financial incentives for higher

The McDonaldization of Society

According to sociologist George Ritzer (1996: 1), the organizational principles that underlie McDonald's, the well-known fast-food chain, are beginning to dominate "more and more sectors of American society as well as of the rest of the world." McDonaldization has four components: efficiency, calculability, predictability, and control.

1 *Efficiency* means that consumers have a quick way of getting meals. In a society where people rush from one place to another and where both parents are likely to work or single parents are pressed for time, McDonald's (and similar franchises) offers an efficient way to satisfy hunger and avoid much "fuss and mess."

Like their customers, McDonald's workers function efficiently: The menu is limited, the registers are automated, and employees perform their tasks rapidly and easily.

2 *Calculability* emphasizes the quantitative aspects of the products sold (portion size and cost) and the time it takes to get the products. Customers often feel that they are getting a lot of food for what appears to be a nominal sum of money, and that a trip to a fast-food restaurant will take less time than eating at home. In reality, soft drinks are sold at a 600 percent markup because most of the space in the cup is taken up by ice. It costs at least twice as much and takes twice as long to get to the restaurant, stand in line, and pick up the food than to prepare a similar meal at home.

3 *Predictability* means that products and services will be the same over time and in all locales. "There is great comfort in knowing that McDonald's offers no surprises" (p. 10). The Quarter Pounder is the same regardless where customers order. Outside of the United States, "homesick American tourists in far-off countries can take comfort in the knowledge that they will likely run into those familiar golden arches and the restaurant they have become so accustomed to" (p. 81).

Workers, like customers, behave in predictable ways: "There are, for example, six steps to window service: greet the customer, take the order, assemble the order, present the order, receive payment, thank the customer and ask for repeat business" (p. 81).

4 *Control* means that technology shapes behavior. McDonald's controls customers subtly by offering limited menus and uncomfortable seats that encourage diners to eat quickly and leave. "Consumers know that they are supposed to line up, move to the counter, order their food, pay, carry the food to an available table, eat, gather up their debris, deposit it in the trash receptacle, and return to their cars. People are moved along in this system not by a conveyor belt, but by the unwritten, but universally known, norms for eating in a fast-food restaurant" (p. 105).

McDonald's controls employees more openly and directly. Workers are trained to do a limited number of things in precisely the same way, managers and inspectors make sure that subordinates toe the line, and McDonald's has steadily replaced human beings with technologies that include soft-drink dispensers that shut off when the glass is full and a machine that rings and lifts the french fries out of the oil when they are crisp. Such technology increases the corporation's control over workers because employees don't have to use their own judgment or need many skills to prepare and serve the food.

Efficiency, calculability, predictability, and control reflect a rational system (remember Weber?) that increases a bureaucracy's efficiency. On the other hand, Ritzer contends, McDonaldization reflects the "irrationality of rationality" because the results can be harmful. For example, the huge farms that now produce "uniform potatoes to create those predictable French fries" of the same size rely on the extensive use of chemicals that then pollute water supplies. And the enormous amount of nonbiodegradable trash that McDonald's produces wastes our money because we—and not McDonald's—pay for landfills.

According to Ritzer (2008: 11, 119), McDonald's is such a powerful model that many businesses have cloned its four dimensions of efficiency, calculability, predictability, and control. Examples include "McDentists" and "McDoctors," drive-in clinics designed to deal quickly with minor dental and medical problems; "McChild" care centers like KinderCare; and "McPaper" newspapers, such as *USA Today*.

JOERG KOCH/AFP/Getty Images

productivity, but the work group pressured people to limit output. The wiremen, for instance, developed the following norms that controlled the group's behavior:

1. You should not turn out too much work. If you do, you are a "rate-buster" and a "speed king."

2. You should not turn out too little work. If you do, you are a "chiseler."

3. You should not tell a supervisor anything that will be detrimental to a coworker. If you do, you are a "squealer."

4. You should not "act officious." If you are an inspector, for example, you should not act like one.

If an individual violated any of these norms, the other workers used "binging" (striking a person on the shoulder) as a form of punishment.

Why did the men control productivity rather than take advantage of the management's promise of higher wages? They feared that if they produced at a high level, they would be required to produce at that level regularly. They also worried that high productivity would lead to layoffs because supervisors would conclude that fewer workers could achieve the same output. In addition, the bank-wiring room men experienced high morale and job satisfaction because they felt they had some control over their work. In contradiction to Taylor's scientific management perspective, then, the Hawthorne studies concluded that there is an important relationship between formal and informal organization.

Modern Work Teams

Since the Hawthorne studies, many managers have recognized that informal groups pervade organizations and affect workers' productivity. As a result, numerous organizations have implemented alternative management strategies.

Today, *self-managing work teams* are the dominant model in most large organizations (Cloke and Goldsmith 2002; Neider and Schriesheim 2005). Contrary to Taylor's notion that workers do and managers think, self-managing work teams, sometimes referred to as *postbureaucratic organizations,* involve groups of 10 to 15 people who take on the duties of their former supervisors. Instead of being told what to do by a boss, self-managing workers gather and interpret information, act on the information, and take collective responsibility for their actions.

Typically, a self-managing work team is responsible for completing a specific, well-defined job function. The team has the authority to make essential decisions to complete the job—whether it's designing a new refrigerator or handling food service for a university. Members of a self-managing team order the materials they need and coordinate with other groups within and outside the organization. Because they're not held back by unresponsive managers, self-managing teams theoretically become committed to the organization and its success (Wellins et al. 1991).

How effective are self-managing work teams? The data are mixed. A number of case studies show that well-designed and well-executed team initiatives improve employee morale and the quality of products and services with relatively small costs. The initiatives that fail are marked by low support from management and union leaders, management's interfering with the group's work, or ineffective team leaders who discourage a team's creativity or autonomy (Manz and Sims 1987; Barker 1993; Lencioni 2002).

3 Sociological Perspectives on Social Groups and Organizations

how do organizations work? And how do social groups affect massive bureaucracies? In answering such questions, functionalism, conflict theory, feminist theories, and symbolic interactionism provide different insights. Taken together, these perspectives provide a multifaceted understanding of groups and organizations (*Table 6.3* summarizes these perspectives).

FUNCTIONALISM: COOPERATION WORKS

Much of what you've read about social groups and formal organizations so far has come from functionalist perspectives, which emphasize that groups and organizations are composed of interrelated, mutually dependent parts. As Weber pointed out, when a bureaucracy operates rationally and efficiently, workers cooperate and maintain the organization's stability and continuity.

Today, many companies still apply Taylor's basic principles of scientific management, especially in industries where the work is routine and monotonous. For example, for workers whose job requires sewing, the labor is broken down into numerous specific tasks, supervisors closely monitor each task, and the more pieces a worker finishes, the higher the pay. In many manufac-

TABLE 6.3
Sociological Perspectives on Groups and Organizations

THEORETICAL PERSPECTIVE	LEVEL OF ANALYSIS	MAIN POINTS	KEY QUESTIONS
Functionalist	Macro	Organizations are made up of interrelated parts and rules and regulations that produce cooperation in meeting a common goal.	• Why are some organizations more effective than others? • How do dysfunctions prevent organizations from being rational and effective?
Conflict	Macro	Organizations promote inequality that benefits elites, not workers.	• Who controls an organization's resources and decision making? • How do those with power protect their interests and privileges?
Feminist	Macro and micro	Organizations tend not to recognize or reward talented women and regularly exclude them from decision-making processes.	• Why do many women hit a glass ceiling? • How do gender stereotypes affect women in groups and organizations?
Symbolic Interactionist	Micro	People aren't puppets but can determine what goes on in a group or organization.	• Why do people ignore or change an organization's rules? • How do members of social groups influence workplace behavior?

turing plants, where wages aren't necessarily based on piecework, workers and bosses must cooperate across a number of sequential steps to turn out a final product, whether it's an automobile or a can of soup.

Functionalists also note that organizations (and especially bureaucracies) can be dysfunctional. Workers may be alienated because of weak reward systems, favoritism, and incompetent supervisors. Such dissatisfaction can result in absenteeism, low morale and productivity, and high resignation rates.

College-educated employees are especially likely to experience "boreout" because they don't have enough to do, are unchallenged, and frustrated by not having opportunities to use their skills and talents. Most Americans suffer from burnout because they're overworked, but an estimated one third of workers are bored because they are underworked. Employers waste more than $5,000 a year per worker on boreout because employees who aren't challenged spend more than two hours a day pretending to work: They shop online, do e-mail, and even surf networking sites hoping to find leads for better jobs (Rothlin and Werder 2008). Do you think it's possible for companies to remedy dysfunctions such as burnout and boreout?

Critical Evaluation

Functionalism has been useful in understanding how groups and organizations fulfill essential functions such as motivating people to get work done and achieving a common goal. For critics, especially conflict theorists, functionalists exaggerate harmony and tend to gloss

Garment work is traditionally piecework, with a worker making only one part of a garment. With piecework, the more you produce, the more you earn.

Neil Beckerman

Some organizations pay to have their products incorporated into the story lines of television programs because many Americans have technology (such as TiVo) that enables them to fast-forward commercials. In one episode of The Office, Michael Scott, the branch manager, introduced casual Fridays and kept proclaiming "I love my new Levi's!" From a conflict perspective, does such product placement manipulate viewers?

over dysfunctions such as worker dissatisfaction and alienation.

A related issue is whether informal social networks improve worker morale and control as much as functionalists claim. After all, a tedious and monotonous job is tedious and monotonous regardless of the degree of informal coworker interaction.

CONFLICT THEORY: SOME BENEFIT MORE THAN OTHERS

Conflict theorists contend that organizations are based on vast differences in power and control. In addition to gender and ethnicity, which we'll examine shortly, social class is important in determining individuals' places in organizations. In many companies, those at the higher levels are more comfortable hiring and promoting others similar to themselves. Phrases such as "fitting the mold" and "having common interests" are often code words for belonging to the in-group, most often higher income white men who share similar recreational activities (like golf or tennis) and political attitudes.

Inequality in income, status, and other rewards means that owners and managers can easily exploit workers. Those at the top dictate to those at the middle and the bottom. Because organizations serve elites, conflict theorists argue, they are usually undemocratic and ignore workers' needs and interests. As a result, workers have little input in deciding how their work is structured.

From a conflict perspective, the corporation's main objective is "to pursue, relentlessly and without ex-

ception, its own self-interest, regardless of the often harmful consequences it might cause to others" (Bakan 2005: 1–2). For example, when a Motorola engineer developed the first mobile phone in the 1960s, he advised, "There should be a lock on the dial so that you couldn't talk while driving." There has been mounting evidence that talking on cell phones (even when they're hands-free) while driving increases the number of fatal car crashes (see Chapter 5). Nonetheless, the communications industry is still not publicizing the dangers of talking on cell phones while driving because "if you're a C.E.O., you don't want to outlaw the thing that's been making a lot of money" (Richtel 2009: 1).

Even when large corporations don't cause harm to workers, consumers, communities, and the environment, they wield enormous power over people and societies. When revenue for the major U.S. airlines dropped in 2008, they started charging fees for baggage, selecting seats more than 24 hours before a flight, and up to $100 each way to fly a child traveling alone, which used to be covered by the price of a ticket. The average American feels powerless about the rising costs because the Transportation Department claims that "it has no authority to regulate the prices that airlines charge for air transportation services" (Maynard 2009: 3).

Critical Evaluation

Among its contributions, conflict theory has underscored the inequality within groups and organizations that saps workers' motivation and limits their economic success. Critics, however, fault conflict theory for assuming that greater equality always leads to a more successful and productive organization. As you saw earlier, even a model of nontraditional organization such as self-managing work teams can fail because of ineffective team leaders or management interference with teams.

In addition, do conflict theorists focus too much on organizational deficiencies? There are, after all, many formal organizations, including some bureaucracies that are efficient and profitable corporations but don't exploit workers (see Kaplan 2010).

FEMINIST THEORIES: MEN BENEFIT MORE THAN WOMEN

Feminist scholars agree with functionalists that organizations can be effective in attaining common goals. They also agree with conflict theorists that those with power protect their self-interests. Feminist analyses differ from those of functionalists and conflict theorists in two ways, however: (1) Feminists emphasize that across all social classes, women (and especially minority women) consistently fare worse than men; and (2) they rely on both macro and micro data to explain why gender is a major variable affecting roles in formal organizations, especially leadership roles.

Women have enjoyed increased success in organizations since the 1980s, but rarely at the highest levels. For example, women hold more than half of all management and professional positions in the United States, but make up less than 2 percent of *Fortune 500* CEOs, 15 percent of board directors at *Fortune 500* companies, and 17 percent of board directors at *Fortune 100* companies (Catalyst 2007; Alliance for Board Diversity 2008).

Large numbers of women still hit a **glass ceiling**—attitudes or organizational biases in the workplace that prevent them from advancing to leadership positions. Organizational barriers reflect, in large part, stereotypes about gender roles. For example, senior-level U.S. executives—both women and men—typically describe women as better at stereotypically feminine "caretaking" skills such as supporting and encouraging others, and men as excelling at stereotypically masculine "taking charge" skills such as influencing superiors and problem solving. Because many promotions are based on taking charge rather than caretaking skills, women often suffer because they are considered too tough (a masculine trait) or too soft (a feminine trait). Thus, women often experience a double bind—that nagging sense that whatever you do, you can do no right (Sabattini et al. 2007; Foust-Cummings et al. 2008).

Critical Evaluation

Feminist theories have expanded conflict explanations of groups and organizations by showing that many talented women are still treated like outsiders. One weakness of feminist theories, however, is that much of the emphasis is still on white and black women in professional and managerial positions, even though Latinas and Asian American women comprise a large segment of these workers and those in the general labor force.

A second limitation is that even when feminist scholars say that both sexes suffer from organizational stereotypes, they offer little data on how such stereotypes affect men. In addition, some female leaders are playing a major role in reshaping organizational structures

because they have good communication skills, know how to increase morale and productivity, and are comfortable with diversity—all assets in today's global economy (Helgesen 2008). The question, then, is whether some feminist scholars are spending too much time focusing on women's ongoing struggles rather than their progress.

SYMBOLIC INTERACTIONISM: PEOPLE DEFINE AND SHAPE THEIR SITUATIONS

While functionalist, conflict, and (some) feminist theorists examine groups and organizations on a macro level, symbolic interactionists focus on interpersonal relationships. Interactionists emphasize that an individual's perception and definition of a situation shape group dynamics and, consequently, organizations. Group leaders or members can create or reinforce conformity (as shown in the Asch and Milgram studies). Informal groups can also determine what goes on in an organization by refusing to obey the rules and implementing their own (as in the Hawthorne studies). Thus, according to symbolic interactionists, individuals make choices, change rules, and mold their own identities instead of being passive members of a group who are manipulated (Kivisto and Pittman 2001).

Employees can make some choices, but symbolic interactionists also note that people's outcomes can be shaped by how coworkers and bosses interpret the same behavior. For example, whether women are supervisors or clerical workers, if they lose their temper, they are overwhelmingly seen as too emotional, incompetent, out of control, weak, and worth less pay. Their angry male counterparts, in contrast, are often viewed as authoritative and in control (Brescoll and Uhlmann 2008). Feminist scholars maintain that a double standard creates inequality between women and men in groups and organizations. Symbolic interactionists go a step further by proposing that a double standard exists because both sexes often stereotype men and women.

Hemera Technologies/Getty Images/Jupiter Images

Critical Evaluation

Symbolic interactionism has made important contributions in describing how members of groups and organizations interpret the world around them and, as a result, affect what goes on. Despite these contributions, the interactionist perspective has several weaknesses. Some scholars have wondered whether results of some of the influential studies (especially Milgram's) reflected the participants' responses to a laboratory situation where they obeyed the experimenter's instructions rather than the way they would have behaved in normal circumstances (Blass 2000).

Because symbolic interactionism is a micro-level theory, it ignores macro-level factors that result in the exploitation of workers and consumers. About 54 percent of young people aged 8 to 21 buy products—whether they need them or not—because of television ads, a macro-level factor (Martin 2006). In addition, and in contrast to interactionists' claims, most people have little control in shaping the situations in which they find themselves. Instead, formal organizations (such as the U.S. government and large companies) often invade the privacy of citizens, workers, or consumers by collecting information and monitoring people's behavior.

We've looked at the general characteristics of social groups and formal organizations, both of which are part of larger structures that sociologists call *social institutions*. The next section introduces you to this important sociological concept and lays the foundation for the discussion of social institutions in later chapters.

4 Social Institutions

a **social institution** (or simply, *institution*) is an organized and established social system that meets one or more of a society's basic needs. Some social institutions are almost universal because they ensure a society's survival and practically all members of a society participate. According to functionalists, there are five major social institutions worldwide:

- The *family* replaces the members of a society through procreation, socializes children, and legitimizes sexual activity between adults.

- The *economy* organizes a society's development, production, distribution, and consumption of goods and services.

- *Political institutions* maintain law and order, pass legislation, and form military groups for internal and external defense.

- *Education* helps to socialize children, transmits knowledge, and provides information and training for jobs and other work-related activities.

- *Religion* encompasses beliefs and practices that offer a sense of meaning and purpose to life.

Besides these core universal institutions (which we'll examine in Chapters 11–15), others that have emerged include law, science, medicine, sports, health care, criminal justice, and the military.

WHY SOCIAL INSTITUTIONS ARE IMPORTANT

Social institutions are abstractions, but they have an organized purpose, weave together norms and values, and, consequently, guide human behavior. No two families are exactly alike, but the family institution reflects broadly shared cultural agreements about what a family should be and do. In the same vein, no two banks are exactly alike, but the economy as an institution creates and perpetuates a variety of rules that usually make banking predictable and fairly stable.

HOW SOCIAL INSTITUTIONS ARE INTERCONNECTED

Social institutions in a society are linked to one another. Through taxes, the economy provides revenues for the political institution, education, and families that need financial support. Education, in turn, trains children (and adults) in the general and

Bill Pugliano/Stringer/Getty Images

Sam Walton, the founder of Wal-Mart, kept in touch with his employees, called them "associates," and promised them "limitless opportunities" in the company. As a result, the employees, despite their low wages, worked hard because they felt that they had a stake in the "Wal-Mart family" (Frank 2006).

specific skills required for productive participation in the economy. The family instills many of the values of hard work and success that educational institutions reinforce. Families and schools could not survive without the goods and services provided by the economy, and the economy needs workers who have been socialized by the family and trained by schools to enter the labor force in adulthood. And in many communities, criminal justice, religious, legal, and political institutions have formed coalitions to decrease substance abuse and other social problems.

Understanding institutions can tell us a lot about how a society functions and how we're connected to each other. Consider, for example, the linkages between six social institutions—the economy, the political system, medicine, education, family, and the media—in addressing Americans' weight. Stated simply, overweight and obesity refer to ranges of weight that are greater than what is generally considered normal for one's height and are measured by the body mass index (BMI), which indicates the amount of body fat (Centers for Disease Control and Prevention 2009).

In 2009, 58 percent of Americans said that their weight was about right, 32 percent said somewhat overweight, only 4 percent said very overweight, and 6 percent said underweight (Gallup Poll 2010). In stark contrast, medical researchers find that about 6 in 10 American adults are either overweight (37 percent) or obese (27 percent), and that the obesity rate has more than doubled since the late 1970s (Pan et al. 2009; Mendes 2010). Media organizations (such as television networks, magazines, and newspapers) routinely broadcast such results and their negative health out-

On average, an 8 ounce soft drink contains at least 3 tablespoons of sugar. Over the course of a year, drinking one soda a day can make you 10 pounds fatter.

comes, including heart disease, strokes, asthma, diabetes, and early death.

By implication, parents are often to blame for adult obesity because being overweight or obese starts in childhood. Among children aged 6 to 17, the percentage of overweight increased only 6 percent between 1976 and 1980, but rose to 15 percent in 2006 (Federal Interagency Forum on Family and Child Statistics 2009). Children who are overweight (because of poor diet and getting little exercise) are likely to be overweight or obese in adulthood.

First lady Michelle Obama recently announced her national initiative to combat childhood obesity "with a show of force that included medical, business and government leaders, grassroots activists, celebrity public service announcement, and cartoon characters as nutrition experts" (Givhan 2010: C1). Earlier in the day, President Obama established for the first time a national task force on childhood obesity that will include members from federal departments, such as the Department of Health and Human Services, Department of Agriculture, and Department of Education. Some schools have already insisted that companies provide lunches that are lower in salt and fat content, and offer more whole grains and more fresh fruit, but the administration will also ask Congress to rid school vending machines of sugary snacks and drinks (Jackson 2010).

As you've seen in this chapter, social groups, formal organizations, and social institutions shape our behavior. Nonetheless, we're not robots who succumb to bureaucracies. Instead, and despite numerous constraints, we can make better decisions if we understand how groups, organizations, and social institutions can help or hinder us in our everyday lives.

5 major social institutions:
- family
- economy
- political system
- education
- religion

All of us violate
some of society's rules.

7 Deviance, Crime, and the Criminal Justice System

what do you think?

There would be less crime if the punishment was more severe.

1	2	3	4	5	6	7
strongly agree					strongly disagree	

Within a week in mid-February 2010, and as I was revising this chapter, the media headlines included the following stories:

- Golfer Tiger Woods publicly apologized for numerous extramarital affairs.

- An irate taxpayer, a software engineer, purposely crashed his plane into a seven-story building in Austin, Texas, that housed Internal Revenue Service offices.

- More than 75,000 computer systems at nearly 2,500 companies in the United States and around the world were hacked into.

All of these incidents are examples of not conforming to societal norms (see Chapter 3).

At one time or another, all of us violate some of society's rules. This chapter explores such violations. We begin by examining the characteristics of deviance and crime, discuss several sociological explanations of why people deviate, and then look at institutional attempts to control and change rule-breaking behavior. First, however, take the brief quiz on page 118 to see how much you know about deviance and crime in the United States.

deviance behavior or trait that violates expected rules or norms.

1 What Is Deviance?

have you ever driven above the speed limit? Cheated on an exam? Are very tall or very short? All are examples of **deviance**, traits or behavior that violate expected rules or norms. The word *deviance* has a derogatory connotation for the general public, but sociologists don't make such value judgments. Instead, they are interested in understanding and explaining deviance.

HOW MUCH DO YOU KNOW ABOUT U.S. DEVIANCE AND CRIME?

True or False?

1. Most crime victims are women.
2. Crime rates have decreased during the last decade.
3. People are more likely to be arrested for a drug violation than for driving while drunk.
4. Serious crimes such as murder and assault are more common than less serious crimes like illegal gambling and prostitution.
5. People in affluent neighborhoods are more likely to experience burglary than those in poor neighborhoods.
6. About 15 percent of all prison inmates are women.
7. Death penalties deter crime.
8. Compared with other nations, the United States has a low number of people in prisons.

The answers for #2 and #3 are true; the rest are false. You'll see why as you read this chapter.

SOME KEY CHARACTERISTICS OF DEVIANCE

Deviance is universal because it exists in every society. Sociologists emphasize, however, that the key characteristics of deviance can vary quite a bit over time, from situation to situation, from group to group, and from culture to culture (Sumner 1906; Schur 1968).

- *Deviance can be a trait or belief rather than a behavior.* People don't necessarily have to do something to be considered deviant. We can be branded as outsiders simply because of our appearance (obese or very thin). In many societies, skin color or sexual orientation can result in being ostracized. We may also be deemed deviant because of our beliefs, such as being a Muslim in a predominantly Christian neighborhood or vice versa (Becker 1963; see also Chapter 15).

- *Deviance is accompanied by social stigmas.* A **stigma** is a negative label that devalues a person and changes her or his self-concept and social identity. Stigmatized individuals may respond to being discredited in many ways: They may alter their appearance (as through cosmetic surgery), associate with others like themselves who accept them (as in gangs), hide information about some aspect of their deviance (as an ex-convict who does not reveal that status), or divert attention from a stigma by excelling in some area (as music or sports) (Goffman 1963).

- *Deviance varies across and within societies.* What is appropriate or tolerated in one society may be deviant in another. For example, in 2007, only 1.6 percent of all births in South Korea were to unmarried women compared with nearly 40 percent in the United States. As a 33-year-old single mother in South Korea explained, "Once you become an unwed mom, you're branded as immoral and a failure. People treat you as if you had committed a crime. You fall to the bottom rung of society" (Sang-Hun 2009: 6). In the United States, in contrast, there's little stigma in having out-of-wedlock children (see Chapters 9 and 13).

- *Deviance varies across situations.* What is seen as normal in one context may be stigmatized in another. Almost 40 percent of Americans ages 18 to 40 years have at least one tattoo, but many employers—especially those in business firms and federal agencies—disapprove of visible "body art" (Hendrix 2009).

- *Deviance is formal or informal. Formal deviance* is behavior that violates laws. A major example is crime, a topic that we'll examine shortly. In contrast, *informal deviance* is behavior that disregards accepted social norms, such as picking one's nose or teeth or scratching one's private parts in public, belching loudly, and not dressing appropriately (e.g., wearing jeans to a wedding reception or job interview). Even when people are no longer formally deviant, they may describe themselves as informally deviant ("I'm a recovering alcoholic").

- *Perceptions of deviance can change over time.* Many behaviors that were acceptable in the past are now seen as deviant. Only during the 1980s and 1990s did U.S. laws define date rape, marital rape, stalking, and child abuse as crimes. Smoking—widely accepted in the past—has been prohibited in practically all U.S. restaurants, airports, colleges, workplaces, and even some public parks.

  On the other hand, most Americans now shrug off behaviors that were stigmatized in the past. Cohabitation and out-of-wedlock births, seen as sinful and immoral only a few decades ago, are now widespread and accepted by most Americans. And Americans' support for legalizing marijuana increased from only 12 percent in 1970 to 44 percent in 2006 (Saad 2009).

© nicholas belton/iStockphoto

More than 1,000 women in Ghana live in exile in witch camps. Most are poor widows or older women who are blamed for outbreaks of disease in their villages and the illness or death of relatives or neighbors (LaFraniere 2007). In the Democratic Republic of Congo, thousands of children whose parents have died in local wars or because of AIDS are living on the streets because their relatives have accused them of witch-craft that caused the parents' deaths. Such charges are usually because of the relatives' living in poverty and not being able to feed the children (Shapiro 2009).

crime a violation of societal norms and rules for which punishment is specified by public law.

criminologists researchers who use scientific methods to study the nature, extent, cause, and control of criminal behavior.

WHO DECIDES WHAT'S DEVIANT?

Because deviance is culturally relative and the standards change over time, who decides what's right or wrong? Those who have authority or power. During our early years, parents and teachers define acceptable and unacceptable behavior in our everyday interactions and behavior. As we get older, we learn that legal institutions also define what is deviant, for example, not allowing us to drive until age 16 or to purchase or consume liquor until age 21.

2 What Is Crime?

What comes to mind when you hear the word *crime*? Most of us typically imagine a murder or a violent physical attack, but such offenses constitute a minority of crimes. **Crime** is a violation of societal norms and rules for which punishment is specified by public law. Many sociologists are **criminologists,** researchers who use scientific methods to study the nature, extent, cause, and control of criminal behavior. Measuring crime may seem straightforward, but the task is not as simple as it appears.

MEASURING CRIME

There are several primary sources of crime statistics, but two of the most important are the FBI's Uniform Crime Report (UCR) and victimization surveys. Each method has its strengths and weaknesses.

Uniform Crime Report

The best known and most widely cited source of official criminal statistics is the UCR, which includes crimes reported to the police and arrests made each year. The UCR divides criminal offenses into two major categories: Part I and Part II. Part I offenses are the eight violations that the FBI considers the most serious: murder, rape, assault, robbery, burglary, arson, larceny, and motor vehicle theft. Part II crimes are all other offenses including minor traffic offenses (such as parking violations).

Because the UCR has been published since 1930, the statistics are useful in examining trends over time. How-

Are any of these people deviant? (Why or why not?)

ever, the UCR doesn't include federal offenses such as corporate crime, kidnapping, and Internet crimes, or any of the roughly 60 percent of all crimes committed in the United States that go unreported to the police (Hart and Rennison 2003).

Also, many crimes don't result in arrests (see *Figure 7.1*): There are no witnesses or the police don't investigate many offenses because they must devote most of their limited resources to violent crimes rather than property crimes. Because of these and other problems, many criminologists also use victimization surveys to measure the extent of crime.

Victimization Surveys

A **victimization survey** involves interviewing people about their experiences as crime victims. Every year, the U.S. Department of Justice sponsors the most widely used survey—the National Crime Victimization Survey (NCVS). Because the response rates are at least 90 percent, the NCVS offers a more accurate picture of offenses than does the UCR. Also, the NCVS includes both reported and unreported crime, and is not affected by police discretion in deciding whether to arrest an offender.

Still, some crimes are underreported because people may not be totally honest. Some don't want to admit having been victims—especially when the perpetrator is a family member or friend. Others may be too embarrassed to tell the interviewer that they were victimized while drunk or engaged in drug sales (Hagan 2008).

HOW MUCH CRIME IS THERE?

No one knows the extent of U.S. crime because even the best sources (like the UCR and NCVS) are only estimates, but some offenses are more common than others. We'll look at UCR crimes here and other offenses, such as white-collar crime and organized crime, later in this chapter.

Incidence of Serious Crimes

Of the more than 14 million crimes in 2008, almost 88 percent were property crimes. Violent crimes are most likely to be covered by the media and, consequently, inspire the greatest fear (Glassner 2010). In reality, Americans are much more likely to be victimized by theft or burglary than to be murdered, raped, robbed, or assaulted with a deadly weapon (see *Table 7.1*). In fact, the average person is 433 times more likely to experience a theft than to be murdered (Federal Bureau of Investigation 2009).

Victimless Crimes

Offenses that are the least likely to be reported—such as illicit drug use, prostitution, drunkenness, and illegal gambling—are called *public order crimes,* or *victimless*

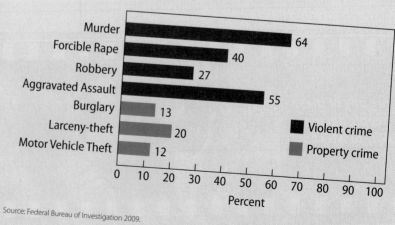

FIGURE 7.1
Percentage of Crimes Cleared by Arrest, 2009

Nationwide, only 44 percent of violent crimes and 16 percent of property crimes are cleared by arrest (someone has been arrested and turned over to the courts for prosecution). So, are arrest rates accurate measures of the prevalence of these crimes? And why are arrest rates much higher for violent crimes than for property crimes?

aggravated assault: an unlawful attack by a person for the purpose of inflicting severe bodily injury.

larceny-theft: stealing or attempting to steal any property or article that is not taken by force or violence (e.g., thefts of bicycles, motor vehicle parts and accessories, shoplifting, pocket-picking).

robbery: taking or attempting to take anything of value by force or threat of force.

burglary: unlawful entry of a structure to commit a theft.

Crime	Percent
Murder	64
Forcible Rape	40
Robbery	27
Aggravated Assault	55
Burglary	13
Larceny-theft	20
Motor Vehicle Theft	12

Violent crime
Property crime

Source: Federal Bureau of Investigation 2009.

TABLE 7.1
Serious Crime in the United States, by Volume and Rate, 2008

CRIMES	VOLUME (NUMBER OF CRIMES)	RATE (PER 100,000 INHABITANTS)
Violent Crime	**1.4 million**	**455**
Murder	16,272	5
Forcible rape	89,000	29
Robbery	441,855	145
Aggravated assault	834,885	275
Property Crime	**9.8 million**	**3,213**
Burglary	2.2 million	731
Larceny-theft	6.6 million	2,167
Motor vehicle theft	956,846	315

Source: Based on Federal Bureau of Investigation 2009, Table 1.

crimes. **Victimless crimes** are acts that violate laws but involve individuals who don't consider themselves victims. For example, prostitutes and sex merchants argue that they are simply providing services to people who want them, and substance abusers claim that they aren't hurting anyone but themselves.

Some contend that this term is misleading because victimless crimes often lead to property and violent crimes, as when addicts commit burglary, rob people at gunpoint, and engage in identity theft to get money for drugs. In a national survey, 70 percent of the respondents said that a family member's drug abuse had a negative effect on the emotional or mental health of at least one other family member, and 39 percent experienced financial problems because they went into debt to pay for treatment for an addict who had no health insurance coverage (Saad 2006).

VICTIMS AND OFFENDERS

A prominent *New York Times* journalist recently described American culture as "soaked in blood" and "insanely violent" because of the widespread availability of guns (Herbert 2009: 19). It's true that we have high violent crime rates compared with most other societies, but as you just saw, the incidence of property crimes is considerably higher than violent crimes.

Perhaps because of media sensationalism, 74 percent of Americans say that there is more crime in the United States, up from 43 percent in 2002 (Jones 2009). In fact, between 1999 and 2008, violent crimes decreased by 41 percent and property crimes by 32 percent (Rand 2009). Also, crime affects some groups much more than others. Let's begin by looking at crime victims.

> **victimless crimes** acts that violate laws but involve individuals who don't consider themselves victims.

Who Are the Victims?

Crime victimization isn't random. Instead, there are trends by sex, race/ethnicity, age, and social class.

1. *Sex.* Most crime victims are men. Except for rape and assaults by intimate partners (such as spouses, ex-spouses, and boyfriends), men are almost twice as likely as women to be victims of violent crimes, such as robbery and assault with a deadly weapon (Harrell 2007).

2. *Race/Ethnicity.* About half of all homicide victims are black men, a majority of them between the ages of 17 and 29 (Harrell 2007). The victimization rates of violent crimes are higher among African Americans at 26 per 1,000 persons age 12 and older than Latinos (16) or whites (18) (Rand 2009).

3. *Age.* Most crime victims are younger than 25. They are 20 more times likely than those age 65 and older to experience nonfatal violent crime (such as robbery). However, crimes against older people are especially traumatic because they are usually physically unable to fight back, and it takes them longer to recover from a crime both physically and emotionally (Klaus 2005; Madigan 2009).

4. *Social Class.* In general, lower income households experience higher victimization rates than their higher income counterparts. In property crimes, for example, and as *Figure 7.2* shows, the poorest households are almost twice as likely as those earning $75,000 or more per year to experience property crime.

Who Are the Offenders?

Most offenders are never caught, but arrest rates show patterns by age, sex, race/ethnicity, and social class.

1. *Age.* Generally, the older Americans get, the less likely they are to engage in crime. Across all racial groups, young males (age 18–24) have the highest arrest rates—making up about 46 percent of all those arrested. Those age 29 and younger constitute

social control the techniques and strategies that regulate people's behavior in society.

54 percent of all arrestees. In contrast, 23 percent of those arrested are 40 or older, and many of their crimes involve drug abuse violations and driving under the influence (Fox and Zawitz 2004; Federal Bureau of Investigation 2009).

2. *Sex.* Of all those arrested in 2008, 75 percent were men. Men make up 82 percent of persons arrested for violent crime and 68 percent of those arrested for property crime. Compared with women, men are 10 times more likely to commit murder. In other crimes, 95 percent of carjackers, 90 percent of those who rob, and 92 percent of those arrested for weapons violations and sexual offenses are men (Rennison 2003; Klaus 2006; Federal Bureau of Investigation 2009).

3. *Race/Ethnicity.* Almost 70 percent of those arrested are white, 28 percent are African American, and the remainder is American Indian or Asian American. (The FBI doesn't provide data on Latinos because it collects information on race but not ethnicity.) Proportionately, African Americans make up about 13 percent of the general population but account for 29 percent of violent crimes (Federal Bureau of Investigation 2009).

4. *Social Class.* Social class also affects crime rates. Offense rates are higher in poor inner-city areas than in suburban and wealthier neighborhoods, and prison statistics consistently show that those incarcerated have low educational levels. For example, 68 percent of state prisoners don't have a high-school diploma, whereas only 11 percent have attended college or have a college degree (Harlow 2003; Federal Bureau of Investigation 2009).

FIGURE 7.2

Property Crimes by Household Income, 2008

Household Income	Victimization rate
Less than $7,500	204
$7,500–$14,999	175
$15,000–$24,999	162
$25,000–$34,999	151
$35,000–$49,999	143
$50,000–$74,999	126
$75,000 or more	133

Victimization rates per 1,000 households

Source: Based on Rand 2009, Table 5.

Men are more likely to be victims of violent crime than women.

Crime rates are higher in low-income areas, but does this mean that poor people are more deviant? Because police devote more resources to poor neighborhoods, those at the lower end of the socioeconomic ladder are more likely to be caught, arrested, prosecuted, and incarcerated. Middle-class criminals are more elusive. For example, the theft of *intellectual property* is a crime that includes offenses such as software piracy, bootlegging musical recordings and movies, selling company trade secrets, and copyright violations. Between 1994 and 2002, less than 1 percent of more than 1 million intellectual property theft suspects were caught, but of those prosecuted, 50 percent were college educated (Motivans 2004).

Most of us don't commit crimes but conform to laws and cultural expectations. We usually conform, however, not because we're innately good, but because of social control.

3 Controlling Deviance and Crime

Social control refers to the techniques and strategies that regulate people's behavior in society. The purpose of social control is to eliminate, or at least reduce, deviance. Ensuring people's conformity to group or societal expectations involves both informal and formal social control.

INFORMAL AND FORMAL SOCIAL CONTROL

Most conformity is due to the internalization of norms during the powerful process of socialization. Because most of us genuinely care about the opinions of family members, friends, and teachers, we try to live up to their expectations (see Chapter 4). In this sense, we conform because of *informal social controls* that we learn and internalize during childhood.

In addition to informal mechanisms, *formal social control* regulates social behavior. Unlike informal social control, formal social control exists outside of the individual. For example, a college dean might threaten a student with suspension or expulsion, or a business might install security cameras. Many formal social control agents, such as police and judges, spend considerable effort trying to prevent or decrease deviance.

POSITIVE AND NEGATIVE SANCTIONS

Most of us conform because of **sanctions,** punishments or rewards for obeying or violating a norm. *Positive sanctions* are rewards for desirable behavior and include a variety of facial expressions (such as smiling), body language (such as hugging), comments (such as "Congratulations!"), and other forms of recognition (such as good grades, trophies, and promotions). Positive sanctions are very effective because they increase our self-confidence, self-esteem, and motivation, especially when the rewards are deserved.

sanctions punishments or rewards for obeying or violating a norm.

Negative sanctions are punishments that convey disapproval for violating a norm. Negative sanctions range from mild and informal expressions (such as frowns and gossip) to more severe and formal reactions (such as fines, arrests, and incarcerations). Some American Indian reservations have revived the traditional penalty of banishment to deal with gangs and drugs. The troublemakers can be ordered off the reservation and stripped of their tribal membership (Snell 2007). The ultimate formal negative sanction in most societies is execution.

The next sections examine four important sociological perspectives—functionalism, conflict theory, feminist theories, and symbolic interactionism—that help us understand why people are deviant (*Table 7.2* summarizes these theories).

TABLE 7.2
Sociological Explanations of Deviance and Crime

THEORETICAL PERSPECTIVE	LEVEL OF ANALYSIS	KEY POINTS
Functionalist	Macro	• Anomie increases the likelihood of deviance. • Crime occurs when people experience blocked opportunities to achieve the culturally approved goal of economic success.
Conflict	Macro	• Laws protect the interests of the few (primarily those in the upper classes) rather than the rights of the many. • Law enforcement is rarely directed at the illegal activities of the powerful.
Feminist	Macro and Micro	• Crimes committed by women reflect their general oppression due to social, economic, and political inequality. • Many women are criminal offenders or victims because of culturally organized beliefs and practices that are sexist and patriarchal.
Symbolic Interactionist	Micro	• People learn deviant and criminal behavior from others—like parents and friends—who are important in their everyday lives. • If people are labeled or stigmatized as deviant, they are likely to develop deviant self-concepts and engage in criminal behavior.

4 Functionalist Perspectives on Deviance and Crime

for functionalists, deviance and crime are normal parts of the social structure. Functionalists don't endorse undesirable behavior, but they view deviance and crime as both functional and dysfunctional.

HOW DEVIANCE AND CRIME CAN BE BOTH DYSFUNCTIONAL AND FUNCTIONAL

Dysfunctions are the undesirable consequences of behavior, but what is functional for one group or individual can be dysfunctional for another. For example, gangs are functional because they provide members with a sense of belonging, identity, and protection. Gangs are dysfunctional, however, because the members often commit violent and property crimes (Egley and O'Donnell 2009).

Crime and deviance are *dysfunctional* when they:

- *Create tension and insecurity.* Crime makes people uneasy. Any violation of norms—a babysitter who cancels at the last minute or the theft of your laptop computer—makes life unpredictable and increases anxiety.

- *Erode trust in personal and formal relationships.* Crimes such as date rape and stalking make many women suspicious of other people. Of the almost 4 million Americans who experienced identity theft in 2004, nearly a third said that they had problems in obtaining banking services or credit cards because financial institutions didn't trust them (Baum 2006).

- *Damage confidence in institutions.* Since the scandals involving Enron and other corporations in 2001, millions of people, even those who didn't lose money, worry that their retirement funds may disappear in the future as a result of similar corporate scams.

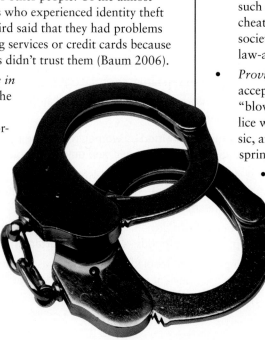

Growing marijuana is moving to the suburbs. Growers pay at least $750,000 for a house in an affluent subdivision, gut the interiors, and install sophisticated artificial lighting and watering systems. Neighbors are rarely aware of what's going on because they assume their communities are safe from crime and rarely know others who live on their street (Blankenstein and Barboza 2007; Ritter 2007).

- *Are costly.* Besides personal costs to victims (such as fear, emotional trauma, and physical injury), deviance is expensive. All of us pay higher prices for consumer goods and services (such as auto and property insurance), as well as taxes for prosecuting criminals, and for building and maintaining prisons.

Deviance and crime can also be *functional* because they provide a number of societal benefits (Durkheim 1893/1964; Erikson 1966; Sagarin 1975):

- *Affirm cultural norms and values.* Negative reactions, such as expelling a college student who's caught cheating or incarcerating a bank robber, assert a society's rules and its values about being honest and law-abiding.

- *Provide temporary safety valves.* Some deviance is accepted under certain conditions, as when people "blow off steam." Typically, a community and its police will tolerate noise, underage drinking, loud music, and obnoxious behavior during college students' spring break because it's a short-lived nuisance.

- *Create social unity.* Some deviant behavior, especially when there is a common enemy, unites a group, community, or society. Following the 9/11 terrorist attacks, most Americans experienced feelings of greater solidarity, despite differences in age, political views, social class, and race and ethnicity.

- *Improve the economy.* Deviance and crime can benefit a community financially. Some

John Lund/Jupiter Images

towns welcome new prisons because they generate jobs and stimulate the economy (Riccardi 2009). Unlike a manufacturing plant that might close down or move to another country, a prison is usually stable.

- *Trigger social change.* Crime and deviance are warning signs that a system isn't working. In response, new laws and rules, such as hate crime legislation and campus sex crime prevention acts, may be established (Carr 2005).

ANOMIE AND SOCIAL STRAIN

Functionalists have offered a variety of explanations for deviance and crime. Two of the most influential are anomie and strain theories, both of which try to seek to explain why so many people commit crimes and engage in deviant behavior even though they share many of the same goals and values as people who conform to social norms.

Durkheim's Concept of Anomie

Émile Durkheim (1893/1964; 1897/1951) introduced the term anomie to describe the condition in which people are unsure of how to behave because of absent, conflicting, or confusing social norms. During periods of rapid social change, such as industrialization in Durkheim's time, societal rules may break down. As many young people moved to the city to look for jobs in the nineteenth century, norms about proper behavior that existed in the countryside crumbled. Even today, as you'll see in Chapter 16, many urban newcomers experience anonymity and miss the neighborliness that was common at home.

Merton's Concept of Social Strain

Robert Merton (1938) elaborated on the concept of anomie to explain how social structure helps to create deviance. According to

Merton, Americans are socialized to believe that anyone can realize the American dream of accumulating wealth and being successful economically. To achieve the *cultural goal* of economic success, society emphasizes legitimate and *institutionalized means* such as education, hard work, saving, starting at the bottom and working one's way up, and making sacrifices instead of seeking pleasures and quick gratifications.

In a highly stratified society like the United States, however, many people don't have access to institutionalized means for financial success. Families may be locked into poverty, and parents may lose their jobs or be unable to afford their children's college education. Thus, the stage is set for anomie—a feeling that one is being denied a chance to become prosperous and successful—which, in turn, ignites anxiety and anger.

How do people respond? Merton's **strain theory** posits that people may engage in deviant behavior when they experience a conflict between goals and the means available to obtain the goals. Not all people turn to deviance in resolving social strain (see *Figure 7.3*). Most of us *conform* by working harder and longer to become successful. The fact that you're reading this textbook shows that, using Merton's language, your mode of adaptation to strain is conformity—one of achieving suc-

anomie the condition in which people are unsure of how to behave because of absent, conflicting, or confusing social norms.

strain theory the idea that people may engage in deviant behavior when they experience a conflict between goals and the means available to obtain the goals.

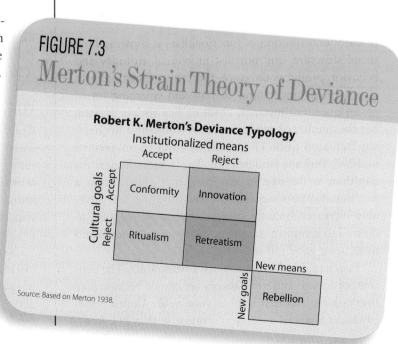

FIGURE 7.3
Merton's Strain Theory of Deviance

Robert K. Merton's Deviance Typology

Source: Based on Merton 1938.

cess through an institutionalized means such as a college education.

Merton's other four modes of adaptation reflect deviance. *Innovation* occurs when people have endorsed the cultural goal of economic success but turn to illegitimate means, especially crime, to achieve their goal. For many people living in inner-city ghettos, education, hard work, and deferred gratification are often unachievable. For others, crime is a quick way to become richer. For innovators, "it's not how you play the game but whether you win or lose."

In *ritualism,* people don't expect to get rich but get the necessary education and experience to obtain or retain their jobs. In many bureaucratic positions, employees don't make decisions and can't move up the ladder, but their jobs are relatively secure. Ritualists aren't criminals, according to Merton, but they are deviant because they have given up on becoming financially successful. Instead, they do what they are told and "go along to get along."

In *retreatism,* people have rejected both the goals and the means for success. Merton used examples like vagrants, alcoholics, and drug addicts, some of whom have given up because they feel it's impossible to succeed.

In *rebellion,* people feel so alienated that they want to change the social structure entirely by substituting new goals and means for the original ones. A contemporary example is paramilitary groups around the United States that oppose the government.

CRITICAL EVALUATION

A major contribution of functionalism is showing how social structure, and not just individual attitudes and behavior, produces deviance and crime. Functionalism also helps us understand current and emerging forms of deviance. For instance, cheating has always existed, but the number of college students who admit to cheating increased from 11 percent in 1963 to 75 percent in 2007. Perhaps students are simply more honest today than in the past in admitting they cheat. From a functionalist perspective, however, cheating has probably increased because students feel more pressure to do well to get into graduate or professional schools and to secure a good job (see Chapter 14).

Functionalist theories also have weaknesses. The concepts of anomie and strain theory are limited because they overlook the fact that not everyone in the United States embraces financial success as a major goal in life. Func-

tionalist theories also don't explain why women's crime rates are much lower than men's (especially since women have fewer legitimate opportunities for financial success) and why people commit some crimes (such as murdering an intimate partner or setting fires just for kicks) that have nothing to do with being successful (Anderson and Dyson 2002; Williams and McShane 2004).

The most consistent criticism is that functionalism typically focuses on lower-class deviance and crime. Conflict theorists have filled this gap by examining middle- and upper-class crime.

5 Conflict Perspectives on Deviance and Crime

f unctionalists ask, "Why do some people commit crimes and others don't?" Most conflict theorists focus on who makes the laws and ask "Why are some acts defined as criminal while others are not?" (Akers 1997).

CAPITALISM, POWER, SOCIAL INEQUALITY, AND CRIME

For conflict theorists, the most powerful groups in society control the law, which defines what's deviant and who will be punished. Because the law embodies the values of those who create it, those outside the power structure (such as youths and members of disadvantaged groups) are more likely to be prosecuted and less likely to have the resources to fight the criminal justice system when they feel that they are treated unjustly (Chambliss 1969; Chambliss and Seidman 1982).

White-Collar Crime

Conflict theorists often focus on white-collar crime to show that most laws protect the interests of the few rather than the many (Sutherland 1949). **White-collar crime** refers to illegal activities committed by high-status individuals in the course of their occupation. There is a wide range of white-collar crimes—from thefts in businesses to high-tech crimes such as Internet fraud.

According to Dutch criminologist Willem Bonger (1916/1969), capitalism is the root cause of criminal behavior because it breeds egoism, or placing one's interests above those of others. That is, workers act and engage in crime because their poverty blunts concern for others;

In 2009, Bernard Madoff—a highly respected stock broker and investment advisor—pleaded guilty to defrauding thousands of investors of almost $170 billion between 1991 and 2008. Madoff was sentenced to 150 years in a federal prison, but his clients haven't recovered their money. His wife and sons continue to lead luxurious lives because Madoff's fraud has left them with millions of dollars in investments and savings.

AP Photo/Kathy Willens

capitalists, competing for profits, are greedy parasites who exploit workers and break the law to become richer.

A number of influential American sociologists have argued, like Bonger, that a strong association exists between capitalism and white-collar crime. Others have expanded Bonger's perspective and maintain that only the behaviors that injure the economic interests or challenge the political power of the dominant class are punished (Vold 1958; Turk 1969, 1976; Quinney 1980). Four of the most common types of white-collar crimes are occupational crimes, corporate crimes, cybercrimes, and organized crime.

Occupational Crimes

Occupational crimes are illegal activities committed in the workplace by individuals acting solely in their own personal interest. Many middle- and upper-class criminals are in positions of trust, have many opportunities for theft, and use rationalizations for committing their crimes (Cressey 1953). Recently, for example, several investigative reports of the Veterans Administration program found that some of its top executives and assistants routinely violated federal laws: They paid themselves $60,000 bonuses, hired unqualified relatives for many positions, and authorized federal money to pay for graduate courses for relatives and friends. Their justification was not being paid enough (Dao 2009).

Corporate Crimes

Corporate crimes (also known as *organizational crimes*) are illegal acts committed by executives to benefit themselves and their companies. Corporate crimes include a vast array of illegal activities such as conspiracies to stifle free market competition, price-fixing, tax evasion, and false advertising. The target of the crime can be the general public, the environment, or even a company's own workers. Often, corporate offenders commit multiple crimes such as stock fraud, insider trading, and perjury.

Corporate crimes are fairly common. For example, Lifestyle Lift, a cosmetic surgery company with 32 centers nationwide, agreed to pay $300,000 in penalties for ordering employees to pretend they were satisfied customers and write glowing reviews of its face-lift procedure on Web sites (Miller 2009).

Cybercrime

Cybercrime, illegal activities that are conducted online, is a new category of white-collar offenses. These high-tech crimes include defrauding consumers with bogus financial investments, embezzling, being paid to recommend stock on chat rooms, and stealing business data. Other offenses include sabotaging computer systems, hacking (gaining unauthorized access to computers), and stealing confidential information.

In 2008 alone, the Internet Crime Complaint Center (2009) received almost 276,000 complaints, an all-time high, amounting to nearly $265 million in reported losses. The most common offenses were Internet auction frauds, undelivered merchandise or payments, and credit/debit card fraud. In addition, every year, nearly 10 million Americans experience identity theft.

Organized Crime

Organized crime refers to activities of individuals and groups that supply illegal goods and services for profit. Organized crime includes drug distribution, loan-sharking

occupational crimes crimes committed in the workplace by individuals acting solely in their own personal interest.

corporate crimes white-collar crimes committed by executives to benefit themselves and their companies (also known as *organizational crimes*).

cybercrime white-collar crimes that are conducted online.

organized crime activities of individuals and groups that supply illegal goods and services for profit.

(lending money at illegal rates), prostitution, illegal gambling, pornography, theft rings, hijacking cargo, and laundering illegal money through legitimate enterprises. The *Godfather* films and the popular television show *The Sopranos* romanticized organized crime and presented the perpetrators as primarily Italian men. Italian-run organized crime exists, but most organized crime is now run by Latino, Asian American, and African American men. Some Russian and other Eastern European groups have been operating on U.S. soil since the 1970s.

LAW ENFORCEMENT AND SOCIAL CLASS

Why do so many people commit white-collar crimes? Because they can, according to conflict theorists. First, most white-collar crimes are *not criminalized* (Turk 1969; Lilly et al. 1995). Because "greed, dubious bookkeeping, and suspiciously timed trading" are unethical but not necessarily criminal, the law is often vague, and prosecutors often find it difficult to demonstrate "not only that an action violated a specific law but also that the executive intentionally committed the bad act" (Sasseen 2005: 60).

Second, there is *minimal enforcement* and few penalties. For example, top officials at the Xerox Corporation agreed to pay $22 million to settle accusations of accounting fraud involving a scam that made $1.4 billion in profits (Norris 2003). Thus, Xerox kept almost 98 percent of the ill-gotten profits. If, using a comparable percentage, you made $35,000 a year illegally and had to pay a fine of $550, what would be the financial incentive for honesty?

Third, white-collar crimes thrive because of *privilege and corruption*. The common cultural background shared by judges and many white-collar defendants leads to greater leniency for these offenders than for street criminals. The federal government continues to award business worth billions to companies that repeatedly violate air and water pollution laws, cause deaths and injuries to their workers because of unsafe equipment, and even defraud the government (Silverstein 2002).

Finally, law enforcement has been inadequate because of a *redistribution of resources*. Federal prosecutions for white-collar crimes have dropped 36 percent since 9/11 because nearly one third of all FBI agents were reassigned to homeland security investigations. As a result, prosecutions of frauds against financial institutions dropped 48 percent from 2000 to 2007, insurance fraud cases plummeted 75 percent, and securities fraud cases dropped 17 percent (Lichtblau et al. 2008).

Anthony Neste/Time Life Pictures/Getty Images

CRITICAL EVALUATION

Conflict theories have been useful in highlighting the linkages between power and social class that may lead to criminal laws that benefit those at the top. Another strength is that conflict theory identifies biases present in the criminal justice system, such as the allocation of more resources to prosecute traditional rather than white-collar offenders.

Critics, however, point to several weaknesses. First, some contend that conflict theory exaggerates the importance of capitalism in explaining white-collar crime. Other capitalistic societies, such as Japan, have much lower crime rates because of greater social solidarity and control of deviant behavior through shaming and restricting individual freedom (Leonardsen 2004). In effect, some critics say, capitalism is not a major reason for crime.

A second criticism is that conflict theory deemphasizes the crimes committed by the poor. The nation's costs of robbery, rape, and other street crimes are almost $4 billion a year in legal expenses, victim injuries, wage losses, and crime prevention activities (Mokhiber 2007). Thus, some critics maintain, low-income people are just as deviant as the rich, and their crimes are costly to society. A related problem is that conflict theories tend to ignore the fact that many affluent people, including corporate executives, don't always get away with their crimes. Conflict theorists counter that the penalties are minimal and that only a handful of corporate criminals ever wind up in prison.

Third, some critics say that conflict theory ignores the ways crime is functional for society as a whole. As

In 2004, a senior FBI official warned that a flood of fraudulent mortgage deals had the potential to become "an epidemic." The next year, as public warnings mounted, the FBI had only 15 full-time agents devoted to mortgage fraud out of a total of 13,000 in the bureau. The number grew to 177 agents in 2008, but it is still hundreds of agents fewer than what is needed (Lichtblau et al. 2008: A1).

you saw earlier, deviance provides jobs and affirms law-abiding cultural norms and values. Finally, many contend, the most influential conflict theories focus almost entirely on men (Moyer 2001; Belknap 2007). Feminist theories have filled this gap.

6 Feminist Perspectives on Deviance and Crime

for much of its history, sociology focused almost entirely on male offenders. As in most other academic disciplines, nearly all sociologists were men who saw women as not worthy of much analytical attention or assumed that explanations of male behavior were equally applicable to females (Flavin 2001; Simpson and Gibbs 2006; Belknap 2007). To remedy such omissions, feminist scholars have concentrated on girls and women as victims and offenders.

WOMEN AS VICTIMS

One of the most publicized events in 2009 was the police's discovery of Jaycee Dugard, a California girl who had been kidnapped in 1991 while waiting for a school bus. The kidnapper was a convicted sex offender who repeatedly raped the girl for 18 years and fathered her two daughters, then ages 11 and 15.

The Dugard case is a recent example of the physi-cal and sexual victimization of women and children. As you saw earlier, many of the serious crimes (such as murder and robbery) are committed by men against other men, but women and girls are commonly the victims of sexual assault, rape, intimate partner violence, stalking, sexual exploitation, female infanticide, and other crimes that degrade women and deny them basic human rights.

Feminist scholars offer several explanations for women's victimization. In patriarchal societies, including the United States, men historically have dominated the government and legal systems. Because women have less access to power, they are at a disadvantage in creating and implementing laws that are more sympathetic to female victims (Price and Sokoloff 2004). For example, of the 193 countries in the world, only 104 have made rape a crime, and the existing laws are rarely enforced (United Nations Development Fund for Women 2007). Such inequity diminishes women's control over their lives and increases their invisibility as victims.

A related reason for female victimization is the effect of culture on gender roles. Many girls and women have

Holding money exchanged for sex, the child of a prostituted woman stands in the doorway of a brothel in Phnom Penh, Cambodia. Children, especially girls, who are raised in brothels, are highly vulnerable to sexual exploitation. Many of the customers are Western men.

been socialized to be victims of male violence because of societal images of women as weaker, less intelligent, and less valued than men: "Girls are rewarded for passivity and feminine behavior, whereas boys are rewarded for aggressiveness and masculine behavior" (Belknap 2007: 243). In effect, then, both sexes internalize the belief that male victimization of females is normal.

But, you might be thinking, there are many strong women who reject sex stereotypes and could, therefore, escape or avoid victimization. Feminist theorists point to several problems with such assumptions. One is that low-income women often believe that leaving an abuser could result in greater economic hardship for themselves and the children. Even among women with college degrees (as you'll see in Chapter 13), many have internalized beliefs that male violence is okay, that women bring the battering on themselves ("I shouldn't have disagreed with him."), or that trying to escape will result in being killed.

Because patriarchal societies often don't enforce laws that punish many male offenders who commit violence against women or give them light sentences, many victims feel trapped. Recently, for example, a judge in Maryland sentenced a 20-year-old man to 3 years in prison for killing his girlfriend's puppy, and 3 years in prison and 5 years of supervised probation for having abused the girlfriend over a 2-year period (Siegel 2009).

WOMEN AS OFFENDERS

Men are more likely than women to commit crimes and to commit more serious crimes, but girls' and women's arrest rates have increased for some offenses. Between 1999 and 2008, for example, female arrests rose 38 percent for robbery, 36 percent for buying and receiving stolen property, 35 percent for drunk driving, and 26 percent for burglary (Federal Bureau of Investigation 2009).

Some analysts propose that girls and women are becoming more deviant because of a breakdown of family, religion, and community; an increase in inadequate schooling that results in high dropout rates; greater assertiveness; and the pervasive violence in much of today's entertainment. Others maintain that the higher arrest rates are a by-product of policy changes, such as more aggressive policing, and the greater likelihood that parents and school officials will call the police to deal with girls' unruly behavior (Alder and Worrall 2004; Prothrow-Stith and Spivak 2005; Steffensmeier et al. 2005).

Some of the explanations of female crime parallel those of women's victimization. According to some feminist criminologists, women who commit crimes experience mistreatment that begins in early childhood:

Girls are more likely than boys to be victims of family-related sexual abuse, the assaults start at a young age, and the abuse lasts longer. These factors can lead to suicide as well as to delinquent or criminal offenses such as running away from home, truancy, drug abuse, and prostitution (Chesney-Lind and Pasko 2004; Snyder and Sickmund 2006; Urbina 2009).

Other feminists emphasize patriarchy and women's limited economic opportunities. Because of their marginalization in the economy, women may resort to criminal activities—especially shoplifting, petty theft, and prostitution—to survive financially or to support a family. Women's offenses are highest in cities, where women's economic oppression and poverty are greatest. To decrease female (and male) crime, feminist scholars propose providing women with greater equality in employment and job training so that they can get a bigger piece of the economic pie (Simon and Landis 1991; Radosh 1993; Heimer et al. 2006).

CRITICAL EVALUATION

Feminist sociologists have been at the forefront of studying women offenders and victims: "The bottom line is that gender shapes human behavior in all arenas, and crime and victimization are no exceptions" (Heimer and Kruttschnitt 2006: 1). If it had not been for feminist scholars, there would probably still be little awareness of crimes such as date rape, stalking, domestic violence, and the international sex trafficking of women and girls.

An estimated 61 percent of rapes and sexual assaults are not reported, but rapes have decreased by almost 41 percent since 1999 (Rand 2009). The reasons for these lower rates are unclear, but much of the decline may be because of feminist activists and scholars who have taught women to avoid drugs and unsafe situations, and more important, who have worked for the passage of tougher rape and domestic violence legislation (Britton 2003; Schulz 2004).

Some critics contend that feminist analyses have not gone far enough in showing how women's experiences as victims and offenders differ because of social class, race, ethnicity, and sexual orientation. Others maintain that because concepts such as patriarchy are difficult to measure, feminist research has yet to show specifically how patriarchy produces crime and affects women. Another criticism is that most feminist analysis emphasizes direct male violence against women (such as partner abuse and rape) and street crime but says little about women's white-collar crimes (Belknap 2001; Moyer 2001; Friedrichs 2004).

7 Symbolic Interaction Perspectives on Deviance and Crime

because we rarely read about white-collar crimes, but watch television dramas such as *CSI*, and receive a constant barrage of crime news on television, in newspapers, and online, many Americans worry about becoming victims of street crimes (Warr 2009). For symbolic interactionists, however, deviance is socially constructed because it's in the eye of the beholder. They offer many theories to explain deviance, but two of the best known are differential association theory and labeling theory.

DIFFERENTIAL ASSOCIATION THEORY

Dale "Rooster" Bogle's family in Oregon is an example of crime running in families. Even though Rooster, the father, served time in prison for theft, he taught his sons and daughters to survive by stealing: "By the time the boys were 10 years old they were breaking into liquor stores for their dad or stealing tractor-trailer trucks, hundreds of them. The girls turned to petty crimes to support their drug addictions" (Butterfield 2002: 1).

The Bogle children's experience illustrates differential association theory. Sociologist Edwin Sutherland coined the term **differential association,** which asserts that people learn deviance through interaction, especially with significant others such as family members and friends. Through such interaction, people learn techniques for committing criminal behavior, and the values, motives, rationalizations, and attitudes that reinforce such behavior. People become deviant, according to Sutherland, if they have more contact with significant others who violate laws than with those who are law-abiding (Sutherland and Cressey 1970). Thus, in Rooster's clan, almost everyone wound up in prison because they grew up in an environment that taught deviance rather than conformity. Sutherland emphasized that differential association doesn't occur overnight. Instead, people are most likely to engage in crime if they are exposed to deviant values (1) early in life, (2) frequently, (3) over a long period of time, and (4) from important people (parents, siblings, close friends, important business associates).

Considerable research supports differential association theory. Almost 47 percent of state prisoners have a parent or other close relative who has also been incarcerated. Parents who abstain from cigarettes and illegal drugs, drink responsibly, and provide loving support and communication are less likely to raise children who use and abuse tobacco, alcohol, or drugs. Even before age 13, children who associate with peers who commit crimes are more likely to do so themselves because they pick up attitudes and values from their friends (Wiig and Widom 2003; *Family Matters* 2005; Conway and McCord 2005). Thus, according to differential association theory, we are products of our socialization.

LABELING THEORIES

Have you ever been accused of something wrong that you didn't do? What about getting credit for something that you and others know you didn't deserve? In either case, did people start treating you differently? The reactions of others are the crux of **labeling theory,** which holds that society's reaction to behavior is a major factor in defining oneself or others as deviant.

A good example of labeling is the American Psychiatric Association's publication *Diagnostic and Statistical Manual of Mental Disorders (DSM),* which essentially defines what behavior is normal or abnormal. Some new disorders in the 2013 edition may include "hypersexuality," especially for men, and "binge eating," especially for women. The *DSM* has far-reaching effects, according to one of the past editors: "Anything you put in that book, any little change you make, has huge implications not only for psychiatry but for pharmaceutical marketing, research, for the legal system, for who's considered to be normal or not, for who's considered disabled. *And it has huge implications for stigma because the more disorders you put in, the more people get labels*" (Carey 2010: 1, emphasis added).

Steve Cole/Photodisc/Getty Images

In some of the earliest sociological studies, researchers found that teenagers who were caught in misbehavior were tagged as delinquents. Such tagging changed the child's self-concept and resulted in more deviance and criminal behavior (Tannenbaum 1938). During the 1950s and 1960s, two influential sociologists—Howard Becker and Edwin Lemert—extended labeling theory.

Becker: Deviance Is in the Eyes of the Beholder

According to Howard Becker (1963), being a deviant or a criminal depends on how others react: "Deviance is *not* a quality of the act the person commits, but rather a consequence of the application by others of rules and sanctions to an 'offender.' The deviant is one to whom that label has successfully been applied; *deviant behavior is behavior that people so label*" (p. 9).

Some people are never caught or prosecuted for crimes they commit, and thus are not labeled as deviant. In other cases, people may be innocent of breaking laws (such as cheating on taxes) but falsely accused and stigmatized. In effect, then, deviance is in the eye of the beholder because societal reaction, rather than an act, labels people as law-abiding or deviant. Moreover, labeling can lead to secondary deviance.

Lemert: Primary and Secondary Deviance

Edwin Lemert (1951, 1967) expanded on the effects of societal reactions by differentiating between primary and secondary deviance. **Primary deviance** is the initial violation of a norm or law. Primary deviance can range from relatively minor offenses, such as not attending a family member's funeral, to serious offenses, such as stealing and murder.

Even if people aren't guilty of primary deviance, labeling can result in **secondary deviance,** rule-breaking behavior that people adopt in response to the reactions of others. A teenager who is caught trying marijuana may be labeled "a druggie." Because the individual is rejected by others, he or she may accept the druggie label, associate with drug users, and become involved in a drug-using subculture. According to Lemert, a single deviant act will rarely result in secondary deviance. The more times that a person is labeled, however, the higher the probability that she or he will accept the label and engage in deviant behavior.

Almost 18 million low-income Americans live in trailer parks because they can't afford other housing. Most realize that they're stigmatized as "trailer trash," but they try to maintain their dignity despite the negative views. For example, they describe themselves as homeowners, differentiate themselves from those who commit crimes, take care of their property, and dress carefully when they're in public (see Kusenbach 2009).

© Colin young-wolff/Alamy

There's considerable evidence that labeling impacts people's lives. For example, nearly half of all Americans who experience severe health problems such as depression, schizophrenia, and eating disorders never seek treatment because they fear being stigmatized as mentally ill (U.S. Department of Health and Human Services 1999).

CRITICAL EVALUATION

Symbolic interactionists' theories are important in understanding the everyday processes that contribute to deviant and criminal behavior. Differential association theory explains how social interaction increases a person's likelihood of engaging in deviant behavior. Labeling theory, by emphasizing the importance of social reactions, shows the dangers of categorizing people negatively because the stigmas can lead to criminal careers.

Despite these contributions, symbolic interactionists' theories have several weaknesses. Differential association theory doesn't explain impulsive crimes of rage (such as domestic murder) committed by people who have grown up in law-abiding families. This theory also ignores the possibility that deviant values and behaviors can be unlearned, as when young children encounter teachers or other adults whom they respect (Anderson and Dyson 2002; Williams and McShane 2004).

Critics have faulted labeling theory on other points: The theory exaggerates the importance of judgments in altering a person's self-concept, doesn't explain why crime rates are higher in the South than in other parts of the United States or at particular times of the year (such as before holidays), and doesn't tell us why people commit crimes. Some critics also contend that social reactions are the *result* rather than the *cause* of deviant behavior, and that social control agents (such as the police) are most likely to label people who have committed serious crimes or who have a long criminal record (Schurman-Kauflin 2000; Benson 2002).

Conflict theorists, in particular, criticize symbolic interactionists for ignoring structural factors—such as poverty and low-paid jobs—that create or reinforce deviance and crime. According to feminist criminologists, symbolic interactionists' theories are limited because, with a few exceptions, they still focus almost exclusively on male criminality (Currie 1985; Belknap 2007).

8 The Criminal Justice System and Social Control

Social institutions such as the family, education, and religion try to maintain social control over moral misbehavior, whereas the criminal justice system has the *legal* power to control crime and punish offenders. The **criminal justice system** refers to government agencies—including the police, courts, and prisons—that are charged with enforcing laws, passing judgment on offenders, and changing criminal behavior. The criminal justice system relies on three major approaches in controlling crime: prevention and intervention, punishment, and rehabilitation. Punishment, as you'll see, is the least effective approach.

PREVENTION AND INTERVENTION

Because most crime first occurs in adolescence (or earlier), criminal justice agencies often focus many of their prevention and intervention efforts on juveniles and their families. The most common sources of prevention and intervention are social service agencies, community outreach programs, and the police.

Social Service Agencies and Community Outreach Programs

Numerous organizations—composed of law enforcement professionals, social workers, and nonprofit groups—try to prevent crime. A typical criminal career that spans one person's juvenile and adult years costs society about $1.5 million. The cost is much higher if we include expenses for foster care for children who have drug-addicted or incarcerated parents. Because of high prison costs, the U.S. Department of Justice, among other federal agencies, funds numerous initiatives that try to decrease youth violence and delinquency, drug dealing, rape, robbery, prostitution, and domestic violence (Burns et al. 2003; Office of Applied Studies 2004; Stephen 2004).

How well do prevention and intervention programs work? The results are mixed, but a national study of adolescents ages 12 to 17 found that the grades of those who participated in a 5-month drug treatment program improved by about 30 percent, often to a level of B or better. In Baltimore, Maryland—one of the cities with the highest drug abuse and crime rates in the nation—a study found that, 1 year after people had entered public residential treatment, their heroin use dropped by 69 percent, cocaine use by 48 percent, and criminal activity by 64 percent (Sugg 2002; Spiess 2003).

Police

The primary role of the police is to enforce society's laws. A more controversial issue is whether the police can prevent crimes. Police can head off some crimes by cruising high-risk areas in patrol cars or by having

> **criminal justice system**
> the government agencies—including the police, courts, and prisons—that are charged with enforcing laws, passing judgment on offenders, and changing criminal behavior.

© porcorex/iStockphoto/Scott Hancock/Rubberball/Jupiter Images

Many crimes involve substance abuse, but the average annual cost per person for treatment of alcohol or drug abuse is much lower than for incarceration (Office of Applied Studies 2004).

more officers on foot patrols. Concentrating on *hot spots*, areas of high criminal activity, reduces crime only temporarily, however, because criminals simply move to other parts of the city (U.S. Department of Justice 1996; Braga 2003). Also, police can't prevent most crimes because they have no control over macro-level factors that lead to criminal behavior—poverty, unemployment, low educational opportunities, and neighborhood deterioration, for example.

PUNISHING CRIME

Those who support a **crime control model** believe that crime rates increase when offenders don't fear apprehension or punishment. This perspective emphasizes protecting society and supports a tough approach toward criminals in sentencing, imprisonment, and capital punishment.

Sentencing

After a defendant has been found guilty of a criminal offense or has pleaded guilty, a judge (and sometimes a jury) imposes a *sentence*, a penalty. A sentence can be a fine, probation (supervision instead of serving time in jail), incarceration, or capital punishment. Those who receive *parole* are released from prison earlier than the sentence with the understanding that she/he will check in regularly with an officer and obey the law.

About 31 percent of those sentenced get probation; the others serve a term in a local jail or a state or federal prison. Many people question the fairness of sentencing because those convicted of similar crimes can receive widely different prison sentences depending, among other factors, on race/ethnicity, social class, variations in state sentencing laws, and how juries and judges evaluate the seriousness of a crime (Durose and Langan 2004; Whelan 2007).

As state and local budgets shrink, even states with reputations for being tough on crime are embracing more lenient punitive policies. Sometimes those arrested for driving while intoxicated avoid jail by attending regular alcohol treatment classes and submitting to random drug tests. Some states have begun to shorten the average number of years on probation and parole, which decreases supervision costs.

Other states are reducing the number of people sent to prison because it costs an average of $79 a day to keep an inmate in prison but about $3.50 a day to monitor the same person on probation (Richburg 2009; Pew Center on the States 2009).

Despite greater leniency, the number of Americans on probation and parole surged from 1.6 million in 1982 to more than 5 million in 2007. If we include those in jail and prison, "a stunning 1 in every 31 adults, or 3.2 percent, is under some form of correctional control. The rates are drastically elevated for men (1 in 18) and blacks (1 in 11) and are even higher in some high-crime inner-city neighborhoods" (Pew Center on the States 2009: 1).

Incarceration

In 2008, and for the first time in history, 1 in every 100 American adults was in prison (see *Figure 7.4*). The United States has less than 5 percent of the world's population, but almost a quarter of the planet's prisoners. Besides the sheer number of inmates, the United States is also the global leader in inmates per capita (751 per 100,000 people), ahead of nations like Russia (627 per 100,000 people) and England (151 per 100,000 people) (Pew Center on the States 2008).

Of all U.S. state and federal prisoners, 93 percent are men. About 34 percent are white, 38 percent are African American, and 20 percent are Latino (Sabol et al. 2009). However, imprisonment rates vary by race/ethnicity and sex. As *Table 7.3* shows, incarceration rates are greatest for African Americans, both women and men.

Capital Punishment

About 65 percent of Americans support *capital punishment* (the death penalty), and this percentage has been fairly consistent since 1937 (Newport 2007, 2009). Since

It's tempting to assume that the more people behind bars, the less crime there will be.

Comstock/Jupiter Images

1990, 108 nations have abolished the death penalty or suspended executions.

In the United States, 35 states have death penalties, but the number of death sentences has declined 63 percent—from a high of 328 in 1994 to 106 in 2009. Nationally, death penalty executions declined from 98 in 1997 to 52 in 2009 (Bureau of Justice Statistics 2009; Death Penalty Information Center 2009).

There are several reasons why death penalty executions have decreased. First, the nation's police chiefs believe that the death penalty doesn't deter crimes. Second, many opponents of the death penalty contend that minorities receive death penalty sentences more often than whites. Third, some argue that the death penalty is a waste of taxpayers' money because inmates can spend 15 to 20 years appealing the death penalty, which is costly. In California, for example, it costs taxpayers $137 million per year for inmates who appeal a death sentence instead of $12 million per year for those serving life sentences (Death Penalty Information Center 2009).

It's tempting to assume that the more people behind bars, the less crime there will be. The national spending on correctional facilities surged from $515 million in 1982 to almost $110 billion in 2005 (Bureau of Justice Statistics 2006). However, *recidivism* (being arrested for committing another offense after being released) has barely changed since 1980: More than half of released prisoners are back behind bars within 3 years (Pew Center on the States 2008).

REHABILITATION

Rehabilitation, a third approach to controlling deviance, maintains that appropriate treatment can change offenders into productive, law-abiding citizens. Advocates argue that public assistance, educational opportunities, job training, and crisis intervention programs can reduce recidivism. According to a criminology professor who served 11 years in a federal prison, "If we really want to lower recidivism rates, prisoners should be released with Social Security cards, current drivers' licenses, and sufficient gate money to cover rent and food

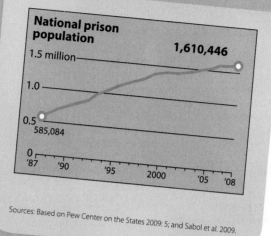

FIGURE 7.4

The Number of U.S. Prisoners Has Nearly Tripled Since 1987

National prison population

1,610,446

585,084

Sources: Based on Pew Center on the States 2009: 5; and Sabol et al. 2009.

> **rehabilitation** a social control approach that holds that appropriate treatment can change offenders into productive, law-abiding citizens.

for three months. They should be provided, upon their request, with professional services (employment assistance, personal and family counseling, drug and alcohol treatment programs, and medical services)" (Ross and Richards 2002: 177).

Are rehabilitation programs successful? Yes, if they provide employment after release. Other effective rehabilitation efforts have offered training for a trade while in prison, earning a high school or college degree while in prison or after release, and services that address several needs (such as housing, employment, and medical services) rather than just one (such as counseling for drug abuse) (Jacobson 2005; Lowenkamp and Latessa 2005).

TABLE 7.3

U.S. Imprisonment Rates by Race/Ethnicity and Sex, 2008

RACE/ETHNICITY	IMPRISONMENT RATE PER 100,000 PEOPLE	
	MALE	FEMALE
Total	952	62
White	487	50
African American	3,161	149
Latino	1,200	75

Total includes American Indians, Alaska Natives, Asians, Native Hawaiians, other Pacific Islanders, and persons identifying as two or more races.

Source: Sabol et al. 2009, Table 2.

Having resources can mean the difference between life and death.

8 Social Stratification

When her toddler wakes up at night thirsty for milk or juice, Christina, a 26-year-old mother, says, "If I don't have it, I take him into bed and try to rock him to sleep." She and her fiancé haven't been able to find jobs, and their gas and electricity were cut off because of unpaid bills (Goldstein 2009: A1).

Christina and her family are trying to survive, but having resources can mean the difference between life and death. This chapter examines stratification, considers why people move up or down the social class ladder, discusses some of the sociological theories that explain why there are haves and have-nots, and looks at global inequality.

what do you think?

Americans who are poor just aren't working hard enough.

1 2 3 4 5 6 7
strongly agree   strongly disagree

1 What Is Social Stratification?

Social stratification is the hierarchical ranking of people in a society who have different access to valued resources, such as property, prestige, power, and status. All societies are stratified, but some more than others. An **open stratification system** is based on individual achievement and allows movement up or down. In a **closed stratification system**, movement from one social position to another is limited by ascribed statuses such as one's sex, skin color, and family background. Closed stratification systems are considerably more fixed than open ones, but no stratification system is completely open or completely closed.

> **social stratification** the hierarchical ranking of people in a society who have different access to valued resources, such as property, prestige, power, and status.
>
> **open stratification system** a system that is based on individual achievement and allows movement up or down.
>
> **closed stratification system** a system in which movement from one social position to another is limited by ascribed statuses such as one's sex, skin color, and family background.

CLOSED STRATIFICATION SYSTEMS

Let's first look at two closed stratification systems: slavery and castes. Both exist today. In *slavery,* an extreme form of inequality, people own others as property and have almost total control over their lives. In *chattel slavery,* people are bought and sold as commodities, sometimes multiple times. Chattel slaves are often abducted from their homes, inherited, or given as gifts to pay a debt. The United Nations banned all forms of slavery worldwide in 1948, but it persists in many countries, including the Middle East, Africa, the Balkans, and Asia (U.S. Department of State 2006; Lampman 2007; Dixon 2009).

Castes, a second type of closed stratification system, are social categories based on heredity. Because social status is ascribed at birth, caste members are severely restricted in their choice of occupations, residence, and social relationships. A good example is India, where a caste system has existed for more than 3,000 years. At the top were the Brahmins (priests, scholars, and educated class), followed by Kshatriyas (kings and warriors), Vaishyas (merchants and farmers), and Sudras (peasants, laborers, and craftspeople). On the bottom rung were the Dalits (formerly referred to as "untouchables"), who were very poor and performed the most menial and unpleasant jobs, such as collecting waste and cleaning streets. Fearing being "polluted," persons of higher castes would not interact with the Dalits (Mendelsohn and Vicziany 1998).

AP Photo/Manish Swarup

India's Dalits, such as those pictured here, still perform unpleasant tasks such as burning corpses and removing carcasses.

India outlawed the caste system in 1949, but social distinctions are deeply entrenched, and most people socialize with and marry within their own castes (Banerjee et al. 2009). In more than half the classrooms across India, Dalit children are often forced to sit in the back and to eat separately, and they are bullied, assaulted, and humiliated. To discourage such discrimination, the government has passed laws to provide lower castes with more educational opportunities (Neelakantan 2008). Still, many Dalit women are married off young, endure abusive marriages, and are not educated (Magnier 2009).

OPEN STRATIFICATION SYSTEMS

In open stratification systems, social classes are relatively fluid because they are based on achieved rather than ascribed statuses. A **social class** is a category of people who have a similar standing or rank in a society based on wealth, education, power, prestige, and other valued resources. Theoretically, people in open stratification systems can move from one class to another. As you'll see throughout much of this chapter, however, the more resources someone has at birth, the greater her or his chance of moving into a higher social class. In effect, then, open stratification systems are not as open as many people believe.

2 Dimensions of Stratification

In the nineteenth century, the English novelist Jane Austen wrote, "A large income is the best recipe for happiness I ever heard of." More than a hundred years later, the late American entertainer Sophie Tucker quipped, "I've been rich and I've been poor. Rich is better." Income is a critical factor of stratification, but it's not the only one. Instead, sociologists use a multidimensional approach that includes wealth, prestige, and power.

WEALTH

Wealth is the money and other economic assets that a person or family owns, including property and income. *Property* comes in many forms, such as buildings, land, stocks and bonds, retirement savings, and personal possessions such as furniture, jewelry, and works of art. *Income* is money a person receives regularly, usually in the form of wages or a salary but also as rents, interest on savings accounts, dividends on stock, royalties, or the proceeds from a business.

Income and wealth are different in several important ways:

- Wealth is *cumulative*. It increases over time, especially through investment, whereas income is usually spent on everyday expenses.

- Because wealth is accumulated over time, much of it can be *passed on to the next generation*. With an estimated $50 billion income in 2009, Bill Gates, co-founder of Microsoft Corporation, is one of the wealthiest people in the world. If each of Gates' three children inherits only 1 percent of his fortune, she or he will get at least $500 million!

- *Wealth produces income* ("It takes money to make money."). For example, a person with substantial stock portfolios can collect several million a year from the dividends.

U.S. wealth and income inequality is staggering. As *Figure 8.1* shows, the top 1 percent of U.S. households owns 35 percent of all wealth, the next two groups hold an additional 39 percent of all wealth, and the bottom 80 percent has only 15 percent of the wealth. Income inequality is even greater: the top 1 percent of households has 43 percent of all income compared with only 7 percent for the bottom 80 percent of Americans.

In 2009, the 400 richest Americans had a collective wealth of almost $1.3 trillion, and the average was $3.2 billion per person (*Forbes* 2009). When the CEO of General Motors was asked if he'd take a cut in his $2.2 million salary as the company was laying off thousands of automotive workers in 2008, he said, "I do have a son in college I have to pay for somehow" (Gilson 2009: 26). In contrast, the median household income plummeted almost 4 percent—from $52,163 in 2007 to $50,303 in 2008, the lowest level since 1997 (DeNavas-Walt et al. 2009).

PRESTIGE

A second dimension of social stratification is **prestige**—respect, recognition, or regard attached to social positions. Prestige is based on many criteria, including wealth, family background, fame, leadership, power, occupation, and accomplishments. For example, every college convocation acknowledges students who graduate *cum laude*, *magna cum laude*, and *summa cum laude*.

We typically evaluate others according to the kind of work they do. *Table 8.1* presents a sample of prestige scores for U.S. occupations. Theoretically, the scores range from 0 to 100, but no occupation is worthless or perfect. As a result, the prestige scores typically range from 20 to 86. In general, non-manual occupations (such as lawyer and optometrist) typically rank higher in prestige than manual jobs (such as bus driver and garbage collector). Studies of occupational prestige in 57 other countries have found results similar to these for the United States (Hauser and Featherman 1977; Treiman 1977).

> **prestige** respect, recognition, or regard attached to social positions.

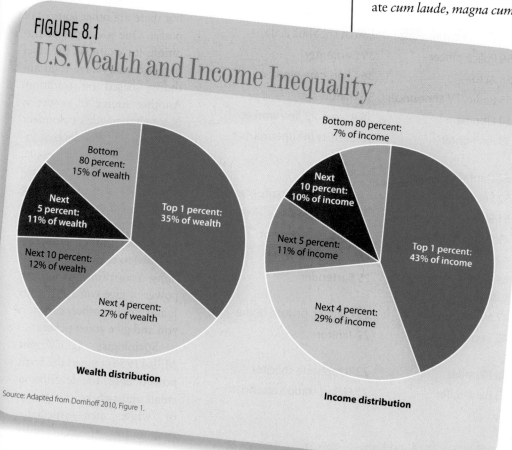

FIGURE 8.1
U.S. Wealth and Income Inequality

Wealth distribution

- Bottom 80 percent: 15% of wealth
- Next 5 percent: 11% of wealth
- Next 10 percent: 12% of wealth
- Next 4 percent: 27% of wealth
- Top 1 percent: 35% of wealth

Income distribution

- Bottom 80 percent: 7% of income
- Next 10 percent: 10% of income
- Next 5 percent: 11% of income
- Next 4 percent: 29% of income
- Top 1 percent: 43% of income

Source: Adapted from Domhoff 2010, Figure 1.

If you examine *Table 8.1*, you'll notice several characteristics of the most prestigious occupations:

- They *require more formal education* (such as college or postgraduate degrees) and/or extensive training. Physicians (86) require from 23 to 28 years of school and then fulfill internship and residency requirements after receiving a medical degree.

- They *pay more*, even though there are some exceptions. A realtor (49) or a truck driver (30) may earn more than a registered nurse (66), but registered nurses are likely to earn more over a lifetime because they have steady employment, good health benefits,

retirement programs, and more opportunities to find jobs during layoffs or career changes.

- They *are seen as more socially important*. An elementary school teacher (64) may earn less than the school's janitor (22), but the teacher's job is more prestigious because of teachers' contributions to reading, writing, and thinking skills.

- They *involve more abstract thought and mental activity*. An architect (73) must use far more imagination in designing a building than a carpenter (39), who performs very specific tasks.

- They *offer greater self-expression, autonomy, and freedom from supervision*. A dentist (72) has considerably more freedom in performing her or his job than a dental hygienist (52). In effect, then, higher prestige occupations provide more privileges.

POWER

A third important dimension of social stratification is **power**, the ability of individuals or groups to achieve goals, control events, and maintain influence over others despite opposition. In every society, power is based on social class, but there are other sources of power. One is custom or tradition; for example, the chief of a tribe may have total authority based on tradition. Another source of power is being charismatic or eloquent or having other traits that inspire large groups of people. Leaders like Mahatma Gandhi and Martin Luther King Jr. motivated millions of people to demand change, peace, and social justice. Power is also tied to particular occupations: Your professor has the power to give you an A or an F, and a police officer can stop you and give you a ticket.

Sociologist C. Wright Mills (1956) coined the term *power elite* to describe a small and tightly knit group of white men—especially corporation heads, politi-

TABLE 8.1
Prestige Scores for Selected Occupations in the United States

Do you agree with these rankings? Are there occupations that you think should rank higher or lower? If so, why?

HIGHER PRESTIGE JOBS	MEDIUM PRESTIGE JOBS	LOWER PRESTIGE JOBS
86 Physician	59 Police officer	39 Carpenter
85 Supreme Court judge	58 Actor	36 Child-care worker
78 Lawyer	55 Radio/TV announcer	36 Hairdresser
74 College professor	54 Librarian	35 Assembly-line worker
74 Computer systems analyst	53 Firefighter	33 Cashier in supermarket
73 Architect	52 Dental hygienist	32 Bus driver
72 Dentist	52 Social worker	31 Auto body repairperson
69 Member of the clergy	51 Electrician	30 Truck driver
67 Optometrist	49 Funeral director	28 Garbage collector
66 Registered nurse	49 Realtor	28 Waiter/waitress
66 High school teacher	48 Manager of a supermarket	25 Bartender
65 Accountant	47 Mail carrier	23 Cleaner, private home
64 Elementary school teacher	46 Secretary	22 Janitor
62 Veterinarian	45 Plumber	22 Telephone solicitor
61 Airline pilot	43 Bank teller	21 Filling station attendant

Sources: Based on Nakao and Treas 1992; and J. Davis et al. 2005.

cal leaders, and high-ranking military officers—who make all the important decisions in U.S. society. More recently, sociologists Richard Zweigenhaft and William Domhoff (1998) have agreed that a socially cohesive and very wealthy group of men continues to be a "ruling class" that dominates much of the American economy and government. (We'll examine power elites in Chapters 11 and 12.)

A person's ranking may be about equal in terms of wealth, prestige, and power. A Supreme Court justice, for instance, is usually affluent, enjoys a great deal of prestige, and wields considerable power. In many cases, however, there can be *status inconsistency,* the condition in which a person ranks differently on various stratification dimensions. Consider funeral directors. Their prestige is relatively low, but most have higher incomes than college professors, who are among the most educated people in U.S. society and have relatively high prestige (see *Table 8.1*). You'll recall that status inconsistency can be stressful and lead to frustration and depression (see Chapter 5).

We've looked at stratification systems and the dimensions of stratification, but how, specifically, do people in different social classes behave? And how does social class affect our behavior?

3 Social Class in America

a good indicator of social class is **socioeconomic status (SES)**, an overall ranking of a person's position in the class hierarchy based on income, education, and occupation. How do sociologists measure social class? Some ask residents to identify the social classes in their communities (reputational approach), some ask people to place themselves in one of a number of classes (subjective approach), but most use SES indicators (objective approach).

Because there are different ways of measuring social class, sociologists don't always agree on the number of social classes in the United States. However, there is consensus that there are four general social classes—upper, middle, working, and lower. Except for the working class, most sociologists often divide these classes further into more specific strata.

Sociologists Dennis Gilbert and Joseph Kahl (1993) developed a teardrop model of the American class structure based, primarily, on income and occupation (see *Figure 8.2*). They caution that social class is a complicated concept, and that specifying the dividing lines between classes is as much art as science, but the model provides an overview of the U.S. social class structure. Besides income, education, and occupation, social classes also differ in values, power, prestige, social networks, and *lifestyles* (tastes, preferences, and ways of living).

THE UPPER CLASS

You saw earlier that very rich Americans control a vastly disproportionate amount of the total U.S. wealth and income. This group comprises two classes in the United

socioeconomic status (SES) an overall ranking of a person's position in the class hierarchy based on income, education, and occupation.

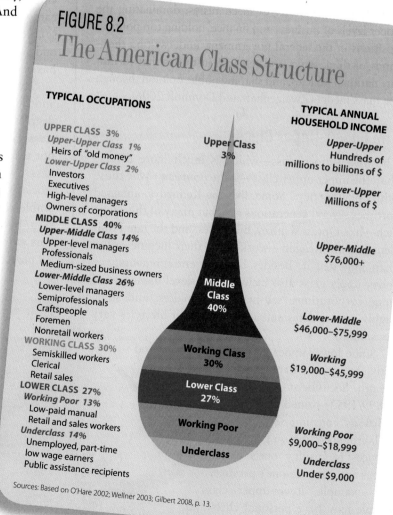

FIGURE 8.2

The American Class Structure

TYPICAL OCCUPATIONS

UPPER CLASS 3%
Upper-Upper Class 1%
  Heirs of "old money"
Lower-Upper Class 2%
  Investors
  Executives
  High-level managers
  Owners of corporations
MIDDLE CLASS 40%
Upper-Middle Class 14%
  Upper-level managers
  Professionals
  Medium-sized business owners
Lower-Middle Class 26%
  Lower-level managers
  Semiprofessionals
  Craftspeople
  Foremen
  Nonretail workers
WORKING CLASS 30%
  Semiskilled workers
  Clerical
  Retail sales
LOWER CLASS 27%
Working Poor 13%
  Low-paid manual
  Retail and sales workers
Underclass 14%
  Unemployed, part-time low wage earners
  Public assistance recipients

Upper Class 3%

Middle Class 40%

Working Class 30%

Lower Class 27%

Working Poor

Underclass

TYPICAL ANNUAL HOUSEHOLD INCOME

Upper-Upper Hundreds of millions to billions of $

Lower-Upper Millions of $

Upper-Middle $76,000+

Lower-Middle $46,000–$75,999

Working $19,000–$45,999

Working Poor $9,000–$18,999

Underclass Under $9,000

Sources: Based on O'Hare 2002; Wellner 2003; Gilbert 2008, p. 13.

States: the upper-upper class and the lower-upper class.

The Upper-Upper Class

Upper-upper class members rarely appear on the lists of wealthiest individuals published by *Forbes* or *Business Week*. Because they value their privacy, some upper-upper class members refuse to be listed even in *The Social Register,* an inventory of America's social elite that has been published since 1887.

Whether the income originally came from legal or illegal activities (Phillipps 2002), most upper-upper class members have enormous wealth that has been passed down through generations. Some of the "old money" families include the Vanderbilts, DuPonts, Rockefellers, and Fords.

Having an inherited fortune brings with it power (McNamee and Miller 1998). Upper-upper class white males, in particular, shape the economic and political climate through a variety of mechanisms: dominating the upper levels of business and finance, holding top political positions in the federal government, underwriting thousands of think tanks and research institutes that formulate national policies, and shaping public opinion through the mass media (Zweigenhaft and Domhoff 2006).

The Lower-Upper Class

The lower-upper class—which is much more diverse than the upper-upper class—is the *nouveau riche,* those with "new money." Some, like the Kennedys, amassed fortunes several generations ago, but many of the newly rich—like Oprah Winfrey, Bill Gates, and the late President Ronald Reagan—worked for their income rather than inherited it. Besides business entrepreneurs, the lower-upper class also includes high-level managers of huge corporations, self-made millionaires, and some highly paid athletes and actors, but their lifestyles vary considerably.

Some lower-upper class members live modestly, but many flaunt their newly earned wealth. Sociologist Thorstein Veblen (1899/1953) coined the term **conspicuous consumption** to refer to lavish spending on goods and services to display one's social status and enhance one's prestige. For example, lower-upper class people may have personal chefs and take exotic vacations (often in private planes). Such conspicuous consumption sends the message "I'm very, very rich."

Because they lack the "right" ancestry and have usually made their money by working for it, lower-uppers are not accepted into "old money" circles that have strong feelings of in-group solidarity. Still, lower-upper class members engage in lifestyles and rituals that try to parallel those of the upper-upper class.

THE MIDDLE CLASS

Most Americans describe themselves as middle class, including 41 percent of those with incomes below $20,000 and 33 percent of those with incomes above $150,000 (Pew Research Center 2008). There are several strata in the middle class (see Morin 2008), but sociologists often distinguish between the *upper middle-class* and the *lower-middle class.*

The Upper-Middle Class

Upper-middle class members, although rich, live on earned income rather than accumulated wealth. Their salaries are high enough to provide economic stability and sizeable savings, but usually because both spouses have careers.

The occupations of this group—mainly professional and managerial—usually require a Ph.D. or advanced degrees in business, law, and medicine. People in this class include corporate executives and managers (but not those at the top), high government officials, business owners, physicians, and successful lawyers and stockbrokers. Many of these occupations have considerable on-the-job autonomy and freedom from supervision, but more than half of upper-middle class members work 50 or more hours per week, compared with 28 percent of the general population (Gardyn 2001).

Status symbols—cars, clothes, vacations, and so on—are not limited to the wealthy. In a recent national poll, 81 percent of Americans said they felt social pressure to buy high-priced goods, even if it meant going into debt, to convey a certain image within their social class (Steinhauer 2005). Many upper-middle class members, in particular, use status symbols to show that they've made it by buying "almost rich" cars (such as Jaguar X-type sedans that start at $30,000), upscale kitchen appliances, designer handbags, and expensive jewelry.

The upper-middle class exercises a large and growing influence in American society. Many of its members vote, volunteer, make campaign donations, run for local offices, and participate in fund-raising activities, especially for their children's schools. Members of this class often spend their leisure time attending arts performances, including classical music concerts, plays, the opera, and the ballet.

The Lower-Middle Class

The lower-middle class, more diverse than the upper-middle class, is composed of people in nonmanual and semiprofessional occupations. Nonmanual jobs include office staff, low-level managers, owners of small businesses, medical and dental technicians, legal and medical secretaries, police officers, sales workers (such as insurance salespeople and real-estate agents), and some highly skilled blue-collar workers (such as building contractors). Examples of semiprofessional occupations are nursing, social work, and teaching. Almost all of these jobs require training beyond high school and many, especially the semiprofessional occupations, require a college degree. Most families in the lower-middle class rely on two incomes to maintain a comfortable standard of living.

Unlike upper-middle class jobs, those in the lower-middle class have less autonomy and freedom from supervision, and there is little chance for advancement. People are more likely to follow orders than to give them. Many lower-middle class jobs are relatively secure, but the workers worry about taxes, inflation, and layoffs as workplaces become more computerized. Except for some retirement funds, most have only modest savings to cover emergencies. Many buy used or inexpensive late-model cars, eat out fairly regularly at middle-income restaurants, and take occasional vacations, but they rarely have the income to buy luxury products without going deeply into debt.

THE WORKING CLASS

The working class consists of skilled and semiskilled laborers, factory employees, and other blue-collar workers in manual occupations. They are construction workers, assembly-line workers, truck drivers, auto mechanics, repair personnel, bartenders, and skilled craft workers like carpenters and electricians. Most of the jobs are blue collar, but some—such as clerks and retail sales workers in the service sector—are white collar.

People who fill working-class jobs often have a high-school degree but no college education, and many

of the positions provide little or no opportunity for advancement. In a weak economy, especially, the bargaining power of working-class people diminishes. Large numbers see their work as boring and routine—a source of income to survive on rather than a means of attaining personal fulfillment. Most of the semiskilled jobs require little training, are mechanized, and closely supervised.

> **working poor** people who work at least 27 weeks a year but receive such low wages that they live in or near poverty.

Working-class people who purchase homes, including mobile homes, may experience foreclosure because of delinquent payments. Many in the working class use credit cards to pay off bills each month but then can barely pay the monthly minimum. Debts become overwhelming when borrowers who live from paycheck to paycheck suffer setbacks such as divorce, illness, or job loss (Mayer 2002).

THE LOWER CLASS

People in the lower class are at the bottom of the economic ladder because they have little education, few occupational skills, work in minimum wage jobs, or are often unemployed. Even though most of the lower class is poor, sociologists often distinguish between the *working poor* and the *underclass.*

The Working Poor

Almost 26 percent of all workers now fall into the category of the **working poor,** people who work at least 27 weeks a year but receive such low wages that they live in or near poverty. Almost half of American families headed by a married couple with at least one full-time, full-year worker are among the working poor (Holzer 2007; "A Profile of the Working Poor..." 2009).

Some sociologists describe the working poor as "the excluded class" who typically "fill the most undesirable jobs in restaurant kitchens or as nighttime cleaners of downtown buildings" (Perrucci and Wysong 1999: 28). Many are the "near poor whose incomes place them above the poverty line, but well below the middle class":

> *Near-poor women work in clothing stores, minimarts, and child-care centers; they clean subway cars on the night shift. Near-poor men often hold down more than one job, working days as aides for the mentally impaired and nights as security guards. (Newman and Chen 2007: B10)*

Up to half of the people who visit food pantries and soup kitchens in some states are the working poor (Ryan 2008). Many attribute their situation to bad luck or fate and feel powerless over their economic insecurity. Like the underclass beneath them, the working poor are generally alienated from political processes.

The Underclass

The **underclass**, which occupies the bottom rung of the U.S. social ladder, consists of people who are persistently poor, segregated residentially, and relatively isolated from the rest of the population. Most rarely work; they are chronically unemployed or drift in and out of jobs. Social scientists commonly use the term *underclass* to describe inner-city minorities, but it applies to people of any race or ethnicity who are locked in destitution and have little chance of moving out of abject poverty. They may work erratically or at part-time jobs, but their lack of skills, low educational levels, and in many cases, disabilities make it difficult for them to find regular, full-time jobs (Beeghley 2000; Gilbert 2008).

For sociologist William Julius Wilson (1996), being in the underclass or one of "the ghetto poor" is the result of joblessness rather than poverty, because the under-

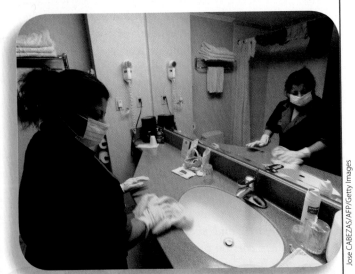

Among America's working poor are hotel housekeepers. On average, those employed even at expensive hotels earn less than $19,000 a year working full time.

Jose CABEZAS/AFP/Getty Images

class grew when most middle-class people—both white and black—moved to the suburbs, the number of factory jobs declined, and the poor became more isolated.

Others argue that the underclass is locked in a "culture of poverty" that has more to do with personal values than with structural factors like unemployment. Most social scientists agree, however, that the underclass experiences a wide range of social problems—crime, welfare, family dissolution, drug abuse, poor health, and domestic violence.

HOW SOCIAL CLASS AFFECTS US

Our social class position, more than any other single variable, affects just about all aspects of our lives. Max Weber referred to the consequences of social stratification as **life chances,** the extent to which people have positive experiences and can secure the good things in life (such as food, housing, education, and good health) because they have economic resources. Regarding health, for example:

- Poor children are less healthy than those at higher SES levels and are more likely to be unhealthy in adulthood. Unhealthy adults earn less, spend less time in the labor force, and must often retire earlier (Cutler et al. 2008).

- Living in a lower SES neighborhood increases biological "wear and tear" due to chronic stress and accelerates the onset of diseases (Bird et al. 2009).

- Thirty percent of Americans making less than $24,000 a year have been diagnosed with depression compared with 13 percent of those who earn $60,000 or more a year (Pelham 2009).

The United States is the richest nation in the world (see Chapter 12), but the gap between the affluent and the poor is increasing.

4 Poverty in America

there is more poverty in the United States today than 35 years ago: almost 40 million Americans were poor in 2008, compared with 23 million in 1973 (DeNavas-Walt et al. 2009). What do sociologists mean by poverty? Who are the poor? And why?

WHAT IS POVERTY?

There are two ways to define poverty: absolute and relative. **Absolute poverty** is not having enough money to afford the most basic necessities of life, such as food, clothing, and shelter ("what I need"). **Relative poverty** is not having enough money to maintain an average standard of living ("what I want").

The Poverty Line

The **poverty line** is the minimal level of income that the federal government considers necessary for basic subsistence. To determine the poverty line, the Department of Agriculture (DOA) estimates the annual cost of food that meets minimum nutritional guidelines and then multiplies this figure by three to cover the minimum cost of clothing, housing, health care, and other necessities. Anyone whose income is below this line is considered officially poor and is eligible for government assistance (such as food stamps).

The poverty line, which in 2008 was $21,834 for a family of four (two adults and two children), is adjusted every year to reflect cost-of-living increases. If a family makes a dollar more than the poverty line figure, they are not officially categorized as poor. Also, many people earn considerably less than the poverty threshold. In 2008, for example, 43 percent of poor families—a group the U.S. Census Bureau refers to as "severely poor"—earned less than half of the poverty threshold (DeNavas-Walt et al. 2009).

Is the Poverty Line Accurate?

Some believe that the official poverty line is too high. They argue, for example, that poverty levels—which were developed in the mid-1960s—don't include the value of noncash benefits such as food stamps, medical services (like Medicare and Medicaid), public housing

As unemployment and poverty rates have increased, "tent cities," such as this one in Sacramento, California, have sprung up across the country.

Justin Sullivan/Getty Images

subsidies, and unreported income (see Eberstadt 2009).

Others claim that the poverty line is unrealistically low because it ignores many current needs of poor people. For example, single mothers require affordable child care so that they can work and pay for transportation costs to child-care centers and jobs. Critics also contend that a poor person who lives in a metropolitan area or in a state such as California and Massachusetts needs more money to survive—often three to four times more than someone who lives in the rural South—primarily because of higher housing costs (Jolliffe 2006). Others argue that poverty estimates are too low because they don't include other measures of economic hardship such as the number of people who aren't defined as poor but depend on food stamps to survive (Mossaad 2009).

> **relative poverty** not having enough money to maintain an average standard of living.
>
> **poverty line** the minimal level of income that the federal government considers necessary for basic subsistence.
>
> **feminization of poverty** the higher likelihood that female heads of households will be poor.

WHO ARE THE POOR?

Poverty isn't random. Both historically and currently, the poor share some common characteristics that include age, gender, family structure, and race and ethnicity.

Age

Children make up only 25 percent of the U.S. population but 35 percent (over 14 million) of the poor. Among older Americans, people 65 and older make up 13 percent of the total population but about 10 percent of the poor (about 4 million) (DeNavas-Walt et al. 2009). Although it is still high, the poverty rate among older Americans is at an all-time low because government programs for the elderly, like Medicare and Medicaid, have kept up with the rate of inflation; in contrast, many programs for children living in poverty have been reduced or eliminated since 1980.

Gender and Family Structure

Of all people 18 years and older who are poor, 57 percent are women (DeNavas-Walt et al. 2009). Researcher Diana Pearce (1978) coined the term **feminization of poverty** to describe the higher likelihood that female heads of households will be poor. Because of increases in divorce and unmarried childbearing, single-mother families are at least five times more likely to be poor than are married-couple families, and they are disproportionately represented among the long-term poor, especially when biological and divorced fathers don't support their children (Grall 2007). Besides marital status, other major reasons for the feminization of poverty are low-paying jobs and wage discrimination, topics that we'll examine in more detail in Chapters 9 and 12.

Race and Ethnicity

Poverty rates for African Americans and Latinos greatly exceed the national average of 13 percent. In 2008, almost 25 percent of blacks and 23 percent of Latinos were poor, compared with 9 percent of whites and 12 percent of Asians. Poverty rates are greatest for families headed by single women, particularly if they are African American or Latino (DeNavas-Walt et al. 2009).

WHY ARE PEOPLE POOR?

In 2008, the nation's poverty rate increased by 1 percent from 2007 (from 37 to almost 40 million Americans), rising to the highest level since 1997 (DeNavas-Walt et al. 2009). Why are people poor? Economists and sociologists have a number of theories (see Cellini et al. 2008 for a nontechnical summary). Many sociologists, however, offer two general explanations for why people are poor: One blames the poor; the other emphasizes societal factors.

Blaming the Poor: Individual Characteristics

About 69 percent of Americans believe that it's possible to start out poor and get rich through hard work. They assert that, since this is a land of opportunity, anyone who doesn't get ahead just isn't working hard enough: "Almost anyone can get rich if they put their mind to it" (Jones 2007; University of Connecticut 2007).

Some researchers see poor people as "deficient" and innately inferior because of genetic factors that produce lower intelligence and cognitive abilities (see Herrnstein and Murray 1994). Proponents of an influential *culture of poverty* perspective contend that the poor are deficient: They share certain values, beliefs, and attitudes about life that differ from those who aren't poor, are more permissive in raising their children, and are more likely to seek immediate gratification instead of planning for the future (Lewis 1966; Banfield 1974). The assertion that these values, beliefs, and attitudes are transmitted from generation to generation implies that the poor create their own problems through a self-perpetuating cycle of poverty ("like father, like son").

SIX BIGGEST MYTHS ABOUT THE POOR

MYTH 1. PEOPLE ARE POOR BECAUSE THEY ARE LAZY AND REFUSE TO WORK. Of poor people 16 years and older, 12 percent work full time year-round, and another 25 percent work part time (Mead 2008).

MYTH 2. MOST POOR PEOPLE ARE MINORITIES. Almost 43 percent of people living in poverty are white (DeNavas-Walt et al. 2009). In proportions, however, African Americans and Latinos are much more likely to be poor than Asian Americans and whites.

MYTH 3. MOST POOR PEOPLE LIVE IN INNER CITIES. A large number (33 percent) of the poor live in inner cities, but the rest live in urban areas outside of inner cities, the suburbs, small towns, and rural communities. In 2008, one third of the nation's poor lived in suburbs (DeNavas-Walt et al. 2009; Kneebone and Garr 2010).

MYTH 4. MOST OF THE POOR ARE SINGLE MOTHERS. Of all families living in poverty, 51 percent are single mothers and their children, but 40 percent of married-couple families and 9 percent of father-headed households are poor (DeNavas-Walt et al. 2009).

MYTH 5. MOST OF THE POOR ARE OLDER AMERICANS. About 10 percent of people 65 years and older are poor, but 35 percent of the poor are children younger than 18 (DeNavas-Walt et al. 2009). Between 2000 and 2008, the incomes of people ages 25 to 54—especially men—decreased about 11 percent but increased by 8 percent for men ages 65 to 74 (Cauchon 2009).

MYTH 6. THE POOR GET SPECIAL ADVANTAGES. The poor pay more for goods and services than do wealthier people. Supermarket chains and discount stores rarely locate in low-income communities, and because the poor have limited access to banks or other financial institutions, they must often rely on "check-cashing stores" that charge high rates for cashing checks or borrowing money (Jeffery 2006).

Blaming Society: Structural Characteristics

In contrast with blaming the poor, most sociologists assert that a society's organization creates and sustains poverty. In a classic article on poverty, sociologist Herbert Gans (1971) maintained that poverty and inequality have many functions:

- The poor ensure that society's dirty yet necessary work gets done (such as dishwashing and cleaning bedpans in hospitals).
- The poor subsidize the middle and upper classes by working for low wages.
- The poor buy goods and services that would otherwise be rejected (such as day-old bread, used cars, and the services of old, retired, or incompetent professionals), and
- The poor absorb the costs of societal change and community growth (as when they are pushed out of their homes by urban renewal and construction of expressways, parks, and stadiums).

Thus, according to Gans, poverty persists in the United States because many people benefit from the consequences.

Which perspective is more accurate: blaming the poor or blaming society? Some people are poor because they're lazy, focus on the present, and would rather get a handout than a job. However, researchers find little support for the argument that poverty is transmitted from generation to generation. Instead, almost 52 percent of Americans experience poverty at some time before age 65 and receive public assistance. Also, about 50 percent of Americans who become poor get out of poverty a year later, and 75 percent experience poverty spells of less than 4 years (McKernan et al. 2009). Thus, most Americans work to escape poverty instead of relying on public assistance.

Most people are poor because of economic conditions (especially low wages), job loss, physical or mental disabilities, or an inability to afford health insurance, which, in turn, can result in acute health problems that interfere with employment. And as more businesses relocate to the suburbs, poor minorities—especially those concentrated in inner cities—are unlikely to hear about employment possibilities or to have the transportation to get to even low-paying jobs (Bernstein et al. 2007; Acs 2009).

social mobility a person's ability to move up or down the class hierarchy.

HOMELESSNESS

One of the most devastating consequences of poverty is homelessness. The uncounted homeless include people who live in automobiles, have makeshift housing (such as boxes and boxcars), or stay with relatives for short periods. An estimated 3.5 million people (about 1 percent of Americans, a third of whom are children) are likely to experience homelessness in a given year (National Coalition for the Homeless 2009a).

Single men comprise 68 percent of the homeless, families with children 23 percent, and single women 9 percent. The homeless population is estimated to be 42 percent African American, 38 percent white, 20 percent Latino, 4 percent American Indian, and 2 percent Asian (National Coalition for the Homeless 2009b).

Homelessness is due to a combination of factors, some of which are beyond the control of individuals. Poverty, lack of education or marketable skills, low-paying jobs, unemployment, domestic violence, substance abuse, the inability of relatives and friends to help during crises, a shortage of affordable housing, and a decline in public assistance are among the most common reasons for homelessness. Young mothers with very young children are especially likely to become homeless. The homeless also include teenage runaways escaping from family violence or incest (Burt et al. 2004; National Coalition for the Homeless 2009b).

In mid-2009, 1 in 84 Americans lost a home to foreclosures, an increase of 15 percent since mid-2008. When the housing market began to decline, many people couldn't sell their homes at the prices they paid for them. Others lost their jobs and couldn't keep up with the monthly mortgage payments (Armour 2009).

Almost one of four of America's homeless are families with children. Because there aren't enough shelters, many live in their cars.

5 Social Mobility

most Americans believe in **social mobility**, a person's ability to move up or down the class hierarchy. The movement results from a variety of factors. Before con-

horizontal mobility moving from one position to another at the same class level.

vertical mobility moving up or down the class hierarchy.

intragenerational mobility moving up or down the class hierarchy over one's lifetime.

intergenerational mobility moving up or down the class hierarchy relative to the position of one's parents.

sidering these factors, let's look at the types of social mobility that sociologists typically examine.

TYPES OF SOCIAL MOBILITY

There are different types of social mobility: horizontal and vertical mobility, and intergenerational and intragenerational mobility.

Horizontal mobility means moving from one position to another at the same class level, or making a lateral move. Tracey, a nurse, might move from the pediatrics to the obstetrics department, but her salary won't change much because the position is similar in responsibilities and qualifications. Sociologists are generally not very interested in horizontal mobility because it involves little change in one's social class.

Vertical mobility refers to moving up or down the class hierarchy. If Tracey wants a higher salary, she may decide to undergo more training and become a physician's assistant (PA). Working under the supervision of a doctor, a PA examines, diagnoses, and treats patients. If Tracey is laid off and can't find another job, she might experience downward mobility. Vertical mobility can be intragenerational and intergenerational.

Intragenerational mobility refers to moving up or down the class hierarchy over one's lifetime. If Tracey begins as a nurse's assistant, becomes a registered nurse, and then a PA, she experiences intragenerational mobility. **Intergenerational mobility** is moving up or down the class hierarchy relative to the position of one's parents. It is a change in social class that occurs across two or more generations. If Tracey's parents were blue-collar workers, her upward movement to the

J. K. Rowling worked as a teacher but was divorced and living on public assistance when she wrote Harry Potter and the Philosopher's Stone during her daughter's naps. The book was published in 1997; by 2007, Rowling, one of the world's richest women and a billionaire, was considerably wealthier than the Queen of England.

middle-class would be an example of intergenerational mobility.

Intragenerational and intergenerational mobility can be downward or upward. Sam Walton, the founder of Wal-Mart, is an example of upward intergenerational mobility. He worked in his father's store while attending high school, graduated from the University of Missouri, and opened his first store, Ben Franklin, with the help of a loan from his father-in-law. When he died in 1992, at the age of 74, Walton was the world's second-richest man, behind Bill Gates. If Walton had lost his fortune and wound up on public assistance, he would have experienced downward intragenerational mobility.

When social mobility occurs, most moves are short (Nichols and Favreault 2009). A child from a working-class family, for example, is more likely to move up to the lower-middle class than to jump to the lower-upper class. The same is true of downward mobility: Someone from the middle class is more likely to slide into the working class than to drop to the underclass.

WHAT AFFECTS SOCIAL MOBILITY?

According to many sociologists, vertical social mobility doesn't always reflect people's talents, intelligence, or hard work. Instead, much social mobility depends on structural, demographic, and individual factors.

Structural Factors

Macro-level variables, over which we have little or no control as individuals, affect social mobility in many ways. First, *changes in the economy* spur upward or downward mobility. During an economic boom, the number of jobs increases, and many people, including those on public assistance, have an opportunity to move up. Second, the *number of available positions* in particular occupations changes over time. The need for agricultural workers dwindled significantly in the United States during the last 100 years, whereas the demand for clerical, technical, and professional workers mushroomed. As a result, an expanding occupational structure created more room in the middle of the social class hierarchy. Third, *immigration* stimulates social mobility. Because most immigrants take low-paying jobs, groups that are already there advance to higher positions. Such upward mobility continues as poor immigrants take the least desirable jobs, allowing others to move into higher-status occupations (Haskins 2007b).

Demographic Factors

Demographic factors, which are usually interrelated, also affect social mobility. Three of the most important are education, gender, and race and ethnicity.

Education is a critical factor in social mobility. Especially when the economy is slumping, people with college and graduate degrees fare better than those with a high-school education or less. Those who don't graduate from high school often face long and frequent bouts of unemployment, must get by with temporary employment, and may move down the socioeconomic ladder (Haskins 2007a).

In terms of *gender,* women's massive entry into the labor force during the 1980s increased family income and many single women's upward mobility. For both sexes, but especially women, whom one marries also affects upward or downward mobility.

Regarding *race and ethnicity,* African Americans and Latinos, especially those from low-income backgrounds, usually experience little upward mobility. Black and Latino middle classes have grown since the 1970s, but both groups still lag significantly behind whites in median family income. A major reason is that white parents have more wealth that they can pass down to their children (Sernau 2001; Isaacs 2007a, 2007b).

Individual Factors

Because family background is a critical factor in social stratification, the best way to be upwardly mobile is to choose the right parents. For example, only 7 of the 44 U.S. presidents came from the lower-middle class or below. Abraham Lincoln, although born in a log cabin, had a father who was one of the wealthiest people in his community. And about a third of the students with low grades at Ivy League universities wouldn't be there if their parents weren't celebrities, well-known politicians, or others who donated at least $25 million to the school (Golden 2006).

Parents tend to *socialize* their children to assume an expected class position. Our upbringing influences interests and activities that determine what French sociologist Pierre Bourdieu (1984) called *habitus*—the habits of speech and lifestyle that determine where one will feel comfortable and knowledgeable. Upper-class parents emphasize flexibility, autonomy, and creativity because they expect their children to step into positions that require such characteristics. Poor and working-class parents stress obedience, honesty, and

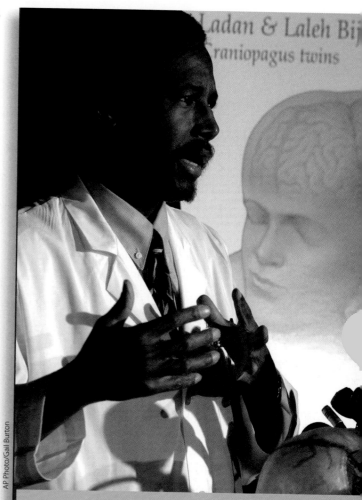

AP Photo/Gail Burton

Children raised in poor families can be upwardly mobile. Dr. Benjamin S. Carson is a world-renowned physician who is currently Director of Pediatric Neurosurgery at the prestigious Johns Hopkins Hospital in Baltimore, Maryland. Benjamin was 8 years old when his mother, who married when she was only 13, divorced his father. Mrs. Carson sometimes worked three jobs at a time to provide for Benjamin and his older brother, Curtis. When the boys' grades fell, Mrs. Carson limited their watching television and wouldn't let them play until they had finished their homework. She required her sons to read two library books a week and to give her written reports, even though she could barely understand the reports because she had left school after third grade. Since the founding of the Carson Scholars Fund in 1994, Dr. Carson and his wife have distributed 3,400 scholarships to graduating high-school seniors to attend college. In 2008, President Bush awarded Dr. Carson a Medal of Freedom, the nation's highest civilian award, for his "groundbreaking contributions to medicine and his inspiring efforts to help America's youth fulfill their potential" (Nitkin 2008: 7B).

appearance—the marks of respectability that many employers expect.

Connections and chance are especially important factors in upward mobility. Many people get jobs by word-of-mouth rather than by searching newspaper ads or Jobs.com. In a candid autobiographical sketch, sociologist S. M. Miller (2001: 1, 3) described his rise in academia, where connections and networking, rather than merit, "made the difference." He concluded that many employment decisions are based not on a person's individual abilities, but on the "social capital of connections—the inequitable distribution of access to people who can help you get a good job."

6 Why There Are Haves and Have-nots

hy are societies stratified? *Table 8.2* summarizes the key points of functionalist, conflict, feminist, and symbolic interactionist theories. Let's begin by looking

at a long-standing debate between functionalists and conflict theorists on why there are haves and have-nots.

FUNCTIONALIST PERSPECTIVES: STRATIFICATION BENEFITS SOCIETY

Functionalists see stratification as both necessary and inevitable because social class provides each individual a place in the social world and motivates people to contribute to society. Without a system of unequal rewards, functionalists argue, many important jobs wouldn't be performed.

The Davis–Moore Thesis

Sociologists Kingsley Davis and Wilbert Moore (1945) developed the most influential functionalist perspective on social stratification that persists today. The **Davis–Moore thesis,** as it is commonly called, asserts that social stratification benefits society. The key arguments of the Davis–Moore thesis can be summarized as follows:

1. **Every society must fill a wide variety of positions and ensure that people accomplish important tasks.** In the United States, we need teachers, doctors, farmers, trash collectors, engineers, secretaries, plumbers, police officers, and so on.

2. **Some positions are more important than others for a society's survival.** Doctors, for example,

TABLE 8.2
Sociological Explanations of Social Stratification

PERSPECTIVE	LEVEL OF ANALYSIS	KEY POINTS
Functionalist	Macro	• Fills social positions that are necessary for a society's survival • Motivates people to succeed and ensures that the most qualified people will fill the most important positions
Conflict	Macro	• Encourages workers' exploitation and promotes the interests of the rich and powerful • Ignores a wealth of talent among the poor
Feminist	Macro and micro	• Constructs numerous barriers in patriarchal societies that limit women's achieving wealth, status, and prestige • Requires most women, not men, to juggle domestic and employment responsibilities that impede upward mobility
Symbolic Interactionist	Micro	• Shapes stratification through socialization, everyday interaction, and group membership • Reflects social class identification through symbols, especially products that signify social status

In 2009, comedian Jerry Seinfeld earned $85 million. Do his earnings reflect his contribution to society, especially compared with teachers, physicians, dentists, trash collectors, computer scientists, and others?

provide more critical services to ensure a society's survival than do lawyers, engineers, or bankers.

3. **The most qualified people must fill the most important positions.** Some jobs require more skill, training, or intelligence than others because they are more demanding, and it's often difficult to replace the workers. Pilots, for example, must have more years of training and aren't replaced as easily as flight attendants.

4. **Society must offer greater rewards to motivate the most qualified people to fill the most important positions.** People won't undergo many years of education or training unless they are rewarded by money, power, status, and/or prestige. If doctors and nurses earned the same salaries, there wouldn't be much incentive for doctors to spend so many years earning a medical degree.

According to the Davis–Moore thesis and other functionalist perspectives, then, stratification and inequality are necessary to motivate people to work hard and to succeed. In open class systems, functionalists claim, inequality reflects the existence of a **meritocracy,** a belief that individuals are rewarded for what they do and how well rather than on the basis of their ascribed status.

Critical Evaluation

Melvin Tumin (1953) was the first sociologist to challenge the Davis–Moore thesis. First, he argued, societies don't always reward the positions that are the most im-

portant for its members' survival. For example, by age 29, golfer Tiger Woods was earning almost $100 million a year. Most doctors don't earn such sums during their entire working lives. If the highest-paid professional athletes, actors, and pop musicians went on strike, many of us would probably barely notice. If, on the other hand, garbage collectors, teachers, doctors, truck drivers, and mail carriers refused to work, society would grind to a halt. Thus, according to Tumin, there's little association between earnings and the jobs that keep a society going.

Second, Tumin argued, Davis and Moore overlook the many ways that stratification limits the discovery of talent. Where wealth is differentially distributed, for instance, access to education, especially higher education, depends on the wealth of one's parents. As a result, large segments of the population are likely to be deprived of the chance to even discover what their talents are, and society loses.

Third, Tumin criticized Davis and Moore for ignoring the critical role of inheritance. In upper social classes, sons and daughters don't have to worry about jobs because their inherited wealth guarantees a lifetime income. Even if class differences were eliminated today, it would take low-income families an average of six generations (about 120 years) to reduce the wealth gap that has accumulated over hundreds of years (Isaacs 2007c).

meritocracy a belief that individuals are rewarded for what they do and how well rather than on the basis of their ascribed status.

bourgeoisie those who own the means of production and can amass wealth and power.

CONFLICT PERSPECTIVES: STRATIFICATION HURTS SOCIETY

Like Tumin, conflict theorists maintain that social stratification is dysfunctional because it harms individuals and societies. In the mid-nineteenth century, Karl Marx spent much of his life in the midst of the enormous and tumultuous changes taking place during the Industrial Revolution in England (see Chapter 1). His analysis (1934) of social class and inequality has had a profound influence on modern sociology, especially conflict theory.

Capitalism Benefits the Rich

Marx was aware that a diversity of classes can exist at any one time, but he predicted that capitalist societies would ultimately be reduced to two social classes: the capitalist class, or bourgeoisie; and the working class, or proletariat. The **bourgeoisie,** those who own the means of production, such as factories, land, banks, and other sources of income, can amass wealth and power. The **proletariat,** workers who sell their labor for wages, earn barely enough to survive.

As the numbers of oppressed and alienated workers increased, Marx said, the proletariat would overthrow the bourgeoisie. "A century after his death, it is apparent that Marx was a better sociologist than he was a prophet" (Gilbert 2008: 7) because revolutions have not occurred in capitalist countries.

Conflict theorists agree with Marx, however, that social stratification benefits the rich at the expense of workers. A major example is **corporate welfare,** an array of direct subsidies, tax breaks, and assistance that the government has created for businesses (see Chapter 11). For example, during the current financial crisis that began in late 2007, so far Americans will have to pay almost $10 trillion to bail out badly managed banks and financial institutions, which comes out to almost $37,000 per person and $88,000 per taxpayer (Barker 2009 and author's calculations). Such estimates are conservative because they don't include inflation and the interest on the debt incurred by the bailout. Some expect the total cost of the bailout to increase to $23 trillion (Javers 2009). Despite the astoundingly huge handouts, the CEOs of the collapsed corporations continue to give themselves bonuses as large as $9 million per person (Hancock 2009).

Critical Evaluation

Some scholars have criticized Marxian and later conflict theories for several reasons. First, even though the concentration of corporate wealth has increased during the last 100 years, the polarization of classes and impoverishment of workers that Marx expected in industrialized countries has not come about. In fact, many people's income has increased considerably since Marx's day, there's an abundance of manufactured goods in capitalist societies, and welfare programs dilute widespread unrest (Glassman 2000).

Second, some question whether people always act primarily out of economic self-interest. For example, Chuck Feeney, the founder of Duty Free Shoppers, has already given $4 billion of his fortune to charities and has instructed his board to donate the rest (another $4 billion) by 2016 (Roosevelt 2008).

Third, functionalists, in particular, criticize conflict theorists for underrating the ability of individuals to be upwardly mobile. They maintain that if people really want to succeed, they can do so by working hard and making sacrifices.

FEMINIST PERSPECTIVES: WOMEN ARE ALMOST ALWAYS AT THE BOTTOM

For feminist scholars, functionalist and conflict theories are limited because they typically focus on men in describing and analyzing social stratification and social class. As a result, women are largely invisible.

Patriarchy Benefits Most Men, Not Women

Patriarchy, according to feminist sociologists, undermines the upward mobility of even the most talented women. For example, of the world's top 20 billionaires, only three were women, and all had inherited their wealth from a father or father-in-law (Kroll and Miller 2010). Of the 39 women among the richest CEOs on the *Forbes 400* list, the majority also inherited their wealth from their fathers or husbands ("Cash Countesses" 2007; "Billionaires 2008" 2008). And among CEOs, the best-paid men earn six times more than the best-paid women, and their bonuses are three times higher (Dobrzynski 2008).

Entertainment is one of the few industries where women have achieved a significant degree of economic success; of the 100 top-paid U.S. celebrities in 2009, 32 were women (Rose 2009). Many (like singers Madonna and Beyoncé) are well-known, but only a few, including Angelina Jolie, also enjoy some measure of political recognition and prestige, not just name recognition, for their humanitarian work in developing countries.

Feminist theorists contend that, in a patriarchal system, men shape the social stratification system because they control a disproportionate share of wealth, prestige, and power. On a micro level, individual women may have more power than men if they earn the major portion of a household's income (Galinsky et al. 2009). On a macro level, however, the feminization of poverty often results in women's downward mobility. In addition, women often have to overcome economic and educational inequities, as well as juggle domestic and workplace responsibilities (see Chapters 9, 12, and 13).

Critical Evaluation

Feminist sociologists point out that patriarchy affects both social stratification and social class, but they typically focus on poor women (see Kendall 2002). A related criticism is that many feminist scholars examine women's and men's income differences and the effects of social stratification on both sexes but say little about social mobility, especially for middle- and working-class women.

SYMBOLIC INTERACTIONIST PERSPECTIVES: PEOPLE CREATE AND SHAPE STRATIFICATION

Symbolic interactionists focus on how people act within social classes rather than why there is stratification. They address micro-level issues such as how people learn their social positions in everyday life and how such learning affects their social class and lifestyles.

People's Beliefs and Actions Reflect Their Social Class

People in upper, middle, working, and lower classes interact and socialize their children differently because of family background, education level, and income. Those in different social classes also acquire and use symbols differently. For example, lower-upper class members may engage in conspicuous consumption to show off their new wealth (by buying a yacht, for example), whereas people in the middle class may go into debt to give an appearance of being richer than they are.

Critical Evaluation

Symbolic interactionists' theories are important in understanding the everyday processes that underlie social stratification, but there are several weaknesses. First, the theories don't explain why—despite the same family background and socialization—one child in a family is upwardly mobile, whereas another plunges into poverty.

Second, it's not clear why some people (across social classes and racial/ethnic groups, and in both sexes) are more obsessed than others with status symbols and visibility. For example, some billionaires live modestly and avoid the media, whereas others, such as billionaire Donald Trump, constantly show off their wealth and even do television commercials to increase their billions.

Finally, conflict theorists, especially, fault symbolic interactionists for ignoring structural factors—including corporate welfare and inherited wealth—that create and reinforce inequality. As you'll see in Chapter 14, for example, many talented and intelligent teenagers drop out of high school because of limited family income and other resources.

For symbolic interactionists, people in lower social classes show deference to those in higher social classes. Doing so confirms the inequality of the relationship and reinforces each person's position in the social hierarchy.

7 Inequality Across Societies

So far, we've focused on U.S. stratification. All societies are stratified, but the inequality varies a great deal. Many people describe our planet as a global village in which societies are connected economically, politically, and socially because of technology. This is true for only a handful at the top of the class hierarchy. Most people live in very different, separate, and unequal worlds.

LIVING WORLDS APART

The richest 2 percent of adults in the world own more than half of global wealth. In contrast, the bottom half of the adult population owns barely 1 percent of global wealth. The top 5 percent of individuals in the world receive about one third of total world income, compared with only 5 percent of world income for the poorest 40 percent (Davies et al. 2006; Milanovic 2006). Such differences in individual wealth are astounding, but what about variations across countries?

The World Bank (2008) describes global stratification in terms of high-income, middle-income, and low-income countries. There are many poor people in high-income countries and some very affluent people in low-income countries, but *Table 8.3* provides an overview of the enormous economic disparities across countries.

High-income countries have a developed industrial economy and an annual gross national income (GNI) of

TABLE 8.3
Global Economic Inequality, 2006

	NUMBER OF COUNTRIES	POPULATION	PERCENTAGE OF WORLD POPULATION	TOTAL GNI	PERCENTAGE OF WORLD GNI	GNI PER CAPITA
Low income	53	2.4 billion	40	$1.6 million	3	$ 649
Middle income	96	3.1 billion	48	$9.4 million	19	$ 3,053
High income	60	1 billion	15	$37.7 billion	78	$36,608
World	209	6.5 billion		$48 billion		$ 7,448
United States		300 million	5	$13 billion	28	$44,710

Note: GNI is the Gross National Income.

Source: Based on material in World Bank 2008.

almost $37,000 per person. The combined population of these countries is only 15 percent of the world's population but enjoys 78 percent of the world's income. The 60 high-income countries include the United States and Canada in North America; Great Britain, France, Germany, Portugal, Norway, Switzerland, and other industrialized nations in Western Europe; Japan in Asia; Australia and New Zealand in Oceania; and Israel. To a greater extent than other countries, high-income countries have access to health services, safe water, and higher education.

Middle-income countries, which comprise about 48 percent of the world's population, have a developing industrial economy and a considerably lower GPI per person than high-income countries. The 96 middle-income countries include most of the European countries that broke away from the Soviet Union in 1991, Russia, Mexico, Latin America, several countries in northern and southern Africa (including Algeria, Libya, and Angola), and many countries in the Middle East (including Turkey, Iran, Iraq, and Saudi Arabia). Most people in middle-income countries have less access to education, health services, food, and amenities such as electricity, automobiles, and telephones than people in high-income countries, but their standard of living is higher than in low-income countries.

Low-income countries are the least industrialized and are largely agricultural. Most people in these countries are peasant farmers or live in villages. The 53 nations in this group, comprising 40 percent of the world's population, have an average GNI of $649 per person. These countries are primarily in Central and East Africa, parts of Asia (Pakistan, India, and China), and Indonesia (Java, Sumatra, and Borneo). People in low-income countries experience a low standard of living, are impoverished, and have little access to health services, education, and safe water.

In 2006, of the world's 6.5 billion people, almost half lived on less than $2 a day and 1.2 billion—almost a fifth—on less than $1 a day, what economists classify as extreme poverty. About 93 percent of those in extreme poverty live in three regions: East Asia, South Asia, and sub-Saharan Africa. In some countries, such as Haiti, where 75 percent of the population earns less than $2 a day, the most destitute feed their children with patties made of mud, oil, and sugar. Those who survive starvation experience stunted physical growth, permanent mental retardation, lower intelligence levels, and a reduced capacity to learn by age 2. Such problems create a vicious cycle: Hunger in childhood can lead to permanently dulled minds, an inability to pursue a livelihood, and having children with a diminished mental capacity (Martens 2005; World Food Program 2006; Lacey 2008).

WHY IS INEQUALITY UNIVERSAL?

Many theories try to explain why inequality is universal, but three of the most influential have been modernization theory, dependency theory, and world-system theory.

Modernization theory claims that low-income countries are poor because the leaders don't have attitudes and values that lead to experimentation and the use of modern technology. Instead, policy makers adhere to traditional customs that isolate them and prevent them from competing in a global economy. In effect, modernization theory blames poor nations for their poverty and other problems. After the key foundations of modernity and capitalism are in place, this perspective maintains, low-income countries will prosper.

Dependency theory contends that the main reason why low-income countries are poor is because they are pawns that high-income countries exploit and dominate. Rich nations wield an enormous amount of power by exporting jobs overseas, manipulating foreign aid, draining less powerful countries of their resources, penetrating other countries with multinational corporations, and coercing national governments to comply with their interests (e.g., by not passing environmental laws). In effect, according to dependency theorists, high-income countries benefit because the poor provide cheap labor and aren't powerful enough to protest even though they work in hazardous conditions and earn less than $1 a day.

More recently, *world-system theory,* similar to dependency theory, argues that "the economic realities of the world system help rich countries stay rich while poor countries stay poor" (Bradshaw and Wallace 1996: 44). That is, those countries that dominate the world economy (like the United States) influence the economies of low-income countries because the workers depend on external markets for jobs. High-income countries can extract raw materials (such as diamonds and oil) with little cost. They can also set the prices for the agricultural products that low-income countries export regardless of market prices, forcing many small farmers to abandon their fields because they can't pay for labor, fertilizer, and other costs (Carl 2002).

None of these perspectives explains inequality across *all* societies. Instead, global inequality is due to a combination of factors, including a country's values and customs, and exploitation by high-income countries.

During the past few years, we've heard about the booming economies of India and China, but not everyone has profited. In India, some people have become enormously wealthy, whereas others remain very poor. A tent city in India houses many of the workers who earn about $1.30 a day building new office towers for the affluent nearby (left). In China, 10 percent of urban households control 40 percent of urban wealth. A man in Shanghai begs as wealthier residents pass by (right).

Gender and gender roles

are social creations.

Chip Wass

9 Gender and Sexuality

How do women and men differ? For the average American male, compared with the average American female, three pairs of shoes are more than enough, he can be showered and ready in 10 minutes, his underwear is $10 for a three pack, a 5-day vacation requires only one carry-on bag, and his bathroom lines in public restrooms are 80 percent shorter. Do such jokes stereotype women and men? Or contain a kernel of truth? This chapter describes how gender, sex, and sexuality shape our lives. We'll examine sexual orientation, some current controversies, and sociological explanations of gender inequality and sexuality. Let's begin by looking at whether women and men are as different as some self-help writers claim.

Key Topics

In this chapter, we'll explore the following topics:

1 Female-Male Similarities and Differences

2 Contemporary Gender Stratification and Inequality

3 Sexuality and Human Development

4 Some Current Controversies about Sexuality

5 Sociological Explanations of Gender Inequality and Sexuality

what do you think?

Having sex is the best way to show one's love.

1	2	3	4	5	6	7
strongly agree						strongly disagree

1 Female-Male Similarities and Differences

many people use the terms *sex* and *gender* interchangeably, but they have distinct meanings. The terms are related, but sex is a biological designation, whereas gender and gender roles are social creations.

SEX AND GENDER

Sex refers to the biological characteristics with which we are born—chromosomes, anatomy, hormones, and other physical and physiological attributes. These attributes *influence* our behavior (such as shaving beards and wearing bras), but do *not determine* how we think, feel, and act. Whether we see ourselves and others as feminine or masculine depends on gender, a considerably more complex concept than sex.

sex the biological characteristics with which we are born.

gender learned attitudes and behaviors that characterize women and men.

Gender refers to learned attitudes and behaviors that characterize women and men. Gender is based on social

gender identity a perception of oneself as either masculine or feminine.

gender roles the characteristics, attitudes, feelings, and behaviors that society expects of females and males.

gender stereotypes expectations about how people will look, act, think, and feel based on their sex.

sexism an attitude or behavior that discriminates against one sex, usually females, based on the assumed superiority of the other sex.

and cultural expectations rather than on physical traits. Thus, most people are *born* either male or female, but we *learn* to be women or men because we associate conventional behavior patterns with each sex. In many societies, for example, women are expected to look young, thin, and attractive, and men are expected to amass as much income and wealth as possible.

GENDER IDENTITY AND GENDER ROLES

Children develop a **gender identity,** or a perception of themselves as either masculine or feminine, early in life. Many Mexican baby girls but not boys have pierced ears, for example, and hairstyles and clothing for American toddlers differ by sex. Gender identity, which typically corresponds to a person's biological sex, usually remains relatively fixed throughout life.

About 90 percent of Americans believe that women are more emotional than men. In fact, both sexes experience emotions such as anger, happiness, and sadness just as deeply. What differs is *how* women and men express their emotions because men are more likely to suppress their feelings, whereas women tend to show their emotions more openly (Newport 2001; Simon and Nath 2004).

Such differences are because of **gender roles**—the characteristics, attitudes, feelings, and behaviors that society expects of females and males. A review of research on the differences between the sexes conducted between 1990 and 2004

Ana Carolina Reston, a 21-year-old Brazilian model, died from complications resulting from anorexia, a dangerous eating disorder characterized by self-starvation and excessive weight loss. She was 5 feet 8 inches tall and weighed 88 pounds. In 2009, American model Kate Moss drew fire from eating disorder experts when she said that her personal motto was "Nothing tastes as good as skinny feels."

concluded that females and males are much more alike than different on a number of characteristics, including cognitive abilities, verbal and nonverbal communication, leadership traits, and self-esteem (Hyde 2005). Still, sociologists often describe our social roles as *gendered*, in that males and females are often treated differently because of their sex (Howard and Hollander 1997).

In the United States, people are more likely now than in the past to pursue jobs and other activities based on their ability and interests rather than their sex. For the most part, however, American society still has fairly rigid gender roles and widespread **gender stereotypes,** expectations about how people will look, act, think, and feel based on their sex.

2 Contemporary Gender Stratification and Inequality

November 2009 *Newsweek* cover featured Sarah Palin, who was governor of Alaska from 2006 to 2009, and the Republican nominee for Vice President of the United States during the 2008 presidential election. Most politicians are delighted to be on a magazine's cover, but Palin complained that the photo was sexist because she's in "sexy" running clothes rather than being portrayed as a serious politician (Orr 2009).

Sexism is an attitude or behavior that discriminates against one sex, usually women, based on the assumed superiority of the other sex. Much sexism, such as that of the Palin photo, is subtle because it diminishes Palin's status as a politician and suggests that she shouldn't be taken as seriously as her male counterparts, none of whom have ever appeared on *Newsweek* covers in sexy poses. Because most people have internalized beliefs that women are inferior to men, we don't notice such discrimination (Benokraitis 1997).

Considerable sexism is still blatant, however, because it's visible, intentional, and easily documented. According to numerous women bloggers, for example, cybersexism (including stalking, death threats, and hate speech) is prevalent, and women whose user names indicate their sex are 25 times more likely than men to experience online harassment (Valenti 2007).

REUTERS/L'Equipe Agence/Landov

Was Sarah Palin justified in complaining that this photo of her on a *Newsweek* **cover was sexist? Have you ever seen any male politicians who have graced newsmagazine covers appear in clothing that reflected their "sexiness" rather than their authority and seriousness in running for a political office?**

Boys and men also experience sexism. One of my students wrote the following during an online discussion of gender roles:

Some parents live their dreams through their sons by forcing them to be in sports. I disagree with this but want my [9-year-old] son to be "all boy." He's the worst player on the basketball team at school and wanted to take dance lessons, including ballet. I assured him that this was not going to happen. I'm going to enroll him in soccer and see if he does better.

Is this mother suppressing her son's natural dancing talent? We'll never know because she, like many parents,

At an early age, sex-appropriate children's toys prepare girls and boys for future adult roles. Do the toys reflect children's own choices or gender socialization by parents, teachers, other adults, and the media?

expects her son to fulfill gender roles that meet with society's approval.

Sexism is widespread due to **gender stratification**—people's unequal access to wealth, power, status, prestige, opportunity, and other valued resources because of their sex. We'll examine some of this stratification in greater depth in later chapters. For now, let's look briefly at gender inequality in the family, education, workplace, and politics.

> **gender stratification**
> people's unequal access to wealth, power, status, prestige, and other valued resources because of their sex.

GENDER AND FAMILY LIFE

Americans have more choices today, but is family life less gendered than in the past? Probably not as much as we think. If Americans were free to do either, half of women and 68 percent of men would prefer to work outside the home rather than stay home to take care of their house and family. Few adults have this either-or choice, however. Instead, nearly three out of four married mothers are in the labor force, compared with two out of four in 1970 (Saad 2007; U.S. Census Bureau 2010).

Having a husband creates an extra 7 hours of housework a week for a woman, but many couples say that they share domestic tasks more equally than their parents or grandparents did. Still, there continues to be a division of labor along traditional gender lines; for example, 68 percent of wives do the laundry (Newport 2008; Stafford 2008).

Men are doing more in the home, but women shoulder twice as much child care and housework as men. Women's domestic work declined from 50 hours in 1965 to 26 hours in 2004, whereas men's increased from 12 to 16 hours. These changes are due partly to men's greater efforts and partly to a decrease in the amount that women do because of having full-time employment (Bianchi et al. 2006; England 2006).

GENDER AND EDUCATION

Many teachers and schools send gendered messages to children that follow them from preschool to college. When children enter kindergarten, they perform similarly on both reading and mathematics tests. By the third grade, however, boys, on average, outperform girls in math and science, whereas girls outperform boys in reading. These gaps increase throughout high school (Dee 2006). Some of the reasons for these differences, as you'll see in Chapter 14, include parental socialization and teacher expectations. Also, many counselors still steer girls and boys into courses that focus on gender-stereotyped disciplines (such as social work for girls and engineering for boys).

In higher education, "women face more obstacles as faculty…than they do as managers and directors in corporate America" (West and Curtis 2006: 4). Even when women earn Ph.D.'s in male-dominated fields, they are less likely to be hired than men. For example, women have received more than 45 percent of all doctorates in biology since 1990, but only 14 percent of full-time biology professors are women (Handelsman et al. 2005). Once hired, women faculty members are less likely than men to be promoted. Since 1982, one third of all recipients of Ph.D. degrees have been women, but men still dominate the rank of full professor (see *Table 9.1*).

GENDER AND THE WORKPLACE

There has been progress toward greater workplace equality, but we still have a long way to go. In the United States (as around the world), many jobs are segregated by sex, there are large gender pay gaps, and

YOSHIKAZU TSUNO/AFP/Getty Images

The Butler Café is very popular in Japan. It's a place for young women to unwind from the stresses of the outside world, including pressure to conform and marry. The only men present are butlers who respond in less than 6 seconds if a customer rings a golden bell located on each table.

numerous women experience sexual harassment and pregnancy discrimination.

Gender-Segregated Work and Gender Pay Gaps

American women still tend to cluster in 21 of 500 occupational categories (WAGE 2006). Generally, women's jobs tend to be "feminine"—those that require nurturing, caregiving, serving others, and working with people. The occupations that men dominate tend to be "masculine"—manual, relatively autonomous, often containing an element of danger, and requiring technical skills or training.

A number of U.S. occupations are almost entirely filled by either women or men. For example, between 92 and 98 percent of all registered nurses, child care workers, receptionists, and preschool and kindergarten teachers are women. At least 98 percent of all steel workers, mechanics, plumbers, and loading machine operators are men. Women have made some progress in the higher paying professional occupations, but 70 percent of physicians, 75 percent of architects, and 78 percent of dentists are men (U.S. Department of Labor 2007).

In 2008, women who worked full-time year-round had a median income of $35,745 compared with $46,367 for men (DeNavas-Walt et al. 2009). This means that women earned 77 cents for every dollar men earned. In effect, *the average woman would have to work almost 4 extra months every year to make the same wages as a man* (Hartmann et al. 2006).

This income difference between women and men is the **gender pay gap** (also called the *wage gap*, *pay gap*, and *gender wage gap*). Over a lifetime, the average

TABLE 9.1
As Rank Increases, the Number of Women Faculty Members Decreases

RANK	PERCENTAGE OF FULL-TIME FEMALE FACULTY MEMBERS
Professor	26
Associate Professor	40
Assistant Professor	47
Instructor	54

Note: Of the almost 704,000 full-time faculty members in 2007, 42 percent were women.
Source: Based on U.S. Department of Education, 2008, Table 249.

woman who works full-time and year-round for 47 years is deprived of a significant amount of money because of the gender pay gap: $700,000 for high-school graduates, $1.2 million for college graduates, and more than $2 million for women with a professional degree, as in business, medicine, or law. Because raises are typically based on a percentage of one's annual income, the lower the wage, the lower the raise. Lower wages and salaries reduce women's savings, as well as their purchasing power and quality of life, and bring them lower Social Security payments after retirement (Murphy and Graff 2005; Soguel 2009).

Not only do women earn less than men at all educational levels, but the gender pay gap increases as the level of educational attainment increases (see *Figure 9.1*).

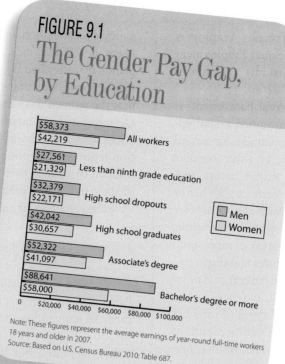

FIGURE 9.1
The Gender Pay Gap, by Education

	Men	Women
All workers	$58,373	$42,219
Less than ninth grade education	$27,561	$21,329
High school dropouts	$32,379	$22,171
High school graduates	$42,042	$30,657
Associate's degree	$52,322	$41,097
Bachelor's degree or more	$88,641	$58,000

Note: These figures represent the average earnings of year-round full-time workers 18 years and older in 2007.
Source: Based on U.S. Census Bureau 2010: Table 687.

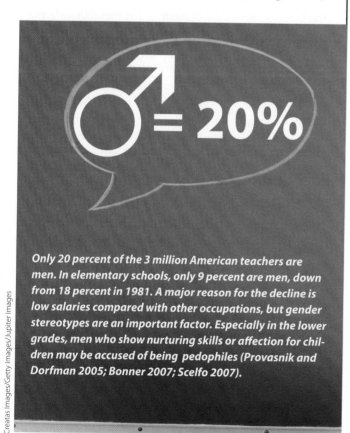

Only 20 percent of the 3 million American teachers are men. In elementary schools, only 9 percent are men, down from 18 percent in 1981. A major reason for the decline is low salaries compared with other occupations, but gender stereotypes are an important factor. Especially in the lower grades, men who show nurturing skills or affection for children may be accused of being pedophiles (Provasnik and Dorfman 2005; Bonner 2007; Scelfo 2007).

Female high-school graduates earn 73 percent of what their male counterparts earn, but women's earnings drop to 65 percent of men's for those with at least a college degree. (Note in *Figure 9.1* that female college graduates earn only slightly more than men with an associate's degree.) As you'll see in Chapter 12, men earn more than women in *every* occupational category, and the gender pay gap increases at the higher paying managerial and professional levels.

The wage gap can be partially explained by differences in education, experience, and time in the labor force, but about 41 percent of the gap is the result of sex discrimination in hiring, promotion and pay, bias against mothers, and occupational segregation. That is, a wage gap remains even when women and men have the same education, occupation, number of years in a job, seniority, marital status, number of children, and are similar on numerous other factors (Boraas and Rodgers 2003; Blau and Kahn 2006).

Why is there a gender pay gap? A common explanation is that women choose fields with lower earnings (such as health care and teaching in elementary and middle schools), whereas men tend to choose higher paying fields (such as engineering, computer science, and the physical sciences). This doesn't explain, however, as you'll see in Chapter 12, why women have lower earnings than men in both high- and low-paying occupations. Second, some scholars maintain that women—especially those in professional, managerial, and executive positions—are getting stuck under glass ceilings. Even in federal agencies, men with much less experience and lower educational levels are routinely promoted over more accomplished women (Stone 2007; Waldref 2008). Third, mothers are more likely than fathers (or women with no children) to work part time, take leaves, or take a break from the workforce to raise children—factors that reduce wages and salaries (Dey and Hill 2007).

Sexual Harassment and Pregnancy Discrimination

Sexual harassment is the fastest-growing type of employment discrimination. Almost 187,000 complaints were filed between 1997 and 2009, 85 percent of them by female employees (U.S. Equal Employment Opportunity Commission 2010b).

Sexual harassment is any unwanted sexual advance, request for sexual favors, or other conduct of a sexual nature that makes a person uncomfortable and interferes with her or his work. It includes *verbal behavior* (such as pressures for dates or demands for sexual favors in return for hiring, promotion, or tenure, as well as the threat of rape), *nonverbal behavior* (such as indecent gestures and displaying posters, photos, or drawings of a sexual nature), and *physical contact* (such as pinching, touching, and rape).

Sexual harassment cuts across all types of jobs but is especially common in male-dominated occupations where female newcomers are unwelcome. Among firefighters, for example, 97 percent of whom are men, many women have complained about offensive behavior such as finding feces in the women's shower stalls, unwanted touching, being referred to as "bitches," and attempted rape (Banks 2006).

The federal Pregnancy Discrimination Act of 1978 makes it illegal for employers with more than 15 workers to fire, demote, or penalize a pregnant employee. Some state laws extend this protection to companies with as few as four employees.

Despite such laws, the Equal Employment Opportunity Commission (EEOC) reports that charges of pregnancy discrimination have increased 33 percent in recent years. In 2009 alone, nearly 6,200 women filed complaints that they had been fired, demoted, or had some of their responsibilities taken away when employers learned that the women were pregnant (U.S. Equal Employment Opportunity Commission 2010a). The EEOC complaints about both sexual harassment and pregnancy discrimination represent only the tip of the iceberg because only a fraction of women ever take action: Many aren't aware of their rights, and others fear losing their jobs or don't have the resources to pursue lengthy lawsuits.

GENDER AND POLITICS

In 1872, Victoria Chaflin Woodhull of the Equal Rights Party was the first female presidential candidate. Since then, 36 women have sought the nation's highest office. In 2007, Senator Hillary Rodham Clinton engaged in a "whisker-close but losing battle to become the first woman major party presidential nominee," a historic run that came close to breaking the glass ceiling of a male-dominated U.S. presidency (Halloran 2008: 34).

Unlike a number of other countries (including Great Britain, Germany, India, Israel, Pakistan, Argentina, Chile, and Philippines), the United States has never had a woman serving as president or even vice-president. In the U.S. Congress, 83 percent of the members are men. In several other important elective offices, only one of four decision makers is a woman (see *Table 9.2*), and this number hasn't changed much since the early 1990s (Center for American Women and Politics 2010).

Worldwide, the United States lags far behind many other countries, including some developing nations, in women's political empowerment (measured by the number of women serving as head of state or in decision-making government positions). Of 128 countries, the United States ranks only 77th in women's political empowerment (Hausmann et al. 2007). According to the president of a U.S. organization working to advance women in political leadership, "It will take [women] till 2063 to reach parity [with men]" (Feldmann 2008: 2).

As you'll see in Chapter 11, women's voting rates in the United States have been higher than men's since 1984. Why, in contrast, are there so few women in political office? One reason may be that women, socialized to be nurturers and volunteers, see themselves as supporters rather than active doers. As a result, they may spend many hours organizing support for a candidate rather than running for a political office themselves.

Second, women are less likely than men to receive encouragement to run for office from a political source

"Are you hiring me because I'm cheap, I'm qualified, or I'm cheap and qualified?"

Liza Donnelly, Women's Enews

(such as a party leader). As a result, even successful women are twice as likely as men to rate themselves as not qualified to run for office. In contrast, men are two-thirds more likely than women with similar credentials to consider themselves qualified or very qualified to run for office (Lawless and Fox 2005).

Third, a lingering sexism is still present in the thinking among both men and women that "from the pulpit to the presidency," men are better leaders (Tucker 2007: A9). The pervasive sexism in media coverage of political candidates was especially evident during the 2008 presidential campaigns. From the beginning, reporters and news commentators criticized Senator Clinton's appearance ("she looked haggard") and voice ("cackling laugh"), described her as a "nagging wife," and referred to her as Hillary but never called Senators Obama and McCain by their first names, or denigrated their appearance or other attributes (Long 2008: 11A; Wakeman 2008: 61).

3 Sexuality and Human Development

i n the movie *Annie Hall,* a therapist asks two lovers how often they have sex. The man rolls his eyes, and complains, "Hardly ever, maybe three times a week!" The woman exclaims, "Constantly, three times a week!" As this exam-ple illustrates, sex is more important for some people than others. Sexuality is considerably more complex than just physical contact because, among other things, it's a product of our sexual identity, sexual orientation, and sexual scripts.

SEXUAL IDENTITY

Our **sexual identity** is our awareness of ourselves as male or female and the ways that we express our sexual values, attitudes, feelings, and beliefs. It involves placing ourselves in a category created by society (such as female and heterosexual) and learning, both consciously and unconsciously, how to act in that category.

Most people's sexual identity corresponds with their biological sex and their gender identity (seeing oneself as feminine or masculine), but not always. As you'll see shortly, some people are transgendered because they feel trapped in the wrong body. Early socialization reinforces children's gender identity because parents treat and interact with their sons and daughters differently (see Chapter 4). Especially in high school, both peers and teachers reinforce a heterosexual and gender identity.

For example, sexuality curricula rarely address homosexuality, teachers and students sometimes exchange jokes about homosexuals, and "You're a faggot" is an epithet that censures male students who behave in any way that can be "defined as unmasculine" (Pascoe 2007: 57).

SEXUAL ORIENTATION

Our sexual identity incorporates a **sexual orientation**, a preference for sexual partners of the same sex, of the opposite sex, of both sexes, or neither sex:

- **Homosexuals** (from the Greek root *homo,* meaning "same") are sexually attracted to people of the same sex. Male homosexuals prefer to be called *gay,* female homosexuals are called *lesbians,* and both gay men and lesbians are often referred to as *gays. Coming out* is a person's public announcement of a gay or lesbian sexual orientation.

sexual identity our awareness of ourselves as male or female and the ways that we express our sexual values, attitudes, feelings, and beliefs.

sexual orientation a preference for sexual partners of the same sex, of the opposite sex, of both sexes, or neither sex.

homosexuals those who are sexually attracted to people of the same sex.

TABLE 9.2
U.S. Women in Elective Offices, 2010

POLITICAL OFFICE	TOTAL NUMBER OF OFFICE HOLDERS	PERCENTAGE WHO ARE WOMEN
U.S. Congress	535	17
Senate	100	16
House of Representatives	436	16
State Elective Offices		
Governor	50	12
Lieutenant Governor	50	12
State Legislator	7,382	24
Attorney General	50	8
Secretary of State	50	24
State Treasurer	50	20
State Comptroller	50	8
Mayor (100 largest cities)	100	15

Source: Based on material at the Center for American Women and Politics 2010.

heterosexuals those who are sexually attracted to people of the opposite sex.

bisexuals those who are sexually attracted to members of both sexes.

asexuals those who lack any interest in or desire for sex.

transgendered people those who are transsexuals, intersexuals, or transvestites.

sexual script specifies the formal or informal norms for legitimate or unacceptable sexual activity, which individuals are eligible sexual partners, and the boundaries of sexual behavior.

- **Heterosexuals,** often called *straight*, are attracted to partners of the opposite sex.

- **Bisexuals,** sometimes called *bis*, are attracted to members of both sexes.

- **Asexuals** lack any interest in or desire for sex.

Heterosexuality is the predominant sexual orientation worldwide, but homosexuality exists in all known cultures.

Transgendered Sexual Orientations

Our cultural expectations dictate that we are female or male, but a number of people are transgendered and are "living on the boundaries of both sexes" (Lorber and Moore 2007: 141). **Transgendered people** encompass several groups:

- *Transsexuals* are people born with one biological sex but choose to live their life as another sex—either by consistently cross-dressing or by having their sex surgically altered.

- *Intersexuals* are people whose medical classification at birth is not clearly either male or female (this term has replaced *hermaphrodites*).

- *Transvestites* are people who cross-dress at times but don't necessarily consider themselves a member of the other sex.

Transgendered people include gays, heterosexuals, bisexuals, and men and women who don't identify themselves with any specific sexual orientation.

Prevalence of Homosexuality

How many Americans are gay men, lesbians, and bisexuals? No one knows for sure, largely because it's difficult to define and measure sexual orientation. For example, are people homosexual if they have ever engaged in same-sex behavior? What about people who have other-sex partners and desire same-sex partners but are afraid to act on this wish?

Researchers generally measure the prevalence of homosexuality by simply asking people whether they identify themselves as heterosexual or gay, lesbian, bi-

sexual, or transgendered (the acronym is GLBT). About 4 percent of Americans identify themselves as homosexual, and almost 5 percent describe themselves as bisexual. However, 18 percent have had same-sex sexual contact (Mosher et al. 2005).

For example, in what one author called being "on the down low," black men who sometimes have sex with other men see themselves as straight and don't disclose their male relationships to their female sex partners, friends, or family members (King 2004). Black men aren't the only ones on the down low: Married white men also frequent chat rooms and use code words such as bimm (bisexual married male) and "m4m" (married male for married male) (Vargas 2004).

SEXUAL SCRIPTS

We like to think that our sexual behavior is spontaneous, but most of us have internalized sexual scripts. A **sexual script** specifies the formal or informal norms for legitimate or unacceptable sexual activity, which individuals are eligible sexual partners, and the boundaries

Meredith (right) and Lynn Bacon remain married despite Meredith's sex change. Meredith, who used to be Wally, is a popular faculty member at the University of Nebraska. Some people were shocked by the transformation, but most students, faculty, and administrators were supportive. Meredith says that since her decision for the sex change at age 59, this is "the first time I've been completely happy" (Wilson 2005: A11).

Lauren Greenfield/INSTITUTE / © iStockphoto.com/Mike Bentley

of sexual behavior. Gender, race, and ethnicity, among other factors, shape our sexual scripts.

Gender and Sexual Scripts

Many sexually healthy men in their 20s to 40s use impotence drugs—such as Viagra and Cialis—because they believe the myth that a "real man" is always interested in sex and always ready to be a sexual superman (Setoodeh 2007). In reality, most women are more concerned about communication, finances, an equal distribution of housework, and sexual fidelity rather the number of times that men have sexual intercourse (see Benokraitis 2011).

Race/Ethnicity and Sexual Scripts

Race and ethnicity also shape sexual scripts. Among many Latinos, for example, "good women" aren't expected to be highly sexual or to take the initiative in sexual relations. Men, on the other hand, are expected to be passionate and to use sexual conquest as proof of masculinity. Whereas 77 percent of black women say they would have sex only if they were in love, only 43 percent of African American men agree. Among whites, boys engage in sex earlier than girls and have more sexual partners (Mahay et al. 2001; Centers for Disease Control and Prevention 2008).

WHAT DETERMINES SEXUAL ORIENTATION?

No one knows why people are heterosexual, homosexual, bisexual, or transgendered. *Biological theories* maintain that sexual orientation has a strong genetic basis because, at least for males, the more genes one shares with a gay male relative, the more likely it is that a male will be gay. Some biologists theorize that brain structure may also be associated with sexual orientation because the size of the hypothalamus—an organ deep in the center of the brain that is believed to regulate the sex drive—differs between heterosexual and gay men. Other scientists have found no evidence of a biological influence on homosexuality. If there's a strong genetic predisposition, gay children would come from gay households and straight children from straight households. This isn't the case, however, because most gay men and lesbians are raised by heterosexuals (Burr 1996; Golombok and Tasker 1996; Rice et al. 1999).

Social constructionist theories hold that sexual behavior is largely the result of social pressure and that culture, not biology, plays a large role in forming sexual identity. For example, and despite their homosexual in-clinations, many straight men who have sex with other men refuse to accept the possibility that they're gay or bisexual. In effect, then, and because of societal pressure to be straight, many gay men and lesbians are living heterosexual lives.

So far, no study has shown conclusively that there is a gay gene or that the environment causes sexual orientation. Instead, many researchers speculate that a combination of genetic and cultural factors may influence sexual orientation.

SOCIETAL REACTIONS TO HOMOSEXUALITY

In much of the Middle East and Africa, gay men and lesbians can be stoned, imprisoned, or killed ("Iranian Gays Present, Hidden" 2007; Londoño 2009). In the United States, the percentage of Americans who believe that homosexuality is an acceptable way of life increased from 43 percent in 1978 to 55 percent in 2008, and 89 percent say that gay men and lesbians should have equal rights in the workplace ("Homosexual Relations" 2008; Saad 2009).

There is growing acceptance of gay rights (except for same-sex marriage, as you'll see shortly), but why do millions of Americans condemn homosexuality? Two concepts—heterosexism and homophobia—provide some answers.

Heterosexism is a belief that heterosexuality is superior to and more natural than homosexuality or bisexuality. Like sexism, heterosexism pervades societal customs,

> **heterosexism** the belief that heterosexuality is superior to and more natural than homosexuality or bisexuality.

laws, and institutions. Examples of heterosexism in the United States include the continuing ban against lesbian and gay military personnel, and widespread hostility toward gay couples who want to formalize their committed relationships through marriage. As a result, many gays and lesbians still hide, deny, or try to suppress their sexual orientation to avoid attacks by heterosexuals.

Homophobia, the fear and hatred of homosexuality, is less overt today than in the past but is still widespread. Homophobia often manifests itself in *gay bashing*—threats, assaults, or acts of violence directed at homosexuals. In 2008, of the almost 9,200 hate crimes reported to law enforcement agencies, 18 percent of all hate crimes were against homosexuals, but much gay bashing is not reported (Federal Bureau of Investigation 2009).

Some Protestant denominations have welcomed gays and lesbians as members and ordained them as ministers and even bishops. Others—Episcopal, Lutheran, Methodist, Presbyterian, and United Church of Christ—find themselves divided over homosexuality. The Catholic Church denounces homosexuality as immoral and contrary to God's law, but many American Catholics believe that the church's view is outdated (Janofsky 2003).

Companies that welcome homosexual workers often enjoy positive public relations and attract well-educated gay men and lesbians. Numerous municipal jurisdictions, corporations, and smaller companies now extend more healthcare coverage and other benefits to their gay and lesbian employees and their partners than to unmarried heterosexuals who live together. In 2008, 125 of the *Fortune* 500 companies included "gender identity" in their nondiscrimination policies, compared with almost none in 2002. And among the largest corporations, 58 percent provided transgender benefits such as regular hormone treatment, psychological counseling, and paying for gender reassignment surgery (Belkin 2008). In effect, then, there is considerably less job discrimination against GLBTs than even 5 years ago.

4 Some Current Controversies about Sexuality

most Americans see sex as a private act, but many also feel that that there should be governmental control of some sexual expressions and decisions. Three of the most controversial issues today are abortion, same-sex marriage, and pornography.

ABORTION

Abortion is the expulsion of an embryo or fetus from the uterus. It can occur naturally—in *spontaneous abortion* (miscarriage)—or it can be induced medically. After the United States outlawed abortion in the nine-

Abortion opponents protesting

Abortion rights advocates protesting

Abortion opponents and abortion-rights proponents are equally passionate. Both sides of this highly controversial issue often stage public demonstrations to support their views. Pictured here are the annual March for Life demonstration in Washington, D.C., and a rally in support of the Jackson Women's Health Organization clinic.

FIGURE 9.2
Who Gets Abortions?

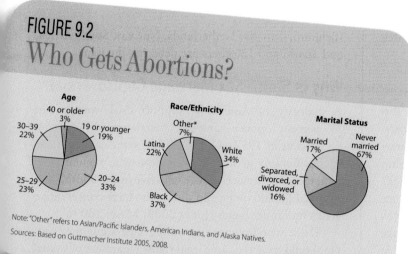

Age
- 40 or older 3%
- 30–39 22%
- 19 or younger 19%
- 25–29 23%
- 20–24 33%

Race/Ethnicity
- Other* 7%
- Latina 22%
- White 34%
- Black 37%

Marital Status
- Married 17%
- Never married 67%
- Separated, divorced, or widowed 16%

Note: "Other" refers to Asian/Pacific Islanders, American Indians, and Alaska Natives.
Sources: Based on Guttmacher Institute 2005, 2008.

teenth century, the procedure was illegal until 1973, when the U.S. Supreme Court legalized abortion (in its *Roe v. Wade* decision).

Trends

Half of all pregnancies in the United States are unintended: Many are unwanted at the time of conception or at any time, whereas others are mistimed because they have occurred sooner than the woman or couple wanted. About 40 percent of the unintended pregnancies and 22 percent of all pregnancies end in abortion. Ultimately, 33 percent of American women have an abortion by age 45 (Jones et al. 2008).

The number of abortions in the United States declined from 1.6 million in 1990 (the all-time high) to 1.2 million in 2005, when 2 percent of all American women had an abortion (Jones et al. 2008). The *abortion rate*, or the number of abortions per 1,000 women aged 15 to 44, was 29 in 1981; it fell steadily and reached an all-time low of 19.4 in 2005 (Guttmacher Institute 2008). Abortion is most common among women who are young (in their 20s), African American or white, and never married (see *Figure 9.2*).

Why Is Abortion Controversial?

Since its legalization, abortion has been one of the most persistently divisive issues in American politics and culture. More Americans describe themselves as pro-life (47 percent) than pro-choice (46 percent) and 7 percent have no opinion. Almost equal numbers hold opposing positions: Abortion should be legal (21 percent) or illegal (18 percent) in all circumstances. These divergent opinions have been fairly consistent since 1975 (Saad 2009).

Anti-abortion groups believe that the embryo or fetus is not just a mass of cells but a human being from the time of conception and, therefore, has a right to live. In contrast, many abortion rights advocates believe that, at the moment of conception, the organism lacks a brain and other specifically and uniquely human attributes, such as consciousness and reasoning. Abortion rights proponents also believe that a pregnant woman has a right to decide what will happen to her body (Almond 2007).

Anti-abortion groups maintain that abortion is immoral and endangers a woman's physical and emotional health. Whether abortion is immoral is a religious and philosophical question. Safety, however, can be measured on two levels: physical and emotional. On the physical level, a legal abortion in the first trimester (up to 12 weeks) is safer than driving a car, using oral contraceptives, undergoing sterilization, or continuing a pregnancy. Abortions performed in the first trimester pose virtually no long-term risk of problems such as miscarriage, birth defects, or preterm or low-birth-weight delivery in future pregnancies. There is also no evidence, despite the claims of abortion opponents, that having an abortion increases the risk of breast cancer, causes infertility, and leads to post-abortion stress disorders or suicide (Boonstra et al. 2006; Guttmacher Institute 2008).

What about emotional health? A team of psychologists who evaluated 73 empirical studies in peer-reviewed journals published between 1990 and 2007 concluded that among adult women who had an unplanned pregnancy, the risk of mental health problems after an abortion was no greater than having a baby and undergoing normal *postpartum depression*—the "blues" that many women experience after the birth of a baby because of a sudden decrease in some hormones (Major et al. 2008).

When women feel sadness, grief, and depression after an abortion, according to the researchers, such feelings are usually due to co-occurring factors including poverty (because low-income mothers worry about providing for a baby), a history of emotional problems and drug or alcohol abuse, or keeping the abortion secret from family and friends who stigmatize abortions. These findings were consistent with previous national studies conducted in the early 1990s (Major et al. 2008).

SAME-SEX MARRIAGE

Same-sex marriage (also called *gay marriage*) is a legally recognized marriage between two people of the same sex. Although still controversial, same-sex marriage is becoming more acceptable in the United States and several other countries.

Trends

Some states have legalized *civil unions* (sometimes also called *domestic partnerships* and *registered partnerships*) that give gay couples the same legal rights as married couples. Some of the rights include joint ownership of homes and other property, a share of the partner's medical or life insurance, and a right to inheritance and to survivors' benefits if a partner dies. However, voters in 31 states have passed laws limiting marriage to a man and a woman, and 29 states have amended their constitutions to explicitly prohibit gay marriage (Drogin 2009; Farrell 2010).

Same-sex marriage is legal in Connecticut, Iowa, Massachusetts, New Hampshire, Vermont and, most recently, the District of Columbia. Worldwide, since 2001, 6 countries have legalized same-sex marriage (Belgium, Canada, Netherlands, Norway, South Africa, and Spain) and 12 others are debating the issue.

Why Is Same-Sex Marriage Controversial?

A majority of Americans support civil unions, but 57 percent oppose same-sex marriages (down from 68 percent in 1997). Opposition to same-sex marriage is considerably greater among those who regularly attend religious services, those who live in the South, people aged 65 and older, and those who have conservative views on family issues (Jones 2009; Masci 2009).

Those who favor same-sex marriage argue that people should have the same legal rights regardless of sexual orientation, and that marriage may increase the stability of same-sex couples and lead to better physical and mental health for gays and lesbians. Those who oppose same-sex marriage contend that such unions are immoral, weaken our traditional notions of marriage, and are contrary to religious beliefs (Sullivan 1997; King and

TABLE 9.3
Why Are People For or Against Same-Sex Marriages?

Many states have passed laws that limit marriage to a man and a woman. What do *you* think? What other reasons can you add for each side of the debate?

SAME-SEX MARRIAGE SHOULD BE LEGAL BECAUSE . . .	SAME-SEX MARRIAGE SHOULD NOT BE LEGAL BECAUSE . . .
• Attitudes and laws change. Until 1967, for example, interracial marriages were prohibited.	• Interracial marriages are between women and men, but gay marriages violate many people's notions about male-female unions.
• Gay marriages would strengthen families and long-term unions that already exist. Children would be better off with parents who are legally married.	• Gay households are not the best place to raise children. Children raised in gay households might imitate their parents' homosexual behavior.
• It would be easier for same-sex couples to adopt children, especially those with emotional and physical disabilities.	• All adopted children—those with and without disabilities—are better off with parents who can provide heterosexual gender role models.
• There are no scientific studies showing that children raised by gay and lesbian parents are worse off than those raised by heterosexual parents.	• There are no scientific studies showing that children raised by gay and lesbian parents are better off than those raised by heterosexual parents.
• Every person should be able to marry someone that she or he loves.	• People can love each other without getting married.
• Same-sex marriages would benefit religious organizations both spiritually and emotionally and bolster membership.	• Same-sex marriages would polarize church members who are opposed to gay unions and decrease the size of congregations.
• Gay marriages are good for the economy because they boost businesses such as restaurants, bakeries, hotels, airlines, and florists.	• What's good for the economy isn't necessarily good for the economy, especially its moral values and religious beliefs.

Sources: Sullivan 2003; "The Merits of Gay Marriage" 2003; LaFraniere and Goodstein 2007; Semuels 2008; Masci 2009; Olson 2010.

Bartlett 2006). *Table 9.3* provides a summary of some of the major pro and con arguments in this debate.

PORNOGRAPHY: EROTIC OR OBSCENE?

Pornography is the graphic depiction of images that cause sexual arousal. The images include photographs, videos (including those on the Internet), and other visual materials. The *pornography industry,* a broader concept, includes massage parlors, prostitution rings, stripping, live sex shows, street prostitution, escort services, peep shows, phone sex, international and domestic trafficking of children but especially girls and women, mail-order bride services, and prostitution tourism (Whisnant and Stark 2004).

Trends

In the United States alone, pornography is a $15 billion a year industry. According to some estimates, 25 percent of Americans look at Internet pornography every day: More than 90 percent of the consumers are men, and despite the costs, they spend at least 6 hours a day viewing these sites. Among American college students, 20 percent of men view online pornographic materials every day or nearly every day, compared with only 3 percent of women (Paul 2005; Carroll et al. 2008).

Why Is Pornography Controversial?

American humorist Mason Cooley once quipped that pornography is the only really safe sex. Some people see adults' viewing of pornography as a harmless erotic recreation, whereas others denounce pornography as debasing and obscene.

Many proponents argue that "because men like to look at naked women, they will inevitably look at pornography." Among other things, some maintain, pornography augments the U.S. economy, enhances some men's sexual lives, and provides a safe outlet for men's sexual fantasies about oppressing women rather than resorting to violence. In addition, pornography can be lucrative for women who strip at expensive casinos and who act in popular adult films. Thus, pornography meets many people's, especially men's, needs. It is also legal under the First Amendment (freedom of speech) (Paul 2005; Urbina 2007).

Others maintain that pornography should be banned because it devalues and exploits women, increases violence against girls and women, and makes people more accepting of rape. Many feminists, in particular, argue

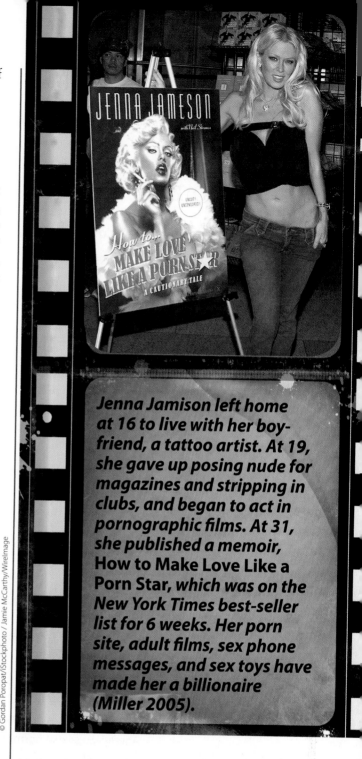

Jenna Jamison left home at 16 to live with her boyfriend, a tattoo artist. At 19, she gave up posing nude for magazines and stripping in clubs, and began to act in pornographic films. At 31, she published a memoir, *How to Make Love Like a Porn Star,* which was on the *New York Times* best-seller list for 6 weeks. Her porn site, adult films, sex phone messages, and sex toys have made her a billionaire (Miller 2005).

© Gordan Poropat/iStockphoto / Jamie McCarthy/WireImage

that there's no scientific evidence that pornography enhances men's lives or improves their sexual relationships. Instead, they believe that women in pornography are debased, exploited, and abused physically and psychologically. Also, according to some researchers, pornography use can increase men's risky sexual behavior, including having multiple sexual partners, which raises the chances of contracting sexually transmitted diseases, includ-

pornography the graphic depiction of images that cause sexual arousal.

ing HIV and AIDS (Carroll et al. 2008; Dines 2008; Attwood 2010).

5 Sociological Explanations of Gender Inequality and Sexuality

Paama Island in the South Pacific has a population of 600 people. A few years ago, the male leaders decided to ban women's wearing trousers "to make sure that western influence does not erode our cultural values." The ban was carried out by the all-male police force, even though many women protested that the policy violated the national constitution and their democratic rights ("Island Women Banned From Wearing Trousers" 2002). Why can a handful of men dictate how women should dress?

The four major sociological perspectives answer this and other questions about gender and sexuality, but somewhat differently. (*Table 9.4* summarizes these perspectives.)

FUNCTIONALISM

Functionalism, you'll recall from Chapter 1, is based on the assumption that society is a complex system of interrelated parts that work together to ensure a society's survival. A division of gender roles, especially within the family, helps society operate smoothly, and sexuality is important for reproduction.

Division of Gender Roles

Some of the most influential functionalist theories, developed during the 1950s, proposed that gender roles differ because women and men have distinct roles and responsibilities. A man (typically a husband and father) plays an *instrumental role* of procreator, protector, and provider. He must produce children, especially boys, to carry on his family name and, as a protector, must ensure his family's physical safety. The provider is competitive and works hard even if he is overwhelmed by multiple roles, such as the responsible breadwinner, the devoted husband, and the dutiful son (Parsons and Bales 1955; Gaylin 1992; Betcher and Pollack 1993).

A woman (typically a wife and mother) plays an *expressive role* by providing the emotional support and nurturance that sustain the family unit and support the father/husband. She should be warm, sensitive, and sympathetic, for example, comforting a husband who

TABLE 9.4
Sociological Explanations of Gender Inequality and Sexuality

THEORETICAL PERSPECTIVE	LEVEL OF ANALYSIS	KEY POINTS
Functionalist	Macro	• Gender roles are complementary and equally important. • Agreed-on sexual norms contribute to a society's order and stability.
Conflict	Macro	• Gender roles give men power to control women's lives instead of allowing the sexes to be complementary and equally important. • Most societies regulate women's, not men's, sexual behavior.
Feminist	Macro and micro	• Women's inequality reflects their historical and current domination by men, especially in the workplace. • Many men use violence—including sexual harassment, rape, and global sex trafficking—to control women's sexuality.
Symbolic Interactionist	Micro	• Gender inequality is a social construction that emerges through day-to-day interactions and reflects people's gender role expectations. • The social construction of sexuality varies across cultures because of societal norms and values.

has had a bad day at work. As expressive role players, women also are the family helper, problem solver, and mediator. For functionalists, the instrumental and expressive roles are complementary. The duties are specialized, but both roles are equally important in meeting a family's needs and ensuring a society's survival.

Why Is Sexuality Important?

For functionalists, sexuality is critical for reproduction, but it should be expressed in an orderly way. For example, many cultures rely on arranged marriages to select the best partners for young unmarried people. Such marriages ensure that the woman's sexual behavior will be confined to her husband, avoiding any doubt about the offspring's parentage.

For functionalists, sex should be practiced within marriage, primarily to encourage the formation of families. Sex outside of marriage is seen as dysfunctional because most unmarried fathers don't support their children, and the offspring often experience instability and poverty, as well as a variety of emotional, behavioral, and academic problems (Seltzer 2004; Avellar and Smock 2005).

Critical Evaluation

The characteristics of the instrumental and expressive roles are useful in understanding some of the differences between traditional and nontraditional gender roles. In traditional roles, because each person knows what is expected of him or her, rights and responsibilities are clear. Men and women don't have to argue over who does what: If the house is clean, she's a "good wife"; if the bills are paid, he's a "good husband."

One of the criticisms of the functionalist perspective is that even during the 1950s, white middle-class male views ignored almost a third of the labor force that was composed of working class, immigrant, and minority women who played *both* instrumental and expressive roles. Thus, the traditional model ignored the experiences of millions of American women.

A related criticism is that functionalists tend to overlook the fact that most people don't have a choice in embracing strictly instrumental and expressive roles. The traditional gender role model seems to work well for some Americans and is common in many countries, but only 19 percent of Americans say that women should return to their traditional roles in society (Parker 2009). This isn't surprising because most families rely on a woman's income for economic survival (see Chapter 12).

Functionalism emphasizes reproduction in contributing to a society's organization and stability over time

and across cultures, but frowns on sexual relationships outside of marriage. For example, even though cohabitation (living together outside of marriage) fulfills many people's sexual and intimacy needs, many functionalists see cohabitation as deviant because it doesn't always result in marriage (Popenoe and Whitehead 2006). As you'll see in Chapter 13, however, marriage doesn't guarantee long or happy relationships.

CONFLICT THEORY

Conflict theorists see gender inequality as built into the social structure, both within and outside the home. In many developing nations, women perform the vast majority of the agricultural work but have virtually no property rights because they aren't allowed, by law, to own land (Seager 2009). In industrialized countries, few women penetrate the top ranks in economic, political, military, and other institutions. In effect, then, most women are still second-class citizens because men control most of a society's resources. Like functionalists, conflict theorists see sexuality as a key component of a society's organization, but they view sexuality as reflecting and perpetuating gender inequality.

Capitalism and Gender Inequality

Unlike functionalists, conflict theorists maintain that capitalism, not complementary roles, explain gender roles and men's social and economic advantages. A full-time stay-at-home American mother would earn at least $135,000 a year if paid for her work (Wulfhorst 2006). In effect, traditional gender roles are profitable for business: Companies can require their male employees to work long hours or make numerous overnight business trips and don't have to worry about workers' demanding child-care services.

Most conflict theorists agree that all men are not equally privileged, and that women in upper classes have more economic power, status, and prestige than men in lower classes. However, within social classes, men typically enjoy more power and control than women.

Is Sexuality Linked to Gender Inequality?

According to conflict theorists, gender inequality has many negative effects on women's sexuality. Most of the victims of domestic violence and rape, in the United States and around the world, are women and girls. In some societies, especially in the Middle East, men dictate how women should dress (even at universities), dismiss women's charges of sexual assaults (including gang rapes), punish real or imagined instances

Since 1995, the number of employed women in India has surged. One of the most difficult tasks for these women is getting to work on crowded trains because men routinely pinch and grope them, or shout insults because the men "feel threatened" by women who work instead of being full-time housewives (Ridge 2009: 4). To decrease the sexual harassment, the railways official, a woman, convinced the government to introduce women-only commuter trains—known as Ladies Specials—in four of India's largest cities. The trains represent a tiny fraction of the nation's commuter trains, but occurrences of vandalism and harassment persist (Yardley 2009: A1).

of women's, but not men's, marital infidelity, and blame girls for child rape because they're "seducing" older men (Neelakantan 2006).

Conflict theorists see men's domination of women, especially in economic terms, as a result of gender power differences. In sexual harassment cases, the offender is typically a male supervisor. In prostitution and sex trafficking, 80 percent of the victims are women and girls who live in poverty (Farr 2005).

Critical Evaluation

Conflict theory is useful in showing how social structures reinforce men's domination in income, the division of domestic work, and access to valued resources. Some have criticized conflict theorists, however, for emphasizing male-female competition rather than cooperation. At home, 31 percent of married couples and those living together say that they make decisions equally—in planning weekend activities, household finances, major purchases for the home, and TV watching. Women (43 percent) have the final say in many decisions, and 80 percent of both sexes report being happy with this situation (Morin and Cohn 2008). Outside the home, women and men often barter with their employers to get what they want ("I'll work late all this week if I can

have Friday off."). A related criticism is that conflict theory emphasizes the differences between women and men rather than their common goals and similar attitudes. Much of our everyday life, after all, involves compromise and negotiation rather than power plays and a struggle for economic dominance.

Conflict theory helps us understand how power over women's sexual lives benefit men personally and economically, but it usually ignores how women use sexuality to exploit other women. During the 1980s, for example, a woman known as the Mayflower Madam (because of her higher class background) ran an elite prostitution ring in New York City. In other cases, women provide men with sexual favors in exchange for resources for themselves or their children (Barrows 1989; Rhoads 2004).

FEMINIST THEORIES

Like conflict theorists, feminists see gender stratification as benefiting men and capitalism. They emphasize, however, that women's subordination also includes their daily vulnerability to violence: "If they are not getting harassed on the street, living in an abusive relationship, recovering from a rape, or in therapy to deal with the sexual abuse they suffered as children, [women] are ordering their daily lives around the *threat* of men's violence" (Katz 2006: 5). Most feminist scholars agree with conflict theorists that sexuality is linked to gender inequality, but they go further in showing that male dominance is especially harmful because it results in men controlling women's sexual behavior.

Living in a Gendered World

Many studies show that women routinely experience inequality and violence because they have little control over their lives. For example:

- In Egypt, only 62 percent of men admit to sexually harassing women, but 83 percent of women report being sexually harassed (Stack 2008).

- In Puebla, Mexico, 35 bright pink and female-only taxis transport women to their destinations to shield women from sexual harassment and kidnapping. Mexico City is considering instituting similar taxis for the same reasons (Llana 2009).

- In Iraq, a young woman's father or maternal uncles often make all the decisions about her life, including how to dress, whom to marry, and forbidding her to go to college (Arraf 2010).

- In the United States, military policy dictates that female soldiers aren't allowed to participate in ground combat (a major requirement for promotions), but many women in the Iraq and Afghanistan wars "have done nearly as much in battle as their male counterparts: patrolled streets with machine guns, served as gunners on vehicles, disposed of explosives, and driven trucks down bomb-ridden roads" (Alvarez 2009: A1).

What do all of these examples have in common? For feminist sociologists, they illustrate women's unequal treatment in society because of our gendered lives.

All feminists (female and male) agree on three general points: (1) men and women should be valued equally; (2) women should have more control over their lives; and (3) gender inequality can be remedied by changing political, economic, family, and other institutions, as well as everyday interactions, attitudes, and behaviors. Feminism has a number of branches, but let's look briefly at three explanations of gender roles.

Liberal feminism maintains that gender equality can be achieved through equal civil rights and equal opportunities. Women and men are more similar than different in their abilities, but liberal feminists maintain that gendered socialization creates inequality by teaching girls and women to be passive and maternal, and by tracking women and men into different educational and employment fields (Jagger and Rothenberg 1984).

Radical feminism contends that patriarchy is the major reason for women's oppression, especially men's control over women's bodies and their sexuality. Men assert their power in the form of rape, intimate partner violence, exploiting women through prostitution and pornography, and sexual harassment. For radical feminists, all women are potential victims of sexual violence and all men are capable of such violence. In this sense, patriarchy is more critical than social class in giving men power over women's lives (MacKinnon 1982; Bart and Moran 1993).

Multiracial feminism (sometimes referred to as *racial ethnic feminism* or *multicultural feminism*) maintains that gender, race, and social class intertwine to form a hierarchical stratification system that shapes women's and men's attitudes, experiences, and behavior. Privileged women have less status than privileged men, but upper-class white men *and* women subordinate lower-class women *and* minority men. In this sense, multiracial feminism addresses the social subordination of both sexes and the oppression that is not only due to race, class, and gender but to sexual orientation and nationality (Collins 1990; Lorber 2005).

Is Sexuality Linked to Social Control?

Feminist theorists often point to sexuality as the root of inequality between women and men, both interpersonally and within economic and other institutions. Among

other things, feminist scholars have demanded an end to sexual slavery, marital rape, and female genital mutilation/cutting (FGM/C). About 140 million girls—usually between the ages of 4 and 12—in Africa and some countries in Asia and the Middle East have experienced FGM/C that involves removing all or part the girl's external genitalia, such as the clitoris, to control a girl's sexual desire and preserve her chastity before marriage. Sometimes the girls hemorrhage and die. In other cases, they become infertile because of infections or experience lifelong problems such as continuous dribbling of urine or feces (Feldman-Jacobs and Clifton 2010; Benokraitis 2011). Thus, feminist scholars maintain that as long as men control women's bodies and behavior, women's sexual well-being will be inferior to men's (hooks 2000).

Feminist scholars emphasize that some sexual groups have power over others. Even though all states have laws against hate crimes, for example, police in many cities are more likely to mistreat lesbians, gay men, bisexuals, and transgendered than heterosexuals.

Feminist theories have also gone much further than conflict theory in documenting men's control of women's sexuality across cultures and over time. Examples include forcing women to marry against their will and *honor killings* (murders committed by male members of a family if they believe that a female relative has

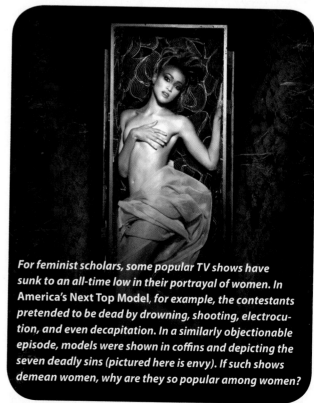

For feminist scholars, some popular TV shows have sunk to an all-time low in their portrayal of women. In America's Next Top Model, for example, the contestants pretended to be dead by drowning, shooting, electrocution, and even decapitation. In a similarly objectionable episode, models were shown in coffins and depicting the seven deadly sins (pictured here is envy). If such shows demean women, why are they so popular among women?

brought shame on the family by refusing an arranged marriage), being the victim of a sexual assault, seeking divorce, or committing adultery (Amnesty International 2006; Magnier 2009).

Critical Evaluation

Feminist perspectives have provided insightful analyses of gender inequality, especially in challenging functionalist views of instrumental and expressive roles as outdated and as reinforcing sexism and patriarchy. Feminist perspectives are not without their weaknesses, however. *Liberal feminism* typically emphasizes women's but not men's oppression in capitalistic societies. *Radical feminism* has been criticized for being too narrow. For example, men are not universally violent or sexually exploitative; many, in fact, respect women and teach their sons to do the same.

Multiracial feminism is very inclusive, but this strength can also be a weakness. When it comes to economic issues such as the gender pay gap, for example, which variable is the most important—race, ethnicity, or social class? Because gender inequality has many causes, it's difficult for multiracial feminists to agree on which factors carry more weight and whether some should be given a priority in implementing social change.

Some feminist scholars are also critical of their colleagues. They contend, for example, that some of the most influential writers haven't focused enough on social interaction (like the everyday communications between women and men) instead of structural factors (such as institutional barriers in employment, education, and politics). Some also maintain that feminist scholars haven't explained why and how women's interaction in everyday relationships has changed since the 1980s, differ across societies and everyday situations, and how people can change "doing gender" (Deutsch 2007; West and Zimmerman 2009).

Feminist theorists have also been criticized for focusing too much on men's sexual domination, while neglecting racial, ethnic, religious, age, and social class differences among women and men. Also, according to some critics, feminist theories tend to minimize the importance of sexuality that reflects love and affection rather than only power.

SYMBOLIC INTERACTIONISM

Whereas functionalist, conflict, and some feminist theories tend to have a macro-level basis, symbolic interactionists focus on the everyday processes that produce and reinforce gender roles. Most of us accommodate

In some parts of Indonesia, the police—who follow religious rules about women's and men's segregation—go after women not properly covered by head scarves and couples engaging in public displays of affection. Pictured here, a policeman lectures a young man for sitting too close to a woman while on an outing at the beach (Glionna, 2009).

our behavior to gender role expectations by "doing gender" (West and Zimmerman 1987). We do gender, sometimes consciously and sometimes unconsciously, by adjusting our behavior and our perceptions depending on the sex of the person with whom we're interacting. Our expression of our sexuality, similarly, is not inborn but reflects socialization processes, and what families and other societal groups decide is appropriate and inappropriate behavior (Hubbard 1990).

Gender Inequality Is a Social Construction

For symbolic interactionists, society is *socially constructed* (see Chapter 1). Because our view of reality is what people agree it is, gender is a social creation, and gender inequality is not shaped by social structures as much as by learning gender roles through daily social interaction. That is, "People act on the basis of their perceptions of equality if and when equality is a relevant concern for them" (Harris 2006: 8). For example, some religious couples try to be equal only in ways that matter to them—such as equality of love or respect—while also interpreting literally the Bible's injunction that "wives should submit to their husbands" (Bartkowski 2001). How Do People Construct Sexuality?

For symbolic interactionists, sexuality is also socially constructed. As with gender roles, we *learn* to be sexual and to express our sexuality differently over time and across cultures. There is no natural human sexuality. Instead, the people around us channel, guide, and limit our sexual behavior. For example, a study of mothers of 3- to 5-year-old children found that most mothers assume that their children are heterosexual. Mothers who are affiliated with conservative Protestant religions try to prevent homosexuality in their children, generally by telling them that being gay is wrong and violates God's laws (Martin 2009).

Because sexual behavior is constructed socially, it can and does change over time. Many Americans have become more comfortable with categories such as bisexual, lesbian, and gay. When I was in college, female premarital virginity was the norm (though often violated). Now, one third of parents of 14-year-olds know that their daughters are sexually active (Albert et al. 2003). In many Middle East countries, men have premarital sex but don't marry women who aren't virgins (Fleishman and Hassan 2009). Thus, sexual double standards are also socially constructed.

Critical Evaluation

Symbolic interactionist theories are useful in explaining how gender and gender roles shape our everyday lives. Through both verbal and nonverbal communication, we learn what behavior is appropriate and how to change it (see Chapter 5). Despite their contributions, interactionists have been criticized for ignoring the social structures that create and maintain gender inequality such as military policies that dictate whether women can participate in combat, an important criterion in military promotions.

Symbolic interactionists have enhanced our understanding of sexuality by showing how behavior is socially constructed and why, consequently, there are cross-cultural variations in sexual attitudes and practices. However, symbolic interactionism doesn't explain why siblings, even identical twins, have different sexual orientations although they were socialized similarly. A related weakness is that symbolic interactionists don't explain why, historically and currently, women around the world are considerably more likely than men to be subjected to sexual control and exploitation. Such analyses require macro-level analyses that examine family, political, and economic institutions.

America's multicultural

umbrella includes at least 150 distinct ethnic or racial groups.

10 Race and Ethnicity

what do you think?

The United States is a melting pot.

1 2 3 4 5 6 7

strongly agree   strongly disagree

Two researchers randomly assigned either a stereotypically African American name (Lakisha Washington or Jamal Jones) or a name that sounded typically white (Emily Walsh or Greg Baker) to both high-quality and low-quality fictitious résumés. They then sent almost 5,000 of the résumés in response to advertisements for a variety of jobs in Chicago and Boston. The results were startling:

- Applicants with white-sounding names received 50 percent more calls for interviews. In fact, a white-sounding name yielded as many more calls as an additional 8 years of work experience for an applicant with a black-sounding name.
- Applicants with black-sounding names received fewer calls across all occupations (from managers to clerical workers) and in all industries (communications, manufacturing, finance, and social services).
- Employers who posted "Equal Employment Opportunity Employer" in their ad discriminated as much as other employers (Bertrand and Mullainathan 2003).

As this example shows, some of us enjoy more opportunities than others simply because of the color of our skin. The situation has improved during the last 50 years or so, but not as much as most people think. This chapter examines the significance of race and ethnicity, their impact on Americans' lives, why racial-ethnic inequality is still widespread, and the growth of interracial and interethnic relationshi

1 Racial and Ethnic Diversity in America

What do you call a person who speaks three languages? Multilingual.
What do you call a person who speaks two languages? Bilingual.
What do you call a person who speaks one language? American.

As this joke suggests, many people stereotype the United States as a single-language and single-culture society. In fact, it's the most multicultural country in the world, a

race a group of people who share physical characteristics, such as skin color and facial features, that are passed on through reproduction.

magnet that draws people from hundreds of nations and that is home to millions of Americans who are bilingual or multilingual.

Of the almost 309 million U.S. population, 13 percent are foreign born. Between 2000 and 2008, the foreign-born population increased by 22 percent compared with only 6 percent of the native born (Dockterman and Velasco 2010). As a result, America's multicultural umbrella includes at least 150 distinct ethnic or racial groups (U.S. Census Bureau 2010). By 2025, only 58 percent of the U.S. population is projected to be white—down from 86 percent in 1950 (see *Figure 10.1*). By 2050—just a few generations away— whites may make up only half of the total population because Latino and Asian populations are expected to triple in size (Population Division, U.S. Census Bureau 2008). One of the most telling examples of our diversity is that the federal government offered online help in filling out the 2010 Census in five languages—English, Spanish, Chinese, Korean, and Russian.

Multiracial people are also increasing. The number of Americans who identify themselves as being two or more races is projected to more than triple—from 5.1 million in 2008 to 16.2 million in 2050 (2 percent and almost 4 percent of the total population, respectively) (U.S. Census Bureau News 2008).

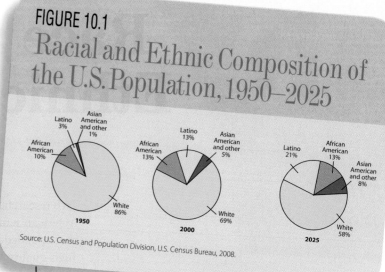

FIGURE 10.1
Racial and Ethnic Composition of the U.S. Population, 1950–2025

1950: African American 10%, Latino 3%, Asian American and other 1%, White 86%

2000: African American 13%, Latino 13%, Asian American and other 5%, White 69%

2025: Latino 21%, African American 13%, Asian American and other 8%, White 58%

Source: U.S. Census and Population Division, U.S. Census Bureau, 2008.

on through reproduction. Contrary to the popular belief that race is determined biologically, it is a *social construction,* a societal invention, that labels people based on physical appearance. Possibly only 6 of the human body's estimated 35,000 genes determine the color of a person's skin. Because all human beings carry 99.9 percent of the same genetic material (DNA), the "racial" genes that makes us look different are miniscule compared with the genes that make us similar (Graves 2001; Pittz 2005).

If our DNA is practically identical, why are we so obsessed with race? People react to the physical char-

2 The Social Significance of Race and Ethnicity

all of us identify with some groups and not others in terms of sex, age, social class, and other factors. Two of the most common and influential sources of self-identification, as well as labeling by others, are race and ethnicity.

RACE

Race refers to a group of people who share physical characteristics, such as skin color and facial features, that are passed

There's much variation in skin color across and within groups. People of African descent have at least 35 different shades of skin tone (Taylor 2003). So, can you determine someone's race by simply looking at her or him?

© Getty Images/Comstock/Jupiter Images

acteristics of others, and those reactions have consequences. Skin color, hair texture, and eye shape, for example, are easily observed and mark groups for unequal treatment. As long as we sort others into racial categories and act on the basis of these characteristics, our life experiences will differ in access to jobs and other resources, how we treat people, and how they treat us (Duster 2005).

ETHNICITY

An **ethnic group** (from the Greek word *ethnos,* meaning "nation") is a group of people who identify with a common national origin or cultural heritage that includes language, geographic roots, food, customs, traditions, and/or religion. Ethnic groups in the United States include Puerto Ricans, Chinese, Serbs, Arabs, Swedes, Hungarians, Jews, and many others. Like race, ethnicity can be a basis for unequal treatment, as you'll see shortly.

RACIAL-ETHNIC GROUP

A group of people who have both distinctive physical and cultural characteristics is a **racial-ethnic group.** Some people use the terms *racial* and *ethnic* interchangeably, but remember that *race* refers to physical characteristics with which we are born, whereas *ethnicity* describes cultural characteristics that we learn. The term *racial-ethnic* includes both physical and cultural traits.

Describing racial-ethnic groups has become more complex because the U.S. government allows people to identify themselves in terms of both race and ethnicity. In the 2000 and 2010 U.S. Census, for example, a Latino/a could check off "Black" for race and "Cuban" for ethnic origin. Such choices generate dozens of racial-ethnic categories.

Most people maintain that they are color-blind, but we learn at an early age that some physical attributes are more valued than others. A notable example is light-colored skin, which confers *white privilege,* the advantages that white people enjoy simply because they happen to be in a particular category. Most white people don't feel privileged because they aren't wealthy. Nonetheless, they enjoy everyday benefits that they take for granted, such as not being followed by store detectives when they shop and being able to buy products—such as greeting cards, dolls, toys, and children's magazines—that represent their own race (McIntosh 1995; Johnson 2008; Rothenberg 2008).

Race, ethnicity, and racial-ethnic aren't fixed in how we identify ourselves or others. Because of the increase of interracial marriages, as you'll see shortly, our definitions and measurements of race and ethnicity are becoming increasingly complex because of people's multiple origins.

> **ethnic group** a group of people who identify with a common national origin or cultural heritage that includes language, geographic roots, food, customs, traditions, and/or religion.
>
> **racial-ethnic group** a group of people who have both distinctive physical and cultural characteristics.

3 Our Changing Immigration Mosaic

the current proportion of foreign-born U.S. residents is 13 percent compared with 15 percent in 1900. Since the turn of the twentieth century, however, there has been a significant shift in immigrants' country of origin and skills. In 1900, almost 85 percent of immigrants came from Europe and with predominately low-level skills; now immigrants come primarily from Asia (mainly China and the Philippines) and Latin America (mainly Mexico), and have varied skills and educational levels (Dockterman and Velasco 2010).

UNDOCUMENTED IMMIGRANTS

The United States admits more than 1 million immigrants every year—more than any other nation. A major change has been the rise of unauthorized (also called *undocumented* and *illegal*) immigrants—from 180,000 in the early 1980s to 11 million in 2009, representing 34 percent of all foreign-born U.S. residents. About 62 percent of undocumented immigrants are from Mexico, 15 percent are from Central and Latin America, 7 percent are from Asia, and 16 percent are from other countries (Capps et al. 2007; Hoefer et al. 2010).

One in three Mexicans say that if they had the means and opportunity to live in the United States, they would do so, and more than half of these individuals would do so illegally. Major reasons for wanting to leave Mexico include crime (81 percent), economic problems (75 percent), illegal drugs (73 percent), and political corruption (68 percent). Most say that life would be better in the United States for themselves and their children, a belief that's similar to those who immigrate legally (Pew Research Center 2009).

ATTITUDES ABOUT IMMIGRATION

Most Americans are ambivalent about legal immigration: 40 percent say that immigrants have made the country better in terms of food, music, and the arts, but a majority feels that immigrants have increased taxes and crime. Especially after the recent economic downturn and high unemployment rates, many Americans want to limit legal immigration to decrease the competition for jobs (Kohut et al. 2007; Keeter 2009). Generally, however, attitudes about legal immigration vary depending on the social context. Shortly after the 9/11 terrorist attacks, for example, 58 percent of Americans favored cutbacks in legal immigration compared with 39 percent in 2008 (Jones 2008).

Illegal immigration is more controversial, but attitudes vary depending on the importance of other issues. In 2006, for instance, 53 percent of Americans contended that illegal immigrants should be required to go home. In 2008—as many Americans focused on other issues such as a struggling economy, healthcare reform, jobs, the war in Afghanistan, and the housing crisis—illegal immigration was not a high priority (Barabak 2006; Keeter 2009). Scholars expect the debates to be ignited, however, because President Obama has reiterated his commitment to pursuing comprehensive immigration reform (Nevins 2010).

Those who want stricter enforcement of current laws and more deportations, now called *removals,* claim that, regardless of legal status, low-skilled immigrants reduce the standard of living and overload schools and welfare systems. They argue that because immigrants are younger, poorer, and less well educated than the native population, they use more government services and pay less in taxes. Especially during recessions, these critics allege, undocumented immigrants take jobs away from U.S.-born Americans, including those at the lower occupational level such as janitors and meat processors (Camarota 2009a, 2009b).

Those who endorse policies that provide a "path to citizenship" for unauthorized immigrants maintain that undocumented immigrants provide numerous economic benefits for their host countries. They clean homes and business offices, toil as nannies and busboys, serve as nurses' aides, and pick fruit—all at low wages and in jobs that most American-born workers don't want. Accounting for 9 percent of the 154 million U.S. workers, unauthorized immigrants comprise 25 percent of all farm workers, 19 percent of the workforce in cleaning occupations, 17 percent of those in construction, and 12 percent in food preparation industries (Passel and Cohn 2009). They are also more likely than U.S.-born people to work in dangerous jobs (such as mining, logging, and construction) that have high fatality rates because of accidents (Orrenius and Zavodny 2009; Zuehlke 2009).

Many scholars argue that, in the long run, easing illegal immigrants' path to citizenship would bring more benefits than costs. For example, they constitute an important labor force for an aging (and primarily white) American population that will require many workers to support Social Security and Medicare payments for the elderly. Naturalized citizens have higher wages, which decreases the likelihood of family poverty; bring billions in taxes at state and federal levels; and contribute to U.S. culture (Mather 2009; Pastor et al. 2010; Shierholz 2010).

4 Dominant and Minority Groups

t he president of the Boston City Council tried, unsuccessfully, to strike the word *minority* from the official city documents because, he argued, the term is insulting and inaccurate in a city whose population is 51 percent people of color (Wiltenburg 2002). For sociologists, *minority*

Guest workers, who are permitted to work in the United States on a temporary basis because of labor shortages, especially in agriculture, often live in little more than shacks (left). Arizona lettuce farmers, some of whom pay their guest workers from Mexico up to $8.50 an hour, don't have enough field hands to harvest the crop (middle). Undocumented immigrants, most of them Latinos, comprised a quarter of the construction workers who helped rebuild parts of New Orleans after Hurricane Katrina (right). Many of these construction workers made an average of $6.50 an hour less than legal workers and had more trouble collecting their wages (Fletcher et al. 2006).

group and *dominant group* are descriptive terms that have little to do with a group's size.

WHAT IS A DOMINANT GROUP?

A **dominant group** is any physically or culturally distinctive group that has the most economic and political power, the greatest privileges, and the highest social status in a society. As a result, it can treat other groups as subordinate. For example, in most societies, men are a dominant group because they have more status, resources, and power than women (see Chapter 9).

Dominant groups aren't necessarily the largest groups in society. From the seventeenth century until 1994, about 10 percent of the population in South Africa was white and had almost complete control of the black population. Because of **apartheid,** a formal system of racial segregation, the black inhabitants couldn't vote, lost their property, and had minimal access to education and politics. Apartheid ended in 1994, but most black South Africans are still a minority because whites "hold the best jobs, live in the most expensive homes, and control the bulk of the country's capital" (Murphy 2004: A4).

WHAT IS A MINORITY?

Sociologists describe Latinos, African Americans, Asian Americans, Middle Eastern Americans, and American Indians as minorities. A **minority** is a group of people who may be subject to differential and unequal treatment because of their physical, cultural, or other characteristics, such as gender, sexual orientation, religion, ethnicity, or skin color. Minorities may be larger than a dominant group, but they have less power, privilege, and social status. For example, American minorities have fewer choices than dominant group members in finding homes and apartments because they are less likely to get help—from either a real-estate agent or a bank—with the intricacies of mortgage financing that most people need or to get the same information about housing possibilities (Massey 2007).

PATTERNS OF DOMINANT-MINORITY GROUP RELATIONS

To understand some of the complexity of dominant-minority group relations, think of a continuum. At one end of the continuum is genocide; at the other end is pluralism (see *Figure 10.2*).

Genocide

Genocide is the systematic effort to kill all members of a particular ethnic, religious, political, racial, or national group. By 1710, for example, the colonists in America had killed thousands of Indians in skirmishes, poisoned others, and promoted scalp bounties. And, in 1851, the governor of California officially called for the extermination of all Indians in the state (de las

dominant group any physically or culturally distinctive group that has the most economic and political power, the greatest privileges, and the highest social status.

apartheid a formal system of racial segregation.

minority a group of people who may be subject to differential and unequal treatment because of their physical, cultural, or other characteristics, such as gender, sexual orientation, religion, ethnicity, or skin color.

genocide the systematic effort to kill all members of a particular ethnic, religious, political, racial, or national group.

FIGURE 10.2
Continuum of Some Dominant-Minority Group Relations

INTOLERANCE
INEQUALITY

ACCEPTANCE
EQUALITY

| **Genocide** Systematic efforts to destroy minorities (e.g., American Indians) | **Internal Colonialism** Subordination of minority groups through exploitation or oppression (e.g., slavery in the United States) | **Segregation** Physical and social separation of dominant and minority groups (e.g., housing segregation) | **Assimilation** A dominant group absorbs minority groups (e.g., through interracial and interethnic marriages) | **Pluralism** There is no dominant group because all groups share power and other resources fairly equally (e.g., possibly Switzerland) |

Casas 1992; Churchill 1997). As *Table 10.1* shows, well over 74 million people have been victims of genocide during the twentieth century alone. The total number of people killed in these countries equals about 24 percent of the current U.S. population.

Internal Colonialism

Internal colonialism refers to the unequal treatment and subordinate status of groups within a country. Sociologist Robert Blauner (1969, 1972) described African Americans as an "internal colony" because blacks entered the United States involuntarily as slaves, were controlled by the dominant group, and were exploited economically and sexually (rapes of slave women, for instance).

Segregation

Segregation is the physical and social separation of dominant and minority groups. In 1954, the Supreme Court's ruling in the *Brown v. the Board of Education* case declared *de jure*, or legal, segregation unconstitutional and

was followed by the passage of a variety of federal laws that prohibited racial segregation in public schools, as well as discrimination in employment, voting, and housing.

De facto, or informal, segregation has replaced *de jure* segregation in the United States. Some *de facto* segregation may be voluntary, as when members of racial or ethnic groups prefer to live among their own group. In most cases, however, *de facto* segregation is due to discrimination, as when realtors steer minorities away from white neighborhoods. Such residential segregation deprives minorities of access to quality schools, retail stores, leisure activities, and jobs that are burgeoning in the suburbs (Farley and Squires 2005; Ledger 2009).

Assimilation

Many minority-group members blend into U.S. society through **assimilation**, the process of conforming to the culture of the dominant group (by adopting its language and values) and intermarrying with that group. Some feel that many newcomers are assimilating less than in the past. For example, many Mexican immigrants aren't learning English, and Cubans have transformed much of Miami, Florida, into an ethnic enclave that tends to exclude whites and African Americans (Huntington 2004).

Others maintain that immigrants who arrived after 1995 are assimilating more rapidly than their predecessors, but that the degree of assimilation varies by

TABLE 10.1
Twentieth-Century Genocide

EVENT	YEARS	ESTIMATED NUMBER OF DEATHS
Turkish government's massacre of Armenians living in Turkey	1915–1918	1.5 million
Joseph Stalin's (Russian dictator) massacre of nearly 25 percent of the population of Ukraine and of many other Eastern European countries (including Latvia, Lithuania, and Estonia)	1932–1953	50+ million
Japanese Imperial Army's murder of inhabitants of China's capital city, Nanking	1937–1938	300,000
Nazi Holocaust in Germany (about 6 million Jews and 11 million Soviet civilians, homosexuals, Romani, political and religious opponents, and others)	1938–1945	17 million
Khmer Rouge leader Pol Pot's slaughter of Cambodians	1975–1979	2+ million
Murders of Muslims by Serb majority in former Yugoslavia	1992–1995	200,000+
Massacres of minority Tutsis by dominant Hutu group in Rwanda, Africa	1994 (nine months)	800,000

Sources: Niewyk and Nicosia 2000; United Human Rights Council 2004.

country of origin, educational level, and the legal status of the immigrant. Mexicans, for example, are considerably less likely to assimilate (than immigrants from the Philippines, Vietnam, or South Korea) because they are more likely to have entered the country illegally, which cuts off the possibility of getting a good job, an education (especially for migrant workers), and becoming a citizen. Still, although most Mexican immigrants speak little English in the first generation, English dominates the second generation, and Spanish fades in the third generation (Vigdor 2008; Telles 2010).

Pluralism

Pluralism, sometimes called *multiculturalism*, is a situation in which minority groups retain their culture but have equal social standing in a society. One historian describes the United States as a pluralistic society because it is multicultural, multicolored, and multilingual. Thus, an American might have diverse neighbors such as a German architect and his Iranian wife, a Palestinian contractor, a Korean scientist, and a car salesman from Madagascar (Karnow 2004).

The United States is pluralistic to some extent because most racial and ethnic communities ("Little Italy," "Greek Town," "Little Korea," Harlem) live peacefully side by side, have numerous ethnic newspapers and radio stations, and have the same constitutional rights (such as the freedom to protest). On the other hand, people of various skin colors and cultures don't always experience the same social standing and there is considerable racial-ethnic friction in the United States.

5 Sources of Racial-Ethnic Friction

On the television program *The View*, Rosie O'Donnell mocked how Chinese Americans speak English (Bonisteel 2006). Such public comments, especially by very visible people, suggest that racism is still common in U.S. culture.

Courtesy of the Cleveland Indians

RACISM

Racism is a set of beliefs that one's own racial group is naturally superior to other groups. It is a way of thinking about racial and ethnic differences that justifies and preserves the social, economic, and political interests of dominant groups (Essed and Goldberg 2002).

Some social scientists have suggested that African Americans are born with lower average intelligence than other groups, especially whites (Herrnstein and Murray 1994). Human intelligence is a product of both genetic and environmental influences, and there is no evidence that one cultural group is more intelligent than another (Montagu 1999). Nonetheless, such racist beliefs fuel prejudice and discrimination.

> **pluralism** minority groups retain their culture but have equal social standing in a society.
>
> **racism** a set of beliefs that one's own racial group is naturally superior to other groups.
>
> **prejudice** an attitude, positive or negative, toward people because of their group membership.

PREJUDICE

Prejudice is an attitude, positive or negative, toward people because of their group membership. We often prejudge those who are different from us in race, ethnic-

A number of colleges and professional teams have replaced their logo, nicknames, and mascots because many American Indians have denounced them as demeaning stereotypes. Some exceptions are the Cleveland Indians in baseball (left) and the Washington Redskins in football (right). Why do many people see the Indian images and team names as offensive? Why do you think that the Minnesota Vikings and University of Notre Dame's Fighting Irish are acceptable?

Photo by Al Messerschmidt/Getty Images

stereotype an oversimplified or exaggerated generalization about a category of people.

ethnocentrism the belief that one's own culture, society, or group is inherently superior to others.

scapegoats individuals or groups whom people blame for their own problems or shortcomings.

discrimination any act that treats people unequally or unfairly because of their group membership.

individual discrimination harmful action directed intentionally, on a one-to-one basis, by a member of a dominant group against a member of a minority group.

ity, or religion ("Asians are really hard workers" or "White people can't be trusted."). Prejudice is not one-sided because *anyone* can be prejudiced, use stereotypes, and exhibit ethnocentric behavior.

A **stereotype** is an oversimplified or exaggerated generalization about a category of people (see, for example, www.stuffwhitepeople-like.com). Stereotypes can be positive ("All African Americans are athletic.") or negative ("All African Americans are lazy."). Whether positive or negative, stereotypes distort reality. Some blacks are great athletes and some are lazy, just like people in other groups. Once established, however, stereotypes are difficult to get rid of because people often dismiss any evidence to the contrary as an exception ("For an Asian, she's really athletic.").

Ethnocentrism is the belief that one's own culture, society, or group is inherently superior to others. If we are ethnocentric, we reject those not from our group as strange, deviant, and inferior: "*Our* customs, *our* laws, *our* food, *our* traditions, *our* music, *our* religion, *our*

beliefs and values, and so forth, are somehow better than those of other societies" (Smedley 2007: 32).

Stereotypes and ethnocentrism can result in a displacement of anger and aggression on **scapegoats,** individuals or groups whom people blame for their own problems or shortcomings ("They didn't hire me because the company wants blacks" or "I didn't get into that college because Asians Americans are at the top of the list."). Minorities are easy targets for scapegoating because they typically differ in physical appearance and are usually too powerless to strike back (Allport 1954; Feagin and Feagin 2008).

At one time or another, almost all newcomers to the United States have been scapegoats. Especially in times of economic hardship, the most recent immigrants often become scapegoats ("Latinos are replacing Americans in construction jobs."). Stereotypes, ethnocentrism, and scapegoating are attitudes, but they often lead to discrimination.

DISCRIMINATION

Discrimination is any act that treats people unequally or unfairly because of their group membership. Discrimination encompasses all sorts of actions, ranging from social slights (such as not inviting minority coworkers to lunch) to rejection of job applications and hate crimes. Discrimination can be subtle (such as not sitting next to someone) or blatant (such as racial slurs), and it occurs at individual and institutional levels.

Individual discrimination is harmful action directed intentionally on a one-to-one basis by a member of

FIGURE 10.3
Relationships between Prejudice and Discrimination

		DOES THE PERSON DISCRIMINATE?	
		Yes	**No**
IS THE PERSON PREJUDICED?	**Yes**	Prejudiced discriminator (e.g., a prejudiced person who attacks minority-group members verbally or physically)	Prejudiced nondiscriminator (e.g., a prejudiced person who goes along with equal employment opportunity policies)
	No	Prejudiced nondiscriminator (e.g., an unprejudiced person who joins a club that excludes minorities)	Unprejudiced nondiscriminator (e.g., an unprejudiced employer who hires minorities)

Source: Based on Merton 1949.

© iStockphoto.com/Junghee Choi

a dominant group against a member of a minority group. In a recent survey, for example, more than half of blacks said that they face everyday discrimination when eating in restaurants, shopping, renting an apartment, buying a house, or applying for a job (Kohut et al. 2007).

In **institutional discrimination** (also called *institutionalized discrimination*), minority-group members experience unequal treatment and opportunities as a result of the everyday operations of a society's laws, rules, policies, practices, and customs. Institutional discrimination is widespread. In health care, for instance, minorities tend to receive lower quality care than whites, even when they have private health insurance and are treated by the same doctors (*National Healthcare Disparities Report* 2003; Sequist et al. 2008).

RELATIONSHIP BETWEEN PREJUDICE AND DISCRIMINATION

About 60 years ago, sociologist Robert Merton (1949) described the relationship between prejudice and discrimination that is still useful today. Merton's model includes four types of people and their possible response patterns (see *Figure 10.3*).

Unprejudiced nondiscriminators, or "all-weather liberals," as Merton called them, are neither prejudiced nor do they discriminate. They sincerely believe in the American creed of freedom and equality for all and cherish egalitarian values, but don't do much, individually or collectively, to change discrimination. In contrast, *prejudiced discriminators* are "active bigots" who are consistent in attitude and action: They are prejudiced and discriminate, and are willing to break laws to express their beliefs and protect their vested interests.

Unprejudiced discriminators are "fair-weather liberals" who aren't prejudiced but discriminate because it's expedient or in their own self-interest to do so. If, for example, an insurance company charges higher automobile insurance premiums to people with low occupational and educational levels (as is often the case for many minorities), agents will implement these policies even though they themselves aren't prejudiced (Florida Office of Insurance Regulation 2007).

Prejudiced nondiscriminators are "timid bigots" who are prejudiced but don't discriminate. Despite their negative attitudes, they hire minorities and are civil in everyday interactions because they feel that they must conform to antidiscrimination laws or situational norms. If, for example, most of their neighbors or coworkers don't discriminate, prejudiced nondiscriminators will go along with them.

> **institutional discrimination** unequal treatment and opportunities that members of minority groups experience as a result of the everyday operations of a society's laws, rules, policies, practices, and customs.

6 Major Racial and Ethnic Groups in the United States

americans absorb many aspects of immigrants' cultures: "Our everyday lexicon is sprinkled with Spanish words. We are now just as likely to grab a burrito as a burger. Hip-hop is tinged with South Asian rhythms. And Chinese New Year and Cinco de Mayo are taking their places alongside St. Patrick's Day as widely celebrated American ethnic holidays" (Jiménez 2007: M1). Of the major U.S. racial-ethnic groups, some experience more constraints than others, but all have numerous strengths that enhance U.S. society.

EUROPEAN AMERICANS: A DECLINING MAJORITY

During the seventeenth century, English immigrants settled the first colonies in Massachusetts and Virginia. Other white Anglo-Saxon Protestants (WASPs), who included people from Wales and Scotland, quickly followed. Most of these groups spoke English. Some of the immigrants were affluent, but many were poor or had criminal backgrounds.

Diversity

About 58 percent of the U.S. population has a European background. The largest groups have ancestors from Germany, Ireland, England, Italy, Poland, and France, and the Scandinavian countries (see *Table 10.2*).

Constraints and Strengths

WASPs generally looked down on later waves of immigrants from southern and eastern Europe. They viewed the newcomers as inferior, dirty, lazy, and uncivilized because they differed in language, religion, and customs. New England, which was 90 percent Protestant,

TABLE 10.2
Americans of European Descent, 2007

Of the many European ancestries that Americans report, the following comprise at least 1 percent of the U.S. population.

ANCESTRY	NUMBER (IN MILLIONS)	PERCENTAGE OF TOTAL U.S. POPULATION
German	35.5	11.9
Irish	22.3	7.4
English	19.1	6.4
Italian	13.9	4.6
Polish	6.8	2.3
French	5.6	1.9
Scottish	3.8	1.3
Norwegian	3.1	1.0

Note: This survey was based on a total estimated population of almost 300 million Americans.
Source: Based on U.S. Census Bureau, 2010, Table 52.

was particularly hostile to Irish Catholics, characterizing them as irresponsible and shiftless (Feagin and Feagin 2008).

All the later waves of European immigrants faced varying degrees of hardship in adjusting to the new land because the first English settlers had a great deal of power in shaping economic and educational institutions. In response to prejudice and discrimination, many of the immigrants founded churches, schools, and recreational activities that maintained their language and traditions (Myers 2007).

Despite stereotypes, prejudice, and discrimination, European immigrants began to prosper within a few generations. They surmounted many barriers and became influential in all sectors of American life. Overall, they now fare much better financially than most other groups in the United States. This doesn't mean that all are rich. In fact, in absolute numbers, poor whites outnumber those of other racial-ethnic groups (see Chapter 12).

LATINOS: A GROWING MINORITY

About one in three Americans is a member of a racial or ethnic minority group, but Latinos are the fastest growing minority group and constitute almost 16 percent of the nation's population. The growth of the Latino population this century is due mainly to births in the United States, not immigration (Passel 2010).

Diversity

Some Latinos trace their roots to the Spanish and Mexican settlers who established homes and founded cities in the Southwest before the arrival of the first English settlers on the East Coast. Other Latinos are recent immigrants or children of the immigrants who arrived in large numbers at the beginning of the twentieth century. Of the almost 47 million Latinos living in the United States, 64 percent were born in Mexico or are of Mexican heritage (U.S. Census Bureau 2010). Spanish-speaking people from Mexico, Puerto Rico, Ecuador, the Dominican Republic, and Spain differ widely in their customs, cuisine, and cultural practices.

Constraints and Strengths

Most Latinos are taking their place in mainstream America, but many still encounter obstacles. The median household income of Latinos is 68 percent of that of white Americans (see *Figure 10.4*). Almost 40 percent of Latino families earn $50,000 a year or more, up considerably from only 7 percent in 1972, but almost 23 percent of Mexican Americans and 25 percent of Puerto Ricans

Dominican-born Alfredo Rodriguez is one of numerous successful Latino businessmen who are rebuilding neglected inner-city neighborhoods. In 1985, Rodriguez bought his first grocery store in Queens, New York, with the $25 a week his mother had been setting aside for him for a decade. In 2002, he purchased a 53,000-square-foot supermarket in Newark, New Jersey, to meet the needs of local Latino shoppers. Five years later, his Xtra Supermarket had annual sales of $9 million (Rayasam 2007).

© Jeffrey MacMillan for U.S. News & World Report

FIGURE 10.4

U.S. Median Household Income, by Race and Ethnicity, 2008

A bar chart titled "U.S. Median Household Income, by Race and Ethnicity, 2008." The vertical axis ranges from 0 to 80,000 in increments of 10,000. The bars show:
- Asian: $65,637
- White: $55,530
- Latino: $37,913
- American Indian/Alaska Native: $37,815
- African American: $34,218

Sources: Based on DeNavas-Walt et al. 2009, Table 1; and "American Indian and Alaska Native..."2009.

live below the poverty line compared with 15 percent of Cuban Americans (U.S. Census Bureau 2010).

As with other groups, the socioeconomic status of Latinos reflects a number of interrelated factors, especially education level, being able to speak English, recency of immigration, and occupation. Many Latinos who were professionals in their native land find only low-paying jobs. They often don't have time to both work and learn English, which would help them gain the accreditation they need to practice as doctors, lawyers, and accountants. In Miami, for example, many Cuban physicians have learned English and obtained licenses to practice medicine. But, says one Cuban American doctor, "I know neurosurgeons who are working in warehouses or factories or as gas attendants" (Ojito 2009: D1).

Only 13 percent of Latinos have a college degree or higher, but there are subgroup variations. For exam-

Among African Americans who have made major contributions, some are better known than others. For example, few people know that Madame C. J. Walker (1867–1919) was a manufacturer of hair care products for African American women and one of the first American women millionaires. Or that Dr. Charles R. Drew (1904–1950) was a renowned surgeon, teacher, and researcher. He was responsible for founding two of the world's largest blood banks, which saved untold lives during and since World War II.

ple, 28 percent of Cuban Americans have at least a bachelor's degree compared with only 9 percent of Mexican Americans (U.S. Census Bureau 2010). Despite a strong familial stress on education, second-generation Latinos have the highest high-school dropout rate—one in seven—of any other U.S.-born racial or ethnic group.

Despite their generally lower economic and educational attainment, many Latinos are successful. They own almost 1.6 million businesses, or 15 percent of all U.S. businesses. Between 1995 and 2005, many foreign-born Latino immigrants earned better hourly wages because they tended to be older, better educated, and more likely to be employed in construction than in agriculture (*Hispanic-Owned Firms*. . . 2006; Kochhar 2007). In addition, many Latino families have strengths such as stability, a commitment to the health and welfare of their children, a strong work ethic, an ability to develop cohesive communities, to cope with economic hardship, and to adjust to a new country (National Council of La Raza 2010).

AFRICAN AMERICANS: A MAJOR SOURCE OF DIVERSITY

The 41 million African Americans are the second largest minority group in the United States, making up more than 13 percent of the population (U.S. Census Bureau 2010). This percentage includes those of more than one race, like President Barack Obama, whose father was Kenyan and whose mother is white.

Michael Ochs Archives/Getty Images

AP Photo

Diversity

Most African Americans share a common characteristic: They are members of the only group ever brought to the United States involuntarily and legally enslaved. Despite a common history of oppression, the term *African American* encompasses tremendous diversity: There are native-born blacks who have black, white, American Indian, and/or Latino ancestors, and recent immigrants who are native-born Africans. Among foreign-born blacks, nearly two thirds are from the Caribbean or a Central or South American country, nearly one third were born in Africa, and the remainder is from Europe and other regions (Kent 2007).

Constraints and Strengths

The effects of 350 years of slavery and legal segregation are still evident. Compared with 12 percent of the U.S. population, 25 percent of African Americans live in poverty (DeNavas-Walt et al. 2009). The median family income of African Americans is the lowest of all racial-ethnic groups (see *Figure 10.4* on p. 187). Especially in the country's inner cities, many young black men are high-school dropouts, jobless, or incarcerated (Mincy 2006; U.S. Census Bureau 2010).

The gap in educational achievement between whites and African Americans has decreased in the last four decades. For example, the proportion of blacks who earned at least a high-school diploma increased from 26 percent in 1964 to 80 percent in 2007. Similarly, during this same period, those with a college degree increased from 4 percent to 17 percent (U.S. Census Bureau 2010). Still, and as you'll see in Chapter 14, many black children receive a lower quality of education through high school, which leaves them unprepared for college and the job market.

Despite centuries of oppression, many African Americans are successful. Many blacks—especially those in higher income groups—are upbeat about their progress and future. In 2009, for example, nearly 65 percent with annual household incomes of $75,000 or more said that African Americans will be better off in the future, up from 50 percent in 2007 (Keeter et al. 2010). Blacks own almost 6 percent of U.S. businesses, generating almost $90 billion in annual sales. African Americans are still rare at the largest *Fortune* 500 corporations, but 84 percent of the top 200 companies have at least one black member on the board of directors, usually a man, a number that has doubled since 1987 (*Black-Owned Firms...* 2006; Crockett 2006).

African Americans have numerous strengths—strong kinship bonds, an ability to adapt family roles to outside pressures, a strong work ethic despite recessions and unemployment, a determination to succeed in education, and an unwavering spirituality that helps people cope with adversity. Single-parent families headed by mothers, especially, show exceptional fortitude and coping skills (Edin and Lein 1997; McAdoo 2002; Peters 2007).

ASIAN AMERICANS: A MODEL MINORITY?

The almost 16 million Asian Americans comprise about 5 percent of the U.S. population. Of this group's most recent population increase, 43 percent is due to births and 57 percent to immigration ("Nation's Population One-Third Minority" 2006; U.S. Census Bureau 2010).

Diversity

Asian Americans encompass a broad swath of cultures and traditions. They come from at least 26 countries in East and Southeast Asia (including China, Taiwan, Korea, Japan, Vietnam, Laos, Cambodia, and the Philippines) and South Asia (especially India, Pakistan, and Sri Lanka), and there are at least 19 Asian languages spoken in the United States ("Asian/Pacific American. . ." 2010). These diverse origins mean that there are tremendous differences in languages and dialects (and even alphabets), religions, cuisines, and customs. Asian Americans also include Native Hawaiian and other Pacific Islanders from Guam and Samoa. Chinese form the largest Asian American group, followed by Filipinos and Asian

Many traditional malls across the United States are struggling to survive, but those catering to Asian Americans are thriving. The malls are successful because they sell familiar food (rather than non-necessities such as diamond necklaces), and provide a sense of community and familiarity with the customers' ethnic origins (Haq 2009).

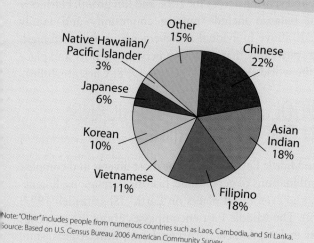

FIGURE 10.5

Asian Americans by Origin

- Chinese 22%
- Asian Indian 18%
- Filipino 18%
- Vietnamese 11%
- Korean 10%
- Japanese 6%
- Native Hawaiian/ Pacific Islander 3%
- Other 15%

Note: "Other" includes people from numerous countries such as Laos, Cambodia, and Sri Lanka.
Source: Based on U.S. Census Bureau 2006 American Community Survey.

Indians (see *Figure 10.5*). Combined, these three groups account for 58 percent of all Asian Americans.

Constraints and Strengths

The most successful Asian Americans are those who speak English relatively well *and* have high educational levels. Asian Americans have the highest median income of all U.S. racial-ethnic groups (see *Figure 10.4* on p. 187). Asian Indians—two thirds of whom have advanced degrees—have the highest annual median household income (almost $74,000) of Asian American subgroups, compared with less than $40,000 for Cambodians, many of whom are less educated, experience language barriers, and have few marketable skills (U.S. Census Bureau 2010).

Overall, Asian Americans have higher educational levels than any other U.S. racial-ethnic group. Half have at least a college degree compared with 28 percent of the white population. There is considerable variation across groups, however.

Because of their educational and economic success, Asian Americans are often hailed as a "model minority." Such labels are misleading, because many households are larger than average and include more workers. Because parents tend to live with their adult children, the latter contribute to the household income (Adler 2003; Aguirre and Turner 2004).

Asian Indians own about 43 percent of the 47,000 U.S. hotels and motels. In many cases, the owners bought run-down lodgings and converted them to upscale Sheraton and Hilton hotels (Yu 2007). Asian Americans have also been more successful than other minority groups in

penetrating corporate suites. In 1995, for example, all of the *Fortune 500* CEOs were white. By 2008, four were black men, five were Latino men, and seven were Asian Americans, two of them women (DiversityInc 2008).

AMERICAN INDIANS: A GROWING NATION

American Indians used to be called the "vanishing Americans," but they have "staged a surprising comeback" due to higher birth rates, a longer life expectancy, and better health services (Snipp 1996: 4). The almost 5 million American Indians and Alaska Natives make up 1.6 percent of the U.S. population but are expected to increase to 2 percent of the population by 2050. Because the median age of this group is only 30 compared with 37 of the population as a whole, some scholars predict that the future population growth of American Indians may outpace that of Latinos (Ogunwole 2006; "American Indian and Alaska Native..." 2009).

Diversity

Like Asian Americans, American Indians are a heterogeneous group. Of the more than 560 federally recognized tribes, those numbering more than 100,000 members include the Cherokee, Navajo, Chippewa, and Sioux. Tribes speak 150 native languages (although many are quickly vanishing), and vary widely in their religious beliefs and cultural practices. Thus, a Comanche-Kiowa educator cautions, "Lumping all Indians together is a mistake. Tribes. . . are sovereign nations and are as different from another tribe as Italians are from Swedes" (Pewewardy 1998: 71; Ashburn 2007).

Constraints and Strengths

American Indians are a unique minority group because they are not immigrants and have been in what is now the United States longer than any other group. Nevertheless, they have experienced centuries of subjugation, exploitation, and political exclusion (such as not having the right to vote until 1924), and have endured a legacy of broken treaties, stolen lands, and tribal extinction (Wilkinson 2006).

American Indians are better off today than they were a decade ago, but long-term institutional discrimination has been difficult to shake. For example, 24 percent of American Indians live below the poverty line compared with 12 percent of the general population ("American Indian and Alaska Native..." 2009). The median household income of American Indians is slightly higher than that of African American households, but lower than other racial-ethnic groups (see *Figure 10.4* on p. 187). On many reservations, where 36 percent of American Indians live, unemployment rates run about 50 percent and some are as high as 90 percent. Substandard housing is common: Many homes on reservations are overcrowded, and lack kitchen facilities (including stoves and refrigerators) and indoor plumbing (Vanderpool 2002; Taylor and Kalt 2005; Ogunwole 2006).

Despite numerous obstacles, American Indians have made considerable economic progress by insisting on self-determination and the rights of tribes to run their own affairs. Since passage of the Indian Gaming Regulatory Act in 1988, the number of casinos owned by American Indian tribes has grown to more than 400, and they account for 37 percent of the U.S. gambling industry. Few tribes have benefited, however, because many casinos are in remote areas that don't attract tourists. Outside of gaming, the number of American Indian–owned businesses grew from fewer than 5 in 1969 to nearly 202,000 in 2002, most of them in construction, retail trade, and health care (Taylor and Kalt 2005; *American Indian- and Alaska Native-Owned Firms. . .* 2006; Kestin and Franceschina 2007).

Mario Tama/Getty Images

Mohegan Sun in southern Connecticut is one of the largest casinos in the United States. It has spent some of its profits on college tuitions, a $15 million senior center, other social programs, and health insurance for tribal members. In contrast, some of the poorest tribes, such as the Navajo and Hopi, who have rejected gaming for religious reasons, have many members who live in poverty.

Regardless of their socioeconomic status, strengths of American Indians include *relational bonding*, a core behavior that is built on values such as respect, generosity, and sharing across the tribe and kin group. Harmony and balance include putting community and family needs above individual achievements. Another strength is a spirituality that sustains a person's identity and place in the world (Stauss 1995; Cross 1998; Cheshire 2006).

MIDDLE EASTERN AMERICANS: AN EMERGING GROUP

The Middle East is "one of the most diverse and complex combinations of geographic, historical, religious, linguistic, and even racial places on Earth" (Sharifzadeh 1997: 442). The Middle East encompasses about 30 countries that include Armenia, Turkey, Israel, Iran, Afghanistan, Pakistan, and 22 Arab nations (such as Algeria, Iraq, Kuwait, Saudi Arabia, and the United Arab Emirates).

Diversity

Those from the Middle East comprise a heterogeneous population that is a "multicultural, multiracial, and multiethnic mosaic" (Abudabbeh 1996: 333). Most are Muslims, but many are Christians or Jews. Arabic is the most common language, but people from the Middle East also speak Turkish, Farsi, Kurdish, and other languages. There is also a multitude of ethnic and linguistic groups with very different customs and cultural practices.

Most Middle Eastern Americans are of Arab ancestry. About 1.2 million Americans, less than 0.5 percent of the total population, report that their ancestry is solely or partly Arab. Almost half were born in the United States, but nearly half arrived during the 1990s (de la Cruz and Brittingham 2003; Brittingham and de la Cruz 2005). Those who classify themselves as Arab Americans come from many Middle Eastern countries (see *Figure 10.6*).

AP Photo/Jeff Robbins

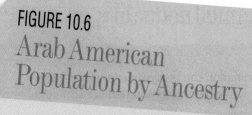

FIGURE 10.6
Arab American Population by Ancestry

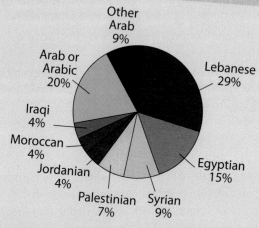

Other Arab 9%

Arab or Arabic 20%

Iraqi 4%

Moroccan 4%

Jordanian 4%

Palestinian 7%

Syrian 9%

Egyptian 15%

Lebanese 29%

Note: "Arab or Arabic" includes people who identify their ancestry as "Arab" or "Arabic" but do not specify a country of origin. "Other Arab" includes Yemeni, Kurdish, Algerian, Saudi, Tunisian, Kuwaiti, Libyan, Berber, United Arab Emirati, Omani, Qatari, Bahraini, Alhuceman, Bedouin, Rio de Oro, and the general terms Middle Eastern and North African.

Source: Based on Brittingham and de la Cruz 2005, Figure 1.

Constraints and Strengths

Middle Eastern Americans tend to be better educated and wealthier than other Americans. Arab Americans are nearly twice as likely as the average U.S. resident to have a college degree: 41 percent compared with 24 percent. As in other groups, there are wide variations. According to the most recent census data, for example, Lebanese have higher median family incomes (almost $61,000) than Moroccans ($41,000). Because of their generally higher educational levels, the proportion of Arab Americans working in management jobs is higher than the proportion of all Americans: 42 percent versus 34 percent (Brittingham and de la Cruz 2005).

Not all Middle Eastern Americans are successful, of course. The proportion living in poverty (17 percent) is greater than that of the general population (12 percent). Lebanese and Syrians have the lowest poverty rates at 11 percent compared with more than 26 percent of those from Iraq and many other Middle East countries (Brittingham and de la Cruz 2005).

Generally, Middle Eastern Americans are well integrated into American life. Besides their high educational levels, three of four speak only English at home or speak English very well, more than half are homeowners, 75 per-

cent of the men are in the labor force, and more than half of those born in another country are U.S. citizens (Brittingham and de la Cruz 2005).

Middle Eastern Americans cope with prejudice and discrimination because they have a strong ethnic identity, close family ties, and religious beliefs that secure children to their communities. Most importantly, perhaps, many families have extended kin networks and relatives on whom they can count for help during hard times (Ajrouch 1999; Hayani 1999).

7 Sociological Explanations of Racial-Ethnic Inequality

a s with other topics, functionalism, conflict theory, feminist theories, and symbolic interactionism help us understand racial-ethnic relations. (*Table 10.3* summarizes the key points of each perspective.) Each has its strengths and weaknesses.

FUNCTIONALISM

Those who criticize immigrants for not becoming Americanized quickly enough reflect a functionalist view of racial-ethnic relations. That is, if a society is to work har-

TABLE 10.3
Sociological Explanations of Racial-Ethnic Inequality

THEORETICAL PERSPECTIVE	LEVEL OF ANALYSIS	KEY POINTS
Functionalist	Macro	• Prejudice and discrimination can be dysfunctional, but they provide benefits for dominant groups and stabilize society.
Conflict	Macro	• Powerful groups maintain their advantages and perpetuate racial-ethnic inequality primarily through economic exploitation.
Feminist	Macro and micro	• Minority women suffer from the combined effects of racism and sexism.
Symbolic Interactionist	Micro	• Hostile attitudes toward minorities, which are learned, can be reduced through cooperative interracial and interethnic contacts.

moniously, newcomers must assimilate by adopting the dominant group's values, goals, and especially, language. Otherwise, the society will experience discord and conflict.

Stability and Cohesion

From a functionalist perspective, racial-ethnic inequality sustains a pool of cheap labor for jobs that require little or no training. Many farmers rely on immigrants to work in fields, orchards, and vineyards at low wages; otherwise, many crops, including lettuce, apples, and grapes would rot in the fields, leading to farmers' economic ruin and increased costs of food (Bustillo 2006). Thus, dominant group members benefit from inequality by avoiding undesirable jobs and minorities with low educational or skill levels find employment.

Racial-ethnic inequality also maintains or increases many dominant group members' current status, power, and profits. Keeping minorities from acquiring higher paying jobs, as well as education and housing, makes more of these scarce resources available to the dominant group. In inner-city neighborhoods, fringe bankers (such as check cashers and pawnshops) profit by offering financial services to low-income residents who can't get bank loans or credit cards (Gans 2005; Squires and Kubrin 2006). Fringe bankers enjoy huge profits (because they charge about 33 percent a *month* in interest vs. about 6 percent a *year* in traditional banks), but they also provide financial stability in poor neighborhoods where people have few borrowing alternatives (see Mahon 2004).

Functionalists acknowledge that discrimination can be dysfunctional. For example, racism prevents a society from recognizing or rewarding talented people who could make important contributions. Recently, anti-Arab visa policies have cost the United States billions in lost tourism and student tuitions to colleges and universities (Smith and Hsu 2007).

Critical Evaluation

Functionalism is useful in understanding how inequality benefits some groups over others and why, as a result, it persists. Functionalists acknowledge that inequality can be dysfunctional, but this is not their major focus. By emphasizing that racial-ethnic inequality maintains a society's stability, functionalists seem to accept inequality as inevitable. Another weakness is that functionalists tend to gloss over the fact that racial-ethnic inequality can lead to tension and violence, which disrupt social solidarity (Chasin 2004).

CONFLICT THEORY

Conflict theorists see ongoing strife between dominant and minority groups. Dominant groups try to protect their power and privilege, whereas subordinate groups struggle to gain a larger share of societal resources. Once a system of racial oppression is in place (e.g., through segregation), racial hierarchies are supported and perpetuated through economic inequality, which reinforces social stratification.

Economic and Social Class Inequality

For most conflict theorists, economic inequality generates racial-ethnic inequality. According to a classic explanation, for example, jobs in the *primary labor market*, held primarily by white workers, provide better wages, health and pension benefits, and some measure of job security. In contrast, workers in the *secondary labor market*, who are largely minorities (such as fast-food workers), are easily replaced. Their wages are low, there are few fringe benefits, and working conditions are generally poor (Doeringer and Piore 1971; Bonacich 1972).

Such economic stratification pits minorities against each other and low-income whites. Because these groups compete with each other instead of uniting against exploitation, capitalists don't have to worry about increasing wages or providing safer work environments. Other conflict theorists maintain that race is a more important factor than social class because even middle-class African Americans (and their counterparts in other racial-ethnic groups) experience discrimination on a daily basis that reminds them of their subordinate place in U.S. society (Feagin and Sikes 1994).

Critical Evaluation

Conflict theories are valuable in explaining why discrimination occurs and persists as when members of privileged groups benefit by subordinating minorities economically. However, conflict theorists often assume that racial inequality is typically conscious, deliberate, widespread, and inescapable. In contrast, 7 in 10 African Americans say that blacks have already reached or will soon attain racial equality. Also, large majorities of both African Americans and Latinos say that immigration and income, not race, are the primary sources of social conflict in the United States (Morin 2009; Agiesta and Cohen 2010). Such data suggest a substantial consensus among minorities that racial inequality is not due entirely to racism.

There is ample evidence that racial inequities persist in employment, but the discrimination isn't always as conscious as some conflict theorists maintain. For example, a study of 700 retail stores found that store managers of different racial and ethnic groups tended to hire employees of the same racial or ethnic group. The researchers attributed the outcomes to factors such as segregated neighborhoods and hiring networks (i.e., institutional discrimination), rather than to prejudice and deliberate discrimination (Giuliano et al. 2009).

FEMINIST THEORIES

Walk through almost any hotel, large discount store, nursing home, or fast-food restaurant in the United States. You'll notice two things: Most of the low-paid employees are women, and they are predominantly minority women. For feminist scholars, such segregation of minority women reflects gendered racism.

Gendered Racism

Gendered racism refers to the combined and cumulative effects of inequality due to racism *and* sexism. Many white women encounter discrimination on a daily basis (see Chapter 9). Minority women, however, are also members of a racial-ethnic group, bringing them a double dose of inequality. If social class is also considered, some minority women experience *triple oppression*. Affluent females, especially, often have no qualms about exploiting recent immigrants, especially Latinas who perform demanding housework at very low wages (Segura 1994; Hondagneu-Sotelo 2001).

Gendered racism also occurs *within* racial-ethnic groups. According to a black male sociologist, for example, scholars rarely discuss black male privilege, which is characterized by having advantages over black women. Examples include being promoted more often and getting higher pay than their black female counterparts who are equally skilled and educated (National Public Radio 2010).

Critical Evaluation

Feminist perspectives have sharpened our understanding of the effects of gendered racism and minority women's subordinate status in U.S. society (Newman 2005). Like conflict theorists, however, feminist scholars often

> **gendered racism** the combined and cumulative effects of inequality due to racism and sexism.

Watch or rewatch the Oscar-winning movie Crash. How does the movie portray some of the benefits and costs of racism, prejudice, and discrimination for both dominant and minority groups?

LIONS GATE/THE KOBAL COLLECTION

contact hypothesis the idea that the more people get to know members of a minority group personally, the less likely they are to be prejudiced against that group.

assume that gendered inequality is deliberate even though it can be unintentional. Because all of us have internalized institutional discrimination, minority-group members may also be guilty of reinforcing inequality in schools, workplaces, and other situations. For example, a black elementary school teacher who assumes that white students will perform better than African American or Latino students may pay more attention to white students. A related weakness is that feminist explanations seldom explore deliberate oppression of minorities by other minorities (such as affluent African American women and men who exploit domestic workers).

SYMBOLIC INTERACTIONISM

According to symbolic interactionists, we learn attitudes, norms, and values throughout the life course (see Chapters 1 and 4). Because, as you saw earlier, race and ethnicity are constructed socially, labeling, selective perception, and social contact can have powerful effects on everyday intergroup relations.

Labeling, Selective Perception, and the Contact Hypothesis

We learn attitudes toward dominant and minority groups through labeling and selective perception, both of which can increase prejudice and discrimination. For example,

a comprehensive study of major U.S. news magazines (such as *Time* and *U.S. News & World Report*) concluded that labeling immigrants as a "problem" and a "menace" ignored "the broader array of Latino roles and contributions to American communities" (Gavrilos 2006: 4; see also "Media Coverage of Hispanics" 2009).

Many popular television shows (such as *CSI: Miami*) portray white characters as more intelligent, attractive, and likeable than black characters. Such images are subtle, but they influence many viewers' perceptions of race and reinforce race bias (Weisbuch et al. 2009).

There are ways to decrease labeling and selective perception. For example, the **contact hypothesis** posits that the more people get to know members of a minority group personally, the less likely they are to be prejudiced against that group. Such contacts are most effective when dominant and minority group members have approximately the same status (such as coworkers or bosses), share common goals (such as working on a project), cooperate rather than compete, and if an authority figure supports intergroup interaction (such as when an employer requires white supervisors to mentor minority workers) (Allport 1954; Kalev et al. 2006).

Critical Evaluation

Symbolic interactionism is valuable in helping us understand how race and ethnicity shape our everyday lives. If we are aware of the negative effects of labeling and selective perception, for example, we can change our attitudes and behavior. It's not clear, however, why exposure to negative images and content—on television and news coverage—increases racial bias among some people but not others, especially when they have similar educational levels (Dovidio 2009).

Another weakness is that symbolic interactionism tells us little about the social structures that create and maintain racial-ethnic inequality. For instance, people who aren't prejudiced can foster discrimination by simply going along with the inequitable policies that have been institutionalized in education, the workplace, and other settings (i.e., the unprejudiced discriminators described earlier).

For symbolic interactionists, images shape our perceptions of racial and ethnic groups.

Looting

After Hurricane Katrina, the caption on a photo of a young black man wading through water described him as "looting".

AP Photo/Dave Martin

Finding

A caption described a white man and a light-skinned woman as "finding" goods at a flooded local grocery store.

©iStockphoto.com / U.P.images / Chris Graythen/Getty Images

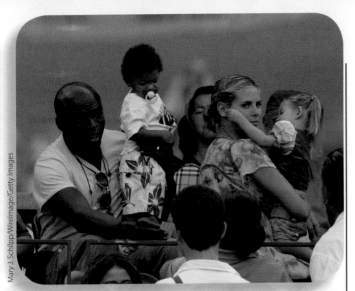

American/German Heidi Klum has a daughter from a previous relationship with an Italian businessman. In 2005, she married musician Seal, the son of Nigerian and Brazilian parents, and they have three children. Do such high-profile people encourage greater acceptance of interracial marriage and multiracial children?

8 Interracial and Interethnic Relationships

i n 1997, professional golfer Tiger Woods said he was "Cablinasian," a word he'd made up as a boy, because he was one-eighth Caucasian, one-fourth black, one-eighth American Indian, one-fourth Thai, and one-fourth Chinese. Many blacks were upset that Woods seemed to downplay his African American roots, but he said that he was embracing all parts of his multicultural heritage.

Interracial relationships are now more acceptable than in the past, but more in principle than as a lived reality. That is, Americans are more likely to approve of interracial dating and intermarriage than to engage in them.

GROWING MULTIRACIAL DIVERSITY

The 2000 U.S. Census allowed people to mark more than one race for the first time because of the growing numbers of interracial dating and marriage, and biracial children. Almost 99 percent of Americans reported only one race, but 1 in 40 is the product of two or more racial groups. Hawaii has the largest percentage of people (21 percent) who identify themselves as two or more races, followed by Alaska and California (5 percent each) (Jones and Smith 2001; Population Division, U.S. Census Bureau 2008).

INTERRACIAL DATING AND MARRIAGE

miscegenation marriage or sexual relations between a man and a woman of different races.

It's now fairly common for people to date someone from a different racial or ethnic group—48 percent of Americans say they have done so, including 69 percent of Latinos, 52 percent of blacks, and 45 percent of whites (Jones 2005). Laws against miscegenation, marriage or sexual relations between a man and a woman of different races, existed in America as early as 1661. It wasn't until 1967, in the U.S. Supreme Court's *Loving v. Virginia* decision, that antimiscegenation laws were overturned nationally. Recently, however, a justice of the peace in Louisiana denied an interracial couple a marriage license: "I'm not a racist. I just don't believe in mixing the races that way" ("Perspectives" 2009: 16).

In 1958, only 4 percent of Americans approved of marriage between blacks and whites. By 2007, 77 percent approved of such unions, but whites were more likely to disapprove (19 percent) than were blacks and Latinos (10 percent each) (Carroll 2007). An overwhelming majority (85 percent) of young adults born in 1981 and later say that they'd be fine with a family member's marriage to someone of a different racial or ethnic group (Keeter et al. 2010).

Attitudes about interracial marriages are changing, but what about behavior? Racial-ethnic intermarriages have increased slowly—from 0.7 percent of all marriages in 1970 to nearly 8 percent in 2010 (Fields and Casper 2001; Frey 2010). Thus, about 92 percent of all Americans still marry someone of the same race.

The increase of intermarriage reflects many interrelated factors—both micro and macro level—that include everyday contact and changing attitudes. For example, we tend to date and marry people we see on a regular basis. The higher the educational level, the greater the potential for intermarriage because educated minority-group members often attend integrated colleges, and their workplaces and neighborhoods are more integrated than in the past (Kalmijn 1998; Qian 2005).

People often marry outside of their racial-ethnic groups because of a shortage of potential spouses within their own group. Because the Arab American population is so small, for example, 80 percent of U.S.-born Arabs have non-Arab spouses. In contrast, intermarriage rates for Latinos and Asian Americans have decreased since 1990—for both women and men—because the influx of new immigrants has provided a larger pool of eligible mates (Kulczycki and Lobo 2002; Qian and Lichter 2007).

Many people

have strong opinions about government
and politics.

11 Government and Politics

In 2008, the election of Barack Obama to the office of President of the United States affirmed many Americans' belief that the United States is a land of political opportunity. On the other hand, two-thirds of Americans are dissatisfied with or angry about the way that government works, the largest number to say so since 1996 (Cohen and Rucker 2010).

Why are many Americans both optimistic and pessimistic about our government and politics? Let's begin by looking at what sociologists mean by these terms. You'll also see that there are many global political systems, interest groups play a major role in elections, many Americans don't participate in the government, and democracies aren't always as open as they seem.

Key Topics

In this chapter, we'll explore the following topics:

1 Government

2 Politics, Power, and Authority

3 Types of Political Systems

4 Power and Politics in U.S. Society

5 Who Votes, Who Doesn't, and Why

6 Who Rules America?

what do you think?

Any child born in America can become President of the United States.

1	2	3	4	5	6	7
strongly agree					strongly disagree	

1 Government

a **government** is a formal organization that has the authority to make and enforce laws. Governments can maintain order, provide social services, regulate the economy, and establish educational systems. Besides maintaining armed forces to discourage (real or imagined) attacks by other countries, governments also try to protect their citizens from internal assaults that range from individual crimes to organized paramilitary groups.

Most governments are huge bureaucracies (see Chapter 6). The U.S. government, for example, consists of executive, legislative, and judicial branches, with numerous departments in the

> **government** a formal organization that has the authority to make and enforce laws.

executive branch alone (see *Figure 11.1*). Among other powers, the president proposes laws, the Congress writes laws, and the judicial system interprets laws and legitimates their enforcement.

Government is often affected by a *civic society*, the nongovernment group of citizens that includes community-based organizations, the media, lobbyists, and voters. If a government seems unjust, a country's civic society can exert considerable power by replacing elected officials or rebelling against appointed leaders.

2 Politics, Power, and Authority

C harles de Gaulle, one of France's past presidents, once remarked, "I have come to the conclusion that politics are too serious a matter to be left to the politicians." All of us should view politics as a serious matter, however, because it can improve or diminish the quality of our everyday lives.

POLITICS AND POWER

Many of us can't discuss politics with relatives or friends without getting into heated debates. Most people feel strongly about **politics,** a social process through which individuals and groups acquire and exercise power and authority, two important concepts (Lasswell 1936).

A neighborhood bully picks on little kids. A bank forecloses on a home mortgage. A government quashes a protest. These are all examples of **power,** the ability of a person or group to affect the behavior of others despite resistance and opposition. There are elements of power in almost all social relationships, such as those between parents and children, students and faculty, officers and soldiers, and employers and employees.

One of the best examples of political power is *earmarks* (known commonly as "pork")—government funds, appointments, or benefits that officials distribute to gain favor with their constituents. More specifically, earmarks are funding requests by lawmakers in Congress to provide federal funding to companies, projects, groups, and organizations, often in their district. Earmarks are inserted into the annual spending bills and don't require competitive bidding.

Despite numerous promises by Congress and President Obama to curb pork spending, the funding has grown considerably—from $10 billion (1,439 projects) in 1995 to $20 billion (10,160 projects) in 2009 (Citizens Against Government Waste 2010). Some examples of pork-barrel projects funded in 2009 included the following:

- $27.8 million to fund three fitness centers at Navy and Air Force military bases in South Carolina

- $4.6 million for 10 states to determine how to use wood

- $3.8 million for tourists to view the site of the Tiger Stadium in Detroit, Michigan, that was demolished in 2009

- $2 million to promote astronomy in Hawaii

FIGURE 11.1
The Government of the United States

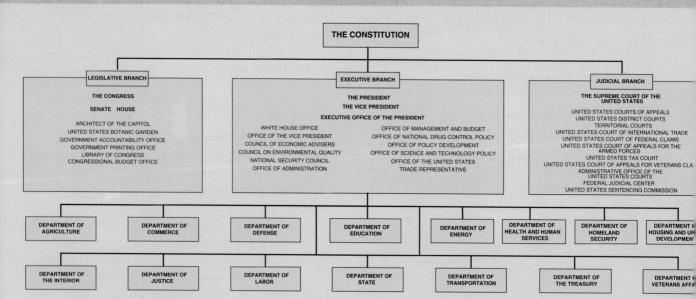

Source: *United States Government Manual, 2005/2006,* p. 21.

TABLE 11.1
Weber's Three Types of Authority

TYPE OF AUTHORITY	DESCRIPTION	SOURCE OF POWER	EXAMPLES
Traditional	Power is based on customs, traditions, and/or religious beliefs.	Personal	Medieval kings and queens, emperors, tribal chiefs
Charismatic	Power is based on exceptional personal abilities or a calling.	Personal	Adolf Hitler, Gandhi, Martin Luther King, Jr.
Rational-legal	Power is based on the rules and laws that are inherent in an elected or appointed office.	Formal	U.S. presidents, Congressional members, state officials, police, judges

- $2.1 million for a grape research center in New York
- $1.8 million each to a honey bee factory in Weslaco, Texas, and for pig odor research in Ames, Iowa (Williams et al. 2010)

Both Democrats and Republicans fight for pork because, they maintain, the money creates jobs and pays for pressing needs, such as maintaining local museums. Critics contend that the earmarks decrease funding for important federal programs, influence re-elections, go to groups that are not at the forefront of research or do not have a good record of completing projects, are typically awarded to high-ranking members of the Appropriations Committee, and are given to companies that, in turn, make generous campaign contributions to the politicians (Brainard and Hermes 2008; Klein 2008; O'Harrow 2008).

Critics also point out that few earmarks create jobs. In Uniontown, Pennsylvania, for example, taxpayers spent $7 million in earmarks to generate four jobs. In West Virginia, a $9.5 million pork-barrel highway project created 60 jobs that lasted less than 2 years, which came out to $175,000 in taxpayer dollars a year for each job created (Leonnig 2009; Williams et al. 2010).

Whether based on persuasion or coercion, power—especially political power—is about controlling others. Because people may revolt against sheer force, many governments depend on authority to establish order, shape people's attitudes, and control their behavior.

AUTHORITY

Authority, the legitimate use of power, has three characteristics. First, people *consent* to authority because they believe that their obedience is for the greater good (e.g., following traffic rules). Second, people see the authority as *legitimate*—valid, justifiable, and necessary (so they pay taxes that support public education, increase national

security, and remove trash and snow). Third, people accept authority because it is *institutionalized* in organizations (such as police departments and government agencies).

Max Weber (1925/1978) described three ideal types of legitimate authority: traditional, charismatic, and rational-legal (see *Table 11.1*). Remember that ideal types are models that describe the basic characteristics of any phenomenon (see Chapters 1 and 5). In reality, the types of authority often overlap.

Traditional Authority

Traditional authority is power based on customs that justify the position of the ruler. The source of power is personal because the ruler inherits authority due to long-standing customs, traditions, or religious beliefs.

Traditional authority is most common in nonindustrialized societies where power resides in kinship groups, tribes, and clans. In the past, kings and emperors ruled because of heredity and the belief that they had a divine right to power, regardless of intelligence or ability. In many African, Middle Eastern, and Asian countries today, power is passed down among men within a family line (Tétreault 2001; see also Chapter 8).

Charismatic Authority

Charismatic authority is power based on exceptional individual abilities and characteristics that inspire devotion, trust, and obedience. Like traditional authority, charismatic authority is personal and reflects extraordinary

> **authority** the legitimate use of power.
>
> **traditional authority** power based on customs that justify the position of the ruler.
>
> **charismatic authority** power based on exceptional individual abilities and characteristics that inspire devotion, trust, and obedience.

deeds or even a belief that a leader has been chosen by God, but the leaders don't pass their power down to their offspring.

Charismatic leaders can inspire loyalty and passion whether they are heroes or tyrants. Examples of the latter include historical figures such as Adolf Hitler, Napoleon, Ayatollah Khomeini, and Fidel Castro. These and other dictators have been spellbinding orators who radiated magnetism, dynamism, tremendous self-confidence, and promised to improve a nation's future (Taylor 1993).

Rational-Legal Authority

Rational-legal authority is power based on the belief that laws and appointed or elected political leaders are legitimate. Unlike traditional and charismatic authority, rational-legal authority comes from rules and regulations that pertain to an office rather than to a person. For example, anyone running for mayor must have specific qualifications (such as U.S. citizenship). When a new mayor (or governor or other politician) is elected, the rules don't change because power is vested in the office rather than the person currently holding the office.

Mixed Authority Forms

Weber's ideal types are useful in identifying the major characteristics of the three types of authority. In reality, people may experience more than one form of author-

ity. For example, some historians believe that presidents Abraham Lincoln, Theodore Roosevelt, John F. Kennedy, and Ronald Reagan enjoyed charismatic appeal beyond their rational-legal authority.

In some countries, such as Japan and England, emperors, kings, and queens have traditional authority and perform symbolic state functions such as attending religious ceremonies and granting titles (like that of Sir Elton John, a singer). Both of these countries also have parliaments that exercise legal-rational authority in determining laws and policies.

We see, then, that political leaders can wield power and authority in many ways. They exert both differently, however, depending on a country's political system.

3 Types of Political Systems

for some years, U.S. and Chinese lawmakers have disagreed about free speech, especially on the Internet. When Secretary of State Hillary Rodham Clinton encouraged "Internet freedom," the Chinese government accused her of "a disguised attempt to impose [American] values on other cultures in the name of democracy" (Mufson 2010: A14). This example illustrates two very different political systems: democracy (in the United States) and totalitarianism (under the Chinese Communist Party [CCP]). Both of these political systems exist in many countries, but there are also totalitarian governments and monarchies.

DEMOCRACY

A **democracy** is a political system in which, ideally, citizens have control over the state and its actions. Democracies are based on several principles:

- Individuals are the best judges of their own interests and participate in governmental decisions.

Joan of Arc (1412–1431) is a well-known example of a charismatic woman who defied the status quo. She was convinced that she was destined by God to lead the French to victory over English invaders. She was burned at the stake as a heretic and witch for claiming that she communicated with God. During the 1960s, California's César Chávez (1927–1993), another charismatic leader, successfully organized a number of strikes to call attention to grape-pickers' and lettuce workers' low wages. Chávez's boycotts and strikes, supported by many consumers nationally, generally improved farm workers' wages and working conditions.

FIGURE 11.2
Political Freedom Around the World 2010

This map shows the degree of political freedom, measured by political rights and civil liberties, in 194 countries around the world. *Political rights* include free and fair elections, competitive parties, and no discrimination against minorities. *Civil liberties* include freedom of speech and the press; freedom to practice one's religion; and the freedom of teachers, professors, and students to discuss political issues without fear of physical violence or intimidation by the government.

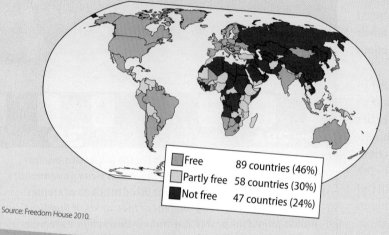

	Free	89 countries (46%)
	Partly free	58 countries (30%)
	Not free	47 countries (24%)

Source: Freedom House 2010.

shortly), U.S. democratic values are endangered because special-interest groups have unprecedented influence on the political process. A minority of hardliners often imposes its views on the majority regarding war, abortion, homosexuality, gun laws, and other social issues, and there is an increased blurring of lines between politics and rigid religious fundamentalism (Carter 2005).

In 2010, 46 percent of the world's population lived in free societies, and another 18 percent lived in partly free societies. About 34 percent of the world's population (almost 2.4 billion people) still lives in authoritarian countries and suffers "intense repression," including "brutal violations of human dignity" and no political freedom (Freedom House 2010). People in sub-Saharan and North Africa, the Middle East, China, and Russia are the least likely to have political freedom (see *Figure 11.2*).

TOTALITARIANISM AND DICTATORSHIPS

At the opposite end of the continuum from democracy is **totalitarianism,** a political system in which the government controls every aspect of people's lives. Totalitarianism has several distinctive characteristics:

- A pervasive ideology that legitimizes state control and instructs people how to act in their public and private lives.

- A single political party controlled by one person, a *dictator*—a supreme, sometimes idolized leader—who stays in office indefinitely.

- A system of terror that relies on secret police and the military to intimidate people into conformity and to punish dissenters.

- Total control by the government over other institutions, including the military, education, family, religion, economy, media, and all cultural activities, including the arts and sports (Taylor 1993; Tormey 1995; Arendt 2004).

- Citizens select leaders who are responsive to the wishes of the majority of the people.

- Suffrage (the right to vote) is universal, and elections are free, fair, secret, and occur frequently.

- The government recognizes individual rights such as freedom of speech (including dissent), press, and assembly, and the right to organize political parties whose members compete for public office.

In reality, democracy doesn't always guarantee equality and respect for human rights. For example, the U.S. Constitution initially limited voting to white male landowners; African American men got the right to vote in 1870, and women of all racial-ethnic groups gained the vote only in 1920. Today, according to some critics (and as you'll see

Contemporary exam-
ples of repressive totalitarian governments include
China, Burma (Myan-
mar), Cuba, Libya, North
Korea, Somalia, Sudan,
Tibet, Turkmenistan, and
Uzbekistan. Within these
countries and territo-
ries, "state control over
daily life is pervasive and
wide-ranging, indepen-
dent organizations and political opposition are banned
or suppressed, and fear of retribution for independent
thought and action is a part of daily life" (Freedom
House 2010).

Whereas democracy assumes that people are rational beings who can manage their own affairs, totalitarian philosophy holds that "humans are by nature either
too irrational or too ignorant to be entrusted with self-
government" (Pauley 1997: 3). Most totalitarian countries have become less successful in controlling people's
actions because their inhabitants are becoming part of
the global economy and the government is less able to
control the media.

Consider China. Since 1949, when the CCP took
power, analysts have consistently described this country
as totalitarian and its government as among the most
repressive in the world. President Hu Jintao, in power
since 2002, is typically on "The World's 10 Worst Dictators" list (Wallechinsky 2010). Citizens cannot vote
against the top leaders or express any opposition to
government policy; journalists who criticize leaders
or their policies are routinely harassed, jailed, or tor-
tured. Freedom of assembly is severely restricted, colleges and universities must support official CCP ideology, and the death penalty can be given for nonviolent
crimes such as burglary, counterfeiting, and bribery. In
addition, although antidiscrimination laws exist, religious groups, minorities, the disabled, and people with
HIV/AIDS suffer severe discrimination (Fowler 2006;
Montlake 2006; Freedom House 2010).

AUTHORITARIANISM AND MONARCHIES

Most nations have some version of democracy or totalitarianism. However, a number of countries are characterized by authoritarianism, a political system in which
the state controls the lives of citizens but permits some
degree of individual freedom. In the Middle East, for

In 2007, pro-democracy activists led the initial demonstrations in Rangoon, Burma, when the military-run government
increased the price of fuel, which hiked the costs of staples
such as rice and cooking oil. Tens of thousands of Buddhist
monks joined the protests, withdrew their religious services
from the military and their families, and issued a statement
denouncing the government as "the enemy of the people."
The monks' participation was significant because they are
highly revered and influential.

Reuters/Landov / © Michael Krinke/iStockphoto.com

example, the ruler of Qatar has absolute power and
discourages public criticism of his policies, but he has
implemented a constitution that specifies that two-
thirds of the officeholders must be elected (rather than
appointed) and has supported numerous progressive
reforms, such as women's active participation in politics (Harman 2007).

A monarchy, the oldest type of authoritarian regime,
is a political system in which power is allocated solely
on the basis of heredity and passes from generation to
generation. In this form of government, a member of
a royal family, usually a king or queen, reigns over a
kingdom. A monarch's power and authority are legiti-
mized by religion (the right to govern is bestowed on
the monarch by God) and tradition.

There are about 29 monarchies around the world.
In some countries—especially in the Middle East and
parts of Africa—monarchs have absolute control.
Those in Norway, Denmark, Belgium, Britain, Japan,
and many other countries have little political power
because they are limited by democratic constitutions.

Instead, many of these modern monarchs serve primarily ceremonial roles, by acting as goodwill ambassadors to other countries, for example.

4 Power and Politics in U.S. Society

President Ronald Reagan once joked, "Politics is not a bad profession. If you succeed, there are many rewards. If you disgrace yourself, well you can always write a book." Despite Reagan's levity, politics plays a critical role in our everyday lives. In the United States, you can contact your government officials, be active in a political party, join a special-interest group, and, of course, vote. Do Americans take advantage of these democratic processes often enough? Let's begin with political parties.

POLITICAL PARTIES

A **political party** is an organization that tries to influence and control government by recruiting, nominating, and electing its members to public office. Political parties provide a legitimate way for citizens to shape public policy at the local, state, and national levels.

Functions of U.S. Political Parties

Political parties are highly organized. They engage in a wide variety of activities—everything from stuffing envelopes and calling voters to drafting laws if a candidate is elected. Through their activities, parties perform a number of vital political functions, especially recruiting candidates for public office, organizing and running elections, and if

© Peter Busomoke/AFP/Getty Images

In 1995, at age 3, Oyo Nyimba Kabamba Iguru became the world's youngest monarch when he was crowned as king of the Ugandan Kingdom of Toro. At age 18, he officially took control of the kingdom.

elected, running the government (Schmidt et al. 2001).

Ideally, that's how political parties *should* work. In reality, parties perform some of these

> **political party** an organization that tries to influence and control government by recruiting, nominating, and electing its members to public office.

functions more effectively than others. For example, parties typically concentrate on winning elections rather than making changes once candidates are in office. In addition, because the United States has a two-party system, many people who don't identify with either group may feel alienated and excluded.

The Two-Party System

Many democracies around the world have a number of major political parties: 3 in Canada, 5 in Germany, 9 in Italy, more than 20 in Israel, and there are 1,050 registered national and regional political parties in India (Yardley, 2009). Iraq, which is trying to establish a democracy, has at least 30 political parties that fielded more than 2,000 candidates in the 2010 elections ("Political Parties" 2010). Thus, compared with many other countries, the two-party system of Democrats and Republicans in the United States is unique.

In the past, the percentage of Americans who identified with either party was about equally divided. In 2009, however, 23 percent identified themselves as Republicans and 35 percent said that they were Democrats. The other 58 percent identified themselves as independent ("Trends in Political Values. . ." 2007; "GOP Party Identification. . ." 2009). Because there's no national Independent Party, independents usually vote for Democrats, Republicans, or not at all.

Those who identify with the Democratic Party typically believe that the government should provide social programs, especially for the poor; those in the Republican Party usually believe that the federal government should be involved in few social programs. *Table 11.2* provides some examples of other major ideological differences between Democrats and Republicans.

Other parties have emerged in the United States, but they usually have little weight. Most third-party candidates have little chance of being elected because the media don't take them seriously and give them little coverage. Sometimes, though, third parties meet with surprising success. In 1998, for example, former wrestler Jesse "The Body" Ventura, a Reform Party candidate, surprised everyone when he was elected governor of Minnesota. More often, however, campaign contributors and voters pay little attention to third-party candidates because they want their donations and ballots to have an effect.

SPECIAL-INTEREST GROUPS

Some people are active in political parties. Others join a **special-interest group** (also called an *interest group*), a voluntary and organized association of people that attempts to influence public policy and policy makers on a particular issue. Political parties often include diverse individuals, whereas special-interest groups are usually made up of people who are very similar in social class and political objectives.

There are thousands of special-interest groups, large and small, in the United States. A few examples include associations of college administrators, farmers, firefighters, bartenders, religious congregations, and a vari-

ety of environmental groups. If you've ever sent a donation to such a group or signed a petition, you're a member of a special-interest group. Special-interest groups use many tactics to influence the government. Three of the most effective—although their aims are rarely representative of the general population—are lobbying,

© AP Images

TABLE 11.2
How Do Democrats and Republicans Differ?

ISSUE	MANY DEMOCRATS BELIEVE THAT . . .	MANY REPUBLICANS BELIEVE THAT . . .
Family	Government programs should implement universal health insurance for all families, especially those with low incomes.	Government should cut all welfare benefits to unwed mothers, stigmatize divorce, and emphasize "traditional" family values.
Abortion	Women should have the right to choose abortion in practically all cases; the government should pay for abortions for low-income women.	The unborn should be protected in all cases; there should be no public money for abortions.
Gay Rights	Gay men and lesbians should have the right to marry and to adopt children. They should be fully accepted in the military and other institutions.	Marriage and adoption should be limited to heterosexuals. Inclusion of gay men and lesbians in the armed forces creates interpersonal problems.
Education	The government should strengthen public schools by raising salaries for teachers and decreasing classroom sizes. It should not use tax dollars to help students attend private schools.	The government should increase state and local control of schools. It should use tax dollars to fund students to attend private schools of their choice if their local school is underperforming.
Environment	The government should provide incentives to promote a clean environment, penalize corporations that pollute, and seek environmental protections in trade agreements.	The government should balance businesses' rights and economic development with environmental protection. Insisting on environmental protection will discourage global trade agreements.

Sources: Based on Benokraitis 2000; Welch et al. 2004.

campaign contributions, and political action committees (PACs).

Lobbyists

A **lobbyist** is a representative of a special-interest group who tries to influence political decisions on the group's behalf. At the federal level alone, more than 64,000 firms, organizations, and individuals lobby about a variety of subjects such as bankruptcy, casinos, immigration, railroads, alcohol, and veterans. In 2009, there were almost 14,000 registered lobbyists who spent $3.5 billion to influence members of Congress, but funding levels vary. Between 1998 and 2009, for example, the finance, insurance, and real-estate sector spent $4 billion on lobbying compared with the labor sector's $392 million (Center for Responsive Politics 2010a).

Nationwide, there is an average of five lobbyists per lawmaker (Political Money Line 2004; Laskow 2006). Some of the best-paid lobbyists are former members of Congress who have retired or lost a re-election. They know how the federal government works and often maintain close ties with incumbents (Kelley 2007). Also, a growing number of lobbyists are relatives of members of Congress.

Between 2000 and 2005, lobbyists paid almost $50 million to send members of Congress, their staffs, and their family members on at least 23,000 "seminars" (actually more like expensive vacations) overseas and across the United States to curry favor with legislators. Such expense is miniscule compared with the benefits. On average, companies generate about $28 in earmarked revenue for every $1 they spend lobbying. In some cases, companies pull in more than $2,000 in earmarks for every lobbying dollar (Morris 2006; Kirkpatrick 2007).

Affluent lobby groups are effective in swaying legislation. In 2009, for example, the beverage industry lobby spent almost $38 million to smother a plan proposed by nutrition scientists to tax sugared beverages (Hamburger and Geiger 2010). A more significant factor is lobbyists' clout in providing campaign contributions.

> **lobbyist** a representative of a special-interest group who tries to influence political decisions on the group's behalf.

Campaign Contributions

Money is the most important factor in winning an election. It doesn't guarantee a victory, but candidates with little financing usually have little public visibility. Among all presidential candidates, the spending soared from $67 million in 1976 to almost $1.4 billion in 2008. Democratic presidential candidate Barack Obama spent almost $730 million, and Republican nominee John McCain spent $333 million (Center for Responsive Politics 2009, 2010b). Billionaire Michael R. Bloomberg spent $74 million of his own money in 2001 to be elected mayor of New York City, $85 million in 2005 for a second term, and $100 million in 2009 for a third term. He spent more out of pocket than any political candidate in U.S. history—about $158 per vote compared with Obama's $12 per vote (Susman and Barabak 2009).

How do most political candidates raise money for their campaigns? There are two types of political contributions: hard money and soft money. *Hard money* refers to political donations that the Federal Election Commission regulates. It's illegal for corporations and labor unions to contribute to campaigns for federal elections, but individuals can contribute up to $25,000 per year to any national party and $10,000 per year to any state or local party.

Soft money is any contribution that is not regulated by federal election laws. Since 1907, corporations and unions had been barred from spending soft money on presidential and congressional elections. In 2010, however, the U.S. Supreme Court voted 5-4 in *Citizens United v. Federal Election Commission* that corporations, trade groups, and unions could use their own money freely to support or oppose individual candidates in federal elections. President Obama condemned the ruling, claiming that it would drown out the voices of everyday citizens. Most Republican lawmakers praised the ruling for giving the same political speech rights to corporations as to individuals (Savage 2010; see also

"Is my face red! — I had so many appointments with lobbyists last session, I forgot to *vote* for anything!"

Baloo-Rex May-, Catalog Reference: rman2238

Krumholz 2010). In contrast, a national poll found that, among voters, 85 percent of Democrats and 76 percent of Republicans strongly opposed the Supreme Court decision (Eggen 2010).

Political Action Committees

A legal but controversial type of special-interest group is a **political action committee (PAC)**, a group that raises money to elect one or more candidates to public office. At the federal level, a PAC can contribute no more than $15,000 to a national party, and an individual's contribution to a PAC is limited to $5,000. Some states have similar limits but others don't. A state can also have many PACs supported by a particular interest group, such as surgeons, that officially have different names (e.g., Baltimore County Surgeons, Howard County Surgeons).

PACs have mushroomed—from 608 in 1974 to almost 4,500 in 2009, 37 percent of them representing corporate interests (U.S. Census Bureau 2010). The top PAC contributors are members of corporations, but professional groups and labor unions are also generous donors (see *Table 11.3*). Notice, also, that some of the PACs give to both parties to cover their bases regardless of who's elected.

Why are PACs controversial? They provide access to politicians and create a sense of obligation, a need to reciprocate, and the larger an organization, the greater its clout. In contrast with small business firms with few resources, national and global corporations can contribute the maximum amount to a similar PAC in every state, increasing their influence. In contrast, low-income and part-time workers aren't likely to have a PAC that represents their interests (Clawson et al. 1998).

Besides lobbying, campaign contributions, and PACs, interest groups and wealthy individuals have other legal ways to buy a lawmaker's goodwill. They can give generous gifts (such as luxurious vacations and tickets to major sports events) to lawmakers' spouses and other family members, donate to the politicians' favorite charities, and hire the lawmakers or their family members as consultants. Many members of Congress routinely use campaign contributions and money from PACs to pay their relatives for fundraising and other campaign work. These payments sometimes amount to hundreds of thousands of dollars per family member (Vogel 2007; Citizens for Responsibility and Ethics in Washington 2007, 2008). Most Americans don't contribute to political campaigns, but many vote.

TABLE 11.3
Top 10 Political Action Committee Contributors to Political Parties, 2009–2010

ORGANIZATION SUPPORTING POLITICAL ACTION COMMITTEES	TOTAL AMOUNT (IN MILLIONS)	PERCENTAGE FOR DEMOCRATS	PERCENTAGE FOR REPUBLICANS
Operating Engineers Union	$2.1	88	12
International Brotherhood of Electrical Workers	$1.7	99	2
AT&T Inc.	$1.7	50	50
National Beer Wholesalers Association	$1.5	59	41
Honeywell International	$1.4	61	39
American Association for Justice	$1.3	96	4
National Community Pharmacists Association	$1.3	65	35
American Bankers Association	$1.3	45	55
Teamsters Union	$1.2	98	2
Boeing Corporation	$1.2	62	38

Source: Center for Responsive Politics, 2010c.

5 Who Votes, Who Doesn't, and Why

The ballot is stronger than the bullet.
—President Abraham Lincoln

Several Democratic and Republican primaries were just held all across the country. It was evenly split between those who forgot to vote and those who chose not to vote.
—Conan O'Brien, comedian

Abraham Lincoln was right about the power of the ballot, but as Conan O'Brien's quote suggests, many Americans are disillusioned with politics. For example:

- Even before the financial meltdown began in 2008, 74 percent of Americans said that they were dissatisfied with the way the nation was being governed, up from 49 percent in 2004 (Jones 2008; Newport 2008).

- In early 2010, fewer than 1 in 10 Americans in a *New York Times*/CBS News poll said that members of Congress deserve re-election; 4 of 5 voters thought that "Congress was more interested in serving special interests than voters" (Nagourney and Thee-Brenan 2010: A1)

- In mid 2010, only 20 percent of Americans approved of the way that Congress was doing its job (Jones 2010).

One might expect that such dissatisfaction would result in higher voter turnout, but this isn't the case. Of 163 countries around the world that hold democratic elections, the United States ranks only 140th in voter turnout. In 34 nations, at least 80 percent of the eligible population votes. More than 90 percent do so in Austria, Italy, and Luxembourg compared, on average, with about half of U.S. citizens (International Institute for Democracy and Electoral Assistance 2007; Thompson 2010).

Some of the high turnout rates in other countries may be partly due to *compulsory voting,* in which the government requires explanations or imposes fines for not voting, may disenfranchise nonvoters (which makes it difficult to get benefits such as public assistance), or requires evidence of voting to get a passport or a driver's license. Generally, these kinds of sanctions send the message that voting is not a privilege but a civic responsibility (Holder 2006; International Institute for Democracy and Electoral Assistance 2007).

In 2008, 64 percent of Americans voted in the presidential election. This was a larger than usual percentage, but lower than the numbers who voted in presidential elections during the 1950s and 1960s (File and Crissey 2010). Who votes, who doesn't, and why reflect demographic characteristics, attitudes about politics, and situational and structural factors. Because presidential elections have the highest turnouts, let's look at some voting patterns in the 2008 election.

DEMOGRAPHIC FACTORS

Many demographic factors influence registration and voting, but the most important are age, marital status, social class, race and ethnicity, and religion. Sex isn't a major variable because in the 2008 presidential election, 66 percent of women and 62 percent of men voted (File and Crissey 2010; unless noted otherwise, much of this section relies on data from this source).

Age

In 2008, as well as historically, the voting rate is routinely higher among older than younger people and generally increases with age (see *Table 11.4a*; voting drops off at age 75 probably because of poor health). Obama captured 66 percent of the vote of people aged 18 to 29. Some political analysts suggest that the higher voting participation of younger people in 2008 may reflect a generally greater interest in civic engagement. Others note that during the 2008 election, among young voters aged 18 to 29, blacks had the highest turnout rate at 58 percent—a historic first (Keeter et al. 2008; Lopez and Taylor 2009).

Why are young adults less likely to vote than their older counterparts? A key factor is registration. Almost half of young people (ages 18–34) are registered to vote compared with 75 percent of those 55 years old and older. Young people have lower registration rates because they are more mobile than older people and are less likely to re-register after a move. They may also be preoccupied with major life events such as going to college and finding jobs. Other young adults don't register or vote because they grew up in homes where their parents paid little attention to politics (60 percent) or believe that lawmakers don't care about their attitudes (38 percent) ("Generational Look at the Public. . ." 2002; Schachter 2004). In effect, then, the low participation rate of young voters means that they have little impact on political processes.

Marital Status

Married people are more likely to vote than those who are widowed, divorced, or have never married (see *Table 11.4b*). People who have not been married tend to be younger, which influences their voting rate, as you've just seen. Married couples are more likely to be registered voters, homeowners, to live in established neighborhoods, to be parents of young children in school, and to be employed (Day and Holder 2004). This combination of characteristics suggests that married people, compared with never-married singles, have a bigger stake in society and, as a result, are more likely to vote.

Social Class

Social class has a significant impact on voting behavior. At each successive level of educational attainment, the voting rate increases. For example, the voting rate of those with a college degree (77 percent) is almost twice as high as for people who have not completed high school, and those with advanced degrees are the most likely to vote (see *Table 11.4c*). People with the highest educational levels are usually more informed about and interested in the political process and feel that their vote counts ("Who Votes. . ." 2006).

Voting rates also increase with income levels. The voting rate of people with annual family incomes of $100,000 or more was 92 percent compared with 56 percent of those with annual incomes under $30,000 (see *Table 11.4d*). People with higher incomes are more likely to be employed, to have assets (such as houses and stock), and, therefore, are more likely to be aware of the costs of not voting to protect or increase their resources. In contrast, people who are unemployed usually have few assets and may be too disillusioned with the political system to vote ("Who Votes. . ." 2006).

Race and Ethnicity

Whites are typically the most likely to vote (see *Table 11.4e*). Here again, a key to voter turnout is registration. Across all racial-ethnic groups—including both native-born and naturalized individuals—the higher the voter registration, the higher the voting rate.

Low voter registration rates among racial-ethnic groups are associated with other demographic and social characteristics. For example, compared with white citizens, minorities tend to be younger, poorer, unemployed, and have lower education levels. Because they are less likely to be homeowners or married, they may be less invested in election outcomes. In addition, minorities are more likely than whites to be pessimistic about government and politics (Frey 2008).

Despite such constraints, during the 2008 election, voters were "the most racially and ethnically diverse in U.S. history, with nearly one-in-four votes cast by non-whites" (Lopez and

TABLE 11.4
Selected Characteristics of Voters in the November 2008 Election

(a) Age

18–24	49%
25–34	57%
35–44	63%
45–54	67%
55–64	72%
65–74	73%
≥75	68%

(b) Marital Status

Married	70%
Widowed	62%
Divorced	59%
Never married	54%

(c) Educational Attainment

Less than high-school graduate	39%
High-school graduate or GED	55%
Some college or associate's degree	68%
Bachelor's degree	77%
Advanced degree	83%

(d) Annual Family Income

Less than $20,000	52%
$15,000–$29,999	56%
$30,000–$39,999	62%
$40,000–$49,999	65%
$50,000–$74,999	71%
$75,000–$99,999	76%
$100,000 and over	92%

(e) Race and Ethnicity

White	66%
Black	65%
Latino	50%
Asian	48%

Source: Based on File and Crissey 2010, Tables 1 and 2.

Taylor 2009: i) and played a large role in the outcome. Nearly all (95 percent) black voters cast their ballot for Barack Obama, as did 67 percent of Latinos, and 62 percent of Asian voters. In contrast, white voters supported John McCain (55 percent) over Obama (43 percent).

Religion

Only 14 percent of Americans say that their religious beliefs influence their politics, but there are strong links between these variables. Among Jews and mainline Protestants (e.g., Lutherans and Methodists), more than 80 percent are registered to vote, compared with 69 percent of Catholics, 48 percent of Muslims, 42 percent of Hindus, and only 13 percent of Jehovah's Witnesses. The low voter registration rates of Muslims and Hindus are primarily due to the fact that many of them are recent immigrants who aren't eligible to vote (Pew Forum on Religion & Public Life 2008).

Religion also shapes political affiliation. Mormons, mainline Protestants, and members of evangelical churches (including born-again Christians) tend to describe themselves as conservative and support the Republican Party. Jews, Buddhists, Hindus, and those not affiliated with a religious group describe their political beliefs as liberal and favor the Democratic Party. The connection between religious affiliation and political opinion appears to be especially strong for certain issues such as abortion and homosexuality (Pew Forum on Religion & Public Life 2008; see also *Table 11.2* on p. 204).

When minorities vote, they can make a huge difference in the results. In 2003, Democratic candidate for governor of Arizona, Janet Napolitano, pictured left, defeated her Republican opponent by about 20,000 votes, most of them from the Navajo reservations. She is currently Secretary of Homeland Security.

ATTITUDES

Of the almost 15.2 million Americans who didn't vote in 2008, 18 percent said they were "too busy" or had "conflicting schedules." Another 32 percent said they weren't interested in the election, didn't like the candidates, forgot to vote, or that the polling place was inconvenient (File and Crissey 2010). Such responses suggest that voting is a low priority, whether because of apathy or other factors.

In October 2008, only 25 percent of Americans said that President Bush was doing a good job, and only 12 percent felt this way about Congress. Two years later, 86 percent of Americans said that federal government was broken and didn't work (West 2010). Many Americans simply don't trust politicians: "They all lie," "I've never met an honest politician," "They're all corrupt," and so on. When Gallup asked people to rate 22 occupations according to honesty and integrity, members of Congress and stockbrokers were among the lowest at 9 percent each (Saad 2009). Whether such cynicism is warranted or not, many people don't vote because they believe that their lives won't improve regardless of who's elected.

SITUATIONAL AND STRUCTURAL FACTORS

There are also a number of situational and structural factors that discourage voting. For example, nearly one in three Americans didn't vote in the 2008 presidential election because of illness, disability, out-of-town travel, and transportation or registration problems (File and Crissey 2010).

Because a key to voter turnout is registration, some states have removed structural barriers to registering. North Dakota, for example, has no voter registration. In other states—Idaho, Maine, Minnesota, New Hampshire, Wisconsin, and Wyoming—people can vote the same day that they register. In Oregon, elections have been conducted by mail since 2000. In all of these states, the voting rates are much higher than the national average, and sometimes well above 72 percent (Welch et al. 2004).

In many European and other countries, where voter turnout is typically high, voters are registered automatically when they pay taxes or receive public services, and elections are held on Saturdays. In the United States, in contrast, the government does little to help people register to vote, and elections are held on a weekday (usually Tuesday). Most of our polls are open from 7:00 a.m. to 8:00 p.m., but voting is still difficult for those with long commutes (see Harder and Krosnick 2008).

pluralism a political system in which power is distributed among a variety of competing groups in a society.

We've seen that officeholders, political parties, and voters participate in a democracy. But who has the most power? And do government leaders represent the average citizen? Such questions have generated considerable debate among sociologists and other social scientists.

6 Who Rules America?

according to symbolic interactionism, whenever there are social interactions, people can assume power and influence social life. And as you saw earlier, people learn to be loyal to a political system—whether it's a democracy or a monarchy—and to show respect for its symbols and leaders. For the most part, however, sociologists rely on macro-level theories to analyze political power. Functionalists argue that the people hold most of the power ("government of the people, by the people, for the people"), conflict theorists maintain that power is concentrated in the hands of a few people at the top, and feminist theorists assert that men have most of the decision-making power (*Table 11.5* summarizes these perspectives).

FUNCTIONALISM: A PLURALIST MODEL

The pluralist model originates from functionalists' theories. For functionalists, the people rule through **pluralism,** a political system in which power is distributed among a variety of competing groups in a society (Riesman 1953; Polsby 1959; Dahl 1961).

Key Characteristics

According to the pluralist model, individuals have little direct power over political decision making but can influence government policies through special-interest groups—trade unions, professional organizations, and so on (see *Figure 11.3*). Because there is so much diversity between and within groups, no single group dominates or controls political life. The various groups rarely join ranks because they concentrate on single issues such as health care, pollution, or education. This focus on different issues fragments groups, but the competition among groups, according to pluralists, also results in a broad representation of a variety of interests and a distribution of power.

Because there are a number of single-issue groups, functionalists maintain, there are multiple leaderships: "Those who exercise power in one kind of decision do not necessarily exercise power in others" (Dye and Ziegler 2003: 12). As a result, many leaders, not just a few, can shape decisions that represent many groups and issues. Pluralists note that people also have power outside of interest groups: They can vote, run for office, contact officeholders, and collect signatures to place specific issues on a ballot. Therefore, there are continuous checks and balances as individuals and groups vie for power and try to influence laws and policies.

Critical Evaluation

Does pluralism work as democratically as functionalists maintain? Critics argue that interest groups have unequal resources. The poor and disadvantaged rarely have the skills and educational backgrounds to organize or to promote their interests. In contrast, wealthy individu-

How Would *You* Describe Congress?

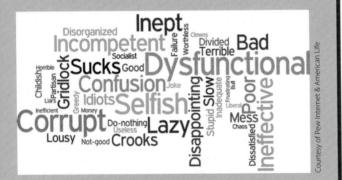

Courtesy of Pew Internet & American Life

In March 2010, the Pew Research Center asked a nationally representative sample of Americans to provide one word that described their impression of Congress. Among all respondents, 86 percent said something negative, 4 percent said something positive, and 10 percent didn't offer an opinion. The responses were entered into Wordle, a website that generates "word clouds" from text, to illustrate the impressions. The larger the word, the more times it was used (Auxier 2010). What one word would *you* use to describe Congress?

Word cloud graphic, created using http://wordle.net, from "Congress in a Wordle," Mar. 22, 2010, The Pew Research Center For the People & the Press, a project of the Pew Research Center

TABLE 11.5
Sociological Explanations of Political Power

	FUNCTIONALISM: A PLURALIST MODEL	CONFLICT THEORY: A POWER ELITE MODEL	FEMINIST THEORIES: A PATRIARCHAL MODEL
Who has political power?	The people	Rich upper-class people—especially those at top levels in business, government, and the military	White men in Western countries; most men in traditional societies
How is power distributed?	Very broadly	Very narrowly	Very narrowly
What is the source of political power?	Citizens' participation	Wealthy people in government, business corporations, the military, and the media	Being white, male, and very rich
Does one group dominate politics?	No	Yes	Yes
Do political leaders represent the average person?	Yes, the leaders speak for a majority of the people.	No, the leaders are most concerned with keeping or increasing their personal wealth and power.	No, the leaders—who are typically white, elite men—are most concerned with protecting or increasing their personal wealth and power.

FIGURE 11.3
Pluralist and Power Elite Perspectives on Political Power

PLURALIST MODEL

Power is dispersed among multiple groups that influence the government. For example,

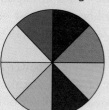

- government employees
- victims' rights groups
- labor unions
- banks and other financial institutions
- realtors and home builders
- teachers
- environmental groups
- women's rights groups

POWER ELITE MODEL

Power is concentrated in a very small group of people who make all the key decisions. For example,

Top level (1 percent)—CEOs of large corporations, high-ranking lawmakers in the executive branch, and top military leaders

Middle level (8 percent)—most members of Congress, lobbyists, entrepreneurs of small businesses, leaders of labor unions and other interest groups (in law, education, medicine, etc.), and influential media commentators

The masses (91 percent)—people who are unorganized and exploited and either don't know or don't care about what's going on in government

als and organizations can influence government through political contributions and personal connections.

Critics also maintain that pluralists aren't realistic about the power of groups to change the status quo. Only 19 percent of Americans register their political opinions with officeholders or government agencies because they don't trust politicians or they believe that lawmakers pay little attention to people's complaints or input (Horrigan 2004).

Reflecting a functionalist view, historian Rich Shenkman (2008) contends that if Americans don't have the government they want, they themselves are to blame. They know little about politics (e.g., only two of every five voters can name the three branches of government), don't question government policies, are easily manipulated because they're uninformed, and don't vote.

CONFLICT THEORY: A POWER ELITE MODEL

In contrast with pluralists, conflict theorists contend that the United States is ruled by a **power elite,** a small group of influential people who make the nation's major political decisions. Sociologist C. Wright Mills (1956) coined the term *power elite* to describe a pyramid of power that he believed characterized American democracy (see *Figure 11.3* on p. 211).

Key Characteristics

According to Mills, the power elite is made up of three small but influential groups of people at the top level who run the country: political leaders (specifically chief executives, who include the president and his top aides), business heads (the corporate rich, who have enormous wealth), and military chiefs (who govern the Pentagon). Practically all of the members of these groups are white, Anglo-Saxon, Protestant men who form an inner circle of power.

For Mills, there are also a number of groups at the middle level of power: Congressional members, lobbyists, influential media commentators, active professionals, leaders of labor unions and other interest groups, and the heads of local and state governments. The bottom level, and the largest and least powerful group, is composed of the masses, consisting of everyone else (see *Figure 11.3*). The power elite tolerates the masses—including their elections and laws—but in the end simply does what it wants, such as declaring wars, decreasing taxes for the rich, and cutting off benefits for the poor (e.g., see Kivel 2004, and Domhoff 2006).

Many contemporary power-elite theorists maintain, like Mills, that the United States is not a democracy because there are close ties between politics, business, and the military. For example, President Obama's top administration includes recent high-ranking employ-

One of the reasons that many Americans are disillusioned with government and politics is because dishonest lawmakers are rarely punished. A recent exception is Rod R. Blagojevich, former governor of Illinois, whom the FBI indicted on 19 felony charges, including racketeering conspiracy, wire fraud, attempted extortion, and lying to federal agents. According to federal prosecutors, Blagojevich used his office for the financial and political benefit of himself, his family, and friends (Davey and Saulny 2009).

ees from corporations such as AT&T, IBM, Allstate Insurance, and Goldman Sachs (a financial corporation that enjoyed a bailout at taxpayers' expense in 2009) (Kalwarski 2010). In addition, the Pentagon often hires retired generals and admirals who work for private defense firms and influence the administration's decisions about funding for the firms (Vanden Brook et al. 2009). In effect, then, there's a "revolving door" between lawmakers, corporate executives, and the military.

Other conflict theorists emphasize that the corporate rich is a more powerful group than Mills originally thought. The owners and top-level managers of corporations, banks, and agribusinesses shape government policies for their own benefit and have "a major impact on the income, job security, and well-being of most other Americans" (Domhoff 2006: xi; Zweigenhaft and Domhoff 2006; see also Chapter 12). According to conflict theorists, the upper classes have enormous power over political institutions because they finance political campaigns and get elected or appointed to political offices. More than half of the members of Congress and the U.S. Supreme Court Justices are multimillionaires. Because many lawmakers are wealthy, they have the power to vote for tax laws and other legislation that promote their own interests (Becker 2001; Becker 2008; Feldmann 2008).

Critical Evaluation

Functionalists maintain that the conflict theorists' claims about the power elite are exaggerated. They point out, for example, that "the masses" aren't just puppets but are very aware of the influence of the power elite. As a result, they vote, mobilize, support particular PACs, and protest current administrative and corporate policies (such as high prescription prices for older people and healthcare reform).

Also, according to critics, the power elite perspective assumes, incorrectly, that the wealthy people at the top are unified in their interests and goals. For example, Vice President Dick Cheney broke away from President Bush's strong endorsement of a constitutional amendment to ban same-sex marriage in 2004 because Cheney's daughter, Mary, is a lesbian who has a life partner and a child. In addition, critics maintain, because the Democratic and Republican political parties and their top officials endorse very different agendas, any power elite that exists is rarely unified.

FEMINIST THEORIES: A PATRIARCHAL MODEL

Feminist theories emphasize that women are generally excluded from the most important political positions. Women's status in the Western world has improved considerably during the last 100 years, but as you saw in Chapter 9, relatively few women, especially minority women, serve in Congress and at the highest levels of government.

Key Characteristics

Of 187 countries worldwide, women occupy only 18 percent of positions in the decision-making bodies that are comparable with our Congress. In Argentina, Cuba, Finland, Sweden, and Rwanda, women make up at least 40 percent of these governing bodies. The United States ranks 81st, well below many African, European, and Asian countries, and even below most of the Arab countries that many Westerners view as repressive toward women (Inter-Parliamentary Union 2008). Thus, U.S. democracy is not as egalitarian as most of us assume.

Feminist theorists maintain that most American women have been shut out of the political process because the United States is still a patriarchal society. Women are successful fund-raisers, vote in higher numbers than men, and often run for office. Compared with men, however, women get considerably less media coverage of their political campaigns or receive coverage that is more disparaging. For example, many commentators, especially feminist scholars, accused the media of sexist attacks that hurt the public's image of then Senator Hillary Clinton in her 2008 bid for a presidential nomination (Kahn 2003; Reed 2008; see also Chapter 9).

Feminist theorists also note that the contributions of women in rank-and-file positions in political organi-

In 2008, Ann E. Dunwoody became the first woman to achieve the rank of four-star general in the U.S. Army. Many hailed the appointment as a major step forward for women. Feminist scholars would ask why it's taken so long to break "the brass ceiling" and why women are still highly underrepresented at top military levels.

zations and campaigns are often undervalued and unrewarded (Kramer 2005). For example, few women are asked to be campaign managers, positions that often lead to political visibility and appointments.

Critical Evaluation

Feminist scholars go further than conflict theorists in showing that most of the powerful elite are typically men. Despite such contributions, critics reject several feminist explanations of political power. They claim, for example, that women aren't elected because they don't venture into political realms. Often, critics say, women work as volunteers rather than seek office. Some critics also argue that most women's organizations typically focus on single issues such as abortion, child care, domestic violence, and so on. Such splintering dilutes women's mobilization within a political party and decreases their chances of winning office.

One might also question many feminists' contention that patriarchy is the root of political power differences between women and men. Some of the most patriarchal societies—those in much of Africa, Latin America, and many Arab countries, for example—have many more women in high-ranking positions in political bodies than does the United States, which professes equality between the sexes. Thus, patriarchy may not be as critical in explaining political power differences between the sexes as many feminist scholars claim.

In addition, some critics point out that American women have made considerable progress in achieving high-level positions. Current examples include Secretary of State Hillary Rodham Clinton; Supreme Court Justices Ruth Bader Ginsburg, Sonia Sotomayor, and Elena Kagan; Secretary of Homeland Security Janet Napolitano; and ambassador to the United Nations Susan Rice.

Money is a major motivator, but work provides other benefits.

12 Work and the Economy

Mark Cooper was the head of security at a *Fortune* 500 company, overseeing a budget of $1.2 million and earning almost $70,000 a year. When the economy began to crash in mid-2008, he lost his job and now makes $12 an hour cleaning an office building for a friend's janitorial services company. Cooper is grateful for the job but says that he fights despair, discouragement, and depression every day because his income has plunged to about $25,000 a year (Luo 2009).

This example illustrates the close linkage between an individual's personal life and the **economy,** a social institution that determines how a society produces, distributes, and consumes goods and services. Let's begin by considering why work is important in our lives.

> **economy** a social institution that determines how a society produces, distributes, and consumes goods and services.
>
> **work** physical or mental activity that accomplishes or produces something, either goods or services.

Key Topics

In this chapter, we'll explore the following topics:

1 Social Significance of Work

2 Global Economic Systems

3 Corporations and Capitalism

4 Work in U.S. Society Today

5 Sociological Explanations of Work and the Economy

what do you think?

Enjoying your work is more important than how much you earn.

1　2　3　4　5　6　7

strongly agree　　strongly disagree

1 Social Significance of Work

Work is physical or mental activity that accomplishes or produces something, either goods or services. Work has many forms: It can be legal or illegal, paid or unpaid (such as raising children and volunteering), and essential for a society's survival (such as producing food) or peripheral (such as creating entertainment). Some work is routine and mechanical, but some involves considerable stress and anxiety.

For most of us, money is a major motivator, but work provides other benefits. Generally, employment leads to better health and a sense of accomplishment and usefulness, and is a major source of social identity. Almost 80 percent of Americans say that having a good relationship with their coworkers is more important than earning a high salary or having a prestigious job because the social contacts often provide friendships and opportunities to participate in mutually satisfying activities. In addition, work provides a sense of stability and order, and a daily rhythm that we don't get from many other activities. Some retirees continue to work part-time or do volunteer work because they enjoy the opportunities for learning and growing (Katzenbach 2003; Mirowsky and Ross 2007).

As with politics (see Chapter 11), societies differ in the kinds of economic systems they develop. Societies worldwide are also experiencing profound changes, as some nations gain unprecedented economic power because of globalization, political transitions, and a revolution in communications technology.

2 Global Economic Systems

t he two major economic systems around the world are capitalism and socialism. In actual operation, economies are usually some mixture of these two types.

CAPITALISM

Capitalism is an economic system in which wealth is in private hands, and is invested and reinvested to produce profits. Ideally, capitalism has four essential characteristics (Smith 1937; Heilbroner and Thurow 1998):

- *Private ownership of property.* Property—such as real estate, banks, and utilities—belongs to individuals or organizations rather than the state or the community.

- *Competition.* Capitalists compete in producing goods and services that offer consumers the greatest value in price and quality.

- *Profit.* Selling something for more than it costs to produce generates profits and an accumulation of wealth for individuals and companies. Profits can invigorate competition because producers create goods and services that consumers want.

- *Investment.* By investing profits, capitalists can increase their own wealth. Workers also can accumulate savings and make investments that augment their income.

In reality, capitalism rarely functions in an ideal way because of abuses, greed, and worker exploitation, and it usually reflects monopoly and oligopoly rather than a free market that encourages competition. A **monopoly** is domination of a particular market or industry by one person or company. With little or no competition, a company can raise prices and reduce production.

An **oligopoly** is a market dominated by a few large producers or suppliers. For example, six companies—including CBS, Time Warner, and the Walt Disney Corporation—now own 90 percent of the U.S. media market. And until fairly recently, a few large American companies dominated the automobile and steel industries.

The companies in an oligopoly often agree to set prices to reduce competition. Such agreements are illegal, but violations are rarely prosecuted. New entrepreneurs have little chance of breaking into an industry dominated by an oligopoly, and consumers have fewer choices in buying products or services (such as fuel and its delivery) because a small number of firms control most of the market. Often, companies involved in an oligopolistic market—such as Barnes and Noble, Comcast, and Microsoft Corporation—continue to grow through mergers and acquisitions of smaller companies.

In 2007, Walt Disney Corporation produced the hit movie **Pirates of the Caribbean: At World's End**, featuring Johnny Depp (top left). Walt Disney is part of an oligopoly. Among other holdings, it owns 4 publishing companies, 11 major television stations (including ABC), 8 major cable stations (including ESPN and the Disney Channel), at least 60 radio stations in major cities, numerous magazines, and 6 theme parks and resorts (in the United States, Tokyo, Paris, and Hong Kong). All of these outlets promote and sell Disney products, increasing the corporation's profits even further.

SOCIALISM

Socialism is an economic and political system based on the principle of the public ownership of the production of goods and services. Ideally, socialism is the opposite of capitalism. A socialistic system has the following characteristics:

- *Collective ownership of property.* The community, rather than the individual, owns property. The government owns utilities, factories, land, and equipment, but distributes them equally among all members of a society.

- *Cooperation.* Working together and providing social services to all people are more important than competition. People get what they need instead of being influenced by advertising.

- *No profit motive.* Goods and services are distributed equally, and private profits that are fueled by greed and exploitation of workers are forbidden.

- *Collective goals rather than individual investments.* The state is responsible for all economic planning and programs. People are discouraged from accumulating individual profits and investments, and are expected to work for the greater good.

There have been many socialist governments during the last 150 years, including those in China, Cuba, and the Soviet Union (before its collapse in the early 1990s). None, however, has reflected pure socialism. Competition and individual profits were officially frowned upon, but there were always considerable differences in social equality. For example, government officials, athletes, and high-ranking party members enjoyed more freedom, larger apartments, higher incomes, and greater access to education and other resources than the rank and file.

MIXED ECONOMIES

After World War II, socialist parties came to power in many nations throughout the world, and much private industry was nationalized. Great Britain, Germany, Sweden, Belgium, the Netherlands, and some countries in Latin America, Asia, and Africa established socialist programs that included national health care and government-owned enterprises (such as education and child-care programs). All of these countries, however, incorporated capitalistic features such as competition, private ownership of property, and free trade in the market.

Karl Marx predicted that **communism,** a political and economic system in which all members of a society are equal, would become dominant around the world because exploited workers would revolt against the yoke of capitalism. His prediction has not come true.

China is a good example of a developing country that espoused communism and practiced socialism but is now endorsing many aspects of capitalism (Becker 2002). In China, many state-owned enterprises are becoming private. Numerous leaders, who see capitalism as a source of economic development, approve foreign-owned factories that produce electronic goods, clothing, toys, and other products for export. As Communist-run industries and unions have dissolved, workers no longer have the security they enjoyed in the past. The income gap between the rich and the poor has increased dramatically, and there has been a surge in corruption, land seizures, arbitrary taxes, and social unrest (Landsberg 2007; Lee 2007).

GLOBAL ECONOMIES

One of the most significant economic changes of the late twentieth century was **globalization,** the growth and spread of investment, trade, production, communication, and new technology around the world. Globalization also changes political systems, culture, language, migration, the environment, and many other aspects of life.

Proponents argue that everyone benefits from globalization because it increases economic freedom and democracy, creates millions of jobs, and brings affordable goods and services (like cell phones) to millions of house-

socialism an economic and political system based on the principle of the public ownership of the production of goods and services.

communism a political and economic system in which all members of a society are equal.

globalization the growth and spread of investment, trade, production, communication, and new technology around the world.

holds around the world. Most people among those polled in 47 industrialized and developing nations were enthusiastic about globalization but also worried that foreign influences and immigration may threaten their traditional cultures and national identities (The Pew Global Attitudes Project 2007).

Critics contend that globalization exploits poor workers, spreads pollution, and destroys indigenous cultures, natural habitats, and animal species (see Chapter 16). They also maintain that many people around the world don't need or benefit from globalization: They have little money to save or invest in global financial industries, consume food they grow, and use products they make rather than acquiring them on global markets, and don't rely on technologies that produce computers, fax machines, or even televisions and refrigerators. Thus, according to opponents, globalization benefits only the world's most powerful companies by expanding their worldwide base of consumers to reap more profits (Hunter and Yates 2002; Schaeffer 2003).

Large companies drive both capitalism and globalization. Major corporations, in particular, wield enormous influence both at home and abroad.

3 Corporations and Capitalism

n 1999, Bob Thompson sold his construction company for $442 million. Because he and his wife believed this was far more than they needed for retirement, Thompson distributed $128 million to his 550 workers, as well as some retirees and widows. About 80 became instant millionaires ("Boss Sells His Company..." 1999).

Unlike Thompson, most corporate heads have luxurious lifestyles, cut their employees' pensions, retire as billionaires, and pass on their massive wealth to their heirs (see Chapter 8). You'll see shortly that corporate and political power are interwoven, but let's begin by looking at some of the characteristics of corporations.

SOME CHARACTERISTICS OF A CORPORATION

A **corporation** is a social entity that has legal rights, privileges, and liabilities apart from those of its members. Until the 1890s, there were only a few U.S. corporations—in textiles, railroads, and the oil and steel industries. Today, there are almost 6 million, most created for profit, and a mere 0.5 percent of corporations bring in 90 percent of all corporate income (U.S. Census Bureau 2010).

Joel Bakan, a legal scholar, describes corporations as governing our lives: "They determine what we eat, what we watch, what we wear, where we work, and what we do." In amassing wealth, corporations exercise more power than do governments: "No internal limits, whether moral, ethical, or legal, limit what or whom corporations can exploit to create wealth for themselves and their owners" (Bakan 2004: 5, 111–112).

The federal government doesn't impose legal limits on corporations but even rewards "bad behavior [which] produces more of the same" (Bauerlein and Jeffery 2010: 4). Beginning in 2008, for example, the Federal Reserve "orchestrated the largest transfer of wealth from the American people to the banking system in the nation's history" (Prins 2009: 2).

The price tag for the Wall Street bailout is often cited as $700 billion—the size of the Troubled Assets Relief Program (TARP). According to some analysts, however, the bailout may cost taxpayers almost $14 trillion because TARP is just one of 30 programs that the federal government has rescued. It has also injected and put aside billions of dollars to bail out numerous financial firms and to pay for the bad loans that banks made (see Prins 2009; Corn 2010; and Wang 2010). Instead of being remorseful about sowing financial destruction or grateful for the taxpayer-financed bailout, in 2009 and 2010, the salaries and bonuses of

China's economic boom has not benefited all of its citizens. Many urban centers are thriving—offering those in upper and middle classes high-rise apartments, stores, and restaurants. In contrast, millions of Chinese, including many older people, like the one pictured here, survive by scouring trash bins for plastic bottles to recycle.

many of the CEOs and employees soared to record levels. At Goldman Sachs, for example (which got a $13 billion bailout), CEO Lloyd Blankfein received almost $43 million in compensation and said he deserved the money because he's not greedy but has "been doing God's work" (Bauerlein and Jeffery 2010: 4; see also Laufer 2010; Shell 2010; and Tse 2010).

CONGLOMERATES

A **conglomerate** is a giant corporation that owns a collection of companies in different industries. Conglomerates emerged during the 1960s and grow by acquiring companies through mergers. Shareholders like mergers because their stock usually increases in value. Investors' choices are often wrong, but mergers make chief executives "truly, titanically, stupefyingly rich" (Morgenson 2004: C1).

One example of a conglomerate is Kraft Foods, which owns companies that produce snacks, beverages, pet foods, a variety of groceries, and convenience foods. Besides owning Maxwell House, Oscar Meyer, Life Savers, Ritz Crackers, and hundreds of other brand names, Kraft produces 23 cereals under the Post label and has ties with other corporations such as Starbucks (see www.kraft.com/brands).

INTERLOCKING DIRECTORATES

Conglomerates aren't the only locus of corporate power and wealth. In an **interlocking directorate**, the same people serve on the boards of directors of several companies or corporations. Some interlocking directorates are especially powerful because they include past U.S. presidents or members of Congress. For example, Sam Nunn was a partner at a prestigious law firm in Atlanta, Georgia, that represented numerous corporations. He was a Democratic senator from Georgia for almost 25 years, chaired several influential Senate committees, and then became a board member at ChevronTexaco Corporation, Coca-Cola, Dell Inc., and Internet Security Systems, Inc., among others. Because they sit on each other's boards, the members of interlocking directorates can set the prices for food, gasoline, automobiles, and even movie tickets (Krugman 2002; Draffan 2003).

TRANSNATIONAL CORPORATIONS AND CONGLOMERATES

Interlocking directorates have become more influential than ever because of the proliferation of transnational corporations. A **transnational corporation** (sometimes called a *multinational corporation* or an *international corporation*) is a large company that is based in one country but operates across international boundaries. By moving production plants abroad, large U.S. corporations can avoid trade tariffs, bypass environmental regulations, and pay low wages. The political leaders of many countries welcome transnational corporations to stimulate their economies, create jobs, and enrich their personal bank accounts (Caston 1998; see also Chapter 16).

The most powerful corporations are **transnational conglomerates,** corporations that own a collection of different companies in various industries in a number of countries. General Electric is a good example of a transnational conglomerate. It owns hundreds of companies in the United States that are involved, among other activities, in manufacturing aircraft engines and parts, engineering consulting, insurance, and financial services. It also owns hundreds of subsidiaries in at least 27 countries and on every continent. These companies provide a wide range of products and services such as manufacturing light bulbs (in Hungary), ultrasound systems (in Germany and Thailand), and chemicals and medical technology systems (in Denmark, France, and Canada) (*LexisNexis Corporate Affiliations* 2003).

Transnational corporations and transnational conglomerates produce goods and services that they can sell to Americans at lower prices, largely because they develop local talent in emerging markets (like India and China) where the pay is 70 to 80 percent lower than in the United States. A small number of U.S. transnational corporations dominate world trade. Of the 25 most profitable companies worldwide, 17 are based in the United States. In effect, then, a very small group of corporations and interlocking directorates holds considerable global economic power (McGregor and Hamm 2008).

conglomerate a giant corporation that owns a collection of companies in different industries.

interlocking directorate a situation in which the same people serve on the boards of directors of several companies or corporations.

transnational corporation (sometimes called a *multinational corporation or an international corporation*) a large company that is based in one country but operates across international boundaries.

transnational conglomerate a corporation that owns a collection of different companies in various industries in a number of countries.

4 Work in U.S. Society Today

Poll after poll now shows that financial hardship is a top issue for many Americans. In 2010, 66 percent said that economic issues were the nation's most important problem, up from 19 percent in 2007. In addition, 6 in 10 Americans reported being worse off than 5 years earlier—the highest number in nearly 50 years (Acs and Nichols 2010; Jones 2010).

Millions of Americans are in debt because they purchase products they don't need or can't pay for, but many are using credit cards to stay afloat financially. During the housing boom between 2005 and 2007, many people took out mortgages they couldn't afford and now owe more than their houses are worth. When the housing bubble burst in 2007 and foreclosures increased, credit counselors were deluged by people, even in the middle-income bracket, who had maxed out their credit cards purchasing everyday necessities such as groceries and gas. In addition, food pantries and homeless shelters report that they've been swamped with unprecedented numbers of Americans, many of them middle-income wage earners, who can't keep up with mounting utility, food, and gas prices (Wolff 2007; Armour 2008).

You may not feel much sympathy toward people who live beyond their means, but even Americans who live modestly are losing economic ground for many reasons. Let's begin with deindustrialization and globalization.

DEINDUSTRIALIZATION AND GLOBALIZATION

Jane Knudsen was a 19-year-old mother of two when she went to work in a textile mill in Mount Airy, North Carolina, in 1973. When the mill shut down in 2008, Knudsen found a job with an auto parts supplier, but was laid off. Now 57 years old, she's a part-time cook at a local jail and has a tough time getting by on $10.39 an hour part-time compared with up to $15 an hour that textile jobs paid. The nation has lost almost 1 million textile and apparel jobs since 2000; the Bureau of Labor Statistics expects the number of these jobs to decline another 48 percent to only 259,000 by 2018 (Wiseman 2010).

James Tucker, a machinist, has lost three full-time jobs in the past 25 years. After the last layoff, and not finding a job after seven months, he takes part in mock interview sessions in Rockford, Illinois. Tucker hopes that the local workforce development office can send him to school so he can learn to program the milling machines he used to run.

Deindustrialization

Jane Knudsen, like many others, is a casualty of **deindustrialization,** a process of social and economic change due to the reduction of industrial activity, especially manufacturing. Between 2000 and 2006 alone, 20 percent of U.S. manufacturing jobs disappeared (Helper 2008). One of the reasons for this decline is that, beginning in the early 1960s, employers easily replaced workers with the lowest level skills, usually those on assembly line, with robots and automation (Lee and Mather 2008). Another reason is globalization.

Globalization

Deindustrialization accelerated because of globalization. One example of globalization is a motor vehicle that is assembled in the United States with practically all of its parts manufactured and produced in Germany, Japan, South Korea, or developing countries. Americans purchase more manufactured goods than in the past, but because people in developing countries work for much lower wages, they are displacing workers in Western economies, including the United States (Bivens 2008). Among other consequences, deindustrialization and globalization have resulted in weaker labor unions and have been accelerated by offshoring.

LABOR UNIONS

Some of your parents and grandparents probably reminisce about the days when labor unions provided job security, good health benefits, pensions, and annual wage increases because of collective bargaining. This was especially true of many blue-collar jobs in manufacturing, transportation (such as truck drivers), and craft trades (such as plumbers and carpenters).

Times have changed. About 38 percent of government employees are unionized, but the rate of unionization among all other workers has been decreasing steadily—from a high of 27 percent in 1953 to 12 percent in 2009 (Eisenbrey et al. 2007; Bureau of Labor Statistics News Release 2010b). Labor union membership has declined for several reasons. First, some groups—such as retail salespeople and office workers, including receptionists—often see their jobs as short-term and hope to be upwardly mobile. Thus, there's little incentive to join a union. Second, many Americans believe that unions aren't effective in protecting the working person (Kohut et al. 2010). Third, many people feel that unions don't have much clout because many jobs are offshored.

OFFSHORING

Offshoring refers to sending work or jobs to another country to cut a company's costs at home. Sometimes called *international outsourcing* or *offshore outsourcing*, the transfer of manufacturing jobs overseas has been going on since at least the 1970s. Labor unions can do little more than watch.

Large percentages of jobs are relocated to Canada, Hungary, the Philippines, Poland, Russia, Egypt, Venezuela, Vietnam, and South Africa, but most of the offshored jobs go to China and India. Between 2001 and 2008, 2.4 million American jobs, most of them in manufacturing, were lost to China: "The impact has affected essentially all production workers with less than a four-year college degree—roughly 70 percent of the private-sector workforce, or about 100 million workers" (Scott 2010: 1).

Initially, most of the offshored jobs were in blue-collar manufacturing jobs. Increasingly, however, U.S. firms have offshored high-level, well-paid information technology (IT) jobs, including those in accounting, computer science, and engineering. A typical accountant in India, for example, earns about $5,000 a year compared with one in the United States who earns about $63,000 a year. These large wage differences make it very attractive for companies to reduce costs by substituting U.S. employees with lower cost overseas workers (Hira 2008).

Some economists maintain that offshoring has few negative effects on American workers because the jobs that are lost are those with the lowest skill levels, offshoring saves taxpayers money, and American consumers benefit by buying products and services at low prices (Liu and Trefler 2008). Others contend that there's something wrong with a government that uses taxpayers' money to create jobs offshore—especially when experienced programmers and analysts are being forced out of the field (Bivens 2006; Whoriskey 2008).

offshoring sending work or jobs to another country to cut a company's costs at home.

HOW AMERICANS' WORK HAS CHANGED

Across the country, many Americans are struggling to survive. They have adopted a variety of techniques, including taking low-paying jobs and working nonstandard hours and part time. If these strategies fail, they find themselves among the unemployed.

Low-Wage Jobs

One researcher has described the United States as "a nation of hamburger flippers" because of the growth of low-wage jobs (Levine 1994: 1E). These are jobs that

IBM Corporation gets tax breaks for creating jobs in the United States, but has been criticized for offshoring many jobs and no longer gives a count of its domestic workers. According to the last public numbers in 2008, of IBM's almost 399,000 employees worldwide, only 29 percent worked in the United States (Wolf 2010). Pictured here are female employees in India attending IBM's leadership conference.

AP Photo/Aijaz Rahi

are safe from offshoring because they must be done on-site, such as child care, security, and hotel and restaurant work.

When a 2009 Gallup poll asked in an open-ended question to name the most important financial problem facing their families today, 1 in 6 Americans (17 percent) said low wages and a lack of money, up from 11 percent in 2008. These responses exceeded other financial concerns such as healthcare costs (14 percent) and not enough money to pay debts (10 percent) (Jacobe and Jones 2009).

The federal minimum wage, which rose from $6.55 to $7.25 an hour in 2009, increased the wages of less than 4 percent of the workforce. When adjusted for inflation, the new federal minimum wage is about 18 percent lower than the minimum wage between 1961 and 1981, and lower than the current minimum wage required by 13 states and the District of Columbia. A person who works full-time at the minimum wage earns $14,500 a year, which is slightly below the 2009 federal poverty level of $14,570 for a family of two (Filion 2009; Orr 2009).

According to the Labor Department, 5 of the 10 occupations expected to add the most jobs through 2016 are very low paying, up to a maximum of $22,000 to $31,000 a year. They include retail sales and home health aide jobs, customer-service representatives, general office clerks, and nurses' aides ("Where the Jobs Are" 2009). Many employers are also shortchanging their low-wage workers by not paying the promised amount or overtime, violating minimum wage laws, and making illegal earnings deductions such as charging employees for using the employers' tools at work (Bernhardt et al. 2009; Kutz and Meyer 2009).

Nonstandard Work Hours

In many countries, workers are needed around the clock because business is being conducted somewhere almost every hour of every day, including weekends. In the United State___ wo in five people work weekends, evenings, or nights (Dohm and Shniper 2007).

These nonstandard work hours (often called *shift work*) are most common among men, African Americans, people in service occupations (such as restaurants), and those who work in hospitality industries, especially in hotels and motels. Except for nurses, shift workers tend to be people with low education levels who have few other choices in making a living

(McMenamin 2007). The demand for nonstandard work hours is expected to increase in the future. The 30 occupations with the largest job growth until 2016 include those outside daytime schedules, such as cashiers, truck drivers, registered nurses, nursing aides and orderlies, security guards, janitors, and people who clean office buildings and hotels (Saenz 2008).

Shift work has both benefits and drawbacks. Some benefits include lower child care costs because parents who work different hours can take turns being at home. Such tag-team parenting also has drawbacks: Even if only one parent works on evenings or weekends, the children tend to do less well in school because a parent is not available to supervise homework. Parents also report more depressive symptoms, such as feeling angry and sometimes withdrawing from family life. These and other strains, especially among low-wage workers, increase the likelihood of parental conflict and divorce (Perry-Jenkins et al. 2007; Davis et al. 2008; Presser et al. 2008).

Contingent Workers and Part-Time Work

Large-scale layoffs, which we'll discuss shortly, have created a large pool of contingent and part-time workers. **Contingent workers** (sometimes called *temporary workers*) are those who don't expect their jobs to last or who say that their jobs are temporary. They make up 4 percent of the American workforce. Across all age groups, contingent workers are more likely than permanent workers to be high-school dropouts, but 52 percent of contingent workers want a permanent job (U.S. Department of Labor 2005). Some contingent workers may work full-time hours, but they usually have month-to-month contracts.

The average number of hours (33) that Americans worked in 2009 was the lowest level since 1964. Of the almost 28 million part-timers (those who work less than 35 hours a week), 32 percent were involuntary because people couldn't find suitable full-time employ-

"The job comes with a thirty-day guarantee."

ment or employers had reduced their hours because of a slowdown in business (Bureau of Labor Statistics 2009; Eisenbrey 2009).

The percentage of contingent workers and part-time employees is likely to increase because employers don't have to pay for health insurance, retirement, sick days, vacations, severance, and unemployment insurance. Companies hold all the power because the workers are disposable ("easy to chuck off when unneeded") (Coy et al. 2010: 35).

Unemployment

The U.S. unemployment rate surged from less than 5 percent in 2007 to 10 percent in early 2010 (Bureau of Labor Statistics 2010). According to economists, the entire growth in jobs since 2001 has been wiped out, unemployed workers have been jobless for longer periods, and the economy has fewer jobs than it did in 2001 (Shierholz 2009; Goodman 2010).

Layoffs have long been fairly common in the workplace. A dramatic recent development, however, is the widespread occurrence of **downsizing,** a euphemism for firing large numbers of employees at once. When a factory closes or a company sends jobs offshore, thousands of people lose their jobs. *Mass layoffs* occur when at least 50 claims for unemployment insurance are filed by former employees of a single establishment during a 5-week period; such layoffs increased from 1,480 in early 2008 to almost 2,800 in mid-2009. The largest mass layoffs were in construction, manufacturing, and wholesale and retail trade (Bureau of Labor Statistics News Release 2010a).

In good times and in bad, African American men have the highest unemployment rates. And compared with their white counterparts, black workers are unemployed long after their unemployment insurance benefits end. Pictured here are laid-off workers examining listings at a job fair.

Unemployment causes widespread hardship, but it hits some groups and sectors harder than others. Some economists refer to the current recession as a "man-cession" because, since 2007, men bore 78 percent of the job losses. The job losses have been greatest among black men, people in construction and manufacturing industries, and those who don't have a college degree (Wall 2009a, 2009b; Jacobsen and Mather 2010). However, layoffs have recently included black professionals, managers, and government workers (White and Lifsher 2009).

According to many economists, today's unemployment rate of 10 percent is misleading because it doesn't include discouraged and underemployed workers. Americans in all racial-ethnic groups, across all ages and education levels, and both women and men are affected by this economic reality. When official statistics include these numbers, the unemployment rate in March 2010 was 17 percent (Bureau of Labor Statistics 2010).

Discouraged and Underemployed Workers

Discouraged workers are unemployed people who want a job and have looked for work in the preceding year but have not searched in the past four weeks because they have given up. In mid-2010, there were 1 million discouraged workers, up from 309,000 a year earlier, comprising about 1 percent of the workforce (Bureau of Labor Statistics 2010). This number may seem small, but the results can be devastating because discouraged workers max out their credit cards to pay for food and utilities, can't afford health care, and often experience foreclosures because they can't keep up with mortgage payments (Haynes 2010).

Why do people give up? Discouraged workers include retirees who believe that they can't find work because of age discrimination, mothers who have been taking care of their kids but can't find a suitable job after entering the job market, those who refuse to work for a minimum wage, and adults younger than 25 who have dropped out of high school and don't have the necessary schooling or job experience that many employers seek (Cohany 2009).

The **underemployed** are people who have part-time jobs but want full-time work or whose jobs are

downsizing a euphemism for firing large numbers of employees at once.

discouraged workers unemployed people who want a job and have looked for work in the preceding year but have not searched in the past four weeks because they have given up.

underemployed people who have part-time jobs but want full-time work or whose jobs are below their experience and education level.

below their experience, skill, and education level. The federal government doesn't track underemployment, but some economists estimate that about 20 percent of Americans are underemployed, and the numbers will probably increase (see Marlar 2010a).

The highest underemployment rates are among young Latinos who are recent immigrants, those who are high-school dropouts, and people in construction and food preparation and serving industries such as fast-food chains. Underemployment is also 13 times greater among workers who earn $13,000 a year or less than those who earn $150,000 or more a year (Sum and Khatiwada 2010a, 2010b). Thus, the underemployed who need better jobs to survive are the least likely to get them.

Some Effects of Unemployment and Underemployment

Since 2007, many Americans—including those in working and middle classes—have experienced drastic changes in lifestyles because of unemployment and underemployment. Most recently, for example, researchers have found that

- Millions of Americans have stopped taking prescription drugs for heart disease, diabetes, and cholesterol because they need the money for groceries and housing. Others take their pills every other day, split them, drop the medical insurance they have, or skip doctors' appointments, all of which can cause major medical problems (Saul 2008; Szabo and Appleby 2009).

- Nearly half (46 percent) of underemployed Americans compared with 29 percent of those who are employed report emotional problems such as sadness, stress, and anger (Marlar 2010b).

- One in eight Americans now receives food stamps because they have no income (Deparle and Gebeloff 2010).

JOB SATISFACTION AND STRESS

In 2009, only 45 percent of Americans said they were satisfied with their jobs, a significant decline from 62 percent in 1987 (Gibbons 2010). Those who say they are very satisfied typically work in occupations that involve teaching, caring for and protecting others, and creativity. The least satisfying jobs are usually in low-skilled manual and service occupations, especially jobs involving customer service and food/beverage preparation and serving (see *Table 12.1*).

Job satisfaction is related to occupational prestige, but the association isn't perfect. For example, 58 percent of physicians, a profession that has a high social

TABLE 12.1
Which Occupations Are the Most and Least Satisfying?

RANK	OCCUPATION	PERCENTAGE VERY SATISFIED	RANK	OCCUPATION	PERCENTAGE LEAST SATISFIED
1	Clergy	87.2	1	Laborers, except construction	21.4
2	Firefighters	80.1	2	Food preparers	23.6
3	Physical therapists	78.1	3	Packers and packagers	23.7
4	Authors	74.2	4	Clothing salespersons	23.9
5	Special education teachers	70.1	5	Cashiers	25.0
6	Teachers	69.2	6	Furniture salespersons	25.2
7	Education administrators	68.4	7	Roofers	25.3
8	Painters, sculptors, and other artists	67.3	8	Freight, stock, and material handlers	25.8
9	Psychologists	66.9	9	Bartenders	26.4
10	Security and financial services salespersons	65.4	10	Waiters/servers	27.0

Source: Based on Smith 2007, Table 2; see also Rosato 2009 for similar results.

standing, report lower job satisfaction than many people in lower prestige occupations (such as clergy and firefighters). It may be that doctors aren't as satisfied with their occupations as one might expect because they often spend less time with patients than on paperwork because health maintenance organizations (HMOs) now dictate a patient's treatment, including hospital admission requirements and length of hospital stay, decreasing many doctors' autonomy.

People define happiness and satisfaction differently, but across all occupations, those who are most satisfied with their jobs are individuals who (in order of importance):

- feel appreciated (being praised or just thanked)
- get respect from workers and supervisors
- feel that they are trusted
- have opportunities to grow and learn on the job
- have a boss who's fair, honest, and listens to them
- feel that the job they're doing—however modest or low-paid—is important (Gardner 2008)

Such factors increase workers' satisfaction and commitment to an organization but don't cost the employer any money.

You may have heard the quip "Europeans work to live; Americans live to work," implying that Americans don't know how to relax and enjoy life. In most European countries, the typical work week is 35 hours—comparable with the definition of part-time work in the United States. The United States is the only industrialized nation in the world that doesn't legally guarantee workers a paid vacation. About 25 percent of American workers in the private sector don't get any paid vacation time or paid holidays. In contrast, the typical worker, especially in Western Europe, has at least 6 weeks of paid vacation, regardless of job seniority or the number of years worked (Ray and Schmitt 2007). Furthermore, even though U.S. workers have the least vacation days in the industrialized world, a third of them don't take all the time they've earned—14 days, on average. In contrast, Europeans use most of their vacation days (Expedia.com 2008).

Why do so many Americans forgo vacations and often work longer (and harder) than their European counterparts? About 60 percent shrink their vaca-

TABLE 12.2
Women and Men in the Labor Force, 1890–2008

YEAR	PERCENTAGE OF ALL MEN AND WOMEN IN THE LABOR FORCE		WOMEN AS A PERCENTAGE OF ALL WORKERS
	MEN	WOMEN	
1890	84	18	17
1900	86	20	18
1920	85	23	20
1940	83	28	25
1960	84	38	33
1980	78	52	42
1990	76	58	45
2008	73	59	43

Source: Bureau of Labor Statistics 2009

tions to a few days or long weekends because they have too much to do on the job, fear being laid off, or worry about not being promoted because their company keeps pushing employees to put in more hours (Alesina et al. 2005; Egan 2006; Joyce 2006). Some corporations encourage their employees to take all of their vacation days to avoid job burnout, reduce stress, and recharge. This isn't typical, however, because U.S. employers save about $65 billion a year when workers don't take the paid vacations they're entitled to (Expedia.com 2008).

WOMEN AND MINORITIES IN THE WORKPLACE

One of the most dramatic changes in the United States during the twentieth century was the increase of women in the workforce (see *Table 12.2*). Many factors contributed to the surge in women's employment, especially since the 1970s. These factors include increases in women's education and job opportunities, an increase in the number of single mothers, the decline in men's wages since 1980 (after accounting for inflation), and the increased costs of homeownership, requiring two incomes. When many men started losing jobs in 2007 and family earnings plummeted, wives' earnings became critical in keeping a family afloat financially (Smith 2009).

Largely because of higher educational attainment, 22 percent of women in two-income marriages bring home the bigger paycheck, up from only 4 percent in 1970 (Fry and Cohn 2010). As a group, however, women have lower earnings than men in both the highest- and lowest-paying occupations, and the wage gaps are greater in high-income jobs (see *Figure 12.1*).

As you saw in Chapter 9, a number of factors help explain the gender pay gap. For example, women are concentrated in fields associated with lower earnings (such as health care and teaching in elementary and middle schools), whereas men tend to dominate the higher paying fields (such as engineering, mathematics, and the physical sciences). In addition, parenthood affects careers differently: Mothers are more likely than fathers (or women with no children) to work part time, take leave, or take a break from the workforce to raise children—factors that reduce wages and salaries (Dey and Hill 2007). Still, a pay gap remains even when women and men have the same education, number of years in a job, seniority, marital status, number of children, and are similar on numerous other factors.

Big disparities in earnings also exist across minority groups, but the differences are especially striking by sex. As you examine *Figure 12.2*, note two general characteristics. First, earnings increase—across all racial-ethnic groups and for both sexes—as people go up the occupational ladder. But across all occupations, men have higher earnings than their female counterparts of the same racial-ethnic group. At the bottom of the occupational ladder are African American women and Latinas, with the latter faring worse than any of the other groups. Thus, both sex *and* race or ethnicity affect the earnings of American workers.

FIGURE 12.1
Women Earn Less Than Men Whether They're Chief Executives or Cooks

These were five of the highest and lowest paid occupations of full-time, year-round workers in the United States in 2007. How might you explain why the earnings differ by sex, especially in the highest paid jobs?

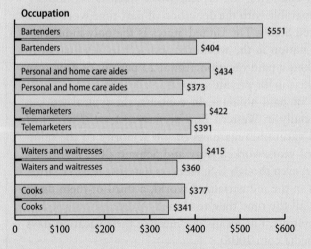

- Median weekly earnings (Men)
- Median weekly earnings (Women)

Men Make More Than Women in Some of the Highest Paying Jobs

Occupation

Chief Executives	$1,918
Chief Executives	$1,536
Pharmacists	$1,887
Pharmacists	$1,603
Physicians and surgeons	$1,796
Physicians and surgeons	$1,062
Lawyers	$1,793
Lawyers	$1,381
Computer and information systems managers	$1,598
Computer and information systems managers	$1,363

0   $500 $1,000 $1,500 $2,000

. . . and in Some of the Lowest Paying Jobs

Occupation

Bartenders	$551
Bartenders	$404
Personal and home care aides	$434
Personal and home care aides	$373
Telemarketers	$422
Telemarketers	$391
Waiters and waitresses	$415
Waiters and waitresses	$360
Cooks	$377
Cooks	$341

0   $100 $200 $300 $400 $500 $600

Note: Some of the differences between men's and women's median weekly earnings may seem small, but multiply each figure by 52 weeks. Thus, in annual earnings, male physicians and surgeons average more than $90,000 a year compared with only about $55,000 for female physicians and surgeons.

Source: Based on U.S. Bureau of Labor Statistics 2008, Table 39.

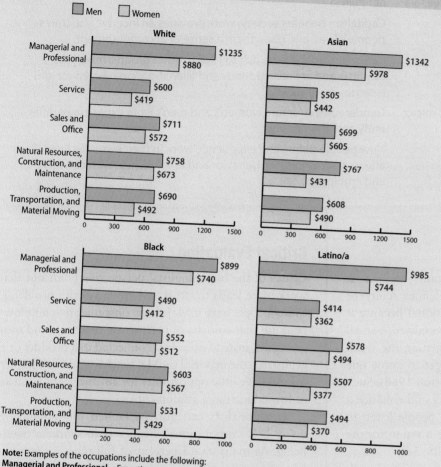

FIGURE 12.2
Median Weekly Earnings of Full-time Workers by Occupation, Sex, and Ethnicity

Legend: ■ Men □ Women

White

Occupation	Men	Women
Managerial and Professional	$1235	$880
Service	$600	$419
Sales and Office	$711	$572
Natural Resources, Construction, and Maintenance	$758	$673
Production, Transportation, and Material Moving	$690	$492

Asian

Occupation	Men	Women
Managerial and Professional	$1342	$978
Service	$505	$442
Sales and Office	$699	$605
Natural Resources, Construction, and Maintenance	$767	$431
Production, Transportation, and Material Moving	$608	$490

Black

Occupation	Men	Women
Managerial and Professional	$899	$740
Service	$490	$412
Sales and Office	$552	$512
Natural Resources, Construction, and Maintenance	$603	$567
Production, Transportation, and Material Moving	$531	$429

Latino/a

Occupation	Men	Women
Managerial and Professional	$985	$744
Service	$414	$362
Sales and Office	$578	$494
Natural Resources, Construction, and Maintenance	$507	$377
Production, Transportation, and Material Moving	$494	$370

Note: Examples of the occupations include the following:
Managerial and Professional—Executives, managers, public administrators
Service—Private household workers, police, firefighters, people in food and health services, janitors
Sales and Office—Supervisors, sales representatives, office administrators
Natural Resources, Construction, and Maintenance—Farmers, fishing industries, construction workers, auto mechanics, machine repairers
Production, Transportation, and Material Moving—Truck drivers, assembly-line workers, equipment cleaners

Source: Based on unpublished data, personal correspondence, U.S. Bureau of Labor Statistics, U.S. Department of Labor, Division of Labor Force Studies, Current Population Survey, Table A-2, 2008.

well-paying job as a corporate accountant and return to college to get a degree in human services, which pays considerably less. According to Matthew,

Accounting provided a steady salary and I made quite a bit of money preparing people's taxes on the side. After the kids graduated from college and we didn't have tuition payments, I became more fidgety. Work seemed more monotonous and I started dreading going to the office every morning. I figure that, after getting my [human services] degree, I can work with kids in low-income neighborhoods and contribute to society. I know my salary will be at least 50 percent lower than it is now, but life is too short to worry about money all the time.

Matthew's comments—about job dissatisfaction and contributing to society—reflect functionalists' view that work provides numerous personal and societal benefits. In contrast, conflict theorists maintain that work is often dangerous to workers' health, feminist thinkers contend that work creates and reinforces sex inequality, and symbolic interactionists focus on how people learn work roles (*Table 12.3* summarizes each perspective's key points).

FUNCTIONALIST THEORIES: WORK PROVIDES MANY SOCIETAL BENEFITS

Functionalists typically emphasize the positive aspects of work rather than its constraints. They also see capitalism as bringing prosperity to society as a whole.

5 Sociological Explanations of Work and the Economy

how do sociological theories help us understand work and the economy? During a recent conversation, I asked Matthew, one of my students, why, at age 51, he had decided to leave his

TABLE 12.3
Sociological Explanations of Work and the Economy

THEORETICAL PERSPECTIVE	LEVEL OF ANALYSIS	KEY POINTS
Functionalist	Macro	Capitalism benefits society; work provides an income, structures people's lives, and gives them a sense of accomplishment.
Conflict	Macro	Capitalism enables the rich to exploit other groups; most jobs pay little and are monotonous and alienating, creating anger and resentment.
Feminist	Macro and micro	Gender roles structure women's and men's work experiences differently and inequitably.
Symbolic Interactionist	Micro	How people define and experience work in their everyday lives affects their workplace behavior and relationships with co-workers and employers.

Key Characteristics

For functionalists, work is important because it enhances a society's economy and defines many of its members' roles. Work is also functional because it bonds people. As jobs become more specialized, a small group of workers is responsible for getting the work done, and coworkers in such groups get to know one another well (Parsons 1954, 1960; Merton 1968). Such networks increase workplace solidarity and enhance a sense of belonging to a group where people listen to each other's ideas, interact, and "share a vision for the work [they] do together" (Gardner 2008: 16).

As you saw earlier, besides providing income, work has social meaning. When asked how much they like their jobs, many Americans see money as the third most important factor: less important than a sense of accomplishment, usefulness, and feeling valued; having a sense of stability, order, and a daily rhythm; and developing interesting social contacts (Katzenbach 2003; Brooks 2007).

From a functionalist perspective, even wars are beneficial during high unemployment periods because they provide jobs for many people with low education levels and few skills. The Department of Defense has experienced high recruitment rates because many of the enrollees have been laid off from construction and other jobs, and get decent military salaries (Peter 2009; Watanabe 2009).

Functionalists also maintain that wage inequities motivate people to persevere and to set higher goals. Low-paying jobs, for example, provide incentives to work harder or obtain further education to move up the economic ladder (see Chapter 8).

Critical Evaluation

Critics of the functionalists' perspective point out that work often leads to stress and myriad health problems. Many people have a McJob, an unstimulating and low-paid job that consists of performing repetitive and routine tasks, instead of feeling connected to a product or a group (see the material on McDonaldization in Chapter 6), and have little opportunity for advancement because of low educational attainment.

Functionalists can also be faulted for minimizing many U.S. corporations' disinterest in workers' well-being. As many as 43 percent of full-time nongovern-

AP Photo/Connecticut Post, Ned Gerard

Many unemployed men—including recent Asian and Latino immigrants—are joining the military because it provides steady work, college education benefits, and an opportunity for career advancement.

ment workers in the United States don't have paid sick days. As a result, "many Americans simply tough it out when ill, going to work with pain, cramps, headaches, fevers, or worse" because they have no choice (Roan 2008).

CONFLICT THEORY: WORK CAN BE HAZARDOUS TO YOUR HEALTH

Whereas functionalists emphasize the benefits of work, conflict theorists argue that capitalism creates social problems. For example, they contend that globalization leads to job insecurity; a handful of transnational conglomerates have enormous power; and many workers have been laid off, especially because of offshoring.

Key Characteristics

Conflict theorists assert that low wages alienate employees rather than motivate them to work harder, because many workers realize that their labor benefits the wealthy and not themselves. Because much work is monotonous, employees arrive late, use company time for personal e-mail and online shopping, or quit. Matthew decided to change jobs because his work had become monotonous, but few people, especially those without college degrees and with heavy family responsibilities, have this option.

Functionalists say that if people have comparable skills, good attitudes, and perseverance, they'll have similar wages and chances for promotion. Conflict theorists challenge such claims because many women and minorities experience pay gaps and do not receive promotions regardless of their skills, attitude, or perseverance (Royster 2003).

Some studies suggest that many Americans agree with conflict theorists that capitalism doesn't benefit most people. In a recent Gallup poll, for example, 33 percent of the respondents said that they have a negative image of capitalism, 49 percent don't trust big business, and 36 percent have a positive image of socialism (Newport 2010).

Besides high unemployment and underemployment rates, many Americans have become disillusioned with capitalism because of the enormous gaps between their pay and that of CEOs—especially those whose companies enjoyed bailouts at taxpayers' expense. Among most industrialized countries, CEOs earn 18 percent more than the average worker. In the United States, CEOs earn 344 percent more than the typical worker (Anderson et al. 2008; Stinson 2008). As mentioned earlier, Lloyd Blankfein, the CEO of Goldman Sachs, whose company got a $13 billion bailout at taxpayers' expense, received almost $43 million in 2009. It would take the average U.S. worker more than 1,000 years to accumulate the amount that Blankfein received during 2009 alone (Sloan 2009).

Critical Evaluation

Are conflict theorists too quick to blame capitalism for economic problems? Critics fault conflict theorists for emphasizing economic constraints rather than choices. For example, middle-class Americans, especially, are borrowing more than they're earning and getting deeper into unmanageable debt, and 35 percent of Americans believe that people are simply living beyond their means—buying luxury products, taking expensive vacations, and often eating at restaurants (Center for American Progress 2006).

Also, deindustrialization and globalization have led to layoffs in assembly-line jobs, but some manufacturers have complained that they turned down business contracts because they experienced a shortage of skilled workers—such as welders, electricians, and machinists—despite offering decent pay (up to $25.00 an hour for a beginner), full health benefits, matching retirement funds, and annual bonuses (Hagenbaugh 2006). Thus, from a functionalist perspective, one might criticize conflict theorists for denouncing capitalism instead of showing how it can benefit many people with low education levels.

FEMINIST THEORIES: THE ECONOMY AND WORK CREATE AND REINFORCE SEX INEQUALITY

Women make up 41 percent of the almost 3 billion workers around the world, but earn at least 20 percent less than men in every country (Hausmann et al. 2007). Feminist scholars agree with conflict theorists that there is widespread inequality in the workplace, but they see gender as a critical factor in explaining this inequality.

Are conflict theorists too quick to blame capitalism for **economic problems?**

Key Characteristics

At all income levels and occupations, women—especially Latinas and black women—earn less than men (see *Figure 12.2* on p. 227). They rarely penetrate the top ranks, often regardless of ability, experience, or educational attainment.

Some national data show that employing women increases sales, generates more customers, and brings more profits to a company because women often offer different ideas and are more creative in providing solutions to workplace problems (Herring 2009). Also, women-owned businesses generate about $3 trillion in revenue and employ 16 percent of the workforce (Center for Women's Business Research 2009).

Despite such accomplishments, college-educated women, on average, still earn only 80 percent of what their male counterparts make in similar positions and with the same level of experience (Bennett et al. 2010). Working mothers, especially, lead harried lives but are often stigmatized for working. Indeed, 42 percent of Americans say that it's best for the mother not to be employed, even part time (Parker 2009).

These views are unrealistic because of today's high unemployment and underemployment rates, but many Americans—both women and men—still see women's roles as caregivers rather than workers who make major contributions to a household's income. Such views increase many working women's guilt in not being full-time homemakers.

Critical Evaluation

Critics of feminist perspectives note that emphasizing men's domination of women in the workplace ignores many situations where high-status women control low-status men and women. Others criticize some feminist scholars for accepting the cultural expectation that mothers, not fathers, are responsible for hearth and home. For example, some critics argue, instead of pushing for paid leave for women to care for sick children or older family members, feminists should insist that men share such burdens, and that the government implement family-friendly policies that reward men who share responsibilities at home (Kramer 2005; Graff 2007).

Some analysts, including women, also fault feminist scholars for being too timid about shaming corporations that

have few female officers at the top. Catalyst, a pioneering women's research organization, used to publish the names of companies that had few or no women at high-level positions. This practice motivated corporations such as General Electric to recruit women into the senior ranks. Recently, however, Catalyst has praised only corporations that have implemented greater diversity. One reason for the change may be that the worst offenders (such as General Electric, Dell, and FedEx) are among the contributors to Catalyst's $11 million annual budget (Brady 2007).

SYMBOLIC INTERACTIONIST THEORIES: WE LEARN WORK ROLES

Unlike the other theorists, symbolic interactionists rely on micro-level approaches to explain the day-to-day meaning of work. They are especially interested in the formal and informal rules that develop in workplaces.

Key Characteristics

Interactionists have provided numerous insights on how people define and experience work. Many low-paid workers who feel disengaged from their jobs tolerate their situations because they have few options. They endure drug tests, constant surveillance, rat- and cockroach-infested buildings, physical pain, and work-related occupational injuries. In many of these jobs, "the trick lies in figuring out how to budget your energy so there'll be some left over for the next day" (Ehrenreich 2001: 195). Still, regardless of the occupation, coworkers may develop close relationships that become friendships outside of work.

Interactionists have also studied professionals to determine how they are socialized into their jobs. For example, sociology professors often encourage graduate students to attend and present papers at conferences to socialize them into becoming professionals. In medicine, surgeons teach their interns and residents that it is normal to make some mistakes, but that carelessness and continued errors are unprofessional (Bosk 1979). Assembly-line workers often control their coworkers who overproduce or underproduce by punishing or rewarding them, especially verbally (see Chapter 6).

Each of the four theoretical perspectives contributes to our understanding of work and the economy. They focus on different aspects but, taken together, provide us with a broad lens on the economic world.

Critical Evaluation

A common criticism is that interactionism, although providing in-depth analyses, sacrifices scope. For example, sociologist Deirdre Royster (2003) studied young men in Baltimore who had graduated from the same vocational high school at about the same time. She found that white male teachers tended to provide the white students, but not black students, with active assistance such as information about job vacancies and job references in trade occupations. We don't know, however, whether these findings are applicable to other cities or other types of jobs because the study was based on a small and nationally nonrepresentative sample of young men.

For symbolic interactionists, cultural expectations shape women's and men's work, as well as determining whether women should even be employed. In Saudi Arabia, one of the world's most patriarchal societies, women are still not permitted to vote, travel abroad, work without the permission of a male relative, or drive, although this ban might soon be lifted ("Saudi Arabia..." 2008). Here, female employees work at the first car showroom in Saudi Arabia where women sell cars, but only to female buyers.

AP Photo/Donna Abu-Nasr

There is no
universal definition of family.

13 Families and Aging

In 2007, 95-year-old Nola Ochs received a college diploma. The mother of 4 and great-grandmother of 15 began taking classes after her husband died in 1972. Instead of viewing aging and her husband's death as setbacks, Ochs forged ahead: She had always yearned for a college education but was too busy raising the children on the family's farm. Ochs may not be typical, but her determination shows that, throughout the life course, we have choices and need not be held back by constraints.

In this chapter, we'll examine some of the most important aspects of families, how they've changed, their diversity, conflict and violence in families, and our aging society. Let's begin by considering what sociologists mean by *family*.

family an intimate group consisting of two or more people who: (1) live together in a committed relationship, (2) care for one another and any children, and (3) share close emotional ties and functions.

what do you think?

It should be much harder to get a divorce.

1   2   3   4   5   6   7

strongly agree   strongly disagree

1 What Is a Family?

Ask five of your friends to define *family*. Their definitions will probably differ not only from each other's but from yours. For our purposes, a **family** is an intimate group consisting of two or more people who: (1) live together in a committed relationship, (2) care for one another and any children, and (3) share close emotional ties and functions. This definition includes households (such as those of foster families and same-sex couples) whose members aren't related by birth, marriage, or adoption.

There is no universal definition of *family* because contemporary household arrangements are complex. Family structures vary across cultures and have changed over time. In some societies, a family includes uncles, aunts, and other relatives. In other societies, only parents and their children are viewed as a family.

HOW FAMILIES ARE SIMILAR

The institution of the family exists in some form in all societies. Worldwide, families are similar in fulfilling some functions, encouraging marriage, and trying to ensure that people select appropriate mates.

incest taboo cultural norms and laws that forbid sexual intercourse between close blood relatives, such as brother and sister, father and daughter, or uncle and niece.

marriage a socially approved mating relationship that people expect to be stable and enduring.

endogamy (sometimes called *homogamy*) the practice of selecting mates from within one's group.

exogamy (sometimes called *heterogamy*) the practice of selecting mates from outside one's group.

Family Functions

Families vary considerably in the United States and globally but must fulfill at least five important functions to ensure a society's survival (Parsons and Bales 1955):

- *Sexual regulation.* Every society has norms regarding who may engage in sexual relations, with whom, and under what circumstances. In the United States, having sexual intercourse with someone younger than 18 (or 16 in some states) is a crime, but some societies permit marriage with girls as young as 8. One of the oldest rules that regulate sexual behavior is the **incest taboo**, a set of cultural norms and laws that forbid sexual intercourse between close blood relatives, such as brother and sister, father and daughter, or uncle and niece.

- *Reproduction and socialization.* Reproduction replenishes a country's population. Through socialization, children acquire language; absorb the accumulated knowledge, attitudes, beliefs, and values of their culture; and learn the social and interpersonal skills needed to function effectively in society (see Chapter 4).

- *Economic security.* Families provide food, shelter, clothing, and other material resources for their members. Increasingly in the United States, as you'll see shortly, both parents must work to purchase life's basic necessities such as housing and food.

- *Emotional support.* Families supply the nurturance, love, and emotional sustenance that people need to be happy, healthy, and secure. Our friends may come and go, but our family is usually our emotional anchor.

- *Social placement.* We inherit a social position based on our parents' social class. Family resources affect children's ability to pursue opportunities such as higher education, but we can move up or down the social hierarchy in adulthood (see Chapter 8).

Many contemporary sociologists now include *recreation* as a basic U.S family function. It's not critical for survival, but since the 1950s, many parents have focused on having fun with their children and spending much more time with them on leisure activities, such as visiting amusements parks and playing video games together (see Coontz 2005).

Marriage

Marriage, a socially approved mating relationship that people expect to be stable and enduring, is also universal. Countries vary in their specific norms and laws dictating who can marry whom and at what age, but marriage everywhere is an important rite of passage that marks adulthood and its related responsibilities, especially providing for a family.

Endogamy and Exogamy

All societies have rules, formal or informal, defining an acceptable marriage partner. **Endogamy** (sometimes called *homogamy*) is the practice of selecting mates from within one's group. The partners are similar in religion, race, ethnicity, social class, and/or age. Across the Arab world and in some African nations, about half of married couples consist of first or second cousins because such unions reinforce kinship ties and increase a family's resources (Aizenman 2005; Bobroff-Hajal 2006).

Exogamy (sometimes called *heterogamy*) is the practice of selecting mates from outside one's group. In the United States, for example, 24 states prohibit marriage between first cousins, even though violations are rarely prosecuted. In some parts of India, where most people still follow strict caste rules, the government is encouraging exogamy by offering a $1,250 cash award to anyone who marries someone from a lower caste. This is a hefty sum in areas where the annual income is less

Nola Ochs, 95, and her 21-year-old granddaughter, Alexandra, were in the same graduating class at Fort Hays State University in Kansas. When she was handed her degree, the crowd gave Nola Ochs a standing ovation, breaking a rule against applauding until the names of all 2,176 graduates had been read.

In China's Himalayas, the Mosuo may be a matriarchal society. For the majority of Mosuo, a family is a household consisting of a woman, her children, and the daughters' offspring. An adult man will join a lover for the night and then return to his mother's or grandmother's house in the morning. Any children resulting from these unions belong to the female, and it is she and her relatives who raise them (Barnes 2006).

than half that amount (Chu 2007; see also discussion of castes in Chapter 8).

HOW FAMILIES DIFFER

There are also considerable worldwide variations in many family characteristics. Some variations affect the structure of the family, whereas others regulate household composition, as well as other behaviors.

Nuclear and Extended Families

In Western societies, the typical family form is a **nuclear family** that is made up of married parents and their biological or adopted children. In much of the world, however, the most common family form is the **extended family,** which consists of parents and children, as well as other kin, such as uncles and aunts, nieces and nephews, cousins, and grandparents.

As the number of single-parent families increases in industrialized countries, extended families are becoming more common. By helping out with household tasks and child care, adult members of extended families make it easier for a single parent to work outside the home. Because the rates of unmarried people who are living together are high, nuclear families now comprise only 23 percent of all U.S. families, down from 40 percent in 1970 (U.S. Census Bureau 2010).

Residence and Authority

Families also differ in their living arrangements, how they trace their descent, and who has the most power. In a **patrilocal residence pattern,** newly married couples live with the husband's family; in a **matrilocal residence pattern,** they live with the wife's family; and in a **neolocal residence pattern,** the newly married couple sets up its own residence.

Around the world, the most common residence pattern is patrilocal. In industrialized societies, married couples are typically neolocal. Since the early 1990s, however, the tendency for young married adults to live with the parents of either the wife or the husband—or sometimes with the grandparents of one of the partners—has increased. At least half of all young American couples can't afford a medium-priced house; others have low-income jobs, are supporting children after a divorce, or just enjoy the comforts of a parental nest.

As a result, a recent phenomenon is the **boomerang generation,** young adults (and twice as many are men compared with women) who move back into their parents' home after living independently for a while or who never leave home in the first place. Parents try to launch their children into the adult world, but like boomerangs, some keep coming back. Some U.S. journalists call this group *adultolescents* because they're still "mooching off their parents" instead of living on their own.

Residence patterns often reflect who has authority within the family. In a **matriarchal family system,** the oldest women (usually grandmothers and mothers) control cultural, political, and economic resources, and consequently, have power over males. Some American Indian tribes were matriarchal, and in some African countries, the eldest women have considerable authority and influence. For the most part, however, matriarchal societies are rare.

nuclear family a form of family consisting of married parents and their biological or adopted children.

extended family a form of family which consists of parents and children, as well as other kin, such as uncles and aunts, nieces and nephews, cousins, and grandparents.

patrilocal residence pattern newly married couples live with the husband's family.

matrilocal residence pattern newly married couples live with the wife's family.

neolocal residence pattern newly married couple sets up its own residence.

boomerang generation young adults who move back into their parents' home after living independently for a while or who never leave it in the first place.

matriarchal family system the oldest women (usually grandmothers and mothers) control cultural, political, and economic resources, and consequently, have power over males.

patriarchal family system the oldest men (grandfathers, fathers, and uncles) control cultural, political, and economic resources, and consequently, have power over females.

egalitarian family system both partners share power and authority fairly equally.

marriage market a courtship process in which prospective spouses compare the assets and liabilities of eligible partners and choose the best available mate.

monogamy one person is married exclusively to another person.

serial monogamy individuals marry several people, but one at a time.

polygamy a marriage form in which a man or woman has two or more spouses.

A more widespread system is a **patriarchal family system,** in which the oldest men control cultural, political, and economic resources, and consequently, have power over females. In some patriarchal societies, women have few rights within the family and none outside the family, such as not being permitted to vote, drive, work outside the home, or attend college (see Chapter 9). In other patriarchal societies, women may have considerable decision-making power in the home, but few legal or political rights, such as the right to obtain a divorce or to run for a political office.

In an **egalitarian family system,** both partners share power and authority fairly equally. Many Americans think they have egalitarian families, but patriarchal families are more common. For example, employed women shoulder twice as much child care as men (see Chapter 9). As you'll see shortly, women are considerably more likely than men to experience intimate partner violence (IPV) and economic hardship after a divorce. Also, employed women are twice as likely as their male counterparts to provide caregiving to aging family members (Houser 2007).

Love and Mate Selection

Sociologists often describe the U.S. dating process as a **marriage market,** a courtship process in which prospective spouses compare the assets and liabilities of eligible partners, and choose the best available mate. Marriage markets don't sound very romantic, but such open dating fulfills several important functions: fun, recreation, and companionship; a socially acceptable way of pursuing love and affection; opportunities for sexual intimacy and experimentation; and finding a spouse (see Benokraitis 2011).

Many societies, in contrast, discourage dating because marriage is seen as a family rather than an individual decision. Children may have veto power, but they believe that if partners are compatible, love will result. In much of India, marriages are usually carefully arranged to ensure a union that the family deems acceptable. In some of India's urban areas, however, arranged marriages also rely on nontraditional methods (such as online dating services) to find prospective spouses (Cullen and Masters 2008).

Monogamy and Polygamy

Several types of marriages are common worldwide. In **monogamy,** one person is married exclusively to another person. Where divorce and remarriage rates are high, as in the United States, people are engaging in **serial monogamy.** That is, they marry several people but one at a time—they marry, divorce, remarry, divorce, and so on. In a classic and often-cited study, a well-known anthropologist concluded that only about 20 percent of societies are strictly monogamous; the others permit either polygamy or combinations of monogamy and polygamy (Murdock 1967).

Polygamy, a form of marriage in which a man or woman has two or more spouses, is subdivided into *polygyny* (one man married to two or more women) and *polyandry* (one woman married to two or more men). Polygyny is common in many societies, especially in Africa, South America, and the Mideast. In Saudi Arabia, for example, Osama bin Laden—who orchestrated the 9/11 terrorist attacks—has 4 wives and 10 children; his father had 11 wives and 54 children. No one knows the incidence of polygamy worldwide, but some observers believe that polygyny is widespread in some regions of Africa and the Middle East (Coll 2008; Grant 2008).

Although rare, polyandry exists. Among the Pimbwe people in western Tanzania, Africa, for example, some women have several husbands because of a shortage of women and the difficulty of one man to provide for a family (Borgerhoff Mulder 2009).

Western and industrialized societies forbid polygamy, but there are pockets of isolated polygynous groups in the United States and Canada. Most are fundamentalists who have broken away from the Church of Jesus Christ of Latter-Day Saints (Mormons); law enforcement agencies rarely prosecute polygamists, but wives who have escaped from these groups have reported forced marriage between men in their 60s and girls as young as 10 years old, sexual abuse, pedophilia, and incest (Janofsky 2003; Madigan 2003).

How much do you know about contemporary U.S. families and aging? Take this quiz to find out.

True	False		
☐	☐	1.	Out-of-wedlock births to teenagers have increased in the United States over the past 20 years.
☐	☐	2.	Cohabitation (unmarried couples living together) decreases the likelihood of divorce.
☐	☐	3.	Almost half of all U.S. children live in one-parent households.
☐	☐	4.	Having children increases marital satisfaction.
☐	☐	5.	About 15 percent of all Americans never marry.
☐	☐	6.	Women and men are equally likely to experience violence by an intimate partner.
☐	☐	7.	Baby boomers (those born between 1946 and 1964) are the fastest-growing segment of the U.S. population.
☐	☐	8.	Most people age 65 and older are isolated and lonely.

Turn the page for the answers.

divorce the legal dissolution of a marriage.

no-fault divorce state laws that do not require either partner to establish guilt or wrongdoing on the part of the other to get a divorce.

2 How U.S. Families Are Changing

t he American family has changed dramatically over the past half century. Noteworthy changes involve divorce, singlehood, cohabitation, unmarried parents, and two-income families.

DIVORCE

Couples of all ages experience **divorce,** the legal dissolution of a marriage. Before the twentieth century, when life spans were much shorter, marriages typically ended with the death of one of the spouses. Now, over a lifetime, between 43 percent and 46 percent of American marriages end in divorce (Schoen and Canudas-Romo 2006). The U.S. divorce rate rose steadily during the twentieth century, peaked in the early 1980s, and then started declining (see *Figure 13.1*). Thus, divorce rates are *lower* today than they were between 1980 and 2005 (Isen and Stevenson 2010).

There are many *micro-level reasons* for divorce. Divorce is easier than in the past be-

cause all states have enacted laws allowing **no-fault divorce,** meaning that neither partner need establish guilt or wrongdoing on the part of the other. Legally valid reasons for divorce range from infidelity and abuse to irreconcilable differences and simple incompatibility. Technological advances, such as the Internet, have also made divorce more accessible than in the past. Some do-it-yourself divorce kits available online cost as little as $50 for all the necessary court forms and documents.

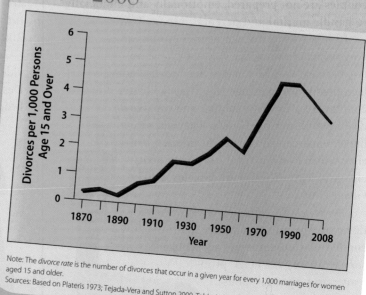

FIGURE 13.1

Divorce Rates in the United States, 1870–2008

Note: The *divorce rate* is the number of divorces that occur in a given year for every 1,000 marriages for women aged 15 and older.

Sources: Based on Plateris 1973; Tejada-Vera and Sutton 2009, Table A; and U.S. Census Bureau 2010, Table 78.

ANSWERS TO THINK YOU KNOW?

If you answered true to any of the statements, you're wrong. Based on material in this chapter, all of the statements are **FALSE**:

1. Out-of-wedlock births to teenagers have decreased over the past 20 years, especially since the early 2000s.
2. Couples who cohabit before marriage have a higher divorce rate than those who don't.
3. A majority of U.S. children (70 percent) live in homes with married parents.
4. Generally, child-rearing decreases marital satisfaction for both partners.
5. At least 90 percent of Americans will marry at least once during their lifetime.
6. Women are almost three times more likely than men to experience violence by an intimate partner.
7. People age 85 and older are the fastest-growing segment of the U.S. population.
8. Most people age 65 and older visit friends and relatives daily, and two-thirds work or engage in numerous volunteer activities.

The economy also affects divorce rates. The recession that began in 2007 has probably increased marital stability because "many couples appear to be developing a new appreciation for the economic and social support that marriages can provide in tough times" (Wilcox 2009: 17). On the other hand, high levels of credit card debt, job losses, and foreclosures can lead to more fighting, interpersonal unhappiness, conflict, and divorce (Dew 2009).

Demographic variables also help explain divorce rates. Marrying at an early age—especially younger than 18—is one of the strongest predictors of divorce. For example, 48 percent of first marriages of females younger than 18 dissolve after 10 years, compared with 24 percent of first marriages of women who are at least 25 at the time of the wedding (Kurdek 1993; Bramlett and Mosher 2002). In most cases, young couples are not prepared, emotionally and financially, to handle marital and parental responsibilities.

People with a college degree are less likely to divorce than those with only a high-school education, not because they're smarter but because going to college postpones marriage. As a result, better educated couples are often more mature and capable of dealing with personal crises. They also have higher incomes and better healthcare benefits, which lessen marital stress over financial problems (Kreider and Fields 2002; Glenn 2005).

There are also interpersonal reasons for divorce. The most common are infidelity, conflict and communication problems, substance abuse, financial problems, and spousal abuse. For example, among those age 40 and older, 23 percent of women, compared with only 8 percent of men, say that verbal, physical, or emotional abuse was "the most significant reason for the divorce" (Montenegro 2004; Glenn 2005).

These and other problems have led to a greater cultural acceptance of divorce. In 2008, 70 percent of Americans said that divorce is "morally acceptable" (up from 56 percent in 2001). In another national survey, 67 percent of Americans said that children are better off if their unhappy parents get a divorce rather than remain married (Taylor et al. 2007; Saad 2008).

The major positive outcome of divorce is that it provides an escape route for people in miserable marriages. Despite the high divorce rate, most people aren't disillusioned about marriage. Indeed, nearly 85 percent of Americans who divorce remarry, half of them within 3 years. Through remarriage, many couples form a **stepfamily,** a household in which two adults are biological or adoptive parents, with a child from a prior relationship, who marry or cohabit. About 17 percent of children live in a stepfamily. African American and American Indian children are most likely to live in stepfamilies, and Asian American children the least likely (Kreider 2008).

Mike Kemp/Rubberball/Jupiter Images

SINGLEHOOD AND POSTPONING MARRIAGE

The number of single Americans increased from 38 million in 1970 to 96 million in 2008, comprising 43 percent of those age 18 and older. Singles include people who are divorced and widowed, but those who never married make up the largest and fastest-growing segment of the single population—30 percent in 2008, up from 22 percent in 1960 (U.S. Census Bureau 2010).

Are Americans giving up on marriage? Not at all, because at least 90 percent will marry at least once during their lifetime. Instead, many people are postponing marriage. In 1960, the median age at first marriage was 20 for women and 23 for men. By 2009, these ages had increased to 26 for women and 28 for men, the oldest average ages for first marriages ever recorded by the U.S. Census Bureau (U.S. Census Bureau News 2010).

Demographic factors also help explain the large number of single people. The longer one waits to marry, the smaller the pool of eligible partners because more of one's peers have paired off. The likelihood of singlehood also varies by education level. For example, 84 percent of unmarried people age 25 and older are high-school graduates compared with 24 percent who have at least a bachelor's degree (U.S. Census Bureau News 2009). More education often means more income, and more income reduces financial barriers to marriage.

Macro-level variables have also increased the number of single people. For example, because it's difficult to juggle a job and a family, many women have chosen to advance their professional careers before marrying and having children. For men, the well-paid blue-collar jobs that once enabled high-school graduates to support families are mostly gone. Also, many young men don't want the responsibility of marriage and children, especially if they are in college or graduate school, or seeking full-time work. Such factors delay marriage and encourage cohabitation.

COHABITATION

Another major change affecting U.S. families is an increase in **cohabitation,** an arrangement in which two unrelated people are not married but live together and have a sexual relationship (shacking up, in plain English). Because it is based on emotional rather than legal ties, "cohabitation is a distinct family form, neither singlehood nor marriage. We can no longer understand American families if we ignore it" (Brown 2005: 33).

The number of heterosexual unmarried couples in the United States has increased more than 12-fold—from 0.4 million in 1960 to almost 7 million in 2009. This number rises by at least another 780,000 if we include same-sex partners, who make up 14 percent of all unmarried-partner households. Keep in mind, however, that only 9 percent of the population is cohabiting at any time, as in 2008 (Simmons and O'Connell 2003; U.S. Census Bureau News 2010).

> **cohabitation** an arrangement in which two unrelated people are not married but live together and have a sexual relationship.

People who cohabit are a diverse age group. Only 20 percent are 24 or younger, whereas more than 60 percent are in their mid-30s to mid-40s (Martinez et al. 2006). Older people sometimes cohabit rather than marry because of financial reasons. A 72-year-old woman who lives with her 78-year-old partner, for example, has no intention of getting married because she'd forfeit her late husband's pension: "My income would be cut by $500 a month if I got married, and we can't afford that" (Silverman 2003).

Does cohabitation lead to a better marriage? No. Generally, couples who live together before marriage have higher divorce rates than those who don't live together before marriage. The probability of a first marriage ending in separation or divorce within 5 years is 20 percent for couples who did not cohabit before a marriage, but 49 percent for those who did. Thus, living together before marriage typically increases a couple's risk for divorce (Bramlett and Mosher 2002; Lichter et al. 2006; Stevenson and Wolfers 2007).

People live together rather than marry for a variety of reasons. Do you think that women or men benefit more from cohabitation? Why?

Why do cohabiters generally experience higher divorce rates? Some are unsuccessful marriage partners because of drug abuse or mental health problems, chronic unemployment, and sexual infidelity. In addition, cohabitants are less likely than noncohabitants to put effort into the relationship, less likely to compromise, more likely to dissolve a relationship than work on it, and more likely to have poorer communication skills—characteristics that tend to lead to divorce (Dush et al. 2003; Tach and Halpern-Meekin 2009). Because of the higher divorce rate it leads to, some social scientists are adamantly opposed to cohabitation, but others see benefits (see *Table 13.1*).

UNMARRIED MOTHERS

In 1950, only 3 percent of all U.S. births were to unmarried women. In 2008, there were more than 1.7 million such births, accounting for 41 percent of all U.S. births. Thus, 4 in 10 American babies are now born outside of marriage, a new record (Hamilton et al. 2010).

Births to unmarried women vary widely across racial-ethnic groups. White women have more out-of-wedlock babies than do other groups. Proportionately, however, nonmarital birth rates are greatest for black women and lowest for Asian American women (see *Figure 13.2*). There is also considerable variation within groups. Among Asian/Pacific Islanders, for example, 6 percent of births to unmarried women are to Chinese women, compared with almost 20 percent to Filipinas and 51 percent to Hawaiian women. Among Latinas, 25 percent of births to unmarried women are to Cuban women and 60 percent to Puerto Rican women (Ventura et al. 2000).

Teenagers accounted for 22 percent of all nonmarital births in 2008 compared with 71 percent for women ages 20 to 34. Thus, the number of births to unmar-

The number of births to unmarried women ages 20 to 34 is almost three times greater than the number **to teenagers.**

TABLE 13.1
Benefits and Costs of Cohabitation

BENEFITS	COSTS
• Couples have the emotional security of an intimate relationship but can also maintain their independence by spending time with their friends separately and visiting family members alone (McRae 1999).	• Unlike married couples, cohabitants enjoy few legal rights. For example, there's no automatic inheritance if a partner dies without a will, and it's more difficult to collect child support from a cohabiting partner than an ex-spouse (Silverman 2003).
• Couples can save money by sharing living expenses, dissolve the relationship without legal problems, and leave the relationship more easily if it becomes abusive (DeMaris 2001; Silverman 2003).	• Women in cohabiting relationships do more of the cooking and other household tasks than do wives (Coley 2002; Ciabattari 2004).
• Couples find out how much they really care about each other when they have to cope with unpleasant realities, such as a partner who doesn't pay bills or has low hygiene standards.	• People who cohabit before marriage tend to have fewer problem-solving skills (such as patience) than those who don't cohabit. In addition, cohabitors are more likely than biological parents to abuse their children sexually, physically, and emotionally (Cohan and Kleinbaum 2002; Popenoe and Whitehead 2002).
• Children in cohabiting households can reap some economic advantages from living with two adult earners instead of a single mother (Kalil 2002; Cabrera et al. 2008).	• Children who grow up in cohabiting households often lack role models for marital success because cohabiting adults don't always respect each other or communicate effectively (Martin et al. 2001).

FIGURE 13.2
Percentages of Births to Unmarried Women, by Race and Ethnicity, 2006

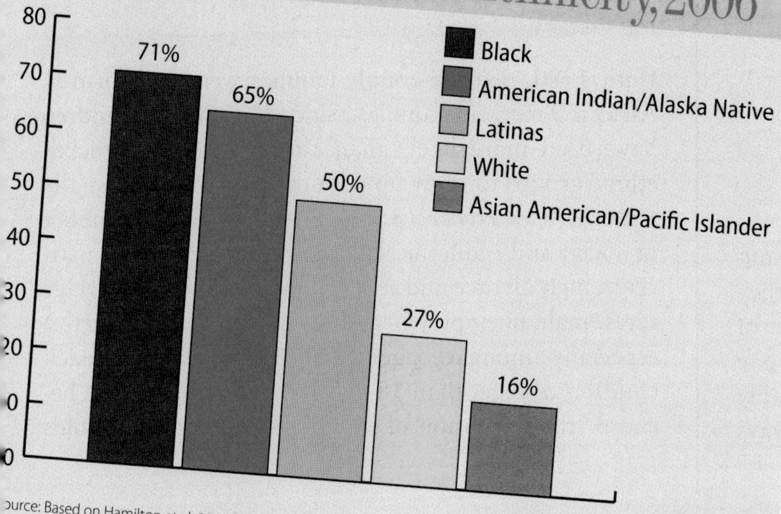

Legend:
- Black
- American Indian/Alaska Native
- Latinas
- White
- Asian American/Pacific Islander

Values: 71%, 65%, 50%, 27%, 16%

Source: Based on Hamilton et al. 2007, Table 1.

Every year, the media feature and applaud stay-at-home dads, but their numbers are negligible. In 2009, about 158,000 American men cared for the family and did the housework while their wives were the wage earners. Among all married two-parent families, about 3 percent of fathers are stay-at-home dads during a given year. The role is usually temporary and undertaken because of unemployment or health problems.

© Getty Images/Comstock/Jupiter Images

ried women ages 20 to 34 is almost three times greater than the number to teenagers. Still, 87 percent of teenage births are nonmarital, compared with 61 percent for women ages 20 to 24, 31 percent for those ages 25 to 29, and 20 percent for those ages 30 to 34 (Hamilton et al. 2010). Because teenage mothers are less likely than their older counterparts to have the resources, parenting skills, and maturity to raise healthy children, their offspring are especially vulnerable to poverty and neglect (Carlson et al. 2005).

Social class, especially education, is an important factor that affects out-of-wedlock births. For example, 63 percent of these births are to women who have not graduated from high school, compared with only 6 percent to women who have either a college or graduate/professional degree. Educated women usually have higher incomes to pay for birth control, more awareness of family planning, and more decision-making power in their relationships, such as insisting that men use condoms (Chandra et al. 2005; Guttmacher Institute 2009).

TWO-INCOME FAMILIES

In the past 50 years, the proportion of married women in the labor force has almost tripled (see Chapter 12). In **dual-earner couples** (also called *dual-income, two-income, two-earner,* or *dual-worker couples*), both partners are employed outside the home. Employed married couples with children younger than 18 make up 66 percent of all married couples (U.S. Census Bureau 2010). When wives work full time outside the home, the median family income can be twice as high, but the couples must also cope with conflicts between domestic and employment responsibilities.

For several decades, a number of sociologists described employed women, especially mothers, as enduring a *second shift*—having to perform housework and child-care tasks after coming home from a job. These days, however, *both* employed partners often experience a second shift. Employed mothers shoulder twice as much child care and housework as their spouses, but employed fathers often work much longer hours than do mothers. Thus, the second shift can be equally stressful for both parents because mothers may feel overwhelmed and fathers may feel guilty for not taking on more domestic tasks and child-rearing responsibilities (Hochschild 1989; Bianchi et al. 2006).

3 Diversity in American Families

i f your ancestors were white ethnic immigrants (such as Irish, Italian, or Polish), they were probably viewed as deviant because of their language, customs, or religion. Despite discrimination, they contributed considerably to contemporary *family diversity,* "the variety of ways that families are structured and function to meet the needs of those defined as family members" (Stewart and Goldfarb 2007: 4). What about minority families? Let's begin with Latinos, the largest racial-ethnic group in the United States.

LATINO FAMILIES

For many Latinos, *familism*—the belief that family relationships take precedence over individual decisions—and the strength of the extended family have traditionally provided emotional and economic support. In a national poll, for example, 82 percent of Latinos, compared with 67 percent of the general U.S. population, said that "relatives are more important than friends" ("The Ties That Bind" 2000).

About 70 percent of Latino children live in two-parent families, down from 78 percent in 1970 (Lugaila 1998; U.S. Census Bureau 2010). Almost 24 percent live in mother-only families (see *Figure 13.3*), and others live with relatives because recent immigrants often depend on family members until they can become self-sufficient (Garcia 2002; Sarmiento 2002).

Latinas, even when they're in the labor force, devote much of their lives to bearing and rearing children. Parental and marital conflicts can erupt, however, because mothers are often overloaded with caring for children, husbands, and elderly relatives, as well as working outside the

home. Fathers don't do nearly as much parenting as mothers, but they're typically warm and loving with children (DeBiaggi 2002; Toth and Xu 2002; Behnke 2004).

AFRICAN AMERICAN FAMILIES

Until 1980, married-couple families were the norm in African American families. Since then, black children have been more likely than children in other racial-ethnic groups to grow up with only one parent, usually a mother (see *Figure 13.3*). This shift reflects a number of social and economic factors: postponement of marriage, high divorce and separation rates, low remarriage rates, male unemployment, and out-of-wedlock births, especially among teenagers. Only 38 percent of all black children younger than 18 live in a two-parent home because "the formation of African-American households

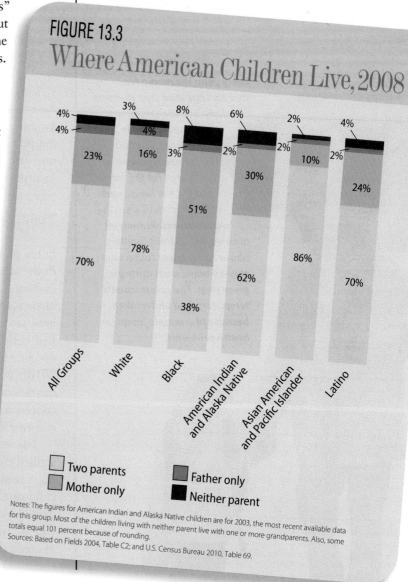

FIGURE 13.3

Where American Children Live, 2008

Notes: The figures for American Indian and Alaska Native children are for 2003, the most recent available data for this group. Most of the children living with neither parent live with one or more grandparents. Also, some totals equal 101 percent because of rounding.
Sources: Based on Fields 2004, Table C2; and U.S. Census Bureau 2010, Table 69.

often originates not in marriage but in the birth of a child" (Barbarin and McCandies 2003: 52).

Some African American nuclear families expand to take in unemployed relatives and become extended families. Others welcome **fictive kin,** nonrelatives who are accepted as part of the family. The ties with fictive kin may be as strong as those established by blood or marriage because these household members provide support—such as caring for children—when parents are employed or negligent (Billingsley 1992; Dilworth-Anderson et al. 1993).

Affluent and middle-class black families, in particular, emphasize success and the accumulation of material wealth through punctuality, hard work, diligence, and saving. Working-class black families also have high aspirations for their children, but they have few resources to achieve their goals. Low-income parents often have few contacts with any community institutions beyond church and school, and depend on both of these to help their children succeed (Willie and Reddick 2003).

AMERICAN INDIAN FAMILIES

About 62 percent of the nation's American Indian/ Alaska Native children live with two parents (see *Figure 13.3*). Compared with 40 percent of the general population, 54 percent of American Indians and Alaska Natives age 30 and older live with their grandchildren and are the primary caretakers ("American Indian and Alaska Native…" 2008).

In many American Indian languages, there is no distinction between blood relatives and relatives by marriage. Sometimes a father's brothers are called "father," uncles and aunts refer to nieces and nephews as "son" or "daughter," and a great-uncle may be referred to as "grandfather" (Sutton and Broken Nose 1996; Yellowbird and Snipp 2002).

American Indian families often emphasize values such as cooperation, sharing, personal integrity, generosity, harmony with nature, and spirituality—which differ from the individual achievement, competitiveness, and drive toward accumulation that many white parents emphasize. Families teach children that men and women may have different roles, but that both should be respected for their contributions to the family (Kawamoto and Cheshire 1997).

ASIAN AMERICAN FAMILIES

Asian American family structures vary widely depending on the members' country of origin, time of arrival, status as either immigrants or refugees, and socio-economic status. Asian American households are likely to be extended families, often including parents, children, unmarried siblings, and grandparents. Most children grow up in two-parent homes. Female-headed households—whether arising from divorce or out-of-wedlock birth—are much less common than in other racial-ethnic groups (see *Figure 13.3*).

> **fictive kin** nonrelatives who are accepted as part of a family.

Many Asian American parents are indulgent, tolerant, and permissive with infants and toddlers. As a child approaches school age, parents expect children to take on more responsibility—such as dressing, completing chores, and doing well in school. Most parents don't tolerate aggressive behavior or sibling rivalry and expect older children to serve as role models for their younger brothers and sisters. Parents also teach their children to conform to societal expectations because they are concerned about what other people—both within and outside of the Asian American community—think. Many Asian American parents not only pressure their children to excel in school but endure hardships—even selling their house—to ensure the best college opportunities for their children (Chan 1997; Fong 2002).

MIDDLE EASTERN AMERICAN FAMILIES

"Wealth and children are the ornaments of this life," says the Qur'an, the sacred book of Islam. Despite the cultural emphasis on large families, U.S.-born Arab American women average just under two children each (which is lower than the average among all U.S. women). Many postpone childbearing and have fewer children because they pursue college and professional degrees and careers (Kulczycki and Lobo 2002; Brittingham and de la Cruz 2005).

Most Middle Eastern American children (84 percent) live with both parents, compared with 70 percent of all U.S. children. Nuclear families are the norm, but extended family ties are important. Households composed of parents and children maintain close contact with their relatives and often provide financial, social, and emotional support. Parents also teach their children to feel a lifelong responsibility to their siblings and parents, and to respect their aunts, uncles, cousins, and grandparents (Phinney et al. 2001).

Because many Middle Eastern American parents see education as critical for success, they expect their children to do well in school. Parents encourage their children to spend time on homework instead of watching television and hanging out with friends. The parents often serve as role models for acquiring education because 41 percent have at least a college degree, compared with 24 percent of the general U.S. adult population (Abu-Laban and Abu-Laban 1999; Brittingham and de la Cruz 2005).

GAY AND LESBIAN FAMILIES

Nationally, an estimated 33 percent of lesbian couples and 22 percent of gay couples are raising children younger than 18 years. More than one in three lesbians has given birth to a child. Gay and lesbian parents are also raising 4 percent of all adopted and 3 percent of all foster children in the United States (Gates and Ost 2004; Gates et al. 2007). Thus, large numbers of lesbians and gay men, single or partnered, are involved in child rearing.

In most respects, lesbian and gay families are like heterosexual families: The parents must make a living, may disagree about finances, and must develop problem-solving strategies. There are three major differences, however. One is that same-sex parents, compared with heterosexual parents, receive less social support from their relatives. Second, gay and lesbian parents face the added burden of raising children who may experience discrimination because of their parents' sexual orientation (Kurdek 2004). A third difference is that banning same-sex marriage denies gay and lesbian parents and their children numerous benefits that married couples and their children enjoy (see *Table 13.2*).

4 Family Conflict and Violence

Conflict is a normal part of family life, but violence is *not* normal. Over a lifetime, we are much more likely to be assaulted or killed by a family member than by a stranger: "That violence and love can coexist in a household is perhaps the most insidious aspect of family violence, because we grow up learning that it is acceptable to hit the people we love" (Gelles 1997: 12).

INTIMATE PARTNER VIOLENCE AND ABUSE

Intimate partner violence (IPV) occurs between people in a close relationship. The term *intimate partner* refers to current and former spouses, couples who live together, and current and former boyfriends or girlfriends. Let's focus on current and former spouses and couples who live together (for a discussion of IPV among current and former boyfriends and girlfriends, see Benokraitis 2011).

IPV is pervasive in U.S. society. In a recent national study, 27 percent of women and 16 percent of men said that they have been victims of IPV at some time in their lives (Black and Breiding 2008). These numbers are conservative because many people are often too ashamed to report the victimization, believe that no one can help, or fear reprisal.

TABLE 13.2
What Are the Legal Benefits of Marriage?

Some states, counties, and cities recognize civil unions and domestic partnerships (see Chapter 9). However, there are more than 1,138 federal benefits and protections tied to marriage that are denied to unmarried couples (U.S. General Accounting Office 2004). For example, partners who aren't married:

- Are not eligible for Social Security benefits if a partner dies
- Are not entitled automatically to a share of the property if there is no will, and even if there is a will, a court can appoint a stranger to administer the estate
- Are unlikely to be required to pay child support or to have visitation rights
- Can't collect a one-time payment of $100,000 in line of duty benefits paid to a surviving spouse of a deceased firefighter, public prosecutor, police officer, or corrections officer
- Are not eligible for veterans' compensation if a partner is killed or disabled in action
- Often pay higher federal and state income taxes because they can't file a joint return
- Don't have automatic privileges for hospital visits, access to intensive care, transferring a partner to a different healthcare facility, making decisions about organ donations, or deciding where the deceased will be buried.

Larry Dale Gordon/Stone/Getty Images

Each year, IPV results in an estimated 1,200 deaths and 2 million injuries among women compared with 330 deaths and nearly 600,000 injuries among men, and is the leading cause of death for women ages 15 to 44 (Catalano 2007; Black and Breiding 2008; Tessier 2008). Indeed, women are much more likely than men to experience IPV over a lifetime, regardless of age, race or ethnicity, annual household income, and education level (Fox and Zawitz 2007).

Aside from being male, there is no "typical" batterer, but some characteristics are common to abusers. Some reflect *macro-level* influences, such as unemployment and poverty. For example, although IPV cuts across all social classes, women living in households with annual incomes less than $7,500 are nearly seven times more likely to be abused than those living in households with an annual income of $75,000 or more because poverty and unemployment increase the likelihood of stress and violence (Thompson et al. 2006).

In addition, cultural factors, such as a strong orientation toward family and community, which is especially common among Latino and Asian American families, increase the likelihood of violence against women who don't "obey" their husbands. Women in Latino or Asian families, especially those who don't speak English well,

may not report marital violence because they fear deportation or being ostracized by their community, are dependent on batterers for economic survival, or don't know about or trust social service organizations that provide help (National Latino Alliance… 2005; Gorman 2010).

Micro-level variables also affect the likelihood of abuse. For example, violence escalates if one or both partners abuse drugs, if they have more children than they can afford (which intensifies financial problems), or if either partner has been raised in a violent household where abuse was a common way to resolve conflict (Benson and Fox 2004). Couples fight about a variety of things, but the most common disagreements have four sources that can escalate into abuse and violence: gender role expectations (such as who does what housework); money (saving and spending); children (especially discipline); and infidelity, both personally and online (Anderson and Sabatelli 2007; Benokraitis 2011).

> **child maltreatment**
> (sometimes called *child abuse*) includes a broad range of behaviors that place a child at serious risk, including physical abuse, sexual abuse, neglect, and emotional mistreatment.

CHILD MALTREATMENT

Child maltreatment (sometimes called *child abuse*) includes a broad range of behaviors that place a child at serious risk or result in serious harm, including death, that include neglect and physical, sexual, and emotional abuse. In 2008, an estimated 772,000 children were victims of child maltreatment, representing 10 per 1,000 children in the U.S. population. Because only a fraction of the total number of child victimization cases is reported, however, federal agencies assume that millions of American children experience abuse and neglect on a daily basis (U.S. Department of Health and Human Services 2010).

Almost 80 percent of the perpetrators are parents, 13 percent are unrelated caregivers (such as foster parents and boyfriends), and 7 percent are relatives. Nearly 80 percent of the children who die of abuse and neglect are younger than 4 years old, and almost 71 percent of the offenders are one or both parents. Victimization rates decline as children get older, presumably because they can protect themselves, run away from home, or adults fear being reported by older children (U.S. Department of Health and Human Services 2010).

About 25 percent of all children live in homes where parents or other adults engage in violence (Finkelhor et al. 2009). Whether children are targets of abuse or see it, a growing body of research has linked violence with lifelong developmental problems, including depression, delinquency, suicide, alcoholism, low academic achievement, unemployment, and medical problems in adulthood (Currie and Tekin 2006; McDonald et al. 2006; Putnam 2006).

ELDER ABUSE AND NEGLECT

Elder abuse (sometimes called *elder mistreatment*) is any knowing, intentional, or negligent act by a caregiver or any other person that causes harm to people age 65 or older. Examples include physical, psychological, and sexual abuse; neglect; isolation from family and friends; deprivation of basic necessities, such as food and heat; and not providing needed medications. Family members and acquaintances mistreat an estimated 5 percent of people age 65 and older every year. Some researchers call elder abuse "the hidden iceberg" because about 93 percent of cases are not reported to police or other protective agencies (National Center on Elder Abuse 2005).

Who are the victims of elder abuse? More than 77 percent are white, 43 percent are 80 years or older, and 66 percent are women; almost 90 percent of cases

The movie Precious (2009) received many awards, but some critics contended that the film stereotyped black female teenagers—especially those living in low-income households—as obese, illiterate, and living with abusive mothers (Amusa 2010). If you've seen the movie, do you agree with such criticism or not? Why?

occur in domestic settings. Whites are more likely to engage in physical abuse of elders, whereas minorities are more likely to be guilty of neglect, emotional abuse, and financial exploitation (such as keeping much of the income from the elderly person's Social Security checks) (Malley-Morrison and Hines 2004; Teaster et al. 2006).

Who are the perpetrators of elder abuse? Most are adult children (53 percent), spouses (19 percent), or other family members (18 percent). Only about 10 percent are friends, neighbors, or nonfamily service providers (Tatara 1998).

Family members neglect or abuse older people for a variety of reasons. On a *micro level,* for example, abuse of alcohol and other drugs is more than twice as likely among family caregivers who abuse elders as among those who do not. On a *macro level,* a shared residence is a major risk factor for elder mistreatment because the caregiver(s) may depend on the older person for housing while the elder is dependent on the caregiver(s) for physical help, increasing the likelihood of everyday tensions and conflict. Also, unlike low-income families, middle-class families are not eligible for admission to public nursing homes, and few can pay for the in-home nursing care and services that upper-class families can afford. As a result, cramped quarters and high expenses increase the caregivers' stress and may lead to elder abuse (Reay and Browne 2001; Bonnie and Wallace 2003).

5 Our Aging Society

many older people are vigorous and productive. The higher life expectancy of recent decades has forged numerous changes for older people and their families, some positive and some negative. (Many researchers use the terms *elderly, aged,* and *older people* interchangeably.) Let's begin by considering what we mean by "old."

WHEN IS "OLD"?

What images come to mind when you hear the word *old*? About a year before my mother died, she remarked, "It's very strange. When I look in the mirror, I see an old woman, but I don't recognize her. I know I'm 86, but I feel at least 30 years younger." She knew her health was failing, yet my mother's identity, like those of many older people, came from within, despite her physical age.

Between the ages of 65 and 91, avid mountaineer Hulda Crooks scaled Mount Whitney (the highest mountain in the continental United States) 23 times. She died at the age of 101 in 1997.

AP Photo/Itsuo Inouye

Age is largely a social construction. In societies where people rarely live past 50 (because of HIV/AIDS in many African nations, for example), 40 is old. In industrialized societies, where the average person lives to at least 75, 40 is considered young. Still, regardless of how we feel, society usually defines *old* in chronological age. In the United States, for instance, people are typically deemed old at age 65, 66, or 67 because they can retire and become eligible for Medicare and Social Security benefits.

Gerontologists—scientists who study the biological, psychological, and social aspects of aging—emphasize that the aging population should not be lumped into one group. Instead, there are significant differences among the *young-old* (65–74 years old), the *old-old* (75–84 years old), and the *oldest-old* (85 years and older) in ability to live independently or to work and in health needs. Generally, for example, a 65-year-old woman is much less likely than an 85-year-old woman to need caregiving from family and friends.

LIFE EXPECTANCY AND MULTIGENERATIONAL FAMILIES

In 1800, the average person's chance of living to 100 was roughly 1 in 20 million; today it's 1 in 500 (Jeune and Vaupel 1995 and author's calculations). More people are reaching age 65 than ever before. For example, American children born in 2006 have a **life expectancy**, the average length of time people of the same age will live, of 78 years (on average, 75 for men and almost 81 for women) compared with 47 years in 1900 and 71 years in 1970 (U.S. Census Bureau 2010). As a result, the number of Americans age 65 and older is booming.

Almost 41 million Americans (13 percent of the total population) are 65 or older, a dramatic increase from just 4 percent in 1900. One of the fastest-growing groups is the oldest-old, whose number increased from 100,000 in 1900 to 4.2 million in 2000. By 2030, this group will constitute almost 3 percent of the U.S. population. By 2020, about 214,000 Americans will be *centenarians*, or people who are 100 years or older (Federal Interagency Forum... 2006; U.S. Census Bureau 2010).

Whereas the number of older Americans has increased, the proportion of young people has decreased. By 2030, there will be more elderly people than young people in the United States (see *Figure 13.4*). One result of longer life spans is the increase of multigenerational families. Many young children enjoy relationships not only with their grandparents, but with their great-grandparents and even great-great-grandparents. On the other hand, millions of adults spend more years caring for frail and elderly parents, grandparents, and other relatives. These adults are often referred to as the **sandwich generation** because they are in the middle of two generations, caring for their own children and their aging parents.

gerontologists scientists who study the biological, psychological, and social aspects of aging.

life expectancy the average length of time people of the same age will live.

sandwich generation people in a middle generation who care for their own children and their aging parents.

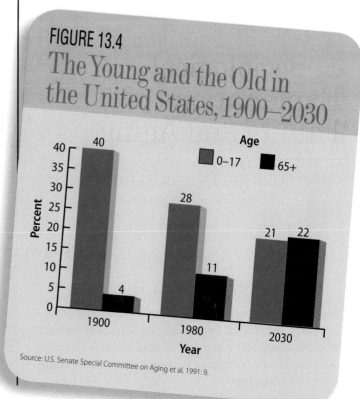

FIGURE 13.4
The Young and the Old in the United States, 1900–2030

Age: 0–17, 65+

(Bar chart values)
- 1900: 0–17 = 40, 65+ = 4
- 1980: 0–17 = 28, 65+ = 11
- 2030: 0–17 = 21, 65+ = 22

Y-axis: Percent (0 to 40)
X-axis: Year

Source: U.S. Senate Special Committee on Aging et al. 1991: 9.

GLOBAL GRAYING

In 2030, 12 percent of the planet's population (about 975 million people) will be 65 years or older, up from 7 percent currently. Industrialized nations have the highest percentages of older people, but the less developed nations in many regions also have large numbers, and the proportions are increasing rapidly (see *Figure 13.5*).

This rapid aging suggests that many countries will face debates—which have already emerged in Europe, the United States, and Canada—over health care, Social Security, and other costs. Consider a few examples:

- Spain, which has a life expectancy of 80 years, has space in nursing homes for only one of every eight seniors who need such care.

- In China, the pension system is already deeply in debt. One demographer predicts that China will soon become a 4-2-1 society in which one child will support two parents and four grandparents.

- In France, despite considerable protests, the government recently passed a law that requires public sector workers (more than 25 percent of the French workforce) to work 40 years instead of 37.5 years before receiving a pension (Sciolino 2003; Longman 2004; French 2007).

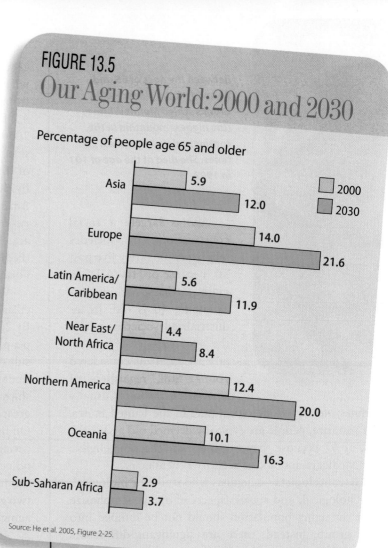

FIGURE 13.5
Our Aging World: 2000 and 2030

Percentage of people age 65 and older

Legend: 2000, 2030

Region	2000	2030
Asia	5.9	12.0
Europe	14.0	21.6
Latin America/Caribbean	5.6	11.9
Near East/North Africa	4.4	8.4
Northern America	12.4	20.0
Oceania	10.1	16.3
Sub-Saharan Africa	2.9	3.7

Source: He et al. 2005, Figure 2-25.

6 Sociological Explanations of Family and Aging

the four sociological perspectives are useful in understanding families and aging (*Table 13.3* summarizes the key points of these theories).

FUNCTIONALISM

Functionalists spotlight the essential tasks that families carry out which benefit society. The performance of these tasks, or *functions,* is critical for a society's survival. Even in our later years, society influences our roles and behavior.

Stability and Activity

We began this chapter by looking at the vital functions that families perform—such as procreation, socialization, and economic security—that promote societal stability and individual well-being. Functionalists recognize that families may differ in structure (e.g., nuclear vs. extended) but believe that the similarities ensure a society's continuity. Social problems arise, for instance, when parents can't or don't provide their children with the necessary financial and emotional support.

The rapid global aging suggests that many countries will face debates over health care, Social Security, and other costs.

Today, you have a 1 in 500 chance of living to be 100.

with their lives (see Atchley and Barusch 2004, for a summary of some of this research).

activity theory proposes that many older people remain engaged in numerous roles and activities, including work.

In the late 1950s, functionalists maintained that, as people age, they withdraw from their social roles and become isolated. This *disengagement theory* was abandoned when many researchers, including gerontologists, found that disengagement was due to age discrimination, not choice, and was limited to older people with disabilities and poor health. Functionalists replaced disengagement theory with **activity theory,** which proposes that many older people remain engaged in numerous roles and activities, including work, and that those who do so adjust better to aging and are more satisfied

Critical Evaluation

For many functionalists, marriage, followed by procreation, are critical in promoting health, social order, and stability. Critics maintain, however, that the functionalist perspective reflects several weaknesses. First, it seems to support traditional family arrangements, such as the nuclear family, but largely devalues other family forms, such as single-parent and same-sex families. Second, it is questionable whether some family functions are as universal or necessary as functionalists claim, because procreation often occurs outside of marriage and because the state has assumed some of the family's functions, such as caring for some children (as in foster homes) and the elderly (by providing Medicare payments, for example) (Lundberg and Pollak 2007). Third, recent data show that never-married Americans are as healthy as their happily-married counterparts; it's

TABLE 13.3
Sociological Perspectives on Family and Aging

THEORETICAL PERSPECTIVE	LEVEL OF ANALYSIS	KEY POINTS
Functionalist	Macro	• Families are important in maintaining societal stability and meeting family members' needs. • Older people who are active and engaged are more satisfied with life.
Conflict	Macro	• Families promote social inequality because of social class differences. • Many corporations view older workers as disposable.
Feminist	Macro and Micro	• Families both mirror and perpetuate patriarchy and gender inequality. • Women have an unequal burden in caring for children as well as older family members and relatives.
Symbolic Interactionist	Micro	• Families construct their everyday lives through interaction and subjective interpretations of family roles. • Many older family members adapt to aging and often maintain previous activities.

the separated, divorced, and widowed who suffer higher rates of illness and disease (Liu and Umberson 2008).

Moreover, is activity theory as representative of older people as some functionalists claim? Many people continue to work, even in their 80s, not because they choose to do so but because they can't afford to retire, even though they are in poor health and unhappy in their low-income jobs. As health deteriorates, many older people tend to become more isolated (Kinsella and Phillips 2005; Lee 2009).

CONFLICT THEORY

Conflict theorists agree that families serve important functions but contend that some groups benefit more than others because families are sources of social inequality that mirror the larger society. The inequities are evident from birth to old age.

Inequality, Social Class, and Power

For conflict theorists, families perpetuate social stratification. Those in high-income brackets have the greatest share of capital, including wealth, that they can pass down to the next generation. Such inheritances reduce the likelihood that all families can compete for resources such as education, decent housing, and health care (see Chapter 8).

There's also a question of whether the government cherishes children as much as it professes. For example, 30 countries—including Cuba, Slovakia, and most of Europe—have lower infant mortality rates than the United States. And of 16 industrialized countries, the United States has the highest rates of child poverty and the lowest rates of spending on children's services (Children's Defense Fund 2008; Haub and Kent 2008).

Unequal power and access to resources continue into old age. Profit-seeking corporations lay off older workers because of their higher salaries and health insurance costs. Some employers insist that they value older workers' loyalty, work ethic, reliability, and experience, but many are less likely to hire or retain older people because they are usually more expensive than younger workers. Because many large companies have cut their pension plans, numerous older workers must work long after they expected to retire (Johnson and Mommaerts 2010; Roscigno 2010).

Critical Evaluation

Conflict theory is useful in highlighting family inequality across social classes, but it often glosses over the ability of low-income families to carry out important

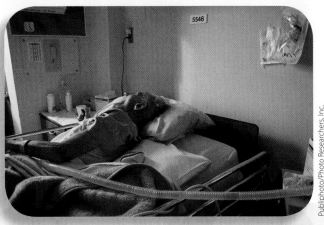

The top U.S. medical centers spend anywhere from $30,000 to almost $94,000 a year per older patient in his or her last two years of life, and all of the costs are covered by Medicare or Medicaid (Wennberg et al. 2008). Is this a good investment of our resources?

functions such as providing children with basic necessities and emotional support. Second, conflict theorists tend to overlook the fact that most of the elderly, especially those in middle and upper classes, don't have to struggle for resources. Between 1960 and 2007, for example, the U.S. government's spending on children declined from 20 percent to 15 percent, but spending on people age 65 and older grew from 22 percent to almost 46 percent because of programs such as Social Security and Medicare. A third weakness is that conflict theory links family inequality to capitalism and social class, but there is also considerable family inequality in countries that are not capitalist.

FEMINIST THEORIES

Feminist scholars agree with conflict theorists that there is considerable inequality between low-income and wealthy families in accessing necessary resources. However, feminist theorists emphasize the inequality of gender roles in families, especially in patriarchal societies (including the United States).

Because employed mothers do twice as much housework and child care as men, many **men benefit from women's unpaid labor at home.**

Gender Roles and Patriarchy

Feminist scholars view the patriarchal family as a major reason for women's inequality. Because employed mothers do twice as much housework and child care as men, many men benefit from women's unpaid labor at home. In most countries, males determine laws about property and inheritance rights, marriage and divorce, and many other regulations that give men authority over women. Men hold most of the power, resources, and privilege, and many feel free to use women and children as targets of sexual and physical abuse, especially when legal systems, religious organizations, and medical institutions don't take violence against women and children as seriously as they should (Lindsey 2005).

Feminist sociologists have for some time challenged popular myths that children of single and employed mothers have emotional, cognitive, and behavioral problems. Feminist scholars have also been the first to document the ways in which sexism, racism, and classism intersect to oppress women and children. For example, the poorest older adults are most likely to be minority women, and caregivers of the old—who are predominantly women—must often leave their jobs or work only part time to accommodate caregiving (Allen and Beitin 2007; Houser 2007).

Critical Evaluation

Feminist theories have called attention to the impact of gender and patriarchy in our family relationships, but some critics question whether feminist perspectives overstate women's oppression. For example, patriarchal family structures limit women's rights, but they also often provide important economic resources for women and children (Benokraitis 2011).

Feminist sociologists have deepened our understanding of family diversity, but some critics believe that feminist scholars have a tendency to view full-time homemakers as victims rather than as individuals who choose the role. Thus, some maintain, feminist scholars are "in danger of refusing to listen to a multiplicity of women's voices" (Johnson and Lloyd 2004: 160).

Some critics also contend that feminist scholars exaggerate many women's subordinate roles in the family and economy. As you saw in Chapter 12, for example, 22 percent of wives earn more than their husbands. Some might assert, justifiably, that even many of these women still shoulder a larger share of the workload at home, but women's higher incomes also mean that they have more domestic decision-making power and don't have to rely on men financially.

SYMBOLIC INTERACTIONISM

For symbolic interactionists, people create subjective meanings of what a family is and what its members' roles are. Thus, people learn, through interaction with others, how to act as a parent, a grandparent, a teenager, a stepchild, and so on throughout the life course.

Learning Family and Aging Roles

Interactionists often use exchange theory to explain mate selection and family roles. The fundamental premise of **exchange theory** is that people seek through their social interactions to maximize their rewards and to minimize their costs. In mate selection, people seek to trade their resources—such as wealth, intelligence, good looks, youth, and/or status—for more, better, or different assets.

Many people stay in unhappy marriages and other intimate relationships because the rewards seem equal to the costs ("It's better than being alone."). Similarly, many female victims tolerate an abusive relationship because they fear loneliness or losing the economic benefits that a man provides. Rewards for perpetrators of family violence include the release of anger and frustration, as well as the accumulation of power and control (Sherman 1992; Choice and Lamke 1997).

A well-known psychologist who interviewed more than 200 couples over a 20-year period found that the

"I distinctly remember you agreeing-if we had them-that you would take blame for the children."

Liza Donnelly

difference between lasting marriages and those that split up was a "magic ratio" of 5 to 1. That is, if there are five positive interactions between partners for every negative one, the marriage is likely to be stable over time (Gottman 1994). Thus, we can improve our family relationships by learning to interact in more positive ways.

Stereotypes about older people are deeply rooted in U.S. society. For example, 84 percent of Americans older than 60 years report one or more incidents of **ageism,** discrimination against older people, including insulting jokes, disrespect, patronizing behavior, and assumptions about being frail or unhealthy (Roscigno 2010). **Continuity theory** posits that older adults can substitute satisfying new roles for those they've lost (Atchley and Barusch 2004). For example, a retired music teacher can offer private lessons. Thus, developing new roles may lessen some of the emotional distress due to ageism.

Critical Evaluation

Symbolic interactionists offer valuable insights on social interaction as a dynamic process in which family members—of all ages—continually modify their behavior throughout the life course. Nonetheless, a common criticism is that interactionism, a micro-level perspective, doesn't address macro-level constraints. For example, families living in poverty, and especially single mothers, are likely to be stigmatized and must often raise their children in unsafe neighborhoods. Such problems increase stress, feelings of helplessness, and family conflict—all of which can derail positive everyday interactions (Seccombe 2007).

Second, exchange theory is useful in explaining why people stay in unhappy or abusive relationships, but individuals don't always calculate the potential costs and rewards of every decision. In the case of women who care for older family members, for example, genuine love and concern can override cost-benefit decisions, especially in many traditional Asian, Latino, and Middle Eastern families, where culturally defined kinship duties take precedence over individual rights (Hurh 1998; Do 1999; see also Chapter 10).

Third, continuity theory neglects societal obstacles that deter older people from engaging in many previous interactions. After retirement, for example, many people must get by on low, fixed incomes and can't afford luxuries such as attending cultural or sports events that they might have enjoyed when they were employed. Also, older people who experience illnesses because of low-quality health care over a lifetime may become too sick to participate in family and community activities or pursue hobbies.

For symbolic interactionists, family traditions and rituals give people an identity and a sense of belonging to a group. Birthday parties (left), an important ritual, commemorate an important event but also unite family members and friends through positive social interaction. In most Latino communities, the quinceañera (pronounced "keen-say-ah-NYAIR-ah") is a coming-of-age rite that celebrates a girl's entrance into adulthood on her fifteenth birthday. The quinceañera, an elaborate and dignified religious (right) and social event, includes a traditional waltz with the father and the tossing of a bouquet to the boys to determine who will win the first dance with the young woman.

Education is an
important source of formal knowledge
and socialization.

DICTIONNAIRE DE LA PEINTURE

L'Architecture

14

Education

When I ask my students why they're in college, about 95 percent say to get a good or better job, 4 percent want an education for its own sake, and 1 percent have other reasons ("My parents are college graduates and expect the same from me."). The reasons may vary, but education comprises a large part of our lives. In this chapter, we'll examine sociological perspectives on the purpose of education in contemporary society and how U.S. education has changed. Let's begin by considering what sociologists mean by *education*.

Key Topics

In this chapter, we'll explore the following topics:

1 What Is Education?

2 Sociological Perspectives on Education

3 Some Problems with U.S. Education

4 New Directions in U.S. Education

what do you think?

People freely decide whether to go to college.

1	2	3	4	5	6	7
strongly agree					strongly disagree	

1 What Is Education?

education is a social institution that transmits attitudes, knowledge, beliefs, values, norms, and skills to its members through formal, systematic training. **Schooling,** a narrower term, is formal training and instruction provided in a classroom setting. U.S. education and schooling have undergone four significant transitions during a relatively short period:

> **education** a social institution that transmits attitudes, knowledge, beliefs, values, norms, and skills to its members through formal, systematic training.
>
> **schooling** formal training and instruction provided in a classroom setting.

- *Universal education has expanded.* By the turn of the twentieth century, elementary schooling was nearly universal in the United States.

- *Community colleges have flourished.* Besides preparing students to transfer to 4-year institutions, the 1,600 community colleges in the United States today educate more than half of the nation's undergraduates, and nearly 1 in 5 Americans who earned doctorates in 2008 attended a community college at some point (Fiegener 2009).

- *Public higher education has burgeoned.* Passage of the GI Bill in 1944 provided those who had served in the military during World War II funds for tuition, fees, books, and living expenses for up to 48 months. In 1947, veterans made up almost half of all college enrollments (Greenberg 2004).

- Especially during the last few decades, *student diversity has increased.* In higher education, for example, racial-ethnic groups and women have accounted for a large proportion of the increases in enrollment at colleges and universities since 1990 (Planty et al. 2009).

Because of these and other changes, 87 percent of Americans 25 or older have completed at least high school, and

31 percent have attained at least a bachelor's degree (see *Figure 14.1*). Both numbers are all-time highs.

2 Sociological Perspectives on Education

Sociologists offer several explanations of education. Functionalists emphasize its benefits, conflict theorists argue that education reinforces a rigid social class structure, feminist theorists maintain that education perpetuates gender inequality, and symbolic interactionists examine how the social context shapes teachers' and students' everyday experiences (*Table 14.1* summarizes these perspectives).

FIGURE 14.1

Educational Attainment of the U.S. Population, 1940–2009

Percent

- High school completion or higher
- Less than high school completion
- Bachelor's or higher degree

1940 1950 1960 1970 1980 1990 2000 2009

Year

Source: Snyder and Dillow 2010, Figure 4.

FUNCTIONALISM: WHAT ARE THE BENEFITS OF EDUCATION?

As in their analyses of other social institutions, functionalists maintain that education contributes to society's stability, solidarity, and well-being. Some of these contributions are manifest functions that are intended and visible. Others, latent functions, are unintended and less visible.

Manifest Functions of Education

For functionalists, education serves several important purposes in society, including the following:

- Schools are *socialization agencies* that teach children how to get along with others and prepare them for adult economic roles (Durkheim 1898/1956; Parsons 1959). Schools have even taken over some socialization functions traditionally handled by the family, such as teaching youngsters basic etiquette rules, self-discipline, anger management, and even acceptable sexual behavior (see Chapters 4 and 9).

- Education *transmits knowledge and culture*. Schools teach children skills such as reading, writing, and counting, but also convey cultural values that encourage competition, achievement, patriotism, and democracy (see Chapters 3 and 11).

- The transmission of cultural values increases *cultural integration*, the social bonds that people have with each other and with the community at large. A major reason for the increase in public schools in the United States was to Americanize the children of immigrants by teaching them English and responsible citizenship. Such schooling increases *societal cohesion* because it instills national values.

- Education encourages *cultural innovation*. For example, faculty at research universities, especially, receive billions of dollars every year to develop computer technology, treatments for diseases, and programs to address social problems such as crime and drug abuse.

- Education *benefits taxpayers*—regardless of whether they have children in school—because more highly educated people tend to pay more in taxes, are less likely to use government support programs, and are less likely to commit crimes (Carroll and Erkut 2009).

BananaStock/Jupiter Images

TABLE 14.1
Major Sociological Perspectives on Education

THEORETICAL PERSPECTIVE	LEVEL OF ANALYSIS	VIEW OF EDUCATION	SOME MAJOR QUESTIONS
Functionalist	Macro	Contributes to society's stability, solidarity, and cohesion	What are the manifest and latent functions of education?
Conflict	Macro	Reproduces and reinforces inequality and maintains a rigid social class structure	How does education limit equal opportunity?
Feminist	Macro and Micro	Produces inequality based on gender	How does gender inequality in education limit women's upward mobility?
Interactionist	Micro	Teaches roles and values through everyday face-to-face interaction and practices	How do tracking, labeling, self-fulfilling prophecies, and engagement affect students' educational experiences?

There's no doubt that education increases job prospects and upward mobility. In 2008, a college graduate earned an average of $57,000 per year compared with only $31,000 for someone with a high-school diploma (U.S. Census Bureau Newsroom 2009). By about age 55, college graduates bring home 90 percent more than people without a degree. Lifetime earnings are even higher for people with advanced degrees (see *Figure 14.2*). And during economic downturns, the more educated people are, the less likely they are to be out of work.

Many Americans seem to agree with functionalists that an education is important. In a national survey, 92 percent of recent graduates of 2- and 4-year institutions said that their education was worth the time and money, 84 percent stated that they were prepared with the skills and knowledge they needed in the workplace, and 50 percent said that they used the critical thinking, research, and communication skills they had learned in college in both their personal life and their work. Furthermore, according to medical researchers, those who are better-educated—regardless of race or ethnicity—live longer because they are better informed about the benefits of healthful behaviors such as keeping weight down, not smoking, and using condoms during sexual intercourse (American Council on Education 2008; Jemal et al. 2008).

Latent Functions of Education

Schools also fulfill many latent, or unintended, functions. For example,

- Schools *provide child care* for the growing number of single-parent and two-income families. Because many

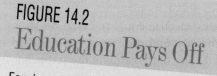

FIGURE 14.2
Education Pays Off

Earnings over a lifetime for full-time, year-round workers (in millions of dollars)

Doctoral degree	$3.4
Professional degree	$4.4
Master's degree	$2.5
Bachelor's degree	$2.1
Associate's degree	$1.6
Some college	$1.5
High school graduate	$1.2
Not high school graduate	$1.0

Source: Day and Newburger 2002, Figure 3.

parents must work shifts or commute long distances to work, preschool, kindergarten, and after-school programs have mushroomed.

- During the current recession, many schools have also become *social service centers* that provide the children of jobless parents with free meals and food to take home, shoes, warm clothes, and school supplies (Chandler 2009).

- High schools and colleges are *matchmaking institutions* that bring together unmarried individuals.

- Education *decreases job competition;* the more time that young adults spend in school, the longer the jobs of older workers they might replace are safe.

- Educational institutions *create social networks.* Especially in college, students can forge relationships with peers that can ultimately lead to jobs or business opportunities.

- Education is *good for business.* Thousands of companies (and jobs) have been created to measure students' intelligence and abilities, and offer services (such as tutoring) to increase scores on standardized tests. In addition, textbook prices rise every year, increasing business profits.

Critical Evaluation

Functionalist analyses are beneficial in highlighting the manifest and latent functions of education, but do functionalists exaggerate its benefits? Those who com-

AP Photo/Josh Reynolds, file

These students are attending a class at Bunker Hill Community College, Massachusetts, from 11:45 p.m. to 2:30 a.m. Other community colleges have added classes as early as 6:00 a.m. to accommodate "a deluge" of part-time students, the jobless, and recent high-school graduates who can't afford more expensive 4-year colleges because of the economic downturn (Goodnough 2009: A1).

plete higher levels of education have, on average, higher vocabulary scores than those with lower educational levels. Over the last 70 years, however, the verbal abilities of graduates at all educational levels have slightly decreased (Nie and Golde 2008). Thus, higher educational attainment doesn't cause better communication skills. Instead, verbal ability reflects other variables such as social class.

Also, according to some critics, functionalists tend to gloss over education's dysfunctional aspects. For instance, schools aren't preparing young adults for the workforce as well as they could: many college graduates aren't punctual, dependable, or industrious; can't solve problems creatively; and don't write and speak well or evaluate information critically. Between 1992 and 2003, there was a 20 percent decline in college graduates' reading literacy, as in understanding news stories, job application forms, transportation schedules, and drug and food labels (EPE Research Center 2007; Kutner et al. 2007).

CONFLICT THEORY: DOES EDUCATION PERPETUATE SOCIAL INEQUALITY?

Whereas functionalists emphasize the advantages of education, conflict theorists ask why education benefits some people more than others. From preschool to graduate school, conflict theorists maintain, education creates and perpetuates social inequality based on social class, race, and ethnicity, and uses results of standardized tests and social control to maintain the status quo.

Social Class, Race, and Ethnicity

One of the best predictors of educational attainment is social class. Wealthy parents have the greatest amount of *economic capital* (such as income and other monetary assets), *cultural capital* (such as an elite education and positive attitudes toward education), and *social capital* (such as social networks that provide support and information about schooling). Differential access to all three types of capital reinforces and reproduces the existing class structure from one generation to the next (Bourdieu 1984; Dickert-Conlin and Rubenstein 2007).

The children—regardless of their intelligence—of influential, celebrity, and wealthy families attend elite elementary and high schools that guarantee them a place in the most prestigious colleges and universities. And affluent families not at that top level tend to live in school districts where public schools enjoy generous funding, up-to-date textbooks and laboratories, small

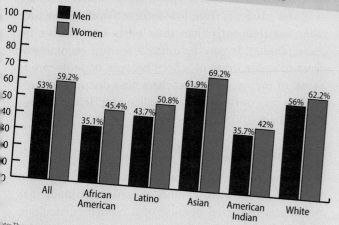

FIGURE 14.3
Racial-Ethnic and Gender Gaps in College Graduation Rates

Men
Women

	All	African American	Latino	Asian	American Indian	White
Men	53%	35.1%	43.7%	61.9%	35.7%	56%
Women	59.2%	45.4%	50.8%	69.2%	42%	62.2%

Note: These are 6-year graduation rates for students who entered college in 2000.
Source: Kevin Carey, 2005, "One Step from the Finish Line: Higher College Graduation Rates Are Within Our Reach," p. 2. Education Trust, Jan. 18, 2005. Reprinted by permission of Education Trust.

classes, experienced teachers, and a high-quality curriculum ("Quality Counts. . ." 2007).

Minority students are enrolling in college in greater numbers than ever before, but graduation rates are higher for whites than for any other group except Asian Americans (see *Figure 14.3*). Why are the attrition rates for some racial-ethnic students so high?

There are many reasons, but most reflect social class (Lopez 2009). Students from lower socioeconomic backgrounds—many of whom are minorities—are less likely to attend high schools that offer high-level courses in mathematics and science that can mean the difference between passing or failing required courses during the first few years of college. Also, many college youths from low-income families face numerous obstacles. For example, they must work part time or full time to pay for tuition, books, and other costs, and therefore often have little time to interact with faculty who might motivate them to continue their studies or to seek financial aid (Chen 2005; Adelman 2006).

Standardized Testing and Gatekeeping

Gatekeeping refers to controlling the access to education or jobs of people from lower socioeconomic levels. Both IQ tests and standardized tests are examples of gatekeeping.

Researchers don't agree on a definition of intelligence but regularly measure an **intelligence quotient**

(IQ), an index of an individual's performance on a standardized test relative to the performance level of others of the same age. Schools typically use the IQ scores to place students into different ability groups.

Numerous scholars have challenged the validity of IQ scores. Among other things, they argue, social and environmental factors have at least as much influence on intelligence as inherited factors. For example, raising a child in an upper-middle-class environment versus a lower-class environment can increase IQ scores by 12 to 18 points. Better schooling (small class sizes, computer access, and teachers' skills) also boost IQ scores, especially for poor and minority children (Nisbett 2009).

What about other standardized tests? The SAT Reasoning Test (called the Scholastic Aptitude Test until 1993, but now known simply as the SAT) includes sections titled "Critical Thinking," "Mathematics," and "Writing." According to the College Board, a nonprofit organization that owns and administers the test, the SAT "is a measure of the critical thinking skills you'll need for academic success in college. [It] assesses how well you analyze and solve problems—skills you learned in school that you'll need in college" (College Board 2006).

Many commercial test preparation providers claim that the courses (which cost $1,000 or more) increase SAT scores by 100 points or more, but research shows that "average gains are more in the neighborhood of 30 points." The increase is negligible, but may fall above a

> **intelligence quotient (IQ)** an index of an individual's performance on a standardized test relative to the performance level of others of the same age.

© Bart Sadowski/iStockPhoto

college's cutoff score for admission (Briggs 2009: 1). Consequently, such coaching gives an advantage to students from higher income families.

SAT defenders claim that scores on the test are accurate predictors of how well a high-school graduate will perform in college (Caperton 2009). Thus, students with higher scores are better bets for institutions that are swamped with admissions applications and shrinking budgets.

Critics contend that the SAT measures social class rather than ability because students at lower socioeconomic levels have less economic, cultural, and social capital. Instead, according to one educator, the admission process should include a broad range of criteria such as personal interviews, letters of recommendation, and a thorough examination of high-school curriculum and grades. "These reveal more about intellectual ability and curiosity than the score on a test administered one Saturday morning" (Tiefenthaler 2009: 25).

Critics also maintain that the SAT and other standardized tests don't measure a variety of skills and abilities such as *creative intelligence* (using skills to create, invent, discover, and deal with novel situations) and *practical intelligence* (the ability to apply knowledge to everyday situations). Because of these and other criticisms, more than 750 four-year colleges and universities in the United States don't use SAT scores in making admissions decisions (Lemann 2000; Sedlacek 2004; Yagelski et al. 2005; FairTest 2007; Soares 2007).

Advanced Placement (AP) courses and exams are also gatekeeping tools. Almost 27 percent of the 3.1 million students who graduated from U.S. public high schools in 2009 took at least one AP exam. However, only 16 percent scored high enough to be able to skip one or more introductory college courses in 37 subjects, ranging from Art History to World History (College Board 2010).

Still, many high-school teachers encourage students to take AP courses and exams because they impress college admissions officers and can enable students to graduate a semester or two early, reducing the cost of a college education. As a result, the number of students taking AP courses has mushroomed. Latino students (54 percent) report taking between 1 and 4 AP classes in high school, as do 50 percent of white and 45 percent of African American students, compared with a low of 39 percent of American Indian students. Asian American students are more than twice as likely to take between 5 and 9 AP courses as white students (34 and 15 percent, respectively) (Pryor et al. 2009).

Many minority, inner-city, and rural students don't have access to AP courses. Even when such courses are available, students from low-income families may take them less frequently than their peers from higher income families. It may be difficult for low-income students to concentrate in school because of problems at home, or they may have teachers who discourage them because the courses are "too challenging" (Klopfenstein and Thomas 2005).

Education and Social Control

Functionalists see education as an avenue for upward mobility. In contrast, conflict theorists maintain that mobility is restricted because of a hidden curriculum, credentialism, and privilege.

Hidden Curriculum. Every school has a formal curriculum that includes reading, writing, and learning other skills. Schools also have a **hidden curriculum,** practices that transmit nonacademic knowledge, values, attitudes, norms, and beliefs that tend to legitimize "economic inequality and the staffing of unequal work roles" (Bowles and Gintis 1977: 108).

Schools in low-income and working-class neighborhoods tend to stress obedience, following directions, and punctuality so that students can fill jobs (as in restaurants, retail stores, and hospitals) that require these characteristics. Instead of preparing students for college or careers, for example, some low-income urban high schools have curricula such as "medical careers and health professions" that focus on training nursing aides, health assistants, and other low-paid personnel for hospitals and nursing homes (Kozol 2005).

Schools in middle-class neighborhoods tend to emphasize proper behavior and appearance, cooperation,

© Rachel Epstein/Photo Edit

following rules, and decision making because many of these students will be working in middle-level bureaucracies that require such attributes. Routine is common because it's good training for many bureaucratic jobs.

In contrast, elite private schools encourage leadership, creativity, independence, and people skills—all prized characteristics in elite circles (see Chapter 8). Teachers may tolerate rule breaking in these schools because their students will probably be making rather than following rules in the future. In effect, then, the hidden curriculum reproduces the existing class structure and provides workers for jobs and occupations in the stratification hierarchy.

According to conflict theorists, corporate values dominate much of higher education. College students are now "consumers," an education is a "product," canceling classes with low enrollments is "cost effective," colleges are "knowledge enterprises," nearly half of the faculty comprises a "contingent labor force" that works part time and for low salaries, and full-time faculty members are "shareholders" who are pressured to pursue "marketable" research, sponsored by corporations and the government, such as developing new drugs and defense technology.

Credentialism. Have you noticed that doctors', lawyers', and dentists' offices are usually wallpapered with framed degrees, certificates, and service awards? Faculty members, similarly, have letterheads and name plates that include their titles to signal their educational achievement. Whether the tangible symbols of people's achievements are framed, hung on office doors, or embellished on business cards, all of them reflect credentialism, an emphasis on certificates or degrees to show that people

have certain skills, educational attainment levels, or job qualifications. Besides conferring social status, credentials connote knowledge or expertise in an area.

Functionalists maintain that credentialism rewards people for their accomplishments, sorts out those who are the most qualified for jobs, and stimulates upward social mobility. Conflict theorists, however, contend that people don't need credentials for many jobs because most can gain skills on the job, during a few weeks of training, or will succeed because of ability or other factors. For example, many successful entrepreneurs such as Ray Kroc, founder of the McDonald's restaurant chain, never attended college. Bill Gates of Microsoft, Steve Jobs of Apple Computers, and Michael Dell of Dell, Inc., were college dropouts. In addition, the brightest students aren't necessarily the only ones who go to college: 78 percent of students from low-income families who rank at the top of their high-school class attend college, but so do 77 percent of students from high-income families who rank at the bottom of their class (Symonds 2003).

Because of a large supply of high-school graduates, employers can demand higher levels of education even though some jobs (such as accounting and law enforcement) don't require a college degree for competent performance, a process called *credential inflation*. As more people acquire a college degree, its value diminishes, and students from low-income families, who are the least likely to have access to a college education, fall further behind (Collins 2002; Bollag 2007).

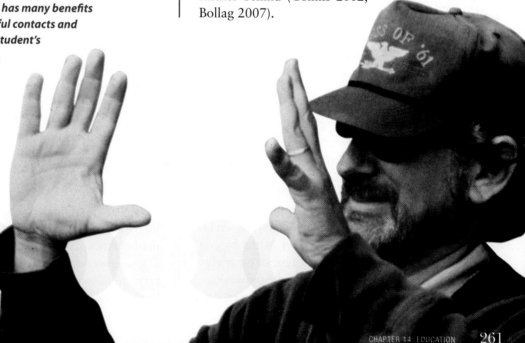

Many sociologists note that graduating from a selective college or university has many benefits that include a network of useful contacts and better job offers. However, a student's motivation, ability, creativity, and ambition may be more important factors than his or her alma mater. Steven Spielberg, the well-known movie producer and director (pictured here while producing Transformers), graduated from California State University at Long Beach after being rejected by the more prestigious University of Southern California and University of California at Los Angeles film schools.

Universal Pictures/Fotos International/Getty Images

Privilege. Many colleges say that they welcome low-income students. In fact, the proportion of financially needy undergraduates at the nation's wealthiest colleges and universities dropped between 2004 and 2007 (Fischer 2008). One reason is the schools' admission of *legacies*, the children of alumni who have "reserved seats" regardless of their accomplishments or ability. For example, President George W. Bush—who had ordinary high-school grades and average standardized test scores—was admitted as a legacy at Yale University, where his father and grandfather attended (Golden 2006; Wickenden 2006; see also Chapter 8).

Another privileged group is *developmental cases*—students with inferior academic records who are children of celebrities, wealthy executives, or influential politicians who make million-dollar donations to the schools they want their children to attend. It is expected that the students will, in turn, also contribute after graduation. Because winning sports teams increase alumni donations, developmental cases also include outstanding athletes, even though athletes' dropout rates are higher than those of other students (Massey 2007).

The Taliban, a conservative religious group in Afghanistan, outlawed all education for girls in 1996, maintaining that educating girls violates Islam. The group was ousted from national power, but its influence is still strong in southern Afghanistan. Gunmen have killed teachers and some schoolgirls, and other men have torched schools to stop girls from learning (Moreau and Yousafzai 2006). Under the Taliban, Afghanistan had only 900,000 students, all boys. Today, 6 million students, boys and girls, attend school, but there's no space for 5.3 million children. About half of Afghanistan's 12,000 schools have no permanent structure, with classes held in tents or in the open air (McCanna 2009).

Critical Evaluation

Conflict theory helps us understand the linkages between education and social inequality. Social class, standardized tests, the hidden curriculum, and credentialism enhance privilege, whose effects continue well after college. Despite their contributions, conflict theorists have been criticized for ignoring the gains that many low-income and minority students have made, including graduating from college and graduate school (Marks 2007).

There is also a question of whether those in the social elite control education and job entry as much as conflict theorists claim they do. For example, several national surveys show that most CEOs of the biggest U.S. corporations didn't attend Ivy League or other elite private colleges. Instead, they went to state universities, big or small, to less well-known private colleges, and to community colleges (Jones 2005; Hymowitz 2006; Sowell 2008).

FEMINIST THEORIES: HOW DOES GENDER AFFECT EDUCATION?

In 1967, the president of Columbia University said, "It would be preposterously naive to suggest that a B.A. can be made as attractive to girls as a marriage license" (Starr 1991: 198). About 35 years later, the president of Harvard University "explained" that fewer women than men have careers in math and science because of "innate ability differences between the sexes" (Margolis and Fisher 2002). Despite significant progress, many women still experience considerable inequality in education.

Gender Gaps from Elementary School to High School

Since 1971, national assessment tests have shown that there is little difference in the average reading and mathematics scores for boys and girls ages 9 to 17. In 2008, however, the reading scores of boys at elementary, middle-school, and high-school levels were lower than those of girls by more than 10 points. In this highly publicized study, the researchers concluded that "the most pressing issue related to gender gaps is the lagging performance of boys in reading" (Chudowsky and Chudowsky 2010: 13).

Is such alarm warranted? The biggest gaps are by ethnicity and social class: students score lower if they are black or Latino, but especially if they come from low-income families that have few resources and lower parental involvement in the children's schooling. Also, in the highest and lowest scoring states, both girls and boys tend to do well or to have low scores. This suggests a connection between achievement scores and a state's population characteristics, such as the proportion of low-income students. Overall, however, girls and boys from similar socioeconomic backgrounds have similar scores (Perie et al. 2005; Lee et al. 2007; Hyde et al. 2008).

Also, since 1972, boys have consistently scored slightly higher than girls on the math and verbal portions of the SAT. In 2008, for example, the overall average for the verbal/critical reading score was 503 for male and 498 for female students. The gender gap was slightly larger in mathematics—534 for male and 499 for female students. As with the elementary- and high-school assessment tests, however, student performance across all racial-ethnic groups was strongly linked to a family's social class, especially income (Corbett et al. 2008; Snyder and Dillow 2010).

Because male students have higher scores than female students in SAT reading and mathematics, it's not clear why some policy analysts are worried about boys' reading scores (but not women's lower math scores) in high school. Feminist scholars are also concerned about some of the gender gaps in higher education.

Gender Gaps in Higher Education

Until the 1840s, U.S. colleges and universities banned women. How do they fare now? If we believe the media, college campuses are becoming all-female enclaves (see Gewertz 2009; Goldrick-Rab 2009; Miners 2009; Whitmire 2010). Across all racial-ethnic groups, women have slightly higher college graduation rates than do men (see *Figure 14.3* on p. 259). As a result, many colleges have been giving men preferential treatment in admissions.

Slightly more women than men enroll in 2- and 4-year U.S. colleges, but more men are earning college degrees today than at any time in history (Snyder and Dillow 2010). The largest gap is not between women and men but between men in low-, middle-, and high-income families. Overall, women have higher educational attainment rates because—in both high school and college—they earn better grades, spend more time studying, hold more leadership posts, and are more involved than men in student clubs and community volunteer work. These gender differences have existed since the early 1980s, probably because many young women realized that even if they married, they would be likely to work outside the home and wanted higher income jobs (Buchmann and DiPrete 2006; Goldin et al. 2006; King 2006).

Another issue is the under-representation of women in the fields of science, technology, engineering, and mathematics (STEM). In elementary, middle, and high school, girls and boys take math and science courses in roughly equal numbers, and about the same numbers leave high school planning to pursue STEM majors in college. By graduation, however, men outnumber women in nearly every STEM field, and in some—such as physics, engineering, and computer science—women earn only 20 percent of the bachelor's degrees. Their numbers decline further at the graduate level and yet again in the transition to the workplace (Hill et al. 2010).

Researchers have attributed this gradual attrition to a number of factors. As early as middle school, teachers and parents are more likely to associate math and science with men than with women. Less encouragement may reduce girls' self-confidence, interest in taking STEM courses and AP exams in high school, and deciding to major in a STEM field in college. In college, female students may initially be as persistent as men in a STEM major and get higher grades, but they are less satisfied than men with the core courses and more likely to doubt

STEM (science, technology, engineering, and mathematics) fields are regarded as critical to the national economy and are among the highest paying occupations. Why, then, are there so few women in these fields? Do you think that one of the reasons is a self-fulfilling prophecy (see Chapter 5)?

their abilities in a male-dominated discipline. The exit from a STEM major is also associated with other factors such as few female faculty role models and mentors, and expectations that they will not be paid or promoted equally with men (Hartman and Hartman 2009; Karukstis 2009; Lord et al. 2009; Hill et al. 2010; Hunt 2010).

Critical Evaluation

Feminist theorists extend conflict theorists' analyses by emphasizing how educational institutions produce gender-based inequity, but some critics fault feminist scholars for being too accepting of the inequality they document. For example, few women, including feminist faculty members, have challenged male privilege in schooling even though feminists have fought for educational equality since 1848 (Rhoads 2004).

Another criticism, although controversial because it seems to blame women, is that female faculty members in women's studies programs focus on topics such as sexual assault, eating disorders, and global women's issues rather than pay inequity in the United States. For example, one year after graduating from college, women earn 80 percent of what their male peers earn, but this percentage drops to 69 percent 10 years out of school, even in the same occupation (Dey and Hill 2007; Seligson 2007). It's not clear, however, whether courses don't address gender pay gaps or whether many female students aren't paying attention to the issue because "It won't happen to me."

SYMBOLIC INTERACTIONISM: HOW DO SOCIAL CONTEXTS AFFECT EDUCATION?

None of us is born a student or a teacher. Instead, these roles, like others, are socially constructed (see Chapters 3–5). For symbolic interactionists, education is an active *process* in which students, teachers, peers, and parents participate, and which often involves tracking, labeling, and student engagement.

Tracking

If a society believes that its education system is based on merit (which includes knowledge and effort), it justifies sorting students by aptitude. Such sorting results

in **tracking** (also called *streaming* or *ability grouping*), assigning students to specific educational programs and classes on the basis of test scores, previous grades, or perceived ability.

Some educators believe that tracking is beneficial because students learn better in groups with others like themselves, and it allows teachers to meet the individual needs of students more effectively. Many symbolic interactionists maintain, however, that tracking creates and reinforces inequality. For example,

- High-track students take classes that involve critical thinking, problem solving, and creativity that high-status occupations require. Low-track students take classes that are limited to simple skills, such as punctuality and conformity, that usually characterize lower status jobs.

- High-track students have more homework, better quality instruction, and more enthusiastic teachers. Moreover, high-track students see themselves as "bright," whereas low-track students see themselves as "dumb" or "slow."

- The effects of tracking are usually cumulative and lasting. Teachers tend to have low expectations for low-track students, who therefore fall further behind every year in reading, mathematics, and interaction skills (Oakes 1985; Riordan 1997; Hanushek and Woessman 2005).

Tracking typically starts in kindergarten when teachers evaluate youngsters' ability to follow directions, to work independently and in a group, and to communicate effectively—skills they'll need in the first grade. Middle school and high school become even more stratified as high-track students are sorted into gifted, honors, or AP programs and courses. In college, students continue to be tracked and sorted as some are accepted into honors' programs and accelerated undergraduate courses.

In 2002, the University of Connecticut received funding to identify and nurture math talent among elementary students, especially those from low-income and minority backgrounds, even with poor language skills. When Project M[3] (Mentoring Mathematical Minds) chose girls who spoke only Spanish at home, one teacher, who had planned to hold a girl back because she wasn't doing well in school, was surprised. After joining Project M[3], the third grader "ended up being one of the top students when she left the fifth grade" (Teicher 2007: 16–17).

Labeling

Tracking often leads to labeling, a serious problem because "there is a widespread culture of disbelief in the learning capacities of many of our children, especially

children of color and the economically disadvantaged" (Howard 2003: 83). Labeling, in turn, can result in a *self-fulfilling prophecy,* whereby students live up or down to teachers' expectations and evaluations that are affected by background, gender, skin color, hygiene, accent, and test scores (see Chapter 5).

Teachers at all educational levels tend to praise and encourage students they consider bright and attentive, but are often disinterested in, critical of, or even impatient with students perceived as less bright, unmotivated, or troublemakers. Students with difficulties often meet their teacher's low expectations by not performing well. Teachers may try to avoid labeling, but they often convey their low expectations and negative attitudes through body language—for example, raising their eyebrows, frowning, or rolling their eyes—and by ignoring the student's accomplishments, however modest. Even very young children pick up on such cues (see Chapters 4 and 5).

Labeling and stereotypes can also affect a student's progress in college. For example, most Americans believe the myth that Asian American students are dominating higher education institutions (especially in science, technology, engineering, and math departments), are enrolled in only the most elite colleges, and are all stellar students (see Chapter 10).

In fact, Asian Americans and Pacific Islanders are evenly distributed in 2-year and 4-year institutions; the majority attend public colleges and universities; they have a wide range of abilities and standardized test scores; and almost 70 percent earn bachelor's degrees in business, the social sciences, humanities, and education. Because of labeling and stereotypes, however, many Asian American college students are less likely to receive mentoring from instructors and are often held to a higher standard than white students (College Board 2008a).

Student Engagement

Many U.S. schools have been assessing performance not only through test results but also by *student engagement,* that is, how involved students are in their own learning. A team of researchers who spent thousands of hours in more than 2,500 first-, third-, and fifth-grade classrooms concluded that the typical U.S. child has only a 1 in 14 chance of being in a school that encourages her or his engagement. Largely because of the federal law called No Child Left Behind (NCLB, which we'll examine shortly),

teachers in public elementary schools spend most of the school day on basic reading and math drills, and little time on problem solving, reasoning, science, and social studies. As a result, the study found, classrooms are often "dull and bleak places" where kids don't get a lot of teacher feedback or face-to-face interaction with their peers (Pianta et al. 2007).

Especially before high school, parental involvement has a strong and positive effect on student engagement. Across public and private schools—and regardless of social class or race and ethnicity—parents can enhance their children's academic performance by frequently discussing what the children study in school, encouraging them to participate in school activities and events, selecting courses, attending school meetings, and volunteering at the school (Houtenville and Conway 2008).

Are most U.S. high-school students engaged in their education? Not as much as they could be. For example, 26 percent admit that they usually don't do their homework, 18 percent come to school without their books or supplies, and 10 percent drop out. The students who are the most likely to be disengaged are from poor or low-income families, African American or Latino, not living with both biological parents, attend financially strapped urban public high schools that are typically overcrowded and understaffed, and have fewer resources such as computers and even textbooks (Finn 2006; Planty et al. 2007).

At the college level, the more engaged students are, the better their grades and their likelihood of graduating. The positive effects of engagement are just as great for lower ability students and for those who attended disadvantaged high schools. But how engaged are most college students? The typical college student spends more time partying and socializing than studying. Some 65 percent of college students say that they study for 10 or fewer hours a week, well below the 24 to 30 hours faculty members say students should be spending on class preparation if they're taking three courses. Also, 32 percent of college students admit playing video games during classes. According to one college instructor, "Education is the only business in which the clients want the least for their money" (Perlmutter 2001: B1; Jones 2003; National Survey of Student Engagement 2006; Saenz and Barrera 2007).

Critical Evaluation

Symbolic interactionists shed considerable light on the process of education and its everyday social context. Their theories show how, through everyday practices (such as tracking and labeling), educational institutions influence people's attitudes, values, and behavior and shape self-identity.

One weakness of this approach is that it deemphasizes individual power in changing the course of events, including overcoming the effects of labeling. For example, in a telephone survey, low-income Latino parents in Chicago, New York, and Los Angeles who were recent immigrants said that they contacted school personnel on a regular basis, despite the language barrier. Other parents said that they went to college open houses and "pushed their way past the crowd" to speak to college representatives, with their children translating the questions and answers (Tornatzky et al. 2002).

Another limitation is that symbolic interactionists, because of their micro-level analysis, neglect the macro-level constraints that are built into society. As conflict and feminist theories show, education in the United States is affected by gatekeeping and control of resources by privileged and powerful groups, which often shape what teachers teach, what students learn, and who will and won't have access to higher education and to particular colleges (Sacks 2007). Such constraints have created numerous problems in U.S. education.

3 Some Problems with U.S. Education

Consider the following:

- 75 percent of Americans 17 to 24 years old who apply aren't eligible to serve in the military; 25 percent don't have a high-school diploma, and many who received a general equivalency degree (GED) don't pass the reading and math tests. Others are disqualified because of obesity, health problems, and criminal records (Christeson et al. 2009).

- 50 percent of Americans can't name the three branches of government, but 80 percent know that Michael Jackson sang "Beat It" (The American Revolution Center 2010; Intercollegiate Studies Institute 2010).

- 45 percent of employers say that public high-school graduates don't have the basic skills to advance beyond entry-level jobs (*Crisis at the Core. . .* 2004).

- 40 percent of students at 4-year colleges and 63 percent at 2-year colleges require remedial coursework ("Rising to the Challenge. . ." 2005).

DO THE MATH

	Students in Asia	American Students
Hours / day	8	5.5
School days / year	220	180

So students in Asia spend about 610 more hours in school per year than American students, which over 12 years means 7.4 more years of school by high-school graduation! (Ornstein 2003: 279)

These statistics and others are bleak, even though the United States produces more college graduates every year than any other nation. Many high-school and college students aren't as engaged in learning as they might be, but the U.S. educational system suffers from other problems, including inadequate schooling, high dropout rates (in both high schools and colleges), and widespread grade inflation and cheating.

QUALITY AND QUANTITY OF SCHOOLING

Fifteen-year-olds in 16 countries outperform their U.S. counterparts in science, and those in 23 countries have much higher scores in math, surpassing even the students in the highest achieving states in the Northeast (Snyder and Dillow 2010). Of the 29 nations, 7 are developing countries such as Turkey and the Slovak Republic.

Furthermore, American 17-year-olds aren't performing any better in reading and math than their counterparts did in the early 1970s. Latino and African American students have improved at greater rates than white students since the 1970s, but have made little progress in narrowing achievement gaps in reading and math. In 2008, for instance, the average mathematics score for white 17-year-olds was 314 (on a 500-point scale)—26 points ahead of black students and 21 points ahead of Latinos (Rampey et al. 2009).

Why are many U.S. students doing so poorly, especially when larger percentages are taking AP courses, as you saw earlier, and have considerably more reading resources than in previous decades? Some believe that the typical curriculum in the United States covers "too many topics too superficially," unlike the curricula in many other countries (Grant and Murray 1999: 25). One reason for the superficiality of coverage may be short school hours. For example, Asian students have longer and more school days than their American counterparts (see the "Do the Math" box).

Not all Americans embrace the idea of longer school days, even if the extra hours offer social studies, art, music, or creative projects like building model houses (to teach fractions). Instead, many parents believe that kids need some time to relax and play, and taxpayers and administrators worry about the additional costs of materials and teachers' salaries. Many Americans complain that the United States is falling behind other nations in academic achievement, but 44 percent say that colleges and universities should not require students to take more math and science courses. Some also contend that locking students in mediocre schools for additional hours would cut into more fruitful after-school learning activities such as participating in sports and community volunteer work (The Winston Group 2006; Gabrieli 2009; Hess 2009).

A number of policy analysts maintain that many U.S. students are performing poorly, in mathematics and other subjects, mainly because of inadequate school funding. As you saw in Chapter 7, on average, states spend almost three times as much on each prisoner as they do on each public school student. However, some educators contend that high funding doesn't guarantee high-quality education, but that good results depend on teachers' effectiveness.

TEACHERS' EFFECTIVENESS

According to most college faculty, and in contrast with many high school teachers' beliefs, many students aren't prepared for college (see *Figure 14.4*). For example, 35 percent of college instructors but only 10 percent of

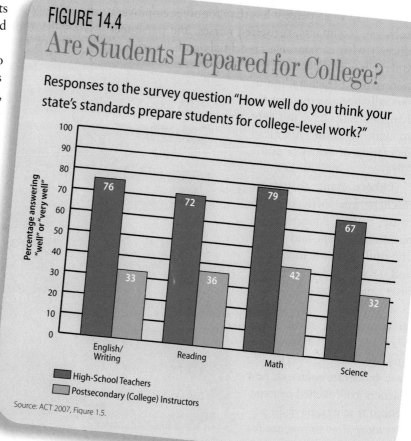

FIGURE 14.4

Are Students Prepared for College?

Responses to the survey question "How well do you think your state's standards prepare students for college-level work?"

Percentage answering "well" or "very well"

	English/Writing	Reading	Math	Science
High-School Teachers	76	72	79	67
Postsecondary (College) Instructors	33	36	42	32

Source: ACT 2007, Figure 1.5.

high-school teachers emphasize knowing the elements of basic grammar and usage, such as sentence structure and punctuation (ACT 2007).

Are many students unprepared for college because the United States does a poor job of educating teachers? Compared with teachers in Europe and elsewhere, many American teachers are out of field; that is, they have neither certification nor a major in the subject they teach. For example, only 8 percent of fourth-grade math teachers in the United States majored or minored in math, compared with 48 percent in Singapore. Furthermore, classes in disadvantaged American schools are 77 percent more likely to be assigned to an out-of-field teacher than are classes in affluent schools (Holt et al. 2006; Levine 2006).

Teachers' unions insist that out-of-field teachers do a good job. However, some research shows that even first- and second-grade female teachers who experience math anxiety have a negative effect on girls' (but not boys') math scores by the end of the school year. The researchers speculate that boys perform better than girls because of many teachers' commonly held stereotype that "boys are good in math, and girls are good at reading," and that girls learn such stereotypes (Beilock et al. 2010).

According to some policy analysts, raising salaries would draw more talented people to teaching. The average starting salary in 2008 was about $42,000 a year and from 15 to 25 percent less than for other employees (such as accountants, registered nurses, and personnel officers) with comparable credentials and experience. And the longer they teach, the more ground teachers lose financially because the cost-of-living increases have not kept up with inflation (American Federation of Teachers 2007; Allegretto et al. 2008).

Others argue that some teachers are ineffective because college education departments accept and graduate students with low GPAs and the students receive little mentoring from the best teachers (Engel 2009). In contrast, in most European and many Asian countries (where teachers also have moderate salaries), new teachers are coached by experienced teachers, have 20 percent more time to prepare for

classes, and receive generous stipends each year to attend professional development workshops and classes (Darling-Hammond et al. 2009).

In the United States, 72 percent of principals say that tenure policies and teachers' unions are obstacles in firing bad teachers (U.S. Chamber of Commerce et al. 2009). Such claims might be warranted, but 40 percent of American teachers, especially those working in low-income neighborhoods, are disheartened because principals don't support them, the schools are decrepit, they can't control misbehaving students, and they have little input on the curriculum (Yarrow 2009).

Control over Curricula

Public school teachers in the United States have less control over their subject matter than ever before. In 2002, President George W. Bush signed, but didn't fund, the No Child Left Behind Act (NCLB) that required all children in the 90,000 public schools to be proficient in reading and math by 2014. The major components of this act included annual student assessments linked to state standards, identification of schools that don't make adequate yearly progress and can be closed, and setting standards for teachers' qualifications.

Some have praised NCLB for making schools more accountable, focusing attention on low-achieving students who had been overlooked (especially poor, minority, and disabled children in urban schools), and

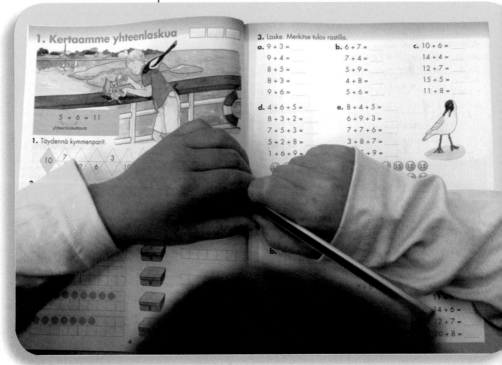

giving principals greater leverage to dismiss teachers whose students have consistently low test scores. Critics, however, have denounced NCLB on numerous grounds, especially that most teachers teach to the test (Spellings 2010; Weingarten 2010). That is, they cover only what they think will be on the test, rather than trying to ignite creativity and keep youngsters interested in school. For example, and using my own example, the tests require memorization ("3 × 4 = 12") rather than the application of information ("If a car has four wheels, how many wheels do three cars have?"). Even worse, according to some critics, students who pass easy tests have an inflated sense of their knowledge and may study less (The Commission on No Child Left Behind 2007; Toch 2007).

A national study found mixed results of the impact of NCLB: Math performances of fourth- and eighth-grade students have increased since NCLB, but reading achievement hasn't changed. It's not clear why there were greater increases in math and not reading (Dee and Jacob 2009). The Obama administration is currently evaluating NCLB, but the major changes might focus on training and hiring highly qualified teachers rather than on teachers' control over the curricula (Nelson 2010).

Some groups have more control over curricula than others. Recently, for example, the 15-member Texas State Board of Education approved revising the high-school social studies curriculum and textbooks,

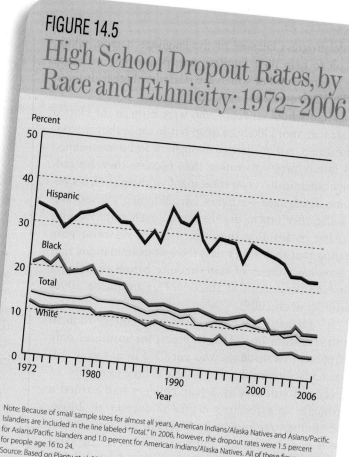

FIGURE 14.5

High School Dropout Rates, by Race and Ethnicity: 1972–2006

Note: Because of small sample sizes for almost all years, American Indians/Alaska Natives and Asians/Pacific Islanders are included in the line labeled "Total." In 2006, however, the dropout rates were 1.5 percent for Asians/Pacific Islanders and 1.0 percent for American Indians/Alaska Natives. All of these figures are for people age 16 to 24.

Source: Based on Planty et al. 2008, Tables 23-1 and 23-2.

which will present Republican political philosophies in a positive light, question the separation of church and state, claim that the U.S. government was infiltrated by Communists during the Cold War, and minimize the role of women and ethnic minorities in American history. More than 1,000 historians, most of them college professors, sent a letter to the board protesting the changes as historically inaccurate and biased. However, according to a leader on the board, a dentist, "Academia is skewed too far to the left" (Birnbaum 2010; McKinley 2010: A1).

Dropping Out

Almost 10 percent of Americans age 16 to 24 are high-school dropouts, down from 15 percent in 1972. Men are more likely to drop out than women. The dropout rate is highest among Latinos, but the gap between that group and others has decreased only slightly, especially since the early 1990s (see *Figure 14.5*).

Foreign-born youths, many of whom were already behind in schooling before arriving in the United States, make up 40 percent of the nation's teenage high-school dropouts. They may attend school briefly but make

In tests administered to students in 40 industrialized nations, Finnish 15-year-olds routinely score at or near the top in reading, science, and math, whereas their U.S. peers rank 18th, 22nd, and 28th, respectively, in those subjects. Finland attributes its success to several factors: Classes average 20 to 25 students (even in high school); local schools have enormous flexibility in choosing textbooks, designing curricula, and allocating funds; and teachers are well-trained. Teachers for all grades must obtain at least a master's degree, education programs at universities are highly competitive, and teachers enjoy high prestige in Finnish society—even those for elementary schoolchildren. "The status of teachers is comparable to doctors and lawyers" (Moore 2007: 55).

little progress because of the language barrier, taking a job to help their families, teen pregnancy, and gang membership, all of which are related to higher dropout rates (Orrenius 2004; Fry 2005).

High-school students who were born in the United States are more likely to drop out because they are unmotivated, not challenged enough, or feel overwhelmed by family problems rather than because they are failing academically. Over time, many of these students become disengaged—arriving late, skipping classes, and leaving after lunch. In other cases, even students with passing grades drop out in their junior or senior year, fearing that they won't pass the exit examinations that a growing number of states require before receiving a diploma (Bridgeland et al. 2006; Dee and Jacob 2006; Grodsky et al. 2008).

It's far easier to be accepted by a college than to graduate from one. After 6 years, for instance, only 58 percent of students who enrolled in a 4-year college had completed a bachelor's degree and only 25 percent of students at 2-year colleges had earned a certificate or associate's degree (Planty et al. 2009). The number one reason students give for leaving college is having to work and go to school at the same time, and not because they're bored or don't want to study. Among students in 4-year schools, 45 percent work more than 20 hours a week. Among those attending community colleges, 60 percent work more than 20 hours a week and 26 percent work more than

35 hours a week. In addition, 23 percent of college students have dependent children, making it difficult to juggle academic and domestic responsibilities (Johnson et al. 2009). Despite such constraints, the high dropout rates of U.S. students are somewhat surprising because there is considerable grade inflation at both high schools and colleges.

Grade Inflation

In 1973, only 20 percent of high-school students earned an A average, compared with 47 percent in 2003. However, standardized tests show that, between 1992 and 2007, the percentage of twelfth-graders who performed at or above a basic level in reading decreased from 80 to 73 percent, whereas the percentage performing at or above a proficient level declined from 40 to 35 percent (Ewers 2004; Lee et al. 2007; Planty et al. 2008). Such data suggest that grades are rising, but learning is lagging.

A professor who tracks GPAs says that grade inflation "has gone wild: When students walk into a classroom knowing that they can go through the motions and get a B+ or better, that's what they tend to do, give minimal effort. Our college classrooms are filled with students who do not prepare for class" (Rojstaczer 2009: 9).

According to one critic, "The demanding professor is close to being extinct" because "professors are under pressure to accommodate students" (Murray 2008: 32). Grade inflation, especially in college, is due to a number of factors, both institutional and individual. Many faculty members give high grades because it decreases student complaints, involves less time and thought in grading exams and papers, and reduces the chances of students' challenging a grade. Some faculty also believe that they can get favorable course evaluations from students by handing out high grades, and others accept students' view of high grades as a reward for simply showing up in class. Moreover, administrators want to keep enrollment up. If students are unhappy with their grades, admission application rates may decrease. Thus, inflating grades satisfies administrators and makes them look good, especially where state legislators base funding on graduation rates (Carroll 2002; Kamber and Biggs 2002; Halfond 2004; Bartlett and Wasley 2008).

Among other problems, grade inflation gives students an exaggerated and unrealistic sense of their ability and accomplishments. Sometimes, for example, students don't understand why their job searches are unsuccessful because "I'm an A student." In fact, many students' incorrect usage of grammar on job applica-

"I got an A for not smoking."

> Would *you* want a military officer, a financial planner, or a dentist who cheated her or his way **through college or graduate school?**

tion forms and résumés, as well as during interviews, turns off prospective employers (Halfond 2004).

Cheating

Despite grade inflation, cheating is common in high school, college, and graduate school. Some 60 percent of high-school students admit to cheating on tests, and 33 percent have plagiarized from the Internet. Between 50 and 75 percent of college students say that they have cheated at least once. Dozens of studies have uncovered cheating at the Air Force Academy and in numerous graduate programs, including those in business administration and dentistry (McCabe et al. 2006; Burrus et al. 2007; Frosch 2007; Wasley 2007; Josephson Institute 2008).

College students who cheat are three times more likely to fail a course than those who don't cheat (Palazzo et al. 2010). There's also evidence that dishonesty isn't a one-time occurrence. In adulthood, those who cheated in high school are two to three times more

Technology has made cheating easier. Students often use cell phones and iPhones to store data, to search for answers on the Internet, and to send text messages to friends for answers (Ford 2009).

likely than non-cheaters to lie to their spouses and intimate partners, bosses, and employees; to inflate an insurance claim; to shoplift; and to lie on their taxes (Josephson Institute 2008).

Grade inflation, cheating, dropping out, and low-quality instruction are serious problems in U.S. education. Because many traditional public schools are failing to educate students adequately, parents and legislators have turned to a variety of alternatives.

vouchers publicly funded payments that parents can apply toward tuition or fees at a public or private school of their choice.

4 New Directions in U.S. Education

Several innovations, some more controversial than others, are transforming traditional education in the United States; they include vouchers, charter schools, and magnet schools. Homeschooling has also expanded.

SCHOOL VOUCHERS

Vouchers are publicly funded payments (up to $7,500 per child a year) that parents can apply toward tuition or fees at a public or private school of their choice. Supporters argue that vouchers provide parents with more options, and thereby equalize the playing field, especially in low-income districts with failing schools. They also claim that the competition will improve public schools.

Opponents maintain that directing public dollars to private schools diverts much-needed resources from public education, and that taxpayers are taxed twice—once to support public schools and a second time to support vouchers for private schools. Also, some object to providing public funds to schools run by religious organizations because this violates the constitutional principle of separation of church and state.

Are vouchers effective? The data are mixed, but there is no significant overall difference in achievement between the children participating in voucher programs and those who remain in public schools, especially if the students have positive attitudes toward education, good teachers, and supportive parents (Heald et al. 2003; Glod and Turque 2008; Miners 2010).

CHARTER SCHOOLS

Charter schools are self-governing public schools that have signed an agreement with their state government to improve students' education. Some see charter schools, in contrast with regular public schools, as providing innovative teaching, offering smaller classrooms, reducing bureaucratic red tape, and having more dedicated teachers. Others maintain that charter schools sometimes avoid accountability by not reporting test scores, drain resources from traditional public schools, hire uncertified teachers, and are more racially segregated than other public schools (Teske et al. 2001; Renzulli and Roscigno 2007).

Do charter schools work? As with school vouchers, the data are mixed. Fourth- and eighth-graders in charter schools trail students in regular public schools in both reading and math, especially in central cities. Students perform about the same, however, if the school has high-quality teachers and curricula (Braun et al. 2006; Dobbie and Fryer 2009; Zimmer et al. 2009; Rettig 2010).

MAGNET SCHOOLS

A **magnet school** is a public school that offers students a distinctive program and specialized curriculum. Magnet schools emphasize particular areas of study, such as business, science, the arts, or technology. Because magnet schools are typically small, there are close student-teacher relationships and a sense of community (Metz 2003). There are magnet schools for middle schoolers, but most are targeted at high-school students.

A major advantage of magnet schools is that, because they focus on specific subject matter areas, students from diverse socioeconomic and ethnic backgrounds have similar opportunities in developing their shared interests. For example, actress Jada Pinkett Smith graduated from the Baltimore School for the Arts, a magnet school in music, theatre, dance, and visual arts. The major disadvantage is that few students can be accepted because enrollments are limited (Rickles et al. 2002).

HOME SCHOOLING

Homeschooling refers to teaching children in the home as an alternative to enrolling them in a public or private elementary, middle, or high school. The number of children who were homeschooled grew from 850,000 in 1999 to 1.5 million in 2007 (about 3 percent of all children age 5–17). Increasingly, parents who homeschool children are white, wealthy, and well-educated. About 81 percent of homeschooled children live in a two-parent home where one parent (usually the mother) is not employed. Some of the major reasons why parents opt for homeschooling are their concerns about negative peer pressure, children's safety, and drugs; their desire to provide religious and moral instruction; and their feeling that schools don't challenge their children academically (Princiotta and Bielick 2006; Planty et al. 2009; Toppo 2009).

How effective is homeschooling? No one knows for sure, because, unlike public school students, children who are homeschooled aren't required by law to undergo either state or national tests. Recently, a California appellate court ruled that only parents with state-recognized credentials can educate their children at home, but reversed this decision after a "nationwide uproar" from homeschoolers, religious activists, and others (Mehta 2008).

As this chapter shows, the United States has high college graduation rates, but public schools, in particular, struggle with serious problems in the quality of schooling. Schools will improve only to the extent that students, teachers, administrators, parents, local communities, and government officials make educational excellence a top priority, and regardless of children's social class, race-ethnicity, and gender.

Religion is an important institution in the United States and around the world.

15 Religion

After the 2010 earthquake in Haiti that killed 300,000 people, a number of inhabitants—whether they believed in voodoo or Christianity—attributed the catastrophe not to geological reasons, such as fault lines, but to God's punishment for people's sins (Mozingo 2010). This chapter examines such otherworldly views, religious behavior, and the relationship between religion and society. Each student reading this chapter probably has a different definition of religion, but what do sociologists mean by this concept?

what do you think?

Religion is what keeps people moral.

1 2 3 4 5 6 7
strongly agree   strongly disagree

1 What Is Religion?

for sociologists, **religion** is a social institution that involves shared beliefs, values, and practices based on the supernatural that unites believers into a community. The notion of community is important because different groups have different beliefs, values, and practices. For example, being Catholic involves confessing (telling one's sins to a priest), a practice that is not followed by Protestants, Jews, Muslims, and other religious groups.

religion a social institution that involves shared beliefs, values, and practices based on the supernatural and unites believers into a community.

sacred anything that people see as mysterious, awe-inspiring, extraordinary and powerful, holy, and not part of the natural world.

profane anything that is not related to religion.

secular the term sociologists use (instead of *profane*) to describe worldly rather than spiritual things.

religiosity the ways people demonstrate their religious beliefs.

THE SACRED AND THE SECULAR

Every society distinguishes between the sacred and the profane (Durkheim 1961). **Sacred** refers to anything that people see as mysterious, awe-inspiring, extraordinary and powerful, holy, and not part of the natural world. **Profane** refers to anything that is not related to religion. Contemporary sociologists typically use **secular** (rather than *profane*) to describe worldly rather than spiritual things. They also differentiate religion from religiosity and spirituality.

RELIGION, RELIGIOSITY, AND SPIRITUALITY

Religion refers to a community of people who have a shared faith, but the frequency and intensity of religious expression can vary. When sociologists examine **religiosity,** the

cult a religious group that is devoted to beliefs and practices that are outside of those accepted in mainstream society.

new religious movement (NRM) term used instead of *cult* by most sociologists.

charismatic leader a religious leader whom followers see as having exceptional or superhuman powers and qualities.

ways people demonstrate their religious beliefs, they often find that religion and religiosity differ. For example, 72 percent of Americans say that they are "deeply religious," but only 44 percent attend worship services once a week. And although 79 percent of college students say that they believe in God, only 40 percent report that religion influences their everyday lives. Especially at schools that are not affiliated with any religion, a majority of students who describe themselves as religious also report engaging in casual sex, attending campus parties with pornographic themes, and cheating on exams (Astin and Astin 2005; Lyons 2005; Freitas 2008).

Spirituality is a personal quest to feel connected to a reality greater than oneself. About 25 percent of Americans who never go to church consider themselves spiritual: They feel united with the people around them, have made personal sacrifices "to make the world a better place" (such as working with others to decrease poverty), and often believe in miracles (Adler 2005; Pew Forum on Religion & Public Life 2008).

People who see themselves as spiritual may not be religious, however. For example, 77 percent of students at one college described themselves as "spiritual," but only 16 percent participated in religious activities on campus (Denton-Borhaug 2004; see also Stanczak 2006). Thus, belonging to a specific religious group, religiosity, and spirituality can involve different behaviors.

AP Photo/The Advocate-Messenger, Clay Jackson

AP Photo/Harry Cabluck

In 2005, the U.S. Supreme Court ruled, 5 to 4, that a 6-foot-high monument containing the Ten Commandments outside the Texas state capitol (bottom) was constitutional and could stay, even though it's on government property. The same day, the Supreme Court barred, in a 5 to 4 vote, displaying the Ten Commandments amid other documents in Kentucky courthouses (top) because doing so promoted religion. Do such rulings seem contradictory? And how do such decisions reflect the overlap between the sacred and the secular?

2 Types of Religious Organization

r eligion is important in all known societies, but there's considerable diversity in its expression. People manifest their religious beliefs most commonly through organized groups, including cults, sects, denominations, and churches.

CULTS (NEW RELIGIOUS MOVEMENTS)

A **cult** is a religious group that is devoted to beliefs and practices that are outside of those accepted in mainstream society. Some sociologists prefer to use **new religious movement (NRM)** rather than *cult* because the latter term has been used by the media in pejorative ways to describe any unfamiliar, new, or seemingly bizarre religious movement (Roberts 2004).

NRMs usually organize around a **charismatic leader** (like Jesus) whom followers see as having exceptional or superhuman powers and qualities. Some NRMs have become established religions. The early Christians were a renegade group that broke away from Judaism. Islam, the second-largest religion in the world today, began as a cult organized around Muhammad, and The Church of Jesus Christ of Latter-day Saints (the Mormon Church) began as a cult around Joseph Smith. Most contemporary cults are fragmentary, loosely organized, and temporary, but others have developed into groups that are more lasting, organized, and highly bureaucratic (such as the Unification Church, or Moonies, and the International Society for Krishna Consciousness, or Hare Krishnas).

SECTS

A **sect** is a religious group that has broken away from an established religion. Those who begin sects are usually dissatisfied members who believe that the parent religion has become too secular and has abandoned key original doctrines. Like cults, some sects are small and disappear after a time, whereas others become established and persist. Examples of sects that have persisted include the Amish, the Jewish Hassidim, Jehovah's Witnesses, Quakers, Seventh Day Adventists, and the Fundamentalist Church of Jesus Christ of Latter Day Saints (FLDS) (Finke and Stark 1992; Bainbridge 1997). Sometimes sects develop into denominations.

DENOMINATIONS

A **denomination** is a subgroup within a religion that shares its name and traditions, and is generally on good terms with the main group. Denominations can form slowly or develop rapidly, depending on factors such as geography, immigration, and culture. Some scholars describe a denomination as somewhere between a sect and a church. Like sects, denominations have a professional ministry. Unlike sects, however, denominations view other religious groups as valid and don't make claims that only they possess the truth (Niebuhr 1929; Hamilton 2001).

Denominations typically accommodate themselves to the larger society instead of trying to dominate or change it. As a result, people may belong to the same denomination as their grandparents or even great-grandparents did. Denominations exist in all religions, including Christianity, Judaism, and Islam. In the United States, for example, the many Protestant denominations include Episcopalians, Baptists, Lutherans, Presbyterians, and Methodists.

CHURCHES

A **church** is a large established religious group that has strong ties to mainstream society. Because leadership of the group is attached to an office rather than a specific leader, new generations of believers replace previous ones, and members follow tradition or authority rather than a charismatic leader. As in a denomination, people are usually born into a church, even though they may decide to withdraw later.

Churches (e.g., Roman Catholic Church, Anglican Church in North America) are typically bureaucratically organized, have formal worship services and trained clergy, and often maintain some degree of control over political or educational institutions (see Chapters 11 and 14). Because churches are an integral part of the social order, they often become dependent on, rather than critical of, the ruling classes (Hamilton 1995).

> **sect** a religious group that has broken away from an established religion.
>
> **denomination** a subgroup within a religion that shares its name and traditions, and is generally on good terms with the main group.
>
> **church** a large established religious group that has strong ties to mainstream society.

3 Some Major World Religions

Worldwide, the largest religious group is Christians, followed by Muslims. If the world's population is represented as an imaginary village of 100 people, it has about

- 33 Christians
- 21 Muslims
- 16 nonreligious individuals (people who may believe in God but are not affiliated with a religious group) or atheists (people who don't believe in God)
- 14 Hindus
- 6 Buddhists
- 6 Chinese Universalists (followers of a complex set of beliefs and practices that combines ancestor cults, elements of Confucianism and Buddhism, Taoism, folk religion, and goddess worship)
- 4 believers in another religion (including Judaism and Sikhism) (based on "Major Religions of the World. . ." 2007)

TABLE 15.1
Characteristics of Some Major World Religions

RELIGION	DATE OF ORIGIN	FOUNDER	PREVALENCE	NUMBER OF FOLLOWERS (IN MID-2007)	CORE BELIEFS
Christianity	0 C.E.	Jesus Christ	All continents, with largest numbers in Latin America and Europe	2.2 billion	Jesus, the son of God, sacrificed his life to redeem humankind. Those who follow Christ's teachings and live a moral life will enter the Kingdom of Heaven. Sinners who don't repent will burn in hell for eternity.
Islam	600 C.E.	Muhammad	Mainly Asia (including Indonesia), but also parts of Africa, China, India, and Malaysia	1.4 billion	God is creator of the universe, omnipotent, omniscient, just, forgiving, and merciful. Those who sincerely repent and submit (the literal meaning of *islam*) to God will attain salvation, while the wicked will burn in hell.
Hinduism	Between 4000 and 1500 B.C.E.	No specific founder	Mainly India, Nepal, Malaysia, and Sri Lanka, but also Africa, Europe, and North America	887 million	Life in all its forms is an aspect of the divine. The aim of every Hindu is to use pure acts, thoughts, and devotion to escape a cycle of birth and rebirth (*samsara*) determined by the purity or impurity of past deeds (*karma*).
Buddhism	525 B.C.E.	Siddhartha Gautama	Throughout Asia, from Sri Lanka to Japan	386 million	Life is misery and decay with no ultimate reality. Meditation and good deeds will end the cycle of endless birth and rebirth, and the person will achieve *nirvana,* a state of liberation and bliss.
Judaism	2000 B.C.E.	Abraham	Mainly Israel and the United States	15 million	God is the creator and the absolute ruler of the universe. God established a particular relationship with the Hebrew people. By obeying the divine law God gave them, Jews bear special witness to God's mercy and justice.

Note: C.E. (Common Era) is the nondenominational abbreviation for A.D. (*Anno Domini,* Latin for "In the year of Our Lord)" and B.C.E. (Before Common Era) is the nondenominational abbreviation for B.C. (Before Christ).

Source: Based on a number of sources including the Center for the Study of Global Christianity 2007 and "Religions of the World ..." 2007.

Note that there is no religious group that comes close to being a global majority, the third-largest group consists of the nonreligious and nonbelievers, and non-Christians outnumber Christians 2 to 1. Five religious groups, especially, have had a worldwide impact on economic, political, and social issues. *Table 15.1* provides a brief overview of these groups.

4 Religion in the United States

lmost 87 percent of Americans believe in God, 11 percent aren't sure, and 2 percent say that "there is no such thing" (Kosmin and Keysar 2009). For sociologists, religiosity is a better measure of being religious than simply asking people whether they believe in God (or a universal spirit) and which religion they follow. Religiosity includes a number of variables, but the most common are religious belief, affiliation, and attendance at services.

RELIGIOUS BELIEF

Some 64 percent of Americans say that religion is important in their lives, down from 75 percent in 1952 (Newport 2006, 2009). Not surprisingly, religion is not very important for those who are agnostics (say that it's impossible to know whether there is a God)

The importance of religion in Americans' lives has declined.

or atheists (believe that there is no God), or for others who are skeptics. Nonetheless, about 25 percent of Americans, including some atheists and agnostics, embrace the tenets of some Eastern religions or elements of New Age spirituality such as reincarnation, meditation, astrology, and the evil eye (casting of harmful curses and spells) (Pew Forum on Religion & Public Life 2009c).

RELIGIOUS AFFILIATION

About 16 percent of Americans say that they have no religious preference or affiliation, up from 8 percent in 1990 (Pew Forum on Religion & Public Life 2008; Kosmin and Keysar 2009). About half of U.S. adults—especially those who were raised as Catholics or Protestants—have changed their religious affiliation since childhood, done so more than once, and 15 percent have opted for no religion at all. The most important reasons for becoming unaffiliated include not believing the teachings, seeing many religious people as hypocritical or judgmental, and losing respect for religious leaders who focus on power and money (Pew Forum on Religion & Public Life 2009a). In 2009, half of Americans rated clerics as dishonest and unethical, the highest negative percentage it has been in the 32 years Gallup has asked the question (J.M. Jones 2009).

Another major change has been the decline of the so-called mainline Protestant groups (especially Methodists and Lutherans) that some sociologists now describe as a "vanishing majority" (Smith and Kim 2004; Pew Forum on Religion & Public Life 2008). There has also been a surge of evangelicals (also called born-again Christians and Pentecostals) who now comprise a significant proportion of Protestants (see *Table 15.2*). Evangelicals believe that the Bible is the literal word of God, that salvation can be attained only through a personal relationship with Jesus Christ, and that every Christian has a responsibility to spread his or her beliefs (to evangelize).

RELIGIOUS PARTICIPATION

Turning to the third measure of religiosity, religious participation, about 4 in 10 Americans attend religious services at least once a week, whereas 27 percent seldom or never attend. Thus, many people are more likely to believe in a religion than to practice it by attending services regularly. Mormons (75 percent), evangelical Protestants (58 percent), and members of historically black churches (59 percent) have greater rates of weekly or almost weekly attendance at religious services than do Catholics (42 percent), Muslims (40 percent), or Jews (16 percent) (Pew Forum on Religion & Public Life 2008).

Of the 72 percent of Americans who attend religious services at least once a year (excluding holidays, weddings, and funerals), 35 percent attend worship services of more than one faith or denomination at churches, synagogues, and mosques (Pew Forum on Religion & Public Life 2009c). Many religious leaders are concerned about such faith-mixing because "it distracts worshipers from the true path and dilutes Christian doctrine." Religion scholars point out, however, that "the cafeteria-style picking of philosophies" dates back centuries and that today's technology, especially the Internet, encourage people's greater spiritual and religious openness (Guarino 2010: 20).

Megachurches—Christian congregations that have a regular weekly attendance of more than 2,000 and tend to be evangelical—represent only 0.5 percent of all U.S. churches, but their number has more than doubled (to more than 1,200) since 2000 (Thumma et al. 2005). Pictured here, the Lakewood Church in Houston, Texas, has the largest congregation in the United States, averaging more than 43,000 in attendance per week.

SOME CHARACTERISTICS OF RELIGIOUS PARTICIPANTS

Americans differ in their beliefs and affiliations, and religious participation varies by one's sex, age, race and ethnicity, and social class.

Sex

Across all age and faith groups and in 145 countries, women tend to be more religious than men in believing in God, praying, attending services, and saying that religion is very important in their lives (Pew Forum on Religion & Public Life 2008; Deaton 2009; Kosmin and Keysar 2009; Taylor et al. 2009). It's not clear why women are more religious than men. It may be that women are expected to be more pious and spiritual because, especially as nurturers, they transmit religious values to their children (see Chapter 9). A related reason may be men's greater involvement in public life (e.g., employment, politics) that demands their time and energy.

Age

Generally, Americans age 65 and older are more likely than younger ones to describe themselves as religious, to say that religion is very important in their lives, and to attend services at least weekly. These age-related differences may reflect several factors: Older Americans grew up decades ago when church attendance was higher for all Americans, they seek spiritual comfort as elderly friends and relatives die, they want to lessen a

TABLE 15.2
Religious Affiliation in the United States

CHRISTIAN	**78.4%**
Protestant	51.3%
Evangelical churches	26.3%
Mainline churches	18.1%
Historically black churches	6.9%
Catholic	23.9%
Mormon	1.7%
Jehovah's Witnesses	0.7%
Other Christian	0.9%
OTHER RELIGIONS	**4.7%**
Jewish	1.7%
Buddhist	0.7%
Muslim	0.6%
Hindu	0.4%
Other	1.5%
UNAFFILIATED	**16.1%**
Atheist	1.6%
Agnostic	2.4%
Nothing in particular	12.1%

Note: Due to rounding and the fact that almost 1% of those polled refused to answer or said "don't know," the numbers may not add to 100%.
Source: Based on Pew Forum on Religion & Public Life 2008: 8.

FIGURE 15.1
Religion and Household Income

Percentage of respondents who said that religion is very important to them

67 65 60 56 45

Less than $20,000 per year | $20,000–$29,999 | $30,000–$49,999 | $50,000–$74,999 | $75,000 or more per year

RELIGION

INCOME

Source: Newport 2006: 6.

sense of isolation or loneliness, and they are preparing for death (Taylor et al. 2009).

Studies show that today's "Millennial" young adults (those born in 1981 and after) are less religious than preceding generations because they are less likely to pray, to regularly attend worship services, or to identify themselves with a religious group. It appears, however, that religiosity increases with age. For example, only 40 percent of Millennials say religion is very important compared with 60 percent of Boomers (those born between 1946 and 1964). In the late 1970s, however, when Boomers were the same age as Millennials, only 39 percent said that religion was very important (Pond et al. 2010).

Race and Ethnicity

In the last decade or so, the group of Americans that is increasing the fastest are those who have no religious affiliation. This group now comprises more than 16 percent of the population: 73 percent of the unaffiliated are white, 11 percent are Latino, 8 percent are black, 4 percent are Asian, and 4 percent are mixed race (Pew Forum on Religion & Public Life 2008).

One reason for greater levels of religious affiliation among minorities may be that religious groups provide important resources (such as housing and finding jobs) to newly arrived immigrants, many of whom are Latino or Asian (see Chapter 10). Some Catholic and evangelical Protestant churches in the United States have been especially successful in attracting recent Latino immigrants because they are more likely to offer services in

Spanish, their services are expressive rather than formal, and the clergy are more responsive to their members' social and economic needs (Campo-Flores 2005; Wolfe 2008).

secularization a process of removing institutions such as education and government from the dominance or influence of religion.

Asian Americans may be the most diverse religious group in America: "Asian Buddhist and Hindu temples, Muslim mosques, and Catholic and Protestant churches have mushroomed in Los Angeles, New York, and other major cities over the past thirty years" (Min 2002: 5). Besides being places of worship, Chinese churches and temples provide weekend language instruction, religious study, and meditation. Similarly, Southeast Asian refugees (primarily Vietnamese, Cambodians, and Laotians) have established churches and temples that teach English, help newcomers find jobs and housing, and maintain their cultural identity and spirituality (Yang 2002; Zhou et al. 2002).

Social Class

People with lower levels of educational attainment are generally more religious than those with higher educational levels. For example, 60 percent of people with a high school degree or less say that religion is very important in their daily lives, compared with 50 percent of college graduates (Pew Forum on Religion & Public Life 2008). Also, because education and income are highly correlated, as income increases, the importance of religion generally decreases (see *Figure 15.1*).

Americans have switched from the religion or denomination in which they were raised, and others are not affiliated with a particular group, but "religion remains a powerful force in the private and public lives of most Americans" (Pew Forum on Religion & Public Life 2008: 19). Many Americans worry, however, that religion is waning in importance and that the United States is becoming a more secularized nation.

5 Secularization: Is Religion Declining?

industrialized nations have been undergoing **secularization,** a process of removing institutions such as education and government from the dominance or influence of religion. Some sociologists maintain that secularization is

fundamentalism the belief in the literal meaning of a sacred text.

increasing rapidly in the United States, but others contend that this claim is greatly exaggerated.

IS SECULARIZATION INCREASING IN THE UNITED STATES?

There is evidence of increased secularization in the United States. For example:

- The U.S. Census Bureau stopped asking questions about religion in the 1950s after opposition from some religious and civil rights groups (Rosen 2010).

- Attendance at religious services has decreased, and fewer Americans say that religion is "very important" in their lives (Kosmin and Keysar 2009).

- Only 52 percent say that they have a "great deal" of confidence in organized religion—down from 66 percent in 1973 (Newport 2007).

- 52 percent of Americans believe that religious groups should keep out of political matters (Pew Research Center 2008).

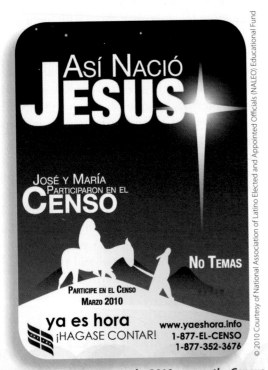

To increase Latino response to the 2010 census, the Census Bureau used this image of Christmas for a poster. It reads, in part, "This is how Jesus was born... Joseph and Mary participated in the census..." Many Latino churches and organizations were enthusiastic about linking the birth of Jesus Christ to the census. Others denounced the poster as sacrilegious and secularizing religion (B. Jones 2009: 2). What do you think?

- 43 percent of the general population (and 68 percent of Mormons) contends that the entertainment industry, especially Hollywood, has damaged religious values (Pew Forum on Religion & Public Life 2008).

In addition, a majority of Americans complain that holy days are anything but religious. For example, secular cards wish "Happy Holidays" (instead of "Merry Christmas"), and radio stations stream songs like "Let It Snow" rather than Christmas carols. Thus, many grumble, Santa Claus and presents have replaced traditional symbols of Christmas, especially images of the birth of Christ.

IS THE EXTENT OF SECULARIZATION EXAGGERATED?

Many sociologists argue that the extent of secularization is greatly overstated. Some point out that **fundamentalism**, the belief in the literal meaning of a sacred text (such as the Christian Bible, the Muslim Qur'an, or the Jewish Torah), has increased in the United States and worldwide (Woolf 2004). There's also evidence that religion has an enormous impact on many Americans' lives. For example:

- Increasing numbers of pharmacists have refused to fill prescriptions for oral contraceptives because doing so violates their religious beliefs (Bergquist 2006).

- 100 million Americans listen to Christian radio stations almost every day, 43 percent more than in 2000 (Piore 2005).

- 59 percent wouldn't vote for a well-qualified presidential candidate who is an atheist (Gibbs and Duffy 2007).

- 69 percent favor using taxpayer money to fund faith-based programs that provide social services such as drug treatment counseling and job training (Pew Forum on Religion & Public Life 2009b).

- 83 percent support Christmas displays on government property (Pew Research Center for the People & the Press 2010).

Over the years, one of the most divisive secularization issues has been the conflict between religion and science. Scientists claim that human beings (and other

TABLE 15.3
Sociological Perspectives on Religion

THEORETICAL PERSPECTIVE	LEVEL OF ANALYSIS	VIEW OF RELIGION	SOME MAJOR QUESTIONS
Functionalist	Macro	Religion benefits society by providing a sense of belonging, identity, meaning, emotional comfort, and social control over deviant behavior.	How does religion contribute to social cohesion?
Conflict	Macro	Religion promotes and legitimates social inequality, condones strife and violence between groups, and justifies oppression of poor people.	How does religion control and oppress people, especially those at lower socioeconomic levels?
Feminist	Macro and Micro	Religion subordinates women, excludes them from decision-making positions, and legitimizes patriarchal control of society.	How is religion patriarchal and sexist?
Symbolic Interactionist	Micro	Religion provides meaning and sustenance in everyday life through symbols, rituals, and beliefs and binds people together in a physical and spiritual community.	How does religion differ within and across societies?

creatures) evolved from earlier animals through a process known as "natural selection" over several million years. In contrast, creationism argues that the earth and the universe were created about 10,000 years ago by God, as described in the Bible. Intelligent design, sometimes described as a watered-down version of creationism, doesn't reject evolution outright but holds that the universe is so complex that it must have been created by a supreme being, not necessarily named God (National Academy of Sciences 2008; Roylance and Hill 2008).

Nearly 87 percent of Americans believe that scientific developments make society better, but many don't want scientific theories about evolution taught in public schools (Masci 2007). This isn't surprising because "more Americans believe in angels than in evolution": 14 percent believe in evolution, 44 percent subscribe to creationism, and 36 percent believe in intelligent design (Dawkins 2009: 53).

Sociologists (and other social scientists) who contend that secularization is not increasing in the United States and other Western countries also cite the prevalence of **civil religion** (sometimes called *secular religion*), practices in which citizenship takes on religious aspects. Examples of civil religion in the United States involve including the phrase "one nation under God" in the Pledge of Allegiance, inscribing coins with the phrase "In God We Trust," routinely asking God to bless the nation in presidential inaugural addresses and annual State of the Union messages, typically beginning a new session of Congress with a prayer, and the closing of the New York Stock Exchange (the country's most capitalistic and secular organization) on Good Friday, a major Christian holy day.

civil religion (sometimes called *secular religion*) practices in which citizenship takes on religious aspects.

6 Sociological Perspectives on Religion

You've seen that religion plays an important role in many people's lives. Why? How does society affect religion? And how does religion influence society? Functionalists view religion as benefiting society, conflict theorists see religion as promoting social inequality, feminist scholars emphasize how religion subordinates and excludes women, and symbolic interactionists focus on everyday religious experiences and processes (*Table 15.3* summarizes these perspectives).

FUNCTIONALISM: WHAT ARE THE BENEFITS OF RELIGION?

Durkheim (1961: 13, 43) described religion as an "essential and permanent aspect of humanity" whose "essential task is to maintain, in a positive manner, the normal course of life." Religion can also be dysfunctional, but first let's consider its positive influence.

Religion as a Societal Glue

Religion fulfills a variety of functions on individual, community, and societal levels. All of the following products of religious practice, according to functionalists, contribute to a society's survival, stability, and solidarity:

- *Belonging and identity.* Communal worship increases social contacts and enhances a sense of acceptance and identity. Rituals for major life events (such as baptisms, weddings, and funerals) and everyday behaviors (such as prayers at meals and bedtime) reinforce the members' feeling of belonging to a group (Christiano 2000; Gruber 2005). Religion also bolsters social cohesion by bringing people together for worship services that strengthen their shared beliefs.

- *Meaning, purpose, and emotional comfort.* Religion provides a sense of meaning in life and offers hope for the future. Religious people are often less likely to despair when they experience injustice, suffering, and illness. Religion also helps people cope with anxiety-producing events. Consider, for example, how often you've prayed (or seen someone pray) in dealing with disappointment, sadness, anxiety (especially before taking an exam), frustration, or the death of a loved one.

- *Social service.* Religions provide numerous social services that benefit their members and others. For example, religious organizations raised millions of dollars for the victims of Hurricane Katrina and the earthquake in Haiti in 2010, distributed food and clothing, and found shelter for displaced families. Also, many people express their religious beliefs by volunteering at soup kitchens and AIDS clinics because they believe that they're delivering God's love in a practical way (Bender 2003; Brown 2005).

  Many religious groups also help immigrants obtain visas, locate housing and jobs, and enroll in schools and English classes, all of which help decrease culture shock by acclimating newcomers to a foreign environment (see Chapter 3 on culture shock). Ethnic churches, especially, offer immigrants services in their own language, which help newcomers maintain continuity with their home culture (Greeley 1972; Ebaugh 2003; McRoberts 2003).

- *Social control.* Because people who are religious internalize rules about right and wrong, and fear damnation in the afterlife, they try to practice self-control, which encourages social conformity and discourages deviant behavior (Durkheim 1961). Religion also legitimizes political leaders and their authority. In some countries, state religions dictate how people should behave; in other countries, such as the United States, political leaders may use religion to justify their decisions. President George W. Bush, for example, defended the 2003 U.S. invasion of Iraq

TIMOTHY A. CLARY/AFP/Getty Images

In 2006, a dairy truck driver burst into an Amish schoolhouse in Lancaster County, Pennsylvania. He killed five girls and wounded three others before shooting himself because, according to his suicide note, he was angry with life and at God. Pictured here, an Amish funeral procession escorts the victims to a burial ground. The Amish community, in which violence is unthinkable, accepted the tragedy as the will of God and started a charity fund to help not only the victims' families but also the gunman's widow and children. From a functionalist perspective, why does their religion help the Amish and other religious people cope with tragedy?

in religious terms ("Liberty is God's gift to every human being in the world") (Milbank 2003; "Faith in the System" 2004).

Religion and Social Change

For functionalists, religion usually supports the status quo, but it can also spearhead social change. Mohandas Gandhi (1869–1948), a spiritual leader in India, worked for his country's independence from Great Britain through nonviolence and peaceful negotiations. In the United States, religious leaders, especially Reverend Martin Luther King, Jr., were at the forefront of the civil rights movement during the late 1960s. Recently, Buddhist religious leaders led hundreds of thousands of people in revolts against what they believed was an unjust authoritarian government in Myanmar (Burma).

Max Weber (1920) maintained that religion sparks economic development. His study of Calvinism, a Christian sect that arose during the sixteenth century, concluded that this belief system supported the dominance of capitalism in the Western world by the nineteenth century. Calvinists believed that people were predestined for salvation or the fires of hell. A sign from God that someone was among the elect (those destined for heaven) was a person's material success on earth. Weber called this view the **Protestant ethic,** a belief that hard work, diligence, self-denial, frugality, and economic success would lead to salvation in the afterlife. For Weber, the Protestant ethic was a self-fulfilling prophecy. That is, the harder that the early Calvinists worked and saved, the more likely they were to accumulate money, to become successful, and to drive the growth of capitalism.

Was Weber right about the relationship between the Protestant ethic and the rise of capitalism? The data are mixed. Some studies show that people are diligent not because of religious beliefs but simply because amassing savings provides resources when disaster strikes (as when crops are lost because of a drought). On the other hand, a study of 59 industrialized and developing countries found that religious beliefs that encourage hard work and thrift spur economic growth (Cohen 2002; Barro and McCleary 2003).

How Is Religion Dysfunctional?

Functionalists emphasize the benefits of religion, but they also recognize that religion can be dysfunctional when it harms individuals, communities, and societies. For example, religious intolerance can lead to conflict between groups (even to vandalizing churches, mosques, and synagogues) and be used to justify attacks on religious minorities. Moreover, many recent investigations have found that since the 1950s, numerous Catholic pastors, bishops, archbishops, and several popes have ignored complaints about priests who have sexually assaulted young boys instead of reporting the crimes to the police (Stobart 2009; De Pommereau 2010; Francis 2010; Llana 2010).

> **Protestant ethic** a belief that hard work, diligence, self-denial, frugality, and economic success will lead to salvation in the afterlife.

Religion helps people deal with misfortune, but it can also heighten anxiety about death and the afterlife. As a result, many elderly and poor people contribute much of their meager income to religious organizations, believing that such donations will help them enter heaven. Also, some groups in the United States have gone to court over the teaching of evolution rather than creationism or intelligent design in science classes, creating considerable conflict in local school districts.

Critical Evaluation

Functionalists' theories are useful in explaining why many people are religious and how religion benefits societies. However, critics accuse functionalists of emphasizing benefits and glossing over the dysfunctional aspects of religion that create and maintain social cleavages. For example, disagreements over whose deity is the "real God" have led to wars, terrorism, and genocide (see Chapter 18 online).

Critics also note that functionalists, by emphasizing the needs that religion fulfills, imply that religion is indispensable to leading a good life. However, people who are not religious donate to many social service organizations, serve as volunteers when disaster strikes, and report having happy and fulfilling lives. In addition, some Catholic priests, presumably very religious people, have admitted to molesting thousands of young boys, and some Protestant pastors and church treasurers have embezzled church funds that have amounted to millions of dollars ("What's That Commandment. . ." 2006; Padgett 2007; Spano 2007). Conflict theorists, especially, maintain that functionalist perspectives focus on social stability rather than addressing discord and social inequality.

CONFLICT THEORY: DOES RELIGION PROMOTE SOCIAL INEQUALITY?

In 2010, and after the District of Columbia's mayor signed a measure recognizing same-sex marriage as legal, Catholic Charities announced that it would not offer health benefits to the same-sex partners of its employees. Catholic Charities also transferred the $22 million that it received from the city to support social service programs such as homeless shelters and foster homes that, presumably, didn't accommodate same-sex couples (Wan 2010). Many functionalists would view such actions as enhancing solidarity among Catholics, but conflict theorists would see them as examples of religious views that create strife and divisiveness.

"The Opium of the People"

Much conflict theory reflects the work of Karl Marx (1845/1972), who described religion as "the sigh of the oppressed creature" and "the opium of the people" because it encouraged passivity and acceptance of class inequality. For Marx, religion taught people to endure suffering and deprivation instead of revolting against injustice. In effect, Marx maintained, religion is like a drug that numbs the poor and downtrodden, and encourages them to tolerate their misery on earth in hope of a better life after death.

Marx viewed religion as a form of **false consciousness**, an acceptance of a system of beliefs that prevents people from protesting oppression. Those who own the means of production (such as factory owners) profit if the masses (the workers) console themselves through religion instead of rising up against exploitation. Contemporary conflict theorists don't view religion as an opiate, but they agree with Marx that religion legitimizes social inequality and sometimes leads to social disruption and violence.

A Source of Social Disruption and Violence

For conflict theorists, religion tends to promote strife because, typically, religious groups differentiate between "we" and "they" ("We're right and they're wrong."). Such distinctions spark numerous disputes within and across societies (Marty 2005). For example, in India, Hindus fight Muslims (and sometimes burn Christian homes and churches), the schism between Iraq's Sunnis and Shiites dates back more than 1,300 years, and there are longstanding conflicts between Muslims and Jews in Israel and Palestine (Ghosh 2007; Ridge 2008).

For thousands of years, many governments and religious leaders have condoned or perpetrated widespread violence in the name of religion. Terrorists who targeted the World Trade Center on 9/11 didn't see themselves as "crazed terrorists" but as "true believers" who were carrying out "God's will" by imposing their religious beliefs on others or destroying their "religious enemies" (Juergensmeyer 2003).

Many conflict theorists point out that religion can be a major source of hatred, prejudice, and discrimination. For example, 43 percent of Americans admit to feeling prejudice toward Muslims—more than twice the number who say the same about Christians (18 percent), Jews (15 percent), and Buddhists (14 percent) (Gallup Center for Muslim Studies 2010). Religious stereotypes are remarkably similar across societies: Many non-Muslims in the West and many Muslims in the Middle East and Asia generally describe people on the other side as immoral, not religious, or fanatical in their religious views and practices (Pew Global Attitudes Project 2006).

"The Anglican Church of Southern Africa has long recognized the value and effectiveness of partnerships. Siyafundisa is a model HIV and AIDS peer education prevention program created by ACSA working together with FreshMinistries. Be The Change International and Be The Change Africa were born out of the energy

In 2003, the Episcopal Church, which is the largest Protestant denomination worldwide, ordained V. Gene Robinson, an openly gay man, as bishop of New Hampshire. The ordination created considerable divisiveness because many of the church's conservative members believe that homosexuality is incompatible with the teachings of the Bible and church doctrine.

Peter Macdiarmid/Getty Images

In Iraq and Afghanistan, Muslims serving in the U.S. military face a double-edged sword. They are prized for their language skills and cultural knowledge by commanders, but may be singled out by insurgents as traitors (Dreazen 2009).

A Legitimation of Social Inequality

Conflict theorists also see religion as a tool dominant groups use to control society and to protect their own interests. In the United States before the Civil War, many churches used a slave catechism "to justify domination by masters, to encourage work, and to attribute lack of work to personal laziness. White pastors told Blacks that God created the masters over them and that the Bible tells them that they must obey their White masters" (Hurst 2001: 310).

In 13 European countries, Muslims experience inequality in employment, education, and housing, and are also the victims of negative stereotyping, especially by the media. Some of the inequality is due to *xenophobia* (the irrational fear and distrust of anything foreign) and factors such as immigrants' not being able to speak the adopted country's language and their lack of higher education. Religious discrimination is also prevalent because a majority of Europeans believes that Muslims isolate themselves from mainstream society and engage in terrorism (European Monitoring Centre on Racism and Xenophobia 2006; Sengupta 2006).

Critical Evaluation

Conflict theory offers valuable insights on how religion creates and maintains social inequality but is criticized on several grounds. Functionalists may overemphasize consensus and harmony, but conflict theorists often ignore the role that religion plays in creating social cohesion and cooperation. For example, many religious people are altruistic, volunteering their time in low-income neighborhoods rather than seeking economic rewards at work or enjoying recreational activities. Some scholars have also criticized Marx (and other conflict theorists) for ignoring the possibility that religious people feel more than a mere opiate-like resignation to difficult circumstances. Instead, many religious people, even among those who are relatively privileged, run charitable organizations and shape public policy to help the poor (Hamilton 2001; Wald 2003; Roberts 2004).

FEMINIST THEORIES: DOES RELIGION SUBORDINATE AND EXCLUDE WOMEN?

Despite criticism from conservatives, the International Bible Society has updated its best-selling modern Bible to include gender-neutral wording. Examples include changing "sons of God" to "children of God" and "a man is justified by faith" to "a person is justified by faith."

Are such changes only cosmetic? Most feminist scholars maintain that gender-neutral language is important because it signals inclusion to female adherents. Feminist theorists agree with conflict theorists that religion can create violence and maintain inequality. They go further, however, by criticizing organized religions for being sexist and patriarchal, and for shutting many women out of leadership positions.

Sexism and Patriarchy

From a feminist perspective, most religions are patriarchal because they emphasize men's experiences and a male point of view, and see women as subordinate to men. According to the apostle Paul, for example, "Wives should submit to their husbands in everything" (*Ephesians* 5: 24). The idea that Eve was created out of Adam's rib is used to justify the domination of men over women. Beliefs such as those of fourth-century theologian Augustine, "We are men, you are women, we are the head, you are the members, we are masters, you are slaves," are reflected today in "even supposedly holy and intelligent men's particularly low opinion of women" (Mananzan 2002: 207).

In Orthodox Judaism, a man's daily prayers include this line: "Blessed are thou, O Lord, our God, King of the Universe, that I was not born a woman." The Qur'an tells Muslims that men are in charge of women and that good women should obey men. Almost all contemporary religions worship a male God, and none of the major world religions—Judaism, Christianity, Islam, Buddhism, Hinduism, or the East Asian philosophical traditions of Confucianism and Taoism—treat women and men equally (Daly 1973; Gross 1996).

Some feminist scholars have charged, however, that the Bible has often been interpreted in a patriarchal manner. For example, Jesus encouraged women's intellectual pursuits when it was not the norm and appeared first to women after his resurrection and told them to report the news to male followers. There are also numerous passages in the Bible about women spreading Jesus' teachings. Muslim feminists similarly note that men have interpreted sacred Islamic texts in ways that ensure male dominance and control. Women were among some of Muhammad's earliest converts, and the Qur'an has numerous passages that establish women's equal rights in inheritance and family roles (Menissi 1991, 1996; Gross 1996). Thus, women's subordination in many Islamic societies is not due to the tenets of the religion but to the men who have interpreted the tenets to maintain their power and privilege (Smith 1994).

Exclusion of Women from Leadership Positions

Since the 1970s, the percentage of Americans who support having women as pastors, ministers, priests, and rabbis has increased from 40 percent to more than 70 percent. Also, the percentage of theology degrees earned by women has risen considerably—from only 2 percent in 1970 to almost 34 percent in 2007. Still, women make up only about 13 percent of the nation's clergy, and only 3 percent of female clergy lead large congregations (i.e., those with more than 350 people) (Winseman 2004; Carroll 2006; U.S. Census Bureau 2010).

Neither Roman Catholicism nor Orthodox Judaism allows women in the clergy because both groups believe that women should serve and not lead. In the United States, Catholic women contribute $6 billion a year during Sunday Masses, but "the presence of women anywhere within the institutional power structure is virtually nil" (Miller 2010: 39). And although nuns dramatically outnumber priests worldwide, they are second-class citizens who are excluded from doctrinal discussions and have little freedom (Briggs 2006).

In other religions, female members of the clergy report that they often encounter a "stained-glass ceiling." The African Methodist Episcopal (AME) Church, the U.S. denomination with the largest number of African Americans, did not elect its first female bishop, Vashti McKenzie, until 2000. According to Bishop McKenzie, "For women, especially for African-American women, you always have to be better than men to get ahead" (Van Biema 2004: 60).

Some Protestant denominations typically justify women's exclusion from leadership positions based on Biblical passages, such as "I permit no woman to teach or have authority over men; she is to keep silent" (*I Timothy* 2: 11–12). Many Protestant groups—including Southern Baptists and especially evangelical groups (such as born-again Christians)—interpret this passage and similar ones to mean that women should never, under any circumstances, instruct men, within or outside of religious institutions. Thus, Southern Baptist seminaries accept women for theological studies, but rarely hire them as faculty members (Bartlett 2007).

Even in liberal Protestant congregations, female clergy tend to be relegated to specialized ministries with responsibilities for music, youth, or Bible studies. The few women who become pastors frequently have small or financially struggling congregations instead of "tall-steeple churches" in affluent neighborhoods. And when women serve as associate pastors, some members of the congregation, especially men, are often unhappy because they prefer male preachers (Banerjee 2006).

AP Photo/Aaron Favila

In the Philippines, a predominantly Catholic country, the Church, supported by the government, has successfully ended campaigns by organizations to distribute free contraceptives and information about birth control methods. According to the Church, "Children are riches, and the more you have, the more blessed you are." Health officials contend that such views have led to overpopulation and poverty. Many poor people have six or seven children they can't afford to feed (Wallace 2008). This pregnant woman holds mock chains during a rally to protest the Church's intrusions on women's lives.

In mid-2005, a Danish newspaper published 12 cartoons lampooning Muslim terrorists, including one of the prophet Muhammad with a bomb in his turban. Many Muslims were furious because Muhammad is a revered symbol of Islamic religious beliefs and mocking him is considered blasphemous (Birch 2006). The cartoons sparked many demonstrations around Europe, including burning Danish flags and products (pictured here). Most European and American commentators agreed that the cartoons were in poor taste but argued that Muslims must learn to accept Western standards of free speech. Some of the commentators also accused the protestors of a double standard, citing Internet videos of radical Muslims slashing the throats of Western journalists and international humanitarian workers, Christians not being permitted to worship openly or to carry a Bible in public in Saudi Arabia, and cartoons by Muslims defaming Jews (Rubin 2006; Van Doorn-Harder 2006).

Critical Evaluation

Feminist scholars have pressed for more rights for women—within Christianity, Islam, and Judaism—and for church leaders to take the religious aspirations and lives of women more seriously (Cooey et al. 1991; Young 1999). However, feminist-oriented theology is still largely a Western movement, and some feminist Muslim scholars have criticized Western feminists for misreading and misinterpreting Islamic and other sacred scriptures, such as reducing practically all discussions on gender to the *hijab* (a veil or scarf that Muslim women wear) instead of focusing on justice for both women and men in marriage, employment, and other areas (Safi 2003; Choudhury et al. 2006; Esposito and Mogahed 2007; Fakhraie 2009).

Another criticism is that feminist scholars sometimes overlook how religious institutions—especially those that are conservative—encourage men to focus on their families. For example, churchgoing men in the United States are generally more involved and affectionate fathers and husbands and have lower rates of domestic violence than their peers who are not regular churchgoers (Bartkowski and Read 2003; Wilcox 2006).

SYMBOLIC INTERACTIONISM: HOW DOES RELIGION PROVIDE MEANING IN EVERYDAY LIFE?

In 2007, a highly respected and experienced British teacher was teaching at an elementary school in Sudan, Africa. She began a project on animals and asked her 7-year-old students to name a teddy bear that the students had to photograph and write about. The class voted resoundingly for Muhammad, the name of Islam's founder and one of the most common names in the Muslim world. Within a few days, some of the children's parents objected because naming the teddy bear

Muhammad violated Islamic beliefs that prohibit using the prophet's name for "idols." There were numerous protests by the Sudanese, many of whom demanded the teacher's execution. The teacher was arrested and went to trial, but the government decided to simply deport her (Crilly 2007; "Crowds Call for Teacher's Death" 2007). Thus, from a symbolic interactionist perspective, not understanding another culture's religion can lead to serious problems.

For symbolic interactionists, religion is a social phenomenon that is taught rather than being innate. Symbols, rituals, and beliefs are three of the most common vehicles for learning and internalizing religion.

Symbols

A *symbol* is anything that stands for or represents something else to which people attach meaning (see Chapter 3). Many religious symbols are objects (a cross, a steeple, a Bible), but they also include behaviors (kneeling and bowing one's head), words ("Holy Father," "Allah," "the Prophet"), and aspects of physical appearance (the wearing of head scarves, skull caps, turbans, clerical collars).

Religious symbols, like all symbols, are shorthand communication tools (see *Figure 15.2*). When people have the same symbols, they share the same definition of reality (including what is acceptable and what is not) and the same *worldview*, a concept of self, society, and the supernatural. Some symbolic interactionists define a religion as "a system of symbols" because it is a community that is unified by its symbols and shares a worldview (Berger and Luckmann 1966; Geertz 1966).

Rituals

A **ritual** (sometimes called a *rite*) is a formal and repeated behavior in which the members of a group regularly engage. There are many secular rituals, such as college graduations and the ceremonies marking the beginning and end of the Olympics.

Religious rituals, like secular ones, strengthen the self-identity of each participant (Reiss 2004). Religious rites of passage—such as the *bat mitzvah* for girls and the *bar mitzvah* for boys in the Jewish community and the first communion and confirmation for Catholic children—reinforce the individual's sense of belonging to a particular religious group. A group's rituals symbolize its spiritual beliefs and include a wide range of practices such as praying, chanting, fasting, singing, dancing, and offering sacrifices.

What Is a Hajj?

Every year, more than 2 million Muslims engage in an important ritual, the Hajj, by making a pilgrimage to Mecca (in Saudi Arabia). The Hajj is one of the five pillars of the Muslim faith that demonstrate the solidarity of Muslims and their submission to God. Every able-bodied follower who can afford it is expected to perform the pilgrimage at least once in a lifetime. The Hajj occurs from the 8th to the 12th days of the last month of the Islamic year (roughly in the November to January period of the Western calendar).

All religions have rituals that mark significant events in a person's life, such as birth, puberty, and marriage (see Chapters 3, 5, and 13). Death rituals are probably the most elaborate and sacred worldwide. They vary across religious groups and societies, but all of them offer comfort to the living and show respect for the dead.

Some traditional rituals are waning. In 2008, for example, 30 percent of American married couples didn't have a religious ceremony and 27 percent of Americans didn't want a religious funeral or service when they died (Kosmin and Keysar 2009). And new rituals are emerging. Atheists claim that rituals are too religious, but some atheists are pioneering a new ritual, "de-baptism." The ceremony involves renouncing their baptism and sending letters to churches requesting that their names be removed from baptismal rolls (MacDonald 2009).

Beliefs

Rituals and symbols come from *beliefs*, convictions about what people think is true. Religious beliefs can be passive (believing in God but never attending formal ser-

FIGURE 15.2
Religious Symbols

From left to right: Buddhist, Christian, Hindu, Indigenous and Ancient Religions, Islam, Judaism,

© Image copyright afalzal, 2009. Used under license from Shutterstock.com

vices) or active (participating in rituals and ceremonies). Beliefs bind people together into a spiritual community.

One of the strongest beliefs around the world is that prayer is important. Islam requires prayer five times a day. In the United States, 58 percent of adult Americans say that they pray more than once a day and do so for a variety of reasons, such as feeling close to God, as well as requesting better health, more money, and cures for sick pets (Pew Forum on Religion & Public Life 2008; Wicker 2009).

Is prayer effective? In a scientifically rigorous study, the researchers followed 1,800 patients who had received heart bypass surgery and concluded that there were no differences in the number of postoperative complications or in the overall recovery rate of those who were and weren't prayed for. In fact, the patients who knew that they were being prayed for fared worse, presumably because they experienced anxiety that their recovery wouldn't live up to the expectations of the people who prayed for them or because the pray-

Spirituality, Lutheran, Confucian, Baha'i, Scientology

ing suggested that the patients were sicker than they thought (Krucoff et al. 2006).

Despite such empirical data, of the physicians who describe themselves as religious, 56 percent believe that religion, including prayer, affects a patient's health, and 33 percent say that religion and spirituality help prevent medical events such as heart attacks, infections, and even death (Curlin et al. 2007). From a symbolic interactionist perspective, prayer provides psychological and spiritual benefits such as comfort and a sense of unity among those who pray together. Still, few Americans would feel comfortable with a physician who recommends prayer rather than aggressive treatment of a life-threatening illness.

Critical Evaluation

A major contribution of symbolic interactionists is that they help explain why religious behaviors vary within and across cultures and provide insights on the reasons for everyday religious practices. A common criticism, however, is that interactionists' focus on micro-level practices ignores the ways that religion promotes social inequality at the macro level. Conflict theorists and feminist thinkers, in particular, maintain that people often use religion to justify violence and women's subordination.

Some critics also wonder if symbolic interactionists are painting too rosy a picture of religion even on a micro level. After all, people's attachment to their religious symbols, rituals, and beliefs can create considerable conflict (as witnessed by the teddy bear incident). In many European and U.S. towns, for example, people often resist religious diversity by opposing proposals to build mosques in their communities, even though the plans include benefits such as housing for Islamic senior citizens and after-school activities for Muslim children (Landler 2006; "Plan to Build. . ." 2006).

Taken together, functionalist, conflict, feminist, and symbolic interactionist perspectives offer a multidimensional understanding of the beneficial and disruptive roles that religion plays on both individual and societal levels. That is, religion is an important institution that has different manifestations across societies.

© iStockphoto.com/Shelly Au

Population growth

and urbanization are changing our lives.

16 Population, Urbanization, and the Environment

what do you think?

Individuals can do little to prevent global warming.

1 2 3 4 5 6 7

strongly agree   strongly disagree

More than 80 percent of all babies are born in developing countries in Africa and Asia. In contrast, some industrialized nations, such as Germany and Italy, are encouraging parenthood because they fear that there won't be enough workers to support a rapidly aging population (Cardwell 2009; see also Chapter 13). This chapter examines population changes, urbanization, and how both affect the environment in the United States and worldwide. Let's begin with population.

1 Population Dynamics

Population growth was one of the most significant changes of the twentieth century. Since 1900, the world's population has more than tripled in size. On a typical day, in fact, the world gains almost 219,000 people (U.S. Census Bureau 2010). Even if most of the births are in other countries, population growth affects all Americans—now and in the future.

> **demography** the scientific study of human populations.
>
> **population** a group of people who share a geographic territory.

Information about population growth comes from **demography,** the scientific study of human populations. Demographers analyze populations in terms of size, composition, distribution, and why they change. A **population** is a group of people who share a geographic territory. A population can inhabit a territory as small as a town or as vast as the planet, depending on a researcher's focus. Demographers also study personal data such as when and where you were born, your probability of getting married or divorced, the kind of job you'll probably have, how many times you'll move, and how long you'll probably live. According to one demographer, "If people are not interested in demographic phenomena, they are not interested in themselves" (McFalls 2007: 3).

WHY POPULATIONS CHANGE

Global population has grown rapidly since 1800 (see *Figure 16.1*). It reached 1 billion in 1804, 5 billion in 1987, 6.5 billion in 2005, and is expected to increase to 9.4 billion by 2050 (U.S. Census Bureau 2010). When demographers examine population changes, they look at the interplay among three key factors: how many people are born (fertility), how many die (mortality), and how many move from one area to another (migration).

Fertility: Adding New People

The study of population changes begins with **fertility,** the number of babies born during a specified period in a particular society. There are several ways to measure fertility, but one of the most general and commonly used is the **crude birth rate,** also known as the *birth rate,* the number of live births for every 1,000 people in a population in a given year.

"Crude" implies that the rate is an imprecise measure of a society's childbearing pattern because it is based on the total population rather than more specific measures such as a woman's age or marital status. However, the crude birth rate allows comparisons for a given year across populations or countries. In 2009, for example, that rate was 20 worldwide, 36 for Africa, 14 for the United States, and 11 for Europe (Haub and Kent 2009).

Birth rates also vary within a country. In the United States, younger women—those between 20 and 34—have higher birth rates than those age 35 to 44, and recent immigrants have higher birth rates than native-born women (Dye 2008). The more affluent, regardless of race and ethnicity, have fewer children than the poor, and people with higher educational levels tend to postpone childbearing and are more likely to use contraceptives. Educated women are likely to delay childbirth until they have completed their education or started a career, which decreases the number of children they will have over a lifetime (Hamilton et al. 2003; see also Chapters 9 and 13).

Mortality: Subtracting People

The second factor in population change is **mortality,** the number of deaths during a specified period in a population. Demographers typically measure mortality by the **crude death rate** (also called the *death rate*), the number of deaths per 1,000 people in a population in a given year. In 2009, for example, the crude death rate was 8 worldwide and for the United States, and 20 in Sierra Leone, Africa (Haub and Kent 2009).

A death rate isn't necessarily the best measure of a population's health, however. Death rates are high in developed countries—even though these nations have better medical services, better nutrition, and healthier environments than most developing countries—because industrialized nations also have large proportions of people who are 65 and older.

A better measure of a population's health is the **infant mortality rate,** the number of deaths of infants younger than 1 year per 1,000 live births. Generally, as the standard of living improves—meaning increased access to

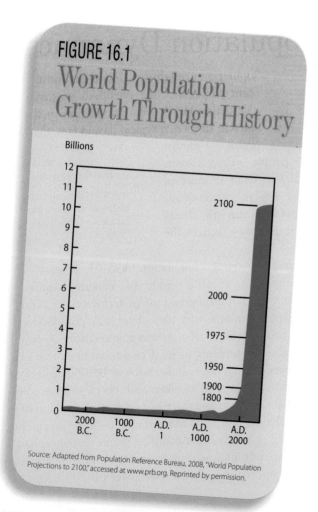

FIGURE 16.1
World Population Growth Through History

Billions

12
11
10 — 2100
9
8
7
6
5 — 2000
4 — 1975
3
2 — 1950
1 — 1900 / 1800
0

2000 B.C.   1000 B.C.   A.D. 1   A.D. 1000   A.D. 2000

Source: Adapted from Population Reference Bureau, 2008, "World Population Projections to 2100," accessed at www.prb.org. Reprinted by permission.

Because of high population growth, the roads in many of India's largest cities, such as this one in New Delhi, are chaotic: "Cars, trucks, buses, motorcycles, taxis, rickshaws, cows, donkeys, and dogs jostle for every inch of the roadway as horns blare and brakes squeal. Drivers run red lights and jam their vehicles into available space, ignoring pedestrians" (Hamm 2007: 49–50).

clean water, adequate sanitation, and medical care—the infant mortality rate decreases. In 2009, the infant mortality rate was 4 in Europe, almost 7 in the United States, and as high as 155 in Afghanistan (Haub and Kent 2009).

Lower infant mortality greatly raises *life expectancy,* the average number of years that people who were born at about the same time can expect to live. Worldwide, in 2009, the average life expectancy was 69 years—67 for men and 71 for women. Again, however, there are considerable variations across countries—from a high of 82 in Switzerland, Italy, and Japan, to a low of 44 in Afghanistan. The United States, with a life expectancy of 78, ranks below at least 25 other industrialized countries and only slightly higher than less developed countries such as Cuba, the Czech Republic, and Uruguay (Haub and Kent 2009).

In general, life expectancy has been increasing worldwide. Much of the increase is due to medical advances that have wiped out many diseases, and the availability of clean drinking water, sanitation, immunization, and antibiotics, all of which tend to prolong life. However, civil wars, genocide, and deaths caused by AIDS have devastated many African countries (Ashford 2006).

U.S. life expectancy soared from 47 years in 1900 to 78 in 2009 (National Center for Health Statistics 2007; U.S. Census Bureau 2010). Still, mortality rates for Americans vary quite a bit by sex, race/ethnicity, and social class. For example, many women live longer than men because they are less likely to work in physically dangerous jobs (such as construction and

law enforcement), to engage in risky behaviors (such as fast driving), to serve in the military, and to commit suicide or to be homicide victims (see Chapters 7 and 9). In virtually every society, people with a higher socioeconomic status live longer and healthier lives: They are more aware of the benefits of nutrition, work in jobs that are relatively safe, and have the resources to access medical services.

> **migration** the movement of people into or out of a specific geographic area.

Migration: Adding and Subtracting People

The third demographic factor in understanding population change is **migration,** the movement of people into or out of a specific geographic area. Migration is the product of both push and pull factors.

Push factors encourage or force people to leave a residence. These factors include war, political or religious persecution, unemployment, high crime rates, and natural disasters. After Hurricanes Katrina and Rita devastated much of the Louisiana-Texas border in 2005, for example, those who were the most disadvantaged—up to 75 percent—moved to other states because they didn't have home insurance policies that covered the costs of the damages (Myers et al. 2010).

Pull factors attract people to a new location. Some of these factors include religious freedom, better schools, lower crime rates, and, especially, economic opportunities. For example, the United States is the destination of most Mexicans (both legal and undocumented) because they see America as a land of opportunity. Such optimism helps explain why 10 percent of Mexicans born in their homeland now live in the United States (Passel and Cohn 2009).

There are two types of migration: international and internal. *International migration* is movement to another country. Such migration includes *emigrants* (people who are moving out of a country) and *immigrants* (people who are moving into a country). You may be a product of international migration, for example, if your great-great-grandparents emi-

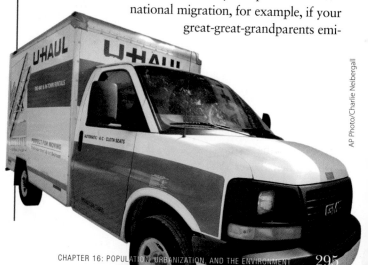

sex ratio the proportion of men to women in a population.

grated from Ireland and immigrated to the United States.

International migration is often in the news, but only about 3 percent of the world's population migrates to a different country and ends up staying for a year or longer. Most emigrants move to a neighboring country (from Mexico to the United States, for example, rather than from Mexico to Canada). International migration is relatively uncommon both because most people have no desire to leave their family and friends, and because governments try to regulate border crossings. However, 20 percent of international migrants live in the United States, higher than any other county in the world (Martin and Zürcher 2008; Bremner et al. 2009).

Of the 700 million adults worldwide who say that they would like to relocate permanently to another country if they could, 24 percent would like to move to the United States to reunite with family members living there, to find jobs, or to provide better lives for their children (Esipova et al. 2010). Thus, the reasons for international migration aren't very different from those of immigrants during the twentieth century.

The second type of migration is *internal migration,* movement within a country. About 40 million Americans move within the United States every year. Most are single and college-educated, and they are more likely to relocate to central cities than suburbs or rural areas because of job prospects (Franklin 2003; U.S. Census Bureau 2010).

POPULATION COMPOSITION AND STRUCTURE

Demographers examine age and sex to understand a population's composition and structure. Two of the most common measures are *sex ratios* and *population pyramids.*

Sex Ratios

The proportion of men to women in a population is a **sex ratio.** A sex ratio of 100 means that there are equal numbers of men and women, whereas a sex ratio of 95 means that there are 95 men for every 100 women (fewer males than females). Sex ratios are important because they affect the availability of marriageable partners, marriage rates, and childbearing (see Chapter 13).

Worldwide, on average, between 103 and 107 boys are born for every 100 girls. This newborn sex ratio decreases throughout life, however, as males experience higher rates of mortality at all stages of life. Although it is not clear why, male fetuses die in miscarriages at a higher rate than female fetuses (Christenson et al. 2004). However, sex ratios are skewed in favor of males in some countries, especially China and India, because of the practice of *female infanticide*—the intentional killing of female infants because of a cultural preference for male offspring (Almond et al. 2009).

FIGURE 16.2
Population Pyramid Projections, 2025

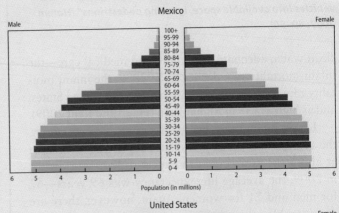

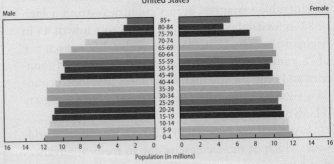

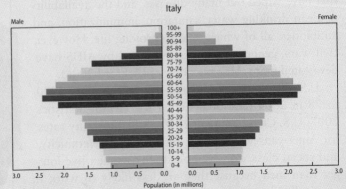

Source: U.S. Census Bureau, International Data Base, www.census.gov/ipc/www/idb/pyramids.html. Accessed January 20, 2007.

Population Pyramids

A **population pyramid** is a visual representation of the makeup of a population in terms of the age and sex of its members at a given point in time. As *Figure 16.2* shows, Mexico is a young country because many of its people are 44 or younger (which also means that many women are in their childbearing years) and there are relatively few people 65 years and older. In contrast, Italy is an old country, and the United States is somewhere in the middle.

The shape of the population pyramid (a triangle for Mexico, a rectangle for the United States, and a diamond for Italy) has future implications for young and old countries. Italy, for example, has a relatively small number of women age 15 to 44 (in their reproductive years) and a bulge of people age 45 to 79. This suggests that there may not be enough workers to support an aging population in the future, and that there will be a greater need for social services for the elderly than for children and adolescents. Thus, population pyramids give us a snapshot of a country's demographic profile, and suggest some of the constraints that people are likely to experience in the future.

POPULATION GROWTH: A TICKING BOMB?

Eight of the countries with the largest populations (many of them in the developing world) will increase even more than they have by 2050 (see *Table 16.1*). So, has population growth gotten out of hand? There are many views on this issue, but two of the most influential have been Malthusian theory (which argues that the world can't sustain its unprecedented population surge) and demographic transition theory (which maintains that population growth is slowing).

population pyramid a visual representation of the makeup of a population in terms of the age and sex of its members at a given point in time.

Malthusian theory the idea that population is growing faster than the food supply needed to sustain it.

Malthusian Theory

For many demographers, population growth is a ticking bomb. They subscribe to **Malthusian theory**, the idea that the population is growing faster than the food supply needed to sustain it. This theory is named after Thomas Malthus (1766–1834)—an English economist, clergyman, and college professor—who maintained that humans are multiplying faster than the ability of the earth to produce sufficient food.

According to Malthus (1798/1965), population grows at a *geometric rate* (2, 4, 8, and so on), whereas the food supply grows at an *arithmetic rate* (1, 2, 3, 4, and so on). That is, two parents can have 4 children and 16 grandchildren within 50 years. The available number of acres of land, farm animals, and other sources of food can increase in that time period, but certainly not quadruple. In effect, then, the food supply will not keep up with population growth. Because there are millions of parents, the results could be catastrophic, such as masses of people living in poverty or dying of starvation.

Malthus first posited that only war, famine, and disease act as *preventive checks* on population growth. In later essays, he also included "moral restraint" as a necessary preventive check, especially for lower classes. The lack of

TABLE 16.1
The World's Largest Countries, 2008 and 2050

COUNTRY	MID-2008 POPULATION (IN MILLIONS)	ESTIMATED 2050 POPULATION (IN MILLIONS)
China	1,325	1,747
India	1,149	1,437
United States	305	420
Indonesia	240	297
Brazil	195	260
Pakistan	173	295
Nigeria	148	282
Bangladesh	147	231

Note: Remember to add six zeros to these figures. For example, China's population in mid-2008 was about 1,325,000,000, or 1.3 billion people.
Sources: Based on Haub 2007, and Haub and Kent 2008.

Hulton Archive/Getty Images

moral restraint characterized people who marry at an early age and don't practice sexual abstinence before and outside of marriage. Such behavior resulted in large families and out-of-wedlock children that the working men couldn't save from "rags and squalid poverty" (Malthus 1872/1991).

Except for the notions about moral restraint, Malthusian theory has had a lasting influence. *Neo-Malthusians* (or New Malthusians) agree that the world population is exploding beyond food supplies. For example, the world population reached its first billion in 1800. In the 200 years that followed, the world added 5 billion people (see *Figure 16.1* on p. 294). Because of this rate of growth, according to some influential neo-Malthusians, the earth has become a "dying planet"—a world with insufficient food and a rapidly expanding population that pollutes the environment (Ehrlich 1971; Ehrlich and Ehrlich 2008).

The number of hungry people in the world, primarily in sub-Saharan Africa and South Asia, increased from 825 million in 1995 to 1.02 billion in 2009. The resources and technical knowledge are available to increase food production by 70 percent in 2050, but poverty and difficult growing conditions plague the countries that need food the most (Food and Agriculture Organization of the United Nations 2009).

Demographic Transition Theory

Some demographers are more optimistic than neo-Malthusians. **Demographic transition theory** maintains that population growth is kept in check and stabilizes as countries experience economic and technological development, which, in turn, affects birth and death rates. According to this theory, population growth changes as societies undergo industrialization, modernization, technological progress, and urbanization. During these processes, a nation goes through four stages (see *Figure 16.3*), from high birth and death rates to low birth and death rates.

- *Stage 1: Preindustrial society.* In this initial stage, there is little population growth. The birth rate is high because people rarely use birth control and they want as many children as possible to

provide unpaid agricultural labor and support their parents in old age. However, a high death rate offsets the high birth rate. Many children don't survive infancy, and mortality is high at all ages because of diseases and minimal access to health care.

- *Stage 2: Early industrial society.* There is a significant population growth because the birth rate is higher than the death rate. The birth rate may even increase over what it was in Stage 1 because mothers and their children enjoy improved health care. Couples may still have large numbers of children because they fear that many of them will die, but the death rate declines because of better sanitation, better nutrition, and medical advances (e.g., immunizations and antibiotics). Most of the world's poorest countries are currently in Stage 2.

- *Stage 3: Advanced industrial society.* As the infant mortality rate declines, parents have fewer children. Effective birth control reduces family size. This decrease in child-care responsibilities, in turn, provides women with time to work outside the home. China and many countries in Latin America are currently in Stage 3 (Gelbard et al. 1999; Brea 2003).

- *Stage 4: Postindustrial society.* In this stage, the demographic transition is complete, because the society has low birth and death rates. Women tend to be well educated and to have full-time jobs or careers. If

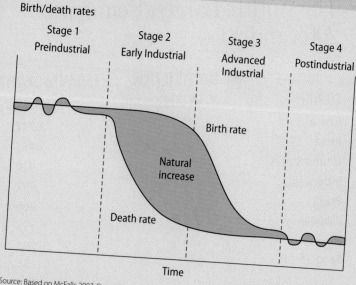

FIGURE 16.3
The Classical Demographic Transition Model

Birth/death rates

Stage 1
Preindustrial

Stage 2
Early Industrial

Stage 3
Advanced Industrial

Stage 4
Postindustrial

Birth rate

Natural increase

Death rate

Time

Source: Based on McFalls 2007, Figure 11.

there is little immigration, the population may even decrease because the birth rate is low. This is the case today in Canada, Japan, Singapore, Hong Kong, Australia, New Zealand, the United States, and many European countries, including Italy and Scotland.

Critical Evaluation

The dire predictions of Malthus and his successors that global population growth would lead to worldwide famine, disease, and poverty have not come true. Still, today more than 20 percent of people live in abject poverty, subsisting on less than $1 a day (World Bank 2008; see also Chapter 8).

Despite neo-Malthusians' fears, global fertility is half of what it was in 1972. The population of some industrialized countries is declining because people aren't having enough babies to replace themselves. These countries are experiencing zero population growth (ZPG), a stable population level that occurs when each woman has no more than two children.

Future population growth is difficult to predict because there are many unknowns. Some low-birth nations with fertility rates below ZPG are now paying women to have more children because there won't be enough young workers to pay for social security systems and the rising cost of health care for aging populations. For example, Russia gives mothers with one child $9,000 for each additional baby; Japan has expanded its day-care facilities and offers families a monthly allowance of $145 per child younger than 15; and China is now encouraging newly married couples to have two children, easing the one-child policy introduced in 1978 (Ford 2010; Haub 2010; Yamazaki and Ito 2010).

Some neo-Malthusians maintain, however, that it's irresponsible for *any* country to encourage higher fertility rates; these demographers worry about the consequences of adding 3 billion more inhabitants to the planet in less than 50 years, especially for many developing countries "with desperate economic outlooks" (Sachs 2005; Shorto 2008).

The birth rate in the United States has declined, but it's third in the world in population growth, behind India and China, largely because of high immigration rates, and many of the immigrants are young women with high fertility rates. Thus, U.S. annual population

During the Industrial Revolution, many cities, such as this one in Hamburg, Germany, in 1864, constructed canals that provided an inexpensive means of transportation and distributing goods.

"is growing by more than all other developed countries *combined*" (Ryerson 2004: 21).

One of the results of population growth is urban growth. Cities attract both immigrants and native-born residents because of jobs and cultural activities, but the population growth of urban areas also creates numerous problems.

> **zero population growth (ZPG)** a stable population level that occurs when each woman has no more than two children.
>
> **city** a geographic area where a large number of people live relatively permanently and secure their livelihood primarily through nonagricultural activities.
>
> **urbanization** population movement from rural to urban areas.

2 Urbanization

I f you've flown over the United States, you've probably noticed that people tend to cluster in and around cities. After sunset, some areas glow with lights, whereas others are engulfed in darkness. The average person, in the United States and worldwide, is more likely to live in a city than a rural area, and this trend is rising.

A **city** is a geographic area where a large number of people live relatively permanently and secure their livelihood primarily through nonagricultural activities. **Urbanization,** which increases the size of cities, is the movement of people from rural to urban areas. Most of this discussion focuses on U.S. cities, but let's begin with a brief look at urbanization globally.

URBANIZATION: A GLOBAL VIEW

In 2008, for the first time in history, a majority of the world's population lived in urban areas. By 2030, urban dwellers will make up roughly 60 percent of the world's

North Wind Picture Archives via AP Images

population (Population Reference Bureau 2007; United Nations Population Division 2008). Why is urbanization increasing? And where is most of it taking place?

Origin and Growth of Cities

Cities are one of the most striking features of modern life, but they have existed for centuries. About 7,000 years ago, for example, people built small cities in the Middle East and Latin America to protect themselves from attackers and to increase trade. By 1800, 56 cities in Western Europe had a population of 40,000 or more (Chandler and Fox 1974; Flanagan 1990; De Long and Shleifer 1992).

Before the Industrial Revolution, which began in the late eighteenth century, urban settlements in Europe, India, and China developed largely because people figured out how to use natural resources (such as mining coal) and transporting water efficiently for irrigation and consumption. The Industrial Revolution spurred ever-increasing numbers of people to move to cities in search of jobs, schooling, and improved living conditions. As a result, the urban population surged—from 3 percent of the world's population in 1800 to 14 percent in 1900 (Sjoberg 1960; Mumford 1961).

World Urbanization Trends

As industrialization advanced, urbanization increased. Between 1920 and 2007, the world's urban population increased from 270 million to 3.3 billion, and it is expected to rise to 9.4 billion by 2050. The pace of urbanization is most rapid in the less developed regions of the world, especially Asia, Africa, and Latin America (see *Table 16.2*). By 2050, most of the world's urban population will be concentrated in Asia and Africa (United Nations Population Division 2008).

Many of the world's largest cities are becoming megacities, metropolitan areas with at least 10 million inhabitants. In 1950, the three largest cities in the world were New York–Newark (12.3 million), Tokyo (11.3 million), and London (8.4 million). By 2025, there will be 27 megacities, but only two in North America (New York–Newark and Los Angeles) and one in Europe (Paris). Besides Tokyo—which will probably be the most populous city in the world, with nearly 36 million inhabitants in 2025—there will be 16 megacities in Asia, 4 in Latin America, and 3 in Africa, and most will be at least twice as large as those in North America and Europe (United Nations Population Division 2008).

Should the explosive growth of cities and megacities concern us? Generally, cities provide jobs, offer better health services, and have more educational opportunities, but not everyone benefits from such advantages. The urban poor are often crowded into slums, where children are less likely to be enrolled in school, there is inadequate

With a population of almost 17.1 million in 2010, Cairo, Egypt, is one of the world's largest cities. Cairo is the cultural center of the Arab world, but millions of Egyptians, including this fisherman, live in dire poverty and don't experience any of the city's cultural benefits. This man sleeps in his boat, makes tea from the water of the Nile River (which is infested with life-threatening parasites), often smiles and waves dutifully as tour boats motor up the river with tourists snapping his picture, and, on a good day, earns a few dollars (Slackman 2007).

© Shawn Baldwin/The New York Times/Redux Pictures

TABLE 16.2
Urbanization Around the World
Percentage of people living in urban areas

REGION	1950	2007	2025 (PROJECTED)
World	29	49	57
Africa	15	39	47
Asia	17	41	51
Latin America and the Caribbean	42	78	84
North America	64	81	86
Europe	51	72	76
Oceania	51	71	72

Source: Based on United Nations Population Division 2008, Table 1.

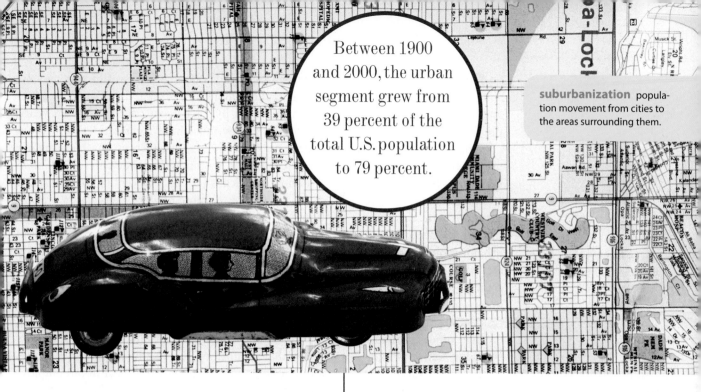

Between 1900 and 2000, the urban segment grew from 39 percent of the total U.S. population to 79 percent.

suburbanization population movement from cities to the areas surrounding them.

sanitation, and a widening economic gap exists between the haves and the have-nots (Cohen 2005).

URBANIZATION IN THE UNITED STATES

Like many other countries, the United States is becoming more urban. During the Industrial Revolution, millions of Americans in agricultural areas migrated to cities to find jobs. Thus, between 1900 and 2000, the U.S. rural population shrank from 61 percent to 21 percent of the total population, whereas the urban segment increased from 39 percent to 79 percent (Riche 2000; U.S. Census Bureau 2010).

Shifts in Urban and Rural Populations

Despite rapid population growth in parts of the South and West, 45 percent of all U.S. counties has lost population since 2000. Of the 1,346 counties that shrank in population between 2000 and 2007, 85 percent were rural. Many rural communities, particularly in the Midwest, have been losing inhabitants for decades and "are on the brink of extinction" (Mather 2008).

The fastest growing counties are located near large metropolitan areas, such as those around Atlanta, Chicago, Dal-las, Houston, Los Angeles, Miami, New York City, and Washington, D.C. Some of this growth is due to migration from rural communities as blacks and whites search for jobs with decent wages. Cities also attract Latinos who seek jobs in rapidly growing economic sectors such as the construction and service industries (see Chapter 12).

The Asian population continues to cluster in traditional immigrant magnet areas (Los Angeles, New York, and San Francisco), but large numbers are also moving to metropolitan areas in Illinois, Maryland, Virginia, and Wisconsin. Overall, a study of population makeup in metropolitan areas concluded that diversity is growing "at a pace that the nation has not seen for many decades" (Frey 2006: 21).

Suburbs and Exurbs

Another major factor in urban growth is **suburbanization,** population movement from cities to the areas surrounding them. When suburbs emerged during the 1930s, only the affluent could afford to commute between work in a congested and polluted city and a home in the tranquility and privacy of the countryside. During the 1950s, suburbs mushroomed, attracting two-thirds of urban dwellers. The federal government, fearful of a return to the economic depression of the 1930s, underwrote the construction of much new housing in the suburbs. The general public obtained low-interest mortgages, veterans were offered the added incentive of being able to purchase a home with a $1 down payment, and massive highway construction programs enabled commuting by car (Rothman 1978). More than 60 percent of Americans live in suburbs (Riche 2000), but, as you'll see shortly, there is still considerable racial and social class segregation in those areas.

Originally, most suburbs were bedroom communities from which commuters went daily to their jobs in the city. Over the last few decades, suburbanization has generated **edge cities,** business centers that are within or close to suburban residential areas and include offices, schools, shopping and entertainment, malls, hotels, and medical facilities. Examples of edge cities include Towson (Maryland), Framingham (Massachusetts), Cherry Hill (New Jersey), Durham-Raleigh (North Carolina), Cool Springs (Tennessee), and Las Colinas (Texas).

People have also created **exurbs,** areas of new development beyond the suburbs that are more rural but on the fringe of urbanized areas. Journalist A. C. Spectorsky introduced the concept in 1955, but it has become popular only recently because about 6 percent of Americans live in exurbs. The average exurbanite is white, a middle-income earner, married with children, a "super commuter" (one who travels two or more hours a day for work), and owns a large house outside of an expensive metropolitan suburb (Berube et al. 2006; Lalasz 2006).

Some Consequences of Urbanization and Suburbanization

Cities offer many benefits. Among other advantages, people can often walk, bicycle, or take a bus or subway to work; they are surrounded by a vast array of restaurants and shops; and they have easy access to numerous cultural activities (such as museums and theaters). Urbanization also creates problems, however, such as urban sprawl, increased traffic congestion, a scarcity of affordable housing, and racial segregation.

Urban sprawl—the rapid, unplanned, and uncontrolled spread of development into regions adjacent to cities—is widespread. Between 1995 and 2002, New Jersey, the nation's most densely populated state, lost 29 percent of its farmland, forests, wildlife habitats, and open recreational areas to urban sprawl (Lathrop and Hasse 2007).

In most cases, the only way to get around in urban sprawl areas is by automobile. This means that most

suburban households face the costs of buying, fueling, insuring, and maintaining several cars. The U.S. population increased by 23 percent over the last 25 years, but total highway miles have increased by only about 5 percent. One of the consequences has been greater traffic congestion within and outside cities. More than 3 million Americans (about 3 percent of workers) now travel 90 minutes or more to work every day, a proportion that has increased by 95 percent since 1990. Traffic snarls and long commutes increase air pollution and stress, and decrease the time that people have for family involvement and leisure pursuits (Sullivan 2007; U.S. Census Bureau 2010).

Urban sprawl has created rapid *job sprawl,* which occurs when companies move jobs from metropolitan areas to suburbs. The more distant the suburb, the less likely that minorities—especially African Americans and Latinos—and the poor are to hear about employment opportunities through informal networks, to afford houses in these areas, and to have transportation to the jobs (Kneebone 2009; Raphael and Stoll 2010).

In other cases, the poor are pushed out through **gentrification,** the process in which middle-class and affluent people buy and renovate houses and stores in downtown urban neighborhoods. Governments in many older cities (including Baltimore, Cincinnati, Detroit, Chicago, and New York City) encourage gentrification to increase dwindling populations, to revitalize urban areas, and to augment tax revenues. However, gentrification often adds to urban problems. For example, when the rent increases, it displaces low-income residents and small businesses.

Racial segregation is another urban and suburban problem. Gentrification displaces many low-income residents, but since the 1970s, some highly educated African Americans migrated to mostly white neighborhoods, whereas others established their own high-income communities, including suburbs (Bayer et al.

Gentrification improves old city neighborhoods and increases property values, but also displaces low-income residents.

FIGURE 16.4
Four Models of City Growth and Change

urban ecology the study of the relationships between people and urban environments.

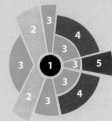
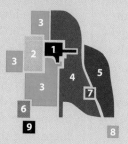
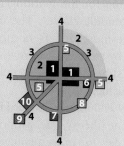

Concentric Zone Theory

1. Central business district
2. Zone in transition
3. Zone of workingmen's homes
4. Residential zone
5. Commuters' zone

Sector Theory

1. Central business district
2. Wholesale, light manufacturing
3. Lower-class residential
4. Middle-class residential
5. Upper-class residential

Multiple Nuclei Theory

1. Central business district
2. Wholesale, light manufacturing
3. Lower-class residential
4. Middle-class residential
5. Upper-class residential
6. Heavy manufacturing
7. Outlying business district
8. Residential suburb
9. Industrial suburb

Peripheral Theory

1. Central city
2. Suburban residential area
3. Circumferential highway
4. Radial highway
5. Shopping mall
6. Industrial district
7. Office park
8. Service center
9. Airport complex
10. Combined employment and shopping center

Sources: Based on Park and Burgess 1921, Hoyt 1939, Harris and Ullman 1945, and Harris 1997.

2005; Booza et al. 2006). Many middle- and upper-class minorities have housing options, but millions of people with low incomes are stuck in inner cities that often have high rents but few jobs that pay above a minimal wage because of job sprawl.

SOCIOLOGICAL EXPLANATIONS OF URBANIZATION

How and why do cities change? And how do these changes affect their populations? In answering these and other questions, functionalists provide insights into urban development, conflict theorists emphasize the impact of capitalism and big business, feminist scholars focus on gender roles and space, and symbolic interactionists examine the quality of city life (*Table 16.3* summarizes these perspectives).

Functionalism: How and Why Cities Change

In the 1920s and 1930s, sociologists at the University of Chicago developed theories of **urban ecology**, the study of the relationships between people and urban environments. Initially, these sociologists based their theories on Chicago, the city in which their university was located, but social scientists later revised the descriptions (see *Figure 16.4*).

Sociologists Robert Park and Ernest Burgess (1921) proposed *concentric zone theory* to explain the distribution of social groups within urban areas. According to this model, a city grows outward from a central point in a series of rings. The innermost ring, the central business district, is surrounded by a zone of transition, which contains industry and poor-quality

---

TABLE 16.3
Sociological Perspectives on Urbanization

PERSPECTIVE	LEVEL OF ANALYSIS	KEY POINTS
Functionalist	Macro	People create urban growth by moving to cities to find jobs and to suburbs to enhance their quality of life.
Conflict	Macro	Driven by greed and profit, large corporations, banks, developers, and other capitalistic groups determine the growth of cities and suburbs.
Feminist	Macro and Micro	Whether they live in cities or suburbs, women generally experience fewer choices and more constraints than do men.
Symbolic Interactionist	Micro	City people are more tolerant of different lifestyles, but they tend to interact superficially and are generally socially isolated.

housing. The third and fourth rings have housing for the working and middle classes. The outermost ring is occupied by people who live in the suburbs and commute daily to work in the central business district.

In developing *sector theory,* economist Homer Hoyt (1939) refined concentric zone theory. He proposed that cities, including Chicago, develop in sectors instead of rings. Pie-shaped wedges radiate from the central business district, their orientation depending on transportation routes (such as rail lines and highways) and various economic and social activities. Thus, some sectors are predominantly industrial, some contain stores and offices, and others, generally farther away from the central business district, are middle- and upper-class residential areas.

Geographers Chauncey Harris and Edward Ullman (1945) developed another influential model, *multiple-nuclei theory,* which proposed that a city contains more than one center around which activities revolve. For example, a "minicenter" often includes an outlying business district with stores and offices that are accessible to middle- and upper-class residential neighborhoods, whereas airports typically attract hotels and warehouses. Thus, heavy industry and high-income housing are rarely in the same part of the city.

As cities grew after World War II, these models no longer fit the changes that occurred in urban spaces. Thus, Chauncey Harris (1997) proposed a *peripheral theory* of urban growth, which emphasized the development of suburbs around a city but away from its center. According to this model, as suburbs and edge cities burgeon, highways that link the city's central business district to outlying areas and beltways that loop around the city provide relatively easy access to airports, the downtown, and surrounding areas.

Conflict Theory: The Impact of Capitalism and Big Business

Functionalists see urban growth as a reflection of people's choices. In contrast, new urban sociology, a perspective heavily influenced by conflict theory, views urban changes as being largely the result of decisions made by powerful capitalists and high-income groups. That is, economic and political factors and the rich, not ordinary citizens, determine urban growth or decline. For example, when a local government wants to rejuvenate parts of the inner city, it typically offers tax breaks, changes zoning laws, and allows real estate, construction, and banking industries to seek profits with little regard for the needs of low-income households or the homeless (Feagin and Parker 1990; Macionis and Parrillo 2007).

Conflict theorists see urban space as a commodity that is bought and sold for profit. It is not the average American, they argue, but bankers, corporate executives, developers, politicians, and influential businesspeople who determine how urban space is used. Increasing the value of some property is a higher priority than respecting community values, considering neighborhood needs, or maintaining a livable city. As a result, poor and low-income people are crowded into dilapidated neighborhoods (Logan and Molotch 1987; Gottdiener and Hutchison 2000).

Feminist Theories: Gender Roles, Space, and Safety

Feminist scholars agree with conflict theorists that many of the problems associated with urbanization reflect macro-level factors—such as the provision of federal funds to developers to build houses regardless of people's needs. However, feminist theories emphasize gender-

Electronics City, India's version of California's Silicon Valley, is an industrial park that spans more than 330 acres and houses more than a hundred businesses, such as Hewlett-Packard, Motorola, and Infosys, as well as a premier graduate school that focuses on information technology (Hamm 2007). If governments and corporations can find the capital to build such facilities, ask conflict theorists, why can't they provide affordable housing for people in surrounding neighborhoods?

related constraints. Whether they live in cities or suburbs, women generally experience more problems than men because living spaces are usually designed by men who have tended to ignore women's changing roles.

In cities, both sexes tend to live in small apartments, but poor women and minorities still have the least access to decent housing. Especially for low-income single mothers, child rearing is difficult because of unsatisfactory schools, few after-school programs, high crime rates, limited recreational facilities, and few safe public places such as parks.

Feminist geographers Mona Domosh and Joni Seager (2001) have observed that many women fear the city, especially urban public spaces such as streets, parks, and public transportation. They see these places as risky for their physical safety, despite the fact that most violence against women occurs at home. A few cities provide public transportation, such as minivans that operate seven nights a week, to prevent crimes against women, usually minorities, who must travel to work after 8:00 p.m. and return home before dawn. For the most part, however, such services are rare (Saegert and Winkel 1981; Hayden 2002).

In the suburbs, both women's and men's physical mobility is limited because of the scarcity of public transportation systems. Consequently, many suburban households have two or more cars, but women living in the suburbs usually experience greater problems than men. For example, there may be fewer job opportunities (especially if women have domestic responsibilities such as being at home when children return from school), and women often spend much of their time maintaining a single-family home, which decreases their time for educational or leisure activities (Cichocki 1981; Hayden 2002).

Symbolic Interactionism: How People Experience City Life

Symbolic interactionists are most interested in the impact of urban life on city residents. In a classic essay, sociologist Louis Wirth (1938: 14) described the city as a place where "our physical contacts are close, but our social contacts are distant."

Wirth defined the city as a large, dense, and socially and culturally diverse area. These characteristics produce *urbanism*, a way of life that differs from that of rural dwellers. Wirth saw urbanites as more tolerant of a variety of lifestyles, religious practices, and attitudes than residents of small towns or rural areas.

He also believed that urbanism has negative consequences, such as alienation, friction because of physical congestion, pursuit of self-interest, impersonal relationships, and a disintegration of kinship and friendship ties. Some studies have supported Wirth's theory of urbanism (see Guterman 1969), but others have challenged his views. According to a recent national study, for example, people living in large metropolitan areas scored higher than those living in small town and rural areas on characteristics such as physical and emotional health, access to basic necessities, and being satisfied with life (Witters 2010).

Critical Evaluation

Some functionalists use multiple nuclei theory and peripheral theory to describe some older industrial cities (such as Cleveland, New York, and Detroit), but patterns of urbanization have become more complex because of gentrification, edge cities, and exurbs. Another limitation, as conflict theorists point out, is that functionalists tend to overlook the negative political and economic impact, especially when profit and greed guide urban planning.

Both functionalist and conflict theories rarely take into account the changing composition of urban populations, especially the increase in the numbers of single mothers who have the least access to affordable housing. Another limitation of conflict theory is the assumption that residents are helpless victims as developers and corporations raze low-income houses. In fact, environmental groups have had considerable success in pushing through legislation to maintain and even increase open public spaces and build energy-saving homes in low-income neighborhoods (Moore 2008).

Recent feminist scholarship on urbanization has come primarily from historians, architects, and geographers, resulting in little sociological analysis. Feminist sociologists have made important contributions through studies of the everyday lives of low-income women, especially in central cities (see Chapter 12), but urbanization has received much less attention.

According to critics, urbanites are more diverse than some symbolic interactionists claim. People living in cities aren't necessarily more self-centered or isolated than those in small towns or rural areas. Instead, many have close family bonds, friends, and satisfying relationships with coworkers (Gans 1962; Crothers 1979; Wilson 1993). Especially since the advent of the Internet and cell phones, people living in cities are interacting with family more than ever before (see Chapter 5). For symbolic interactionists, people interpret and actively shape their urban environment. However, this perspective does not show how social, political, cultural,

ecosystem an area in which all forms of life live in relation to one another and a shared physical environment.

educational, religious, and economic factors shape urban inhabitants' experiences of city life (Hutter 2007).

You've seen that the world's population is growing rapidly and becoming more urbanized. Many scholars worry that population increases are permanently damaging the earth because people are changing the environment through their high consumption of food, energy, water, and land. Others dismiss such concerns as alarmist; they maintain that natural resources are replaceable and technology will solve environmental problems. What do the data tell us?

3 Environmental Issues

Consider the following:

- Most of us have at least 116 toxic chemicals in our bodies that did not exist in the environment (much less in humans) just 75 years ago ("Second National Report..." 2003).
- Every American now produces, on average, 5 pounds of garbage a day compared with 2.7 pounds a day in 1960 (U.S. Environmental Protection Agency 2009).
- Commercial logging—spurred by high U.S. demand for hardwoods such as teak, mahogany, and rosewood—destroys 50,000 species every year, including plants that produce life-saving Western medicines (Raintree Nutrition, Inc. 2008).
- Coastal counties comprise less than 25 percent of the land area of the United States but are home to more than 52 percent of the total population. Coastal development destroys wildlife habitat and degrades water quality (Bourne 2006).
- As many as 7 million Americans get sick every year from swimming in water contaminated with bacteria, viruses, or parasites that cause a wide range of diseases, including ear, nose, and eye infections; hepatitis; skin rashes; and respiratory illnesses (Natural Resources Defense Council 2007).

Such examples of environmental problems are important because every person on the planet is part of an **ecosystem,** an area in which all forms of life live in relation to one another and a shared physical environment. This means that plants, animals, and humans depend on each other for survival. Because the ecosys-

tem is interconnected worldwide, what happens in one country affects others. Let's look more closely at clean water, air pollution, and global warming—three interrelated environmental problems that are threatening the ecosystem in the United States and globally.

WATER

"By means of water," says the Qur'an, "we give life to everything." In 1746, Benjamin Franklin noted, "When the well is dry, we learn the worth of water." Indeed, water has an enormous impact on human life. More than 1 billion people worldwide don't have clean water, and water-related diseases cause 50 percent of illnesses and deaths worldwide every year (United Nations World Water. . . 2006).

The introduction of water filtration and chlorination in major U.S. cities between 1900 and 1940 was responsible for about 43 percent of the total decline in mortality over that period (Scommegna 2005). Few Americans die because of contaminated water, but as many as 19 million become sick each year because of the parasites, viruses, and bacteria in drinking water (Duhigg 2009b).

Nearly half the world's population still drinks contaminated water, and diarrheal diseases kill more than 3 million children every year (Water Quality & Health Council 2005). In some developing countries, families often spend up to 25 percent of their income to purchase water, and many women and children spend up to 6 hours per day carrying it home (United Nations Development Programme 2006).

In much of India, residents don't know when the next water delivery will arrive. They spend days waiting for, and often fighting over, the shipments.

Consumption and Availability

A United Nations report predicts that water will become the dominant global problem in this century because the world's demand for water has tripled over the last half century. Some refer to water as "blue gold" because it's becoming one of the earth's most precious and scarce commodities. Water shortages—rather than oil or diamonds—are behind conflicts and even wars in a number of countries. According to the Secretary-General of the United Nations, "Too often, where we need water, we find guns. . ." (World Water Assessment Programme 2009: 20). By 2050, about 7 billion people in 60 countries may experience water scarcity, with the worst shortages occurring in poor countries (United Nations World Water. . . 2006).

Industrialized nations not only have greater access to clean water than the developing world, they use more and pay less for it. The average person in the United States uses about 151 gallons of water per day (for drinking, cooking, bathing, flushing toilets, and watering a yard), compared with 101 gallons in Italy, 23 in China, and less than 3 in Mozambique. Among people living in industrialized countries, Americans pay the lowest rate for water ($2.49 a gallon), whereas Danes and Germans pay the most (almost $9.00 a gallon). In the developing world, people typically pay five times as much as Europeans (United Nations Development Programme 2006; Lavelle 2007). Thus, in many countries, clean water is a luxury rather than a basic human right.

Just 3 percent of the earth's water is fresh, and two-thirds of that water is locked up in the ground, glaciers, and ice caps. That leaves about 1 percent of freshwater for the world's almost 7 billion people (Schirber 2007).

Threats to Water Supplies

Precipitation (in the form of rain, snow, sleet, or hail) is the main source of water for the ecosystem. Clean water has been depleted for many reasons, including pollution, privatization, and mismanagement.

1. **Pollution.** Toxins from cities, factories, and farms are spoiling U.S. freshwater supplies. Every year, more than 860 billion gallons of sewage, pesticides, fertilizers, automotive chemicals, and trash enter the country's rivers (Gurwitt 2005).

   In 1972, Congress passed the Clean Water Act to eliminate water pollution. The Act has been violated more than 500,000 times since 2004 by more than 23,000 companies. About 60 percent of the polluters have been deemed in "significant noncompliance" because they dumped chemicals that can contribute to mental retardation and cancer. Fewer than 3 percent of the violations resulted in fines or other punishment by state officials (Duhigg 2009a).

   The 1974 Safe Water Drinking Act requires communities to deliver safe tap water to local residents. Since 2004, however, the water provided to more than 49 million Americans has contained illegal concentrations of chemicals (e.g., arsenic) or radioactive substances (e.g., uranium). Fewer than 6 percent of the violators were ever fined or punished by state or federal officials (Duhigg 2009b).

2. **Privatization.** Water is a big business because of *privatization*, transferring some or all of the assets or operations of public systems into private hands. Perrier, Evian, Coca-Cola, PepsiCo—and particularly the French giants Vivendi and Suez—have been buying the rights to extract water in the United States and other countries at will from aquifers (underground layers of rock that hold water), then bottling and selling it around the world.

   About 70 percent of Americans say they drink bottled water, almost 9 billion gallons in 2008 (Mui 2009). Bottling water is lucrative for corporations, but there are many environmental drawbacks. For example:

   - It depletes local water supplies, whether the water comes from municipal sources (40 percent) or local springs (60 percent) (Velasquez-Manoff 2009).

   - It takes 3 liters of water to produce 1 liter of bottled water (Food & Water Watch 2007).

   - About 86 percent of the empty plastic bottles in the United States clog landfills instead of being recycled (Food & Water Watch 2007).

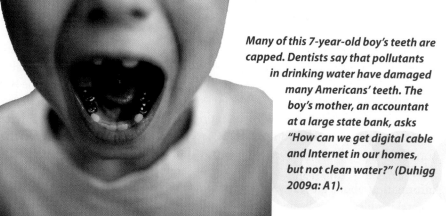

Many of this 7-year-old boy's teeth are capped. Dentists say that pollutants in drinking water have damaged many Americans' teeth. The boy's mother, an accountant at a large state bank, asks "How can we get digital cable and Internet in our homes, but not clean water?" (Duhigg 2009a: A1).

Damon Winter/The New York Times/Redux Pictures

3. **Mismanagement.** Most water pollution problems are due to human mismanagement, not nature. In China and India, for example, many government officials support economic growth and rarely punish local or international polluters who dump chemicals and waste into rivers and lakes (Carmichael 2007; Ford 2007).

Of all available water worldwide, agriculture consumes about 70 percent, industry uses 20 percent, and 10 percent is residential (World Water Assessment Programme 2009). In all cases, there's been considerable waste. In agriculture, many irrigation systems are inefficient, farmers often grow water-hungry crops (e.g., cotton and sugarcane) in arid areas, and use pesticides and chemical fertilizers that runoff from fields and pollute streams, rivers, and lakes. Some Americans are trying to conserve water, but they're probably a minority. For example, nearly 75 percent of residential water use in California—which has experienced numerous water emergencies—goes to outdoor purposes, mostly land-scaping (Goodale 2009; Clayton 2010).

In the United States, a significant water pipe bursts, on average, every 2 minutes somewhere in the country (Duhigg 2010). The Environmental and Protection Agency (EPA) estimates that it would cost from $17 billion to $23 billion per year for the next 20 years to replace the country's substandard sewage pipes, especially in cities along the eastern seaboard. Most of the pipes in those cities are nearly 200 years old, and some are made of wood. A water pipe that leaks or bursts wastes huge amounts of drinking water, damages streets and homes, and seeps dangerous pollutants into drinking water (American Rivers 2005; Lavelle 2007). Some environmentalists wonder why the federal government spent more than $700 billion to bail out bankers (see Chapter 12) but less than $2 billion a year to replace aging sewage pipes that affect millions of Americans.

AIR POLLUTION AND GLOBAL WARMING

In 2007, the Intergovernmental Panel on Climate Change, an international panel representing more than a thousand scientists, shared the Nobel Peace Prize with former Vice-President Al Gore (who narrated the documentary *An Inconvenient Truth*), for disseminating information about global warming, a critical environmental problem. Let's begin by looking at air pollution, the major cause of global warming.

Air Pollution: Some Sources and Causes

More than 188 hazardous air pollutants can have negative effects on human health or the environment ("Hazardous Air Pollution. . ." 2005). There are many sources and causes of air pollution, but four are among the most common. First, a major source of air pollution is the burning of *fossil fuels,* substances obtained from the earth, including coal, petroleum, and natural gas. The exhaust gases of cars, trucks, and buses contain poisons—sulfur dioxide, nitrogen oxide, carbon dioxide (CO_2), and carbon monoxide. Power plants that produce electricity by burning coal or oil also spew pollutants.

Second, manufacturing plants that produce consumer goods pour pollutants into the air. Formaldehyde-based vapors that can lead to cancer and respiratory problems are emitted by many household and personal care products: pressed wood (often used in furniture), permanent-press clothes, grocery bags, waxed paper, latex paints, detergents, nail polish, cosmetics, shampoos, bubble baths, and hair conditioners ("Formaldehyde" 2004).

Third, winds blow contaminants in the air across borders and oceans. For example, air pollution from Asia, especially China, has affected the air quality in the Sequoia and Kings Canyon national parks in California. Air pollution originating in Europe has been tracked to Asia, the Arctic, and the United States (Spotts 2004; Lamb 2009). Many of the smog-producing gases that come from Asia have also increased pollution in rural areas in the western United States where there is little industry or automobile traffic, increasing serious health problems such as asthma and premature death in people with heart or lung disease (Cooper et al. 2010).

Finally, government policies that affect air pollution vary from one administration to another. Between 2002 and 2006, for example, lawsuits by the Justice Department against polluters declined by 70 percent, and criminal and civil fines for polluting decreased by more than half, compared with the period from 1996 to 2000. The Bush administration blocked the efforts of 18 states to cut emissions from cars and trucks because it judged current standards good enough and believed that tougher regulations would hurt the U.S. economy (Environmental Integrity Project 2007; Pelton 2007; "No Action on Greenhouse Gases" 2008). The Obama administration has promised to decrease air pollution, but influential petroleum and coal companies have been lobbying "fast and furious" to defeat any future legislation that might decrease their profits (Broder and Mouawad 2009: A1; see also Morris 2009).

One of the most dangerous effects of air pollution is climate change, especially global warming. As air pollution increases, it disrupts Earth's temperature and, as a result, the global ecosystem.

Global Warming and the Greenhouse Effect

Global warming is an increase in the average temperature of Earth's atmosphere. The warming has resulted from numerous factors. Some are natural, such as changes in solar radiation, the Earth's orbit, and the frequency or intensity of volcanic activity. Most of the factors underlying global warming, however, are due to human industrial activity (Intergovernmental Panel on Climate Change 2007).

Global warming begins with the **greenhouse effect,** the heating of Earth's atmosphere because of the presence of certain atmospheric gases. Heat from the Sun passes into the atmosphere: Some of it is absorbed by Earth's surface, and some of it is reflected back to space. The presence of greenhouse gases in the atmosphere traps some of this heat. Heat is necessary to support life, but when greenhouse gases increase in the atmosphere, Earth becomes warmer than it would be otherwise, and endangers public health and the welfare of current and future generations (Fagan 2008; U.S. Environmental Protection Agency 2009).

Air pollutants, especially CO_2, ignite the greenhouse effect. Every year, humans release at least 1 billion tons

In 2007, the prestigious American Institute of Architects chose a Seattle branch of a public library as one of its "Top Ten Green Projects." The library has 4 inches of soil planted with native grasses and succulent ground covers designed to absorb and filter rainwater, remove CO_2 from the atmosphere, and insulate the building in both summer and winter. The roof also lasts longer than a traditional hard roof (Adler 2007).

of CO_2 into the atmosphere, primarily from coal-fired power plants. In mid-2007, the United States, which has only 5 percent of the world's population, was responsible for 25 percent of all CO_2 emissions. Since then, China's CO_2 emissions have exceeded those of the United States by 8 percent (Netherlands Environmental Assessment Agency 2007).

A few years after the influential Intergovernmental Panel on Climate Change report was published, some questions arose, especially among skeptics, about the panel's accuracy in describing global warming (Rosenthal 2010). Because of these or other reasons, the percentage of Americans who said that the seriousness of global warming was exaggerated increased from 33 percent in 2007 to 48 percent in 2010 (Newport 2010). Despite doubts about global warming, 55 percent of Americans believe that the United States should curb its CO_2 emissions, regardless of what other countries do (Eilperin 2009).

Some Effects of Climate Change

Climate change is a change of overall temperatures and weather conditions over time. Since such record keeping began in 1850, the years 1995 to 2006 have been the warmest. Some scientists argue that global warming began thousands of years ago when "humans began changing the planet [by] clearing land to grow food by cutting down and burning forests" (Fischman 2009: B11). Such *deforestation,* clearing massive amounts of forests, affects global climate changes because forests recycle carbon dioxide into oxygen.

According to many scientists, changes have already occurred because of global warming and climate change. For example:

- Higher CO_2 levels are turning oceans more acidic, resulting in some shellfish (e.g., clams and crabs) dying or not developing (Spotts 2009).

- In Syria, more than 800,000 people have lost their livelihoods and had to abandon their homes because of a 4-year dry spell, increased by climate change, and can't afford rising food prices (Akkad 2009).

- On Alaska's coasts, ice shelves that acted as shields against storms and tidal forces are melting. As waters advance 80 feet a year because of coastal erosion, more than 180 Alaskan villages are in danger of be-

global warming the increase in the average temperature of Earth's atmosphere.

greenhouse effect the heating of Earth's atmosphere because of the presence of certain atmospheric gases.

climate change a change of overall temperatures and weather conditions over time.

vertical
Photo courtesy of American Hydrotech, Inc.

ing engulfed unless they relocate (Tizon 2008).

• In the United States, climate-related changes have resulted in heavy downpours and floods in some states, drought in others, alterations in river flows (that affect agriculture), and harmful health effects on people because of heat stress and poor air quality (Karl et al. 2009).

Such data suggest that our planet is ailing. Nonetheless, many individuals and groups are hoping to change the situation, in the United States and globally, by better environmental policies and practices. One such endeavor is sustainable development.

IS SUSTAINABLE DEVELOPMENT POSSIBLE?

Sustainable development refers to economic activities that meet the needs of the present without threatening the environmental legacy of future generations. Is there an inherent contradiction between "sustainable" and "development"? There are reasons to be both pessimistic and optimistic about achieving sustainable development.

Reasons to Be Pessimistic

Which country is the greenest? A recent study of environmental performance ranked 149 countries on factors such as maintaining and improving air and water quality, cooperating with other countries on environmental problems, overfishing, and emitting greenhouse gases. Switzerland, Sweden, Norway, Finland, and Costa Rica were the top five. The United States ranked 39th, well below a number of developing countries, including Slovakia and Albania (Esty et al. 2008).

Why, compared with other industrialized and even some developing countries, does the United States rank so low in environmental performance? There are many reasons, but two may be especially important. First, lawmakers often accommodate business. During 2006 and 2007, for instance, oil and utilities industries were successful in pressuring Congress to drop laws that would have required them to provide renewable energy sources (such as wind and solar) and to pay $13 billion more in taxes for using only fossil fuels (Broder 2007; see also Chapter 11 on the close ties between the government and corporations).

Second, environmental issues are a low priority for some administrations. Since 2000, for example, the

Most Americans want fluffy and ultra-plush toilet paper. Environmentalists complain that such products are a menace because they're made by chopping down and grinding up the pulp of trees that are decades or even a century old, a threat to the world's trees. Big U.S. toilet-paper makers say that they've introduced "Earth-friendly" toilet paper, but "customers are unwavering in their desire for the softest paper possible" (Fahrenthold 2009: A1).

EPA hasn't enforced many environmental laws because of funding cuts, which resulted in the agency's having fewer staff members to investigate polluters and to apply penalties (Stephenson 2007). And some environmentalists are especially dismayed by *greenwashers*, companies and other organizations that pollute the planet while presenting an environmentally responsible public image (Elgin 2008).

Reasons to Be Optimistic

Is there hope for the environment? There has been some progress since 1970, when the United States implemented and celebrated its first Earth Day: Most cars no longer burn leaded gasoline; ozone-destroying chlorofluorocarbons (CFCs) have been generally phased out; and total emissions of the six major air pollutants declined by 54 percent during the same period as the U.S. population increased by 47 percent (Hayward and Kaleita 2007; Sperry 2008). And since 2005, there has been an explosion of interest in improving the environment.

Unlike the federal government, many companies are finding that being green is good for their profits and image, as well as the environment. For example, Wal-Mart has slashed its electricity usage by 17 percent since 2002 by switching to more efficient lightbulbs and adding skylights to its stores for natural light (Carey 2007).

And Johnson & Johnson, the world's largest manufacturer of health care products, now relies on renewable energy sources, such as wind and solar, for 30 percent of its electricity (Cohn 2007).

How much are Americans willing to sacrifice for a cleaner environment? Recent surveys show that Americans today are no more environmentally friendly than they were in 2000. For example, 90 percent say that they recycle paper, glass, aluminum, or other items. However, only 38 percent say that protecting the environment should be as important as economic growth, down from 71 percent in 1991 (Morales 2010; Saad 2010). Americans also say that they want cleaner energy, but most oppose wind farms, for example, because the 40-foot windmills would "disturb our views of the landscape" (Dunlap 2007). Thus, are Americans eco-friendly only when it's convenient?

Are Americans eco-friendly only when it's convenient?

Many groups are contributing to sustainable development. In the Netherlands, an oil refinery owned by Shell (one of Europe's largest corporations responsible for emitting tons of CO$_2$ into the air) pipes CO$_2$ gas into greenhouses. The CO$_2$ bolsters rose growers' crops and decreases the refinery's emission of greenhouse gases (left). In Vermont, a dairy farmer sells "poop power" by converting cow manure to electricity (right). Consumers pay about 4 percent more for the electricity, but the manure is abundant and endlessly renewable, and its conversion to power decreases air pollution and practically eliminates the smell of cow dung in rural areas (Moore 2006).

Herman Wouters/The New York Times/Redux Pictures

AP Photo/Alden Pellett, File

Every society

experiences change.

17 Social Change: Collective Behavior, Social Movements, and Technology

Key Topics

In this chapter, we'll explore the following topics:

1 Collective Behavior

2 Social Movements

3 Technology and Social Change

what do you think?

Facebook and similar networking sites do more harm than good.

1   2   3   4   5   6   7
strongly agree   strongly disagree

For the most part, as you've seen throughout this textbook, sociologists examine behavior and social processes that are relatively institutionalized, routine, stable, and highly predictable. This chapter examines **social change**, the transformations of societies and social institutions over time. Some collective behavior is short-lived with few long-term changes; others, particularly social movements, can have lasting effects. Technology has also played a critical role in sparking social change. Let's begin with the concept of collective behavior.

> **social change** the transformations of societies and social institutions over time.
>
> **collective behavior** the spontaneous and unstructured behavior of a large number of people.

1 Collective Behavior

do you have several boxes crammed with collectibles such as Barbie dolls or baseball cards? A tattoo? Ever signed a petition? Joined a club? Posted on Facebook or sent text messages? If so, you've engaged in collective behavior.

WHAT IS COLLECTIVE BEHAVIOR?

Collective behavior is the spontaneous and unstructured behavior of a large number of people. Collective behavior encompasses a wide range of actions, including riots, fads, fashion, panic, rumors, and responses to disasters.

Sociologists emphasize two important characteristics of collective behavior. First, it is an act rather than a state of mind. For example, you may *feel* panic when a hurricane threatens your town, but you don't engage in collective behavior until you actually *leave* your home and head for a safer location.

Second, collective behavior varies in its degree of spontaneity and structure. The residents of New Orleans who jammed highways to escape Hurricane Katrina demonstrated the least structured form of collective behavior, which came close to panic and was short-lived. Fads—like collecting baseball cards—are more structured. They may last several years, and many people carefully wrap and store their collectibles hoping to make money in the future. Other forms of collective behavior—such as pro- and anti-abortion groups—become highly institutionalized social movements that involve a staff, budget, and lobbying.

WHEN DOES COLLECTIVE BEHAVIOR OCCUR?

One of the biggest media stories in 2005 involved Cindy Sheehan. Her 24-year-old son and six other soldiers were killed in Sadr City in 2004, almost a year after President Bush had declared the end of major

In 2005, groups such as the Gold Star Families for Peace and the Vietnam Veterans for Peace supported Cindy Sheehan's protest of the Iraq war by pitching tents in front of President George W. Bush's ranch in Crawford, Texas.

combat operations in Iraq. Sheehan pitched a tent near the president's ranch in Crawford, Texas, protesting the continuing war and demanding a face-to-face meeting with the president, but he refused to do so.

Sheehan's stance elicited widespread national and international coverage. Gold Star Families for Peace, a coalition of military families whose relatives died in the war, aired a television ad in which Sheehan accused the president of dishonesty about the weapons of mass destruction: "You lied to us and because of your lies, my son died" (Madigan 2005: 1D). Some situations, such as Sheehan's, are more likely to encourage collective behavior than others. Why?

Structural Strain Theory

According to sociologist Neil Smelser (1962), there are six macro-level conditions that encourage or discourage collective behavior. Smelser described these conditions as "value-added." That is, each condition leads to the next one, ending in an episode of collective behavior.

1. **Structural conduciveness.** Structural conduciveness consists of social conditions that allow a particular kind of collective behavior to occur. When channels for expressing a grievance either are not available or fail, for instance, like-minded people may resort to protests to voice their complaint. In Sheehan's case, the families who lost members in the Iraq war supported Sheehan because they felt that the Bush administration was insensitive to their personal losses.

2. **Structural strain.** Structural strain occurs when an important aspect of a social system is seen as discriminatory or unjust, creates problems, or interferes with people's everyday lives. Many of the families that sided with Sheehan, for example, did so because they believed that the administration, by not moving to end the war in Iraq, increased the number of U.S. casualties.

3. **Growth and spread of a generalized belief.** In the course of social interaction, people begin to see a situation as a widespread problem instead of just a personal experience. Along with this generalized belief that there is a problem is a general recognition that something should be done about it. In the Sheehan case, many mothers, especially, supported Sheehan and were the most vocal leaders of a number of antiwar protests because they felt that their children were dying "for nothing" (Bumiller 2005).

4. **Precipitating factors.** Some incident or behavior triggers an event and inspires action. Sheehan's pitching a tent outside of President Bush's ranch spurred many other antiwar advocates to support her accusations on radio talk shows and in letters to the editor.

AP Photo/J. Scott Applewhite

5. **Mobilizing people for action.** Mobilization often requires leaders who encourage agitation to change the status quo. Sheehan was the leader in agitating for peace in Iraq, but antiwar groups supported her efforts through television ads.

6. **Social control.** In this stage, opposing groups may try to prevent, interrupt, or repress those advocating social change. Government officials, the police, community and business leaders, courts, the mass media, and other social control agents—all of whom benefit from the status quo—may quash, ridicule, or challenge the emerging collective behavior. In Sheehan's case, the administration and right-wing political commentators on television and radio dismissed Sheehan as a "crackpot" and described her protests as "treasonous" (Madigan 2005).

Critical Evaluation

Smelser's model contributed to an understanding of the emergence and development of collective behavior by helping to predict when and where episodes of such behavior might break out, and providing insights on why, at every stage, collective behavior may either fade or escalate (Locher 2002). If, for instance, the president had met with Sheehan to discuss the general anxiety surrounding the war (reducing structural strain), the initial criticisms of his administration would probably have died down (halting the spread of a generalized belief), and the antiwar groups would not have run the television ads (limiting the mobilization of participants).

Smelser's model doesn't explain all forms of collective behavior, however. With fads and rumors, as you'll see shortly, all six stages don't necessarily occur. A second criticism is that the sequence of the stages is not necessarily the same as Smelser outlined (Berk 1974).

A third criticism is that the determinants don't always spark collective behavior. For example, many groups—such as college students who complain about the price of textbooks and tuition costs—experience structural strain and are free to protest and mobilize, but rarely engage in collective behavior to change a situation that they complain about.

VARIETIES OF COLLECTIVE BEHAVIOR

There are many types of collective behavior; some are more fleeting or harmful than others (Turner and Killian 1987). Let's begin by looking at some of the most common types—rumors, gossip, and urban legends.

Rumors, Gossip, and Urban Legends

> **rumor** unfounded information that people spread quickly.

There were widespread rumors that on January 1, 2000, a glitch (Y2K) in operating systems would cause computers around the world to crash, leading to global power outages, banks losing all of their customers' statements, and even airplanes falling from the skies. None of this occurred.

A **rumor** is unfounded information that people spread quickly. Through modern communication technology, a rumor can spread to millions of people over the Internet within seconds, especially when the subject line says something like "THIS IS REALLY TRUE!" Rumors can incite riots, panic, or widespread anxiety. Because of the Y2K rumor, thousands of people built underground shelters, and millions of others stocked up on bottled water, canned food, batteries, and medical supplies.

Most rumors (that rock stars Elvis Presley and John Lennon are alive, for example) are harmless. Others can wreak considerable damage. After a patron in northern California claimed that she found part of a human finger in her cup of Wendy's beef chili, the restaurant's business dropped by half nationally and rumors warning people to stop eating fast-food altogether spread over the Internet (Richtel and Barrionuevo 2005). Ultimately, the woman admitted that she had planted the finger to try to get a lucrative settlement. However, rumors can have a long life, as evidenced by customers who are still leery about eating at fast-food restaurants.

Rumors are typically false, so why do so many people believe them? First, rumors often deal with an important

During the recently proposed healthcare reform, many opponents spread the rumor that the new bill would result in "death panels" that would deny care to older people and children born with birth defects. Neither was true (Snow et al. 2009).

AP Photo/Coeur d'Alene Press, Jerome A. Pollos

subject about which—especially during uncertain economic times or natural disasters—people are anxious, insecure, or stressed. This makes people especially suggestible. In Hurricane Katrina's aftermath, for example, the media reported numerous rumors of carjacking, murders, thefts, and rapes, the overwhelming majority of which subsequently proved to be false. Second, there is often little factual information to counter a rumor, or people distrust the sources of such information. During Y2K, the people who stockpiled groceries and so forth didn't believe computer scientists or federal officials who said that there would not be a major calamity on January 1, 2000. Third, rumors offer entertainment, diversion, and drama in otherwise mundane daily lives (Turner and Killian 1987; Marx and McAdam 1994; Campion-Vincent 2005; Heath 2005).

There are two types of rumors: gossip and urban legends. **Gossip** is the act of spreading rumors, often negative, about other people's personal lives. Someone once said that "no one gossips about other people's virtues." Because of its tendency to be derogatory, gossip makes us feel superior ("Did you know that Margie just had breast implants? Isn't she pathetic?"). Some Web sites (such as www.campusgossip.com) urge visitors to post gossip because the comments are always "100% anonymous." Sometimes, people gossip to control other people's behavior and to reinforce a community's moral standards. For example, comments about someone's drug abuse or marital infidelity reinforce notions of what's deviant or unacceptable (see Chapter 4). In other cases, people gossip because they resent or envy someone's success or accomplishments, or because the gossip reinforces what people think they already know (Sunstein 2009).

Another form of rumor is **urban legends** (also called *contemporary legends* and *modern legends*), stories—funny, horrifying, or just odd—that supposedly happened somewhere. Some of the most common and enduring urban legends, but with updated variations, deal with food contamination, such as the finger at Wendy's. Others have targeted politicians. We still hear, for example, false allegations that George W. Bush had the lowest IQ of all presidents of the past 50 years, and that President Obama is a radical Muslim who refuses to recite the Pledge of Allegiance.

Why do urban legends persist much longer than gossip? First, they reflect contemporary anxieties and fears—about contaminated food, unscrupulous companies, and corrupt and unresponsive governments. Second, urban legends are cautionary tales that warn us to watch out in a dangerous world. For example, there have been tales that sunscreens cause blindness, that Mountain Dew (a soft drink) decreases sperm count, and that women have died sniffing perfume samples sent to them in the mail. Third, we tend to believe urban legends because we hear them from people we trust—family members, coworkers, and friends. Finally, urban legends—such as the one about alligators living in New York City's sewage system—are fun to tell and "too beguiling to fade away" (Kapferer 1992; Brunvand 2001; Ellis 2005).

Panic and Mass Hysteria

In 2003, an indoor fireworks display meant to kick off a heavy metal concert in West Warwick, Rhode Island, set off a fire that killed 100 people and injured 200 others. Panic ensued as thick black smoke poured through the audience and hundreds of patrons stampeded for the front door (even though there were three other exits), trampling and crushing those who had fallen beneath them.

Most of the deaths in West Warwick were due not to the fire, but to **panic,** a collective flight, typically irratio-

BETTY CROCKER MAKEOVER

1936 **1955** **1965** **1968**

1972 **1980** **1986** **1996**

In 1921, General Mills created Betty Crocker, a fictitious woman, to answer thousands of questions about baking that came in from consumers every year. As fashions and hairstyles changed, so did Betty Crocker's image. The original image of a stern, gray-haired older woman has morphed over the years so that, by 1996, she had a darker complexion and was dressed in casual attire. Can you think of other brands that have changed their image over the years to keep up with changing trends?

nal, from a real or perceived danger. The danger seems so overwhelming that people desperately jam an escape route, jump from high buildings, leap from a sinking ship, or sell off their stock. Fear drives panic: "Each person's concern is with his [or her] own safety and personal security, whether the danger is physical, psychological, social, or financial" (Lang and Lang 1961: 83).

Panic can result in hundreds or thousands of casualties, but it's a relatively rare type of collective behavior (Smelser 1962). Most people try to rescue loved ones rather than fleeing a dangerous situation (such as a flood or hurricane), and many leave a life-threatening situation in an orderly fashion (as in the World Trade Center on 9/11).

Panic is similar to **mass hysteria,** an intense, fearful, and anxious reaction to a real or imagined threat by large numbers of people. A recent example of mass hysteria is the scare over the H1N1 flu ("swine flu"). In mid-2009, the World Health Organization issued an alert that H1N1 would become a pandemic (worldwide

epidemic) and result in the death of otherwise healthy people. Millions of Americans stood in line for hours, sometimes

> **mass hysteria** an intense, fearful, and anxious reaction to a real or imagined threat by large numbers of people.
>
> **fashion** a standard of appearance that enjoys widespread but temporary acceptance within a society.

overnight, because the vaccine was initially in short supply, but the swine flu never materialized on the scale that was predicted (Witters 2010).

Unlike panic, which usually subsides quickly, mass hysteria may last longer. Alarms similar to that in response to the swine flu will probably continue to occur in the future because urban legends—especially about health and food—reinforce our general fears and anxieties about life's dangers.

Fashions, Fads, and Crazes

Fashions, fads, and crazes are three more kinds of collective behavior that encompass broad geographical areas and involve large numbers of people. Of the three, fashion is the most structured and changes most slowly.

A **fashion** is a standard of appearance that enjoys widespread but temporary acceptance within a society. Whether they last for years or change after a few months, fashions are highly institutionalized products and styles that are popular among a large number of people (Smelser 1962; Blumer 1969). For example, African American women's hairstyles have changed—from Afros in the late 1960s, to straightened hair during the 1980s, to braids, cornrows, dreadlocks, hair extensions, and coloring more recently—to reflect gender politics, racial solidarity, generational differences, power, identity, and images of beauty (Banks 2000; Desmond-Harris 2009).

Fashion also involves periodic changes in the popularity of clothes, architecture, furniture, music, language usage, books, automobiles, sports, recreational activities, the names parents give their children, and even the dogs that people own. Teenagers who want to be fashionable buy clothes with prominent labels such as American Eagle, Hollister, Sean John, Abercrombie and Fitch, and Under Armour, but what's fashionable changes from year to year.

Why do fashions, especially in clothes, change fairly quickly? One reason is that designers, manufacturers,

fad a form of collective behavior that spreads rapidly and enthusiastically but lasts only a short time.

craze a fad that becomes an all-consuming passion for many people for a short time.

and retailers must continuously create demand for new fashions to maintain their profits. Second, many people keep up with fashion because they don't want to seem different or they fear being perceived as out-of-date or dowdy. Third, shopping for new clothes and other products decreases the boredom of everyday routine. Also, clothes and other products are status symbols that signal being an insider: "Others. . . will admire me for being the kind of person who makes stylish choices" (Best 2006: 85–86; for classic analyses of fashion and collective behavior, see Veblen 1899/1953; Barber and Lobel 1952; Packard 1959; and Bourdieu 1984).

A **fad** is a form of collective behavior that spreads rapidly and enthusiastically but lasts only a short time (Turner and Killian 1987; Lofland 1993). Fads that have arisen and faded fairly quickly include *products* (such as the Rubik's cube, bean bag chairs, and Crocs), *activities* (such as disco dancing and a variety of diets, including Atkins and South Beach), and widespread enthusiasm for *popular personalities and television characters* (such as the Lone Ranger during the 1950s, and more recently, Britney Spears and the Backstreet Boys).

Why do fads sprout? A major reason is profit. Because children and adolescents are especially likely to adopt fads, manufacturers create numerous products and activities that they hope will catch on. Many of these products include toys, sportswear, and new cereals. The hottest fads are usually the must-have Christmas toys that children plead for (such as Cabbage Patch dolls, PlayStation, and Zhu Zhu pets). When such a fad arises, parents may stand in line for hours, drive to nearby cities, and scour the Internet to get the product. A few months later, the toy may be thrown away or stuffed in the back of a closet.

Some people dismiss fads as "ridiculous" or "silly," but they serve several functions. In a mass society, where people often feel anonymous, a fad can develop strong in-group feelings and a sense of belonging, especially among people who share similar interests and attitudes. Fads can also be fun, promise to resolve a nagging problem (such as being overweight), and help us keep up with technological changes (Marx and McAdam 1994; Best 2006).

> Crazes involving ways to make easy money are most common in capitalistic societies.

Most fads are soon forgotten, but some become established. For example, Pez candy dispensers, which originated in 1952 and cost 49 cents, are still inexpensive (about $1.49), are sold in more than 60 countries, and have been continuously updated to include popular television characters such as the Simpsons (Paul 2002). Other fads, such as streaking (running around nude in public places), reemerge from time to time. Streaking appeared on some college campuses during the early 1970s and may have been a way of releasing stress during the Vietnam War. After dying down for a time, it made a comeback during the late 1990s ("Streaking" 2005).

Some fads are **crazes,** forms of collective behavior that become all-consuming passions for a short time. The Beanie Babies fad of the late 1990s turned into a craze. After an entrepreneur published a highly successful magazine on these stuffed toys, there was a mad rush to buy them. The creator limited the sales in many stores to generate demand and retired earlier models to make them more sought after by collectors. The strategies worked and the entrepreneur became one of richest people on Earth. What about the collectors? According to an owner of a large toy store, "[Beanie Babies] make great insulation if you stick them in the walls" (Mulligan 2004: 3C).

Crazes involving ways to make easy money are most common in capitalistic societies where many people want to make as much money as possible and as quickly as possible. Such crazes often involve investments in high-risk ventures. The problem with economic crazes is that they may end quite suddenly and with very disappointing results, as we saw during the recent home mortgage boom and collapse. Ten years earlier, most of the fast-growing dot-com businesses collapsed after 2000. Investors' portfolios fell by as much as 50 percent, thousands of workers were laid off, and almost all of the "hot" Internet sites disappeared nearly overnight (van Ginneken 2003; McCarthy 2004).

Disasters

Whereas people choose to participate in fashion, fads, and crazes, a **disaster** is an unexpected event that causes widespread damage, destruction, distress, and loss. Some disasters are due to *social causes,* such as war, genocide, terrorist attacks, and civil strife. Some are due to *technological causes,* including oil spills, nuclear accidents, burst dams, building collapses, and mine explosions. Others are the result of *natural causes,* such as fires, floods, landslides, earthquakes, hurricanes, tsunamis, and volcanic eruptions (Marx and McAdam 1994).

Resulting in an estimated 1,800 deaths, Hurricane Katrina was one of the worst natural disasters that occurred in the United States. The number of casualties was small, however, compared with many other natural disasters around the world. For example, floods in China killed an estimated 4 million people in 1931 and 2 million in 1959 (Crossley 2008).

Disasters often inspire organized behavior rather than chaos. Instead of panicking, most people are rational, cooperative, and altruistic. They often care for family members instead of fleeing, for example, and thousands of volunteers offer financial, medical, and other help. Days before the federal government responded to the Hurricane Katrina disaster, numerous individuals and organizations set up Web sites that offered the evacuees jobs and housing (Noguchi 2005).

Publics, Public Opinion, and Propaganda

A **public** is a collection of people, not necessarily in direct contact with each other, who are interested in a particular issue. A public is not the same as the general public, which consists of everyone in a society.

There are as many publics as there are issues—abortion, education, gun control, pollution, health care, and gay marriage, to name just a few. Even within one organization or institution, there may be several publics that are concerned about entirely different issues. At a college, for instance, students may be most concerned about the cost of tuition, faculty may spend much time discussing instructional technology, and maintenance employees may be most interested in wages.

In most cases, the interaction within a public is carried on indirectly through the mass media (newspapers, books, radio, television, and motion pictures), social media (online), newsletters, or professional journals. Because publics aren't organized groups with memberships, they're often transitory. Publics expand or contract as people lose or develop interest in an issue. For example, a public may surge during a highly publicized and controversial incident, such as removing a patient's life support, but then evaporate quickly. In some cases, however, publics organize and become enduring social movements (a topic we'll examine shortly).

Some publics express themselves through **public opinion,** widespread attitudes on a particular issue. Public opinion has three components: It (1) is a verbalization rather than an action, (2) it is about a matter that is of concern to many people, and (3) it involves a controversial issue (Turner and Killian 1987). Like pub-

disaster an unexpected event that causes widespread damage, destruction, distress, and loss.

public a collection of people, not necessarily in direct contact with each other, who are interested in a particular issue.

public opinion widespread attitudes on a particular issue.

Copyright by Leslie-Judge Co., N.Y./Library of Congress

Propaganda tries to influence people's attitudes and behavior. One of the best-known examples of propaganda in the United States is this Uncle Sam poster, designed in 1917 and used to recruit soldiers for World Wars I and II. Opponents of the Vietnam War used it as an anti-war poster during the 1960s and 1970s.

propaganda the presentation of information to influence people's opinions or actions.

crowd a temporary gathering of people who share a common interest or participate in a particular event.

lics, public opinions wax and wane over time. People's interest in crime and education, for example, decreases when they are more concerned about pressing events such as an economic crisis.

Public opinion can be swayed through **propaganda,** the presentation of information to influence people's opinions or actions. Propaganda isn't a type of collective behavior, but it affects collective behavior in several important ways. First, it may create attitudes that will inspire collective outbursts such as strikes or riots. Second, propaganda may be used to try to prevent collective outbursts, as when corporations try to convince employees that the loss of jobs is due to the economy rather than to offshoring (see Chapter 12). Third, propaganda is often used to try to gain adherents for a cause, whatever it might be (Smelser 1962).

Propaganda is institutionalized in advertising, political campaign literature, and government policies. It is conveyed to people in many ways: the mass media, social media, political speeches, religious groups, rumor, and symbols (such as flags). Much propaganda presents misinformation intended to sway an audience toward a particular viewpoint, but propaganda isn't necessarily good or bad. Instead, it's a means of influencing people.

Crowds

Much collective behavior is scattered geographically, but crowds are concentrated in a limited physical space. After Pope John Paul II died in 2005, more than 4 million people viewed his body at St. Peter's Basilica in Rome, one of the largest religious gatherings in the history of Christianity. This is an example of a **crowd,** a temporary gathering of people who share a common interest or participate in a particular event. Regardless of size—whether it's a few dozen people or millions—crowds come together for a specific reason, such as a religious leader's death, a concert, or a riot.

Crowds differ in their motives, interests, and emotional level:

- A *casual crowd* is a loose collection of people who have little in common except for being in the same place at the same time and participating in a common activity or event. There is little, if any, interaction, the gathering is temporary, and there is little emotion. Examples include people watching a street performer, spectators at the scene of a fire, and shoppers at a busy mall.

- A *conventional crowd* is a group of people that assembles for a specific purpose and follows established norms. Unlike casual crowds, conventional crowds are structured; their members may interact, and they conform to rules that are appropriate for the situation. Examples include people attending religious services, funerals, graduation ceremonies, and parades.

- An *expressive crowd* is a group of people who exhibit strong emotions toward some object or event. The feelings—which can range from joy to grief—pour out freely as the crowd reacts to a stimulus. Examples include attendees at religious revivals, revelers during Mardi Gras, and enthusiastic fans at a football game.

- An *acting crowd* is a group of people who are motivated by intense, powerful emotions and have a single-minded purpose. The event may be planned, but acting crowds can also involve spontaneous demonstrations or other focused group behavior. Examples of acting crowds include people fleeing a burning building, soccer fans storming a field, and students engaged in water balloon fights.

- A *protest crowd* is a group of people who assemble in public to achieve a specific goal. Protest crowds demonstrate their support of or opposition to an idea or event. Most demonstrations—such as anti-war protests, civil rights marches, boycotts, and labor strikes—are usually peaceful. Peaceful protesters can become aggressive, however, resulting in destruction and violence (Blumer 1946; McPhail and Wohlstein 1983).

In 2006 and 2010, hundreds of thousands of Latinos and their supporters participated in demonstrations and rallies in Washington, D.C. and other cities, calling on Congress to offer citizenship to illegal immigrants. Is this kind of collective behavior an example of an expressive, acting, or protest crowd?

One type of crowd can easily change into another. A conventional crowd at a nightclub can turn into an acting crowd if a fire causes people to panic and flee for safety. Indeed, any of the five types of crowds—from casual to protest—can become a mob or a riot.

Mobs

A **mob** is a highly emotional and disorderly crowd that uses force or violence against a specific target. The target can be a person, a group, or a property. In the Oakland neighborhood of Chicago, a van veered off the street and struck a group of people sitting on a stoop of a home. Seven male spectators, ranging in age from 16 to 47, mobbed the van. They pulled the driver and passenger from the car, stomping and beating them to death with bricks and stones ("7 People Charged. . ." 2002).

Mobs often arise in situations where people are demanding radical societal changes, like the removal of corrupt government officials. In other cases, especially when authority breaks down, people who are desperate may engage in mob behavior. For example, after the earthquake in Port-au-Prince, Haiti, most of the city's 3 million survivors focused on clearing the streets of debris and pulling bodies out of the rubble. However, dozens of armed men—some wielding machetes, others with sharpened pieces of wood—"dodged from storefront to storefront, battering down doors and hauling away whatever they could carry: shoes, luggage, rolls of carpet. . ." (Romero and Lacey 2010: A1). After attacking, a mob tends to dissolve quickly.

Riots

Compared with mobs, riots usually last longer. A **riot** is a violent crowd that directs its hostility at a wide and shifting range of targets. Unlike mobs, which usually have a specific target, rioters unpredictably attack whomever or whatever gets in their way during a rampage. Most riots arise out of longstanding anger, frustration, or dissatisfaction that may have smoldered for years or even decades. Some of the long-term tensions arise from discrimination, poverty, poor housing conditions, unemployment, economic deprivation, or other unaddressed grievances.

There are numerous protests in the United States every year, but race riots have been the most violent and destructive. More than 150 U.S. cities experienced such riots after the assassination of Martin Luther King, Jr. in 1968. In 1992, riots broke out in 11 cities after the acquittal of police officers involved in the beating of Rodney King, a black motorist, in Los Angeles.

That violence resulted in deaths and considerable property damage because of fires and looting.

Riots are usually expressions of deep-seated hostility, but this isn't always the case. Sports celebration riots, such as the one that followed the Red Sox victory over the Yankees in the 2004 American League Championship Series, occur because of extreme enthusiasm and excitement rather than anger or frustration: "Participants smash, trample, and knock things down to express their ecstasy. Celebration riots are an orgy of gleeful destruction" (Locher 2002: 95).

Much collective behavior, such as a mob or riot, is spontaneous and short-lived. Bringing about long-term social changes, especially at a macro level, requires collective behavior that is structured and enduring. Social movements are important vehicles for creating or suppressing societal changes.

mob a highly emotional and disorderly crowd that uses force or violence against a specific target.

riot a violent crowd that directs its hostility at a wide and shifting range of targets.

social movement a large and organized activity to promote or resist a particular social change.

2 Social Movements

there are hundreds of social movements in the United States alone. Why are they so widespread? And how important are they in changing society?

WHAT IS A SOCIAL MOVEMENT?

A **social movement** is a large and organized activity to promote or resist a particular social change. Examples of social movements include groups that focus on the rights of the disabled, crime victims, gun control, and drunk driving, to name just a few. "Social movements are as American as apple pie," notes sociologist Lynda Ann Ewen (1998: 81–82). "The abolition of slavery, women's right to vote, legal unions, open admissions to public colleges and student aid, and Head Start are all changes in our society that were won through social movements."

Unlike other forms of collective behavior, social movements are organized, goal-oriented, deliberate, structured, and can have a lasting impact on a society. And unlike many other forms of collective behavior (such as crowds, mobs, and riots), the people who make up a social movement are dispersed over time and space, and usually have little face-to-face interaction (Turner and Killian 1987; Lofland 1996).

Some social movements in the United States, such as those focusing on white supremacy, are relatively small. Others are large and have subgroups that appeal to different segments of the population. For example, the U.S. environmental movement has at least 50 subgroups, including Earth First!, Greenpeace, the National Audubon Society, Union of Concerned Scientists, and the Wilderness Society.

TYPES OF SOCIAL MOVEMENTS

Sociologists generally classify social movements according to their goals (changing some aspect of society or resisting such a change) and the amount of change that they seek (limited or widespread) (Aberle 1982). As *Table 17.1* suggests, some social movements may be perceived as more threatening than others because they challenge the existing social order.

Alternative social movements focus on changing some people's attitudes or behavior in a specific way. These movements typically emphasize spirituality, self-improvement, or physical well-being. They are the least threatening to the status quo because they seek limited change and only for some people. For example, millions of non-Asian Americans, influenced by Asian religions, have embraced yoga, meditation, and healing practices such as acupuncture (Cadge and Bender 2004).

Redemptive social movements (also called *religious* or *expressive movements*) offer a dramatic change, but only in some peoples' lives. Redemptive movements are typically based on spiritual or supernatural beliefs, promising to renew people from within and to guarantee some form of salvation or rebirth. Examples include any religious movements that actively seek converts, such as the Jehovah's Witnesses and certain Christian evangelical groups (see Chapter 15).

Reformative social movements want to change everyone, but only with regard to a particular topic or issue. These movements, the most

common type of social movement in U.S. society, do not want to remove or replace the existing economic, political, or social class arrangements, but to change society in some specific way. Examples include civil rights groups, gay rights activists, labor unions, and animal rights groups.

Resistance social movements (also called *reactionary movements*) try to preserve the status quo by blocking change or undoing change that has already occurred. Resistance movements are often called *countermovements* because they usually form immediately after an earlier movement has succeeded in creating change within a society. For example, anti-abortion groups that arose in the United States shortly after the Supreme Court decision in *Roe v. Wade* (1973), which legalized abortion, seek to reverse that decision.

Revolutionary social movements want to completely destroy the existing social order and replace it with a new one. Their goal is the total transformation of society. Revolutionary movements range from utopian groups that withdraw from society and try to create their own to radical terrorists who use violence and intimidation. Examples of the latter include militia groups in the United States that believe the federal government is evil and want to overthrow it. Fidel Castro's socialist movement in Cuba, the French Revolution, and

©iStockphoto.com/Feng Yu

TABLE 17.1
Five Types of Social Movements

MOVEMENT	GOAL	EXAMPLES
Alternative	Change some people in a specific way	Alcoholics Anonymous, transcendental meditation
Redemptive	Change some people, but completely	Jehovah's Witnesses, born-again Christians
Reformative	Change everyone, but in specific ways	Gay rights advocates, Mothers Against Drunk Driving (MADD)
Resistance	Preserve status quo by blocking or undoing change	Anti-abortion groups, white supremacists
Revolutionary	Change everyone completely	Right-wing militia groups, Communism

the Communist Revolution in China all succeeded in replacing the existing social order with a new one.

WHY SOCIAL MOVEMENTS EMERGE

A social movement is "an answer either to a threat or a hope" (Touraine 2002: 89). Yet not everyone who feels threatened or hopeful joins a social movement. Why not? Let's look at four explanations, beginning with the oldest.

Mass Society Theory

Early on, sociologists believed that the people who formed social movements felt powerless, insignificant, and isolated in modern mass societies, which are impersonal, industrialized, and highly bureaucratized. Thus, according to *mass society theory*, social movements offer a sense of belonging to people who feel alienated and disconnected from others (Kornhauser 1959).

Critical Evaluation

Mass society theory may explain why some people form extreme political movements, like Fascism and Nazism, but subsequent research has shown that movement organizers are typically not isolated but well-integrated into their families and communities. Also, historically, many political activists in the United States, such as those behind the civil rights and women's rights movements during the late 1960s, were not powerless but came from relatively privileged backgrounds (Davis 1991; McAdam and Paulsen 1994).

Relative Deprivation Theory

Relative deprivation theory is broader than mass society theory. **Relative deprivation** is a gap between what people have and what they think they should have compared with other people in a society. According to *relative deprivation theory*, what matters is not what people actually have—whether it's money, social status, power, or privilege—but what they *think* they should have.

Relative deprivation theorists note two other elements. First, people often feel that they *deserve* better than they have ("I've worked hard all my life."). Second, they believe that *they cannot attain their goals through conventional channels* ("I've written people in Congress, and they just ignore me."). Thus, shared beliefs combined with unfulfilled expectations can trigger change-oriented social movements, as witnessed by the gay rights and civil rights movements (Davies 1962, 1979; Morrison 1971).

Critical Evaluation

Because relative deprivation theory is more general than mass society theory, it provides a better explanation of why some social movements emerge. Critics point out, however, that there is a certain amount of relative deprivation in all societies, but that people don't always form social movements in reaction to it. In addition, relative deprivation theory doesn't explain why some people join movements even though they don't see themselves as deprived and don't expect to gain anything personally if the movement is successful (Gurney and Tierney 1982; Johnson and Klandermans 1995; Orum 2001).

relative deprivation a gap between what people have and what they think they should have compared with other people in a society.

Resource Mobilization Theory

It takes more than feeling alienated (mass society theory) or disadvantaged (relative deprivation theory) to sustain a social movement. Instead, according to *resource mobilization theory*, a social movement will succeed if it can put together (or mobilize) an organization and leadership dedicated to advancing its cause (Oberschall

© Jim Parkin/Alamy

The "Tea Party" is an emerging social movement in U.S. politics. It originated in early 2010, has an estimated 500 local groups, and has attracted more Republicans than Democrats. No single person leads the movement, so far, but its supporters are motivated by safeguarding individual liberty, cutting taxes, and ending bailouts for business while the American taxpayer gets burdened with more and more debt (Jonsson 2010; O'Hara 2010).

1973, 1995; McCarthy and Zald 1977; Gamson 1990).

Organization and leadership are critical resources for a social movement. Other resources include money, dedicated volunteers, paid staff, access to the media, effective communication systems, contacts, special technical or legal knowledge and skills, equipment, physical space, alliances with like-minded groups, and a positive public image. Many labor unions have fewer members than in the past, but those of teachers and police officers remain strong. This is because such unions have millions of members who pay dues, much of which goes to lobbyists who represent their interests in Congress (see Chapter 11). Further, these unions are well organized at state and national levels, and enjoy widespread support from the general public.

Critical Evaluation

One of the major contributions of resource mobilization theory is its emphasis on structural factors (such as organization and leadership) in explaining why some social movements thrive whereas others disappear. However, a major criticism is that resource mobilization theory largely ignores the role of relative deprivation in the formation of a social movement. If there aren't large numbers of dissatisfied people to initiate a movement, even plentiful resources will not be able to sustain it (Jenkins 1983; Klandermans 1984; Scott 1995; Buechler 2000).

New Social Movements Theory

New social movements theory, which became prominent during the 1970s, emphasizes the linkages between culture, politics, and ideology. Unlike the earlier perspectives, new social movements theory proposes that many recent movements (such as those that work for peace and environmental protection) promote the rights and welfare of *all* people rather than specific groups in particular countries (Touraine 1981; Laraña et al. 1994; Melucci 1995). Thus, new social movements theory is especially interested in "the struggle to liberate the voices of the dispossessed" (Schehr 1997: 6).

For these theorists, recent social movements differ from older ones in two ways. First, they attract a disproportionate number of members who are well-educated and relatively affluent, represent a wide variety of professions (such as educators, scientists, actors, businesspeople, and political leaders), and share a broad goal—improving the quality of life for all people around the world. Second, recent social movements pursue goals or advance values that may have no immediate personal benefit to the participants,

such as eradicating measles or tuberculosis in developing countries (Obach 2004).

Critical Evaluation

Unlike earlier perspectives, new social movements theory contributes to our understanding of collective behavior that crosses international boundaries. According to some critics, however, neither this perspective nor the groups that it examines are novel. For example, some social movements (like feminism and environmentalism) have been around for a long time and still focus on the same basic issues, such as women's second-class citizenship and population growth. In addition, some scholars point out that educated, middle-class or wealthy activists were as common in the old social movements as in more recent ones (Rose 1997; Buechler 2000; Sutton 2000).

Critics also contend that new social movements theory often overstates people's altruistic motivations for forming or participating in social movements. For example, many people who join environmental groups do so for reasons referred to as NIMBY (not in my backyard). That is, they are concerned about some undesirable environmental condition in their own community but show little interest in environmental threats to people elsewhere (Obach 2004).

These four theories, despite their limitations, help us understand social movements because "no single theory is sufficient to explain the complexities of any social movement" (Blanchard 1994: 8). The next question is why some social movements thrive and others fail.

THE STAGES OF SOCIAL MOVEMENTS

Most social movements are short-lived. Some never really get off the ground; others meet their goals and disband. Social movements generally go through four stages—emergence, organization, institutionalization, and decline (see *Figure 17.1*) (King 1956; Mauss 1975; Spector and Kitsuse 1977; Tilly 1978).

"If there aren't large numbers of dissatisfied people to initiate a movement, **even plentiful resources will not be able to sustain it.**"

FIGURE 17.1
Typical Stages of a Social Movement

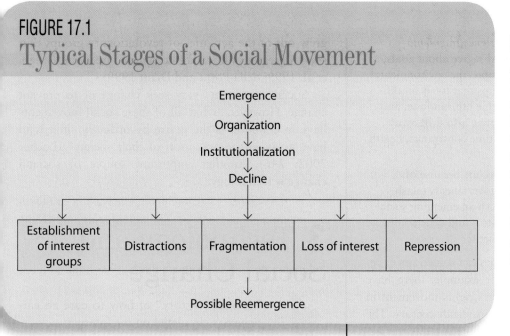

Emergence
↓
Organization
↓
Institutionalization
↓
Decline

| Establishment of interest groups | Distractions | Fragmentation | Loss of interest | Repression |

↓
Possible Reemergence

Emergence

During *emergence,* the first stage of a social movement, a number of people are upset about some condition and want to change it. One or more individuals, serving as agitators or prophets, emerge as leaders. They verbalize the feelings of the discontented, crystallize the issues, and push for taking action. If leaders don't get support after the initial interest, the movement may die. If, on the other hand, the discontent resonates among growing numbers of people, public awareness increases and the movement attracts like-minded people. For example, many scholars attribute the rise of the women's movement during the 1960s to the popularity of *The Feminine Mystique,* a book in which Betty Friedan (1963), then a full-time housewife, questioned whether educated women should give up careers to be full-time homemakers.

Organization

Once people's consciousness has been raised, the second stage of a social movement is *organization.* The most active members form alliances, seek media coverage, develop strategies and tactics, recruit members, and acquire the necessary resources. A division of labor is established in which the leaders make policy decisions and the followers perform necessary tasks such as preparing mass mailings, developing Web sites, and responding to phone calls or e-mail messages. At this stage, the movement may develop chapters at local, regional, national, and international levels.

Institutionalization

As a movement grows, it becomes *institutionalized* and more bureaucratic: The number of staff positions increases, members draw up by-laws governing the organization's activities, the organization may hire outsiders (such as writers, attorneys, and lobbyists) to handle some of the necessary tasks, and the charismatic leaders may spend more of their time on speaking tours, in media interviews, and at national or international meetings. As the social movement grows and becomes more bureaucratic and self-sufficient, the original leaders may move on to better-paying and more influential positions in government or the private sector.

Decline

All social movements end sooner or later. Their *decline,* the last stage, reflects a number of factors:

- If a social movement is successful, it can become an *interest group* and a part of society's fabric. For example, a small anti-smoking movement that began in the mid-1970s now has the enthusiastic support of numerous prestigious organizations, such as the American Cancer Society, the American Heart Association, the American Medical Association, the World Health Organization, and governing bodies within and outside the United States (Wolfson 2001).

- Those involved in a social movement may *become distracted* because the group loses sight of its original goals, their enthusiasm diminishes, or both. For example, when Ralph Nader first criticized the automobile industry for car safety defects, he gained a large following. As Nader and his consumer rights groups expanded their focus to include environmental issues and corporate crimes, many of the initial followers lost interest.

Smoking Deaths This Year 30,077 And Counting

American Heart Association   AMERICAN CANCER SOCIETY   American Lung Association

- A social movement may experience *fragmentation* because the participants disagree about goals, strategies, or tactics. For example, the environmental movement has numerous groups that focus on different issues—air quality, marine life, land use, and global warming. Participants may also drift away from a movement because of time constraints, health problems, or other reasons.

- Social movements may also decline because of *repression*. Many autocratic governments quash dissent. A government can crush an emerging social movement by arresting protestors and imprisoning or even executing leaders (see Chapter 11).

A social movement that declines can sometimes experience a resurgence later on. For example, there have been several waves of the women's rights movement in the United States since the mid-nineteenth century. The first wave ensured women's right to vote in 1920; the second wave expanded employment and educational rights during the 1960s and 1970s; and the third wave, during the 1990s, focused on economic and other inequalities experienced by women of different social classes, sexual orientations, and nationalities (Kramer 2005).

Many people avoid getting involved in social movements because "they don't make any difference." Are these people right?

WHY SOCIAL MOVEMENTS MATTER

As you've seen, social movements can either create or resist change. On an *individual level,* many of us enjoy a variety of rights as workers, consumers, voters, and even victims—rights that we owe to highly dedicated people who were determined to change inequitable laws and practices (e.g., see Jenness and Grattet 2001; and Switzer 2003).

On an *institutional level,* social movements can change general practices. For example, shopping for healthy food is much easier today than before the 1990s, when veggie burgers, tofu, and organic produce were practically nonexistent. Now, mainstream grocery stores have large natural food sections, a much greater variety of fruits and vegetables, and breads and cereals that are made with whole grains, nuts, and less salt, sugar, and chemical additives. In effect, then, vegetarian and consumer groups have had a major impact on industries that control the choice of food products.

On a *societal level,* social movements have had a major effect in the United States and around the world. Most of the world's great religions began as protest movements (see Chapter 15). Also, democratic forms of government in the United States and other countries

grew out of the activities of revolutionary groups that sought greater political and economic freedom (Giugni et al. 1999; della Porta and Diani 1999).

Social movements may seek change or to prevent change. However, "what all of these social movements have in common is the desire by ordinary citizens to have a say in the operation of their society" (Locher 2002: 246). Another important source of societal change is technology.

3 Technology and Social Change

*t*his brief "history" of how to cure an earache has circulated on the Internet:

- 2000 B.C.—Here, eat this root.
- 1000 A.D.—That root is heathen, say this prayer.
- 1850 A.D.—That prayer is superstition, drink this potion. • 1940 A.D.—That potion is snake oil, swallow this pill.
- 1985 A.D.—That pill is ineffective, take this antibiotic.

AP Photo/Tina Fineberg

"Freeganism" is a social movement that began in the mid-1960s but has gained momentum and positive media exposure since the 1990s. In a practice that Americans call "dumpster diving," freegans get free, unspoiled food in the garbage of restaurants, grocery stores, and other food-related industries. Some freegans live on the food, whereas others give it to the poor. Such foraging, according to freegans, keeps perfectly edible food from adding to landfill clutter and unnecessarily depleting the environment.

- 2000 A.D.—That antibiotic is artificial. Here, eat this root.

As this anecdote suggests, despite technological progress over the centuries, some of the old remedies are enjoying renewed popularity (e.g., see The People's Pharmacy, www.peoplespharmacy.com, which offers home remedies for treating everything from arthritis to toenail fungus). Still, technological advances have brought enormous social changes. What are some of the major recent technological advances, their benefits and costs, and the ethical issues that they've generated?

SOME RECENT TECHNOLOGICAL ADVANCES

Technology, the application of scientific knowledge for practical purposes, is a vital aspect of human life: "For good or ill, [technologies] are woven inextricably into the fabric of our lives, from birth to death, at home, in school, in paid work" (MacKenzie and Wajcman 1999: 3).

In the next 75 years, technology is likely to change our lives more dramatically than ever before. Several companies are working on "smart" pills that will presumably improve mental ability and restore brains that are impaired by disease or injury. Our houses may be built with sensors that will automatically test for carbon dioxide, anthrax, environmental contaminants, allergens, and radioactivity, and with devices that will defend against the release of chemical and biological agents (Rubin 2004; Murphy 2005). Whether such predictions will become reality is anyone's guess. In the meantime, technological advances continue to affect our lives. Let's look briefly at a few of the most influential.

Computer Technology

In 1887, English mathematician Charles Babbage designed the first programmable computer. Since then, computers have gone through seven genera-

tions of evolution. One of the most practical aspects of computer technology is the development of *robots*, machines that are programmed to perform human-like functions. Robots are typically used for tasks that are too dull, dirty, or dangerous for humans—such as auto assembly, toxic waste cleanup, mining, minefield sweeping, and underwater and space exploration. Since 2001, American doctors have used a combination of computers, telecommunications, videoconferencing, and advanced robots to guide surgery that is carried out thousands of miles away (Rosen and Hannaford 2006).

> **technology** the application of scientific knowledge for practical purposes.

In time, robots may be able to discuss stock market investment strategies, give you advice about a personal problem, read a book to you in any desired language or in a voice of either sex, and be emotionally savvy companions who cheer you up when you're unhappy (Breazeal 2002; Bar-Cohen and Breazeal 2003). On the negative side, computer scientists worry that the technology is already being used for criminal activities such as identity theft (see Chapter 7), and that robots will threaten even more jobs in the future (Markoff 2009).

Biotechnology

Biotechnology is a broad term that applies to all practical uses of living organisms. It covers anything from the use of microorganisms (e.g., yeast) to ferment beer to

Japan leads the world in robotics, especially in developing intelligent robots that are useful in the real world. Wakamaru (pictured left), which is 3 feet tall and costs about $14,000, wakes up and follows its owner around, keeps her/him on a schedule, recites the day's news headlines, and alerts friends or relatives if the owner doesn't respond to a message. AIBO (pictured right), which sells for about $2,000, seems to be almost as effective as a live dog in relieving the loneliness of nursing home residents. When petted or talked to, AIBO responds by wagging its tail, barking, and blinking its lights (Banks et al. 2008).

© Purdue University News Service/David Umberger/Junko Kimura/Getty Images

genetic engineering, sophisticated techniques that can change the makeup of cells and move genes across species boundaries to produce new organisms.

One form of genetic engineering focuses on producing genetically modified (GM) crops to increase production and to make agriculture less costly, especially by developing new varieties of plants that can tolerate herbicides, resist pests, or both (like the cotton bollworm). The three main GM crops in the United States are corn (45 percent of all corn acreage is planted with GM varieties), soybeans (85 percent of acreage), and cotton (76 percent of acreage) (Pew Initiative on Food and Biotechnology 2004).

Another application of biotechnology that is more controversial than GM crops is stem cell research. A *stem cell* is a building block of the human body. It can replicate indefinitely, and thus serves as a continuous source of new cells. These self-regenerating cells are found in embryos and umbilical cords, but also in parts of adult bodies, including the brain, blood, heart, skin, bone marrow, intestines, and other organs. Embryonic stem cells are more valuable in research because they can produce any cell type of the body, whereas adult stem cells are generally limited to the cell types of their tissue of origin such as a liver or kidney (National Institutes of Health 2006).

Opponents of stem cell research argue that all embryos deserve protection. Proponents maintain that the tissue that yields stem cells doesn't constitute an embryo because it is not implanted in a woman's uterus. These scientists also argue that hundreds of thousands of embryos that fertility clinics dispose of every year are a wasted resource that could be used to treat heart disease, leukemia and other cancers, diabetes, Parkinson's disease, and numerous other health problems (Slevin 2005; Weiss 2005).

Nanotechnology

Another promising recent technology is *nanotechnology,* the ability to build objects one atom or molecule at a time. The key characteristic of these objects is tiny size. Nanotechnology is based on structures measured in nanometers, a unit of measurement equal to 1 billionth of a meter, or 1/80,000th the width of a human hair.

Nanotechnology will probably result in computer chips that are barely visible to the human eye. In medicine, researchers

foresee the day when thousands of nanotubes could potentially be packed into a hair-like capsule the size of a splinter, which could be painlessly implanted under the skin to continuously monitor blood sugar, cholesterol, and hormone levels. Some ongoing research also suggests that nanotechnology might be able to destroy tumors in the body without also frying the adjacent healthy cells, one of the negative effects of current chemotherapy and radiation treatments for cancer (Weiss 2004, 2005).

These and other technological innovations promise longer and healthier lives in the future, but what about the present? What are some of the current benefits and costs of technological changes?

SOME BENEFITS AND COSTS OF TECHNOLOGY

The ever-accelerating pace of change means that most U.S. children born after 2000 are now using technologies that didn't exist just a decade ago. Indeed, much of this "iGeneration" views even those in their 20s as outdated in their tech skills (Rosen 2010).

Technology may be creating greater generation gaps than in the past, but many Americans view the major technological and communications advances in a positive light. There is a greater division of opinion, however, over whether social networking sites or Internet blogs have been changes for the better (see *Table 17.2*). According to another recent national survey, 68 percent of Americans see technology companies as having a positive impact on the country, compared with large corporations and the federal government (25 percent each), Congress (24 percent), and banks and financial institutions (22 percent) (Allen 2010).

Should the average American be less upbeat about technology changing for the better? Let's first look at some of its benefits.

Some Benefits

Technological advances have for some time offered benefits such as performing surgery, tracking people's medications, and monitoring children and older family members from afar using webcams. In other cases, robotic devices have performed repetitive, dirty, or dangerous tasks, including digging deep wells, testing military equipment, and locating bombs.

DNA testing has provided millions of people with information about their genetic predispositions for diseases such as emphysema, cancer, and Huntington's disease (an incurable neurological disorder). Having

Image Source/Jupiter Images

NOW REMEMBER THIS FORMULA, IT'S GOING TO BE ON THE TEST.

CLICK CLICK CLICK CLICK CLIC CLICK

© Ralph Hagen. Reproduction rights obtainable from www.cartoonstock.com

such information has helped doctors and patients make more informed healthcare decisions (Harmon 2008).

More than one-third of Americans age 65 or older falls each year. The economic cost of falls, including hip fractures and replacements, is about $75 billion a year. Low-cost wireless sensors in carpets, clothing, and rooms allow doctors to monitor an older person's walking and activity. As a result, physicians are reducing falls by devising exercise programs for specific muscles or changing medications to eliminate dizziness (Lohr 2009).

Some scientists also maintain that use of the Internet has enhanced human intelligence: As people have more access to information, they become smarter and make better decisions. In effect, as the digital systems that people rely on become faster and more sophisticated, so will our capabilities in working on solutions for problems such as the growing population density, the spread of pandemics, and global pollution (Cascio 2009).

Some Costs

Cell phones, the Internet, and other forms of telecommunication bring people together and provide quick access to a wealth of information. Some argue, however, that the Internet, especially, has made us more sedentary and lazy, and that the ease of online searching and browsing has limited our ability to concentrate, to read without distractions, and to think (Carr 2008). Others worry that the iGeneration expects an instant response from everyone they communicate with, and has little patience for anything else (Rosen 2010). A more common concern is that virtually every techno-

logical advance in telecommunications reduces privacy.

Many companies routinely collect information about people as they click from site to site on the Internet. Much of this Web tracking is done anonymously, but a new crop of "snooper" sites is making it easier than ever before for anyone with Internet access to assemble and sell the information, including your name, Social Security number, address, and which sites you've visited on almost any topic, product, or service. The data come from a variety of sources, including public records on campaign contributions, property sales, and court cases; networking sites where people provide information about themselves, their jobs, relatives, and friends; and even Netflix, where marketers can track the movies that customers have watched and rated (Sarno 2009; Singer 2009, 2010).

Many Americans are vulnerable because they're not very knowledgeable about privacy laws. For example, only 22 percent know that if a Web site has a privacy policy, the site can share information about you with other companies without your permission (Turow et al. 2009).

Another increasingly common intrusion on privacy is by health and life insurance companies that pay only about $15 per search to other companies that prepare health "credit reports." They have accessed at least 200 million Americans' 5-year history of purchases of pre-

TABLE 17.2
Opinions of Technological Changes

TECHNOLOGICAL CHANGES	PERCENTAGE SAYING THAT THE CHANGE HAS BEEN "FOR THE BETTER"
Cell phones	69
E-mail	68
Internet	65
Increased surveillance/security	58
BlackBerrys/iPhones	56
Online shopping	54
Social networking sites	35
Internet blogs	29

Sources: Based on Kohut et al. 2009, p. 2.

In 2005, after being mauled by her Labrador retriever, this French woman (who underwent several operations) became the world's first face transplant patient, receiving lips, a chin, and a nose from a brain-dead donor. Some doctors were appalled when they learned that she signed a film deal 3 months before the operation. However, an American bioethicist defended the woman. Even if her medical expenses were fully covered by the French national health system, he said, she might not find employment in the future (Victory 2005). Was signing the film deal ethical? Also, do you think that the success of such surgery will encourage wealthy people to trade their faces for those that are younger or prettier?

scription drugs, the dosages and refills, and possible medical conditions. With such reports, insurance companies' can charge some customers higher premiums or exclude some medical conditions from policies. Even worse, according to some health experts, some insurance companies have misinterpreted the information and denied coverage (Nakashima 2008; Terhune 2008).

SOME ETHICAL ISSUES

As you saw in Chapter 13, most Americans yearn to be young. As a result, RealAge (www.realage.com), which promises to shave years off your biological age, has become one of the most popular quizzes on the Internet. More than 27 million people have taken the test, which asks about 150 questions about lifestyle and family medical history, and then recommends how to become younger. Throughout the test, RealAge prompts people to become free subscribers. Millions have done so, and their test results go into a marketing database, a clearinghouse for drug corporations. The corporations then suggest new medications that people don't need and for problems that a doctor hasn't even diagnosed. The RealAge privacy policy states, in part, that it will share members' personal data with third parties, but few people read the policy statement (Clifford 2009). Thus, RealAge and similar sites profit by preying on people's anxieties and creating huge databases on private health information.

Biotechnology sparks some of the most intense ethical controversies. One ethical dilemma, for example, is that biotechnological advances, like other technological developments, are most readily available to the wealthy, especially to prolong life. For example, nearly 90,000 Americans are on lists for organ transplants, mostly kidneys and livers. Because of the scarcity of organs, many patients have turned to the Internet in search of donors. Proponents argue that the Web sites used by these people save lives because they motivate others to donate organs when they are touched by heart-wrenching personal stories. Opponents maintain that such pleas give an edge to those who are affluent, educated, and computer-literate (Stearns 2006; Morais 2007). Thus, technological advances are fraught with both promise and ethical pitfalls.

The references that are new to this edition are printed in red.

"7 People Charged in Fatal Mob Attack." 2002. *Baltimore Sun*, August 4, 2A.

AAA Foundation for Traffic Safety. 2008. "Cell Phones and Driving: Research Update." Retrieved December 15, 2009 (www.AAAfoundation.org).

Aberle, David. 1982. *The Peyote Religion among the Navaho*, 2nd ed. Chicago, IL: Aldine.

Abudabbeh, Nuha. 1996. "Arab Families." Pp. 333-346 in *Ethnicity and Family Therapy*, 2nd edition, edited by Monica McGoldrick, Joe Giordano, and John K. Pearce. New York: The Guilford Press.

Abu-Laban, Sharon M., and Baha Abu-Laban. 1999. "Teens Between: The Public and Private Spheres of Arab-Canadian Adolescents." Pp. 113-148 in *Arabs in America: Building a New Future*, edited by Michael W. Suleiman. Philadelphia: Temple University Press.

Acs, Gregory. 2009. "Poverty in the United States, 2008." Urban Institute, September 10. Retrieved March 6, 2010 (www.urban.org).

_____ and Austin Nichols. 2010. "Changes in the Economic Security of American Families." Urban Institute, February. Retrieved April 4, 2010 (www.urban.org).

ACT. 2007. *ACT National Curriculum Survey 2005-2006*. Retrieved July 29, 2007 (www.act.org).

Adams, Bert N. and R. A. Sydie. 2001. *Sociological Theory*. Thousand Oaks, CA: Pine Forge Press.

Adamson, David M. 2009. "Health Care on Aisle 7: The Growing Phenomenon of Retail Clinics." Rand Health. Retrieved February 14, 2010 (www.rand.org).

Adelman, Clifford. 2006. *The Toolbox Revisited: Paths to Degree Completion from High School Through College*. Washington, DC: U.S. Department of Education.

Adler, Jerry. 2005. "In Search of the Spiritual." *Newsweek*, August 20-September 5, 44-64.

_____. 2007. "How to Design a Healthier Planet." *Newsweek*, March 6, 66-70.

Adler, Patricia. A. and Paul Adler. 1994. "Observational Techniques." Pp. 377-392 in *Handbook of Qualitative Research*, edited by Norman K. Denzin and Yvonna S. Lincoln. Thousand Oaks, CA: Sage.

Adler, Susan M. 2003. "Asian-American Families." Pp. 82-91 in *International Encyclopedia Of Marriage And Family*, 2nd ed., volume 2, edited by J. J. Ponzetti, Jr. New York: Macmillan.

Agence France Presse. 2001. "Nigerian Girl to Be Lashed 180 Times." *Christian Science Monitor*, January 4, 7.

Agiesta, Jennifer and Jon Cohen. 2010. "Fewer Americans Think Obama Has Advanced Race Relations, Poll Says." *Washington Post*, January 18, A3.

Aguirre, Adalberto Jr. and Jonathan H. Turner. 2004. *American Ethnicity: The Dynamics and Consequences of Discrimination*, 4th ed. Boston, MA: McGraw Hill.

Aizenman, N. C. 2005. "In Afghanistan, New Misgivings about an Old but Risky Practice." *Washington Post*, April 17. A16.

Ajrouch, Kristine. 1999. "Family and Ethnic Identity in an Arab-American Community." Pp. 129-139 in *Arabs in America: Building a new future*, edited by Michael W. Suleiman. Philadelphia: Temple University Press.

Akers, Ronald L. 1997. *Criminological Theories: Introduction and Evaluation*, 2nd edition. Los Angeles, CA: Roxbury.

Akkad, Dania. 2009. "Mass Emigration Compounds Iraqi Refugee Crowding." *Christian Science Monitor*, September 18. Retrieved May 2, 2010 (www.csmonitor.com).

Albert, Bill, Sarah Brown, and Christine M. Flanigan, eds. 2003. *14 and Younger: The Sexual Behavior of Young Adolescents*. The National Campaign to Prevent Teen Pregnancy. Retrieved June 10, 2003 (www.teenpregnancy.org).

Alder, Christine and Anne Worrall, eds. 2004. *Girls' Violence: Myths and Realities*. Albany: State University of New York Press.

Alesina, Alberto, Edward Glaeser, and Bruce Sacerdote. 2005. "Work and Leisure in the U.S. and Europe: Why So Different?" National Bureau of Economic Research, April. Retrieved June 2, 2007 (www.nber.org).

Allegretto, Sylvia A., Sean P. Corcoran, and Lawrence Mishel. 2008. *The Teaching Penalty: Teacher Pay Losing Ground*. Washington, DC: Economic Policy Institute.

Allen, Jodie T. 2010. "United We Stand. . . On Technology." Pew Research Center, May 5. Retrieved May 6, 2010 (pewresearch.org).

Allen, Katherine R., and Ben K. Beitin. 2007. "Gender and Class in Culturally Diverse Families." Pp. 63-79 in *Cultural Diversity and Families: Expanding Perspectives*, edited by Bahira Sherif Trask and Raeann R. Hamon. Thousand Oaks, CA: Sage, pp. 63-79.

Alliance for Board Diversity. 2008. "Women and Minorities on Fortune 100 Boards." *Catalyst*. Retrieved April 28, 2008 (www.catalyst.org).

Allport, Gordon. W. 1954. *The Nature of Prejudice*. Reading, MA: Addison-Wesley.

Almeida, R. V., ed. 1994. *Expansions of Feminist Family Theory through Diversity*. New York: Haworth Press.

Almond, Douglas, Lena Edlund, and Kevin Milligan. 2009. "Son Preference and the Persistence of Culture: Evidence from Asian Immigrants to Canada." National Bureau of Economic Research, October. Retrieved May 1, 2010 (www.nber.org).

Almond, Lucinda. 2007. *The Abortion Controversy*. Farmington Hills, MI: Greenhaven Press.

Alvarez, Lizette. 2005. "Got 2 Extra Hours for Your E-Mail?" *New York Times* (November 10): E1-E2.

_____. 2009. "Women at Arms: G.I. Jane Breaks the Combat Barrier." *New York Times*, August 16, A1.

American Academy of Pediatrics. "Children, Adolescents, and Television." 2001. *Pediatrics* 109 (November): 423-426.

American Association of Suicidology. 2009. "Elderly Suicide Fact Sheet." June 23. Retrieved December 17, 2009 (www.suicidology.org).

American Council on Education. 2008. "Recent Graduates Give Alma Maters High Grades." May 20. Retrieved July 18, 2008 (www.solutions forourfuture.org).

American Federation of Teachers. 2007. "Survey and Analysis of Teacher Salary Trends 2005." Retrieved July 13, 2008 (www.aft.org).

"American Indian and Alaska Native Heritage Month: November 2008." 2008. U. S. Census Bureau News, Facts for Features, October 16, CB08-FF.18. Retrieved March 10, 2009 (www.census.gov).

"American Indian and Alaska Native Heritage Month: November 2009." 2009. U.S. Census Bureau News, October 15, CB09-FF.20. Retrieved March 13, 2010 (www.census.gov).

American Indian- and Alaska Native-Owned Firms: 2002. 2006. U.S. Census Bureau, SB02-00CS-AIAN (RV). Retrieved May 1, 2007 (www.census.gov).

American Library Association. 2010. "Frequently Challenged Books." Retrieved June 3, 2010 (www.ala.org).

"American Manners Poll." 2005. *USA Today*, October 14. Retrieved October 15, 2005 (www.usatoday.com).

American Revolution Center, The. 2010. "The American Revolution. Who Cares?" Retrieved April 20, 2010 (www.americanrevolutioncenter.org).

American Rivers. 2005. "America's Most Endangered Rivers of 2005." Retrieved June 22, 2005 (www.americanrivers.org).

American Society for Aesthetic Plastic Surgery. 2010. "Cosmetic Procedures in 2008." Retrieved January 27, 2010 (www.cosmeticplasticsurgerystatistics.com).

American Sociological Association. 1999. *Code of Ethics and Policies and Procedures of the ASA Committee on Professional Ethics*. Retrieved January 10, 2010 (www.asanet.org).

_____. 2006. "What Can I Do with a Bachelor's Degree in Sociology?": A National Survey of Seniors Majoring in Sociology: First Glances: What Do They Know and Where Are They Going?" Washington, DC: American Sociological Association.

Amnesty International. 2006. *Stonewalled: Police Abuse and Misconduct against Lesbian, Gay, Bisexual, and Transgender People in the U.S.* London: Amnesty International Publications.

Amusa, Malena. 2010. "'Precious' Pushes Past Controversy to Oscar Night." Women's E-News, March 5. Retrieved March 8, 2010 (www.womensenew.org).

Anderson, Craig A., et al. 2003. "The Influence of Media Violence on Youth." *Psychological Science in the Public Interest* 4 (December): 81-110.

Anderson, David A. 1999. "The Aggregate Burden of Crime." *Journal of Law and Economics* 42 (October): 611-42.

Anderson, Elijah. 1999. *Code of the Street: Decency, Violence, and the Moral Life of the Inner City*. New York: W.W. Norton.

Anderson, James F. and Laronistine Dyson. 2002. *Criminological Theories: Understanding Crime in America*. Lanham, MD: University Press of America.

Anderson, John W. 2001. "Iran's Cultural Backlash." *Washington Post*, August 16, A1, A20.

Anderson, Sarah, John Cavanagh, Chuck Collins, Dedrick Muhammad, and Sam Pizzigati. 2008. "Analysis of Treasury Department Rules on Executive Compensation for Bailout Firms." Institute for Policy Studies, October 15. Retrieved November 7, 2008 (www.ips-dc.org).

Anderson, Sarah, John Cavanagh, Chuck Collins, Sam Pizzigati, and Mike Lapham. 2008. "Executive Excess 2008." Institute for Policy Studies and United for a Fair Economy, August 25. Retrieved November 7, 2008 (www.faireconomy.org).

Anderson, Sarah, John Cavanagh, Chuck Collins, Sam Pizzigati, and Mike Pelham. 2008. "Executive Excess 2008. How Average Taxpayers Subsidize Runaway Pay." Institute for Policy Studies and United for a Fair Economy, August 25. Retrieved March 11, 2010 (www.faireconomy.org).

Anderson, Stephen A. and Ronald M. Sabatelli. 2007. *Family Interaction: A Multicultural Developmental Perspective*, 4th ed. Boston, MA: Allyn & Bacon.

Arendt, Hannah. 2004. *The Origins of Totalitarianism*. New York: Schocken.

Ariès, Phillippe. 1962. *Centuries of Childhood*. New York: Vintage.

Armour, Stephanie. 2008. "Day Care's New Frontier: Your Baby at Your Desk." *USA Today*, March 30. Retrieved July 16, 2009 (www.usatoday.com).

_____. 2008. "Hitting Home: New Faces Join Ranks of the Homeless." *USA Today*, June 15. Retrieved June 17, 2008 (www.usatoday.com).

_____. 2009. "Foreclosures Up: 1 in 84 Homes Affected in First Half of Year." *USA Today*, July 15. Retrieved July 20, 2009 (www.usatoday.com).

Arnoldy, Ben. 2009. "For Laid-Off IBM Workers, a Job in India?" *Christian Science Monitor*, March 26 (http://www.csmonitor.com/Money/2009/0326/for-laid-off-ibm-workers-a-job-in-india).

Arraf, Jane. 2010. "Nada Won't Leave, But She Can't Fully Participate." *Christian Science Monitor*, March 1, 27.

Asch, Solomon. 1952. *Social Psychology*. Englewood Cliffs, NJ: Prentice-Hall, Inc.

Ashburn, Elyse. 2007. "A Race to Rescue Native Tongues." *Chronicle of Higher Education*, September 28, B15.

Ashford, Lori. S. 2006. "How HIV and AIDS Affect Populations." Population Reference Bureau. Retrieved February 1, 2008 (www.prb.org).

"Asian/Pacific American Heritage Month: May 2010." 2010. U.S. Census Bureau News, March 2, CB10-FF.07. Retrieved March 13, 2010 (www.census.gov).

Astin, Alexander, and Helen Astin. 2005. "Spirituality in Higher Education." Higher Education Research Institute. Retrieved December 15, 2005 (www.gseis.ucla.edu).

Atchley, Robert C., and Amanda S. Barusch. 2004. *Social Forces and Aging: An Introduction to Social Gerontology*, 10th ed. Belmont, CA: Wadsworth.
Attinasi, John J. 1994. "Racism, Language Variety, and Urban U.S. Minorities: Issues in Bilingualism and Bidialectalism." Pp. 319-347 in *Race*, edited by Steven Gregory and Roger Sanjek. New Brunswick, NJ: Rutgers University Press.
Attwood, Feona, ed. 2010. *Porn.com: Making Sense of Online Pornography*. New York: Peter Lang Publishing.
Aunola, Kaisa, and Jari-Erik Nurmi. 2005. "The Role of Parenting Styles in Children's Problem Behavior." *Child Development* 76 (November/December): 1144-1159.
Austen, Ian. 2002. "A Leg with a Mind of Its Own." *New York Times*, January 3, G1.
Auxier, Richard. 2010. "Congress in a Wordle." Pew Research Center, March 22. Retrieved March 26, 2010 (http://pewresearch.org).
Avellar, Sarah, and Pamela Smock. 2005. "The Economic Consequences of the Dissolution of Cohabiting Unions." *Journal of Marriage and Family* 67 (May): 315-327.
Axtell, Roger E., Tami Briggs, Margaret Corcoran, and Mary Beth Lamb. 1997. *Do's and Taboos Around the World for Women in Business*. New York: John Wiley & Sons, Inc.
Babbie, Earl. 2002. *The Basics of Social Research*, 2nd edition. Belmont, CA: Wadsworth.
Bailey, Carol A. 2007. *A Guide to Qualitative Field Research*, 2nd ed. Thousand Oaks, CA: Pine Forge Press.
Bainbridge, William S. 1997. *The Sociology of Religious Movements*. New York: Routledge.
Bakan, Joel. 2004. *The Corporation: The Pathological Pursuit of Profit and Power*. New York: Free Press.
____. 2005. *The Corporation: The Pathological Pursuit of Profit and Power*. New York: Free Press.
Bandura, Albert and Richard H. Walters. 1963. *Social Learning and Personality Development*. New York: Holt, Rinehart & Winston.
Banerjee, Abhijit, Esther Duflo, Maitreesh Ghatak, and Jeanne Lafortune. 2009. "Marry for What: Caste and Mate Selection in Modern India." National Bureau of Economic Research, May. Retrieved March 2, 2010 (www.nber.org).
Banerjee, Neela. 2006. "Clergywomen Find Hard Path to Bigger Pulpit." *New York Times*, August 26, A1, A12.
Banfield, Edward C. 1974. *The Unheavenly City Revisited*. Boston, MA: Little, Brown.
Banks, Ingrid. 2000. *Hair matters: Beauty, Power, and Black Women's Consciousness*. New York: New York University Press.
Banks, Marian R., Lisa M. Willoughby, and William A. Banks. 2008. "Animal-Assisted Therapy and Loneliness in Nursing Homes: Use of Robotic versus Living Dogs." *Journal of the American Medical Directors Association* 9 (March): 173-177.
Banks, Sandy. 2006. "Firehouse Culture and Ordeal for Women." *Los Angeles Times*, December 3. Retrieved December 4, 2006 (www.latimes.com).
Barabak, Mark Z. 2006. "Guest-Worker Proposal Has Wide Support." *Los Angeles Times*, April 30. Retrieved May 2, 2006 (www.latimes.com).
Barash, David P. 2002. "Evolution, Males, and Violence." *Chronicle of Higher Education*, May 24, B7-B9.
Barbarin, Oscar A., and Terry McCandies. 2003. "African-American Families." Pp. 50-56 in *International Encyclopedia Of Marriage And Family*, 2nd ed., volume 1, edited by James J. Ponzetti Jr., 50-56. New York: Macmillan.
Barber, Bernard, and Lyle S. Lobel. 1952. "Fashion in Women's Clothes and the American Social System." *Social Forces* 31 (December): 124-131.
Bar-Cohen, Yoseph and Cynthia Breazeal. 2003. *Biologically Inspired Intelligent Robots*. Bellingham, WA: Spie Press.
Barker, Christopher. 2009. "$8.6 Trillion Was a Drop in the Bucket." *The Motley Fool*, February 19. Retrieved March 5, 2009 (www.fool.com).
Barker, James B. 1993. "Tightening the Iron Cage: Concertive Control in Self-Managing Teams." *Administrative Science Quarterly* 38 (September): 408-437.
Barnard, Chester. 1938. *The Functions of the Executive*. Cambridge, MA: Harvard University Press.
Barnes, Cynthia. 2006. "China's 'Kingdom of Women'." *Slate*, November 17. Retrieved June 12, 2007 (www.slate.com).
Barnett, Rosalind and Caryl Rivers. 2004. *Same Difference: How Gender Myths Are Hurting Our Relationships, Our Children, and Our Jobs*. New York: Basic Books.
Barro, Robert J., and Rachel M. McCleary. 2003. "Religion and Economic Growth across Countries." *American Sociological Review* 68 (October): 760-781.
Barrows, Sydney B. 1989. *Mayflower Madam: The Secret Life of Sydney Biddle Barrows*. Westminster, MD: Arbor House.
Bart, Pauline B. and Eileen Geil Moran, eds. 1993. *Violence Against Women: The Bloody Footprints*. Thousand Oaks, CA: Sage.
Bartkowski, John P. 2001. *Remaking the Godly Marriage: Gender Negotiation in Evangelical Families*. New Brunswick, NJ: Rutgers University Press.
Bartkowski, John P., and Jen'nan Ghazal Read. 2003. "Veiled Submission: Gender, Power, and Identity among Evangelical and Muslim Women in the United States." *Qualitative Sociology* 26 (Spring): 71-92.
Bartlett, Thomas, and Paula Wasley. 2008. "Just Say 'A': Grade Inflation Undergoes Reality Check." *Chronicle of Higher Education*, September 5, A1, A10.
Bartlett, Thomas. 2007. "'I Suffer Not a Woman to Teach'." *Chronicle of Higher Education*, April 13, A10-A12.
Barton, Allen H. 1980. "A Diagnosis of Bureaucratic Maladies." Pp. 27-26 in *Making Bureaucracies Work*, edited by Carol H. Weiss and Allen H. Barton. Beverly Hills, CA: Sage.
Basken, Paul. 2009a. "Ghostwriters Haunt the Integrity of Medical Journals." *Chronicle of Higher Education*, September 18, A10.
____. 2009b. "University Doctors Got Paid in Drug Sales Campaign." *Chronicle of Higher Education*, October 30, A1, A8.
Bauerlein, Monika, and Clara Jeffery. 2010. "Too Big to Jail?" *Mother Jones*, January/February, 4.
Baum, Katrina. 2006. "Identity Theft, 2004." Bureau of Justice Statistics Bulletin, April. Retrieved March 10, 2008 (wwwl.ojp.usdoj.gov).
Baumrind, Diana. 1968. "Authoritarian versus Authoritative Parental Control." *Adolescence* 3 (11); 255-72.
____. 1989. "Rearing Competent Children." Pp. 349-378 in *Child Development Today and Tomorrow*, edited by William Damon. San Francisco, CA: Jossey-Bass.
Bayer, Patrick, Hanming Fang, and Robert McMillan. 2005. "Separate When Equal? Racial Inequality and Residential Inequality." National Bureau of Economic Research. Retrieved January 22, 2008 (www.nberl.org).
Becker, Bernice. 2008. "Justices List Their Assets; Wide Range of Wealth." *New York Times*, June 7, 12.
Becker, Elizabeth. 2001. "Some Who Vote on Farm Subsidies Get Them as Well." *New York Times*, September 1, 10.
Becker, Howard S. 1963. *Outsiders: Studies in the Sociology of Deviance*. New York: Free Press.
Becker, Jasper. 2002. "China's Workers—No Longer a Privileged Class." *Christian Science Monitor*, October 21, 7-8.
Beeghley, Leonard. 2000. *The Structure of Social Stratification in the United States*, 3rd ed. Boston, MA: Allyn and Bacon.
Behnke, Andrew. 2004. "Latino Dads: Structural Inequalities and Personal Strengths." *Report: National Council on Family Relations* 49 (September): F6-F7.
Beilock, Sian L., Elizabeth A. Gunderson, Gerardo Ramirez, and Susan C. Levine. 2010. "Female Teachers' Math Anxiety Affects Girls' Math Achievement." *Proceedings of the National Academy of Sciences* 107 (February 2): 1860-1863.
Belkin, Lisa. 2008. "Smoother Transitions." *New York Times*, September 4, 2.
Belknap, Joanne. 2001. *The Invisible Woman: Gender, Crime, and Justice*, 2nd edition. Belmont, CA: Wadsworth.
____. 2007. *The Invisible Woman: Gender, Crime, and Justice*, 3rd edition. Belmont, CA: Wadsworth Press.
Bender, Courtney. 2003. *Heaven's Kitchen: Living Religion at God's Love We Deliver*. Chicago, IL: The University of Chicago Press.
Bennett, J. 2009. "Tales of a Modern Diva." *Newsweek*, April 6, 42-43.
Bennett, Jessica, Jesse Ellison, and Sarah Ball. 2010. "Are We There Yet?" *Newsweek*, March 29, 42-46.
Benokraitis, Nijole V. 1997. *Subtle Sexism: Current Practices and Prospects for Change*. Thousand Oaks, CA: Sage.
____, ed. 2000. *Feuds about Families: Conservative, Centrist, Liberal, and Feminist Perspectives*. Upper Saddle River, NJ: Prentice Hall.
Benokraitis, Nijole V. 2011. *Marriages & Families: Changes, Choices, and Constraints*, 7th ed. Upper Saddle River, NJ: Prentice Hall.
Benson, Michael L. 2002. *Crime and the Life Course*. Los Angeles, CA: Roxbury.
Benson, Michael L., and Greer Litton Fox. 2004. "When Violence Hits Home: How Economics and Neighborhood Play a Role." National Institute of Justice, September. Retrieved October 1, 2004 (www.ojp.usdoj.gov).
Bergen, Raquel K., Jeffrey L. Edleson, and Claire M. Renzetti, eds. 2005. *Violence against Women: Classic Papers*. Boston, MA: Allyn and Bacon.
Berger, Peter L. and Thomas Luckmann. 1966. *The Social Construction of Reality: A Treatise in the Sociology of Knowledge*. New York: Doubleday & Company.
Bergquist, Amy. 2006. "Pharmacist Refusals: Dispensing (With) Religious Accommodation under Title VII." *Minnesota Law Review* 90 (April): 1073-1106.
Berk, Richard A. 1974. *Collective Behavior*. Dubuque, Iowa: Wm. C Brown Company.
Berkos, Kristen M., Terre H. Allen, Patricia Kearney, and Timothy G. Plax. 2001. "When Norms are Violated: Imagined Interactions as Processing and Coping Mechanisms." *Communication Monographs* 68 (September): 289-300.
Berman, Greg, and Aubrey Fox. 2009. "Lessons from the Battle over D.A.R.E.: The Complicated Relationship between Research and Practice." U.S. Department of Justice, Bureau of Justice Assistance, Center for Court Innovation. Retrieved May 16, 2010 (www.ojp.usdoj.gov).
Bernhardt, Annette, et al. 2009. "Broken Laws, Unprotected Workers" Violations of Employment and Labor Laws in America's Cities." Center for Urban Economic Development, National Employment Law Project, and UCLA Institute for Research on Labor and Employment. Retrieved April 8, 2010 (www.nelp.org).
Bernstein, Jared, Elise Gould, and Lawrence Mishel. 2007. "Poverty, income, and health insurance trends in 2006." Economic Policy Institute, August 28. Retrieved August 29, 2008 (www.epi.org).
Berrey, Ellen. 2009. "Sociology Finds Discrimination in the Law." *Contexts* 8 (Spring): 28-32.
Bertrand, Marianne, and Sendhil Mullainathan. 2003. "Are Emily and Greg More Employable than Lakisha and Jamal? A Field Experiment on Labor Market Discrimination." Massachusetts Institute of Technology, Department of Economics. Retrieved May 3, 2004 (http://papers.ssrn.com).
Berube, Alan, Audrey Sinter, Jill H. Wilson, and William H. Frey. 2006. "Finding Exurbia: America's Fast-Growing Communities at the Metropolitan Fringe." Brookings Institution. Retrieved February 2, 2008 (www.brookings.edu).
Best, Joel. 2001. *Damned Lies and Statistics: Untangling Numbers from the Media, Politicians, and Activists*. Berkeley: University of California Press.
____. 2006. *Flavor of the Month: Why Smart People Fall for Fads*. Berkeley: University of California Press.
Betcher, R. William and William S. Pollack. 1993. *In a Time of Fallen Heroes: The Re-Creation of Masculinity*. New York: Atheneum.
Bianchi, Suzanne M., John P. Robinson and Melissa A. Milkie. 2006. *Changing Rhythms of American Family Life*. New York: Russell Sage Foundation.
Billingsley, Andrew. 1992. *Climbing Jacob's Ladder: The Enduring Legacy of African-American Families*. New York: Simon & Schuster.
"Billionaires 2008." 2008. *Forbes*, March 24, 80-86.
Binder, Amy. 1993. "Constructing Racial Rhetoric: Media Depictions of Harm in Heavy Metal and Rap Music." *American Sociological Review* 58 (December): 753-767.
Bingham, Shawn C., and Alexander A. Hernandez. 2009. "'Laughing Matters': The Comedian as Social Observer, Teacher, and Conduit of the Sociological Perspective." *Teaching Sociology* 37 (October): 335-352.
Birch, Douglas. 2006. "Deep Anger, Not Cartoons, Spurred Muslim Protests." *Baltimore Sun*, February 9, 1A, 13A.
Bird, Chloe E., et al. 2009. "Neighborhood Socioeconomic Status and Biological 'Wear & Tear' in a Nationally Representative Sample of U.S. Adults." *Journal of Epidemiology and Community Health*, September 16. Retrieved March 5, 2010 (http://jech.bmj.com).
Birnbaum, Michael. 2010. "Historians Speak Out Against Proposed Texas Textbook Changes." *Washington Post*, March 18, A3.
Bivens, L. Josh. 2006. "Offshoring." Economic Policy Institute, May. Retrieved June 1, 2007 (www.epinet.org).
____. 2008. "Trade, Jobs, and Wages: Are the Public's Worries about Globalization Justified?" Economic Policy Institute, May 6. Retrieved July 4, 2008 (www.epi.org).
Black, M. C., and M. J. Breiding. 2008. "Adverse Health Conditions and Health Risk Behaviors Associated with Intimate Partner Violence—United States, 2005." *MMWR Weekly*, 57 (February 8): 113-117.

Black-Owned Firms: 2002. 2006. U.S. Census Bureau, SB02-00CS-BLK (RV). Retrieved May 1, 2007 (www.census.gov).

Blanchard, Dallas A. 1994. *The Anti-Abortion Movement and the Rise of the Religious Right: From Polite to Fiery Protest*. New York: Twayne Publishers.

Blankenstein, Andrew, and Tony Barboza. 2007. "More Pot House Busts Revealed." *Los Angeles Times*, April 12. Retrieved April 19, 2007 (www.latimes.com).

Blass, Thomas. 2000. "The Milgram Paradigm After 35 Years: Some Things We Now Know About Obedience to Authority." In Thomas Blass (Ed.), *Obedience to Authority: Current Perspectives on the Milgram Paradigm*. Mahwah, NJ: Lawrence Erlbaum Associates, pp. 35-59.

Blau, Francine B., and Lawrence M. Kahn. 2006. "The Gender Pay Gap: Going, Going . . . but Not Gone." Pp. 37-66 in *The Declining Significance of Gender?* edited by Francine D. Blau, Mary C. Brinton, and David B. Grutsky. New York: Russell Sage Foundation.

Blau, Peter M. 1986. *Exchange and Power in Social Life*, revised ed. New Brunswick, NJ: Transaction.

Blau, Peter M. and Marshall W. Meyer. 1987. *Bureaucracy in Modern Society*, 3rd edition. New York: Random House.

Blauner, Robert. 1969. "Internal Colonialism and Ghetto Revolt." *Social Problems* 16 (Spring): 393-408.

———. 1972. *Racial Oppression in America*. New York: Harper and Row.

Blumenstyk, Goldie. 2009. "Company Says Research It Sponsored at Pitt and Hopkins Was Fraudulent." *Chronicle of Higher Education*, September 4. Retrieved September 6, 2009 (www.chronicle.com).

Blumer, Herbert. 1946. "Collective Behavior." Pp. 65-121 in *New Outline of the Principles of Sociology*, edited by Alfred M. Lee (Ed.). New York: Barnes & Noble.

———. 1969. *Symbolic Interactionism: Perspective and Method*. Englewood Cliff, NJ: Prentice Hall.

Boak, Joshua. 2009. "Layoffs Are Driving Change Among the Amish." *Los Angeles Times,* April 20. Retrieved April 22, 2009 (www.latimes.com).

Bobroff-Hajal, Anne. 2006. "Why Cousin Marriage Matters in Iraq." *Christian Science Monitor*, December 26, 9.

Bogle, Kathleen A. 2008. *Hooking Up: Sex, Dating, and Relationships on Campus*. New York: New York University Press.

Bohannon, Lisa. 2000. "Is Your Body Language on Your Side?" *Career World* 29 (November/December): 21-23.

Bollag, Burton. 2007. "Credential Creep." *Chronicle of Higher Education*, June 22, A10-A12.

Bonacich, Edna. 1972. "A Theory of Ethnic Antagonism: The Split Labor Market." *American Sociological Review* 37 (October): 547-559.

Bonger, Willem A. 1916/1969. *Criminality and Economic Conditions*. Bloomington: Indiana University Press.

Bonisteel, Sara. 2006. "Asian Leaders Angered by Rosie O'Donnell's 'Ching Chong' Comments." Fox News, December 11. Retrieved September 10, 2008 (www.foxnews.com).

Bonner, Robert. 2007. "Research—Male Elementary Teachers: Myths and Realities." Men Teach. Retrieved June 12, 2008 (www.menteach.org).

Bonnie, Richard J., and Robert B. Wallace, eds. 2003. *Elder Mistreatment: Abuse, Neglect, and Exploitation in an Aging America*. Washington, DC: The National Academies Press.

Boonstra, Heather D., Rachel B. Gold, Cory L. Richards, and Lawrence B. Finer. 2006. "Abortion in Women's Lives." Guttmacher Institute. Retrieved December 21, 2006 (www.guttmacher.org).

Booza, Jason C., Jackie Cutsinger, and George Galster. 2006. "Where Did They Go? The Decline of Middle-Income Neighborhoods in Metropolitan America." Brookings Institution. Retrieved January 21, 2008 (www.brookings.edu).

Boraas, Stephanie, and William M. Rodgers III. 2003. "How Does Gender Play a Role in the Earnings Gap? An Update." *Monthly Labor Review* 126 (March): 9-15.

Borgerhoff Mulder, Monique. 2009. "Serial Monogamy as Polygyny or Polyandry?" *Human Nature* 20 (Summer): 130-150.

Borzekowski, Dina L., and Thomas N. Robinson. 2005. "The Remote, the Mouse, and the No. 2 Pencil." *Archives of Pediatrics & Adolescent Medicine* 159 (July): 607-613.

Bosk, Charles. 1979. *Forgive and Remember: Managing Medical Failure*. Chicago, IL: University of Chicago Press.

"Boss Sells His Company, Shares Proceeds." 1999. *Baltimore Sun*, September 12, 24A.

Boucher, Geoff. 2007. "You Too Can Rent a Rock Star." *Los Angeles Times*, January 11. Retrieved January 12, 2007 (www.latimes.com).

Bourdieu, Pierre. 1984. *Distinction: A Social Critique of the Judgement of Taste*. Trans. Richard Nice. Cambridge, MA: Harvard University Press.

Bourne, Joel K. Jr. 2006. "Loving Our Coasts to Death." *National Geographic* 210 (July): 60-87.

Bowles, Samuel and Herbert Gintis. 1977. *Schooling in Capitalist America: Educational Reform and the Contradictions of Economic Life*. New York: Basic Books.

Bradshaw, York W. and Michael Wallace. 1996. *Global Inequalities*. Thousand Oaks, CA: Pine Forge Press.

Bradsher, Keith. 2005. "More Than a Billion Chinese but So Few Coffins." *New York Times*, November 10, C1, C6.

Brady, Diane. 2007. "A Little Shame Goes a Long Way." *Business Week*, April 16, 34-35.

Braga, Anthony A. 2003. "Systematic Review of the Effects of Hot Spots Policing on Crime." Unpublished paper. Retrieved May 14, 2005 (www.campbellcollaboration.org/doc-pdf/hotspots.pdf).

Brainard, Jeffery, and J. J. Hermes. 2008. "Colleges' Earmarks Grow, Amid Criticism." *Chronicle of Higher Education*, March 28, A1, A8-A11.

Bramlett, Mosher D., and William D. Mosher. 2002. *Cohabitation, Marriage, Divorce, and Remarriage in the United States*. Centers for Disease Control and Prevention, *Vital and Health Statistics* (Series 23, No. 25). Hyatsville, MD: National Center for Health Statistics.

Braun, Henry, Frank Jenkins, and Wendy Grigg. 2006. *A Closer Look at Charter Schools Using Hierarchical Linear Modeling* (NCES 2006-460). National Center for Education Statistics, U.S. Department of Education. Washington, DC: U.S. Government Printing Office.

Brea, Jorge A. 2003. "Population Dynamics in Latin America." *Population Bulletin* 58 (March): 1-36.

Breazeal, Cynthia L. 2002. *Designing Sociable Robots*. Cambridge, MA: MIT Press.

Bremner, Jason, Carl Haub, Marlene Lee, Mark Mather, and Eric Zuehlke. 2009. "World Population Highlights: Key Findings from PRB's 2009 World Population Data Sheet." *Population Bulletin* 64 (September): 1-12.

Brescoll, Victoria L., and Eric L. Uhlmann. 2008. "Can An Angry Woman Get Ahead? Status Conferral, Gender, and Expression of Emotion in the Workplace." *Psychological Science* 19 (March): 268-275.

Bricher, R. Marie. 1992. "Teaching Introductory Sociology: Using Aspects of the Classroom as Sociological Events." *Teaching Sociology* 20 (October): 270-275.

Bridgeland, John M., John J. DiIulio, Jr., and Karen Burke Morison. 2006. "The Silent Epidemic: Perspectives of High School Dropouts." Civic Enterprises, March. Retrieved July 21, 2007 (www.civicenterprises.net).

Briggs, Derek C. 2009. "Preparation for College Admission Exams." National Association for College Admission Counseling. Retrieved April 16, 2010 (www.nacacnet.org).

Briggs, Kenneth. 2006. *Double Crossed: Uncovering the Catholic Church's Betrayal of American Nuns*. New York: Doubleday.

Brittingham, Angela, and G. Patricia de la Cruz. 2005. "We the People of Arab Ancestry in the United States." Census 2000 Special Reports, CENSR-21, March. Retrieved March 26, 2007 (www.census.gov).

Britton, Dana M. 2003. *At Work in the Iron Cage: The Prison as a Gendered Organization*. New York: New York University Press.

Britz, Jennifer D. 2006. "To All the Girls I've Rejected." *New York Times*, March 23, A27.

Broder, John, and Jad Mouawad. 2009. "Energy Firms Find No Unity on Climate Bill." *New York Times*, October 19, A1.

Broder, John M. 2007. "Industry Flexes Muscle, Weaker Energy Bill Passes." *New York Times*, December 14, 29.

Brody, Gene H., Shannon Dorsey, Rex Forehand, and Lisa Armistead. 2002. "Unique and Protective Contributions of Parenting and Classroom Processes to the Adjustment of African American Children Living In Single-Parent Families." *Child Development* 73 (January-February): 274-286.

Brooks, Arthur C. 2007. "I Love My Work." *The American* (online): September-October. Retrieved September 30, 2007 (www.theamericanmag.com).

Brouillette, John R., and Ronny E. Turner. 1992. "Creating the Sociological Imagination on the First Day of

Class: The Social Construction of Deviance." *Teaching Sociology* 20 (October): 276-279.

Brown, David. 2005. "Polio Outbreak Occurs Among Amish Families in Minnesota." *Washington Post*, October 14, A3.

Brown, Matthew Hay. 2005. "Storm Victims Rely on Faith to Help Them Through Crisis." *Baltimore Sun*, September 12, 6A.

Brown, Susan I. 2005. "How Cohabitation Is Reshaping American Families." *Contexts* 4 (Summer): 33-37.

Brunvand, Jan H. 2001. *The Truth Never Stands in the Way of a Good Story*. Urbana and Chicago, IL: University of Illinois Press.

Buchmann, Claudia, and Thomas A. DiPrete. 2006. "The Growing Female Advantage in College Completion: The Role of Family Background and Academic Achievement." *American Sociological Review* 71 (August): 515-541.

Buechler, Steven M. 2000. *Social Movements in Advanced Capitalism: The Political Economy and Cultural Construction of Social Activism*. New York: Oxford University Press.

Bulik, Beth S. 2009. "How the U.S. Census is Reading Your Mind." *Advertising Age,* October 26, 6.

Bullock, Karen. 2005. "Grandfathers and the Impact of Raising Grandchildren." *Journal of Sociology and Social Welfare* 32 (March): 43-59.

Bumiller, Elisabeth. 2005. "In the Struggle over the Iraq War, Women Are On the Front Line." *New York Times*, August 29, 11.

Bureau of Justice Statistics. 2006. "Expenditures: National Estimates." Retrieved February 25, 2010 (http://bjs.ojp.usdoj.gov/dataonline).

———. 2009. "Capital Punishment." Retrieved February 25, 2010 (bjs.ojp.usdoj.gov).

Bureau of Labor Statistics. 2009. "Occupational Employment and Wages, May 2008." U.S. Department of Labor. Retrieved July 14, 2009 (www.bls.gov).

———. 2010. "Employment Situation Summary." April 2. Retrieved April 6, 2010 (www.bls.gov).

Bureau of Labor Statistics News Release. 2010a. "Mass Layoffs—February 2010." March 23. Retrieved April 6, 2010 (www.bls.gov).

———. 2010b. "Union Members, 2009." January 22. Retrieved April 6, 2010 (www.bls.gov).

Burns, Barbara J., et al. 2003. "Treatment, Services, and Intervention Programs for Child Delinquents." Washington, DC: U.S. Department of Justice, Office of Juvenile Justice and Delinquency Prevention.

Burr, Chandler. 1996. *A Separate Creation: The Search for the Biological Origins of Sexual Orientation*. New York: Hyperion.

Burrus, Robert T., KimMarie McGoldrick, and Peter W. Schuhmann. 2007. "Self-Reports of Student Cheating: Does a Definition of Cheating Matter?" *Journal of Economic Education* 38 (Winter): 3-16.

Burt, Martha R., John Hedderson, Janine M. Zweig, Mary Jo Ortiz, Laudan Y. Aron, and Sabrina M. Johnson. 2004. "Strategies for Reducing Chronic Street Homelessness." Urban Institute, January 15. Retrieved January 12, 2007 (www.urban.org).

"Bush's Cooks Get Queen Boiling Mad." 2003. *Baltimore Sun*, November 22, 2D.

Bustillo, Miguel. 2006. "Farmers Say They've Got Fruit but No Labor." *Los Angeles Times*, April 17. Retrieved April 28, 2006 (www.latimes.com).

———. 2007. "Ethnicity is No Bar to Jindal's Dream." *Los Angeles Times*, October 24. Retrieved October 25, 2008 (www.latimes.com).

Butterfield, Fox. 2002. "Father Steals Best: Crime in an American Family." *New York Times* (August 15): 1A.

Cabrera, Natasha J., Jay Fagan, and Danielle Farrie. 2008. "Explaining the Long Reach of Fathers' Prenatal Involvement on Later Paternal Engagement." *Journal of Marriage and Family* 70 (December): 1094-1107.

Cadge, Wendy, and Courtney Bender. 2004. "Yoga and Rebirth in America: Asian Religions are Here to Stay." *Contexts* 3 (Winter): 45-51.

Camarota, Steven A. 2009a. "Immigration's Impact on Public Coffers in the United States." Pp. 29-39 in *The Effects of Mass Immigration*. Fraser Institute. Retrieved March 15, 2010 (www.fraserinstitute.org).

———. 2009b. "Immigration's Impact on U.S. Workers." Center for Immigration Studies, November. Retrieved March 15, 2010 (cis.org).

Cameron, Deborah. 2007. *The Myth of Mars and Venus*. Oxford, NY: Oxford University Press.

Campaign Finance Institute. 2008. "Inside Fundraising for the 2008 Party Conventions: Party Surrogates Gather Soft Money While Federal Regulators Turn a Blind Eye." Retrieved June 26, 2008 (www.cfinst.org).

Campion-Vincent, Véronique. 2005. "From Evil Others to Evil Elites: A Dominant Pattern in Conspiracy Theories Today." Pp. 103-122 in *Rumor Mills: The Social Impact of Rumor and Legend*, edited by Gary Alan Fine, Véronique Campion-Vincent, and Chip Heath. New Brunswick, NJ: Transaction Publishers.

Campo-Flores, Arian. 2005. "The Battle for Latino Souls." *Newsweek*, March 31, 50-51.

Cantor, Paul A. 2001. *Gilligan Unbound: Pop Culture in the Age of Globalization*. Lanham, MD: Rowman & Littlefield.

Cantril, Hadley, Hazel Gaudet, and Herta Herzog. 1952. *The Invasion from Mars*. Princeton, NJ: Princeton University Press.

Caperton, Gaston. 2009. "Test Data Allow Better Decisions." *U.S. News & World Report*, September, 24.

Capps, Randy, Rosa Maria Castañeda, Ajay Choudry, and Robert Santos. 2007. *Paying the Price: The Impact of Immigration Raids on America's Children*. Washington, DC: National Council of La Raza.

Card, Josefina J., Marvin B. Eisen, James L. Peterson, and Bonnie Sherman-Williams. 1994. "Evaluating Teenage Pregnancy Prevention and Other Social Programs: Ten Stages of Program Assessment." *Family Planning Perspectives* 26 (May): 116-131.

Cardwell, Sarah. 2009. "Where Do Babies Come From?" *Newsweek*, October 19, 56.

Carey, Benedict. 2004. "Long After Kinsey, Only the Brave Study Sex." *New York Times*, November 9, F1.

_____. 2010. "Revising Book on Disorders of the Mind." *New York Times*, February 10, 1.

Carey, John. 2007. "Big Strides to Become the Jolly Green Giant." *Business Week*, January 29, 57.

Carey, Kevin. 2005. "One Step from the Finish Line: Higher College Graduation Rates are Within Our Reach." Education Trust. Retrieved January 18, 2005 (www2.edtrust.org).

Carl, Traci. 2002. "Amid Latte, Mocha Craze, Coffee Growers Go Hungry in Paradise." Retrieved September 19, 2002 (http://story.news.yahoo.com).

Carlson, Marcia, Sara McLanahan, Paula England, and Barbara Devaney. 2005. "What We Know about Unmarried Parents: Implications for Building Strong Families Programs." Mathematica Policy Research, Inc., January. Retrieved June 5, 2007 (www.mathematica-mpr.com).

Carmichael, Mary. 2007. "Troubled Waters." *Newsweek*, June 4, 52-56.

Carnagey, Nicholas L., and Craig A. Anderson. 2005. "The Effects of Reward and Punishment in Violent Video Games on Aggressive Affect, Cognition, and Behavior." *Psychological Science* 16 (November): 882-889.

Carney, Ginny. 1997. "Native American Loanwords in American English." *Wicazo SA Review*, 12 (Spring): 189-203.

Carr, J. L. 2005. *American College Health Association Campus Violence White Paper*. Baltimore MD: American College Health Association.

Carr, Nicholas. 2008. "Is Google Making Us Stupid?" *Atlantic Monthly*, July/August. Retrieved May 11, 2010 (www.theatlantic.com).

Carroll, Jason S., Laura M. Padilla-Walker, Larry J. Nelson, Chad D. Olson, Carolyn McNamara Barry, and Stephanie D. Madsen. 2008. "Generation XXX: Pornography Acceptance and Use Among Emerging Adults." *Journal of Adolescent Research* 23 (January): 6-30.

Carroll, Jill. 2002. "Getting Good Teaching Evaluations Without Stand-Up Comedy." *Chronicle of Higher Education*, April 15. Retrieved April 15, 2002 (http://chronicle.com).

Carroll, Joseph. 2006. "Americans Prefer Male Boss to a Female Boss." Gallup Organization. Retrieved September 3, 2006 (www.gallup.com).

_____. "Most Americans Approve of Interracial Marriages." Gallup News Service, July 6. Retrieved October 10, 2007 (www.galluppoll.com).

Carroll, Stephen J., and Emre Erkut. 2009. *The Benefits to Taxpayers from Increases in Students' Educational Attainment*. Santa Monica, CA: Rand.

Carter, Jimmy. 2005. *Our Endangered Values: America's Moral Crisis*. New York: Simon & Schuster.

Cascio, Jamais. 2009. "Get Smarter." *Atlantic Monthly*, July/August. Retrieved May 11, 2010 (www.theatlantic.com).

"Cash Countesses." 2007. *Forbes*, October 8, 312, 316-317.

Caston, Richard J. 1998. *Life in a Business-Oriented Society: A Sociological Perspective*. Boston, MA: Allyn & Bacon.

Catalano, Shannan. 2007. "Intimate Partner Violence in the United States." Bureau of Justice Statistics. Retrieved April 9, 2010 (www.ojp.usdoj.gov/bjs).

Catalyst. 2007. "2007: Board Directors." Retrieved April 28, 2008 (www.catalyst.org).

Cauchon, Dennis. 2009. "Incomes of Young in 8-Year Nose Dive." *USA Today*, September 17. Retrieved September 18, 2010 (www.usatoday.com).

Cawthorne, Alexandra. 2009. "Weathering the Storm: Black Men in the Recession." Center for American Progress, April 15. Retrieved April 20, 2009 (www.americanprogress.com).

Cellini, Stephanie R., Signe-Mary McKernan, and Caroline Ratcliffe. 2008. "The Dynamics of Poverty in the United States: A Review of Data, Methods, and Findings." *Journal of Policy Analysis and Management* 27 (Summer): 577-605.

Center for American Progress. 2006. "Public Recognizes Debt as a Fast Growing Problem in U.S." July 19. Retrieved June 3, 2007 (www.americanprogress.org).

Center for American Women and Politics. 2008. "Women in Elective Office 2008." Retrieved June 5, 2008 (www.cawp.rutgers.edu).

_____. 2010. "Women in Elective Office 2010." Retrieved March 5, 2010 (www.cawp.rutgers.edu).

Center for Responsive Politics. 2009. "Presidential Fundraising and Spending, 1976-2008." Retrieved March 25, 2010 (www.opensecrets.org).

_____. 2010a. "Lobbying Database." Retrieved March 25, 2010 (www.opensecrets.org).

_____. 2010b. "Most Expensive Races." Retrieved March 25, 2010 (www.opensecrets.org).

_____. 2010c. "Top PACs." Retrieved March 25, 2010 (www.opensecrets.org).

Center for the Study of Global Christianity. 2007. "Global Table 5: Status of Global Mission, Presence and Activities, AD 1800-2005." Gordon-Conwell Theological Seminary. Retrieved August 24, 2007 (www.gcts.edu).

Center for Women's Business Research. 2009. "The Economic Impact of Women-Owned Businesses in the United States." October. Retrieved April 9, 2010 (www.womensbusinessresearch.org).

Centers for Disease Control and Prevention. 2008. *Sexually Transmitted Disease Surveillance, 2007*. Atlanta, GA: U.S. Department of Health and Human Services.

Chambliss, William J., and Robert B. Seidman. 1982. *Law, Order, and Power*, 2nd edition. Reading, MA: Addison-Wesley.

Chambliss, William J., ed. 1969. *Crime and the Legal Process*. New York: McGraw-Hill.

Chan, Sam. 1997. "Families with Asian Roots." Pp. 251-344 in *Developing Cross-Cultural Competence: a Guide for Working with Children and Their Families*, 2nd edition, edited by Eleanor W. Lynch and Marci J. Hanson. Baltimore, MD: Paul H. Brookes Publishing.

Chandler, Michael Alison. 2009. "Joblessness at Home a Burden on Schools." *Washington Post*, November 27, B2.

Chandler, Tertius and Gerald Fox. 1974. *3000 Years of Urban Growth*. New York: Academic Press.

Chandra, A., G. A. Martinez, W. D. Mosher, J.C. Abma, and J. Jones. 2005. "Fertility, Family Planning, and Reproductive Health of U.S. Women: Data from the 2002 National Survey of Family Growth." *Vital and Health Statistics* (Series 23, No. 25). Hyatsville, MD: National Center for Health Statistics.

Chang, Andrea. 2008. "Couples Are Finding Ways to Cut Wedding Costs." *Los Angeles Times*, August 27. Retrieved August 28, 2008 (www.latimes.com).

Chapman, Tony, and Jenny Hockey, eds. 1999. *Ideal Homes? Social Change and Domestic Life*. New York: Routledge.

Chasin, Barbara H. 2004. *Inequality & Violence in the United States: Casualties of Capitalism*, second edition. Amherst, NY: Humanity Books.

Chelala, César. 2002. "World Violence against Women A Great Unspoken Pandemic." *Philadelphia Inquirer*, November 4. Retrieved November 7, 2002 (www.commondreams.org).

Chen, Xianglei. 2005. *First Generation Students in Postsecondary Education: A Look at Their College Transcripts* (NCES 2005-17). U.S. Department of Education, National Center for Education Statistics. Washington, DC: U.S. Government Printing Office.

Cheshire, Tamara. 2006. "American Indian Families: Strength and Answers from Our Past." Pp. 315-327 in *Families in Global and Multicultural Perspective*, 2nd ed., edited by Bron B. Ingoldsby and Suzanna D. Smith. Thousand Oaks, CA: Sage.

Chesler, Phyllis. 2006. "The Failure of Feminism." *Chronicle of Higher Education*, February 26, B12.

Chesney-Lind, Meda and Lisa Pasko. 2004. *The Female Offender: Girls, Women, and Crime*, 2nd edition. Thousand Oaks, CA: Sage.

Child Welfare Information Gateway. 2009. "Foster Care Statistics." U.S. Department of Health and Human Services, Administration for Children and Families. Retrieved January 10, 2010 (www.childwelfare.gov).

Children's Defense Fund. 2008. *The State of America's Children 2008*. Retrieved July 12, 2009 (www.unicef.org).

Choice, Pamela, and Leanne K. Lamke. 1997. "A Conceptual Approach to Understanding Abused Women's Stay/Leave Decisions." *Journal of Family Issues* 18 (May): 290-314.

Choudhury, Tufyal, Mohammed Aziz, Duaa Izzidien, Intissar Khreeji, and Dilwar Hussein. 2006. "Perceptions of Discrimination and Islamophobia: Voices from Members of Muslim Communities in the European Union." Retrieved September 1, 2007 (www.eumc.eu).

Christensen, Kim, and Garrett Therolf. 2009. "California Falls Short in Examining Deaths of Children." *Los Angeles Times*, November 5. Retrieved November 6, 2009 (www.latimes.com).

Christenson, Matthew, Thomas M. McDevitt, and Karen A. Stanecki. 2004. *Global Population Profile: 2002*. U.S. Census Bureau, International Population Reports WP/02. Washington, DC: Government Printing Office.

Christeson, William, Amy Dawson Taggart, Ted Eismeier, and Soren Messner-Zidell. 2009. "Ready, Willing, and Unable to Serve: 75 Percent of Young Adults Cannot Join the Military; Early Ed in Pennsylvania Is Needed to Ensure National Security." Mission: Readiness. Retrieved April 22, 2010 (www.missionreadiness.org).

Christiano, Kevin J. 2000. "Religion and the Family in Modern American Culture." Pp. 43-78 in *Family, Religion, and Social Change in Diverse Societies*, edited by Sharon K. Houseknecht and Jerry G. Pankhurst. New York: Oxford University Press.

Chu, Henry. 2007. "A Gift for India's Inter-Caste Couples." *Los Angeles Times*, November 4. Retrieved November 6, 2007 (www.latimes.com).

Chudowsky, Naomi, and Victor Chudowsky. 2010. "Are There Differences in Achievement Between Boys and Girls?" *Center on Education Policy*, March. Retrieved April 20, 2010 (www.cep-dc.org).

Churchill, Ward. 1997. *A Little Matter of Genocide: Holocaust and Denial in the Americas, 1492 to the Present*. San Francisco: City Lights Books.

Ciabattari, Teresa, 2004. "Cohabitation and Housework: The Effects of Marital Intentions." *Journal of Marriage and Family* 66 (February): 118-125.

Cichocki, Mary K. 1981. "Women's Travel Patterns in a Suburban Development." Pp. 151-163 in *New Space for Women*, edited by Gerda R. Wekerle, Rebecca Peterson, and David Morley. Boulder, CO: Westview Press.

Citizens Against Government Waste. 2010. "Pork-Barrel Report." Retrieved March 25, 2010 (www.cagw.org).

Citizens for Responsibility and Ethics in Washington (CREW). 2007. "CREW Releases 'Family Affair' Detailing how 96 House Members Used Campaign Funds to Financially Benefit Family Members." June 17. Retrieved June 27, 2008 (www.citizensforethics.org).

_____. 2008. "CREW Releases New Report Detailing Senators' Use of Positions to Benefit Family Members." February 24. Retrieved June 27, 2008 (www.citizensforethics.org).

Clawson, Dan, Alan Neustadtl and Mark Weller. 1998. *Dollars and Votes: How Business Campaign Contributions Subvert Democracy*. Philadelphia, PA: Temple University Press.

Clayton, Mark. 2010. "Earth's Growing Nitrogen Threat." *Christian Science Monitor*, January 10, 36-37.

Clifford, Stephanie. 2009. "Online Age Quiz is a Window for Drug Makers." *New York Times*, March 26, 1.

Cloke, Kenneth and Joan Goldsmith. 2002. *End of Management and the Rise of Organizational Democracy*. San Francisco: Jossey-Bass.

Cohan, Catherine I., and Stacey Kleinbaum. 2002. "Toward a Greater Understanding of the Cohabitation Effect: Premarital Cohabitation and Marital Communication." *Journal of Marriage and Family* 64 (February): 180-192.

Cohany, Sharon. 2009. "Ranks of Discouraged Workers and Others Marginally Attached to the Labor Force Rise During Recession." Issues in Labor Statistics, U.S. Bureau of Labor Statistics, April. Retrieved August 9, 2009 (www.bls.gov).

Cohen, Harry. 1981. *Connections: Understanding Social Relationships*. Ames: Iowa State University Press.

Cohen, Jere. 2002. *Protestantism and Capitalism: The Mechanisms of Influence.* New York: Aldine de Gruyter.

Cohen, Joel E. 2005. "Human Population Grows Up." *Scientific American* 293 (September): 48-56.

Cohen, Jon, and Philip Rucker. 2010. "Poll Finds Most Americans Are Unhappy with Government." *Washington Post*, February 11, A3.

Cohn, Meredith. 2007. "Green." *Baltimore Sun*, March 11, 1A, 18A.

Colapinto, John. 1997. "The True Story of John/Joan." *Rolling Stone* (December 11): 54-73, 92-97.

———. 2001. *As Nature Made Him: The Boy Who Was Raised as a Girl.* New York: Harper Perennial.

———. 2004. "What Were the Real Reasons Behind David Reimer's Suicide?" *Slate*, June 3. Retrieved April 24, 2008 (www.slate.com).

Coley, Rebekah L. 2002. "What Mothers Teach, What Daughters Learn: Gender Mistrust And Self-Sufficiency Among Low-Income Women." Pp. 97-106 in *Just Living Together: Implications of Cohabitation on Families, Children, And Social Policy*, edited by Alan Booth and Ann C. Crouter. Mahwah, NJ: Lawrence Erlbaum Associates.

Coll, Steve. 2008. *The Bin Ladens: An Arabian Family in the American Century.* New York: Penguin.

College Board. 2006. "2006 College-Bound Seniors: Total Group Profile Report." Retrieved July 29, 2007 (www.collegeboard.com).

———. 2008a. "Asian Americans and Pacific Islanders: Facts, not Fiction: Setting the Record Straight." Retrieved July 12, 2008 (www.collegeboard.com).

———. 2008b. "The 4th Annual AP Report to the Nation." February. Retrieved July 15, 2008 (professionals.collegeboard.com).

———. 2010. "The 6th Annual AP Report to the Nation." February 10. Retrieved April 15, 2010 (www.collegeboard.com).

Collins, Patricia Hill. 1990. *Black Feminist Thought: Knowledge, Consciousness, and the Politics of Empowerment.* New York: Routledge.

Collins, Randall. 2002. "Credential Inflation and the Future of Universities." Pp. 23-46 in *The Future of the City of Intellect: The Changing American University*, edited by Steven Brint. Stanford, CA: Stanford University Press.

Commission on No Child Left Behind, The. 2007. *Beyond NCLB: Fulfilling the Promise to Our Nation's Children.* Retrieved July 21, 2007 (www.aspeninstitute.org).

Conger, Rand D., and Glen H. Elder, eds. 1994. *Families in Troubled Times: Adapting to Change in Rural America.* New York: Aldine.

Conley, Dalton. 2004. *The Pecking Order: Which Siblings Succeed And Why.* New York: Pantheon.

Conlin, M. 2007. "The Kids Are All Right." *Business Week*, October 8, 18.

Connolly, Frank W. 2001. "My Students Don't Know What They're Missing." *Chronicle of Higher Education*, December 21, B5.

Consumer Electronics Association. 2007. "The Energy and Greenhouse Gas Emissions Impact of Telecommuting and e-Commerce." July. Retrieved October 17, 2007 (www.cea.org).

Conway, Kevin P., and Joan McCord. 2005. "Co-Offending and Patterns of Juvenile Crime." Washington, DC: National Institute of Justice. Retrieved October 12, 2006 (www.ojp.usdoj.gov/nij).

Cooey, Paula M., William R. Eakin, and Jay B. McDaniel, eds. 1991. *After Patriarchy: Feminist Transformations of the World Religions.* Maryknoll, NY: Orbis Books.

Cook, Thomas D. and Donald T. Campbell. 1979. *Quasi-Experimentation: Design and Analysis Issues for Field Settings.* Chicago, IL: Rand McNally.

Cooley, Charles Horton. 1909/1983. *Social Organization: A Study of the Larger Mind.* New Brunswick, NJ: Transaction Books.

Coontz, Stephanie. 2005. *Marriage: A History: How Love Conquered Marriage.* New York, Penguin.

Cooper, O. R., et al. 2010. "Increasing Springtime Ozone Mixing Ratios in the Free Troposphere over Western North America." *Nature* 463 (January 21): 344-348.

Corbett, Christianne, Catherine Hill and Andresse St. Rose. 2008. *Where the Girls Are: The Facts about Gender Equity in Education.* Washington, DC: American Association of University Women.

Corn, David. 2010. "Thank You, Sir. May We Have Another?" *Mother Jones*, January/February, 31-33.

Corporation for National and Community Service, Office of Research and Policy Development. 2007. *Volunteering in America: 2007 State Trends and Rankings in Civic Life.* Washington, DC.

Cose, Ellis. 1999. "Deciphering the Code of the Street." *Newsweek*, August 30, 33.

Coser, Lewis. 1956. *The Functions of Social Conflict.* New York: Free Press.

Coy, Peter, Michelle Conlin, and Moira Herbst. 2010. "The Disposable Worker." *Bloomburg Businessweek*, January 18, 33-39.

Cressey, Donald R. 1953. *Other People's Money: A Study in the Social Psychology of Embezzlement.* Glencoe, IL: Free Press.

Crilly, Rob. 2007. "In Sudan, a Blasphemous Teddy Bear." *Christian Science Monitor*, November 29, 7.

Crisis at the Core: Preparing All Students for College and Work. 2004. American College Testing. Retrieved January 5, 2005 (www.act.org).

Crockett, Roger O. 2006. "The Rising Stock of Black Directors." *Business Week*, February 27, 34.

Cross, Terry L. 1998. "Understanding Family Resiliency from a Relational World View." Pp. 143-157 in *Resiliency in Native American and immigrant families*, edited by Hamilton I. McCubbin, Elizabeth A. Thompson, Anne I. Thompson, and Julie E. Fromer. Thousand Oaks, CA: Sage.

Crossley, David. 2008. "The Worst Natural Disasters Ever." LiveScience, May 6. Retrieved August 4, 2008 (www.livescience.com).

Crothers, Charles. 1979. "On the Myth of Rural Tranquility: Comment on Webb and Collette." *American Journal of Sociology.* 84 (May): 1441-1445.

"Crowds Call for Teacher's Death." 2007. *Baltimore Sun*, December 1, 3A.

Cullen, Lisa T., and Coco Masters. 2008. "We Just Clicked." *Time*, January 28, 86-89.

Curlin, Farr A., Sarah A. Sellergren, John D. Lantos, and Marshall H. Chin. 2007. "Physicians' Observations and Interpretations of the Influence of Religion and Spirituality on Health." *Archives of Internal Medicine* 167 (April 9): 649-654.

Currie, E. 1985. *Confronting Crime: An American Challenge.* New York: Pantheon.

Currie, Janet, and Erdal Tekin. 2006. "Does Child Abuse Cause Crime?" Cambridge, MA: National Bureau of Economic Research, Working Paper 12171. Retrieved June 12, 2006 (http://papers.nber.org).

Curtiss, Susan. 1977. *Genie.* New York: Academic Press.

Cutler, David M., Adriana Lleras-Muney, and Tom Vogl. 2008. "Socioeconomic Status and Health: Dimensions and Mechanisms." National Bureau of Economic Research, September. Retrieved March 2, 2010 (www.nber.org).

Dahl, Robert A. 1961. *Who Governs? Democracy and Power in an American City.* New Haven. CT: Yale University Press.

Dalton, Madeline A., et al. 2005. "Use of Cigarettes and Alcohol by Preschoolers While Role-Playing as Adults." *Archives of Pediatrics & Adolescent Medicine* 159 (September): 854-859.

Daly, Mary. 1973. *Beyond God the Father.* Boston, MA: Beacon Press.

Dandaneau, Steven P. 2001. *Taking It Big: Developing Sociological Consciousness in Postmodern Times.* Thousand Oaks, CA: Pine Forge Press.

Danziger, S. 2008. "The Price of Independence: The Economics of Early Adulthood." *Family Focus* 53 (March): F7-F8.

Dao, James. 2009. "At V.A., Scrutiny over Abuses and $24 Million in Bonuses." *New York Times*, August 22, A11.

Darling-Hammond, Linda, Ruth Chung Wei, Alethea Andree, Nikole Richardson, and Stelios Orphanos. 2009. *Professional Learning in the Learning Profession: A Status Report on Teacher Development in the United States and Abroad.* Retrieved April 20, 2010 (www.nsdc.org).

Davey, Monica, and Susan Saulny. 2009. "Blagojevich Charged with 16 Corruption Felonies." *New York Times*, April 3, A1.

Davies, James B., Susanna Sandstrom, Anthony Shorrocks, and Edward N. Wolff. 2006. "The World Distribution of Household Wealth." World Institute for Development Economic Research, United Nations University, December 5. Retrieved March 23, 2007 (www.wider.unu.edu).

Davies, James C. 1962. "Toward a Theory of Revolution." *American Sociology Review* 27 (February): 5-19.

———. 1979. "The J-Curve of Rising and Declining Satisfaction as a Cause of Revolution and Rebellion." Pp. 413-436 in *Violence in America: Historical and Comparative Perspectives*, edited by Hugh D. Graham and Ted R. Gurr. Beverly Hills, CA: Sage.

Davis, F. J. 1991. *Who is Black?* University Park: Pennsylvania State University Press.

Davis, James A., Tom W. Smith and Peter V. Marsden. 2005. *General Social Surveys, 1972-2004: Cumula-*

tive Codebook. Chicago, IL: National Opinion Research Center.

Davis, Kelly D., W. Benjamin Goodman, Amy E. Pirretti, and David M. Almeida. 2008. "Nonstandard Work Schedules, Perceived Family Well-Being, and Daily Stressors." *Journal of Marriage and Family* 70 (November): 991-1003.

Davis, Kingsley, and Wilbert E. Moore. 1945. "Some Principles of Stratification." *American Sociological Review* 10 (April): 242-49.

Dawkins, Richard. 2009. "The Angry Evolutionist." *Newsweek*, October 5, 51-53.

Day, Jennifer Cheeseman, and Eric C. Newburger. 2002. "The Big Payoff: Educational Attainment and Synthetic Estimates of Work-Life Earnings." U.S. Census Bureau, Current Population Reports, P23-210. Retrieved December 5, 2004 (www.census.gov).

Day, Jennifer Cheeseman, and Kelly Holder. 2004. "Voting and Registration in the Election of November 2002." U.S. Census Bureau, Current Population Reports, P20-552. Retrieved August 2, 2004 (www.census.gov).

de la Cruz, G. Patricia, and Angela Brittingham. 2003. "The Arab Population: 2000." U.S. Census Bureau. Retrieved May 3, 2004 (www.census.gov).

de las Casas, Bartolome. 1992. *The Devastation of the Indies: A Brief Account.* Baltimore, Maryland: Johns Hopkins University Press.

De Long, J. Bradford, and Andrei Shleifer. 1992. "Princes and Merchants: European City Growth Before the Industrial Revolution." National Bureau of Economic Research, December. Retrieved January 10, 2008 (www.nper.org).

Death Penalty Information Center. 2009. "The Death Penalty in 2009: Year End Report." Retrieved February 25, 2010 (www.deathpenaltyinfo.org).

Deaton, Angus S. 2009. "Aging, Religion, and Health." National Bureau of Economic Research, August. Retrieved April 26, 2010 (www.nber.org).

DeBiaggi, Sylvia D. 2002. *Changing Gender Roles: Brazilian Immigrant Families in the U.S.* New York: LFB Scholarly Publishing LLC.

Dee, Thomas, and Brian Jacob. 2009. "The Impact of No Child Left Behind on Student Achievement." National Bureau of Economic Research, November. Retrieved April 20, 2010 (www.nber.org).

Dee, Thomas S. 2006. "The Why Chromosome." *Education Next* No 4. (Fall): 69-75.

Dee, Thomas S., and Brian A. Jacob. 2006. "Do High School Exit Exams Influence Educational Attainment or Labor Market Performance?" National Bureau of Economic Research, April. Retrieved, www.nber.org (accessed July 25, 2007).

Deegan, Mary Jo. 1986. *Jane Addams and the Men of the Chicago School, 1892-1918.* New Brunswick, NJ: Transaction Books.

"Defining Overweight and Obesity." 2009. Centers for Disease Control and Prevention, August 12. Retrieved August 23, 2009 (www.cdc.gov).

Degler, Carl. 1981. *At Odds: Women and the Family in America from the Revolution to the Present.* New York: Oxford University Press.

della Porta, Donatella and Mario Diani. 1999. *Social Movements: An Introduction.* Malden, MA: Blackwell Publishers.

DeMaris, Alfred. 2001. "The Influence of Intimate Violence on Transitions Out Of Cohabitation." *Journal of Marriage and Family* 63 (February): 235-246.

Demick, Barbara. 2002. "Where Dogs Are Diners or Dinners." *Baltimore Sun*, January 26, 2A.

Demos, John. 1986. *Past, Present, and Personal: The Family and the Life Course in American History.* New York: Oxford University Press.

DeNavas-Walt, Carmen, Bernadette D. Proctor, and Jessica C. Smith. 2009. *Income, Poverty, and Health Insurance Coverage in the United States: 2008.* Washington, DC: U.S. Government Printing Office.

Denton-Borhaug, Kelly. 2004. "The Complex and Rich Landscape of Student Spirituality: Findings from the Goucher College Spirituality Survey." *Religion & Education* 31 (Fall): 41-61.

DeParle, Jason, and Robert Gebeloff. 2010. "The Safety Net—Living on Nothing but Food Stamps." *New York Times*, January 3, 1.

De Pommereau, Isabelle. 2010. "Germany Faces Up to Abuse." *Christian Science Monitor*, April 26, 13.

Deresiewicz, William. 2009. "Faux Friendship." *The Chronicle Review*, December 11, B6-B10.

Desmond-Harris, Jenee. 2009. "Why Michelle's Hair Matters." *Time*, September 7, 55-57.

Deutsch, Francine M. 2007. "Undoing Gender." *Gender & Society* 21 (February): 106-127.

Deveny, Kathleen. 2008. "They're No Baby Einsteins." *Newsweek*, January 14, 61.

Dew, Jeffrey. 2009. "Bank on It: Thrifty Couples Are the Happiest." Pp. 23-30 in *The State of Our Union, Marriage in America 2009: Money & Marriage,* edited by W. Bradford Wilcox and Elizabeth Marquardt. Charlottesville, VA: The National Marriage Project.

Dey, Judy Goldberg, and Catherine Hill. 2007. "Behind the Pay Gap." American Association of University Women Educational Foundation. Retrieved March 1, 2008 (www.aauw.org).

Diamond, Milton, and H. Keith Sigmundson. 1997. "Sex Reassignment at Birth: Long-Term Review and Clinical Implications." *Archives of Pediatrics & Adolescent Medicine* 15 (March): 298-304.

Dickert-Conlin, Stacy and Ross Rubenstein. 2007. *Economic Inequality and Higher Education: Access Persistence and Success*. New York: Russell Sage Foundation.

Dilworth-Anderson, Peggye, Linda M. Burton, and William L. Turner. 1993. "The Importance of Values in the Study of Culturally Diverse Families." *Family Relations* 42 (July): 238–242.

Dines, Gail. 2008. "Yale Sex Week Glosses over Porn's Dark Side." *Hartford Courant*, February 11. Retrieved June 1, 2008 (www.courant.com).

Dinkes, Rachel, Jana Kemp, Katrina Baum, and Thomas D. Snyder. 2010. *Indicators of School Crime and Safety: 2009* (NCES 2010-012/NCJ 228478). National Center for Education Statistics, Institute of Education Sciences, U.S. Department of Education, and Bureau of Justice Statistics, Office of Justice Programs, U.S. Department of Justice, Washington, DC.

DiversityInc. 2008. "Fortune 500 Black, Latino, Asian CEOs." July 22. Retrieved September 11, 2008 (www.diversity.com).

Dixon, Robyn. 2009. "Africa's Bitter Cycle of Child Slavery." *Los Angeles Times,* July 12. Retrieved July 13, 2009 (www.latimes.com).

Do, Hien Duc. 1999. *The Vietnamese Americans*. Westport, CT: Greenwood Press.

Dobbie, Will, and Roland G. Fryer, Jr. 2009. "Are High Quality Schools Enough to Close the Achievement Gap? Evidence from a Social Experiment in Harlem." National Bureau of Economic Research, November. Retrieved April 20, 2010 (www.nber.org).

Dobrzynski, Judith. 2008. "The Highest Paid Women in Corporate America." *ForbesLife Executive Woman*, Fall, 76, 111.

Dockterman, Daniel, and Gabriel Velasco. 2010. "Statistical Portrait of the Foreign-Born Population in the United States, 2008." Pew Hispanic Center, January 21. Retrieved March 15, 2010 (pewhispanic.org).

Doeringer, Peter B. and Michael J. Piore. 1971. *Internal Labor Markets and Manpower Analysis*. Lexington, MA: Heath-Lexington Books.

Dohm, Arleen, and Lynn Shniper. 2007. "Occupational Employment Projections to 2016." *Monthly Labor Review* 130 (November): 86-125.

Domhoff, G. William. 2006. *Who Rules America? Power, Politics, & Social Change*, 5th ed. Boston, MA: McGraw Hill.

____. 2010. "Power in America: Wealth, Income, and Power." Retrieved March 3, 2010 (http://sociology.ucsc.edu/whorulesamerica/power/wealth.html).

Domosh, Mona and Joni Seager. 2001. *Feminist Geographers Make Sense of the World*. New York: The Guilford Press.

Dorius, Cassandra J., Stephen J. Bahr, John P. Hoffman, and Elizabeth L. Harmon. 2004. "Parenting Practices as Moderators of the Relationship between Peers and Adolescent Marijuana Use." *Journal of Marriage and Family* 66 (February): 163-178.

Douglas, Susan J. and Meredith W. Michaels. 2004. *The Mommy Myth: The Idealization of Motherhood and How It Has Undermined Women*. New York: Free Press.

Dovidio, John F. 2009. "Racial Bias, Unspoken but Heard." *Science* 326 (December 18): 1641-1642.

Draffan, George. 2003. "Profile of Boeing." Retrieved September 5, 2004 (www.endgame.org).

Dreazen, Yochi J. 2009. "Muslim Population in the Military Raises Difficult Issues." *Wall Street Journal*, November 9. Retrieved November 12, 2009 (http://online.wsj.com).

Drogin, Bob. 2009. "Same-Sex Vote Draws U.S. Focus." *Baltimore Sun,* November 4, 10.

Du Bois, W. E. B. 1986. *The Souls of Black Folk*. New York: Library of America.

Duhigg, Charles. 2009a. "Clean Water Laws Are Neglected, at a Cost of Suffering." *New York Times,* August 10, A1.

____. 2009b. "Millions in U.S. Drink Dirty Water, Records Show." *New York Times,* December 8, A1.

____. 2010. "Saving U.S. Water and Sewer Systems Would Be Costly." *New York Times*, March 14, A1.

Dunifon, Rachel and Lori Kowaleski-Jones. 2007. "The Influence of Grandparents in Single-Mother Families." *Journal of Marriage and Family* 69 (May): 465-481.

Dunlap, Riley E. 2007. "The State of Environmentalism in the U.S." Gallup Poll, April 19. Retrieved March 27, 2007 (www.gallup.com).

Durkheim, Emile. 1893/1964. *The Division of Labor in Society*. New York: Free Press.

____. 1897/1951. *Suicide: A Study in Sociology*. (John A. Spaulding and George Simpson, trans,; George Simpson, ed., 1951). New York: Free Press.

____. 1898/1956. *Education and Sociology*. Trans. Sherwood D. Fox. Glencoe, IL: Free Press.

____. 1961. *The Elementary Forms of the Religious Life*. New York: Collier Books.

Durose, Matthew R., and Patrick A. Langan. 2004. "Felony Sentences in State Courts, 2002." Washington, DC: U.S. Department of Justice, Bureau of Justice Statistics.

Dush, Kamp, Catherine Cohan, and Paul Amato. 2003. "The Relationship between Cohabitation and Marital Quality and Stability: Change Across Cohorts?" *Journal of Marriage and Family* (August): 539-549.

Duster, Troy. 2005. "Race and Reification in Science." *Science* 307, February 18, 1050-1051.

Dye, Jane Lawler. 2008. *Fertility of American Women: 2006*. Current Population Reports, P20-558. Washington, DC: U.S. Census Bureau.

Dye, Thomas R. and Harmon Ziegler. 2003. *The Irony of Democracy: An Uncommon Introduction to American Politics*, 12th ed. Belmont, CA: Wadsworth.

Eaton, Leslie. 2007. "In Mississippi, Poor Lag in Hurricane Aid." *New York Times,* November 16, 1.

Ebaugh, Helen Rose. 2003. "Religion and the New Immigrants." Pp. 225-239 in *Handbook of the Sociology of Religion*, edited by Michele Dillon. New York: Cambridge University Press,

Eberstadt, Nicholas. 2009. "Poor Statistics." *Forbes,* March 2, 26.

Eckstein, Rick, Rebecca Schoenike, and Kevin Delaney. 1995. "The Voice of Sociology: Obstacles to Teaching and Learning the Sociological Imagination." *Teaching Sociology* 23 (October): 353-363.

Edin, Kathryn and Laura Lein. 1997. *Making Ends Meet: How Single Mothers Survive Welfare And Low-Wage Work*. New York: Russell Sage Foundation.

Egan, Timothy. 2006. "The Rise of Shrinking-Vacation Syndrome." *New York Times*, August 20, A18.

Eggen, Dan. 2010. "Corporate Sponsorship is Campaign Issue on Which Both Parties Can Agree." *Washington Post,* February 18, A15.

Egley, Arlen Jr., and Christina E. O'Donnell. 2009. "Highlights of the 2007 National Youth Gang Survey." Office of Justice Programs, April. Retrieved February 22, 2010 (www.ojp.usdoj.gov).

Ehrenreich, Barbara. 2001. *Nickel and Dimed: On (Not) Getting by in America*. New York: Metropolitan Books.

Ehrlich, Paul. 1971. *The Population Bomb*, 2nd ed. San Francisco: Freeman.

Ehrlich, Paul R. and Anne H. Ehrlich. 2008. *The Dominant Animal: Human Evolution and the Environment*. Washington, DC: Island Press.

Eilperin, Juliet. 2009. "Fewer Americans Believe in Global Warming, Poll Shows." *Washington Post,* November 25, A4.

Eisenberg, Abne M. and Ralph R. Smith, Jr. 1971. *Nonverbal Communication*. Indianapolis: The Bobbs-Merrill Company, Inc.

Eisenberg, Nancy, et al., 2005. "Relations among Positive Parenting, Children's Effortful Control, And Externalizing Problems: A Three-Wave Longitudinal Study." *Child Development* 76 (September/October): 1055-1071.

Eisenbrey, Ross. 2009. "Downtime: Workers Forced to Settle for Fewer Hours." Economic Policy Institute, January 14. Retrieved July 26, 2009 (www.epi.org).

——. Mark Levinson, and Lawrence Mishel. 2007. "The Agenda for Shared Prosperity." *EPI Journal* 17 (Winter): 1-8.

Ekman, Paul. 1985. *Telling Lies: Clues to Deceit in the Marketplace, Politics, and Marriage*. New York: W.W. Norton & Company.

Ekman, Paul and Wallace V. Friesen. 1984. *Unmasking the Face: A Guide to Recognizing Emotions from Facial Clues*. Palo Alto, CA: Consulting Psychologists Press, Inc.

Elgin, Ben. 2008. "Green—Up to a Point." *Business Week*, March 3, 25-26.

Ellingwood, Ken. 2009. "Not Being on Time a High Art in Mexico." *Los Angeles Times,* September 12. Retrieved September 22, 2009 (www.latimes.com).

Ellis, Bill. 2005. "Legend/AntiLegend: Humor as an Integral part of the Contemporary Legend Process." Pp. 123-140 in *Rumor Mills: The Social Impact of Rumor and Legend*, edited by Gary Alan Fine, Véronique Campion-Vincent, and Chip Heath. New Brunswick, NJ: Transaction Publishers.

Engel, Susan. 2009. "Teach Your Teachers Well." *New York Times,* November 2, 21.

Engemann, Kristie M. and Michael T. Owyang. 2005. "So Much for That Merit Raise: The Link between Wages and Appearance." *Regional Economist* (April): 10-11.

England, Paula. 2006. "Toward Gender Equality: Progress and Bottlenecks." Pp. 245-264 in *The Declining Significance of Gender?* edited by Francine D. Blau, Mary C. Brinton, and David B. Grutsky. New York: Russell Sage Foundation.

____, Emily Fitzgibbons Shafer, and Alison C. K. Fogarty. 2007. "Hooking Up and Forming Romantic Relationships on Today's College Campuses." Pp. 531-547 in *The Gendered Society Reader,* 3rd edition, edited by Michael Kimmel. New York: Oxford University Press.

____, and Reuben J. Thomas. 2009. "The Decline of the Date and the Rise of the College Hook Up." Pp. 141-152 in *Family in Transition,* 15th ed., edited by Arlene S. Skolnick and Jerome H. Skolnick. Boston: Pearson Higher Education.

Environmental Integrity Project. 2007. "Paying Less to Pollute: Environmental Enforcement Under the Bush Administration." Retrieved February 12, 2008 (www.enrironmentalintegrity.org).

EPE Research Center. 2007. "More Than 1.2 Million Students Will Not Graduate in 2007; Detailed Graduation Data Available for Every U.S. District and State." *Education Week*, June 12. Retrieved July 23, 2007 (www.edweek.org).

Erikson, Kai T. 1966. *Wayward Puritans: A Study in the Sociology of Deviance*. New York: John Wiley & Sons.

Esipova, Neli, Julie Ray, and Rajesh Srinivasan. 2010. "Young, Less Educated Yearn to Migrate to the U.S." *Gallup,* April 30. Retrieved April 30, 2010 (www.gallup.com).

Esposito, John L. and Dalia Mogahed. 2007. *Who Speaks for Islam? What a Billion Muslims* Really *Think*. New York: Gallup Press.

Essed, Philomena, and David Theo Goldberg, eds. 2002. *Race Critical Theories: Text and Context*. Malden, MA: Blackwell Publishers.

Esty, Daniel C., M. A. Levy, C. H. Kim, A. de Sherbinin, T. Srebojnak, and V. Mara. 2008. *2008 Environmental Performance Index*. New Haven: Yale Center for Environmental Law and Policy.

European Monitoring Centre on Racism and Xenophobia. 2006. "Muslims in the European Union: Discrimination and Islamophobia." Retrieved September 1, 2007 (www.eumc.eu).

Evans, Harold, Gail Buckland, and David Lefer. 2006. *They Made America: From the Steam Engine to the Search Engine: Two Centuries of Innovators*. New York: Little, Brown.

Ewen, Lynda Ann. 1998. *Social Stratification and Power in America: A View from Below*. Six Hills, NY: General Hall, Inc.

Ewers, Justin. 2004. "Drowning in Applications." *U.S. News & World Report* (December 20): 64-65.

Expedia.com. 2008. "2008 International Vacation Deprivation Survey Results." Retrieved July 4, 2008 (www.expedia.com).

Fagan, Brian. 2008. *The Great Warming: Climate Change and the Rise and Fall of Civilizations*. New York: Bloomsbury Press.

Fahrenthold, David A. 2009. "Environmentalists Seek to Wipe Out Plush Toilet Paper." *Washington Post,* September 24, A1.

FairTest. 2007. "Test Scores Do Not Equal Merit." August. Retrieved July 14, 2008 (www.fairtest.org).

"Faith in the System." 2004. *Mother Jones*, September/October, 26-27.

Fakhraie, Fatemeh. 2009. "Feminists Don't Understand Muslim Women." Double X, May 20. Retrieved April 26, 2010 (www.doublex.com).

Falah, Ghazi-Wald, and Caroline Nagel, eds. 2005. *Geographies of Muslim Women: Gender, Religion, and Space*. New York: The Guilford Press.

Fallows, Deborah. 2005. "How Women and Men Use the Internet." PEW Internet & American Life Project. Retrieved February 12, 2006 (www.pewinternet.org).

____. 2008. "Most Chinese Say They Approve of Government Internet Control." Pew Internet &

American Life Project, March 27. Retrieved June 12, 2000 (www.pewinternet.org).
Family Matters: Substance Abuse and the American Family. 2005. The National Center on Addiction and Substance Abuse at Columbia University, March. Retrieved May 3, 2005 (www.casacolumbia.org).
Farley, John E., and Gregory D. Squires. 2005. "Fences and Neighbors: Segregation in 21st-century America." *Contexts* 4 (Winter): 33-39.
Farley, Melissa. 2001. "Prostitution: The Business of Sexual Exploitation." Pp. 879-891 in *Encyclopedia of Women and Gender*, Vol. 2, edited by Judith Worrell. New York: Academic Press.
Farr, Kathryn. 2005. *Sex Trafficking: The Global Market in Women and Children*. New York: Worth.
Farrell, Michael B. 2010. "Trial Raises Stakes in Gay-Marriage Debate." *Christian Science Monitor,* January 24, 19-20.
Feagin, Joe R. 2001. "Social Justice and Sociology: Agendas for the Twenty-First Century." *American Sociological Review* 66 (February): 1-20.
Feagin, Joe R. and Clairece Booher Feagin. 2008. *Racial and Ethnic Relations*, 8th ed. Upper Saddle River, NJ: Prentice Hall.
Feagin, Joe R. and Melvin P. Sikes. 1994. *Living with Racism: The Black Middle-Class Experience*. Boston, MA: Beacon Press.
Feagin, Joe R. and Robert Parker. 1990. *Building American Cities: The Urban Real Estate Game*, 2nd ed. Englewood Cliffs, NJ: Prentice Hall.
Federal Bureau of Investigation. 2009. *Crime in the United States 2008*. Retrieved February 12, 2010 (www.fbi.gov).
____. 2009. "Family Child Abductions." Retrieved December 18, 2009 (www.fbi.gov).
____. 2009. "Hate Crime Statistics, 2008." U.S. Department of Justice. Retrieved March 4, 2010 (www.fbi.gov).
Federal Interagency Forum on Aging-Related Statistics. 2006. *Older Americans Update 2006: Key Indicators of Well-Being*. Washington, DC: Government Printing Office.
____. 2009. *America's Children: Key National Indicators of Well-Being, 2009*. Washington, DC: U.S. Government Printing Office.
Feldmann, Linda. 2008. "How Voters May React to Clintons' $109 Million Income." *Christian Science Monitor*, April 7, 4.
____. 2008. "Women Make Modest Gains in Election 2008." *Christian Science Monitor,* November 17, 2.
Feldman-Jacobs, Charlotte, and Donna Clifton. 2010. "Female Genital Mutilation/Cutting: Data and Trends Update 2010." Population Reference Bureau, February. Retrieved March 12, 2010 (www.prb.org).
Ferree, Myra M. 2005. "It's Time to Mainstream Research on Gender." *The Chronicle Review*, August 12, B10.
Fiegener, Mark K. 2009. "Doctorate Recipients from U.S. Universities: Summary Report 2007-08." National Science Foundation, December. Retrieved April 21, 2010 (www.nsf.gov).
Fields, Jason. 2004. "America's Families and Living Arrangements: 2003." U.S. Census Bureau, Current Population Reports, P20-553. Retrieved November 30, 2004 (www.census.gov).
Fields, Jason, and Lynne. M. Casper. 2001. "America's Families and Living Arrangements: 2000." U.S. Census Bureau, Current Population Reports, P20-537. Retrieved February 12, 2003 (www.census.gov).
File, Thom, and Sarah Crissey. 2010. "Voting and Registration in the Election of November 2008: Population Characteristics." U.S. Census Bureau, May, Current Population Reports, P20-572. Retrieved May 15, 2010 (www.census.gov).
Filion, Kai. 2009. "Minimum Wage Issue Guide." Economic Policy Institute, July 21. Retrieved April 4, 2010 (www.epi.org).
Finke, Roger and Rodney Stark. 1992. *The Churching of America, 1776-1990: Winners and Losers in Our Religious Economy*. New Brunswick, NJ: Rutgers University Press.
Finkelhor, David, Heather Turner, Richard Ormrod, Sherry Hamby, and Kristen Kracke. 2009. "Children's Exposure to Violence: A Comprehensive National Survey." Office of Justice Programs, October. Retrieved April 8, 2010 (www.ojp.usdoj.gov).
Finn, Jeremy D. 2006. *The Adult Lives of At-Risk Students: The Roles of Attainment and Engagement in High School* (NCES 2006-328). Washington, DC: U.S. Department of Education.
Fischer, Karin. 2008. "Top Colleges Admit Fewer Low-Income Students." *Chronicle of Higher Education,* May 2, A1, A19-A20.
Fischman, Josh. 2009. "Global Warming Before Smokestacks." *Chronicle Review,* November 6, B11-B12.
Flanagan, William G. 1990. *Urban Sociology: Images and Structure*. Boston, MA: Allyn & Bacon.
Flavin, Jeanne. 2001. "Feminism for the Mainstream Criminologist: An Invitation." *Journal of Criminal Justice* 29 (July/August): 271-285.
Flegal, Katherine M., Margaret D. Carroll, Cynthia L. Ogden, and Lester R. Curtin. 2010. "Prevalence and Trends in Obesity among U.S. Adults, 1999-2008." *JAMA* 303 (January 20): 235-241.
Fleishman, Jeffrey, and Amro Hassan. 2009. "Gadget to Help Women Feign Virginity Angers Many in Egypt." *Los Angeles Times,* October 7. Retrieved October 28, 2009 (www.latimes.com).
Fletcher, Douglass Scott and Ian M. Taplin. 2002. *Understanding Organizational Evolution: Its Impact on Management and Performance*. Westport, CT: Quorum Books.
Fletcher, Laurel E., Phuong Pham, Eric Stover, and Patrick Vinck. 2006. "Rebuilding After Katrina: A Population-Based Study of Labor and Human Right in New Orleans." Retrieved June 25, 2006 (www.hrcberkeley.org).
Florida Office of Insurance Regulation. 2007. "The Use of Occupation and Education as Underwriting/Rating Factors for Private Passenger Automobile Insurance." March. Retrieved April 15, 2007 (www.floir.com).
Fogg, Piper. 2005. "Don't Stand So Close to Me." *Chronicle of Higher Education*, April 29, A10-A12.
Fong, Timothy P. 2002. *The Contemporary Asian American Experience: Beyond the Model Minority,* 2nd ed. Upper Saddle River, NJ: Prentice Hall.
Food and Agriculture Organization of the United Nations. 2009. "Hunger in the Face of Crisis." Policy Brief No. 6. Retrieved May 2, 2010 (ftp.fao.org).
Food & Water Watch. 2007. "Take Back the Tap: Why Choosing Tap Water over Bottled Water Is Better for Your Health, Your Pocketbook, and the Environment." Retrieved May 1, 2010 (www.foodandwaterwatch.org).
Ford, Carin. 2009. "The Top 5 Ways Students Use Technology to Cheat." HigherEd Morning, September 3. Retrieved September 10, 2009 (www.higheredmorning.com).
Ford, Peter. 2007. "Pollution Puts China Lake Off Limits." *Christian Science Monitor,* June 4, 7.
____. 2010. "China's Crib Conundrum." *Christian Science Monitor,* December 27, 23, 27.
"Formaldehyde." 2004. Environmental Defense. Retrieved July 10, 2005 (www.scorecard.org).
Forsberg, Hannele. 2005. "Finland's Families." Pp. 262-282 in *Handbook of World Families,* edited by Bert N. Adams and Jan Trost. Thousand Oaks, CA: Sage.
Foster, Andrea L. 2006. "Student Who Sued Operator of Term-Paper Sites Settles Her Case Out of Court." *Chronicle of Higher Education* 52, January 20, A41.
Foust-Cummings, Heather, Laura Sabattini, and Nancy Carter. 2008. "Women in Technology: Maximizing Talent, Minimizing Barriers." *Catalyst*. Retrieved April 28, 2008 (www.catalyst.org).
Fowler, Geoffrey A. 2006. "An Arrest in China Spotlights Limits to Artistic Freedom." *Wall Street Journal*, July 3, A1, A8.
Fox, James Alan, and Marianne W. Zawitz. 2004. "Homicide Trends in the United States: 2002 Update." Washington, DC: U.S. Department of Justice, Bureau of Justice Statistics.
____, and Marianne W. Zawitz. 2007. "Homicide Trends in the United States." Bureau of Justice Statistics. Retrieved April 8, 2010 (www.ojp.usdoj.gov/bjs).
Fox, Susannah. 2006. "Are 'Wired Seniors' Sitting Ducks?" April, Pew Internet & American Life Project, April. Retrieved September 20, 2007 (www.pewinternet.org).
Fox, Susannah, and Sydney Jones. 2009. "The Social Life of Health Information." Pew Internet & American Life Project, February 3. Retrieved February 5, 2010 (www.pewinternet.org).
Francis, David. 2010. "German Catholics Under Fire." *Christian Science Monitor,* March 22, 13.
Frank, T. A. 2006. "A Brief History of Wal-Mart." CorpWatch. Retrieved February 19, 2007 (www.corpwatch.org).
Franklin, Rachel S. 2003. "Migration of the Young, Single, and College Educated: 1995 to 2000." U.S. Census Bureau, Census 2000 Special Reports CENSR-12. Washington, DC: Government Printing Office.
Freedom House. 2010. "Freedom in the World 2010: Global Erosion of Freedom." Retrieved March 26, 2010 (www.freedomhouse.org).
Freese, Jeremy. 2008. "Genetics and the Social Science Explanation of Individual Outcomes." *American Journal of Sociology* 114 (Suppl.): S1-S35.
Freitas, Donna. 2008. *Sex & the Soul: Juggling Sexuality, Spirituality, Romance, and Religion on America's College Campuses*. New York: Oxford University Press.
French, Howard W. 2007. "China Scrambles for Stability as Its Workers Age." *New York Times*, March 22, A1, A8.
Frey, William H. 2006. "Diversity Spreads Out: Metropolitan Shifts in Hispanic, Asian, and Black Populations Since 2000." Brookings Institution. Retrieved February 2, 2008 (www.brookings.edu).
____. 2008. "Race, Immigration, and America's Changing Electorate." Brookings Institution, February 18. Retrieved June 23, 2008 (www.brookings.edu).
____. 2010. "Five Myths about the 2010 Census and the U.S. Population." *Washington Post,* February 14, B3.
Friedan, Betty. 1963. *The Feminine Mystique*. New York: Norton.
Friedrichs, David O. 2004. *Trusted Criminals: White Collar Crime in Contemporary Society*, 2nd edition. Belmont, CA: Wadsworth.
Frosch, Dan. 2007. "18 Air Force Cadets Exit Over Cheating." *New York Times*, May 2, 18.
Fry, Richard. 2005. "The Higher Dropout Rate of Foreign-born Teens: The Role of Schooling Abroad." Pew Hispanic Center, November 1. Retrieved July 20, 2007 (www.pewhispanic.org).
Gabrieli, Chris. 2009. "Expand Hours, Expand Learning." *U.S. News & World Report,* May, 12.
Galinsky, Ellen, Kersten Aumann, and James T. Bond. 2009. "Times Are Changing: Gender and Generation at Work and at Home." Families and Work Institute. Retrieved April 2, 2010 (www.familiesandwork.org).
Gallup Center for Muslim Studies. 2010. "In U.S., Religious Prejudice Stronger Against Muslims." *Gallup,* January 21. Retrieved April 27, 2010 (www.gallup.com).
Gallup Poll. 2010. "Personal Weight Situation." *Gallup News,* February 9. Retrieved February 14, 2010 (www.gallup.com).
Gamson, William. 1990. *The Strategy of Social Protest*, 2nd ed. Belmont, CA: Wadsworth.
Gans, Herbert J. 1962. "Urbanism and Suburbanism as Ways of Life: A Reevaluation of Definitions." Pp. 625-48 in *Human Behavior and Social Processes: An Interactionist Approach*, edited by Arnold M. Rose. Boston, MA: Houghton Mifflin.
____. 1971. "The Uses Of Poverty: The Poor Pay All." *Social Policy* (July/August): 78–81.
____. 2005. "Race as Class." *Contexts* 4 (Fall): 17-21.
____. 2005. "Wishes for the Discipline's Future." *The Chronicle Review*, August 12, B9.
Garcia, Alma M. 2002. *The Mexican Americans*. Westport, CT: Greenwood Press.
Gardner, Marilyn. 2008. "Happiness is a Warm 'Thank You'." *Christian Science Monitor*, January 28, 13, 16.
Gardyn, Rebecca. 2001. "A League of Their Own." *American Demographics* 23 (March): 12-13.
Garfinkel, Harold. 1967. *Studies in Ethnomethodology*. Englewood Cliffs, NJ: Prentice-Hall, Inc.
Garrison, Michelle M., and Dimitri A. Christakis. 2005. "A Teacher in the Living Room? Educational Media for Babies, Toddlers and Preschoolers." Henry J. Kaiser Family Foundation, December. Retrieved April 12, 2008 (www.kff.org).
Gates, Gary, L. M. V. Badgett, Jennifer E. Macomber, and Kate Chambers. 2007. "Adoption and Foster Care by Gay and Lesbian Parents in the United States." Urban Institute, March. Retrieved April 10, 2010 (www.urban.org).
Gates, Gary J., and Jason Ost. 2004. *The Gay & Lesbian Atlas*. Washington, DC: The Urban Institute Press.
Gavrilos, Dina. 2006. "U.S. News Magazine Coverage of Latinos: 2006 Report." National Association of Hispanic Journalists, June. Retrieved April 2, 2007 (www.nahj.org).
Gaylin, Willard. 1992. *The Male Ego*. New York: Viking.
Geertz, Clifford. 1966. "Religion as a Cultural System." Pp. 1-46 in *Anthropological Approaches to the Study of Religion*, edited by Michael Banton. London: Tavistock.
Gelbard, Alene, Carl Haub, and Mary M. Kent. 1999. "World Population Beyond Six Billion." *Population Bulletin* 54 (March): 1-44.
Gelles, Richard J. 1997. *Intimate Violence in Families,* 3rd ed. Thousand Oaks, CA: Sage.
"Generational Look at the Public: Politics and Policy, A." 2002. *Washington Post*/Kaiser Family Foundation/Harvard University, October. Retrieved August 14, 2004 (www.kff.org).
Gerth, H.H. and C. Wright Mills, eds. 1946. *Max Weber: Essays in Sociology*. Oxford University Press.
Gewertz, Catherine. 2009. "Do Men Deserve A Break in College Admissions?" *Education Week* online, December 9. Retrieved December 13, 2010 (http://blogs.edweek.org).

Ghosh, Bobby. 2007. "Why They Hate Each Other." *Time*, March 5, 29-40.

Gibbons, John M. 2010. "I Can't Get No. . . Job Satisfaction, That Is." The Conference Board, January. Retrieved April 8, 2010 (www.conferene-board.org).

Gibbs, Nancy. 2008. "College Confidential." *Time*, April 14, 80.

——, and Michael Duffy. 2007. "Leveling the Praying Field." *Time*, July 23, 28-34.

Gilbert, Dennis and Joseph A. Kahl. 1993. *The American Class Structure: A New Synthesis*, 4th ed. Homewood, IL: Dorsey Press.

Gilbert, Dennis. 2008. *The American Class Structure in an Age of Growing Inequality*, 7th ed. Belmont, CA: Wadsworth Press.

Gilligan, Carol. 1982. *In a Different Voice: Psychological Theory and Women's Development*. Cambridge, MA: Harvard University Press.

Gilson, Dave. 2009. "The Trickle-Up Economy." *Mother Jones*, March-April, 26-28.

Giugni, Marco, Doug McAdam, and Charles Tilley, eds. 1999. *How Social Movements Matter*. Minneapolis: University of Minnesota Press.

Giuliano, Laura, David I. Levine, and Jonathan Leonard. 2009. "Manager Race and the Race of New Hires." *Journal of Labor Economics* 27 (October): 589-631.

Givhan, Robin. 2005. "Dick Cheney, Dressing Down." *Washington Post*, January 28, C1.

——. 2010. "First Lady Michelle Obama: 'Let's Move' and Work on Childhood Obesity Problem." *Washington Post*, February 10, C1.

Glassman, Ronald M. 2000. *Caring Capitalism: A New Middle-Class Base for the Welfare State*. New York: St. Martin's Press.

Glassner, Barry. 2010. "Still Fearful After All These Years." *Chronicle Review*, January 22, B11-B12.

Glenn, Norval D. 2001. "Social Science Findings and the 'Family Wars'." *Society* 38 (May/June): 13-19.

——. 2005. "With This Ring . . . : A National Survey on Marriage in America." National Fatherhood Initiative. Retrieved April 2, 2006 (www.fatherhood.org).

Glionna, John M. 2009. "Aceh's Morality Police on the Prowl for Violators." *Los Angeles Times*, November 8. Retrieved November 28, 2009 (www.latimes.com).

——. 2009. "South Korean Kids Get a Taste of Boot Camp." *Los Angeles Times*, August 22, A1.

Glod, Maria, and Bill Turque. 2008. "Report Finds Little Gain from Vouchers." *Washington Post*, June 17, A1.

Goffman, Erving. 1959. *The Presentation of Self in Everyday Life*. New York: Doubleday Anchor Books.

——. 1961. *Asylums: Essays on the Social Situation of Mental Patients and Other Inmates*. Garden City, NY: Anchor Books.

——. 1963. *Stigma: Notes on the Management of Spoiled Identity*. Englewood Cliffs, NJ: Prentice-Hall.

——. 1967. *Interaction Ritual: Essays on Face-to-Face Behavior*. New York: Anchor Books.

——. 1969. *Strategic Interaction*. Philadelphia, PA: University of Pennsylvania Press.

Goldberg, Jonah. 2009. "America Through the Reality Lens." *Los Angeles Times*, December 15. Retrieved December 22, 2009 (www.latimes.com).

Golden, Daniel. 2006. *The Price of Admission: How America's Ruling Class Buys Its Way into Elite Colleges—and Who Gets Left Outside the Gates*. New York: Crown.

Goldin, Claudia, Lawrence F. Katz, and Ilyana Kuziemko. 2006. "The Homecoming of American College Women: The Reversal of the College Gender Gap." National Bureau of Economic Research. Retrieved July 25, 2007 (www.nber.org/papgers/w12139).

Goldrick-Rab, Sara. 2009. "The So-Called Boy Mystery." *Chronicle of Higher Education*, December 6. Retrieved December 14, 2009 (http://chronicle.com/blog).

Goldstein, Amy. 2009. "Missing More Than a Meal." *Washington Post*, December 12, A1.

Golombok, Susan, and Fiona Tasker. 1996. "Do Parents Influence The Sexual Orientation Of Their Children? Findings from a Longitudinal Study of Lesbian Families." *Developmental Psychology* 32 (1): 3–11.

Goodale, Gloria. 2009. "A Wake-Up Call on Water Use." *Christian Science Monitor*, June 10. Retrieved June 12, 2009 (www.csmonitor.com).

Goodkin, Kerala. 2005. "Smelling the Roses." *Glimpse* (Winter): 6-13.

Goodman, Peter S. 2010. "Despite Signs of Recovery, Chronic Joblessness Rises." *New York Times*, February 20, 1.

Goodnough, Abby. 2009. "New Meaning for Night Class at 2-Year Colleges." *New York Times*, October 28, A1.

"GOP Party Identification Slips Nationwide and in Pennsylvania." 2009. Pew Research Center, April 29. Retrieved March 29, 2010 (http://pewresearch.org).

Gopnik, Alison, Andrew N. Meltzoff and Patricia K. Kuhl. 2001. *The Scientist in the Crib: What Early Learning Tells Us about the Mind*. New York: Perennial.

Gorman, Anna. 2010. "Immigrants Often See Peril in Reporting Domestic Abuse." *Los Angeles Times*, January 25. Retrieved January 26, 2010 (www.latimes.com).

Gottdiener, Mark and Ray Hutchison. 2000. *The New Urban Sociology*, 2nd ed. New York: McGraw-Hill.

Gottman, John M. 1994. *What Predicts Divorce? The Relationships between Marital Processes and Marital Outcome*. Hillsdale, NJ: Lawrence Erlbaum Associates.

Gouldner, Alvin W. 1962. "Anti-Minotaur: The Myth of a Value-Free Sociology." *Social Problems* 9 (Winter): 199-212.

Grabe, S., L. M. Ward, and J. S. Hyde. 2008. "The Role of the Media in Body Image Concerns Among Women: A Meta-Analysis of Experimental and Correlational Studies." *Psychological Bulletin* 134 (May): 460-476.

Graff, E. J. 2007. "The Opt-Out Myth." *Columbia Journalism Review* 45 (March/April): 51-54.

Grall, Timothy S. 2007. "Custodial Mothers and Fathers and Their Child Support: 2005." U.S. Census Bureau, Current Population Reports, August, P60-234. Retrieved July 1, 2009 (www.census.gov).

Grant, Alexis. 2008. "In Cameroon, Polygamy Doesn't Pay." *Christian Science Monitor*, November 13, 20.

Grant, Gerald and Christine E. Murray. 1999. *Teaching in America: The Slow Revolution*. Cambridge, MA: Harvard University Press.

Grauerholz, Liz and Sharon Bouma-Holtrop. 2003. "Exploring Critical Sociological Thinking." *Teaching Sociology* 31 (October): 485-496.

Graves, Joseph. L. Jr. 2001. *The Emperor's New Clothes: Biological Theories of Race at the Millennium*. New Brunswick, NJ: Rutgers University Press.

Gray, Paul S., John B. Williamson, David R. Karp, and John R. Dalphin. 2007. *The Research Imagination: An Introduction to Qualitative and Quantitative Methods*. New York: Cambridge University Press.

Grazian, David. 2008. *On the Make: The Hustle of Urban Nightlife*. Chicago: University of Chicago Press.

Greeley, Andrew M. 1972. *The Denominational Society*. Glenview, IL: Scott, Foresman.

Greenberg, Milton. 2004. "How the GI Bill Changed Higher Education." *Chronicle of Higher Education*, June 18, B9-B11.

Grodsky, Eric, John Robert Warren, and Demetra Kalogrides. 2008. "State High School Exit Examinations and NAEP Long-Term Trends in Reading and Mathematics, 1971-2004." *Education Policy* 22 (June). Retrieved July 17, 2008 (online.sagepub.com).

Gross, Rita M. 1996. *Feminism and Religion: An Introduction*. Boston, MA: Beacon Press.

Gruber, Jonathan. 2005. "Religious Market Structure, Religious Participation, and Outcomes: Is Religion Good for You?" National Bureau of Economic Research, May. Retrieved August 28, 2007 (www.nber.org).

Guarino, Mark. 2010. "Faith-Mixing Common in US." *Christian Science Monitor*, January 24, 20-21.

Guo, Guang, Michael E. Roettger, and Tanji Cai. 2008a. "The Integration of Genetic Propensities into Social-Control Models of Delinquency and Violence among Male Youths." *American Sociological Review*, 73 (August): 543-568.

——, Yuying Tong, and Tanji Cai. 2008b. "Gene by Social Context Interactions for Number of Sexual Partners among White Male Youths: Genetics-Informed Sociology." *American Journal of Sociology* 114 (Suppl.): S36-S66.

Gurney, Joan M., and Kathleen T. Tierney. 1982. "Relative Deprivation and Social Movements: A Critical Look at Twenty Years of Theory and Research." *Sociological Quarterly* 23 (Winter): 33-47.

Gurwitt, Rob. 2005. "The Nose That Knows." *Mother Jones*, March/April, 24.

Guterman, Lila. 2005. "Lost Count." *Chronicle of Higher Education*, February 4, A10-A13.

Guterman, Stanley S. 1969. "In Defense of Wirth's 'Urbanism as a Way of Life'." *American Journal of Sociology* 74 (March): 492-499.

Guttmacher Institute. 2005. "Facts on Induced Abortion in the United States. Retrieved December 21, 2006 (www.guttmacher.org).

——. 2008. "Facts on Induced Abortion in the United States." July. Retrieved August 15, 2008 (www.guttmacher.org).

——. 2009. "A Real-Time Look at the Impact of the Recession on Women's Family Planning and Pregnancy Decisions." September. Retrieved April 12, 2010 (www.guttmacher.org).

Hagan, Frank E. 2008. *Introduction to Criminology: Theories, Methods, and Criminal Behavior*, 6th edition. Thousand Oaks, CA: Sage.

Hagenbaugh, Barbara. 2006. "U.S. Manufacturers Getting Desperate for Skilled People." *USA Today*, December 5, 1.

Halfond, Jay A. 2004. "Grade Inflation is Not a Victimless Crime." *Christian Science Monitor*, May 3, 9.

Hall, Edward T. 1959. *The Silent Language*. New York: Doubleday & Company, Inc.

——. 1966. *The Hidden Dimension*. Garden City, NY: Doubleday & Company, Inc.

Halloran, Liz. 2008. "An Uncertain Legacy." *U.S. News & World Report*, September, 34-37.

Hamburger, Tom, and Kim Geiger. 2010. "Beverage Industry Douses Tax on Soft Drinks." *Los Angeles Times*, February 7. Retrieved February 10, 2010 (www.latimes.com).

Hamby, Sherry L. and David Finkelhor. 2001. "Choosing and Using Child Victimization Questionnaires." *OJJDP Juvenile Justice Bulletin*. Washington, DC: U.S. Department of Justice.

Hamermesh, Daniel S. and Amy W. Parker. 2003. "Beauty in the Classroom: Professors' Pulchritude and Putative Pedagogical Productivity." Working Paper 9853, July. Cambridge, MA: National Bureau of Economic Research.

Hamilton, Brady E., Joyce A Martin, and Stephanie J. Ventura. 2007. "Births: Preliminary Data for 2006." *National Vital Statistics Reports*, vol. 56, no 7. Hyattsville, MD: National Center for Health Statistics.

——. 2010. "Births: Preliminary Data for 2008." *National Vital Statistics Reports* 58 (April 16): 1-18.

Hamilton, Brady E., Paul D. Sutton, and Stephanie J. Ventura. 2003. "Revised Birth and Fertility Rates for the 1990s and New Rates for Hispanic Populations, 2000 and 2001: United States." *National Vital Statistics Reports*, 51, no 12. Retrieved August 25, 2003 (www.cdc.gov).

Hamilton, Malcolm B. 1995. *The Sociology of Religion: Theoretical and Comparative Perspectives*. New York: Routledge.

——. 2001. *The Sociology of Religion*, 2nd ed. New York: Routledge.

Hamm, Steve. 2007. "The Trouble with India." *Business Week*, March 19, 49-58.

Hampton, Keith N., Lauren Fl. Sessions, Eun Ja Her, and Lee Rainie. 2009. "Social Isolation and New Technology." Pew Internet & American Life Project, November. Retrieved February 5, 2010 (www.pewinternet.org).

Hamre, Bridget K., and Robert C. Pianta. 2001. "Early Teacher-Child Relationships and the Trajectory of Children's School Outcomes Through Eighth Grade." *Child Development* 72 (March/April): 625-38.

Hancock, Jay. 2009. "Push to Give Shareholders Say on CEO Pay Rankles GOP." *Baltimore Sun*, August 12, 2.

Handelsman, Jo et al. 2005. "Careers in Science." *Science* 309 (August 19): 1190-1191.

Hanes, Stephanie. 2009. "Risky Business: Driving While Distracted." *Christian Science Monitor*, November 1, 2009.

Haney, Craig, Curtis Banks, and Philip Zimbardo. 1973. "Interpersonal Dynamics in a Simulated Prison." *International Journal of Criminology and Psychology* 1: 69-97.

Hanowski, Rich. 2009. "New Data from VTTI Provides Insight into Cell Phone Use and Driving Distraction." Virginia Tech Transportation Institute. Retrieved December 15, 2009 (www.vtti.vt.edu).

Hanushek, Eric A., and Ludger Woessman. 2005. "Does Educational Tracking Affect Performance and Inequality? Differences-in-Differences Evidence Across Countries." National Bureau of Economic Research, February. Retrieved July 25, 2007 (www.nber.org).

Haq, Husna. 2009. "Ethnic Malls are Buzzing." *Christian Science Monitor*, August 30, 30-31.

Harder, Joshua, and Jon A. Krosnick. 2008. "Why Do People Vote? A Psychological Analysis of the Causes of Voter Turnout." *Journal of Social Issues*, 64 (September): 525-549.

Hare, Mary Gail. 2009. "Census Officials Call Strategy Best Ever." *Baltimore Sun*, December 10, 6.

Harlow, Caroline Wolf. 2003. "Education and Correctional Populations." U.S. Department of Justice, Bureau of Justice Statistics. Retrieved January 16, 2003 (www.ojp.usdoj.gov/bjs).

Harlow, Harry E., and Margaret K. Harlow. 1962. "Social Deprivation in Monkeys." *Scientific American*, 206 (November): 137–146.

Harman, Danna. 2007. "Qatar Reformed by a Modern Marriage." *Christian Science Monitor*, March 6, 20.
Harmon, Amy. 2008. "The DNA Age—Insurance Fears Lead Many to Shun DNA Tests." *New York Times*, February 24, 1.
Harrell, Andrew. 2005. "Are Prettier Kids Protected Better? A Field Observational Study of Child Safety in Grocery Carts." Population Research Laboratory, University of Alberta. Unpublished manuscript.
Harrell, Erika. 2007. "Black Victims of Violent Crime." Washington, DC: U.S. Department of Justice, Bureau of Justice Statistics.
Harris, Chauncey D. 1997. "'The Nature of Cities' and Urban Geography in the Last Century." *Urban Geography* 18: 15-35.
Harris, Chauncey D., and Edward L. Ullman. 1945. "The Nature of Cities." *Annals* 242: 7-17.
Harris, Gardiner. 2008. "Cigarette Company Paid for Lung Cancer Study." *New York Times*, March 26, 6.
Harris, Scott R. 2006. *The Meanings of Marital Equality*. Albany: State University of New York Press.
Hart, Timothy C., and Callie Rennison. 2003. "Reporting Crime to the Police, 1992-2000." Washington, DC: U.S. Department of Justice, Bureau of Justice Statistics.
Hartman, Harriet, and Moshe Hartman. 2009. "Do Gender Differences in Undergraduate Engineering Orientations Persist When Major Is Controlled?" *International Journal of Gender, Science and Technology* 1 (1): 61-82. Retrieved April 12, 2010 (http://genderandset.open.ac.uk).
Hartmann, Heidi, Olga Sorokina, and Erica Williams. 2006. *The Best and Worst State Economies for Women*. Washington, DC: Institute for Women's Policy Research.
Haskins, Rob. 2007a. "Education and Economic Mobility." Pp. 91-104 in *Getting Ahead or Losing Ground: Economic Mobility in America*, edited by Julia B. Isaacs, Isabel V. Sawhill, and Ron Haskins. Washington, DC: The Brookings Institution.
____. 2007b. "Immigration: Wages, Education, and Mobility." Pp. 81-90 in *Getting Ahead or Losing Ground: Economic Mobility in America*, edited by Julia B. Isaacs, Isabel V. Sawhill, and Ron Haskins. Washington, DC: The Brookings Institution.
Haub, Carl. 2007. "2007 World Population Data Sheet." Population Reference Bureau, Washington, DC, wall chart.
____. 2010. "Russia's Population Now Increasing?" Population Reference Bureau, January 8. Retrieved April 30, 2010 (http://prbblog.org).
Haub, Carl, and Mary Mederios Kent. 2008. "2008 World Population Data Sheet." Population Reference Bureau, Washington, DC, wall chart.
____. 2009. "2009 World Population Data Sheet." Washington, DC: Population Reference Bureau (wall chart).
Hauser, Robert M. and David L. Featherman. 1977. *The Process of Stratification: Trends and Analysis*. New York: Academic Press.
Hausmann, Ricardo, Laura D. Tyson, and Saadia Zahidi. 2007. "The Global Gender Report 2007." World Economic Forum. Retrieved June 25, 2008 (www.weforum.org).
Hayani, Ibrahim. 1999. "Arabs in Canada: Assimilation or Integration?" Pp. 284-303 in *Arabs in America: Building a New Future,* edited by Michael W. Suleiman. Philadelphia: Temple University Press.
Hayden, Dolores. 2002. *Redesigning the American Dream: Gender, Housing, and Family Life*. New York: W.W. Norton & Company.
Haynes, V. Dion. 2010. "Jobless Rate May Rise as Many Are Drawn Back to Labor Force." *Washington Post,* April 5, A1.
Hayward, Steven F. and Amy Kaleita. 2007. *Index of Leading Environmental Indicators: 2007, Twelfth Edition*. Pacific Research Institute. Retrieved February 15, 2008 (www.aconvenientfiction.com).
"Hazardous Air Pollution—A National Overview." 2005. Environmental Defense. Retrieved July 10, 2005 (www.scorecard.org).
He, Wan, Manisha Sengupta, Victoria A. Velkoff, and Kimberly A. DeBarros. 2005. *65+ in the United States: 2005*. U.S. Census Bureau, Current Population Reports, P23-209. Washington, DC: Government Printing Office.
Heald, Anne, et al. 2003. "A Conversation on School Vouchers." Washington, DC: Economic Policy Institute, June 12. Retrieved January 20, 2005 (www.epinet.org).
Heath, Chip. 2005. "Introduction." Pp. 81-85 in *Rumor Mills: The Social Impact of Rumor and Legend*, edited by Gary Alan Fine, Véronique Campion-Vincent, and Chip Heath. New Brunswick, NJ: Transaction Publishers.
Heath, Jennifer. 2008. *The Veil: Women Writers on Its History, Lore, and Politics*. Berkeley: University of California Press.
Hechter, Michael and Karl-Dieter Opp. 2001. "Introduction." Pp. xi-xx in *Social Norms*, edited by Michael Hechter and Karl-Dieter Opp. New York: Russell Sage Foundation.
Heilbroner, R. L. and L. C. Thurow. 1998. *Economics Explained: Everything You Need to Know about How the Economy Works and Where It's Going*. New York: Touchstone.
Heimer, Karen, and Candace Kruttschnitt. 2006. "Introduction: New Insights into the Gendered Nature of Crime and Victimization." Pp. 1-14 in *Gender and Crime: Patterns of Victimization and Offending*, edited by Karen Heimer and Candace Kruttschnitt. New York: New York University Press.
Heimer, Karen, Stacy Wittrock, and Halime Ünal. 2006. "The Crimes of Poverty: Economic Marginalization and the Gender Gap in Crime." Pp. 115-126 in *Gender and Crime: Patterns of Victimization and Offending*, edited by Karen Heimer and Candace Kruttschnitt. New York: New York University Press.
Helgesen, Sally. 2008. "Female Leadership: Changing Business for the Better." *Christian Science Monitor*, January 17, 9.
Helper, Susan. 2008. "Renewing U.S. Manufacturing: Promoting a High-Road Strategy." Economic Policy Institute, February 13. Retrieved July 4, 2008 (www.epi.org).
Hendrix, Steve. 2009. "Fewer People Are Sending Holiday Cards Via Snail Mail in 2009." *Washington Post,* December 19, A1.
____. 2009. "In D.C., Tattoos Are Largely Taboo from 9 to 5." *Washington Post,* December 10, A1.
Henschke, Claudia I., David F. Yankelevitz, Daniel M. Libby, Mark W. Pasmantier, and James Posit. 2006. "Survival of Patients with Stage 1 Lung Cancer Detected on CT Screening." *New England Journal of Medicine* 355 (October 26): 1763-1771.
Herbert, Bob. 2009. "A Culture Soaked in Blood." *New York Times,* April 25, 19.
Heritage, John. 1984. *Garfinkel and Ethnomethodology.* New York: Basil Blackwell, Inc.
Herod, Andrew. 1993. "Gender Issues in the Use of Interviewing As a Research Method." *The Professional Geographer* 45 (August): 305-17.
Heron, Melonie, Donna L. Hoyert, Sherry L. Murphy, Jaquan Xu, Kenneth D. Kochanek, and Betzaida Tejada-Vera. 2009. "Deaths: Final Data for 2006." *National Vital Statistics Reports* 57 (April 17): 1-135.
Herring, Cedric. 2009. "Does Diversity Pay?: Race, Gender, and the Business Case for Diversity." *American Sociological Review* 74 (April): 208-224.
Herrnstein, Richard J. and Charles Murray. 1994. *The Bell Curve: Intelligence and Class Structure in American Life*. New York: Free Press.
Hess, Frederick M. 2009. "Time Needs to Be Better Spent. *U.S. News & World Report,* May, 13.
Hetherington, E. Mavis, Ross D. Parke, and Virginia Otis Locke. 2006. *Child Psychology: A Contemporary Viewpoint*, 6th edition. Boston, MA: McGraw-Hill.
Heubeck, Elizabeth. 2005. "Pressure Grows To Telecommute." *Baltimore Sun*, October 26, K1-K2.
Hilbert, Richard A. 1992. *The Classical Roots of Ethnomethodology: Durkheim, Weber, and Garfinkel.* Chapel Hill: The University of North Carolina Press.
Hill, Catherine, Christianne Corbett, and Andresse St. Rose. 2010. *Why So Few? Women in Science, Technology, Engineering, and Mathematics.* Washington, DC: American Association of University Women.
Hillaker, B. D., H. E. Brophy-Herb, F. A. Villarruel, and B. E. Hass. 2008. "The Contributions of Parenting to Social Competencies and Positive Values in Middle School Youth: Positive Family Communication, Maintaining Standards, and Supportive Family Relationships." *Family Relations* 57 (December): 591-601.
Hinkle, Stephen, and John Schopler. 1986. "Bias in the Evaluation of In-Group and Out-Group Performance." Pp. 196-212 in *Psychology of Everyday Intergroup Relations*, 2nd ed., edited by Stephen Worchel and William. G. Austin. Chicago, IL: Nelson-Hall.
Hira, Ron. 2008. "An Overview of the Offshoring of U.S. Jobs." *Population Bulletin* 63 (June): 14-15.
"Hispanic Heritage Month 2009: Sept. 15-Oct. 15." 2009. U.S. Census Bureau News, October 15, CB09-FF.17. Retrieved March 13, 2010 (www.census.gov).
Hispanic-Owned Firms: 2002. 2006. U.S. Census Bureau, SB02-00CS-HISP (RV). Retrieved May 1, 2007 (www.census.gov).
Hochschild, Arlie Russell. 1983. *The Managed Heart: Commercialization of Human Feeling*. Berkeley: University of California Press.
____. 1989. *The Second Shift: Working Parents and the Revolution At Home*. New York: Penguin.
Hoecker-Drysdale, Susan. 1992. *Harriet Martineau: First Woman Sociologist*. Providence, RI: Berg.
Hoefer, Michael, Nancy Rytina, and Bryan C. Baker. 2010. "Estimates of the Unauthorized Immigrant Population Residing in the United States: January 2009." Homeland Security, Office of Immigration Statistics, January. Retrieved March 12, 2010 (www.dhs.gov).
Holder, Kelly. 2006. "Voting and Registration in the Election of November 2004." U.S. Census Bureau, March, Current Population Reports, P20-556. Retrieved May 15, 2007 (www.census.gov).
Holt, Emily W., Daniel J. McGrath, and Marilyn M. Seastrom. 2006. "Qualifications of Pubic Secondary School History Teachers, 1999-2000." U.S. Department of Education, National Center for Education Statistics, NCES 2006-004. Retrieved July 12, 2007 (http://nces.ed.gov).
Holzer, Harry. 2007. "Better Workers for Better Jobs: Improving Worker Advancement in the Low-Wage Labor Market." Urban Institute, December 12. Retrieved May 18, 2008 (www.urban.org).
Homans, George. 1974. *Social Behavior: Its Elementary Forms*, revised ed. New York: Harcourt Brace Jovanovich.
"Homosexual Relations." 2008. *Gallup*. Retrieved May 21, 2009 (www.gallup.com).
Hondagneu-Sotelo, Pierrette. 2001. *Doméstica: Immigrant Workers Cleaning and Caring in the Shadows of Affluence*. Berkeley: University of California Press.
hooks, bell. 2000. *Feminism is for Everybody: Passionate Politics*. Cambridge, MA: South End Press.
Horrigan, John B. 2004. "How Americans Get in Touch with Government." Pew Internet & American Life, May 24. Retrieved September 9, 2004 (www.pewinternet.org).
Horrigan, John B., and Lee Rainie. 2006. "The Internet's Growing Role in Life's Major Moments." April, Pew Internet & American Life Project, April. Retrieved September 20, 2007 (www.pewinternet.org).
Horwitz, Allan V. and Jerome C. Wakefield. 2006. "The Epidemic in Mental Illness: Clinical Fact or Survey Artifact?" *Contexts* 5 (Winter): 19-23.
Houser, Ari. 2007. "Women & Long-Term Care." AARP Public Policy Institute. Retrieved April 10, 2010 (http://assets.aarp.org).
Houtenville, Andrew J., and Karen Smith Conway. 2008. "Parental Effort, School Resources, and Student Achievement." *Journal of Human Resources* 43 (Spring): 437-453.
Howard, Jeff. 2003. "Still at Risk: The Causes and Costs of Failure to Educate Poor and Minority Children for the Twenty-First Century." Pp. 81-97 in *A Nation Reformed? American Education 20 Years after A Nation at* Risk, edited by David T. Gordon and Patricia A. Graham. Cambridge, MA: Harvard Education Press.
Howard, Judith A. and Jocelyn A. Hollander. 1997. *Gendered Situations, Gendered Selves: A Gender Lens On Social Psychology.* Thousand Oaks, CA: Sage.
Hoyt, Homer. 1939. *The Structure and Growth of Residential Neighborhoods in American Cities*. Washington, DC: Federal Housing Administration.
Hubbard, Ruth. 1990. *The Politics of Women's Biology.* New Brunswick, NJ: Rutgers University Press.
Hughes, Everett C. 1945. "Dilemmas and Contradictions of Status." *American Journal of Sociology* 50: 353-359.
Hunt, Jennifer. 2010. "Why Do Women Leave Science and Engineering?" National Bureau of Economic Research, March. Retrieved April 20, 2010 (www.nber.org).
Hunter, James Davison, and Joshua Yates. 2002. "In the Vanguard of Globalization: The World of American Globalizers." Pp. 323-357 in *Many Globalizations: Cultural Diversity in the Contemporary World*, edited by Peter L. Berger and Samuel P. Huntington. New York: Oxford University Press.
Huntington, Samuel P. 2004. "The Hispanic Challenge." *Foreign Policy* Issue # 141 (March/April): 30-45.
Hurh, Won Moo. 1998. *The Korean Americans*. Westport, CT: Greenwood Press.
Hurst, Charles E. 2001. *Social Inequality: Forms, Causes, and Consequences*, 4th ed. Boston, MA: Allyn and Bacon.

Hutter, Mark. 2007. *Experiencing Cities*. Boston, MA: Allyn & Bacon.
Hyde, Janet S. 2005. "The Gender Similarities Hypothesis." *American Psychologist* 60 (September): 581-592.
Hyde, Janet S., Sara M. Lindberg, Marcia C. Linn, Amy B. Ellis, and Caroline C. Williams. 2008. "Gender Similarities Characterize Math Performance." *Science* 321 (July): 494-495.
Hymowitz, Carol. 2006. "'Any College Will Do'." *Wall Street Journal*, September 18. Retrieved November 8, 2007 (online.wsj.com).
Independent Sector. 2006. "Value of Volunteer Time." Retrieved September 7, 2006 (www.independent sector.org).
____. 2009. "Value of Volunteer Time." Retrieved February 13, 2010 (www.independentsector.org).
Institute of Medicine. 2006. *Food Marketing to Children and Youth: Threat or Opportunity?* Washington, DC: National Academy of Sciences.
Insurance Institute for Highway Safety. 2008. "Q&As: Teenagers—General." March. Retrieved March 26, 2008 (www.iihs.org).
Intercollegiate Studies Institute. 2010. "Americans are Getting F's." March 3. Retrieved March 10, 2010 (www.isi.org).
Intergovernmental Panel on Climate Change. 2007. "Fourth Assessment Report." Retrieved February 12, 2008 (www.ipcc.ch).
International Institute for Democracy and Electoral Assistance. 2007. "Turnout over Time: Advances and Retreats in Electoral Participation." Retrieved May 24, 2007 (www.idea.int).
Internet Crime Complaint Center. 2009. "2008 Internet Crime Report." Retrieved February 25, 2010 (www.ic3.gov).
Inter-Parliamentary Union. 2008. "Women in National Parliaments." April 30. Retrieved June 28, 2008 (www.ipu.org).
Ioannidis, John. 2005. "Contradicted and Initially Stronger Effects in Highly Cited Clinical Research." *Journal of the American Medical Association* 294 (July 13): 218-228.
"Iranian Gays Present, Hidden." 2007. *Baltimore Sun*, September 30, 16A.
Isaacs, Julia B. 2007a. "Economic Mobility of Black and White Families." Pp. 71-80 in *Getting Ahead or Losing Ground: Economic Mobility in America*, edited by Julia B. Isaacs, Isabel V. Sawhill, and Ron Haskins. Washington, DC: The Brookings Institution.
____. 2007b. "Economic Mobility of Men and Women." Pp. 61-70 in *Getting Ahead or Losing Ground: Economic Mobility in America*, edited by Julia B. Isaacs, Isabel V. Sawhill, and Ron Haskins. Washington, DC: The Brookings Institution.
____. 2007c. "International Comparisons of Economic Mobility." Pp. 37-46 in *Getting Ahead or Losing Ground: Economic Mobility in America*, edited by Julia B. Isaacs, Isabel V. Sawhill, and Ron Haskins. Washington, DC: The Brookings Institution.
Isen, Adam, and Betsey Stevenson. 2010. "Women's Education and Family Behavior: Trends in Marriage, Divorce, and Fertility." National Bureau of Economic Research, February. Retrieved April 15, 2010 (www.nber.org).
"Island Women Banned From Wearing Trousers." 2002. *Ananova News*, January 4. Retrieved January 5, 2002 (www.ananova.com/news).
Jackson, C. Kirabo. 2010. "A Stitch in Time: The Effects of a Novel Incentive-Based High-School Intervention on College Outcomes." National Bureau of Economic Research, February. Retrieved May 15, 2010 (www.nber.org).
Jackson, D. D. 1998. "'This Hole in Our Heart': Urban Indian Identity and the Power of Silence." *American Indian Culture and Research Journal* 22 (4): 227-54.
Jackson, Henry C. 2010. "Ag Secretary Pushes School Nutrition Plan." *Washington Post,* February 8. Retrieved February 15, 2010 (www.washingtonpost.com).
Jacobe, Dennis, and Jeffrey M. Jones. 2009. "Lack of Money/Wages Top Family Financial Problem in the U.S." *Gallup,* November 19. Retrieved April 6, 2010 (www.gallup.com).
Jacobs, Jerry A. 2005. "Multiple Methods in *ASR*." *Footnotes* 33 (December): 1, 4.
Jacobsen, Linda A., and Mark Mather. 2010. "U.S. Economic and Social Trends since 2000." *Population Bulletin* 65 (February): 1-16.
Jacobson, Michael. 2005. *Downsizing Prisons: How to Reduce Crime and End Mass Incarceration.* New York: New York University Press.
Jagger, Alison M., and Paula S. Rothenberg, eds. 1984. *Feminist Frameworks*, 2nd ed. New York: McGraw-Hill.
Jandt, Fred E. 2001. *Intercultural Communication: An Introduction*. Thousand Oaks, CA: Sage.
Janis, Irving L. 1972. *Victims of Groupthink: A Psychological Study of Foreign-Policy Decisions and Fiascoes*. Boston, MA: Houghton Mifflin Company.
Janofsky, Michael. 2003. "Amid Acceptance of Gays, a Split on Marriage Issue." *New York Times*, November 23, A12.
____. 2003. "Young Brides Stir New Outcry on Utah Polygamy." *New York Times,* February 28, 1.
Jaschik, Scott. 2009. "Protecting His Sources." Inside Higher Ed, December 4. Retrieved December 5, 2009 (www.insidehightered.com).
Javers, Eamon. 2009. "Bailouts Could Cost U.S. $23 Trillion." July 20. Retrieved March 5, 2010 (http://dyn.politico.com).
Jeffery, Clara. 2006. "Poor Losers." *Mother Jones*, July/August, 20-21.
Jemal, A., R. Siegel, E. Ward, Y. Hao, J. Xu, T. Murray, and M. J. Thun. 2008. "Cancer Statistics, 2008." *CA: Cancer Journal for Clinicians* 58 (March-April): 71-96.
Jenkins, J. Craig. 1983. "Resource Mobilization Theory and the Study of Social Movements." *Annual Review of Sociology* 9 (August): 527-553.
Jenness, Valerie and Ryken Grattet. 2001. *Making Hate a Crime: From Social Movement to Law Enforcement*. New York: Russell Sage Foundation.
Jeune, Bernard and James W. Vaupel, eds. 1995. *Exceptional Longevity: From Prehistory to the Present.* Denmark: Odense University Press.
Jiménez, Tomás R. 2007. "The Next Americans." *Los Angeles Times*, May 27, M1.
Johnson, Allan G. 2008. "Our House is on Fire." Paper presented, March 17. Retrieved June 17, 2008 (http://uhavax.hartford.edu/agjohnson/kellogg.htm).
Johnson, Hank, and Bert Klandermans, eds. 1995. *Social Movements and Culture*. Minneapolis: University of Minnesota Press.
Johnson, Jean, and Jon Rochkind. 2009. *With Their Whole Lives Ahead of Them: Myths and Realities about Why so Many Students Fail to Finish College.* Public Agenda. Retrieved April 20, 2010 (www.publicagenda.org).
Johnson, Leslie and Justine Lloyd. 2004. *Sentenced to Everyday Life: Feminism and the Housewife*. New York: Berg.
Johnson, Rachel L., Debra Roter, Neil R. Powe, and Lisa A. Cooper. 2004. "Patient Race/Ethnicity and Quality of Patient-Physician Communication during Medical Visits." *American Journal of Public Health* 94 (December): 2084-2090.
Johnson, Richard W., and Corina Mommaerts. 2010. "How Did Older Workers Fare in 2009?" Urban Institute, March. Retrieved April 12, 2010 (www.urban.org).
Johnston, Pamela. 2005. "Dressing the Part." *Chronicle of Higher Education*, August 10. Retrieved Augusts 11, 2005 (http://chronicle.com/jobs).
Jolliffe, Dean. 2006. "The Cost of Living and the Geographic Distribution of Poverty." U.S. Department of Agriculture, Economic Research Service, September. Retrieved November 10, 2006 (www.ers.usda.gov).
Jones, Brent. 2009. "Latino Groups at Odds Over Poster Urging Census Participation." *Baltimore Sun,* December 25, 2.
Jones, Del. 2005. "Wanted: CEO, no Ivy Required." *USA Today*, April 7. Retrieved November 8, 2007 (www.usatoday.com).
Jones, Jeffrey M. 2005. "Most Americans Approve of Interracial Dating." Gallup News Service, October 7. Retrieved October 10, 2005 (www.galluppoll.com).
____. 2006. "One In Three U.S. Workers Have 'Telecommuted' To Work." Gallup Organization, August 16. Retrieved September 28, 2006 (www.galluppoll.com).
____. 2007. "Public: Family of Four Needs to Earn Average of $52,000 to Get By." Gallup News Service, February 9. Retrieved June 2, 2007 (www.galluppoll.com).
____. 2008. "Confidence in Congress: Lowest Ever for Any U.S. Institution." Gallup, June 20. Retrieved August 20, 2008 (www.gallup.com).
____. 2008. "Fewer Americans Favor Cutting Back Immigration." Gallup poll, July 10. Retrieved September 9, 2008 (www.gallup.com).
Jones, Jeffrey M. 2009. "Americans Perceive Increased Crime in U.S." *Gallup,* October 14. Retrieved October 16, 2009 (www.gallup.com).
____. 2009. "Majority of Americans Continue to Oppose Gay Marriage." *Gallup,* May 27. Retrieved March 12, 2010 (www.gallup.com).
____. 2009. "U.S. Clergy, Bankers See New Lows in Honesty/Ethics Ratings." *Gallup,* December 9. Retrieved April 27, 2010 (www.gallup.com).
____. 2010. "Americans Say Jobs Top Problem Now, Deficit in Future." *Gallup,* March 12. Retrieved April 6, 2010 (www.gallup.com).
Jones, Nicholas A., and Amy S. Smith. 2001. "*The Two or More Races Population: 2000*. "U.S. Census Bureau. Retrieved April 16, 2003 (www.census.gov).
Jones, Rachel K., Mia R. S. Zolna, Stanley K. Henshaw, and Lawrence B. Finer. 2008. "Abortion in the United States: Incidence and Access to Services, 2005." *Perspectives on Sexual and Reproductive Health* 40 (March): 6-16.
Jones, Steve. 2003. "Let the Games Begin: Gaming Technology and Entertainment among College Students." Pew Internet & American Life Project. Retrieved December 12, 2004 (www.pewinternet.org).
Jones, Susan S., and Hye-Won Hong. 2001. "Onset of Voluntary Communication: Smiling Looks to Mother." *Infancy* 2 (3): 353-70.
Jones, Vanessa J. 2008. "Coffee and Yoga and Prius and 'Juno'." *Boston Globe,* March 24. Retrieved November 6, 2008 (www.boston.com).
Jonsson, Patrik. 2007. "In US Justice, How Much Bias?" *Christian Science Monitor*, September 21, 1, 10.
____. 2010. "'Tea Party' Activists: Who They Are, What They Want." *Christian Science Monitor,* January 31, 21.
Josephson Institute. 2008. "Josephson Institute's Report Card on American Youth: There's a Hole in Our Moral Ozone and It's Getting Bigger." November 30. Retrieved April 19, 2010 (www.josephsoninstitute.org).
Joyce, Amy. 2006. "Vacation Deprivation." *Washington Post*, June 25, D4.
Juergensmeyer, Mark. 2003. "Thinking Globally about Religion." Pp. 3-13 in *Global Religions: An Introduction*, edited by Mark Juergensmeyer. New York: Oxford University Press.
Kaestner, Robert, and Benjamin Yarnoff. 2009. "Long Term Effects of Minimum Legal Drinking Age Laws on Adult Alcohol Use and Driving Fatalities." National Bureau of Economic Research, October. Retrieved January 5, 2010 (www.nber.org).
Kahn, Kim Fridkin. 2003. "Assessing the Media's Impact on the Political Fortunes of Women." Pp. 173-189 in *Women and American Politics: New Questions, New Directions*, edited by Susan J. Carroll. Oxford, NY: Oxford University Press.
Kalev, Alexandra, Frank Dobbin, and Erin Kelly. 2006. "Best Practices or Best Guesses? Assessing the Efficacy of Corporate Affirmative Action and Diversity Policies." *American Sociological Review* 71 (August): 589-617.
Kalil, Ariel. 2002. "Cohabitation and Child Development." Pp. 153-160 in *Just Living Together: Implications Of Cohabitation On Families, Children, And Social Policy*, edited by Alan Booth, Ann C. Crouter, and Nancy S. Landale. Mahwah, NJ: Lawrence Erlbaum Associates.
Kalmijn, Matthijs. 1998. "Intermarriage and Homogamy: Causes, Patterns, Trends." *Annual Review of Sociology* 24 (August): 395–421.
Kalwarski, Tara. 2010. "The Business of Politics." *Bloomburg Businessweek*, February 1 and 8, 36.
Kamber, Richard, and Mary Biggs. 2002. "Grade Conflation: A Question of Credibility." *Chronicle of Higher Education*, April 12, B14.
Kane, Emily. W., and Laura J. Macaulay. 1993. "Interviewer Gender and Gender Attitudes." *Public Opinion Quarterly* 57 (Spring): 1 -28.
Kapferer, Jean-Noel. 1992. "How Rumors are Born." *Society* 29 (July/August): 53-60.
Kaplan, David A. 2010. "The Best Company to Work For." *Fortune,* February 8, 57-72.
Karch, Debra L., et al. 2009. "Surveillance for Violent Deaths—National Violent Death Reporting System, 16 States, 2006." Centers for Disease Control and Prevention. *MMWR* 58 (SS-1): 1-44.
Karl, Thomas R., Jerry M. Melillo, and Thomas C. Petersen, eds. 2009. *Global Climate Change Impacts in the United States.* Cambridge, MA: Cambridge University Press.
Karnow, Stanley. 2004. "Keep Your Tired, Poor Stereotypes About Immigrants." *Baltimore Sun*, March 5, 13A.
Karukstis, Kerry K. 2009. "Women in Science, Beyond the Research University: Overlooked and Undervalued." *Chronicle of Higher Education,* July 10, A23.
Katz, Jackson. 2006. *The Macho Paradox: Why Some Men Hurt Women and How All Men Can Help.* Naperville, IL: Sourcebooks, Inc.
Katzenbach, Jon. 2003. *Why Pride Matters More Than Money: The Power of the World's Greatest Motivational Force*. New York: Crown Business.

Kawamoto, Walter T., and Tamara C. Cheshire. 1997. "American Indian Families." Pp. 15-34 in *Families in Cultural Context: Strengths and Challenges in Diversity,* edited by Mary Kay DeGenova. Mountain View, CA: Mayfield Publishing Company.

Keeter, Scott. 2009. "New Tricks for Old—and New—Dogs: Challenges and Opportunities Facing Communications Research." Pew Research Center Publications, March 3. Retrieved December 31, 2009 (http://pewresearch.org).

____. 2009. "Where the Public Stands on Immigration Reform." Pew Research Center, November 23. Retrieved March 15, 2010 (pewresearch.org).

Keeter, Scott, Juliana Horowitz, and Alec Tyson. 2008. "Young Voters in the 2008 Election." Pew Research Center, November 12. Retrieved November 14, 2008 (www.pewresearch.org).

Keeter, Scott, et al. 2010. "A Year after Obama's Election: Blacks Upbeat about Black Progress, Prospects." Pew Research Center, January 12. Retrieved March 13, 2010 (www.pewresearchcenter.org).

Kelley, Matt. 2007. "Ex-lawmakers Find Work with Lobbyists." *USA Today,* February 21, 1A.

Kempner, Joanna, Clifford S. Perlis, and Jon F. Merz. 2005. "Ethics: Forbidden Knowledge." *Science* 307 (February 11): 854.

Kendall, Diana. 2002. *The Power of Good Deeds: Privileged Women and the Social Reproduction of the Upper Class.* Lanham, MD: Rowman & Littlefield.

Kennedy, Tracy L. M., Aaron Smith, Amy Tracy Wells, and Barry Wellman. 2008. "Networked families." Pew Internet & American Life Project, October 19. Retrieved September 20, 2008 (www.pewinternet.org).

Kent, Mary Mederios. 2007. "Immigration and America's Black Population." *Population Bulletin* 62 (December): 1-16.

Kestin, Sally, and Peter Franceschina. 2007. "Federal Watchdog Examines Seminoles' Gambling Profits." *South Florida Sun-Sentinel,* December 8. Retrieved December 10, 2007 (www.sun-sentinel.com).

Kilbourne, Jean. 1999. *Deadly Persuasion: Why Women and Girls Must Fight the Addictive Power of Advertising.* New York: Free Press.

Kim, Victoria. 2009. "For Students, a Right to Be Mean Online?" *Los Angeles Times,* December 13. Retrieved December 15, 2009 (www.latimes.com).

King, C. Wendell. 1956. *Social Movements in the United States.* New York: Random House.

King, J. L. 2004. *On the Down Low: A Journey into the Lives of "Straight" Black Men Who Sleep with Men.* New York: Broadway Books.

King, Jacqueline E. 2006. *Gender Equity in Higher Education: 2006.* Washington, DC: American Council on Education.

King, Michael, and Annie Bartlett. 2006. "What Same Sex Civil Partnerships May Mean for Health." *Journal of Epidemiology and Community Health* 60 (March): 188-191.

Kinsella, Kevin, and David R. Phillips. 2005. "Global Aging: The Challenge of Success." *Population Bulletin* 60 (March): 1-40.

Kirkpatrick, David D. 2007. "Congress Finds Ways to Avoid Lobbyist Limits." *New York Times,* February 11, 1.

Kivel, Paul. 2004. *You Call This a Democracy? Who Benefits, Who Pays and Who Really Decides.* New York: Apex Press.

Kivisto, Peter and Dan Pittman. 2001. "Goffman's Dramaturgical Sociology: Personal Sales and Service in a Commodified World." Pp. 311-334 in *Illuminating Social Life: Classical and Contemporary Theory Revisited,* 2nd edition. Thousand Oaks, CA: Pine Forge Press.

Klandermans, Bert. 1984. "Mobilization and Participation: Social Psychological Explanations of Resource Mobilization Theory." *American Sociological Review* 49 (October): 583-600.

Klaus, Marshall H., John H. Kennell, and Phyllis H. Klaus. 1995. *Bonding: Building the Foundations of Secure Attachment and Independence.* Reading, MA: Addison-Wesley.

Klaus, Patsy. 2005. "Crimes against Persons Age 65 or Older, 1993-2002." Washington, DC: U.S. Department of Justice, Bureau of Justice Statistics.

____. 2006. "Crime and the Nation's Households, 2004." Washington, DC: U.S. Department of Justice, Bureau of Justice Statistics.

Klein, Alyson. 2008. "Education Earmarks Get Scrutiny." *Education Week,* February 29. Retrieved March 1, 2008 (www.edweek.org).

Klopfenstein, Kristin, and M. Kathleen Thomas. 2005. "The Advance Placement Performance Advantage: Fact or Fiction?" Retrieved February 10, 2005 (www.utdallas.edu).

Kneebone, Elizabeth. 2009. "Job Sprawl Revisited: The Changing Geography of Metropolitan Employment." Brookings Institute, Metropolitan Policy Program, April. Retrieved May 1, 2010 (www.brookings.edu).

Kneebone, Elizabeth, and Emily Garr. 2010. "The Suburbanization of Poverty: Trends in Metropolitan America, 2000 to 2008." Brookings Institute, January. Retrieved Mach 8, 2010 (www.brookings.edu).

Knickerbocker, Brad. 2005. "Fallout of Marijuana Verdict." *Christian Science Monitor,* June 8, 3.

Kochhar, Rakesh. 2007. "1995-2005: Foreign-Born Latinos Make Progress on Wages." Pew Hispanic Center, August 21. Retrieved October 10, 2007 (www.pewhispanic.org).

Kohut, Andrew, et al. 2007. "Blacks See Growing Values Gap between Poor and Middle Class." Pew Research Center, November 13. Retrieved December 10, 2007 (www.pewsocialtrends.org).

____, et al. 2010. "Favorable Ratings of Labor Unions Fall Sharply." Pew Research Center, February 23. Retrieved April 5, 2010 (www.pewresearch.org).

____, Carroll Doherty, Michael Dimock, and Scott Keeter. 2009. "Current Decade Rated as Worst in 50 Years." Pew Research Center for the People & the Press, December 21. Retrieved May 6, 2010 (www.people-press.org).

____. 2010. "Public's Priorities for 2010: Economy, Jobs, and Terrorism." Pew Research Center for the People & the Press, January 25. Retrieved May 2, 2010 (www.people-press.org).

Kornhauser, William. 1959. *The Politics of Mass Society.* New York: Free Press.

Kosmin, Barry A., and Ariela Keysar. 2009. *American Religious Identification Survey [ARIS 2008].* Summary Report, March. Retrieved April 25, 2010 (www.americanreligionsurvey-aris.org).

Kosova, Weston, and Pat Wingert. 2009. "Crazy Talk." *Newsweek,* June 8, 54-62.

Koss-Feder, L. 2009. "Bunking in with Mom and Dad." *Time,* March 2, 45-46.

Kozol, Jonathan. 2005. *The Shame of the Nation: The Restoration of Apartheid Schooling in America.* New York: Crown.

Krache, D. 2008. "How to Ground a 'Helicopter Parent'." CNN, August 19. Retrieved July 10, 2009 (www.cnn.com).

Kramer, Laura. 2005. *The Sociology of Gender: A Brief Introduction,* 2nd ed. Los Angeles, CA: Roxbury.

Kreider, Rose M. 2008. *Living Arrangements of Children: 2004.* Current Population Reports, P70-114. Washington, DC: U.S. Census Bureau.

Kreider, Rose M., and Jason M. Fields. 2002. "Number, Timing, and Duration of Marriages and Divorces: 1996." U.S. Census Bureau, Current Population Reports, P70-80. Retrieved March 1, 2003 (www.census.gov).

Kreps, Gary L. 2006. "Communication and Racial Inequities in Health Care." *American Behavioral Scientist* 49 (February): 760-774.

Krucoff, Mitchell W, Suzanne W. Crater, and Kerry L. Lee. 2006. "From Efficacy to Safety Concerns: A STEP Forward or a Step Back for Clinical Research and Intercessory Prayer: The Study of Therapeutic Effects of Intercessory Prayer (STEP). *American Heart Journal* 151 (April): 762-4.

Krugman, Paul. 2002. "Crony Capitalism, U.S.A." *New York Times,* January 15, 21.

Krumholz, Sheila. 2010. "Prepare for Turbulent Political Season as Courts Issue New Campaign Finance Decisions." Center for Responsive Politics, March 26. Retrieved March 29, 2010 (www.opensecrets.org).

Kuhn, Manford H., and Thomas. S. McPartland. 1954. "An Empirical Investigation of Self-Attitudes." *American Sociological Review* 19 (February): 68-76.

Kulczycki, Andrei and Arun P. Lobo. 2002. "Patterns, Determinants, and Implications of Intermarriage among Arab Americans." *Journal of Marriage and the Family* 64 (February): 202-210.

Kurdek, Lawrence A. 1993. "Predicting Marital Dissolution: A 5-Year Prospective Longitudinal Study of Newlywed Couples." *Journal of Personality and Social Psychology* 64 (February): 221-42.

____. 2004. "Are Gay and Lesbian Cohabiting Couples *Really* Different from Heterosexual Married Couples?" *Journal of Marriage and Family* 66 (November): 880-900.

Kusenbach, Margarethe. 2009. "Salvaging Decency: Mobile Home Residents' Strategies of Managing the Stigma of 'Trailer' Living." *Qualitative Sociology* 32 (December): 399-428.

Kutner, Lawrence, and Cheryl Olson. 2008. *Grand Theft Childhood.* New York: Simon & Schuster.

Kutner, M., E. Greenberg, Y. Jin, B. Boyle, Y. Hsu, and E. Dunleavy. 2007. *Literacy in Everyday Life: Results from the 2003 National Assessment of Adult Literacy* (NCES 2007-480). Washington, DC: U.S. Department of Education.

Kutz, G. D., and J. T. Meyer. 2009. "Wage and Hour Division's Complaint Intake and Investigative Processes Leave Low Wage Workers Vulnerable to Wage Theft." GAO, March 25, GAO-09-458T. Retrieved April 4, 2010 (www.gao.gov).

Lacey, Marc. 2008. "Across Globe, Empty Bellies Bring Rising Anger." *New York Times,* April 18, 1.

LaFraniere, Sharon. 2007. "African Crucible: Cast as Witches. Then Cast Out." *New York Times,* November 15, 1.

LaFraniere, Sharon, and Laurie Goodstein. 2007. "Anglicans Rebuke U.S. Branch on Blessing Same-Sex Unions." *New York Times,* February 20, A1, A11.

Lakoff, Robin. T. 1990. *Talking Power: The Politics of Language.* New York: Basic Books.

Lalasz, Robert. 2006. "Americans Flocking to Outer Suburbs in Record Numbers." Population Reference Bureau. Retrieved January 24, 2008 (www.prg.org).

Lamb, Gregory M. 2009. "National Parks Face New Threats." *Christian Science Monitor,* September 27, 36-37.

____. 2009. "Rise of the Public You." *Christian Science Monitor,* August 30, 13-16.

Lampman, Jane. 2007. "New Fight, Old Foe: Slavery." *Christian Science Monitor,* February 21, 13-14.

Landler, Mark. 2006. "In Munich, Provocation in a Symbol of Foreign Faith." *New York Times,* December 8, A3.

Landsberg, Mitchell. 2007. "They're More Interested in Money Than Mao." *Los Angeles Times,* June 26, A1.

Landsberger, Henry A. 1958. *Hawthorne Revisited.* Ithaca, NY: Cornell University Press.

Lang, Kurt, and Gladys Engel Lang. 1961. *Collective Dynamics.* New York: Thomas Y. Crowell.

Lannutti, Pamela J., Melanie Laliker, and Jerold L. Hale. 2001. "Violations of Expectations and Social-Sexual Communication in Student/Professor Interactions." *Communication Education* 50 (January): 69-82.

Laraña, Enrique, Hank Johnston, and Joseph R. Gusfield, eds. 1994. *New Social Movements: From Ideology to Identity.* Philadelphia, PA: Temple University Press.

LaRossa, Ralph and Donald C. Reitzes. 1993. "Symbolic Interactionism and Family Studies." Pp. 135–63 in *Sourcebook of Family Theories and Methods: A Contextual Approach,* edited by Pauline G. Boss, William J. Doherty, Ralph LaRossa, Walter R. Schumm, and Suzanne K. Steinmetz. New York: Plenum Press.

Larson, Jeffry and Rachel Hickman. 2004. "Are College Marriage Textbooks Teaching Students the Premarital Predictors of Marital Quality?" *Family Relations* 53 (July): 385-392.

Laskow, Sarah. 2006. "Hired Guns: State Lobbying Becomes Billion-Dollar Business." Center for Public Integrity, December 20. Retrieved May 23, 2007 (www.publicintegrity.org).

Lasswell, Harold. 1936. *Politics: Who Gets What, When and How.* New York: McGraw-Hill.

Lathrop, Richard G., and John Hasse. 2007. "Tracing New Jersey's Dynamic Landscape: A Municipal Report Card on Urban Grown and Open Space Loss." Retrieved January 28, 2008 (www.crssa.rutgers.edu).

Laufer, Prakash. 2010. "The Earning Report for Main Street: A Sorry Account, Indeed." New Jersey News Room, January 28. Retrieved April 5, 2010 (www.newjerseynewsroom.com).

Lavelle, Marianne. 2007. "Water Woes." *U.S. News & World Report,* June 4, 37-46.

Lawless, Jennifer L. and Richard L. Fox. 2005. *It Takes a Candidate: Why Women Don't Run for Office.* New York: Cambridge University Press.

Leaper, Campbell, and Melanie M. Ayres. 2007. "A Meta-Analytic Review of Gender Variations in Adults' Language Use: Talkativeness, Affiliative Speech, and Assertive Speech." *Personality and Social Psychology Review* 11 (November): 328-363.

Ledger, Kate. 2009. "Sociology and the Gene." *Contexts* 8 (Summer): 16-20.

____. 2009. "The Moynihan Report, a Retrospective." *Contexts* 8 (Fall): 49-52.

Lee, Don. 2007. "In China, Income Disparity Takes a Great Leap." *Los Angeles Times,* June 10, C1.

Lee, J., W. Grigg, and G. Dion. 2007. *The Nation's Report Card: Mathematics 2007* (NCES 2007-494). Washington, DC: National Center for Education Statistics, Institute of Education Sciences, U.S. Department of Education.

Lee, Marlene. 2009. "Aging, Family Structure, and Health." Population Reference Bureau, October. Retrieved April 10, 2010 (www.prb.org).

Lee, Marlene A., and Mark Mather. 2008. "U.S. Labor Force Trends." *Population Bulletin* 63 (June): 1-17.

Lemann, Nicholas. 2000. *The Big Test: The Secret History of the American Meritocracy.* New York: Farrar, Straus, and Giroux.

Lemert, Edwin M. 1951. *Social Pathology: A Systematic Approach to the Theory of Sociopathic Behavior.* New York: McGraw-Hill.

____. 1967. *Human Deviance, Social Problems and Social Control.* Englewood Cliffs, NJ: Prentice Hall.

Lencioni, Patrick. 2002. *The Five Dysfunctions of a Team: A Leadership Fable.* San Francisco, CA: Jossey-Bass.

Lengermann, Patricia Madoo and Jill Niebrugge-Brantley. 1992. "Contemporary Feminist Theory." Pp. 308-357 in *Contemporary Sociological Theory*, 3rd edition, edited by George Ritzer. New York: McGraw-Hill.

Lenhart, Amanda. 2007. "Cyberbullying and Online Teens." June, Pew Internet & American Life Project, April. Retrieved September 20, 2007 (www.pewinternet.org).

____. 2009. "Adults and Social Network Websites." Pew Internet & American Life Project, January 14. Retrieved February 5, 2010 (www.pewinternet.org).

____, Kristen Purcell, Aaron Smith, and Kathryn Zickuhr. 2010. "Social Media & Mobile Internet Use Among Teens and Young Adults." Pew Internet & American Life Project, February 3. Retrieved February 5, 2010 (www.pewinternet.org).

Leonardsen, Dag. 2004. *Japan as a Low-Crime Nation.* New York: Palgrove Macmillan.

Leonnig, Carol D. 2009. "Rep. Murtha's Earmarks Lead to Fewer Jobs Than Promised." *Washington Post,* December 31, A3.

Lessig, Lawrence. 2001. "The Internet under Siege," *Foreign Policy,* Issue 127 (November/December): 56-66.

Levine, Arthur. 2006. "Educating School Teachers." The Education Schools Project, September. Retrieved March 15, 2010 (www.edschools.org).

Levine, Marc V. 1994. "A Nation of Hamburger Flippers?" *Baltimore Sun,* July 31, 1E, 4E.

Lewin, Tamar. 2009. "No Einstein in Your Crib? Get a Refund." *New York Times,* October 24, 1.

Lewis, David Levering. 1993. *W. E. B. Du Bois: Biography of a Race, 1868-1919.* New York: Henry Holt.

Lewis, Oscar. 1966. "The Culture of Poverty." *Scientific American* 115 (October): 19-25.

LexisNexis Corporate Affiliations. 2003. New Providence, NJ: LexisNexis Group.

Lichtblau, Eric, David Johnson, and Ron Nixon. 2008. "F.B.I. Struggles to Handles Financial Fraud Cases." *New York Times,* October 19, A1.

Lichter, Daniel T., Zhenchao Qian, and Leanna M. Mellott. 2006. "Marriage or Dissolution? Union Transitions among Poor Cohabiting Women." *Demography* 43 (May): 223-240.

Lilly, J. Robert, Francis T. Cullen and Richard A. Ball. 1995. *Criminological Theory: Context and Consequences,* 2nd edition. Thousand Oaks, CA: Sage.

Lindsey, Linda L. 2005. *Gender Roles: A Sociological Perspective,* 4th ed. Upper Saddle River, NJ: Prentice Hall.

Lino, Mark, and Andrew Carlson. 2009. *Expenditures on Children by Families, 2008.* U.S. Department of Agriculture, Center for Nutrition Policy and Promotion, July. Retrieved January 25, 2010 (www.cnpp.usda.gov).

Linton, Ralph. 1936. *The Study of Man.* New York: Appleton-Century-Crofts.

____. 1964. *The Study of Man: An Introduction.* New York: Appleton-Century-Crofts.

Liu, Hui, and Debra J. Umberson. 2008. "The Times They Are a Changin': Marital Status and Health Differentials from 1972 to 2003." *Journal of Health and Social Behavior* 49 (September): 239-253.

Liu, Runjuan, and Donald Trefler. 2008. "Much Ado about Nothing: American Jobs and the Rise of Service Outsourcing to China and India." National Bureau of Economic Research, Working Paper 14061, June. Retrieved April 6, 2010 (www.nber.org).

Livingston, Gretchen, Kim Parker, and Susannah Fox. 2009. "Latinos Online, 2006-2008: Narrowing the Gap." Pew Hispanic Center, December 22. Retrieved February 5, 2010 (www.pewhispanic.org).

Llana, Sara Miller. 2005. "Can a $103 Fine Stop Students from Swearing?" *Christian Science Monitor,* December 7, 1-2.

____. 2009. "Finding Safety in the Pink." *Christian Science Monitor,* December 20, 4.

____. 2010. "Church Faces Backlash on Scandal." *Christian Science Monitor,* April 19, 14.

Locher, David A. 2002. *Collective Behavior.* Upper Saddle River, NJ: Prentice Hall.

Lofland, John. 1993. "Collective Behavior: The Elementary Forms." Pp. 70-75 in *Collective Behavior and Social Movements,* edited by Russell L. Curtis, Jr. and Benigno E. Aguirre. Boston, MA: Allyn & Bacon.

____. 1996. *Social Movement Organizations: Guide to Research on Insurgent Realities.* New York: Aldine De Gruyter.

Logan, John and Harvey Molotch. 1987. *Urban Fortunes: The Political Economy of Place.* Berkeley: University of California Press.

Lohr, Steve. 2009. "Watch the Walk and Prevent a Fall." *New York Times,* November 8, 4.

Londoño, Ernesto. 2009. "Gay Men Targeted in Iraq, Report Says: Militias Blamed for Scores of Killings." *Washington Post,* August 17, A6.

Long, Lynette. 2008. "Painful Lessons." *Baltimore Sun,* May 18, 11A.

Longman, Phillip. 2004. "Which Nations Will Go Forth and Multiply?" *Fortune,* April 12, 60-61.

Lopez, Mark Hugo. 2009. "Latinos and Education: Explaining the Attainment Gap." Pew Hispanic Center, October 7. Retrieved April 2, 2010 (www.pewhispanic.org).

Lopez, Mark Hugo, and Susan Minushkin. 2008. *2008 National Survey of Latinos: Hispanic Voter Attitudes.* Washington, DC: Pew Hispanic Center.

Lopez, Mark Hugo, and Paul Taylor. 2009. "Dissecting the 2008 Electorate: Most Diverse in U.S. History." Pew Research Center, April 30. Retrieved March 26, 2010 (www.pewhispanic.org).

Lopez, Shane. 2009. "Americans Keep Volunteering During Tough Economic Times." *Gallup News,* November 24. Retrieved February 13, 2010 (www.gallup.com).

Lorber, Judith. 2005. *Gender Inequality: Feminist Theories and Politics,* 3rd ed. Los Angeles, CA: Roxbury.

Lorber, Judith and Lisa Jean Moore. 2007. *Gendered Bodies: Feminist Perspectives.* Los Angeles, CA: Roxbury.

Lord, Susan M., Michelle M. Camacho, Richard A. Layton, Russell A. Long, Matthew W. Ohland, and Mara H. Wasburn. 2009. "Who's Persisting in Engineering? A Comparative Analysis of Female and Male Asian, Black, Hispanic, Native American, and White Students." *Journal of Women and Minorities in Science and Engineering* 15 (September): 167-190.

Louw, P. Eric. 2001. *The Media and Cultural Production.* Thousand Oaks, CA: Sage.

Lowenkamp, Christopher T., and Edward J. Latessa. 2005. "Developing Successful Reentry Programs: Lessons Learned from the 'What Works' Research." *Corrections Today* 67 (April): 72-77.

Lugaila, Terry. A. 1998. "Marital Status and Living Arrangements: March 1998 (Update)." Current Population Reports, P20-514. Retrieved August 8, 2000 (www.census.gov).

Lukemeyer, Anna, Marcia K. Meyers, and Timothy Smeeding. 2000. "Expensive Children In Poor Families: Out-Of-Pocket Expenditures for the Care of Disabled and Chronically Ill Children in Welfare Families." *Journal of Marriage and the Family* 62 (May): 399-415.

Lundberg, Shelly, and Robert A. Pollak. 2007. "The American Family and Family Economics." *Journal of Economic Perspectives* 21 (Spring): 3-26.

Luo, Michael. 2009. "Forced from Executive Pay to Hourly Wage." *New York Times,* March 1, 1.

Lutz, William. 1989. *Doublespeak.* New York: Harper & Row.

Lynch, Eleanor W., and Marci J. Hanson, eds. 1999. *Developing Cross-Cultural Competence: A Guide for Working with Children and Their Families,* 2nd ed. Baltimore, MD: Paul H. Brookes Publishing Co.

Lynn, David B. 1969. *Parental and Sex Role Identification: A Theoretical Formulation.* Berkeley, CA: McCutchen.

Lynn, M. and M. Todoroff. 1995. "Women's Work and Family Lives." Pp. 244-71 in *Feminist Issues: Race, Class, and Sexuality,* edited by Nancy Mandell. Scarborough, Ontario: Prentice Hall Canada.

Lyons, Linda. 2005. "Tracking U.S. Religious Preferences Over the Decades." The Gallup Poll, May 24. Retrieved August 25, 2007 (www.galluppoll.com).

Maccoby, Eleanor E., and John A. Martin. 1983. "Socialization in the Context of the Family: Parent-Child Interaction." Pp. 1-101 in *Socialization, Personality, and Social Development: Vol. 4. Handbook of Child Psychology,* edited by E. Mavis Hetherington. New York: Wiley.

MacDonald, Jeffrey G. 2009. "Ranks of Atheists Grow, Get Organized." *Christian Science Monitor,* June 28. Retrieved July 1, 2009 (www.csmonitor.com).

Macionis, John J. and Vincent N. Parrillo. 2007. *Cities and Urban Life,* 4th ed. New Jersey: Upper Saddle River.

MacKenzie, Donald, and Judy Wajcman, eds. 1999. *The Social Shaping of Technology,* 2nd ed. Philadelphia, PA: Open University Press.

MacKinnon, Catharine. 1982. "Feminism, Marxism, Method, and the State: An Agenda for Theory." *Signs* 7 (Spring): 515-544.

Madigan, Nick. 2003. "Suspect's Wife Is Said To Cite Polygamy Plan." *New York Times,* March 15, 1.

____. 2005. "Sheehan's Ad Says Bush Lied About Iraq War." *Baltimore Sun,* August 27, 1D, 4D-5D.

____. 2009. "Seniors Increasingly Targeted by Con Artists; Police 'Struggling to Keep Up'." *Baltimore Sun,* January 14, 3.

Magnier, Mark. 2009. "Dalit Women Find Their Voice Through a Newspaper." *Los Angeles Times,* October 14. Retrieved October 16, 2009 (www.latimes.com).

____. 2009. "In Northern India, Village Elders Order 'Honor Killings'." *Los Angeles Times,* September 26. Retrieved September 28, 2009 (www.latimes.com).

Mahay, Jenna, Edward O. Laumann, and Stuart Michaels. 2001. "Race, Gender, and Class in Sexual Scripts." Pp. 197-238 in *Sex, Love, and Health in America,* edited by Edward O. Laumann and Robert T. Michael. Chicago: University of Chicago Press.

Mahon, Joe. 2004. "Banking on the Fringe." The Federal Reserve Bank of Minneapolis, July. Retrieved September 10, 2008 (www.minneapolisfed.org).

Maines, David R. 2001. *The Faultline of Consciousness: A View of Interactionism in Sociology.* New York: Aldine De Gruyter.

Major, Brenda, Mark Appelbaum, Linda Beckman, Mary Ann Dutton, Nancy Felipe Russo, and Carolyn West. 2008. "Report of the APA Task Force on Mental Health and Abortion." August 13, American Psychological Association. Retrieved September 5, 2008 (www.apa.org).

"Major Religions of the World Ranked by Number of Adherents." 2007. Retrieved August 24, 2007 (www.adherents.com).

Makino, Catherine. 2009. "Rape Victim Presses Case of Police Abuse in Japan." Women's eNews, May 5. Retrieved May 7, 2009 (www.womensenews.org).

Malley-Morrison, Kathleen and Denise A. Hines. 2004. *Family Violence in a Cultural Perspective: Defining, Understanding, and Combating Abuse.* Thousand Oaks, CA: Sage.

Malthus, Thomas Robert. 1798/1965. *An Essay on Population.* New York: Augustus Kelley.

____. 1872/1991. *An Essay on the Principle of Population,* 7th ed. London: Reeves & Turner.

Mananzan, Mary John. 2002. "Theological Reflections on Violence against Women (A Catholic Perspective)." Pp. 205-212 in *Gendering the Spirit: Women, Religion & the Post-Colonial Response,* edited by Durre S. Ahmed. New York: Zed Books.

Manz, Charles C., and Henry P. Sims. 1987. "Leading Workers to Lead Themselves: The External Leadership of Self-Managing Work Teams." *Administrative Science Quarterly* 32: 106-108.

Margolis, Jane, and Allan Fisher. 2002. *Unlocking the Clubhouse: Women in Computing.* Cambridge, MA: MIT Press.

Markoff, John. 2009. "Scientists Worry Machines May Outsmart Man." *New York Times,* July 26, 1.

Marks, Joseph L. 2007. *Fact Book on Higher Education 2007.* Atlanta, GA: Southern Regional Education Board.

Marlar, Jenny. 2010a. "The Emotional Cost of Underemployment." *Gallup,* March 9. Retrieved April 6, 2010 (www.gallup.com).

____. 2010b. "Underemployment Rises to 20.3% in March." *Gallup,* April 1. Retrieved April 6, 2010 (www.gallup.com).

Martens, Jens. 2005. "A Compendium of Inequality." Global Policy Forum. Retrieved October 25, 2006 (www.globalpolicy.org).

Martin, Karin A. 2009. "Normalizing Heterosexuality: Mothers' Assumptions, Talk, and Strategies with Young Children." *American Sociological Review* 74 (April): 190-207.

Martin, Molly A. 2008. "The Intergenerational Correlation in Weight: How Genetic Resemblance Reveals the Social Role of Families." *American Journal of Sociology* 114 (suppl.): S67-S105.

Martin, Paige D., Don Martin, and Maggie Martin. 2001. "Adolescent Premarital Sexual Activity, Cohabitation, and Attitudes toward Marriage." *Adolescence* 36 (Fall): 601-609.

Martin, Philip, and Gottfried Zürcher. 2008. "Managing Migration: The Global Challenge." *Population Bulletin* 63 (March): 1-20.

Martin, Suzanne. 2006. "Advertising to Youth: What Youth Want and What Advertisers Need to Know." *Trends and Tudes* 5 (August): 1-5.

Martinez, G. M., A. Chandra, J. C. Abma, J. Jones, and W. D. Mosher. 2006. "Fertility, Contraception, and Fatherhood: Data on Men and Women from Cycle 6 (2002) of the National Survey of Family Growth. *Vital Health Statistics* 23 (26). Retrieved June 3, 2007 (www.cdc.gov/nchs).

Marty, Martin E. 2005. *When Faiths Collide*. Malden, MA: Blackwell.

Marx, Eric. 2008. "Time to Go on a Carbon Diet?" *Christian Science Monitor,* November 10, 2008, 13, 16.

Marx, Gary T. and Douglas McAdam. 1994. *Collective Behavior and Social Movements: Process and Structure*. Upper Saddle River, NJ: Prentice Hall.

Marx, Karl. 1844/1964. *Economic and Philosophic Manuscripts of 1844*. New York: International Publishers.

____. 1845/1972. "The German Ideology." Pp. 110-164 in *The Marx-Engels Reader*, edited by Robert C. Tucker. New York: W. W. Norton.

____. 1867/1967. *Capital*. Friedrich Engels, ed. New York: International Publishers.

____. 1934. *The Class Struggles in France*. New York: International Publishers.

____. 1964. *Karl Marx: Selected Writings in Sociology and Social Philosophy*. T. B. Bottomore, trans. New York: McGraw-Hill.

Masci, David. 2007. "How the Public Resolves Conflicts Between Faith and Science." Pew Forum on Religion & Public Life, August 27. Retrieved September 3, 2007 (www.pewforum.org).

____. 2009. "A Contentious Debate: Same-Sex Marriage in the U.S." Pew Research Center, July 9. Retrieved March 12, 2010 (http://pewforum.org).

Massey, Douglas S. 2007. *Categorically Unequal: The American Stratification System*. New York: Russell Sage Foundation.

Mather, Mark. 2008. "Population Losses Mount in U.S. Rural Areas." March, Population Reference Bureau. Retrieved July 29, 2008 (www.prb.org).

____. 2009. *Children in Immigrant Families Chart New Path*. Washington, DC: Population Reference Bureau.

Mauss, Armand. 1975. *Social Problems as Social Movements*. Philadelphia, PA: Lippincott.

Mayer, Caroline E. 2002. "Stuck Under a Load of Debt." *Washington Post*, November 9, E01.

Maynard, Micheline. 2009. "Even as Fares Creep Up, Airlines Tack on Fees, Too." *New York Times,* October 16, 3.

Mayo, Elton. 1945. *The Problems of an Industrial Civilization*. Cambridge, MA: Harvard University Press.

McAdam, Doug, and Ronnelle Paulsen. 1994. "Specifying the Relationship between Social Ties and Activism." *American Journal of Sociology* 99 (November): 640-67.

McAdoo, Harriette P. 2002. "African American Parenting." Pp. 47-58 in *Handbook of Parenting,* 2nd ed., Volume 4: *Social Conditions and Applied Parenting,* edited by Marc H. Bornstein. Mahwah, NJ: Lawrence Erlbaum Associates.

McCabe, Donald L., Kenneth D. Butterfield, and Linda K. Treviño. 2006. "Academic Dishonesty in Graduate Business Programs: Prevalence, Causes, and Proposed Action." *Academy of Management Learning Education* 5 (September): 294-305.

McCanna, Shaun. 2009. "New Afghan Crisis: No Room in Schools." *Christian Science Monitor,* December 6, 11.

McCarthy, Ellen. 2004. "Md. Professor Archives History of Dot-Com Bombs." *Washington Post*, October 28, E1.

McCarthy, John, and Mayer Zald. 1977. "Resource Mobilization and Social Movements: A Partial Theory." *American Journal of Sociology* 82 (May): 1212–1241.

McCoy, J. Kelly, Gene H. Brody, and Zolinda Stoneman. 2002. "Temperament and the Quality of Best Friendships: Effect of Same-Sex Sibling Relationships." *Family Relations* 51 (July): 248-255.

McCrummen, Stephanie. 2009. "'I Will Only Wear Pants'." Women's eNews, November 14. Retrieved November 17, 2009 (www.womensenews.org).

McDonald, Renee, Ernest N. Jouriles, Suhasini Ramisetty-Mikler, Raul Caetano, and Charles E. Green. 2006. "Estimating the Number of American Children Living in Partner-Violent Families." *Journal of Family Psychology* 20 (March): 137-142.

McFadden, Robert D., and Angela Macropoulos. 2008. "Wal-Mart Employee Trampled to Death." *New York Times,* November 29, A16.

McFalls, Joseph A., Jr. 2007. "Population: A Lively Introduction," 5th ed. *Population Bulletin* 62 (March): 1-31.

McGregor, Jena, and Steve Hamm. 2008. "Managing the Workforce." *Business Week*, January 28, 34-43.

McHale, Susan M. 2001. "Free-Time Activities in Middle Childhood: Links with Adjustment in Early Adolescence." *Child Development* 76 (November/December): 1764-78.

McIntosh, Peggy. 1995. "White Privilege and Male Privilege: A Personal Account of Coming to See Correspondences through Work in Women's Studies." Pp. 76-87 in *Race, Class, and Gender: An Anthology*, 2nd ed., edited by Margaret L. Andersen and Patricia Hill Collins. Belmont, CA: Wadsworth.

McKernan, Signe-Mary, Caroline Ratcliffe, and Stephanie R. Cellini. 2009. "Transitioning in and out of Poverty." Urban Institute, September. Retrieved March 6, 2010 (www.urban.org).

McKinley, James C., Jr. 2010. "Texas Conservatives Win Curriculum Change." *New York Times,* March 12, A10.

McKinley, Jesse, and Kirk Johnson. 2008. "Mormons Tipped Scale in Ban on Gay Marriage." *New York Times,* November 15, 1.

McLaughlin, Kathleen E. 2005. "With Woofs and Wet Noses, Dogs Help Heal in China." *Christian Science Monitor,* June 1, 7.

McMenamin, Terence M. 2007. "A Time to Work: Recent Trends in Shift Work and Flexible Schedules." *Monthly Labor Review* 130 (December): 3-14.

McNamee, Stephen J., and Robert K. Miller Jr. 1998. "Inheritance and Stratification." Pp. 193-213 in *Inheritance and Wealth in America*, edited by Robert K. Miller Jr. and Stephen J. McNamee. New York: Plenum Press.

McPhail, Clark, and Ronald T. Wohlstein. 1983. "Individual and Collective Behavior within Gatherings, Demonstrations, and Riots." *Annual Review of Sociology*, 9 (August): 579-600.

McRae, Susan. 1999. "Cohabitation or Marriage?" Pp. 172-190 in *The Sociology of the Family*, edited by Graham Allan. Malden, MA: Blackwell Publishers.

McRoberts, Omar M. 2003. *Streets of Glory: Church and Community in a Black Urban Neighborhood*. Chicago, IL: The University of Chicago Press.

Mead, George Herbert. 1934. *Mind, Self, and Society.* Chicago, IL: University of Chicago Press.

____. 1964. *On Social Psychology.* Chicago, IL: University of Chicago Press.

Mead, Lawrence M. 2008. "Comment on 'Helping Poor Working Parents Get Ahead'." Urban Institute, July 17. Retrieved August 25, 2008 (www.urban.org).

Mead, Margaret. 1935. *Sex and Temperament in Three Primitive Societies*. New York: Morrow.

"Media Coverage of Hispanics." 2009. Pew Hispanic Center Project for Excellence in Journalism, December 7. Retrieved March 12, 2010 (pewhispanic.org).

Medina, Jennifer. 2008. "Next Question: Can Students Be Paid to Excel?" *New York Times,* March 5, 1.

Mehl, Matthias R., Simine Vazire, Nairán Ramírez-Esparza, Richard B. Slatcher, and James W. Pennebaker. 2007. "Are Women Really More Talkative Than Men?" *Science* 317 (July): 82.

Mehta, Seema. 2008. "Parents May Home-School Children Without Teaching Credential, California Court Says." *Los Angeles Times*, August 9. Retrieved August 14, 2008 (www.latimes.com).

Mello, Michelle M., Brian R. Clarridge, and David M. Studdert. 2005. "Academic Medical Centers' Standards for Clinical-Trial Agreements with Industry." *New England Journal of Medicine* 352 (May 26): 2202-2210.

Melucci, Alberto. 1995. "The New Social Movements Revisited: Reflections on a Sociological Misunderstanding." Pp. 107-119 in *Social Movements and Social Classes: The Future of Collective Action*, edited by Louis Maheu. Thousand Oaks, CA: Sage.

Menchik, Daniel A., and Xiaoli Tian. 2008. "Putting Social Context into Text: The Semiotics of E-mail Interaction." *American Journal of Sociology* 114 (September): 332-370.

Mendelsohn, Oliver and Maria Vicziany. 1998. *The Untouchables, Subordination, Poverty and the State in Modern India.* New York: Cambridge University Press.

Mendes, Elizabeth. 2010. "Six in 10 Overweight or Obese in U.S., More in '09 Than in '08." *Gallup News,* February 9. Retrieved February 14, 2010 (www.gallup.com).

Menifield, Charles E., Winfield H. Rose, John Homa, and Anita B. Cunningham. 2001. "The Media's Portrayal of Urban and Rural School Violence: A Preliminary Analysis." *Deviant Behavior: An Interdisciplinary Journal*, 22 (September/October): 447-64.

Menissi, Fatima. 1991. *The Veil and the Male Elite: A Feminist Interpretation of Women's Rights in Islam*. Reading, MA: Addison-Wesley.

____. 1996. *Women's Rebellion and Islamic Memory*. Atlantic Highlands: Zed Books.

"The Merits of Gay Marriage." 2003. Editorial, *Washington Post,* November 20, A40.

Mertens, Richard. 2009. "Indiana's Amish Return to Their Plows." *Christian Science Monitor,* May 24, 23.

Merton, Robert K. 1938. "Social Structure and Anomie." *American Sociological Review* 3 (December): 672-682.

____. 1948/1996. "The Self-Fulfilling Prophecy." Pp. 183-201 in *Robert K. Merton: On Social Structure and Science*, edited by Piotr Sztompka. Chicago, IL: University of Chicago Press.

____. 1949. "Discrimination and the American Creed." Pp. 99-126 in *Discrimination and National Welfare*, edited by Robert M. MacIver. New York: Harper.

____. 1968. *Social Theory and Social Structure*. New York: Free Press.

Merton, Robert K., and Alice K. Rossi. 1950. "Contributions to the Theory of Reference Group Behavior." Pp. 40-105 in *Continuities in Social Research*, edited by Robert K. Merton and Paul L. Lazarsfeld. New York: Free Press.

Metz, Mary Haywood. 2003. *Different by Design: The Context and Character of Three Magnet Schools*. New York: Teachers College, Columbia University.

Meyer, Cheryl L. and Michelle Oberman. 2001. *Mothers Who Kill Their Children: Understanding the Acts of Moms from Susan Smith to the "Prom Mom."* New York: New York University Press.

Michels, Robert. 1911/1949. *Political Parties*. Glencoe, IL: Free Press.

Mikkelson, Barbara, and David Mikkelson. 2005. "Super Bull Sunday." Retrieved August 14, 2009 (www.snopes.com).

Milanovic, Branko. 2006. "Global Income Inequality: What It Is and Why It Matters." World Bank.Retrieved October 20, 2006 (siteresources.worldbank.org).

Milbank, Dana. 2003. "Bush Delivers Religious Address." *Washington Post*, February 10, A2.

Milgram, Stanley. 1963. "Behavioral Study of Obedience." *Journal of Abnormal and Social Psychology* 67: 4 (371-378).

____. 1965. "Some Conditions of Obedience and Disobedience to Authority." *Human Relations* 18 (February): 57-76.

Miller, Claire C. 2009. "Company Settles Case of Reviews It Faked." *New York Times,* July 15, 5.

Miller, D. W. 2001. "DARE Reinvents Itself—With Help From Its Social-Scientist Critics." *Chronicle of Higher Education*, October 16, A12-A-14.

Miller, Lisa. 2010. "A Woman's Place Is in the Church." *Newsweek,* April 12, 34-41.

Miller, Matthew. 2005. "The (Porn) Player." *Forbes*, July 4, 124, 126, 128.

Miller, S. M. 2001. "My Meritocratic Rise." *Tikkun* (March/April): 1-3. Retrieved January 20, 2003 (www.tikkun.org).

Mills, C. Wright. 1956. *The Power Elite*. New York: Oxford University Press.

____. 1959. *The Sociological Imagination*. New York: Oxford University Press.

Min, Pyong Gap. 2002. "Introduction." Pp. 1-14 in *Religions in Asian America: Building Faith Communities*, edited by Pyong Gap Min and Jung Ha Kim. Walnut Creek, CA: AltaMira Press.

Mincy, Ronald, ed. 2006. *Black Males Left Behind*. Washington, DC: Urban Institute Press.

Miners, Zach. 2009. "A New Look at Why Girls Don't Get In." *U.S. News Weekly,* November 13, 8.

____. 2010. "Washington's Voucher Program Dilemma." *U.S. News & World Report,* January, 39-40.

Mirowsky, John, and Catherine E. Ross. 2007. "Creative Work and Health." *Journal of Health and Social Behavior* 48 (December): 385-403.

Mischel, Walter. 1966. "A Social Learning View of Sex Differences." Pp. 57-81 in *The Development of Sex Differences,* edited by Eleanor E. Maccoby. Stanford, CA: Stanford University Press.

Mitchell, Josh. 2002. "Hot Rod as Hobby, and Obsession." *Baltimore Sun*, July 24, 1A, 6A.

Mokhiber, Russell. 2007. "Twenty Things You Should Know about Corporate Crime." *Corporate Crime Reporter* 21 (June 12). Retrieved February 25, 2010 (corporatecrimereporter.com).

Money, John and Anke A. Ehrhardt. 1972. *Man & Woman, Boy & Girl: The Differentiation and Dimorphism of Gender Identity from Conception to*

Maturity. Baltimore, MD: Johns Hopkins University Press.
Montagu, Ashley, ed. 1999. *Race and IQ: Expanded Edition*. New York: Oxford University Press.
Montenegro, Xenia P. 2004. "The Divorce Experience: A Study of Divorce at Midlife and Beyond." *AARP the Magazine* (May): 40-79.
Montlake, Simon. 2006. "China Reins in Reach of Foreign News." *Christian Science Monitor*, September 13, 6.
Mooney, Carolyn. 2007. *The Myth of Mars and Venus: Do Men and Women Really Speak Different Languages?* New York: Oxford University Press.
Moore, Elizabeth S. 2006. "It's Child's Play: Advergaming and the online Marketing of Food to Children." Henry J. Kaiser Family Foundation, July. Retrieved April 12, 2008 (www.kff.org).
Moore, Kathleen. 2008. "Low-income Homes Green—and Affordable." *Daily Gazette*, July 1. Retrieved September 21, 2008 (www.dailygazette.com).
Moore, Lisa. 2007. "The Secret to Smarter Schools." *U.S. News & World Report*, March 26-April 7, 54-55.
Moore, Martha T. 2006. "Cows Power Plan for Alternative Fuel." *USA Today*, December 3, 11A.
Morais, Richard C. 2007. "Desperate Arrangements." *Forbes*, January 29, 72-79.
Morales, Lymari. 2010. "Green Behaviors Common in U.S., but Not Increasing." *Gallup*, April 9. Retrieved April 30, 2010 (www.gallup.com).
Moreau, Ron, and Sami Yousafzai. 2006. "A War on Schoolgirls." *Newsweek*, June 26, 34-35.
Morgenson, Gretchen. 2004. "No Wonder C.E.O.'s Love Those Mergers." *New York Times*, July 18, C1.
Morin, Richard. 2008. "America's Four Middle Classes." Pew Research Center, July 29. Retrieved July 23, 2009 (pewresearch.org).
____. 2009. "What Divides America?" Pew Research Center, September 24. Retrieved March 2, 2010 (pewresearch.org).
____, and D'Vera Cohn. 2008. "Women Call the Shots at Home; Public Mixed on Gender Roles in Jobs." Pew Research Center, September 28. Retrieved November 20, 2008 (pewresearch.org).
____, and Paul Taylor. 2009. "Suburbs Not Most Popular, But Suburbanites Most Content." Pew Research Center, February 26. Retrieved May 1, 2010 (www.pewresearch.org).
Morris, Desmond. 1994. *Bodytalk: The Meaning of Human Gestures*. New York: Crown Trade Paperbacks.
Morris, Jim. 2006. "Power Trips: Privately Sponsored Trips Hot Tickets on Capitol Hill." Center for Public Integrity, June 5. Retrieved May 23, 2007 (www.publicintegrity.org).
Morris, Rachel. 2009. "Agents of Climate Change." *Mother Jones*, November/December, 36.
Morrison, Denton E. 1971. "Some Notes toward Theory on Relative Deprivation, Social Movements, and Social Change." *The American Behavioral Scientist* 14 (May-June): 675-690.
Mosher, William D., Anjani Chandra, and Jo Jones. 2005. "Sexual Behavior and Selected Health Measures: Men and Women 15-44 Years of Age, United States, 2002." National Center for Health Statistics, *Vital and Health Statistics*, No. 362, September 15. Retrieved January 10, 2006 (www.cdc.gov/nchs).
Mossaad, Nadwa. 2009. "U.S. Food Stamp Enrollment Rises." Population Reference Bureau, October. Retrieved March 2, 2010 (www.prb.org).
Motivans, Mark. 2004. "Intellectual Property Theft, 2002." Washington, DC: U.S. Department of Justice, Bureau of Justice Statistics.
Moyer, Imogene L. 2001. *Criminological Theories: Traditional and Nontraditional Voices and Themes*. Thousand Oaks, CA: Sage.
____. 2003. "Jane Addams: Pioneer in Criminology." *Women & Criminal Justice* 14 (3/4): 1-14.
Mozingo, Joe. 2010. "In Haiti, Some See the Spirit World Behind the Quake." *Los Angeles Times*, January 22. Retrieved January 23, 2010 (www.latimes.com).
Mufson, Steven. 2010. "Chinese Government Sharply Criticizes Clinton's Speech Urging Internet Freedom." *Washington Post*, January 23, A14.
Mui, Ylan Q. 2009. "Bottled Water Boom Appears Tapped Out." *Washington Post*, August 13, A10.
Mulac, Anthony. 1998. "The Gender-Linked Language Effect: Do Language Differences Really Make a Difference?" Pp. 127-153 in *Sex Differences and Similarities in Communication: Critical Essays and Empirical Investigations of Sex and Gender in Interaction*, edited by Daniel J. Canary and Kathryn Dindia. Mahwah, NJ: Lawrence Erlbaum Associates.
Mulligan, Thomas S. 2004. "Beanie Babies Rode Own Bubble." *Baltimore Sun*, August 31, 1C, 3C.
Mumford, Lewis. 1961. *The City in History: Its Origins, Transformations, and Its Prospects*. New York: Harcourt, Brace.
Mumola, Christopher J. 2000. "Incarcerated Parents and Their Children." U.S. Department of Justice, November. Retrieved July 14, 2002 (www.ojp.usdoj.gov/bjs).
"Municipal Solid Waste." 2005. U.S. Environmental Protection Agency. Retrieved June 30, 2005 (www.epa.gov).
Murdock, George P. 1940. "The Cross-Cultural Survey." *American Sociological Review*, 5: 361-70.
____. 1945. "The Common Denominator of Cultures." Pp. 123-142 in *The Science of Man in the World Crisis*, edited by Ralph Linton. New York: Columbia University Press.
____. 1967. "Ethnographic Atlas: A Summary." *Ethnology* 6, 109–236.
Murphy, Cait. 2005. "Fast-Forward to the Future." *Fortune*, September 19, 271.
Murphy, Caryle. 2009. "Behind the Veil." *Christian Science Monitor*, December 13, 12-17.
Murphy, Evelyn and E. J. Graff. 2005. *Getting Even: Why Women Don't Get Paid Like Men—And What To Do About It*. New York: Simon & Schuster.
Murphy, John. 2004. "S. Africa's New Goal: Economic Equality." *Baltimore Sun*, April 27, 1A, 4A.
Murray, Charles. 2008. "College Daze." *Forbes*, September 1, 32.
Myers, Candice A., Tim Slack, and Joachim Singelmann. 2010. "Understanding the Aftermath of Hurricanes Katrina and Rita." Population Reference Bureau, February. Retrieved April 30, 2010 (www.prb.org).
Myers, John P. 2007. *Dominant-Minority Relations in America: Convergence in the New World*, 2nd ed. Boston, MA: Allyn & Bacon.
Nagourney, Adam, and Megan Thee-Brenan. 2010. "Poll Finds Edge for Obama Over G.O.P. Among the Public." *New York Times*, February 12, A1.
Naisbitt, John, Nana Naisbitt, and Douglas Philips. 1999. *High Tech/High Touch: Technology and Our Search for Meaning*. New York: Broadway Books.
Nakao, Keiko and Judith Treas. 1992. "The 1989 Socioeconomic Index of Occupations: Construction from the 1989 Occupational Prestige Scores," GSS Methodological Report No. 74. Chicago, IL: National Opinion Research Center.
Nakashima, Ellen. 2008. "Prescription Data Used to Assess Consumers." *Washington Post*, August 4, A1.
National Academy of Sciences. 2007. *Treatment of PTSD: An Assessment of the Evidence*. Washington, DC: National Academies Press.
____. 2008. *Science, Evolution, and Creationism*. Washington, DC: National Academy of Sciences.
National Center on Addiction and Substance Abuse. 2008. "National Survey of American Attitudes on Substance Abuse XIII: Teens and Parents." Retrieved January 10, 2010 (www.casacolumbia.org).
National Center on Elder Abuse. 2005. "Elder Abuse Prevalence and Incidence." Retrieved June 23, 2007 (www.elderabusecenter.org).
National Center for Health Statistics. 2007. *Health, United States, 2007 with Chartbook on Trends in the Health of Americans*. Washington, DC: U.S. Government Printing Office.
National Coalition for the Homeless. 2009a. "How Many People Experience Homelessness?" July. Retrieved March 4, 2010 (www.nationalhomeless.org).
____. 2009b. "Who Is Homeless?" July. Retrieved March 4, 2010 (www.nationalhomeless.org).
National Council of La Raza. 2010. "The State of Latino Children and Youth in the United States." Retrieved March 18, 2010 (www.nclr.org).
National Council of Teachers of English Committee on Public Doublespeak. 2005. Retrieved February 12, 2006 (www.ncte.org).
National Healthcare Disparities Report. 2003. U.S. Department of Health and Human Services. Retrieved April 20, 2004 (www.qualitytools.ahrq.gov).
National Institutes of Health. 2006. "Stem Cell Information." Retrieved August 6, 2008 (www.stemcells.nih.gov/info).
National Latino Alliance for the Elimination of Domestic Violence. 2005. "Domestic Violence Affects Families of All Racial, Ethnic, and Economic Backgrounds." Retrieved June 20, 2007 (www.dvalianza.org).
National Public Radio. 2010. "Black Male Privilege?" Interview transcript, March 4. Retrieved March 10, 2010 (www.npr.org).
National Research Council. 2001. *Informing America's Policy on Illegal Drugs: What We Don't Know Keeps Hurting Us*. Washington, DC: National Academy Press.
National Survey of Student Engagement. 2006. "Engaged Learning: Fostering Success for All Students, Annual Report 2006." National Survey of Student Engagement. Retrieved August 5, 2007 (http://nsse.iub.edu).
"Nation's Population One-Third Minority." 2006. U.S. Census Bureau News, May 10. Retrieved July 28, 2006 (www.census.gov).
Natural Resources Defense Council. 2007. "Beach Pollution." Retrieved February 8, 2008 (www.ndrc.org).
Neelakantan, Shailaja. 2006. "In India, Conservatives Want Women Under Wraps." *Chronicle of Higher Education*, May 26, A47-A48.
____. 2008. "India Expands Quota System for Lower-Caste Students." *Chronicle of Higher Education* (April 25): A31.
Neider, Linda L. and Chester A. Schriesheim, eds. 2005. *Understanding Teams*. Greenwich, CT: Information Age.
Nelson, Libby. 2010. "Obama's Efforts to Improve Teachers' Training Stir Old Debates." *Chronicle of Higher Education*, February 19, A19.
Netherlands Environmental Assessment Agency. 2007. "China Now No. 1 in CO_2 Emissions; USA in Second Position." Retrieved February 12, 2008 (www.mnp.nl).
Nevins, Joseph. 2010. "Security First: The Obama Administration and Immigration 'Reform'." *NACLA Report on the Americas* 43 (January/February): 32-36.
Newman, David M. 2005. *Identities and Inequalities: Exploring the Intersections of Race, Class, Gender, and Sexuality*. New York: McGraw-Hill.
Newman, Katherine S., and Victor Tan Chen. 2007. "The Crisis of the Near Poor." *Chronicle of Higher Education*, October 5, B10-B11.
Newport, Frank. 2001. "Americans See Women as Emotional and Affectionate, Men as More Aggressive." *Gallup Poll Monthly* No. 425 (February, 2001): 34-38.
____. 2006. "Who Believes in God and Who Doesn't?" The Gallup Poll, June 23. Retrieved June 24, 2006 (www.galluppoll.com).
____. 2007. "Just Why Do Americans Attend Church?" The Gallup Poll, April 6. Retrieved August 27, 2007 (wwww.galluppoll.com).
____. 2007. "Sixty-Nine Percent of Americans Support Death Penalty." Gallup News Service, October 12. Retrieved May 12, 2008 (www.gallup.com).
____. 2008. "Bush Job Approval at 25%, His Lowest Yet." Gallup, October 6. Retrieved October 14, 2008 (www.gallup.com).
____. 2008. "Wives Still Do Laundry, Men Do Yard Work." Gallup News Service, April 4. Retrieved June 2, 2008 (www.gallup.com).
____. 2009. "Despite Recession, No Uptick in Americans' Religiosity." Gallup, March 23. Retrieved April 26, 2010 (www.gallup.com).
____. 2009. "In U.S., Two-Thirds Continue to Support Death Penalty." *Gallup*, October 13, Retrieved February 19, 2010 (www.gallup.com).
____. 2010. "Americans' Global Warming Concerns Continue to Drop." *Gallup*, March 11. Retrieved April 30, 2010 (www.gallup.com).
____. 2010. "Socialism Viewed Positively by 36% of Americans." *Gallup*, February 4. Retrieved April 6, 2010 (www.gallup.com).
Nichols, Austin, and Melissa Favreault. 2009. "A Detailed Picture of Intergenerational Transmission of Human Capital." Urban Institute, May 22. Retrieved March 6, 2010 (www.urban.org).
Nie, Norman H., and Saar D. Golde. 2008. "Does Education Really Make You Smarter?" *Miller-McCune* 1 (June/July): 56-64.
Niebuhr, H. Richard. 1929. *The Social Sources of Denominationalism*. New York: Meridian.
Nielsen Company, The. 2008. "College Spring Break Study." February 27. Retrieved April 10, 2008 (www.alcoholstats.com).
Niewyk, Donald L., and Francis R. Nicosia. 2000. *The Columbia Guide to the Holocaust*. New York: Columbia University Press.
Nisbett, Richard E. 2009. *Intelligence and How to Get It: Why Schools and Cultures Count*. New York: W. W. Norton.
Nitkin, David. 2008. "Hopkins' Carson to Get Medal of Freedom." *Baltimore Sun*, June 12, 7B.
"No Action on Greenhouse Gases." 2008. *Baltimore Sun*, July 12, 2A.
Noguchi, Yuki. 2005. "Good Samaritans Turn to Web to Help Victims." *Washington Post*, September 2, D4.
Norris, Pippa. 2003. "The Gender Gap: Old Challenges, New Approaches." Pp. 146-170 in *Women and American Politics: New Questions, New Directions*, edited by Susan J. Carroll. Oxford, NY: Oxford University Press.

Nossiter, Adam. 2007. "A Son of Immigrants Rises in a Southern State." *New York Times*, October 22, 1.

Nunberg, Geoffrey. 2007. "The Language of Death." *Los Angeles Times*, February 12. Retrieved February 14 (www.latimes.com).

O'Brien, Jodi and Peter Kollock. 2001. *The Production of Reality: Essays and Readings on Social Interaction*, 3rd ed. Thousand Oaks, CA: Pine Forge.

O'Brien, Rourke. 2008. "Paying City Students is a Wise Investment." *Baltimore Sun*, June 27, 19A.

O'Donnell, Victoria. 2007. *Television Criticism*. Thousand Oaks, CA: Sage.

O'Hara, John M. 2010. *A New American Tea Party: The Counterrevolution against Bailouts, Handouts, Reckless Spending, and More Taxes*. Hoboken, NJ: John Wiley & Sons.

O'Hare, William P. 2002. "Tracking the Trends in Low-Income Working Families," *Population Today* 30 (August/September): 1-3.

O'Harrow, Jr., Robert. 2008. "Earmark Spending Makes a Comeback." *Washington Post*, June 13, A1.

O'Neill, Brendan. 2007. "Gaelic-Only Laws: Linguistic Apartheid?" *Christian Science Monitor*, February 6, 20.

Oakes, Jeannie. 1985. *Keeping Track: How Schools Structure Inequality*. New Haven, CT: Yale University Press.

Obach, Brian K. 2004. *Labor and the Environmental Movement: The Quest for Common Ground*. Cambridge, MA: MIT Press.

Oberschall, Anthony. 1973. *Social Conflict and Social Movements*. Englewood Cliffs, NJ: Prentice Hall.

____. 1995. *Social Movements: Ideologies, Interests, and Identities*. New Brunswick, NJ: Transaction.

Office of Applied Studies. 2004. "Alcohol and Drug Services Study (ADSS) Cost Study." Substance Abuse and Mental Health Services Administration (SAMSA), June 18. Retrieved May 14, 2005 (oas.samhsa.gov).

Office of the Deputy Chief of Staff for Intelligence. 2006. "Arab Cultural Awareness: 58 Factsheets." U.S. Army Training and Doctrine Command, Ft. Leavenworth, Kansas, January. Retrieved February 15, 2006 (www.fas.org).

Ogburn, William F. 1922. *Social Change with Respect to Culture and Original Nature*. New York: Dell.

Ogden, Cynthia L., Margaret D. Carroll, and Katherine M. Flegal. 2008. "High Body Mass Index for Age among US Children and Adolescents, 2003-2006." *JAMA* 299 (May 28): 2401-2405.

Ogunwole, Stella U. 2006. "We the People: American Indians and Alaska Natives in the United States." Census 2000 Special Reports, CENSR-28. Retrieved March 26, 2007 (www.census.gov).

Ojito, Mirta. 2009. "Doctors in Cuba Start Over in the U.S." *New York Times*, August 4, D1.

Olson, Theodore B. 2010. "The Conservative Case for Gay Marriage." *Newsweek*, January 18, 48-53.

Onishi, Norimitsu. 2007. "Corporate Korea Corks the Bottle as Women Rise." *New York Times*, June 10, 1.

Opsahl, Kurt. 2010. "Six Things You Need to Know about Facebook Connections." Electronic Frontier Foundation, May 4. Retrieved May 11, 2010 (www.eff.org).

Ornstein, Allan C. 2003. *Pushing the Envelope: Critical Issues in Education*. Upper Saddle River, NJ: Prentice Hall.

Orr, Andrea. 2009. "Minimum Wage Still Low by Historic Measures." Economic Policy Institute. Retrieved April 2, 2010 (www.epi.org).

Orr, Jimmy. 2009. "Is Sarah Palin *Newsweek* Cover Sexist?" *Christian Science Monitor*, November 17. Retrieved November 18, 2009 (features.csmonitor.com).

Orrenius, Pia. 2004. "Immigrant Assimilation: Is the U.S. Still a Melting Pot?" *Southwest Economy*, Federal Reserve Bank of Dallas, May/June. Retrieved January 3, 2005 (www.dallasfed.org).

Orrenius, Pia M., and Madeline Zavodny. 2009. "Do Immigrants Work in Riskier Jobs?" *Demography* 46 (August): 535-551.

Orum, Anthony M. 2001. *Introduction to Political Sociology*, 4th ed. Upper Saddle River, NJ: Prentice Hall.

Packard, Vance. 1959. *The Status Seekers*. New York: David McKay.

Padgett, Tim. 2007. "Pilfering Priests." *Time*, February 26, 46-47.

Palazzo, David J., Young-Jin Lee, Rasil Warnakulasooriya, and David E. Pritchard. 2010. "Patterns, Correlated, and Reduction of Homework Copying." *Physics Education Research*. Vol. 6. Retrieved April 22, 2010 (www.prst-per.aps.org).

Pan, L., et al. 2009. "Differences in Prevalence of Obesity among Black, White, and Hispanic Adults—United States, 2006-2008." *MMWR Weekly*, 58 (July 17): 740-744.

Parents Television Council. 2010. "Best and Worst TV Shows of the Week." Retrieved January 24, 2010 (www.parentstv.org).

Park, Robert and Ernest Burgess. 1921. *Introduction to the Science of Sociology*. Chicago, IL: University of Chicago Press.

Parker, Kim. 2009. "The Harried Life of the Working Mother." Pew Research Center, October 1. Retrieved March 11, 2010 (http://pewresearch.org).

Parkinson, C. Northcote. 1962. *Parkinson's Law*, 2nd ed. Boston, MA: Houghton Mifflin.

Parsons, Talcott. 1954. *Essays in Sociological Theory*, revised edition. New York: Free Press.

____. 1959. "The School Class as a Social System: Some of its Functions in American Society." *Harvard Educational Review* 29 (Fall): 297-313.

____. 1960. *Structure and Process in Modern Societies*. New York: Free Press.

Parsons, Talcott, and Robert F. Bales, eds. 1955. *Family, Socialization and Interaction Process*. New York: Free Press.

Pascoe, C. J. 2007. *Dude, You're a Fag: Masculinity and Sexuality in High School*. Berkeley: University of California Press.

Passel, Jeffrey S. 2010. "Census History: Counting Hispanics." Pew Hispanic Center, March 3. Retrieved March 19, 2010 (www.pewhispanic.org).

Passel, Jeffrey S., and D'Vera Cohn. 2009. "A Portrait of Unauthorized Immigrants in the United States." Pew Research Center, April 14. Retrieved March 16, 2010 (pewresearch.org).

____. 2009. "Mexican Immigrants: How Many Come? How Many Leave?" Pew Hispanic Center, July 22. Retrieved July 25, 2009 (www.pewhispanic.org).

Pastor, Manuel, Justin Scoggins, Jennifer Tran, and Rhonda Ortiz. 2010. "The Economic Benefits of Immigrant Authorization in California." Center for the Study of Immigrant Integration, January. Retrieved March 14, 2010 (http://csii.usc.edu).

Paul, Noel. C. 2002. "The Birth of a Would-Be-Fad." *Christian Science Monitor*, September 23, 11, 14-16.

Paul, Pamela. 2005. *Pornified: How Pornography is Transforming Our Lives, Our Relationships, and Our Families*. New York: Henry Holt.

Paul, Richard and Linda Elder. 2007. *The Miniature Guide to Critical Thinking: Concepts and Tools*. Dillon Beach, CA: The Foundation for Critical Thinking.

Pauley, Bruce F. 1997. *Hitler, Stalin, and Mussolini: Totalitarianism in the Twentieth Century*. Wheeling, IL: Harlan Davidson, Inc.

Pearce, Diana. 1978. "The Feminization of Poverty: Women, Work, and Welfare." *Urban and Social Change Review* 11, 28–36.

Pedersen, Paul. 1995. *The Five Stages of Culture Shock: Critical Incidents around the World*. Westport, CT: Greenwood Press.

Pelham, Brett W. 2009. "About One in Six Americans Report History of Depression." *Gallup*, October 22. Retrieved March 2, 2010 (www.gallup.com).

Pelton, Tom. 2007. "U.S. Blocks States on Emissions." *Baltimore Sun*, February 20, A7.

Perie, Marianne, Rebecca Moran, and Anthony D. Lutkus. 2005. "NAEP 2004 Trends in Academic Progress: Three Decades of Student Performance in Reading and Mathematics (NCES 2005-464). U.S. Department of Education, Institute of Education Sciences, National Center for Education Statistics. Washington, DC: U.S. Government Printing Office.

Perlmutter, David D. 2001. "Students are Blithely Ignorant; Professors are Bitter." *Chronicle of Higher Education*, July 27, B20.

Perloff, Richard M., Bette Bonder, George B. Ray, Eileen B. Ray, and Laura A. Siminoff. 2006. "Doctor-Patient Communication, Cultural Competence, and Minority Health." *American Behavioral Scientist* 49 (February): 835–852.

Perrucci, Robert and Earl Wysong. 1999. *The New Class Society*. Lanham, MD: Rowman & Littlefield Publishers.

Perry-Jenkins, Maureen, Abbie E. Goldberg, Courtney P. Pierce, and Aline G. Sayer. 2007. "Shift Work, Role Overload, and the Transition to Parenthood." *Journal of Marriage and Family* 69 (February): 123-138.

"Perspectives." 2009. *Newsweek*, October 26, 16.

Pescosolido, Bernice A., Brea L. Perry, J. Scott Long, Jack K. Martin, John I. Nurnberger, Jr., and Victor Hesselbrock. 2008. "Under the Influence of Genetics: How Transdisciplinary Leads Us to Rethink Social Pathways to Illness." *American Journal of Sociology* 114 (Suppl.): S171-S201.

Peter, Lawrence J., and Raymond Hull. 1969. *The Peter Principle*. New York: Morrow.

Peter, Tom A. 2009. "It's Not Just an Adventure, It's a Job—A Much Needed One." *Christian Science Monitor*, November 1, 17.

Peters, Marie F. 2007. "Parenting of Young Children in Black Families: A Historical Note." Pp. 203-218 in *Black Families*, 4th ed., edited by Harriette Pipes McAdoo. Thousand Oaks, CA: Sage.

Peterson, Scott. 2008. "In Iran, Barbie Seen as Cultural Invader." *Christian Science Monitor*, September 15, 4.

Pew Center on the States. 2008. "One in 100: Behind Bars in America 2008." February. Retrieved May 11, 2008 (www.pewcenteronthestates.org).

____. 2009. *One in 31: The Long Reach of American Corrections*. Washington, DC: The Pew Charitable Trusts.

Pew Forum on Religion & Public Life. 2008. "U.S. Religious Landscape Survey: Religious Beliefs and Practices: Diverse and Politically Relevant." June. Retrieved June 26, 2008 (religions.pewforum.org).

____. 2009a. "Faith in Flux: Changes in Religious Affiliation in the U.S." April. Retrieved April 25, 2010 (www.pewforum.org).

____. 2009b. "Faith-Based Programs Still Popular, Less Visible." November 16. Retrieved April 25, 2010 (www.pewforum.org).

____. 2009c. "Many Americans Mix Multiple Faiths." December. Retrieved April 25, 2010 (www.pewforum.org).

Pew Global Attitudes Project. 2006. "The Great Divide: How Westerners and Muslims View Each Other." June 22. Retrieved August 15, 2007 (www.pewglobal.org).

____. 2007. "World Publics Welcome Global Trade—But Not Immigration." October 4. Retrieved November 25, 2007 (www.pewglobal.org).

Pew Initiative on Food and Biotechnology. 2004. "Genetically Modified Crops in the United States." August. Retrieved September 30, 2005 (www.pewagbiotech.org).

Pew Internet & American Life Project. 2010. "Internet User Profiles Reloaded." January 5. Retrieved February 5, 2010 (http://pewresearch.org).

Pew Research Center. 2008. "Inside the Middle Class: Bad Times Hit the Good Life." April 9. Retrieved April 10, 2008 (pewresearch.org).

____. 2008. "Public Support Falls for Religion's Role in Politics." August 21. Retrieved September 18, 2008 (www.pewresearch.org).

____. 2009. "Troubled by Crime, the Economy, Drugs and Corruption: Most Mexicans See Better Life in U.S.—One-in-Three Would Migrate." Pew Global Attitudes Project, September 23. Retrieved March 12, 2010 (www.perglobal.org).

Pew Research Center for the People & the Press. 2010. "83%—Support Christmas Displays in Public." Retrieved April 26, 2010 (http://pewresearch.org).

Pewewardy, Cornel. 1998. "Fluff and Feathers: Treatment of American Indians in the Literature and the Classroom." *Equity & Excellence in Education* 31 (April): 69–76.

Phillips, Kevin. 2002. *Wealth and Democracy: A Political History of the American Rich*. New York: Broadway Books.

Phinney, Jean S., Irma Romero, Monica Nava, and Dan Huang. 2001. "The Role of Language, Parents, and Peers in Ethnic Identity among Adolescents in Immigrant Families." *Journal of Youth and Adolescence* 30 (April): 135-153.

Pianta, Robert C., Jay Belsky, Renate Houts, Fred Morrison, and The National Institute of Child Health and Human Development (NICHD) Early Child Care Research Network. 2007. "Teaching: Opportunities to Learn in America's Elementary Classrooms." *Science* 315 (March 30): 1795-6.

Piore, Adam. 2005. "A Higher Frequency." *Mother Jones*, December, 47-51, 80-81.

Pipher, Mary. 1994. *Reviving Ophelia: Saving the Selves of Adolescent Girls*. New York: Putnam.

Pittz, Will. 2005. "Closing the Gap: Solutions to Race-Based Health Disparities." Applied Research Center & Northwest Federation of Community Organizations, June. Retrieved April 20, 2007 (www.arc.org).

"Plan to Build Texas Mosque Sends Neighbors Into Uproar." 2006. *Baltimore Sun*, December 8, 2A.

Planty, M. W. Hussar, T. Snyder, S. Provasnik, G. Kena, R. Dinkes, A. KewalRamani, and J. Kemp. 2008. *The Condition of Education 2008* (NCES 2008-031). Washington, DC: National Center for Education Statistics, Institute of Education Sciences, U.S. Department of Education.

Planty, Michael, et al. 2007. *The Condition of Education 2007* (NCES 2007-064). Washington, DC: U.S. Government Printing Office.

____, et al. 2009. *The Condition of Education 2009*. National Center for Education Statistics, Institute of Education Sciences, U.S. Department of Education. Washington, DC.

Plateris, Alexander A. 1973. *100 Years of Marriage and Divorce Statistics: 1867-1967*. Rockville, MD: National Center for Health Statistics.

Political Money Line. 2004. "Money in Politics Databases." Retrieved August 18, 2004 (www.fecinfo.com).

"Political Parties." 2010. Global Security. Retrieved March 25, 2010 (www.globalsecurity.org).

Polsby, Nelson W. 1959. "Three Problems in the Analysis of Community Power." *American Sociological Review* 24 (December): 796-803.

Pond, Allison, Gregory Smith, and Scott Clement. 2010. "Religion Among the Millenials: Less Religiously Active than Older Americans, but Fairly Traditional in Other Ways." Pew Research Center. Retrieved April 25, 2010 (www.pewforum.org).

Pong, Suet-ling, Lingxin Hao, and Erica Gardner. 2005. "The Roles of Parenting Styles and Social Capital in the School Performance of Immigrant Asian and Hispanic Adolescents." *Social Science Quarterly* 86 (December): 928-950.

Popenoe, David and Barbara D. Whitehead. 2002. *Should We Live Together? What Young Adults Need To Know About Cohabitation Before Marriage—A Comprehensive Review Of Recent Research*, 2nd ed. New Brunswick, NJ: The National Marriage Project, Rutgers University. Retrieved July 12, 2003 (marriage.rutgers.edu).

____. 2006. *The State of Our Unions: 2006*. Rutgers, the State University of New Jersey, The National Marriage Project. Retrieved July 28, 2006 (http://marriage.rutgers.edu).

Population Division, U.S. Census Bureau. 2008. "Projections of the Population by Race and Hispanic Origin for the United States: 2208 to 2050" and "Percent of the Projected Population by Race and Hispanic Origin for the United States: 2008 to 2050." August 14. Retrieved September 8, 2008 (www.census.gov).

Population Reference Bureau. 2007. "World Population Highlights." *Population Bulletin* 62 (September): 1-12.

____. 2008. "World Population Projections to 2100." Retrieved May 3, 2010 (www.prb.org/publications/graphicsbank/populationtrends.aspx).

Powell, Lisa M., Glen Szczypka, Frank J. Chaloupka, and Carol L. Braunschweig. 2007. "Nutritional Content of Television Food Advertisements Seen by Children and Adolescents in the United States." *Pediatrics* 120 (September): 576-583.

Powers, Charles H. 2004. *Making Sense of Social Theory: A Practical Introduction*. Lanham, MD: Rowman & Littlefield.

Presser, Harriet B., Janet C. Gornick, and Sangeeta Parashar. 2008. "Gender and Nonstandard Work Hours in 12 European Countries." *Monthly Labor Review* 131 (February): 83-103.

Price, Barbara Raffel, and Natalie J. Sokoloff, eds. 2004. *The Criminal Justice System and Women: Offenders, Prisoners, Victims, & Workers*, 3rd edition. New York: McGraw-Hill.

Price, J. A. 1981. "North American Indian Families." Pp. 245–68 in *Ethnic Families in America: Patterns and Variations*, 2nd ed., edited by Charles H. Mindel and Robert W. Habenstein. New York: Elsevier.

Princiotta, Daniel, and Stacey Bielick. 2006. *Homeschooling in the United States: 2003* (NCES 2006-042). National Center for Education Statistics, U.S. Department of Education. Washington, DC: U.S. Government Printing Office.

Prins, Nomi. 2009. *It Takes a Pillage: Behind the Bailouts, Bonuses, and Backroom Deals from Washington to Wall Street*. Hoboken, New Jersey: John Wiley & Sons.

"A Profile of the Working Poor, 2007." 2009. U.S. Department of Labor, U.S. Bureau of Labor Statistics, March, Report 1012. Retrieved August 5, 2009 (www.dol.gov).

Prothrow-Stith, Deborah and Howard R. Spivak. 2005. *Sugar and Spice and No Longer Nice: How We Can Stop Girls' Violence*. San Francisco, CA: Jossey-Bass.

Provasnik, Stephen and Scott Dorfman. 2005. *Mobility in the Teacher Workforce* (NCES 2005-114). U.S. Department of Education, National Center for Education Statistics. Washington, DC: U.S. Government Printing Office.

Pryor, J. H., S. Hurtado, L. DeAngelo, L. Palucki Blacke, and S. Tran. 2009. *The American Freshman: National Norms Fall 2009*. Los Angeles: Higher Education Research Institute, UCLA.

Pryor, John H., Sylvia Hurtado, Victor B. Saenz, José Louis Santos, and William S. Korn. 2007. *The American Freshman: Forty Year Trends*. Los Angeles: Higher Education Research Institute, UCLA.

Putnam, Frank W. 2006. "The Impact of Trauma on Child Development." *Juvenile and Family Court Journal* 57 (Winter): 1-11.

Qian, Zhenchao. 2005. "Breaking the Last Taboo: Interracial Marriage in America." *Contexts* 4 (Fall): 33-37.

Qian, Zhenchao, and Daniel T. Lichter. 2007. "Social Boundaries and Marital Assimilation: Interpreting Trends in Racial and Ethnic Intermarriage." *American Sociological Review* 72 (February): 68-94.

"Quality Counts 2007: From Cradle to Career." 2007. *Education Week*, January 4. Retrieved July 23, 2007 (www.edweek.org).

Quinney, Richard. 1980. *Class, State, and Crime*. Boston, MA: Little, Brown.

Radosh, Polly F. 1993. "Women and Crime in the United States: A Marxian Explanation." Pp. 263-289 in *Female Criminality: The State of the Art*, edited by Concetta C. Culliver. New York: Garland.

Radwin, David. 2009. "High Response Rates Don't Ensure Survey Accuracy." *The Chronicle Review*, October 9, B8-B9.

Raintree Nutrition, Inc. 2008. "Rainforest Facts." Retrieved February 12, 2008 (www.rain-tree.com).

Rampey, B. D., G. S. Dion, and P. L. Donahue. 2009. *NAEP 2008 Trends in Academic Progress*. National Center for Education Statistics, Institute of Education Sciences, U.S. Department of Education. Washington, DC.

Rand, Michael R. 2009. "Criminal Victimization, 2008." Bureau of Justice Statistics Bulletin, September. Retrieved February 25, 2010 (http://bjs.ojp.usdoj.gov).

Raphael, Steven, and Michael A. Stoll. 2010. "Job Sprawl and the Suburbanization of Poverty." Brookings Institute, Metropolitan Policy Program, March. Retrieved May 1, 2010 (www.brookings.edu).

Ray, Rebecca, and John Schmitt. 2007. "No-Vacation Nation." Center for Economic and Policy Research, May. Retrieved July 4, 2008 (www.cepr.net).

Rayasam, Renuka. 2007. "Immigrants: The Unsung Heroes of the U.S. Economy." *U.S. News & World Report*, February 26, 58.

Reay, Campbell A. M., and K. D. Browne. 2001. "Risk Factor Characteristics for Carers Who Physically Abuse or Neglect Their Elderly Dependents." *Aging and Mental Health* 5 (February): 56-62.

Reed, Betsy. 2008. "Race to the Bottom." *The Nation*, May 1. Retrieved June 25, 2008 (www.thenation.com).

Reeves, Mary E. 1999. "School Is Hell: Learning with (and from) *The Simpsons*." Pp. 55-82 in *Popular Culture and Critical Pedagogy: Reading, Constructing, Connecting*, edited by Toby Daspit and John A. Weaver. New York: Garland Publishing.

Reiss, Steven. 2004. "The Sixteen Strivings for God." *Zygon* 39 (June): 303-320.

"Religions of the World: Number of Adherents, Names of Houses of Worship . . .". 2007. Religious Tolerance. Retrieved August 24, 2007 (www.religioustolerance.org).

Rennison, Callie M. 2003. *Intimate Partner Violence, 1993-2001*. Washington, DC: U.S. Department of Justice.

Renzulli, Linda A., and Vincent J. Roscigno. 2007. "Charter Schools and the Public Good." *Contexts* 6 (Winter): 31-36.

Rettig, Jessica. 2010. "How to Choose a Charter School." *U.S. News & World Report*, January, 48-49.

Rhoads, Steven E. 2004. *Taking Sex Differences Seriously*. San Francisco, CA: Encounter Books.

Rice, George, Carol Anderson, Neil Risch, and George Ebers. 1999. "Male Homosexuality: Absence of Linkage to Microsatellite Markers at Xq28." *Science* 284 (April 23): 665-667.

Richburg, Keith B. 2009. "States Seek Less Costly Substitutes for Prison." *Washington Post*, July 13, A1.

Riche, Martha Farnsworth. 2000. "America's Diversity and Growth: Signposts for the 21st Century." *Population Bulletin* 55 (June): 1-41.

"The Richest People in America." 2009. *Forbes*, October 19, 36-37.

Richtel, Matt. 2009. "Driven to Distraction—Promoting the Car Phone, Despite Risks." *New York Times*, December 17, 1.

Richtel, Matt, and Alexei Barrionuevo. 2005. "Wendy's Restaurants." *New York Times*, April 22, A9.

Rickles, Jordan, Paul M. Ong, and Doug Houston. 2002. "The Integrating (and Segregating) Effect of Charter, Magnet, and Traditional Elementary Schools: The Case of Five California Metropolitan Areas."

UCLA School of Public Policy and Social Research, October 11. Retrieved January 2, 2005 (http://lewis.sppsr.ucla.edu).

Rideout, Victoria. 2007. "Parents, Children & Media." Henry J. Kaiser Family Foundation, June. Retrieved April 12, 2008 (www.kff.org).

____, Ulla G. Foehr, and Donald F. Roberts. 2010. *Generation M²: Media in the Lives of 8- to 18-Year-Olds*. Kaiser Family Foundation, January. Retrieved January 30, 2010 (www.kff.org).

Ridge, Mian. 2008. "Anti-Christian Attacks Flare in India." *Christian Science Monitor*, September 24, 7.

____. 2009. "A Peaceful Train for Women." *Christian Science Monitor*, November 1, 4.

Riesman, David. 1953. *The Lonely Crowd*. New York: Doubleday.

Riordan, Cornelius. 1997. *Equality and Achievement: An Introduction to the Sociology of Education*. New York: Addison-Wesley Longman.

"Rising to the Challenge: Are High School Graduates Prepared for College and Work? A Study of Recent High School Graduates, College Instructors, and Employers." 2005. Achieve, Inc., February. Retrieved February 10, 2005 (www.achieve.org).

Ritter, John. 2007. "Pot Growing Moves to Suburbs." *USA Today*, February 7, 3A.

Ritzer, George. 1992. *Contemporary Sociological Theory*, 3rd ed. New York: McGraw-Hill.

____. 1996. *The McDonaldization of Society: An Investigation into the Changing Character of Contemporary Social Life*. Thousand Oaks, CA: Pine Forge Press.

____. 2008. *The McDonaldization of Society*, 5th edition. Los Angeles, CA: Pine Forge Press.

Roan, Shari. 2008. "Cut in Paid Sick Days Leave Unhealthy Employees Stuck in the Workplace." *Los Angeles Times*, July 7. Retrieved July 7, 2008 (www.latimes.com).

Roberts, Keith A. 2004. *Religion in Sociological Perspective*, 4th ed. Belmont, CA: Wadsworth.

Robey, Elizabeth B., Daniel J. Canary, and Cynthia S. Burggraf. 1998. "Conversational Maintenance Behaviors of Husbands and Wives: An Observational Analysis." Pp. 373-92 in *Sex Differences and Similarities in Communication: Critical Essays and Empirical Investigations of Sex and Gender in Interaction*, edited by Daniel J. Canary and Kathryn Dindia. Mahwah, NJ: Lawrence Erlbaum Associates.

Roethlisberger, F. J., and William J. Dickson. 1939/1942. *Management and the Worker: An Account of a Research Program Conducted at the Western Electric Company, Hawthorne Works, Chicago*. Cambridge, MA: Harvard University Press.

Rohde, David. 2007. "Army Enlists Anthropology in War Zones." *New York Times*, October 5, 1.

Rojstaczer, Stuart. 2009. "Grade Inflation Gone Wild." *Christian Science Monitor*, March 24, 9.

Romero, Simon, and Marc Lacey. 2010. "Looting Flares Where Authority Breaks Down." *New York Times*, January 17, A1.

Roosevelt, Margot. 2008. "An Elusive Billionaire Gives Away His Good Fortune." *Los Angeles Times*, March 8. Retrieved March 9, 2008 (www.latimes.com).

Rosato, Donna. 2009. "The 50 Best Jobs in America." *Money*, November, 88-96.

Roscigno, Vincent J. 2010. "Ageism in the American Workplace." *Contexts* 9 (Winter): 16-21.

Rose, Fred. 1997. "Toward a Class-Cultural Theory of Social Movements: Reinterpreting New Social Movements." *Sociological Forum* 12 (September): 461-494.

Rose, Lacey. 2009. "100 Celebrity." *Forbes*, June 22, 81, 88-89.

Rose, Peter I. 1997. *They and We: Racial and Ethnic Relations in the United States*, 5th edition. New York: McGraw-Hill.

Rosen, Anne Farris. 2010. "A Brief History of Religion and the U.S. Census." January 26. Retrieved April 26, 2010 (http://pewresearch.org).

Rosen, Jacob, and Blake Hannaford. 2006. "Doc at a Distance." *IEEE Spectrum* (October): 34-39.

Rosen, Larry D. 2010. *Rewired: Understanding the iGeneration and the Way They Learn*. New York: Palgrave Macmillan.

Rosenberg, Janice. 1993. "Just the Two of Us." Pp. 301-307 in *Reinventing Love: Six Women Talk About Lust, Sex, And Romance*, edited by Laurie Abraham, Laura Green, Magda Krance, Janice Rosenberg, Janice Somerville, and Carroll Stoner. New York: Plume.

Rosenthal, Elisabeth. 2010. "Skeptics Find Fault with U.N. Climate Panel." *New York Times*, February 9, A1.

Rosenthal, Robert, and Lenore Jacobson. 1968. *Pygmalion in the Classroom: Teacher Expectation and Pupils' Intellectual Development*. New York: Holt, Rinehart, and Winston.
Ross, Jeffrey Ian and Stephen C. Richards. 2002. *Behind Bars: Surviving Prison*. Indianapolis, IN: Alpha Books.
Rothenberg, Paula S. 2008. *White Privilege: Essential Reading on the Other Side of Racism*, 3rd ed. New York: Worth.
Rothlin, Phillippe, and Peter R. Werder. 2008. *Boreout! Overcoming Workplace Demotivation*. Philadelphia: Kogan Page.
Rothman, Sheila M. 1978. *Women's Proper Place: A History of Changing Ideals and Practices, 1870 To the Present*. New York: Basic Books.
Rowe, Meredith L., and Susan Goldin-Meadow. 2009. "Differences in Early Gesture Explain SES Disparities in Child Vocabulary Size at School Entry." Science 323 (February 13): 951-953.
Rowe-Finkbeiner, Kristin. 2004. *The F-Word: Feminist in Jeopardy, Women, Politics, and the Future*. Emeryville, CA: Seal Press.
Roylance, Frank D., and Michael Hill. 2008. "Scientists Say Evolution Fits." *Baltimore Sun*, January 5, 1A, 5A.
Royster, Deirdre A. 2003. *Race and the Invisible Hand: How White Networks Exclude Black Men from Blue-Collar Jobs*. Berkeley: University of California Press.
Rubin, Kenneth, William Bukowski, and Jeffrey G. Parker. 1998. "Peer Interactions, Relationships, and Groups." Pp. 619-700 in *Handbook of Child Psychology: Vol. 3. Social, Emotional, and Personality Development*, edited by William Damon and Nancy Eisenberg. New York: Wiley.
Rubin, Rita. 2004. "'Smart Pills' Make Headway." *USA Today*, July 7, 1D.
Rubin, Trudy. 2006. "Reaction to Cartoons Shows Lack of Understanding." *Baltimore Sun*, February 7, 13A.
Rutherford, Markella B. 2009. "Children's Autonomy and Responsibility: An Analysis of Childrearing Advice." *Qualitative Sociology* 32 (December): 337-353. Unpublished manuscript.
Ryan, Missy. 2008. "In US, Record Numbers Seeking Food Stamps." *Christian Science Monitor*, May 8, 4.
Ryerson, William. 2004. "Responses to: Demographic 'Bomb' May Only Go 'Pop!'" *Pop!ulation Press* 10 (Fall): 21.
Saad, Lydia. 2001. "Majority Considers Sex Before Marriage Morally Okay." *The Gallup Poll Monthly*, No. 428 (May): 46–48.
____ . 2006. "Families of Drug and Alcohol Abusers Pay an Emotional Toll." August 25, Gallup News Service. Retrieved August 27, 2006 (www.galluppoll.com).
____. 2007. "Women Slightly More Likely to Prefer Working to Homemaking." Gallup News Service, August 31. Retrieved September 3, 2007 (www.gallup.com).
____. 2008. "Cultural Tolerance for Divorce Grows to 70%." Gallup News Service, May 19. Retrieved July 8, 2008 (www.gallup.com).
____. 2008. "Telecommuting Still a Rare Perk." Gallup, August 15. Retrieved August 17, 2008 (www.gallup.com).
____. 2009. "Honesty and Ethics Poll Finds Congress' Image Tarnished." *Gallup*, December 9. Retrieved March 26, 2010 (www.gallup.com).
____. 2009. "Republicans Move to the Right on Several Moral Issues." Gallup News Service, October 19. Retrieved January 14, 2010 (www.gallup.com).
____. 2009. "U.S. Abortion Attitudes Closely Divided." *Gallup*, August 4. Retrieved March 10, 2010 (www.gallup.com).
____. 2009. "U.S. Support for Legalizing Marijuana Reaches New High." Gallup News Service, October 19. Retrieved January 17, 2010 (www.gallup.com).
____. 2010. "Americans Firm in Prioritizing Economy over Environment." *Gallup*, March 18. Retrieved April 30, 2010 (www.gallup.com).
Sabattini, Laura, Nancy M. Carter, Jeanine Prime, and David Megathlin. 2007. "The Double-Bind Dilemma for Women in Leadership: Damned if You Do, Doomed if You Don't." *Catalyst*. Retrieved April 28, 2008 (www.catalyst.org).
Sabol, William J., Heather C. West, and Matthew Cooper. 2009. "Prisoners in 2008." Bureau of Justice Statistics Bulletin, December. Retrieved February 25, 2010 (http://bjs.ojp.usdoj.gov).
Sachs, Jeffrey S. 2005. "Confusion over Population: Growth or Dearth?" *Pop!ulation Press* 11 (Winter/Spring): 17.
Sacks, Peter. 2007. *Tearing Down the Gates: Confronting the Class Divide in American Education*. Berkeley: University of California Press.
Saegert, Susan, and Gary Winkel. 1981. "The Home: A Critical Problem for Changing Sex Roles." Pp. 41-63 in *New Space for Women*, edited by Gerda R. Wekerle, Rebecca Peterson, and David Morley. Boulder, CO: Westview Press.
Saenz, Rogelio. 2008. "A Demographic Profile of U.S. Workers Around The Clock." Population Reference Bureau, September. Retrieved July 31, 2009 (www.prb.org).
Saenz, Victor B. and Douglas S. Barrera. 2007. "Findings from the 2005 College Student Survey (CSS): National Aggregates." UCLA Graduate School of Education Information Studies. Retrieved August 5, 2007 (www.gseis.ucla.edu).
Safi, Omid. 2003. "Introduction: The Times They Are A-Changin'—A Muslim Quest for Justice, Gender, Equality, and Pluralism." Pp. 1-29 in *Progressive Muslims: On Justice, Gender, and Pluralism*, edited by Omid Safi. Oxford, England: Oneworld Publications.
Sagarin, Edward. 1975. *Deviants and Deviance*. New York: Praeger.
Sandstrom, Kent L., Daniel D. Martin and Gary Alan Fine. 2006. *Symbols, Selves, and Social Reality: A Symbolic Interactionist Approach to Social Psychology and Sociology*, 2nd edition. Los Angeles, CA: Roxbury.
Sang-Hun, Choe. 2009. "Group Resists Korean Stigma for Unwed Mothers." *New York Times*, October 8, 6.
Sarmiento, Soccorro T. 2002. *Making Ends Meet: Income-Generating Strategies among Mexican Immigrants*. New York: LFB Scholarly Publishing LLC.
Sarno, David. 2009. "Online, Your Private Life Is Searchable." *Los Angeles Times*, August 16. Retrieved August 18, 2009 (www.latimes.com).
Sasseen, Jane. 2005. "White-Collar Crime: Who Does It?" *Business Week*, February 6, 60-61.
"Saudi Arabia: Women without the Vote." 2008. International Museum of Women, September. Retrieved September 17, 2008 (www.imow.org).
Saul, Stephanie. 2008. "In Sour Economy, Some Scale Back On Medications." *New York Times*, October 22, 1.
Savage, David G. 2010. "Court Opens Up Election Spending." *Baltimore Sun*, January 22, 1, 14.
Scarlett, W. George, Sophie Naudeau, Dorothy Salonius-Pasternak and Iris Ponte. 2005. *Children's Play*. Thousand Oaks, CA: Sage.
Scelfo, Julie. 2007. "Come Back, Mr. Chips." *Newsweek*, September 17, 44.
Schachter, Jason P. 2004. "Geographical Mobility: 2002 to 2003." U.S. Census Bureau, March, Current Population Reports, P20-549. Retrieved May 15, 2007 (www.census.gov).
Schaeffer, Robert K. 2003. *Understanding Globalization: The Social Consequences of Political, Economic, and Environmental Change*, 2nd edition. Lanham, MD: Rowman & Littlefield Publishers.
Schehr, Robert C. 1997. *Dynamic Utopia: Establishing Intentional Communities as a New Social Movement*. Westport, CT: Bergin & Garvey.
Schirber, Michael. 2007. "Why Desalination Doesn't Work (Yet)." June 25, *Live Science*. Retrieved February 7, 2008 (www.livescience.com).
Schmall, Emily. 2007. "The Cult of Chick-fil-A." *Forbes*, July 23, 80, 83.
Schmidt, Peter. 2008. "2 Studies Raise Questions about Research Based on Student Surveys." *Chronicle of Higher Education*, November 6. Retrieved November 9, 2008 (http://chronicle.com).
Schmidt, Steffen W., Mack C. Shelley and Barbara A. Bardes. 2001. *American Government and Politics Today*. Belmont, CA: Wadsworth.
Schnittker, Jason. 2008. "Happiness and Success: Genes, Families, and the Psychological Effects of Socioeconomic Position and Social Support." *American Journal of Sociology* 114 (Suppl.): S233-S259.
Schoen, Robert, and Vladimir Canudas-Romo. 2006. "Timing Effects on Divorce: 20th Century Experience in the United States." *Journal of Marriage and Family*, 68 (August): 749-758.
Schuckit, Marc A. 1999. "New Findings in the Genetics of Alcoholism." *JAMA* 281 (May 26): 1875-1876.
Schulz, Dorothy M. 2004. *Breaking the Brass Ceiling: Women Police Chiefs and Their Paths to the Top*. Westport, CT: Praeger.
Schur, Edwin M. 1968. *Law and Society: A Sociological View*. New York: Random House.
Schurman-Kauflin, Deborah. 2000. *The New Predator: Women Who Kill*. New York: Algora.
Schutz, Alfred. 1967. *The Phenomenology of the Social World*. Evanston, IL: Northwestern University Press.
Schwalbe, Michael. 2001. *The Sociologically Examined Life: Pieces Of the Conversation*, 2nd ed. Mountain View, CA: Mayfield.
Schwartz, Marlene B. Lenny R. Vartanian, Brian A. Nosek, and Kelly D. Brownwell. 2006. "The Influence of One's Own Body Weight on Implicit and Explicit Anti-fat Bias." *Obesity* 14 (July): 440-447.
Sciolino, Elaine. 2003. "France Makes Major Changes in Pension Law." *New York Times*, July 25, 7.
Scommegna, Paola. 2005. "Clean Water's Historic Effect on U.S. Mortality Rates Provides Hope for Developing Countries." Population Reference Bureau. Retrieved June 25, 2005 (www.prb.org).
Scott, Katherine V. 1995. *Gender and Development: Rethinking Modernization and Dependency Theory*. Boulder, CO: Lynne Rienner.
Scott, Robert E. 2010. "Unfair China Trade Costs Local Jobs." Economic Policy Institute, March 23. Retrieved April 4, 2010 (www.epi.org).
Seager, Joni. 2009. *The Penguin Atlas of Women in the World*, 4th ed. New York: Penguin Books.
Search Institute, Center for Spiritual Development in Childhood and Adolescence. 2008. "With Their Own Voices: A Global Exploration of How Today's Young People Experience and Think about Spiritual Development." November 5. Retrieved November 21, 2008 (www.spiritualdevelopmentcenter.org).
Seccombe, Karen. 2007. *Families in Poverty*. New York: Allyn & Bacon.
"Second National Report on Human Exposure to Environmental Chemicals." 2003. Centers for Disease Control and Prevention, January. Retrieved June 25, 2005 (www.cdc.gov).
Sedlacek, William E. 2004. *Beyond the Big Test: Noncognitive Assessment in Higher Education*. San Francisco, CA: Jossey-Bass.
Segura, Denise. A. 1994. "Working at Motherhood: Chicana and Mexican Immigrant Mothers and Employment." Pp. 211-33 in *Mothering: Ideology, Experience, And Agency*, edited by Evelyn N. Glenn, Grace Chang, and Linda R. Forcey. New York: Routledge.
Seligson, Hannah. 2007. "Colleges Go Light on Women's Pay Inequity." Women's e-news, April 25. Retrieved April 26, 2007 (www.womensenews.org).
Seltzer, Judith A. 2004. "Cohabitation and Family Change." Pp. 57-78 in *Handbook of Contemporary Families: Considering The Past, Contemplating the Future*, edited by Marilyn Coleman and Lawrence H. Ganong. Thousand Oaks, CA: Sage.
Semuels, Alana. 2008. "Gay Marriage May Be a Gift to California's Economy." *Los Angeles Times*, June 2. Retrieved June 9, 2008 (www.latimes.com).
Sengupta, Somini. 2006. "Report Shows Muslims Near Bottom of Social Ladder." *New York Times*, November 29, A4.
Sequist, Thomas D., Garrett M. Fitzmaurice, Richard Marshall, Shimon Shaykevich, Dena Gelb Safran, and John Z. Ayanian. 2008. "Physical Performance and Racial Disparities in Diabetes Mellitus Care." *Archives of Internal Medicine* 168 (June 9): 1145-1151.
Sernau, Scott. 2001. *Worlds Apart: Social Inequalities in a New Century*. Thousand Oaks, CA: Pine Forge Press.
Setoodeh, Ramin. 2007. "Need a Lift?" *Newsweek*, February 26, 12.
Shanahan, Michael J., Stephen Vaisey, Lance D. Erickson, and Andrew Smolen. 2008. "Environmental Contingencies and Genetic Propensities: Social Capital, Educational Continuation, and Dopamine Receptor Gene DRD2." *American Journal of Sociology* 114 (Suppl.): S260-S286.
Shapiro, Danielle. 2009. "Children Targeted as Witches in the Congo." Women's E-News, November 22. Retrieved November 23, 2009 (www.womensenews.org).
Sharifzadeh, Virginia-Shirin. 1997. "Families with Middle Eastern Roots." Pp. 441-482 in *Developing Cross-Cultural Competence: a Guide for Working with Children and Families*, edited by Eleanor W. Lynch and Marci J. Hanson. Baltimore, MD: Paul H. Brookes Publishing.
Shaw-Taylor, Yoku and Nijole V. Benokraitis. 1995. "The Presentation of Minorities in Marriage and Family Textbooks." *Teaching Sociology* 23 (April): 122-35.
Shell, Adam. 2010. "Despite Recession, Average Wall Street Bonus Leaps 25%." *USA Today*, February 23. Retrieved February 25, 2010 (www.usatoday.com).
Shenkman, Rick. 2008. *Just How Stupid Are We? Facing the Truth about the American Voter*. New York: Basic Books.
Sherman, Lawrence. 1992. *Policing Domestic Violence: Experiment and Dilemmas*. New York: Free Press.
Shibutani, Tamotsu. 1986. *Social Process: An Introduction to Sociology*. Berkeley, CA: University of California Press.

Shierholz, Heidi. 2009. "Nine Years of Job Growth Wiped Out." Economic Policy Institute, July 2. Retrieved August 9, 2009 (www.epi.org).

____. 2010. "The Effects of Citizenship on Family Income and Poverty." Economic Policy Institute, February 24. Retrieved March 15, 2010 (www.epi.org).

Shorto, Russell. 2008. "No Babies?" *New York Times,* June 29, 34.

Siegel, Andrea F. 2009. "Dog Killer Gets 3 Years." *Baltimore Sun,* August 21, 10.

Siegman, Aron W., and Stanley Feldstein, eds. 1987. *Nonverbal Behavior and Communication.* Hillsdale, NJ: Lawrence Erlbaum Associates.

Silverman, Rachel E. 2003. "Provisions Boost Rights of Couples Living Together." *Wall Street Journal,* March 5, D1.

Silverstein, Ken. 2002. "Unjust Rewards." *Mother Jones,* May/June, 69-86.

Simmons, Tavia, and Martin O'Connell. 2003. "Married-couple and Unmarried-partner Households: 2000." U.S. Census Bureau. Retrieved April 20, 2003 (www.census.gov).

Simon, Rita J. and Jean Landis. 1991. *The Crimes Women Commit, the Punishments They Receive.* Lexington, MA: Lexington Books.

Simon, Robin W., and Leda E. Nath. 2004. "Gender and Emotion in the United States: Do Men and Women Differ in Self-Reports of Feelings and Expressive Behavior." *American Journal of Sociology* 109 (March): 1137-76.

Simpson, Sally S., and Carole Gibbs. 2006. "Making Sense of Intersections." Pp. 269-302 in *Gender and Crime: Patterns of Victimization and Offending,* edited by Karen Heimer and Candace Kruttschnitt. New York: New York University Press.

Singer, Natasha. 2009. "When 2+2 Equals a Privacy Question." *New York Times,* October 18, 4.

____. 2010. "Shoppers Who Can't Have Secrets." *New York Times,* April 30, 5.

Sjoberg, Gideon. 1960. *The Preindustrial City: Past and Present.* Glencoe, IL: Free Press.

Skerry, Peter. 2002. "Beyond Sushiology: Does Diversity Work?" *Brookings Review* 20 (Winter): 20-23.

Slackman, Michael. 2007. "In Arab Hub, Poor are Left in Dire Straits." *New York Times,* March 1, A1, A4.

Slevin, Peter. 2005. "In Heartland, Stem Cell Research Meets Fierce Opposition." *Washington Post,* August 10, A1.

Sloan, Allan. 2009. "What's *Still* Wrong with Wall Street?" *Time,* November 9, 24-29.

Smedley, Audrey. 2007. *Race in North America: Origin and Evolution of a Worldview,* 3rd ed. Boulder, CO: Westview Press.

Smelser, Neil J. 1962. *Theory of Collective Behavior.* New York: Free Press.

____. 1988. "Social Structure." Pp. 103-129 in *Handbook of Sociology,* edited by Neil J. Smelser. Newbury Park, CA: Sage.

Smith, Adam. 1937. *An Inquiry into the Nature and Causes of the Wealth of Nations.* New York: The Modern Library, orig. 1776.

Smith, Dorothy E. 1987. *The Everyday World as Problematic: A Feminist Sociology.* Toronto: University of Toronto Press.

Smith, Grant F., and Tanya Carina Hsu. 2007. "Visa Denied: How Anti-Arab Visa Policies Destroy US Export, Jobs and Higher Education." Institute for Research: Middle Eastern Policy. Retrieved May 7, 2007 (www.irmep.org).

Smith, Jane I. 1994. "Women in Islam." Pp. 303-325 in *Today's Woman in World Religions,* edited by Arvind Sharma. Albany: State University of New York Press.

Smith, Kristin. 2009. "Increased Reliance on Wives as Breadwinners during the First Year of the Recession." Carsey Institute, University of New Hampshire, Fall. Retrieved April 2, 2010 (www.carseyinstitute.unh.edu).

Smith, Tom W. 2007. "Job Satisfaction in the United States." April 17, NORC/University of Chicago. Retrieved June 1, 2007 (www-news.uchicago.edu).

Smith, Tom W., and Seokho Kim. 2004. "The Vanishing Protestant Majority." NORC/University of Chicago, July. Retrieved March 3, 2005 (www-news.uchicago.edu).

Snell, Marilyn B. 2007. "The Talking Way." *Mother Jones,* January/February, 30-35.

Snipp, C. Matthew. 1996. "A Demographic Comeback for American Indians." *Population Today* 24 (November): 4-5.

Snow, Kate, John Gever, and Dan Childs. 2009. "Experts Debunk Health Care Reform Bill's 'Death Panel' Rule." ABC News, August 11. Retrieved May 9, 2010 (abcnews.go.com).

Snyder, Howard N., and Melissa Sickmund. 2006. *Juvenile Offenders and Victims: 2006 National Report.* Washington, DC: U.S. Department of Justice, Office of Justice Programs, Office of Juvenile Justice and Delinquency Prevention.

Snyder, Leslie B., Frances Fleming Milici, Michael Slater, Helen Sun, and Yulija Strizhakova. 2006. "Effects of Alcohol Advertising Exposure on Drinking among Youth." *Archives of Pediatrics & Adolescent Medicine* 160 (January): 18-24.

Snyder, Thomas D., and Sally A. Dillow. 2010. *Digest of Education Statistics 2009.* National Center for Education Statistics, Institute of Education Sciences, U.S. Department of Education. Washington, DC.

Soares, Joseph A. 2007. *The Power of Privilege: Yale and America's Elite Colleges.* Stanford, CA: Stanford University Press.

Soguel, Dominique. 2009. "Wage Gap Study Arrives in Time for Equal Pay Day." Women's eNews, April 28. Retrieved April 28, 2009 (www.womensenews.org).

Sowell, Thomas. 2008. "A Prestigious Degree Doesn't Always Equal Success." *Chronicle of Higher Education,* January 18, A34.

Spalter-Roth, Roberta, and Nicole Van Vooren. 2008. "What Are They Doing with a Bachelor's Degree in Sociology? Data Brief on Current Jobs." January, American Sociological Association, Department of Research and Development. Retrieved March 27, 2008 (www.asanet.org).

Spano, John. 2007. "Abuse Deal Reached in L.A." *Baltimore Sun,* July 15, 3A.

Spector, Malcolm and John Kitsuse. 1977. *Constructing Social Problems.* Menlo Park, CA: Cummings.

Spectorsky, A. C. 1955. *The Exurbanites.* Philadelphia, PA: J. B. Lippincott.

Spellings, Margaret. 2010. "Measuring the Value of Accountability." *U.S. News & World Report,* January, 33-34.

Spencer, Herbert. 1862/1901. *First Principles.* New York: P. F. Collier & Son.

Sperry, Shelley. 2008. "Ozone Defense." *National Geographic* 214 (October): no page given.

Spiess, Michele. 2003. "Juveniles and Drugs." Rockville, MD: ONDCP Drug Policy Information Clearinghouse.

Spotts, Peter N. 2004. "Blowing in the Wind: Transatlantic Pollution." *Christian Science Monitor,* August 5, 14, 17.

____. 2009. "New Climate Change Signal: Oceans Turning Acidic." *Christian Science Monitor,* December 9. Retrieved December 12, 2010 (www.csmonitor.com).

Spradley, J.P. and M. Phillips. 1972. "Culture and Stress: A Quantitative Analysis." *American Anthropologist* 74 (3): 518-529.

Squires, Gregory D., and Charis E. Kubrin. 2006. *Privileged Places: Race, Residence, and the Structure of Opportunity.* Boulder, CO: Lynne Rienner.

Stack, Liam. 2008. "In Egypt, Chorus of Catcalls Grows." *Christian Science Monitor,* September 23, 7.

Stafford, Frank. 2008. "Exactly How Much Housework Does a Husband Create?" University of Michigan News Service, April 3. Retrieved June 2, 2008 (www.ns.umich.edu).

Stanczak, Gregory C. 2006. *Social Change and American Religion.* New Brunswick, NJ: Rutgers University Press.

Stanley, Thomas J. and William D. Danko. 1996. *The Millionaire Next Door: The Surprising Secrets of America's Wealthy.* Atlanta, GA: Longstreet Press.

Starr, Tama. 1991. *The "Natural Inferiority" of Women.* New York: Poseidon Press.

Stauss, Joseph H. 1995. "Reframing and Refocusing American Indian Family Strengths." Pp. 105-18 in *American Families: Issues in Race and Ethnicity,* edited by Cardell K. Jacobson. New York: Garland

Stead, D. 2008. "What Mom and Dad Are Buying." *Business Week,* December 15, 19.

Stearns, Matt. 2006. "Organ Transplants Called Biased for the Well-To-Do." *Philadelphia Inquirer,* June 7, A10.

Steffensmeier, Darrell, Jennifer Schwartz, Hua Zhong, and Jeff Ackerman. 2005. "An Assessment of Recent Trends in Girls' Violence Using Diverse Longitudinal Sources: Is the Gender Gap Closing?" *Criminology* 43 (May): 355-405.

Steinhauer, Jennifer. 2005. "When the Joneses Wear Jeans." *New York Times,* May 29, 1.

Stephen, J. 2004. *State Prison Expenditures, 2001.* Bureau of Justice Statistics Special Report. Washington, DC: U.S. Department of Justice.

Stephenson, John B. 2007. "Environmental Protection: EPA-State Enforcement Partnership Has Improved, but EPA's Oversight Needs Further Enhancement." United States Government Accountability Office,

July, GAO—07-883. Retrieved February 12, 2008 (www.gao.gov).

Sternbergh, Adam. 2008. "Why White People Like 'Stuff White People Like'." *The New Republic,* March 17. Retrieved November 6, 2008 (www.tnr.com).

Sternheimer, Karen. 2007. "Do Video Games Kill?" *Contexts* 6 (Winter): 13-17.

Stevenson, Betsey, and Justin Wolfers. 2007. "Marriage and Divorce: Changes and Their Driving Forces." *Journal of Economic Perspectives* 21 (Spring): 27-52.

Stewart, Pearl, and Katia Paz Goldfarb. 2007. "Historical Trends in the Study of Diverse Families." Pp. 3-19 in *Cultural Diversity and Families: Expanding Perspectives,* edited by Bahira Sherif Trask and Raeann R. Hamon. Thousand Oaks, CA: Sage, pp. 3-19.

Stillars, Alan L. 1991. "Behavioral Observation." Pp. 197-218 in *Studying Interpersonal Interaction,* edited by B. M. Montgomery and S. Duck. New York: Guilford Press.

Stinson, Jeffrey. 2008. "As CEO Pay in Europe Rises, So Does Talk of Curbing It." *USA Today,* June 30. Retrieved November 7, 2009 (www.usatoday.com).

Stobart, Jane. 2009. "Irish Catholic Church Covered Up Abuse, Report Finds." *Los Angeles Times,* November 27. Retrieved November 30, 2009 (www.latimes.com).

Stolley, Giordano, and Somchai Taphaneeyapan. 2002. "Stomaching Bugs in Thailand." *Baltimore Sun,* June 20, 2A.

Stone, Brad. 2009. "Breakfast Can Wait. The Day's First Stop is Online." *New York Times,* August 10, 1.

Stone, Pamela. 2007. *Opting out? Why Women Really Quit Careers and Head Home.* Berkeley: University of California Press.

Strasburger, Victor C. and Barbara J. Wilson. 2002. *Children, Adolescents, & the Media.* Thousand Oaks, CA: Sage Publications.

Strasburger, Victor C., et al. 2006. "Children, Adolescents, and Advertising." *Pediatrics* 118 (December 6): 2563-2569.

"Streaking." 2005. Wikipedia Encyclopedia. Retrieved September 8, 2005 (www.en.wikipedia.org/wiki).

Strean, William B. 2009. "Remembering Instructors: Play, Pain, and Pedagogy." *Qualitative Research in Sport and Exercise,* 1 (November): 210-220.

Stroebe, Margaret, Maarten van Son, Wolfgang Stroebe, Rolf Kleber, Henk Schut, and Jan van den Bout. 2000. "On the Classification and Diagnosis of Pathological Grief." *Clinical Psychology Review* 20 (January): 57-75.

"Study Shows Positive Results from Early Head Start Program." 2002. U.S. Department of Health and Human Services, June 3. Retrieved July 10, 2002 (www.hhs.gov).

Sugg, Diana K. 2002. "Baltimore Drug Programs are Effective, Study Says." *Baltimore Sun,* January 31, 7A.

Sullivan, Andrew, ed. 1997. *Same-Sex Marriage,* Pro and Con: A Reader. New York: Vintage.

____. 2003. "The Conservative Case for Gay Marriages." *Time,* June 30, 76.

Sullivan, Evelin. 2001. *The Concise Book of Lying.* New York: Farrar, Straus and Giroux.

Sullivan, Will. 2007 "Road Warriors." *US News & World Report,* May 7, 40-49.

Sum, Andrew, and Ishwar Khatiwada. 2010a. "Labor Underutilization Problems of U.S. Workers Across Household Income Groups at the End of the Great Recession: A Truly Great Depression among the Nation's Low Income Workers Amidst Full Employment among the Most Affluent." Center for Labor Market Studies, Northeastern University, February. Retrieved April 1, 2010 (www.clms.neu.edu).

____. 2010b. "Underemployment Problems in U.S. Labor Markets in 2009: Predicting the Probabilities of Underemployment for Key Age, Gender, Race-Ethnic, Nativity, Educational Attainment, and Occupational Subgroups of U.S. Workers." Center for Labor Market Studies, Northeastern University, February. Retrieved April 1, 2010 (www.clms.neu.edu).

Sumner, William G. 1906. *Folkways.* New York: Ginn.

Sunstein, Cass R. 2009. *On Rumors: How Falsehoods Spread, Why We Believe Them, What Can Be Done.* New York: Farrar, Straus & Giroux.

Susman, Tina, and Mark Z. Barabak. 2009. "New York's Bloomberg Spent Big, for Small Return." *Los Angeles Times,* November 6. Retrieved November 8, 2009 (www.latimes.com).

Sutherland, Edwin H. 1949. *White Collar Crime.* New York: Holt, Rinehart, and Winston.

Sutherland, Edwin H., and D. R. Cressey. 1970. *Criminology,* 8th edition. Philadelphia, PA: Lippincott.

Sutton, Charles T., and Mary A. Broken Nose. 1996. "American Indian Families: An Overview." Pp. 31-54 in *Ethnicity and Family Therapy,* 2nd ed., edited by Monica McGoldrick, Joe Giordano, and John K. Pearce. New York: The Guilford Press.

Sutton, Philip W. 2000. *Explaining Environmentalism: In Search of a New Social Movement.* Burlington, VT: Ashgate Publishing Company.

Switzer, Jacqueline V. 2003. *Disabled Rights: American Disability Policy and the Fight for Equality.* Washington, DC: Georgetown University Press.

Symonds, William C. 2003. "College Admissions: The Real Barrier is Class." *Business Week* (April 14): 66, 68.

Szabo, Liz, and Julie Appleby. 2009. "21% of Americans Scramble to Pay Medical, Drug Bills." *USA Today,* March 10. Retrieved July 7, 2009 (www.usatoday.com).

Tach, Laura, and Sarah Halpern-Meekin. 2009. "How Does Premarital Cohabitation Affect Trajectories of Marital Quality?" *Journal of Marriage and Family,* 71 (May): 298-317.

Tajfel, Henri. 1982. "Social Psychology of Intergroup Relations." *Annual Review of Psychology.* Palo Alto, CA: Annual Reviews, 1-39.

Tannen, Deborah. 1990. *You Just Don't Understand: Women And Men In Conversation.* New York: Ballantine.

Tannenbaum, Frank. 1938. *Crime and the Community.* New York: Columbia University Press.

Tanur, Judith M. 1994. "The Trustworthiness of Survey Research." *Chronicle of Higher Education,* May 25, B1–B3.

Tatara, Toshio. 1998. "The National Elder Abuse Incidence Study." The National Center on Elder Abuse and the American Public Humane Services Association. Retrieved October 19, 2000 (www.aoa.gov).

Tate, Ryan. 2010. "Facebook Crushes Privacy with Impunity." Retrieved May 8, 2010 (http://gawker.com).

Taylor, Frederick W. 1911/1967. *The Principles of Scientific Management.* New York: W. W. Norton & Company.

Taylor, Jay. 1993. *The Rise and Fall of Totalitarianism in the Twentieth Century.* New York: Paragon House.

Taylor, Jonathan B. and Joseph P. Kalt. 2005. *American Indians on Reservations: A Databook of Socioeconomic Change between the 1990 and 2000 Censuses.* Harvard Project on American Indian Economic Development, January. Retrieved April 20, 2007 (www.ksg.harvard.edu).

Taylor, Paul, Cary Funk, and April Clark. 2007. "As Marriage and Parenthood Drift Apart, Public as Concerned about Social Impact." Pew Research Center, July 1. Retrieved June 15, 2009 (www.pewresearch.org).

Taylor, Paul, Rich Morin, Kim Parker, and D'Vera Cohn. 2009. "Growing Old in America: Expectations vs. Reality." Pew Research Center, June 29. Retrieved April 30, 2010 (http://pewsocialtrends.org).

Taylor, Susan C. 2003. *Brown Skin: Dr. Susan Taylor's Prescription for Flawless Skin, Hair, and Nails.* New York: HarperCollins.

Teaster, Pamela B., Tyler A. Dugar, Marta S. Mendiondo, Erin L. Abner, Kara A. Cecil, and Joanne M. Otto. 2006. "The 2004 Survey of State Adult Protective Services: Abuse of Adults 60 Years of Age and Older." National Center on Elder Abuse. Retrieved June 27, 2007 (www.elderabusecenter.org).

Teicher, Martin. 2000. "Wounds That Time Won't Heal: The Neurobiology of Child Abuse." *Cerebrum* 2 (Fall), The Dana Foundation. Retrieved July 7, 2002 (www.dana.org).

Teicher, Stacy A. 2007. "Closing the Gaps." *Christian Science Monitor,* April 5, 16-17.

Tejada-Vera, B., and P. D. Sutton. 2009. "Births, Marriages, Divorces, and Deaths: Provisional Data for 2008." *National Vital Statistics Reports* 57 (July 29): 1-6.

Telles, Edward E. 2010. "Mexican Americans and Immigrant Incorporation." *Contexts,* 9 (Winter): 28-33.

Terhune, Chad. 2008. "They Know What's in Your Medicine Cabinet." *Business Week,* August 4, 48-52.

Teske, Paul, Mark Schneider, Jack Buckley, and Sara Clark. 2001. "Can Charter Schools Change Traditional Public Schools?" Pp. 188-214 in *Charters, Vouchers, and Public Education,* edited by Paul E. Peterson and David E. Campbell. Washington, D.C.: Brookings Institution Press.

Tessier, Marie. 2008. "Intimate Violence Remains a Big Killer of Women." Women's e-News, August. Retrieved April 11, 2010 (www.womensenews.org).

Tétreault, Mary Ann. 2001. "A State of Two Minds: State Cultures, Women, and Politics in Kuwait." *International Journal of Middle East Studies* 33 (May): 203-220.

Thibaut, John W. and Harold H. Kelley. 1959. *The Social Psychology of Groups.* New York: Wiley.

Thomas, W. I. and Dorothy Swaine Thomas. 1928. *The Child in America.* New York: Alfred A. Knopf.

Thompson, Michael. 2010. "Voter Turnout: Other Nations Overshadow U.S." Associated Content. Retrieved March 29, 2010 (www.associatedcontent.com).

Thompson, Robert S., et al. 2006. "Intimate Partner Violence: Prevalence, Types, and Chronicity in Adult Women." *American Journal of Preventive Medicine* 30 (June): 447-57.

Thumma, Scott, Dave Travis, and Warren Bird. 2005. "Megachurches Today 2005." Hartford Institute for Religion Research. Retrieved August 14, 2007 (http://hirr.hartsem.edu).

Tiefenthaler, Jill. 2009. "A Student Is More Than Numbers." *U.S. News & World Report,* September, 25.

"Ties that Bind, The." 2000. *Public Perspective* 11 (May–June): 10.

Tilly, Charles. 1978. *From Mobilization to Revolution.* Reading, MA: Addison-Wesley.

Tizon, Tomas. 2008. "An Alaskan Village Prepares to Move." *Christian Science Monitor,* January 10, 17.

Tobar, Hector. 2009. "Language as a Bridge and an Identity." *Los Angeles Times,* September 22. Retrieved September 24, 2009 (www.latimes.com).

Toch, Thomas. 2007. "In Testing, the Infrastructure is Buckling." *Education Week,* July 24. Retrieved July 11, 2007 (www.edweek.org).

Toder, Eric J. 2005. "What Will Happen To Poverty Rates Among Older Americans In The Future And Why?" The Urban Institute, November. Retrieved August 16, 2002 (www.urban.org).

Toppo, Gregg. 2009. "More Higher-Income Families Are Home Schooling Their Children." *USA Today,* June 6. Retrieved April 16, 2010 (www.usatoday.com).

Tormey, Simon. 1995. *Making Sense of Tyranny: Interpretations of Totalitarianism.* New York: Manchester University Press.

Tornatzky, Louis G., Richard Cutler, and Jongho Lee. 2002. "College Knowledge: What Latino Parents Need to Know and Why They Don't Know It." The Tomás Rivera Policy Institute. Retrieved January 2, 2005 (www.trpi.org).

Toth, John F., and Xiaohe Xu. 2002. "Fathers' Child-Rearing Involvement in African American, Latino, and White Families." Pp. 130-140 in *Contemporary Ethnic Families in the United States: Characteristics, Variations, And Dynamics,* edited by Nijole V. Benokraitis. Upper Saddle River, NJ: Prentice Hall.

Touraine, Alain. 1981. *The Voice and the Eye: An Analysis of Social Movements.* Cambridge: Cambridge University Press.

____. 2002. "The Importance of Social Movements." *Social Movement Studies* 1 (April): 89-96.

Treiman, Donald. 1977. *Occupational Prestige in Comparative Perspective.* New York: Academic Press.

"Trends in Political Values and Core Attitudes: 1987-2007." 2007. Pew Research Center for the People & the Press, March 22. Retrieved May 10, 2007 (www.people-press.org).

Tse, Tomoeh Murakami. 2010. "Goldman Sachs CEO Blankfein Get Stock-Based $9 Million Bonus." *Washington Post,* February 6, A8.

Tucker, Cynthia. 2007. "Lingering Sexism Impedes Women's Path to Highest Level of Power." *Baltimore Sun,* January 8, A9.

Tumin, Melvin M. 1953. "Some Principles of Stratification: A Critical Analysis." *American Sociological Review* 18 (August): 387-393.

Turk, Austin T. 1969. *Criminality and the Legal Order.* Chicago, IL: Rand-McNally.

____. 1976. "Law as a Weapon in Social Conflict." *Social Problems* 23 (February): 276-291.

Turner, Ralph H., and Lewis M. Killian. 1987. *Collective Behavior,* 3rd ed. Englewood Cliffs, NJ: Prentice Hall.

Turow, Joseph, Jennifer King, Chris Jay Hoofnagle, Amy Bleakley, and Michael Hennessy. 2009. "Americans Reject Tailored Advertising." Social Science Research Network, September. Retrieved May 11, 2010 (papers.ssrn.com).

Twitchell, Geoffrey R., Gregory L. Hanna, Edwin H. Cook, Scott F. Stoltenberg, Hiram E. Fitzgerald, and Robert A. Zucker. 2001. "Serotonin Transporter Promoter Polymorphism Genotype Is Associated With Behavioral Disinhibition and Negative Affect in Children of Alcoholics." *Alcoholism: Clinical and Experimental Research* 25 (July): 953-959.

U.S. Bureau of Labor Statistics. 2008. Table 39: Median Weekly Earning of Full-Time Wage and Salary Workers by Detailed Occupation and Sex. Retrieved July 2, 2008 (www.bls.gov).

U.S. Census Bureau. 2006. American Community Survey. "General Demographic Characteristics." Retrieved May 3, 2007 (http://factfinder.census.gov).

____. 2008. *Statistical Abstract of the United States,* 127th ed. Washington, DC: U.S. Government Printing Office.

____. 2010. "Voting and Registration in the Election of November 2008—Detailed Tables." Retrieved March 26, 2010 (www.census.gov).

____. 2010. *Statistical Abstract of the United States: 2010,* 129th ed. Washington, DC: Government Printing Office.

____, Current Population Survey, 2009. "2008 Annual Social and Economic Supplement," January. Retrieved June 6, 2009 (www.census.gov).

____, International Data Base. Available at: www.census.gov/ipc/www/idb/pyramids.html. Accessed January 20, 2007.

U.S. Census Bureau News. 2008. "An Older and More Diverse Nation by Midcentury." August 14. Retrieved August 18, 2008 (www.census.gov).

____. 2009. "Unmarried and Single Americans Week Sept. 20-16, 2009." July 21. Retrieved April 10, 2010 (www.census.gov).

____. 2010. "Census Bureau Reports Families with Children Increasingly Face Unemployment." January 15. Retrieved April 14, 2010 (www.census.gov).

U.S. Census Bureau Newsroom. 2009. "Census Bureau Releases Data Showing Relationship Between Education and Earnings." April 27. Retrieved April 16, 2010 (www.census.gov).

U.S. Census and Population Division, U.S. Census Bureau. 2008. "2008 National Population Projections Tables and Charts." August 14. Retrieved September 9, 2008 (www.census.gov/population/www/projections/tablesandcharts.html).

U.S. Chamber of Commerce, Center for American Progress, and Frederick M. Hess. 2009. *Leaders and Laggards: A State-by-State Report Card on Educational Innovation.* November. Retrieved April 22, 2010 (www.americanprogress.org).

U.S. Department of Education. 2008. *Digest of Education Statistics 2005.* National Center for Education Statistics. Retrieved March 8, 2010 (nces.ed.gov/programs).

U.S. Department of Health and Human Services. 1999. *Mental Health: A Report of the Surgeon General.* Rockville, MD: U.S. Department of Health and Human Services, National Institutes of Health, National Institute of Mental Health.

____. 2009. *Child Maltreatment 2007.* Washington, DC: U.S. Government Printing Office.

____. 2010. *Child Maltreatment 2008.* Washington, DC: Government Printing Office.

U.S. Department of Justice. 1996. "Policing Drug Hot Spots." National Institute of Justice, January. Retrieved May 3, 2005 (www.ncjrs.org).

U.S. Department of Labor. 2002. *Working in the 21st Century.* Washington, DC: U.S. Government Printing Office.

____. 2005. "Occupational Employment Statistics." Bureau of Labor Statistics. Retrieved October 15, 2006 (www.bls.gov).

____. 2005. "Workers on Flexible and Shift Schedules in 2004 Summary." July 1. Retrieved June 4, 2007 (www.bls.gov).

____. 2007. "Women in the Labor Force: A Databook." U.S. Bureau of Labor Statistics, September. Retrieved July 2, 2008 (www.bls.gov).

U.S. Department of State. 2006. *Trafficking in Persons Report.* June. Retrieved November 1, 2006 (www.state.gov).

U.S. Environmental Protection Agency. 2009. "EPA's Endangerment Finding." December 7. Retrieved May 1, 2010 (www.epa.gov).

____. 2009. "Municipal Solid Waste Generation, Recycling, and Disposal in the United States: Facts and Figures for 2008." Retrieved May 2, 2010 (www.epa.gov).

U.S. Equal Employment Opportunity Commission. 2010a. "Pregnancy Discrimination Charges EEOC & FEPAs Combined: FY 1997-FY 2007." Retrieved March 3, 2010 (www.eeoc.gov).

____. 2010b. "Sexual Harassment Charges EEOC & FEPAs Combined: FY 1997-FY 2007." Retrieved March 3, 2010 (www.eeoc.gov).

U.S. General Accounting Office. 2004. "Defense of Marriage Act: Update to Prior Report." www.gao.gov (accessed July 5, 2007).

U.S. Senate Special Committee on Aging, American Association of Retired Persons, Federal Council on the Aging, and U.S. Administration on Aging. 1991. *Aging America: Trends and projections, 1991.* Washington, DC: Department of Health and Human Services.

United Human Rights Council. 2004. "History of Genocide." Retrieved April 29, 2004 (www.unitedhumanrights.org).

United Nations Development Fund for Women. 2007. "Violence against Women—Facts and Figures." March. Retrieved March 11, 2007 (www.unifem.org).

United Nations Development Programme. 2006. *Human Development Report 2006: Beyond Scarcity: Power, Poverty, and the Global Water Crisis*. New York: United Nations Development Programme.

United Nations Population Division. 2008. "An Overview of Urbanization, Internal Migration, Population Distribution and Development in the World." Population Division. Retrieved January 20, 2008 (www.un.org).

United Nations World Water Development Report 2. 2006. "Water: A Shared Responsibility." Retrieved February 3, 2008 (www.unesco.org).

United States Government Manual, 2005/2006, The. 2006. Washington, DC: U.S. Government Printing Office.

United States Senate. 2004. *Report on the U.S. Intelligence Community's Prewar Intelligence Assessments on Iraq*. Retrieved September 13, 2006 (www.gpoaccess.gov).

University of Connecticut, Center for Survey Research & Analysis. 2007. "Two Americas but One American Dream." July 6. Retrieved May 25, 2008 (www.csra.uconn.edu).

Urbina, Ian. 2006. "In Online Mourning, Don't Speak Ill of the Dead." *New York Times*, November 5, 1.

———. 2007. "Court Rejects Law Limiting Pornography on Internet." *New York Times*, March 23, A11.

———. 2009. "For Runaways, Sex Buys Survival." *New York Times*, October 27, A1.

Valenti, Jessica. 2007. "How the Web Became a Sexists' Paradise." *The Guardian*, April 6. Retrieved April 9, 2007 (www.guardian.co.uk).

Van Biema, David. 2004. "Rising Above the Stained-Glass Ceiling." *Time*, June 28, 58-61.

Van Doorn-Harder, Nelly. 2006. "Behind the Cartoon War: Radical Clerics Competing for Followers." *Christian Science Monitor*, February 23, 9.

van Ginneken, Jaap. 2003. *Collective Behavior and Public Opinion: Rapid Shifts in Opinion and Communication*. Mahwah, NJ: Lawrence Erlbaum Associates.

Vanden Brook, Tom, Ken Dilanian, and Ray Locker. 2009. "Military 'Senior Mentors' Cashing In." *USA Today*, November 18, 1A, 10A.

Vanderpool, Tim. 2002. "Tribes Move Beyond Casinos to Malls and Concert Halls." *Christian Science Monitor*, October 22, 2-3.

Vandewater, Elizabeth A., Victoria J. Rideout, Ellen A. Wartella, Xuan Huang, June H. Lee, and Mi-suk Shim. 2007. "Digital Childhood: Electronic Media and Technology Use Among Infants, Toddlers, and Preschoolers." *Pediatrics* 119 (May): e106-e1015.

Vargas, Jose A. 2004. "Married Men with Another Life to Live." *Washington Post*, August 14, C1.

Veblen, Thorstein. 1899/1953. *The Theory of the Leisure Class*. New York: New American Library.

Vedantam, Shankar. 2002. "Negative View? It May Be Brain 'Knob'." *Seattle Times*, February 12. Retrieved February 13, 2002 (http://seattletimes.nwsource.com).

Velasquez-Manoff, Moises. 2009. "Pressure Builds over Bottled Water." *Christian Science Monitor*, October 18, 36-37.

Venkatesh, Sudhir. 2008. *Gang Leader for a Day: A Rogue Sociologist Takes to the Streets*. New York: Penguin Press.

Ventura, S. J., J. A. Martin, S. C. Curtin, T. J. Mathews, and M. M. Park. 2000. "Births: Final Data for 1998." *National Vital Statistics Reports* 48, March 28, Centers for Disease Control and Prevention. Retrieved September 22, 2000 (www.cdc.gov).

Victory, Joy. 2005. "Face Transplant Patient Signed Movie Deal." ABC News, December 8. Retrieved September 18, 2008 (www.abcnews.go.com).

Vigdor, Jacob L. 2008. "Measuring Immigrant Assimilation in the United States." Center for Civic Innovation, May. Retrieved June 6, 2008 (www.manhattan-institute.org).

Violence Policy Center. 2008. "When Men Murder Women: An Analysis of 2006 Homicide Data." September. Retrieved April 12, 2010 (www.vpc.org).

Vitullo, Margaret Weigers. 2009. "Searching for a Job with an Undergraduate Degree in Sociology." *Footnotes*, September/October, 8.

Vogel, Nancy. 2007. "Donor Money Talks, Often in a Whisper." *Los Angeles Times*, December 27. Retrieved December 28, 2007 (www.latimes.com).

Vold, George B. 1958. *Theoretical Criminology*. New York: Oxford University Press.

WAGE. 2006. "Occupational segregation." WAGE: Women are Getting Even." Retrieved May 9, 2006 (www.wageproject.org).

Wakeman, Jessica. 2008. "Misogyny's Greatest Hits." *Extra!* Fairness & Accuracy and Reporting. May/June, pp. 6-7.

Wald, Kenneth D. 2003. *Religion and Politics in the United States*, 4th ed. Lanham, MD: Rowman & Littlefield.

Waldref, J. 2008. "Women at Work Find Reinforced Glass Ceilings." Women's eNews, August. Retrieved September 2, 2008 (www.womensenews.org).

Walker, Lenore E. 2000. *The Battered Woman Syndrome*, 2nd ed. New York: Springer.

Wall, Howard J. 2009a. "The Effects of Recessions across Demographic Groups." Federal Reserve Bank of St. Louis, September. Retrieved April 8, 2010 (www.stlouisfed.org).

———. 2009b. "The 'Mann-Cession' of 2008-09: It's Big, But It's Not Great." *The Regional Economist*, October, 4-9. Retrieved April 8, 2010 (www.stlouisfed.org).

Wallace, Bruce. 2006. "Japanese Schools to Teach Patriotism." *Los Angeles Times*, December 16. Retrieved December 18, 2006 (www.latimes.com).

———. 2008. "Debate Grows with Philippine Population." *Los Angeles Times*, May 7. Retrieved May 9, 2008 (www.latimes.com).

Wallechinsky, David. 2010. "The World's Worst Dictators." *Parade*, March 22. Retrieved March 28, 2010 (www.parade.com).

Wan, William. 2010. "Same-Sex Marriage Leads Catholic Charities to Adjust Benefits." *Washington Post*, March 2, A1.

Wang, Marian. 2010. "What Else Could $14 Trillion Buy?" *Mother Jones*, January/February, 31-33.

Warr, Mark. 2009. "Safe at Home." *Contexts* 8 (Summer): 46-51.

Wartzman, Rick. 2008. "Put a Cap on CEO Pay." *Business Week*, September 12. Retrieved November 7, 2008 (www.businessweek.com).

Wasley, Paula. 2007. "46 Students are Disciplined for Cheating at Indiana University's Dental School." *Chronicle of Higher Education*, May 9. Retrieved May 10, 2007 (www.chronicle.com).

———. 2008. "The Syllabus Becomes a Repository of Legalese." *Chronicle of Higher Education* 54, March 14, A1, A8-A11.

Watanabe, Teresa. 2009. "Asian Americans Drive Army Recruiting Boom in L.A." *Los Angeles Times*, December 16. Retrieved December 17, 2009 (www.latimes.com).

Water Quality & Health Council. 2005. "Facts About Chlorine and Drinking Water." Retrieved July 3, 2005 (www.waterandhealth.org).

Watson, C. W. 2000. *Multiculturalism*. Philadelphia, PA: Open University Press.

Weber, Lynn, Tina Hancock, and Elizabeth Higginbotham. 1997. "Women, Power, and Mental Health." Pp. 380-96 in *Women's Health: Complexities And Differences*, edited by Sheryl B. Ruzek, Virginia L. Olesen, and Adele E. Clarke. Columbus: Ohio State University Press.

Weber, Max. 1920. *The Protestant Ethic and the Spirit of Capitalism*. 1904-1905. (Talcott Parsons, Trans., 1958). New York: Charles Scribner's Sons.

———. 1925/1947. *The Theory of Social and Economic Organization*. New York: Free Press.

———. 1925/1978. *Economy and Society*. Guenther Roth and Claus Wittich, eds. Berkeley: University of California Press.

———. 1946. *From Max Weber: Essays in Sociology*, translated and edited by H. H. Gerth and C. Wright Mills. Berkeley: University of California Press.

Weil, Elizabeth. 2006. "What if It's (Sort of) a Boy and (Sort of) a Girl?" *New York Times Magazine* (September 24): 48-53.

Weingarten, Randi. 2010. "Good Objectives Weighed Down by Fatal Flaws." *U.S. News & World Report*, January, 36-37.

Weisbuch, Max, Kristin Pauker, and Nalini Ambady. 2009. "The Subtle Transmission of Race Bias via Televised Nonverbal Behavior." *Science* 326 (December 18): 1711-1714.

Weiss, Carol H. 1998. *Evaluation: Methods for Studying Programs and Policies*, 2nd edition. Upper Saddle River, NJ: Prentice Hall.

Weiss, Rick. 2004. "Nanomedicine's Promise is Anything but Tiny." *Washington Post*, January 31, A8.

———. 2005. "The Power to Divide." *National Geographic* 208 (July): 3-27.

Welch, Susan, John Gruhl, John Comer, and Susan Rigdon. 2004. *Understanding American Government*, 7th ed. Belmont, CA: Wadsworth.

Wellins, Richard S., William C. Byham, and Jeanne M. Wilson. 1991. *Empowered Teams: Creating Self-Directed Work Groups that Improve Quality, Productivity, and Participation*. San Francisco, CA: Jossey-Bass.

Wellner, Alison Stein. 2003. "The Wealth Effect." *American Demographics* 24 (January): 35-47.

Wells, H. G. 1898. *The War of the Worlds*. New York: Harper & Brothers.

Wendler, David, et al. 2006. "Are Racial and Ethnic Minorities Less Willing to Participate in Health Research?" *PLOS Medicine* 3 (December 6): 202-210. Retrieved July 31, 2006 (www.plosmedicine.org).

Wennberg, J. E., E. S. Fisher, D. C. Goodman, and J. S. Skinner. 2008. *Tracing the Care of Patients with Severe Chronic Illness*. Dartmouth Institute for Health Policy and Clinical Practice. Retrieved April 9, 2010 (www.dartmouthatlas.org).

Wenneras, Christine and Agnes Wold. 1997. "Nepotism and Sexism in Peer Review." *Nature* 387 (May 22): 341-43.

West, Candace, and Don H. Zimmerman. 1987. "Doing Gender." *Gender and Society* 1 (June): 125-51.

———. 2009. "Accounting for Doing Gender." *Gender & Society* 23 (February): 112-122.

West, Darrell M. 2010. "Broken Politics." Governance Studies at Brookings, March. Retrieved March 27, 2010 (www.brookings.edu).

West, Martha S., and John W. Curtis. 2006. *AAUP Faculty Gender Equity Indicators 2006*. Washington, DC: American Association of University Professors.

"What's That Commandment against Stealing?" 2006. *Forbes*, December 25, 36.

Whelan, Christine B. 2009. "A Feminist-Friendly Recession?" Pp. 55-62 in *The State of Our Unions, Marriage in America 2009: Money & Marriage*, edited by W. Bradford Wilcox, The National Marriage Project and the Institute for American Values. Retrieved December 20, 2009 (www.stateofourunions.org).

Whelan, David. 2007. "The Sentencing Game." *Forbes*, February 12, 40.

"Where the Jobs Are." 2009. *New York Times*, July 10, 24 (editorial).

Whisnant, Rebecca, and Christine Stark, eds. 2004. *Not for Sale: Feminists Resisting Prostitution and Pornography*. North Melbourne, Australia: Spinifex Press.

White, James W. 2005. *Advancing Family Theories*. Thousand Oaks, CA: Sage.

White, Ronald D., and Marc Lifsher. 2009. "Blacks Lose Ground in Job Slump." *Los Angeles Times*, March 21, B1.

Whitelaw, Kevin. 2000. "But What to Call It?" *U.S. News & World Report*, October 16, 42.

Whitmire, Richard. 2010. "How 9th-Grade Gridlock Keeps Boys out of College." *Chronicle of Higher Education*, February 12, A35.

Whoriskey, Peter. 2008. "Skilled-Worker Visa Demand Expected to Far Exceed Supply." *Washington Post*, April 1, D3.

"Who Votes, Who Doesn't, and Why: Regular Voters, Intermittent Voters, and Those Who Don't." 2006. Pew Research Center for the People & the Press, October 18. Retrieved May 3, 2007 (www.people-press.org).

Wickenden, Dorothy. 2006. "Top of the Class." *The New Yorker*, October 2. Retrieved July 26, 2007 (www.newyorker.com).

Wicker, Christine. 2009. "How Spiritual Are We?" *Parade*, October 4, 4-5.

Wiehe, Vernon R. 1997. *Sibling Abuse: Hidden Physical, Emotional, And Sexual Trauma*, 2nd edition. Thousand Oaks, CA: Sage Publications.

Wiig, Janet and Cathy Spatz Widom. 2003. *Understanding Child Maltreatment & Juvenile Delinquency*. Washington, DC: Child Welfare League of America.

Wilcox, W. Bradford. 2006. "Religion and the Domestication of Men." *Contexts* 5 (Fall): 42-46.

———. 2009. "The Great Recession's Silver Lining?" Pp. 15-21 in *The State of Our Union, Marriage in America 2009: Money & Marriage*, edited by W. Bradford Wilcox and Elizabeth Marquardt. Charlottesville, VA: The National Marriage Project.

Wilkinson, Charles. 2006. *Blood Struggle: The Rise of Modern Indian Nations*. New York: W.W. Norton & Company.

Williams III, Frank P. and Marilyn D. McShane. 2004. *Criminological Theory*, 4th edition. Upper Saddle River, NJ: Prentice Hall.

Williams, David E., Sean Kennedy, and Kerrie Rushton. 2010. *2009 Congressional Pig Book Summary*. Citizens Against Government Waste. Retrieved March 27, 2010 (www.cagw.org).

Williams, Dmitri, and Marko Skoric. 2005. "Internet Fantasy Violence: A Test of Aggression in an Online Game." *Communication Monographs* 27 (June): 217-33.

Williams, Robin M. Jr. 1970. *American Society: A Sociological Interpretation*, 3rd edition. New York: Knopf.

Willie, Charles Vert, and Richard J. Reddick. 2003. *A New Look at Black Families*, 5th ed. Walnut Creek, CA: AltaMira Press.

Willoughby, Brian J., and Jason S. Carroll. 2009. "The Impact of Living in Co-ed Resident Halls on Risk-Taking among College Students." *Journal of American College Health,* 58 (November-December): 241-246.

Wilson, Robin. 2005. "Second Sex." *Chronicle of Higher Education,* October 7, A10.

Wilson, Thomas C. 1993. "Urbanism and Kinship Bonds: A Test of Four Generalizations." *Social Forces* 71 (March): 703-712.

Wilson, William Julius. 1996. *When Work Disappears: The World of the New Urban Poor.* New York: Knopf.

Wilt, G. E. 1998. "Vote Early And Often." *American Demographics* 20 (December): 23.

Wiltenburg, Mary. 2002. "Minority." *Christian Science Monitor,* January 31, 14.

Winseman, Albert L. 2004. "Women in the Clergy: Perception and Reality." Gallup Organization, March 30. Retrieved March 30, 2004 (www.gallup.com).

Winston Group, The. 2006. "Math and Science Education and United States Competitiveness: Does the Public Care?" Retrieved July 15, 2007 (www.solutionsforourfuture.org).

Wirth, Louis. 1938. "Urbanism as a Way of Life." *American Journal of Sociology* 44 (July): 1-24.

Wiseman, Paul. 2010. "When the Textile Mill Goes, So Does a Way of Life." *USA Today,* March 10, 1A.

Witters, Dan. 2010. "The Flu Season That Wasn't." *Gallup,* May 6. Retrieved May 6, 2010 (www.gallup.com).

____. 2010. "Large Metro Areas Top Small Towns, Rural Areas in Wellbeing." *Gallup,* May 17. Retrieved May 20, 2010 (www.gallup.com).

Wolf, Craig. 2010. "Amid Offshoring, IBM to Stop Reporting U.S. Worker Count." *Poughkeepsie Journal,* March 18. Retrieved April 7, 2010 (www.poughkeepsiejournal.com).

Wolfe, Alan. 2008. "Pew in the Pews." *Chronicle of Higher Education,* March 21, B5-B6.

Wolff, Edward N. 2007. "Recent Trends in Household Wealth in the United States: Rising Debt and the Middle-Class Squeeze." The Levy Economics Institute, June. Retrieved May 20, 2008 (www.levy.org).

Wolfson, Mark. 2001. *The Fight Against Big Tobacco: The Movement, the State, and the Public's Health.* New York: Aldine de Gruyter.

Wood, Daniel B. 2009. "Medical Pot Gains Momentum." *Christian Science Monitor,* November 22, 22.

Woolf, Alex. 2004. *Fundamentalism.* Chicago, IL: Raintree.

World Bank. 2008. *World Development Indicators 2008.* Washington, DC: The International Bank.

World Food Program. 2006. *World Hunger Series 2006: Hunger and Learning.* United Nations. Retrieved November 3, 2006 (www.wfp.org).

World Health Organization. 2005. *WHO Multi-country Study on Women's Health and Domestic Violence against Women: Summary Report of Initial Results on Prevalence, Health Outcomes and Women's Responses.* Geneva: World Health Organization.

World Water Assessment Programme. 2009. *The United Nations World Water Development Report 3: Water in a Changing World.* Paris: UNESCO, and London: Earthscan.

Wright, Wynne, and Elizabeth Ransom. 2005. "Stratification on the Menu: Using Restaurant Menus to Examine Social Class." *Teaching Sociology* 33 (July): 310-316.

Wulfhorst, Ellen. 2006. "US Mothers Deserve $134,121 In Salary." May 3. Retrieved May 10, 2006 (http://today.reuters.com).

Wyatt, Edward. 2009. "More Than Ever, You Can Say That on Television." *New York Times,* November 14, A1.

Yagelski, Robert, et al. 2005. "The Impact of the SAT and ACT Timed Writing Tests." National Council of Teachers of English, April 16. Retrieved July 4, 2007 (www.ncte.org).

Yamazaki, Tomoko, and Komaki Ito. 2010. "Japan: Boosting Growth with Day Care." *Bloomburg Businessweek,* December 28, 2009 and January 4, 2010, 96-97.

Yan, Sophia. 2009. "Anonymous Gossip Sites." *Time,* December 7, 97-98.

Yang, Fenggang. 2002. "Religious Diversity among the Chinese in America." Pp. 71-98 in Religions *in Asian America: Building Faith Communities,* edited by Pyong Gap Min and Jung Ha Kim. Walnut Creek, CA: AltaMira Press.

Yardley, Jim. 2009. "Indian Women Find New Peace in Rail Commute." *New York Times,* September 16, A1.

____. 2009. "On Cluttered Ballots of India, Families Proliferate." *New York Times,* October 12, 1.

Yarrow, Andrew L. 2009. "State of Mind." *Education Week,* October 21. Retrieved April 21, 2010 (www.edweek.org).

Yellowbird, Michael, and C. Matthew Snipp. 2002. "American Indian Families." Pp. 227-249 in *Minority Families in The United States: A Multicultural Perspective,* 3rd ed., edited by Ronald L. Taylor. Upper Saddle River, NJ: Prentice Hall.

Yokota, Fumise and Kimberly M. Thompson. 2000. "Violence in G-rated Animated Films." *JAMA: Journal of the American Medical Association* 283 (May 24/31): 2716-20.

Young, Katherine K. 1999. "Introduction." Pp. 1-24 in *Feminism and World Religions,* edited by Arvind Sharma and Katherine K. Young. Albany: State University of New York Press.

Yu, Roger. 2007. "Indian-Americans Book Years of Success." *USA Today,* April 18, 1B-2B.

Zahedi, Ashraf. 2008. "Concealing and Revealing Female Hair: Veiling Dynamics in Contemporary Iran." Pp. 250-265 in *The Veil: Women Writers on Its History, Lore, and Politics,* edited by Jennifer Heath. Berkeley: University of California Press.

Zajonc, Robert B., and Gregory B. Markus. 1975. "Birth Order and Intellectual Development." *Psychological Review* 82 (January): 74-88.

Zhou, Min, Carl L. Bankston III, and Rebecca Y. Kim. 2002. "Rebuilding Spiritual Lives in the New Land: Religious Practices among Southeast Asian Refugees in the United States." Pp. 37-70 in *Religions in Asian America: Building Faith Communities,* edited by Pyong Gap Min and Jung Ha Kim. Walnut Creek, CA: AltaMira Press.

Zimbardo, Philip G., Christina Maslach, and Craig Haney. 2000. "Reflections on the Stanford Prison Experiment: Genesis, Transformations, Consequences." Pp. 193-237 in *Obedience to Authority: Current Perspectives on the Milgram Paradigm,* edited by Thomas Blass. Mahwah, NJ: Lawrence Erlbaum Associates.

Zimbardo, Philip. G. 1975. "Transforming Experimental Research into Advocacy for Social Change." Pp. 33-66 in *Applying Social Psychology: Implications for Research, Practice, and Training,* edited by Morton Deutsch and Harvey A. Hornstein. Hillsdale, NJ: Erlbaum.

Zimmer, Ron, Brian Gill, Kevin Booker, Stephane Lavertu, Tim R. Sass, and John Witte. 2009. *Charter Schools in Eight States: Effects on Achievement, Attainment, Integration, and Competition.* Santa Monica, CA: Rand.

Zimmerman, F. J., D. A. Christakis, and A. N. Meltzoff. 2007. "Associations Between Media Viewing and Language Development in Children under Age 2 Years." *Journal of Pediatrics* 151 (October): 364-368.

Zuehlke, Eric. 2009. "Immigrants Work in Riskier and More Dangerous Jobs in the United States." Population Reference Bureau, November. Retrieved March 15, 2010 (www.prb.org).

Zweigenhaft, Richard L. and G. William Domhoff. 1998. *Diversity in the Power Elite: Have Women and Minorities Reached the Top?* New Haven: Yale University Press.

____. 2006. *Diversity in the Power Elite: How It Happened, Why It Matters.* Lanham, MD: Rowman & Littlefield.

SUBJECT INDEX

Note: Italic page numbers indicate material in tables or figures. Bold page numbers indicate definitions.

CHAPTER 1 TOPICS

1 What Is Sociology?

Sociology is the systematic study of social interaction—how we act toward and react to people around us—at a variety of levels. Sociologists use scientific research to discover patterns and create theories about who we are, how we interact with others, and why we do what we do. Sociology goes beyond common sense in understanding our social world, including small groups (e.g., families and friends), large organizations and institutions (e.g., your college), and entire societies (e.g., the United States).

2 What Is the Sociological Imagination?

Sociology helps us understand diversity within the community, make socially conscious decisions, evaluate public policy, and explain how we fit into the big picture. The *sociological imagination,* which emphasizes the intersection between individual lives and external social influences, relies on both micro-level and macro-level approaches in examining the social world. *Microsociology* concentrates on the relationships between individual characteristics, whereas *macrosociology* examines social dynamics across the breadth of a society. Macro-level systems and institutions shape society, often limiting our personal options on the micro level.

3 Some Origins of Sociological Theory

Sociologists use *theories,* also called *theoretical perspectives,* to explain why a phenomenon occurs among people, institutions, and societies. Why is society structured like it is? What holds society together? What pulls it apart? Theories answer these and many other questions. Theories produce knowledge, but they can also offer solutions to everyday social problems. New theories build on older ones and are tested through ongoing research. Some of the most influential theorists have included Auguste Comte, Harriet Martineau, Émile Durkheim, Karl Marx, Max Weber, Jane Addams, and W. E. B. Du Bois. Each brought to sociology a new level of understanding about our world.

4 Contemporary Sociological Theories

Sociologists typically use more than one theory in explaining human behavior. The fullest understanding of society comes from using all four theories:

- *Functionalism explains society as interconnected social systems.* Critics contend that functionalism ignores social inequality and social conflict.
- *Conflict theory developed as opposition to functionalism grew, and sees disagreement and the resulting changes in society as natural, inevitable, and even desirable.* Critics argue that conflict theory ignores the importance of harmony and cooperation.
- *Feminist theories, which build on conflict theory, maintain that gender inequality is central to all conflict.* Critics claim that feminism is too narrowly focused.
- *Symbolic interactionism focuses on the symbolic meanings of micro-level interactions.* Critics claim that symbolic interactionism overlooks the impact of macro-level factors on our everyday behavior.

Example: *Critical Thinking & Common Sense*

When thinking critically, it's important to differentiate between common sense myths and facts. Here are a few examples:

Myth: Older people make up the largest group of those who are poor.
Fact: Children younger than 6, and not older people, make up the largest group of those who are poor (see Chapters 8 and 11).
Myth: Divorce rates are higher today than ever before.
Fact: Divorce rates are lower today than they were between 1980 and 2005 (see Chapter 13).
Myth: Most of the poor live in inner cities.
Fact: Almost 67 percent of poor Americans live in urban areas outside of inner cities, in the suburbs, in small towns, and in rural communities (see Chapter 8).

KEY TERMS

sociology the systematic study of social interaction at a variety of levels.

sociological imagination the intersection between individual lives and larger social influences.

microsociology the study of small-scale patterns of individuals' social interaction in specific settings.

macrosociology the study of large-scale patterns and processes that characterize society as a whole.

theory a set of statements that explains why a phenomenon occurs.

empirical information that is based on observations, experiments, or experiences rather than on ideology, religion, or intuition.

social facts aspects of social life, external to the individual, that can be measured.

social solidarity social cohesiveness and harmony.

division of labor an interdependence of different tasks and occupations, characteristic of industrialized societies, that produce social unity and facilitate change.

capitalism an economic system in which the ownership of the means of production—like land, factories, large sums of money, and machines—is in private hands.

alienation the feeling of separation from one's group or society.

value free separating one's personal values, opinions, ideology, and beliefs from scientific research.

functionalism *(structural functionalism)* an approach that maintains that society is a complex system of interdependent parts that work together to ensure a society's survival.

dysfunctional social patterns that have a negative impact on a group or society.

manifest functions functions that are intended and recognized; they are present and clearly evident.

latent functions functions that are unintended and unrecognized; they are present but not immediately obvious.

conflict theory an approach that examines the ways in which groups disagree, struggle over power, and compete for scarce resources (such as property, wealth, and prestige).

feminist theories approaches that try to explain the social, economic, and political position of women in society with a view to freeing women from traditionally oppressive expectations, constraints, roles, and behavior.

symbolic interactionism *(interactionism)* a micro-level perspective that looks at individuals' everyday behavior through the communication of knowledge, ideas, beliefs, and attitudes.

interaction action in which people take each other into account in their own behavior.

TEST YOUR LEARNING

1. _____ looks at the relationship between individual characteristics; _____ examines the relationships between institutional characteristics.
   a. Microsociology; macrosociology
   b. Macrosociology; microsociology
   c. Metasociology; macrosociology
   d. Metasociology; microsociology

2. Which social class, as identified by Karl Marx, includes the ruling elite who own the means of production?
   a. Capitalists
   b. Communists
   c. Power elite
   d. Proletariat

3. James saw Julie laughing in the hallway with a friend and assumes that Julie is feeling happy. James is using Weber's
   a. explanatory understanding.
   b. surveillance understanding.
   c. common understanding.
   d. direct observational understanding.

4. Jeremy views society as a system of interrelated parts, but Tom sees society as composed of groups competing for scarce resources. Jeremy would be considered a _____ theorist, and Tom would be seen as a _____ theorist.
   a. symbolic interactionist; functionalist
   b. conflict; functionalist
   c. functionalist; symbolic interactionist
   d. functionalist; conflict

5. Many people buy designer clothes that they can't afford. The clothes are an example of a status symbol that reflects a
   a. latent function.
   b. manifest function.
   c. dysfunction.
   d. social system.

6. **True or False** In the definition of sociology, "systematic" means behavior that is built into the larger social structure of society.

7. **True or False** Émile Durkheim saw sociology as the scientific study of two aspects of society: social statics and social dynamics.

8. **True or False** Jane Addams was an early sociologist who published extensively on topics such as social disorganization, immigration, and urban neighborhoods.

9. **True or False** Much of contemporary functionalism grew out of the work of Auguste Comte and Émile Durkheim.

10. **True or False** Conflict theorists see society as cooperative and harmonious.

1. a 2. a 3. d 4. d 5. a 6. False 7. False 8. False 9. True 10. False

For full table, see Table 1.1 on page 19.

TABLE 1.1
Leading Contemporary Perspectives in Sociology

THEORETICAL PERSPECTIVE	FUNCTIONALIST	CONFLICT	FEMINIST	SYMBOLIC INTERACTIONIST
Level of Analysis	Macro	Macro	Macro and Micro	Micro
Key Points	• Society is composed of interrelated, mutually dependent parts • Structures and functions maintain a society's or group's stability, cohesion, and continuity • Dysfunctional activities that threaten a society's or group's survival are controlled or eliminated	• Life is a continuous struggle between the "haves" and the "have nots" • People compete for limited resources that are controlled by a small number of powerful groups • Society is based on inequality in terms of ethnicity, race, social class, and gender	• Women experience widespread inequality in society because, as a group, they have little power • Gender, ethnicity, race, age, sexual orientation, and social class—rather than a person's intelligence and ability—explain many of our social interactions and lack of access to resources • Social change is possible only if we change our institutional structures and our day-to-day interactions	• People act on the basis of the meaning they attribute to others Meaning grows out of the social interaction that we have with others • People continuously reinterpret and reevaluate their knowledge and information in their everyday encounters

CHAPTER 2 TOPICS

1 Doing Sociology: What Is Social Research?

Social research requires curiosity and imagination, but also an understanding of the rules and procedures that govern careful scientific study. The process involves choosing a socially relevant topic, asking a research question, developing and testing a hypothesis, and analyzing the findings. In contrast, many opinions in self-help publications often ignore the scientific method

2 Why Is Sociological Research Important in Our Everyday Lives?

Much of our knowledge is based on tradition and authority. In contrast, sociological research creates new knowledge that helps us understand social life, exposes myths, affects social policies, sharpens our critical thinking skills, and helps us make informed decisions about our everyday lives.

3 The Scientific Method

The *scientific method* incorporates careful data collection, exact measurement, accurate recording and analysis of findings, thoughtful interpretation of results, and, when appropriate, a generalization of the findings to a larger group. Sociologists use the scientific method to measure the relationships between *variables*. A research question or a *hypothesis* examines the association between an *independent variable* and the *dependent variable*. Sociologists use both *qualitative* and *quantitative* approaches, and are always concerned about the *reliability* and *validity* of their measures.

4 Some Major Data Collection Methods

Six data collection methods are especially common in sociology. Sociologists weigh the advantages and limitations of each data collection method in designing their studies (see Table 2.2). Because sociologists don't conduct research in a cultural vacuum, many groups use the findings to change current policies and practices.

Example: *The Complicated Relationship between Research and Practice*

Many supporters of the DARE (Drug Abuse Resistance Education) program were unhappy when more than 30 research studies showed that DARE had negligible long-term impacts on reducing teen drug use. Nonetheless, about 75 percent of U.S. school districts used the findings to revise the DARE curriculum. Police officers were retrained to engage young people in a conversation about the consequences of using illegal drugs rather than preaching at them. Many communities altered but continued DARE because they believed that the program built a positive relationship between police, students, parents, and educators (Berman and Fox 2009).

5 Ethics, Politics, and Sociological Research

Sociological research demands a strict code of ethics throughout every research step to avoid exploitation and maltreatment of participants. For example, participants must give informed consent and must not be harmed, humiliated, abused, or coerced; researchers must honor their guarantees of privacy, confidentiality, and/or anonymity. Still, sociologists often encounter pressure from policy makers and others to limit their research to topics that won't stir controversy on sensitive issues.

KEY TERMS

social research research that examines human behavior.

scientific method the steps in the research process that include careful data collection, exact measurement, accurate recording and analysis of the findings, thoughtful interpretation of results, and, when appropriate, a generalization of the findings to a larger group.

variable a characteristic that can change in value or magnitude under different conditions.

hypothesis a statement of a relationship between two or more variables that researchers want to test.

independent variable a characteristic that determines or has an effect on the dependent variable.

dependent variable the outcome, which may be affected by the independent variable.

reliability the consistency with which the same measure produces similar results time after time.

validity the degree to which a measure is accurate and really measures what it claims to measure.

deductive reasoning an inquiry process that begins with a theory, prediction, or general principle that is then tested through data collection.

inductive reasoning an inquiry process that begins with a specific observation, followed by data collection, a general conclusion, or theory construction.

population any well-defined group of people (or things) about whom researchers want to know something.

sample a group of people (or things) that are representative of the population that researchers wish to study.

probability sample a sample for which each person (or thing, such as an e-mail address) has an equal chance of being selected because the selection is random.

nonprobability sample a sample for which little or no attempt is made to get a representative cross section of the population.

qualitative research research that examines non-numerical material and interprets it.

quantitative research research that focuses on a numerical analysis of people's responses or specific characteristics.

surveys a systematic method for collecting data from respondents, including questionnaires, face-to-face or telephone interviews, or a combination of these.

secondary analysis examination of data that have been collected by someone else.

field research data collection by systematically observing people in their natural surroundings.

content analysis a method of studying social behavior that systematically examines some form of communication.

experiment a carefully controlled artificial situation that allows researchers to manipulate variables and measure the effects.

experimental group the group of subjects in an experiment who are exposed to the independent variable.

control group the group of subjects in an experiment who are not exposed to the independent variable.

evaluation research research that uses all of the standard data collection techniques to assess the effectiveness of social programs in both the public and the private sectors.

TEST YOUR LEARNING

1. Sociological research is important in our daily lives for a number of reasons. Which of the following is NOT one of those reasons?
   a. It exposes myths.
   b. It challenges the findings of psychology researchers.
   c. It affects social policy.
   d. It sharpens our critical thinking skills.

2. What is a hypothesis?
   a. A theory based on one's opinions.
   b. A measure of how accurate a study is.
   c. A statement of a relationship between two or more variables.
   d. An analysis of multiple studies that researchers use to make generalizations.

3. Alexandra notices that she tends to perform best on tests that are given in the afternoon. She then begins to collect data of her test performances and asks close friends and classmates to do the same. In trying to understand whether test scores and test times are related, Alexandra is using
   a. intuition.
   b. inferences.
   c. deductive reasoning.
   d. inductive reasoning.

4. Which of the following data collection methods is the most likely to suggest a cause-and-effect relationship?
   a. Experiment
   b. Survey
   c. Field research
   d. Content analysis

5. There are three golden rules that apply to all sociological research. Which of the following is NOT one of those three rules?
   a. Do no harm.
   b. Be fully transparent with the subject.
   c. Get the subject's informed consent.
   d. Protect the subject's confidentiality.

6. *True or False* Social researchers continuously challenge the quality of existing studies.

7. *True or False* If researchers use a nonprobability sample, they can generalize the results to a larger population.

8. *True or False* Validity is the consistency that a measure produces similar results over time; reliability is the degree to which the measure is accurate and really measures what it claims to measure.

9. *True or False* Observing second graders interact with one another in their classroom is an example of field research.

10. *True or False* Correlation equals causation.

1. b 2. c 3. d 4. a 5. b 6. True 7. False 8. False 9. True 10. False

For full table, see Table 2.2 on page 34.

TABLE 2.2
Some Data Collection Methods in Sociological Research

METHOD	ADVANTAGES	DISADVANTAGES
Surveys	Questionnaires are fairly inexpensive and simple to administer; interviews have high response rates; findings are often generalizable	Mailed questionnaires may have low response rates; respondents may be self-selected; interviews are usually expensive
Secondary analysis	Usually accessible, convenient and inexpensive; often longitudinal and historical	Information may be incomplete; some documents may be inaccessible; some data can't be collected over time
Field research	Flexible; offers deeper understanding of social behavior; usually inexpensive	Difficult to quantify and to maintain observer/subject boundaries; the observer may be biased or judgmental; findings are not generalizable
Content analysis	Usually inexpensive; can recode errors easily; unobtrusive; permits comparisons over time	Can be labor-intensive; coding is often subjective (and may be distorted); may reflect social class biases
Experiments	Usually inexpensive; plentiful supply of subjects; can be replicated	Volunteers and paid subjects aren't representative of a larger population; the laboratory setting is artificial
Evaluation research	Usually inexpensive; valuable in real-life applications	Often political; findings might be rejected

Culture

CHAPTER 3 TOPICS

1 Culture and Society

Culture is learned, transmitted from one generation to another, adaptive, and always changing. A *society* shares a culture and sees itself as a social unit. People construct a *material culture* (such as buildings) and *nonmaterial culture* (such as rules for behavior) that influence each other (such as forbidding smoking in public buildings).

2 The Building Blocks of Culture

The following are some of the fundamental building blocks of culture:

- *Symbols* that take many forms, can change over time, can unify or divide a society, and can affect cross-cultural views
- *Language,* a system of shared symbols that enables social interaction, can change over time, and can affect perceptions of gender, race, class, and ethnicity
- *Values,* which provide general guidelines for behavior, are usually emotion laden, vary across cultures, and change over time
- *Norms*—whether they are folkways, mores, or laws—regulate our behavior; they vary across cultures and are subject to sanctions ranging from mild to severe

Example: *Sanctions for Violating the Dead*

Sanctions are more severe for violating laws than folkways. Legacy.com, which carries a death notice or obituary for virtually all of the roughly 2.4 million Americans who die each year, dedicates at least 30 percent of its budget to weeding out comments (a relatively mild punishment) that "diss the dead" (Urbina 2006). In contrast, when there's no prior criminal record, the penalties in many states for vandalizing a tombstone, a property crime, can result in a fine up to $1,000, up to a year in jail, or both.

3 Some Cultural Similarities

Although many cultural characteristics vary across countries, *cultural universals* are common to all societies, such as some form of food taboo. People who encounter

an unfamiliar way of life or environment may experience *culture shock.*

4 Some Cultural Variations

Subcultures and *countercultures* account for some of the complexity within a society. The former differ from people of the larger society in some ways, whereas the latter oppose or reject some of the dominant culture's basic beliefs, values, and norms. *Ethnocentrism* has its benefits but can also lead to conflict and discrimination. *Cultural relativism,* the opposite of ethnocentrism, encourages cross-cultural understanding and respect. In *multiculturalism,* many cultures coexist without trying to dominate one another.

5 Popular Culture

Popular culture, which is widely shared among a population, includes television, music, radio, advertising, sports, hobbies, fads, fashions, and movies, as well as the food we eat, the people with whom we spend time, the gossip we share, and the jokes we pass along. Popular culture is typically spread through *mass media,* including television and the Internet, and has enormous power in shaping our perceptions and opinions.

6 Cultural Change and Technology

Some societies are relatively stable because of *cultural integration,* but all societies change over time because of diffusion, innovation and invention, discovery, external pressures, and changes in the physical environment. A *cultural lag* occurs when a culture's material side changes more rapidly than its nonmaterial side.

7 Sociological Perspectives on Culture

KEY TERMS

culture the learned and shared behaviors, beliefs, attitudes, values, and material objects that characterize a particular group or society.

society a group of people who have lived and worked together long enough to become an organized population and to think of themselves as a social unit.

material culture the tangible objects that members of a society make, use, and share.

nonmaterial culture the shared set of meanings that people in a society use to interpret and understand the world.

symbol anything that stands for something else and has a particular meaning for people who share a culture.

language a system of shared symbols that enables people to communicate with one another.

values the standards by which members of a particular culture define what is good or bad, moral or immoral, proper or improper, desirable or undesirable, beautiful or ugly.

norms a society's specific rules concerning right and wrong behavior.

folkways norms that members of a society (or a group within a society) see as not being critical and that may be broken without severe punishment.

mores norms that members of a society consider very important because they maintain moral and ethical behavior.

laws formal rules about behavior that are defined by a political authority that has the power to punish violators.

sanctions rewards for good or appropriate behavior and/or penalties for bad or inappropriate behavior.

cultural universals customs and practices that are common to all societies.

ideal culture the beliefs, values, and norms that people in a society say they hold or follow.

real culture the actual everyday behavior of people in a society.

ethnocentrism the belief that one's culture and way of life are superior to those of other groups.

KEY TERMS

cultural relativism the belief that no culture is better than another and that a culture should be judged by its own standards.

subculture a group or category of people whose distinctive ways of thinking, feeling, and acting differ somewhat from those of the larger society.

counterculture a group of people who deliberately oppose and consciously reject some of the basic beliefs, values, and norms of the dominant culture.

multiculturalism *(cultural pluralism)* the coexistence of several cultures in the same geographic area, without one culture dominating another.

culture shock a sense of confusion, uncertainty, disorientation, or anxiety that accompanies exposure to an unfamiliar way of life or environment.

popular culture the beliefs, practices, activities, and products that are widely shared among a population in everyday life.

mass media forms of communication designed to reach large numbers of people.

cultural imperialism the cultural values and products of one society that influence or dominate those of another.

cultural integration the consistency of various aspects of society that promotes order and stability.

cultural lag the gap when nonmaterial culture changes more slowly than material culture.

TEST YOUR LEARNING

1. Society and culture are mutually
   a. dependent.
   b. exclusive.
   c. destructive.
   d. diversified.

2. _____ stand for something else and have a particular meaning for people who share a culture.
   a. Mores
   b. Symbols
   c. Values
   d. Norms

3. At a party, George was eating nachos and salsa. He took a bite of his chip and then dipped what was left of his chip back into the large bowl of salsa. His friend Brett gave him a disgusted look. Which of the following did George break?
   a. A more
   b. A cultural universal
   c. A folkway
   d. A law

4. Which of the following is an example of a subculture?
   a. A group of adolescent Goths
   b. Roman Catholics
   c. A 40-and-over women's bridge club
   d. All of the above

5. Anaz is an 8-year-old Iranian girl who loves the female fashions she sees in American films and television shows. Lately she's been questioning why her mother wears a burka. Anaz's questioning of her family's traditions could best be explained by
   a. cultural relativism.
   b. multiculturalism.
   c. cultural imperialism.
   d. ethnocentrism.

6. *True or False* Culture is adapting and always changing.

7. *True or False* Language helps communicate ideas, but it's not considered a symbol.

8. *True or False* In most societies, the real culture matches the ideal culture.

9. *True or False* The legal controversy over file sharing and downloading music off the Web is an example of cultural lag.

10. *True or False* Symbolic interactionists take a macro approach in examining culture.

1. a   2. b   3. c   4. d   5. c   6. true   7. False   8. False   9. True   10. False

TABLE 3.3
Sociological Explanations of Culture

THEORETICAL PERSPECTIVE	FUNCTIONALIST	CONFLICT	FEMINIST	SYMBOLIC INTERACTIONIST
Level of Analysis	Macro	Macro	Macro and Micro	Micro
Key Points	• Similar beliefs bind people together and create stability. • Sharing core values unifies a society and promotes cultural solidarity.	• Culture benefits some groups at the expense of others. • As powerful economic monopolies increase worldwide, the rich get richer and the rest of us get poorer.	• Women and men often experience culture differently. • Cultural values and norms can increase inequality because of gender, race/ethnicity, and social class.	• Cultural symbols forge identities (that change over time). • Culture (such as norms and values) helps people merge into a society despite their differences.

Socialization

CHAPTER 4
IN REVIEW

CHAPTER 4 TOPICS

1 Socialization: Its Purpose and Importance

Socialization, a lifelong process, teaches us to be human. Socialization fulfills four key purposes: It establishes our social identity, teaches us role taking, controls our behavior (through *internalization*), and transmits culture to the next generation.

2 Nature and Nurture

Biologists tend to focus on the role of heredity (or genetics) in human development. In contrast, most social scientists, including sociologists, underscore the role of learning, socialization, and culture. This difference of opinion is often called the *nature-nurture debate. Sociobiologists* argue that genetics (nature) can explain much of our behavior, whereas most sociologists maintain that socialization and culture (nurture) shape even biological inputs.

3 Sociological Explanations of Socialization

Sociologists have offered many explanations of socialization, but two of the most influential, both at the micro level, have been social learning and symbolic interaction theories.

4 Primary Socialization Agents

Parents are the first and most important *agents of socialization*, but siblings, grandparents, and other family members also play important roles. Other important socialization agents include play and peer groups, teachers and schools, popular culture, and the media. Advertising is an especially powerful force in socialization.

Example: *Are Parents Realistic in Socializing Their Children?*

Many parents tell their offspring that the children are very intelligent. In fact, only about 5 percent of American kids can be considered "gifted" (endowed with significantly higher than average intellectual or other abilities), even though many are enrolled in gifted classes. Some educators argue that telling average—or even above average—children that they're superior does them a disservice: It gives them false expectations on how the world will treat them, encourages being self-centered, and increases anger and unhappiness when they don't succeed in college or the workplace (Deveny 2008).

5 Socialization Throughout Life

As we progress through the life course, we learn culturally approved norms, values, and roles. Infants are born with an enormous capacity for learning that parents and other caregivers can enrich and shape. In adolescence, these and other socialization agents teach children how to form relationships on their own, to get along with others, and to develop their social identity through play and peer groups. In adulthood, people must learn new roles that include singlehood, marriage, parenthood, divorce, work, and experiencing the death of a loved one. Socialization continues in later life when many people learn still new roles such as grandparents, retirees, older workers, and being widowed.

6 Resocialization

Much of *resocialization*, which can be voluntary or involuntary, takes place in *total institutions*, where people are isolated from the rest of society, stripped of their former identities, and required to conform to new rules and behavior.

KEY TERMS

socialization the lifelong process of social interaction in which the individual acquires a social identity and ways of thinking, feeling, and acting that are essential for effective participation in a society.

internalization the process of learning cultural behaviors and expectations so deeply that we assume they are correct and accept them without question.

sociobiology a theoretical approach that applies biological principles to explain the behavior of animals, including human beings.

social learning theories approaches whose central notion is that people learn new attitudes, beliefs, and behaviors through social interaction, especially during childhood.

self an awareness of one's social identity.

looking-glass self a self-image based on how we think others see us.

role taking learning to take the perspective of others.

significant others the people who are important in one's life, such as parents or other primary caregivers and siblings.

anticipatory socialization the process of learning how to perform a role one doesn't yet occupy.

generalized other people who don't have close ties to a child but who influence her or his internalization of society's norms and values.

impression management the process of providing information and cues to others to present oneself in a favorable light while downplaying or concealing one's less appealing qualities.

reference groups groups of people who shape an individual's self-image, behavior, values, and attitudes in different contexts.

agents of socialization the individuals, groups, or institutions that teach us what we need to know to participate effectively in society.

peer group people who are similar in age, social status, and interests.

resocialization the process of unlearning old ways of doing things and adopting new attitudes, values, norms, and behavior.

total institutions places where people are isolated from the rest of society, stripped of their former identities, and required to conform to new rules and behavior.

TEST YOUR LEARNING

1. Emma learned from her mother that girls can do anything that boys can do in getting a good education. This is an example of the _____ process.

   a. multicultural
   b. ethnocentric
   c. socialization
   d. hereditary

2. "Human development is fairly fixed." This statement is an example of which side of the nature/nurture debate?

   a. Nature side of the debate
   b. Nurture side of the debate
   c. Neither the nature nor nurture side of the debate
   d. Both the nature and nurture side of the debate

3. According to social learning theory, the greatest impact of social interaction occurs during

   a. childhood.
   b. adolescence.
   c. early adulthood.
   d. middle adulthood.

4. What are the three stages of Mead's role-taking theory?

   a. Prework stage, work stage, postwork stage
   b. Anal stage, phallic stage, postphallic stage
   c. Mirror stage, active stage, passive stage
   d. Preparatory stage, play stage, game stage

5. According to Mead, children learn how to perform a role they don't yet occupy. Mead referred to this process as

   a. a developing self.
   b. anticipatory socialization.
   c. role taking.
   d. the generalized other.

6. **True or False** Institutionalization is the process of learning cultural behaviors and expectations so deeply that we assume they are correct and accept them without question.

7. **True or False** Charles Horton Cooley proposed that the looking-glass self develops in five phases.

8. **True or False** According to Erving Goffman, social life mirrors theatrical performance.

9. **True or False** Healthy child development is most likely in authoritative homes.

10. **True or False** Resocialization is the process of reinforcing the established values and beliefs of an individual.

1. c 2. a 3. a 4. d 5. b 6. False 7. False 8. True 9. True 10. False

For full table, see Table 4.2 on p. 67.

TABLE 4.2
Key Elements of Socialization Theories

SOCIAL LEARNING THEORIES	SYMBOLIC INTERACTION THEORIES
• Social interaction is important in learning appropriate and inappropriate behavior. • Socialization relies on direct and indirect reinforcement.	• The self emerges through social interaction with significant others. • Socialization includes role taking and controlling the impression we give to others.

Social Interaction and Social Structure

CHAPTER 5 TOPICS

1 Social Structure

Social interaction, central to all social activity, affects people's behavior. Our interaction is part of the *social structure,* which guides our actions and gives us a feeling that life is orderly and predictable. Every society has a social structure that encompasses statuses and roles.

2 Status

A *status* is a social position that an individual occupies in a society. Every person has many statuses that form her or his *status set,* which include both ascribed and achieved statuses. An *ascribed status* is a social position that a person is born into and can't control, change, or choose (such as age, race, and being male or female). An *achieved status* is a social position that a person attains through personal effort or assumes voluntarily (such as college student or wife). Because we hold many statuses, some clash and result in *status inconsistency* because we occupy social positions that are ranked differently (such as being a low-paid college professor).

3 Role

A *role* defines how we are expected to behave in a particular status, but people vary considerably in fulfilling the responsibilities associated with their roles. These differences reflect *role performance,* the actual behavior of a person who occupies a status. A *role set* encompasses different roles attached to a single status (such as a parent who is a teacher, chauffeur, and PTA member). Playing many roles often leads to *role conflict,* because it's difficult to meet the requirements of two or more statuses, and *role strain,* the stress that arises because of incompatible demands among roles within a single status.

Some common ways to resolve role conflict include compromising, negotiating, setting priorities, compartmentalizing, not taking on more roles, and exiting one or more current roles.

Example: *Exiting a Marriage*

Divorce is a good example of role exit, but often involves a long process of five stages that may last several decades (Bohannon 1971). The "emotional divorce" begins when one or both partners feel disillusioned or unhappy. The "legal divorce" is the formal dissolution of the marriage during which the partner who does not want the divorce may try to stall the end of the marriage. During the "economic divorce" stage, the partners may argue about who should pay past debts, property taxes, and unforeseen expenses (such as moving costs). The "coparental divorce" stage involves parents' agreeing on issues such as child support and visitation rights. During the "community divorce" stage, partners inform friends, family, and others that they are no longer married. Finally, the couple goes through a "psychic divorce," in which the partners separate from each other emotionally. In many cases, one or both spouses never complete this stage because they can't let go of their pain, anger, and resentment—even if they remarry.

4 Explaining Social Interaction

Please see Table 5.2 on next page.

5 Nonverbal Communication

Our *nonverbal communication* includes gestures, facial expressions, eye contact, and silence. Touching and how we use space are also important forms of nonverbal communication because they send powerful messages about our feelings and power.

6 Online Interaction

Many people interact in *cyberspace,* an online world of computer networks. Internet usage varies by gender, age, ethnicity, and social class. Cyberspace can be impersonal and socially isolating, but it can also save time, foster closer relationships among family members and friends, and facilitate working from home.

KEY TERMS

social interaction the process by which we act toward and react to people around us.

social structure an organized pattern of behavior that governs people's relationships.

status a social position that a person occupies in a society.

status set a collection of social statuses that a person occupies at a given time.

ascribed status a social position that a person is born into.

achieved status a social position that a person attains through personal effort or assumes voluntarily.

master status an ascribed or achieved status that determines a person's identity.

status inconsistency the conflict that arises from occupying social positions that are ranked differently.

role the behavior expected of a person who has a particular status.

role performance the actual behavior of a person who occupies a status.

role set the different roles attached to a single status.

role conflict the frustrations and uncertainties a person experiences when confronted with the requirements of two or more statuses.

role strain the stress that arises from incompatible demands among roles within a single status.

self-fulfilling prophecy a situation where if we define something as real and act on it, it can, in fact, become real.

ethnomethodology the study of how people construct and learn to share definitions of reality that make everyday interactions possible.

dramaturgical analysis a technique that examines social interaction as if occurring on a stage where people play different roles and act out scenes for the audiences with whom they interact.

social exchange theory the perspective whose fundamental premise is that social interaction is based on each person's trying to maximize rewards (or benefits) and minimize punishments (or costs).

nonverbal communication messages that are sent without using words.

TEST YOUR LEARNING

1. Jenna is the youngest of three girls in her family. Being the youngest sister is an example of a(n)
   a. achieved status.
   b. ascribed status.
   c. problematic status.
   d. interchangeable status.

2. Jake has a full-time course load while also working 30 hours a week. Given the demands of both work and school, Jake might be likely to experience
   a. role set.
   b. role strain.
   c. role conflict.
   d. role exchange.

3. According to _____, social interaction is based on trying to maximize rewards for oneself while minimizing costs.
   a. ethnomethodology theory
   b. feminist theory
   c. conflict theory
   d. social exchange theory

4. Gestures, eye contact, and silence are all examples of
   a. emotional language.
   b. punishment.
   c. healthy relationship interaction.
   d. nonverbal communication.

5. A disadvantage of telecommuting is that that it
   a. pays less than working on site at the office.
   b. blurs the line between home life and work.
   c. is more available to men than women.
   d. all of the above are disadvantages of telecommuting

6. *True or False* In sociology, status signifies prestige.

7. *True or False* A master status is based on one's achieved status.

8. *True or False* We can minimize role conflict and role strain by not setting priorities.

9. *True or False* If we define something as real and act on it, it can, in fact, become real. This is known as the self-fulfilling prophecy.

10. *True or False* Being an African American college student is an example of having two ascribed statuses.

1. b 2. c 3. d 4. d 5. b 6. False 7. False 8. False 9. True 10. False

TABLE 5.2
Sociological Explanations of Social Interaction

PERSPECTIVE	KEY POINTS
Symbolic Interactionist	• People create and define their reality through social interaction. • Our definitions of reality, which vary according to context, can lead to self-fulfilling prophecies.
Social Exchange	• Social interaction is based on a balancing of benefits and costs. • Relationships involve trading a variety of resources, such as money, youth, and good looks.
Feminist	• The sexes act similarly in many interactions but often differ in communication styles and speech patterns. • Men are more likely to use speech that's assertive (to achieve dominance and goals), while women are more likely to use language that connects with others.

Social Groups, Organizations, and Social Institutions

CHAPTER 6 TOPICS

1 Social Groups

A *social group* gives us a common identity and a sense of belonging (such as friends or work groups). Social groups include *primary groups* (such as family members) that shape our social and moral development, and *secondary groups* (such as the students in your sociology class) that pursue a specific goal or activity. Members of an *in-group* share a sense of identity and "we-ness," whereas *out-groups* are viewed and treated negatively because they are seen as having values, beliefs, and other characteristics different from those of the in-group. We also have *reference groups* who influence who we are, what we do, and who we'd like to be in the future. Groups often form a *social network*, a web of social ties that links an individual to others (such as members of a local hiking group).

Example: *Secondary Groups Can Replace Primary Groups*

In 1864, an alcoholic who had ruined a promising career on Wall Street because of his constant drunkenness cofounded Alcoholics Anonymous (AA), a program that would enable people to stop drinking by undergoing a spiritual awakening and seeking help from a buddy to stay sober. Initially, AA was a secondary group that tried to beat alcoholism by encouraging its members to attend regular meetings where alcoholics talked about their accomplishments in staying sober. Over the years, however, AA has become a primary group for many members because it offers a relatively small group of people who engage in face-to-face interaction over an extended period, especially when their family and friends have rejected them.

2 Formal Organizations

We depend on a variety of *formal organizations* to provide goods and services in a stable and predictable way. Two of the most widespread and important types of formal organizations in the United States are *voluntary associations* (such as charitable groups) whose members share a common set of interests and are not paid for their participation, and *bureaucracies* (such as your college) that are supposed to accomplish goals and tasks in the most efficient and rational way possible.

3 Sociological Perspectives on Social Groups and Organizations

See Table 6.3 on the next page.

4 Social Institutions

A *social institution* meets a society's basic needs to survive. Functionalists identify five core social institutions—family, economy, political institutions, education, and religion—that are universal and interconnected.

KEY TERMS

social group two or more people who interact with one another, and who share a common identity and a sense of belonging or "we-ness."

primary group a relatively small group of people who engage in intimate face-to-face interaction over an extended period.

secondary group a large, usually formal, impersonal, and temporary collection of people who pursue a specific goal or activity.

ideal types general traits that describe a social phenomenon rather than every case.

in-groups people who share a sense of identity and "we-ness" that typically excludes and devalues outsiders.

out-groups people who are viewed and treated negatively because they are seen as having values, beliefs, and other characteristics different from those of an in-group.

reference group a group of people who shape our behavior, values, and attitudes.

groupthink a tendency of in-group members to conform without critically testing, analyzing, and evaluating ideas, which results in a narrow view of an issue.

social network a web of social ties that links an individual to others.

formal organization a complex and structured secondary group that has been deliberately created to achieve specific goals in an efficient manner.

voluntary association a formal organization created by people who share a common set of interests and who are not paid for their participation.

bureaucracy a formal organization that is designed to accomplish goals and tasks through the efforts of a large number of people in the most efficient and rational way possible.

alienation a feeling of isolation, meaninglessness, and powerlessness that may affect workers in a bureaucracy.

iron law of oligarchy the tendency of a bureaucracy to become increasingly dominated by a small group of people.

glass ceiling attitudes or organizational biases in the workplace that prevent women from advancing to leadership positions.

social institution an organized and established social system that meets one or more of a society's basic needs.

TEST YOUR LEARNING

1. A(n) _____ is a small group of people who engage in frequent and intimate face-to-face interaction.
   a. out-group
   b. reference group
   c. secondary group
   d. primary group

2. _____ conducted experiments that used "teachers" who administered electric shocks to "learners."
   a. Solomon Asch
   b. Stanley Milgram
   c. Philip Zimbardo
   d. Irving Janis

3. Max Weber outlined the characteristics of an efficient and productive bureaucracy. Which of the following was NOT one of those characteristics?
   a. High degree of specialization
   b. Explicit rules and regulations
   c. Qualifications-based employment
   d. Decentralized authority

4. Regarding social groups and organizations, symbolic interactionists maintain that
   a. some people benefit more than others.
   b. cooperation works.
   c. men benefit more than women.
   d. people define and shape their situations.

5. _____ contend that organizations are based on vast differences in power and control.
   a. Functionalists
   b. Conflict theorists
   c. Symbolic interactionists
   d. Exchange theorists

6. **True or False** A high-school football team is a good example of a primary group.

7. **True or False** Groupthink occurs most often when in-group members discuss a diversity of ideas.

8. **True or False** The proper functioning of a bureaucracy might result in an alienation of individual workers.

9. **True or False** The iron law of oligarchy states that bureaucracies have a tendency to become increasingly dominated by a small group of people.

10. **True or False** The glass ceiling refers to organizational barriers, but not attitudes, in the workplace.

1. d 2. b 3. d 4. d 5. b 6. False 7. False 8. True 9. True 10. False

TABLE 6.3
Sociological Perspectives on Groups and Organizations

THEORETICAL PERSPECTIVE	LEVEL OF ANALYSIS	MAIN POINTS	KEY QUESTIONS
Functionalist	Macro	Organizations are made up of interrelated parts and rules and regulations that produce cooperation in meeting a common goal.	• Why are some organizations more effective than others? • How do dysfunctions prevent organizations from being rational and effective?
Conflict	Macro	Organizations promote inequality that benefits elites, not workers.	• Who controls an organization's resources and decision making? • How do those with power protect their interests and privileges?
Feminist	Macro and micro	Organizations tend not to recognize or reward talented women and regularly exclude them from decision-making processes.	• Why do many women hit a glass ceiling? • How do gender stereotypes affect women in groups and organizations?
Symbolic Interactionist	Micro	People aren't puppets but can determine what goes on in a group or organization.	• Why do people ignore or change an organization's rules? • How do members of social groups influence workplace behavior?

CHAPTER 7 TOPICS

1 What Is Deviance?

Deviance, the violation of social norms, is usually punished by a *stigma,* a negative label. Perceptions of deviance vary across and within societies, and can change over time. Those in authority or power decide what's right or wrong.

Example: *Deviance and College Drinking*

According to many college presidents, alcohol abuse is the most serious problem on campus because it results in alcohol poisoning and blackouts, and leads to sexual assault, violent behavior, injuries, and academic problems. Because drinking laws are rarely enforced, some college presidents have proposed that the drinking age be lowered from 21 to 18. Others argue that doing so would increase traffic fatalities and drinking problems. Young people can get a driver's license at 16 and vote and enlist in the military at 18. Should they be the ones, then, to decide whether drinking laws should be changed?

2 What Is Crime?

Crime violates societal norms and rules. *Criminologists* study the nature, extent, cause, and control of criminal behavior. Violent crimes are most likely to be covered by the media, but Americans are much more likely to be victimized by theft or burglary than to be murdered, raped, robbed, or assaulted with a deadly weapon. *Victimless crimes* violate laws, but the parties involved don't consider themselves victims.

3 Controlling Deviance and Crime

The purpose of *social control* is to eliminate, or at least reduce, deviance and crime. Formal social control is administered by those in authority or power. Informal social control is internalized from childhood. Most people conform because of positive and negative *sanctions*.

Table 7.2 on the next page summarizes the approaches for key topics 4 through 7.

8 The Criminal Justice System and Social Control

The *criminal justice system* relies on three major approaches in controlling crime: prevention and intervention, punishment, and rehabilitation. A *crime control model* supports a tough approach toward criminals in sentencing, imprisonment, and capital punishment. In contrast, many people believe that *rehabilitation* can change offenders into productive and law-abiding citizens.

KEY TERMS

deviance behavior or trait that violates expected rules or norms.

stigma a negative label that devalues a person and changes her or his self-concept and social identity.

crime a violation of societal norms and rules for which punishment is specified by public law.

criminologists researchers who use scientific methods to study the nature, extent, cause, and control of criminal behavior.

victimization survey involves interviewing people about their experiences as crime victims.

victimless crimes acts that violate laws but involve individuals who don't consider themselves victims.

social control the techniques and strategies that regulate people's behavior in society.

sanctions punishments or rewards for obeying or violating a norm.

anomie the condition in which people are unsure of how to behave because of absent, conflicting, or confusing social norms.

strain theory the idea that people may engage in deviant behavior when they experience a conflict between goals and the means available to obtain the goals.

white-collar crime illegal activities committed by high-status individuals in the course of their occupation.

occupational crimes crimes committed in the workplace by individuals acting solely in their own personal interest.

corporate crimes white-collar crimes committed by executives to benefit themselves and their companies (also known as *organizational crimes*).

cybercrime white-collar crimes that are conducted online.

organized crime activities of individuals and groups that supply illegal goods and services for profit.

differential association people learn deviance through interaction, especially with significant others.

labeling theory a perspective which holds that society's reaction to behavior is a major factor in defining oneself or others as deviant.

primary deviance the initial violation of a norm or law.

secondary deviance rule-breaking behavior that people adopt in response to the reactions of others.

criminal justice system the government agencies—including the police, courts, and prisons—that are charged with enforcing laws, passing judgment on offenders, and changing criminal behavior.

crime control model an approach that believes that crime rates increase when offenders don't fear apprehension or punishment.

rehabilitation a social control approach that holds that appropriate treatment can change offenders into productive, law-abiding citizens.

TEST YOUR LEARNING

1. Which of the following statements about deviance is incorrect?
    a. Deviance can be a trait or a behavior.
    b. Informal deviance violates laws.
    c. Deviance is usually accompanied by social stigmas.
    d. Deviance varies across situations.

2. Who of the following is most likely to be the victim of a crime?
    a. A black man
    b. A black woman
    c. A white man
    d. A white woman

3. When 3-year-old Kyle colored the kitchen table blue with his new crayons, his mother frowned and scolded him. Kyle's mother used _____ to control his behavior?
    a. punishment
    b. negative sanctions
    c. behavior modification
    d. positive sanctions

4. Merton proposed four deviant modes by which people adapted to social strain. Which of the following was NOT one of Merton's modes?
    a. Innovation
    b. Retreatism
    c. Ritualism
    d. Recidivism

5. What is a fundamental question that a conflict theorist would ask regarding crime?
    a. "Why do some people commit crimes whereas others do not?"
    b. "Why are some acts defined as criminal whereas others are not?"
    c. "Why do men commit more violent crimes than women?"
    d. "How does one's social context impact deviant behavior?"

6. **True or False** Female crime rates have decreased.

7. **True or False** Differential association theory claims that people learn deviant behaviors through interaction with others.

8. **True or False** Labeling theory claims that society's reaction to a behavior is a major factor in defining oneself or others as deviant.

9. **True or False** Capital punishment decreases crime.

10. **True or False** The crime control model stresses that rehabilitation is the best way to decrease the frequency of crime.

1. b 2. a 3. b 4. d 5. b 6. False 7. True 8. True 9. False 10. False

TABLE 7.2
Sociological Explanations of Deviance and Crime

THEORETICAL PERSPECTIVE	KEY POINTS
4. Functionalist	• Anomie increases the likelihood of deviance. • Crime occurs when people experience blocked opportunities to achieve the culturally approved goal of economic success.
5. Conflict	• Laws protect the interests of the few (primarily those in the upper classes) rather than the rights of the many. • Law enforcement is rarely directed at the illegal activities of the powerful.
6. Feminist	• Crimes committed by women reflect their general oppression due to social, economic, and political inequality. • Many women are criminal offenders or victims because of culturally organized beliefs and practices that are sexist and patriarchal.
7. Symbolic Interactionist	• People learn deviant and criminal behavior from others—like parents and friends—who are important in their everyday lives. • If people are labeled or stigmatized as deviant, they are likely to develop deviant self-concepts and engage in criminal behavior.

Social Stratification

CHAPTER 8 TOPICS

1 What Is Social Stratification?

Social stratification is a hierarchical ranking of people who have different access to valued resources. In a *closed stratification system*, movement from one social position to another is very limited. An *open stratification system* allows more movement up or down because people can move from one *social class* to another.

2 Dimensions of Stratification

In explaining stratification, sociologists use a multidimensional approach that includes *wealth, prestige*, and *power*. People are more likely to experience status inconsistency if they rank differently on these three dimensions, such as a football player who has great wealth but little power.

3 Social Class in America

A good indicator of social class is *socioeconomic status (SES)*, an overall rank based on a person's income, education, and occupation. Using SES and other variables (such as values, power, and *conspicuous consumption*), most sociologists agree that there are at least four social classes in the United States: upper, middle, working, and lower. These groups can be divided further into upper-upper, lower-upper, upper-middle, lower-middle, and the working class. The lower class includes the *working poor* and the *underclass*. A major outcome of social stratification is *life chances*.

Example: *Restaurant Menus and Stratification*

Two sociologists—in Iowa and Virginia—asked their students in introductory sociology classes to do a content analysis (see Chapter 1) of 10 menus that represented a cross-sampling of restaurants by social class. The students found that the restaurants that catered to upper-class clientele had higher than average entrée prices, described the entrées in foreign languages, used fancy sauces, recommended expensive wines, and had few illustrations. Middle-class menus emphasized "value for the dollar," presented photos of entrées with "bountiful plates overflowing with appetizing food," and popular items such as quesadillas. Menus at lower-class restaurants featured low prices ($3 to $10 entrées), the items were numbered, none of the entrées had "pretentious names," and the typesetting was simple (Wright and Ransom 2005). In effect, then, even menus denote social class and social status.

4 Poverty in America

Absolute poverty is a serious social problem compared with *relative poverty* because millions of Americans live below the *poverty line*. Explanations for poverty vary, but two perspectives propose that individual characteristics lead to poverty or that a society's organization creates and sustains poverty.

5 Social Mobility

Social mobility can be *horizontal, vertical, intragenerational*, or *intergenerational*. Structural, demographic, and individual factors affect a person's social mobility.

6 Why There Are Haves and Have-nots

7 Inequality Across Societies

Global inequality is widespread, but some societies are much wealthier than others. Sociologists use *modernization theory, dependency theory*, and *world-system theory* to explain why inequality is universal.

KEY TERMS

social stratification the hierarchical ranking of people in a society who have different access to valued resources, such as property, prestige, power, and status.

open stratification system a system that is based on individual achievement and allows movement up or down.

closed stratification system a system in which movement from one social position to another is limited by ascribed statuses such as one's sex, skin color, and family background.

social class a category of people who have a similar standing or rank in a society based on wealth, education, power, prestige, and other valued resources.

wealth the money and other economic assets that a person or family owns, including property and income.

prestige respect, recognition, or regard attached to social positions.

power the ability of individuals or groups to achieve goals, control events, and maintain influence over others despite opposition.

socioeconomic status (SES) an overall ranking of a person's position in the class hierarchy based on income, education, and occupation.

conspicuous consumption lavish spending on goods and services to display one's social status and to enhance one's prestige.

working poor people who work at least 27 weeks a year but receive such low wages that they live in or near poverty.

underclass people who are persistently poor and seldom employed, segregated residentially, and relatively isolated from the rest of the population.

life chances the extent to which people have positive experiences and can secure the good things in life because they have economic resources.

absolute poverty not having enough money to afford the most basic necessities of life.

relative poverty not having enough money to maintain an average standard of living.

poverty line the minimal level of income that the federal government considers necessary for basic subsistence.

feminization of poverty the higher likelihood that female heads of households will be poor.

social mobility a person's movement up or down the class hierarchy.

horizontal mobility moving from one position to another at the same class level.

vertical mobility moving up or down the class hierarchy.

intragenerational mobility moving up or down the class hierarchy over one's lifetime.

intergenerational mobility moving up or down the class hierarchy relative to the position of one's parents.

KEY TERMS

Davis–Moore thesis the functionalist view that social stratification benefits a society.

meritocracy a belief that individuals are rewarded for what they do and how well rather than on the basis of their ascribed status.

bourgeoisie those who own the means of production and can amass wealth and power.

proletariat workers who sell their labor for wages.

corporate welfare an array of direct subsidies, tax breaks, and assistance that the government has created for businesses.

TEST YOUR LEARNING

1. Slavery and castes are _____ systems.
   a. capitalist
   b. open stratification
   c. closed stratification
   d. socialist

2. A person's socioeconomic status (SES) is based on
   a. income, education, and occupation.
   b. wealth, prestige, and power.
   c. wealth, prestige, and lifestyle.
   d. education, income, and age.

3. The economic gap between the wealthy and the poor
   a. fluctuates from year to year.
   b. is about the same as during the 1990s.
   c. is decreasing.
   d. is increasing.

4. Which of the following is NOT a major structural factor in social mobility?
   a. Changes in the economy
   b. Immigration patterns
   c. Consumer confidence
   d. Number of available positions in given occupations

5. _____ claim that social stratification ultimately benefits society.
   a. Functionalists
   b. Conflict theorists
   c. Feminist theorists
   d. Symbolic interactionists

6. **True or False** One of the criticisms of conflict theory is that it ignores structural factors in explaining stratification.

7. **True or False** Conspicuous consumption displays one's social status and enhances one's prestige.

8. **True or False** Intergenerational mobility refers to moving up or down the class hierarchy over one's lifetime.

9. **True or False** The Davis–Moore thesis is a symbolic interactionist perspective.

10. **True or False** According to world systems theory, equality exists throughout the world because the global economic system helps richer countries stay rich while poorer countries remain poor.

1. c 2. a 3. d 4. c 5. a 6. False 7. True 8. False 9. False 10. True

For full table, see Table 8.2 on page 150.

TABLE 8.2
Sociological Explanations of Social Stratification

PERSPECTIVE	KEY POINTS
Functionalist	• Fills social positions that are necessary for a society's survival • Motivates people to succeed and ensures that the most qualified people will fill the most important positions
Conflict	• Encourages workers' exploitation and promotes the interests of the rich and powerful • Ignores a wealth of talent among the poor
Feminist	• Constructs numerous barriers in patriarchal societies that limit women's achieving wealth, status, and prestige • Requires most women, not men, to juggle domestic and employment responsibilities that impede upward mobility
Symbolic Interactionist	• Shapes stratification through socialization, everyday interaction, and group membership • Reflects social class identification through symbols, especially products that signify social status

Self-Assessment Exam

Take the quiz on this card to test your knowledge of the concepts from Chapters 1–8

1. _____ looks at the relationship between individual characteristics; _____ examines the relationships between institutional characteristics.
   a. Microsociology; macrosociology
   b. Macrosociology; microsociology
   c. Metasociology; macrosociology
   d. Metasociology; microsociology

2. Many people buy designer clothes that they can't afford. The clothes are an example of a status symbol that reflects a
   a. latent function.
   b. manifest function.
   c. dysfunction.
   d. social system.

3. Jeremy views society as a system of interrelated parts, but Tom sees society as composed of groups competing for scarce resources. Jeremy would be considered a _____ theorist, and Tom would be seen as a _____ theorist.
   a. symbolic interactionist; functionalist
   b. conflict; functionalist
   c. functionalist; symbolic interactionist
   d. functionalist; conflict

4. **True or False.** Émile Durkheim saw sociology as the scientific study of two aspects of society: social statics and social dynamics.

5. **True or False.** Jane Addams was an early sociologist who published extensively on topics such as social disorganization, immigration, and urban neighborhoods.

6. **True or False.** In the definition of sociology, "systematic" means behavior that is built into the larger social structure of society.

7. **True or False.** Much of contemporary functionalism grew out of the work of Auguste Comte and Émile Durkheim.

8. Sociological research is important in our daily lives for a number of reasons. Which of the following is NOT one of those reasons?
   a. It exposes myths.
   b. It challenges the findings of psychology researchers.
   c. It affects social policy.
   d. It sharpens our critical thinking skills.

9. What is a hypothesis?
   a. A theory based on one's opinions.
   b. A measure of how accurate a study is.
   c. A statement of a relationship between two or more variables.
   d. An analysis of multiple studies that researchers use to make generalizations.

10. Alexandra notices that she tends to perform best on tests that are given in the afternoon. She then begins to collect data of her test performances and asks close friends and classmates to do the same. In trying to understand whether test scores and test times are related, Alexandra is using
    a. intuition.
    b. inferences.
    c. deductive reasoning.
    d. inductive reasoning.

11. **True or False.** If researchers use a nonprobability sample, they can generalize the results to a larger population.

12. **True or False.** Correlation equals causation.

13. **True or False.** Validity is the consistency that a measure produces similar results over time; reliability is the degree to which the measure is accurate and really measures what it claims to measure.

14. At a party, George was eating nachos and salsa. He took a bite of his chip and then dipped what was left of his chip back into the large bowl of salsa. His friend Brett gave him a disgusted look. Which of the following did George break?
    a. A more
    b. A cultural universal
    c. A folkway
    d. A law

15. Anaz is an 8-year-old Iranian girl who loves the female fashions she sees in American films and television shows. Lately she's been questioning why her mother wears a burka. Anaz's questioning of her family's traditions could best be explained by
    a. cultural relativism.
    b. multiculturalism.
    c. cultural imperialism.
    d. ethnocentrism.

16. Which of the following is an example of a subculture?
    a. A group of adolescent Goths
    b. Roman Catholics
    c. A 40-and-over woman's bridge club
    d. All of the above

17. **True or False.** Language helps communicate ideas, but it's not considered a symbol.

18. **True or False.** In most societies, the real culture matches the ideal culture.

19. **True or False.** The legal controversy over file sharing and downloading music off the Web is an example of cultural lag.

20. Emma learned from her mother that girls can do anything that boys can do in getting a good education. This is an example of the _____ process.
    a. multicultural
    b. ethnocentric
    c. socialization
    d. hereditary

21. "Human development is fairly fixed." This statement is an example of which side of the nature-nurture debate?
    a. Nature side of the debate
    b. Nurture side of the debate
    c. Neither the nature nor nurture side of the debate
    d. Both the nature and nurture side of the debate

22. What are the three stages of Mead's role-taking theory?
    a. Prework stage, work stage, postwork stage
    b. Anal stage, phallic stage, postphallic stage
    c. Mirror stage, active stage, passive stage
    d. Preparatory stage, play stage, game stage

23. **True or False.** Institutionalization is the process of learning cultural behaviors and expectations so deeply that we assume they are correct and accept them without question.

24. **True or False.** Charles Horton Cooley proposed that the looking-glass self develops in five phases.

25. **True or False.** According to Erving Goffman, social life mirrors theatrical performance.

26. Jake has a full-time course load while also working 30 hours a week. Given the demands of both work and school, Jake might be likely to experience
   a. role set.
   b. role strain.
   c. role conflict.
   d. role exchange.

27. Gestures, eye contact, and silence are all examples of
   a. emotional language.
   b. punishment.
   c. healthy relationship interaction.
   d. nonverbal communication.

28. A disadvantage of telecommuting is that that it
   a. pays less than working on site at the office.
   b. blurs the line between home life and work.
   c. is more available to men than women.
   d. all of the above are disadvantages of telecommuting

29. According to _____, social interaction is based on trying to maximize rewards for oneself while minimizing costs.
   a. ethnomethodology theory
   b. feminist theory
   c. conflict theory
   d. social exchange theory

30. True or False. If we define something as real and act on it, it can, in fact, become real. This is known as the self-fulfilling prophecy.

31. True or False. Being an African American college student is an example of having two ascribed statuses.

32. A(n) _____ is a small group of people who engage in frequent and intimate face-to-face interaction.
   a. out-group
   b. reference group
   c. secondary group
   d. primary group

33. _____ conducted experiments that used "teachers" who administered electric shocks to "learners."
   a. Solomon Asch
   b. Stanley Milgram
   c. Philip Zimbardo
   d. Irving Janis

34. Max Weber outlined the characteristics of an efficient and productive bureaucracy. Which of the following was NOT one of those characteristics?
   a. High degree of specialization
   b. Explicit rules and regulations
   c. Qualifications-based employment
   d. Decentralized authority

35. True or False. A high-school football team is a good example of a primary group.

36. True or False. Groupthink occurs most often when there is a diversified collection of ideas discussed among the in-group members.

37. True or False. The iron law of oligarchy states that bureaucracies have a tendency to become increasingly dominated by a small group of people.

38. True or False. The glass ceiling refers to organizational barriers, but not attitudes, in the workplace.

39. Who of the following is most likely to be the victim of a crime?
   a. A black man
   b. A black woman
   c. A white man
   d. A white woman

40. When 3-year-old Kyle colored the kitchen table blue with his new crayons, his mother frowned and scolded him. Kyle's mother used _____ to control his behavior?
   a. punishment
   b. negative sanctions
   c. behavior modification
   d. positive sanctions

41. Merton proposed four deviant modes by which people adapted to social strain. Which of the following was NOT one of Merton's modes?
   a. Innovation
   b. Retreatism
   c. Ritualism
   d. Recidivism

42. What is a fundamental question that a conflict theorist would ask with regard to crime?
   a. "Why do some people commit crimes whereas others do not?"
   b. "Why are some acts defined as criminal whereas others are not?"
   c. "Why do men commit more violent crimes than women?"
   d. "How does one's social context impact deviant behavior?"

43. True or False. Labeling theory claims that society's reaction to a behavior is a major factor in defining oneself or others as deviant.

44. True or False. The crime control model stresses that rehabilitation is the best way to decrease the frequency of crime.

45. Which of the following is NOT a major structural factor in social mobility?
   a. Changes in the economy
   b. Immigration patterns
   c. Consumer confidence
   d. Number of available positions in given occupations

46. Slavery and castes are _____ systems.
   a. capitalist
   b. open stratification
   c. closed stratification
   d. socialist

47. True or False. One of the criticisms of conflict theory is that it ignores structural factors in explaining stratification.

48. True or False. Conspicuous consumption displays one's social status and enhances one's prestige.

49. True or False. Intergenerational mobility refers to moving up or down the class hierarchy over one's lifetime.

50. True or False. The Davis–Moore thesis is a symbolic interactionist perspective.

Gender and Sexuality

CHAPTER 9 TOPICS

1 Female-Male Similarities and Differences

Sex refers to biological characteristics, whereas *gender* refers to learned attitudes and behaviors. *Gender identity* and *gender roles* differ depending on whether people perceive themselves as masculine or feminine, and because a society expects women and men to think and behave differently. Many Americans still have *gender stereotypes* about how people will look, act, think, and feel.

2 Contemporary Gender Stratification and Inequality

Sexism is widespread because of *gender stratification,* which can lead to inequality in the family, education, the workplace (as in the case of a *gender pay gap*), and politics. *Sexual harassment* and *pregnancy discrimination* are also common in the workplace.

3 Sexuality and Human Development

Our sexual identity incorporates a *sexual orientation* that can be *homosexual, heterosexual, bisexual,* or *asexual. Transgendered* people include those living on the boundaries of the sexes. Many biological theories maintain that sexual orientation has a strong genetic basis, but social constructionists argue that culture, not biology, plays a large role in forming sexual identity.

4 Some Current Controversies about Sexuality

Abortion is controversial because almost equal percentages of Americans support or condemn the practice. Those who favor same-sex marriage argue that people should have the same legal rights regardless of sexual orientation; those who oppose same-sex marriage contend that such unions are immoral and contrary to religious beliefs. Some people view *pornography* as erotic recreation, whereas others denounce it as obscene and as debasing women.

5 Sociological Explanations of Gender Inequality and Sexuality

See Table 9.4 on the next page.

Example: *Gender Roles and Hooking Up—Are Women the Losers?*

Hooking up refers to physical encounters, no strings attached, and can mean anything from kissing and genital fondling to oral sex and sexual intercourse. At many high schools, hooking up is more common than dating. At some college campuses, 76 percent of the students have hooked up 5 times, on average, and 28 percent have had 10 or more such encounters (England et al. 2007). Hooking up has its advantages. It's much cheaper than dating. Also, it's assumed that hooking up requires no commitment of time or emotion. In addition, hookups remove the stigma from those who can't get dates but can experience sexual pleasure, and they make people feel sexy and desirable (Bogle 2008). Hooking up also has disadvantages, especially for women, because women who hook up generally get a bad reputation as being "easy" (England and Thomas 2009). In effect, then, and despite the advantages of hooking up, the sexual double standard persists.

KEY TERMS

sex the biological characteristics with which we are born.

gender learned attitudes and behaviors that characterize women and men.

gender identity a perception of oneself as either masculine or feminine.

gender roles the characteristics, attitudes, feelings, and behaviors that society expects of females and males.

gender stereotypes expectations about how people will look, act, think, and feel based on their sex.

sexism an attitude or behavior that discriminates against one sex, usually females, based on the assumed superiority of the other sex.

gender stratification people's unequal access to wealth, power, status, prestige, and other valued resources because of their sex.

gender pay gap the overall income difference between women and men in the workplace (also called the *wage gap, pay gap,* and *gender wage gap*).

sexual harassment any unwanted sexual advance, request for sexual favors, or other conduct of a sexual nature that makes a person uncomfortable and interferes with her or his work.

sexual identity our awareness of ourselves as male or female and the ways that we express our sexual values, attitudes, feelings, and beliefs.

sexual orientation a preference for sexual partners of the same sex, of the opposite sex, of both sexes, or neither sex.

homosexuals those who are sexually attracted to people of the same sex.

heterosexuals those who are sexually attracted to people of the opposite sex.

bisexuals those who are sexually attracted to members of both sexes.

asexuals those who lack any interest in or desire for sex.

transgendered people those who are transsexuals, intersexuals, or transvestites.

sexual script specifies the formal or informal norms for legitimate or unacceptable sexual activity, which individuals are eligible sexual partners, and the boundaries of sexual behavior.

heterosexism the belief that heterosexuality is superior to and more natural than homosexuality or bisexuality.

homophobia the fear and hatred of homosexuality.

abortion the expulsion of an embryo or fetus from the uterus.

pornography the graphic depiction of images that cause sexual arousal.

TEST YOUR LEARNING

1. _____ refers to learned attitudes and behaviors, whereas _____ refers to biological characteristics with which we are born.
   a. Sex; gender
   b. Gender; sex
   c. Sex; gender roles
   d. Sexual identity; gender stereotypes

2. Generally, the gender pay gap increases as the level of educational attainment
   a. increases.
   b. decreases.
   c. neither of the above because it depends on how hard a person works
   d. neither a nor b because such data are not available

3. Sean, age 16, lies to his friends about the frequency of his sexual activity and new sexual exploits every week. Sean is
   a. being a normal male.
   b. adhering to a sexual script.
   c. falling into a pathologic life course.
   d. challenging gender norms.

4. _____ is the belief that heterosexuality is superior to and more natural than homosexuality or bisexuality.
   a. Heterobiology
   b. Homosexism
   c. Heterosexism
   d. Bisexism

5. _____ posit that gender inequality and sexuality are socially constructed.
   a. Functionalists
   b. Conflict theorists
   c. Feminist theorists
   d. Symbolic interactionists

6. **True or False** Sexism can only be enacted by men against women.

7. **True or False** Sexual harassment is the fastest growing type of employment discrimination.

8. **True or False** U.S. abortion rates have been increasing.

9. **True or False** A majority of Americans support same-sex marriage.

10. **True or False** Conflict theorists believe that capitalism increases gender inequality.

1. b 2. a 3. b 4. c 5. d 6. False 7. True 8. False 9. False 10. True

---

TABLE 9.4
Sociological Explanations of Gender Inequality and Sexuality

THEORETICAL PERSPECTIVE	KEY POINTS
Functionalist	• Gender roles are complementary and equally important. • Agreed-on sexual norms contribute to a society's order and stability.
Conflict	• Gender roles give men power to control women's lives instead of allowing the sexes to be complementary and equally important. • Most societies regulate women's, not men's, sexual behavior.
Feminist	• Women's inequality reflects their historical and current domination by men, especially in the workplace. • Many men use violence—including sexual harassment, rape, and global sex trafficking—to control women's sexuality.
Symbolic Interactionist	• Gender inequality is a social construction that emerges through day-to-day interactions and reflects people's gender role expectations. • The social construction of sexuality varies across cultures because of societal norms and values.

Race and Ethnicity

CHAPTER 10 TOPICS

1 Racial and Ethnic Diversity in America

Perhaps the most multicultural country in the world, the United States includes about 150 distinct ethnic or racial groups among more than 309 million inhabitants. By 2025, only 58 percent of the U.S. population will be white—down from 86 percent in 1950.

2 The Social Significance of Race and Ethnicity

Race refers to physical characteristics, whereas an *ethnic group* identifies with a common national origin or cultural heritage. A *racial-ethnic group* has both distinctive physical and cultural characteristics.

3 Our Changing Immigration Mosaic

In 1900, almost 85 percent of immigrants came from Europe; now immigrants come primarily from Asia and Latin America. Many Americans are ambivalent about immigrants, especially those who are in the country illegally, but most scholars argue that, in the long run, both legal and undocumented immigrants bring more benefits than costs.

4 Dominant and Minority Groups

A *dominant group* has the most economic and political power and the greatest privileges. A *minority*, which may be larger in number than a dominant group, may be subject to differential and unequal treatment because of its physical, cultural, or other characteristics, such as sexual orientation or religion. The pattern of dominant-minority group relations includes *genocide, internal colonialism, segregation, assimilation,* and *pluralism.*

5 Sources of Racial-Ethnic Friction

Racism justifies and preserves the social, economic, and political interests of dominant groups. *Prejudice* is an attitude; *discrimination* is an act that occurs at both the individual and institutional level. All of us can be prejudiced, but minorities are typically targets of *stereotypes* and *ethnocentrism* that often lead to *scapegoating.*

6 Major Racial and Ethnic Groups in the United States

European Americans, who settled the first colonies, are declining in population, whereas Latinos now comprise 15 percent of the population. Other large racial and ethnic populations are African Americans (13 percent), Asian Americans (5 percent), and American Indians (less than 2 percent). Middle Eastern Americans, who comprise less than 0.05 percent of the population, come from more than 30 countries. All of these groups have experienced prejudice and discrimination, but they have enhanced U.S. society and culture.

Example: *Stuff White People Like*

The popular blog *Stuff White People Like* has generated clones (e.g., *Stuff Educated Black People Like* and *Stuff Asian People Like*). Why are these sites so popular? Many fans say that the descriptions are funny because they're true. According to some critics, however, by poking fun at privileged upper-middle-class people, the sites fuel stereotypes instead of having painfully frank discussions about U.S. race and racism. In addition, sites such as *Stuff White People Like* allow readers to feel superior because the entries don't reflect their own lifestyles or because it's comforting to recognize oneself as a member of a comfortable middle class (Jones 2008; Sternbergh 2008). Do you agree?

7 Sociological Explanations of Racial-Ethnic Inequality

8 Interracial and Interethnic Relationships

Almost 99 percent of Americans report being only one race, but the numbers of biracial children are increasing because of interracial dating and marriage. The rise of racial-ethnic intermarriage reflects many micro and macro factors that include greater acceptance of integration, and interethnic and interracial contact.

KEY TERMS

race a group of people who share physical characteristics, such as skin color and facial features, that are passed on through reproduction.

ethnic group a group of people who identify with a common national origin or cultural heritage that includes language, geographic roots, food, customs, traditions, and/or religion.

racial-ethnic group a group of people who have both distinctive physical and cultural characteristics.

dominant group any physically or culturally distinctive group that has the most economic and political power, the greatest privileges, and the highest social status.

apartheid a formal system of racial segregation.

minority a group of people who may be subject to differential and unequal treatment because of their physical, cultural, or other characteristics, such as gender, sexual orientation, religion, ethnicity, or skin color.

genocide the systematic effort to kill all members of a particular ethnic, religious, political, racial, or national group.

internal colonialism the unequal treatment and subordinate status of groups within a country.

segregation the physical and social separation of dominant and minority groups.

assimilation the process of conforming to the culture of the dominant group (by adopting its language and values) and intermarrying with that group.

pluralism minority groups retain their culture but have equal social standing in a society.

racism a set of beliefs that one's own racial group is naturally superior to other groups.

prejudice an attitude, positive or negative, toward people because of their group membership.

KEY TERMS

stereotype an oversimplified or exaggerated generalization about a category of people.

ethnocentrism the belief that one's own culture, society, or group is inherently superior to others.

scapegoats individuals or groups whom people blame for their own problems or shortcomings.

discrimination any act that treats people unequally or unfairly because of their group membership.

individual discrimination harmful action directed intentionally, on a one-to-one basis, by a member of a dominant group against a member of a minority group.

institutional discrimination unequal treatment and opportunities that members of minority groups experience as a result of the everyday operations of a society's laws, rules, policies, practices, and customs.

gendered racism the combined and cumulative effects of inequality due to racism and sexism.

contact hypothesis the idea that the more people get to know members of a minority group personally, the less likely they are to be prejudiced against that group.

miscegenation marriage or sexual relations between a man and a woman of different races.

TEST YOUR LEARNING

1. What is the difference between race and ethnicity?
   a. Race is a negative term that refers to difference; ethnicity is the politically correct term that refers to difference.
   b. Race refers to the physical characteristics of a group of people; ethnicity refers to the cultural heritage of a people.
   c. Race refers to people around the world; ethnicity refers only to a group of people within a specific nation.
   d. There is no difference between race and ethnicity; the terms are synonymous.

2. Today most immigrants to the United States come from which of the following countries?
   a. China and Mexico
   b. Mexico and Canada
   c. England and Canada
   d. Japan and Russia

3. _____ is the unequal treatment and subordinate status of groups within a country.
   a. Hegemony
   b. Internal colonialism
   c. Genocide
   d. Assimilation

4. Tyrone and Jeanette were up for the same job, which Jeanette ultimately won. Tyrone told his friends that he didn't get the job not because Jeanette was more qualified but because "women always get hired first now." This is an example of
   a. scapegoating.
   b. pluralism.
   c. stereotyping.
   d. prejudice.

5. Laws against miscegenation were overturned nationally in
   a. 1807.
   b. 1867.
   c. 1907.
   d. 1967.

6. **True or False** On the continuum of dominant versus minority group relations, genocide reflects the least tolerance, whereas pluralism illustrates the greatest tolerance.

7. **True or False** Ethnocentrism is the belief that one's own racial group is naturally inferior to others.

8. **True or False** The fastest growing ethnic minority in the United States is Asian Americans.

9. **True or False** American Indians are on the verge of vanishing from the American landscape.

10. **True or False** The lower the educational level, the greater the likelihood that a person will have an interracial marriage.

1. b 2. a 3. b 4. a 5. d 6. True 7. False 8. False 9. False 10. False

TABLE 10.3
Sociological Explanations of Racial-Ethnic Inequality

THEORETICAL PERSPECTIVE	KEY POINTS
Functionalist	• Prejudice and discrimination can be dysfunctional, but they provide benefits for dominant groups and stabilize society.
Conflict	• Powerful groups maintain their advantages and perpetuate racial-ethnic inequality primarily through economic exploitation.
Feminist	• Minority women suffer from the combined effects of racism and sexism.
Symbolic Interactionist	• Hostile attitudes toward minorities, which are learned, can be reduced through cooperative interracial and interethnic contacts.

Government and Politics

CHAPTER 11 TOPICS

1 Government

A *government* maintains order, provides welfare services, regulates the economy, and establishes educational systems. The U.S. government, like many other democracies, is also affected by a civic society, the media, lobbyists, and voters.

2 Politics, Power, and Authority

Politics includes *power* and *authority*. Authority can be based on tradition, charisma, rational-legal power, or a combination of these sources.

Example: *Rational-Legal Authority*

In societies based on rational-legal authority, people obey the rules even when they disagree. Americans don't revolt, for instance, if candidates they support lose an election. Nor do they question the authority of police, social workers, judges, and other state employees even if they dislike them. On the other hand, leaders who violate laws can lose their authority and office. For example, President Richard Nixon was forced to resign during the 1970s when it became apparent that he had approved a break-in at the Democratic Party's National Committee offices in Washington, D.C.

3 Types of Political Systems

In a *democracy*, citizens, ideally, have a high degree of control over the state because they can elect leaders, and the government recognizes individual rights, such as freedom of speech, press, and assembly. *Totalitarianism* is a political system in which the government controls people's lives, and one person, a dictator, stays in office indefinitely. *Authoritarianism* is a political system in which the state controls the lives of its citizens but generally permits some degree of individual freedom. A *monarchy* is the oldest type of authoritarian regime.

4 Power and Politics in U.S. Society

A *political party* tries to influence and control government by recruiting, nominating, and electing its members to public office. Unlike the two-party system in the United States, many democratic countries around the world have numerous parties. A *special-interest group* attempts to influence policy makers on a particular issue. Some of the most influential special-interest groups include *lobbyists*, wealthy campaign contributors, and *political action committees (PACs)*.

Example: *How Corporations Influence Politics*

In 2008, corporations spent at least $112 million on the Democratic and Republican conventions. Some of the largest included reduced-fare tickets by United Airlines; use of "plush new vehicles" by General Motors; state-of-the-art technology underwritten by Microsoft, Google, AT&T, and other companies; and corporate-funded events for convention members. Donors who contributed $250,000 or more enjoyed private meetings with top government officials (Campaign Finance Institute 2008). A major benefit is that the biggest donors, regardless of who wins an election, have greater access to elected officials than does the average citizen.

5 Who Votes, Who Doesn't, and Why

Typically, only about half of eligible Americans vote in national elections, and only 25 percent vote in local elections. The voting rate is much greater among older than younger people; married people than those who are divorced, never married, or widowed; those with at least a college degree; people with higher incomes; and white Americans than racial-ethnic groups. Religion often affects who votes and for whom. Situational and structural factors, such as convenience, can also encourage or discourage voting.

6 Who Rules America?

Please see Table 11.5 on the next page.

KEY TERMS

government a formal organization that has the authority to make and enforce laws.

politics a social process through which individuals and groups acquire and exercise power and authority.

power the ability of a person or group to affect the behavior of others despite resistance and opposition.

authority the legitimate use of power.

traditional authority power based on customs that justify the position of the ruler.

charismatic authority power based on exceptional individual abilities and characteristics that inspire devotion, trust, and obedience.

rational-legal authority power based on the belief that laws and appointed or elected political leaders are legitimate.

democracy a political system in which, ideally, citizens have control over the state and its actions.

totalitarianism a political system in which the government controls every aspect of people's lives.

authoritarianism a political system in which the state controls the lives of citizens but generally permits some degree of individual freedom.

monarchy a political system in which power is allocated solely on the basis of heredity and passes from generation to generation.

political party an organization that tries to influence and control government by recruiting, nominating, and electing its members to public office.

special-interest group (sometimes called an *interest group*) a voluntary and organized association of people that attempts to influence public policy and policy makers on a particular issue.

lobbyist a representative of a special-interest group who tries to influence political decisions on the group's behalf.

political action committee (PAC) a special-interest group that raises money to elect a candidate to public office.

pluralism a political system in which power is distributed among a variety of competing groups in a society.

power elite a small group of influential people who make the nation's major political decisions.

TEST YOUR LEARNING

1. According to Max Weber, which one of the following types of authority is most characteristic of the majority of U.S. presidents?
   a. Charismatic
   b. Absolute
   c. Traditional
   d. Rational-legal

2. _____ is a political system in which the state controls the lives of citizens but generally permits some degree of freedom.
   a. Democracy
   b. Totalitarianism
   c. Dictatorship
   d. Authoritarianism

3. What is typically the most important factor in winning elections in the United States?
   a. Money
   b. Public sentiment
   c. Political platform
   d. Charisma

4. Voter turnout is greater in many countries than in the United States. Which of the following does NOT explain why this is the case?
   a. Some countries impose fines for not voting.
   b. Citizens of other countries are more patriotic.
   c. Elections in other countries are often conducted on weekends.
   d. Other countries believe that voting is a responsibility.

5. _____ claim that the U.S. political structure is patriarchal.
   a. Functionalists
   b. Conflict theorists
   c. Feminist theorists
   d. Symbolic interactionists

6. **True or False** According to the pluralism model, a small group of influential people make the major political decisions in the United States.

7. **True or False** In the United States, most Republicans believe that the federal government should provide social programs for its citizens.

8. **True or False** Firefighters, farmers, and environmentalists are examples of special-interest groups.

9. **True or False** Married people are more likely to vote than people who are not married.

10. **True or False** Some of the best-paid lobbyists are retired corporate executives (CEOs).

1. d 2. d 3. a 4. b 5. c 6. False 7. False 8. True 9. True 10. False

TABLE 11.5
Sociological Explanations of Political Power

	FUNCTIONALISM: A PLURALIST MODEL	CONFLICT THEORY: A POWER ELITE MODEL	FEMINIST THEORIES: A PATRIARCHAL MODEL
Who has political power?	The people	Rich upper-class people—especially those at top levels in business, government, and the military	White men in Western countries; most men in traditional societies
What is the source of political power?	Citizens' participation	Wealthy people in government, business corporations, the military, and the media	Being white, male, and very rich
Does one group dominate politics?	No	Yes	Yes
Do political leaders represent the average person?	Yes, the leaders speak for a majority of the people.	No, the leaders are most concerned with keeping or increasing their personal wealth and power.	No, the leaders—who are typically white, elite men—are most concerned with protecting or increasing their personal wealth and power.

Work and the Economy

CHAPTER 12 TOPICS

1 Social Significance of Work

The *economy* determines how a society produces, distributes, and consumes goods and services. *Work* provides a sense of stability, accomplishment, and social identity, but is also a major source of stress.

2 Global Economic Systems

Capitalism frequently spawns *monopolies* and *oligopolies*, which dominate the market and discourage competition. Ideally, *socialism* emphasizes cooperation, a collective ownership of property, and forbids private profits; in reality, there is considerable economic inequality. The late twentieth century experienced *globalization*, which has affected political systems, culture, and other aspects of life.

3 Corporations and Capitalism

A *corporation*, usually created for profit, often forms *conglomerates*, giant corporations that own a collection of companies in different industries. Both corporations and conglomerates are governed by *interlocking directorates*, in which the same people serve on the boards of directors. Interlocking directorates have become more powerful than ever because of the growth of *transnational corporations* and *transnational conglomerates*, both of which own and operate a variety of companies in a number of countries.

Example: *Runaway CEO Pay*

U.S. CEOs, even during hard economic times, enjoy huge pay packages. In 2007, the average CEO pay was almost $11 million, 344 times the pay of the typical American worker. The top 50 private fund managers averaged $588 million each, more than 19,000 times as much as typical U.S. workers earned (Anderson et al. 2008b). Management consultant Peter Drucker has proposed that top CEOs shouldn't get more than 20 times the average salary in the company, but some Americans see such proposals as "nothing but Communist rhetoric" (Wartzman 2008). In 2008, after the federal government's $100 billion bailout of a number of corporations with taxpayer money, the new legislation for executive pay did not set any monetary limits on the pay of top executives at bailed out companies (Anderson et al. 2008a).

4 Work in U.S. Society Today

Many American workers have been casualties of *deindustrialization,* especially in manufacturing. Others have lost their jobs to *offshoring.* Because globalization, deindustrialization, and offshoring have decreased job security, many Americans have had to take low-wage jobs and work shifts. Widespread *downsizing* has created a large pool of *contingent workers* who can find only temporary jobs and part-time work. In addition, millions of Americans are *underemployed* because their jobs are below their experience and education level.

5 Sociological Explanations of Work and the Economy

Please see Table 12.3 on the next page.

KEY TERMS

economy a social institution that determines how a society produces, distributes, and consumes goods and services.

work physical or mental activity that accomplishes or produces something, either goods or services.

capitalism an economic system in which wealth is in private hands, and is invested and reinvested to produce profits.

monopoly domination of a particular market or industry by one person or company.

oligopoly a market dominated by a few large producers or suppliers.

socialism an economic and political system based on the principle of the public ownership of the production of goods and services.

communism a political and economic system in which all members of a society are equal.

globalization the growth and spread of investment, trade, production, communication, and new technology around the world.

corporation a social entity that has legal rights, privileges, and liabilities apart from those of its members.

conglomerate a giant corporation that owns a collection of companies in different industries.

interlocking directorate a situation in which the same people serve on the boards of directors of several companies or corporations.

transnational corporation (sometimes called a *multinational corporation* or an *international corporation*) a large company that is based in one country but operates across international boundaries.

transnational conglomerate a corporation that owns a collection of different companies in various industries in a number of countries.

deindustrialization a process of social and economic change due to the reduction of industrial activity, especially manufacturing.

offshoring sending work or jobs to another country to cut a company's costs at home.

contingent workers (sometimes called *temporary workers*) people who don't expect their jobs to last or who say that their jobs are temporary.

downsizing a euphemism for firing large numbers of employees at once.

discouraged workers unemployed people who want a job and have looked for work in the preceding year but have not searched in the past four weeks because they have given up.

underemployed people who have part-time jobs but want full-time work or whose jobs are below their experience and education level.

TEST YOUR LEARNING

1. _____ is a physical or mental activity that accomplishes or produces something, either goods or services.
   a. Economy
   b. Industry
   c. Labor
   d. Work

2. _____ is a market system dominated by a few large producers or suppliers.
   a. Capitalism
   b. Monopoly
   c. Oligopoly
   d. Socialism

3. Socialism is characterized by all of the following *except*
   a. cooperation.
   b. investment.
   c. collective ownership of property.
   d. collective goals.

4. Felipe serves on the board of directors of several different companies. He is part of
   a. an interlocking directorate.
   b. a transnational corporation.
   c. a conglomerate.
   d. a monopoly.

5. The dramatic surge in women's employment since the 1970s can be attributed to many factors. Which of the following is NOT one of those factors?
   a. The falling wages of men
   b. Women's increased education
   c. Rising cost of home ownership
   d. Decrease in sexism

6. *True or False* Compared with low-wage U.S. jobs, high-wage jobs are relatively safe from offshoring.

7. *True or False* Deindustrialization has spread because of globalization.

8. *True or False* U.S. unionization rates have been gradually increasing since 1980.

9. *True or False* A common criticism of functionalist explanations of work and the economy is that functionalists overlook macro-level variables.

10. *True or False* Sayid got laid off from his job two months ago and has given up looking for work. Sayid is what is known as a discouraged worker.

1. d 2. c 3. b 4. a 5. d 6. False 7. True 8. False 9. False 10. True

TABLE 12.3
Sociological Explanations of Work and the Economy

THEORETICAL PERSPECTIVE	KEY POINTS
Functionalist	Capitalism benefits society; work provides an income, structures people's lives, and gives them a sense of accomplishment.
Conflict	Capitalism enables the rich to exploit other groups; most jobs pay little and are monotonous and alienating, creating anger and resentment.
Feminist	Gender roles structure women's and men's work experiences differently and inequitably.
Symbolic Interactionist	How people define and experience work in their everyday lives affects their workplace behavior and relationships with co-workers and employers.

Families and Aging

CHAPTER 13 TOPICS

1 What Is a Family?

Among other activities, a *family* cares for one another and any children. Worldwide, however, there are variations in many family characteristics such as whether the family structure is a *nuclear* or an *extended* family, living arrangements (*patrilocal, matrilocal,* or *neolocal*), who has authority (*matriarchal, patriarchal,* or *egalitarian*), and how many marriage mates a person can have (*monogamy* or *polygamy*).

2 How U.S. Families Are Changing

Divorce is easier to obtain than in the past because all states have *no-fault divorce* laws. The number of single people has risen greatly, primarily because many people are postponing marriage. There has also been a striking increase in *cohabitation* and out-of-wedlock births. In *dual-earner couples,* median income can be twice as high when wives work full time, but there are many conflicts between domestic and employment responsibilities.

3 Diversity in American Families

Among many racial-ethnic populations, extended families are common and provide considerable emotional and economic support. However, family structures can vary widely depending on the members' time of arrival to the United States and socioeconomic status. Middle Eastern American families tend to have fewer children than the average American family. Gay and lesbian families are very similar to heterosexual families but often lack the legal rights and benefits that married couples enjoy.

4 Family Conflict and Violence

We are more likely to experience violence with an intimate partner or family member than with a stranger. Nationally, 27 percent of women and 16 percent of men say that they have been victims of *intimate partner violence* at some time in their lives. *Child maltreatment* is common, and 25 percent of all children live in homes where parents or other adults engage in violence. In the case of *elder abuse,* similarly, most of the offenders are adult children, spouses, or other family members.

5 Our Aging Society

How people define "old" varies across societies depending on *life expectancy. Gerontologists* emphasize that the aging population should not be lumped into one group because, for example, there are significant differences between the young-old and the oldest-old. The United States, like many other countries, is rapidly graying, which has put a significant strain on the nation's health care and other resources.

Example: *"He Gets Prettier; I Get Older"*

When comparing her own public image with that of her actor husband, the late Paul Newman, actress Joanne Woodward once remarked, "He gets prettier; I get older." Was she right? If aging gracefully is acceptable, why does Dove, among other companies, tout antiaging products? And why are the products targeted only at women?

6 Sociological Explanations of Family and Aging

KEY TERMS

family an intimate group consisting of two or more people who: (1) live together in a committed relationship, (2) care for one another and any children, and (3) share close emotional ties and functions.

incest taboo cultural norms and laws that forbid sexual intercourse between close blood relatives, such as brother and sister, father and daughter, or uncle and niece.

marriage a socially approved mating relationship that people expect to be stable and enduring.

endogamy (sometimes called *homogamy*) the practice of selecting mates from within one's group.

exogamy (sometimes called *heterogamy*) the practice of selecting mates from outside one's group.

nuclear family a form of family consisting of married parents and their biological or adopted children.

extended family a form of family which consists of parents and children, as well as other kin, such as uncles and aunts, nieces and nephews, cousins, and grandparents.

patrilocal residence pattern newly married couples live with the husband's family.

matrilocal residence pattern newly married couples live with the wife's family.

neolocal residence pattern newly married couple sets up its own residence.

boomerang generation young adults who move back into their parents' home after living independently for a while or who never leave it in the first place.

matriarchal family system the oldest women (usually grandmothers and mothers) control cultural, political, and economic resources, and consequently, have power over males.

patriarchal family system the oldest men (grandfathers, fathers, and uncles) control cultural, political, and economic resources, and consequently, have power over females.

egalitarian family system both partners share power and authority fairly equally.

marriage market a courtship process in which prospective spouses compare the assets and liabilities of eligible partners and choose the best available mate.

monogamy one person is married exclusively to another person.

serial monogamy individuals marry several people, but one at a time.

polygamy a marriage form in which a man or woman has two or more spouses.

divorce the legal dissolution of a marriage.

no-fault divorce state laws that do not require either partner to establish guilt or wrongdoing on the part of the other to get a divorce.

stepfamily a household in which two adults are biological or adoptive parents, with a child from a prior relationship, who marry or cohabit.

cohabitation an arrangement in which two unrelated people are not married but live together and have a sexual relationship.

dual-earner couples both partners are employed outside the home (also called *dual-income, two-income, two-earner,* or *dual-worker couples*).

fictive kin nonrelatives who are accepted as part of a family.

KEY TERMS

intimate partner violence (IPV) abuse that occurs between people in a close relationship.

child maltreatment (sometimes called *child abuse*) includes a broad range of behaviors that place a child at serious risk, including physical abuse, sexual abuse, neglect, and emotional mistreatment.

elder abuse (sometimes called *elder mistreatment*) any knowing, intentional, or negligent act by a caregiver or any other person that causes harm to people age 65 or older.

gerontologists scientists who study the biological, psychological, and social aspects of aging.

life expectancy the average length of time people of the same age will live.

sandwich generation people in a middle generation who care for their own children and their aging parents.

activity theory proposes that many older people remain engaged in numerous roles and activities, including work.

exchange theory posits that people seek through their interactions with others to maximize their rewards and to minimize their costs.

ageism discrimination against older people.

continuity theory posits that older adults can substitute satisfying new roles for those they've lost.

TEST YOUR LEARNING

1. The textbook defines a *family* as two or more people who adhere to three criteria. Which of the following is NOT one of those criteria?
   a. Are legally sanctioned by the state
   b. Live together in a committed relationship
   c. Care for one another and any children
   d. Share close emotional ties and bonds

2. The family serves many important functions in a society. Which of the following functions does the family NOT serve?
   a. Sexual regulation   b. Social placement
   c. Peer approval   d. Economic security

3. Around the world, the most common residence pattern is
   a. patriarchal.   b. matriarchal.
   c. neolocal.   d. egalitarian.

4. Which of the following is NOT a common factor in intimate partner violence (IPV)?
   a. Income level
   b. Employment status
   c. Drug abuse
   d. Number of children

5. _____ use both a macro and a micro approach in examining families and aging.
   a. Functionalists
   b. Conflict theorists
   c. Feminist theorists
   d. Symbolic interactionists

6. **True or False** Jack marries several people, but one at a time. Jack is a serial monogamist.

7. **True or False** U.S. divorce rates have decreased since 1980.

8. **True or False** Couples who live together before marriage have lower divorce rates than those who don't cohabit before marriage.

9. **True or False** Most offenders of child maltreatment are relatives and unrelated caregivers such as foster parents and boyfriends.

10. **True or False** So far, the world's aging population characterizes industrialized and not developing countries.

1. a 2. c 3. a 4. d 5. c 6. c 7. True 8. False 9. False 10. False

Please see Table 13.3 on page 249 in your text.

TABLE 13.3
Sociological Perspectives on Family and Aging

THEORETICAL PERSPECTIVE	KEY POINTS
Functionalist	• Families are important in maintaining societal stability and meeting family members' needs. • Older people who are active and engaged are more satisfied with life.
Conflict	• Families promote social inequality because of social class differences. • Many corporations view older workers as disposable.
Feminist	• Families both mirror and perpetuate patriarchy and gender inequality. • Women have an unequal burden in caring for children as well as older family members and relatives.
Symbolic Interactionist	• Families construct their everyday lives through interaction and subjective interpretations of family roles. • Many older family members adapt to aging and often maintain previous activities.

Education

CHAPTER 14 TOPICS

1 What Is Education?

In the United States, both *education* and *schooling* have changed in four important ways: Education has expanded and mass schooling is universal, community colleges have flourished, public higher education has burgeoned, and student diversity has greatly increased.

2 Sociological Perspectives on Education

Please see Table 14.1 on the next page.

3 Some Problems with U.S. Education

Despite numerous strengths, the U.S. educational system suffers from serious problems. Compared with many other countries, large numbers of students are performing poorly in elementary and high schools—especially in mathematics and the sciences. Most public schools, particularly in low-income communities, are struggling to survive financially because of inadequate funding. Compared with countries in Europe and elsewhere, American teachers' salaries are low, many teachers are out of field, and they have less control over curricula than ever before. And despite widespread grade inflation, high school and college dropout rates are high.

4 New Directions in U.S. Education

Because many traditional public schools are failing to educate students adequately, parents and legislators have turned to a variety of alternatives. Some states offer *vouchers*, but there is no significant overall difference in achievement between the children participating in voucher programs and those who remain in public schools. *Charter schools* promise to improve students' education, but students perform about the same as in traditional public schools. A *magnet school* offers students a distinctive program and specialized curriculum, but few students can be accepted because enrollments are limited. *Homeschooling* has grown, but there are no national data on whether this alternative is more successful in improving the quality of students' schooling than attending a traditional public or private school.

Example: *Paying Students to Excel*

There's an emerging trend at some public schools to reward student progress on standardized test scores with cash, certificates, gift certificates, McDonald's meals, and so on (Medina 2008; O'Brien 2008). In a study of Texas high-school students, those who earned cash for passing AP examinations showed not only better GPAs, but also higher college attendance, performance, and the likelihood of earning their degrees. The effects were most pronounced among minorities (Jackson 2010). Is paying students for their performance a good idea in motivating high school students to study harder?

KEY TERMS

education a social institution that transmits attitudes, knowledge, beliefs, values, norms, and skills to its members through formal, systematic training.

schooling formal training and instruction provided in a classroom setting.

intelligence quotient (IQ) an index of an individual's performance on a standardized test relative to the performance level of others of the same age.

hidden curriculum school practices that transmit nonacademic knowledge, values, attitudes, norms, and beliefs that legitimize economic inequality and fill unequal work roles.

credentialism an emphasis on certificates or degrees to show that people have certain skills, educational attainment levels, or job qualifications.

tracking (also called *streaming* or *ability grouping*) assigning students to specific educational programs and classes on the basis of test scores, previous grades, or perceived ability.

vouchers publicly funded payments that parents can apply toward tuition or fees at a public or private school of their choice.

charter schools self-governing public schools that have signed an agreement with their state government to improve students' education.

magnet school a public school that offers students a distinctive program and specialized curriculum in a particular area, such as business, science, the arts, or technology.

homeschooling teaching children in the home as an alternative to enrolling them in a public or private elementary, middle, or high school.

TEST YOUR LEARNING

1. _____ maintain that the education system creates and perpetuates social inequality.
   a. Functionalists
   b. Conflict theorists
   c. Feminist theorists
   d. Symbolic interactionists

2. An emphasis on certificates or degrees is called
   a. meritocracy.
   b. tracking.
   c. the hidden curriculum.
   d. credentialism.

3. According to recent research studies, which one of the following statements about gender and higher education is FALSE?
   a. Many colleges have been giving men preferential treatment in admission.
   b. Women are underrepresented in STEM fields.
   c. Across all racial-ethnic groups, women have slightly higher college graduation rates than men.
   d. Fewer men than ever before are earning college degrees.

4. In examining educational outcomes, _____ are the most likely to focus on process.
   a. functionalists
   b. conflict theorists
   c. feminist theorists
   d. symbolic interactionists

5. A _____ school is a self-governing public school that has signed an agreement with their state's government to improve student's education.
   a. magnet
   b. private
   c. charter
   d. parochial

6. **True or False** Cultural innovation is one of the latent functions of education.

7. **True or False** According to conflict theorists, education benefits even taxpayers who don't have children in schools.

8. **True or False** IQ tests are good examples of gatekeeping.

9. **True or False** U.S. high-school dropout rates have been increasing.

10. **True or False** There is little basis for claims that grade inflation is a problem in our educational system.

1. b 2. d 3. d 4. d 5. c 6. d 7. False 8. False 9. False 10. False

TABLE 14.1
Major Sociological Perspectives on Education

THEORETICAL PERSPECTIVE	VIEW OF EDUCATION	SOME MAJOR QUESTIONS
Functionalist	Contributes to society's stability, solidarity, and cohesion	What are the manifest and latent functions of education?
Conflict	Reproduces and reinforces inequality and maintains a rigid social class structure	How does education limit equal opportunity?
Feminist	Produces inequality based on gender	How does gender inequality in education limit women's upward mobility?
Interactionist	Teaches roles and values through everyday face-to-face interaction and practices	How do tracking, labeling, self-fulfilling prophecies, and engagement affect students' educational experiences?

Religion

CHAPTER 15 TOPICS

1 What Is Religion?

Religion unites believers into a community, and every known society distinguishes between *sacred* (spiritual) and *secular* (nonspiritual) activities. Religion, *religiosity*, and spirituality differ because, for example, people who describe themselves as religious may not attend services.

Example: *Sacred vs. Secular*

S. Truett Cathy, the founder and chairman of Chick-fil-A (a franchise that prepares sandwiches), says that serving chicken is God's work. The corporate mission, as stated on a plaque at company headquarters, is "to glorify God." Chick-fil-A is the only national fast-food chain that closes on Sunday so employees can go to church and prospective employees are asked about their religious activities. Some franchise operators are delighted with the religious emphasis; others believe that a business should stay out of its workers' personal lives (Schmall 2007). What do *you* think?

2 Types of Religious Organization

People express their religious beliefs most commonly through organized groups, including *cults* (also called *new religious movements [NRMs]*), *sects*, *denominations*, and *churches*. Some NRMs, which usually organize around a *charismatic leader*, have been short-lived, whereas others have become established religions with highly organized bureaucracies. Sometimes sects develop into denominations, which typically accommodate themselves to the larger society.

3 Some Major World Religions

Worldwide the largest religious group is Christians, followed by Muslims, but there is no religious group that comes close to being a global majority. The third largest group is nonreligious persons. The number of followers varies, but five religions—Christianity, Islam, Hinduism, Buddhism, and Judaism—have had an impact on economic, political, and social issues since their origin.

4 Religion in the United States

About 87 percent of Americans believe in God, but religion in the United States is complex and diverse. The number of Americans who say that religion is "very important in their lives" has decreased since the 1950s. About half of U.S. adults have changed their religion since childhood, many opting for no religion at all. A major change has been the decline of the so-called mainline Protestant groups and the surge of evangelicals. Many Americans are more likely to believe in a religion than to practice it by attending formal services regularly. Religious participation varies by sex, age, race and ethnicity, and social class.

5 Secularization: Is Religion Declining?

Many European countries are undergoing *secularization*, but such trends are less clear in the United States. Some sociologists maintain that secularization is increasing rapidly in the United States, but others contend that this claim is greatly exaggerated, especially as witnessed by the growth of *fundamentalism* and the prevalence of *civil religion*.

6 Sociological Perspectives on Religion

Please see Table 15.3 on the next page.

KEY TERMS

religion a social institution that involves shared beliefs, values, and practices based on the supernatural and unites believers into a community.

sacred anything that people see as mysterious, awe-inspiring, extraordinary and powerful, holy, and not part of the natural world.

profane anything that is not related to religion.

secular the term sociologists use (instead of *profane*) to describe worldly rather than spiritual things.

religiosity the ways people demonstrate their religious beliefs.

cult a religious group that is devoted to beliefs and practices that are outside of those accepted in mainstream society.

new religious movement (NRM) term used instead of *cult* by most sociologists.

charismatic leader a religious leader whom followers see as having exceptional or superhuman powers and qualities.

sect a religious group that has broken away from an established religion.

denomination a subgroup within a religion that shares its name and traditions, and is generally on good terms with the main group.

church a large established religious group that has strong ties to mainstream society.

secularization a process of removing institutions such as education and government from the dominance or influence of religion.

fundamentalism the belief in the literal meaning of a sacred text.

civil religion (sometimes called *secular religion*) practices in which citizenship takes on religious aspects.

Protestant ethic a belief that hard work, diligence, self-denial, frugality, and economic success will lead to salvation in the afterlife.

false consciousness an acceptance of a system of beliefs that prevents people from protesting oppression.

ritual (sometimes called a *rite*) a formal and repeated behavior in which the members of a group regularly engage.

TEST YOUR LEARNING

1. A _____ is a religious group that is devoted to beliefs and practices that are outside of those accepted in mainstream society.
   a. cult
   b. sect
   c. denomination
   d. church

2. Which of the following is the world's oldest religion?
   a. Christianity
   b. Judaism
   c. Islam
   d. Hinduism

3. Which U.S. racial-ethnic group has the most diverse religious affiliations?
   a. Whites
   b. Blacks
   c. Latinos
   d. Asians

4. What evidence is there that the United States is becoming more secular?
   a. More than half of the population doesn't believe in a higher power.
   b. Divorce rates have dramatically increased over the past decade.
   c. Attendance at religious services has decreased
   d. About 10 percent of teenagers are self-claimed Satan worshippers.

5. According to _____, religion is taught and not innate.
   a. functionalists
   b. conflict theorists
   c. feminist theorists
   d. symbolic interactionists

6. *True or False* Every known society distinguishes between what is sacred and secular.

7. *True or False* Both religion and religiosity are social institutions.

8. *True or False* Ninety percent of people who are born into a particular religious affiliation maintain that affiliation.

9. *True or False* The Protestant work ethic is a belief that hard work, diligence, self-denial, frugality, and economic success will lead to salvation in the afterlife.

10. *True or False* One of the criticisms of functionalist theories on religion is that they often ignore the role that religion plays in creating social cohesion and harmony.

1. a 2. d 3. d 4. c 5. d 6. True 7. False 8. False 9. True 10. False

TABLE 15.3
Sociological Perspectives on Religion

THEORETICAL PERSPECTIVE	VIEW OF RELIGION	SOME MAJOR QUESTIONS
Functionalist	Religion benefits society by providing a sense of belonging, identity, meaning, emotional comfort, and social control over deviant behavior.	How does religion contribute to social cohesion?
Conflict	Religion promotes and legitimates social inequality, condones strife and violence between groups, and justifies oppression of poor people.	How does religion control and oppress people, especially those at lower socioeconomic levels?
Feminist	Religion subordinates women, excludes them from decision-making positions, and legitimizes patriarchal control of society.	How is religion patriarchal and sexist?
Symbolic Interactionist	Religion provides meaning and sustenance in everyday life through symbols, rituals, and beliefs and binds people together in a physical and spiritual community.	How does religion differ within and across societies?

Population, Urbanization, and the Environment

CHAPTER 16 TOPICS

1 Population Dynamics

Demography examines the interplay between *fertility, mortality,* and *migration.* The *crude death rate* and the *infant mortality rate* measure a population's life expectancy and health. Push and pull factors affect international migration and internal migration. Demographers also use *sex ratios* and *population pyramids* to understand a population's composition and structure.

Demographers who believe that population growth is a ticking bomb subscribe to *Malthusian theory,* which argues that the world's food supply will not keep up with population growth. *Demographic transition theory,* in contrast, maintains that population growth is kept in check and stabilizes as countries experience greater economic and technological development.

2 Urbanization

Globally and in the United States, *cities* and *urbanization* mushroomed during the twentieth century and are expected to increase. As more people move from rural to urban areas, many of the world's largest cities are becoming *megacities.* In the United States, urban growth has led to *suburbanization, edge cities, exurbs, gentrification,* and *urban sprawl.*

Sociologists offer several perspectives on how and why cities change, and how these changes affect people: See Table 16.3 on the next page.

3 Environmental Issues

Population growth and urbanization are changing the planet's *ecosystem* and, many argue, endangering plants, animals, and humans that affect survival. Water and air pollution and global warming are good examples of threats to the ecosystem in the United States and globally. Clean water has been depleted for many reasons, including pollution, privatization, and mismanagement.

Four of the most common sources and causes of air pollution are the burning of fossil fuels, manufacturing plants that spew pollutants into the air, winds that carry contaminants across borders and oceans, and lax governmental policies. Air pollution, which can lead to the *greenhouse effect,* is a major cause of *climate change* and *global warming.*

The rise of environmental problems has sparked a concern about *sustainable development.* Those who are pessimistic about achieving sustainable development show that, worldwide, the United States has one of the worst records on environmental performance, largely because of the close ties between government officials and corporations. Others are optimistic about achieving sustainable development and point to examples such as decreases of the emissions of major air pollutants and some large U.S. corporations' switching to practices that decrease pollution and energy consumption.

KEY TERMS

demography the scientific study of human populations.

population a group of people who share a geographic territory.

fertility the number of babies born during a specified period in a particular society.

crude birth rate (also known as the *birth rate*) the number of live births per 1,000 people in a population in a given year.

mortality the number of deaths during a specified period in a population.

crude death rate (also called the *death rate*) the number of deaths per 1,000 people in a population in a given year.

infant mortality rate the number of deaths of infants (younger than 1 year) per 1,000 live births in a population.

migration the movement of people into or out of a specific geographic area.

sex ratio the proportion of men to women in a population.

population pyramid a visual representation of the makeup of a population in terms of the age and sex of its members at a given point in time.

Malthusian theory the idea that the population is growing faster than the food supply needed to sustain it.

demographic transition theory the idea that population growth is kept in check and stabilizes as countries experience economic and technological development.

zero population growth (ZPG) a stable population level that occurs when each woman has no more than two children.

city a geographic area where a large number of people live relatively permanently and secure their livelihood primarily through nonagricultural activities.

urbanization population movement from rural to urban areas.

megacities metropolitan areas with at least 10 million inhabitants.

suburbanization population movement from cities to the areas surrounding them.

edge cities business centers that are within or close to suburban residential areas.

exurbs areas of new development beyond the suburbs that are more rural but on the fringe of urbanized areas.

urban sprawl the rapid, unplanned, and uncontrolled spread of development into regions adjacent to cities.

gentrification the process in which middle-class and affluent people buy and renovate houses and stores in downtown urban neighborhoods.

urban ecology the study of the relationships between people and urban environments.

new urban sociology urban changes are largely the result of decisions made by powerful capitalists and high-income groups.

ecosystem an area in which all forms of life live in relation to one another and a shared physical environment.

global warming the increase in the average temperature of Earth's atmosphere.

greenhouse effect the heating of Earth's atmosphere because of the presence of certain atmospheric gases.

climate change a change of overall temperatures and weather conditions over time.

sustainable development economic activities that meet the needs of the present without threatening the environmental legacy of future generations.

TEST YOUR LEARNING

1. _____ is the study of human populations.
   a. Sociology
   b. Demography
   c. Ecology
   d. Zero population growth (GPG)

2. Emma is comparing the number of deaths per 1,000 people in Spain and Russia for 2011. She is measuring
   a. fertility.
   b. mortality.
   c. the crude birth rate.
   d. the crude death rate.

3. Which one of the following is NOT one of the phases of demographic transition theory?
   a. Preindustrial society
   b. Early industrial society
   c. Advanced industrial society
   d. Declining industrial society

4. Maleek and Shonda live in a newly developed area that's rural but on the fringe of an urbanized region. They live in
   a. an exurb.
   b. a suburb.
   c. a gentrified area.
   d. an edge city.

5. Why do many feminist scholars maintain that women suffer more problems than men when living in urban areas?
   a. Women don't have the natural aggressive instinct that men have.
   b. Husbands tend to maintain tighter controls over their wives in urban areas.
   c. Urban areas have typically been designed by men and for men.
   d. All of the above explain why women suffer more problems in urban areas.

6. *True or False* Malthusian theory claims that population growth is kept in check and stabilizes as developing countries experience economic and technological development.

7. *True or False* Population pyramids are visual representations of a population's makeup in terms of the age and sex of its members at a given point in time.

8. *True or False* Concentric zone theory emphasizes the development of suburbs around a city but away from its center.

9. *True or False* A sex ratio of 115 means that there are 115 women for every 100 men in a population.

10. *True or False* Global warming begins with the greenhouse effect.

1. b   2. d   3. d   4. a   5. c   6. False   7. True   8. False   9. False   10. True

TABLE 16.3
Sociological Perspectives on Urbanization

PERSPECTIVE	KEY POINTS
Functionalist	People create urban growth by moving to cities to find jobs and to suburbs to enhance their quality of life.
Conflict	Driven by greed and profit, large corporations, banks, developers, and other capitalistic groups determine the growth of cities and suburbs.
Feminist	Whether they live in cities or suburbs, women generally experience fewer choices and more constraints than do men.
Symbolic Interactionist	City people are more tolerant of different lifestyles, but they tend to interact superficially and are generally socially isolated.

Social Change: Collective Behavior, Social Movements, and Technology

CHAPTER 17 TOPICS

1 Collective Behavior

According to an influential sociological theory, six macro-level conditions can encourage or discourage *collective behavior*—structural conduciveness, structural change, the growth and spread of a generalized belief, precipitating factors, mobilization, and social control. There are many types of collective behavior, some more short-lived or harmful than others. *Rumors, gossip,* and *urban legends* are typically untrue, but many people believe and pass them on for a number of reasons, such as anxiety or to reinforce a community's moral standards. In contrast, *panic* and *mass hysteria* can have dire consequences, including death.

Fashions, fads, and *crazes* are harmless because they usually last only a short time and change over time. People choose to participate in fashions, fads, and crazes, whereas a *disaster* is an unexpected event due to social, technological, and natural causes.

Publics, public opinion, and *propaganda* also affect large numbers of people, and some of these types of collective behavior are more harmful than others. *Crowds* vary in their motives, interests, and emotional level. A casual crowd, for example, has little, if any, interaction, the gathering is temporary, and there is little emotion. On the other hand, protest crowds, especially *mobs* and those involved in a *riot,* can wreak considerable havoc on property and result in death.

Example: *Crowds Can Be Deadly*

On Thanksgiving, 2008, crowds started gathering at 9:00 p.m. outside of the Wal-Mart store in Valley Stream, New York, for a bargain-hunting ritual known as Black Friday, the day after Thanksgiving. By 4:55 a.m. the next morning, the crowd had grown to more than 2,000 people and could no longer be held back. Suddenly, according to witnesses, the glass doors shattered and "the shrieking mob surged through in a blind rush for holiday bargains." A 34-year-old male temporary worker, who had been hired for the holiday season, was trampled to death, and four other people, including a 28-year-old woman who was eight months pregnant, were treated for injuries (McFadden and Macropoulos 2008). Review the types of crowds in Chapter 17. Which type of crowd do you think is most representative of this Wal-Mart incident?

2 Social Movements

Unlike collective behavior, *social movements* are typically organized and have long-lasting effects. Some of the most common social movements are alternative, redemptive, reformative, resistance, and revolutionary (see Table 17.1 on the next page). Sociologists have offered several explanations for the emergence of social movements that include *mass society theory, relative deprivation theory, resource mobilization theory,* and *new social movements theory.* Each theory has strengths and weaknesses in helping us understand social movements.

Social movements generally go through four stages: emergence, organization, institutionalization, and decline. Decline is most likely when a social movement is successful and becomes a part of society's fabric; when the members become distracted because the group loses sight of its original goals and/or their enthusiasm diminishes; the membership fragments because the participants disagree about goals, strategies, or tactics; and when a government quashes dissent. Social movements are important because they can create or resist change on the individual, institutional, and societal level.

3 Technology and Social Change

Technology also generates changes. Some of the most important technological advances have included computer technology, biotechnology, and nanotechnology—all of which have changed our lives dramatically. Technology has both benefits and costs, however. For example, the Internet and other forms of telecommunication technology can bring people together but can also intrude on our privacy. In addition, technological advances raise numerous ethical questions, such as their greater availability to the wealthy and educated.

KEY TERMS

social change the transformations of societies and social institutions over time.

collective behavior the spontaneous and unstructured behavior of a large number of people.

rumor unfounded information that people spread quickly.

gossip rumors, often negative, about other people's personal lives.

urban legends (also called *contemporary legends* and *modern legends*) a type of rumor consisting of stories that supposedly happened.

panic a collective flight, typically irrational, from a real or perceived danger.

mass hysteria an intense, fearful, and anxious reaction to a real or imagined threat by large numbers of people.

fashion a standard of appearance that enjoys widespread but temporary acceptance within a society.

fad a form of collective behavior that spreads rapidly and enthusiastically but lasts only a short time.

craze a fad that becomes an all-consuming passion for many people for a short time.

disaster an unexpected event that causes widespread damage, destruction, distress, and loss.

public a collection of people, not necessarily in direct contact with each other, who are interested in a particular issue.

public opinion widespread attitudes on a particular issue.

propaganda the presentation of information to influence people's opinions or actions.

crowd a temporary gathering of people who share a common interest or participate in a particular event.

mob a highly emotional and disorderly crowd that uses force or violence against a specific target.

riot a violent crowd that directs its hostility at a wide and shifting range of targets.

social movement a large and organized activity to promote or resist a particular social change.

relative deprivation a gap between what people have and what they think they should have compared with other people in a society.

technology the application of scientific knowledge for practical purposes.

TEST YOUR LEARNING

1. According to sociologist Neil Smelser, which one of the following does NOT encourage collective behavior?
   a. Structural strain
   b. Growth and spread of a generalized belief
   c. Social control
   d. Personal dissatisfaction at work or home

2. A major difference between panic and mass hysteria is that
   a. panics are typically not as severe as mass hysteria.
   b. panics don't usually last as long as mass hysteria.
   c. panics stem from imagined events, whereas mass hysteria arises from real events.
   d. panics tend to occur less today, whereas mass hysteria occurs more frequently.

3. The "amazing ball" was a toy that became incredibly popular and sold for a very high price, but its popularity dropped off very quickly. This is an example of a
   a. fashion.
   b. fad.
   c. craze.
   d. disaster.

4. _____ maintains that social movements emerge because there's a gap between what people have and what they think they should have compared with other people.
   a. Mass society theory
   b. Relative deprivation theory
   c. Resource mobilization theory
   d. New social movements theory

5. Which of the following is NOT one of four stages of a social movement?
   a. Emergence
   b. Conflict
   c. Institutionalization
   d. Decline

6. **True or False** During the organization stage of social movements, the movement becomes more bureaucratic.

7. **True or False** Gossip and urban legends are types of rumors.

8. **True or False** Mobs typically last longer than riots.

9. **True or False** Environmentalism is an example of the new social movements theory.

10. **True or False** A positive trend in technology is that the advances are now available to most low-income people.

1. d 2. b 3. c 4. b 5. b 6. b 7. False 8. False 9. True 10. False

TABLE 17.1
Five Types of Social Movements

MOVEMENT	GOAL	EXAMPLES
Alternative	Change some people in a specific way	Alcoholics Anonymous, transcendental meditation
Redemptive	Change some people, but completely	Jehovah's Witnesses, born-again Christians
Reformative	Change everyone, but in specific ways	Gay rights advocates, Mothers Against Drunk Driving (MADD)
Resistance	Preserve status quo by blocking or undoing change	Anti-abortion groups, white supremacists
Revolutionary	Change everyone completely	Right-wing militia groups, Communism

For practice tests, printable flash cards, and more, visit **4ltrpress.cengage.com/soc.**

Take the quiz on this card to test your knowledge of the concepts from Chapters 9–17

1. _____ refers to learned attitudes and behaviors, whereas _____ refers to biological characteristics with which we are born.
   a. Sex; gender
   b. Gender; sex
   c. Sex; gender roles
   d. Sexual identity; gender stereotypes

2. _____ is the belief that heterosexuality is superior to and more natural than homosexuality or bisexuality.
   a. Heterobiology
   b. Homosexism
   c. Heterosexism
   d. Bisexism

3. _____ posit that gender inequality and sexuality are socially constructed.
   a. Functionalists
   b. Conflict theorists
   c. Feminist theorists
   d. Symbolic interactionists

4. **True or False.** U.S. abortion rates have been increasing.

5. **True or False.** A majority of Americans support same-sex marriage.

6. **True or False.** Conflict theorists believe that capitalism increases gender inequality.

7. What is the difference between race and ethnicity?
   a. Race is a negative term that refers to difference; ethnicity is the politically correct term that refers to difference.
   b. Race refers to the physical characteristics of a group of people; ethnicity refers to the cultural heritage of a people.
   c. Race refers to people around the world; ethnicity refers only to a group of people within a specific nation.
   d. There is no difference between race and ethnicity; the terms are synonymous.

8. Today most immigrants to the United States come from which of the following countries?
   a. China and Mexico
   b. Mexico and Canada
   c. England and Canada
   d. Japan and Russia

9. _____ is the unequal treatment and subordinate status of groups within a country.
   a. Hegemony
   b. Internal colonialism
   c. Genocide
   d. Assimilation

10. **True or False.** On the continuum of dominant versus minority group relations, genocide reflects the least tolerance, whereas pluralism illustrates the greatest tolerance.

11. **True or False.** Ethnocentrism is the belief that one's own racial group is naturally inferior to others.

12. **True or False.** The lower the educational level, the greater the likelihood that a person will have an interracial marriage.

13. Voter turnout is higher in many countries than in the United States. Which of the following does NOT explain why this is the case?
    a. Some countries impose fines for not voting.
    b. Citizens of other countries are more patriotic.
    c. Elections in other countries are often conducted on weekends.
    d. Other countries believe that voting is a responsibility.

14. According to Max Weber, which one of the following types of authority is most characteristic of the majority of U.S. presidents?
    a. Charismatic
    b. Absolute
    c. Traditional
    d. Rational-legal

15. _____ claim that the U.S. political structure is patriarchal.
    a. Functionalists
    b. Conflict theorists
    c. Feminist theorists
    d. Symbolic interactionists

16. **True or False.** According to the pluralism model, a small group of influential people make the major political decisions in the United States.

17. **True or False.** In the United States, most Republicans believe that the federal government should provide social programs for its citizens.

18. **True or False.** Firefighters, farmers, and environmentalists are examples of special-interest groups.

19. _____ is a market system dominated by a few large producers or suppliers.
    a. Capitalism
    b. Monopoly
    c. Oligopoly
    d. Socialism

20. Socialism is characterized by all of the following except
    a. cooperation.
    b. investment.
    c. collective ownership of property.
    d. collective goals.

21. Felipe serves on the board of directors of several different companies. He is part of
    a. an interlocking directorate.
    b. a transnational corporation.
    c. a conglomerate.
    d. a monopoly.

22. **True or False.** Deindustrialization has spread because of globalization.

23. **True or False.** U.S. unionization rates have been gradually increasing since 1980.

24. **True or False.** A common criticism of functionalist explanations of work and the economy is that functionalists overlook macro-level variables.

25. The family serves many important functions in a society. Which of the following functions does the family NOT serve?
    a. Sexual regulation
    b. Social placement
    c. Peer approval
    d. Economic security

26. Around the world, the most common residence pattern is
   a. patriarchal.
   b. matriarchal.
   c. neolocal.
   d. egalitarian.

27. Which of the following is NOT a common factor in intimate partner violence (IPV)?
   a. Income level
   b. Employment status
   c. Drug abuse
   d. Number of children

28. True or False. U.S. divorce rates have decreased since 1980.

29. True or False. Most offenders of child maltreatment are relatives and unrelated caregivers such as foster parents and boyfriends.

30. True of False. So far, the world's aging population characterizes industrialized and not developing countries.

31. An emphasis on certificates or degrees is called
   a. meritocracy.
   b. tracking.
   c. the hidden curriculum.
   d. credentialism.

32. _____ maintain that the education system creates and perpetuates social inequality.
   a. Functionalists
   b. Conflict theorists
   c. Feminist theorists
   d. Symbolic interactionists

33. True or False. Cultural innovation is one of the latent functions of education.

34. True or False. According to conflict theorists, education benefits even taxpayers who don't have children in schools.

35. True or False. There is little basis for claims that grade inflation is a problem in our educational system.

36. Which of the following is the world's oldest religion?
   a. Christianity
   b. Judaism
   c. Islam
   d. Hinduism

37. What evidence is there that the United States is becoming more secular?
   a. More than half of the population doesn't believe in a higher power.
   b. Divorce rates have dramatically increased over the past decade.
   c. Attendance at religious services has decreased
   d. About 10 percent of teenagers are self-claimed Satan worshippers.

38. According to _____, religion is taught and not innate.
   a. functionalists
   b. conflict theorists
   c. feminist theorists
   d. symbolic interactionists

39. True or False. Every known society distinguishes between what is sacred and secular.

40. True or False. The Protestant work ethic is a belief that hard work, diligence, self-denial, frugality, and economic success will lead to salvation in the afterlife.

41. Emma is comparing the number of deaths per 1,000 people in Spain and Russia for 2011. She is measuring
   a. fertility.
   b. mortality.
   c. the crude birth rate.
   d. the crude death rate.

42. Why do many feminist scholars maintain that women suffer more problems than men when living in urban areas?
   a. Women don't have the natural aggressive instinct that men have.
   b. Husbands tend to maintain tighter controls over their wives in urban areas.
   c. Urban areas have typically been designed by men and for men.
   d. All of the above explain why women suffer more problems in urban areas.

43. True or False. Malthusian theory claims that population growth is kept in check and stabilizes as developing countries experience economic and technological development.

44. True or False. Concentric zone theory emphasizes the development of suburbs around a city but away from its center.

45. True or False. A sex ratio of 115 means that there are 115 women for every 100 men in a population.

46. According to sociologist Neil Smelser, which one of the following does NOT encourage collective behavior?
   a. Structural strain
   b. Growth and spread of a generalized belief
   c. Social control
   d. Personal dissatisfaction at work or home

47. The "amazing ball" was a toy that became incredibly popular and sold for a very high price, but its popularity dropped off very quickly. This is an example of a
   a. fashion.
   b. fad.
   c. craze.
   d. disaster.

48. _____ maintains that social movements emerge because there's a gap between what people have and what they think they should have compared with other people.
   a. Mass society theory
   b. Relative deprivation theory
   c. Resource mobilization theory
   d. New social movements theory

49. True or False. Gossip and urban legends are types of rumors.

50. True or False. Environmentalism is an example of the new social movements theory.

Answers:
1. b 2. c 3. d 4. False 5. False 6. True 7. b 8. a 9. b 10. True
11. False 12. False 13. b 14. d 15. c 16. False 17. False 18. True 19. c 20. b
21. a 22. True 23. False 24. False 25. c 26. a 27. d 28. True 29. False 30. False
31. d 32. b 33. False 34. True 35. False 36. d 37. c 38. d 39. True 40. True
41. d 42. c 43. False 44. False 45. False 46. d 47. c 48. b 49. True 50. True

Self-Assessment Comprehensive Exam

Take the quiz on this card to test your knowledge of the concepts from Chapters 1–17

1. _____ looks at the relationship between individual characteristics; _____ examines the relationships between institutional characteristics.
   a. Microsociology; macrosociology
   b. Macrosociology; microsociology
   c. Metasociology; macrosociology
   d. Metasociology; microsociology

2. Many people buy designer clothes that they can't afford. The clothes are an example of a status symbol that reflects a
   a. latent function.
   b. manifest function.
   c. dysfunction.
   d. social system.

3. **True or False.** Much of contemporary functionalism grew out of the work of Auguste Comte and Émile Durkheim.

4. Alexandra notices that she tends to perform best on tests that are given in the afternoon. She then begins to collect data of her test performances and asks close friends and classmates to do the same. In trying to understand whether test scores and test times are related, Alexandra is using
   a. intuition.
   b. inferences.
   c. deductive reasoning.
   d. inductive reasoning.

5. **True or False.** If researchers use a nonprobability sample, they can generalize the results to a larger population.

6. **True or False.** Correlation equals causation.

7. At a party, George was eating nachos and salsa. He took a bite of his chip and then dipped what was left of his chip back into the large bowl of salsa. His friend Brett gave him a disgusted look. Which of the following did George break?
   a. A more
   b. A cultural universal
   c. A folkway
   d. A law

8. Anaz is an 8-year-old Iranian girl who loves the female fashions she sees in American films and television shows. Lately she's been questioning why her mother wears a burka. Anaz's questioning of her family's traditions could best be explained by
   a. cultural relativism.
   b. multiculturalism.
   c. cultural imperialism.
   d. ethnocentrism.

9. **True or False.** The legal controversy over file sharing and downloading music off the Web is an example of cultural lag.

10. What are the three stages of Mead's role-taking theory?
    a. Prework stage, work stage, postwork stage
    b. Anal stage, phallic stage, postphallic stage
    c. Mirror stage, active stage, passive stage
    d. Preparatory stage, play stage, game stage

11. **True or False.** Charles Horton Cooley proposed that the looking-glass self develops in five phases.

12. **True or False.** According to Erving Goffman, social life mirrors theatrical performance.

13. Jake has a full-time course load while also working 30 hours a week. Given the demands of both work and school, Jake might be likely to experience
    a. role set.
    b. role strain.
    c. role conflict.
    d. role exchange.

14. According to _____, social interaction is based on trying to maximize rewards for oneself while minimizing costs.
    a. ethnomethodology theory
    b. feminist theory
    c. conflict theory
    d. social exchange theory

15. **True or False.** If we define something as real and act on it, it can, in fact, become real. This is known as the self-fulfilling prophecy.

16. Max Weber outlined the characteristics of an efficient and productive bureaucracy. Which of the following was NOT one of those characteristics?
    a. High degree of specialization
    b. Explicit rules and regulations
    c. Qualifications-based employment
    d. Decentralized authority

17. **True or False.** Groupthink occurs most often when there is a diversified collection of ideas discussed among the in-group members.

18. **True or False.** The glass ceiling refers to organizational barriers, but not attitudes, in the workplace.

19. Who of the following is most likely to be the victim of a crime?
    a. A black man
    b. A black woman
    c. A white man
    d. A white woman

20. What is a fundamental question that a conflict theorist would ask with regard to crime?
    a. "Why do some people commit crimes whereas others do not?"
    b. "Why are some acts defined as criminal whereas others are not?"
    c. "Why do men commit more violent crimes than women?"
    d. "How does one's social context impact deviant behavior?"

21. **True or False.** Labeling theory claims that society's reaction to a behavior is a major factor in defining oneself or others as deviant.

22. Which of the following is NOT a major structural factor in social mobility?
    a. Changes in the economy
    b. Immigration patterns
    c. Consumer confidence
    d. Number of available positions in given occupations

23. **True or False.** One of the criticisms of conflict theory is that it ignores structural factors in explaining stratification.

24. **True or False.** The Davis–Moore thesis is a symbolic interactionist perspective.

25. _____ is the belief that heterosexuality is superior to and more natural than homosexuality or bisexuality.
    a. Heterobiology
    b. Homosexism
    c. Heterosexism
    d. Bisexism

26. _____ posit that gender inequality and sexuality are socially constructed.
   a. Functionalists
   b. Conflict theorists
   c. Feminist theorists
   d. Symbolic interactionists

27. **True or False.** U.S. abortion rates have been increasing.

28. What is the difference between race and ethnicity?
   a. Race is a negative term that refers to difference; ethnicity is the politically correct term that refers to difference.
   b. Race refers to the physical characteristics of a group of people; ethnicity refers to the cultural heritage of a people.
   c. Race refers to people around the world; ethnicity refers only to a group of people within a specific nation.
   d. There is no difference between race and ethnicity; the terms are synonymous.

29. **True or False.** Ethnocentrism is the belief that one's own racial group is naturally inferior to others.

30. **True or False.** The lower the educational level, the greater the likelihood that a person will have an interracial marriage.

31. According to Max Weber, which one of the following types of authority is most characteristic of the majority of U.S. presidents?
   a. Charismatic
   b. Absolute
   c. Traditional
   d. Rational-legal

32. _____ claim that the U.S. political structure is patriarchal.
   a. Functionalists
   b. Conflict theorists
   c. Feminist theorists
   d. Symbolic interactionists

33. **True or False.** Firefighters, farmers, and environmentalists are examples of special-interest groups.

34. Felipe serves on the board of directors of several different companies. He is part of
   a. an interlocking directorate.
   b. a transnational corporation.
   c. a conglomerate.
   d. a monopoly.

35. **True or False.** Deindustrialization has spread because of globalization.

36. **True or False.** A common criticism of functionalist explanations of work and the economy is that functionalists overlook macro-level variables.

37. The family serves many important functions in a society. Which of the following functions does the family NOT serve?
   a. Sexual regulation
   b. Social placement
   c. Peer approval
   d. Economic security

38. Which of the following is NOT a common factor in intimate partner violence (IPV)?
   a. Income level
   b. Employment status
   c. Drug abuse
   d. Number of children

39. **True or False.** U.S. divorce rates have decreased since 1980.

40. _____ maintain that the education system creates and perpetuates social inequality.
   a. Functionalists
   b. Conflict theorists
   c. Feminist theorists
   d. Symbolic interactionists

41. **True or False.** Cultural innovation is one of the latent functions of education.

42. **True or False.** There is little basis for claims that grade inflation is a problem in our educational system.

43. Which of the following is the world's oldest religion?
   a. Christianity
   b. Judaism
   c. Islam
   d. Hinduism

44. According to _____, religion is taught and not innate.
   a. functionalists
   b. conflict theorists
   c. feminist theorists
   d. symbolic interactionists

45. **True or False.** The Protestant work ethic is a belief that hard work, diligence, self-denial, frugality, and economic success will lead to salvation in the afterlife.

46. Why do many feminist scholars maintain that women suffer more problems than men when living in urban areas?
   a. Women don't have the natural aggressive instinct that men have.
   b. Husbands tend to maintain tighter controls over their wives in urban areas.
   c. Urban areas have typically been designed by men and for men.
   d. All of the above explain why women suffer more problems in urban areas.

47. **True or False.** Malthusian theory claims that population growth is kept in check and stabilizes as developing countries experience economic and technological development.

48. **True or False.** A sex ratio of 115 means that there are 115 women for every 100 men in a population.

49. _____ maintains that social movements emerge because there's a gap between what people have and what they think they should have compared with other people.
   a. Mass society theory
   b. Relative deprivation theory
   c. Resource mobilization theory
   d. New social movements theory

50. **True or False.** Environmentalism is an example of the new social movements theory.

Students: Accessing a CourseMate Website and Enrolling in an Instructor-Led Course

Prepared by the Cengage Learning CourseMate Team

Introduction

The purpose of this document is to give step-by-step instructions on accessing a CourseMate website and enrolling in a course led by your instructor.

This document includes three sections, only one of which will be appropriate for you.

- If You Purchased CourseMate Access in Your School Bookstore and Don't Have an Account at http://login.cengagebrain.com

Or

- If You Purchased CourseMate Access in Your School Bookstore and Already Have an Account at http://login.cengagebrain.com

Or

- If You Want to Purchase CourseMate Access via http://www.cengagebrain.com

Finally, note that there are hundreds of different CourseMate sites, and many of them have different visual designs. So, if what you are seeing as you travel the registration and enrollment path does not exactly *look like* the screen captures shown in this document, note that the *functionality* described in this document is common to all CourseMate sites.

If You Purchased CourseMate Access in Your School Bookstore and Don't Have an Account at http://login.cengagebrain.com

What is http://login.cengagebrain.com? Imagine that you are using multiple applications from Cengage Learning (CourseMate and other applications). Rather than having credentials to sign into each of these applications, Cengage Learning offers a single location. With one set of Sign On credentials, then, at http://login.cengagebrain.com you can access all of your Cengage Learning tools.

When you access http://login.cengagebrain.com, you will see the following.

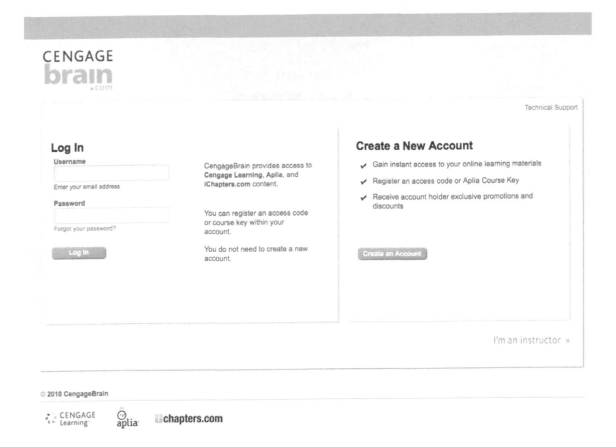

This section you are currently reading assumes that you do not already have an account at this location.

1. Click the "Create a New Account" button.

2. The following will load.

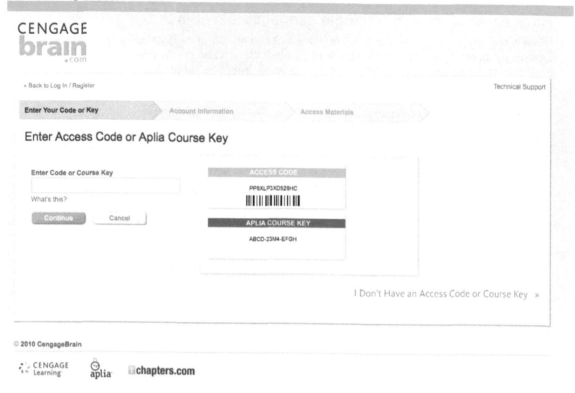

3. Provide the *access code* you find on the printed access card you received with your bookstore purchase, and click "Continue." A page like the following will appear (where not all of the page is shown in the following).

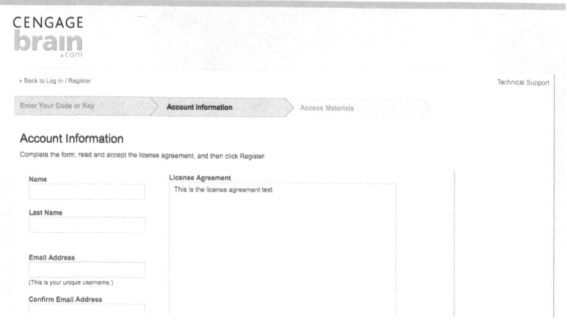

4. Provide First Name, Last Name, Email Address, etc., confirm that you are at least 13 years of age, and click "Register." You will be taken to a page that prompts you to identify the school where you are studying.

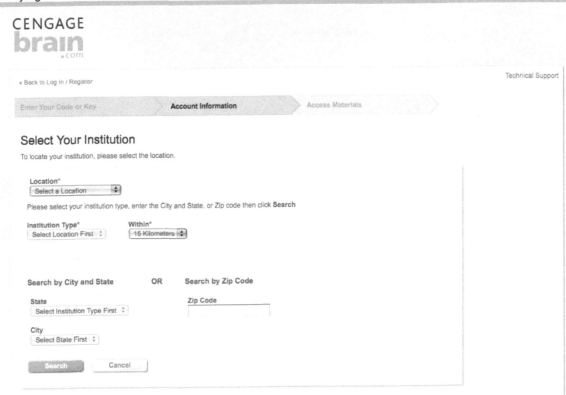

5. Complete the fields on this page, providing the information unique to you, and then click the "Search" button. Something like the following will appear.

CENGAGE
brain
.com

| Enter Your Code or Key | **Account Information** | Access Materials |

Select Your Institution

54 institutions were found in your search of 4-Year College within **25 miles of San Francisco, CA**. Select your institution from the list below, then click **Register**.

Select	Institution Name	City	State/Province	Country
○	University of California San Francisco	San Francisco	CA	US
○	Academy of Art University	San Francisco	CA	US
○	Art Institute of California, San Francisco	San Francisco	CA	US
○	California Culinary Academy	San Francisco	CA	US
○	San Francisco State Univeristy	San Francisco	CA	US
○	Golden Gate University	San Francisco	CA	US
○	San Francisco Art Institute	San Francisco	CA	US
○	School for Self Healing	San Francisco	CA	US
○	University of California Hastings	San Francisco	CA	US
○	University of San Francisco	San Francisco	CA	US

[Register]   [Cancel]

6. Select the proper institution and click the "Register" button. Something like the following will appear.

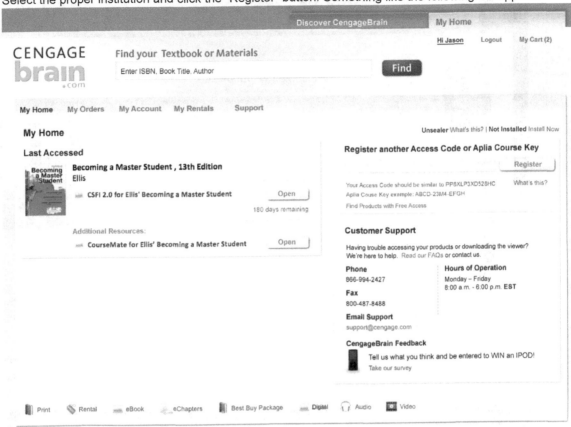

7. There are hundreds of CourseMate sites, and which one you access when you click the "Open" link for the CourseMate resource depends on the textbook you are using. For example, the "Open" link in the example above would take you to the landing page in a College Success CourseMate site, whereas the example below is the landing page on an Art Study CourseMate website.

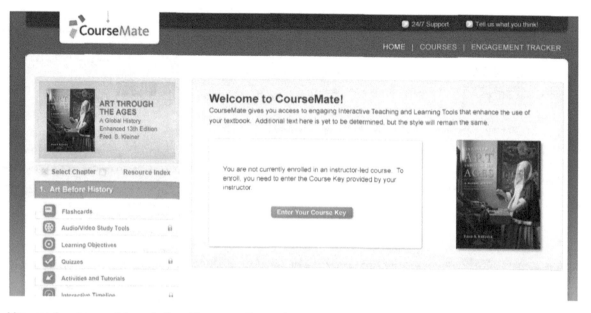

8. You are free to use this website without enrollment in an instructor-led course. If you do so and then later enroll in an instructor-led course, all activity before enrollment will appear to the instructor once enrolled (as will all activity after enrollment).

At the point you wish to enroll in an instructor-led course, you will need to have from the instructor a "Course Key." With this Course Key in hand, click the **Enter Your Course Key** button. An overlay will appear, on top of the current screen.

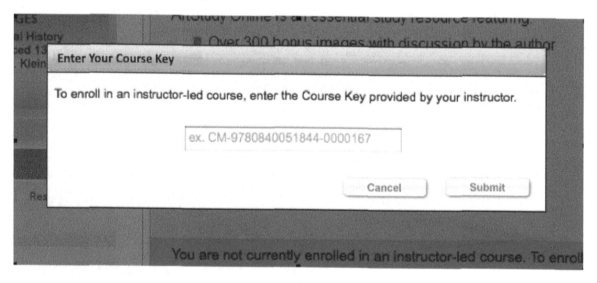

9. Provide the Course Key your instructor gave to you, and click the Submit button. The overlay will disappear, and the Home page of the site will have changed as follows.

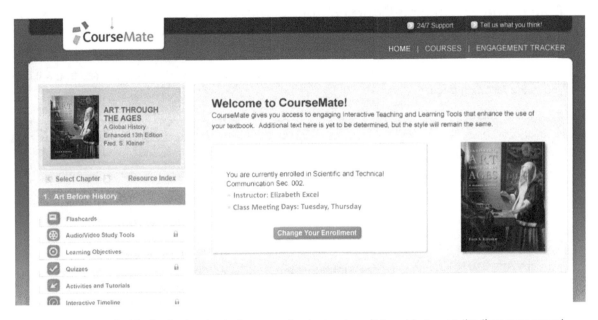

Now that you are enrolled in the instructor-led course, the instructor will be able to see the time you spend on all resources in the CourseMate site, and will also be able to see your scores for the graded quizzes in the site.

Else If You Purchased CourseMate Access in Your School Bookstore and Already Have an Account at http://login.cengagebrain.com

This section assumes you have an existing account at login.cengage.com, a web address that will bring you to the following page.

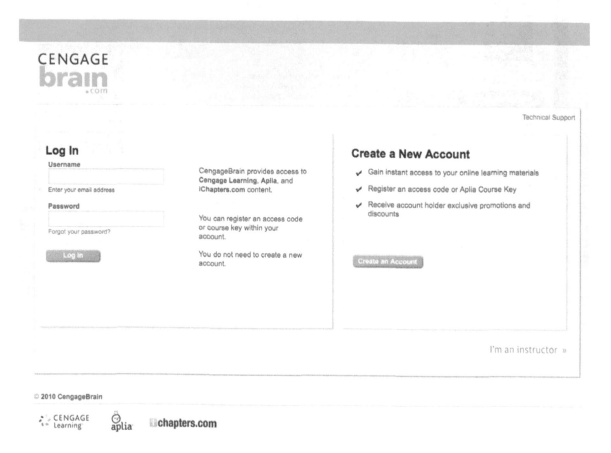

1. Provide the credentials to your existing account, and click the **Log In** button. Your Dashboard will appear, similar to the following.

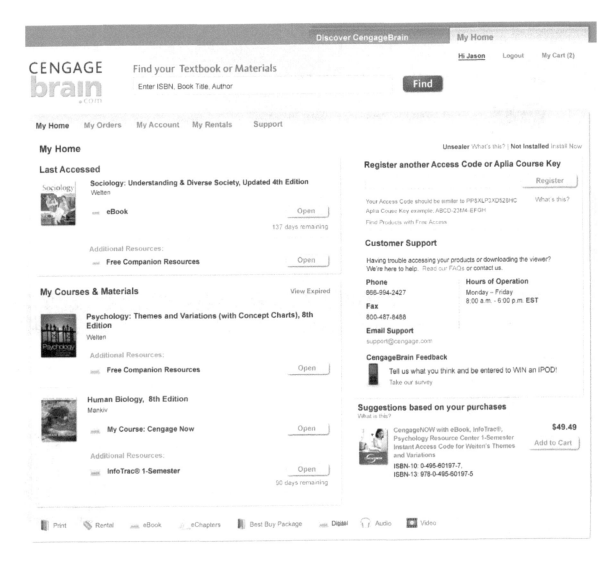

2. Locate the **Register another Access Code or Aplia Course Key** field.

Register another Access Code or Aplia Course Key

Register

3. Provide the *access code* you find on the printed access card you received with your bookstore purchase, and click "Continue." The Dashboard's **Last Accessed** area will update with your new

product.

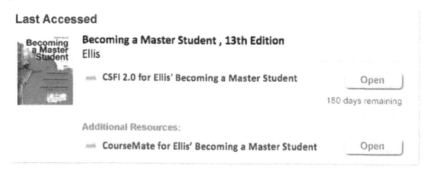

4. There are hundreds of CourseMate sites, and which one you access when you click the "Open" link for the CourseMate resource depends on the textbook you are using. For example, the "Open" link in the example above would take you to the landing page in a College Success CourseMate site, whereas the example below is the landing page on an Art Study CourseMate website.

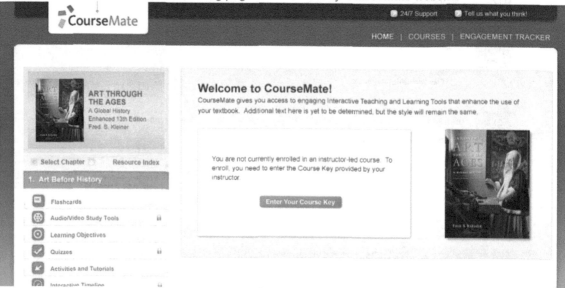

5. You are free to use this website without enrollment in an instructor's course. If you do so and then later enroll in an instructor-led course, all activity before enrollment will appear to the instructor once enrolled (as will all activity after enrollment).

    At the point you wish to enroll in an instructor-led course, you will need to have from the instructor a "Course Key." With this Course Key in hand, click the **Enter Your Course Key** button. An overlay will appear, on top of the current screen.

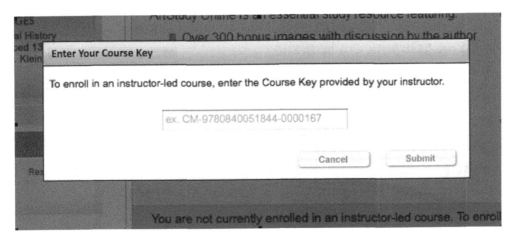

6. Provide the Course Key your instructor gave to you, and click the Submit button. The overlay will disappear, and the Home page of the site will have changed as follows.

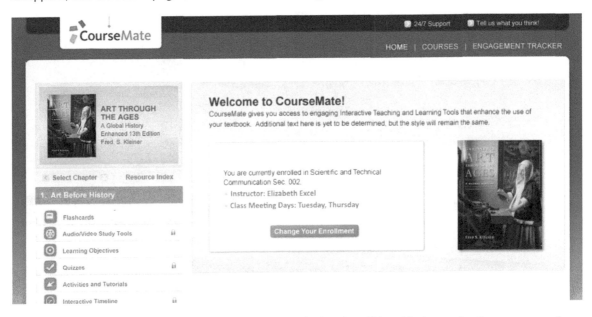

Now that you are enrolled in the instructor-led course, the instructor will be able to see the time you spend on all resources in the CourseMate site, and will also be able to see your scores for the graded quizzes in the site.

Else If You Want to Purchase CourseMate Access via the http://www.cengagebrain.com Website

At http://www.cengagebrain.com, you can use a credit card to purchase Cengage Learning products, such as CourseMate websites. If you are interested in this route, the following steps will guide you.

1. Point your browser to http://www.cengagebrain.com.

CENGAGE brain .com	**Find your Textbook or Materials** Enter ISBN, Book Title, Author	**Find**

Welcome

Log In   Sign Up   My Cart(0)

username

password   Password?

☐ Remember Me   log in

Save on Textbooks!

hardbound
up to 70% off

rentals
save up to 60%

ebooks
always 50% off

echapters
as low as $1.99

bundles
save up to 60%

Register
Access Code or Aplia Course Key

Enter Code

what's this?   register

FORMAT OPTIONS   IMMEDIATE ACCESS   FREE ECHAPTER   YOUR DIGITAL HUB

Follow CengageBrain
on Twitter & Facebook

Get the latest access to promotions, new products and services. Find out more...

RSS and more
Access free streaming audio

Lorem ipsum dolor sit amet, consecr Lorem ipsum dor sit amet, consectur Lorem sum dolor sit amet, consectetur. Find out more...

FAQ
Frequently Asked Questions

Learn about eBooks, eChapters and other CengageBrain features. Find out more...

© 2010 CengageBrain

CENGAGE Learning

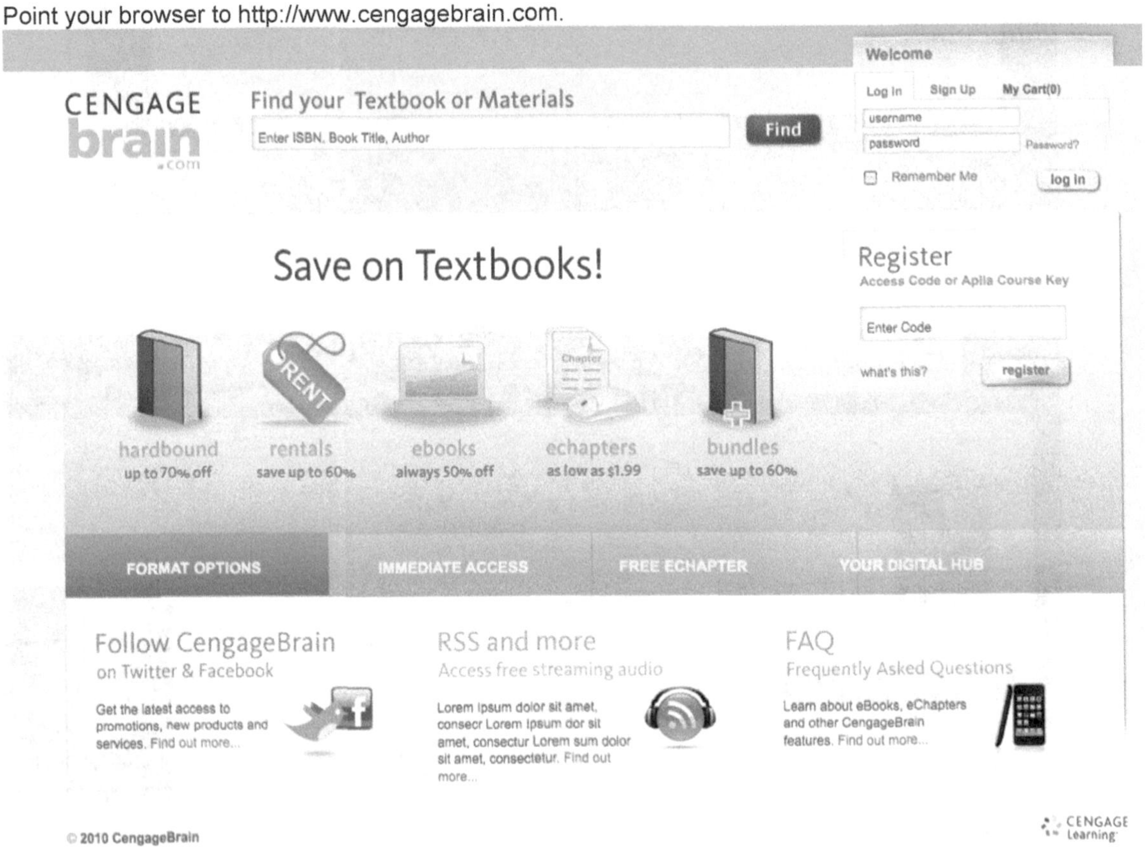

2. In the **Search** box, search for the product you seek. If you want to use the name or ISBN of your textbook, that will work, or you can just search for *CourseMate*.

3. Upon click of "Find," something like the following will appear.

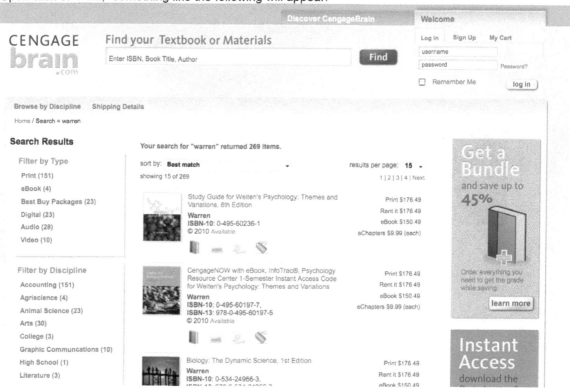

4. Find the product you are interested in, and click on it. Something like the following will appear.

Find your Textbook or Materials

Enter ISBN, Book Title, Author

Find

Discover CengageBrain

Welcome

Log In   Sign Up   My Cart

username

password   Password?

☐ Remember Me   log in

« Back

Psychology: Themes and Variations (with Concept Charts), 8th Edition

Weiten

ISBN-10: 0-534-24966-3, **ISBN-13**: 978-0-534-24966-3

© 2010 | Hardcover | 1456 Pages

Available

New edition available: Click here to view

Preview the 1st chapter FREE

See Description +   ✓ Send to a Friend

Only available at CengageBrain

Gain instant access to free study tools for this book

Quizzing	Flashcards
Glossary	Data sets
Learning Objectives	and more ...

Access Now   Save to Home »

*available content varies title by title

Purchase Options

List Price: $168.99

Print

• Hardcover	$151.99	**Why Hardcover?**
Rental 60 Day	$67.49	Save up to 15%. New Book. Ships in 3-5 days. Free shipping on $25.
Rental 90 Day	$83.99	
Rental 130 Day	$83.99	Eligible for Free Shipping
Paperback	$68.46	**Add to Cart**
Closeout	68.46	

Digital

• Integrated eBook + Study Tools	$109.49	**Why CourseMate?**
eChapters	$5.99 (EA)	eBook integrated with online study tools like video, audio, flashcards, quizzes and more.

Add to Cart

Related Products

5. If you want to buy the product, click on the "Add to Cart" button.

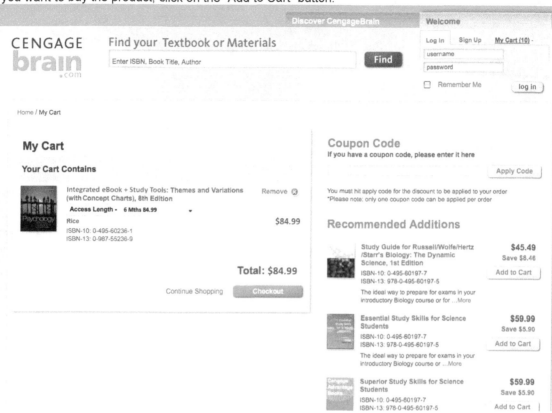

6. Click the "Checkout" button.

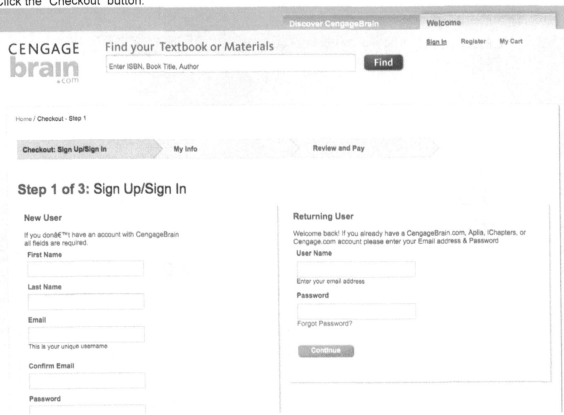

If you have an existing account with Cengage Learning, travel that path. This document, though, focuses on the other path: "New User."

7. Provide all the requested information and click “Continue.”

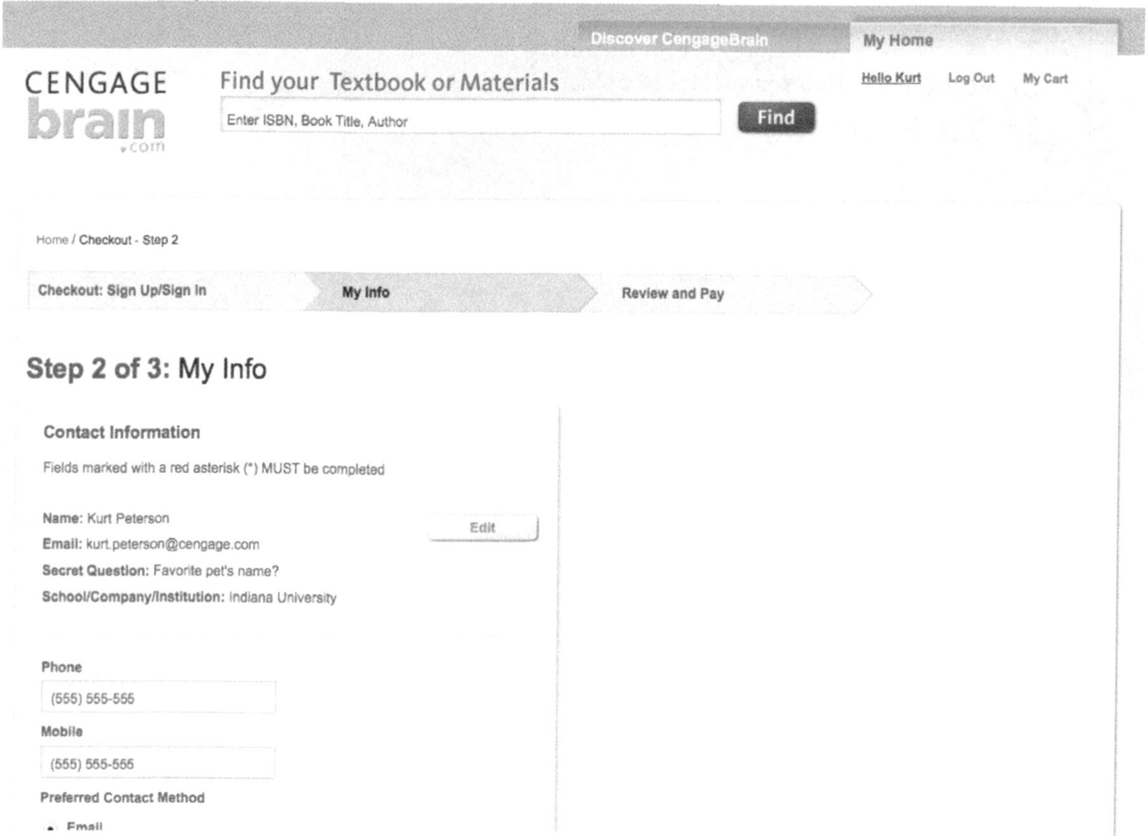
Discover CengageBrain
My Home
CENGAGE brain .com
Find your Textbook or Materials
Enter ISBN, Book Title, Author
Find
Hello Kurt
Log Out
My Cart
Home / Checkout - Step 2
Checkout: Sign Up/Sign In
My Info
Review and Pay
Step 2 of 3: My Info
Contact Information
Fields marked with a red asterisk (*) MUST be completed
Name: Kurt Peterson
Email: kurt.peterson@cengage.com
Secret Question: Favorite pet's name?
School/Company/Institution: Indiana University
Edit
Phone
(555) 555-555
Mobile
(555) 555-555
Preferred Contact Method
Email

8. Provide the requested information and click "Continue."

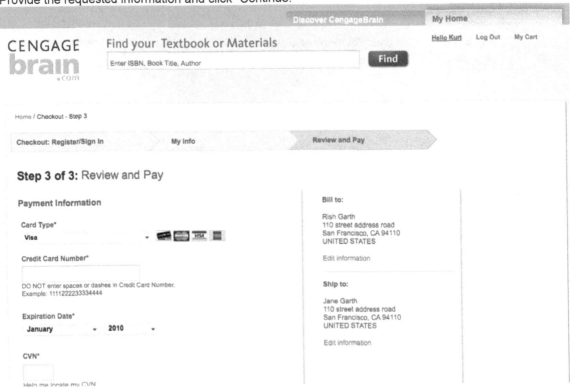

9. Provide payment information, review your order (not seen in the screen capture snippet above), OK the user agreement, and click the "Finish Purchase" button.

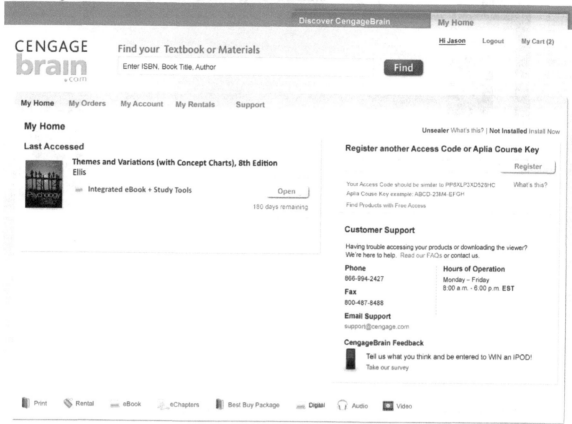

7. There are hundreds of CourseMate sites, and which one you access when you click the "Open" link for the CourseMate resource depends on the textbook you are using. For example, the "Open" link in the example above would take you to the landing page in a Psychology CourseMate site, whereas the example below is the landing page on an Art Study CourseMate website.

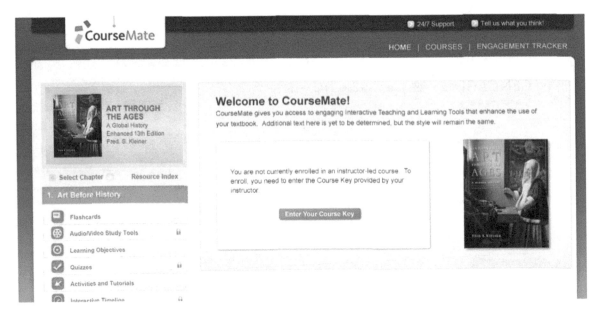

8. You are free to use this website without enrollment in an instructor's course. If you do so and then later enroll in an instructor-led course, all activity before enrollment will appear to the instructor once enrolled (as will all activity after enrollment).

   At the point you wish to enroll in an instructor-led course, you will need to have from the instructor a "Course Key." With this Course Key in hand, click the **Enter Your Course Key** button. An overlay will appear, on top of the current screen.

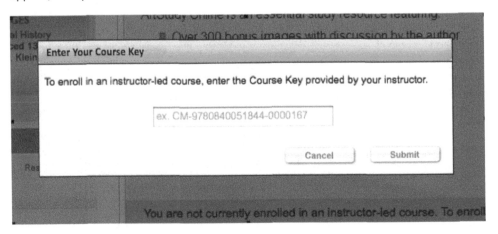

9. Provide the Course Key your instructor gave to you, and click the Submit button. The overlay will disappear, and the Home page of the site will have changed as follows.

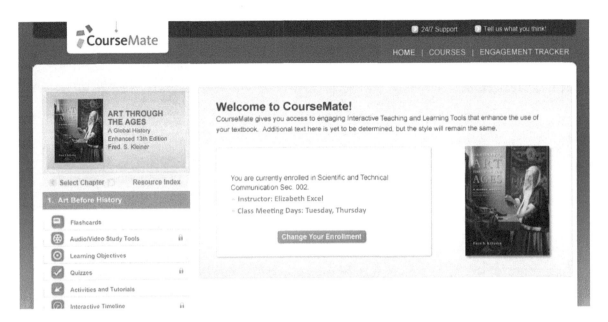

Now that you are enrolled in the instructor-led course, the instructor will be able to see the time you spend on all resources in the CourseMate site, and will also be able to see your scores for the graded quizzes in the site.

Betty Crocker's

SOUTHWEST COOKING

▲▲▲▲▲▲▲▲▲

Prentice Hall

▲▲▲▲▲▲▲▲▲

New York   London   Toronto   Sydney   Tokyo   Singapore

Prentice Hall General Reference
15 Columbus Circle
New York, NY 10023

Published simultaneously in Canada by Prentice Hall Canada, Inc.

PRENTICE HALL and colophon are registered trademarks of Simon & Schuster, Inc.

BETTY CROCKER is a registered trademark of General Mills, Inc.

Library of Congress Cataloging-in-Publication Data
Crocker, Betty.
[Southwest cooking]
Betty Crocker's Southwest cooking.—1st ed.
p.   cm.
Includes index.
ISBN 0-671-86818-7
1. Cookery, American—Southwestern style.   2. Cookery, Mexican,
I. Title.   II. Title: Southwest cooking,
TX715.2.S69C76   1989
641.5979—dc19   88-29014
CIP

Manufactured in the United States of America

10   9   8   7   6   5   4   3

First Edition

Preceding pages:
A chili party: Texas Red Chili (page 75), White Bean
Chili (page 75) and Vegetable Cornmeal Muffins
(page 181). See page 212 for a complete chili
party menu.

A formal dinner: Spicy Pork Roast (page 120),
Spinach Budin (page 173) and Jicama Citrus Salad
with Sangria Dressing (page 169). See page 212 for a
complete formal dinner menu.

Introduction

The cuisine of the Southwest changes continuously, its evolution a result of cultural mélange and the introduction of "new" foods. It is a growing cuisine based on a brilliant variety of ingredients and native cooking techniques, and it is where the cookery of Spaniards, Mexicans and Native Americans has come together.

Southwest cooking has just recently enjoyed wide appreciation that has traveled far beyond the borders of New Mexico and Texas. Today, many of the ingredients that once were difficult to find anywhere but in the Southwest can be purchased in supermarkets across the country. What isn't to be found at the grocery store is available from Mexican specialty shops and through the dozens of mail-order houses that pepper the United States. Refer to the Glossary of Ingredients for a brief introduction to scores of typical southwestern ingredients. There you will find easy directions for such techniques as roasting tomatoes and chiles, too. And, on pages 212–213 is your key to true Southwestern Hospitality: a dozen suggestions for deliciously different, complete menus. Turn there for a guide to entertaining with flair on any occasion.

Many of the recipes in this volume are southwestern basics, featured as ingredients in other recipes. Sauces of all kinds—smooth and spicy, fresh and long-simmered—are among those basics that can be put to countless delicious uses. On pages 214–216 is a listing of those recipes that are called for as ingredients in other recipes, convenient when you are looking to satisfy a craving or looking for a way to use some extra sauce you have on hand. We hope you enjoy this introduction to southwest cooking, a glorious tradition that is the oldest, and nevertheless among the freshest and most exciting, in the land.

THE BETTY CROCKER EDITORS

Contents

Southwest Cooking

The region known as the Southwest, with its somewhat indefinite boundaries, owes its culture and history to many: Spanish missionaries and fortune hunters, Americans pushing westward, and the numerous Indian tribes of Mexico and territories to the north. Three states make up the American Southwest—Arizona, Texas and New Mexico—and they have brought to the rest of the nation a style of cooking that is at once brilliant and modest. The birthplace of southwestern cuisine is a patchwork of mesa and mountain, semiarid and with an unforgiving climate. Yet out of this stern land has come delicious food painted bright with bold sauces, colored with the true red, emerald, purple and yellow of hardy vegetables, and fiery with the temperamental flavor of chiles.

The maxim "less is more" has no bearing on southwestern cuisine. Served with every dish, even with every bread, is an array of piquant condiments and sauces in an atmosphere of plenty. And if tortillas are not an ingredient in a dish, then stacks of them are served right up alongside of it at the table. Even the recipes themselves seem designed to feed larger-than-average crowds. Cooking in the Southwest seems to be especially democratic, too. Everybody sits down to pretty much the same sort of fare. Southwest cooking is not a restrictive discipline. There are only a couple of rules when it comes to cooking southwestern-style: Make sure the food packs a wallop of flavor, and make sure there is more than enough to go around.

From the coastal shores fish and seafood are brought inland by truck. The culinary traditions, though, rest on game, beef, pork and chicken. It is thought by some, perhaps too simply, that southwest cooking today is the result of continental technique applied to local produce. In fact, if there is any culinary debt to pay, it is to the Native American. Regardless of who lays claim to the original technique of grilling, it is wildly popular far and wide. Among the most frequently used woods for fuel are mesquite, hickory, oak, almond, pecan, piñon and such fruitwoods as cherry and peach. In the Southwest, far from the Carolina vinegar-based barbecues, the preference is for "moppin' and soppin' " sauces liberally slapped on during cooking and brought to the table for "soppin'," too.

It was the Native American cultivation of corn that allowed many Indian societies to thrive generation after generation. For thousands of years Indians have planted, and in cases irrigated, corn crops not only for subsistence but for stockpiling, too, against harder times. They developed resilient corn hybrids, and the Pueblo Indians in particular were renowned for their forty-some ways to use this grain. The Hopi Indians of Arizona are similarly celebrated for their ingenuity with beans—more than twelve varieties—in addition to corn. Southwestern-style sauces have their origin in the spicy chile and tomato sauces of the Pueblos, whose chile stews with meat or beans are not very different from those enjoyed throughout the Southwest today.

Southwest cooking continues to enjoy coast-to-coast popularity that is nothing short of sensational. It has become quite easy to find ingredients that once were nearly impossible to locate any distance from Santa Fe, and thanks are due in part to this demand for true southwestern flavor. Items not available at local supermarkets are usually to be found at specialty or gourmet shops. Beyond that, at least a dozen mail-order stores featuring southwestern ingredients have cropped up across the country like desert flowers after a rain. It is often convenient to purchase nonperishable groceries in quantity, to eliminate repetitive shopping. The advantage of mail-order buying is delivery direct to your door.

A last word, about chiles. Chiles are vegetables, but they are a fantastically versatile seasoning, too. No other vegetable has had greater effect on a way of cooking—or a way of life—than the chiles of the Southwest. Use them fresh, canned, dried, puréed, roasted, minced, whole . . . but use them. Chiles are simple things, obligingly easy to cook with and powerfully evocative. The confidence of the chile will take even the most timid cooks in hand and lead them to delicious success. In their nearly limitless variety is the romance, the savor, and the bravado of the food of the Southwest.

Glossary of Ingredients

ACHIOTE SEED: The dried, reddish seeds of the annatto tree give food a bright orange-yellow tint when they are cooked first in hot fat; then, the seeds themselves are discarded. Sometimes they are ground to a powder and stirred into such foods as butter for color. They impart a flavor that is gentle and hard to describe; like that of saffron, it has an earthy quality.

ADOBO: A piquant sauce of tomato, vinegar and spices.

ANISE SEED: This small, elongated seed tastes sharply of licorice.

ATOLE BLUE CORNMEAL: This is blue corn that has been dried, roasted, and ground specifically to be used in making *atole*, a cornmeal gruel. Blue corn, unlike ordinary field corn, is always dried and ground before use. Cornmeal, blue, yellow or white, can be used as a thickener.

AVOCADO: This fruit is ripe when the flesh under the leathery skin yields to light pressure. A hard avocado will ripen if left at room temperature for two or three days. The Haas or California type is smaller and darker green than the emerald type grown in Florida, and some say it is more flavorful as well. Keep avocado flesh from discoloring by brushing it with lemon juice as it is peeled.

BEANS: It takes time to prepare dried beans, but the result is a tender bean that is still firm. Canned beans are sometimes mushy, but they are convenient to keep on hand and are packed in liquid that adds flavor to many recipes. Dried beans keep almost indefinitely. Before cooking dried beans, rinse them well and pick them over for stones or inferior beans.

BLACK BEANS (*frijoles negros*, turtle beans), though small, have a hearty flavor. South American cooking makes great use of them. With their dramatic dark purple-blue color, they lend themselves nicely to garnishes.

BLACK-EYED PEAS (cowpeas) are the seeds of the cowpea, an annual vine. They are tan with a blackish stain, hence "black-eyed."

GARBANZO BEANS (chickpeas) are Spanish in origin. These rounded, beige beans have a nutty flavor.

NORTHERN BEANS are white, relatively large and mild.

PINTO BEANS (*frijoles*) are charmingly speckled with brown on a pale or pinkish background.

RED BEANS are favorites in the southern states. Pinto beans may be substituted.

BUFFALO: This commercially raised red meat is lower in cholesterol and fat than beef. Unlike beef, it isn't marbled with fat. Accustomed as we are today to tender cuts of meat, buffalo is best enjoyed ground rather than as steaks.

CAPERS: These are the pickled, green buds from the prickly caper bush. They are somewhat smaller than raisins and are bottled in brine.

CAYENNE: See Chile (page 14).

CHAYOTE (christophine, mirliton, vegetable pear): Related to gourds, chayote squash have none of their brilliant decoration. Light green skin encases firm flesh of an even paler green. Chayote may be baked, steamed, stuffed and sautéed. A 1-pound chayote makes a nice serving for two or three people.

CHEESE: Traditional Mexican cheeses were made with goat's or sheep's milk. The recipes that follow use these cheeses.

A variety of beans used in southwest cooking (clockwise from spoon): Pinto beans, black-eyed peas, red beans, garbanzo beans, black beans and great northern beans.

CHEDDAR is a mild firm cheese of English origin that becomes more sharp with age. It melts beautifully.

CHIHUAHUA (*Asadero* or *Oaxaca*) is white, creamy and tangy. Sometimes it is sold braided. Mozzarella or Monterey Jack may be substituted.

CO-JACK is an American invention, block cheese marbled with Colby and Monterey Jack.

COLBY is a slightly sharp cheese with a flavor similar to that of Cheddar. This American cheese has a rather soft, open texture.

MONTEREY JACK is a mild cheese usually sold in blocks. It softens at room temperature.

QUESO AÑEJO is an aged, hard grating cheese. It ranges from pale cream to white in color and is quite salty. Romano or Parmesan may be substituted.

QUESO FRESCO (*ranchero seco*) can be compared to a very salty farmer's cheese. A reasonable substitute for this crumbly cheese is feta.

SIERRA is another rather dry, sharp cheese that grates easily. Romano or Parmesan may be substituted.

CHILE: Chiles are native to the Americas. They have been known in North America for some time but are said to have traveled north by a circuitous route; apparently they found their way from Mexico to the Western world with Christopher Columbus, then to the East and finally back to North America. New strains of chiles are developed frequently, bred for hardiness, sweetness, hotness and so forth. But chiles are full of surprises; two chiles picked from the same plant may vary widely in hotness. To quench the fire of a too-spicy mouthful, do not reach for a water glass. Water will only spread the capsaicin (the compound that our tongues register as "hot") around. Instead, take a large mouthful of something starchy: corn chips, beans, bread or rice. Sometimes finding fresh chiles is difficult. This probably isn't a question of distribution, but of perishability. Canned and dried chiles are usually available.

ANAHEIM CHILES (California green chiles) are slim, between five and eight inches long, and of various light shades of green. These mildly hot chiles are sometimes twisted in appearance. They are occasionally stuffed, but their flesh is thin and more fragile than that of poblano chiles. The Anaheims cultivated in New Mexico—where the name is *chile verde*—are reputedly hotter. A ripe, red Anaheim is sometimes known as a *chile Colorado*. Anaheim chiles are dried and tied in wreathes (*ristras*) and ground and blended in commercial chile powder mixtures. They may be purchased in cans as "mild green chiles." These chiles were named after the town that, at the turn of the century, was the site of a chile cannery.

ANCHO refers to a ripened, dried poblano chile.

CASCABEL CHILES, true ones, are scarcer than hens' teeth in most parts of the United States. Sometimes dried Anaheim chiles are labeled "cascabel," but they are very different from the authentic item. Fresh cascabel chiles are hot and have a distinctive flavor. They are round, and 1½ inches in diameter. Dried, the cascabel chile has a nutlike flavor.

CAYENNE CHILES are thin and tapered, three to seven inches long. Dark green (unripe) or bright red (ripe), the cayenne is incendiary and well known to Asian kitchens. The red ones are dried and ground to make cayenne pepper (here, "ground red pepper"). This product adds heat and just a little chile flavor.

CHIPOTLE CHILES are smoked, dried jalapeños with a very wrinkled appearance. Fresh jalapeños are vibrant green but they turn brown when smoked. Chipotles can be purchased loose (dry) or canned in adobo sauce. The canned variety is especially convenient as it saves having to soak and soften them.

GUAJILLO CHILES (MIRASOL CHILES) have a vegetal flavor that shines even through the drying process. Guajillos are orange-red, skinny and about two to three inches long.

JALAPEÑO CHILES range from hot to very hot. They are dark green, fat and about two to three inches long with a characteristically rounded tip. Watch out for the little ones, which are hottest. Jalapeños ripen to red. Use them fresh or pickled.

PASILLA CHILES are hot and brown (almost black when dried, which is how they are commonly found). They have a dusky flavor.

POBLANO is the chile most frequently used for *chiles rellenos*. It is a suave dark green and ranges from mild to hot. Shaped like a long bell pepper, the poblano has a nice shape for stuffing.

RED PEPPER FLAKES are just that: flaked, dried ripe chiles. Most red pepper flake mixtures are quite hot.

SERRANO CHILES are a sort of middling green, developing to brilliant red when ripe. Extremely hot (as hot as any chile), this chile is usually shorter and thinner than the jalapeño.

Chile safety: The flesh, ribs and seeds of chiles are rich in irritating, burning oils. When preparing chiles, always wash hands and utensils in soapy water. Be especially careful not to rub your face—eyes in particular—until the oils have been thoroughly washed away. When processing chiles in a blender or food processor, avert your face as even the fumes are burning. Some cooks who work with chiles for any extended length of time wear plastic gloves. There is a higher concentration of capsaicin in the ribs of chiles; remove them for a milder chile.

Roasting chiles: Recipes often call for chiles to be roasted. This enhances the flavor and makes them a snap to peel. Roasted chiles may be frozen before peeling, a convenience if you roast a big batch at once; wrap them airtight in plastic wrap.

Broiler method: Set oven control to broil. Arrange whole chiles with their top surfaces about 5 inches from the heat. (Some people cut a small slit in the shoulder of each chile, to prevent it from bursting.) Broil, turning occasionally, until the skin is blistered and evenly browned (*not* burned). Remove chiles to a plastic bag and close tightly; let chiles sit for 20 minutes, then peel.

Anaheim and poblano chiles will roast in 12 to 17 minutes; jalapeño and serrano chiles, in about 5 minutes.

Gas stove-top method: Spear a whole chile on a long-handled metal fork and hold it about 5 inches from the flame. Turn the chile so that it roasts evenly. Place roasted chiles in a plastic bag and close tightly; let chiles sit for 20 minutes, then peel. The disadvantage of this method is of course that you can't roast a number of chiles at once.

Electric stove-top method: This involves a little ingenuity on the part of the cook. Arrange a sturdy, heatproof metal rack (such as a cake rack) so that the grill sits about 4 to 5 inches above the electric burner. Place whole chiles on the rack over high heat. Turn the chiles occasionally so that they roast evenly. Remove chiles to a plastic bag and close tightly; let chiles sit for 20 minutes, then peel.

CHILE POWDER: This is a mixture of ground, dried red chiles blended with other spices and herbs. It is said to have been invented by Willie Gebhardt, a Texan, in 1892. Most brands include cumin and oregano. Often chile powder formulas contain paprika, coriander and salt. Chile powder is not to be confused with ground red chiles (page 18).

CHOCOLATE: The Aztecs are credited with the discovery of chocolate. It was probably first used to flavor a bitter drink favored by their mystics. Another Mexican invention, the molinillo, is a wooden whisk used to whip hot chocolate. The handle is rolled between the palms of the hands, whipping the mixture until it is frothy. Today, block Mexican chocolate frequently contains cinnamon, vanilla, clove and ground almonds.

Following pages: Assorted chiles (clockwise from top of photograph): Jalapeño (green and red, in spoon), poblano, ancho, pasilla, serrano, cascabel, guajillo, jalapeño (red), serrano (yellow and orange), jalapeño (green and red), Anaheim (green and red, in bag), serrano and chipotle.

CHORIZO: This spicy smoked pork (or pork and beef) sausage is available both in links and in bulk.

CILANTRO (Mexican parsley, Chinese parsley, fresh coriander): This herb bears a resemblance to flat-leaf parsley, but the flavor is entirely different: strong, fresh, acid. Cilantro is perishable; store it in the refrigerator with the stems in water and plastic loosely covering the leafy tops.

CINNAMON: This is truly a spice of Mexican cuisine, used in dishes sweet and savory. It is available ground as a powder or in tightly rolled dry quills. Sometimes the bark of the cassia tree is sold as cinnamon; the flavor is similar, but neither as true nor as intense. Look for authentic cinnamon.

CORIANDER: This spice is the seed of the plant that gives us cilantro. It has a dusky flavor that is often associated with Eastern cooking. It may be purchased ground or as whole, dried seeds.

CORN HUSKS: Dried corn husks, softened by soaking, are used to wrap food before it is cooked. They make a sort of natural jacket that holds a mixture together as it steams. Remove any silk clinging to the dried husk before using. Several small corn husks may be overlapped for a larger wrapping, as for a tamale.

CORNMEAL: Dried corn is of course the staple of southwestern larders. When cornmeal is called for, use yellow or white, coarsely or finely ground.

CUMIN: This is the powerful, sometimes dominating spice so often used in traditional southwest cooking. Recipes may call for whole cumin seed or ground cumin.

DUCK: This bird is considered "game" less and less, perhaps because it is widely available, frozen, in supermarkets. Wild duck indeed tastes gamy, and in fact the flesh of water fowl may take on a distinctly fishy taint. Commercially bred ducks, though, are well fed and succulent.

FRIJOLE: Spanish for "bean." See Beans, page 12.

GAME: Americans tend to consider the following animals game: buffalo, duck, goose, pheasant, quail, rabbit and venison. Generally speaking, a farm-raised game animal hasn't had to scratch for a living and so is meatier and has a flavor somewhat less "gamy." It is traditional to serve any game with the foods upon which it feeds. For example, serve game birds with berry sauces and wild rice.

GROUND RED CHILES: This is pure chile powder from finely ground, dried red chiles. It is not blended chile powder.

GROUND RED PEPPER: From ground, dried cayenne chiles, this is often called "cayenne pepper." See Chile, Cayenne, page 14.

GUAVA: These yellow-green fruits with pale, faintly pink flesh are about the size of plums. They are intensely fragrant when ripe. Guava paste is only one of the fruit pastes beloved of Hispanics, often served with cream cheese as dessert. The fruit is cooked with sugar until thick, then canned or shaped into blocks.

HOMINY: These corn kernels have been soaked and lightly cooked so that the outer coating can be removed.

INSTANT CORN FLOUR TORTILLA MIX (*masa*): This commercial product is the shortcut in making fresh corn tortillas. It is fresh corn *masa* (see right) that has been dried and ground.

JERUSALEM ARTICHOKE (sunchoke): This knobbed root keeps well in the refrigerator or other cold place. Jerusalem artichokes discolor after peeling. Dip them in acidulated water as the flesh is exposed. Enjoy Jerusalem artichokes raw in salads, or broiled, sautéed, mashed or in a gratin.

JÍCAMA: The flesh of the jícama root is often compared to that of the water chestnut, both for flavor and crunch. Jícama is related to the sharp-tasting turnip but is so mild in flavor that, when eaten raw, it is usually sprinkled with lemon or lime juice and chile powder. After the brown fibrous skin has been pared away, jícama flesh does not discolor. Look for smallish jícama, which will be sweet and moist.

JUNIPER BERRIES: The fruit of an evergreen,

juniper berries give gin its distinctive flavor. They are sometimes used to flavor game dishes. These blue-green berries are purchased dried. Add them (sparingly) whole to saucy foods for subtle flavor or slightly crushed for more impact.

LARD: This has been perhaps the most frequently used cooking fat south of the border since it was introduced by the Spaniards. For tender, flaky pastries, lard can't be beat. It is little known that lard, for all its reputation, has approximately half the cholesterol of butter.

MANGO: The skin of this oval fruit is washed in gold, pink, red and parrot green. The flesh is deep yellow, juicy and richly perfumed. Mangoes have flat, oval pits. To slice the fruit, free it from the pit in large pieces.

MASA: Literally, "dough" in Spanish. *Masa* is cornmeal dough made from dried corn kernels that have been softened in a lime (calcium hydroxide) solution, then ground. Fresh *masa* is commercially available in Mexico, but it is tricky to work with and dries out quickly. *Masa* comes finely ground, for tortillas, and coarsely ground, for tamales. It is easier to use Instant Corn Flour Tortilla Mix (page 18) when making tortillas.

NOPALES: These leaves of the prickly pear (*nopal*) cactus are firm, crunchy pads. Let size be your guide in buying them; the smaller the pad, the more likely it is to be tender. Use tweezers to remove spines, a sharp paring knife or vegetable peeler to remove their bases. With a flavor similar to green beans, *nopales* are eaten both raw and cooked.

NUTS: In southwest cooking, nuts are sometimes ground and stirred into sauces as a thickening agent. In addition to giving the sauce more body, raw nuts add, of course, their own particular flavor. Toasted nuts are more often used as a garnish or in baking.

Toasting enhances the flavor of the nut. To toast nuts, spread them in a single layer in an ungreased pan; bake at 350°, stirring and checking for doneness frequently. Nuts are toasted when they are lightly browned. Let almonds, pecans and walnuts bake for 7 to 12 minutes. Pine nuts toast more rapidly, in 5 to 7 minutes.

To grind nuts, place ⅓ to ½ cup at a time in the workbowl of a food processor or blender. Process them in short pulses just until ground (longer, and you will have nut butter).

PAPAYA: A nearly oval fruit with creamy golden yellow skin, orange yellow flesh and scores of shiny black seeds conveniently packed in its center. When slightly underripe, the flesh is firm (perfect for making into relishes); when ripe, it is so juicy as to be almost melting.

PECAN: This oil-rich nut is an American native. See Nuts, left, for toasting and grinding.

PEPITA: See Pumpkin Seed, page 20.

PEPPER: There is *Piper nigrum*, peppercorn, and the *Capsicum frutescens* and *Capsicum annuum*, the families of vegetables known variously as peppers and chiles. Peppercorns came to the Western world originally from Madagascar. The success of medieval spice traders made black pepper more widely available and only a little less precious than it had previously been.

Representing the *frutescens* contingent, bell peppers are related to chiles but lack capsaicin (the compound that makes them hot). Bell peppers are therefore known as "sweet." Until recently, bell peppers of any color other than green were an oddity at many markets; today there is a profusion of yellow, red and purple ones. Red and yellow are acknowledged to be the sweetest. Roast bell peppers as for chiles, page 15.

PHEASANT: This game bird fares equally well when cooked with a bravely seasoned sauce or a mild, creamy one. Serve it with a grain side dish; see Game, page 18.

PILONCILLO: This unrefined sugar is purchased in hard cones. Like other "raw" sugars, piloncillo is beige to brown; the deeper the color, the more pronounced the molasses flavor.

PINE NUTS: (*piñons*, *pignolis*): Pine nuts are the seeds of the piñon pine. They are delicious raw or toasted. Store them tightly covered and either refrigerated or frozen, depending on how quickly they are to be used. See Nuts, left, for toasting and grinding.

PLANTAIN: This relative of the banana boasts a thick skin and large size. The fruit itself tends to be a deeper yellow than that of the banana. Cooked unripe, plantain is eaten as one would a potato. Plantains are sweetest when ripe, which isn't until their skins are an alarming, thorough black. Like bananas, plantains will ripen after they have been harvested.

POSOLE: Sometimes hominy is called "posole," but the word authentically refers to a dish made with hominy as an ingredient. See Hominy, page 18.

PRICKLY PEAR: This is the diminutive (egg-size) fruit of the cactus of the same name. It is nearly impossible to avoid the prickles when peeling to reveal the garnet-colored flesh. Prickly pears are sometimes sold with the prickles removed.

PUMPKIN SEED: With the shells or husks removed, pumpkin seeds are known as *pepitas*. Store them in a cool, dry place. To toast pumpkin seeds, spread them in a single layer in an ungreased pan. Bake at 350° for 13 to 15 minutes, stirring and checking for doneness frequently.

QUAIL: These little birds usually weigh in at about ¼ pound. They have richly flavored meat, what there is of it. Quail are most commonly available frozen. See Game, page 18.

QUESO: Spanish for "cheese."

QUESO AÑEJO: The name means "aged cheese," in Spanish. See Cheese, page 14.

QUESO FRESCO: The name means "fresh cheese." See Cheese, page 14.

RABBIT: Rabbits are raised commercially. As with many uncommon meats, it is said of rabbit that it "tastes like chicken." It doesn't; it tastes like rabbit. Large rabbits aren't as tender as the little ones; it is well to marinate or stew older ones, or make rabbit sausage. See Game, page 18.

RED PEPPER: See Ground Red Pepper, page 18.

RED PEPPER SAUCE: This commercially bottled condiment is made from vinegar, spices and hot chiles. It adds heat but little in the way of flavor.

RICE: Mexican cooking calls for long-grain or medium-grain white rice. The occasional southwestern dish uses wild rice, which really isn't rice. It is the fruit of an aquatic grass once harvested only by Native Americans who lived by the Great Lakes.

SQUASH BLOSSOMS: Contrary to popular belief, the blossoms used in southwest cooking are those of winter squashes such as pumpkin, not zucchini. They are a perishable item and are best used the day they are bought.

TAMARIND: This is an intensely pungent, tart pod about four inches long. Tamarind is usually bought packaged in a tightly compressed, sticky, plastic-wrapped lump. The flesh is riddled with fibers and seeds—not what you want in your food—and must be soaked before using. Separate the tamarind pods, pulling away and discarding as much of the pod as you reasonably can. Cover with water and let the pulp soak for at least an hour (overnight, if time permits). Then, squeeze the pulp well to extract the juice, or rub as much pulp as you can through a fine-mesh sieve.

TEQUILA: A pale, sharp-tasting liquor distilled from the agave plant, which thrives in an arid, hot climate. The stem of the agave, known also as the "century plant," is used in making both *pulque* and tequila.

TOMATILLO: These fat little vegetables are the size of robust cherry tomatoes. They grow in papery husks reminiscent of Japanese lanterns and taste best when they are brilliant green in color. By the time they begin to turn yellow, they have lost some of their acid freshness. This happens when they are lightly cooked too, but then, although they relinquish their vibrant color, they develop a gentler flavor and become more luscious. Uncooked, chopped tomatillos are the basis for chunky green salsas. Select tomatillos with their husks still drawn tightly around them. Husk and rinse off the sticky residue before using them.

TOMATO: Roasting tomatoes gives them a faintly mysterious flavor. It works best with truly ripe, red tomatoes.

To roast and peel tomatoes: Set oven control to broil. Arrange cored tomatoes with their top surfaces about 5 inches from the heat. Broil, turning occasionally, until the skin is blistered and evenly browned, 5 to 8 minutes. The skins will be easy to remove. If the tomatoes are roasted on aluminum foil, clean-up will be easy and you'll be able to save any juice they give off as they roast.

TORTILLA: Tortillas are round, flat unleavened breads made from ground wheat or corn. They are the basis of Mexican cookery. Tortillas are rolled, folded, used as dippers, fried crisp and munched fresh. Corn tortillas are cut into wedges and fried for chips. For the best chips, fry tortillas that are at least one day old. Flour tortillas, softer than those made from corn, are more popular in northern Mexico where corn does not flourish; wheat was brought there by the Spanish. Commercially made tortillas of both kinds are best stored in the freezer until needed.

To soften tortillas, warm them on a hot, ungreased skillet or griddle for about 30 seconds to 1 minute. They can be warmed in a 250° oven for 15 minutes. Or, wrap several in dampened, microwavable paper toweling or microwave plastic wrap and microwave on high (100% power) for 15 to 20 seconds.

TRIPE: Usually what is meant by tripe is the lining of pig and sheep stomachs. Tripe is the identifying ingredient of traditional *menudo*, a hearty soup. Tripe needs to be thoroughly rinsed, often in three or four changes of cold water, before it can be used.

VENISON: Venison is deer meat. Because it is lean, venison needs moist heat to keep it tender. See Game, page 18.

WALNUTS: The flavor of this nut is delicious with corn. See Nuts, page 19, for toasting and grinding.

WILD RICE: See Rice, page 20.

Condiments and Sauces

Spicy, flavorful sauces and fresh relishes and salsas are essential elements of southwestern cuisine. Rarely are they mere optional features of traditional dishes. Recipes in this chapter are intended to accompany a good number of the fish, meat and tortilla dishes that follow. They are delicious with many, many more, so experiment to your heart's content. The relishes and salsas are chunky mixtures of fruits, vegetables, herbs and spices. The sauces are smoother and usually pack a punch.

A variety of southwestern sauces, shown with grilled chicken (clockwise from top): Chipotle Mayonnaise (page 28), Apricot Basting Sauce (page 29), Tomatillo Sauce (page 27), Red Pepper–Sour Cream Sauce (page 28) and Jalapeño Cream Sauce (page 28).

Cucumber Salsa

This recipe makes a good quantity of sauce: three cups. It is extremely versatile. Try it with Southwest Beef Fajitas (page 92). It plays a major role in Salmon with Cucumber Salsa (page 130) and would be delicious with poached or grilled chicken.

1 cup dairy sour cream
1 cup plain yogurt
1/4 cup snipped parsley
1/4 cup snipped fresh cilantro
1 teaspoon ground cumin
1/2 teaspoon salt
2 medium cucumbers, pared, seeded and coarsely shredded

Mix all ingredients. Cover and refrigerate until chilled, about 2 hours.

ABOUT 3 CUPS SALSA

Corn Salsa

Chiles and vinegar turn a can of corn into a quick relish. This is a piquant southwestern variation on an old American classic.

1 can (16 ounces) whole kernel corn, drained
1 can (4 ounces) chopped green chiles
1 jalapeño chile, seeded and finely chopped
1/4 cup chopped green bell pepper
1/4 cup sliced green onions (with tops)
2 tablespoons white wine vinegar
1 tablespoon vegetable oil
1/4 teaspoon salt

Mix all ingredients. Cover and refrigerate until chilled, about 1 hour.

ABOUT 2 1/3 CUPS SALSA

Fresh Tomato Salsa

Here is the all-purpose southwestern favorite. This simple salsa is unbeatable when tomatoes are at their brilliant best. If time permits, refrigerate the salsa for two or three hours before serving, so that the flavors of individual ingredients "marry." Serve it with any of the tortilla dishes, grilled chicken or hamburger, or tortilla chips.

3 medium tomatoes, seeded and chopped (about 3 cups)
1/2 cup sliced green onions (with tops)
1/2 cup chopped green bell pepper
2 to 3 tablespoons lime juice
2 tablespoons snipped fresh cilantro
1 tablespoon finely chopped jalapeño chile
1 teaspoon finely chopped garlic (about 3 cloves)
1/2 teaspoon salt

Mix all ingredients.

ABOUT 3 1/2 CUPS SALSA

Basic Red Sauce

This smooth sauce has a gentle ancho flavor. It is a superb all-around tomato sauce, perfect for serving with tacos and enchiladas.

8 ancho chiles
3 1/2 cups warm water
1 medium onion, chopped (about 1/2 cup)
2 cloves garlic, chopped
1/4 cup vegetable oil
1 can (8 ounces) tomato sauce
1 tablespoon dried oregano leaves
1 tablespoon cumin seed
1 teaspoon salt

Cover chiles with warm water. Let stand until softened, about 30 minutes; drain. Strain liquid; reserve. Remove stems, seeds and membranes from chiles.

Cook and stir onion and garlic in oil in 2-quart saucepan until onion is tender. Stir in chiles, 2 cups of the reserved liquid and the remaining ingredients. Heat to boiling; reduce heat. Simmer uncovered 20 minutes; cool.

Pour into food processor workbowl fitted with steel blade or into blender container; cover and process until smooth. Cover and refrigerate up to 10 days.

ABOUT 2½ CUPS SAUCE

Roasted Tomato Sauce

Roasting tomatoes is easy. Turn to the entry on tomatoes in the Glossary of Ingredients (page 20) for information on how it's done.

1 medium onion, chopped (about ½ cup)
¼ cup finely chopped carrot
1 tablespoon vegetable oil
2 pounds tomatoes, roasted and peeled (page 20)
1 tablespoon snipped fresh basil leaves
2 teaspoons sugar
1 teaspoon snipped fresh oregano leaves
¼ teaspoon salt
¼ teaspoon ground red pepper

Cook onion and carrot in oil over medium heat, stirring occasionally, until tender. Cut tomatoes into fourths; drain.

Place onion, carrot, tomatoes and remaining ingredients in food processor workbowl fitted with steel blade or in blender container; cover and process until well blended. Serve warm or cold.

ABOUT 3½ CUPS SAUCE

Casera Sauce

From spicing soups to saucing seafood, Casera Sauce is delicious anywhere the zing of cilantro and jalapeño is welcome.

2 medium tomatoes, finely chopped (about 1½ cups)
1 medium onion, chopped (about ½ cup)
1 small clove garlic, finely chopped
1 canned jalapeño chile, seeded and finely chopped
½ teaspoon canned jalapeño chile liquid
1 tablespoon finely snipped fresh cilantro
1 tablespoon lemon juice
½ teaspoon dried oregano leaves
1½ teaspoons vegetable oil

Mix all ingredients in glass or plastic bowl. Cover and refrigerate up to 7 days.

ABOUT 2 CUPS SAUCE

Almond Red Sauce

Almond Red Sauce is especially good with beef and poultry. The almonds give it body and a sophisticated, toasted flavor.

½ cup slivered almonds, toasted (page 19)
1 large onion, finely chopped (about 1 cup)
1 clove garlic, crushed
2 tablespoons vegetable oil
1 can (8 ounces) tomato sauce
2 teaspoons paprika
1 teaspoon ground red chiles
¼ teaspoon ground red pepper

Place almonds in food processor workbowl fitted with steel blade or in blender container; cover and process until finely ground.

Cook onion and garlic in oil over medium heat, stirring frequently, until onion is tender. Stir in remaining ingredients except almonds.

Heat to boiling; reduce heat. Simmer 1 minute, stirring constantly; stir in almonds. Serve hot.

ABOUT 1¾ CUPS SAUCE

Hot Chile Sauce

Here is a powerful sauce, a homemade condiment to rival commercial chile sauces. If cascabel chiles are hard to find, ancho chiles may be substituted for a slightly less fiery result.

2 cups water
6 to 8 dried cascabel chiles or ¹/₂ medium ancho chile
¹/₄ cup red wine vinegar
1 teaspoon dry mustard
1 clove garlic
¹/₄ cup olive oil

Heat water to boiling; stir in chiles. Boil uncovered 5 minutes; drain. Remove stems.

Place chiles, vinegar, mustard and garlic in blender container; cover and blend until chiles are finely chopped. Gradually pour in oil, blending until smooth.

ABOUT ¹/₂ CUP SAUCE

Chipotle Sauce

Chipotle chiles (smoked, dried jalapeños), bacon and beef broth give this unusual tomato-based sauce its deep flavor. Use it in Braised Meat Loaf and, of course, Meatballs in Chipotle Sauce (page 118).

2 to 4 dried chipotle chiles
2 slices bacon, finely cut up
1 small onion, finely chopped (about ¹/₄ cup)
4 medium tomatoes, finely chopped (about 3 cups)
1 cup beef broth
¹/₄ cup finely chopped carrot
¹/₄ cup finely chopped celery
¹/₄ cup snipped fresh cilantro
¹/₂ teaspoon salt
¹/₄ teaspoon pepper

Cover chiles with warm water. Let stand until softened, about 1 hour. Drain and finely chop.

Cook and stir bacon and onion in 2-quart saucepan until bacon is crisp; stir in chiles and remaining ingredients.

ABOUT 4 CUPS SAUCE

Basic Green Sauce

This emerald sauce is basic to Green Enchiladas (page 101). Serve it with Egg and Spinach Casserole (page 141) for a luxurious late breakfast.

2 medium onions, chopped (about 1 cup)
¹/₂ cup vegetable oil
10 ounces fresh spinach, chopped
¹/₂ pound tomatillos, coarsely chopped
1 can (4 ounces) chopped green chiles
2 cloves garlic, crushed
1 tablespoon dried oregano leaves
1 cup chicken broth
2 cups dairy sour cream

Cook and stir onions in oil in 3-quart saucepan until tender. Stir in remaining ingredients except broth and sour cream. Cover and cook over medium heat 5 minutes, stirring occasionally.

Place mixture in food processor workbowl fitted with steel blade or in blender container; cover and process until smooth, about 1 minute. Return mixture to saucepan; stir in broth.

Heat to boiling; reduce heat. Simmer uncovered 10 minutes. Stir in sour cream. Cover and refrigerate any remaining sauce.

ABOUT 4 CUPS SAUCE

New Mexico Green Sauce

This is a suave chile sauce, slightly chunky and rich with cream. It dresses up Chicken Chilaquiles Casserole (page 85) and can be substituted for any green sauce where a touch of elegance is preferred.

1 large onion, finely chopped (about 1 cup)
4 poblano chiles, roasted, peeled (page 15), seeded and finely chopped (about 1/2 cup)
1 jalapeño chile, seeded and finely chopped
1 clove garlic, finely chopped
2 tablespoons vegetable oil
1/2 cup whipping cream
1/4 teaspoon salt

Cook onion, chiles and garlic in oil over medium heat, stirring occasionally, until onion is tender, about 8 minutes. Stir in whipping cream and salt.

ABOUT 1 1/3 CUPS SAUCE

Tomatillo Sauce

Use this citric, fresh sauce as a dip for tortilla chips or whenever an uncooked green sauce is wanted.

1/4 cup chopped red onion
1/4 cup snipped fresh cilantro
1/4 teaspoon salt
1/2 pound tomatillos, cut into halves
2 canned serrano chiles, rinsed and seeded, or 1 fresh serrano chile, seeded

Place all ingredients in food processor workbowl fitted with steel blade or in blender container; cover and process until well blended.

ABOUT 1 1/4 CUPS SAUCE

Pumpkin Seed Sauce

Rich Pumpkin Seed Sauce is served with Pepita Vegetable Burritos (page 102) and Pumpkin Ravioli (page 146). The sauce may be kept warm over medium-low heat.

1 cup shelled pumpkin seeds
1 small onion, chopped (about 1/4 cup)
1 slice white bread, torn into small pieces
1 clove garlic, crushed
2 tablespoons vegetable oil
2 tablespoons canned chopped green chiles
1 can (14 ounces) chicken broth
1/2 cup whipping cream
Dash of salt

Cook pumpkin seeds, onion, bread and garlic in oil, stirring frequently, until bread is golden brown. Stir in chiles.

Place mixture in food processor workbowl fitted with steel blade; cover and process until smooth. Stir in broth, whipping cream and salt.

ABOUT 3 CUPS SAUCE

Blender Method: Place pumpkin seed mixture and about half of the broth in blender container; cover and blend until smooth. Stir in remaining broth, the whipping cream and salt.

Cilantro Pesto

Use this southwestern pesto anywhere you would use traditional basil pesto: with pasta or on simply cooked chicken or fish. Cilantro Pesto is called for in Ricotta Cheese Enchiladas (page 102) and, of course, in Halibut with Cilantro Pesto (page 130).

1½ cups firmly packed fresh cilantro
½ cup firmly packed fresh parsley
½ cup grated Parmesan cheese
½ cup vegetable oil
¼ teaspoon salt
3 cloves garlic
¼ cup pine nuts (1 ounce)

Place all ingredients in food processor workbowl fitted with steel blade or in blender container; cover and process until well blended.

ABOUT 1¼ CUPS PESTO

Chipotle Mayonnaise

This is beautiful—pale orange with intense orange flecks. It is delicious served with cold grilled beef, as a dip for raw vegetables or as a dressing for salads. Chipotle Mayonnaise is used in Sole Steamed in Corn Husks (page 128).

½ cup mayonnaise
½ cup dairy sour cream
⅛ teaspoon dried oregano leaves, if desired
2 canned chipotle chiles in adobo sauce, finely chopped

Mix all ingredients. Cover and refrigerate until chilled, about 1 hour.

ABOUT 1 CUP MAYONNAISE

Red Pepper–Sour Cream Sauce

This is another pretty sauce, soft pink in color. It flavors the Stacked New Mexico Quesadilla (page 84) and would be nice accompanying any tortilla dish that isn't brutally spicy.

3 red bell peppers, roasted and peeled (page 15)
1 red jalapeño chile, roasted and peeled (page 15)
½ cup dairy sour cream
1 teaspoon sugar

Place bell peppers and chile in food processor workbowl fitted with steel blade or in blender container; cover and process until well blended. Stir in sour cream and sugar.

ABOUT 2 CUPS SAUCE

Jalapeño Cream Sauce

Here is a refreshing sauce, great for dipping appetizers. Serve a cooling dollop with Baked Chimichangas (page 89).

1 to 2 jalapeño chiles, seeded and finely chopped
1 clove garlic, finely chopped
2 teaspoons vegetable oil
1 container (10 ounces) crème fraîche or Quick Crème Fraîche (below)
⅛ teaspoon salt
Dash of pepper

Cook chiles and garlic in oil over low heat, stirring frequently, until tender, about 4 minutes. Remove from heat; stir in remaining ingredients.

ABOUT 1¼ CUPS SAUCE

QUICK CRÈME FRAÎCHE

⅓ cup whipping cream
⅔ cup dairy sour cream

Gradually stir whipping cream into sour cream. Cover and refrigerate up to 48 hours.

Lime Butter Sauce

Make this lime hollandaise with butter only. It is delicious on seafood and cooked vegetables and as a sauce for egg dishes in the tradition of Eggs Benedict. Lime Butter Sauce is a natural with Grilled Red Snapper (page 128).

2 egg yolks
1 tablespoon lime juice
1/2 cup firm butter*
1/2 teaspoon grated lime peel

Stir egg yolks and lime juice vigorously in 1½-quart saucepan. Add ¼ cup of the butter. Heat over very low heat, stirring constantly, until butter is melted.

Add remaining butter. Continue heating, stirring vigorously, until butter is melted and sauce is thickened. (Be sure butter melts slowly so that sauce will thicken without curdling.) Stir in lime peel. Serve hot or at room temperature. Cover and refrigerate any remaining sauce.

ABOUT ¾ CUP SAUCE

* Margarine not recommended.

Apricot Basting Sauce

Like the barbecue sauces that follow, Apricot Basting Sauce is brushed on food both before and during cooking, then served at the table as a dipping sauce. This apricot version is used with Breakfast Fruit Chimichangas (page 100), Duck with Pine Nut Wild Rice (page 111) and Apricot-basted Quail (page 106).

1/2 cup apricot jam
1/4 cup dried apricots, finely chopped
1/4 cup dry white wine
1 tablespoon honey
1 teaspoon Worcestershire sauce

Heat all ingredients over low heat, stirring occasionally, until jam is melted.

ABOUT 1 CUP SAUCE

Citrus Barbecue Sauce

This sauce is the perfect basting mixture for grilled fish. For no-fuss fish steaks in the oven, see Baked Citrus Swordfish (page 125).

1 large onion, finely chopped (about 1 cup)
1 tablespoon ground red chiles
1/4 teaspoon ground red pepper
1 ancho chile, seeded and finely chopped
1 tablespoon vegetable oil
1 cup orange juice
1/2 cup lime juice
2 tablespoons sugar
2 tablespoons lemon juice
1 tablespoon snipped fresh cilantro
1 teaspoon salt

Cook onion, ground red chiles, red pepper and ancho chile in oil, stirring frequently, until onion is tender, about 5 minutes. Stir in remaining ingredients.

Heat to boiling; reduce heat to low. Simmer uncovered 10 minutes, stirring occasionally.

ABOUT 2⅓ CUPS SAUCE

Plum Barbecue Sauce

All manner of game, four-footed and winged alike, are delicious with this sweet-sour sauce.

1 small onion, finely chopped (about 1/4 cup)
1/4 cup margarine or butter
1/4 cup chile sauce
2 teaspoons Dijon-style mustard
1 can (16½ ounces) purple plums, drained, pitted and
  finely chopped
1 can (6 ounces) frozen lemonade concentrate, thawed

Cook onion in margarine in 2-quart saucepan, stirring occasionally, until tender, about 2 minutes. Stir in remaining ingredients.

Heat to boiling; reduce heat to low. Simmer uncovered 15 minutes, stirring occasionally.

ABOUT 2 CUPS SAUCE

Spicy Texas Barbecue Sauce

Here is a gutsy sauce made especially for beef and pork. Like all barbecue sauces, it is meant to be used generously.

1 cup catsup
1/2 cup packed brown sugar
1/4 cup lime juice
2 to 3 tablespoons ground red chiles
1 tablespoon vegetable oil
1 tablespoon Worcestershire sauce
3 medium onions, chopped (about 1 1/2 cups)
2 jalapeño chiles, seeded and finely chopped
2 cloves garlic, finely chopped
1 can (12 ounces) tomato paste
1 can or bottle (12 ounces) beer

Heat all ingredients to boiling in a 2-quart saucepan; reduce heat to low. Cover and simmer 1 hour, stirring occasionally.

ABOUT 5 CUPS SAUCE

Black Bean Relish

This is a dramatic relish: dark, with bright red pieces of bell pepper and tomato. It is the basis for Layered Mexican Salad (page 164) and is a bright-tasting accent to Santa Fe Chicken (page 111). Serve it with tortillas, salads, and simple grilled chicken or poached fish.

1 can (15 ounces) black beans, rinsed and drained
1 medium tomato, finely chopped (about 3/4 cup)
1 serrano chile, seeded and finely chopped
1/2 cup chopped red bell pepper
1/4 cup finely chopped red onion
2 tablespoons white wine vinegar
1 tablespoon vegetable oil
1/4 teaspoon salt

Mix all ingredients. Cover and refrigerate until chilled, about 1 hour.

2 1/2 CUPS RELISH

Hot Pickled Vegetables

Serve this fresh vegetable relish as a hot and spicy complement to any grilled meat or simple fish.

4 ounces whole green beans
3 stalks celery, cut into 2 x 1/4-inch strips (about 1 1/2 cups)
2 medium carrots, cut diagonally into thin slices (about 1 cup)
1 1/2 cups cauliflowerets
1 cup broccoli flowerets
1 cup pearl onions
1/2 cup sliced fresh or canned serrano or jalapeño chiles
1/2 cup coarse salt
2 cups cider vinegar
2 cups water
2 tablespoons black peppercorns
3/4 teaspoon ground cloves

Mix all ingredients in large glass or plastic container. Cover and refrigerate at least 48 hours but no longer than 2 weeks.

ABOUT 10 CUPS VEGETABLES

Radish and Cilantro Relish

This relish is a great head start for Pork Chops in Radish Sauce (page 122).

2 cups thinly sliced radishes (about 24)
1 medium onion, chopped (about ½ cup)
3 tablespoons orange juice
2 tablespoons lime juice
2 tablespoons finely snipped fresh cilantro
2 tablespoons vegetable oil
¼ teaspoon salt
⅛ teaspoon freshly ground pepper

Mix all ingredients in glass or plastic bowl. Cover and refrigerate at least 1 hour.

3 CUPS RELISH

Southwest Relish

This beautiful relish is a classic complement to Southwest Beef Fajitas (page 92). Like Black Bean Relish (page 30), Corn Salsa (page 24) and Cucumber Salsa (page 24), it would be equally good served with grilled chicken, cold poached fish or seafood, salads or tortillas.

6 ounces tomatillos, chopped (about 1 cup)
1 medium tomato, seeded and chopped (about ¾ cup)
1 small green bell pepper, diced (about ¾ cup)
1 small red bell pepper, diced (about ¾ cup)
1 small yellow bell pepper, diced (about ¾ cup)
¼ cup pine nuts (1 ounce), toasted (page 19)
2 cloves garlic, finely chopped
1 tablespoon snipped fresh sage leaves
1 tablespoon lemon juice
¼ teaspoon salt

Mix all ingredients. Cover and refrigerate at least 1 hour.

4 CUPS RELISH

Zucchini Relish

The principal ingredient of the relish is zucchini, but the principal flavor is cilantro. A hint of sugar brings out the flavor of the squash.

2 cups shredded zucchini
¼ cup snipped fresh cilantro
2 tablespoons lime juice
2 tablespoons olive or vegetable oil
1 teaspoon salt
¼ teaspoon sugar
¼ teaspoon pepper

Mix all ingredients in glass or plastic bowl. Cover and refrigerate at least 1 hour.

1¼ CUPS RELISH

Papaya Relish

Another superb relish to accompany grilled meats, Papaya Relish is delicious with dishes of more complex flavors (Grilled Pork Tacos, page 94, for example).

½ cup chopped red onion
½ cup chopped red bell pepper
1 small red chile, seeded and finely chopped
1 tablespoon vegetable oil
¼ cup snipped fresh mint leaves
2 tablespoons lime juice
1 papaya, pared, seeded and cut into ½-inch cubes

Cook onion, bell pepper and chile in oil over medium heat, stirring frequently, until tender. Stir in remaining ingredients. Cover and refrigerate until chilled, about 2 hours.

3 CUPS RELISH

Following pages: A variety of southwestern relishes, shown with a grilled swordfish steak (clockwise from top): Papaya Relish (in bowl, page 31), Southwest Relish (page 31), Hot Pickled Vegetables (page 30), Radish and Cilantro Relish (page 31) and Zucchini Relish (in bowl, page 31).

Appetizers, Snacks and Beverages

A profusion of appetizers is typical of the southwestern table, where a generous and colorful spread speaks of welcome and hospitality. Sometimes the difference between an appetizer and a main dish is just the size of the serving. Relishes have a place on the appetizer table, too, whether they are spread on or scooped up with crisp tortilla chips. The following pages feature dips sparked with citrus or cilantro, stuffed vegetables to nibble chilled or piping hot and classic cheese savories.

What should be drunk with southwestern food? Honest beer is often a good choice, but not the only one. Try a refreshing Southwest Smoothie (page 56) or Mexican Tea Punch (page 56), exotic Tamarind Cooler (page 55) or spicy-rich Fiesta Hot Chocolate (page 62) to accompany sweets. Here are the time-honored formulas for such traditional favorites as Sangria Blanco (page 58), Café Diablo (page 62), and the sophisticated Chartreuse Cocktail (page 58) . . . in short, a drink for every taste and every occasion.

Double Cheese Wheel

Double Cheese Wheel

1 whole, firm round Chihuahua cheese or Monterey
Jack cheese (1 pound)
1 package (3 ounces) cream cheese, softened
¼ cup chopped marinated artichoke hearts, drained
¼ cup pine nuts (1 ounce), toasted (page 19)
1½ teaspoons snipped fresh basil leaves or ½ teaspoon
dried basil leaves

Remove any wax coating or rind from Chihuahua cheese. Hollow out cheese with knife or spoon, leaving a shell ½-inch thick on side and bottom; reserve cheese shell. Finely chop enough of the scooped-out cheese to measure 1 cup (reserve any extra for another use).

Place 1 cup chopped cheese, the cream cheese, artichoke hearts, 3 tablespoons of the pine nuts and the basil in food processor workbowl fitted with steel blade; cover and process until well mixed.

Pack mixture into cheese shell. Sprinkle with remaining 1 tablespoon pine nuts; press lightly. Cover and refrigerate until filling is firm, about 3 hours.

Cut into thin wedges. Serve with assorted crackers if desired.

24 SERVINGS

Bean and Garlic Dip

2 cups Pinto Beans (page 12)
¼ cup mayonnaise or salad dressing
1 clove garlic, finely chopped
1½ teaspoons ground red chiles
¼ teaspoon salt
Dash of pepper

Mix all ingredients. Cover and refrigerate 1 hour. Serve with tortilla chips.

ABOUT 2 CUPS DIP

Corn and Walnut Dip

2 packages (8 ounces each) cream cheese, softened
¼ cup vegetable oil
¼ cup lime juice
1 tablespoon ground red chiles
1 tablespoon ground cumin
½ teaspoon salt
Dash of pepper
1 can (8¾ ounces) whole kernel corn, drained
1 cup chopped walnuts
1 small onion, chopped (about ¼ cup)

Beat all ingredients except corn, walnuts and onion in large bowl on medium speed until smooth. Stir in corn, walnuts and onion. Serve with tortilla chips.

4 CUPS DIP

Avocado and Raisin Dip

Raisins give deep background flavor to the light, fruity avocado. Fresh lime juice does more than add a sharp note of citrus; it keeps the dip fresh looking, even at room temperature.

2 avocados, peeled and chopped
½ cup raisins
½ cup vegetable oil
¼ cup lime juice
1 teaspoon sugar
1 teaspoon salt
¼ teaspoon freshly ground pepper

Place all ingredients in blender container. Cover and blend on high speed until smooth, about 45 seconds. Serve with raw vegetables, assorted crackers or fried tortillas.

1⅔ CUPS DIP

Corn and Walnut Dip

Chile con Queso

1 cup shredded Cheddar or Monterey Jack cheese
  (4 ounces)
1 can (4 ounces) chopped green chiles, drained
1/4 cup half-and-half
2 tablespoons finely chopped onion
2 teaspoons ground cumin
1/2 teaspoon salt

Heat all ingredients over low heat, stirring constantly, until cheese is melted. Serve warm with tortilla chips.

1¼ CUPS DIP

Southwest Guacamole

5 ripe avocados, peeled and pitted
4 cloves garlic, finely chopped
1 medium tomato, chopped (about 1 cup)
1/4 cup lime juice
1/2 teaspoon salt

Mash avocados in a medium bowl until slightly lumpy. Stir in remaining ingredients. Cover and refrigerate 1 hour.

3 CUPS GUACAMOLE

Cowboy Caviar

Black beans and olives, rather than sturgeon roe, take prize of place here. After the big taste of southwestern "caviar," it's hard to go back to the itty-bitty stuff city folk call caviar.

1 can (15 ounces) black beans, rinsed and drained
1 can (4 ounces) chopped ripe olives, drained
1 small onion, finely chopped (about 1/4 cup)
1 clove garlic, finely chopped
2 tablespoons vegetable oil
2 tablespoons lime juice
1/4 teaspoon salt
1/4 teaspoon crushed red pepper
1/4 teaspoon ground cumin
1/8 teaspoon pepper
1 package (8 ounces) cream cheese, softened
2 hard-cooked eggs, peeled and chopped
1 green onion (with top), sliced

Mix all ingredients except cream cheese, eggs and green onion. Cover and refrigerate at least 2 hours.

Spread cream cheese on serving plate. Spoon bean mixture evenly over cream cheese. Arrange eggs on bean mixture in ring around edge of plate; sprinkle with green onion.

ABOUT 12 SERVINGS

Cowboy Caviar

Cheese Chiles

This spicy appetizer is strictly for fun. Shredded chile-spiked cheese is molded into chile shapes, complete with cilantro stalks to imitate chile stems. Cheese Chiles can be prepared several days ahead of time; replace the cilantro "stems" before serving.

1 cup shredded Cheddar cheese (4 ounces)
1 cup shredded Colby cheese (4 ounces)
1 teaspoon ground red chiles
1 bunch cilantro stems, cut into ¹/₂-inch pieces
Paprika

Place all ingredients except cilantro and paprika in food processor workbowl fitted with steel blade; cover and process until smooth, about 1 minute. Roll mixture by teaspoonfuls into chile shapes.

Insert cilantro pieces in wide ends of shapes for stems. Sprinkle with paprika. Cover and refrigerate until serving time.

48 APPETIZERS

Nachos

Vegetable oil
6 flour or corn tortillas (6 to 8 inches in diameter)
1¹/₂ cups shredded Cheddar cheese (6 ounces)
6 jalapeño chiles, seeded and each cut into 6 strips

Heat oil (¹/₂ inch) to 365° in 8- to 10-inch skillet. Cook tortillas, one at a time, in oil: hold tortilla down in oil with tongs until light brown, about 1 minute; drain.

Place tortillas on ungreased cookie sheet. Sprinkle each with ¹/₄ cup of the cheese. Arrange chile strips on cheese.

Set oven control to broil. Broil tortillas with tops 3 to 4 inches from heat until cheese is melted. Cut each tortilla into 6 wedges.

36 NACHOS

Cheese Chiles

Jícama Appetizer

1 jícama (about 2 pounds)
¹/₄ cup lemon juice
1 teaspoon salt
1 teaspoon ground red chiles

Pare jícama; cut into fourths. Cut each fourth into ¹/₄-inch slices. Arrange slices on serving plate. Drizzle with lemon juice; sprinkle with salt and ground red chiles. Refrigerate until chilled, at least 2 hours.

ABOUT 3¹/₂ DOZEN APPETIZERS

Breaded Plantain Rounds

Use only fully ripe plantains for this appetizer. To ripen plantains, store them at room temperature until their skins are black and they give slightly when gently pressed. A ripe plantain isn't as soft as a ripe banana (but it shouldn't be hard, either).

¹/₄ cup margarine or butter
1 tablespoon lemon juice
¹/₃ cup fine dry bread crumbs
¹/₃ cup freshly grated queso añejo or Parmesan cheese
¹/₂ teaspoon ground red chiles
¹/₈ teaspoon pepper
2 ripe plantains, peeled and cut into ¹/₂-inch slices

Heat oven to 375°. Heat margarine and lemon juice until margarine is melted. Mix together remaining ingredients except plantains. Dip plantain slices into margarine mixture; coat with crumb mixture.

Place on greased cookie sheet. Carefully spoon any remaining margarine mixture over slices. Bake until tender and golden brown, 20 to 25 minutes.

ABOUT 30 APPETIZERS

Plantain Chips

Vegetable oil
4 plantains, cut into 1/4-inch slices
1 tablespoon chile powder
1/2 teaspoon salt

Heat oil (1 inch) to 350° in 3-quart saucepan or 4-quart Dutch oven. Fry plantains in oil, turning once, until golden brown, about 2 minutes; drain. Toss with chile powder and salt.

ABOUT 5 CUPS CHIPS

Stuffed Mushrooms

24 medium mushrooms
2 tablespoons margarine or butter
1 medium onion, chopped (about 1/4 cup)
2 tablespoons dry white wine
1/4 cup dry bread crumbs
1/4 cup finely chopped fully cooked smoked ham
2 tablespoons snipped parsley
1 tablespoon lime juice
1 clove garlic, finely chopped
1 teaspoon dried oregano leaves
Dash of pepper
1/2 cup finely shredded Monterey Jack cheese (2 ounces)

Cut stems from mushrooms; finely chop enough stems to measure 1/4 cup. Heat margarine in 10-inch skillet just until bubbly. Place mushroom caps, top sides down, in margarine. Cook uncovered until mushrooms are light brown; remove mushrooms with slotted spoon.

Cook and stir onion in same skillet until tender; stir in wine. Simmer uncovered 2 minutes. Mix in chopped mushroom stems and remaining ingredients except cheese and mushroom caps; cool slightly.

Shape mixture into 24 small balls; place 1 in each mushroom cap. Sprinkle with cheese. Set oven control to broil. Place mushrooms caps on rack in broiler pan. Broil with tops 3 to 4 inches from heat until cheese is melted, about 3 minutes.

24 APPETIZERS

Bell Pepper Rajas

Rajas ("strips") usually refers to ribbons of chiles. To prepare *rajas* in the microwave oven, arrange strips on a microwave-safe serving plate. Sprinkle with toppings and cover loosely with waxed paper. Microwave on high (100% power) 1 minute; rotate plate one quarter turn. Microwave 30 to 60 seconds longer, until the cheese has melted.

1/2 green bell pepper, seeded and cut into 6 strips
1/2 red bell pepper, seeded and cut into 6 strips
1/2 yellow bell pepper, seeded and cut into 6 strips
3/4 cup shredded Monterey Jack cheese (3 ounces)
2 tablespoons chopped ripe olives
1/4 teaspoon crushed red pepper

Cut bell pepper strips crosswise into halves. Arrange in ungreased broilerproof pie pan, 9 x 1 1/4 inches, or round pan, 9 x 2 inches. Sprinkle with cheese, olives and red pepper.

Set oven control to broil. Broil peppers with tops 3 to 4 inches from heat until cheese is melted, about 3 minutes.

6 SERVINGS

Avocado Toast

1/2 cup margarine or butter, softened
1/2 cup mashed avocado
2 teaspoons lime juice
1 1/2 teaspoons snipped fresh oregano leaves or
  1/2 teaspoon dried oregano leaves
1 clove garlic, finely chopped
12 slices French bread, cut diagonally 1/2 inch thick

Beat all ingredients except bread on medium speed until smooth. Set oven control to broil. Place bread on ungreased cookie sheet. Broil with tops about 4 inches from heat until light brown, 2 to 3 minutes.

Spread each slice bread generously with avocado mixture. Broil until bubbly, about 2 minutes.

12 SERVINGS

Snappy Stuffed Tomatillos

20 tomatillos or cherry tomatoes (1¼ to 1½ inches)
⅔ cup shredded Cheddar cheese
½ cup whole kernel corn
2 packages (3 ounces each) cream cheese, softened
2 green onions (with tops), sliced
1 teaspoon ground red chiles
Ground red chiles

Cut thin slice from stem ends of tomatillos. Remove pulp and seeds with melon baller or small spoon.

Mix Cheddar cheese, corn, cream cheese, onions and 1 teaspoon ground red chiles. Fill tomatillos with cheese mixture; sprinkle with ground red chiles. Cover and refrigerate until serving time.

20 APPETIZERS

Corn and Onion Fritters

1 large onion, chopped (about 1 cup)
2 tablespoons margarine or butter
1 can (16½ ounces) whole kernel corn, drained
1 jar (4 ounces) chopped pimientos, drained
¾ teaspoon salt
¼ teaspoon pepper
Vegetable oil
1 cup all-purpose flour
½ cup shredded Colby cheese (2 ounces)
1 teaspoon baking powder
½ cup milk
2 eggs, separated

Cook and stir onion in margarine until tender. Stir in corn, pimiento, salt and pepper; cool.

Heat oil (1 inch) to 375° in 4-quart Dutch oven. Mix corn mixture, flour, cheese and baking powder. Stir in milk and egg yolks. Beat egg whites in small bowl until stiff but not dry. Fold corn mixture into egg whites.

Drop batter by rounded teaspoonfuls into oil. Fry until golden brown, turning once, about 1 minute; drain.

ABOUT 48 FRITTERS

Flautas

1 cup finely chopped cooked chicken
12 flour tortillas (7 to 8 inches in diameter)
Vegetable oil

Spoon 1 rounded tablespoon of the chicken across bottom of each tortilla. Roll up tightly; secure with wooden picks.

Heat oil (1 inch) to 350° in 4-quart Dutch oven. Cook tortillas in oil, turning once, until golden brown, about 2 minutes; drain. Remove wooden picks. Serve with Southwest Guacamole (page 38) or a salsa.

12 FLAUTAS

Blue Cornmeal Chicken Wings

¼ cup lime juice
¼ cup vegetable oil
½ teaspoon crushed red pepper
10 chicken wings (about 2 pounds)
2 tablespoons margarine or butter
½ cup blue or yellow cornmeal
2 tablespoons all-purpose flour
½ teaspoon salt
½ teaspoon ground cumin
⅛ teaspoon pepper

Mix lime juice, oil and red pepper in large glass or plastic bowl. Cut each chicken wing at joints to make 3 pieces; discard tip. Cut off and discard excess skin. Place wings in oil mixture; stir to coat. Cover and refrigerate at least 3 hours, stirring occasionally; drain.

Heat oven to 425°. Heat margarine in rectangular pan, 13 x 9 x 2 inches, in oven until melted. Shake remaining ingredients in plastic bag, or mix in bowl. Shake wings in cornmeal mixture to coat; place in pan. Bake uncovered 20 minutes; turn. Bake until golden brown, 20 to 25 minutes longer.

20 APPETIZERS

Snappy Stuffed Tomatillos

Western Swing Pâté

½ pound bacon
1 pound ground turkey
½ pound ground pork
1 egg
2 cloves garlic, finely chopped
1 medium onion, chopped (about ½ cup)
½ cup diced red bell pepper
½ cup diced yellow bell pepper
½ cup unsweetened corn bread crumbs
2 tablespoons tequila
2 tablespoons snipped fresh cilantro
1 teaspoon salt
½ teaspoon ground coriander

Heat oven to 350°. Line bottom of loaf pan, 8½ x 4½ x 2½ or 9 x 5 x 3 inches, crosswise with bacon, bringing slices up sides and over edge of pan.

Mix remaining ingredients. Spoon into pan; smooth top. Fold bacon ends over top of meat mixture. Place remaining slices bacon lengthwise on top. Cover with aluminum foil. Bake 1½ to 2 hours; drain carefully, leaving pâté in pan. Let stand uncovered 1 hour.

Cover with plastic wrap. Refrigerate until cold, at least 5 hours but no longer than 3 days. Loosen pâté from bottom of pan if necessary; invert on serving platter. Cut into thin slices.

16 SERVINGS

Tex-Mex Peanuts

2 cloves garlic, crushed
1 teaspoon vegetable oil
1 cup unsalted dry-roasted peanuts
1 tablespoon chile powder
½ teaspoon salt

Cook and stir garlic in oil in 8-inch skillet over medium heat until golden brown; discard garlic. Stir peanuts and chile powder into skillet. Cook and stir over medium heat until peanuts are warm, about 2 minutes; drain. Sprinkle with salt.

1 CUP PEANUTS

Blue Cornmeal Mini Muffins

Tiny muffins make wonderful appetizers. These little gems are just two bites each. Make the larger muffins in the variation below for brunch or dinner. Serve with green-flecked Chile Butter.

Chile Butter (below)
2 eggs
1½ cups milk
3 tablespoons vegetable oil
2 tablespoons finely chopped canned green chiles, drained
1¼ cups blue cornmeal
¾ cup all-purpose flour
2 teaspoons baking powder
½ teaspoon salt

Prepare Chile Butter. Heat oven to 400°. Generously grease 12 miniature muffin cups, 1¾ x ¾ inch. Beat eggs in large bowl; stir in milk, oil and chiles. Stir in remaining ingredients, all at once, just until cornmeal is moistened (batter will be lumpy). Fill muffin cups about ⅘ full. Cover and refrigerate remaining batter.

Bake until light golden brown, about 15 minutes. Loosen edges with knife; immediately remove from pan. Repeat twice with remaining batter. Serve with Chile Butter.

36 MINI MUFFINS

Blue Cornmeal Muffins: Generously grease about 18 medium muffin cups, 2½ x 1¼ inches. Fill cups about ¾ full. Bake about 20 minutes.

ABOUT 18 MUFFINS

CHILE BUTTER

½ cup margarine or butter
2 tablespoons finely chopped canned green chiles

Mix margarine and chiles until well blended. Cover, and refrigerate. Remove from refrigerator 15 minutes before serving time.

Western Swing Pâté

Empanaditas

Empanaditas ("little *empanadas*") are baked or fried pastries stuffed with savory or sweet fillings. These little *empanadas* are just right for dipping into Jalapeño Cream Sauce (page 28) or Almond Red Sauce (page 25).

½ pound ground beef
1 small onion, finely chopped (about ¼ cup)
2 tablespoons raisins, chopped
2 tablespoons chopped green olives
¼ teaspoon salt
⅛ teaspoon pepper
¼ cup small curd creamed cottage cheese
1 hard-cooked egg, peeled and chopped
1 egg, separated
1 teaspoon water
Pastry dough for 10-inch 2-crust pie
2 teaspoons milk

Cook and stir ground beef in 10-inch skillet, breaking up into small pieces, until brown; drain, reserving 1 tablespoon fat and the beef in skillet. Stir in onion, raisins, olives, salt and pepper. Cover and cook over low heat 5 minutes. Stir in cottage cheese and hard-cooked egg.

Heat oven to 400°. Mix egg white and water until slightly foamy; reserve. Prepare pastry dough; gather into a ball. Divide into halves. Shape into 2 flattened rounds on lightly floured cloth-covered surface. Roll 1 round of pastry into circle, about 14 inches in diameter. Cut into 11 or 12 circles, 3½ inches in diameter.

Spoon 2 teaspoons beef mixture onto center of each circle; brush edge of pastry with egg white mixture. Fold pastry circle up over filling; press edge with fork to seal. Place empanaditas on ungreased cookie sheet. Repeat with remaining round of pastry and filling. Gather any remaining pastry; shape into another round. Repeat rolling, cutting and filling.

Beat egg yolk and milk until well blended; brush over tops of empanaditas. Bake until golden brown, 15 to 20 minutes. Serve warm.

ABOUT 34 EMPANADITAS

Southwest Riblets

Pork ribs are cut in half to make bite-size appetizers. Unsweetened chocolate smooths the assertive flavor of garlic and the punch of ground red chiles. These riblets are luscious; don't forget to put out lots of paper napkins.

1 medium onion, chopped (about ½ cup)
2 tablespoons vegetable oil
1 tablespoon ground red chiles
6 dried juniper berries, crushed
3 cloves garlic, finely chopped
½ teaspoon salt
½ ounce unsweetened chocolate, grated
1 cup water
2 tablespoons cider vinegar
1 can (6 ounces) tomato paste
2 tablespoons sugar
3-pound rack fresh pork back ribs, cut lengthwise across bones into halves

Cook and stir onion in oil in 2-quart saucepan 2 minutes. Stir in ground red chiles, juniper berries, garlic and salt. Cover and cook 5 minutes, stirring occasionally. Stir in chocolate until melted.

Pour water, vinegar and tomato paste into food processor workbowl fitted with steel blade or into blender container. Add onion mixture and sugar; cover and process until well blended.

Heat oven to 375°. Cut between pork back ribs to separate. Place in single layer in roasting pan; pour sauce evenly over pork. Bake uncovered 30 minutes; turn pork. Bake until done, about 30 minutes longer.

ABOUT 28 APPETIZERS

Southwest Riblets

Preceding pages: Empanaditas

Meatballs in Chile Sauce

3 corn tortillas (6 inches in diameter), cut into small
  pieces
1/2 cup milk
1/2 pound ground beef
1/2 pound ground pork
1/2 pound finely chopped fully cooked smoked ham
1 small onion, chopped (about 1/4 cup)
1 clove garlic, finely chopped
1 teaspoon ground cumin
1 teaspoon dried oregano leaves
1/2 teaspoon salt
1/4 teaspoon pepper
1 cup Basic Red Sauce (page 24)
1 cup beef broth

Place tortilla pieces and milk in large bowl; let
stand 15 minutes. Mix in remaining ingredients
except Basic Red Sauce and broth. Shape into
1-inch balls.

Heat Basic Red Sauce and broth to boiling in 10-
inch skillet; reduce heat. Add meatballs. Cover
and simmer until done, 15 to 20 minutes.

ABOUT 42 MEATBALLS

Southwest Ham and Cheese

6 thin slices fully cooked smoked ham
6 flour tortillas (7 inches in diameter)
3 slices Muenster or mild Cheddar cheese
6 tablespoons vegetable oil

Place 1 slice ham on each of 3 tortillas. Top each
with cheese, another slice ham and a tortilla.

Heat 2 tablespoons of the oil in 10-inch skillet
over medium heat until hot. Cook 1 sandwich in
oil, turning once, until golden brown and cheese
is melted, about 3 minutes. Cut into 4 wedges.
Repeat with remaining oil and sandwiches.

12 APPETIZERS

Caramelized Carnitas

Traditional recipes for carnitas ("little pieces of
meat") require threading thin strips of meat on
skewers before broiling or grilling them. This
easy stove-top method eliminates that step.

1 1/2-pound pork boneless shoulder, cut into 1-inch
  cubes
2 tablespoons packed brown sugar
1 tablespoon tequila
1 tablespoon molasses
1/2 teaspoon salt
1/4 teaspoon pepper
2 cloves garlic, finely chopped
1/3 cup water
1 green onion (with top), sliced

Place pork cubes in single layer in 10-inch skillet.
Top with remaining ingredients except green
onion. Heat to boiling; reduce heat.

Simmer uncovered, stirring occasionally, until
water is evaporated and pork is slightly caramelized, about 35 minutes. Sprinkle with green
onion and serve with wooden picks.

10 SERVINGS

Mexican Shrimp Cocktail

1 cup water
⅓ cup lime juice
1 clove garlic, finely chopped
2 teaspoons salt
Dash of pepper
24 raw medium shrimp, peeled and deveined
1 avocado, peeled and chopped
2 jalapeño chiles, seeded and finely chopped
¼ cup chopped tomato
2 tablespoons chopped onion
2 tablespoons finely chopped carrot
2 tablespoons snipped fresh cilantro
2 tablespoons olive or vegetable oil
1½ cups finely shredded lettuce
Lemon or lime wedges

Heat water, lime juice, garlic, salt and pepper to boiling in 4-quart Dutch oven; reduce heat. Simmer uncovered until reduced to ⅔ cup. Add shrimp. Cover and simmer 3 minutes; do not overcook. Immediately remove shrimp from liquid with slotted spoon; place in bowl of iced water. Simmer liquid until reduced to 2 tablespoons; cool.

Mix reduced liquid, shrimp and remaining ingredients except shredded lettuce and lemon wedges in glass or plastic bowl. Cover and refrigerate at least 1 hour.

Just before serving, place ¼ cup lettuce on each of 6 serving dishes. Divide shrimp mixture among dishes. Garnish with lemon wedges.

6 SERVINGS

Crab and Avocado Cocktail

1 cup cooked crabmeat
2 avocados, peeled and chopped
2 jalapeño chiles, seeded and finely chopped
1 small tomato, chopped (about ¼ cup)
¼ cup lime juice
2 tablespoons olive or vegetable oil
2 tablespoons chopped onion
2 tablespoons snipped fresh cilantro
1 clove garlic, finely chopped
¾ teaspoon salt
Dash of pepper
1½ cups finely shredded lettuce
Lime or lemon wedges

Mix all ingredients except lettuce and lime wedges. Place ¼ cup of the lettuce on each of 6 serving dishes. Divide crabmeat mixture among dishes. Garnish with lime wedges.

6 SERVINGS

Fish en Escabeche

Escabeche and *ceviche*, pickled fish dishes popular throughout the Southwest, differ primarily in that *ceviche* is made with marinated, raw fish. For *escabeche*, use a firm white-fleshed fish that will hold together during cooking. The traditional cracker to serve with fish *en escabeche* is the saltine.

1 pound firm white fish fillets (orange roughy, haddock
* or mackerel), cut into ¹/₂-inch cubes*
¹/₃ cup lemon juice
¹/₃ cup lime juice
¹/₄ cup olive or vegetable oil
1 tablespoon snipped fresh cilantro or 1 teaspoon dried
* cilantro leaves*
1 teaspoon snipped fresh oregano or ¹/₄ teaspoon dried
* oregano leaves*
³/₄ teaspoon salt
¹/₄ teaspoon pepper
12 small pimiento-stuffed green olives
2 jalapeño chiles, seeded and chopped
1 small onion, finely chopped (about ¹/₄ cup)
1 clove garlic, finely chopped
1 large tomato, seeded and chopped (about 1 cup)
1 avocado, peeled and chopped

Heat ¾ inch water to boiling in 10-inch skillet; carefully place fish in water. Heat to boiling; reduce heat. Simmer uncovered just until fish is opaque, about 30 seconds (do not overcook, or fish will fall apart); drain carefully.

Mix remaining ingredients except tomato and avocado in glass or plastic dish. Stir in fish. Cover and refrigerate 2 days, stirring occasionally.

Just before serving, gently stir in tomato and avocado; drain. Serve fish mixture with crackers or tortilla chips if desired.

12 SERVINGS

Fresh Fruit Frappé

1 cup cut-up watermelon
1 cup cut-up cantaloupe or honeydew melon
1 cup cut-up pineapple
1 cup cut-up mango
1 cup strawberry halves
¹/₄ cup sugar
1 cup orange juice
Crushed ice

Mix all ingredients except ice. Fill blender container ¹/₂ full of mixture; add crushed ice to fill to top. Cover and blend on high speed until of uniform consistency.

Repeat with remaining mixture. Serve immediately; garnish with fruit if desired.

7 SERVINGS (ABOUT 1 CUP EACH)

Tamarind Cooler

Tamarind Cooler looks like iced tea, and takes just a little more effort to make. This is a citric, sweet-tart drink. Garnish with fresh mint.

1 pound whole tamarind pods
Hot water
2 quarts water
1 to 1¹/₃ cups sugar

Cover tamarind pods with hot water. Let stand 5 minutes; drain. Rinse and drain. Remove pods, stems and strings from tamarinds. Place tamarinds in 2 quarts water. Let stand 4 hours; drain, reserving liquid.

Press as much tamarind pulp as possible through sieve. Mix pulp, reserved liquid and the sugar. Cover and refrigerate until chilled. Serve over ice if desired.

8 SERVINGS (1 CUP EACH)

Fish en Escabeche

Pineapple Limeade

1/2 cup sugar
3 cups pineapple juice
1/2 cup lime juice
1 quart sparkling water, chilled

Mix all ingredients except sparkling water; refrigerate until chilled. Just before serving, stir in sparkling water. Serve over ice. Garnish with lime slices if desired.

8 SERVINGS (ABOUT 1 CUP EACH)

Sangria

1 bottle (25 ounces) dry red wine
1/2 can (6-ounce size) frozen lemonade concentrate, thawed, (about 1/3 cup)
1/2 cup brandy
1/2 cup orange-flavored liqueur
1/3 cup orange juice
1/4 cup lemon juice
2 cups chilled ginger ale

Mix all ingredients except ginger ale; refrigerate until chilled. Just before serving, stir in ginger ale. Garnish with fruit if desired.

12 SERVINGS (ABOUT 2/3 CUP EACH)

Mexican Tea Punch

2 cups tequila
2 cups cold strong tea
1 cup pineapple juice
1/4 cup honey
1/4 cup water
1/4 cup lemon juice
1/4 cup lime juice
1 1/2 teaspoons ground cinnamon
1 1/2 teaspoons aromatic bitters

Mix all ingredients; refrigerate until chilled. Stir before serving. Serve over ice.

9 SERVINGS (ABOUT 2/3 CUP EACH)

Piña Colada

1/4 cup crushed ice
2 tablespoons light rum (1 ounce)
2 tablespoons pineapple juice (1 ounce)
1 tablespoon cream of coconut (1/2 ounce)

Place all ingredients in blender container. Cover and blend on high speed until foamy, about 30 seconds. Garnish with fruit if desired.

1 SERVING

Margarita Sunrise

1 lime, cut into halves
Granulated sugar
3 cups cracked ice
1/4 cup powdered sugar
1 cup tequila
1 can (6 ounces) frozen orange juice concentrate, thawed

Rub rims of 4 stemmed glasses with 1 lime half; dip rims of glasses in granulated sugar. Squeeze juice from both lime halves into blender container. Add remaining ingredients. Cover and blend on high speed until foamy.

6 SERVINGS (ABOUT 2/3 CUP EACH)

Southwest Smoothie

1/2 cup sliced banana
1/2 cup chopped mango, papaya or guava
2 cups milk
1 tablespoon honey

Place all ingredients in food processor workbowl fitted with steel blade or in blender container; cover and process on high speed until smooth. Strain if using mango.

3 SERVINGS (ABOUT 1 CUP EACH)

Margarita Sunrise

Sangria Blanco

¼ cup sugar
½ cup water
2 sticks cinnamon, broken into halves
1 cup sparkling water
1 cup apple juice
½ cup orange juice
1 bottle (25 ounces) Chardonnay or dry white wine,
  chilled
1 medium unpared orange, cut into halves and thinly
  sliced
1 medium unpared eating apple, cut into thin wedges
1 medium banana, sliced
Ice cubes

Heat sugar, water and cinnamon to boiling in 1-quart saucepan; reduce heat. Simmer uncovered 5 minutes. Cover and refrigerate at least 2 hours but no longer than 1 week.

Remove cinnamon sticks from sugar mixture. Mix sugar mixture, sparkling water, apple juice, orange juice and wine in large pitcher. Gently stir in fruit and ice. Serve with several pieces fruit in each glass.

8 SERVINGS (ABOUT 1 CUP EACH)

Chartreuse Cocktail

Chartreuse is a liqueur flavored with herbs. This distinctive, brilliantly colored cordial was developed by French monks hundreds of years ago. It is made today from the same, unchanged and closely guarded formula.

3 tablespoons tequila (1½ ounces)
2 parts green Chartreuse liqueur (1 ounce)
1 tablespoon lime juice (½ ounce)
¼ cup crushed ice

Pour all ingredients over ice in tightly covered container. Shake until very cold. Pour into serving glass; garnish with lime slice if desired.

1 SERVING

Atole

This thin gruel was introduced to the Spaniards by the Aztec Indians. White or yellow cornmeal may be used if blue cornmeal is not available. Flavored with cocoa, *atole* becomes *champurrado*.

1 cup atole blue cornmeal*
½ teaspoon ground cinnamon
¼ teaspoon salt
2 cups water
3 cups milk
½ cup honey

Mix cornmeal, cinnamon, salt and water in 3-quart saucepan. Heat to boiling, stirring constantly; reduce heat to low. Stir in milk and honey. Heat to simmering, stirring constantly (do not boil).

6 SERVINGS (ABOUT 1 CUP EACH)

Champurrado: Stir in ¼ cup cocoa with the cornmeal. (Mixture will be very thick when heated to boiling.) Gradually stir in milk.

* Regular blue cornmeal can be substituted for the *atole* blue cornmeal. Heat oven to 400°. Spread cornmeal in ungreased shallow baking pan. Bake, stirring occasionally, until light brown, about 10 minutes.

Sangria Blanco

Fiesta Hot Chocolate

½ cup cocoa
1 tablespoon all-purpose flour
⅓ cup grated piloncillo or ¼ cup packed dark brown
* sugar*
4 cups milk
3 whole cloves
1 stick cinnamon, broken into halves
2 tablespoons powdered sugar
1½ teaspoons vanilla
Whipped cream
4 sticks cinnamon

Mix cocoa and flour in 2-quart saucepan. Stir in piloncillo, milk, cloves and 1 stick cinnamon. Heat just to boiling over medium heat, stirring constantly; reduce heat. Simmer uncovered 5 minutes (do not boil). Remove from heat; remove cloves and cinnamon. Stir in powdered sugar and vanilla.

Beat with molinillo, wire whisk or hand beater until foamy. Pour into 4 cups or mugs. Serve with whipped cream and cinnamon sticks.

4 SERVINGS (ABOUT 1 CUP EACH)

Café Mexicano

8 cups cold water
½ cup grated piloncillo or ⅓ cup packed dark brown
* sugar*
½ ounce unsweetened chocolate, finely chopped
2 whole cloves
1 stick cinnamon, broken into halves
1 cup regular-grind coffee (dry)
1 teaspoon vanilla

Heat water, piloncillo, chocolate, cloves, and cinnamon to boiling in 3-quart saucepan; reduce heat. Simmer uncovered 15 minutes.

Stir in coffee. Remove from heat; cover and let stand 5 minutes. Stir in vanilla. Strain coffee through 4 thicknesses cheesecloth.

7 SERVINGS (ABOUT 1 CUP EACH)

Café Diablo

Café Mexicano (above)
¼ cup brandy
Whipped cream
8 tablespoons coffee liqueur

Prepare Café Mexicano; keep hot in saucepan after straining. Heat brandy just until warm in small, long-handled saucepan. Remove from heat; ignite. Pour flaming brandy over coffee. Allow flame to burn out; stir.

Pour coffee into cups or mugs. Top each with whipped cream and 1 tablespoon liqueur. Garnish with cinnamon stick if desired.

8 SERVINGS (ABOUT 1 CUP EACH)

Preceding pages: Fiesta Hot Chocolate (shown with Churros, page 210)

Soups
and Stews

Generally speaking, southwestern soups are hearty. There is little place here for the likes of a thin broth with lonely snips of vegetable set adrift. Much more typical are Southwest Black Bean Soup with ham (page 66) and silky Butternut Squash Soup (page 68). Chicken Tortilla Soup (page 68) indeed has a base of chicken broth, but it is thick with sweet bell pepper, chunks of avocado and chicken and quickly fried strips of flour tortillas. As for stews, Beef and Tequila Stew (page 76), White Bean Chili (page 75) and Pork Stew with Corn Bread Topping (page 76) are practically meals in themselves. Warm a stack of tortillas, corn muffins or a crusty loaf of bread to serve with any of these soups and stews for a substantial lunch or simple supper.

Posole

In Mexico, *posole* is traditionally made on New Year's Day. This stew is thick with hominy, beans and pork.

¼ cup vegetable oil
1 clove garlic, finely chopped
½ pound pork boneless shoulder, cut into ½-inch cubes
¼ cup all-purpose flour
1 medium onion, choppped (about ½ cup)
1 can (15 ounces) pinto beans, drained
1 can (30 ounces) hominy, drained
¼ cup chopped carrot
¼ cup chopped celery
¼ cup chopped green chiles
1 tablespoon ground red chiles
3 cups chicken broth
1 teaspoon salt
¼ teaspoon pepper
1½ teaspoons dried oregano leaves
1 small onion, chopped (about ¼ cup)
¼ cup snipped fresh cilantro
Lime wedges
Tortilla chips

Heat oil and garlic in 3-quart saucepan until oil is hot. Coat pork with flour. Cook and stir pork in oil over medium heat until brown; remove pork with slotted spoon and drain.

Cook and stir ½ cup onion in same saucepan until tender. Stir in beans, hominy, carrot, celery, green chiles, ground red chiles and broth. Heat to boiling; reduce heat. Cover and simmer 10 minutes.

Stir pork, salt and pepper into vegetable mixture. Heat to boiling; reduce heat. Cover and simmer 30 minutes. Sprinkle with oregano, ¼ cup onion and the cilantro. Serve with lime wedges and tortilla chips.

6 SERVINGS (ABOUT 1 CUP EACH)

Southwest Black Bean Soup

1 large onion, chopped (about 1 cup)
4 cloves garlic, finely chopped
2 tablespoons vegetable oil
1 pound dried black beans
2 cups cubed fully cooked smoked ham
6 cups chicken broth
2 tablespoons ground red chiles
2 tablespoons snipped fresh cilantro
1 tablespoon dried oregano leaves
2 teaspoons ground cumin
1 can (28 ounces) whole tomatoes, undrained
1 canned chipotle chile in adobo sauce
Quick Crème Fraîche (page 28)
Chopped red bell pepper

Cook and stir onion and garlic in oil in 4-quart Dutch oven until onion is tender. Stir in remaining ingredients except Quick Crème Fraîche and bell pepper; heat to boiling. Boil 2 minutes; reduce heat. Cover and simmer until beans are tender, about 2¼ hours.

Pour ¼ of the soup into food processor workbowl fitted with steel blade or into blender container; cover and process until smooth. Repeat with remaining soup. Serve with Quick Crème Fraîche and bell pepper.

8 SERVINGS (ABOUT 1⅓ CUPS EACH)

Southwest Black Bean Soup

Chicken Tortilla Soup

Based on the traditional Mexican soup *sopa azteca*, this rich broth features crisp fried tortilla strips and creamy slices of avocado.

1 medium onion, finely chopped (about ½ cup)
1 clove garlic, finely chopped
2 tablespoons vegetable oil
4 cups chicken broth
¼ cup chopped red bell pepper
1 teaspoon ground red chiles
¾ teaspoon dried basil leaves
½ teaspoon salt
¼ teaspoon pepper
1 can (15 ounces) tomato purée
½ cup vegetable oil
10 corn tortillas (6 inches in diameter), cut into
    ½-inch strips
2 cups cut-up cooked chicken breasts
Shredded Monterey Jack or Chihuahua cheese
Avocado slices

Cook and stir onion and garlic in 2 tablespoons oil in 4-quart Dutch oven until onion is tender. Stir in broth, bell pepper, ground red chiles, basil, salt, pepper and tomato puree. Heat to boiling; reduce heat. Simmer uncovered 30 minutes.

Heat ½ cup oil in 10-inch skillet until hot. Cook tortilla strips in oil until light golden brown, 30 to 60 seconds; drain. Divide tortilla strips and chicken among 6 bowls; pour broth over chicken. Top with cheese and avocado slices.

6 SERVINGS (ABOUT 1½ CUPS EACH)

Butternut Squash Soup

1 medium onion, chopped (about ½ cup)
2 tablespoons margarine or butter
2 cups chicken broth
1 pound butternut squash, pared, seeded and cut into
    1-inch cubes
2 pears, pared and sliced
1 teaspoon snipped fresh thyme leaves
¼ teaspoon salt
¼ teaspoon white pepper
¼ teaspoon ground coriander
1 cup whipping cream
1 unpared pear, sliced
½ cup chopped pecans, toasted (page 19)

Cook and stir onion in margarine in 4-quart Dutch oven until tender. Stir in broth, squash, 2 sliced pears, thyme, salt, white pepper and coriander. Heat to boiling; reduce heat. Cover and simmer until squash is tender, 10 to 15 minutes.

Pour about half of the soup into food processor workbowl fitted with steel blade or into blender container; cover and process until smooth. Repeat with remaining soup. Return to Dutch oven; stir in whipping cream. Heat, stirring frequently, until hot. Serve with sliced pear and pecans.

6 SERVINGS (ABOUT 1 CUP EACH)

Butternut Squash Soup

Beer Soup with Cheese

1 medium onion, chopped (about 1/2 cup)
2 tablespoons margarine or butter
1 can or bottle (12 ounces) beer
1/2 cup finely chopped carrot
1/2 cup finely chopped celery
2 cups chicken broth
1 teaspoon salt
1 teaspoon ground cumin
1/4 teaspoon ground nutmeg
Dash of ground cloves
Dash of pepper
1 cup dairy sour cream
4 ounces Cheddar or Monterey Jack cheese, cut into
   1/4-inch cubes (about 1 cup)

Cook and stir onion in margarine in 2-quart saucepan until tender. Stir in beer, carrot and celery. Heat to boiling; reduce heat. Cover and simmer 10 minutes.

Stir in remaining ingredients except sour cream and cheese. Heat to boiling; reduce heat. Cover and simmer 30 minutes. Remove from heat; stir in sour cream. Sprinkle with cheese.

5 SERVINGS (ABOUT 1 CUP EACH)

Shrimp Soup

1/2 pound shelled small raw shrimp, chopped
4 cups chicken broth
1/4 cup Casera Sauce (page 25)
1/2 teaspoon salt
1/8 teaspoon ground saffron
Dash of pepper
1 tablespoon cold water
1 teaspoon cornstarch
1/2 cup half-and-half
1/4 cup snipped parsley

Place shrimp, 1 cup of the broth and the Casera Sauce in blender container. Cover and blend on high speed until smooth. Heat shrimp mixture, remaining broth, the salt, saffron and pepper to boiling in 3-quart saucepan.

Mix water and cornstarch; stir into shrimp mixture. Heat to boiling, stirring constantly. Boil and stir 1 minute. Remove from heat; stir in half-and-half. Sprinkle with parsley.

5 SERVINGS (ABOUT 1 CUP EACH)

Spinach and Potato Soup

2 slices bacon, cut up
1 medium onion, chopped (about 1/2 cup)
2 cups chicken broth
2 cups diced potatoes
1/4 cup finely chopped carrot
1/4 cup finely chopped celery
1/4 cup dry white wine
1 teaspoon salt
1 1/2 teaspoons snipped fresh thyme leaves or 1/2
   teaspoon dried thyme leaves
1 1/2 teaspoons snipped fresh sage leaves or 1/2 teaspoon
   dried sage leaves
1/2 teaspoon pepper
2 pounds fresh spinach, chopped
2 cups milk
1/2 cup snipped parsley
1/4 pound chorizo sausage links, cooked and sliced

Cook and stir bacon in 3-quart saucepan until crisp. Remove bacon with slotted spoon and drain; reserve fat in saucepan. Cook and stir onion in fat until tender.

Stir in broth, potatoes, carrot, celery, wine, salt, thyme, sage and pepper. Heat to boiling; reduce heat. Cover and simmer 30 minutes.

Stir in half of the spinach; cover and cook 2 minutes. Stir in remaining spinach; cover and cook just until spinach is wilted, about 2 minutes.

Stir in milk, parsley and bacon; heat just until hot. Serve with sausage.

6 SERVINGS (ABOUT 1 CUP EACH)

Tortilla Dumpling Soup

¼ cup Casera Sauce (page 25)
4 cups chicken broth
½ cup instant corn flour tortilla mix
½ teaspoon baking powder
½ teaspoon ground red chiles
¼ teaspoon salt
2 tablespoons chopped onion
1 tablespoon snipped parsley
1 egg
2 tablespoons milk

Heat Casera Sauce and broth to boiling in 3-quart saucepan. Mix remaining ingredients except milk; stir in milk. Shape dough by teaspoonfuls into small balls; add to broth mixture. Cover and cook over medium heat 15 minutes. Sprinkle with chopped green onion if desired.

8 SERVINGS (½ CUP EACH)

Zucchini Soup

1 small onion, chopped (about ¼ cup)
1 tablespoon margarine or butter
2 cups chicken broth
2 tablespoons finely chopped canned green chiles
½ teaspoon salt
⅛ teaspoon pepper
2 small zucchini, chopped
1 can (8¾ ounces) whole kernel corn, drained
1 cup milk
2 ounces Monterey Jack cheese, cut into ¼-inch cubes (about ½ cup)
Ground nutmeg
Snipped parsley

Cook and stir onion in margarine in 2-quart saucepan until tender. Stir in broth, chiles, salt, pepper, zucchini and corn. Heat to boiling; reduce heat. Cover and simmer until zucchini is tender, about 5 minutes. Stir in milk; heat until hot. Stir in cheese. Garnish with nutmeg and parsley.

5 OR 6 SERVINGS (ABOUT 1 CUP EACH)

Garlic Soup

This simple, straightforward soup features garlic's gentler side. With longer cooking, garlic loses its sharpness and mellows. Garlic soup, thickened slightly with egg, would be a nice first course to precede a hearty main dish.

3 cloves garlic, crushed
2 tablespoons vegetable oil
2 slices white bread, cut into small pieces
4 cups chicken broth
½ teaspoon salt
¼ teaspoon pepper
1 egg, slightly beaten

Cook and stir garlic in oil in 3-quart saucepan until brown. Stir in bread; cook and stir until light brown. Stir in broth, salt and pepper. Heat to boiling; reduce heat. Cover and simmer 20 minutes.

Stir at least half of the hot mixture gradually into egg. Stir back into hot mixture in saucepan. Boil and stir 1 minute. Sprinkle with snipped parsley if desired.

8 SERVINGS (ABOUT ½ CUP EACH)

Gazpacho

1 can (28 ounces) whole tomatoes, undrained
1 cup finely chopped green bell pepper
1 cup finely chopped cucumber
1 cup croutons
1 medium onion, chopped (about ½ cup)
2 tablespoons white wine
2 tablespoons olive or vegetable oil
1 tablespoon ground cumin
1 tablespoon vinegar
½ teaspoon salt
¼ teaspoon pepper

Place tomatoes, ½ cup each of the bell pepper, cucumber and croutons, ¼ cup of the onion, the wine, oil, cumin, vinegar, salt and pepper in blender container or food processor workbowl fitted with steel blade.

Cover and blend on medium speed until smooth. Cover and refrigerate at least 1 hour. Serve with remaining ingredients as accompaniments.

8 SERVINGS (ABOUT ½ CUP EACH)

Avocado Soup

3 cups chicken broth
1 cup half-and-half
1 tablespoon chopped onion
¾ teaspoon salt
¼ teaspoon snipped fresh cilantro
Dash of pepper
2 large avocados, peeled and cut up
1 clove garlic, crushed

Place 1½ cups of the broth and the remaining ingredients in blender container or food processor workbowl fitted with steel blade. Cover and process on medium speed until smooth. Stir in remaining broth.

Cover and refrigerate until chilled, about 2 hours. Garnish with sour cream and paprika or avocado slices if desired.

6 SERVINGS (ABOUT ¾ CUP EACH)

Santa Fe Melon Soup

1 large cantaloupe (about 4 pounds), pared, seeded and chopped
3 tablespoons sugar
2 tablespoons snipped fresh mint leaves
½ cup dairy sour cream
¼ cup dry white wine
2 teaspoons grated orange peel
Fresh mint leaves

Place cantaloupe, sugar and 2 tablespoons mint in food processor workbowl fitted with steel blade or in blender container; cover and process until smooth. Stir in sour cream, wine and orange peel. Garnish with mint leaves.

6 SERVINGS (ABOUT ⅔ CUP EACH)

Santa Fe Melon Soup

White Bean Chili

1 large onion, chopped (about 1 cup)
1 clove garlic, finely chopped
¼ cup margarine or butter
4 cups ½-inch cubes cooked chicken
3 cups chicken broth
2 tablespoons snipped fresh cilantro
1 tablespoon dried basil leaves
2 teaspoons ground red chiles
¼ teaspoon ground cloves
2 cans (16 ounces each) great northern beans
1 medium tomato, chopped (about ¾ cup)
Blue or yellow corn tortilla chips

Cook and stir onion and garlic in margarine in 4-quart Dutch oven until onion is tender. Stir in remaining ingredients except chopped tomato and tortilla chips.

Heat to boiling; reduce heat. Cover and simmer 1 hour, stirring occasionally. Serve with tomato and tortilla chips.

6 SERVINGS (ABOUT 1½ CUPS EACH)

Texas Red Chili

3 pounds beef boneless round steak, cut into 1-inch cubes
1 large onion, finely chopped (about 1 cup)
4 cloves garlic, finely chopped
¼ cup vegetable oil
2 cups tomato purée
2 to 3 tablespoons ground red chiles
1 teaspoon cumin seed, ground
1 teaspoon ground coriander
4 Anaheim chiles, seeded and chopped
4 jalapeño chiles, seeded and chopped
Shredded Cheddar cheese
Flour tortillas
Cooked pinto beans

Cook and stir beef, onion and garlic in oil in 4-quart Dutch oven until beef is brown. Stir in remaining ingredients except cheese, tortillas and beans.

Heat to boiling; reduce heat. Cover and simmer, stirring occasionally, until beef is tender, about 2 hours. Serve with cheese, tortillas and beans.

6 SERVINGS (ABOUT 1¼ CUPS EACH)

Green Chile Stew

Substitute Anaheim chiles for the poblano chiles to moderate the "heat" of the dish. This is a very fragrant stew, rich with the flavor of lamb and the accents of lemon peel and juniper berries.

3 pounds lamb boneless shoulder
1 large onion, chopped (about 1 cup)
3 cloves garlic, finely chopped
¼ cup vegetable oil
2 cups chicken broth
1 teaspoon salt
1 teaspoon dried juniper berries, crushed
¾ teaspoon pepper
1 tablespoon all-purpose flour
¼ cup water
4 medium poblano chiles, roasted, peeled (page 15), seeded and cut into 2 x ¼-inch strips
2 tablespoons finely shredded lemon peel

Trim excess fat from lamb shoulder; cut lamb into 1-inch cubes. Cook and stir lamb, onion and garlic in oil in 4-quart Dutch oven until lamb is no longer pink; drain.

Stir in broth, salt, juniper berries and pepper. Heat to boiling; reduce heat. Cover and simmer, stirring occasionally, until lamb is tender, about 1 hour.

Shake flour and water in tightly covered container; stir into lamb mixture. Heat to boiling, stirring constantly. Boil and stir 1 minute. Stir in chiles. Sprinkle each serving with lemon peel.

4 SERVINGS (ABOUT 1¼ CUPS EACH)

Green Chile Stew

Pork Stew with Corn Bread Topping

1 small red bell pepper
1 small yellow bell pepper
1 pound pork boneless loin, cut into 1-inch cubes
1/2 pound bulk chorizo sausage
1 large onion, chopped (about 1 cup)
2 cloves garlic, finely chopped
1 cup beef broth
1 tablespoon dried basil leaves
1 tablespoon dried cilantro leaves
2 teaspoons ground red chiles
1 cup whole kernel corn
1 medium tomato, chopped (about 1 cup)
1 small butternut or acorn squash, pared and cut into
    1/2-inch cubes (about 1 cup)
1 can (2 1/4 ounces) sliced ripe olives, drained (about
    1/2 cup)
Corn Bread Topping (right)
Fresh Tomato Salsa (page 24)

Cut 5 thin slices from each bell pepper; reserve slices. Chop remaining bell peppers (about 1/2 cup each). Cook pork, sausage, onion and garlic in 4-quart Dutch oven over medium heat, stirring occasionally, until pork is no longer pink; drain. Stir in chopped bell peppers, broth, basil, cilantro and ground red chiles. Heat to boiling; reduce heat. Cover and simmer 30 minutes, stirring occasionally. Stir corn, tomato, squash and olives into meat mixture; cook 15 minutes longer.

Heat oven to 425°. Prepare Corn Bread Topping. Pour meat mixture into ungreased rectangular baking dish, 13 x 9 x 2 inches, or 3-quart shallow casserole. Pour Corn Bread Topping over meat mixture; carefully spread to cover, sealing to edge of dish. Arrange reserved bell pepper slices on top. Bake until topping is golden brown, 15 to 20 minutes. Serve with Fresh Tomato Salsa.

8 SERVINGS (ABOUT 1 1/2 CUPS EACH)

CORN BREAD TOPPING

1 1/2 cups yellow cornmeal
1/2 cup all-purpose flour
1 cup dairy sour cream
2/3 cup milk
1/4 cup vegetable oil
2 teaspoons baking powder
1/2 teaspoon baking soda
1/2 teaspoon salt
1 egg

Mix all ingredients; beat vigorously 30 seconds.

Beef and Tequila Stew

2 pounds beef boneless chuck, tip or round, cut into
    1-inch cubes
1/4 cup all-purpose flour
1/4 cup vegetable oil
1 medium onion, chopped (about 1/2 cup)
2 slices bacon, cut up
1/4 cup chopped carrot
1/4 cup chopped celery
1/4 cup tequila
3/4 cup tomato juice
2 tablespoons snipped fresh cilantro
1 1/2 teaspoons salt
1 can (15 ounces) garbanzo beans
4 medium tomatoes, chopped (about 4 cups)
2 cloves garlic, finely chopped

Coat beef with flour. Heat oil in 10-inch skillet until hot. Cook and stir beef in oil over medium heat until brown. Remove beef with slotted spoon and drain. Cook and stir onion and bacon in same skillet until bacon is crisp.

Stir in beef and remaining ingredients. Heat to boiling; reduce heat. Cover and simmer until beef is tender, about 1 hour.

6 SERVINGS (ABOUT 1 CUP EACH)

Pork Stew with Corn Bread Topping (shown with Fresh Tomato Salsa, page 24)

Beef and Plantains

Plantains take the place of potatoes in this tomato-beef stew. Rather than cooking with the meat and vegetables, the plantains are fried separately and added to the stew just before serving.

Vegetable oil
2 plantains, peeled and cut into 1/4-inch slices
1 teaspoon ground red chiles
2 pounds beef for stew, cut into 1-inch cubes
8 whole cloves
4 medium tomatoes, chopped (about 4 cups)
2 medium onions, each cut into fourths
2 cloves garlic, finely chopped
1/4 cup chopped celery
1/4 cup chopped carrot
4 cups water
2 tablespoons snipped fresh cilantro
2 teaspoons salt
1 teaspoon ground thyme
1 teaspoon ground oregano
1/4 teaspoon pepper
1 cup chopped green bell pepper

Heat oil (1 inch) to 350°. Fry plantains, a few slices at a time, in oil until golden brown, about 2 minutes; drain. Toss with ground red chiles; reserve.

Heat remaining ingredients except bell pepper to boiling in 4-quart Dutch oven; reduce heat. Cover and simmer until the beef is tender, 2 to 2½ hours.

Remove beef with slotted spoon and drain. Cook broth uncovered over high heat until reduced to 3 cups. Stir in beef, plantains and bell pepper. Simmer uncovered 10 minutes.

6 TO 8 SERVINGS (ABOUT 1¼ CUPS EACH)

Baja Seafood Stew

1 medium onion, chopped (about 1/2 cup)
1/2 cup chopped green chiles
2 cloves garlic, finely chopped
1/4 cup olive oil
2 cups dry white wine
1 tablespoon grated orange peel
1 1/2 cups orange juice
1 tablespoon sugar
1 tablespoon snipped fresh cilantro
1 teaspoon dried basil leaves
1 teaspoon salt
1/2 teaspoon pepper
1/2 teaspoon dried oregano leaves
1 can (28 ounces) whole Italian plum tomatoes, undrained and cut into halves
24 soft-shell clams (steamers), scrubbed
1 1/2 pounds shelled medium raw shrimp
1 pound cod, sea bass, mahimahi or red snapper fillets, cut into 1-inch pieces
1 package (6 ounces) frozen crabmeat, thawed, drained and cartilage removed

Cook and stir onion, chiles and garlic in oil in 6-quart Dutch oven until onion is tender. Stir in remaining ingredients except the seafood. Heat to boiling; reduce heat. Simmer uncovered 15 minutes.

Add clams; cover and simmer until clams open, 5 to 10 minutes. (Discard any clams that have not opened.) Carefully stir in shrimp, cod and crabmeat. Heat to boiling; reduce heat. Cover and simmer until shrimp are pink and cod flakes easily with fork, 4 to 5 minutes.

6 TO 8 SERVINGS (ABOUT 1½ CUPS EACH)

Baja Seafood Stew

Zuni Vegetable Stew

The Zuni, a tribe of Pueblo Indians, live in New Mexico. The fresh ingredients that make up this hearty stew (various chiles and squashes, corn and beans) are representative of that region's native bounty. Hot Navajo Fry Breads (page 163) would be delicious served with this one.

3/4 cup chopped onion
1 clove garlic, finely chopped
2 tablespoons vegetable oil
1 large red bell pepper, cut into 2 x 1/2-inch strips
2 medium poblano or Anaheim chiles, seeded and cut
  into 2 x 1/2-inch strips
1 jalapeño chile, seeded and chopped
1 cup cubed Hubbard or acorn squash (about
  1/2 pound)
2 cans (14 1/2 ounces each) chicken broth
1/2 teaspoon salt
1/2 teaspoon pepper
1/2 teaspoon ground coriander
1 cup thinly sliced zucchini
1 cup thinly sliced yellow squash
1 can (17 ounces) whole kernel corn, drained
1 can (16 ounces) pinto beans, drained

Cook and stir onion and garlic in oil in 4-quart Dutch oven over medium heat until onion is tender. Stir in bell pepper, poblano and jalapeño chiles. Cook 15 minutes.

Stir in Hubbard squash, broth, salt, pepper and coriander. Heat to boiling; reduce heat. Cover and simmer until squash is tender, about 15 minutes. Stir in remaining ingredients. Cook uncovered, stirring occasionally, until zucchini is tender, about 10 minutes.

6 SERVINGS (ABOUT 1 1/3 CUPS EACH)

Zuni Vegetable Stew

Menudo

This is a filling soup traditionally stewed all day long, often with beef shanks or veal bones, always with tripe. Robust versions tend to include some corn, whether in hominy form or as *nixtamal* (partially cooked, dried corn). *Menudo* is informal fiesta fare.

2 pounds honeycomb tripe
4 whole cloves
1 medium onion, cut into fourths
3 cups chicken broth
2 cups water
1/2 cup chopped carrot
1/2 cup chopped celery
1 can (16 ounces) whole tomatoes, undrained
3 cloves garlic, finely chopped
1 teaspoon salt
1/2 teaspoon ground oregano
1/2 teaspoon ground sage
1/2 teaspoon pepper
1 tablespoon olive or vegetable oil

Rinse tripe under cold running water. Place tripe and enough water to cover in 4-quart Dutch oven. Let stand 2 hours; drain and repeat. Cut tripe into strips, 2 x 1/4 inches.

Insert 1 clove into each onion fourth. Heat tripe, onion and remaining ingredients except oil to boiling; reduce heat. Cover and simmer until tripe is tender, about 4 hours. Stir in oil. Sprinkle with finely chopped green onions and snipped cilantro if desired.

8 SERVINGS (ABOUT 1 CUP EACH)

Tortilla and Masa Specialties

These are the dishes that most characteristically represent the cooking of the Southwest. Tortillas, made with corn or flour, are the basis of the southwestern meal. They are served as bread, of course, but beyond that they are the definitive ingredient in each of the following dishes:

- A *burrito* is a flour tortilla folded like an envelope around a filling.
- *Chilaquiles* is a casserole of fried tortilla strips baked with sauces and fillings.
- A *chimichanga* is a *burrito* that traditionally is deep-fat fried after it has been filled.
- An *enchilada* is a filled corn tortilla served with a sauce.
- *Fajitas* are flour tortillas filled with slices of steak and various condiments.
- A *flauta* ("flute") is a very tightly rolled *enchilada*.
- *Nachos* are crisp chips of corn tortillas served with cheese and salsa or chiles, usually as an appetizer (page 41).
- A *quesadilla* is a tortilla, filled principally with cheese, then folded or stacked.
- And, a *taco* is a tortilla, crisp or soft, folded in half around a filling.

Masa dishes are made with cornmeal. Some contemporary *masa* recipes included here are Shrimp with Cornmeal Pancakes, (page 96), Southwest Torte (page 100) and a spectacular, simplified tamale: Turkey Tamale Pie (page 90).

Stacked New Mexico Quesadilla (shown with sour cream and Fresh Tomato Salsa, page 24)

Stacked New Mexico Quesadilla

Red Pepper–Sour Cream Sauce (page 28)
Fresh Tomato Salsa (page 24)
3 cups shredded cooked chicken
1 medium zucchini, chopped
1 medium red bell pepper, chopped
2 tablespoons margarine or butter
8 flour tortillas (8 inches in diameter)
Margarine or butter, softened
1 cup shredded Monterey Jack cheese (4 ounces)

Prepare Red Pepper Sour Cream Sauce and Fresh Tomato Salsa; reserve. Cook chicken, zucchini and bell pepper in 2 tablespoons margarine in 3-quart saucepan over medium heat, stirring occasionally, until pepper is tender, about 10 minutes. Stir in ½ cup of the Red Pepper Sour Cream Sauce.

Heat oven to 350°. Place 2 tortillas on cookie sheet; spread with margarine. Spoon about ⅔ cup of the chicken mixture onto each tortilla; spread to edge of tortilla. Top each with tortilla, and spread with margarine and ⅔ cup of the chicken mixture; repeat. Top each stack with tortilla and ½ cup cheese.

Bake until cheese is melted and filling is hot, 10 to 15 minutes. Cut quesadilla into wedges; serve with remaining Red Pepper–Sour Cream Sauce and the Fresh Tomato Salsa or with sour cream if desired.

6 TO 8 SERVINGS

Corn Tortillas

2 cups instant corn flour tortilla mix
1¼ cups warm water

Mix tortilla mix and water with hands until all of tortilla mix is moistened and dough cleans side of bowl (add 1 to 2 teaspoons water if neccessary). Cover with damp towel; let rest 10 minutes. Divide dough into twelve 1-inch balls.

For each tortilla, place 1 ball on waxed paper square; flatten slightly. Cover with second waxed paper square. Roll into 6-inch circle. Peel off top waxed paper square.

Heat ungreased skillet or griddle over medium-high heat until hot. Place tortilla in skillet, waxed paper side up. Cook 30 seconds; immediately remove waxed paper. Continue cooking tortilla until dry around edge, about 1 minute. Turn and cook other side until dry, about 2 minutes. Stack tortillas, placing waxed paper between each. Cover with damp towel.

TWELVE 6-INCH TORTILLAS

Flour Tortillas

2 cups all-purpose flour
1 teaspoon salt
3 tablespoons lard or shortening
½ cup warm water
Lard or shortening

Mix flour and salt; cut in lard until particles are size of fine crumbs. Sprinkle in water, one tablespoon at a time, until all flour is moistened and dough almost cleans side of bowl. Gather dough into a ball; divide into 12 equal parts for 6-inch tortillas, 8 equal parts for 8-inch tortillas or 6 equal parts for 10-inch tortillas. Shape each part into ball; brush lightly with lard. Cover and let rest 20 minutes.

For each tortilla, roll 1 ball on floured surface into 6-, 8- or 10-inch circle. Heat ungreased griddle or skillet over medium-high heat until hot. Cook tortilla until dry around edge and blisters appear on surface, about 2 minutes. Turn and cook other side until dry, about 1 minute. Stack tortillas, placing waxed paper between each. Cover with damp towel.

12, 8 OR 6 TORTILLAS

Bean Tortilla Casserole

4 cups water
*1 pound dried pinto beans**
1 medium onion, finely chopped (about ½ cup)
2 cloves garlic
⅓ to ½ cup canned chipotle chiles in adobo sauce
1½ teaspoons instant chicken bouillon
⅛ teaspoon ground cumin
½ cup vegetable oil
2½ cups diced cooked chicken
12 flour tortillas (8 inches in diameter), warmed
1½ cups dairy sour cream
1½ cups shredded Monterey Jack cheese (6 ounces)
¼ cup sliced green onions (with tops)

Mix water, beans, chopped onion and garlic in 4-quart Dutch oven. Heat to boiling; reduce heat. Simmer uncovered until beans are tender, about 3 hours (add water if necessary).

Place half of the beans, ½ cup bean liquid, the chipotle chiles, bouillon (dry) and cumin in food processor workbowl fitted with steel blade or in blender container. Cover and process until smooth; pour into large bowl. Place remaining beans with just enough liquid to cover in work-bowl. Cover and process until smooth; add to bean mixture in bowl. Heat oil in 10-inch skillet until hot; stir in bean mixture. Cook uncovered, stirring frequently, until mixture is consistency of cake batter.

Heat oven to 350°. Spoon scant ¼ cup chicken onto half of each tortilla; fold tortillas into halves. Arrange in greased 3-quart round shallow casse-role or rectangular baking dish, 13 x 9 x 2 inches; spoon bean mixture over tortillas. Top with sour cream, cheese and green onions. Bake uncovered until hot and bubbly, 15 to 20 minutes.

10 SERVINGS

* 4 cans (15 ounces each) pinto beans may be substituted for the 4 cups water and dried pinto beans. Drain pinto beans, reserving 1 cup liquid. Cook onion and chopped garlic in 2 tablespoons vegetable oil until tender. Place 2 cans of the beans and ½ cup of the reserved liquid in food processor workbowl fitted with steel blade or in blender container; continue as directed.

Chicken Chilaquiles Casserole

Chilaquiles is a word that refers to the ragged straws of a broken sombrero. This casserole is layered with tortilla strips, hence its name. The strips are fried first, ideal for using up leftover tortillas.

New Mexico Green Sauce (page 27)
½ cup vegetable oil
10 flour or corn tortillas (6 to 7 inches in diameter), cut into ½-inch strips
2 cups shredded cooked chicken or turkey
2 cups shredded Chihuahua or mozzarella cheese (8 ounces)

Prepare New Mexico Green Sauce; reserve. Heat oil in 10-inch skillet until hot. Cook tortilla strips in oil until light golden brown, 30 to 60 seconds; drain.

Heat oven to 350°. Layer half of the tortilla strips in bottom of greased 2-quart casserole; top with chicken, half of the New Mexico Green Sauce (about ⅔ cup) and 1 cup of the cheese. Gently press layers down into casserole. Repeat with remaining tortilla strips, sauce and cheese. Bake until cheese is melted and golden brown, about 30 minutes.

6 TO 8 SERVINGS

Following pages: Chicken Chilaquiles Casserole

Baked Chimichangas

Chimichangas, traditionally fried, have a tempting, even, golden brown color. The *picadillo* filling combines warm spices, nuts and dried fruits.

Almond Red Sauce (page 25)
Jalapeño Cream Sauce (page 28)
1 pound ground beef
1 small onion, finely chopped (about ¼ cup)
1 clove garlic, finely chopped
¼ cup slivered almonds
¼ cup raisins
1 tablespoon red wine vinegar
1 teaspoon ground red chiles
½ teaspoon salt
¼ teaspoon ground cinnamon
⅛ teaspoon ground cloves
1 can (4 ounces) chopped green chiles
1 medium tomato, chopped (about 1 cup)
8 flour tortillas (10 inches in diameter), warmed
1 egg, beaten
2 tablespoons margarine or butter, softened

Prepare Almond Red Sauce and Jalapeño Cream Sauce; reserve. Cook and stir ground beef, onion and garlic in 10-inch skillet over medium heat until beef is brown; drain.

Stir in remaining ingredients except tortillas, egg and margarine. Heat to boiling; reduce heat. Simmer uncovered 20 minutes; stir occasionally.

Heat oven to 500°. Spoon about ½ cup beef mixture onto center of each tortilla. Fold one end of tortilla up about 1 inch over beef mixture; fold right and left sides over folded end, overlapping. Fold remaining end down; brush edges with egg to seal. Brush each chimichanga with margarine.

Place seam sides down in ungreased jelly roll pan, 15½ x 10½ x 1 inch. Bake until tortillas begin to brown and filling is hot, 8 to 10 minutes. Serve with Almond Red Sauce and Jalapeño Cream Sauce.

4 SERVINGS

Fried Chimichangas (shown with Almond Red Sauce, page 25, and Jalapeño Cream Sauce, page 28)

Fried Chimichangas: Omit 2 tablespoons margarine or butter. Heat vegetable oil (about 1 inch) to 365°. Fry chimichangas, 2 or 3 at a time, in oil, turning once, until golden brown, 3 to 4 minutes. Keep warm in 300° oven.

Fold up 1 end of tortilla about 1 inch over beef mixture.

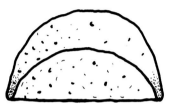

Fold right and left sides over folded end, overlapping.

Fold down remaining end.

Beef Burritos

2 cups shredded cooked beef
1 cup Refried Beans (page 152)
8 flour tortillas (about 10 inches in diameter), warmed
2 cups shredded lettuce
2 medium tomatoes, chopped (about 2 cups)
1 cup shredded Cheddar cheese (4 ounces)

Heat beef and Refried Beans separately. Place about ¼ cup of the beef on center of each tortilla. Spoon about 2 tablespoons beans onto beef. Top with ¼ cup of the lettuce and about 2 tablespoons each of the tomatoes and cheese.

Fold one end of tortilla up about 1 inch over filling; fold right and left sides over folded end, overlapping. Fold down remaining end.

8 SERVINGS

Turkey Tamale Pie

Tamales are individually wrapped corn husk packets filled with savory mixtures. This recipe for a "pie" calls for one large corn husk package, rather than a score of little ones. The dry corn husks must be softened first. Weight them to keep them submerged while they soak.

4 to 6 dried corn husks
Almond Red Sauce (page 25)
¾ pound cooked turkey breast, cut into ½-inch cubes
  (about 2 cups)
1 cup slivered almonds, toasted
1 cup golden raisins
½ cup chopped red bell pepper
2 cans (4 ounces each) chopped green chiles
Tamale Dough (right)
Dairy sour cream

Rinse corn husks and remove silk; cover husks with warm water and let stand until softened, at least 2 hours.

Prepare Almond Red Sauce. Mix ½ cup of the sauce and the remaining ingredients except Tamale Dough and sour cream; reserve. Prepare Tamale Dough; reserve.

Heat oven to 350°. Drain corn husks; pat dry. Line greased springform pan, 10 x 3 inches, with corn husks, extending pointed ends of husks over side of pan. Spread half of the Tamale Dough over husks on bottom of pan; cover with turkey mixture. Spread remaining dough over turkey mixture up to edge of pan. Cover top of pan with piece of heavy-duty aluminum foil, 15 inches long, shaping down over side of pan (pointed ends of corn husks will bend down against outside of pan).

Bake until dough is set and slightly dry, about 1½ hours. Carefully remove side of pan. Serve with remaining warm Almond Red Sauce and the sour cream.

8 SERVINGS

TAMALE DOUGH

2 cups instant corn flour tortilla mix
½ cup shortening
2 cups chicken broth
2 teaspoons baking powder
½ teaspoon salt

Beat all ingredients in large bowl on low speed, scraping bowl constantly, until well blended. Beat on medium speed 1 minute.

Mixed Tostadas

1½ cups Refried Beans (page 152)
1½ cups Casera Sauce (page 25)
Vegetable oil
6 corn tortillas (6 to 7 inches in diameter)
2 cups cut-up cooked chicken
¾ cup shredded Monterey Jack cheese (3 ounces)
3 cups shredded lettuce
1 avocado, cut into 12 slices
Dairy sour cream

Prepare Refried Beans and Casera Sauce; heat separately until hot. Heat ⅛ inch oil in skillet over medium heat just until hot. Cook tortillas, one at a time, in the hot oil until crisp, about 1 minute; drain.

Spread each tortilla with ¼ cup of the beans. Top with 2 tablespoons of the sauce, ⅓ cup of the chicken and 2 more tablespoons of the sauce. Sprinkle each with 2 tablespoons of the cheese. Set oven control to broil. Place tortillas on rack in broiler pan. Broil with tops 2 to 3 inches from heat until cheese is melted, about 3 minutes. Top each tortilla with ½ cup lettuce, 2 avocado slices and sour cream.

6 SERVINGS

Soft Tacos

Vegetable oil
12 corn tortillas (6 inches in diameter)
1½ cups shredded cooked beef, pork or chicken

Heat ⅛ inch oil in skillet until hot. Cook tortillas, one at a time, in the hot oil until soft, about 30 seconds; drain.

Spoon 2 tablespoons meat slightly below center of each tortilla. Roll tortilla over meat; secure with wooden pick.

Heat ⅛ inch oil until hot. Cook each taco in oil, turning once, until light golden brown, about 2 minutes; drain. Remove wooden picks. Garnish with 2 or 3 of the following if desired: chopped tomatoes, shredded lettuce, chopped onion, chopped green chiles, chopped avocado, shredded cheese.

6 SERVINGS

Texas Breakfast Tacos

Southwest Guacamole (page 38)
Fresh Tomato Salsa (page 24)
1 pound bulk chorizo sausage
1 large onion, finely chopped (about 1 cup)
1 medium green bell pepper, cut into strips
1 tablespoon margarine or butter
12 eggs, beaten
10 flour tortillas (7 to 8 inches in diameter), warmed
1½ cups shredded Co-Jack cheese (6 ounces)
2 tablespoons margarine or butter, melted

Prepare Southwest Guacamole and Fresh Tomato Salsa; reserve. Cook and stir sausage, onion and bell pepper in 10-inch skillet over medium heat, stirring frequently, until sausage is done, about 10 minutes; drain and reserve.

Heat 1 tablespoon margarine in skillet over medium heat until hot and bubbly. Pour eggs into skillet. As eggs begin to set at bottom and side, gently lift cooked portions with spatula so that thin, uncooked portion can flow to bottom. Avoid constant stirring. Cook until eggs are thickened throughout but still moist, about 5 minutes.

Heat oven to 450°. Spoon about ¼ cup sausage mixture onto each tortilla; top each with about ¼ cup eggs and 2 tablespoons cheese. Fold tortillas into halves. Arrange 5 assembled tacos in ungreased jelly roll pan, 15½ x 10½ x 1 inch; brush with melted margarine. Bake until light golden brown, 10 to 12 minutes. Repeat with remaining tacos. Serve with guacamole and salsa.

5 SERVINGS

Southwest Beef Fajitas

Set out the beef and tortillas together with all the condiments, and let guests roll their own *fajitas*.

Cucumber Salsa (page 24)
Southwest Relish (page 31)
Southwest Guacamole (page 38)
1 pound beef boneless top round steak, about ½ inch thick
¼ cup lime juice
2 tablespoons vegetable oil
2 teaspoons ground red chiles
2 cloves garlic, finely chopped
8 flour tortillas (10 inches in diameter), warmed

Prepare Cucumber Salsa, Southwest Relish and Southwest Guacamole; reserve. Cut beef steak diagonally across grain into thin slices, each 2 x ⅛ inch. Mix remaining ingredients except tortillas in glass or plastic bowl; stir in beef until well coated. Cover and refrigerate 1 hour.

Set oven control to broil. Place beef slices on rack in broiler pan. Broil with tops 2 to 3 inches from heat until brown, about 5 minutes.

Place ⅛ of the beef, some Cucumber Salsa, Southwest Relish and Southwest Guacamole on center of each tortilla. Fold one end of tortilla up about 1 inch over beef mixture; fold right and left sides over folded end, overlapping. Fold down remaining end. Serve with remaining salsa, relish and guacamole.

8 SERVINGS

Southwest Beef Fajitas (shown with Southwest Guacamole, page 38, Cucumber Salsa, page 24 and Southwest Relish, page 31)

Beef Tortilla Casserole

Basic Red Sauce (page 24)
Southwest Guacamole (page 38)
½ cup vegetable oil
10 corn tortillas (6 to 7 inches in diameter), cut into
  2-inch-wide strips
1 pound ground beef
2 Anaheim chiles, seeded and finely chopped
1 medium onion, chopped (about ½ cup)
1 can (15 ounces) pinto beans, drained
2 cups shredded Cheddar cheese (8 ounces)
Dairy sour cream

Prepare Basic Red Sauce and Southwest Guacamole; reserve. Heat oil in 10-inch skillet until hot. Cook tortilla strips in oil until light golden brown, about 1 minute; drain. Cook and stir ground beef, chiles and onion until beef is brown; drain.

Heat oven to 350°. Arrange tortilla strips in bottom of greased rectangular baking dish, 13 x 9 x 2 inches. Top with beef mixture, Basic Red Sauce, beans and cheese. Bake until hot and bubbly, 25 to 30 minutes. Serve with Southwest Guacamole and sour cream.

8 SERVINGS

Pork Carnitas

Southwest Guacamole (page 38)
4 poblano chiles, roasted, peeled (page 15) and seeded
1 medium onion, cut lengthwise into halves
1 pound pork boneless center loin roast, cut into
  2 x ¼-inch strips
1 clove garlic, finely chopped
2 tablespoons vegetable oil
2 tablespoons tomato paste
1 tablespoon red wine vinegar
¼ teaspoon salt
½ pound Italian plum tomatoes, finely chopped (about
  1⅓ cups)
Flour or corn tortillas
Dairy sour cream

Prepare Southwest Guacamole; reserve. Cut chiles and onion halves lengthwise into ¼-inch strips. Cook pork, chiles, onion and garlic in oil in 10-inch skillet over medium heat, stirring occasionally, until pork is no longer pink, about 12 minutes.

Stir in tomato paste, vinegar, salt and tomatoes; cook until hot. Serve with tortillas, Southwest Guacamole and sour cream.

4 SERVINGS

Grilled Pork Tacos

Papaya Relish (page 31)
1 tablespoon margarine or butter
1 pound pork boneless center loin roast, cut into
  2 x ¼-inch strips
½ cup chopped fresh papaya
½ cup chopped fresh pineapple
10 flour tortillas (6 to 7 inches in diameter), warmed
1½ cups shredded Monterey Jack cheese (6 ounces)
2 tablespoons margarine or butter, melted

Prepare Papaya Relish; reserve. Heat 1 tablespoon margarine in 10-inch skillet over medium heat until hot and bubbly. Cook pork in margarine, stirring occasionally, until no longer pink, about 10 minutes; drain. Stir in papaya and pineapple. Heat, stirring occasionally, until hot.

Heat oven to 425°. Spoon about ¼ cup pork mixture onto half of each tortilla; top with about 2 tablespoons cheese. Fold tortillas into halves. Arrange five assembled tacos in ungreased jelly roll pan, 15½ x 10½ x 1 inch; brush with melted margarine. Bake until light golden brown, about 10 minutes. Repeat with remaining tacos. Serve with Papaya Relish and, if desired, dairy sour cream.

5 SERVINGS

Grilled Pork Tacos (shown with Papaya Relish,
page 31)

Shrimp with Cornmeal Pancakes

These buttermilk pancakes are made with crunchy cornmeal. Use blue cornmeal for a darker, more dramatic pancake. The sauce for the shrimp isn't too spicy—full of roasted chile flavor and not too hot.

3 poblano chiles, roasted, peeled (page 15) and seeded
2 medium tomatoes, roasted (page 20), peeled, cut into
   halves and seeded
1 medium onion, cut into fourths
1 clove garlic
¼ cup dry white wine
1 teaspoon sugar
¼ teaspoon salt
⅛ teaspoon ground red pepper
½ cup dairy sour cream
1 pound cooked medium shrimp
Cornmeal Pancakes (below)
½ cup shredded Monterey Jack cheese (2 ounces)

Place chiles, tomatoes, onion and garlic in food processor workbowl fitted with steel blade or in blender container; cover and process until smooth.

Pour into 2-quart saucepan; stir in wine, sugar, salt and red pepper. Heat to boiling; reduce heat to low. Cook uncovered, stirring occasionally, until thickened, about 15 minutes. Stir in sour cream and shrimp; heat just until hot. Spoon over Cornmeal Pancakes; top with cheese.

6 SERVINGS (6 OR 7 PANCAKES EACH)

CORNMEAL PANCAKES

2 eggs
1 cup yellow or blue cornmeal
¼ cup all-purpose flour
2 cups buttermilk
¼ cup margarine or butter, melted
2 teaspoons baking powder
1 teaspoon baking soda

Beat eggs in medium bowl until fluffy; beat in remaining ingredients just until smooth. For each pancake, pour about 2 tablespoons batter onto hot greased griddle. Cook until pancakes are dry around edges; turn and cook other sides until golden brown.

Grilled Seafood Flautas

Roasted Tomato Sauce (page 25)
1 package (8 ounces) frozen salad-style imitation
   crabmeat, thawed (about 1½ cups)
½ cup sliced green onions (with tops)
1 tablespoon margarine or butter
½ cup dairy sour cream
½ cup shredded Monterey Jack cheese (2 ounces)
1 can (14 ounces) artichoke hearts, drained and cut
   into fourths
10 flour tortillas (7 to 8 inches in diameter), warmed
4 tablespoons margarine or butter

Prepare Roasted Tomato Sauce; reserve. Cook crabmeat and onions in 1 tablespoon margarine over medium heat, stirring frequently, until onions are tender. Mix in sour cream, cheese and artichoke hearts.

Spoon about ⅓ cup mixture onto one end of each tortilla. Roll up tightly into cylinder shape; secure with wooden picks.

Heat 2 tablespoons margarine in 10-inch skillet over medium heat until hot and bubbly. Cook 3 or 4 flautas in margarine, turning frequently, until golden brown, about 5 minutes. Keep warm in 300° oven. Repeat with remaining flautas, adding remaining margarine as needed. Serve with warm Roasted Tomato Sauce.

5 SERVINGS

Shrimp with Cornmeal Pancakes

Seafood Chilaquiles Casserole

1/2 cup vegetable oil
10 flour or corn tortillas (6 to 7 inches in diameter),
*   cut into 1/2-inch strips*
1/2 cup sliced green onions (with tops)
1/4 cup margarine or butter
1/4 cup all-purpose flour
1/2 teaspoon salt
1/4 teaspoon pepper
2 cups half-and-half
1 canned chipotle chile in adobo sauce, finely chopped
1 pound bay scallops
1 pound shelled medium raw shrimp
4 slices bacon, crisply cooked and crumbled

Heat oil in 10-inch skillet until hot. Cook tortilla strips in oil until light golden brown, 30 to 60 seconds; drain and reserve.

Cook onions in margarine in 3-quart saucepan over low heat until tender; stir in flour, salt and pepper. Cook, stirring constantly, until mixture is bubbly. Remove from heat; stir in half-and-half. Heat to boiling, stirring constantly. Boil and stir 1 minute; reduce heat. Stir in remaining ingredients except bacon. Cook over medium heat, stirring frequently, just until shrimp are pink, about 9 minutes.

Heat oven to 350°. Layer half of the tortilla strips in bottom of greased 3-quart casserole; top with half of the seafood mixture. Repeat with remaining tortilla strips and seafood mixture; top with bacon. Bake until hot, 15 to 20 minutes.

6 SERVINGS

Filled Tortillas

1 medium onion, thinly sliced
4 radishes, thinly sliced
2 tablespoons vinegar
1 tablespoon orange juice concentrate
6 drops red pepper sauce
1/2 teaspoon salt
Flour Tortillas (page 84)
2 cups Refried Beans (page 152)
Vegetable oil
2 cups shredded lettuce
2 cups shredded cooked chicken
2 jalapeño chiles, thinly sliced
2 medium tomatoes, sliced

Mix onion, radishes, vinegar, orange juice concentrate, pepper sauce and salt in glass or plastic bowl. Cover and refrigerate 30 minutes; drain.

Prepare Flour Tortillas as directed in recipe for 6-inch tortillas except divide dough into 6 equal parts. Carefully split each tortilla, using a knife, to form a pocket. Spread about 2 tablespoons Refried Beans in each pocket; press gently to close pockets.

Heat oil (1½ inches) in 4-quart Dutch oven to 365°. Fry tortillas, one at a time, in oil until crisp and golden brown, about 1 minute on each side; drain. Top each with lettuce, onion mixture, chicken, chiles and tomatoes.

6 SERVINGS

Filled Tortilla

Breakfast Fruit Chimichangas

Any flour tortilla that is stuffed, folded like a burrito and deep fried may be called a *chimichanga*. This sweet-tart apricot version is lighter (it's baked instead of fried in oil) and would make a very satisfying snack.

Apricot Basting Sauce (page 29)
1 package (8 ounces) cream cheese, softened
1/2 cup ricotta cheese
1/4 cup sugar
1 teaspoon grated orange peel
6 flour tortillas (8 inches in diameter), warmed
1/4 cup apricot preserves
1 egg, beaten
2 tablespoons margarine or butter, softened
1 cup sliced apricots

Prepare Apricot Basting Sauce; reserve. Heat oven to 500°. Mix cream cheese, ricotta cheese, sugar and orange peel thoroughly. Spoon about 1/4 cup mixture onto center of each tortilla; top with 1 tablespoon preserves.

Fold one end of tortilla up about 1 inch over mixture; fold right and left sides over folded end, overlapping. Fold remaining end down; brush edges with egg to seal. Brush each *chimichanga* with margarine.

Place seam sides down in ungreased jelly roll pan, 15½ x 10½ x 1 inch. Bake until *chimichangas* begin to brown and filling is hot, 8 to 10 minutes. Serve with apricots and Apricot Basting Sauce.

6 SERVINGS

Southwest Torte

Cornmeal Pastry (below)
1 cup shredded Cheddar cheese (4 ounces)
1/4 cup sliced ripe olives
4 slices bacon, crisply cooked and crumbled
1/2 cup chopped red bell pepper
1/2 cup whole kernel corn
3 eggs
1½ cups half-and-half
1/4 teaspoon ground red pepper

Place oven rack in lowest position. Heat oven to 450°. Prepare Cornmeal Pastry; gather into a ball. Press in bottom and 2 inches up side of ungreased springform pan, 9 x 3 inches. Sprinkle cheese, olives, bacon, bell pepper and corn in pastry-lined pan. Beat eggs slightly; beat in remaining ingredients. Pour into pan. Bake uncovered on lowest oven rack 20 minutes.

Reduce oven temperature to 300°. Bake until knife inserted in center comes out clean, 30 to 35 minutes longer. Let torte stand 10 minutes before cutting.

6 SERVINGS

CORNMEAL PASTRY

1 cup all-purpose flour
1/3 cup yellow cornmeal
1 tablespoon dried oregano leaves
1/2 teaspoon salt
1/2 cup shortening
3 to 4 tablespoons cold water

Mix flour, cornmeal, oregano and salt in small bowl; cut in shortening until particles are size of fine crumbs. Sprinkle in water, 1 tablespoon at a time, tossing with fork until flour is moistened and pastry almost cleans side of bowl (add 1 to 2 teaspoons water if necessary).

Red Enchiladas with Cheese

1 large onion, finely chopped (about 1 cup)
2 cloves garlic, finely chopped
¼ cup vegetable oil
½ cup chicken broth
4 medium tomatoes, chopped (about 4 cups)
1 tablespoon ground red chiles
1 teaspoon salt
1 teaspoon ground cumin
1 teaspoon dried oregano leaves
⅛ teaspoon pepper
12 corn or flour tortillas (6 to 7 inches in diameter)
3 cups shredded mozzarella cheese (12 ounces)
Dairy sour cream

Cook and stir onion and garlic in oil in 10-inch skillet over medium heat until onion is tender. Stir in remaining ingredients except tortillas, cheese and sour cream. Heat to boiling; reduce heat. Simmer uncovered 30 minutes, stirring occasionally.

Heat oven to 350°. Dip each tortilla into sauce to coat both sides. Spoon 2 tablespoons of the cheese onto each tortilla; roll up. Place seam sides down in ungreased rectangular baking dish, 13 x 9 x 2 inches. Pour remaining sauce over enchiladas; sprinkle with remaining cheese. Bake uncovered until cheese is melted, about 15 minutes. Serve with sour cream.

6 SERVINGS

Green Enchiladas

2 cups Basic Green Sauce (page 26)
1 cup dairy sour cream
*10 corn or flour tortillas (6 inches in diameter),
    warmed*
*3 cups shredded cooked chicken or Refried Beans
    (page 152)*
1 cup shredded Monterey Jack cheese (4 ounces)
Dairy sour cream

Prepare Basic Green Sauce; stir in 1 cup sour cream. Heat oven to 350°. Dip each tortilla into sauce to coat both sides.

Spoon ¼ cup of the chicken onto each tortilla; roll up. Place seam sides down in ungreased rectangular baking dish, 13 x 9 x 2 inches. Pour remaining sauce over enchiladas; sprinkle with cheese. Bake uncovered until cheese is melted, about 15 minutes. Serve with sour cream.

5 SERVINGS

Red Enchiladas: Substitute 2 cups Basic Red Sauce (page 24) for the Basic Green Sauce. Substitute 3 cups shredded cheese or cooked beef for the chicken.

Ricotta Cheese Enchiladas

These enchiladas are a southwestern version of manicotti. The cilantro and nut sauce is a nice counterpoint to the rich ricotta filling.

Roasted Tomato Sauce (page 25)
1 container (15 ounces) ricotta cheese
1 cup shredded Monterey Jack cheese (4 ounces)
¼ cup grated Sierra or Romano cheese (1 ounce)
2 tablespoons snipped fresh cilantro
1 small onion, finely chopped (about ¼ cup)
2 eggs
10 flour tortillas (8 inches in diameter), warmed
½ cup shredded Monterey Jack cheese (2 ounces)
Cilantro Pesto (page 28)

Prepare Roasted Tomato Sauce; reserve. Heat oven to 350°. Mix ricotta cheese, 1 cup Monterey Jack cheese, the Sierra cheese, cilantro, onion and eggs. Spoon about ⅓ cup mixture onto each tortilla; roll up. Place seam sides down in greased rectangular pan, 13 x 9 x 2 inches. Pour Roasted Tomato Sauce over top.

Bake uncovered until filling is set, about 40 minutes. Sprinkle with ½ cup Monterey Jack cheese; bake until cheese is melted, 3 to 4 minutes. Serve with Cilantro Pesto.

5 SERVINGS

Tortilla Skillet

½ cup vegetable oil
12 corn or flour tortillas (6 to 7 inches in diameter),
   cut into ½-inch strips
½ cup chopped green onions (with tops)
1 can (16 ounces) whole tomatoes, drained
½ teaspoon ground oregano
½ teaspoon salt
⅛ teaspoon pepper
1 cup shredded Monterey Jack cheese (4 ounces)
Dairy sour cream

Heat oil in 10-inch skillet until hot. Cook tortilla strips and onions in oil, turning occasionally, until tortillas are crisp, about 10 minutes.

Stir in tomatoes, oregano, salt and pepper. Sprinkle with cheese; heat just until cheese is melted. Serve with sour cream.

4 TO 6 SERVINGS

Pepita Vegetable Burritos

Burritos ("little burros") are a very common use of flour tortillas. Here the bundles are stuffed with garlicky, crisp-tender vegetables: broccoli, summer squash and sweet red bell pepper, and served with a rich pumpkin seed sauce.

Pumpkin Seed Sauce (page 27)
1 cup chopped broccoli
1 medium onion, finely chopped (about ½ cup)
2 cloves garlic, finely chopped
2 tablespoons vegetable oil
1 cup 2 x ¼-inch strips yellow squash
1 cup 2 x ¼-inch strips zucchini
½ cup finely chopped red bell pepper
¼ cup shelled pumpkin seeds, toasted (page 20)
1 tablespoon lemon juice
1 teaspoon ground red chiles
¼ teaspoon salt
¼ teaspoon ground cumin
6 flour tortillas (10 inches in diameter), warmed

Prepare Pumpkin Seed Sauce; reserve. Cook broccoli, onion and garlic in oil in 10-inch skillet, stirring frequently, until tender. Stir in remaining ingredients except tortillas. Cook, stirring occasionally, until squash is crisp-tender, about 2 minutes; keep warm.

Spoon about ½ cup of the vegetable mixture onto center of each tortilla. Fold one end of tortilla up about 1 inch over mixture; fold right and left sides over folded end, overlapping. Fold remaining end down. Serve with Pumpkin Seed Sauce.

6 SERVINGS

Pepita Vegetable Burrito

Poultry, Meats and Seafood

Southwest cooking has made great use of the chicken, perhaps the most versatile of birds. Game birds historically had their place too, but by the late nineteenth century wild turkeys, quail, pheasant and squab had grown somewhat scarce in the Southwest. Today farm-raised game birds are available nationwide, and because they don't have to scratch for a living, they are meatier than the wild birds.

The grasslands of the Southwest fostered a booming cattle industry. Beef, together with the sheep and pigs kept by Navajo Indians and Basque settlers, became important contributions to regional dishes. With the abundance of meat, the southwestern barbecue came into its own. Some say the word *barbecue* is derived from *barbacoa*, the Spanish translation of an Indian word meaning a cooking grill of green wood. Others insist it comes from the French expression for roasting a whole animal, *de barbe á queue*, "from beard to tail." Whatever the derivation, barbecues today feature buffalo, rabbit, venison and game birds in addition to lamb, pork and beef.

The importance of seafood in the southwestern repertory is somewhat recent, except around the Gulf of Mexico where the availability of fish has never been in question. Fish lends itself nicely to the Southwest's flamboyant flavors and uncomplicated cooking techniques.

Apricot-basted Quail

Apricot-basted Quail

Apricot Basting Sauce (page 29)
6 quail (about 6 ounces each)
6 slices bacon

Prepare Apricot Basting Sauce; reserve. Heat oven to 400°. Wrap each quail in 1 slice bacon. Place breast sides up, at least 1 inch apart, on rack in shallow roasting pan. Roast uncovered 30 minutes.

Brush generously with Apricot Basting Sauce. Roast until done, 15 to 20 minutes longer. Heat remaining sauce, and serve with quail.

4 TO 6 SERVINGS

Mexican Chicken

1 medium onion, thinly sliced
½ cup vegetable oil
12 pitted green olives
4 medium tomatoes, chopped (about 4 cups)
2 stalks celery, chopped
2 cloves garlic, finely chopped
2 bay leaves
½ cup water
2 tablespoons capers
1 tablespoon dried oregano leaves
1 teaspoon salt
¼ teaspoon pepper
6 boneless chicken breast halves
8 ounces mushrooms, sliced

Cook and stir onion in oil in 10-inch skillet until tender. Stir in remaining ingredients except chicken breasts and mushrooms. Heat to boiling; reduce heat. Simmer uncovered 30 minutes.

Place chicken, skin sides up, in single layer in skillet. Cover and cook over medium-low heat 30 minutes. Add mushrooms; cover and cook until chicken is done, about 15 minutes longer.

6 SERVINGS

Chicken Almendrado

This one-skillet version of "almond chicken" could hardly be easier. Ground almonds thicken a cinnamon-chile sauce nicely.

1 medium onion, chopped (about ½ cup)
2 tablespoons margarine or butter
1 tablespoon vegetable oil
1 cup chicken broth
¼ cup slivered almonds
1 tablespoon ground red chiles
1 teaspoon vinegar
½ teaspoon sugar
½ teaspoon ground cinnamon
4 boneless chicken breast halves
Slivered almonds

Cook and stir onion in margarine and oil in 10-inch skillet until tender. Stir in broth, ¼ cup almonds, the ground red chiles, vinegar, sugar and cinnamon. Heat to boiling; reduce heat. Simmer uncovered 10 minutes.

Spoon mixture into blender container; cover and blend on low speed until smooth, about 1 minute. Return sauce to skillet.

Dip chicken breasts into sauce to coat both sides. Place skin sides up in single layer in skillet. Heat to boiling; reduce heat. Cover and simmer until done, about 45 minutes. Serve sauce over chicken; sprinkle with almonds.

4 SERVINGS

Chicken Almendrado

Grilled Chicken Adobo

The Achiote Sauce Base (below) makes more than enough for two recipes. Store the remainder in the freezer for a shortcut Chicken Adobo another time.

10 boneless, skinless, chicken breast halves (about 3½ pounds)
¼ cup Achiote Sauce Base (below)
1 cup orange juice
2 tablespoons lemon juice
2 tablespoons vegetable oil
1 teaspoon dried basil leaves
1 teaspoon ground cinnamon
½ teaspoon salt

Place chicken breasts in shallow glass or plastic dish. Mix remaining ingredients; pour over chicken. Cover and refrigerate 2 hours.

Remove chicken from marinade; reserve marinade. Cover and grill chicken 5 to 6 inches from medium coals 10 to 20 minutes.

Turn chicken. Cover and grill, turning and brushing with marinade 2 or 3 times, until done, 10 to 20 minutes longer.

Heat remaining marinade to boiling. Boil uncovered until thickened, 8 to 10 minutes. Serve with chicken.

6 SERVINGS

ACHIOTE SAUCE BASE

⅓ cup achiote seeds (annatto seeds)
⅓ cup orange juice
⅓ cup white vinegar
1 teaspoon ground red chiles
½ teaspoon pepper
1 clove garlic

Cover achiote seeds with boiling water. Cover; let stand at least 8 hours. Drain seeds. Place seeds and remaining ingredients in food processor workbowl fitted with steel blade. Cover and pro-

cess until seeds are coarsely ground; strain. Store in refrigerator up to 1 week or in freezer up to 2 months.

ABOUT ⅔ CUP SAUCE BASE

Broiled Chicken Adobo: Set oven control to broil. Remove chicken from marinade; reserve marinade. Place chicken in greased rectangular pan, 13 x 9 x 2 inches; pour half of the marinade over chicken. Broil chicken with tops about 4 inches from heat until light brown, about 10 minutes. Turn chicken; pour remaining marinade over chicken. Broil until done, about 6 minutes longer.

Chicken and Orange Salad

2 tablespoons finely chopped scallions or green onions (with tops)
2 tablespoons lime juice
¼ teaspoon salt
2 cups cut-up cooked chicken
1 cup cooked green peas
1 cup mayonnaise or salad dressing
¼ cup finely chopped carrot
¼ cup finely chopped celery
¼ cup finely snipped fresh cilantro
3 tablespoons orange juice
½ teaspoon salt
½ teaspoon ground cinnamon
¼ teaspoon freshly ground pepper
Lettuce leaves
3 oranges, pared and sectioned or unpared and cut into wedges
2 avocados, peeled and cut into wedges

Sprinkle scallions with lime juice and ¼ teaspoon salt; cover and refrigerate. Mix remaining ingredients except lettuce, oranges and avocados; cover and refrigerate at least 1 hour.

Spoon chicken mixture onto lettuce. Garnish with oranges and avocados; sprinkle with scallions.

6 SERVINGS

Chicken and Orange Salad

Chicken in Mole Sauce

Mole comes from the Aztec word *molli*, meaning a saucy dish. The best-known versions of *mole* are dark and highly spiced sauces for poultry and include unsweetened chocolate as an ingredient. The chocolate flavor is indistinct—unrecognizable to most people as chocolate—but adds a smooth, mysterious background note to *mole*.

1 dried chipotle chile
¼ cup shortening or lard
2 tablespoons ground red chiles
2 cups chicken broth
4 flour tortillas, (7 to 8 inches in diameter), cut into small pieces
¼ cup tomato sauce
1 small onion, chopped (about ¼ cup)
1 clove garlic, finely chopped
1 tablespoon raisins
1 tablespoon chopped almonds or walnuts
1 tablespoon sesame seed
1 tablespoon shelled pumpkin seeds
1 tablespoon peanut butter
1½ teaspoons sugar
1½ teaspoons ground oregano
1½ teaspoons cocoa
½ teaspoon anise seed
¼ teaspoon ground cinnamon
¼ teaspoon ground cloves
¼ teaspoon ground nutmeg
¼ teaspoon ground allspice
¼ teaspoon ground ginger
¼ teaspoon ground cumin or ½ teaspoon cumin seed
1 cup chicken broth
8 boneless chicken breast halves (about 4 pounds)

Cover chile with warm water. Let stand until softened, about 1 hour. Drain and finely chop.

Heat shortening in 3-quart saucepan over medium heat until hot. Cook and stir ground red chiles in shortening until brown (add about ¼ teaspoon water to prevent scorching if necessary); cool.

Stir in 2 cups broth. Stir in remaining ingredients except remaining 1 cup broth and the chicken.

Heat to boiling; reduce heat. Cover and simmer 30 minutes, stirring occasionally; cool.

Pour a small amount of sauce into blender container. Cover and blend on high speed until smooth. Repeat with remaining sauce.

Heat 1 cup of the sauce and the remaining broth to boiling in 12-inch skillet; reduce heat. Place chicken, skin sides up, in single layer in skillet. Cover and simmer until done, about 1 hour. Remove chicken to serving dish; keep warm. Measure cooking liquid. In skillet combine 1 cup of cooking liquid with the remaining sauce. Heat to boiling, stirring constantly; pour over chicken.

8 SERVINGS

Mexican Chicken Salad

2 cups cut-up cooked chicken
¼ cup dairy sour cream
¼ cup mayonnaise or salad dressing
¼ cup finely chopped carrot
2 tablespoons snipped fresh cilantro
2 tablespoons capers
2 tablespoons chopped pimiento
2 tablespoons lime juice
½ teaspoon ground cumin
½ teaspoon dried oregano leaves
1 small onion, chopped (about ¼ cup)
Lettuce leaves
1 avocado, peeled and cut into wedges
Paprika

Toss all ingredients except lettuce, avocado and paprika. Serve on lettuce with avocado; sprinkle with paprika.

4 SERVINGS

Santa Fe Chicken

Black Bean Relish (page 30)
8 boneless, skinless, chicken breast halves
¼ cup vegetable oil
2 tablespoons lime juice
½ teaspoon salt
¼ teaspoon pepper
2 cloves garlic, finely chopped
1 medium onion, chopped (about ½ cup)
1 can (14 ounces) artichoke hearts, drained and cut
  into fourths

Prepare Black Bean Relish; reserve. Place chicken breasts in shallow glass or plastic dish. Mix remaining ingredients except artichoke hearts; pour over chicken. Cover and refrigerate 1 hour.

Set oven control to broil. Remove chicken from marinade; reserve marinade. Place chicken in greased broiler pan (without rack); brush with marinade. Broil chicken with tops about 4 inches from heat until light brown, about 10 minutes.

Turn chicken; brush with marinade. Arrange artichoke hearts around chicken. Broil until chicken is done, 8 to 11 minutes longer. Serve with Black Bean Relish.

8 SERVINGS

Grilled Cornish Hens

Plum Barbecue Sauce (page 29)
3 Rock Cornish hens (about 1¼ pounds each)

Prepare Plum Barbecue Sauce; reserve. Cut hens lengthwise into halves. Place bone sides down on grill. Cover and grill 5 to 6 inches from medium coals 35 minutes.

Turn hens. Cover and grill, turning and brushing with Plum Barbecue Sauce 2 or 3 times, until done, 25 to 35 minutes longer. Heat any remaining sauce, and serve with hens.

6 SERVINGS

Roast Cornish Hens: Heat oven to 350°. Place cut hens, bone sides down, on rack in shallow roasting pan. Roast uncovered 30 minutes. Brush hens generously with Plum Barbecue Sauce. Roast uncovered, brushing hens with sauce 2 or 3 times, until done, about 45 minutes longer.

Duck with Pine Nut Wild Rice

Apricot Basting Sauce (page 29)
4½- to 5-pound duckling
Pine Nut Wild Rice (below)

Prepare Apricot Basting Sauce. Heat oven to 350°. Place duckling, breast side up, on rack in shallow roasting pan. Brush with Apricot Basting Sauce. Insert meat thermometer so tip is in thickest part of inside thigh muscle and does not touch bone. Do not add water. Do not cover.

Roast, brushing with sauce 2 or 3 times, until thermometer registers 180° to 185° or drumstick meat feels very soft when pressed between fingers, 2 to 2½ hours. Serve with Pine Nut Wild Rice.

4 SERVINGS

PINE NUT WILD RICE

½ cup uncooked wild rice
2 tablespoons sliced green onions (with tops)
1 teaspoon margarine or butter
1½ cups chicken broth
½ cup pine nuts (2 ounces), toasted (page 19)
½ cup chopped dried pears
½ cup currants

Cook and stir wild rice and onions in margarine in 2-quart heavy saucepan over medium heat until onions are tender, about 3 minutes. Stir in broth. Heat to boiling, stirring occasionally; reduce heat. Cover and simmer until wild rice is tender, 40 to 50 minutes. Stir in pine nuts, pears and currants.

Turkey with Southwest Stuffing

Turkey is a native American bird. One of its great virtues is that, with relatively little effort in preparation, it serves many. The rich corn bread stuffing boasts an untraditional, delicious combination of sage, cilantro and pecans. Chayote guarantees that it will be moist.

Southwest Stuffing (right)
10- to 12-pound turkey
Margarine or butter, melted

Prepare Southwest Stuffing. Fill wishbone area of turkey with stuffing. Fasten neck skin to back with skewer. Fold wings across back with tips touching. Fill body cavity lightly. (Do not pack—stuffing will expand.) Tuck drumsticks under band of skin at tail, or skewer to tail.

Spoon any remaining stuffing into ungreased 1-quart casserole; cover. (Refrigerate until about 30 minutes before turkey is done. Bake covered until hot, about 45 minutes.)

Heat oven to 325°. Place turkey, breast side up, on rack in shallow roasting pan. Brush with margarine. Insert meat thermometer so tip is in thickest part of inside thigh muscle or thickest part of breast meat and does not touch bone. (Tip of thermometer can be inserted in center of stuffing.) Do not add water. Do not cover. Roast until done, 3½ to 4 hours.

Place a tent of aluminum foil loosely over turkey when it begins to turn golden. After 2½ hours, cut band or remove skewer holding legs. Turkey is done when thermometer placed in thigh muscle registers 185° or drumstick meat feels very soft when pressed between fingers. (Thermometer inserted in stuffing will register 165°.)

Let stand about 20 minutes before carving. As soon as possible after serving, remove every bit of stuffing from turkey. Cool stuffing and turkey promptly; refrigerate separately, and use within 2 days.

8 TO 10 SERVINGS

SOUTHWEST STUFFING

1 cup chopped chayote (about 1 small)
4 jalapeño chiles, seeded and finely chopped
2 cloves garlic, finely chopped
1 large onion, finely chopped (about 1 cup)
1 cup margarine or butter
1 tablespoon snipped fresh cilantro
1 teaspoon salt
½ teaspoon dried thyme leaves
½ teaspoon dried sage leaves
9 cups ½-inch cubes corn bread
1 cup chopped pecans

Cook and stir chayote, chiles, garlic and onion in margarine in 10-inch skillet until chayote is tender. Stir in cilantro, salt, thyme and sage until well blended. Stir in about ⅓ of the corn bread cubes. Turn mixture into deep bowl. Add remaining corn bread cubes and the pecans; toss.

Turkey in Jalapeño Cream Sauce

Jalapeño Cream Sauce (page 28)
2 large boneless, skinless turkey breasts (about 1 pound each), each cut into 3 slices
¼ cup all-purpose flour
½ teaspoon cracked black pepper
¼ teaspoon salt
¼ cup margarine or butter

Prepare Jalapeño Cream Sauce; reserve. Flatten each turkey breast slice to ¼-inch thickness between plastic wrap or waxed paper.

Mix flour, pepper and salt. Coat turkey with flour mixture. Heat margarine in 10-inch skillet until melted. Cook turkey in margarine, turning once, until done, about 8 minutes. Serve with Jalapeño Cream Sauce.

6 SERVINGS

Turkey with Southwest Stuffing

Venison with Plum Sauce

Plum Barbecue Sauce (page 29)
6 venison steaks, 1 inch thick (about 4 ounces each)

Prepare Plum Barbecue Sauce. Set oven control to broil. Place venison steaks in greased broiler pan (without rack); spoon ½ cup of the sauce evenly over venison.

Broil venison with tops about 4 inches from heat until light brown, about 10 minutes. Turn venison; spoon ½ cup of the sauce evenly over venison. Broil until rare to medium-rare doneness, about 5 minutes longer. Heat remaining sauce, and serve with venison.

6 SERVINGS

Pheasant in Almond Red Sauce

Pheasant is a deep-flavored meat and delicious cooked simply, with a minimum of fuss. Almond Red Sauce is equally simple to prepare. It is thick with nuts, which always go well with game.

Almond Red Sauce (page 25)
2½- to 3-pound pheasant, cut up
2 tablespoons vegetable oil
½ cup chicken broth

Prepare Almond Red Sauce; reserve. Cook pheasant in oil in 10-inch skillet until light brown, 15 to 18 minutes; drain.

Stir in broth and Almond Red Sauce. Heat to boiling; reduce heat. Cover and simmer until pheasant is done, about 30 minutes longer. Skim fat from sauce.

6 SERVINGS

Spicy Brisket

Spicy Texas Barbecue Sauce (page 30)
4- to 5-pound well-trimmed beef brisket

Prepare Spicy Texas Barbecue Sauce. Heat oven to 325°. Place beef brisket in ungreased rectangular baking dish, 13 x 9 x 2 inches. Pour sauce over beef.

Cover and bake 2 hours. Turn beef over; cover and bake until tender, about 2 hours longer. Serve with warmed flour tortillas if desired.

12 SERVINGS

Broiled Steak

2 beef flank steaks (1 to 1½ pounds each)
½ cup lime juice
2 tablespoons dried oregano leaves
2 tablespoons olive or vegetable oil
2 teaspoons salt
½ teaspoon pepper
4 cloves garlic, crushed

Place beef steaks in shallow glass or plastic dish. Mix remaining ingredients; pour over beef. Cover and refrigerate at least 8 hours, turning beef occasionally.

Set oven control to broil. Place beef on rack in broiler pan. Broil with tops about 3 inches from heat until brown, about 5 minutes. Turn beef; broil 5 minutes. Cut beef diagonally across grain into thin slices. Serve with tortillas and guacamole if desired.

8 SERVINGS

Venison with Plum Sauce

Santa Fe Flank Steak

3 guajillo chiles
2 cloves garlic, finely chopped
1 tablespoon packed brown sugar
1 teaspoon dried thyme leaves
¼ teaspoon salt
¼ teaspoon freshly ground pepper
2 pounds beef flank steak

Place chiles and enough water to cover chiles in 2-quart saucepan. Heat to boiling. Boil uncovered 5 minutes; drain. Remove stems; finely chop chiles. Mix chiles and remaining ingredients except beef steak. Rub mixture on both sides of beef. Cover and refrigerate 1 hour.

Set oven control to broil. Place beef on rack in broiler pan. Broil with top about 3 inches from heat until brown, about 5 minutes. Turn beef; broil until of medium-rare doneness, 4 to 6 minutes longer. Cut beef diagonally across grain into very thin slices.

8 SERVINGS

Grilled Jalapeño Buffalo Burgers

Hot Chile Sauce (page 26)
1½ pounds ground buffalo or ground beef
1 medium onion, finely chopped (about ½ cup)
2 to 3 jalapeño chiles, seeded and finely chopped
1 clove garlic, finely chopped

Prepare Hot Chile Sauce; reserve. Mix remaining ingredients. Shape into 6 patties, each about ½ inch thick.

Brush grill with vegetable oil. Grill patties about 4 inches from medium coals, turning once, until of desired doneness, 4 to 6 minutes on each side for medium. Serve with Hot Chile Sauce.

6 SERVINGS

Broiled Jalapeño Buffalo Burgers: Set oven control to broil. Place patties on rack in broiler pan. Broil with tops about 3 inches from heat, turning once, until of desired doneness, 4 to 6 minutes on each side for medium.

Mexican Pot Roast

6-pound beef arm, blade or cross-rib pot roast
8 cloves garlic
4 slices bacon, cut into halves
2 teaspoons salt
½ teaspoon pepper
½ cup prepared mustard
¼ cup vegetable oil
½ cup chopped carrot
½ cup chopped celery
½ cup sliced mushrooms
2 tablespoons snipped fresh cilantro
1 teaspoon ground nutmeg
1 teaspoon ground thyme
2 jalapeño chiles, seeded and finely chopped
2 bay leaves
1 medium onion, chopped (about ½ cup)
1 bottle or can (12 ounces) beer

Make a 1½-inch-deep cut across beef roast. Wrap each clove garlic in 1 piece bacon; insert in cut. Sprinkle beef with salt and pepper; spread with mustard. Cover and refrigerate at least 4 hours.

Cook beef in oil in 4-quart Dutch oven over medium heat until brown. Stir in remaining ingredients. Heat to boiling; reduce heat. Cover and simmer until beef is tender, about 2½ hours.

Remove beef to warm platter. Remove bay leaves from broth. Skim fat from broth. Place 2 cups of the broth and vegetables in blender container; cover and blend on medium speed until smooth. Serve with beef.

12 SERVINGS

Santa Fe Flank Steak

Southwest Burgers

Fresh Tomato Salsa (page 24)
1½ pounds ground beef
1 can (4 ounces) chopped green chiles, drained
½ cup diced Monterey Jack cheese
½ teaspoon pepper
¼ teaspoon salt

Prepare Fresh Tomato Salsa; reserve. Mix remaining ingredients. Shape into 6 patties, each about ½ inch thick.

Set oven control to broil. Place patties on rack in broiler pan. Broil with tops of burgers about 3 inches from heat until of desired doneness, 5 to 7 minutes on each side for medium. Serve with Fresh Tomato Salsa.

6 SERVINGS

Meatballs in Chipotle Sauce

Chipotle Sauce (page 26)
1 pound ground beef
1 pound ground pork
2 eggs
½ cup dry bread crumbs
½ cup milk
2 tablespoons finely chopped onion
2 tablespoons snipped fresh cilantro
2 teaspoons salt
½ teaspoon pepper

Prepare Chipotle Sauce. Mix remaining ingredients; shape into 1½-inch balls. Heat sauce and meatballs to boiling; reduce heat. Cover and simmer until meatballs are done, about 20 minutes. Serve with hot cooked rice or noodles, if desired.

8 SERVINGS

Braised Meat Loaf

1 pound ground beef
1 pound fully cooked smoked ham, finely chopped
1 pound ground pork
3 eggs
2 teaspoons salt
½ teaspoon pepper
¼ teaspoon ground nutmeg
Chipotle Sauce (page 26)
½ cup dry bread crumbs
¼ cup instant corn flour tortilla mix
½ cup vegetable oil

Mix ground beef, ham, ground pork, eggs, salt, pepper and nutmeg; shape into loaf. Cover and refrigerate 1 hour. Prepare Chipotle Sauce.

Mix bread crumbs and tortilla mix. Coat meat loaf with bread crumb mixture. Heat oil in 10-inch skillet until hot. Cook meat loaf in oil over medium heat until brown on all sides; drain. Pour Chipotle Sauce over meat loaf. Heat to boiling; reduce heat. Cover and simmer until done, about 1 hour.

12 SERVINGS

Chiles in Walnut Sauce

Poblano chiles lend themselves to stuffing. Chiles in Walnut Sauce are filled with a sweet-and-sour beef mixture, then fried in the manner of traditional Chiles Rellenos (page 174).

8 poblano chiles, roasted and peeled (page 15)
1 pound ground beef
1 small onion, chopped (about ¼ cup)
2 medium tomatoes, chopped (about 2 cups)
1 unpared all-purpose apple, chopped
1 banana, peeled and sliced
1 jalapeño chile, seeded and finely chopped
1 clove garlic, finely chopped
1 cup raisins
⅓ cup slivered almonds
2 tablespoons chopped green olives
1 tablespoon capers
¾ teaspoon ground cinnamon
½ teaspoon salt
¼ teaspoon cumin seed
¼ teaspoon ground oregano
⅛ teaspoon freshly ground pepper
4 eggs, separated
Flour
Vegetable oil
Walnut Sauce (right)
Pomegranate seeds or raisins
Snipped fresh cilantro

Cut lengthwise slit down one side of each poblano chile. Carefully remove seeds and membranes; reserve chiles.

Cook and stir ground beef and onion in 10-inch skillet until beef is brown; drain. Stir in remaining ingredients except eggs, flour, oil, Walnut Sauce, pomegranate seeds and cilantro. Cover and simmer 15 minutes. Fill chiles with beef mixture. Cover and refrigerate 1 hour.

Beat egg whites in large bowl until stiff. Beat egg yolks; fold into egg whites. Coat filled chiles with flour; dip into egg mixture. Heat ¼ inch oil in 8-inch skillet until hot. Cook chiles, one at a time, in oil, turning once, until puffy and golden, about 2 minutes on each side; drain. Place on cookie sheet; keep warm in 200° oven.

Prepare Walnut Sauce; spoon over chiles. Sprinkle with pomegranate seeds and cilantro.

8 SERVINGS

WALNUT SAUCE

1 cup ground walnuts
1 cup dairy sour cream
½ cup chicken broth

Mix all ingredients.

Roast Loin of Pork

5-pound pork boneless top loin roast
2 to 4 tablespoons ground red chiles
½ cup lime juice
1 teaspoon salt
1 teaspoon ground cumin
1 teaspoon dried oregano leaves
½ teaspoon pepper
2 cloves garlic, crushed
1 can (6 ounces) frozen orange juice concentrate, thawed
¼ cup dry white wine
½ cup dairy sour cream
½ teaspoon salt

Place pork roast in shallow glass or plastic dish. Mix ground red chiles, lime juice, 1 teaspoon salt, the cumin, oregano, pepper, garlic and ¼ cup of the orange juice concentrate; brush on pork. Cover and refrigerate at least 8 hours.

Heat oven to 325°. Place pork, fat side up, on rack in shallow roasting pan. Insert meat thermometer so tip is in center of thickest part of pork and does not rest in fat. Roast uncovered until thermometer registers 170°, 2 to 2½ hours.

Remove pork and rack from pan. Strain drippings from pan; reserve. Add enough water to remaining orange juice concentrate to measure ¾ cup; stir juice and wine into drippings. Stir in sour cream and salt. Serve with pork.

12 TO 15 SERVINGS

Spicy Pork Roast

1/4 cup sugar
1 teaspoon ground red chiles
1 teaspoon dried oregano leaves
1/2 teaspoon pepper
2-pound pork boneless loin roast

Mix sugar, ground red chiles, oregano and pepper; rub over pork roast. Cover and refrigerate 30 minutes.

Heat oven to 325°. Place pork, fat side up, on rack in shallow roasting pan. Insert meat thermometer so tip is in thickest part of pork and does not rest in fat. Roast uncovered until thermometer registers 170°, about 2 hours.

6 SERVINGS

Pork with Cumin

2 pounds pork boneless shoulder, cut into 1-inch cubes
1/4 cup all-purpose flour
1/2 cup vegetable oil
1 medium onion, chopped (about 1/2 cup)
2 slices bacon, cut up
1/2 cup water
2 tablespoons orange juice
2 tablespoons lime juice
2 teaspoons instant chicken bouillon (dry)
2 teaspoons cumin seed
1 teaspoon dried oregano leaves
1/2 teaspoon salt
1/4 teaspoon pepper
4 medium tomatoes, chopped (about 4 cups)
2 medium pared or unpared potatoes, diced
1/2 cup dairy sour cream

Coat pork with flour. Heat oil in 10-inch skillet until hot. Cook and stir pork in oil over medium heat until brown. Remove pork with slotted spoon; drain.

Cook and stir onion and bacon in same skillet until bacon is crisp. Stir in pork and remaining ingredients except sour cream. Heat to boiling; reduce heat. Cover and simmer until pork is done, about 45 minutes. Stir in sour cream; heat until hot.

7 SERVINGS

Pork Tenderloin in Tequila

1/4 cup prepared mustard
2 pounds pork tenderloin
1/4 cup vegetable oil
2 cloves garlic, cut into halves
1/4 cup chopped carrot
1/4 cup chopped celery
1/4 cup lime juice
1/4 cup tequila
1 tablespoon ground red chiles
1 teaspoon salt
1 teaspoon dried oregano leaves
1 teaspoon dried thyme leaves
1/4 teaspoon pepper
4 medium tomatoes, chopped (about 4 cups)
1 small onion, chopped (about 1/4 cup)
1 bay leaf
1/4 cup snipped parsley

Spread mustard over pork tenderloin. Heat oil and garlic in 10-inch skillet until hot. Cook pork in oil over medium heat until brown. Remove garlic.

Stir in remaining ingredients except parsley. Heat to boiling; reduce heat. Cover and simmer until pork is done, about 30 minutes. Remove bay leaf. Sprinkle with parsley.

6 SERVINGS

Pork Tenderloin in Tequila

Pork Chops in Radish Sauce

Radish and Cilantro Relish (page 31)
2 tablespoons vegetable oil
6 pork loin or rib chops, about ½ inch thick
1 teaspoon salt
¼ teaspoon pepper
2 medium tomatoes, chopped (about 2 cups)
Hot cooked rice

Prepare Radish and Cilantro Relish; reserve. Heat oil in 10-inch skillet until hot. Cook pork chops in oil over medium heat until brown; sprinkle with salt and pepper. Remove pork from skillet.

Cook and stir relish and tomatoes in same skillet 5 minutes. Add pork. Heat to boiling; reduce heat. Cover and simmer until pork is done, about 45 minutes. Serve with rice. Garnish with snipped fresh cilantro if desired.

6 SERVINGS

Spicy Texas Spareribs

Spicy Texas Barbecue Sauce (page 30)
4½ pounds fresh pork spareribs, cut into serving pieces
1 lemon, sliced
1 large onion, sliced

Prepare Spicy Texas Barbecue Sauce; reserve. Heat oven to 325°. Place pork spareribs, meaty sides up, on rack in shallow roasting pan. Place lemon and onion slices on pork. Cover and bake 2 hours.

Pour 2 cups of the Spicy Texas Barbecue Sauce over pork. Bake uncovered, brushing with sauce 2 or 3 times, until done, about 2 hours longer. Heat any remaining sauce, and serve with pork.

6 SERVINGS

Citrus-marinated Pork Chops

2 dried chipotle chiles
6 pork loin or rib chops, about ½ inch thick
½ cup orange juice concentrate, thawed
¼ cup vegetable oil
¼ cup lemon juice
2 tablespoons grated orange peel
1 teaspoon salt
1 clove garlic
1 medium orange, cut into 6 slices

Cover chiles with warm water. Let stand until softened, about 1 hour. Drain and finely chop.

Place pork chops in shallow glass or plastic dish. Place chiles and remaining ingredients except orange in blender container. Cover and blend on low speed until smooth; pour over pork. Cover and refrigerate at least 3 hours, spooning marinade over pork occasionally.

Set oven control to broil. Remove pork from marinade; reserve marinade. Place pork on rack in broiler pan. Broil with tops 3 to 5 inches from heat until light brown, about 10 minutes.

Turn pork; brush with marinade. Broil until done, about 5 minutes longer. Garnish with orange slices.

6 SERVINGS

Citrus-marinated Pork Chops

Pecan-breaded Lamb Chops

These chops are irresistible. The mustard coating is a piquant French touch that holds the crusty nut coating in place and ensures juicy meat.

1 egg white
1 tablespoon Dijon-style mustard
1/2 cup finely chopped pecans
1/2 cup soft bread crumbs (about 1 1/3 slices bread)
1 clove garlic, finely chopped
6 lamb loin or shoulder chops, about 3/4 inch thick
2 tablespoons vegetable oil
2 tablespoons brandy

Beat egg white slightly in small bowl; stir in mustard. Mix pecans, bread crumbs and garlic. Dip lamb chops into mustard mixture; coat with pecan mixture.

Heat oil in 10-inch skillet until hot. Cook lamb in oil over low heat until deep golden brown, about 10 minutes on each side. Remove from heat; immediately sprinkle brandy around lamb in skillet.

6 SERVINGS

Baked Citrus Swordfish

Citrus Barbecue Sauce (page 29)
6 swordfish or salmon steaks, 1 inch thick (about 5 ounces each)

Prepare Citrus Barbecue Sauce. Heat oven to 450°. Place fish steaks in ungreased rectangular baking dish, 13 x 9 x 2 inches. Pour 1 cup of the sauce over fish.

Bake uncovered until fish flakes easily with fork, 20 to 25 minutes. Serve with remaining Citrus Barbecue Sauce.

6 SERVINGS

Baked Red Snapper

2 pounds red snapper fillets, cut into 8 serving pieces
1 cup milk
1 teaspoon dried oregano leaves
1 medium onion, sliced
1/4 cup olive or vegetable oil
1/2 cup pitted ripe olives
1/4 cup dry white wine
1/4 cup lemon juice
2 tablespoons capers
1 teaspoon ground cumin
1/2 teaspoon salt
1/4 teaspoon pepper
4 large tomatoes, chopped (about 4 cups)
2 cloves garlic, finely chopped

Place fish fillets in shallow glass or plastic dish. Mix milk and oregano; pour over fish. Cover and refrigerate 1 hour.

Cook and stir onion in oil in 10-inch skillet until tender. Stir in remaining ingredients except fish. Simmer uncovered until thickened, about 15 minutes.

Heat oven to 350°. Drain fish; pat dry. Place 1 piece fish on each of eight 12-inch squares heavy-duty aluminum foil. Spoon some tomato mixture onto fish. Fold foil over fish; seal securely. Place foil packets in ungreased jelly roll pan, 15½ x 10½ x 1 inch. Bake until fish flakes easily with fork, about 30 minutes. Serve with snipped fresh cilantro and lemon wedges if desired.

8 SERVINGS

Pecan-breaded Lamb Chops

Sea Bass in Cilantro

2 pounds sea bass or red snapper fillets, cut into 8
  serving pieces
1 cup milk
1 teaspoon ground cumin
1 large onion, finely chopped (about 1 cup)
1/4 cup vegetable oil
1 cup finely chopped canned green chiles
1/4 to 1/2 cup snipped fresh cilantro
3/4 teaspoon salt
1/4 teaspoon pepper
Lime or lemon wedges

Place fish fillets in shallow glass or plastic dish.
Mix milk and cumin; pour over fish. Cover and
refrigerate 1 hour.

Cook and stir onion in oil in 2-quart saucepan
until tender. Stir in remaining ingredients except
fish and lime wedges. Heat to boiling; reduce
heat. Simmer uncovered until thickened, about
10 minutes.

Heat oven to 350°. Drain fish; pat dry. Place 1
piece fish on each of eight 12-inch squares heavy-
duty aluminum foil. Spoon some onion mixture
onto fish. Fold foil over fish; seal securely. Place
foil packets in ungreased jelly roll pan, 15½ x
10½ x 1 inch. Bake until fish flakes easily with
fork, 25 to 30 minutes. Serve with lime wedges.

8 SERVINGS

Paella-stuffed Snapper

A whole stuffed fish makes a stunning presentation, and this one feeds a crowd. Paella is a Spanish invention that combines seafood and meats
with saffron-scented rice. Serrano chiles give the
paella stuffing a Mexican kick.

Paella Stuffing (below)
6- to 8-pound red snapper, cod or lake trout, cleaned
  and dressed
Lime juice
1/4 cup margarine or butter, melted
2 tablespoons lime juice
Lime wedges

Prepare Paella Stuffing. Heat oven to 350°. Rub
cavity of fish with lime juice; fill with Paella Stuffing. Close opening with skewers; lace with string.
Place in large ungreased broiler pan (without
rack) or in shallow roasting pan.

Mix margarine and 2 tablespoons lime juice.
Bake fish uncovered, brushing with margarine
mixture occasionally, until fish flakes easily with
fork, about 1½ hours. Serve with lime wedges.

10 SERVINGS

PAELLA STUFFING

1/2 pound chorizo sausage links, chopped
1 large onion, chopped (about 1 cup)
2 cloves garlic, finely chopped
2 serrano chiles, seeded and chopped
2 tablespoons margarine or butter
2 cups cooked rice
1/2 cup slivered almonds, toasted
1/4 cup snipped fresh cilantro
1/4 cup tomato sauce
1/4 teaspoon ground saffron
1 package (6 ounces) frozen cooked medium shrimp

Cook sausage, onion, garlic and chiles in margarine in 10-inch skillet over medium heat, stirring
frequently, until sausage is done, about 10 minutes; drain. Stir in remaining ingredients.

Paella-stuffed Snapper (shown before cooking)

Sole Steamed in Corn Husks

Chipotle Mayonnaise (page 28)
12 dried corn husks
2 poblano chiles, roasted, peeled (page 15), seeded and
    chopped
2 red bell peppers, chopped
1 medium tomato, seeded and chopped (about ¾ cup)
2 cloves garlic, finely chopped
¼ teaspoon salt
2 pounds sole or orange roughy fillets

Prepare Chipotle Mayonnaise; reserve. Rinse corn husks and remove silk; cover with boiling water. Let stand until softened, at least 1 hour; drain, and pat dry. Mix remaining ingredients except fish fillets and Chipotle Mayonnaise.

Cut fish into 1-inch pieces; divide evenly among corn husks. Place 2 to 3 tablespoons of the chile mixture on fish. Roll corn husks lengthwise around filling. Fold ends up toward center; secure with string.

Place corn husk packets on rack in 6-quart Dutch oven or steamer. Pour boiling water into Dutch oven to just below rack level. Cover; simmer until fish flakes easily with fork, about 25 minutes. Serve with Chipotle Mayonnaise.

6 SERVINGS

Roll corn husks lengthwise around filling.

Fold up ends toward center; secure with string.

Grilled Red Snapper with Vegetable Sauté

Southwest Vegetable Sauté (including Lime Butter
    Sauce) (page 176)
8 red snapper or cod fillets (about 5 ounces each)
¼ cup vegetable oil
Salt and pepper

Prepare Southwest Vegetable Sauté and Lime Butter Sauce; keep warm. Generously brush fish fillets with oil; sprinkle with salt and pepper.

Grill over medium coals until fish flakes easily with fork, 10 to 12 minutes. Serve with Southwest Vegetable Sauté and Lime Butter Sauce.

8 SERVINGS

Broiled Red Snapper: Set oven control to broil. Place fish on rack in broiler pan. Broil with tops about 4 inches from heat until fish flakes easily with fork, 10 to 12 minutes.

Cod with Garlic

2 pounds cod or scrod fillets, cut into 8 serving pieces
8 cloves garlic, finely chopped
2 tablespoons margarine or butter
2 tablespoons vegetable oil
¼ cup lemon juice
1 teaspoon salt
Snipped fresh cilantro

Place fish fillets on rack in broiler pan. Cook and stir garlic in margarine and oil until golden brown. Remove garlic; reserve. Drizzle margarine mixture and lemon juice over fish; sprinkle with salt.

Set oven control to broil. Broil fish with tops about 3 inches from heat until fish flakes easily with fork, 10 to 12 minutes. Sprinkle with garlic and cilantro. Serve with lemon wedges if desired.

8 SERVINGS

Grilled Red Snapper with Vegetable Sauté

Halibut with Cilantro Pesto

Cilantro Pesto (page 28)
6 halibut steaks, 1 inch thick (about 5 ounces each)
2 tablespoons margarine or butter, melted
2 tablespoons lemon juice

Prepare Cilantro Pesto; reserve. Heat oven to 450°. Place fish steaks in ungreased rectangular baking dish, 13 x 9 x 2 inches. Mix margarine and lemon juice; pour over fish.

Bake uncovered until fish flakes easily with fork, 20 to 25 minutes. Serve with Cilantro Pesto.

6 SERVINGS

Salmon with Cucumber Salsa

One classic sauce for poached salmon is a creamy one thick with cucumbers. Here, a livelier version benefits from the tang and reduced calories of yogurt.

Cucumber Salsa (page 24)
2 cups water
1 cup dry white wine
1 teaspoon salt
¼ teaspoon dried thyme leaves
¼ teaspoon dried oregano leaves
⅛ teaspoon ground red pepper
4 black peppercorns
4 cilantro sprigs
1 small onion, sliced
2 pounds salmon fillets, cut into 6 serving pieces

Prepare Cucumber Salsa; reserve. Heat remaining ingredients except fish fillets to boiling in 12-inch skillet; reduce heat. Cover and simmer 5 minutes.

Place fish in skillet; if necessary, add water so that fish is covered. Heat to boiling; reduce heat. Simmer uncovered until fish flakes easily with fork, about 14 minutes.

Carefully remove fish from skillet with slotted spatula; drain on wire rack. Cover and refrigerate until cold, about 2 hours. Serve with Cucumber Salsa.

6 SERVINGS

Salmon with Cucumber Salsa

Shrimp and Potato Salad

Cool shrimp salad is made even more refreshing with the snap of fresh lime juice and cilantro. This would be a substantial luncheon dish, doubly welcome because it can be made ahead.

2½ cups cooked small shrimp
2 cups cubed cooked potatoes
1 cup cooked green peas
¼ cup chopped celery
2 tablespoons lime juice
1 teaspoon ground cumin
¼ teaspoon salt
⅛ teaspoon freshly ground pepper
¾ cup mayonnaise or salad dressing
4 tablespoons snipped fresh cilantro
Lettuce leaves
3 tomatoes, cut into wedges

Mix shrimp, potatoes, peas, celery, lime juice, cumin, salt and pepper. Cover and refrigerate at least 2 hours.

Just before serving, toss shrimp mixture, mayonnaise and 3 tablespoons of the cilantro until potatoes are well coated. Serve on lettuce with tomatoes and remaining cilantro.

6 SERVINGS

Grilled Texas Shrimp

¼ cup vegetable oil
¼ cup tequila
¼ cup red wine vinegar
2 tablespoons lime juice
1 tablespoon ground red chiles
½ teaspoon salt
2 cloves garlic, finely chopped
1 red bell pepper, finely chopped
24 large raw shrimp, peeled and deveined (leave tails intact)

Mix all ingredients except shrimp in shallow glass or plastic dish; stir in shrimp. Cover and refrigerate 1 hour.

Remove shrimp from marinade; reserve marinade. Thread 4 shrimp on each of six 8-inch metal skewers. Grill over medium coals, turning once, until pink, 2 to 3 minutes on each side.

Heat marinade to boiling in nonaluminum saucepan; reduce heat to low. Simmer uncovered until bell pepper is tender, about 5 minutes. Serve with shrimp.

6 SERVINGS

Broiled Texas Shrimp: Set oven control to broil. Place skewered shrimp on rack in broiler pan. Broil with tops about 4 inches from heat, turning once, until pink, 2 to 3 minutes on each side.

Grilled Texas Shrimp

Shrimp Cilantro

1 medium onion, chopped (about ½ cup)
2 cloves garlic, finely chopped
2 tablespoons margarine or butter
2 tablespoons vegetable oil
16 large raw shrimp, peeled and deveined
2 tablespoons snipped fresh cilantro
Lemon slices

Cook and stir onion and garlic in margarine and oil in 10-inch skillet until tender. Add shrimp; cook 1 minute.

Turn shrimp; cook until pink, about 2 minutes longer. (Do not overcook.) Remove shrimp to serving dish; sprinkle with cilantro. Pour pan juices over shrimp; serve with lemon slices.

4 SERVINGS

Shrimp Cilantro (shown with a Margarita Sunrise, page 56)

Southwest Sautéed Scallops

2 cups water
1 dried Anaheim chile
¼ cup sliced green onions (with tops)
2 tablespoons margarine or butter
2 tablespoons lime juice
2 pounds sea scallops
2 cups cubed fresh pineapple
1 cup Chinese pea pod halves (about 3 ounces)
3 cups hot cooked fettuccine

Heat water to boiling in 1-quart saucepan. Add chile. Boil 5 minutes; drain. Remove stem and seeds; finely chop chile.

Cook and stir onions, margarine, lime juice and chile in 10-inch skillet until margarine is melted. Carefully stir in scallops. Cook over medium heat, stirring frequently, until scallops turn white, about 12 minutes.

Stir in the pineapple and pea pods; heat until hot. Remove scallop mixture with slotted spoon; keep warm.

Heat liquid in skillet to boiling. Boil until slightly thickened and reduced by half. Spoon scallop mixture onto fettuccine; pour liquid over scallop mixture.

6 SERVINGS

Eggs and Pasta

The handy, ubiquitous hen's egg was brought to Mexico by the Spanish. South of the border, it is most often found scrambled, but in this chapter there are some rustic classics made with whole eggs. Without them a collection of southwestern recipes would be incomplete.

Pasta is certainly not a native invention, nor did it play a part in early southwest cooking. Yet few other foods are as easy to combine with the gifts of the southwestern kitchen. Tossed with any number of savory sauces and morsels of simply cooked meat or fish, pasta proves itself as obliging as the tortilla. Homemade pasta opens up fresh vistas, for the dough itself can be deliciously flavored with chiles and vegetables. Making pasta fresh at home isn't at all difficult, as Chipotle Fettuccine (page 145) and Pumpkin Ravioli (page 146) show.

Huevos Rancheros (shown with a Mexican Sweet Bun, page 206)

Huevos Rancheros

Huevos Rancheros ("ranch-style eggs") in fact refers to any egg dish served on tortillas. Spicy sausage makes this version a hearty one.

8 ounces bulk chorizo sausage
Vegetable oil
6 corn tortillas (6 to 7 inches in diameter)
1¼ cups warm Casera Sauce (page 25)
6 fried eggs
1½ cups shredded Cheddar cheese (6 ounces)

Cook and stir sausage until done; drain. Heat ⅛ inch oil in 8-inch skillet over medium heat just until hot. Cook tortillas, one at a time, in oil until crisp, about 1 minute; drain.

Spread each tortilla with 1 tablespoon Casera Sauce to soften. Place 1 egg on each tortilla; top each with scant tablespoon Casera Sauce, ¼ cup sausage, another tablespoon sauce and ¼ cup cheese.

6 SERVINGS

Mexican Omelet

Casera Sauce (page 25)
2 eggs
2 tablespoons half-and-half
½ teaspoon dried oregano leaves
¼ teaspoon salt
Dash of pepper
1 tablespoon margarine or butter
¼ cup shredded Monterey Jack cheese (1 ounce)
2 tablespoons chopped green chiles
Dairy sour cream

Prepare Casera Sauce; reserve. Mix eggs, half-and-half, oregano, salt and pepper with fork just until whites and yolks are blended. Heat margarine in 8-inch skillet or omelet pan over medium-high heat. As margarine melts, tilt skillet to coat bottom completely. When margarine just begins to brown, skillet is hot enough to use.

Quickly pour egg mixture into skillet. Slide skillet back and forth rapidly over heat, and, at the same time, stir quickly with fork to spread eggs continuously over bottom of skillet as they thicken. Let stand over heat a few seconds to lightly brown bottom of omelet. (Do not overcook; omelet will continue to cook after folding.)

Tilt skillet; run fork under edge of omelet, then jerk skillet sharply to loosen eggs from bottom of skillet. Sprinkle with cheese and chiles. Fold portion of omelet nearest you just to center. (Allow for portion of omelet to slide up sides of skillet.)

Turn omelet onto warm plate, flipping folded portion of omelet over so far side is on bottom. Tuck sides of omelet under if necessary. Top with Casera Sauce and sour cream; sprinkle with snipped fresh cilantro if desired.

1 SERVING

Eggs and Chorizo

1 small onion, chopped (about ¼ cup)
2 tablespoons vegetable oil
8 ounces bulk chorizo sausage
8 eggs
¼ cup half-and-half
½ teaspoon dried oregano leaves

Cook and stir onion in oil in 10-inch skillet until tender. Add sausage; cook and stir until sausage is done; drain.

Mix eggs, half-and-half and oregano thoroughly with fork. Pour into sausage mixture in skillet. Cook over medium heat. As mixture begins to set at bottom and side, gently lift cooked portion with spatula so that thin, uncooked portion can flow to bottom. Avoid constant stirring. Cook until eggs are cooked throughout but still moist, 3 to 5 minutes.

6 SERVINGS

Mexican Omelet

Festival Eggs

1/4 cup margarine or butter
1/4 cup vegetable oil
6 flour tortillas (7 to 8 inches in diameter), cut into
    thin strips
1 medium onion, chopped (about 1/2 cup)
6 eggs, beaten
2 medium tomatoes, chopped (about 2 cups)
1 jalapeño chile, seeded and chopped
2 tablespoons snipped fresh cilantro
3/4 teaspoon salt
1/4 teaspoon pepper
1/2 cup shredded Colby cheese (2 ounces)

Heat margarine and oil in 10-inch skillet over
medium heat until hot. Add tortilla strips and
onion; cook, turning occasionally, until tortillas
are brown.

Mix remaining ingredients except cheese; pour
into skillet. As mixture begins to set at bottom
and side, gently lift cooked portions with spatula
so that thin uncooked portion can flow to bottom.
Avoid constant stirring. Turn egg mixture; cook
until eggs are cooked throughout but still moist,
3 to 5 minutes. Sprinkle with cheese.

6 SERVINGS

Sweet Potato Scrambled Eggs

The native sweet potato adds a touch of sweetness to this savory dish. To trim preparation time
in the morning, cook sweet potatoes the night
before; cover and refrigerate until needed.
Then, simply add them to the skillet after cooking the bacon and proceed as directed.

1 1/2 cups diced uncooked sweet potatoes
4 slices bacon, cut up
6 eggs, beaten
1 teaspoon ground red chiles
1/4 teaspoon salt
2 green onions (with tops), sliced

Heat enough salted water to cover sweet potatoes
(1/4 teaspoon salt to 1 cup water) to boiling. Add
potatoes. Cover and heat to boiling; reduce heat.
Simmer until potatoes are tender, about 6 minutes; drain.

Cook bacon in 10-inch skillet until crisp; remove
bacon and drain. Drain fat, reserving 1 tablespoon in skillet. Stir potatoes into fat in skillet.
Cook over medium heat, stirring frequently,
until golden brown.

Mix eggs, ground red chiles and salt; pour into
skillet. Sprinkle with bacon and onions. As mixture begins to set at bottom and side, gently lift
cooked portions with spatula so that thin, uncooked portion can flow to bottom. Avoid constant stirring. Cook until eggs are cooked
throughout but still moist, 3 to 5 minutes.

4 SERVINGS

Yucatán Poached Eggs

1 small onion, chopped (about 1/4 cup)
2 tablespoons margarine or butter
1 tablespoon vegetable oil
2 medium tomatoes, chopped (about 2 cups)
1 jalapeño chile, seeded and finely chopped
2 tablespoons snipped fresh cilantro
4 eggs
Salt and pepper to taste
1/2 cup shelled pumpkin seeds, toasted (page 19) and
    ground

Cook and stir onion in margarine and oil in
10-inch skillet until tender. Stir in tomatoes, chile
and cilantro. Cover and cook over low heat 10
minutes, stirring occasionally.

Break each egg into measuring cup or saucer;
holding cup close to skillet, slip 1 egg at a time
onto tomato mixture. Cover and cook until desired doneness, 3 to 5 minutes. Season to taste
with salt and pepper; sprinkle with ground
pumpkin seeds.

4 SERVINGS

Mexican Deviled Eggs

12 hard-cooked eggs, peeled
1/4 cup mayonnaise or salad dressing
1 tablespoon ground cumin
1 tablespoon finely chopped capers
1 tablespoon prepared mustard
1/2 teaspoon salt
1 jalapeño chile, seeded and finely chopped
Ground red chiles
Finely snipped fresh cilantro

Cut eggs lengthwise into halves. Slip out yolks; mash with fork. Mix yolks, mayonnaise, cumin, capers, mustard, salt and jalapeño chile well.

Fill egg whites with egg yolk mixture, heaping lightly. Sprinkle with ground red chiles; garnish with cilantro.

12 SERVINGS

Quiche in Green Chile Shell

This quiche uses split chiles for a crust. Serve it with a crisp green salad and Vegetable Cornmeal Muffins (page 181).

1/2 pound bulk chorizo sausage
2 cans (4 ounces each) whole green chiles, drained
1 cup shredded Monterey Jack cheese (4 ounces)
5 eggs
1/2 cup milk
1/4 teaspoon pepper

Heat oven to 350°. Generously grease pie plate, 9 x 1 1/4 inches. Cook and stir sausage in skillet until done; drain. Cut lengthwise slit in each chile. Open chiles; arrange on bottom and against side of pie plate, forming a shell. Sprinkle with sausage and cheese.

Beat eggs slightly; beat in milk and pepper. Pour into chile-lined pie plate. Bake uncovered until knife inserted halfway between center and edge comes out clean, about 30 minutes. Let stand 10 minutes before cutting.

6 SERVINGS

Egg and Spinach Casserole

Vegetable oil
6 corn tortillas (6 to 7 inches in diameter)
2 slices bacon, cut up
1 small onion, chopped (about 1/4 cup)
1 clove garlic, finely chopped
2 tablespoons margarine or butter
1 tablespoon vegetable oil
2 medium tomatoes, chopped (about 2 cups)
1 teaspoon salt
1/2 teaspoon pepper
1/4 teaspoon ground nutmeg
1 pound fresh spinach, chopped
8 hard-cooked eggs, peeled
1 cup Basic Green Sauce (page 26)
1 cup shredded Chihuahua or Monterey Jack cheese (4 ounces)

Heat oven to 400°. Heat 1/8 inch oil in 8-inch skillet over medium heat just until hot. Cook tortillas, one at a time, in oil until crisp, about 1 minute; drain. Cut into small pieces.

Cook and stir bacon, onion and garlic in margarine and 1 tablespoon oil in 10-inch skillet until onion is tender. Stir in tomatoes, salt, pepper and nutmeg. Simmer uncovered 3 minutes, stirring occasionally. Add spinach; cover and cook until wilted, about 3 minutes.

Line bottom of ungreased square pan, 8 x 8 x 2 inches, with tortilla pieces. Spread spinach mixture over tortilla pieces. Cut eggs lengthwise into halves; arrange on spinach mixture. Pour Basic Green Sauce over eggs; sprinkle with cheese. Bake uncovered until cheese is melted, about 15 minutes.

8 SERVINGS

Mexicali Pasta Salad

8 ounces uncooked tricolor pasta spirals (about 3 cups)
6 small tomatillos, each cut into 8 wedges
½ jalapeño chile, seeded and finely chopped
1 can (20 ounces) pineapple chunks in juice, drained (reserve 2 tablespoons juice)
1 tablespoon snipped fresh cilantro
2 tablespoons vegetable oil
½ teaspoon grated lime peel
¼ teaspoon salt

Cook pasta as directed on package; drain. Rinse with cold water; drain. Mix pasta, tomatillos, chile and pineapple.

Mix reserved pineapple juice and the remaining ingredients. Pour over pasta mixture; toss. Cover and refrigerate until chilled, at least 2 hours.

6 SERVINGS

Baja Chicken Pasta Salad

1 boneless, skinless whole chicken breast (about ¾ pound)
1 package (6 ounces) diced dried mixed fruit (about 1½ cups)
1 cup uncooked orzo or ring macaroni
1 cup cubed jícama
2 green onions (with tops), sliced
½ cup mayonnaise or salad dressing
2 tablespoons plain yogurt or dairy sour cream
1 teaspoon ground red chiles
¼ teaspoon salt

Heat enough salted water to cover chicken breast (¼ teaspoon salt to 1 cup water) to boiling in 4-quart Dutch oven. Add chicken breast. Cover and heat to boiling; reduce heat. Simmer until chicken is done, 15 to 20 minutes.

Remove chicken with slotted spoon. Heat water in Dutch oven to boiling; add fruit and orzo gradually so that water continues to boil. Boil uncovered, stirring occasionally, just until orzo is tender, about 10 minutes (6 to 8 minutes for ring macaroni); drain. Rinse with cold water; drain.

Cut chicken into ½-inch pieces. Mix chicken, fruit, orzo, jícama and onions. Mix remaining ingredients; toss with chicken mixture. Cover and refrigerate until chilled, at least 2 hours.

6 SERVINGS

Pasta Shells in Bell Pepper Sauce

3 red bell peppers, chopped
1 medium onion, chopped (about ½ cup)
1 clove garlic, finely chopped
2 tablespoons vegetable oil
1 teaspoon instant chicken bouillon
¼ teaspoon salt
¼ teaspoon ground red chiles
1 pound bulk chorizo sausage
2 cups whole kernel corn
6 ounces shredded Monterey Jack cheese (1½ cups)
5 ounces queso fresco, crumbled (about 1 cup)
1 egg
8 ounces uncooked jumbo pasta shells
¼ cup pine nuts (1 ounce), toasted (page 19)

Cook and stir bell peppers, onion and garlic in oil in 10-inch skillet until tender. Stir in bouillon (dry), salt and ground red chiles. Heat to boiling; reduce heat. Cover and simmer 5 minutes.

Pour mixture into food processor workbowl fitted with steel blade or into blender container; cover and process until smooth. Pour into ungreased rectangular baking dish, 13 x 9 x 2 inches.

Cook and stir sausage until done; drain. Mix sausage, corn, cheeses and egg; reserve. Cook shells as directed on package; drain.

Heat oven to 350°. Fill each shell with about 2 tablespoons sausage mixture; place on sauce in baking dish. Cover and bake until hot, about 30 minutes. Sprinkle with pine nuts.

6 SERVINGS

Mexicali Pasta Salad

Chipotle Fettuccine

Three ingredients much favored in southwest cooking (corn, chiles and smoked meat) are incorporated here in a maverick, contemporary dish. Adding ground or finely chopped chiles to any homemade pasta heightens both the color and flavor of the finished dish. Chipotle in adobo sauce adds a smokey note all its own.

Chipotle Fettuccine (right)
1½ cups whole kernel corn
½ cup water
1 small onion, chopped (about ¼ cup)
2 tablespoons margarine or butter
2 tablespoons all-purpose flour
½ teaspoon salt
¼ teaspoon pepper
1 cup milk
½ cup half-and-half
2 cups cut-up smoked turkey breast (about 12 ounces)

Prepare Chipotle Fettuccine. Heat corn, water and onion to boiling; reduce heat. Cover and simmer 5 minutes. Pour into food processor workbowl fitted with steel blade or into blender container; cover and process until almost smooth.

Heat margarine in 2-quart saucepan over low heat until melted. Stir in flour, salt and pepper. Cook over low heat, stirring constantly, until smooth and bubbly. Remove from heat; stir in corn mixture, milk, half-and-half and turkey. Heat to boiling, stirring constantly. Boil and stir 1 minute.

Break fettuccine into desired size pieces. Cook fettuccine in 3 quarts boiling salted water (1 tablespoon salt) until tender, 8 to 10 minutes; drain. Toss with turkey mixture.

6 SERVINGS

CHIPOTLE FETTUCCINE

2 cups all-purpose flour
½ teaspoon salt
1 tablespoon vegetable oil
2 eggs
1 to 2 canned chipotle chiles in adobo sauce, finely chopped

Mix flour and salt in large bowl; make well in center. Beat oil, eggs and chiles; pour into well. Stir with fork, gradually bringing flour mixture to center, until dough forms a ball. If dough is too dry, mix in up to 2 tablespoons water. Roll and cut as directed below. (Use additional flour when rolling and cutting noodles.) Place fettuccine strips on towel; let stand 30 minutes.

Hand Rolling Method: Knead dough on lightly floured surface until smooth and elastic, about 5 minutes. Divide into 4 equal parts. Roll dough, one part at a time, into paper-thin rectangle, about 14 x 10 inches (keep remaining dough covered). Loosely fold rectangle lengthwise into thirds; cut crosswise into ¼-inch strips. Unfold, and separate strips.

Manual Pasta Machine Method: Knead dough on a lightly floured surface about 2 to 3 minutes. Divide dough into 4 equal parts. Feed dough, one part at a time, through smooth rollers set at widest setting (keep remaining dough covered). Sprinkle with flour if dough becomes sticky. Fold lengthwise into thirds. Repeat feeding dough through rollers and folding into thirds until dough is firm and smooth, 8 to 10 times. Feed dough through progressively narrower settings until dough is paper thin. (Dough will lengthen as it becomes thinner; it may be cut crosswise at any time for easier handling.) Feed through fettuccine cutting rollers.

Chipotle Fettuccine

Pumpkin Ravioli

1 cup ricotta cheese
½ cup canned pumpkin
½ teaspoon salt
¼ teaspoon ground nutmeg
2 cups all-purpose flour
½ teaspoon salt
¼ cup tomato paste
1 tablespoon olive or vegetable oil
2 eggs
Pumpkin Seed Sauce (page 27)

Mix cheese, pumpkin, ½ teaspoon salt and the nutmeg; reserve.

Mix flour and ½ teaspoon salt in large bowl; make well in center. Beat tomato paste, oil and eggs until well blended; pour into well. Stir with fork, gradually bringing flour mixture to center, until dough forms a ball. If dough is too dry, mix in up to 2 tablespoons water. Knead on lightly floured cloth-covered surface, adding flour if dough is sticky, until smooth and elastic, about 5 minutes. Cover; let rest 5 minutes.

Divide dough into 4 equal parts. Roll dough, one part at a time, into rectangle, about 12 x 10 inches (keep remaining dough covered). Drop pumpkin mixture by 2 level teaspoonfuls onto half of the rectangle about 1½ inches apart in 2 rows of 4 mounds each. Moisten edges of dough and dough between rows of pumpkin mixture with water. Fold other half of dough up over pumpkin mixture, pressing dough down around mixture. Trim edges with pastry wheel or knife. Cut between rows of filling to make ravioli; press edges with fork to seal. Repeat with remaining dough and pumpkin mixture. Place ravioli on towel; let stand, turning once, until dry, about 30 minutes.

Prepare Pumpkin Seed Sauce. Heat until hot; keep warm. Cook ravioli in 4 quarts boiling salted water (2 teaspoons salt) until tender, 10 to 15 minutes; drain carefully. Serve ravioli with sauce.

6 SERVINGS

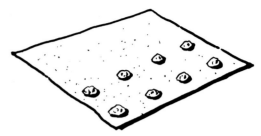

Drop pumpkin mixture by 2 level teaspoonfuls onto half of the rectangle about 1½ inches apart in 2 rows of 4 mounds each.

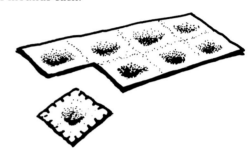

Cut between rows of filling to make ravioli; press edges with fork to seal.

Macaroni con Queso

Chile con Queso (page 38)
½ cup milk
4 ounces uncooked elbow macaroni or macaroni shells (about 1 cup)
1 large tomato, chopped (about 1 cup)
1 tablespoon snipped fresh cilantro
1 cup shredded Cheddar or Monterey Jack cheese (4 ounces)
¼ cup crushed tortilla chips

Heat oven to 375°. Prepare Chile con Queso as directed except stir in milk with the half-and-half; reserve. Cook macaroni as directed on package; drain.

Mix macaroni, Chile con Queso, tomato and cilantro in ungreased 1½-quart casserole. Sprinkle with cheese and tortilla chips. Bake uncovered until hot, about 30 minutes.

4 SERVINGS

Pumpkin Ravioli

Beans, Corn and Rice

Where would southwestern food be without beans, corn and rice? Each one of these staples was a food of the earliest inhabitants of the Southwest. The very name of the class of bean "haricot"—which includes all dried beans—comes from the Aztec word *ayacotl*. Pinto beans are the most prevalent, with red and black beans the basis of those dishes from the Sonoran and Yucatán regions of Mexico.

The gathering of corn continues to be an event celebrated by the Hopi Indians of Arizona. Traditionally the Hopis planted corn of four colors: yellow, blue, red and white. Each color represented a virtue: knowledge, patience, respect and purity respectively. Dried corn kernels thousands of years old, found in Mayan and other ruins, are testimony to the history of man's dependence on this virtually life-sustaining vegetable.

The Spanish brought rice with them to Mexico, and from there it spread throughout the Southwest. Rice is usually prepared as part of a mild dish in order to complement (and quench the fire of) hot foods. Red Rice is a rather spicy exception.

Corn-stuffed Poblano Chiles

Corn-stuffed Poblano Chiles

6 poblano chiles
2 eggs
1 1/2 cups whole kernel corn
1/2 cup shredded Cheddar cheese (2 ounces)
1/2 cup chopped pecans
1/2 cup finely chopped red bell pepper
1/4 cup finely chopped onion
1/2 teaspoon salt
1/8 teaspoon ground red pepper

Set oven control to broil. Cut chiles lengthwise into halves; carefully remove seeds. Place cut sides down on rack in broiler pan. Broil with tops about 4 inches from heat until skin blisters. Place chiles in plastic bag 15 minutes. Carefully remove as much skin as possible.

Heat oven to 375°. Beat eggs in medium bowl until thick and lemon colored, about 4 minutes; stir in remaining ingredients. Place chiles in greased rectangular baking dish, 13 x 9 x 2 inches. Spoon about 1/4 cup of the corn mixture into each chile half. Cover and bake until corn mixture is hot, about 25 minutes.

6 SERVINGS

Frontier Beans

1 cup sliced green onions (with tops)
1/2 pound chorizo sausage links, chopped
2 cans (16 ounces each) pinto beans, 1 can drained
3 small poblano chiles, roasted, peeled, (page 15)
  seeded and chopped
1 large tomato, chopped (about 1 cup)
1/4 teaspoon salt

Heat oven to 350°. Cook and stir onions and sausage until sausage is done; drain.

Mix sausage mixture and remaining ingredients in ungreased 2-quart casserole. Bake uncovered until hot and bubbly, about 30 minutes.

6 SERVINGS

Frontier Beans

Spicy Garbanzos

1 teaspoon whole mustard seed
1 medium onion, chopped (about 1/2 cup)
1 tablespoon vegetable oil
2 cans (15 ounces each) garbanzo beans, drained
1/2 cup chicken broth
2 tablespoons tomato paste
1/2 teaspoon salt
1/4 teaspoon ground cinnamon
1/8 teaspoon ground cloves

Cook and stir mustard seed and onion in oil in 2-quart saucepan until onion is tender. Stir in remaining ingredients; cook, stirring occasionally, until beans are heated through, 5 minutes.

6 SERVINGS

Pinto Beans

Every Old West chuck wagon was outfitted with large cast-iron kettles, used to cook everything from sourdough bread to beans. Dried beans (usually pinto beans) were a cowboy's bland staple. Chiles, meats, vinegar and oftentimes beer were added to give the beans flavor.

4 cups water
1 pound dried pinto or black beans (about 2 cups)
1 medium onion, chopped (about 1/2 cup)
1/4 cup vegetable oil
1 teaspoon salt
1 teaspoon cumin seed
2 cloves garlic, crushed
1 slice bacon

Mix water, beans and onion in 4-quart Dutch oven. Cover and heat to boiling. Boil 2 minutes. Remove from heat; let stand 1 hour.

Add just enough water to beans to cover. Stir in remaining ingredients. Heat to boiling; reduce heat. Cover and boil gently, stirring occasionally, until beans are very tender, about 2 hours (add water during cooking if necessary); drain. Beans can be covered and refrigerated up to 10 days.

ABOUT 8 SERVINGS

Refried Beans

Of course these beans aren't "refried" at all. They are simmered, then fried. Refried Beans are basic to many enchiladas, tostadas, burritos and tortillas. Refer to page 216 for a list of recipes featuring Refried Beans.

1/2 cup lard or vegetable oil
2 cups cooked Pinto Beans (page 12)
2 tablespoons chile powder
1 tablespoon ground cumin
1 teaspoon salt
1/8 teaspoon pepper

Heat lard in 10-inch skillet over medium heat until hot. Add Pinto Beans; cook 5 minutes, stirring occasionally.

Mash beans; stir in remaining ingredients. Add oil to skillet if necessary; cook and stir until smooth paste forms, about 5 minutes. Garnish with shredded cheese if desired.

4 SERVINGS

Refried Black Beans

1 small onion, chopped (about 1/4 cup)
2 jalapeño chiles, seeded and finely chopped
2 cloves garlic, finely chopped
2 tablespoons vegetable oil
2 cans (15 ounces each) black beans, undrained
1 canned chipotle chile in adobo sauce, chopped
1 teaspoon ground red chiles
1/2 teaspoon salt

Cook and stir onion, jalapeño chiles and garlic in oil in 10-inch skillet over medium heat until onion is tender. Stir in remaining ingredients; mash beans.

Cook uncovered, stirring occasionally, until thick, about 15 minutes.

6 SERVINGS

Frijoles Rancheros

8 slices bacon, cut up
2 jalapeño chiles, seeded and chopped
2 cloves garlic, finely chopped
1 large onion, chopped (about 1 cup)
3/4 cup beer
1 tablespoon vinegar
2 to 3 teaspoons ground red chiles
2 cans (16 ounces each) pinto beans, drained
1 can (6 ounces) tomato paste

Heat oven to 375°. Cook bacon in 10-inch skillet until crisp; stir in jalapeño chiles, garlic and onion. Cook and stir until onion is tender; drain.

Mix bacon mixture and remaining ingredients in ungreased 2-quart casserole. Bake uncovered, stirring once, until beans are hot and bubbly, about 45 minutes.

6 SERVINGS

Marinated Black-eyed Peas

1/2 cup olive oil
1/4 cup red wine vinegar
1 teaspoon salt
1/4 teaspoon pepper
1 clove garlic, crushed
1 cup chopped celery
1/2 cup chopped red onion
1/2 cup chopped green bell pepper
1 jalapeño chile, chopped
2 cans (15 ounces each) black-eyed peas, drained

Mix oil, vinegar, salt, pepper and garlic; pour over remaining ingredients in large bowl. Cover and refrigerate at least 2 hours but no longer than 24 hours, stirring occasionally.

8 SERVINGS

Serrano Grits with Cheese

White hominy is ground into grits, and cooked grits becomes thick like pudding. Grits makes a rib-sticking side dish, and this version featuring fiery serranos would deliciously hold its own with steak or venison.

1/2 cup chopped red bell pepper
1/2 cup sliced green onions (with tops)
2 serrano chiles, seeded and chopped
2 tablespoons margarine or butter
1 1/2 cups milk
1 1/2 cups water
1/2 teaspoon salt
1/4 teaspoon pepper
3/4 cup white hominy quick grits
1 1/2 cups shredded Monterey Jack cheese (6 ounces)

Cook and stir bell pepper, onions and chiles in margarine in 10-inch skillet until pepper is tender.

Heat milk, water, salt and pepper to boiling in 2-quart saucepan. Gradually add grits, stirring constantly; reduce heat. Simmer uncovered, stirring frequently, until thick, about 5 minutes. Stir in bell pepper mixture and cheese.

6 SERVINGS

Zucchini and Hominy

1 small onion, chopped (about 1/4 cup)
2 tablespoons margarine or butter
2 tablespoons vegetable oil
3 medium zucchini, cut into 1/2-inch pieces
2 medium tomatoes, chopped (about 2 cups)
1 can (20 ounces) hominy, drained
2 tablespoons lime juice
1 tablespoon chile powder
1 teaspoon salt
Dash of pepper

Cook and stir onion in margarine and oil in 10-inch skillet over medium heat until tender. Stir in remaining ingredients. Cook uncovered, stirring occasionally, until zucchini is tender, 10 to 15 minutes.

5 OR 6 SERVINGS

Mexican Corn and Potatoes

1 to 2 serrano chiles, seeded and chopped
1 large onion, chopped (about 1 cup)
2 tablespoons margarine or butter
2 cups whole kernel corn
2 cups cubed cooked potatoes
1 1/2 teaspoons ground red chiles
1/2 teaspoon salt

Cook and stir serrano chiles and onion in margarine in 10-inch skillet until onion is tender. Stir in remaining ingredients; cook, stirring occasionally, until heated through, about 4 minutes.

6 SERVINGS

Corn Fritters

1/2 recipe Roasted Tomato Sauce (page 25)
Vegetable oil
1 cup all-purpose flour
1/2 cup milk
1 teaspoon baking powder
1 teaspoon vegetable oil
1/4 teaspoon salt
2 eggs
1 cup whole kernel corn

Prepare Roasted Tomato Sauce; keep warm. Heat oil (1 inch) in deep fryer or 4-quart Dutch oven to 375°. Beat remaining ingredients except corn with hand beater until smooth; stir in corn.

Drop by level tablespoonfuls into hot oil. Fry until completely cooked, about 5 minutes; drain. Serve with Roasted Tomato Sauce.

9 SERVINGS

Corn Soufflé

Both this mild soufflé and the accompanying Green Chile Cheese Sauce feature a hint of cumin, the spice many associate with the flavor of the Southwest.

3 tablespoons margarine or butter
3 tablespoons all-purpose flour
1/4 teaspoon sugar
1/4 teaspoon ground cumin
1/4 teaspoon ground nutmeg
1/4 teaspoon ground red pepper
1 cup milk
3 eggs, separated
2 tablespoons finely chopped onion
2 tablespoons finely chopped green chiles
1 can (8 3/4 ounces) whole kernel corn, drained
Green Chile Cheese Sauce (right)

Heat oven to 350°. Butter 1-quart soufflé dish or casserole. Heat margarine in 2-quart saucepan over low heat until melted. Stir in flour, sugar, cumin, nutmeg and red pepper. Cook over low heat, stirring constantly, until mixture is smooth and bubbly. Stir in milk; heat to boiling, stirring constantly. Boil and stir 1 minute.

Beat egg yolks slightly in medium bowl. Stir at least half of the hot mixture gradually into egg yolks. Stir back into hot mixture in saucepan. Boil and stir 1 minute. Remove from heat; stir in onion, chiles and corn.

Beat egg whites in medium bowl on high speed until stiff. Stir about one-fourth of the egg whites into corn mixture. Fold corn mixture into remaining egg whites. Carefully pour mixture into soufflé dish.

Bake uncovered until knife inserted in center comes out clean, about 50 minutes. Prepare Green Chile Cheese Sauce. Serve soufflé immediately with sauce.

6 SERVINGS

GREEN CHILE CHEESE SAUCE

1/2 cup shredded Cheddar cheese (2 ounces)
1/4 cup finely chopped green chiles
1/3 cup half-and-half
1 tablespoon finely chopped onion
1 teaspoon ground cumin
1/4 teaspoon salt

Heat all ingredients over low heat, stirring constantly, until cheese is melted.

Corn Fritters with Roasted Tomato Sauce

Grilled Corn with Chile-Lime Spread

No other method of cooking can quite match the outdoors flavor of fresh corn grilled in its husk. Before it is cooked, the corn is slathered with Chile-Lime Spread.

½ cup margarine or butter, softened
½ teaspoon grated lime peel
3 tablespoons lime juice
1 to 2 teaspoons ground red chiles
6 ears corn (with husks)

Mix all ingredients except corn. Remove large outer husks from each ear corn; turn back inner husks, and remove silk. Spread each ear corn with about 2 teaspoons margarine mixture; reserve remaining margarine mixture.

Pull husks up over ears; tie with fine wire to secure. Grill corn 3 inches from medium coals, turning frequently, until done, 20 to 30 minutes. Serve with remaining margarine mixture.

6 SERVINGS

Roast Corn with Chile-Lime Spread: Heat oven to 475°. Prepare corn as directed. Roast in ungreased jelly roll pan, 15½ x 10½ x 1 inch, turning frequently, until done, 30 to 35 minutes.

Southwest Green Rice

2 large poblano chiles, roasted, peeled (page 15) and seeded
2 cloves garlic, finely chopped
1 medium onion, chopped (about ½ cup)
1 cup uncooked regular rice
2 cups chicken broth
¼ teaspoon salt
¼ cup snipped parsley

Place chiles, garlic and onion in food processor workbowl fitted with steel blade or in blender container; cover and process until smooth.

Mix chile mixture and remaining ingredients except parsley in 3-quart saucepan. Heat to boiling, stirring once or twice; reduce heat. Cover and simmer 16 minutes. (Do not lift cover or stir.) Remove from heat; fluff rice lightly with fork. Cover and let steam 10 minutes. Stir in parsley.

6 SERVINGS

Red Rice

1 large red bell pepper, roasted, peeled (page 15) and seeded
1 to 2 red jalapeño chiles, roasted, peeled (page 15) and seeded
1 small onion, chopped (about ¼ cup)
1 clove garlic, finely chopped
2 tablespoons margarine or butter
1 cup uncooked regular rice
2 cups chicken broth
¼ teaspoon salt
⅛ teaspoon red pepper sauce

Place bell pepper and chiles in food processor workbowl fitted with steel blade or in blender container; cover and process until smooth.

Cook and stir onion and garlic in margarine in 3-quart saucepan until onion is tender. Stir in remaining ingredients except bell pepper mixture. Heat to boiling, stirring once or twice; reduce heat. Cover and simmer 16 minutes. (Do not lift cover or stir.) Remove from heat; stir in bell pepper mixture. Cover and let steam 10 minutes.

6 SERVINGS

Grilled Corn with Chile-Lime Spread

Pine Nut and Green Onion Pilaf

A pilaf (pilau, pilaw, pilaff) calls for sautéing the rice in hot fat prior to actually cooking it in broth. Green onions and lemon peel give this pilaf a gentle flavor that is superb with any saucy fish.

1 cup uncooked regular rice
½ cup sliced green onions (with tops)
½ cup pine nuts (2 ounces)
2 tablespoons margarine or butter
2½ cups chicken broth
1 teaspoon grated lemon peel
¼ teaspoon salt
¼ cup sliced green onion tops

Cook and stir rice, ½ cup onions and the pine nuts in margarine in 3-quart saucepan until nuts are light brown, about 5 minutes. Stir in remaining ingredients except ¼ cup onion tops.

Heat to boiling, stirring once or twice; reduce heat. Cover and simmer 14 minutes. (Do not lift cover or stir.) Remove from heat; fluff rice lightly with fork. Cover and let steam 5 to 10 minutes. Sprinkle with onion tops.

6 SERVINGS

Baked Rice with Green Chiles

3 cups cooked white rice
1 cup dairy sour cream
½ cup shredded Monterey Jack cheese (2 ounces)
½ cup shredded Cheddar cheese (2 ounces)
1 to 2 teaspoons ground red chiles
2 cans (4 ounces each) chopped green chiles, drained

Heat oven to 350°. Mix all ingredients in ungreased 2-quart casserole. Bake uncovered 30 minutes.

8 SERVINGS

Mexican Rice

1 clove garlic, cut into halves
2 tablespoons vegetable oil
1 cup uncooked long-grain regular rice
2 cups chicken broth
¼ cup Casera Sauce (page 25)

Cook and stir garlic in oil in 2-quart saucepan over medium heat until brown; discard garlic. Cook and stir rice in oil until golden, about 5 minutes.

Stir in broth and Casera Sauce. Heat to boiling, stirring occasionally; reduce heat. Cover and simmer 20 minutes. (Do not lift cover or stir.)

8 SERVINGS

Mexican Rice with Peas: Prepare Mexican Rice; gently stir in 1 cup cooked green peas. Cover and let steam 3 minutes.

Mexican Cinnamon Rice

1 medium onion, chopped (about ½ cup)
1 clove garlic, finely chopped
2 tablespoons margarine or butter
1 cup uncooked regular rice
½ cup currants
2¼ cups chicken broth
2 teaspoons ground cinnamon
¼ teaspoon salt
1 to 2 tablespoons snipped fresh cilantro

Cook and stir onion and garlic in margarine in 3-quart saucepan until onion is tender. Stir in remaining ingredients except cilantro.

Heat to boiling, stirring once or twice; reduce heat. Cover and simmer 16 minutes. (Do not lift cover or stir.) Remove from heat; fluff rice lightly with fork. Cover and let steam 10 minutes. Stir in cilantro.

6 SERVINGS

Salads, Vegetables and Breads

The splendid variety of southwestern vegetables is due not only to the changing seasons, but to the patchwork of climates that covers this territory. Even semiarid ranges have, with irrigation, been coaxed into farmland. Jícama, *nopales*, chayote and of course chiles are featured in the recipes that follow, as well as the more widely familiar squashes, corn and sweet potatoes.

The truly authentic breads of the Southwest are those handed down from Native Americans. Navajo Fry Bread (page 163), Pueblo Adobe Bread (page 181), and corn breads are among them. Anise rolls (*semitas*), for example, are a New Mexican sweet bread traditionally baked to signal feast days.

Navajo Fry Bread

Navajo Fry Breads

Navajo Fry Bread is a Santa Fe specialty that has become popular throughout the Southwest. A hole is always poked through the center of each round of dough so that the bread puffs spectacularly when cooked in hot oil.

2 cups all-purpose flour
2 teaspoons baking powder
1 teaspoon salt
2 tablespoons shortening
2/3 cup warm water
Vegetable oil

Mix flour, baking powder and salt; cut in shortening until mixture resembles fine crumbs. Sprinkle in water, 1 tablespoon at a time, tossing with fork until all flour is moistened and dough almost cleans side of bowl. Gather into ball; cover and refrigerate 30 minutes.

Heat oil (1 inch) to 400° in 4-quart Dutch oven. Divide dough into 12 equal pieces. Roll each piece into 6-inch circle on lightly floured surface. Let rest a few minutes.

Make a hole about ½ inch in diameter in center of each circle. Fry circles, turning once, until puffed and golden, about 1 minute on each side; drain. Serve warm.

12 BREADS

Mexican Flag Salad

6 cups water
2 tablespoons lime juice
1 pound whole green beans
1 small jícama, pared and cut into ¼-inch strips (about 2 cups)
2 red bell peppers, cut into ¼-inch strips
Herbed Vinaigrette (below)
Lettuce leaves
6 to 8 ripe olives, finely chopped

Heat water and lime juice to boiling. Place green beans in wire strainer; lower into boiling water. Cover and cook 5 minutes. Immediately rinse under running cold water; drain.

Place beans, jícama and bell peppers in separate bowls. Pour ¼ cup Herbed Vinaigrette over each vegetable. Cover and refrigerate at least 1 hour.

Arrange beans, jícama and bell peppers on lettuce leaves in Mexican flag design. Place olives in center of rectangle formed by jícama.

6 TO 8 SERVINGS

HERBED VINAIGRETTE

½ cup olive or vegetable oil
2 tablespoons lemon juice
2 tablespoons lime juice
1 tablespoon wine vinegar
1 teaspoon snipped parsley
1 teaspoon chile powder
½ teaspoon dry mustard
¼ teaspoon salt
¼ teaspoon dried basil leaves
¼ teaspoon dried oregano leaves
¼ teaspoon ground sage
⅛ teaspoon freshly ground pepper
1 clove garlic, finely chopped

Shake all ingredients in tightly covered container.

Mexican Flag Salad

Layered Mexican Salad

1 cup shredded iceberg lettuce
¼ cup chopped green bell pepper
1¼ cups Black Bean Relish (page 30)
½ cup whole kernel corn
1 small avocado, peeled and sliced
Lime Vinaigrette (below)

Layer lettuce, bell pepper, ¾ cup of the Black Bean Relish and the corn in medium bowl. Arrange remaining ½ cup relish and the avocado slices on top. Serve with Lime Vinaigrette.

6 SERVINGS

LIME VINAIGRETTE

½ teaspoon grated lime peel
2 tablespoons lime juice
1 tablespoon snipped fresh cilantro
¼ teaspoon salt
1 small clove garlic, crushed
½ cup olive oil

Place all ingredients except oil in food processor workbowl fitted with steel blade or in blender container; cover and process until mixed. Gradually pour in oil, processing until thick.

Texas Slaw with Cumin Dressing

Cumin Dressing (right)
1 small head green cabbage, finely shredded (about 3 cups)
1 small head red cabbage, finely shredded (about 3 cups)
1 small red bell pepper, thinly sliced
1 small yellow bell pepper, thinly sliced
1 to 2 jalapeño chiles, seeded and finely chopped
2 tablespoons snipped fresh cilantro

Prepare Cumin Dressing. Mix remaining ingredients. Just before serving, toss with Cumin Dressing.

10 TO 12 SERVINGS

CUMIN DRESSING

½ cup dairy sour cream
½ cup plain yogurt
2 teaspoons sugar
½ teaspoon salt
½ teaspoon ground cumin
¼ teaspoon pepper

Mix all ingredients. Refrigerate covered 1 hour.

Tossed Romaine Salad

Tossed Romaine Salad is a spicy relative of the Caesar salad.

Cayenne Croutons (below)
1 clove garlic, cut into halves
2 anchovy fillets
¼ cup olive or vegetable oil
¼ cup grated Parmesan cheese
1 tablespoon lime juice
1 teaspoon Worcestershire sauce
½ teaspoon salt
⅛ teaspoon freshly ground pepper
1 large or 2 small bunches romaine, torn into bite-size pieces (about 8 cups)

Prepare Cayenne Croutons. Rub large wooden bowl with cut clove of garlic; discard garlic. Mash anchovy fillets in bowl with fork. Stir in remaining ingredients except romaine. Add romaine and Cayenne Croutons; toss until leaves glisten.

6 SERVINGS

CAYENNE CROUTONS

2 tablespoons margarine or butter, melted
¼ teaspoon ground red pepper
3 or 4 slices bread, crusts trimmed and cut into ½-inch cubes

Heat oven to 400°. Mix margarine and red pepper; pour over bread cubes and toss to coat. Bake in ungreased pan, stirring occasionally, until golden brown and crisp, 10 to 15 minutes.

Layered Mexican Salad

Cauliflower and Avocado Salad

1 medium head cauliflower (about 2 pounds),
   separated into flowerets
2 tablespoons vinegar
2 tablespoons vegetable oil
1/2 teaspoon salt
Dash of pepper
Southwest Guacamole (page 38)
Romaine
2 tablespoons slivered almonds

Heat 1 inch water to boiling. Add cauliflower. Cover and heat to boiling; reduce heat. Boil 4 minutes; drain. Immediately rinse under cold running water; drain.

Mix vinegar and oil in large glass or plastic bowl. Add cauliflower, salt and pepper; toss. Cover and refrigerate at least 1 hour. Prepare Southwest Guacamole.

Just before serving, arrange cauliflower on romaine; top with Southwest Guacamole. Sprinkle with almonds.

6 TO 8 SERVINGS

Cactus, Zucchini and Red Pepper Salad

Cactus "paddles" (*nopales*) are covered with little spines. Usually they are sold cleaned (see page 19 for instructions on cleaning them). *Nopales* have a flavor variously described as that of okra, squash or green beans. To combat their slippery tendencies, they may be blanched in salted water and then rinsed thoroughly.

8 cups water
1 tablespoon salt
1/2 pound prickly pear cactus pads, peeled and cut into
   1/2-inch pieces
2 small zucchini, thinly sliced
1 red bell pepper, cut into 1/4-inch strips
Cilantro Vinaigrette (below)

Heat water and salt to boiling in 3-quart saucepan. Add cactus pads. Heat to boiling; reduce heat. Boil uncovered 5 minutes; drain. Immediately rinse under cold running water, or plunge into large bowl of ice and water; drain. Repeat rinsing and draining twice.

Mix cactus, zucchini and bell pepper; toss with Cilantro Vinaigrette.

6 SERVINGS

CILANTRO VINAIGRETTE

1/2 cup olive or vegetable oil
1/4 cup white wine vinegar
1 tablespoon snipped fresh cilantro
1/2 teaspoon salt
1 clove garlic, crushed
Generous dash of freshly ground pepper

Shake all ingredients in tightly covered container.

Cactus, Zucchini and Red Pepper Salad

Jícama Citrus Salad with Sangria Dressing

3 large oranges, pared and sectioned
2 red grapefruit, pared and sectioned
1 medium jícama (about 1 pound), pared and cut into
   ½-inch cubes
Sangria Dressing (below)

Arrange oranges, grapefruit and jícama on 8 salad plates or mix together. Serve with Sangria Dressing.

8 SERVINGS

SANGRIA DRESSING

¼ cup vegetable oil
¼ cup dry red wine
2 tablespoons honey
2 tablespoons orange juice

Shake all ingredients in tightly covered container.

Orange Salad with Pecan Dressing

4 oranges, pared
1 head lettuce, torn into bite-size pieces
Pecan Dressing (below)

Cut oranges crosswise into slices; cut slices into fourths. Mix oranges and lettuce. Toss with Pecan Dressing.

6 SERVINGS

PECAN DRESSING

¼ cup ground pecans
2 tablespoons mayonnaise or salad dressing
2 tablespoons dairy sour cream
1 tablespoon lime juice
½ teaspoon sugar
½ teaspoon salt
⅛ teaspoon ground cinnamon
Dash of pepper

Mix all ingredients.

Jícama Citrus Salad with Sangria Dressing

Rio Grande Melon Salad

2 cups watermelon balls
2 mangoes or papayas, pared and sliced
1/2 honeydew melon, pared, seeded and thinly sliced
3/4 cup seedless red grape halves
1 large bunch watercress
Honey-Lime Dressing (below)

Arrange fruits on watercress. Drizzle with Honey-Lime Dressing.

6 SERVINGS

HONEY-LIME DRESSING

1/3 cup vegetable oil
1/4 teaspoon grated lime peel
2 tablespoons lime juice
1 tablespoon honey

Shake all ingredients in tightly covered container.

Stuffed Red Chiles

6 red Anaheim chiles or 3 red bell peppers
1 large onion, finely chopped (about 1 cup)
1 serrano chile, seeded and finely chopped
1 clove garlic, finely chopped
2 tablespoons vegetable oil
1 cup whole kernel corn
1 cup shredded Chihuahua or Monterey Jack cheese (4 ounces)
1/2 cup dairy sour cream
Fresh cilantro leaves

Heat oven to 375°. Cut Anaheim chiles lengthwise into halves; remove seeds. Cook onion, serrano chile and garlic in oil in 10-inch skillet until onion is tender. Stir in corn, shredded cheese and sour cream.

Fill each chile half with cheese mixture; place in ungreased rectangular pan, 13 x 9 x 2 inches. Cover and bake until crisp-tender, chiles about 25 minutes, bell peppers about 35 minutes. Garnish with cilantro leaves.

6 SERVINGS

Spicy Baked Cauliflower

1 medium head cauliflower (about 2 pounds), separated into flowerets
1 medium onion, chopped (about 1/2 cup)
2 tablespoons vegetable oil
1 medium green bell pepper, chopped
1 large tomato, chopped (about 1 cup)
1 jalapeño chile, seeded and finely chopped
1 clove garlic, finely chopped
1 tablespoon coarsely chopped green olives
1 tablespoon snipped parsley
1 teaspoon capers
1/2 teaspoon salt
1/4 cup dry bread crumbs
1/2 cup shredded Cheddar cheese (2 ounces)

Heat oven to 350°. Heat 1 inch salted water (1/2 teaspoon salt to 1 cup water) to boiling. Add cauliflower. Cover and boil 5 minutes; drain. Arrange cauliflower in ungreased rectangular baking dish, 10 x 6 x 1 1/2 inches.

Cook and stir onion in oil in 10-inch skillet until tender. Stir in remaining ingredients except bread crumbs and cheese; cook uncovered 5 minutes. Spoon over cauliflower. Sprinkle with bread crumbs and cheese. Bake uncovered until cheese is melted, about 15 minutes.

5 SERVINGS

Rio Grande Melon Salad

Cinnamon Squash Rings

2 tablespoons packed brown sugar
2 tablespoons milk
1 egg
3/4 cup soft bread crumbs (about 2 1/2 slices bread)
1/4 cup yellow or white cornmeal
2 teaspoons ground cinnamon
1 large acorn squash (about 1 1/2 pounds), cut crosswise
    into 1/2-inch slices and seeded
1/3 cup margarine or butter, melted

Heat oven to 400°. Mix brown sugar, milk and egg. Mix bread crumbs, cornmeal and cinnamon. Dip squash slices into egg mixture, and coat with bread crumb mixture; repeat.

Place in ungreased rectangular pan, 13 x 9 x 2 inches; drizzle with margarine. Bake uncovered until squash is tender, 30 to 35 minutes.

6 SERVINGS

Baked Chayotes with Tomatoes

4 medium chayotes
2 slices bacon, cut into 1/2-inch pieces
2 tablespoons vegetable oil
1/2 teaspoon salt
1/2 teaspoon dried oregano leaves
1/4 teaspoon ground nutmeg
1/4 teaspoon pepper
4 medium tomatoes, chopped (about 4 cups)
1 large onion, chopped (about 1 cup)
1 clove garlic, finely chopped
1 cup shredded Monterey Jack cheese (4 ounces)

Pare chayotes; cut lengthwise into fourths. Remove seeds. Heat enough salted water to cover chayotes (1/2 teaspoon salt to 1 cup water) to boiling. Add chayotes. Cover and boil until crisp-tender, 15 to 20 minutes; drain. Arrange chayotes in ungreased rectangular baking dish, 13 x 9 x 2 inches.

Cook and stir bacon in 2-quart saucepan until crisp. Stir in remaining ingredients except cheese. Heat to boiling; reduce heat. Simmer uncovered 15 minutes.

Heat oven to 350°. Pour vegetable mixture over chayotes; sprinkle with cheese. Bake uncovered until hot and bubbly and cheese is melted, about 15 minutes.

8 SERVINGS

Spinach Budín

A budín ("pudding") is a popular way to prepare vegetables in the Southwest. Budín denotes a soufflélike dish, frequently made with spinach, zucchini or carrots.

2 poblano chiles, roasted, peeled (page 15), seeded and
    chopped
1 medium onion, finely chopped (about 1/2 cup)
2 packages (10 ounces each) frozen chopped spinach,
    thawed and drained
2 tablespoons margarine or butter
1/2 cup half-and-half
1/2 cup tomato sauce
1/4 teaspoon salt
3 eggs, separated
1/4 cup finely shredded Monterey Jack cheese (2 ounces)

Heat oven to 350°. Cook and stir chiles, onion and spinach in margarine in 10-inch skillet until onion is tender. Stir in half-and-half, tomato sauce and salt.

Beat egg whites in large bowl until stiff. Beat egg yolks in small bowl until thick and lemon colored; stir into spinach mixture. Fold egg whites into spinach mixture.

Carefully pour into greased 2-quart soufflé dish. Bake until knife inserted in center comes out clean, about 30 minutes. Sprinkle with cheese.

6 SERVINGS

Cinnamon Squash Rings

Chiles Rellenos

Chiles Rellenos ("stuffed chiles") are a Mexican classic familiar to Americans across the country. Poblano chiles are stuffed with cheese and then fried with a puffed, golden coating. They make a piquant main dish all by themselves.

8 poblano chiles, roasted and peeled (page 15)
1 cup shredded Monterey Jack cheese (4 ounces)
1 cup shredded Cheddar cheese (4 ounces)
1 cup dry bread crumbs
4 eggs, separated
¼ teaspoon salt
¼ teaspoon cream of tartar
Vegetable oil
1 cup tomato juice
½ cup Casera Sauce (page 25)
1 tablespoon finely chopped fully cooked smoked ham
Dairy sour cream
Snipped fresh cilantro

Cut a slit lengthwise down side of each chile. Carefully remove seeds and membranes; rinse. Mix Monterey Jack and Cheddar cheeses. Fill each chile with ¼ cup cheese mixture; coat with bread crumbs. Cover and refrigerate 20 minutes.

Beat egg whites, salt and cream of tartar in large bowl until stiff. Beat egg yolks until thick and lemon colored, about 5 minutes; fold into egg whites.

Heat oil (1 to 1½ inches) to 375° in 4-quart Dutch oven. Dip each chile into egg mixture. Fry chiles, one at a time, turning once, until puffy and golden brown, about 3 minutes. Place chiles on cookie sheet; keep warm in 200° oven.

Heat tomato juice, Casera Sauce and ham to boiling. Pour over chiles. Garnish with sour cream and cilantro.

8 SERVINGS

Red Onion–topped Potatoes

These savory potatoes would be delicious with any grilled main dish. Fresh, acid cilantro sparks the rich topping of cheese and onions.

3 large baking potatoes (about 1½ pounds)
Salt and pepper to taste
1 cup grated queso añejo or Romano cheese
¾ cup finely chopped red onion
1 tablespoon snipped fresh cilantro
1 clove garlic, finely chopped

Heat oven to 375°. Bake potatoes until tender, about 1 hour.

Cut potatoes lengthwise into halves; score top of potatoes crisscross fashion, being careful not to cut through skin. Sprinkle with salt and pepper.

Mix remaining ingredients. Divide mixture among potatoes. Press into scores and on top of each potato. Bake until hot, about 5 minutes.

6 SERVINGS

Caramelized Sweet Potatoes

1½ pounds sweet potatoes, pared and coarsely shredded
½ pound Jerusalem artichokes, pared and coarsely shredded
½ cup margarine or butter, melted
¼ cup sugar

Mix potatoes, artichokes and margarine; reserve. Heat sugar in 10-inch skillet over medium heat until melted and light brown, about 10 minutes.

Stir in potato mixture; cook, stirring occasionally, until potatoes are tender, about 15 minutes.

8 SERVINGS

Red Onion–topped Potatoes

Mustard Artichoke Hearts

1 small onion, chopped (about ¼ cup)
2 tablespoons margarine or butter
2 tablespoons brandy
1 tablespoon prepared mustard
½ teaspoon ground cumin
¼ teaspoon salt
⅛ teaspoon pepper
1 clove garlic, finely chopped
2 cans (14 ounces each) artichoke hearts, drained and cut into halves
¼ cup snipped parsley

Cook and stir onion in margarine in 10-inch skillet over medium heat until tender. Stir in brandy; simmer uncovered 2 minutes.

Stir in remaining ingredients except artichoke hearts and parsley. Stir in artichoke hearts; cook uncovered 5 minutes, stirring occasionally. Stir in parsley.

6 SERVINGS

Wilted Spinach

Fresh, lightly cooked spinach is a treat. Nutmeg is a heady, traditional seasoning for spinach, here tossed briefly in hot bacon fat.

1 medium onion, chopped (about ½ cup)
1 slice bacon, cut up
1 clove garlic, finely chopped
2 tablespoons margarine or butter
2 tablespoons olive or vegetable oil
½ teaspoon salt
¼ teaspoon pepper
¼ teaspoon ground nutmeg
1 pound fresh spinach
2 tablespoons lime juice

Cook and stir onion, bacon and garlic in margarine and oil in 4-quart Dutch oven over medium heat until bacon is crisp; reduce heat. Stir in salt, pepper and nutmeg. Add spinach; toss just until spinach is wilted. Drizzle with lime juice.

6 SERVINGS

Southwest Vegetable Sauté

Lime Butter Sauce (page 29)
1 medium onion, finely chopped (about ½ cup)
2 cloves garlic, finely chopped
¼ cup margarine or butter
4 very small pattypan squash (about 4 ounces each), cut into halves
2 small zucchini, cut into ¼-inch strips
2 small yellow squash, cut into ¼-inch strips
1 medium chayote, pared, seeded and cut into ½-inch cubes
1 small red bell pepper, cut into thin rings
1 small yellow bell pepper, cut into thin rings
½ teaspoon salt
¼ teaspoon ground red pepper
8 fresh squash blossoms, if desired

Prepare Lime Butter Sauce; reserve. Cook and stir onion and garlic in margarine in 4-quart Dutch oven until onion is tender.

Stir in remaining ingredients except squash blossoms. Cook over medium heat, stirring occasionally, until vegetables are crisp-tender; stir in squash blossoms. Serve with Lime Butter Sauce.

8 SERVINGS

Southwest Vegetable Sauté

Mexican-style Green Beans

1 pound green beans
4 slices bacon, cut up
1 medium onion, chopped (about ½ cup)
1 medium tomato, chopped (about 1 cup)
1 clove garlic, finely chopped
½ teaspoon dried oregano leaves
¼ teaspoon salt
Dash of pepper
2 tablespoons lemon juice

Heat green beans and 1 inch salted water (½ teaspoon salt to 1 cup water) to boiling; reduce heat. Boil uncovered 5 minutes. Cover and boil until tender, 5 to 10 minutes longer. Immediately rinse under cold running water; drain.

Cook bacon in 10-inch skillet until crisp. Remove bacon with slotted spoon and drain; reserve fat in skillet. Cook and stir onion in fat until tender; stir in tomato, garlic, oregano, salt and pepper. Cook 5 minutes, stirring frequently. Stir in beans; heat until hot. Drizzle with lemon juice; sprinkle with bacon.

4 SERVINGS

Eggplant with Cheese

1 medium eggplant (about 1½ pounds)
1 teaspoon salt
½ cup vegetable oil
1 cup ricotta cheese
1 cup shredded Cheddar cheese (4 ounces)
¼ cup grated Parmesan cheese

Pare eggplant; cut lengthwise into ¼-inch slices. Cut each slice into strips, about 2 inches wide. Sprinkle with salt; let stand 30 minutes.

Rinse eggplant; pat dry. Cook eggplant in oil in 10-inch skillet, turning occasionally, until light golden brown; drain. Mix ricotta and Cheddar cheese; place 1 rounded teaspoonful cheese mixture on one end of each eggplant piece. Roll up, beginning at end with cheese.

Set oven control to broil. Place filled eggplant pieces seam-sides up on rack in broiler pan; sprinkle with Parmesan cheese. Broil with tops 3 to 4 inches from heat until golden brown, about 5 minutes.

4 OR 5 SERVINGS

Mexican Zucchini and Corn

1 medium onion, chopped (about ½ cup)
2 tablespoons vegetable oil
3 medium zucchini, cut into ½-inch slices
1 package (10 ounces) frozen whole kernel corn
½ teaspoon salt
1 teaspoon dried oregano leaves
Dash of pepper
1 can (28 ounces) Italian plum tomatoes

Cook and stir onion in oil in 10-inch skillet over medium heat until tender. Stir in zucchini; cook and stir 1 minute.

Stir in remaining ingredients. Heat to boiling; reduce heat. Cover and simmer until zucchini is tender, about 15 minutes.

6 SERVINGS

Carrots with Green Grapes

8 medium carrots
2 tablespoons margarine or butter
1 tablespoon sugar
½ teaspoon salt
2 cups seedless green grapes
¾ teaspoon snipped fresh tarragon leaves or ¼
   teaspoon dried tarragon leaves
½ cup dairy sour cream
2 tablespoons water

Cut carrots crosswise into halves. Cut each half lengthwise into ½-inch strips. Heat 1 inch salted water (½ teaspoon salt to 1 cup water) to boiling. Add carrots. Cover and heat to boiling; reduce heat. Boil until carrots are crisp-tender, about 5 minutes; drain.

Heat margarine in 10-inch skillet over medium-high heat until melted. Stir in carrots, sugar and salt; cook and stir 5 minutes. Stir in grapes and tarragon; heat until hot. Remove from heat; stir in sour cream and water.

6 SERVINGS

New Mexico Anise Rolls

5¾ to 6 cups all-purpose flour
¾ cup packed brown sugar
½ cup margarine or butter, softened
1½ teaspoons salt
1 teaspoon anise seed, crushed
2 packages active dry yeast
¾ cup very warm water (120° to 130°)
5 eggs
1 egg
1 tablespoon anise seed

Mix 2 cups of the flour, the brown sugar, margarine, salt, crushed anise seed and yeast in large bowl; stir in warm water and 5 eggs. Beat on low speed 1 minute, scraping bowl frequently. Beat on medium speed 1 minute, scraping bowl frequently. Stir in enough remaining flour, 1 cup at a time, to make dough easy to handle.

Turn dough onto lightly floured surface; knead until smooth and elastic, about 10 minutes. Place in greased medium bowl; turn greased side up. Cover and let rise in warm place until double, about 1 hour. (Dough is ready if indentation remains when touched.)

Punch down dough. Turn onto lightly floured surface; knead until smooth. Divide dough into 18 equal pieces. Shape each piece into a smooth oval, 3 to 4 inches long; flatten slightly. Place on greased cookie sheets. Cover and let rise until double, about 45 minutes.

Heat oven to 350°. Beat 1 egg; brush over rolls. Sprinkle with 1 tablespoon anise seed. Bake until golden brown, about 20 minutes. Cool rolls on wire rack.

18 ROLLS

Adobe Bread

This crusty bread of the Pueblo Indians is still baked today in beehive-shaped ovens called *hornos*. Often the round loaves of the Indians are decorated with symbols (bear paws or squash blossoms, for example) for special occasions. Authentic Pueblo bread can't be duplicated in ordinary ovens; the *horno* bakes the bread with heat that slowly decreases as the wood fire dies.

2 cups whole wheat flour
¼ cup sugar
¼ cup shortening or lard
2 teaspoons salt
2 packages active dry yeast
2 cups very warm water (120° to 130°)
3 to 4 cups all-purpose flour
2 teaspoons all-purpose flour

Mix whole wheat flour, sugar, shortening, salt and yeast in large bowl; stir in warm water. Beat on low speed 1 minute, scraping bowl frequently. Beat on medium speed 1 minute, scraping bowl frequently. Stir in enough all-purpose flour, 1 cup at a time, to make dough easy to handle.

Turn dough onto lightly floured surface; knead until smooth and elastic, about 10 minutes. Place in greased medium bowl; turn greased side up. Cover and let rise in warm place until double, 40 to 60 minutes. (Dough is ready if indentation remains when dough is touched.)

Punch down dough; divide into halves. Let rest 5 minutes. Shape each half into a round, slightly flat loaf. Place loaves on opposite corners of greased large cookie sheet. Cover and let rise until double, 40 to 50 minutes.

Heat oven to 375°. Make ½-inch-deep slashes across top of each loaf in lattice design. Sprinkle each loaf with 1 teaspoon all-purpose flour. Bake until loaves are deep golden brown and sound hollow when tapped, 35 to 40 minutes. Cool on wire rack.

2 LOAVES

Adobe Bread

Vegetable Cornmeal Muffins

1¼ cups yellow cornmeal
¾ cup all-purpose flour
¼ cup shortening
1½ cups buttermilk
2 teaspoons baking powder
1 teaspoon sugar
1 teaspoon salt
½ teaspoon baking soda
2 eggs
1 cup shredded zucchini, drained
½ cup chopped red bell pepper
2 tablespoons chopped jalapeño or serrano chiles

Heat oven to 450°. Grease 16 medium muffin cups, 2½ x 1¼ inches, or line muffin cups with paper baking cups.

Mix all ingredients except zucchini, bell pepper and chiles; beat vigorously 30 seconds. Stir in remaining ingredients.

Fill muffin cups about ⅞ full. Bake until light golden brown, 20 to 25 minutes. Remove from pan immediately.

16 MUFFINS

Desserts and Sweets

Southwestern desserts reflect the region's Mexican and Indian heritage. They are quite sweet and very substantial. Puddings, custards, deep-fried pastries and pralines are favorites. Fresh fruit is the original Mexican dessert, a refreshing finale to a spicy meal. "New" southwestern desserts are often wildly innovative, inspired by local color and motifs.

Southwest Lemon Fruit Tart

Southwest Lemon Fruit Tart

A soothing pecan crust filled with lemon mousse and topped with fresh fruit: a perfect contrast to a spicy southwestern meal. This is a beautiful tart, sensational with its glistening arrangement of different fruits. It would be an elegant finish to any dinner party.

Pecan Crust (below)
1 teaspoon unflavored gelatin
1 tablespoon cold water
1/2 cup sugar
2 eggs
2 tablespoons grated lemon peel
1/4 cup lemon juice
1/2 cup whipping cream
1 cup strawberry halves
1 cup raspberries
1/2 cup blackberries or blueberries
1 mango or papaya, pared and sliced
1/3 cup guava jelly or apricot jam, melted

Prepare Pecan Crust; cool. Sprinkle gelatin on cold water in 1½-quart saucepan to soften. Beat sugar and eggs until thick and lemon colored; stir into gelatin mixture. Heat just to boiling over low heat, stirring constantly, about 15 minutes. Remove from heat; stir in lemon peel and juice.

Beat whipping cream in chilled medium bowl until soft peaks form. Fold in lemon mixture; pour into Pecan Crust. Refrigerate 2 hours. Arrange fruits on top; drizzle with jelly. Refrigerate any remaining tart.

8 SERVINGS

PECAN CRUST

1 cup all-purpose flour
1/2 cup finely chopped pecans
1/4 cup sugar
1/4 cup margarine or butter, softened
1 egg

Heat oven to 375°. Mix flour, pecans and sugar; mix in margarine and egg until crumbly. Press in bottom and up side of greased tart pan, 9 x 1 inch. Bake until light golden brown, 15 to 20 minutes.

Date-Pecan Upside-down Cake

1/4 cup plus 2 tablespoons margarine or butter
2/3 cup packed brown sugar
12 pitted dates
1 cup coarsely chopped pecans
1 cup all-purpose flour
3/4 cup granulated sugar
1/3 cup shortening
3/4 cup milk
1 1/2 teaspoons baking powder
1 teaspoon vanilla
1/2 teaspoon salt
1 egg
Whipped cream

Heat oven to 350°. Heat margarine in 10-inch ovenproof skillet or square pan, 9 x 9 x 2 inches, in oven until melted. Sprinkle evenly with brown sugar. Arrange dates on top so that each serving will include one date; sprinkle with pecans.

Beat remaining ingredients except whipped cream in large bowl on low speed, scraping bowl constantly, 30 seconds. Beat on high speed, scraping bowl occasionally, 3 minutes. Pour evenly over dates and pecans.

Bake until wooden pick inserted in center comes out clean, 40 to 45 minutes. Loosen edge of cake with knife. Invert on heatproof platter; leave skillet over cake a few minutes. Serve warm with whipped cream.

12 SERVINGS

Date-Pecan Upside-down Cake

Tucson Lemon Cake

Lemon cakes are very popular in Arizona, thanks to the profusion of local lemon groves. This lemony cake is dramatically shot through with poppy seeds. A lemon glaze soaks into the cake while it is still hot from the oven.

1½ cups sugar
½ cup margarine or butter, softened
3 eggs
2½ cups all-purpose flour
1 teaspoon baking soda
½ teaspoon salt
1 cup buttermilk
¼ cup poppy seed
2 tablespoons grated lemon peel
2 tablespoons lemon juice
Lemon Glaze (below)

Heat oven to 325°. Grease and flour 12-cup bundt cake pan or tube pan, 10 x 4 inches. Beat sugar and margarine in large bowl on medium speed until light and fluffy. Beat in eggs, 1 at a time.

Mix flour, baking soda and salt; beat into sugar mixture alternately with buttermilk until well blended. Stir in poppy seed, lemon peel and lemon juice. Spread in pan.

Bake until wooden pick inserted in center comes out clean, 50 to 55 minutes. Immediately poke holes in top of cake with long-tined fork; pour about ⅔ of the Lemon Glaze over top. Cool 20 minutes. Invert on heatproof serving plate; remove pan. Spread with remaining glaze.

16 SERVINGS

LEMON GLAZE

2 cups powdered sugar
¼ cup margarine or butter, melted
2 tablespoons grated lemon peel
¼ cup lemon juice

Mix all ingredients.

Tucson Lemon Cake

Toasted Almond Pound Cake

2¾ cups sugar
1¼ cups margarine or butter
5 eggs
3 cups all-purpose flour
2 teaspoons ground cinnamon
1 teaspoon baking powder
¼ teaspoon salt
1 cup evaporated milk
1½ cups chopped blanched almonds, toasted
Cinnamon-Chocolate Sauce (below)
Whipped cream

Heat oven to 350°. Grease and flour 12-cup bundt cake pan or tube pan, 10 x 4 inches. Beat sugar, margarine and eggs in large bowl on low speed, scraping bowl constantly, 30 seconds. Beat batter on high speed, scraping bowl occasionally, 5 minutes.

Beat in flour, cinnamon, baking powder and salt alternately with milk, on low speed. Fold in almonds. Spread in pan.

Bake until wooden pick inserted in center comes out clean, 70 to 80 minutes. Cool 20 minutes. Invert on heatproof serving plate; remove pan. Serve with Cinnamon-Chocolate Sauce and whipped cream.

16 SERVINGS

CINNAMON-CHOCOLATE SAUCE

1 cup whipping cream
½ cup sugar
3 ounces unsweetened chocolate
1 tablespoon margarine or butter
1 teaspoon ground cinnamon

Heat whipping cream, sugar and chocolate to boiling over medium heat, stirring constantly. Boil and stir until chocolate is well blended, about 30 seconds. Remove from heat; stir in margarine and cinnamon.

Orange-Pecan Pie

Orange-Pecan Pie is a luxurious twist on the nut-studded classic: there is a hint of citrus in the crust and a liqueur-laced sauce to pass separately.

Orange Pastry (below)
2/3 cup sugar
1/3 cup margarine or butter, melted
1 cup corn syrup
1 to 2 tablespoons orange liqueur
1/2 teaspoon salt
3 eggs
1 cup pecan halves
1/4 cup semisweet chocolate chips
1 teaspoon shortening
Orange Sauce (right)

Heat oven to 375°. Prepare Orange Pastry. Gather into ball; shape into flattened round on lightly floured cloth-covered board. Roll 2 inches larger than inverted pie plate, 9 x 1¼ inches, with floured cloth-covered rolling pin. Ease pastry into plate, pressing firmly against bottom and side. Trim overhanging edge of pastry 1 inch from rim of plate. Fold and roll pastry under, even with plate; flute.

Beat sugar, margarine, corn syrup, liqueur, salt and eggs with hand beater until smooth; stir in pecans. Pour into pastry-lined pie plate. Cover edge with 2- to 3-inch strip of aluminum foil to prevent excessive browning; remove foil during last 15 minutes of baking.

Bake until set, 40 to 50 minutes. Cool 15 minutes. Heat chocolate chips and shortening until melted; drizzle over top of pie. Serve with Orange Sauce.

8 SERVINGS

ORANGE PASTRY

1 cup all-purpose flour
1 tablespoon grated orange peel
1/2 teaspoon salt
1/3 cup plus 1 tablespoon shortening or 1/3 cup lard
2 to 3 tablespoons cold water

Mix flour, orange peel and salt; cut in shortening until size of small peas. Sprinkle in water, 1 tablespoon at a time, tossing with fork until pastry is moistened and almost cleans side of bowl.

ORANGE SAUCE

1/4 cup sugar
1 tablespoon cornstarch
3/4 cup orange juice
2 tablespoons orange liqueur
1 tablespoon grated orange peel

Mix sugar and cornstarch in 1-quart saucepan. Stir in orange juice and liqueur. Cook over medium heat, stirring constantly, until mixture thickens and boils. Boil and stir 1 minute; stir in orange peel.

Almond Torte

1 cup blanched whole almonds, toasted (page 19)
1/4 cup all-purpose flour
5 eggs, separated
1/2 cup sugar
1 tablespoon brandy
1 teaspoon almond extract
Sweetened whipped cream
Sliced almonds, toasted (page 19)

Heat oven to 350°. Place whole almonds and flour in blender container; cover and blend on high speed until finely ground.

Beat egg whites in large bowl on medium speed until foamy. Beat in sugar, 1 tablespoon at a time, on high speed; continue beating until stiff and glossy. Do not underbeat. Beat in egg yolks, one at a time. Beat in brandy and almond extract. Fold in ground almond mixture.

Pour into greased and floured springform pan, 9 x 3 inches. Bake until top springs back when touched lightly, about 50 minutes. Cool 10 minutes; remove from pan. Serve with whipped cream and sliced almonds.

10 TO 12 SERVINGS

Orange-Pecan Pie

Peach Cobbler

¹⁄₄ cup packed brown sugar
1 tablespoon lemon juice
¹⁄₂ teaspoon ground cinnamon
*3 pounds peaches, sliced, or 2 packages (16 ounces
    each) frozen sliced peaches, thawed and drained*
³⁄₄ cup all-purpose flour
¹⁄₂ cup granulated sugar
2 teaspoons baking powder
¹⁄₄ teaspoon salt
³⁄₄ cup whipping cream
¹⁄₄ cup margarine or butter, melted
Caramel Sauce (below)

Heat oven to 375°. Mix brown sugar, lemon juice, cinnamon and peaches; place in greased shallow 2¹⁄₂-quart casserole. Mix flour, granulated sugar, baking powder and salt; stir in whipping cream and margarine until well blended. Spoon batter over fruit.

Bake until crust is deep golden brown, 40 to 45 minutes. Serve warm with warm Caramel Sauce.

8 SERVINGS

CARAMEL SAUCE

1 cup packed brown sugar
¹⁄₂ cup whipping cream
¹⁄₄ cup corn syrup
1 tablespoon margarine or butter
2 teaspoons ground cinnamon

Heat all ingredients to boiling over medium heat, stirring constantly; reduce heat to low. Simmer uncovered 5 minutes.

Rich Chocolate-Banana Cake

6 ounces sweet cooking chocolate
³⁄₄ cup margarine or butter
4 eggs, separated
¹⁄₈ teaspoon salt
³⁄₄ cup sugar
³⁄₄ cup ground pecans
¹⁄₂ cup mashed banana (about 1 medium)
Creamy Banana Sauce (below)
Pecan halves, toasted

Heat oven to 375°. Grease and flour springform pan, 8 x 2¹⁄₂ inches. Heat chocolate and margarine in 1¹⁄₂-quart saucepan until melted; cool 5 minutes.

Beat egg whites and salt in medium bowl on high speed until stiff but not dry. Beat egg yolks and sugar on medium speed until lemon colored; stir into chocolate. Stir in ground pecans and banana. Gradually fold chocolate mixture into egg whites; pour into pan.

Bake until top is dry and knife inserted in center comes out slightly wet, 40 to 45 minutes. (Do not overbake.) Cool completely; remove from pan. Serve with Creamy Banana Sauce; garnish with pecan halves.

12 SERVINGS

CREAMY BANANA SAUCE

1 cup mashed bananas (about 2 medium)
¹⁄₄ cup whipping cream
2 tablespoons powdered sugar
¹⁄₈ teaspoon ground cinnamon

Beat all ingredients until well blended.

Mexican Bread Pudding

3 cups soft bread crumbs (about 4 slices bread)
½ cup margarine or butter, softened
1 cup packed brown sugar
1 cup water
2 teaspoons brandy
¼ teaspoon ground cinnamon
⅛ teaspoon ground cloves
1 cup shredded Cheddar cheese (4 ounces)
1 cup chopped dried apples
½ cup raisins
½ cup chopped walnuts

Heat oven to 300°. Place bread crumbs in jelly roll pan, 15½ x 10½ x 1 inch. Dot with ¼ cup of the margarine. Bake uncovered, stirring occasionally, until golden brown, about 20 minutes; cool crumbs.

Heat brown sugar, water, brandy, cinnamon and cloves over medium heat, stirring constantly, until sugar is dissolved. Place 1 cup of the bread crumbs in ungreased round pan, 9 x 1½ inches. Pour ⅓ cup of the syrup over crumbs; sprinkle with cheese. Top with 1 cup of the crumbs; sprinkle with apples, raisins, and walnuts. Top with ⅓ cup of the syrup and remaining crumbs. Pour remaining syrup over crumbs; dot with remaining margarine.

Bake uncovered in 300° oven until hot and bubbly, about 30 minutes. Let stand 10 minutes before serving. Garnish with sweetened whipped cream if desired.

8 SERVINGS

Chocolate Ranch Pudding

¼ cup margarine or butter
2 ounces semisweet chocolate
1 cup packed brown sugar
¾ cup corn syrup
¼ cup bourbon
3 eggs, slightly beaten
1½ cups chopped pecans, toasted (page 19)
1 cup whipping cream
1 teaspoon bourbon, if desired

Heat oven to 400°. Heat margarine and chocolate in 1½-quart saucepan over low heat, stirring constantly, until chocolate is melted and mixture is smooth. Remove from heat; stir in brown sugar, corn syrup, ¼ cup bourbon and the eggs.

Sprinkle pecans over bottom of greased 2-quart casserole; pour chocolate mixture over pecans. Bake uncovered 10 minutes. Reduce oven temperature to 350°. Bake until pudding is set, 20 to 25 minutes longer.

Beat whipping cream in chilled bowl until stiff; fold in 1 teaspoon bourbon. Serve pudding warm with whipped cream.

8 TO 10 SERVINGS

Baked Indian Pudding

¼ cup sugar
1 teaspoon ground cinnamon
½ teaspoon ground ginger
¼ teaspoon salt
¼ teaspoon ground nutmeg
4 cups milk
½ cup yellow cornmeal
½ cup golden raisins
½ cup maple syrup
2 tablespoons margarine or butter, softened
2 eggs, beaten
Whipped cream

Heat oven to 350°. Mix sugar, cinnamon, ginger, salt and nutmeg until well blended; reserve.

Heat milk to scalding in 3-quart saucepan; stir in cornmeal. Cook over low heat, stirring constantly, until very thick, about 20 minutes. Remove from heat; stir in sugar mixture and remaining ingredients except whipped cream.

Pour into greased 2-quart casserole. Place casserole in rectangular pan, 13 x 9 x 2 inches, on oven rack. Pour very hot water into pan to depth of 1 inch. Bake until knife inserted in center comes out clean, 55 to 60 minutes. Serve warm with whipped cream.

8 SERVINGS

Brandy Flan

Flan is the quintessential Spanish and Mexican dessert. It may be dense or light, depending on custom and region, but it is always rich in eggs.

¾ cup sugar
2 tablespoons water
2 eggs
½ cup sugar
2 tablespoons brandy
½ teaspoon vanilla
¼ teaspoon ground nutmeg
¼ teaspoon ground cinnamon
¼ teaspoon ground allspice
Dash of salt
2 cups lukewarm milk (scalded then cooled)

Heat ¾ cup sugar in heavy 1-quart saucepan over low heat, stirring constantly, until melted and golden brown. Gradually stir in water. Divide syrup evenly among six 6-ounce custard cups. Let stand until hard, about 10 minutes.

Heat oven to 350°. Beat eggs slightly in medium bowl; mix in remaining ingredients except milk. Gradually stir in milk; pour over syrup in each cup. Place cups in rectangular pan, 13 x 9 x 2 inches, on oven rack. Pour very hot water into pan to within ½ inch of tops of cups.

Bake until knife inserted in center comes out clean, about 45 minutes. Remove cups from water. Refrigerate until chilled; unmold.

6 SERVINGS

Pumpkin Flan

¾ cup sugar
¼ cup water
1 cup canned pumpkin
¾ cup sugar
1 teaspoon ground cinnamon
½ teaspoon ground ginger
¼ teaspoon ground allspice
¼ teaspoon ground nutmeg
6 eggs
1 cup half-and-half
1 cup whipping cream

Heat oven to 350°. Heat ¾ cup sugar and the water to boiling in heavy 2-quart saucepan over low heat, stirring constantly. Boil, without stirring, until mixture is deep golden brown.

Place quiche dish, 9 x 1½ or 10 x 1¼ inches, in hot water until warm (to prevent dish from cracking when pouring hot syrup into it); dry completely. Pour syrup into dish; immediately rotate dish until syrup covers bottom.

Beat remaining ingredients except half-and-half and whipping cream in large bowl until well blended; beat in half-and-half and whipping cream. Pour over syrup. Place quiche dish in shallow roasting pan on oven rack. Pour very hot water into pan to depth of 1 inch. Bake flan until knife inserted in center comes out clean, 1 to 1¼ hours.

Remove dish from water; cool 15 minutes. Refrigerate until chilled, at least 3 hours. Loosen side of flan from dish, using knife; unmold. Refrigerate any remaining flan.

10 SERVINGS

Tangerine Soufflé

This brilliant dessert recalls the painted dessert: pale orange and fuchsia, sunset sky and the desert flowers that suddenly appear after a hard rain. Sweet prickly pears taste something like watermelon. Select prickly pears that are tender (not squishy) and free of soft or moldy spots, and strain out the numerous, hard seeds.

¾ cup sugar
1 cup water
¾ cup tangerine juice
¼ teaspoon salt
2 envelopes unflavored gelatin
4 eggs, separated
1 tablespoon grated tangerine peel
½ cup sugar
1 cup whipping cream
Prickly Pear Sauce (right)

Mix ¾ cup sugar, the water, tangerine juice, salt and gelatin in 2-quart saucepan. Beat egg yolks slightly; stir into gelatin mixture. Heat just to boiling over medium heat, stirring constantly. Remove from heat; stir in tangerine peel. Refrigerate, stirring occasionally, just until mixture mounds slightly when dropped from a spoon, 20 to 30 minutes. (If mixture becomes too thick, place pan in bowl of hot water; stir constantly until mixture is of proper consistency.)

Make a 4-inch band of triple-thickness aluminum foil 2 inches longer than the circumference of 6-cup soufflé dish. Extend dish by securing band around outside edge.

Beat egg whites in large bowl until foamy. Beat in ½ cup sugar, 1 tablespoon at a time; continue beating until stiff and glossy. Do not underbeat. Fold gelatin mixture into egg whites.

Beat whipping cream in chilled large bowl until stiff. Fold whipped cream into egg white mixture. Carefully turn into soufflé dish. Refrigerate until set, about 8 hours.

Prepare Prickly Pear Sauce; cool. Just before serving, carefully remove foil band from soufflé. Serve with Prickly Pear Sauce. Refrigerate any remaining soufflé immediately.

12 SERVINGS

PRICKLY PEAR SAUCE

6 prickly pears, peeled and cut into about 1-inch pieces
2 tablespoons honey
1 teaspoon cornstarch
1 teaspoon grated tangerine peel, if desired

Place prickly pears in food processor workbowl fitted with steel blade or in blender container; cover and process until smooth. Press through sieve to remove seeds. Mix pears, honey and cornstarch in 1-quart saucepan. Cook over medium heat, stirring constantly, until mixture thickens and boils. Boil and stir 1 minute; stir in tangerine peel.

Tangerine Soufflé

Mango Mousse

½ cup sugar
2 envelopes unflavored gelatin
4 eggs
3 egg yolks
2 cups mashed ripe mangoes (about 3 mangoes)
¼ cup brandy
¼ teaspoon almond extract
2 cups whipping cream
Sweetened whipped cream

Mix sugar and gelatin in 2-quart saucepan. Beat eggs and egg yolks until thick and lemon colored, about 5 minutes.

Stir eggs into gelatin mixture. Heat just to boiling over medium heat, stirring constantly. Remove from heat; stir in mangoes, brandy and almond extract. Refrigerate just until gelatin mixture mounds slightly when dropped from a spoon, about 1½ hours.

Beat whipping cream in chilled bowl until stiff. Fold mango mixture into whipped cream. Pour into 8-cup mold. Refrigerate until firm, about 4 hours; unmold. Serve with sweetened whipped cream. Garnish with mango slices if desired.

12 SERVINGS

Apricot Mousse: Substitute 1 can (30 ounces) apricot halves, drained, for the mangoes. Place apricots in blender container; cover and blend on high speed until smooth, about 1 minute. Decrease sugar to ¼ cup.

Peach Mousse: Substitute 1 can (29 ounces) sliced peaches, drained, for the mangoes. Place peaches in blender container; cover and blend on high speed until smooth, about 1 minute. Decrease sugar to ¼ cup.

Natillas

Natillas

Natillas are a southwestern version of floating island: little meringues set adrift on a pool of thin custard. Just before serving, run the dessert under the broiler for a pretty, golden effect.

4 eggs, separated
½ teaspoon cream of tartar
1 cup granulated sugar
4 cups milk
½ cup granulated sugar
1 teaspoon vanilla
¼ teaspoon salt
⅛ teaspoon ground cinnamon
Powdered sugar, sifted

Beat egg whites and cream of tartar in small bowl until foamy. Beat in 1 cup granulated sugar, 1 tablespoon at a time; continue beating until stiff and glossy. Do not underbeat.

Heat milk to simmering in 10-inch skillet over medium heat; reduce heat just until bubbles form around edge of skillet. Drop 12 mounds of egg white mixture, 3 or 4 at a time, into hot milk. Cook uncovered 2 minutes; turn gently. Cook uncovered 2 minutes longer. Remove meringues with slotted spoon and drain.

Strain milk; reserve 2¼ cups. Mix egg yolks, ½ cup granulated sugar, the vanilla, salt and cinnamon in heavy 2-quart nonaluminum saucepan.

Gradually stir in reserved milk. Cook over low heat, stirring constantly, until mixture coats a metal spoon, about 20 minutes. Remove from heat; place saucepan in cold water, stirring occasionally, until cool.

Place meringues in shallow 3-quart nonaluminum casserole. Pour custard over meringues; refrigerate 1 hour.

Just before serving, set oven control to broil. Sprinkle custard and meringues with powdered sugar. Broil with tops of meringues about 4 inches from heat until light brown, about 2 minutes. Refrigerate any remaining dessert.

6 SERVINGS

Mango-Honey Ice Cream

Here is a luscious combination that could only be homemade: cream, honey, mango and cinnamon. This dessert captures an impossibly fragrant tropical fruit in a rich, pastel-pale frozen base. Mango-Honey Ice Cream would be especially welcome after hot, spicy foods.

2 eggs
¾ cup sugar
½ cup milk
2 tablespoons honey
½ teaspoon ground cinnamon
¼ teaspoon salt
2 cups whipping cream
½ teaspoon vanilla
3 cans (15 ounces each) sliced mangoes, drained and mashed

Beat eggs in 2-quart saucepan; mix in sugar, milk, honey, cinnamon and salt. Heat just to simmering over medium heat, stirring constantly. Cover and refrigerate 1 hour or until cool. Stir in whipping cream, vanilla and mangoes. Freeze according to ice cream maker manufacturer's directions.

2 QUARTS ICE CREAM

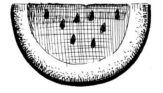

Sautéed Strawberries

½ cup margarine or butter
1 quart strawberries, cut into halves
¼ cup sugar
2 tablespoons orange-flavored liqueur
1 teaspoon grated lime peel
2 tablespoons brandy
Vanilla ice cream

Heat margarine in 10-inch skillet over medium heat until melted. Stir in strawberries; cook and stir 1 minute. Stir in sugar, liqueur and lime peel; cook and stir 1 minute.

Heat brandy in long-handled saucepan until warm; ignite and pour over strawberries. Serve hot over ice cream.

6 SERVINGS

Oranges and Cinnamon

4 chilled large oranges
1 teaspoon ground cinnamon
½ cup flaked or shredded coconut

Pare and thinly slice oranges. Arrange each orange on crushed ice in each of 4 serving dishes. Sprinkle each with ¼ teaspoon cinnamon and 2 tablespoons coconut.

4 SERVINGS

Fruit Compote

1 pineapple, cut into fourths and pared
2 cups sugar
2 cups water
6 whole cloves
1 stick cinnamon
3 apples, cut into fourths
3 peaches, cut into fourths
3 pears, cut into fourths
1 tablespoon grated lime peel
¼ cup lime juice

Cut each piece of pineapple into ½-inch slices. Mix sugar, water, cloves and cinnamon in 4-quart Dutch oven. Heat to boiling; stir in pineapple and remaining ingredients.

Heat to boiling; reduce heat. Cover and simmer 10 minutes. Remove from heat; cool slightly. Cover and refrigerate until cold.

8 SERVINGS

Bananas Flambé

½ cup margarine or butter
4 large bananas, cut into ¼-inch slices (about 3¼ cups)
¼ cup sugar
¼ cup banana-flavored liqueur
½ teaspoon ground cinnamon
¼ cup brandy
Vanilla ice cream

Heat margarine in 10-inch skillet over medium heat until melted. Stir in bananas; cook and stir 1 minute. Stir in sugar, liqueur and cinnamon; cook and stir 1 minute.

Heat brandy in long-handled saucepan until warm; ignite and pour over bananas. Serve hot over ice cream.

6 SERVINGS

Pears Stuffed with Dates

¼ cup brandy
1 cup pitted dates
6 pears (with stems)
2 cups water
⅓ cup sugar
2 tablespoons lime juice
4 whole cloves
1 stick cinnamon
¼ cup grenadine syrup

Pour brandy over dates; let stand 2 hours.

Pare and core pears from the bottom (do not remove stems). Heat water, sugar, lime juice, cloves and cinnamon to boiling in 3-quart saucepan, stirring occasionally; reduce heat. Add pears. Simmer uncovered, turning pears occasionally, until soft when pierced with a sharp knife, about 5 minutes. Remove pears with slotted spoon; cool.

Simmer syrup until reduced to ½ cup; remove cinnamon and cloves. Stir in grenadine. Fill pear cavities with dates; place in serving dishes. Spoon about 2 tablespoons syrup onto each pear. Cover and refrigerate until cold, at least 3 hours.

6 SERVINGS

Following pages: Pears Stuffed with Dates

Crepes with Caramel Filling

The caramel filling for these crepes is so rich and full-flavored that no one will guess it is so simply made. Turning this canned milk into caramel is a trick that's been around as long as they've been canning the milk. The silky filling is a perfect foil to the tender crepes, but you can gild the lily and serve a little vanilla ice cream on the side.

Caramel Custard (right)
1 cup all-purpose flour
1 tablespoon powdered sugar
1 teaspoon baking powder
½ teaspoon salt
1 cup milk
½ teaspoon vanilla
2 eggs, slightly beaten
¼ cup brandy
2 tablespoons powdered sugar
½ teaspoon ground cinnamon

Prepare Caramel Custard. Mix flour, 1 tablespoon powdered sugar, the baking powder and salt in medium bowl; stir in milk, vanilla and eggs. Beat with hand beater until smooth.

Lightly butter 6- to 8-inch skillet; heat over medium heat until bubbly. For each crepe, pour scant ¼ cup of the batter into skillet; immediately rotate skillet until thin film covers bottom. Cook until light brown. Run wide spatula around edge to loosen; turn and cook other side until light brown. Stack crepes, placing waxed paper between each. Keep covered.

Spread about 2 tablespoons custard on each warm crepe; roll up. Drizzle each crepe with 1 teaspoon brandy; sprinkle with powdered sugar and cinnamon.

12 CREPES

CARAMEL CUSTARD

Heat oven to 425°. Pour 1 can (14 ounces) sweetened condensed milk into 8-inch pie plate. Cover tightly with aluminum foil. Place pie plate in square pan, 9 x 9 x 2 inches, on oven rack. Pour very hot water into pan to within ½ inch of top of pie plate. Bake until thick and golden brown, about 1 hour. Carefully remove pie plate from hot water. Remove foil; cool.

Guava Paste and Cream Cheese

1 package (3 ounces) cream cheese
4 ounces guava paste

Cut cream cheese into fourths. Cut guava paste into 8 thin slices. Place each piece cream cheese between 2 slices guava paste. Serve with cookies if desired.

4 SERVINGS

Fresh Fruit Tostadas

This original, light dessert looks impressive but is deceptively easy to prepare. Crisp tortilla shells are painted with chocolate and filled with a sweet-tart fresh fruit mixture and whipped cream. Any combination of seasonal fresh fruit would be delightful.

Tostada Shells (below)
1 can (17 ounces) apricot halves, drained
2 tablespoons honey
1 cup strawberry halves
1 cup sliced peaches or apricots
1 cup quartered fresh figs or plums
1/2 cup whipping cream
2 tablespoons powdered sugar

Prepare Tostada Shells. Place apricot halves and honey in food processor workbowl fitted with steel blade or in blender container; cover and process until smooth.

Mix apricot mixture, strawberries, peaches and figs. Spoon about 1/2 cup mixture into each tostada shell.

Beat whipping cream and powdered sugar in chilled bowl until stiff. Serve with tostadas.

6 SERVINGS

TOSTADA SHELLS

6 flour tortillas (6 to 7 inches in diameter), warmed
   (page 84)
Margarine or butter, softened
1/2 cup semisweet chocolate chips
1 teaspoon shortening

Heat oven to 400°. Spread one side of each tortilla with margarine. Press each tortilla, margarine side down, in ungreased 10-ounce custard cup. Place custard cups in jelly roll pan, 15½ x 10½ x 1 inch. Bake until light golden brown, about 10 minutes. Remove shells from custard cups. Heat chocolate chips and shortening until melted; drizzle over insides of tostada shells. If necessary, refrigerate until chocolate is firm, 3 to 4 minutes.

Pumpkin Empanaditas

Pastry (below)
1 cup canned pumpkin
1/2 cup golden raisins
1/2 cup packed brown sugar
1/2 teaspoon ground cinnamon
1/4 teaspoon ground ginger
Granulated sugar

Prepare Pastry. Gather into ball; divide into halves. Divide each half into 16 equal pieces. Roll each piece between plastic wrap into 3½-inch circle. (Keep pastry covered before and after rolling to prevent drying.)

Heat remaining ingredients except granulated sugar to boiling, stirring constantly; reduce heat. Simmer uncovered until brown sugar is dissolved, about 5 minutes; cool.

Heat oven to 400°. Spoon 2 teaspoons pumpkin mixture onto center of each circle; brush edge of pastry with water. Fold pastry up over filling; press edge with fork to seal. Place empanaditas on ungreased cookie sheet; sprinkle with granulated sugar. Bake until light golden brown, 20 to 25 minutes. Serve warm.

32 EMPANADITAS

PASTRY

2 cups all-purpose flour
1 teaspoon salt
2/3 cup plus 2 tablespoons shortening
4 to 5 tablespoons cold water

Mix flour and salt; cut in shortening until particles are size of small peas. Sprinkle in water, 1 tablespoon at a time, tossing with fork until all flour is moistened and pastry almost cleans side of bowl (add 1 to 2 teaspoons water if necessary).

Following pages: Fresh Fruit Tostadas

Mexican Sweet Buns

Sweet-topped buns, or *conchas*, are named for the seashell design drawn in the flavored topping. Mexican bakers use a small metal cutter to stamp the design into the topping, but the pattern is easily drawn freehand with a knife.

1 package regular active dry yeast
½ cup warm water (105° to 115°)
½ cup lukewarm milk (scalded then cooled)
⅓ cup sugar
⅓ cup margarine or butter, softened
1 teaspoon salt
1 egg
3½ to 4 cups all-purpose flour
Flavored Topping Dough (right)

Dissolve yeast in warm water in large bowl. Stir in milk, sugar, margarine, salt, egg and 2 cups of the flour. Beat until smooth. Stir in enough remaining flour to make dough easy to handle.

Turn onto lightly floured surface; knead until smooth and elastic, about 5 minutes. Place in greased large bowl; turn greased side up. Cover and let rise in warm place until double, about 1½ hours. (Dough is ready if indentation remains when touched.)

Prepare Flavored Topping Dough; cover with plastic wrap to prevent from drying. Punch down sweet bun dough. Divide into 12 equal pieces; shape each piece into ball. Place on greased cookie sheet. Divide each part topping dough into 4 equal pieces. Pat each piece into 3-inch circle. Place 1 circle on each ball of dough, shaping down over ball. Make 5 or 6 cuts across topping, using a table knife, to form a shell pattern. Cover and let rise until double, about 40 minutes.

Heat oven to 375°. Bake until golden brown, about 20 minutes.

1 DOZEN ROLLS

FLAVORED TOPPING DOUGH

⅓ cup sugar
¼ cup margarine or butter
½ cup all-purpose flour
1 teaspoon ground cinnamon
¼ teaspoon vanilla
1½ teaspoons grated orange peel

Beat sugar and margarine until light and fluffy. Stir in flour until mixture is consistency of thick paste. Divide into 3 equal parts. Stir cinnamon into one part, vanilla into one part and orange peel into one part.

Place 1 circle of topping on each ball of dough, shaping down over ball.

Make 5 or 6 cuts across topping, using table knife, to form shell pattern.

Mexican Sweet Buns

New Mexico Piñon Candy

2 cones piloncillo, shredded (about 1¼ cups), or 1 cup
  packed dark brown sugar
1 cup water
2 tablespoons butter*
1½ cups toasted pine nuts or pecan halves (page 19)
1 teaspoon vanilla

Heat piloncillo and water to boiling in 2-quart saucepan, stirring constantly; reduce heat slightly. Cook, without stirring, to 236° on candy thermometer or until small amount of mixture dropped into very cold water forms a soft ball that flattens when removed from water; remove from heat. Immediately remove thermometer; stir in butter. Cool 8 minutes without stirring.

Stir in pine nuts and vanilla. Beat with spoon until slightly thickened and mixture just coats pine nuts but remains glossy, about 1 minute. Drop by rounded teaspoonfuls onto waxed paper. Let stand until candies are firm. Store tightly covered at room temperature.

ABOUT 24 CANDIES

* Margarine not recommended.

New Mexico Biscochitos

Biscochitos are Mexico's answer to the Old World seed cookie. Rich with the flavor of anise, these holiday cookies were cut into *fleur de lis* shapes for Christmas. *Biscochitos* are quite short— traditionally a high ratio of lard to flour and sugar—and are as easy to roll out and cut as sugar cookies. Biscochitos are the official state cookie of New Mexico.

1 cup sugar
1 cup margarine or butter, softened
3 tablespoons sweet sherry
1 egg
3 cups all-purpose flour
2 teaspoons baking powder
2 teaspoons anise seed, crushed
¼ teaspoon salt
¼ cup sugar
1 teaspoon ground cinnamon

Heat oven to 350°. Mix sugar, margarine, sherry and egg in large bowl. Stir in remaining ingredients except ¼ cup sugar and the cinnamon. Divide dough into halves. Roll each half ¼ inch thick on lightly floured board.

Cut into desired shapes with cookie cutters; place on ungreased cookie sheet. Mix ¼ cup sugar and the cinnamon; sprinkle on cookies. Bake until light golden brown, 10 to 12 minutes.

ABOUT 4 DOZEN 2-INCH COOKIES

*New Mexico Biscochitos and New Mexico Piñon
Candy*

Churros

The batter for this version of *churros* is prepared using the same technique as that for cream puff dough. Piped into ragged, crispy oblongs, these deep-fried cakes are named for the shaggy, long-haired Mexican sheep they resemble.

Vegetable oil
1 cup water
½ cup margarine or butter
1 cup all-purpose flour
¼ teaspoon salt
3 eggs
Powdered sugar or cinnamon-sugar mixture

Heat oil (1½ inches) to 375° in 4-quart Dutch oven or deep saucepan. Heat water and margarine to rolling boil in 3-quart saucepan. Remove from heat; quickly stir in flour and salt. Stir vigorously over low heat until mixture forms a ball. Remove from heat; beat in eggs, 1 at a time, until smooth and glossy.

Spoon mixture into pastry bag fitted with star tip #6. Squeeze 5-inch strips of dough into hot oil. Cook, turning frequently, until deep golden brown; drain. Sprinkle generously with powdered sugar. Serve warm.

ABOUT 2 DOZEN CHURROS

Buñuelos

½ cup water
2 tablespoons packed brown sugar
1 egg, slightly beaten
2 cups all-purpose flour
½ teaspoon baking powder
¼ teaspoon salt
2 tablespoons margarine or butter
Vegetable oil
Granulated sugar and ground cinnamon or honey

Heat water and brown sugar to boiling in 1-quart saucepan, stirring constantly. Boil and stir 2 minutes; cool. Stir in egg.

Mix flour, baking powder and salt; cut in margarine until mixture resembles fine crumbs. Stir in egg mixture until dough forms. Turn onto lightly floured surface; knead until elastic, about 5 minutes. Shape dough into roll, about 20 inches long. Cover and let rest 1 hour.

Heat oil (1 inch) to 365° in 4-quart Dutch oven. Cut dough into 1-inch slices. Roll each slice into 5-inch circle on lightly floured surface. Fry circles, turning once, until golden brown, about 2 minutes; drain. Sprinkle with granulated sugar and cinnamon, or serve with honey.

20 BUÑUELOS

Sopaipillas

2 cups all-purpose flour
2 teaspoons baking powder
1 teaspoon salt
2 tablespoons lard or shortening
⅔ cup lukewarm water
Vegetable oil

Mix flour, baking powder and salt; cut in lard until mixture resembles fine crumbs. Sprinkle in water, 1 tablespoon at a time, tossing with fork until all flour is moistened and pastry almost cleans side of bowl. Gather pastry into ball. Cover and refrigerate 30 minutes.

Heat oil (1 to 2 inches) to 400° in 4-quart Dutch oven. Turn pastry onto lightly floured surface. Roll into rectangle, 12 x 10 inches. Cut into rectangles, 3 x 2 inches. Fry 3 or 4 rectangles at a time, turning once, until puffed and golden, about 2 minutes; drain. Sprinkle with powdered sugar or granulated sugar if desired.

20 SOPAIPILLAS

Southwestern Hospitality: Menus for all Occasions

Southwest Thanksgiving
Butternut Squash Soup
Turkey with Southwest Stuffing
Corn Relish
Southwest Vegetable Sauté
Caramelized Sweet Potatoes
Pumpkin Flan
Sangria Blanco

New Mexico Christmas Dinner
Blue Cornmeal Chicken Wings
Posole
Orange Salad with Pecan Dressing
Sopaipillas
New Mexico Bizcochitos
Fiesta Hot Chocolate

Cinco de Mayo Celebration
Snappy Stuffed Tomatillos
Turkey Tamale Pie
Mexican Flag Salad with Herb Vinaigrette
Fresh Fruit Tostadas
Sangria

Southwest Buffet Dinner
Western Swing Pâté
Flour Tortillas and Salsa
Ricotta Cheese Enchiladas
Santa Fe Chicken
Layered Mexican Salad
Tucson Lemon Cake

Formal Dinner
Stuffed Mushrooms
Pumpkin Ravioli
Spicy Pork Roast
Spinach Budín
Jícama Citrus Salad with Sangria Dressing
Orange-Pecan Pie
Café Mexicana

Texas Barbecue
Cowboy Caviar
Corn Tortillas
Spicy Texas Ribs
Texas Slaw with Cumin Dressing
Ranch Beans
Peach Cobbler

Native American Dinner
Zuni Vegetable Stew
Navajo Fry Bread
Rio Grande Melon Salad
Baked Indian Pudding

Chili Party
Nachos
Texas Red Chili
White Bean Chili
Vegetable Cornmeal Muffins
Tossed Romaine Salad
Chocolate Ranch Pudding
Cold Beer and Iced Tea

Summer Brunch

Santa Fe Melon Soup
Mexican Omelet
Breakfast Fruit Chimichangas
Serrano Grits with Cheese
Mexican Sweet Buns
Buñuelos
Margarita Sunrise

Fourth of July Picnic

Grilled Cornish Hens
Grilled Corn with Chile-Lime Spread
Adobe Bread
Cactus, Zucchini and Red Pepper Salad
Southwest Lemon Fruit Tart
Pineapple Limeade

Southwestern Luncheon

Gazpacho
Baja Pasta Chicken Salad
Blue Cornmeal Muffins
Tangerine Soufflé

Cocktail Party for a Crowd

Southwest Guacamole with Tortilla Chips
Cheese Chiles
Bell Pepper Rajas
Double Cheese Wheel
Southwest Riblets
Grilled Seafood Flautas
Fish en Escabeche
Southwest Smoothies
Sangria
Margarita Sunrise

Recipe Cross-reference Guide

Relishes
Black Bean Relish

Radish and Cilantro Relish
Southwest Relish
Papaya Relish

Salsas
Cucumber Salsa

Fresh Tomato Salsa

Red Sauces
Basic Red Sauce

Casera Sauce

Roasted Tomato Sauce

Almond Red Sauce

Hot Chile Sauce

Chipotle Sauce

Used In
Layered Mexican Salad
Santa Fe Chicken

Pork Chops in Radish Sauce
Southwest Beef Fajitas
Grilled Pork Tacos

Used In
Salmon with Cucumber Salsa
Southwest Beef Fajitas

Pork Stew with Corn Bread Topping
Southwest Burgers
Stacked New Mexico Quesadilla
Texas Breakfast Tacos

Used In
Beef Tortilla Casserole
Meatballs in Chile Sauce
Red Enchiladas

Chiles Rellenos
Huevos Rancheros
Mexican Omelet
Mexican Rice
Mixed Tostadas
Shrimp Soup
Tortilla Dumpling Soup

Corn Fritters
Grilled Seafood Flautas
Ricotta Cheese Enchiladas

Baked Chimichangas
Pheasant in Almond Red Sauce
Turkey Tamale Pie

Grilled Jalapeño Buffalo Burgers

Braised Meat Loaf
Meatballs in Chipotle Sauce

Green Sauces

Basic Green Sauce

New Mexico Green Sauce

Cilantro Pesto

Pumpkin Seed Sauce

Used In

Egg and Spinach Casserole
Green Enchiladas

Chicken Chilaquiles Casserole

Halibut with Cilantro Pesto
Ricotta Cheese Enchiladas

Pepita Vegetable Burritos
Pumpkin Ravioli

Creamy Sauces

Chipotle Mayonnaise

Red Pepper–Sour Cream Sauce

Jalapeño Cream Sauce

Lime Butter Sauce

Quick Crème Fraîche

Used In

Sole Steamed in Corn Husks

Stacked New Mexico Quesadilla

Baked Chimichangas
Turkey in Jalapeño Cream Sauce

Grilled Red Snapper with Vegetable Sauté
Southwest Vegetable Sauté

Jalapeño Cream Sauce
Southwest Black Bean Soup

Basting Sauces

Apricot Basting Sauce

Citrus Barbecue Sauce

Plum Barbecue Sauce

Spicy Texas Barbecue Sauce

Used In

Apricot-basted Quail
Breakfast Fruit Chimichangas
Duck with Pine Nut Wild Rice

Baked Citrus Swordfish

Grilled Cornish Hens
Venison with Plum Sauce

Spicy Brisket
Spicy Texas Spareribs

Dips and Spreads

Chile con Queso

Southwest Guacamole

Used In

Macaroni con Queso

Beef Tortilla Casserole
Cauliflower and Avocado Salad
Pork Carnitas
Southwest Beef Fajitas
Texas Breakfast Tacos

Beverages

Café Mexicano

Used In

Café Diablo

Beans
Pinto Beans

Refried Beans

Vegetables
Southwest Vegetable Sauté

Tortillas
Flour Tortillas

Used In
Bean and Garlic Dip
Refried Beans

Beef Burritos
Filled Tortillas
Green Enchiladas
Mixed Tostadas
Red Enchiladas

Used In
Grilled Red Snapper with Vegetable Sauté

Used In
Filled Tortillas

Index

GENERAL MILLS, INC.

Editor: Karen Couné
Associate Food Editor: Julie H. Turnbull
Test Kitchen Home Economist: Mary Hallin Johnson
Recipe Copy Editor: Lauren Long
Administrative Assistant: Phyllis Weinbender
Food Stylists: Cindy Lund, Katie W. McElroy, Mary Sethre
Photographer: Nanci E. Doonan
Photography Assistant: Carolyn Luxmoore
Director, Betty Crocker Food and Publications Center: Marcia Copeland
Assistant Manager, Publications: Lois Tlusty

Many of the plates featured in *Betty Crocker's Southwest Cooking* were commissioned especially for this book. Artists: Nina Duran (front cover, pages 23, 33, 83, 95, 105, 114, 200–201); Patricia Fabricant (page 79); Jillene Kingstedt (pages 4, 121, 133); Tomar Levine (pages 77, 97, 123, 124, 129, 155, 177, 195); Helène Maumy-Florescu (pages 69, 80, 131); J. C. Suarès (pages 51, 137, 150, 167); Christina Sun (pages 54, 109, 149); and Ardith Truhan (back cover, pages 86–87, 88, 99, 116, 144, 171).

You may find these other Betty Crocker cookbooks useful for international cooking:

Betty Crocker's Cookbook
Betty Crocker's New Chinese Cookbook
Betty Crocker's Italian Cooking
Betty Crocker's New International Cookbook